THE
WRITER'S
HANDBOOK
1996

EDITOR

BARRY TURNER

MACMILLAN

First published 1988
This edition published by Macmillan Reference Books
a division of Macmillan Publishers Ltd
25 Eccleston Place, London SW1W 9NF
and Basingstoke
Associated companies around the world

10 9 8 7 6 5 4 3 2 1

A CIP catalogue record for this book is available from the British Library

ISBN 0–333–63832–8

Typeset by Heronwood Press
Printed and bound in Great Britain
by Hazell Books Ltd, Aylesbury

If you would like an entry in *The Writer's Handbook
1997*, please write or send a fax to:
The Writer's Handbook, 45 Islington Park Street,
London N1 1QB.
Fax 0171 359 6026.

Contents

Preface

With the next edition, *The Writer's Handbook* enters its second decade. It all started with Julian Ashby, Macmillan's reference book publisher. When the idea was put to me I was dubious. Was the writers' market strong enough to sustain two yearbooks? Our prospective rival, the name of which escapes me, had been around for a long time and would not take kindly to an intruder. I should not have worried. It soon became clear that the demand for insider information on the publishing trade far outpaces supply. Every year *The Writer's Handbook* has increased in size and scope.

But there is a limit to the quantity of new material that can be encompassed within a single volume. This is why we are launching *The Writer's Companion* which will bring together the feature material of the *Handbook* with expanded and updated intelligence on writing in all its manifestations, from old-fashioned print to the superhighway.

The ineffable Jill Fenner, researcher and database manipulator, is working on both *The Writer's Handbook* and *The Writer's Companion*. Her energy and dedication knows no bounds and her skill is evident at every stage of the compilation. Our overseer at Macmillan is Dominic Taylor who juggles his responsibilities with enviable dexterity.

As ever, we are grateful to the Society of Authors, the Writers' Guild, PEN and the National Union of Journalists for their generous permission to quote from their publications but more especially for their prompt and constructive response to a succession of individual queries.

But, need I add? It is the Editor, alone and palely loitering who must take the full force of criticism for any errors or omissions.

Barry Turner

THE WRITER'S COMPANION

The essential guide to being published

Barry Turner

The Writer's Companion is a route map through the media jungle, an indispensable guide for established writers and newcomers alike who seek to make best commercial use of their talents.

Drawing on the cumulative experiences of its sister volume, *The Writer's Handbook*, which is now in its ninth year, *The Writer's Companion* is packed with a wealth of practical advice taking in:

- book publishing
- freelance journalism
- film and televison
- radio drama
- theatre and poetry

Everyday concerns, financial and legal, from how to avoid contractual pitfalls to minimising the risks of libel are given full coverage and there is up-to-date advice on raising funds for creative projects on stage and screen.

Published in 1996 by Macmillan

Little Acorns

Barry Turner explores the pleasures of writing and the practicalities of getting into print

One of the virtues of getting older is the chance to work more by choice than by compulsion. The rule is not infallible, of course. I assume a fair trade wind to take care of the mortgage and to put the children in the way of gainful employment. But with average luck, advanced maturity brings happy diversions from the pursuit of profit.

My own recent example is a venture into live theatre. I have written for television and radio but never hitherto for the stage. It happened this way. I had put together a proposal for a biography of the great Victorian actor, Sir Henry Irving. This in itself was a labour of love. Nobody earns big money from books about long-dead actors. In the event, I was not able to earn even small money since every publisher I approached gave me that thin smile of polite but irrevocable dismissal. I had almost given up on Irving when I was introduced to the renowned director, James Roose-Evans who turned out to be an authority on Victorian drama. He it was who suggested a collaborative effort to put Irving back on stage. And so we did an entertainment based on Irving's life and work.

It must be clear that I am not talking of a triumph to match *Phantom of the Opera*. Indeed, poor Irving is destined for no more than a single night in the West End – and that a charity performance. Its audience is limited to the festival circuit and maybe, just maybe, an adaptation to radio. The odds are against us earning more than a few pounds for our efforts.

But that is not the point. The point for me is that the project has brought enormous pleasure, the opportunity to work in a medium new to me, to try out ideas, a few of which have succeeded, and to meet creative people who might otherwise have remained beyond my range of experience.

It is commonplace for writers to complain that their's is a hard and often agonising discipline with few compensations beyond the purely mercenary. It was Dr Johnson, no less, who said that no one but a fool writes for aught but money. Heresy it may be to contradict the good doctor but I believe this to be one of his sillier aphorisms. Aside from money,

'For a writer, success is always temporary. Success is only failure – delayed.'
Graham Greene

'. . . there is a single material factor linking Joyce, Woolf and Conrad it is that they all at one time or another in their literary career submitted work to *Titbits*.'
D. J. Taylor, *After the War, The Novel in England Since 1945*

'The most essential gift for a good writer is a built-in shock proof shit-detector.'
Ernest Hemingway

'We have hardly begun to grasp the extent to which radio, the cinema and, first and foremost, television are appropriating the resources of time and of perception which were once the domain of the book. Most new homes have bulging shelves of cassettes, records and videos instead of books.'
George Steiner

'I always knew that a good writer was one who threw out what most other people kept, but then it occurred to me that a good writer is also one who keeps what most other people throw out.'
David Mamet

there are many good reasons for writing, not least a deep sense of personal fulfilment.

A recent survey for the BBC2 programme *Bookworm* found that one in ten of those questioned felt they had a book in them. Moreover, one in fifty had actually written a book.

Add to this the wealth of letters from aspiring writers I receive at *The Writer's Handbook*, and we can safely assume that the desire to write is widespread and deep rooted. Few, if any, of these correspondents reveal an ambition to become a bestselling author or a lion of the literary circuit. It is enough that they see their words in print and earn some appreciation for their efforts.

But here's the rub. How does one achieve the transition from words on a scrap of paper or on a typewriter or computer to words in real print? It is nonsense to argue that publication is incidental to the art of writing – that mere composition should bring its own reward. This is like asking an artist to paint without a canvas.

On the face of it, publication is more difficult now than almost at any time in the history of printing. We have seen, in the last ten years, the rise of the publishing conglomerates – media empires that dominate not simply the publication of books but the dissemination of all information – by print, sound and screen. To break into one of these charmed circles takes enormous application and a thick slice of luck. Do not be misled by newspaper stories of first time authors walking away with multi-million pound contracts. The chances of this happening are on par with engaging the fickle finger of the national lottery. At *The Writer's Handbook* we hear tales galore of manuscripts returned unread, of manuscripts read but not returned, of manuscripts circulating a company's internal postal system in an everlasting game of pass the parcel.

The sad fact is that the media barons are not too interested in new talent. What they want is names – big names. If a celeb happens to have written a book or two, so much the better. Hence, for example, the value put on the Amis's – father and son – whose talent for self-publicity enhances their market appeal. But literary qualifications are not essential. A book can always be found to match up with a personality.

So it is that super model Naomi Campbell makes £100,000 plus for a novel written by an anonymous ghost. Celebrity sagas crowd the front counters of high street bookshops. Edwina Currie, Jill Gascoine, Kirk Douglas,

Martine Navratilova, Eddie Shah, Tim Waterstone – all have thrived on the pulling power of their names. In terms of publishers' return on investment, the only hint of failure I can detect is the advance Joan Collins has been asked to return Random House for failing to measure up to their expectations.

What we are into is a business dominated by marketing. And if marketing people have a weakness it is their tendency to play safe. They have little time for newcomers – however talented – who are unable to boast a track record.

If mass marketing counts against the newcomer, so too does the old boy network. In this book publishing is no different from any other business, certainly no different from newspapers or television or radio or cinema or computer games. In industries which have become highly centralised, everybody who is anybody knows anybody who is somebody. Unknowns tend to stay that way.

To make any sort of impact can take years of dedicated socialising. Being there helps; being part of a media enterprise where young ones line up to be talent spotted by kindly mentors. Many of the television writers in regular employment started as set builders, or prop movers or window cleaners. Famous dramatists recall, none too fondly, their days as stage managers. But when the moment came to present a manuscript they knew who to go to; a director or producer with whom they were on first name terms.

It cannot be said too often: on spec submissions to big companies have little chance of serious, let alone sympathetic consideration. There is no future in head banging against an immovable object.

Let journalist John Diamond speak for all those disillusioned freelancers, many of them products of the writing schools, who have lined their walls with rejection slips. Here he is writing in *The Spectator*:

'I have spent long hours turning commissioned and subliterate copy from household named journalists into something that stands a chance of getting read, and then minutes writing rejection slips to competent amateurs who have sent in entirely readable, but unsuitable, pieces on spec.'

What then is the way forward for the novice writer who, for one reason or another, is in no position to throw himself into the murky shallows of editorial networking? The

'If I were on the Booker organising committee, I should make a rule that no judge should be over 60 years old. This is not ageist, just as veterans' sports events are not ageist. An enlightened institution – Saga Holidays, *The Oldie* - might inaugurate a book to be judged *only* by the over-sixties. The truth is that few older people, even those who are dedicated readers, really enjoy new fiction, or not the kind that the clever young are reading. Most prefer to read history and biography, or to re-read the novels they enjoyed in the past. This is not a fault, it is a fact of nature.' **Victoria Glendinning**

'They don't give a heck for the futures and livelihoods of writers, yet they expect loyalty in return.' Booker nominee, **Jill Paton Walsh,** whose *Knowledge of Angels* was initially rejected by 14 publishers

'A great writer creates a world of his own and his readers are proud to live in it. A lesser writer may entice them in for a moment, but soon he will watch them filing out.' **Cyril Connolly** *Enemies of Promise*

'Everyone involved with the production of a book - the editors and publishers, the manufacturers of paper, the binders, the van drivers, the accountants, the publicists, the booksellers, the office cleaners - makes a reasonable living except the majority of starry-eyed masochists who actually provide the words without which all the others would have to be doing something else.'
Milton Shulman

'The most insidious influence on the young is not violence, drugs, tobacco, drink or sexual perversion, but our pursuit of the trivial and our tolerance of the third rate.'
Dr Eric Anderson, Headmaster of Eton

answer is to think small. Steer clear, for now, and possibly for ever, of the senior league of publishers, broadcasters and producers. Instead, go for the independents who serve regional or local markets.

It is one of the paradoxes of modern publishing that while the move towards centralisation grabs the headlines on the city and media pages, the advance in communication technology has spawned a multitude of small publishers who are on the lookout for ideas and talent. There are now around 6000 small presses and publishers operating in the UK. Some are way out, financial misfits. Many are well managed businesses with clever and imaginative editors. They do not pay out vast sums but to get rich quick is not the prime objective. Experience, the essential learning process, has a value and it is at grass roots that it can be best acquired.

But why limit the argument to publishers? Local radio is often more exciting and innovative than national radio; provincial theatre thrives while the West End lurches from crisis to crisis. Before long, community based television will extend the range of programming and open the way for untried talent. Every year, there are more literary and drama festivals crying out for inspiration. At this level opportunities abound for writers to enjoy the satisfaction of having their work read or performed.

Fame and fortune may follow. Victories in the second division can lead to promotion. But this is not a universal ambition. Most writers would subscribe to the more modest principle – to stay small is beautiful.

UK Publishers

AA Publishing

The Automobile Association, Fanum House, Basingstoke, Hampshire RG21 2EA
☎01256 491574   Fax 01256 492440

Managing Director *John Howard*
Editorial Director *Michael Buttler*
Approx. Annual Turnover £22 million

Publishes maps, atlases and guidebooks, motoring and leisure. About 100 titles a year.

Authors' Rating Benefiting from a clearly defined market, the AA has advanced strongly in the publication of maps and tour guides. Travel writers who really know their stuff are among the beneficiaries.

Abacus

See **Little, Brown & Co (UK)**

ABC – All Books For Children (a division of The All Children's Co. Ltd)

33 Museum Street, London WC1A 1LD
☎0171 436 6300   Fax 0171 240 6923

Managing Director *Sue Tarsky*

Publishes children's titles only, including the successful *Angelina Ballerina* and *Ned* books and toys. About 40 titles a year. *Specialises* in co-editions worldwide. **SoftbABCks** paperback imprint launched 1991 and **FactbABCks** non-fiction imprint launched 1995. Unsolicited material welcome but no novels. All material should be addressed to the Editorial Department; s.a.e. essential for return.
Royalties paid twice yearly.

ABC-Clio Ltd

Old Clarendon Iron Works, 35a Great Clarendon Street, Oxford OX2 6AT
☎01865 311350   Fax 01865 311358

Managing Director *Tony Sloggett*
Editorial Director *Dr Robert G. Neville*

Formerly Clio Press Ltd. *Publishes* academic reference work, social sciences and humanities. Markets, outside North America, the CD-ROM publications of the American parent company. Art Bibliographies *S. Pape.* SERIES *World Bibliographical; International Organisations; World Photographers; Clio Montessori.*
Royalties paid twice yearly.

Aberdeen University Press

See **Mercat Press**

Abington Publishing

See **Woodhead Publishing Ltd**

Absolute Press

14 Widcombe Crescent, Bath, Avon BA2 6AH
☎01225 316013   Fax 01225 445836

Managing/Editorial Director *Jon Croft*

FOUNDED 1980. *Publishes* food and wine-related subjects as well as travel guides. About 10 titles a year.
Also publishes English translations of plays and theatre considered to be world masterpieces under the **Absolute Classics** imprint. No unsolicited mss. Synopsis and ideas for books welcome.
Royalties paid twice yearly.

Academic Press

See **Harcourt Brace and Company Ltd**

Academy Books

35 Pretoria Avenue, London E17 7DR
☎0181 521 7647   Fax 0181 503 6655

Chairman/Managing Director *Tony Freeman*
Approx. Annual Turnover £150,000

FOUNDED 1990 as a self-publishing venture for specialist transport titles. *Publishes* non-fiction, mostly historical and technological, with a strong bias towards transport. TITLES *Humber, an Illustrated History; Lost Voice of Queen Victoria; How To Trace the History of Your Car; Daimler: An Illustrated History; Lanchester Cars 1895–1956; Sir Joseph Bradney's History of Monmouthshire; The Godfather of Rolls Royce; Edsel, The Motor Industry's Titanic; Bentley, The Overdrive Cars; The Nyasaland Survey Papers; The Culwick Papers.* Unsolicited mss, synopses and ideas welcome. Synopses should be accompanied by sa.mple chapter or example of previously published work. Mss must be supplied on computer disk prior to acceptance. Packaging undertaken on specialist academic and specialist transport titles for some clients. Several magazines handled on a contract basis.
Royalties paid monthly.

Academy Group Ltd
42 Leinster Gardens, London W2 3AN
☎0171 402 2141   Fax 0171 723 9540
Chairman *H. D. Köhler*
Managing Director *John Stoddart*
Approx. Annual Turnover £3 million
FOUNDED 1969. Part of VCH Verlagsgesellschaft mbh, Germany. *Publishes* architecture,
art and design. Welcomes unsolicited mss, synopses and ideas. Contacts: *Michael Spens* Architecture; *Maggie Toy* Architectural Design;
Nicola Kearton Art & Design.
Royalties paid annually.

Acair Ltd
Unit 7, 7 James Street, Stornoway, Isle of
Lewis, Scotland PA87 2QA
☎01851 703020   Fax 01851 703294
Manager *Joan Morrison*
Specialises in matters pertaining to the Gaidheal-
tachd, Acair publishes books on history, culture
and the Gaelic language. 75% of their children's
books are targeted at primary school usage and
are published exclusively in Gaelic.
Royalties paid twice yearly.

Ace Books
1268 London Road, London SW16 4ER
☎0181 679 8000   Fax 0181 679 6069
Approx. Annual Turnover £500,000
Publishing arm of Age Concern England.
Publishes related non-fiction only. No fiction.
About 18 titles a year. Unsolicited mss, syn-
opses and ideas welcome.

Acropolis Books
See **Anness Publishing Ltd**

Actinic Press
See **Cressrelles Publishing Co. Ltd**

Addison–Wesley Publishers Ltd
Finchampstead Road, Wokingham, Berkshire
RG11 2NZ
☎01734 794000   Fax 01734 794035
President, UK/Europe/Australia *Derek Hall*
Editorial Director *Andrew Ware*
A division of the Addison–Wesley European
Publishing Group, owned by Pearson since
1988, making it part of one of the largest book
publishers in the world. *Publishes* scientific, tech-
nical, academic and senior school books, and is
one of the leading computer science publishers.
Several series covering computer science, micro-

electronics and international business, for the
international market. Unsolicited mss, synopses
and ideas for books welcome.
Royalties paid twice yearly.

Authors' Rating Set for growth now that it has
taken over from Longman all the rest of the educational output controlled by the Pearson
Group. A first acquisition is Nelson's ELT list
which comes over from Thomson. Many blockbuster texts benefiting from strong marketing.

Adlard Coles Ltd
See **A & C Black (Publishers) Ltd**

Adlib
See **Scholastic Publications Ltd**

African Books Collective
The Jam Factory, 27 Park End Street, Oxford
OX1 1HU
☎01865 726686   Fax 01865 793293
FOUNDED 1990. Collectively owned by its 18
founder member publishers. Exclusive distribution in N. America, UK, Europe and Commonwealth countries outside Africa for 42
African member publishers. Aims to promote
and disseminate African-published material
outside Africa. No unsolicited mss.

Airlife Publishing Ltd
101 Longden Road, Shrewsbury, Shropshire
SY3 9EB
☎01743 235651   Fax 01743 232944
Chairman/Managing Director
    A. D. R. Simpson
Editorial Head *John Beaton*
Approx. Annual Turnover £3 million
IMPRINTS
Airlife *Publishes* specialist aviation titles, both
technical and general, for pilots, historians and
enthusiasts. About 35 titles a year. TITLES *Air
Pilot's Manuals; The Source Book of the RAF; Diary
of an Aviator; Jets: Airliners of the Golden Age.*
Swan Hill Press covers country sport, natural
history, travel and adventure, wildlife art.
About 25 titles a year. TITLES *The Whitehead
Encyclopedia of Deer; Minton – The First 200 Years;
Salmon Flyfishing – The Dynamics Approach; Voice
From the Wilderness.*
    About 12 sailing and yachting titles a year are
published under the **Waterline Books** imprint.
TITLES *Hand Reef & Steer; High Performance
Sailing; Dinghy Systems; Voyaging on a Small
Income.*

Unsolicited mss, synopses and ideas for books welcome.

Royalties paid annually or twice yearly by arrangement.

Ian Allan Ltd

Coombelands House, Coombelands Lane, Addlesdown, Surrey KT15 1HY
☎01932 855909   Fax 01932 854750
Chairman *David Allan*
Managing Director *Martin Kenny*
Publishing Director *S. Forty*

Publishes atlases and maps, aviation, biography and autobiography, hobbies, guidebooks, defence and militaria, nautical, reference and dictionaries, transport, travel and topography. About 100 titles a year. Send sample chapter and synopsis (with s.a.e.). Manages distribution and sales for third party publishers.

IMPRINT **Dial House** sport, leisure, cookery, gardening.

J. A. Allen & Co. Ltd

1 Lower Grosvenor Place, Buckingham Palace Road, London SW1W 0EL
☎0171 834 0090   Fax 0171 976 5836
Chairman/Managing Director *Joseph A. Allen*
Publishing Director *Caroline Burt*
Editor *Jane Lake*
Approx. Annual Turnover £700,000

FOUNDED 1926 as part of J. A. Allen & Co. (The Horseman's Bookshop) Ltd, and became a separate independent company in 1960. *Publishes* equine and equestrian non-fiction and fiction. About 20 titles a year. Mostly commissioned, but willing to consider unsolicited mss of technical/instructional material related to all aspects of horses and horsemanship.

Royalties paid twice yearly.

Allen Lane The Penguin Press

See **Penguin Books Ltd**

Allison & Busby

179 King's Cross Road, London WC1X 9BZ
☎0171 833 1042   Fax 0171 833 1044
Managing Director/Editor *Peter Day*
Rights *Sarah Fulford*

FOUNDED 1967. *Publishes* literary fiction and non-fiction, including 20th-century classics, writers' guides and crime. About 36 titles a year. Send synopses with two sample chapters. No replies without s.a.e.

The Amaising Publishing House Ltd

Beech Cottage, Ecclesmachan, By Broxburn, West Lothian EH52 6NJ
☎01506 853875   Fax 01506 853875
Managing Director *Mrs Katrena M. Allan*
Approx. Annual Turnover £60,000

FOUNDED 1983. *Publishes* children's picture books only. 4 titles in 1994. Began as an avenue for author and director Aileen Paterson to publish her works. Her *Masie* series consistently no. 1 in the Scottish bestsellers. Send synopsis and sample pictures with s.a.e. or return postage. No unsolicited mss, poetry or novels.

Amber Lane Press Ltd

Cheorl House, Church Street, Charlbury, Oxfordshire OX7 3PR
☎01608 810024   Fax 01608 810024
Chairman *Brian Clark*
Managing Director/Editorial Head *Judith Scott*

FOUNDED 1979 to publish modern play texts. *Publishes* plays and books on the theatre. About 4 titles a year. TITLES *After Aida; The Best of Friends; The Dresser* (play texts); *Patterns of Postwar British Drama* Colin Chambers & Mike Prior; *The Sound of One Hand Clapping: A Guide to Writing for the Theatre* Sheila Yeger. No unsolicited mss. Synopses and ideas welcome.

Royalties paid twice yearly.

Amsco

See **Omnibus Press**

Andersen Press Ltd

20 Vauxhall Bridge Road, London SW1V 2SA
☎0171 973 9720   Fax 0171 233 6263
Managing Director/Publisher *Klaus Flugge*
Editorial Director *Denise Johnstone-Burt*
Editor, Fiction *Audrey Adams*

FOUNDED 1976 by Klaus Flugge and named after Hans Christian Andersen. *Publishes* children's hardback fiction. Seventy per cent of their books are sold as co-productions abroad. TITLES *Not Now Bernard* David McKee; *A Dark, Dark Tale* Ruth Brown; *I Want My Potty* Tony Ross; *Badger's Parting Gift* Susan Varley. Unsolicited mss welcome for picture books and young readers up to age 12.

Royalties paid twice yearly.

Anness Publishing Ltd

Boundary Studios, 1–7 Boundary Row,
London SE1 8HP
☎0171 401 2077   Fax 0171 633 9499

Chairman/Managing Director *Paul Anness*
Publisher/Partner *Joanna Lorenz*

FOUNDED 1989. Successful, small entrepreneurial company: international packager and publisher of highly illustrated co-edition titles. *Publishes* illustrated general non-fiction: cookery, crafts, interior design, gardening, photography, decorating, lifestyle and children's. About 30 titles a year. Unsolicited summaries and proposals welcome, no manuscripts.

IMPRINTS **Lorenz Books; Acropolis Books; Anness Publishing.**

Antique Collectors' Club

5 Church Street, Woodbridge, Suffolk
IP12 1DS
☎01394 385501   Fax 01394 384434

Managing Director *Diana Steel*
Editorial Adviser *John Steel*

FOUNDED 1966. Has a five-figure membership spread over the United Kingdom and the world. The Club's magazine *Antique Collecting* is sold on a subscription basis (currently £19.50 *p.a.*) and is published 10 times a year. It is sent free to members who may also buy the Club's books at special pre-publication prices. *Publishes* specialist books on antiques and collecting. The price guide series was introduced in 1968 with the first edition of *The Price Guide to Antique Furniture*. Subject areas include furniture, silver/jewellery, metalwork, glass, textiles, art reference, ceramics, horology. Also books on architecture and gardening. TITLES *Dictionary of Worcester* John & Henry Sandon; *Travels in China – A Plantsman's Paradise* Roy Lancaster; *Dictionary of British 20th Century Painters* Frances Spalding; *Jewellery 1789–1910* Shirley Bury; *Old Roses and English Gardens* David Austin. Unsolicited synopses and ideas for books welcome. No mss.

Royalties paid quarterly as a rule, but can vary.

Anvil Press Poetry Ltd

69 King George Street, London SE10 8PX
☎0181 858 2946   Fax 0181 858 2946

Editorial Director *Peter Jay*

FOUNDED 1968 to promote English and foreign poetry, both classic and contemporary, in translation. English list includes Peter Levi and Carol Ann Duffy. Anvil has now developed to the point at which most of its new titles are new volumes by their regulars. Preliminary enquiry required for translations. Unsolicited book-length collections of poems are welcome from writers whose work has appeared in poetry magazines.

Authors' Rating Distancing himself from the aggressive marketing tactics paraded by some other houses, Peter Jay is said to be the least likely of all publishers to sign a fashionable poet for merely commercial reasons but he has had great success with younger poets.

Apollos

See **Inter-Varsity Press**

Apple

See **Quarto Publishing** under **UK Packagers**

Appletree Press Ltd

19–21 Alfred Street, Belfast BT2 8DL
☎01232 243074   Fax 01232 246756

Managing Director *John Murphy*
Senior Editor *Douglas Marshall*
Cookery Editor *Pat Scott*

FOUNDED 1974. *Publishes* cookery and other small-format gift books, plus general non-fiction of Irish and Scottish interest. TITLES *Little Cookbook* series (about 40 titles); *Ireland: The Complete Guide; Northern Ireland: The Background to the Conflict.* No unsolicited mss; send initial letter or synopsis. Appletree's London office is at 10 Barley Mow Passage, London W4 4PH (Tel: 0181–994 6477), but all editorial approaches should be sent to Belfast.

Royalties paid twice yearly in the first year, annually thereafter. For the *Little Cookbook* Series, a standard fee is paid.

Arc Publications

Nanholme Mill, Shaw Wood Road,
Todmorden, Lancashire OL14 6DA
☎01706 812338   Fax 01706 818948

Publishers *Rosemary Jones, Angela Jarman, Tony Ward*
General Editor *Tony Ward*
Associate Editors *Michael Hulse* (International), *David Morley* (UK)

FOUNDED in 1969 to specialise in the publication of contemporary poetry from new and established writers both in the UK and abroad. Runs the annual **Northern Short Story Competition** and *publishes* an anthology of winning entries. AUTHORS include Dinah Hawken (New Zealand), W.N. Herbert, Jonathan Davidson, Rose Ausländer (Austria),

Robert Gray (Australia), John Hartley Williams, Jackie Wills and Don Coles (Canada). 8 titles a year. Authors submitting material should ensure that it is compatible with the current list and should enclose s.a.e. if they wish mss to be returned.

Arena
See **Ashgate Publishing Co. Ltd**

Argus Books
See **Nexus Special Interests**

Aris & Phillips Ltd
Teddington House, Warminster, Wiltshire BA12 8PQ
☎01985 213409   Fax 01985 212910
Managing/Editorial Director *Adrian Phillips*
Editor, Hispanic Classics *Lucinda Phillips*
FOUNDED 1972 to publish books on Egyptology. A family firm which has remained independent. *Publishes* academic, classical, oriental and hispanic. About 20 titles a year. With such a highly specialised list, unsolicited mss and synopses are not particularly welcome, but synopses will be considered.
Royalties paid twice yearly.

Arkana
See **Penguin Books Ltd**

Armada
See **HarperCollins Publishers Ltd**

Arms & Armour Press
See **Cassell**

Arnefold
See **George Mann Books**

Edward Arnold
See **Hodder Headline plc**

Arrow
See **Random House UK Ltd**

Artech House
Portland House, Stag Place, London SW1E 5XA
☎0171 973 8077   Fax 0171 630 0166
Managing Director (USA) *William M. Bazzy*
Commissioning Editor *Dr Julie Lancashire*
FOUNDED 1969. European office of Artech House Inc., Boston. *Publishes* electronic engineering, especially telecommunications, computer communications, computer science,

optoelectronics and solid-state materials and devices (books, software and videos). 50–60 titles a year. Unsolicited mss and synopses considered.
Royalties paid twice yearly.

Ashford, Buchan & Enright
PO Box 20, Leatherhead, Surrey KT24 5HH
☎01483 282991   Fax 01483 281121
Managing Director *John Mole*
Approx. Annual Turnover £300,000
FOUNDED 1984. Taken over by Martins Printing Group in 1987 and became independent in January 1991. *Specialises* in travel, military history, field sports and nautical. About 10 titles a year. Unsolicited mss welcome if return postage included. Synopses and ideas for books considered.
Royalties paid twice yearly.

Authors' Rating An exciting young company with a strong sense of marketing and promotion.

Ashgate Publishing Co. Ltd
Gower House, Croft Road, Aldershot, Hampshire GU11 3HR
☎01252 331551   Fax 01252 344405
Chairman/Managing Director *Nigel Farrow*
FOUNDED 1967. *Publishes* professional and academic books in social sciences, arts and humanities. Associated companies include **Dartmouth Publishing Co. Ltd** and **Edward Elgar Publishing Ltd.**

IMPRINTS
Arena *Jo Gooderham* Social work and policy; *John Hindley* Aviation, construction and technical. **Avebury** *Sarah Markham* Research monographs on social science. **Gower** *Christopher Simpson* Business and management titles. **Scolar Press** *Nigel Farrow* Academic and specialist books on fine art, music studies, books about books, bibliographies, etc. **Variorum** *John Smedley* Collected studies on history. Unsolicited mss welcome. Synopses and ideas for books considered.
Royalties paid as per contract.

Ashmolean Museum Publications
Ashmolean Museum, Beaumont Street, Oxford OX1 2PH
☎01865 278009   Fax 01865 278018
Publisher/Editorial Head *Ian Charlton*
Approx. Annual Turnover £200,000
The Ashmolean Museum, which is wholly owned by Oxford University, was founded in 1683. The first publication appeared in 1890

but publishing did not really start in earnest until the 1960s. *Publishes* European and Oriental fine and applied arts, European archaeology and ancient history, Egyptology and numismatics, for both adult and children's markets. About 8 titles a year. No fiction, American/African art, ethnography, modern art or post-medieval history.

IMPRINTS
Ashmoleum Museum Publications and **Griffith Institute** (Egyptology imprint). TITLES *Old Master Drawings; The Ancient Romans; Principles of Egyptian Art; Camille Pissarro and His Family* and *Indian Art in Oxford* (the two most recent in the *Ashmolean Handbook Series*). No unsolicited mss; synopses and ideas welcome. *Royalties* paid annually.

Associated University Presses (AUP)
See **Golden Cockerel Press Ltd**

The Athlone Press
1 Park Drive, London NW11 7SG
☎0181 458 0888
Managing Director *Doris Southam*
Editorial Head *Brian Southam*
FOUNDED 1949 as the publishing house of the University of London. Now wholly independent, but preserves links with the University via an academic advisory board. *Publishes* archaeology, architecture, art, economics, history, medical, music, Japan, oriental, philosophy, politics, religion, science, sociology, zoology, women's/feminist issues. Anticipated developments in the near future: more emphasis on women's/feminist studies and environmental/Green issues, including medicine. About 35 titles a year. Unsolicited mss, synopses and ideas for academic books welcome. *Royalties* paid annually/twice yearly by arrangement. *Overseas associates* The Athlone Press, Atlantic Highlands, New Jersey, USA.

Atlantic Europe Publishing Co. Ltd
Greys Court Farm, Greys Court, Nr Henley on Thames, Oxon RG9 4PG
☎01491 628188   Fax 01491 628189
Directors *Dr B. J. Knapp, D. L. R. McCrae*
Closely associated, since 1990, with Earthscape Editions packaging operation. *Publishes* full-colour, highly illustrated children's non-fiction in hardback for international co-editions. Not interested in any other material. Main focus is on National Curriculum titles, especially in the fields of mathematics, science, technology, social history and geography. About 15 titles a

year. Unsolicited synopses and ideas for books welcome but s.a.e. essential for return of submissions. *Royalties* or fees paid depending on circumstance.

Attic Books
The Folly, Rhosgoch, Painscastle, Builth Wells, Powys LD2 3JY
☎01497 851205
Managing Director/Editorial Head *Jack Bowyer*
FOUNDED 1984 by its architect owners. *Publishes* books on building crafts, architecture and engineering. Mostly technical books for the industry, dealing mainly with restoration and conservation. *Royalties* paid annually.

AUP (Associated University Presses)
See **Golden Cockerel Press Ltd**

Aurum Press Ltd
25 Bedford Avenue, London WC1B 3AT
☎0171 637 3225   Fax 0171 580 2469
Chairman *André Deutsch*
Managing Director *Bill McCreadie*
Editorial Director *Piers Burnett*
FOUNDED 1977. Formerly owned by Andrew Lloyd Webber's Really Useful Group, now owned jointly by Piers Burnett, Bill McCreadie and Sheila Murphy (Marketing & Rights Director), all of whom worked together in the 70s for André Deutsch. Committed to producing high-quality, illustrated/non-illustrated adult non-fiction in the areas of general human interest, art and craft, lifestyle and travel. About 40 titles a year. *Royalties* paid twice yearly.

Authors' Rating After the buyout from Andrew Lloyd Webber's Really Useful Group in 1992, Aurum did well enough to attract outside interest. The aim now is to double the size of the business without increasing overheads.

Autumn Publishing Ltd
First Floor, North Barn, Appledram Barns, Birdham Road, Near Chichester, West Sussex PO20 7EQ
☎01243 531660   Fax 01243 774433
Managing Director *Campbell Goldsmid*
Editorial Director *Ingrid Goldsmid*
FOUNDED 1976. Publisher and packager of highly illustrated non-fiction: mainly children's, including activity books. About 20 titles

a year. Unsolicited synopses and ideas for books welcome if they come within relevant subject areas.

Payment varies according to contract; generally a flat fee.

Avebury
See **Ashgate Publishing Co. Ltd**

Babbage Press
See **Headstart History**

Baillière Tindall
See **Harcourt Brace and Company Ltd**

Balch Institute Press
See **Golden Cockerel Press Ltd**

Balnain Books
Druim House, Lochloy Road, Nairn
IV12 5LF
☎01667 452940   Fax 01667 455099
Editorial Director *Sarah Fraser*

FOUNDED 1983. Independent Scottish publishing house. *Publishes* literature, fiction, sport, holistic, horses and biography in trade hardback and paperback format. About 8 titles a year. TITLES *The Sea-King's Daughter* George Mackay Brown; *'Flower of Scotland'*, Roy Williamson, *My Father* Karen Williamson; *Thoughts of Murdo* Iain Crichton Smith; *The Key Above the Door* Maurice Walsh. No children's, educational, crime, political, military, wildlife, academic or poetry. Unsolicited mss only accepted on request following preliminary enquiry regarding suitability. Currently expanding the list into areas of non-fiction (e.g. biography, horses). Editorial consultant and packaging services offered.

Royalties paid twice yearly.

Bantam/Bantam Press
See **Transworld Publishers Ltd**

Barefoot Books Ltd
PO Box 95, Kingswood, Bristol, Avon
BS15 5BH
☎0117 9328885   Fax 0117 9328887
Managing Director *Nancy Traversy*
Publisher *Tessa Strickland*
Approx. Annual Turnover £250,000

FOUNDED in 1993. *Publishes* children's picture books, particularly stories from other cultures, myths, legends and fairy tales. 11 titles in 1994. No unsolicited mss.

Royalties paid twice yearly.

Barny Books
The Cottage, Hough on the Hill, Near
Grantham, Lincolnshire NG32 2BB
☎01400 250246
Managing Director/Editorial Head *Molly Burkett*
Business Manager *Ian Smith*
Approx. Annual Turnover £10,000

FOUNDED with the aim of encouraging new writers and illustrators. *Publishes* mainly children's books. TITLES *A Raven Called Charlie; Happy Birthday Bonko; Once Upon a Wartime* (2 vols) Molly Burkett; *Terrific Teachers* The Downs School, Compton; *The Big Sneeze* Joy Mellins; *Images; Time Call* Keith West. Too small a concern to have the staff/resources to deal with unsolicited mss. Writers with strong ideas should approach Molly Burkett by letter in the first instance. Also runs a readership and advisory service for new writers (£10 fee).

Royalties division of profits 50/50.

Authors' Rating Molly Burkett reports on a busy year culminating in the totally unexpected - a call from the Cabinet Office to say that *Jessica's Garden* and *Sheep Shandy* were 'two of the most delightful children's stories they'd seen'. There followed an invitation to Molly and all the children who had worked with her to come to London, a fitting tribute to this friendliest and gentlest of small publishers.

Baron Birch
See **The Barracuda Collection/Quotes Ltd**

The Barracuda Collection/ Quotes Ltd
The Book Barn, Church Way, Whittlebury,
Northamptonshire NN12 8XS
☎01327 858301   Fax 01327 858302
Publisher *Clive Birch*

Barracuda was formed in 1974, Quotes in 1985. *Publishes* local and natural history, country and sporting life, military, transport, church, family and institutional histories. About 30 titles a year.

IMPRINTS
The Barracuda Collection TITLES *The Book of Bacup; The Book of Aylesbury.* **Quotes in Camera** TITLES *Essex Buses; Northampton.* **Saga** launched 1987. TITLES *Murder in Old Buckinghamshire.* **Sporting & Leisure Press** launched 1976. TITLES *Palace Parade.* **Baron Birch** launched 1992. TITLES *Brighton's Music Halls; Eagles Over Water.* Synopses and ideas for

books welcome with sample mss page, extent of words and pictures.
Royalties paid annually.

Barrie & Jenkins Ltd
See **Random House UK Ltd**

Bartholomew
See **HarperCollins Publishers Ltd**

B. T. Batsford Ltd
4 Fitzhardinge Street,
London W1H 0AH
☎0171 486 8484   Fax 0171 487 4296
President *Peter Kemmis Betty*
Chief Executive *Bobby Cox*
Editorial Director *Timothy Auger*
Approx. Annual Turnover £5 million

FOUNDED in 1843 as a bookseller, and began publishing in 1874. An independent company and world leader in books on chess, arts and craft. *Publishes* non-fiction: archaeology, school reference, cinema, crafts and hobbies, numismatics, equestrian, fashion and costume, graphic design, horticulture, botany and gardening. Acquired Faber chess list in 1994. About 130 titles a year.

DIVISIONS
Arts & Crafts; **Archaeology & Ancient History**; **Chess**; **Horticulture**; **Country Sports**; **Graphic Design**.
Royalties paid twice in first year, annually thereafter.

Authors' Rating One of the last of the old independents, Batsford has survived by concentrating on its core list. Not a source of huge advances but plenty of strong sellers in the crafts and hobbies market.

Bay View Books Ltd
The Red House, 25–26 Bridgeland Street,
Bideford, Devon EX39 2PZ
☎01237 479225/421285
Fax 01237 421286
Managing Directors *Charles Herridge, Bridgid Herridge*

FOUNDED 1986. *Publishes* transport books only, including series: all-colour classic car restoration guides; A–Zs of cars, motorcycles and racing cars. About 10 titles a year.
Payment varies according to contract.

BBC Books
80 Wood Lane, London W12 0TT
☎0181 576 2399   Fax 0181 576 2858
Director Books/Audio Publishing
Christopher Weller
Editorial Directors *Sheila Ableman, Suzanne Webber*
Approx. Annual Turnover £25 million

BBC Books is a division of BBC Worldwide Publishing. *Publishes* TV tie-in titles, including books which, though linked with BBC television or radio, may not simply be the 'book of the series'. Books with no television or radio link are of little interest. About 150 titles a year.
TITLES *Delia Smith's Summer Collection; Have I Got News For You; Troubleshooter 2*.

Unsolicited mss (which come in at the rate of about 15 weekly) are rarely read. However, strong ideas well expressed will always be considered, and promising letters stand a chance of further scrutiny.

IMPRINTS
Network Books A new range of non-fiction tie-ins to TV programmes broadcast on channels other than BBC1 or BBC2. Includes cookery, gardening, crafts, plus some children's fiction. 4 titles in 1994.
BBC Penguin Launched November 1993. A co-publishing deal which gives BBC Books a mass-market paperback outlet. Output is expected to be in the region of 18–24 tie-in titles a year, in A or B format.
Royalties paid twice yearly.

Authors' Rating A safe bet for authors with accompanying television series. BBC marketing has improved out of all recognition in recent years, benefiting authors with other publishers whose works transfer to television or radio. BBC Books is the leader in the fast expanding talking books market (see article, pages 102–3, and listing under **Audio Books**).

BBC Penguin
See **BBC Books Ltd**

Bedford Square Press
See **NCVO Publications**

Bellew Publishing Co. Ltd
Nightingale Centre, 8 Balham Hill,
London SW12 9EA
☎0181 673 5611   Fax 0181 675 3542

Chairman *Anthony Rainbird*
Managing Director *Ib Bellew*
Approx. Annual Turnover £600,000

FOUNDED 1983. Publisher and packager. *Publishes* craft, art and design, fiction, illustrated non-fiction, general interest, religion and politics. About 25 titles a year. TITLES *Sagebrush & Spurs* ed. Eric Tripp; *Sing & Shout* Jim Cozens; *The Awakening of Willie Ryland* Tom Hart; *On Depiction: Critical Essays on Art* Avigdor Arikha; *Quaker Symbols* Kathleen Thomas. No unsolicited mss. Synopses with specimen chapters welcome.
Royalties paid annually.

Benn Technical Books
See **Tolley Publishing Co. Ltd**

Berg Publishers Ltd
150 Cowley Road, Oxford OX4 1JJ
☎01865 245104   Fax 01865 791165
Managing Director *Peter Cowell*
Commissioning Editor *Kathryn Earle*
Approx. Annual Turnover £600,000

Also **Oswald Wolff Books** imprint. *Publishes* scholarly books in the fields of history, social sciences and humanities. About 70 titles a year. No unsolicited mss. Synopses and ideas for books welcome.
Royalties paid annually.

Berkswell Publishing Co. Ltd
PO Box 420, Warminster, Wiltshire
BA12 9XB
☎01985 840189   Fax 01985 840189
Managing Director *John Stidolph*
Approx. Annual Turnover £250,000

FOUNDED 1974. *Publishes* illustrated books, royalty, heritage, country sports, biography and books about Wessex. No fiction. About 4 titles a year. Unsolicited mss, synopses and ideas for books welcome.
Royalties paid according to contract.

BFI Publishing
British Film Institute, 21 Stephen Street, London W1P 1PL
☎0171 255 1444   Fax 0171 436 7950
Head of Publishing *Edward Buscombe*
Approx. Annual Turnover £400,000

FOUNDED 1982. Part of the **British Film Institute**. *Publishes* academic and general film/television-related books. About 30 titles a year. TITLES *Film Classics* (series); *Script Girls* Lizzie Francke; *Encyclopedia of Indian Cinema* ed.

by Ashish Rajadhyaksha and Paul Willemen; *David Lynch* Michel Chion. Unsolicited synopses and ideas preferred to complete mss.
Royalties paid annually.

Bible Society
Stonehill Green, Westlea, Swindon, Wiltshire SN5 7DG
☎01793 418100   Fax 01793 418118
Executive Director *Neil Crosbie*
Approx. Annual Turnover £4 million

The Bible Society was founded in 1804 and was granted a royal charter in 1948. It is now part of a worldwide fellowship of Bible Societies, working in over 180 countries. A mission agency with the specific task of enabling the Church to use the Bible in her mission. *Publishes* Bibles, Bible-related resources, group study, religious education and video materials. TITLES *The Good News Bible; Just Looking; Learn New Testament Greek; Finding Faith Today.* 32 titles in 1994. Unsolicited synopses and ideas welcome. No Christian biography, fiction, poetry, general religious or commentaries.
Royalties paid twice yearly.

Clive Bingley Books
See **Library Association Publishing Ltd**

A. & C. Black (Publishers) Ltd
35 Bedford Row, London WC1R 4JH
☎0171 242 0946   Fax 0171 831 8478
Chairman *Charles Black*
Deputy Chairman *David Gadsby*
Managing Directors *Charles Black, Jill Coleman*
Approx. Annual Turnover £6.5 million

Publishes children's and educational books, including music, for 3–15-year-olds, arts and crafts, ceramics, fishing, ornithology, nautical, reference, sport, theatre and travel. About 125 titles a year. Acquisitions brought the Adlard Coles sailing list and Christopher Helm's natural history and ornithology lists into A. & C. Black's stable.

IMPRINTS **Adlard Coles; Christopher Helm**. TITLES *New Mermaid* drama series; *Who's Who; Writers' & Artists' Yearbook; Know the Game* sports series; *Blue Guides* travel series. Initial enquiry appreciated before submission of mss.
Royalties payment varies according to contract.

Black Dagger Crime
See **Chivers Press Ltd**

Black Lace
See **Virgin Publishing**

Black Spring Press Ltd
63 Harlescott Road, Nunhead, London
SE15 3DA
☎0171 639 2492   Fax 0171 639 2508
Managing Director/Editor *Simon Pettifar*
FOUNDED 1986. *Publishes* fiction, literary criticism, biography, theatre and cinema studies. About 5 titles a year. TITLES *And the Ass Saw the Angel* Nick Cave; *The Favourite Game* Leonard Cohen; *My Original Sin* Marie-Victoire Rouillier; *The Terrible News* collection of Russian short stories; *The Mordecai Trilogy* Kyril Bonfiglioli. Send proposals rather than completed mss.
Royalties paid twice yearly.

Black Swan
See **Transworld Publishers Ltd**

Blackie
See **Penguin Books Ltd**

Blackstaff Press Ltd
3 Galway Park, Dundonald, Belfast BT16 0AN
☎01232 487161   Fax 01232 489552
Director/Editorial Head *Anne Tannahill*
FOUNDED 1971. Changed hands in 1980. *Publishes* mainly, but not exclusively, Irish interest books, fiction, poetry, history, politics, illustrated and fine editions, natural history and folklore. About 25 titles a year. Unsolicited mss considered, but preliminary submission of synopsis plus short sample of writing preferred. Return postage *must* be enclosed.
Royalties paid twice yearly.

Authors' Rating Past winner of the *Sunday Times* Small Publisher of the Year Award, this Belfast publisher is noted for a strong backlist, 'wonderfully well-presented catalogues and promotional material'.

Blackwell Publishers Ltd
108 Cowley Road, Oxford OX4 1JF
☎01865 791100   Fax 01865 791347
Chairman *Nigel Blackwell*
Managing Director *René Olivieri*
FOUNDED 1922. Rapid growth since the 1970s included the establishment of a wholly owned distribution company, Marston Book Services, joint ventures with **Polity Press** and the National Computing Centre in Manchester. The focus is on international research journals and undergraduate textbooks in social sciences, business and humanities; computer-aided instruction on p.c. applications; corporate training. About 300 titles a year and over 100 journals.

DIVISIONS/IMPRINTS
Books *Philip Carpenter, Stephan Chambers, John Davey* **Business** *Richard Burton* **Journals** *Sue Corbett, Claire Andrews* **Shakespeare Head Press** *John Davey* **New Business** *Stephan Chambers.* Unsolicited synopses with specimen chapter and table of contents welcome.
Royalties paid annually. *Overseas associates* Blackwell Publishers Inc., Cambridge, Mass.; InfoSource Inc., Orlando, Fl.

Authors' Rating The nature of the business continues to change with Blackwell's takeover of fast growing finance and economics list based in the US. Gone are the days of school texts, weighty monographs and library reference. Now it is the non-academic business sector that is getting all the attention. One aim is to make an early start on electronic delivery.

Blackwell Science Ltd
Osney Mead, Oxford OX2 0EL
☎01865 206206   Fax 01865 721205
Chairman *Nigel Blackwell*
Managing Director *Robert Campbell*
Editorial Director *Peter Saugman*
Approx. Annual Turnover £60 million (Group)
FOUNDED 1939. Part of the Blackwell Group, Oxford, which has seen rapid growth since the 1970s, culminating in expansion into Europe in the late 1980s with the acquisition of Medizinische Zeitschriften Verlagsgesellschaft (MZV), Vienna; Ueberreuter Wissenschaft Verlag (now Blackwell Wissenschafts-Verlag), Berlin; Arnette, Paris; more recently, Grosse Verlag, Germany; and the academic publishing of Paul Parey. *Publishes* medical, professional and science. About 230 titles a year, plus 160 journals. TITLES *Diseases of the Liver and Biliary System* Sherlock; *Essential Immunology* Roitt; *Textbook of Dermatology* Rook. Unsolicited mss and synopses welcome.
Royalties paid annually. *Overseas subsidiaries* in USA, Australia, Paris, Berlin and Vienna; editorial offices in London and Edinburgh.

Authors' Rating Best known for publishing journals for learned societies and for highly specialist texts on subjects most of us would rather not know about, Blackwell Science has come up with an international bestseller – *Miss Smilla's Feeling for Snow* – from Danish subsidiary, Munksgaard – though here the book is published by Harvill. But don't let one swallow fool you. The core business is targeted at the higher reaches of academia with electronic projects a priority.

Blake Publishing
3 Bramber Court, 2 Bramber Road, London W14 9PB
☎0181 381 0666   Fax 0181 381 6868
Chairman *David Blake*
Managing Director *John Blake*
Approx. Annual Turnover £1 million
FOUNDED 1991 and rapidly expanding. *Publishes* fiction and mass-market non-fiction. No cookery, children's, specialist or non-commercial. 20 titles in 1994. No unsolicited mss; synopses and ideas welcome. Please enclose s.a.e.
Royalties paid twice yearly.

Authors' Rating Tabloid version of book publishing with an 'unashamedly mass-market' list. Strong on sale of serial rights.

Blandford Press
See **Cassell**

Bloodaxe Books Ltd
PO Box 1SN, Newcastle upon Tyne NE99 1SN
☎0191 232 5988   Fax 0191 222 0020
Chairman *Simon Thirsk*
Managing/Editorial Director *Neil Astley*

Publishes poetry, literature and criticism, and related titles by British, Irish, European, Commonwealth and American writers. 95 per cent of their list is poetry. About 50 titles a year. TITLES include two major anthologies, *The New Poetry* Hulse, Kennedy and Morley (eds); *Sixty Women Poets* Linda France (ed); *The Gaze of the Gorgon* Tony Harrison – winner of the **Whitbread Award** for poetry in 1992. Unsolicited poetry mss welcome. Authors of other material should write first with details of their work.
Royalties paid annually.

Authors' Rating 'The liveliest and most innovative poetry house', according to the editor of *Poetry Review*. Strong on women's poetry and on translations.

Bloomsbury Publishing Plc
2 Soho Square, London W1V 5DE
☎0171 494 2111   Fax 0171 434 0151
Chairman/Managing Director *Nigel Newton*
Publishing Directors *Liz Calder, David Reynolds, Kathy Rooney*
FOUNDED 1986 by Nigel Newton, David Reynolds, Alan Wherry and Liz Calder. Over

the following years Bloomsbury titles were to appear regularly on *The Sunday Times* bestseller list and many of its authors have gone on to win prestigious literary prizes. In 1991 Nadine Gordimer won the **Nobel Prize for Literature**, Michael Ondaatje's *The English Patient* won the 1992 **Booker Prize** and Tobias Wolff's *In Pharaoh's Army* won the 1994 **Esquire/Volvo/Waterstone's Non-Fiction Award**. *Publishes* literary fiction and non-fiction, including general reference and children's books. TITLES *The Best of Friends* Joanna Trollope; *Debatable Land* Candia McWilliam; *The Piano* Jane Campion; *Crossing the River* Caryl Phillips; *The Robber Bride* Margaret Atwood; *Thomas Hardy: The Definitive Biography* Martin Seymour-Smith; *The Unlikely Spy* Paul Henderson; *Bloomsbury Thesaurus; Guide to Human Thought; Guide to Women's Literature; Bloomsbury Classics.* Unsolicited mss and synopses welcome; no poetry.
Royalties paid twice yearly.

Authors' Rating A successful flotation brought windfalls to authors benefiting from the Bloomsbury Trust. But of longer term significance, the injection of cash via the Stock Exchange has released a wave of expansion which takes in paperback publishing and home reference. Title output is expected to increase by a third this year.

Blueprint Monographs
See **Fourth Estate Ltd**

Boatswain Press
See **Kenneth Mason Publications Ltd**

Bobcat
See **Omnibus Press**

Bodley Head
See **Random House UK Ltd**

The Book Guild Ltd
Temple House, 25–26 High Street, Lewes, East Sussex BN7 2LU
☎01273 472534   Fax 01273 476472
Chairman *George M. Nissen CBE*
Managing Director *Carol Biss*
FOUNDED 1982. *Publishes* fiction, academic, general, naval and military, biography, art, children's. Expanding paperback list. About 75 titles a year.

DIVISIONS/TITLES
Fiction *An Unreadable Love Letter* Daniel; *The Passion Principle* Lucy Abelson; *The Golden Imp*

John Atkins. **Academic** *The Odyssey* R.D. Dawe; *Monsters in the Mind* Frank Cawson; *Muse in Torment* Alex Mezey. **Art** *The Life and Work of James Ward* Oliver Beckett; *Blake, Palmer, Linnell & Co.* David Linnell. **General** *Shroud Mafia* Noel Currer-Briggs; *Tom Sayers: The Last Great Bareknuckle Champion* Alan Wright. **Naval & Military:** *All Muck, No Medals* Joan Mant; *Accidental Warrior* Geoffrey Picot; *Aegean Adventures* Michael Woodbine Parish; *At Sea Level* Geoffrey Searle. **Biography** *Voices From the Past* Herbert Levy; *View From the Shore* Roger Pilkington; *Century Story* Claudia Parsons. **Children's** *Spuddy* Pat Hill.

IMPRINTS **Temple House Books** Fiction: *Drug Squad* Brian Windmill. Non-fiction: *Colditz, Last Stop* Jack Pringle; *The Fitzroy* Sally Fiber. **Seagull Books** *Aspects of a Sculptor's Practice* Tim Threlfall. Unsolicited mss. Ideas and synopses welcome.
Royalties paid twice yearly.

Authors' Rating Trawls for authors in the small ads columns of the literary pages who may be asked to cover their own production costs.

Bookmarks Publications
265 Seven Sisters Road, Finsbury Park, London N4 2DE
☎0181 802 6145   Fax 0181 802 3835
Managing Director *Lee Humber*
Approx. Annual Turnover £75,000
FOUNDED 1979 to promote the international socialist movement. Has close links with the Socialist Workers Party and its internationally related organisations. *Publishes* politics, economics, labour history, trade unionism, international affairs. About 7 titles a year. TITLES *A Nation of Change and Novelty; Marxism and Imperialism Today; Rosa Luxemburg.* Unsolicited synopses and ideas welcome as long as they are compatible with existing policy. No unsolicited mss.
Royalties paid annually. *Overseas associates* Chicago, USA; Melbourne, Australia.

Boulevard Books
8 Aldbourne Road, London W12 0LN
☎0181 743 5278   Fax 0181 743 5278
Managing Director *Ray Keenoy*
Sales & Rights *Siân Williams*
Established to publish younger contemporary foreign writers* in translation. Currently expanding the list to include readers' guides to literature in translation. 6 titles in 1994.

DIVISONS
Latin American *Ray Keenoy* TITLES *Dragons* Caio Abreu; *Tattoo* Ednodio Quintero. **Italian** *Fiorenza Conte* TITLES *The Toy Catalogue* Sandra Petrignani; *Run!* Valeria Viganò; *Old Heaven, New Earth* Ginevra Bompiani. **Other** *Lola Rinvolucri.* **Babel Guides to Fiction in Translation** *David Treece* (Brazil & Portugal); *Tom MacCarthy* (France).
Suggestions and proposals for translations of contemporary fiction welcome. Also seeking contributors to forthcoming Babel Guides (all literatures). Foreign Film Guides in preparation.
Royalties paid twice yearly.

Bowker–Saur Ltd
Maypole House, Maypole Road, East Grinstead, West Sussex RH19 1HH
☎01342 323650   Fax 01342 330191
Managing Director *Charles Halpin*
Publishers *Geraldine Turpie*
Publisher, Electronics *John Sands*
Owned by Reed Elsevier, Bowker-Saur is the UK division of Reed Reference Publishing. *Publishes* library reference, library science, bibliography, biography, African studies, politics and world affairs. Unsolicited mss will not be read. Approach with ideas only.
Royalties paid annually.

Boxtree
2nd Floor, Broadwall House, 21 Broadwall, London SE1 9PL
☎0171 928 9696   Fax 0171 928 5632
Chairman *Peter Roche*
Managing Director *Sarah Mahaffy*
Deputy Managing Director *David Inman*
Publishing Directors *Adrian Sington, Michael Alcock*
Editorial Directors *Humphrey Price, Susanna Wadeson*
Approx. Annual Turnover £7.5 million
FOUNDED 1987. *Publishes* books linked to and about television; also video and music. About 200 titles a year. New non-fiction list added in 1992. TITLES *McCartney, Yesterday and Today* Ray Coleman; *Autobiography* Joan Collins; *Jimi Hendrix: The Ultimate Experience; Divine Magic* (Channel 4); *Turning Points; Paul Merton; Oliver Otter and His Friends* Kate Veale.
Royalties paid twice yearly.

Authors' Rating The box in Boxtree is a small screen. The living proof that publishing and television can work in harmony, Boxtree has by far the strongest list of TV tie-in books with comedians Rowan Atkinson (soon to be fronting a Mr Bean stationery range) and Paul Merton leading the bestsellers.

Marion Boyars Publishers Ltd
24 Lacy Road, London SW15 1NL
☎0181 788 9522   Fax 0181 789 8122
Managing Director/Editorial Director
Marion Boyars
Editor, Non-fiction *Ken Hollings*
FOUNDED 1975, formerly Calder and Boyars. *Publishes* architecture and design, biography and autobiography, business and industry, economics, fiction, law, literature and criticism, medical, music, philosophy, poetry, politics and world affairs, psychology, religion and theology, sociology and anthropology, theatre and drama, film and cinema, travel, women's studies. About 30 titles a year. AUTHORS include Georges Bataille, Ingmar Bergman, Heinrich Böll, Jean Cocteau, Clive Collins, Julian Green, Ivan Illich, Pauline Kael, Ken Kesey, Kenzaburo Oe, Michael Ondaatje, Hubert Selby, Igor Stravinsky, Frederic Tuten, Eudora Welty, Judith Williamson. Unsolicited mss not welcome for fiction; submissions from agents preferred. Unsolicited synopses and ideas welcome for non-fiction.
Royalties paid annually. *Overseas associates* Marion Boyars Publishers Inc., 237 East 39th Street, New York, NY 10016, USA.

Authors' Rating Where have all the intellectuals gone? Maybe not every one to Marion Boyars but her list is cerebral, to put it mildly. So beset is she by unsolicited mss that she has a mind to charge an administration fee 'by arrangement'. Who can blame her?

Boydell & Brewer Ltd
PO Box 9, Woodbridge, Suffolk IP12 3DF
☎01394 411320

Publishes non-fiction only. All books commissioned. No unsolicited material.

BPS Books
St Andrews House, 48 Princess Road East, Leicester LE1 7DR
☎0116 2549568   Fax 0116 2470787
Publications Manager *Joyce Collins*
Editor *Susan Pacitti*
Book publishing division of the British Psychological Society. *Publishes* a wide range of academic and applied psychology, including specialist monographs, textbooks for teachers, managers, doctors, nurses, social workers, and schools material; plus general psychology. 10–15 titles a year. Proposals considered.

Bracken Books
See **Studio Editions Ltd**

Brampton Publications
See **SB Publications**

Brassey's (UK) Ltd
33 John Street, London WC1N 2AT
☎0171 753 7777   Fax 0171 753 7794
Chairman *Lord Rippon*
Managing Directors *A. J. Trythan, Jenny Shaw*
Publishing Director *Jenny Shaw*
Approx. Annual Turnover £2.65 million
Began life as *Brassey's Naval Annual* in 1886 to become the most important publisher of serious defence-related material in the world. Changed hands in 1993 following the collapse of the Maxwell empire of which it was formerly part. Now owned by Robert Stephens Holdings. There are plans to build upon Brassey's well-established lists, as well as opening up new lines of activity. *Publishes* books and journals on defence, international relations, military history, maritime and aeronautical subjects and defence technology.
IMPRINTS **Brassey's (UK)**; **Brassey's (US)**; **Conway Maritime Press** naval history and ship modelling; **Putnam Aeronautical Books** technical and reference.
Royalties paid annually.

Nicholas Brealey Publishing Ltd
21 Bloomsbury Way, London WC1A 2TH
☎0171 430 0224   Fax 0171 404 8311
Managing Director *Nicholas Brealey*
FOUNDED 1992 with a backlist of major titles from The Industrial Society. Independent non-fiction publisher focusing on high-profile, practical books for business that enable, inform, entertain. *Publishes* 'readable reference' on management, law, training and human resources. TITLES *Coaching for Performance; Head to Head; Reengineering the Corporation; Global Paradox; The Frontiers of Excellence; The Fifth Discipline Fieldbook; China Wakes; Russia 2010; Snapshots from Hell.* No fiction, poetry or leisure titles. No unsolicited mss; synopses and ideas welcome.
Royalties paid twice yearly.

Authors' Rating A recent entry into the booming management book market, Nicholas Brealey looks to be succeeding in breaking away from the usual computer speak business manuals to publish information and literate texts. Lead titles have a distinct trans-Atlantic feel.

Breese Books Ltd

164 Kensington Park Road, London W11 2ER
☎0171 727 9426   Fax 0171 229 3395
Chairman/Managing Director *Martin Breese*

FOUNDED 1975 to produce specialist conjuring books and then went on to establish a more general list, linking up with German, Italian, French and US publishers. *Publishes* fiction, crime, biography, self-hypnosis, bibliography, meditation, ESP and related fields, music and conjuring titles. About 20 titles a year.

IMPRINTS
Breese Books TITLES *Even if They Fail* David Holbrook; *Exit Mr Punch* Mignon Warner; *Foxtrot, Oscar, X-Ray* James Neat. **Breese Books Paperbacks** TITLES *Self-hypnosis and Other Mind Expanding Techniques* Charles Tebbetts; *The Gourmet Detective* Peter King; *The Dreamer's Guide* series.

Unsolicited mss not welcome but synopses plus 10 sample mss pages will be considered; if rejected and time allows reasons will be given. 'Sadly we cannot afford to promote first novelists unless the material is of the quality of Graham Greene's writing – before submitting anything writers should consider whether their work can be so compared!'

Royalties paid twice yearly. *Distributed* by Clipper Distribution.

Authors' Rating Quality publisher with a clear idea of what it wants to achieve.

Brimax Books

See **Reed International Books**

Bristol Classical Press

See **Gerald Duckworth & Co. Ltd**

British Academic Press

See **I. B. Tauris & Co. Ltd**

The British Academy

20–21 Cornwall Terrace, London NW1 4QP
☎0171 487 5966   Fax 0171 224 3807
Publications Officer *J. M. H. Rivington*

FOUNDED 1901. The primary body for promoting scholarship in the humanities, the Academy publishes many series stemming from its own long-standing research projects, or series of lectures and conference proceedings. Main subjects include history, philosophy and archaeology. About 10–15 titles a year.

SERIES *Auctores Britannici Medii Aevi; Early English Church Music; Fontes Historiae Africanae; Records of Social and Economic History.* Proposals for these series are welcome and are forwarded to the relevant project committees. The British Academy is a registered charity and does not publish for profit.

Royalties paid only when titles have covered their costs.

British Association for Local History

See **Phillimore & Co. Ltd**

The British Library

Marketing & Publishing Office, 41 Russell Square, London WC1B 3DG
☎0171 412 7704   Fax 0171 412 7768
Managing Director *Jane Carr*
Publishing Manager *David Way*
Approx. Annual Turnover £750,000

FOUNDED 1979 as the publishing arm of The British Library's London Collections to publish works based on the historic collections and related subjects. *Publishes* bibliographical reference, manuscript studies, illustrated books based on the Library's collections, and book arts. TITLES *Russian Avant-Garde Books 1917–34; Discoveries and Inventions* series; *Medieval Maps; A History of Writing; Anglo-Saxon Manuscripts; The Doves Bindery*. About 30 titles a year. Unsolicited mss, synopses and ideas welcome if related to the history of the book, book arts or bibliography. No fiction or general non-fiction.

Royalties paid annually.

British Museum Press

46 Bloomsbury Street, London WC1B 3QQ
☎0171 323 1234   Fax 0171 436 7315
Managing Director *Patrick Wright*
Head of Publishing *Emma Way*

The book publishing division of British Museum Publications Ltd. FOUNDED 1973; relaunched 1991 as British Museum Press. *Publishes* ancient history, archaeology, ethnography, art history, exhibition catalogues, guides, children's books, and all official publications of the British Museum. Around 50 titles a year. TITLES *Masks, the Art of Expression; Magic in Ancient Egypt; The Decorated Style; The Parthenon Frieze; 8000 Years of Ornament; French Porcelain*. Synopses and ideas for books welcome.

Royalties paid twice yearly.

The Brockhampton Press

See **Hodder Headline plc**

W. C. B. Brown

See **Times Mirror International Publishers Ltd**

Brown, Son & Ferguson Ltd
4–10 Darnley Street, Glasgow G41 2SD
☎0141 429 1234   Fax 0141 420 1694
Chairman/Joint Managing Director
T. Nigel Brown
FOUNDED 1850. *Specialises* in nautical textbooks, both technical and non-technical. Also Boy Scout/Girl Guide books, and Scottish one-act/three-act plays. Unsolicited mss, synopses and ideas for books welcome.
Royalties paid annually.

Brown Watson Ltd
The Old Mill, 76 Fleckney Road, Kibworth Beauchamp, Leicestershire LE8 0HG
☎0116 2796333   Fax 0116 2796303
Managing Director *Michael B. McDonald*
FOUNDED 1980. *Publishes* children's books only. About 150 titles a year. Most books are commissioned. Unsolicited mss and synopses are not welcome.

Authors' Rating Children's books for the cheaper end of the market. Authors must work fast to make money.

Bucknell
See **Golden Cockerel Press Ltd**

Burns & Oates
See **Search Press**

Business Education Publishers Ltd
Leighton House, 10 Grange Crescent, Sunderland, Tyne & Wear SR2 7BN
☎0191 567 4963   Fax 0191 514 3277
Managing Director *P. M. Callaghan*
Approx. Annual Turnover £350,000
FOUNDED 1981. *Publishes* business education, economics and law for BTEC and GNVQ reading. Currently expanding into further and higher education, computing, community health services, travel and tourism, occasional papers for institutions and local government administration. Unsolicited mss and synopses welcome.
Royalties paid annually.

Butterworth
See **Reed International Books**

Cadogan Books plc
London House, Park Gate Road, London SW11 4NQ
☎0171 738 1961   Fax 0171 924 5491
Chairman *Bill Colegrave*
Publisher *Rachel Fielding*

Approx. Annual Turnover £1.2 million
Publishes the *Cadogan Travel Guide* series, and chess and bridge titles. About 55 titles a year. No unsolicited mss; send introductory letter with synopsis only. Synopses and ideas welcome.
Royalties paid twice yearly.

Calder Publications Ltd
179 Kings Cross Road, London WC1X 9BZ
☎0171 833 1300
Chairman/Managing Director/Editorial Head *John Calder*
Formerly John Calder (Publishers) Ltd. A publishing company which has grown around the tastes and contacts of John Calder, the iconoclast of the literary establishment. The list has a reputation for controversial and opinion-forming publications; Samuel Beckett is perhaps the most prestigious name. The list includes all of Beckett's prose and poetry. *Publishes* autobiography, biography, drama, literary fiction, literary criticism, music, opera, poetry, politics, sociology. AUTHORS Marguerite Duras, Erich Fried, Trevor Hoyle, P. J. Kavanagh, Robert Pinget, Alain Robbe-Grillet, Nathalie Sarraute, Julian Semyonov, Claude Simon, Howard Barker (plays), ENO opera guides. All approaches must be accompanied by s.a.e. if a reply is required. No unsolicited material.
Royalties paid annually.

Authors' Rating Operating in Paris and London and points between, John Calder is said to be 'overflowing with geniuses and eccentric talents'. But according to the publisher, times are hard and there is never enough money to pay all the bills. He is much revered in France as a free and far-ranging intellectual.

California University Press
See **University Presses of California, Columbia & Princeton Ltd**

Cambridge University Press
The Edinburgh Building, Shaftesbury Road, Cambridge CB2 2RU
☎01223 312393   Fax 01223 315052
Chief Executive *A. K. Wilson*
Managing Director, Publishing *R. J. Mynott*
The oldest press in the world. Over the last few years CUP has been diversifying into reference, electronic, legal and medical publishing and has expanded its activities in Europe, the Far East, Latin America, Australia and the USA. Recent developments include a CUP bookshop in central Cambridge; editorial offices at Stanford University, California, Cape Town, South

Africa and Barcelona; new offices in Bologna and Mexico; the acquisition of **Grotius Publications** (International Law); major National Curriculum and ELT course publications; Cambridge Encyclopedia programme; the Cambridge International Dictionary of English; low price editions for the developing world; new Cambridge Guides and Illustrated Histories; the new paperback imprint **Canto**. *Publishes* academic/educational books for international English-language markets, at all levels from primary school to postgraduate. Also bibles and over 100 academic journals. Over 20,000 authors in 100 different countries, and about 1500 new titles a year. No fiction or poetry.

GROUPS
Bibles *L. M. Hieatt* **ELT** *C. J. F. Hayes* **Humanities** *A. M. C. Brown* **Journals** *C. Guettler* **Reference** *A. du Plessis* **Education** *S. A. Seddon* **Social Sciences** *M. Y. Holdsworth* **Sciences and Electronics Publishing** *S. Mitton.* No unsolicited mss; synopses and ideas for books considered.
Royalties paid twice yearly.

Authors' Rating Welcome news for authors is that CUP has now moved to twice yearly royalty payments and is showing greater flexibility on the touchy question of copyright. Famed for its international distribution network (170 countries), CUP is exploiting its formidable backlist with modestly-priced reprints of revered titles.

Camden Large Print
See **Chivers Press Ltd**

David Campbell Publishers Ltd
79 Berwick Street, London W1V 3PF
☎0171 287 0035   Fax 0171 287 0038
Chairman *Alewyn Birch*
Managing Director *David Campbell*
Approx. Annual Turnover £2.4 million

Independent publishing house. FOUNDED 1990 with the acquisition of **Everyman's Library** (established 1906) bought from **J. M. Dent**. *Publishes* classics of world literature and travel guides. AUTHORS include Austen, Bulgakov, Coward, Forster, Joyce, Mann, Nabokov, Orwell, Tolstoy, Waugh and Yeats. No unsolicited mss; ideas welcome.
Royalties paid annually.

Authors' Rating Everyman Library, founded to produce cheap, pocket-size volumes of classic literature for every kind of reader, ended up

on a backwater under Weidenfeld until David Campbell and Mark Bicknell raised £1 million to fund its acquisition and relaunch. The publishing brief obviously excludes new authors – unless they feel themselves to be associated with instant classical status.

Campbell Books
See **Macmillan Publishers Ltd**

Canongate Books Ltd
14 High Street, Edinburgh EH1 1TE
☎0131 557 5111   Fax 0131 557 5211
Joint Managing Directors *Jamie Byng, Hugh Andrew*
Approx. Annual Turnover £500,000

FOUNDED 1973. Independent again, following a management buyout in September 1994. *Publishes* general fiction and non-fiction, children's fiction (age 8+), and Scottish interest. Also have an audio list (see under **Audio Books**).
IMPRINTS **Canongate Classics** adult paperback series; **Kelpie** children's paperback fiction series; **Payback Press** Afro-American, Black orientated fiction and non-fiction; music, history, etc. About 40 titles a year. Synopses preferred to complete mss.
Royalties paid twice yearly.

Authors' Rating There were worries about Canongate after serious losses in 1993 and the decision of its parent company, the distributor Albany, to leave publishing to the publishers. But a buyout from receivership led by Jamie Byng and Hugh Andrew has led to some promising early results. If there is any justice, this independent Scottish publisher will survive and thrive.

The Canterbury Press Norwich/Chansitor Publications
St Mary's Works, St Mary's Plain, Norwich, Norfolk NR3 3BH
☎01603 616563/Chansitor 615995
Fax 01603 624483
Chairman *Very Revd Dr Henry Chadwick KBE*
Publisher *G. A. Knights*

Canterbury Press Norwich is an imprint of **Hymns Ancient & Modern Ltd**, which owns the weekly publication *Church Times*. *Publishes* Church of England doctrine, theology, history and associated topics, music and liturgy. About 20 titles a year. Also publishes the *Church Pulpit Year Book* and *The Sign* (a monthly insert for the Church of England parish magazines) under the aegis of **Chansitor Publications**. Synopses and ideas welcome. No complete mss.

Royalties paid annually.

Canto
See **Cambridge University Press**

Jonathan Cape Ltd
See **Random House UK Ltd**

Carcanet Press Ltd
402 Corn Exchange Buildings, Manchester M4 3BQ
☎0161 834 8730   Fax 0161 832 0084
Chairman *Kate Gavron*
Managing Director/Editorial Director *Michael Schmidt*

Since 1969 Carcanet has grown from an undergraduate hobby into a substantial venture. Robert Gavron bought the company in 1983 and has established strong Anglo-European links. *Publishes* poetry, academic, literary biography, fiction in translation, memoirs and translations. About 40 titles a year, including the *P. N. Review* (six issues yearly). AUTHORS John Ashbery, Edwin Morgan, Elizabeth Jennings, Iain Crichton Smith, Natalia Ginzburg, Stuart Hood, Leonardo Sciascia, Christine Brooke-Rose, Pier Paolo Pasolini, C. H. Sisson, Donald Davie.

Royalties paid annually.

Authors' Rating One of the leaders of the poetry revival in the eighties, Carcanet shows how quality can be profitable. William Boyd says of Carcanet that it is 'everything an independent publisher should be'.

Carlton Books Ltd
20 St Anne's Court, Wardour Street, London W1V 3AW
☎0171 734 7338   Fax 0171 434 1196
Managing Director *Jonathan Goodman*

FOUNDED 1992. Owned by Carlton Communications, Carlton books are aimed at the mass market for subjects such as computer games, popular science and rock'n'roll. *Publishes* illustrated leisure and entertainment. Prime UK customers include the Book Club and W H Smith. A second arm of the company, established late 1992, was set up to create a promotional books business. No unsolicited mss; synopses and ideas welcome.

Royalties paid twice yearly.

Frank Cass & Co Ltd
Newbury House, 890–900 Eastern Avenue, Newbury Park, Ilford, Essex IG2 7HH
☎0181 599 8866   Fax 0181 599 0984
Managing Director *Frank Cass*
Editorial Head *David Michael*

Publishes Africa, development, strategic and military studies, education, history, literature, Middle East, politics and world affairs plus over 40 academic journals. TITLES *Anwar Sadat: Visionary Who Dared* Joseph Finklestone; *The Global Sports Arena: Athletic Talent Migration in an Interdependent World* eds. John Bale and Joseph Maguire; *Policing Politics: Security Intelligence and the Liberal Democratic State* Peter Gill.

DIVISIONS
Woburn Press Educational list. TITLES *Educational Reconstruction: The 1944 Education Act and the 21st Century* Gary McCulloch; *The State and Higher Education* eds. Brian Salter and Ted Tapper.
　　Vallentine Mitchell/Jewish Chronicle Publications Books of Jewish interest. TITLES *Will We Have Jewish Grandchildren? Jewish Continuity and How to Achieve It* Chief Rabbi Dr Jonathan Sacks; *A World Apart: The Story of the Chasidim in Britain* Rabbi Harry Rabinowicz; *Library of Holocaust Testimonies* series: *A Cat Called Adolf* Trude Levi; *Jewish Year Book; Jewish Travel Guide*. Unsolicited mss considered but synopsis with covering letter preferred.

Royalties paid annually.

Cassell
Wellington House, 125 Strand, London WC2R 0BB
☎0171 420 5555   Fax 0171 240 7261
Chairman/Managing Director *Philip Sturrock*
Approx. Annual Turnover £20 million

FOUNDED 1848 by John Cassell. Bought by Collier Macmillan in 1974, then by CBS Publishing Europe in 1982. Finally returned to independence in 1986 as Cassell plc and a string of acquisitions followed: Tycooly's book publishing division; Link House Books (now Blandford Publishing Ltd); Mansell; then Mowbray and Ward Lock, publisher of Mrs Beeton (in print continuously since 1861); and finally Victor Gollancz Ltd in 1992. *Publishes* business, education and academic, general non-fiction, primary and secondary school books, poetry, religion. About 600 titles a year.

DIVISIONS
General *Alan Gordon Walker*, Managing Director
Academic & Religious *Stephen Butcher*

IMPRINTS

Cassell *Clare Howell* (general books) TITLES *Cassell Concise English Dictionary; French Country Crafts* Marie-Pierre Moine; *Brewer's Politics – A Dictionary of Phrase and Fable* Nicholas Comfort; *Wisley Handbooks.*

Cassell (academic books) and **Mansell** TITLES *Reflective Teaching in Primary Schools* Pollard; *Practical Counselling Skills* Nelson-Jones; *Index of English Literary Manuscripts* Peter Beal.

Arms & Armour Press *Roderick Dymott* TITLES *The Royal Air Force: An Illustrated History* Michael Armitage; *Waterloo: New Perspectives* David Hamilton-William.

Blandford Press *Alison Goff* TITLES *Insects in Flight* John Brackenbury; *A Dictionary of Dream Symbols* Eric Ackroyd; *Play the Game Series.*

Studio Vista *Clare Howell* TITLES *The Beginner's Guide to Painting in Watercolour* Jenny Rodwell.

Ward Lock *Alison Goff* TITLES *How to be a Supergardener* Alan Titchmarsh; *Mrs Beeton's Book of Cookery and Household Management* Bridget Jones (ed.).

Victor Gollancz *Liz Knight* TITLES *Fever Pitch* Nick Hornby; *Men at Arms* Terry Pratchett; *Official and Confidential* A. Summers.

Geoffrey Chapman *Ruth McCurry* TITLES *Cardinal Hume and the Changing Face of English Catholicism* Peter Stanford; *New Jerome Biblical Commentary* Brown, Fitzmyer, Murphy (eds.).

Mowbray *Ruth McCurry* TITLES *Robert Runcie* Adrian Hastings; *Celebrating Common Prayer.*

New Orchard Editions *Alan Smith* TITLES *Natural History of Britain's Coasts* Eric Foothill; *One Hour Garden* Laurence Fleming.

Leicester University Press *Janet Joyce* (history archaeology, museum and cultural studies) TITLES *The Origins of Anglo Saxon Kingdoms; The Archaeology of Society in the Holy Land.*

Pinter Publishers Ltd *Janet Joyce* (social sciences and humanities) TITLES *Globalisation and Interdependence in the International Political Economy; An Introduction to Systemic Functional Linguistics.*

Royalties payment depends on sales potential and varies between imprints; generally twice yearly, but annually for Arms & Armour Press.

Authors' Rating Dedicated to growth by acquisition, Cassell has a formidable reputation for reviving companies once thought to be on their last legs. Ward Lock, Gollancz and Blandford are among the famous names now recovering under Cassell management. Publishing policy is aimed towards a higher proportion of general non-fiction titles.

Catesby Press
See **Headstart History**

Kyle Cathie Ltd
20 Vauxhall Birdge Road, London SW1V 2SA
☎0171 973 9710   Fax 0171 821 9258
Publisher/Managing Director *Kyle Cathie*
FOUNDED 1990 to publish and promote 'books we have personal enthusiasm for'. *Publishes* non-fiction: history, natural history, health, biography, food and drink, craft, gardening and reference. TITLES *50 Great Curries of India* Camellia Panjabi; *Jekka's Complete Herb Book* Jekka McVicar; *The Complete Verse of Rudyard Kipling.* About 40 titles a year. No unsolicited mss. 'Synopses and ideas are considered in the fields in which we publish.'
Royalties paid twice yearly.

Authors' Rating A refugee from big-time publishing who has made good as a small independent producing books which really matter.

Catholic Truth Society
192 Vauxhall Bridge Road, London SW1V 1PD
☎0171 834 4392   Fax 0171 630 1124
Chairman *Rt. Rev. Mgr. Peter Smith*
Managing Director *David Murphy*
Approx. Annual Turnover £500,000
FOUNDED originally in 1869 and re-founded in 1884. *Publishes* religious books – Roman Catholic and ecumencial. 35 titles in 1994. TITLES *My Lourdes Diary* Ellen Ryder; *The Human Face of Jesus* Bernard O'Connor; *Saints' Names for Boys and Girls* J. J. Dwyer; *Prayer in a Busy Life* Bishop John Crowley; *The Second World War* Pope John Paul II. Unsolicited mss, synopses and ideas welcome if appropriate to their list.
Royalties paid annually.

Causeway Press Ltd
PO Box 13, 129 New Court Way, Ormskirk, Lancashire L39 5HP
☎01695 576048   Fax 01695 570714
Chairman/Managing Director
    M. Haralambos
Approx. Annual Turnover £1.4 million
FOUNDED in 1982. *Publishes* educational textbooks only. 15 titles in 1994. TITLES *Causeway*

Maths Series; Discovering History Series; Economics/Business Studies; Sociology: A New Approach; Causeway GNVQ: Intermediate Business. Unsolicited mss, synopses and ideas welcome.
Royalties paid annually.

CBA Publishing

Bowes Morrell House, 111 Walmgate, York YO1 2UA
☎01904 671417   Fax 01904 671384

Managing Editor *Christine Pietrowski*
Approx. Annual Turnover £25,000

Publishing arm of the **Council for British Archaeology**. *Publishes* academic archaeology reports, practical handbooks, yearbook, *British Archaeology* (monthly newsletter), monographs, archaeology and education. TITLES *The Spitalfields Project; Roman Towns: The Wheeler Inheritance; Environment and Economy in Anglo-Saxon England; The Jewish Burial Ground at Jewbury; Fixtures and Fittings in Dated Buildings 1567–1763.*
Royalties not paid.

CBD Research Ltd

Chancery House, 15 Wickham Road, Beckenham, Kent BR3 2JS
☎0181 650 7745   Fax 0181 650 0768

Chairman *G. P. Henderson*
Managing Director *S. P. A. Henderson*
Approx. Annual Turnover £300,000

FOUNDED 1961. *Publishes* directories and other reference/guides to sources of information. Increased output over the last few years. About 8 titles a year planned. No fiction.
IMPRINT **Chancery House Press** non-fiction of an esoteric/specialist nature for 'serious researchers and the dedicated hobbyist'. Unsolicited mss, synopses and ideas welcome.
Royalties paid quarterly.

Centaur Press

Fontwell, Arundel, West Sussex BN18 0TA
☎01243 543302

Managing Director *Jon Wynne-Tyson*

FOUNDED 1954. A one-man outfit publishing some 20 titles a year at its peak. Then became increasingly preoccupied with humane education and has reduced output to around 5 titles a year. After a semi-dormant period in the 1980s, Centaur went on to launch *The Kinship Library*, a series on the philosophy, politics and application of humane education, with special focus on the subject of animal rights and its relevance to the human condition.

IMPRINT **Linden Press** (no connection with **Simon & Schuster**'s later adoption). TITLES *Victims of Science; The Universal Kinship; Publishing Your Own Book.* No unsolicited mss. New titles are commissioned.

Authors' Rating Given the limited range of its own output it may seem appropriate that Centaur offers a useful guide to *Publishing Your Own Book* (£3.50, revised edition).

Century Books

See **Random House UK Ltd**

Chadwyck-Healey Ltd

The Quorum, Barnwell Road, Cambridge CB5 8SW
☎01223 215512   Fax 01223 215513

Chairman *Sir Charles Chadwyck-Healey*
Editorial Head *Alison Moss*

FOUNDED 1973. Expansion into Europe and the USA followed in the 1970s and 1980s. *Publishes* on microform and CD-ROM, with a few reference works/guides to their own microform collections. No monographs. About 50 titles a year. TITLES *The English Satirical Print; Theatre in Focus; Index of Manuscripts in The British Library.* No unsolicited mss. Synopses and ideas welcome for reference works only.
Royalties paid annually.

Authors' Rating More than half the business is electronic with output ranging from a four CD collection of all published English poets from Saxon times to 1900 (at £25,000) to a forthcoming complete works of Goethe, the equivalent of 142 volumes. Courting other publishers to bring out electronic editions of modern literature.

Chambers Harrap Ltd

See **Larousse plc**

Chancery House Press

See **CBD Research Ltd**

Chansitor Publications Ltd

See **The Canterbury Press Norwich/Chansitor Publications**

Chapman

4 Broughton Place, Edinburgh EH1 3RX
☎0131 557 2207   Fax 0131 556 9565

Managing Editor *Joy Hendry*

A venture devoted to publishing works by the best of the Scottish writers, both up-and-coming and established, published in *Chapman*

magazine, Scotland's leading literary quarterly. 'We intend to expand publishing activities considerably over the next two years and are now publishing a wider range of works though the broad policy stands.' *Publishes* poetry, drama, short stories, books of contemporary importance in 20th-century Scotland. About 4 titles a year. TITLES *Carlucco and the Queen of Hearts; The Blasphemer* George Rosie; *Gold of Kildonan; Songs of the Grey Coast* George Gunn; *The Collected Shorter Poems* Tom Scott. No unsolicited mss; synopses and ideas for books welcome.
Royalties paid.

Geoffrey Chapman
See **Cassell**

Paul Chapman Publishing Ltd
144 Liverpool Road, London N1 1LA
☎0171 609 5315   Fax 0171 700 1057
Managing Director *Paul R. Chapman*
Editorial Director *Marianne Lagrange*

Publishes business, management, accountancy and finance, education, geography, environment, planning and economics, for the academic and professional markets.
Royalties paid twice yearly.

Chapmans Publishers
See **Orion Publishing Group**

Chatto & Windus Ltd
See **Random House UK Ltd**

Cherrytree Press Children's Books
See **Chivers Press Ltd**

Child's Play (International) Ltd
Ashworth Road, Bridgemead, Swindon, Wiltshire SN5 7YD
☎01793 616286   Fax 01793 512795
Chairman *Michael Twinn*

FOUNDED 1972. This Swindon-based publisher has pioneered learning-through-play since the early days of its inception. *Publishes* children's books: picture books, fiction, science, art, activity books and dictionaries. TITLES *Dear Santa; Big Hungry Bear; Percy's Face Paint Party; Ten in a Bed; Wally Whale; One Odd Old Owl.* Unsolicited mss welcome. Send s.a.e. for return or response. Expect to wait 1–2 months for a reply.
Royalties payment varies according to contract.

Chivers Press Ltd
Windsor Bridge Road, Bath, Avon BA2 3AX
☎01225 335336   Fax 01225 443005
Chairman *Roger H. Lewis*
Managing Director *Simon D. Gibbs*

Part of the Gieves Group. *Publishes* reprints for libraries mainly, in large print editions, including biography and autobiography, children's, crime, fiction, complete and unabridged, and spoken word cassettes. No unsolicited material.

IMPRINTS
Chivers Large Print; Gunsmoke Westerns; Galaxy Children's Large Print; Camden Large Print; Paragon Softcover Large Print; Cherrytree Press Children's Books; Windsor Large Print; Black Dagger Crime. Chivers Audio Books (see under Audio Books.
Royalties paid twice yearly.

Christian Focus Publications
Geanies House, Fearn, Tain, Ross-shire IV20 1TW
☎01862 87541   Fax 01862 87699
Chairman *R. W. M. Mackenzie*
Managing Director *William Mackenzie*
Editorial Head *Malcolm Maclean*
Approx. Annual Turnover £500,000

FOUNDED 1979 to produce children's books for the co-edition market. Now a major producer of Christian books. *Publishes* Christianity, adult and children's, including some fiction. About 30 titles a year. Unsolicited mss, synopses and ideas welcome from Christian writers. Now entering other English-speaking markets, for example, Australia, USA, Canada, South Africa.
Royalties paid twice yearly.

Churchill Livingstone
Robert Stevenson House, 1–3 Baxter's Place, Leith Walk, Edinburgh EH1 3AF
☎0131 556 2424   Fax 0131 558 1278
Managing Director *Andrew Stevenson*
Publishing Director *Jennifer Mitchell*
Director, Nursing and Allied Health *Peter Shepherd*
Publishing Manager *Timothy Horne*

Formed from the amalgamation of E. & S. Livingstone and J. & A. Churchill in the early 1970s. Now part of Pearson Professional. *Publishes* books, journals and loose-leaf material in medicine, nursing and allied health matters, plus complementary therapies. About 150 titles a year. No unsolicited mss. Synopses and ideas welcome.

Royalties paid annually. *Overseas associates* worldwide.

Authors' Rating Churchill Livingstone remains the leading medical publisher.

Cicerone Press

2 Police Square, Milnthorpe, Cumbria
LA7 7PY
☎015395 62069   Fax 015395 63417
Managing Director *Dorothy Unsworth*
Editorial Director *Walt Unsworth*

FOUNDED 1969. Guidebook publisher for outdoor enthusiasts. About 30 titles a year. No fiction or poetry. TITLES *Mountain Walks on the Costa Blanca; Border Pubs & Inns – A Walker's Guide; London Theme Walks; The High Tatras.* No unsolicited mss; synopses and ideas considered.
Royalties paid twice yearly.

Clarendon Press
See **Oxford University Press**

Claridge Press

33 Canonbury Park South, London N1 2JW
☎0171 226 7791   Fax 0171 354 0383
Chairman/Managing Director/Editorial Head *Roger Scruton*

FOUNDED 1987. Developed from the quarterly *Salisbury Review* (see under **Magazines**). *Publishes* current affairs – political, philosophical and sociological – from a right-wing viewpoint. SERIES *Thinkers of our Time.* TITLES *Falsification of the Good; Measure of Man; Understanding Youth; Some Turn to Mecca to Pray: Islamic Values in the Modern World.* Unsolicited mss welcome within given subject areas.
Royalties paid according to contract.

Authors' Rating As the only house devoted to publishing the works of conservative thinkers, Claridge proclaims itself to be 'Britain's most backward-looking publisher'.

Robin Clark
See **Quartet Books**

T. & T. Clark

59 George Street, Edinburgh EH2 2LQ
☎0131 225 4703   Fax 0131 220 4260
Managing Director/Editorial Head *Geoffrey Green*

FOUNDED 1821. *Publishes* religion, theology, law and philosophy, for academic and professional markets. About 35 titles a year, including journals. TITLES *Church Dogmatics* Karl Barth; *A*

Textbook of Christian Ethics ed. Robin Gill; *Scottish Law Directory; The Law of Arbitration in Scotland* R. L. C. Hunter. Unsolicited mss, synopses and ideas for books welcome.
Royalties paid annually.

James Clarke & Co.

PO Box 60, Cambridge CB1 2NT
☎01223 350865   Fax 01223 66951
Managing Director *Adrian Brink*

Parent company of **Lutterworth Press**. *Publishes* scholarly and academic works, mainly theological, directory and reference titles. TITLES *The Encyclopedia of the Early Church; The Libraries' Directory.* Approach in writing with ideas in the first instance.

Clever Clogs
See **Henderson Publishing plc**

Clio Press Ltd
See **ABC–Clio International**

Richard Cohen Books Ltd

The Basement Offices, 7 Manchester Square, London W1M 5RE
☎0171 935 2099   Fax 0171 935 2199
Chairman/Managing Director *Richard Cohen*
Approx. Annual Turnover £1 million

FOUNDED in 1994. *Publishes* fiction, biography, current affairs, travel, history, politics, the arts, and sport. First titles published in 1995 with plans to expand from 20 books a year to 30. No erotica, DIY, children's, reference, science fiction, fantasy, or historical romance.

DIVISIONS **RCB General Books** *Richard Cohen* TITLES *Michael Redgrave, My Father* Corin Redgrave; *Autobiography* David Platt; *Lucien Freud* Nigel Jones; *Mrs Rochester* Emma Tennant; *John Osborne* Peter Whitebrook. No unsolicited mss; synopses and ideas welcome.
Royalties paid twice yearly.

Authors' Rating A brave venture – a new general publishing house set up by an editor who inspires author loyalty. Indeed, eight of his authors have actually invested in the company. Up to 20 titles are promised for the first year.

Frank Coleman Publishing Ltd

Enterprise Way, Maulden Road, Flitwick, Bedfordshire MK45 5BW
☎01525 712261   Fax 01525 718205
Managing Director *Neil Goldman*
Approx. Annual Turnover £100,000

Publishes children's books. Unsolicited mss, synopses and ideas welcome.
Royalties paid annually.

Peter Collin Publishing Ltd
1 Cambridge Road, Teddington, Middlesex TW11 8DT
☎0181 943 3386   Fax 0181 943 1673
Chairman *P. H. Collin*
FOUNDED 1985. *Publishes* dictionaries only, including specialised dictionaries in English for students and specialised bilingual dictionaries for translators (French, German, Swedish, Spanish, Greek). About 5 titles a year. Synopses and ideas welcome. No unsolicited mss; copy must be supplied on disk.
Royalties paid twice yearly.

Collins
See **HarperCollins Publishers Ltd**

Collins & Brown
London House, Great Eastern Wharf, Parkgate Road, London SW11 4NQ
☎0171 924 2575   Fax 0171 924 7725
Chairman *Cameron Brown*
Managing Director *Mark Collins*
Approx. Annual Turnover £4.75 million
FOUNDED 1989. Independent publisher. *Publishes* illustrated non-fiction: practical photography, crafts, gardening, illustrated letters and history. No fiction, children's, poetry or local interest. About 50 titles a year.
    No unsolicited mss; outlines with s.a.e. only.
Royalties paid twice yearly.

Columbia University Press
See **University Presses of California, Columbia & Princeton Ltd**

Condor
See **Souvenir Press Ltd**

Conran Octopus
See **Reed International Books**

Constable & Co. Ltd
3 The Lanchesters, 162 Fulham Palace Road, London W6 9ER
☎0181 741 3663   Fax 0181 748 7562
Chairman/Managing Director *Benjamin Glazebrook*
Editorial Director *Carol O'Brien*
Approx. Annual Turnover £3.3 million
FOUNDED in 1890 by Archibald Constable, a grandson of Walter Scott's publisher. Controlling interest was bought by Benjamin

Glazebrook in 1967 and the remaining 48% was purchased by Hutchinson, now owned by **Random House**, in 1968. A small but select publisher whose list includes Muriel Spark and John Julius Norwich. *Publishes* archaeology, architecture and design, biography and autobiography, cookery, fiction, guidebooks, history and antiquarian, natural history, psychology, sociology and anthropology, travel and topography, wines and spirits. About 75 titles a year. TITLES *Curriculum Vitae* Muriel Spark; *The Catholic Families* Mark Bence-Jones; *Yesterday Came Suddenly* Francis King. Unsolicited mss, synopses and ideas for books welcome.
Royalties paid twice yearly.

Authors' Rating Said by the **Society of Authors** to be the only publisher ready to take on the entire cost of having an index professionally prepared. Usually the cost is shared with an author. Also distinguished by paying authors at least two-thirds of income from the sale of paperback rights.

Consultants Bureau
See **Plenum Publishing Ltd**

Consumers' Association
See **Which? Books/Consumers' Association**

Conway Maritime Press
See **Brassey's (UK) Ltd**

Leo Cooper/Pen & Sword Books Ltd
190 Shaftesbury Avenue, London WC2H 8JL
☎0171 836 3141   Fax 0171 240 9247
Chairman *Sir Nicholas Hewitt*
Managing Director *Leo Cooper*
FOUNDED 1990 following the acquisition of the Leo Cooper imprint from Octopus Publishing. *Publishes* military history, naval and aviation history, autobiography and biography. About 40 titles a year. Unsolicited synopses and ideas welcome; no unsolicited mss.
Royalties paid twice yearly. *Associated company* **Wharncliffe Publishing Ltd**.

Corgi
See **Transworld Publishers Ltd**

Cornerhouse Publications
70 Oxford Street, Manchester M1 5NH
☎0161 237 9662   Fax 0161 237 9664
Publications Manager *Alison Buchan*

Approx. Annual Turnover £150,000

Publishing activity of Manchester's film and visual arts centre, Cornerhouse. FOUNDED 1987. Winner of *The Sunday Times* Small Publisher of the Year Award in 1990. *Publishes* illustrated books and critical texts on the visual arts, photography, design and media. About 12 titles a year. Unsolicited approaches welcome though 'we rarely commission work'. Not interested in anything outside its subject areas.

Royalties paid annually.

Cornwall Books
See **Golden Cockerel Press Ltd**

Coronet Books
See **Hodder Headline plc**

Countryside Books
2 Highfield Avenue, Newbury, Berkshire RG14 5DS
☎01635 43816   Fax 01635 551004

Publisher *Nicholas Battle*

FOUNDED 1976. *Publishes* mainly paperbacks on regional subjects, generally by county. Local history, genealogy, walking and photographic, some transport. Over 250 titles available in 1994. Unsolicited mss and synopses welcome but, regretfully, no fiction, poetry or personal memories.

Royalties paid twice yearly.

Crabtree Publishing
73 Lime Walk, Headington, Oxford OX3 7AD
☎01865 67575   Fax 01865 750079

President *Peter Crabtree*
Editorial Director *Bobbie Kalman*

FOUNDED 1980. *Publishes* ecological and educational books in series. About 12 titles a year. SERIES *Animals and Their Ecosystems; Lands, Peoples and Culture; The Arctic World; Endangered Animals; Historic Communities; Crabtree Environment; Primary Ecology* and for 1995, *The Crabapple Series* – 'exciting non-fiction books for beginning readers'.

Royalties paid twice yearly.

CRC Press
See **Times Mirror International Publishers Ltd**

Cressrelles Publishing Co. Ltd
10 Station Road Industrial Estate, Colwall, Malvern, Worcestershire WR13 6RN
☎01684 540154

Managing Director *Leslie Smith*

Publishes a range of general books, drama and chiropody titles.

IMPRINTS **Actinic Press** specialises in chiropody; **J. Garnet Miller Ltd** plays and theatre texts; **Kenyon-Deane** plays and drama textbooks.

Croom Helm
See **Routledge**

Crossway
See **Inter-Varsity Press**

The Crowood Press Ltd
The Stable Block, Crowood Lane, Ramsbury, Marlborough, Wiltshire SN8 2HR
☎01672 20320   Fax 01672 20280

Chairman *John Dennis*
Managing Director *Ken Hathaway*

Publishes sport and leisure titles, including animal and land husbandry, climbing and walking, maritime, country sports, equestrian, fishing and shooting; also chess and bridge, crafts, dogs, gardening, natural history and motoring. About 70 titles a year. Preliminary letter preferred in all cases.

Royalties paid annually.

James Currey Publishers
54B Thornhill Square, London N1 1BE
☎0171 609 9026   Fax 0171 609 9605

Chairman/Managing Director *James Currey*

FOUNDED 1985. A small specialist publisher. *Publishes* academic books on Africa, the Caribbean and Third World: history, anthropology, economics, sociology, politics and literary criticism. Approach in writing with synopsis if material is 'relevant to our needs'.

Royalties paid annually.

Curzon Press Ltd
St John's Studios, Church Road, Richmond, Surrey TW9 2QA
☎0181 948 5322   Fax 0181 332 6735

Managing Director *Martina B. Campbell*

Specialised scholarly publishing house. *Publishes* academic/scholarly books on history and archaeology, languages and linguistics, philosophy, religion and theology, sociology and anthropology, cultural studies and reference, all in the context of Africa and Asia. IMPRINT **Japan Library**.

Cygnus Arts
See **Golden Cockerel Press Ltd**

Dalesman Publishing Co. Ltd

Stable Courtyard, Broughton Hall, Skipton,
West Yorkshire BD23 3AE
☎01756 701381   Fax 01756 701326

Editor (books) *Robert Flanagan*
Editor (magazines) *Terry Fletcher*

Publishers of *Dalesman*, *Cumbria* and *Pennine* magazines and regional books covering Yorkshire and the Lake District. Subjects include crafts and hobbies, geography and geology, guidebooks, history and antiquarian, humour, travel and topography. Unsolicited mss considered on all subjects. About 20 titles a year.
Royalties paid annually.

Terence Dalton Ltd

Water Street, Lavenham, Sudbury, Suffolk
CO10 9RN
☎01787 247572   Fax 01787 248247

Director/Editorial Head *Elisabeth Whitehair*

FOUNDED 1967. Part of Lavenham Holdings plc, a family company. *Publishes* non-fiction: aviation and maritime history, river series and East Anglian interest. 3 titles in 1994. TITLES *East Anglia 1945* R. Douglas Brown; *The Lost City of Dunwich* Nicholas Comfort; *A Month of Summers* Ian Stott. No unsolicited mss; send synopsis with two or three sample chapters. Ideas welcome.
Royalties paid annually.

The C. W. Daniel Co. Ltd

1 Church Path, Saffron Walden, Essex
CB10 1JP
☎01799 521909   Fax 01799 513462

Managing Director *Ian Miller*
Approx. Annual Turnover £1,000,000

FOUNDED in 1902 by a man who knew Tolstoy, the company was taken over by its present directors in 1973. Output has increased following the acquisition in 1980 of health and healing titles from the Health Science Press, and the purchase of Neville Spearman Publishers' metaphysical list in 1985. *Publishes* New Age: alternative healing and metaphysical. About 15 titles a year. No fiction, diet or cookery. Unsolicited synopses and ideas welcome; no unsolicited mss.
Royalties paid annually.

Darf Publishers Ltd

277 West End Lane, London NW6 1QS
☎0171 431 7009   Fax 0171 431 7655

Chairman/Managing Director
M. B. Fergiani

Editorial Head *A. Bentaleb*
Approx. Annual Turnover £500,000

FOUNDED 1982 to publish books and reprints on the Middle East, history, theology and travel. *Publishes* geography, history, language, literature, oriental, politics, theology, travel and cricket. About 50 titles a year. TITLES *Moslems in Spain; Travels of Ibn Battuta; The Barbary Corsairs; Elementary Arabic; Travels in Syria and the Holy Land* Burckhardt. Unsolicited mss, synopses and ideas for books welcome.
Royalties paid annually. *Overseas associates* Dar Al-Fergiani, Cairo and Tripoli.

Dartmouth Publishing Co. Ltd

Gower House, Croft Road, Aldershot,
Hampshire GU11 3HR
☎01252 331551   Fax 01252 344405

Managing Director *John Irwin*

FOUNDED 1989. *Publishes* books and reference works on law, international relations, politics and management. Unsolicited mss, synopses and ideas welcome.
Royalties paid according to contract.

Darton, Longman & Todd Ltd

1 Spencer Court, 140–42 Wandsworth High
Street, London SW18 4JJ
☎0181 875 0155   Fax 0181 875 0133

Editorial Director *Morag Reeve*
Approx. Annual Turnover £1 million

FOUNDED by Michael Longman, who broke away from Longman Green in 1959 when they decided to cut their religious list. In July 1990 DLT became a common ownership company, owned and run by staff members. The company is a leading ecumenical, predominantly Christian, publisher, with a strong emphasis on spirituality and the ministry and mission of the Church. About 50 titles a year. TITLES include *Jerusalem Bible; New Jerusalem Bible; God of Surprises; Audacity to Believe.* Sample material for books on theological or spiritual subjects considered.
Royalties paid twice yearly.

David & Charles Publishers

Brunel House, Forde Road, Newton Abbot,
Devon TQ12 4PU
☎01626 61121   Fax 01626 64463

Managing Director *Terry Stubbs*
Publishing Director *Piers Spence*

FOUNDED 1960 as a specialist company. Family controlled until 1990 when it was acquired by the **Reader's Digest Association Ltd.**

Publishes crafts and hobbies, art techniques, gardening, equestrian and countryside, natural history and field guides. No fiction, poetry, memoirs or children's. About 50 titles a year. TITLES *The Ehrman Tapestry Book; Decorative Folk Art; Hillier Gardener's Guide to Trees and Shrubs; The Encyclopedia of Fungi; Tales of the Old Gamekeepers.* Unsolicited mss will be considered if return postage is included, synopses and ideas welcome.

Royalties paid twice yearly.

Authors' Rating Restructured and relaunched under Reader's Digest ownership, David & Charles had reduced its publishing programme from 100 to around 60 titles a year. With Reader's Union book clubs as part of the company package, a bright future is likely for this once ailing company.

Christopher Davies Publishers Ltd

PO Box 403, Swansea, West Glamorgan SA1 4YF
☎01792 648825   Fax 01792 648825
Managing Director/Editorial Head
   Christopher T. Davies
Approx. Annual Turnover £100,000
FOUNDED 1949 to promote and expand Welsh-language publications. By the 1970s the company was publishing over 50 titles a year but a subsequent drop in Welsh sales led to the establishment of a small English list which has continued. *Publishes* biography, cookery, history and literature of Welsh interest. About 4 titles a year. TITLES *English/Welsh Dictionaries; Chronicle of Welsh Events; Swansea in the Golden Age of Postcards.* No unsolicited mss. Synopses and ideas for books welcome.

Royalties paid twice yearly.

Authors' Rating A favourite for Celtic readers and writers.

Debrett's Peerage Ltd

73–77 Britannia Road, PO Box 357, London SW6 2JY
☎0171 736 6524   Fax 0171 731 7768
Chairman *Ian McCorquodale*
Managing Director *R. M. Summers*
General Manager *Jonathan Parker*
FOUNDED 1769. The company's main activity (in conjunction with **Macmillan**) is the quinquennial *Debrett's Peerage and Baronetage* (published in 1995) and annual *Debrett's People of Today.* Debrett's general books are published under licence through **Headline**.

Royalties paid twice yearly.

Dedalus Ltd

Langford Lodge, St Judith's Lane, Sawtry, Cambridgeshire PE17 5XE
☎01487 832382   Fax 01487 832382
Chairman *Juri Gabriel*
Managing Director *George Barrington*
Approx. Annual Turnover £175,000
FOUNDED 1983. *Publishes* contemporary European fiction and classics, literary fantasy anthologies and original literary fantasy in the fields of magic realism, surrealism, the grotesque and bizarre. 16 titles in 1995.

TITLES *The Confessions of a Flesh-Eater Cookbook; The Arabian Nightmare* Robert Irwin; *Pfitz* Andrew Crumey; *Memoirs of a Gnostic Dwarf* David Madsen; *Music in a Foreign Language* Andrew Crumey (winner of the **Saltire Best First Book Award** in 1994); Welcomes submissions for original fiction and books suitable for its list but 'most people sending work in have no idea of what kind of books Dedalus publishes and merely waste their efforts'. Particularly interested in intellectually clever and unusual fiction. A letter about the author should always accompany any submission. No replies without s.a.e.

DIVISIONS/IMPRINTS **Original Fiction in Paperback; Contemporary European Fiction 1992–1995; Dedalus European Classics; Surrealism; Empire of the Senses.**

Royalties paid annually. *Overseas associates* Hippocrene Books, Inc., New York; Ariadne Press, California.

Authors' Rating A small publisher triumphing against powerful competition by the simple expedient of putting quality first.

Delaware

See **Golden Cockerel Press Ltd**

J. M. Dent

See **Orion Publishing Group**

André Deutsch Children's Books

See **Scholastic Publications Ltd**

André Deutsch Ltd

106 Great Russell Street, London WC1B 3LJ
☎0171 580 2746   Fax 0171 631 3253
Chairman/Managing Director
   T. G. Rosenthal
Submissions *Laura Morris*
Approx. Annual Turnover £2.5 million
FOUNDED in 1950 by André Deutsch, who sold the company between 1984 and 1987 and

ended his long association with it in 1991. By then a major fiction list had been established, with writers like V. S. Naipaul, Philip Roth and Norman Mailer among the *literati*. *Publishes* fiction, poetry and non-fiction, particularly biography, current affairs, history, cricket, politics and photographic. About 60 titles a year now following the sale of Deutsch's children's list to **Scholastic Publications Ltd** in 1991.

AUTHORS Malcolm Bradbury, Joan Brady, Paul Erdman, Carlos Fuentes, William Gaddis, Gail Godwin, George V. Higgins, Bohumil Hrabal, Dan Jacobson, Molly Keane, Penelope Lively, Clive Sinclair, David Thomson, John Updike, Gore Vidal. Unsolicited mss, synopses and ideas for books considered.

Royalties paid twice yearly.

Authors' Rating Now back on course after several troubled years. Very much at the quality end of the market.

Dial House
See **Ian Allan Ltd**

Disney
See **Ladybird Books Ltd**

Eric Dobby Publishing
12 Warnford Road, Orpington, Kent BR6 6LN
☎01689 862855   Fax 01689 861256
Chairman/Managing Director
E. R. Dobby
Approx. Annual Turnover £500,000
FOUNDED 1993. *Publishes* non-fiction: reference, dictionaries, hobbies (specialising in dolls and dolls' houses), gift stationery, sport, travel and true crime. About 35 titles a year. No unsolicited mss; synopses and ideas welcome. Not interested in anything outside current areas of publishing.
Royalties paid twice yearly.

Dolphin Book Co. Ltd
Tredwr, Llangrannog, Llandysul, Dyfed SA44 6BA
☎01239 654404   Fax 01239 654002
Managing Director Martin L. Gili
Approx. Annual Turnover £5000
FOUNDED 1957. A small publishing house specialising in Catalan, Spanish and South American books for the academic market. TITLES *Letters and Society in Fifteenth-Century Spain; Introductory Catalan Grammar* J. Gili (5th ed.); *The Late Poetry of Pablo Neruda* Christopher Perriam; *Hispanic Linguistic Studies*

in Honour of F. W. Hodcroft; Salvatge cor/Savage Heart Carles Riba; Catalan text with English translations by J. L. Gili. Unsolicited mss not welcome. Approach by letter.
Royalties paid annually.

John Donald Publishers Ltd
138 St Stephen Street, Edinburgh EH3 5AA
☎0131 225 1146   Fax 0131 220 0567
Publishing & Production *Donald Morrison*
Acquisition Editor *Russell Walker*
Publishes academic and scholarly, agriculture, archaeology, architecture and design, business and industry, economics, educational and textbooks, guidebooks, history and antiquarian, languages and linguistics, military, music, religious, sociology and anthropology, transport. About 30 titles a year. Unsolicited mss considered.
Royalties paid annually.

Donhead Publishing Ltd
28 Southdean Gardens, Wimbledon, London SW19 6NU
☎0181 789 0138   Fax 0181 789 9114
Contact *Jill Pearce*
FOUNDED 1990 to specialise in publishing how-to books for building practitioners; particularly interested in building conservation material. *Publishes* building and architecture only. 6 titles a year. TITLES *Encyclopaedia of Architectural Terms; A Good Housekeeping Guide to Churches and their Contents; Cleaning Historic Buildings; Brickwork; Journal of Architectural Conservation* (3 issues yearly). Unsolicited mss, synopses and ideas welcome.

Dorling Kindersley Ltd
9 Henrietta Street, London WC2E 8PS
☎0171 836 5411   Fax 0171 836 7570
Chairman *Peter Kindersley*
Deputy Chairman *Christopher Davis*
FOUNDED 1974. Packager and publisher of illustrated non-fiction: cookery, crafts, gardening, health, natural history and children's information books. Launched a US imprint in 1991. About 175–200 titles a year.

DIVISIONS
Adult; Children's; Direct; Education; Multimedia; Vision (video). TITLES *Eyewitness Guides; BMA Complete Family Health Encyclopaedia; RHS Gardener's Encyclopedia of Plants and Flowers; Reader's Digest Complete Guide to Cookery.* Unsolicited synopses/ideas for books welcome.

Authors' Rating Investing heavily in multimedia, Dorling Kindersley is achieving the level of sales for its early titles to justify a rapid expansion of its CD-ROM list. Meanwhile, highly illustrated reference books continue to sell in massive numbers across the world. Authors must expect to work as part of a team, with the designer taking precedence, and many writers are hired on straight fees.

Doubleday
See **Transworld Publishers Ltd**

DP Publications Ltd
Aldine Place, 142–144 Uxbridge Road, London W12 8AW
☎0181 746 0044   Fax 0181 743 8692
Managing Director *R. J. Chapman*
Publishing Director *Catherine Tilley*
FOUNDED 1972. Part of BPP Holdings plc. *Publishes* accounting, business, computing and mathematics textbooks for higher and further education. Unsolicited synopses and ideas for books welcome. Authors sought for active learning material in business, accounting and computing in further and higher education.
Royalties paid twice yearly.

Dragon's World
7–9 St Georges Square, London SW1V 2HX
☎0171 630 9955   Fax 0171 630 9921
Managing Director *Hubert Schaafsma*
FOUNDED 1975. *Publishes* fantasy art, natural history, children's non-fiction (ages 7–11), contemporary album cover art, fine art, design, craft, photography, DIY, folklore, illustrated children's classics and fables. About 50 titles a year.
IMPRINTS **Dragon's World** General illustrated non-fiction, notably natural history, with a major pocket guide series. **Paper Tiger Books** Fantasy art. Unsolicited mss, synopses and ideas for books welcome.

Drake Educational Associates
St Fagans Road, Fairwater, Cardiff CF5 3AE
☎01222 560333   Fax 01222 554909
Contact *R. G. Drake*
Academic book publishers.

Dryden Press
See **Harcourt Brace and Company Limited**

Gerald Duckworth & Co. Ltd
The Old Piano Factory, 48 Hoxton Square, London N1 6PB
☎0171 729 5986   Fax 0171 729 0015
Managing Director *Robin Baird-Smith*

Editorial Director *Deborah Blake*
FOUNDED 1898. A joint ownership company. Some of the company's early credits include authors like Hilaire Belloc, August Strindberg, Henry James and John Galsworthy. *Publishes* academic material in the main, and some fiction. A recent acquisition was the Bristol Classical Press list in 1991. About 80 titles a year.
IMPRINTS **Bristol Classical Press** Classical texts and modern languages; **Paperduck** Paperback imprint. No unsolicited mss; synopses and sample chapters only. Enclose s.a.e. or return postage for response/return.
Royalties paid twice yearly at first, annually thereafter.

Authors' Rating When Colin Haycraft died everyone thought it was the end of Duckworth but swift action by Anna Haycraft, alias Alice Thomas Ellis and author and shareholder Stephen Hill led to a buyout and a new management structure. The aim is for Duckworth to 'remain a strong and independent force in British publishing'. New fiction plus some classics are promised.

Martin Dunitz Ltd
The Livery House, 7–9 Pratt Street, London NW1 0AE
☎0171 482 2202   Fax 0171 267 0159
Chairman/Managing Director *Martin Dunitz*
FOUNDED 1978. Dunitz sold the successful *Positive Health Guides* series to former Macdonald in the 80s and now concentrates solely on specialist medical and dental titles aimed at an international market, with co-editions for the USA and Europe. The company won the Queen's Award for Export Achievement (1991). 20–30 titles a year. Unsolicited synopses and ideas welcome but no mss. Co-publisher of *Journal of Cytokines and Molecular Therapy*.
Royalties paid twice yearly.

Dunrod Press
8 Brown's Road, Newtownabbey, Co. Antrim BT36 8RN
☎01232 832362   Fax 01232 848780
Managing Director/Editorial Head *Ken Lindsay*
FOUNDED 1979. *Publishes* politics and world affairs. About 3 titles a year. Preliminary letter essential. Synopses and ideas for books welcome.
Royalties paid annually.

Dutton
See **Penguin Books**

Eagle
See **Inter Publishing Ltd**

Earthscan Publications Ltd
See **Kogan Page Ltd**

East-West Publications
8 Caledonia Street, London N1 9DZ
☎0171 837 5061   Fax 0171 278 4429
Chairman L. W. Carp
Managing Director B. G. Thompson
Approx. Annual Turnover £250,000

FOUNDED in the early 1970s. *Publishes* Eastern religions/philosophy and children's books. No unsolicited material. Enquiries in writing only.
    DIVISIONS **East-West Publications** L. W. Carp TITLES *The Sacred Mountain; Nirvana Tao; Nada Brahma*; **Gallery Children's Books** B. G. Thompson TITLES *A Child's Garden of Verses; Our Old Nursery Rhymes; Baby's Album*.
    Royalties paid twice yearly.

Ebury Press
See **Random House UK Ltd**

Economist Books
See **Penguin Books Ltd**

Edinburgh University Press Ltd
22 George Square, Edinburgh EH8 9LF
☎0131 650 4218/Polygon: 650 4689
Fax 0131 662 0053
Chief Editor Vivian Bone

Publishes academic and scholarly books and journals: archaeology, botany, history, Islamic studies, law and jurisprudence, linguistics, literary criticism, philosophy, environment, social sciences, Scottish studies, theology. About 100 titles a year.
    IMPRINT **Polygon** Creative writing and Scottish studies. *Publishes* international fiction and poetry. SERIES include *Sigma* (aphorisms, anarchisms and surreal); *Determinations* (Scottish cultural polemics); *Living Memory* (oral history). No unsolicited mss for EUP titles; mss welcome for Polygon but must be accompanied by s.a.e. for reply/return; letter/synopsis preferred in the first instance, particularly for EUP.
    Royalties paid annually.

Element Books
The Old School House, The Courtyard, Bell Street, Shaftesbury, Dorset SP7 8BP
☎01747 851448   Fax 01747 855721
Chairman/Publisher Michael Mann
Managing Director David Alexander
Approx. Annual Turnover £4 million

FOUNDED 1978. An independent general publishing house whose policy is 'to make available knowledge and information to aid humanity in a time of major transition'. *Publishes* general non-fiction in hardback and paperback, including full-colour, illustrated and gift books. TITLES *Iron John; The Dead Sea Scrolls Uncovered; Positive Thinking; I Ching; Nostradamus; When Men Believe in Love*. SERIES Elements Of; Little Books; The Natural Way; Self Help; Health Essentials; Health Workbooks; Earth Quest; Sacred Arts. Unsolicited mss, synopses and ideas welcome. No fiction.
    Royalties paid twice yearly.

Authors' Rating Very popular with way-out authors. Books about 'black magic or witchcraft or psychic phenomena' are turned away but Michael Mann does want to hear from authors who are 'concerned about ... the heart of religion, the mystical side of the great traditions. There have been some problems with royalties – but more a case of late payment than no payment at all.

Edward Elgar Publishing Ltd
8 Lansdown Place, Cheltenham, Gloucestershire GL50 2HU
☎01242 226934   Fax 01242 262111
Managing Director Edward Elgar

FOUNDED 1986. *Publishes* books and reference material on economics and other social sciences. Unsolicited mss, synopses and ideas welcome.
    Royalties paid according to contract.

Elliot Right Way Books
Kingswood Buildings, Lower Kingswood, Tadworth, Surrey KT20 6TD
☎01737 832202   Fax 01737 830311
Managing Directors Clive Elliot, Malcolm G. Elliot

FOUNDED 1946 by Andrew G. Elliot. *Publishes* how-to titles and instruction books on a multifarious list of subjects including cookery, DIY, family financial and legal matters, family health and fitness, fishing, looking after pets and horses, motoring, popular education, puzzles, jokes and quizzes. All the early books were entitled *The Right Way to . . .* but this format became too restrictive. No fiction.
    IMPRINTS **Paperfronts** Mass-market how-to paperbacks in A format; **Right Way** More specialised instructional paperbacks in B format. Unsolicited mss, synopses and ideas for books welcome.
    Royalties paid annually.

Ellipsis London Ltd
55 Charlotte Road, London EC2A 3QT
☎0171 739 3157   Fax 0171 739 3175
Contact *Tom Neville*
FOUNDED 1992. A subsidiary of Zurich-based
Artemis Verlags AG following a management
buyout in 1994. *Publishes* architecture. About
8–10 titles a year. No unsolicited mss, synopses
or ideas.
Royalties paid once yearly.

Aidan Ellis Publishing
Cobb House, Nuffield, Henley on Thames,
Oxfordshire RG9 5RT
☎01491 641496   Fax 01491 641678
Partners/Editorial Heads *Aidan Ellis,*
Lucinda Ellis
Approx. Annual Turnover £220,000
FOUNDED in 1971. *Publishes* fiction and general
trade books. About 12 titles a year.
DIVISIONS **Non-Fiction** TITLES *The Royal*
Gardens at Windsor Roddy Llewellyn; *Look Back*
and Laugh Alan Bloom; *How Many Years*
Marguerite Yourcenar; *The Bodleian Library and*
Its Treasures The Keepers; *Fifty Years of Red*
Cross Tracing Elizabeth Fidderman. **Fiction**
AUTHORS include David MacSweeney and José
Miguel Roig. No unsolicited mss.
Royalties paid twice yearly. *Overseas associates*
worldwide.

Elm Publications
Seaton House, Kings Ripton, Huntingdon,
Cambridgeshire PE17 2NJ
☎01487 773254   Fax 01487 773359
Managing Director *Sheila Ritchie*
FOUNDED 1977. *Publishes* textbooks, teaching
aids, educational resources, educational software and languages, in the fields of business
and management for adult learners. Books and
teaching/training resources are generally commissioned to meet specific business, management and other syllabuses. About 30 titles a
year. Ideas are welcome for new textbooks –
first approach in writing with outline or by a
brief telephone call.
Royalties paid annually.

Elsevier Science Ltd
The Boulevard, Longford Lane, Kidlington,
Oxford OX5 1GB
☎01865 843000   Fax 01865 843010
Managing Director *Michael Boswood*
Parent company **Elsevier**, Amsterdam. Now
incorporates **Pergamon Press**. *Publishes* aca-
demic and professional reference books, scien-
tific, technical and medical books, journals and
magazines.
DIVISIONS **Advanced Technology** *Nick*
Baker; **Elsevier Trends Journals** *David*
Bousfield; **Pergamon Press** *Barbara Barrett,*
Michael Mabe, Chris Lloyd, Peter Shepherd, Jim
Gilgunn-Jones. Unsolicited mss, synopses and
ideas for books welcome.
Royalties paid annually.

Authors' Rating An offshoot of the largest
Dutch publisher. Refreshingly open with
authors in the tradition of northern European
publishers – early news on print runs and royalties paid promptly.

Elvendon Press
See **William Reed Directories**

Emissary Publishing
PO Box 33, Bicester, Oxfordshire OX6 7PP
☎01869 323447   Fax 01869 324096
Editorial Director *Val Miller*
FOUNDED 1992. *Publishes* humorous books.
About 12 titles a year. Expansion planned over
the next couple of years. No unsolicited mss or
synopses. Contact by letter in the first instance
(with s.a.e. for reply).
Royalties paid twice yearly.

Enitharmon Press
36 St George's Avenue, London N7 0HD
☎0171 607 7194   Fax 0171 607 8694
Director *Stephen Stuart-Smith*
FOUNDED 1969 by Alan Clodd. An independent company with an enterprising editorial
policy, Enitharmon has established itself as one
of Britain's leading poetry presses. Patron of
'the new and the neglected', Enitharmon
prides itself on the success of its collaborations
between writers and artists. *Publishes* poetry,
literary criticism, fiction, art and photography.
About 20 titles a year. TITLES include new
poetry collections by Jane Duran, Hubert
Moore, Jeremy Reed and David Gascoyne's
Selected Verse Translations. Among the limited
editions are *Shakespeare's Ovid* by Ted Hughes
and Christopher Le Brun, published in aid of
the Shakespeare Globe Theatre; *In the Twilight*
Slot by Thom Gunn and Attila Richard
Lukacs; and Shinro Ohtake's *Poems and*
Etchings. No unsolicited mss.
Royalties paid according to contract.
Distribution in the UK and Ireland by Password
(Books) Ltd, Manchester; in the USA by Dufour
Editions Inc., Chester Springs, PA 19425.

Epworth Press

Hartley Victoria College, Luther King House, Brighton Grove, Manchester M14 5JP
☎0161 224 2215   Fax 0161 248 9201
Chairman *Graham Slater*
Editor *Dr C. S. Rodd*

Formerly based in Cambridge, Epworth now operates from Manchester. *Publishes* Christian books only: philosophy, theology, biblical studies, pastoralia and social concern. No fiction, poetry or children's. Launched a new series in the early 1990s based on the text of the *Revised English Bible* and entitled *Epworth Commentaries*. About 10 titles a year. TITLES *The Epistle of James* M. J. Townsend; *Purge This Realm: A Life of Joseph Rayner Stephens* Michael S. Edwards; *Companion to the Lectionary, Vol. 5; All Together for Worship* Peter Sheasby; *The Flight of the Crane: Harry Vine Norman (1868–1900)* Elisabeth Green. Unsolicited mss considered but write to enquire in the first instance. Authors wishing to have their mss returned must send sufficient postage.
Royalties paid annually.

Eros Plus

See **Titan Books**

ESC

See **Sweet & Maxwell Ltd**

Euromonitor

60–61 Britton Street, London EC1M 5NA
☎0171 251 8024   Fax 0171 608 3149
Chairman *R. N. Senior*
Managing Director *T. J. Fenwick*
Approx. Annual Turnover £4.5 million

FOUNDED 1972. International business information publisher specialising in library and professional reference books, market reports, electronic databases and journals. *Publishes* business reference, market analysis and information directories only. About 80–85 titles a year.
DIVISIONS **Market Direction** *S. Holmes*; **Reference Books & Reports** *S. Leckey*; **Directories** *M. McGrath*. TITLES *Credit & Charge Cards: The International Market*; *Europe in the Year 2000*; *European Marketing Handbook*; *European Directory of Trade and Business Associations*; *World Retail Directory and Sourcebook*.
Royalties payment is generally by flat fee.

Europa Publications Ltd

18 Bedford Square, London WC1B 3JN
☎0171 580 8236   Fax 0171 636 1664
Chairman *C. H. Martin*
Managing Director *P. A. McGinley*

Approx. Annual Turnover £5 million

Owned by Staples Printers Ltd. FOUNDED 1926 with the publication of the first edition of *The Europa Year Book*. *Publishes* annual reference books on political, economic and commercial matters. About 3 titles a year. No fiction, biography or poetry. Enquiries in writing only.
Royalties paid annually.

Evangelical Press of Wales

Bryntirion House, Bridgend, Mid-Glamorgan CF31 4DX
☎01656 655886   Fax 01656 656095
Chairman *Reverend S. Jones*
Chief Executive *G. Wyn Davies*
Approx. Annual Turnover £85,000

Owned by the Evangelical Movement of Wales. *Publishes* Christian books. 7 titles in 1994. TITLES *Christian Handbook; The Welsh Revival of 1904; Why Does God Allow War?; I Will Never Become a Christian; Social Issues and the Local Church*. No unsolicited mss; synopses and ideas welcome.
Royalties paid twice yearly.

Evans Brothers Ltd

2A Portman Mansions, Chiltern Street, London W1M 1LE
☎0171 935 7160   Fax 0171 487 5034
Managing Director *Stephen Pawley*
International Publishing Director *Brian Jones*
Commissioning Editor *Sue Swallow*
Approx. Annual Turnover £3 million

FOUNDED 1908 by Robert and Edward Evans. Originally published educational journals, books for primary schools and teacher education. After rapid expansion into popular fiction and drama, both were sacrificed to a major programme of educational books for schools in East and West Africa. A new UK programme was launched in 1986 followed by the acquisition of **Hamish Hamilton**'s non-fiction list for children in 1990. *Publishes* UK children's and educational books, and educational books for Africa, the Caribbean and Far East. About 70 titles a year.
DIVISIONS **Overseas** TITLE *National History of Nigeria*. **UK Publishing** SERIES: *Science Spotlight; Stage and Screen; Holy Cities; Rainbows*. Unsolicited mss, synopses and ideas for books welcome.
Royalties paid annually. *Overseas associates* in Kenya, Cameroon, Sierra Leone; Evans Bros (Nigeria Publishers) Ltd.

Everyman

See **Orion Publishing Group**

Everyman's Library
See **David Campbell Publishers Ltd**

University of Exeter Press
Reed Hall, Streatham Drive, Exeter, Devon
EX4 4QR
☎01392 263066   Fax 01392 263064
Publisher *Simon Baker*

FOUNDED 1956. *Publishes* academic books:
archaeology, classical studies, mining, history,
maritime studies, English literature (especially
medieval), linguistics, European studies, modern languages and literature, American studies,
cultural studies, Arabic studies and books on
Exeter and the South West. About 25 titles a
year. Unsolicited mss welcomed in the subject
areas mentioned above.
Royalties paid annually.

Exley Publications Ltd
16 Chalk Hill, Watford, Hertfordshire
WD1 4BN
☎01923 248328   Fax 01923 818733
Managing/Editorial Director *Helen Exley*

FOUNDED 1976. Independent family company.
Publishes gift books, quotation anthologies,
social stationery and humour. All in series only
– no individual titles. Has a substantial children's non-fiction list. About 65 titles a year.

DIVISIONS
Children's TITLES *The World's Greatest
Composers; Organisations That Help the World;
Women Achievers; Great Business Stories;
Understanding Differences;* **Gift Series** TITLES *To
a Very Special Friend, Daughter, Son, ...; The
Fanatics Guide to Golf, Cats, Dads, etc; The
Crazy World of Aerobics, Golf, Learning to Drive;
Golf Quotations; Book Lovers; So-Much-More-
Than-A-Card Collection.* No unsolicited mss but
proposals for series (accompanied by s.a.e.)
welcome. 'Joke and gag writers are very badly
needed. Also writers who can create personal
"messages" rather like not-too-sugary greetings
cards.'

Faber & Faber Ltd
3 Queen Square, London WC1N 3AU
☎0171 465 0045   Fax 0171 465 0034
Chairman/Managing Director *Matthew
Evans*
Approx. Annual Turnover £8.8 million

Geoffrey Faber and Richard de la Mare
founded the company in the 1920s, with T.S.
Eliot as an early recruit to the board. The original list was based on contemporary poetry and
plays (the distinguished backlist includes Eliot,
Auden and MacNeice). *Publishes* poetry and
drama, art, children's, fiction, film, music, politics, biography, specialist cookery and wine.
Unsolicited mss will be considered; synopses
and ideas for books welcome. Return postage
required.

DIVISIONS
Children's *Janice Thomson* AUTHORS Gene
Kemp, Russell Stannard, Susan Price; **Cookery
and Wine** *Belinda Matthews* TITLES *Simple
French Cuisine; Pastability; Cuisine Grandmère;*
Fiction *Robert McCrum, Nicholas Pearson*
AUTHORS P. D. James, Peter Carey, William
Golding, Milan Kundera, Mario Vargas Llosa,
Garrison Keillor, Paul Auster; **Plays** *Peggy
Butcher;* **Film** *Walter Donohue.* AUTHORS
Samuel Beckett, Alan Bennett, David Hare,
Tom Stoppard, John Boorman, Woody Allen,
Martin Scorsese, Quentin Tarantino; **Poetry**
Christopher Reid AUTHORS Seamus Heaney,
Ted Hughes, Douglas Dunn, Tom Paulin,
Simon Armitage; **Non-fiction** *Julian Loose*
TITLES *Elizabeth Gaskell; On Flirtation.*
Royalties paid twice yearly. *Overseas office*
Boston.

Authors' Rating Maintains a quality output
with a little help from one of the strongest literary backlists in the business and royalties from
Cats.

Fairleigh Dickinson
See **Golden Cockerel Press**

Falmer Press
4 John Street, London WC1N 2ET
☎0171 400 3500   Fax 0171 831 2035
Managing/Editorial Director *Malcolm
Clarkson*

Part of **Taylor & Francis**. *Publishes* educational books/materials for all levels. Largely
commissioned. Unsolicited mss considered.
Royalties paid annually.

Farming Press Books & Videos
Wharfedale Road, Ipswich, Suffolk IP1 4LG
☎01473 241122   Fax 01473 240501
Manager *Roger Smith*

Owned by United Newspapers plc. *Publishes*
specialist books/videos on farming, plus a range
of humorous and countryside titles. About 15
titles a year. No unsolicited mss; synopses and
ideas welcome provided material is suitable for
their list.
Royalties paid twice yearly.

Fernhurst Books
Duke's Path, High Street, Arundel,
West Sussex BN18 9AJ
☎01903 882277   Fax 01903 882715
Chairman/Managing Director *Tim Davison*
FOUNDED 1979. For people who love water-sports. *Publishes* practical, highly illustrated hand-books on sailing, watersports and skiing. No unsolicited mss; synopses and ideas welcome.
Royalties paid twice yearly.

Finborough Services
See **Tolley Publishing Co. Ltd**

First & Best in Education Ltd
34 Nene Valley Business Park, Oundle,
Peterborough PE8 4HL
☎01832 275285   Fax 01832 278281
Publisher *Tony Attwood*
Senior Editor *Keith Buckby*
Publishes educational books of all types for all ages as well as business books. Currently launching 40 new titles a month and 'keenly looking for new authors all the time'. TITLES *Getting Ready to Start School; Primary School Curriculum Policy; The Job Desert; Electricity and Magnetism.* In the first instance send s.a.e. for details of requirements and current projects.
Royalties normally 12% paid twice yearly.

Fitzjames Press
See **Motor Racing Publications**

Flamingo
See **HarperCollins Publishers Ltd**

Flicks Books
29 Bradshaw Road, Trowbridge, Wiltshire
BA14 9AN
☎01225 767728   Fax 01225 760418
Managing Director *Matthew Stevens*
FOUNDED 1986. Devoted solely to publishing books on the cinema and related media. 5 titles in 1994. Unsolicited mss, synopses and ideas within the subject area are welcome.
Royalties twice yearly.

Floris Books
15 Harrison Gardens, Edinburgh EH11 1SH
☎0131 337 2372   Fax 0131 346 7516
Managing Director *Christian Maclean*
Editor *Christopher Moore*
Approx. Annual Turnover £350,000
FOUNDED 1977. *Publishes* books related to the Steiner movement, including arts & crafts, children's, the Christian Community, history, religious, science, social questions and Celtic studies. No unsolicited mss. Synopses and ideas for books welcome.
Royalties paid annually.

Fodor's
See **Random House UK Ltd**

Folger Shakespeare Library
See **Golden Cockerel Press Ltd**

Fontana
See **HarperCollins Publishers Ltd**

Forest Books
20 Forest View, Chingford,
London E4 7AY
☎0181 529 8470   Fax 0181 524 7890
Managing Director *Brenda Walker*
Approx. Annual Turnover £70,000
FOUNDED 1984 to promote international cultural links through publishing. *Publishes* literary translations, poetry, anthologies, fiction and plays. Particularly keen to publish works from minority languages and ethnic groups. *Specialises* in books from Eastern Europe. A number of books are published in collaboration with UNESCO. TITLES *Young Poets of A New Poland* ed. Donald Pirie; *Route Tournante* Espmark; *Days of the Consuls* Andric. No unsolicited material.

G. T. Foulis & Co Ltd
See **Haynes Publishing**

W. Foulsham & Co.
The Publishing House, Bennetts Close,
Cippenham, Berkshire SL1 5AP
☎01753 526769   Fax 01753 535003
Chairman *R. S. Belasco*
Managing Director *B. A. R. Belasco*
Approx. Annual Turnover £2.2 million
FOUNDED 1816 and now one of the few remaining independent family companies to survive takeover. *Publishes* non-fiction on most subjects including astrology, gardening, cookery, DIY, business, hobbies, sport, health, marriage and New Age. No fiction. Unsolicited mss, synopses and ideas welcome. Around 60 titles a year.
Royalties paid twice yearly.

Fount
See **HarperCollins Publishers Ltd**

Fountain Press Ltd

2 Gladstone Road, Kingston-upon-Thames,
Surrey KT1 3HD
☎0181 541 4050   Fax 0181 547 3022
Managing Director *H. M. Ricketts*
Approx. Annual Turnover £600,000

FOUNDED 1923 when it was part of the
Rowntree Trust Group. Owned by the British
Electric Traction Group until 1982 when it was
bought out by the present managing director.
Publishes mainly photography, cookery, health,
music, natural history and travel. About 25 titles
a year. TITLES *Photography Yearbook; Wildlife
Photographer of the Year; Antique and Collectable
Cameras; Camera Manual* (series). Unsolicited mss
and synopses are welcome.
Royalties paid twice yearly.

Authors' Rating Highly regarded for production values, Fountain has the reputation for
involving authors in every stage of the publishing process.

Fourmat Publishing

See **Tolley Publishing Co. Ltd**

Fourth Estate Ltd

6 Salem Road, London W2 4BU
☎0171 727 8993   Fax 0171 792 3176
Chairman/Managing Director *Victoria
Barnsley*
Publishing Director *Christopher Potter*
Approx. Annual Turnover £2.5 million

FOUNDED 1984. Independent publisher with
strong reputation for literary fiction and up-to-
the-minute non-fiction. *Publishes* fiction, popular science, current affairs, biography,
humour, self-help, travel, design and architecture, reference. About 75 titles a year.

DIVISIONS
Literary Fiction/Non-fiction *Christopher
Potter* TITLES *Wonder Boys* Michael Chabon;
The Stone Diaries Carol Shields; *The Shipping
News* E. Annie Proulx; *The Loves of Faustyna*
Nina Fitzpatrick; *Coltrane in a Cadillac* Robbie
Coltrane; *Revolution in the Head* Ian MacDonald;
Spying in Guru Land William Shaw; *Ha Bloody
Ha* William Cook; **General Fiction/Non-
Fiction** TITLES *The Revised Kama Sutra* Richard
Castra. No unsolicited mss; synopses welcome.

IMPRINTS
Guardian Books in association with *The
Guardian*; **Observer Books** in association with
The Observer; **Blueprint Monographs** books in
association with *Blueprint* Magazine.
Royalties paid twice yearly.

Authors' Rating Marking up a second
Pulitzer Prize winner (Carol Shields, *The
Stone Diaries*), Fourth Estate is confirmed in its
reputation as an imaginative publisher ready to
tackle controversial issues. Now carries all its
major authors in paperback as well as hardback
editions.

Free Association Books Ltd

39–41 North Road, London N7 9DP
☎0171 609 5646   Fax 0171 700 0330
Chairman/Finance Director *T. E. Brown*
Managing Director *Gill Davies*

Publishes psychoanalysis and psychotherapy, cul-
tural studies, sexuality and gender, women's
studies, applied social sciences. Very selective.
TITLES *Clinical Klein; In the Best Interests of the
Child; Cultural Collapse; Femininities, Masculinities,
Sexualities.* Always write a letter in the first
instance accompanied by a book outline.
Royalties paid twice yearly. *Overseas associates*
New York University Press, USA; Astam,
Australia.

W. H. Freeman & Co. Ltd

20 Beaumont Street, Oxford OX1 2NQ
☎01865 726975   Fax 01865 790391
President *Robert Beiwen* (New York)
Managing Director *Elizabeth Warner*

Part of W. H. Freeman & Co., USA. *Publishes*
academic, agriculture, animal care and breeding,
archaeology, artificial intelligence, biochemistry,
biology and zoology, chemistry, computer science, economics, educational and textbooks,
engineering, geography and geology, mathematics and statistics, medical, natural history, neuroscience, palaeontology, physics, politics and
world affairs, psychology, sociology and anthropology, and veterinary. Freeman's editorial office
is in New York (Oxford is a sales and marketing
office only) but unsolicited mss can go through
Oxford. Those which are obviously unsuitable
will be sifted out; the rest will be forwarded to
New York.
Royalties paid annually.

Samuel French Ltd

52 Fitzroy Street, London W1P 6JR
☎0171 387 9373   Fax 0171 387 2161
Chairman *Charles R. Van Nostrand*
Managing Director *John Bedding*

FOUNDED 1830 with the object of acquiring
acting rights and publishing plays. Part of
Samuel French Inc., New York. *Publishes*
plays only. About 50 titles a year. Unsolicited
mss considered only after initial submission of

synopsis and specimen scene. Such material should be addressed to the Performing Rights Department.

Royalties paid twice yearly.

Authors' Rating The darling of amdram (a booming specialist market), Samuel French has cornered the publication of play texts and the permissions (around £50 a night for amateurs) for their performance. Editorial advisers give serious attention to new material but a high proportion of the list is staged before it goes into print. Non-established writers are advised to try one-act plays, much in demand by the amateur dramatic societies but rarely turned out by well-known playwrights.

David Fulton (Publishers) Ltd
2 Barbon Close, Great Ormond Street, London WC1N 3JX
☎0171 405 5606   Fax 0171 831 4840
Chairman/Managing Director *David Fulton*
Editorial Director *John Owens*
Approx. Annual Turnover £600,000

FOUNDED 1987. *Publishes* non-fiction: teacher training at B.Ed and PGCE levels for primary, secondary and special education; geography for undergraduate and professional. In 1995 David Fulton set up a Fulton Fellowship (see under **Bursaries, Fellowships and Grants**). About 50 titles a year. No unsolicited mss; synopses and ideas for books welcome.

Royalties paid twice yearly.

Funfax/Junior Funfax
See **Henderson Publishing Ltd**

Gaia Books Ltd
66 Charlotte Street, London W1P 1LR
☎0171 323 4010   Fax 0171 323 0435
Also at: 20 High Street, Stroud, Gloucestershire GL5 1AS
☎01453 752985   Fax 01453 752987
Managing Director *Joss Pearson*

FOUNDED 1983. *Publishes* ecology, health, natural living and mind, body & spirit, mainly in practical self-help illustrated reference form. About 10 titles a year. TITLES *Gaia: The Practical Science of Planetary Medicine; Step-by-Step Tai Chi; The Gaia Atlas of Planet Management.* Outlines and mss with s.a.e. considered. Most projects conceived in-house.

Royalties paid.

Gairm Publications
29 Waterloo Street, Glasgow G2 6BZ
☎0141 221 1971   Fax 0141 221 1971

Chairman *Prof. Derick S. Thomson*

FOUNDED 1952 to publish the quarterly Gaelic periodical *Gairm* and soon moved into publishing other Gaelic material. Acquired an old Glasgow Gaelic publishing firm, Alexander MacLaren & Son, in 1970. *Publishes* a wide range of Gaelic and Gaelic-related books: dictionaries, grammars, handbooks, children's, fiction, poetry, music and song.

Galaxy Children's Large Print
See **Chivers Press Ltd**

Gallery Children's Books
See **East-West Publications**

J. Garnet Miller Ltd
See **Cressrelles Publishing Co. Ltd**

Garnet Publishing Ltd
8 Southern Court, South Street, Reading, Berkshire RG1 4QS
☎01734 597847   Fax 01734 597356
Managing Director *Ken Banerji*

FOUNDED 1992 and purchased Ithaca Press in the same year. *Publishes* art, architecture, photography, archive photography, cookery, travel classics, travel, comparative religion, Islamic culture and history, Arabic fiction in translation. Core subjects are Middle Eastern but list is rapidly expanding to be more general. Published 48 titles 1994.

IMPRINTS **Ithaca Press** *Adel Kamal* TITLES *Nasser: The Final Years; Handshake in Washington: The Beginning of Middle East Peace; Through Secret Channels – Water Resources Development in Ethiopia; Dilemma of Development;* **Garnet Publishing** *Anna Watson* TITLES *Traditional Arabic Cooking; Flavours of Madras; The Hindu Pantheon; Freya Stark in Persia; Freya Stark in Iraq and Kuwait; Freya Stark in the Levant; Japan Caught in Time: Great Photographic Archives China, Sudan, Bukhara* (Series); *A Lebanese Harvest* (cookery book). Unsolicited mss not welcome – write with outline and ideas first. Not interested in sport or general fiction.

Royalties paid twice yearly. *Sister companies:* All Prints, Beirut; EdiFra, Paris.

The Gay Men's Press (GMP Publishers Ltd)
PO Box 247, London N6 4BW
☎0181 341 7818   Fax 0181 341 7467
Managing Director *Aubrey Walter*

Publishes primarily books by gay authors about gay-related issues: art, photography, biography and autobiography, literary fiction and popular (historical romance to crime and science fiction), health and leisure. No poetry. Works should generally be submitted by the author on disk.

DIVISIONS **Art & Photography** *Aubrey Walter*, **General Books** *David Fernbach*. TITLES *Mother Clap's Molly House* Rictor Norton; *Halfway Home* Paul Monette; *Gaveston* Chris Hunt; *Trouble with the Law?* Caroline Gooding; *Rodeo Pantheon* Delmas Hale; *Younger Days* Ian David Baker. Send synopsis with sample chapters rather than complete mss. *Royalties* negotiable.

Stanley Gibbons Publications
5 Parkside, Christchurch Road, Ringwood, Hampshire BH24 3SH
☎01425 472363   Fax 01425 470247
Chairman *P. I. Fraser*
Managing Director *A. J. Pandit*
Editorial Head *D. Aggersberg*
Approx. Annual Turnover £3 million

Long-established force in the philatelic world with over a hundred years in the business. *Publishes* philatelic reference catalogues and handbooks. Approx. 15 titles a year. Reference works relating to other areas of collecting may be considered. TITLES *Stanley Gibbons British Commonwealth Stamp Catalogue; Collect British Stamps; How to Arrange and Write Up a Stamp Collection; Stamps of the World; Collect Aircraft on Stamps.* Monthly publication *Gibbons Stamp Monthly* (see under **Magazines**). Unsolicited mss, synopses and ideas welcome.
Royalties by negotiation.

Robert Gibson & Sons
17 Fitzroy Place, Glasgow G3 7SF
☎0141 248 5674   Fax 0141 221 8219
Chairman/Managing Director
R. G. C. Gibson

FOUNDED 1850 and went public in 1886. *Publishes* educational books only, and has been agent for the Scottish Certificate of Education Examination Board since 1902. About 40 titles a year. Unsolicited mss preferred to synopses/ideas.
Royalties paid annually.

Ginn
See **Reed International Books**

Mary Glasgow Publications
See **Stanley Thornes (Publishers) Ltd**

Golden Cockerel Press Ltd
25 Sicilian Avenue, London WC1A 2QH
☎0171 405 7979   Fax 0171 405 7979
Chairman/Managing Director *Thomas Yoseloff* (USA)
Editorial Head UK *Tamar Yoseloff*

FOUNDED 1980 to distribute titles for US-based Associated University Presses Inc., New Jersey. *Publishes* academic titles mostly: art, film, history, literary criticism, music, philosophy, sociology and special interest. About 80 titles a year.

IMPRINTS
AUP: Bucknell; Delaware; Fairleigh Dickinson; Folger Shakespeare Library; Cygnus Arts non-academic books on the arts; **Cornwall Books** (trade hardbacks); **Balch Institute Press; Lehigh University Press; Susquehanna University Press.** Unsolicited mss, synopses and ideas for academic books welcome.

Authors' Rating Very much attuned to American interests with trans-Atlantic spelling and punctuation predominating. Purists may find the process wearisome but those who persevere win through to a wider market.

Victor Gollancz
See **Cassell**

Gomer Press
Wind Street, Llandysul, Dyfed SA44 4BQ
☎01559 362371   Fax 01559 363758
Chairman/Managing Director *J. H. Lewis*

FOUNDED 1892. *Publishes* adult fiction and non-fiction, children's fiction and educational material in English and Welsh. About 100 titles a year (80 Welsh; 20 English).

IMPRINTS **Gomer Press** *Dr D. Elis-Gruffydd*; **Pont Books** *Mairwen Prys Jones*. No unsolicited mss, synopses or ideas.
Royalties paid twice yearly.

Gower
See **Ashgate Publishing Co. Ltd**

GPC Books
See **University of Wales Press**

Grafton
See **HarperCollins Publishers Ltd**

Graham & Trotman Ltd
See **Kluwer Law International**

Graham & Whiteside Ltd

Tuition House, 5–6 Francis Grove,
London SW19 4DT
☎0181 947 1011   Fax 0181 947 1163
Managing Director *Alastair M. W. Graham*

FOUNDED 1995. *Publishes* annual directories for
the business and professional market with titles
dating back to 1975 originally published by
Graham & Trotman. TITLES *Major Companies of
Europe; Major Companies of the Arab World;
Major Companies of the Far East and Australasia.*
Proposals for new projects welcome.
Royalties paid once yearly.

Graham-Cameron Publishing

The Studio, 23 Holt Road, Sheringham,
Norfolk NR26 8NB
☎01263 821333   Fax 01263 821334
Editorial Director *Mike Graham-Cameron*
Art Director *Helen Graham-Cameron*

FOUNDED 1984 as a packaging operation.
Publishes illustrated books for children, institu-
tions and business; also biography, education
and social history. TITLES *Up From the Country;
In All Directions; The Holywell Story; Let's Look
at Dairying.* Please do not send unsolicited mss.
Royalties paid annually. *Subsidiary company*:
Graham-Cameron Illustration (agency).

Granta Publications

2–3 Hanover Yard, Noel Road, London
N1 8BE
☎0171 704 9776   Fax 0171 704 0474
Managing Director *Frances Coady*

FOUNDED 1979. *Publishes* literary magazines, literary fiction, reportage and travel, and general
non-fiction.

Granville Publishing

102 Islington High Street, London N1 8EG
☎0171 226 2904
Managing Director *John Murray-Browne*
Approx. Annual Turnover 'very small'

FOUNDED 1983. *Publishes* literature reprints only.
No unsolicited mss.

Green Books

Foxhole, Dartington, Totnes, Devon
TQ9 6EB
☎01803 863843   Fax 01803 863843
Chairman *Satish Kumar*
Managing Editor *John Elford*
Approx. Annual Turnover £80,000

FOUNDED in 1987 with the support of a number
of Green organisations. Closely associated with

Resurgence magazine. *Publishes* high-quality books
on a wide range of Green issues, particularly with
ideas, philosophy and the practical application of
Green values. No fiction or books for children.
TITLES *Forest Gardening* Robert A. de J. Hart;
Eco-Renovation Edward Harland; *The Growth
Illusion* Richard Douthwaite; *The Living Tree*
John Lane; *Tongues in Trees* Kim Taplin. No un-
solicited mss. Synopses and ideas welcome.
Royalties paid twice yearly.

Green Print

See **Merlin Press Ltd**

Greenhill Books/ Lionel Leventhal Ltd

Park House, 1 Russell Gardens, London
NW11 9NN
☎0181 458 6314   Fax 0181 905 5245
Managing Director *Lionel Leventhal*

FOUNDED 1984 by Lionel Leventhal (ex-**Arms
& Armour Press**). *Publishes* aviation, military
and naval books, and its Napoleonic Library
series. Synopses and ideas for books welcome.
No unsolicited mss.
Royalties paid twice yearly.

Greenpeace Books Ltd

See under **UK Packagers**

Gresham Books

See **Woodhead Publishing Ltd**

Gresham Books Ltd

PO Box 61, Henley on Thames, Oxfordshire
RG9 3LQ
☎01734 403789   Fax 01734 403789
Managing Director *Mary V. Green*
Approx. Annual Turnover £150,000

Bought by Mary Green from Martins Publishing Group in 1980. A small specialist publishing
house. *Publishes* hymn and service books for
schools and churches, also craftbound choir and
orchestral folders and Records of Achievement.
TITLES include music and melody editions of
*Hymns for Church and School; The School Hymnal;
Praise and Thanksgiving.* No unsolicited material
but ideas welcome.

Grey Seal Books

28 Burgoyne Road,
London N4 1AD
☎0181 340 6061   Fax 0181 340 6061
Chairman *John E. Duncan*

FOUNDED 1990. *Publishes* comparative religion,
Islam, history, politics and futures studies. About

6 titles a year. No unsolicited mss; synopses and ideas welcome.
Royalties paid annually.

Griffith Institute
See **Ashmolean Museum Publications Ltd**

Grisewood & Dempsey
See **Larousse plc**

Grosvenor Books
54 Lyford Road, Wandsworth, London SW18 3JJ
☎0181 870 2124   Fax 0181 871 9239
Managing Director *David W. Locke*
FOUNDED 1964. Owned by Grosvenor Productions Ltd. *Publishes* biography, contemporary issues, and religious. TITLES *Hope For A Change* Michael Henderson; *Poet Against The Lie* Irina Ratushinskaya; *Forgiveness in International Affairs* Bryan Hamlin; *Rediscovering Freedom* John Lester & Pierre Spoerri; *The Missing Dimension of Statecraft* D. Johnstone and others; *Forward to Basics* Kenneth Nobel; *Handing Out Change* Frank Cooney. No unsolicited mss.
Royalties paid yearly. *Overseas associates* in Australia, New Zealand, USA, Canada.

Grove's Dictionaries of Music
See **Macmillan Publishers Ltd**

Grub Street
The Basement, 10 Chivalry Road, London SW11 1HT
☎0171 924 3966   Fax 0171 738 1009
Managing Directors *John Davies, Anne Dolamore*
FOUNDED 1982. *Publishes* cookery, health, cartoon, humour and aviation history books. About 20 titles a year. TITLES *Buyer's Guide to Olive Oil; Everyday Light-hearted Cookbook; Aces High; War Diaries of Neville Duke*. Unsolicited mss and synopses welcome.
Royalties paid twice yearly.

Grune & Stratton
See **Harcourt Brace and Company Limited**

Guardian Books
See **Fourth Estate Ltd**

Guild of Master Craftsmen Publications
166 High Street, Lewes, East Sussex BN7 1XU
☎01273 477374   Fax 01273 478606
Chairman *A.E. Phillips*
Managing Director *John Kelsey*

Approx. Annual Turnover £2 million
FOUNDED 1979. Part of G.M.C. Services Ltd. *Publishes* woodworking and craft books. 20 titles in 1995. Unsolicited mss, synopses and ideas for books welcome. No fiction.
Royalties paid twice yearly.

Guinness Publishing Ltd
33 London Road, Enfield, Middlesex EN2 6DJ
☎0181 367 4567   Fax 0181 367 5912
Chairman *Ian Chapman, CBE*
Managing Director *Christopher Irwin*
Publishing Director *Stephen Adamson*
Editor *(Guinness Book Of Records)* *Peter Matthews*
FOUNDED 1954 to publish *The Guinness Book of Records*, now the highest-selling copyright book in the world, published in 35 languages. In the late 1960s the company set about expanding its list with a wider range of titles. About 50 titles a year. Ideas and synopses for books welcome if they come within their fields of sport, human achievement (with the emphasis on facts and feats), popular music and family reference.

Authors' Rating Said by *The Bookseller* to be 'a strong contender for the title of most profitable adult trade publisher', all activity is centred on the founding title. The emphasis now is on using the Guinness name to broaden the publishing base.

Gunsmoke Westerns
See **Chivers Press Ltd**

Gwasg Prifysgol Cymru
See **University of Wales Press**

Peter Haddock Ltd
Pinfold Lane Industrial Estate, Bridlington, East Yorkshire YO16 5BT
☎01262 678121   Fax 01262 400043
Managing Director *Peter Haddock*
Contact *Pat Hornby*
FOUNDED 1952. *Publishes* children's picture story and activity books. About 200 series a year. Ideas for picture books welcome.
Royalties payments vary according to contract.

Authors' Rating Cheap end of the market. Writers need to work fast to make a living.

Peter Halban Publishers
42 South Molton Street, London W1Y 1HB
☎0171 491 1582   Fax 0171 629 5381
Directors *Peter Halban, Martine Halban*
FOUNDED 1986. Independent publisher. *Publishes* biography, autobiography and memoirs, history,

philosophy, theology, politics, literature and criticism, Judaica and world affairs. 4–5 titles a year. No unsolicited material. Approach by letter in first instance.

Royalties paid twice yearly for first two years, thereafter annually in December.

Robert Hale Ltd

Clerkenwell House, 45–47 Clerkenwell Green, London EC1R 0HT
☎0171 251 2661   Fax 0171 490 4958
Chairman/Managing Director *John Hale*

FOUNDED 1936. Family-owned company. *Publishes* adult fiction (but not interested in category crime, romance or science fiction) and non-fiction. No specialist material (education, law, medical or scientific). Over 300 titles a year. TITLES *World History* Bruce Wetterau; *A History of English Country Sports* Michael Billett; *Homosexuality* Dr Joan Gomez; *The Popular Guide to Classical Music* Dr Anne Gray; *The Fireside Book of Deadly Diseases* Robert Wilkins; *Old Houses and Cottages of Kent* R. J. Brown. Unsolicited mss, synopses and ideas for books welcome.

Royalties paid twice yearly.

Authors' Rating Takes good care of authors but can be tough on advances. Favours the popular end of the fiction market.

The Hambledon Press

102 Gloucester Avenue, London NW1 8HX
☎0171 586 0817   Fax 0171 586 9970
Chairman/Managing Director/Editorial Head *Martin Sheppard*

FOUNDED 1980. *Publishes* English and European history from post-classical to modern. Currently expanding its list to include history titles with a wider appeal. 25–30 titles a year. TITLES *Jane Austen and Food* Maggie Lane; *Dilke, The Lost Prime Minister* David Nicholls; *Channel Tunnel Visions* Keith Wilson. No unsolicited mss; send preliminary letter. Synopses and ideas welcome.

Royalties paid annually. *Overseas associates* **The Hambledon Press (USA)**, Ohio.

Hamish Hamilton Ltd

See **Penguin Books Ltd**

Hamlyn/Hamlyn Children's Books

See **Reed International Books**

Harcourt Brace and Company Limited

24–28 Oval Road, London NW1 7DX
☎0171 267 4466 Fax 0171 482 2293/485 4752
Managing Director *Bill Barnett*

Owned by US parent company. *Publishes* scientific, technical and medical books, college textbooks, educational & occupational test. No unsolicited mss. IMPRINTS **Academic Press; Baillière Tindall; Dryden Press; Grune & Stratton; Holt Rinehart and Winston; W. B. Saunders & Co. Ltd.; Saunders Scientific Publications**.

Harlequin Mills & Boon Ltd

Eton House, 18–24 Paradise Road, Richmond, Surrey TW9 1SR
☎0181 948 0444   Fax 0181 940 5899
Chairman *John T. Boon*
Managing Director *A. Flynn*
Editorial Director *Karin Stoecker*

FOUNDED 1908. Owned by the Canadian-based Torstar Group. *Publishes* romantic fiction and historical romance. Over 600 titles a year.

IMPRINTS **Mills & Boon Romances** (50–55,000 words) contemporary romances with international settings, focusing intensely on hero and heroine, with happy endings assured. **Mills & Boon Temptation** *Linda Fildew* (60–65,000 words) Modern, sensual love stories where characters face dilemmas and choices in fast-paced plots. **Love On Call** *Elizabeth Johnson* (50–55,000 words) Modern medical practice provides a unique background to love stories. **Legacy of Love** *Elizabeth Johnson* (75–80,000 words) Historical romances. **Mira** *Linda Fildew* (minimum 100,000 words) Individual women's fiction.

Silhouette Desire, Special Edition, Sensation and **Intrigue** imprints are handled by US-based **Silhouette Books** (see **US Publishers**). Unsolicited mss welcome for imprints other than Silhouette.

Tip sheets and guidelines for the Harlequin Mills & Boon series available from Harlequin Mills & Boon Editorial Dept. (please send s.a.e.). Also available (at £9.99 inc. VAT, p&p): *And Then He Kissed Her*, a 40-minute audio cassette with advice on characterisation, plot, dialogue, etc plus *Behind The Hearts and Flowers*, a 28-page booklet containing practical advice on preparing a manuscript.

Royalties paid twice yearly.

Authors' Rating Harlequin Mills & Boon is the only top name publisher readers can immediately identify with its product. But romantic fiction has become racier of late with more dynamic female characters who enjoy sex as much as a successful business deal. Mills & Boon do more than most to attract new writers. What with a helpful guide to the romantic novel, workshops for aspiring authors and a promise to read unsolicited mss, it is hard to imagine what else they could do to nurture talent. But this is still a woman's world. In the Mills & Boon list, male writers are as rare as a sad ending.

Harley Books

Martins, Great Horkesley, Colchester, Essex CO6 4AH
☎01206 271216   Fax 01206 271182
Managing Director *Basil Harley*

FOUNDED 1983. Natural history publishers specialising in entomological books. Definitive, high-quality illustrated reference works. TITLES *The Moths and Butterflies of Great Britain and Ireland; Spiders of Great Britain and Ireland; Dragonflies of Europe.*

Royalties paid twice yearly in the first year, annually thereafter.

HarperCollins Publishers Ltd

77–85 Fulham Palace Road, London W6 8JB
☎0181 741 7070   Fax 0181 307 4440
Also at: Freepost PO Box, Glasgow G4 0NB
☎0141 772 3200 Fax 0141 306 3119
Executive Chairman/Publisher *Eddie Bell*
Managing Director, Trade Group *Adrian Bourne*
Managing Director, Reference Group *Roy Davey*
Approx. Annual Turnover £200 million

Publisher of high-profile authors like Jeffrey Archer, James Herbert, Fay Weldon and Len Deighton. Owned by News Corporation. Since 1991 there has been a period of consolidated focus on key management issues within the HarperCollins empire. This has led to various imprints being phased out in favour of others, among them Grafton and Fontana, which have been merged under the HarperCollins paperback imprint. Title output has been reduced by about 20%.

DIVISIONS
Trade *David Young*, Deputy Managing Director; *Stuart Profitt*, Publisher; **Fiction** *Malcolm Edwards, Nick Sayers*; **Non-Fiction** *Michael Fishwick.* IMPRINTS **Collins Crime; Flamingo** (literary fiction, both hardback and paperback); **HarperCollins   Paperbacks;   Tolkein;**

HarperCollins Science Fiction and Fantasy; **Fontana Press; HarperCollins**. Over 650 titles a year, hardback and paperback. No longer accepts unsolicited submissions.

Thorsons *Eileen Campbell*, Deputy Managing Director.   IMPRINTS   **Pandora   Press**; **Thorsons** Health, nutrition, business, parenting, popular psychology, positive thinking, self-help, divination, therapy, recovery, feminism, women's issues, mythology, religion, yoga, tarot, personal development, sexual politics, biography, history, popular culture. About 250 titles a year.

Children's *Roy Davey* IMPRINTS **Picture Lions; HarperCollins Audio** (see under **Audio Books); Jets; Young Lions; Lions; Armada; Tracks; Collins Non-Fiction** Quality picture books and book and tape sets for under 7s; all categories of fiction for the 6–14 age group; dictionaries and general reference for pre-school and primary. About 250 titles a year.

Reference *Robin Wood* IMPRINTS **Collins New Naturalist Library; Collins Gems; Collins Willow** (sport); **HarperCollins; Janes** (military) Encyclopedias, guides and handbooks, phrase books and manuals on popular reference, art instruction, cookery and wine, crafts, DIY, gardening, military natural history, pet care, Scottish, sports and pastimes. About 120 titles a year.

Educational *Roy Davey* Textbook publishing for schools and FE colleges (5–18-year-olds): all subjects for primary education; strong in English, history, geography, science and technology for secondary education; and sociology, business studies and economics in FE. (Former Holmes McDougall, Unwin Hyman, Mary Glasgow Primary Publications and part of Harcourt, Brace & Co. educational imprints have been incorporated under Collins Educational.) About 90 titles a year.

Dictionaries *Richard Thomas* IMPRINTS **Collins; Collins Cobuild; Collins Gem** Includes the *Collins English Dictionary* range with dictionaries and thesauruses, *Collins Bilingual Dictionary* range (French, German, Spanish, Italian, etc.), and the *Cobuild* series of English dictionary, grammars and EFL books. About 50 titles a year.

HarperCollege *Kate Harris* IMPRINT **HarperCollins College** Selected US academic titles, mostly imported from College Division, Basic Books, Harper Business and Harper Perennial.

Most of the titles stocked are university-level texts, previously published under the Harper & Row and Scott Foresman imprints. A programme to publish UK editions of some of these commenced in 1994. Strength areas are economics, psychology, allied health and business. About 550 titles stocked in the UK.

HarperCollins World *Roy Davey*. IMPRINTS **HarperCollins US**; **Australia**; **New Zealand**; **Canada**; **India** General trade titles imported into the UK market.

Religious *Eileen Campbell* A broad-based religious publisher across all denominations. IMPRINTS **HarperCollins**; **Fount**; **Marshall Pickering** Extensive range covering both popular and academic spirituality, music and reference. Marshall Pickering, bibles, missals, prayer books, and hymn books. About 150 titles a year.

HarperCartographic *Jeremy Westwood* The cartographic division, with Bartholomew and Times Books now joined as one division, but operating from two addresses: Bartholomew from Edinburgh (12 Duncan Street, Edinburgh EH9 1TA. Tel: 0131–667 9341. Fax: 0131–662 4282); Times Books from Fulham Palace Road (as above). IMPRINTS **Bartholomew**; **Collins HarperCollins Audiobooks** (see under **Audio Books**); **Invincible Press**; **Longman**; **Nicholson**; **Nicholson/Ordnance Survey**; **Sun Crosswords**; **Times Atlases**; **Times Books**; **Times Crosswords**. Maps, atlases and guides (Bartholomew; Collins; Collins Longman; Times Atlases); leisure maps; educational titles (Collins Longman); London titles (Nicholson); waterway guides (Nicholson/Ordnance Survey); sports titles for *The Sun* and *News of the World* (Invincible Press); reference and non-fiction (Times Books). About 30 titles a year.

HarperCollins Interactive *Steve Paul* Supports the company's electronic publishing activities on CD-ROM, floppy disk and on-line. *Specialises* in special interest, children's, reference and interactive fiction.

Broadcasting Consultancy *Cresta Norris* Newly formed to exploit TV and film rights across the country.

Authors' Rating A good measure of the generation gap is to ask if anyone remembers the days when Rupert Murdoch bought into Collins promising not to make too many changes. Only the young and innocent will look blank. Today, HarperCollins is so much the modern, state of the art company that staff are said to have to do

physical jerks and undertake voluntary work on behalf of the less privileged – not necessarily other publishers. After an extensive reorganisation, in what is now frequently described as the most successful publisher in Britain, 'commitment' is the word to savour – commitment to best selling authors who are famed the length and breadth of the high street (17 titles in the Guardian 100 Fastseller list) but commitment also to that profitable core of reference and theological books, the only reminder that the old Collins was actually quite a successful publisher. HarperCollins shares with Hodder Headline the Society of Authors accolade for 'the clearest and most informative royalty statements'.

Harrap Publishing Group Ltd
See **Larousse plc**

Harvard University Press
Fitzroy House, 11 Chenies Street,
London WC1E 7ET
☎0171 306 0603   Fax 0171 306 0604
Director *William Sisler*
General Manager *Ann Sexsmith*

Part of **Harvard University Press**, USA. *Publishes* academic and scholarly works in history, politics, philosophy, economics, literary criticism, psychology, sociology, anthropology, women's studies, biological sciences, astronomy, history of science, art, music, film, reference. All mss go to the American office: 79 Garden Street, Cambridge, MA 02138.

The Harvill Press Ltd
84 Thornhill Road, London N1 1RD
☎0171 609 1119   Fax 0171 609 2019
Chairman *Christopher MacLehose*
Managing Director *John Mitchinson*

FOUNDED in 1947, the list was bought by Collins in 1959, of which it remained an imprint until returning to its original independent status in early 1995. *Publishes* literature in translation (especially Russian, Italian and French), literature, quality thrillers, illustrated books and Africana, plus an occasional poetry anthology. 50–60 titles in 1994. TITLES *Fields of Glory* (Jean Rouaud - winner of the Prix Goncourt; *The Leopard* Giuseppe Tomasi di Lampedusa; *Will You Please Be Quiet, Please* Raymond Carver; *The Sportswriter* Richard Ford; *A Void* Georges Perec. Mss usually submitted by foreign publishers and agents.

Synopses and ideas welcome. No educational or technical books.

Royalties paid twice yearly.

Authors' Rating Back as an independent publisher after a management buyout from HarperCollins, the aim is to produce some 50 titles in the first year with a mix of quality fiction and monographs. Some top names are going elsewhere – Gerald Seymour, George Macdonald Fraser and Martin Cruz Smith among them – but money saved on big advances will make for a more balanced list.

Haynes Publishing

Sparkford, Near Yeovil, Somerset BA22 7JJ
☎01963 440635   Fax 01963 440825
Chairman *John H. Haynes*
Approx. Annual Turnover £20 million

FOUNDED in 1960 by John H. Haynes. A family-run business. The mainstay of its programme has been the *Owners' Workshop Manual*, first published in the mid 1960s and still running off the presses today. Indeed the company maintains a strong bias towards motoring and transport titles. *Publishes* DIY workshop manuals for cars and motorbikes, railway, aviation, military, maritime, model making, and general leisure under imprints.

IMPRINTS **G. T. Foulis & Co.** cars and motoring-related books; **J. H. Haynes & Co. Ltd** *Scott Mauck* workshop manuals; **Oxford Illustrated Press** photography, sports and games, gardening, travel and guidebooks; **Oxford Publishing Co.** railway titles; **Patrick Stephens Ltd** *Darryl Reach* motoring, rail, aviation, military, maritime, model making. Unsolicited mss welcome if they come within the subject areas covered.

Royalties paid annually. *Overseas associates* Haynes Publications Inc., California, USA.

Authors' Rating Having a hard time of it throughout the recession, Haynes is back on form after a severe cutback in non-core publishing. If you are into workshop manuals, Haynes is your publisher.

Hazar Publishing Ltd

147 Chiswick High Road, London W4 2DT
☎0181 742 8578   Fax 0181 994 1407
Managing Director *Gregory Hill*
Editorial Head (Adult) *Marie Clayton*
Editorial Head (Children's) *Rio Brown*
Approx. Annual Turnover £700,000

FOUNDED 1993, Hazar is a new independent publisher of high quality illustrated books. *Publishes* children's fiction and adult non-fiction: design and architecture. Planning to expand the children's list. 15 titles in 1994. Welcome unsolicited mss, synopses and ideas.

Royalties paid twice yearly.

Hazleton Publishing

3 Richmond Hill, Richmond, Surrey TW10 6RE
☎0181 948 5151   Fax 0181 948 4111
Chairman/Managing Director *R. F. Poulter*

Publisher of the leading Grand Prix annual *Autocourse*, now in its 45th edition. *Publishes* high-quality motor sport titles including annuals. About 13 titles a year. No unsolicited mss; synopses and ideas welcome. Interested in all motor sport titles.

Royalties payment varies.

Headline

See **Hodder Headline plc**

Headstart

See **Hodder Headline plc**

Headstart History

PO Box 41, Bangor, Gwynedd LL57 1GB
☎01248 351816   Fax 01248 362115
Publisher *Judith Loades*

FOUNDED 1990 to publish the *Medieval History* journal. *Publishes* academic history: student history papers and learned books, including reprints; historical novels and history books for the general market. 30 titles a year planned. No unsolicited mss; sample chapter only.

IMPRINTS **Catesby Press** historical novels; **Babbage Press** showbusiness; **Headstart History Papers** TITLES *The Tudor Court* D. M. Loades; *The Last Plantagenet* Hazel Bird; *Victorian Nonconformity* D. Bebbington; *The Diary of John Evelyn* ed. Guy de la Bedoyère; **The Phoenix Press (Swansea)** *Tractarian Grass Roots* Denison & Jones; *Dietrich Bonhoeffer: The Ethics* H. R. Lockley; **The Umberleigh Press** *A Diversity of Birds* George Stebbing-Allen.

Royalties paid annually.

Headway

See **Hodder Headline plc**

Heinemann

See **Reed International Books**

Helicon Publishing

42 Hythe Bridge Street, Oxford OX1 2EP
☎01865 204204   Fax 01865 204205
Managing Director *David Attwooll*
Editorial Director *Michael Upshall*
Acquisition Director *Anne-Lucie Norton*

FOUNDED 1992 from the management buy-out of former Random Century's reference division. Led by David Attwooll, the buy-out (for an undisclosed sum) included the Hutchinson Encyclopedia titles and databases, along with other reference titles. Random maintain a close relationship, representing Helicon to the trade. Helicon is increasing the range of reference titles, particularly in history, science and current affairs and is maintaining its lead in electronic publishing. TITLES *History of the World* J. M. Roberts; *Enquire Within* Moira Bremner.

Christopher Helm Publishers Ltd

See **A. & C. Black (Publishers) Ltd**

Henderson Publishing plc

The Salt House, Tide Mill Way, Woodbridge, Suffolk IP12 1BY
☎01394 380622   Fax 01394 380618
Managing Director *Barrie Henderson*
Commissioning Editor *Hazel Jones*

FOUNDED 1990. *Publishes* non-fiction novelty and information books for children. Most ideas are generated in-house to specific formats across the range of imprints. Unsolicited mss, synopses and ideas for books welcome. Maximum length 7500 words; 3500 for Junior Funfax titles. No poetry, long fiction or teenage subject matter. IMPRINTS **Funfax; Junior Funfax; My Little Funfax; Clever Clogs; Know-Alls**.

Ian Henry Publications Ltd

20 Park Drive, Romford, Essex RM1 4LH
☎01708 749119   Fax 01621 850862
Managing Director *Ian Wilkes*

FOUNDED 1976. *Publishes* local history, transport history and Sherlockian pastiches. 8–10 titles a year. TITLES *Baker Street Irregular; Ghost Hunter's Guide to Essex; The Hampstead Poisonings; Secret Essex*. No unsolicited mss. Synopses and ideas for books welcome.
Royalties paid twice yearly.

The Herbert Press Ltd

46 Northchurch Road, London N1 4EJ
☎0171 254 4379   Fax 0171 254 4332
Managing Director/Editorial Director
David Herbert

Publishes archaeology, architecture and design, botanical art, crafts and hobbies, exhibition catalogues, fashion and costume, fine art and art history, photography. About 8 titles a year. Unsolicited mss welcome.
Royalties paid twice yearly.

Nick Hern Books

14 Larden Road, London W3 7ST
☎0181 740 9539   Fax 0181 746 2006
Chairman/Managing Director *Nick Hern*
Approx. Annual Turnover £200,000

FOUNDED 1988 by Nick Hern, under the aegis of Walker Books, then under **Random House**. Fully independent since 1992. *Publishes* books on theatre: from how-to and biography to plays. About 25 titles a year. No unsolicited playscripts. Scripts, ideas and proposals for other theatre material welcome. Not interested in material unrelated to the theatre.

Authors' Rating Winner of the 1994 *Sunday Times* Small Publishers Award, Nick Hern Books is the leading specialist publisher of plays and theatrical biographies. *The Sunday Times* judges were impressed with 'the coherence of its list and the evident firmness of purpose behind the company'.

High Risk Books

See **Serpent's Tail**

Highland Books

See **Inter Publishing Ltd**

Hippo

See **Scholastic Publications Ltd**

HMSO Books

St Crispins, Duke Street, Norwich, Norfolk NR3 1PD
☎01603 622211   Fax 01603 695582
Controller *Dr Paul Freeman*

FOUNDED 1786. Government publisher of material sponsored by Parliament, government departments and other official bodies. No unsolicited material. The Controller is responsible for the administration of Crown and parliamentary copyright. The contact point for any copyright queries is 01603 695506.

Hobsons Publishing

Bateman Street, Cambridge CB2 1LZ
☎01223 354551   Fax 01223 323154
Chairman *Charles Sinclair*
Managing Director *Martin Morgan*

Approx. Annual Turnover £11 million
FOUNDED 1973. A division of Harmsworth Publishing Ltd, part of the Daily Mail & General Trust. *Publishes* course and career guides, under exclusive licence and royalty agreements for CRAC (Careers Research and Advisory Bureau); computer software; directories and specialist titles for employers, government departments and professional associations. TITLES *Graduate Employment and Training; Casebooks; Graduate Studies; The Student HelpBook Series; Degree Course Guides; The Which Degree Series; The Directory of Higher Education; The Directory of Further Education; CRAC GNVQ Assignment Series.* Also publisher of *Johansens Hotel Guides.*

Authors' Rating Formula publishing based on a close and shrewd analysis of the education and business markets.

Hodder & Stoughton
See **Hodder Headline plc**

Hodder Headline plc
338 Euston Road, London NW1 3BH
☎0171 873 6000   Fax 0171 873 6024
Group Chief Executive *Tim Hely Hutchinson*
Deputy Chief Executive *Mark Opzoomer*
Approx. Annual Turnover £80 million
Formed in June 1993 through the merger of **Headline Book Publishing** and **Hodder & Stoughton**. Headline was formed in 1986 and had grown dramatically, whereas Hodder & Stoughton was 125 years old with a diverse range of publishing.

DIVISIONS
Headline Book Publishing Managing Director *Sian Thomas*. **Non-fiction** *Alan Brooke*; **Fiction** *Jane Morpeth. Publishes* commercial fiction (hardback and paperback) and popular non-fiction including biography, cinema, design and film, food and wine, countryside, TV tie-ins and sports yearbooks. IMPRINTS **Headline**; **Headline Feature**; **Headline Review**; **Headline Delta**; **Liaison** (erotic fiction). AUTHORS Raymond Blanc, Harry Bowling, Martina Cole, Josephine Cox, John Francome, Dean Koontz, Richard Laymon, Lyn Macdonald, Ellis Peters and Peter Scudamore.

Hodder & Stoughton General Managing Director *Martin Nield*, Deputy Managing Director *Sue Fletcher*. **Non-fiction** *Roland Philipps*; **Horror** *Nick Austin*; **Sceptre** *Carole Welch*; **Fiction** *Carolyn Mays, Carolyn Caughey*; **Audio** (See **Audio Books**). *Publishes* com-

mercial and literary fiction; biography, autobiography, history, self-help, humour, travel and other general interest non-fiction; audio. IMPRINTS **Hodder & Stoughton**; **Coronet**; **New English Library**; **Sceptre**. AUTHORS Elizabeth Adler, Melvyn Bragg, John le Carré, James Clavell, Edwina Currie, Stephen King, Stephen Leather, Gavin Lyall, Ed McBain, Hilary Norman and Mary Stewart, Terry Waite.

Hodder & Stoughton Educational Managing Director *Brian Steven*. **Humanities, Science & Mathematics** *David Lea*; **Language, Business and Psychology** *Tim Gregson-Williams*. Textbooks for the primary, secondary, tertiary and further education sectors and for self-improvement. IMPRINTS **Hodder & Stoughton Educational**; **Teach Yourself**; **Headway**.

Hodder Children's Books Managing Director *Mary Tapissier*, Publishing Director *Fiona Kenshole*. IMPRINTS **Hodder & Stoughton**; **Knight**; **Picture Knight**; **Hodder Dargaud**; **Headstart**; **Test Your Child**. AUTHORS Goscinny & Uderzo (*Asterix*), Rolf Harris, Mick Inkpen, Christopher Pike.

Hodder & Stoughton Religious Managing Director *Eric Major*. **Bibles & Liturgical** *Emma Sealey*; **Christian paperbacks** *James Catford*. Bibles, commentaries, liturgical works (both printed and software), and a wide range of Christian paperbacks. IMPRINTS **New International Version of the Bible**; **Hodder Christian paperbacks**.

Edward Arnold Managing Director *Richard Stileman*. **Humanities** *Chris Wheeler*; **Medical, Science and Engineering** *Nicki Dennis*. Academic and professional books and journals.
The Brockhampton Press Managing Director *John Maxwell*. Promotional books.
Royalties paid twice yearly.

Authors' Rating Having advanced to become the largest independent book publisher (Macmillan was the first until the recent sale) Hodder Headline is set to expand its list to at least 2500 titles a year. Unashamedly populist, Hodder Headline's commissioning policy is driven by marketing 'the kind of books people want to read'. This covers a huge range including latterly, a talking books division. Advantage points for authors include regular and frequent updates on sales figures. The restructured children's list, led by Mary Tapissier, thrives on imaginative design and packaging. Quote of the year from chief executive Tim Hely Hutchinson: 'We love and pay our best authors to the very best of our ability ... In the 12 years

I have been running publishing companies I have never lost a single best-selling author.'

Holmes McDougall
See **HarperCollins Publishers Ltd**

Holt Rinehart & Winston
See **Harcourt Brace and Company Limited**

Honeyglen Publishing Ltd
56 Durrels House, Warwick Gardens, London W14 8QB
☎0171 602 2876
Directors *N. S. Poderegin, J. Poderegin*

FOUNDED 1983. *Publishes* history, philosophy of history, biography and selective fiction. No children's or science fiction. TITLES *The Soul of India; A Child of the Century* Amaury de Riencourt; *With Duncan Grant in South Turkey* Paul Roche; *Vladimir, The Russian Viking* Vladimir Volkoff; *The Dawning* Milka Bajic-Poderegin; *Quicksand* Louise Hide. Unsolicited mss welcome. No synopses or ideas.

Authors' Rating Highly commended in *The Sunday Times* survey of small independent publishers.

How To Books Ltd
Plymbridge House, Estover Road, Plymouth, Devon PL6 7PZ
☎01752 735251/695745   Fax 01752 695699
Publisher/Managing Director *Roger Ferneyhough*

The first titles were published in 1987 by **Northcote House Publishers**. By 1991 the list had grown so much and was expanding at such a rate that Roger Ferneyhough set up a separate company, with 25 titles in print and a programme of some 20 new titles a year. There are now 100 titles in the series, many in revised and updated new editions. TITLES take the form of 'how to achieve a specific goal or benefit' in the areas of employment, business, education, international opportunities and self-development: *How to Become an Au Pair; How to Survive Divorce; How to Lose Weight & Keep Fit; How to Master Languages*. Well-structured proposals from qualified and experienced professionals welcome.
Royalties paid annually.

The University of Hull Press/ The Lampada Press
Cottingham Road, Hull, North Humberside HU6 7RX
☎01482 465322   Fax 01482 465936
Chairman *Dr P. A. Holmes*

Secretary *Miss J.M. Smith*

The University of Hull Press *publishes* books of academic merit and those that command a wide general market. TITLES *The Diary of Sir Edward Walter Hamilton 1885–1906* ed. Dudley W.R. Bahlman; *Pugin's Builders: The Life and Work of George Myers* Patricia Spencer-Silver. The Lampada Press *publishes* well-researched popular works, mainly of local interest. Welcomes unsolicited mss, synopses and ideas for books.
Royalties paid annually. *Overseas representatives*: Paul & Company Publishers Consortium Inc., USA; St Clair Press, Australia.

Human Horizons
See **Souvenir Press Ltd**

Human Science Press
See **Plenum Publishing Ltd**

Hunt & Thorpe
Bowland House, off West Street, Alresford, Hampshire SO23 9AT
☎01962 735633   Fax 01962 735320
Approx. Annual Turnover £1.5 million
Publishes children's and religious titles only. About 25 titles a year. Unsolicited material welcome.

C. Hurst & Co.
38 King Street, London WC2E 8JZ
☎0171 240 2666   Fax 0171 240 2667
Chairman/Managing Director *Christopher Hurst*
Editorial Heads *Christopher Hurst, Michael Dwyer*

FOUNDED 1967. An independent company, cultivating a concern for literacy, detail and the visual aspects of the product. *Publishes* contemporary history, politics and social science. About 20 titles a year. TITLES *A History of Mozambique; Resistance and Reform in Tibet; Bosnia and Hercegovina – A Tradition Betrayed; Who Are the Macedonians; Following Ho Chi Minh – Memoirs of a North Vietnamese Colonel; Sex, Culture and Modernity in China*. No unsolicited mss. Synopses and ideas welcome.
Royalties paid twice in first year, annually thereafter.

Hutchinson Books
See **Random House UK Ltd**

Hymns Ancient & Modern Ltd
St Mary's Works, St Mary's Plain, Norwich, Norfolk NR3 3BH
☎01603 616563   Fax 01603 624483

Chairman *Very Rev. Dr Henry Chadwick KBE*
Publisher *G.A. Knights*

Publishes hymn books for churches, schools and other institutions. All types of religious books, both general and educational.

IMPRINTS **The Canterbury Press Norwich** (see entry); **Religious and Moral Education Press** moral, personal and social education list of books and videos for primary and secondary schools; **Church Times**. TITLES *Tradition and Exploration; City Prayers; Christian Perspectives; Life Beyond Death.* Ideas welcome; no mss.
Royalties paid annually.

Hymns Ancient & Modern Ltd
St Mary's Works, St Mary's Plain, Norwich, Norfolk NR3 3BH
☎01603 616563   Fax 01603 624483
Chairman *Very Rev. Dr Henry Chadwick KBE*
Publisher *G. A. Knights*

Publishes hymn books for churches, schools and other institutions. IMPRINTS **Canterbury Press Norwich** (see entry); **Religious and Moral Education Press; Church Times** TITLES *Prayers for Everyday Use; New Springtime in the Church; Revised Common Lectionary.* Ideas welcome; no mss.
Royalties paid annually.

IBC Publishing
57–61 Mortimer Street, London W1N 7TD
☎0171 637 4383   Fax 0171 636 6414
Managing Director *Tony Powell*

Owned by International Business Communications (Holdings) plc. *Publishes* the *Banking Technology* magazine and a range of legal, tax, financial, management and business to business books, newsletters and directories, aimed at senior management and professional practices. About 50 titles a year. Unsolicited synopses and ideas welcome, but initial approach in writing preferred.
Royalties paid twice yearly.

Impact Books Ltd
Axe and Bottle Court, 70 Newcomen Street, London SE1 1YT
☎0171 403 3541   Fax 0171 407 6437
Managing Director *Jean-Luc Barbanneau*
Approx. Annual Turnover £150,000

FOUNDED 1985 by Jean-Luc Barbanneau, formerly Deputy Managing Director and Publisher of Harrap Publishing Group. *Publishes* travel, practical guides, reference, illustrated books, children's books, fiction. About 20 titles a year.

TITLES *The Drive-Thru Museum* A. Soutter (Travellers' Tales series); *It's Never Too Late* J Perkin (a guide to returning to education for women); *Life on the Floor* Biff; *French Glossary for Bilingual Secretaries.* Unsolicited mss not welcome – send detailed synopses and sample chapters first.
Royalties paid twice yearly.

Inter Publishing Ltd
St Nicholas House, The Mount, Guildford, Surrey GU2 4NH
☎01483 306309   Fax 01483 579196
Managing Director *David Wavre*
Approx. Annual Turnover £400,000

FOUNDED 1990. *Publishes* religious books only. About 24 titles a year. IMPRINTS **Eagle, Highland Books.** Unsolicited mss, synopses and ideas for books welcome.
Royalties paid quarterly.

Inter-Varsity Press
38 De Montfort Street, Leicester LE1 7GP
☎0116 2551754   Fax 0116 2542044
Chairman *Ralph Evershed*
Chief Executive *Frank Entwistle*

FOUNDED mid-30s as the publishing arm of Universities and Colleges Christian Fellowship, it has expanded to wider Christian markets worldwide. *Publishes* Christian belief and lifestyle, reference and bible commentaries. About 50 titles a year. No secular material or anything which fails to empathise with orthodox Protestant Christianity.
IMPRINTS **IVP, Apollos, Crossway** TITLES *The Bible Speaks Today; Sociology through the Eyes of Faith* Campolo & Fraser. No unsolicited mss; synopses and ideas welcome.
Royalties paid twice yearly.

Intrigue
See **Harlequin Mills & Boon Ltd**

Invincible Press
See **HarperCollins Publishers Ltd**

Richard D. Irwin/Irwin Professional Publishers
See **Times Mirror International Publishers Ltd**

Isis Publishing Limited
7 Centremead, Osney Mead, Oxford OX2 0ES
☎01865 250333   Fax 01865 790358
Managing Director *John Durrant*

Publishes large print books – fiction and non-fiction; audio books (see under **Audio Books**).

TITLES *The Colour of Magic* Terry Pratchett; *The Book of Guys* Garrison Keillor; *The Rise and Fall of the House of Windsor.* No unsolicited mss as Isis undertake no original publishing.
Royalties paid twice yearly.

Ithaca Press
See **Garnet Publishing Ltd**

IVP
See **Inter-Varsity Press**

JAI Press Ltd
The Courtyard, 28 High Street, Hampton Hill, Middlesex TW12 1PD
☎0181 943 9296   Fax 0181 943 9317
Chairman *Herbert M. Johnson*
Managing Director *Piers R. Allen*
FOUNDED 1976. Owned by JAI Press, Inc., USA. *Publishes* research-level scholarly publications in business, economics, social sciences, computer sciences, chemistry and life sciences, spanning the complete range of social and economic sciences, natural, pure and applied physical sciences. *Specialises* in the publication of research serials and monograph series, as well as journals. About 140 titles a year. TITLES *Advances in Biosensors; Research in Organizational Behavior; Research in Third World Accounting; Advances in Solid-State Chemistry.* No undergraduate texts. Unsolicited mss discouraged. Synopses and ideas welcome.
Royalties paid annually. *Overseas associates* JAI Press, Inc., Greenwich, Connecticut, USA.

Arthur James Ltd
4 Broadway Road, Evesham, Worcestershire WR11 6BH
☎01386 446566   Fax 01386 446717
Editorial Office: Deershot Lodge, Park Lane, Ropley, Nr Alresford, Hampshire SO24 0BE
Managing Director *Ian Carlile*
Editorial Director *Mr J. Hunt*
Approx. Annual Turnover £165,000
FOUNDED 1944 by a Fleet Street journalist, A. J. Russell. *Publishes* day books, devotional classics, psychological, religious, social work and *New Testament* translations. AUTHORS include William Barclay, George Bennett, Howard Booth, Stanley Booth-Clibborn, Betty Brooke, Denis Duncan, J. B. Phillips, Leslie Weatherhead. No unsolicited mss.
Royalties paid annually. *Overseas associates* Buchanan, Australia; Omega, New Zealand.

Jane's Information Group
163 Brighton Road, Coulsdon, Surrey CR5 2NH
☎0181 763 1030   Fax 0181 763 1005
Managing Director *Alfred Rolington*
Approx. Annual Turnover £25 million
FOUNDED 1898 by Fred T. Jane with the publication of *All The World's Fighting Ships.* Now part of The Thomson Corporation. For the last few years management has been focusing on growth opportunities in its core business and in enhancing the performance of initiatives like Jane's yearbooks on CD-ROM. *Publishes* reviews and yearbooks on defence, aerospace and transport topics, with details of equipment and systems; plus directories and strategic studies. Also *Jane's Defence Weekly* (see under **Magazines**).

DIVISIONS
Defence Magazines *Simon Kay* TITLES *Jane's Defence Weekly; International Defence Review; Jane's Intelligence Review; Defence Systems Modernisation; International Defence Review; Navy International;* **Data Division** *Gina Dawkins* TITLES *Defence Aerospace Yearbooks* (hard copy and CD-ROM); *Defence Aerospace Directories/ Binders; Jane's Airport Review; Sentinel* (threat analysis). Unsolicited mss, synopses and ideas for books welcome.
Royalties paid twice yearly. *Overseas associates* Jane's Information Group Inc., USA.

Janus Publishing Company Ltd
Edinburgh House, 19 Nassau Street, London W1N 7RE
☎0171 580 7664   Fax 0171 636 5756
Managing Director *Ronald Ross Stanton*
Publishes fiction, human interest, memoirs/biography, mind, body and spirit, religion and theology, social questions, popular science, history, spiritualism and the paranormal, poetry, children and young adults. About 50 titles a year. TITLES *Ghosts at Cockcrow* June Barraclough; *A Doctor in the Wilderness* Dr Walter Yellowlees; *Chronicles of Alston* Joan Rockwell; *China and its Religious Inheritance* John H. Chamberlayne; *If Only Toads Could Fly* John Gilmore. Unsolicited mss welcome.
Royalties paid twice yearly. Agents in USA, Australia, South Africa and Asia.

Authors' Rating Authors may be asked to cover their own production costs.

Japan Library
See **Curzon Press Ltd**

Jarrold Publishing
Whitefriars, Norwich, Norfolk NR3 1TR
☎01603 763300   Fax 01603 662748
Managing Director *Antony Jarrold*

Part of Jarrold & Sons Ltd, long-established printing/publishing company. *Publishes* travel, leisure, light poetry and calendars. Material tends to be of a high pictorial content. No novels or biography, unless of specific local interest. About 30 titles a year. Unsolicited mss, synopses and ideas welcome but approach by phone or in writing before submitting anything.
Royalties paid twice yearly.

Jets
See **HarperCollins Publishers Ltd**

Jewish Chronicle Publications
See **Frank Cass & Co Ltd**

Michael Joseph Ltd
See **Penguin Books Ltd**

Kahn & Averill
9 Harrington Road, London SW7 3ES
☎0181 743 3278   Fax 0181 743 3278
Managing Director *Mr M. Kahn*

FOUNDED 1967 to publish children's titles but now specialises in music titles. A small independent publishing house. *Publishes* music and general non-fiction. No unsolicited mss; synopses and ideas for books considered.
Royalties paid twice yearly.

Karnak House
300 Westbourne Park Road, London W11 1EH
☎0171 221 6490   Fax 0171 221 6490
Chairman *Dada Imarogbe*
Managing Director *Amon Saba Saakana*
Approx. Annual Turnover £75,000

FOUNDED 1979. *Publishes* anthropology, education, Egyptology, history, language and linguistics, literary criticism, music, parapsychology, prehistory, fiction and education for children. No poetry, humour or sport. About 12 titles a year. No unsolicited mss; send introduction or synopsis with one sample chapter. Synopses and ideas welcome.
Royalties paid twice yearly. *Overseas subsidiaries*: The Antef Institute, and Karnak House, Illinois, USA.

Richard Kay Publications
80 Sleaford Road, Boston, Lincolnshire PE21 8EU
☎01205 353231
Managing Editor *Richard Allday*

FOUNDED 1970. Non-profit motivated publisher of local interest (Lincs.) material: dialect, history, autobiography and biography, philosophy, medico-political and contemporary dissent on current affairs. About 6 titles a year. TITLES *Winceby and the Battle; Alcoholism: A Terminal Disease; William Brewster: The Father of New England; Royal Navy in Lincolnshire.* No unsolicited mss; synopses and ideas welcome.
Royalties paid if appropriate.

Kelpie
See **Canongate Books Ltd**

Kenilworth Press Ltd
Addington, Buckingham, Buckinghamshire MK18 2JR
☎01296 715101   Fax 01296 715148
Chairman/Managing Director *David Blunt*
Approx. Annual Turnover £500,000

FOUNDED 1989 with the acquisition of Threshhold Books. The UK's principal instructional equestrian publisher, producing the official books of the British Horse Society, the famous *Threshold Picture Guides*, and a range of authoritative titles sold around the world. About 15 titles a year. IMPRINTS **Kenilworth Press** TITLES *British Horse Society Manuals*; *The International Warmblood Horse*; *Course Design & Construction for Horse Trials*; *Eventing Insights*; *Lungeing and Long-Reining.* **Threshold Books** TITLES *Threshold Picture Guides 1–33.* Unsolicited mss, synopses and ideas welcome but only for titles concerned with the care or riding of horses or ponies.
Royalties paid twice yearly.

Kenyon-Deane
See **Cressrelles Publishing Co. Ltd**

Laurence King
71 Great Russell Street, London WC1B 3BN
☎0171 831 6351   Fax 0171 831 8356
Chairman *Robin Hyman*
Managing Director *Laurence King*

FOUNDED 1991. Publishing imprint of UK packager **Calmann & King Ltd** (see under **UK Packagers**). *Publishes* colour illustrated books on art history, the decorative arts, photography and design. Unsolicited material welcome.
Royalties paid twice yearly.

Kingfisher
See **Larousse plc**

Jessica Kingsley Publishers Ltd
116 Pentonville Road, London N1 9JB
☎0171 833 2307   Fax 0171 837 2917
Managing Director *Jessica Kingsley*
Production Manager *Anna French*
Approx. Annual Turnover £700,000
FOUNDED 1987. Independent publisher of social and behavioural sciences, including arts therapies, psychotherapy (especially forensic psychotherapy), social work, regional studies and higher education policy. Approx. 50 titles in 1995. TITLES include the *Journal of Access Studies; Forensic Psychotherapy: Crime, Psychodynamics and the Offender Patient* (major two-volume reference work); three dictionaries of psychology. The first issue of a new journal, *Tertiary Education and Management* was published in 1995.

Kingsway Communications
Lottbridge Drove, Eastbourne, East Sussex BN23 6NT
☎01323 410930   Fax 01323 411970
Chairman *Peter Fenwick*
Joint Managing Directors *John Paculabo, Brian Davies*
Editorial Contact *Mrs J. Oldroyd*
Approx. Annual Turnover £1.3 million
Part of Kingsway Trust Group Ltd, a charitable trust with Christian objectives. *Publishes* Christian books: bibles, Christian testimonies, church growth, devotional, biblical reference tools. No poetry please. About 50 titles a year. IMPRINTS **Kingsway; Minstrel; Phoenix.** TITLES *The Life Application Bible; The Father Heart of God* Floyd McClung; *Rolling in the Aisles* Murray Watts; *Hagbane's Doom* John Houghton. Unsolicited mss welcome, but partial submissions/synopses preferred. Return postage appreciated; all submissions should be addressed to the Editorial Department.
Royalties paid annually.

Kluwer Academic Publishers
PO Box 55, Lancaster LA1 1PE
☎01524 34996   Fax 01524 32144
Managing Director *Mr A. Visser*
Publishing Director *Dr Peter Clarke*
Approx. Annual Turnover £1.5 million
A member of the Dutch Kluwer Group, publisher of approximately 200 scholarly journals and 500 titles a year across an extensive range of scientific disciplines. Kluwer Academic (UK) specialises in medical, scientific and technical publishing at the postgraduate level. *Publishes* research monographs, postgraduate textbooks, colour atlases and texts for family physicians. Particular areas of medical specialisation include cardiology, nephrology, radiology, oncology, pathology, neurosciences and immunology.

Kluwer Law International
Sterling House, 66 Wilton Road, London SW1V 1DE
☎0171 821 1123   Fax 0171 630 5229
Director of Operations *Marcel Nieuwenhuis*
FOUNDED 1995. Parent company: Wolters Kluwer Group. Kluwer Law International consists of three components: the law list of Graham & Trotman, Kluwer Law and Taxation and Martinus Nyhoff. *Publishes* international law. Plans to publish 200 titles a year. Unsolicited synopses and ideas for books on law at an international level welcome.
Royalties paid once yearly. North American sales and marketing: Kluwer Law International, 675 Massachusetts Avenue, Cambridge, MA 02139.

Knight
See **Hodder Headline plc**

Charles Knight Publishing
See **Tolley Publishing Co Ltd**

Know-Alls
See **Henderson Publishing plc**

Kogan Page Ltd
120 Pentonville Road, London N1 9JN
☎0171 278 0433   Fax 0171 837 3768/6348
Managing Director *Philip Kogan*
Approx. Annual Turnover £7 million
FOUNDED 1967 by Philip Kogan to publish *The Industrial Training Yearbook*. Member of the Euro Business Publishing Network. Following the acquisition in 1992 of Earthscan Publications, Kogan Page went on to form a co-publishing deal with the publishers of the *World of Information* and launched a new management research series. *Publishes* business and management reference books and monographs, education and careers, marketing, personal finance, personnel, small business, training and industrial relations, transport, plus journals. Further expansion is planned, particularly in the professional and human resource areas, yearbooks and directories, and international business reference.

DIVISIONS
Kogan Page *Pauline Goodwin, Philip Mudd, Peter Chadwick, Dolores Black.* TITLES *Training and Enterprise Directory; British Vocational Qualifications.* SERIES *Working for Yourself; Careers; Better Management Skills.* **Earthscan Publications** *Jonathan Sinclair Wilson* Has close associations with the International Institute for Environment and Development and with the Worldwide Fund for Nature. *Publishes* Third World issues and their global implications, and general environmental titles, both popular and academic. About 30 titles a year. TITLES *European Environmental Technology Directory.* Unsolicited mss, synopses and ideas for books welcome.
Royalties paid twice yearly.

Authors' Rating Now the largest independent publisher of business books, Kogan Page rewards good ideas with strong marketing, particularly in airports and other gathering points for young executives.

Labyrinth Publishing (UK) Ltd
See under **UK Packagers**

Ladybird Books Ltd
Beeches Road, Loughborough, Leicestershire LE11 2NQ
☎01509 268021   Fax 01509 234672
Chair *Peter Mayer*
Managing Director *A. D. Forbes Watson*
Publishing Director *M. H. Gabb*
International Director *B.D.L. Cotton*
Approx. Annual Turnover £19 million
FOUNDED in the 1860s. Introduced just before the First World War, the Ladybird name and format was fully established as a result of the development of a children's list during the Second World War. In the early 1960s the commercial print side of the operation was abandoned in favour of publishing Ladybird titles only and in 1971 the company was bought by the Pearson Longman Group. From 1st January 1995, Ladybird has been integrated into the Penguin Group. *Publishes* children's trade books for the mass market internationally. About 200 titles a year.
IMPRINTS **Ladybird; Disney.** TITLES *Favourite Tales; Read it Yourself; Say The Sounds Reading Scheme; Read With Me Reading Scheme; Disney; Beatrix Potter; Dennis the Menace and Friends; Mumfie; Spot; Activity Books; Practice at Home National Curriculum Series; Learning at Home; First Focus* range; *Toddler Books;* plus the Ladybird audio cassette/book series. Although most material is generally commissioned once

publication programme has been determined, unsolicited mss relating to published areas are welcome. *Overseas associates* Ladybird Books Inc, Auburn, Maine, USA.

Authors' Rating Having dumped its old-fashioned 'tat for tots' philosophy, Ladybird is promoting high-quality product at prices that appeal to the mass market. Education, primarily early learning books, is a growing sector.

The Lampada Press
See **The University of Hull Press**

Larousse plc
Elsley House, 24–30 Great Titchfield Street, London W1P 7AD
☎0171 631 0878   Fax 0171 323 4694
Managing Director *John Clement*
FOUNDED 1994 when owners, Groupe de la Cité (also publishers of the Larousse dictionaries in France), merged their UK operations of **Grisewood & Dempsey** and **Chambers Harrap Ltd.** Larousse will continue to publish under the **Kingfisher** and **Chambers** imprints and have started a new **Larousse** imprint.

IMPRINTS
Chambers *Robert Allen, Min Lee* Editorial offices: 43–45 Annandale Street, Edinburgh EH7 4AZ. ☎0131 557 4571 Fax: 0131 557 2936. *Publishes* dictionaries, reference, and local interest. The imprint was founded in the early 1800s to publish self-education books, but soon diversified into dictionaries and other reference works. Acquired by Groupe de la Cité in 1989. The acquisition of **Harrap Publishing Group's** core business strengthened its position in the dictionary market, adding bilingual titles, covering almost all the major European languages, to its English-language dictionaries. Send synopsis with accompanying letter rather than completed mss.

Kingfisher *Vanessa Clark* (Based at London address above.) Founded in 1973 by **Grisewood & Dempsey Ltd.** *Publishes* children's fiction and non-fiction in hardback and paperback: story books, rhymes and picture books, fiction and poetry anthologies, young non-fiction, activity books, general series and reference.

Larousse *Jim Miles* (illustrated reference) *Robert Allen, Min Lee* (dictionaries and reference). Editorial offices in London and Edinburgh. *Publishes* adult reference and dictionaries.
Royalties paid bi-annually where applicable.

Lawrence & Wishart Ltd
144A Old South Lambeth Road, London
SW8 1XX
☎0171 820 9281   Fax 0171 587 0469
Managing Director *Sally Davison*
Editors *Sally Davison, Ruth Borthwick*
FOUNDED 1936. An independent publisher
with a substantial backlist. *Publishes* current
affairs, cultural politics, economics, history, politics and education. 15–20 titles a year. TITLES
*Reclaiming Reality: A Contribution to a Critique of
Cultural Relativism; Romance Revisited; Behind the
Screens: The Structure of British Television in the
Nineties; Leadership and Democracy: The History of
NUPE, Vol. 2, 1928–93.* Synopses preferred to
complete mss. Ideas welcome.
Royalties paid annually, unless by arrangement.

Authors' Rating One of the few genuine
left-wing publishers. Authors should expect to
surrender profit to principles.

Legacy of Love
See **Harlequin Mills & Boon Ltd**

Legend
See **Random House UK Ltd**

Lehigh University Press
See **Golden Cockerel Press Ltd**

Leicester University Press
See **Cassell**

Lennard Publishing
See **Lennard Associates Ltd** under **UK
Packagers**

Charles Letts & Co. Ltd
See **New Holland (Publishers) Ltd**

John Libbey & Co. Ltd
13 Smiths Yard, Summerley Street, London
SW18 4HR
☎0181 947 2777   Fax 0181 947 2664
Chairman/Managing Director *John Libbey*
FOUNDED 1979. *Publishes* media and medical
books only. TITLES *Progress in Obesity Research
1990; Television and the Gulf War.* About 50
titles a year. Unsolicited mss normally welcome
for media titles. Synopses and ideas welcome
for both specialist areas.
    Overseas subsidiaries John Libbey Eurotext
Ltd, France; John Libbey-Cic, Italy.

Library Association Publishing Ltd
7 Ridgmount Street, London WC1E 7AE
☎0171 636 7543   Fax 0171 636 3627
Chairman *E. M. Broome*
Managing Director *Janet Liebster*
Publishing arm of **The Library Association**.
Publishes library and information science,
monographs, reference, textbooks and bibliography. About 30 titles a year.
    IMPRINTS **Library Association Publishing**;
Clive Bingley Books Over 200 titles in print,
including *Walford's Guide to Reference Material*
and *AACR2*. Unsolicited mss, synopses and
ideas welcome provided material falls firmly
within the company's specialist subject areas.
    Royalties paid annually.

Frances Lincoln Ltd
4 Torriano Mews, Torriano Avenue,
London, NW5 2RZ
☎0171 284 4009   Fax 0171 267 5249
Managing Director *Frances Lincoln*
FOUNDED 1977. *Publishes* highly illustrated
non-fiction: gardening, interiors, health, crafts,
cookery; children's picture and information
books; and stationery. About 45 titles a year.
    DIVISIONS **Adult Non-fiction** *Erica
Hunningher* TITLES *Penelope Hobhouse On
Gardening; The Swedish Room* Lars and Ursula
Sjöberg; **Children's** *Janetta Otter-Barry Black
Ships Before Troy* Rosemary Sutcliffe (winner of
the 1994 Kate Greenaway Medal); *Pepi and the
Secret Names* Jill Paton Walsh, illus. Fiona French.
Synopses and ideas for books considered.
    Royalties paid twice yearly.

Liaison
See **Hodder Headline plc**

Linden Press
See **Centaur Press**

Lion Publishing
Peter's Way, Sandy Lane West,
Oxford OX4 5HG
☎01865 747550   Fax 01865 747568
Approx. Annual Turnover £7 million
FOUNDED 1971. A Christian book publisher,
strong on illustrated books for a popular international readership, with rights sold in 88 languages worldwide. *Publishes* a diverse list with
Christian viewpoint the common denominator. All ages, from board books for children to
multi-contributor adult reference, children's
fiction and non-fiction, educational, paperbacks and colour co-editions.

DIVISIONS **Adult** *Lois Rock*; **Children's** *Su Box*; **Lynx Communications** *Robin Keeley* new imprint publishing training resources for churches. Unsolicited mss welcome provided they have a positive Christian viewpoint intended for a wide general and international readership. Synopses, proposals and ideas also welcome.

Royalties paid twice yearly.

Authors' Rating A fall back in overseas markets has caused a few wobbles but Lion now looks to be back on course. Authors remain impressed with editorial courtesy and straight dealing.

Lions
See **HarperCollins Publishers Ltd**

Little, Brown & Co. (UK)
Brettenham House, Lancaster Place, London WC2E 7EN
☎0171 911 8000   Fax 0171 911 8100
Managing Director *Philippa Harrison*
Approx. Annual Turnover £23 million

FOUNDED 1988. Part of Time-Warner Inc. Began by importing its US parent company's titles and in 1990 launched its own illustrated non-fiction list. Two years later the company took over former Macdonald & Co. *Publishes* hardback and paperback fiction, literary fiction, crime, science fiction and fantasy; and general non-fiction, including illustrated: architecture and design, fine art, photography, biography and autobiography, cinema, gardening, history, humour, travel, crafts and hobbies, reference, cookery, wines and spirits, DIY, guidebooks, natural history, nautical, alternative health, ecology and popular psychology.

IMPRINTS **Abacus** *Richard Beswick* literary fiction and non-fiction paperbacks; **Optima** *Martin Bryant* alternative health, women's and popular psychology, mostly in B-format paperbacks; **Orbit** *Colin Murray* science fiction and fantasy; **Little Brown/Warner** *Alan Samson, Barbara Boote, Hilary Hale* mass-market fiction and non-fiction; **Warner-Futura** *Hilary Hale, Barbara Boote* crime paperbacks; **X Libris** *Helen Goodwin* women's erotica; **Illustrated** *Vivien Bowler* hardbacks. Approach in writing in the first instance. No unsolicited mss.

Royalties paid twice yearly.

Authors' Rating Thriving on a mix of popular fiction and non-fiction, attention is focused on the new X Libris list of women's erotica where sales are high but uninhibited writers are hard to find.

Liverpool University Press
Senate House, Abercromby Square,
PO Box 147, Liverpool L69 3BX
☎0151 794 2232/37   Fax 0151 708 6502
Managing Director/Editorial Head *Robin Bloxsidge*

The principal activity of LUP, since its foundation in 1899, has been in the humanities and social sciences. *Publishes* academic and scholarly hardback and paperback books in the fields of archaeology, education, geography, ancient and modern history, science fiction criticism, modern French literature, English literature, Hispanic languages and literature, town planning and veterinary medicine. 15–20 titles a year. TITLES *Excavations in Castletown, Isle of Man, 1989–1992; Documentation for Ancient Arabia; Joseph Beuys: Diverging Critiques; Culture, Tourism and Development: The Case of Ireland; A Stone in Spain's Shoe: The Search for a Solution to the Problem of Gilbraltar; Weathering the Storm: The Mersey Docks Financial Crisis 1970–1974; Statecraft and Diplomacy in the Twentieth Century; Autobiography and the Existential Self: Studies in Modern French Writing; Anticipations: Essays on Early Science Fiction and its Precursors; Utopian and Science Fiction by Women.* Unsolicited mss, synopses and ideas for books welcome.

Royalties paid annually.

Livewire Books for Teenagers
See **The Women's Press**

Longman Group UK Ltd
Edinburgh Gate, Harlow,
Essex CM20 2JE
☎01279 623623   Fax 01279 431059
Contracts & Copyrights Department *Brenda Gvozdanovic*

FOUNDED 1724 by Thomas Longman. Restructured in 1994 to focus solely on educational publishing. A subsidiary of Pearson plc. *Publishes* a range of curriculum subjects, including English language teaching for students at primary and secondary school level, college and university. All unsolicited mss should be addressed to the Manager, Contracts and Copyrights Department.

Royalties twice yearly. *Overseas associates* worldwide.

Authors' Rating The conglomerate has exploded with bits and pieces landing all over the Pearson empire. Business and professional books have merged with the *Financial Times* business publishing division, education is now part of Addison–Wesley and Ladybird has gone to Penguin. The Longman name will survive in conjunction with Addison–Wesley on books for schools and colleges with English Language Teaching as the likely money-spinner. The good news for Longman authors is that henceforth they will receive royalties twice a year instead of annually.

Lorenz Books
See **Anness Publishing Ltd**

Love on Call
See **Harlequin Mills & Boon Ltd**

Peter Lowe (Eurobook Ltd)
PO Box 52, Wallingford, Oxfordshire OX10 0XU
☎01865 749033   Fax 01865 749044

Managing Director *Peter Lowe*

FOUNDED 1968. *Publishes* children's natural history, animal-based fiction, popular science and illustrated adult non-fiction. No unsolicited mss; synopses and ideas welcome. No adult fiction.

Lund Humphries Publishers Ltd
Park House, 1 Russell Gardens, London NW11 9NN
☎0181 458 6314   Fax 0181 905 5245

Chairman *Lionel Leventhal*
Editor *Lucy Myers*

Publisher of fine art books. First title appeared in 1895. *Publishes* art, architecture, design and graphics. Publishers of exhibition catalogues in association with museums and galleries, and of the annual *Calendar of Art Exhibitions*. About 20 titles a year. There are plans to expand the graphic arts and design list in the years to come. Unsolicited mss welcome but initial introductory letter preferred. Synopses and ideas for books considered.
Royalties paid twice yearly.

The Lutterworth Press
PO Box 60, Cambridge CB1 2NT
☎01223 350865   Fax 01223 66951

Managing Director *Adrian Brink*
Editorial Director *Colin Lester*

The Lutterworth Press dates back to the 18th century when it was founded by the Religious Tract Society. In the 19th century it was best known for its children's books, both religious and secular, including *The Boys' Own Paper*. Since 1984 it has been part of **James Clarke &**

Co. *Publishes* general non-fiction: antiques and collecting, architecture and design, biography, children's books, educational and textbooks, fine art and art history, environmental, natural history, religion and theology. Sponsored and non-sponsored books. About 25 titles a year.

DIVISIONS **Children's**, **Adult**. TITLES *My Puppy is Born*; *The Birds of CITES*; *When Lion Could Fly*; *The Archaeology of the Land of the Bible*; *Journey Round the Arctic Circle*; *Hogarth (vol. 3)*. Initial letter with s.a.e. advised before submitting mss.
Royalties paid annually.

Authors' Rating The list is expanding but it still has its anchor in evangelical publishing. Imaginative children's list.

Lynx Communications
See **Lion Publishing**

M & N Publishing
Keighley Business Centre, Knowle Mill, South Street, Keighley, West Yorks BD21 1AG
☎01535 690090   Fax 01535 690090

Chairman/Managing Director *Malcolm Naismith*
Editorial Head *Claire Phillips*

FOUNDED 1994. New company with three partners. *Publishes* fiction, children's, literature, millenium/New Age, biography, religion/devotional, cookery, health and some poetry. Unsolicited mss welcome – return postage essential. Synopses and ideas welcome.

Authors' Rating Authors may be asked to cover their own production costs.

Macdonald & Co.
See **Little, Brown & Co. (UK)**

Macmillan Publishers Ltd
25 Eccleston Place, London SW1W 9NF
☎0171 881 8000   Fax 0171 881 8001

Chairman *Nicholas Byam Shaw*
Group Managing Director *Iain Burns*
Managing Director, Book Publishing Group *Adrian Soar*
Approx. Annual Turnover £50 million (Book Publishing Group)

FOUNDED 1843. Macmillan is one of the largest publishing houses in Britain, publishing approximately 1400 titles a year. In 1986 it bought Sidgwick & Jackson and in 1987 completed the buy-out of Pan Books. In May 1994 the two UK book publishing companies, Pan Macmillan and Macmillan Press, were reorganised into a unified structure which, with Grove's Dictionaries of Music and The Dictionary of Art, comprises seven divisions. In 1995, Verlagsgruppe Georg von Holtzbrinck, a major German publisher, acquired a majority stake in the Macmillan Group. Unsolicited proposals, synopses and mss are welcome in all divisions of the company (with the exception of Macmillan Children's Books). Authors who wish to send material to Macmillan General Books and Macmillan Reference Books should note that there is a central submissions procedure in operation. For these divisions, send a synopsis and the first 3–4 chapters with a covering letter and return postage to the Submissions Editor, 25 Eccleston Place, London SW1W 9NF.

DIVISIONS

Macmillan Press Ltd Brunel Road, Houndmills, Basingstoke, Hampshire RG21 6XS ☎01256 29242   Fax 01256 479476 Managing Director *Dominic Knight*. **Journals** *H. Holt*; **Scholarly** *T. M. Farmiloe*; **Higher Education** *S. Kennedy*; **Further Education** *J. Winckler*; **Academic and Professional Reference** *S. O'Neill* (Eccleston Place, address as above) *Publishes* textbooks, monographs and works of reference in academic, professional and vocational subjects; medical and scientific journals; directories.

Macmillan Education Basingstoke (address as for Macmillan Press). Managing Director *Chris Harrison*, Publishing Director *Alison Hubert*. *Publishes* regional ELT titles and a wide list for the international education market.

Macmillan General Books (Eccleston Place). Managing Director *Ian S. Chapman*. **Non-Fiction** *William Armstrong, Georgina Morley, Catherine Hurley* IMPRINTS **Macmillan, Pan, Sidgwick & Jackson**. *Publishes* a comprehensive range of subjects in hardback and paperback, including: autobiography, biography, business and industry, cinema and video, crafts and hobbies, economics, gift books, health and beauty, history, humour, medical, military and war, music, politics and world affairs, pop and rock, drama, travel, wines and spirits. TITLES *Grand Prix Year* Damon Hill; *Take it Like a Man* Boy George; *Last Letters Home* Tamasin Day-Lewis; *Summer of Love* George Martin; *The Lonely Leader* Alistair Horne and David Montgomery; *The Last of the Duchess* Caroline Blackwood; *Now and Then* Roy Castle; *Fabulous Figures* Rachel Swift. **Fiction** *Suzanne Baboneau, Maria Rejt, Peter Lavery*. IMPRINTS **Macmillan, Pan**. TITLES *The Seventh Scroll* Wilbur Smith; *A Place Called Freedom* Ken Follett; *Casting Off* Elizabeth Jane

Howard; *Cold Shoulder* Lynda La Plante; *Perfect Love* Elizabeth Buchan; *The Dark Room* Minette Walters; *The Daughters of Cain* Colin Dexter; *L is for Lawless* Sue Grafton. AUTHORS Douglas Adams, Stephen Humphrey Bogart, Simon Brett, Jackie Collins, Shirley Conran, Colin Forbes, Dick Francis, Rumer Godden, James Herriot, Carl Hiaasen, Deirdre Purcell.

Literary Group *Peter Straus, Jon Riley, Georgia Garrett*. IMPRINTS **Picador, Papermac** Picador specialises in outstanding international writing in both hardcover and paperback. The list began in 1972 publishing fiction and non-fiction in paperback from Herman Hesse, Angela Carter to Jorge Luis Borges. From 1990 it has also been publishing hardbacks. *Publishes* fiction and non-fiction: history, contemporary affairs, humour, politics, travel, philosophy, psychology, science, music, film, theatre and *occasionally* poetry and plays. Papermac specialises in serious non-fiction: history, biography, cultural criticism and art history. AUTHORS Julian Barnes, Roland Barthes, Harold Bloom, Bruce Chatwin, Umberto Eco, Brett Easton Ellis, John Fowles, Norman Lewis, Noel Malcolm, Gabriel Garcia Marquez, Patrick McCabe, Cormac McCarthy, Ian McEwan, Toni Morrison, Eric Newby, P. J. O'Rourke, Oliver Sacks, Graham Swift, Hunter Thompson, Edmund White, Tom Wolfe.

Macmillan Reference Books Eccleston Place (as above) *Julian Ashby, Judith Hannam*. *Publishes* encyclopedias, subject dictionaries, consumer guides, astronomy, cinema, health, history, language, military and war, natural history, science and technology, travel guides, cookery and gardening. TITLES *The Macmillan Encyclopedia*; *The Good Deal Directory*; *The Good English Guide*; *The RSPB Book of British Birds*; *The Writer's Handbook*; *The Gardener's Yearbook*; *The Macmillan International Film Encyclopedia*; *Essentials of Classic Italian Cooking, Let's Go* series.

Macmillan Children's Books Eccleston Place (address as above) *Kate Wilson*; **Fiction** *Marion Lloyd*; **Non-fiction** *Susie Gibbs*; **Picture Books & Properties** *Alison Green*. IMPRINTS **Macmillan, Pan, Campbell Books**. *Publishes* board books, fiction and picture books, non-fiction (illustrated and non-illustrated) and novelty books in paperback and hardback.

Grove's Dictionaries of Music 3 Dyer's Buildings, Holborn, London EC1N 2JT. Tel: 0171 405 5730 Fax: 0171 405 6510. Publishing Director *Margot Levy*. *Publishes The New Grove Dictionary of Music and Musicians* ed. Stanley Sadie; and associated works.

The Dictionary of Art Eccleston Place (as above). Managing Director *Ian Jacobs*. *Publishes The Dictionary of Art* (1996) ed. Jane Shoaf Turner.

Royalties paid annually or twice yearly depending on contract.

Authors' Rating And as the convoy of security vans, stuffed with used fivers, recedes slowly into the west, we say goodbye to the Macmillan family. Well, not quite. The sale of this, the last of the great British privately owned publishing houses, to German media conglomerate Holtzbrinck for undisclosed millions, still leaves the Macmillan Trust with a thirty per cent share of the company. Moreover, since Holtzbrinck is not quoted on the Stock Exchange, Macmillan remains privately owned, part of one of the largest companies of its sort in the world. Management has been quick to reassure authors of Holtzbrinck's good intentions. 'Greater resources' will be available for 'good ideas and good authors' says a round robin letter. A pointer to the future is Holtzbrinck's expertise in electronic delivery.

Julia MacRae Books
See **Random House UK Ltd**

Magi Publications
112 Whitfield Street, London W1P 5RU
☎0171 387 0610   Fax 0171 383 5003
Postal address only: 55 Crowland Avenue, Hayes, Middlesex UB3 4JP
Publisher *Monty Bhatia*
Editor *Linda Jennings*
Approx. Annual Turnover £500,000
FOUNDED 1987. *Publishes* children's picture books only. About 24 titles a year. Unsolicited mss, synopses and ideas welcome, but please telephone first.
Royalties paid annually.

Mainstream Publishing Co. (Edinburgh) Ltd
7 Albany Street, Edinburgh EH1 3UG
☎0131 557 2959   Fax 0131 556 8720
Directors *Bill Campbell, Peter MacKenzie*
Approx. Annual Turnover £2.2 million
Publishes art, autobiography/biography, current affairs, fiction, health, history, illustrated and fine editions, photography and sport, politics and world affairs, popular paperbacks. Over 60 titles a year. Ideas for books considered, but they should be preceded by a letter, synopsis and s.a.e. or return postage.
Royalties paid twice yearly.

Authors' Rating A Scottish company aiming for a British profile. Keen on finding authors who 'can develop with us'.

Mammoth Paperbacks
See **Reed International Books**

Management Books 2000 Ltd
125A The Broadway, Didcot, Oxfordshire OX11 8AW
☎01235 815544   Fax 01235 817188
Managing Director *Nicholas Dale-Harris*
Editorial Director *Robert Postema*
Approx. Annual Turnover £500,000
FOUNDED 1993 to develop a range of books for executives and managers working in the modern world of business, supplemented with information through other media like seminars, audio and video. *Publishes* business and management, company histories and sponsored titles. About 30 titles a year. Unsolicited mss, synopses and ideas for books welcome.

Manchester University Press
Oxford Road, Manchester M13 9NR
☎0161 273 5539   Fax 0161 274 3346
Publisher/Chief Executive *Francis Brooke*
Approx. Annual Turnover £1.4 million
FOUNDED at the turn of the century and now Britain's third largest university press, with a list marketed and sold internationally. Originally based on history, MUP's list has expanded to cover the humanities, social sciences and academic books from A-level texts to research monographs. *Publishes* academic and educational books in literature, cultural and media studies, history, art and architecture, politics, international law, economics, modern languages, anthropology and special education. Also more general books, notably on genealogy, history and the North-west of England. About 100 titles a year, plus journals.
DIVISIONS **Humanities** *Anita Roy*; **History** *Jane Thorniley-Walker*; **Politics** *Richard Purslow*; **Economics** *Francis Brooke*; **Arts** *Katharine Reeve*. Unsolicited mss welcome.
Royalties paid annually.

Mandarin
See **Reed International Books**

George Mann Books
PO Box 22, Maidstone, Kent ME14 1AH
☎01622 759591   Fax 01622 721953
Chairman *George Mann*
Managing Director *John Arne*

FOUNDED 1972, originally as library reprint publishers, but has moved on to other things with the collapse of the library market. *Publishes* fiction, non-fiction and selected reprints. Launched a new imprint called Recollections in 1992 for subsidised publication of books of an autobiographical/biographical nature, for which unlimited editorial advice and assistance can be made available. In the same year a new pamphlet series, Polemical Pamphlets, was begun.

IMPRINTS **Arnefold; Recollections; George Mann; Polemical Pamphlets**. The latter is a paperback platform for controversial views on matters of public interest, local or national. 'Within the law, and supported by the best legal and editorial advice, we will enable anyone to disseminate to the widest possible readership, a well-written and well-presented opinion.' Length 20–30,000 words. Production costs are generally shared. No unsolicited mss; send preliminary letter with synopis. Material not accompanied by return postage will be neither read nor returned.
Royalties paid twice yearly.

Mansell
See **Cassell**

Manson Publishing Ltd
73 Corringham Road, London NW11 7DL
☎0181 905 5150   Fax 0181 201 9233
Chairman/Managing Director *Michael Manson*
Approx. Annual Turnover £400,000
FOUNDED 1992. *Publishes* scientific, technical, medical and veterinary. 8 titles in 1994. No unsolicited mss; synopses and ideas will be considered.
Royalties paid twice yearly.

Marc
See **Monarch Publications**

Marshall Pickering
See **HarperCollins Publishers Ltd**

Marston House
Marston House, Marston Magna, Yeovil, Somerset BA22 8DH
☎01935 850511   Fax 01935 816717
Managing Director/Editorial Head
Anthony Birks-Hay
Approx. Annual Turnover £200,000
FOUNDED 1989. Publishing imprint of book packager **Alphabet & Image Ltd**. *Publishes* archaeology, fine art, architecture, ceramics.

4 titles a year. Unsolicited synopses and ideas for books welcome.
Royalties paid twice yearly, or flat fee in lieu of royalties.

Masks/Mask Noir
See **Serpent's Tail**

Kenneth Mason Publications Ltd
Dudley House, 12 North Street, Emsworth, Hampshire PO10 7DQ
☎01243 377977   Fax 01243 379136
Chairman *Kenneth Mason*
Managing Director *Piers Mason*
Approx. Annual Turnover £500,000
FOUNDED 1958. *Publishes* diet, health, fitness, nutrition, family, women's topics and nautical. No fiction. 15 titles in 1994. Initial approach by letter with synopsis preferred. IMPRINT **Boatswain Press**.
Royalties paid twice yearly (Jun/Dec) in first year, annually (Dec) thereafter.

Kevin Mayhew Ltd
Rattlesden, Bury St Edmunds, Suffolk IP30 0SZ
☎01449 737978   Fax 01449 737834
Chairman *Kevin Mayhew*
Managing Director *Gordon Carter*
Approx. Annual Turnover £2 million
FOUNDED in 1976. One of the leading sacred music and Christian book publishers in the UK. *Publishes* religious titles – liturgy, sacramental, humour, also children's books and school aids. 50 titles in 1994. Unsolicited mss, synopses and ideas within the subject areas listed are welcome.

IMPRINT **Palm Tree Press** *Kevin Mayhew* bibles and bible stories.
Royalties paid annually.

McGraw-Hill Book Co. Europe
McGraw-Hill House, Shoppenhangers Road, Maidenhead, Berkshire SL6 2QL
☎01628 23432   Fax 01628 770224
Group Vice President (Europe/Middle East/Africa) *Fred J. Perkins*
Editorial Director *Andrew Phillips*
FOUNDED 1899. Owned by US parent company. Began publishing in Maidenhead in 1965. *Publishes* business and economics, engineering, computer science, business computing and secretarial studies for the academic, student and professional markets. Around 100 titles a year. Unsolicited mss, synopses and ideas welcome.
Royalties paid twice yearly.

The Medici Society Ltd
34–42 Pentonville Road, London
N1 9HG
☎0171 837 7099   Fax 0171 837 9152
Art Director *Charles Howell*

FOUNDED 1908. *Publishes* illustrated children's
fiction, art and nature. About 6 titles a year. No
unsolicited mss; send synopses with specimen
illustrations only.
Royalties paid annually.

Melrose Press Ltd
3 Regal Lane, Soham, Ely, Cambridgeshire
CB7 5BA
☎01353 721091   Fax 01353 721839
Chairman *Richard A. Kay*
Managing Director *Nicholas S. Law*
Approx. Annual Turnover £1.5 million

FOUNDED 1960. Took on its present name in
1969. *Publishes* biographical who's who reference only (not including the famed *Who's
Who*, which is published by **A. & C. Black**).

DIVISIONS
International Biographical Centre *Jocelyn
Timothy*. TITLES *International Authors and Writers
Who's Who; International Who's Who in Music;
Who's Who in Australasia and the Far East; World
Who's Who of Women*. Ideas welcome.

Mercat Press
c/o James Thin Booksellers, 53 South Bridge,
Edinburgh EH1 1YS
☎0131 556 6743   Fax 0131 557 8149
Chairman/Managing Director *D. Ainslie
Thin*
Editorial Heads *Tom Johnstone, Seán Costello*

FOUNDED 1971 as an adjunct to the large Scottish bookselling chain of James Thin. Began by
publishing reprints of classic Scottish literature
but has since expanded into publishing new
work. In 1992 the company acquired the bulk
of the stock of Aberdeen University Press, a
victim of the collapse of the Maxwell empire.
The backlist has expanded five-fold as a result
to just under 300 titles and new titles are added
regularly. *Publishes* Scottish classics reprints and
non-fiction of Scottish interest, mainly historical and literary. TITLES *The Fall of the Tay
Bridge* David Swinfen; *Scotland and Ulster* ed.
Ian S. Wood; *The Scots Kitchen* F. Marion
McNeill; *Scotichronicon* Walter Bower, ed.
D.E.R. Watt. Unsolicited synopses and ideas
for non-fiction books, preferably with sample
chapters, are welcome. No complete mss.
Royalties paid annually.

Merehurst Ltd
Ferry House, 51–57 Lacy Road, London
SW15 1PR
☎0181 780 1177   Fax 0181 780 1714
Chief Executive Officer *Graham Fill*
Publishing Director *Shirley Patton*
Approx. Annual Turnover £3.5 million

Owned by Australian media group J. B. Fairfax
International Ltd. *Publishes* full-colour non-
fiction: cake decorating, cookery, craft, gardening, homes and interiors, children's crafts and
hobbies. About 80 titles a year. Synopses and
ideas for books welcome; no unsolicited mss.
Royalties paid twice yearly.

Merlin Press Ltd
10 Malden Road, London NW5 3HR
☎0171 267 3399   Fax 0171 284 3092
Directors *Martin Eve, P. M. Eve*

FOUNDED 1956. *Publishes* ecology, economics,
history, philosophy, left-wing politics. AUTHORS
Georg Lukacs, Ernest Mandel, Istvan Meszaros,
Ralph Miliband, E. P. Thompson. About 20
titles a year. No fiction. IMPRINTS **Green Print**,
Seafarer Books sailing titles, with an emphasis
on the traditional. No unsolicited mss; preliminary letter essential before making any type of
submission.
Royalties paid twice yearly.

Mermaid Books
See **Penguin Books Ltd**

Methuen & Co.
See **Routledge**

Methuen/Methuen Children's Books
See **Reed International Books**

Michelin Tyre plc
The Edward Hyde Building, 38 Clarendon
Road, Watford, Hertfordshire WD1 1SX
☎01923 415000   Fax 01923 415250

FOUNDED 1900 as travel publisher. *Publishes*
travel guides, maps and atlases, children's I-Spy
books. 20 titles in 1994. Travel-related synopses and ideas welcome; no mss.

Midland Publishing Ltd
24 The Hollow, Earl Shilton, Leicester
LE9 7NA
☎01455 847256   Fax 01455 841805
Director *N. P. Lewis*

Publishes aviation, military and railways. No

wartime memoirs. No unsolicited mss; synopses and ideas welcome.

Royalties paid quarterly.

Milestone Publications
See **Scope International Ltd**

Millenium
See **Orion Publishing Group**

Harvey Miller Publishers
Knightsbridge House, 8th Floor,
197 Knightsbridge, London SW7 1RB
☎0171 584 7676   Fax 0171 823 7969
Director *Harvey Miller*
Editorial Director *Mrs Elly Miller*
FOUNDED 1974. *Publishes* serious studies in the history of art only. 6 titles in 1994. No unsolicited mss; synopses and ideas welcome.

Royalties paid annually.

Mills & Boon Ltd
See **Harlequin Mills & Boon Ltd**

Minerva
See **Reed International Books**

Minstrel
See **Kingsway Communications**

Mira
See **Harlequin Mills & Boon Ltd**

The MIT Press Ltd
Fitzroy House, 11 Chenies Street, London
WC1E 7ET
☎0171 306 0603   Fax 0171 306 0604
Director *F. Urbanowski*
General Manager *A. Sexsmith*
Part of **The MIT Press**, USA. *Publishes* academic, architecture and design, art history and theory, bibliography, biography, business and industry, cinema and media studies, computer science, cultural studies and critical theory, economics, educational and textbooks, engineering, environment, linguistics, medical, music, natural history, philosophy, photography, physics, politics and world affairs, psychology, reference, scientific and technical, neurobiology and neuroscience. All mss go to the American office: 55 Hayward Street, Cambridge, Mass. 02142.

Mitchell Beazley
See **Reed International Books**

Mitre
See **Monarch Publications**

Monarch Publications
Broadway House, The Broadway,
Crowborough, East Sussex TN6 1HQ
☎01892 652364   Fax 01892 663329
Directors *Tony & Jane Collins*
Formerly part of **Kingsway Publications** but broke away from that company in 1992 to publish an independent list of Christian books across a wide range of concerns. About 30 titles a year. In 1994 took on *Renewal* and *Healing and Wholeness* magazines.

IMPRINTS **Monarch** upmarket, social concern issues list covering a wide range of areas from psychology to future studies, politics, etc., all with a strong Christian dimension; **Marc** leadership, mission and church growth titles; **Mitre** creative writing imprint: humour and drama with a Christian dimension. Unsolicited mss, synopses and ideas welcome. 'Regretfully no poetry or fiction.'

Mondo
See **Titan Books**

Moorland Publishing Co. Ltd
Moorfarm Road, Airfield Estate, Ashbourne,
Derbyshire DE6 1HD
☎01335 344486   Fax 01335 346397
Managing Director *Mr C. L. M. Porter*
Editorial Head *Mrs Tonya Monk*
Approx. Annual Turnover £1 million
FOUNDED 1971. *Publishes* travel guides and gardening titles only. SERIES *Visitor's Guide*; *Off The Beaten Track*; *Independent Travellers*; *Insiders Guides*; *Spectrum Guides*. Agents for Little Hills Press travel titles. Unsolicited mss will be considered, but synopses accompanied by letters of introduction preferred.

Royalties paid annually.

Mosby/Mosby Wolf Publishing
See **Times Mirror International Publishers Ltd**

Motor Racing Publications
Unit 6, The Pilton Estate, 46 Pitlake,
Croydon, Surrey CR0 3RY
☎0181 681 3363   Fax 0181 760 5117
Chairman/Editorial Head *John Blunsden*
Approx. Annual Turnover £500,000
FOUNDED soon after the end of World War II to concentrate on motor-racing titles. Fairly dormant in the mid 60s but was reactivated in 1968 by a new shareholding structure. John Blunsden later acquired a majority share and

major expansion followed in the 70s. About 15 titles a year. *Publishes* motor-sporting history, classic car collection and restoration, road transport, motorcycles, off-road driving and related subjects.

IMPRINTS **Fitzjames Press**; **Motor Racing Publications** TITLES *Ayrton Senna: Goodbye Champion, Farewell Friend* Karin Sturm; *BRM* Doug Nye; *The Complete Mini* Chris Rees; *Bedford to Berlin* Robert Coates; *Porsche 911 Collector's Guide (2 vols.)* Michael Cotton; *Suzuki Vitara Enthusiast's Companion* Nigel Fryatt. Unsolicited mss, synopses and ideas in specified subject areas welcome.
Royalties paid twice yearly.

Mowbray
See **Cassell**

Multi-Sensory Learning Ltd
34 Nene Valley Business Park, Oundle, Peterborough PE8 4HL
☎01832 275285   Fax 01832 275281
Publisher *Philippa Attwood*
Course Co-ordinator *Karen Robinson*

Publishes materials and books related to dyslexia; the multi-learning course for teachers of dyslexic children, plus numerous other items on assessment, reading, maths, music, etc. for dyslexics. Keen to locate authors able to write materials for dyslexic people and for teachers of dyslexics.

Multimedia Books Ltd
Unit L, 32–34 Gordon House Road, London NW5 1LP
☎0171 482 4248   Fax 0171 482 4203
Managing Director *Barry Winkleman*

Formerly a packaging operation but began publishing under the Prion imprint in 1987. *Publishes* illustrated non-fiction: wildlife and nature, Americana, cinema and photography, cars, history and places, guidebooks, food, psychology and health. In 1991 started a small fiction list. About 20 titles a year. Unsolicited mss, synopses and ideas welcome.
Royalties paid twice yearly.

John Murray (Publishers) Ltd
50 Albemarle Street, London W1X 4BD
☎0171 493 4361   Fax 0171 499 1792
Chairman *John R. Murray*
Managing Director *Nicholas Perren*

FOUNDED 1768. Independent publisher. *Publishes* general trade books, educational (secondary school and college textbooks) and Success Studybooks.

DIVISIONS **General Books** *Grant McIntyre*; **Educational Books** *Nicholas Perren*. Unsolicited material discouraged.
Royalties paid annually.

Authors' Rating After heavy losses in the late 80s, there was a serious risk that this grand old house would fall to the City demolition squad. But cost cutting and efficiency controls have brought their reward and there is now talk of expansion. Education may be dodgy – it is with everyone else – but the general list remains strong with no sacrifice of traditional quality.

My Little Funfax
See **Henderson Publishing plc**

Navigator Books
Moorhouse, Kingston, Ringwood, Hampshire BH24 3BJ
☎01425 476708   Fax 01425 480075
Managing Director *Philip Bristow*

FOUNDED 1964. *Publishes* nautical, war, achievements of older folk, nostalgia plus some fiction and children's. 18 titles in 1994. TITLES *Jump On, Jump On* (colour history of fairground rides); *H.M.S. Bedouin; A Tramp About the World; Old Time Characters of the Isle of Wight; Across Africa and Beyond; Wiltshire Farmer's Story; A Walk About England.* Prefers to hear from authors of completed works – send synopsis and sample chapter. No religious, gardening, domestic, art or technical.
Royalties paid twice yearly.

NCVO Publications
Regent's Wharf, 8 All Saints Street, London N1 9RL
☎0171 713 6161   Fax 0171 713 6300
Commissioning Editor *Jackie Sallon*
Approx. Annual Turnover £140,000

FOUNDED 1992. Publishing imprint of the National Council for Voluntary Organisations, embracing former **Bedford Square Press** titles and NCVO's many other publications. The list reflects NCVO's role as the representative body for the voluntary sector. *Publishes* directories, management and trustee development, legal, finance and fundraising titles of primary interest to the voluntary sector. TITLES *The Voluntary Agencies Directory; Grants from Europe; Planning for the Future: An Introduction to Business; Planning for Voluntary Organisations.* Unsolicited mss, synopses and ideas for books welcome.
Royalties paid twice yearly.

Thomas Nelson & Sons Ltd
Nelson House, Mayfield Road, Walton on
Thames, Surrey KT12 5PL
☎01932 252211   Fax 01932 246109
Managing Director *Rod Gauvin*
Development Director *Pamela Hutchinson*
Approx. Annual Turnover £30 million
FOUNDED 1798. Part of the Thomson
Corporation. Major school book publisher cov-
ering all levels for students aged 5–19 in full and
part-time education – National Curriculum,
GNVQ, NVQ – for the home market, and a
range for the Caribbean market. Also publishes
Multimedia product (CD-ROM) for school
and home learning. TITLES *Gaia: Geography, An
Integrated Approach; Nelson English; Route
Nationale; Maths Chest; Tricolore; Zickzack;
Deutsch Heute; Route Nationale; Balanced Science.*
Unsolicited mss and synopses welcome.
Royalties paid twice yearly.

Network Books
See **BBC Books Ltd**

New English Library
See **Hodder Headline plc**

New Holland (Publishers) Ltd
24 Nutford Place, London W1H 6DQ
☎0171 724 7773   Fax 0171 724 6184
Chairman *Gerry Struik*
Managing Director *John Beaufoy*
Editorial Head *Charlotte Parry-Crooke*
Approx. Annual Turnover £3.5 million
FOUNDED 1956. Relaunched 1987 with new
name and editorial identity. New directions
and rapid expansion transformed the small specialist imprint into a publisher of illustrated
books for the international market. In 1993,
they diversified further with the acquisition of
the **Charles Letts Publishing Division** list.
Publishes non-fiction, specialising in natural his-
tory, travel, cookery, cake decorating, crafts,
gardening and DIY. TITLES *Field Guide to the
Birds of Britain and Europe, Australia; Wild
Malaysia, New Zealand; Globetrotter Travel Guide
Series.* No unsolicited mss; synopses and ideas
welcome.
Royalties paid twice yearly.
Authors' Rating New Holland can thank Sir
John Harvey-Jones for their acquisition of Letts
general trade publishing. It was he who advised
Letts to concentrate on its core diary business.
But if diversification was a problem for Letts, it
seems to act as a stimulus on New Holland.
Expansion in general non-fiction is impressive.

New Left Books Ltd
See **Verso**

New Naturalist Library
See **HarperCollins Publishers Ltd**

New Orchard Editions
See **Cassell**

Nexus
See **Virgin Publishing**

Nexus Special Interests
Nexus House, Boundary Way, Hemel
Hempstead, Hertfordshire HP2 7ST
☎01442 66551   Fax 01442 66998
General Manager *Beverley Laughlin*
Argus Consumer Magazines and Argus Books
were bought out by Nexus Media Communications in 1995 and the Nexus Special Interests
imprint was established in the spring of that
year. *Publishes* aviation, leisure and hobbies,
modelling, electronics, health, wine and beer
making, woodwork. Send synopses rather than
completed mss.
Royalties paid twice yearly.

NFER-NELSON Publishing Co. Ltd
Darville House, 2 Oxford Road East,
Windsor, Berkshire SL4 1DF
☎01753 858961   Fax 01753 856830
Managing Director *Michael Jackson*
Publishing Director *Keith Nettle*
Editorial Coordinator *Carolyn Richardson*
FOUNDED 1981. Jointly owned by the Thomson
Corporation and the National Foundation for
Educational Research. *Publishes* educational
and psychological tests and training materials.
Main interest is in educational, clinical and
occupational assessment and training material.
Unsolicited material welcome.
Royalties vary according to each contract.

Nicholson
See **HarperCollins Publishers Ltd**

James Nisbet & Co. Ltd
78 Tilehouse Street, Hitchin, Hertfordshire
SG5 2DY
☎01462 438331   Fax 01462 431528
Chairman *E. M. Mackenzie-Wood*
FOUNDED 1810 as a religious publisher and expanded into more general areas from around
1850 onwards. The first educational list appeared
in 1926 and the company now specialises in edu-

cational material and business studies. About 5 titles a year. No fiction, leisure or religion. No unsolicited mss; synopses and ideas welcome.

Royalties paid twice yearly.

No Exit Press
See **Oldcastle Books Ltd**

Nonesuch Press
See **Reinhardt Books Ltd**

Northcote House Publishers Ltd
Plymbridge House, Estover Road, Plymouth, Devon PL6 7PZ
☎01752 735251   Fax 01752 695699
Managing Director *Brian Hulme*

FOUNDED 1985. Recently launched a new series of literary critical studies called *Writers and their Work*. *Publishes* careers, education management, literary criticism, educational dance and drama. 30 titles in 1995. 'Well-thought-out proposals with strong marketing arguments welcome.'

Royalties paid annually.

W. W. Norton & Co. Ltd
10 Coptic Street, London WC1A 1PU
☎0171 323 1579   Fax 0171 436 4553
Managing Director *R. A. Cameron*

Owned by US parent company. *Publishes* non-fiction, academic and nautical. No unsolicited material. Enquiries only in writing.

Nottingham University Press
Manor Farm, Thrumpton, Nottingham NG11 0AX
☎0115 9831011   Fax 0115 9831003
Managing Editor *Dr D. J. A. Cole*
Approx. Annual Turnover £150,000

A newly formed company which intends to publish across a broad range of subjects. Initially concentrating on agricultural and food sciences. 10 titles in 1994 with 20 planned for 1995. TITLES *Resource Capture by Crops; Issues in Agricultural Bioethics; Biotechnology in the Feed Industry; High Pressure Processing of Foods; Principles of Rig Science.* Unsolicited mss, synopses and ideas welcome.

Royalties paid twice yearly.

Michael O'Mara Books Ltd
9 Lion Yard, Tremadoc Road, London SW4 7NQ
☎0171 720 8643   Fax 0171 627 8953
Chairman *Michael O'Mara*
Managing Director *Lesley O'Mara*
Editorial Director *David Roberts*

Approx. Annual Turnover £5 million

FOUNDED 1985. Independent publisher. *Publishes* general non-fiction, royalty, history, humour, anthologies and reference. TITLES *Diana: Her True Story* Andrew Morton; *The Rape of Tutankhamun* John Romer; *The ITN Book of the Queen Mother.* Unsolicited mss, synopses and ideas for books welcome.

Royalties paid twice yearly.

Authors' Rating Reports of a sharp drop in turnover suggest heavy reliance on a few mega-selling royal books which are now fading from the list. But authors know that Michael O'Mara, though a smallish publisher, can handle big ideas.

Oak
See **Omnibus Press**

Oast Books
See **Parapress Ltd**

Oberon Books
521 Caledonian Road, London N7 9RH
☎0171 607 3637   Fax 0171 607 3629
Publishing Director *James Hogan*
Managing Director *Charles D. Glanville*

Publishes play texts (usually in conjunction with a production) and theatre books. *Specialises* in contemporary plays and translations of European classics. AUTHORS/TRANSLATORS Marguerite Duras, Dic Edwards, Graham Greene, Giles Havergal, Robert David MacDonald, Adrian Mitchell, Stephen Mulrine, Meredith Oakes, David Pownall, Roland Rees, Colin Winslow.

Observer Books
See **Fourth Estate Ltd**

Octagon Press Ltd
PO Box 227, London N6 4EW
☎0181 348 9392   Fax 0181 341 5971
Managing Director *George R. Schrager*
Approx. Annual Turnover £100,000

FOUNDED 1972. *Publishes* philosophy, psychology, travel, Eastern religion, translations of Eastern classics and research monographs in series. 4–5 titles a year. Unsolicited material not welcome. Enquiries in writing only.

Royalties paid annually.

Oldcastle Books Ltd
18 Coleswood Road, Harpenden, Hertfordshire AL5 1EQ
☎01582 712244   Fax 01582 712244
Managing Director *Ion S. Mills*

FOUNDED 1985. *Publishes* crime fiction and gambling non-fiction. 15 titles in 1994. No unsolicited mss; synopses and ideas for books within the two areas of interest welcome.
IMPRINTS **No Exit Press** TITLES *Burglar Who Traded; Killing Suki Flood; No Beast So Fierce*; **Oldcastle Books** TITLES *Biggest Game in Town* Al Alvarez.
Royalties paid twice yearly.

OM Publishing
See **STL Ltd**

Omnibus Press
Book Sales/Music Sales Ltd, 8–9 Frith Street, London W1V 5TZ
☎0171 434 0066   Fax 0171 734 2246
Editorial Head *Chris Charlesworth*
FOUNDED 1971. Independent publisher of music books, rock and pop biographies, song sheets, educational tutors, cassettes, videos and software.
IMPRINTS **Amsco**; **Bobcat**; **Oak**; **Omnibus**; **Proteus**; **Wise**; **Zomba**. Unsolicited mss, synopses and ideas for books welcome.
Royalties paid twice yearly.

Oneworld Publications
185 Banbury Road, Oxford OX2 7AR
☎01865 310597   Fax 01865 310598
Managing Director *Juliet Mabey*
FOUNDED 1986. Distributed worldwide by **Penguin Books**. *Publishes* adult non-fiction, world religions, psychology, social issues. 21 titles in 1994. TITLE *Islam and the West* Norman Daniel. No unsolicited mss; synopses and ideas welcome. No fiction or poetry.
Royalties paid annually.

Onlywomen Press Ltd
40 St Lawrence Terrace, London W10 5ST
☎0181 960 7122   Fax 0181 960 7122
Editorial Director *Lilian Mohin*
FOUNDED 1974. *Publishes* radical feminist lesbian books only: fiction, poetry and non-fiction, including anthologies. About 6 titles a year. In 1995, published the first three titles in a new crime novel list, original paperbacks set in contemporary England with lesbian protagonists. TITLES *Burning Issues* Maggie Kelly; *Dirty Work* Vivien Kelly; *A Fearful Symmetry* Tash Fairbanks. Unsolicited mss, synopses and ideas welcome. Submissions should be accompanied by s.a.e. for return of material and/or notification of receipt.

Open Books Publishing Ltd
Beaumont House, Wells, Somerset BA5 2LD
☎01749 677276   Fax 01749 670760
Managing Director *Patrick Taylor*
FOUNDED 1974. *Publishes* academic and general. No unsolicited material. All books are commissioned.
Royalties paid twice yearly.

Open Gate Press
51 Achilles Road, London NW6 1DZ
☎0171 431 4391   Fax 0171 431 5088
Managing Directors *Jeannie Cohen, Elisabeth Petersdorff*
FOUNDED 1989 to provide a forum for psychoanalytic social and cultural studies. *Publishes* psychology, philosophy, social sciences, politics. 5–6 titles a year. SERIES *Psychoanalysis and Society*. Synopses and ideas for books welcome.
Royalties paid twice yearly.

Open University Press
Celtic Court, 22 Ballmoor, Buckingham, Buckinghamshire MK18 1XW
☎01280 823388   Fax 01280 823233
Managing Director *John Skelton*
Approx. Annual Turnover £3 million
FOUNDED 1977 as an imprint independent of the Open University's course materials. *Publishes* academic and professional books in the fields of education, management, sociology, health studies, politics, psychology, women's studies. No economics or anthropology. Not interested in anything outside the social sciences. About 100 titles a year. No unsolicited mss; enquiries/proposals only.
Royalties paid annually.

Optima
See **Little, Brown & Co. (UK)**

Orbit
See **Little, Brown & Co. (UK)**

Orchard Books
See **The Watts Publishing Group**

Orion Publishing Group
Orion House, 5 Upper St Martin's Lane, London WC2H 9EA
☎0171 240 3444   Fax 0171 240 4822
Chairman *Sir John Cuckney*
Chief Executive *Anthony Cheetham*
Managing Director *Peter Roche*
FOUNDED 1992 by Anthony and Rosemary Cheetham and Peter Roche. Incorporates

Weidenfeld & Nicolson, J. M. Dent and Chapmans Publishers.

DIVISIONS
Orion *Rosemary Cheetham, Jane Wood* Hardcover fiction and non-fiction. IMPRINTS **Millenium** *Caroline Oakley* Science fiction and fantasy.

Weidenfeld & Nicolson *Ion Trewin* General non-fiction, biography and autobiography, history and travel. IMPRINTS **General Books**; **Phoenix House** *Maggie McKernan* Literary fiction.

Illustrated *Michael Dover* Illustrated non-fiction with a strong emphasis on the visual and upmarket design, cookery, wine, gardening, art and architecture, natural history and personality-based books.

Orion Children's Books *Judith Elliott* Children's fiction and non-fiction.

Mass Market *Susan Lamb* IMPRINTS **Orion**; **Phoenix**; **Everyman** *Hilary Laurie*.

Authors' Rating The brainchild of one-time Random Century boss, Anthony Cheetham, Orion has responded quickly to market forces by dropping academic and heavy non-fiction books to concentrate on strong selling trade titles with paperback potential. Expect a Stock Exchange flotation in 1996 and rapid expansion thereafter.

Osprey
See **Reed International Books**

Peter Owen Ltd
73 Kenway Road, London SW5 0RE
☎0171 373 5628/370 6093
Fax 0171 373 6760
Chairman *Peter Owen*
Senior Editor *Jill Foulston*
FOUNDED 1951. *Publishes* biography, general non-fiction, English literary fiction and translations, sociology. 'No middlebrow romance, thrillers or children's.' AUTHORS Jane Bowles, Paul Bowles, Shusaku Endo, Anna Kavan, Fiona Pitt-Kethley, Anaïs Nin, Jeremy Reed, Peter Vansittart. 35–40 titles a year. Unsolicited synopses welcome for non-fiction material; mss should be preceded by a descriptive letter or synopsis with s.a.e.
Royalties paid twice yearly. *Overseas associates* worldwide.

Authors' Rating According to *The Guardian*, 'a publisher of the old and idiosyncratic school', Peter Owen works out of an Earls Court basement and claims not to draw a salary – 'We couldn't keep going if I did'. Certainly, his books are not great money spinners but they are the stuff of learned treatises and academic seminars. He has seven Nobel prizewinners on his list.

Oxford Illustrated Press/Oxford Publishing Co.
See **Haynes Publishing**

Oxford University Press
Walton Street, Oxford OX2 6DP
☎01865 56767   Fax 01865 56646
Chief Executive *James Arnold-Baker*
Approx. Annual Turnover £200 million
A department of the university for several hundred years, OUP grew from the university's printing works and developed into a major publishing business in the 19th century. *Publishes* academic books in all categories: student texts, scholarly journals, schoolbooks, ELT material, dictionaries, reference, music, bibles, electronic publishing, imported titles from the USA and beyond, as well as paperbacks, poetry, general non-fiction and children's books. Around 3000 titles a year.

DIVISIONS
Arts and Reference *I. S. Asquith* TITLES *Concise Oxford Dictionary*; **Educational** *F. E. Clarke* courses for the National Curriculum; **ELT** *P. R. Mothersole* ELT courses and dictionaries; **Science, Medical & Journals** *J. R. Manger* TITLES *Birds of the Western Paleartic*.

IMPRINTS **Clarendon Press** monographs in humanities, science and social science; **Oxford Paperbacks** trade paperbacks; **Oxford Science Publications, Oxford Medical Publications, Oxford Electronic Publications**. OUP welcomes first-class academic material in the form of proposals or accepted theses.
Royalties paid twice yearly. *Overseas subsidiaries* Sister company in USA; also branches in Australia, Canada, East Africa, Hong Kong, India, Japan, New Zealand, Pakistan, Singapore, South Africa. Offices in Argentina, Brazil, France, Germany, Greece, Italy, Mexico, Spain, Taiwan, Thailand, Turkey, Uruguay. Joint companies in Malaysia, Nigeria and Germany.

Authors' Rating Having survived the recession in great style, OUP is the largest publisher of ELT and a market leader in the teaching of reading, though academic and reference books are the core of the business. Authors invariably have close connections with the university. New translations of great European works are appearing and the price war with Wordsworth and Penguin has brought down the price of best selling classics. The next stage of development is electronic publishing with easy access to an intellectual powerhouse.

Palm Tree Press
See **Kevin Mayhew Ltd**

Pan Books Ltd
See **Macmillan Publishers Ltd**

Pandora Press
See **HarperCollins Publishers Ltd**

Paper Tiger Books
See **Dragon's World**

Paperduck
See **Gerald Duckworth & Co Ltd**

Paperfronts
See **Elliot Right Way Books**

Papermac
See **Macmillan Publishers Ltd**

Paragon Softcover Large Print
See **Chivers Press Ltd**

Parapress Ltd
12 Dene Way, Speldhurst, Nr Tunbridge Wells, Kent TN3 0NX
☎01892 862860   Fax 01892 863861
Managing Director *Ian W. Morley-Clarke*
FOUNDED 1993. *Publishes* autobiography, biography, diaries, journals of military personnel and sportsmen. Also books on local history. About 12 titles a year. Largely self-publishing. IMPRINT: **Oast Books**.

Partridge Press
See **Transworld Publishers Ltd**

The Paternoster Press
See **STL Ltd**

Pavilion Books Ltd
26 Upper Ground, London SE1 9PD
☎0171 620 1666   Fax 0171 620 1314
Chairmen *Tim Rice, Michael Parkinson*
Managing Director *Colin Webb*
Publishes biography, children's, cookery, gardening, humour, art, sport and travel. About

70 titles a year. Unsolicited mss not welcome. Synopses and ideas for non-fiction titles and children's fiction considered.
Royalties paid twice yearly.

Payback Press
See **Canongate Books Ltd**

Pelham Books
See **Penguin Books Ltd**

Pen & Sword Books Ltd
See **Leo Cooper**

Penguin Books Ltd
27 Wrights Lane, London W8 5TZ
☎0171 416 3000   Fax 0171 416 3099
Chief Executive *Peter Mayer*
Managing Director *Trevor Glover*
Editor-in-Chief, Adult Publishing
     Peter Carson
Publisher, Children's *Elizabeth Attenborough*

Owned by Pearson plc. For more than 60 years the publisher of one of the largest paperback lists in the English language, the Penguin list embraces fiction, non-fiction, poetry, drama, classics, reference and special interest areas. Reprints and new work. In 1995, Penguin restructured its adult book publishing, creating three divisions issuing both hardback and paperback editions.

DIVISIONS
General Adult fiction and non-fiction. Publisher *Tony Lacey*, Associate Publisher *Clare Alexander* IMPRINTS **Hamish Hamilton Ltd**; **Penguin**; **Viking**. Non-fiction synopses and ideas welcome; no unsolicited fiction; no poetry.

Penguin Press Serious adult non-fiction, reference and classics. Director *To be appointed*. IMPRINTS **Allen Lane**; **Arkana** Mind, body and spirit; **Buildings of England**; **Classics**; **Economist Books**; **Penguin Press**. Approach in writing only.

Michael Joseph Ltd Publishing Director *Susan Watt* IMPRINTS **Michael Joseph** Popular fiction; **Pelham**; **Pelham Studio** Illustrated books; **ROC** Science fiction and fantasy; **Signet** Mass-market fiction and non-fiction. Unsolicited mss discouraged; synopses and ideas welcome.

Frederick Warne *Sally Floyer* Classic children's publishing and merchandising including *Beatrix Potter*™; *Flower Fairies; Orlando;* **Ventura** *Sally Floyer* Producer and packager of *Spot* titles by Eric Hill.

Children's Hardback IMPRINTS **Blackie**

Rosemary Stones Mainly *Topsy & Tim* titles; **Dutton** *Rosemary Stones* Novelty, picture books and fiction; **Hamish Hamilton Children's** *Jane Nissen* Fiction and picture books. Unsolicited mss, synopses and ideas welcome; **Viking Children's** *Rosemary Stones.* Fiction, non-fiction, picture books and poetry. Unsolicited mss discouraged; synopses and ideas welcome.

Children's Paperbacks IMPRINTS **Puffin** *Philippa Milnes-Smith* Leading children's paperback list publishing in virtually all fields including fiction, non-fiction, poetry and picture books, media-related titles.

Royalties paid twice yearly. *Overseas associates* worldwide.

Authors' Rating A sixtieth birthday is a good excuse for a party and, in the case of a publishing company, an even better excuse for a public relations assault on the media. 1995 was Penguin's year for grabbing attention and congratulations for six decades of quality publishing during which time it became one of the largest and most successful English Language publishers in the world. It has not been an entirely easy ride. Arrogance and a misplaced feeling of invulnerability led to near disaster in the early seventies. But since 1978, when Peter Mayer joined the company, Penguin has responded to all challenges including, latterly, competition from Wordsworth Classics, pile 'em high and sell 'em cheap publisher of many of Penguin's standard titles, with a series of 60p mini books which took over the bestseller list. With a list that is marvellously varied there is a niche somewhere for any writer who can match readability with sales potential. The shortest jump on to the paperback shelves is from one of Penguin's hardback divisions. Children's books account for around half of all Penguin sales. No infant's bookshelf is complete without its collection of Puffins.

Pergamon Press
See **Elsevier Science Ltd**

Phaidon Press Limited
Regent's Wharf, All Saints Street, London N1 9PA
☎0171 843 1000   Fax 0171 843 1010
Chairman *Richard Schlagman*
Editorial Heads *M. Jordan, D. Jenkins, R. Sears, I. Blazwick*

Publishes quality books on the visual arts, including fine art, art history, architecture, design, practical art, photography, decorative arts and performing arts. About 100 titles a year. Unsolicited mss welcome but 'only a small amount of unsolicited material gets published'.

Royalties paid twice yearly.

Authors' Rating High production values, and the Phaidon catalogue is an art book in itself – but this publisher has come up against the **Society of Authors** for insisting that authors give up moral rights. Other contract clauses which give offence to the Society include tight delivery dates ('the publisher could cancel the contract and get the advance back if delivery is a day late') and a condition on royalty payments that they should add up to more than £100 a year. Anything less is held over to the next accounting year.

George Philip
See **Reed International Books**

Phillimore & Co. Ltd
Shopwyke Manor Barn, Chichester, West Sussex PO20 6BG
☎01243 787636   Fax 01243 787636
Chairman *Philip Harris*
Managing Director *Noel Osborne*
Approx. Annual Turnover £1 million

FOUNDED 1870 by W. P. W. Phillimore, Victorian campaigner for local archive conservation in Chancery Lane, London. Became the country's leading publisher of historical source material and local histories. Somewhat dormant in the 1960s, it was revived by Philip Harris in 1968. *Publishes* British local and family history, including histories of institutions, buildings, villages, towns and counties, plus guides to research and writing in these fields. About 70 titles a year. No unsolicited mss; synopses/ideas welcome for local or family histories.

IMPRINTS **Phillimore** *Noel Osborne* TITLES *Domesday Book; A History of Essex; Carlisle; The Haberdashers' Company; Channel Island Churches;* **British Association for Local History** *Noel Osborne* TITLES *Running a Local History Society; Writing Local History.*

Royalties paid annually.

Phoenix (Kingsway)
See **Kingsway Communications**

The Phoenix Press (Swansea)
See **Headstart History**

Phoenix/Phoenix House
See **Orion Publishing Group**

Piatkus Books

5 Windmill Street, London W1P 1HF
☎0171 631 0710   Fax 0171 436 7137
Managing Director *Judy Piatkus*
Approx. Annual Turnover £4.75 million

FOUNDED 1979 by Judy Piatkus, the company is committed to continuing independence. Piatkus Books almost doubled its turnover and output in the last two years. *Specialises* in self-help, personal growth, business and management, careers, cookery, health and beauty, healing, mind, body and spirit, women's interests, popular psychology and fiction. About 180 titles a year (50 of which are fiction).

DIVISIONS **Fiction** *Judy Piatkus* TITLES *Houses of Stone* Barbara Michaels; *Happy are the Peacemakers* Andrew M. Greeley; *Kernow and Daughter* Malcolm Ross. **Non-fiction** *Gill Cormode* TITLES *Curry Club Balti Curry Cookbook* Pat Chapman; *The Complete Style Guide* Colour Me Beautiful Organisation; *The Perfect CV* Tom Jackson; *The Reflexology Handbook* Laura Norman; *Nostradamus: The Next Fifty Years* Peter Lemesurier; *Living Magically* Gill Edwards. Piatkus are expanding their range of books and welcome synopses and ideas.
Royalties paid twice yearly.

Authors' Rating Piatkus Books has grown from a one-room band to a thriving independent list. The company claims to give commitment to each book they take on and to treat every non-fiction title as a lead. Authors are cheered by fast decision-making and by the policy of frequent small reprints which keeps titles in print for much longer than average.

Picador
See **Macmillan Publishers Ltd**

Pictorial
See **Souvenir Press Ltd**

Picture Knight
See **Hodder Headline plc**

Picture Lions
See **HarperCollins Publishers Ltd**

Pimlico
See **Random House UK Ltd**

Pinter Publishers Ltd
See **Cassell**

Pitkin Pictorials
See **Reed International Books**

Pitman Publishing

128 Long Acre, London WC2E 9AN
☎0171 379 7383   Fax 0171 240 5771
Managing Director *Rod Bristow*
Publishing Director *Mark Allin*

Part of Pearson Professional. Publisher and supplier of business education and management development materials. Portfolio of products and services includes books, journals, directories, looseleafs, CD-ROMS, conferences and seminars aimed at business education and management development in both private and public sectors. About 250 titles a year.

IMPRINTS **Pitman Publishing; Financial Times; Institute of Management; M & E Handbooks; NatWest Business Handbooks**. Unsolicited mss, synopses and ideas for books and other materials welcome.
Royalties paid annually.

Plenum Publishing Ltd

88–90 Middlesex Street, London E1 7EZ
☎0171 377 0686   Fax 0171 247 0555
Chairman *Martin E. Tash* (USA)
Managing Director *Dr Ken Derham*
Editor *Joanna Lawrence*

FOUNDED 1966. A division of **Plenum Publishing**, New York. The London office is the editorial and marketing base for the company's UK and European operations. *Publishes* postgraduate, professional and research-level scientific, technical and medical monographs, conference proceedings and reference books. About 300 titles (worldwide) a year.

IMPRINTS **Consultants Bureau; IFI Plenum Data Company; Plenum Insight; Plenum Medical Company; Plenum Press; Human Science Press**. Proposals for new publications will be considered, and should be sent to the editor.
Royalties paid annually.

Pluto Press Ltd

345 Archway Road, London N6 5AA
☎0181 348 2724   Fax 0181 348 9133
Managing Director *Roger Van Zwanenberg*
Editorial Director *Anne Beech*

FOUNDED 1970. Has developed a reputation for innovatory publishing in the field of non-fiction. *Publishes* academic and scholarly books across a range of subjects including cultural studies, politics and world affairs, social sciences and socialist, feminist and Marxist books; plus self-help guides on all aspects of the media.

About 50–60 titles a year. Synopses and ideas welcome.

Authors' Rating Is now out of theatre, cinema and literary criticism. Much more interested in political and social themes.

Point
See **Scholastic Publications Ltd**

Polemical Pamphlets
See **George Mann Books**

Polity Press
65 Bridge Street, Cambridge CB2 1UR
☎01223 324315   Fax 01223 461385

FOUNDED 1984. All books are published in association with **Blackwell Publishers**. *Publishes* archaeology and anthropology, criminology, economics, feminism, general interest, history, human geography, literature, media and cultural studies, medicine and society, philosophy, politics, psychology, religion and theology, social and political theory, sociology. Unsolicited mss, synopses and ideas for books welcome.
Royalties paid annually.

Polygon
See **Edinburgh University Press Ltd**

Pont Books
See **Gomer Press**

Pop Universal
See **Souvenir Press Ltd**

Porpoise
See **Random House UK Ltd**

Portland Press Ltd
59 Portland Place, London W1N 3AJ
☎0171 580 5530   Fax 0171 323 1136
Chairman *Professor A.J. Turner*
Managing Director *S.D. Jones*
Editorial Director *Rhonda Oliver*
Approx. Annual Turnover £2.5 million
FOUNDED 1990 to expand the publishing activities of the Biochemical Society (1911). *Publishes* biochemisty and medicine for graduate, postgraduate and research students. Expanding the list to include schools and general readership. 11 titles in 1994. TITLES *Essays in Biochemistry; Molecular Botany; Temperature Adaptation of Biological Membranes*. New series *Making Sense of Science* being launched 1995/96. Unsolicited mss, synopses and ideas welcome. No fiction.
Royalties paid twice yearly. *Overseas subsidiary* Portland Press Inc.

Presentations
See **Souvenir Press Ltd**

Princeton University Press
See **University Presses of California, Columbia & Princeton Ltd**

Prion
See **Multimedia Books Ltd**

Prism Press Book Publishers Ltd
The Thatched Cottage, Partway Lane, Hazelbury Bryan, Sturminster Newton, Dorset DT10 2DP
☎01258 817164   Fax 01258 817635
Managing Director *Julian King*
FOUNDED 1974. *Publishes* alternative medicine, conservation, environment, farming, health, mysticism, philosophy, politics and cookery. About 6 titles a year at present. TITLES *Boundaries of the Soul* June Singer; *Environmental Impact Assessments* Diane Wiesner; *Complete Home Winemaking* Brian Leverett. Synopses and ideas welcome.
Royalties paid twice yearly. *Overseas associates* Prism Press, USA.

Proteus
See **Omnibus Press**

Puffin
See **Penguin Books Ltd**

Putnam Aeronautical Books
See **Brassey's (UK) Ltd**

Quartet Books
27 Goodge Street, London W1P 1FD
☎0171 636 3992   Fax 0171 637 1866
Chairman *Naim Attallah*
Editorial Director *Jeremy Beale*
Approx. Annual Turnover £1 million
FOUNDED 1972. Part of the Namara Group which includes **The Women's Press**. *Publishes* classical music books, fiction, jazz, literary biography, literature in translation (most European languages including East European), photography and popular non-fiction. About 50 titles a year. IMPRINTS **Robin Clark**, **Quartet Encounters** (foreign literature in translation series). Unsolicited mss, synopses and ideas for books welcome. No crime fiction.
Royalties paid twice yearly.

Authors' Rating A high-profile company riding on the flamboyant reputation of its owner, Naim Attallah, whose publishing interests include the best of the book journals, *The Literary Review*.

Queen Anne Press
See **Lennard Associates Ltd** under **UK Packagers**

Quiller Press
46 Lillie Road, London SW6 1TN
☎0171 499 6529   Fax 0171 381 8941
Managing/Editorial Director *Jeremy Greenwood*

Specialises in sponsored books and publications sold through non-book trade channels as well as bookshops. *Publishes* architecture, biography, business and industry, children's, cookery, DIY, gardening, guidebooks, humour, reference, sports, travel, wine and spirits. About 15 titles a year. TITLES *Novelty Teapots* Edward Bramah; *Crash the Ash* Auberon Waugh; *Monkey Business* Gen. Sir Cecil Blacker; *Water: The Book* Hugh Barty-King. Most ideas originate in-house – unsolicited mss not welcome unless the author sees some potential for sponsorship or guaranteed sales.
Royalties paid twice yearly.

Quotes Ltd
See **The Barracuda Collection**

RAC Publishing
RAC House, Bartlett Street, South Croydon, Surrey CR2 6XW
☎0181 686 0088   Fax 0181 688 2882
Publisher *Alan Wakeford*

Publishes accommodation guides. Synopses and ideas for books considered.

Authors' Rating Way behind the AA as a publishing enterprise, the RAC has raised its profile by joining up with HarperCollins to publish high quality road maps. Guide books are aimed at the popular end of the market.

Radcliffe Medical Press Ltd
18 Marcham Road, Abingdon, Oxon OX14 1AA
☎01235 528820   Fax 01235 528830
Managing Director *Andrew Bax*
Editorial Head *Gillian Nineham*
Approx. Annual Turnover £1.5 million

FOUNDED 1985. Medical publishers which began by specialising in books for general practice. *Publishes* clinical, management, health policy books and CD-ROM. 35 titles in 1994. Unsolicited mss, synopses and ideas welcome.

No non-medical or medical books aimed at lay audience.
Royalties paid twice yearly. *Overseas subsidiary* Radcliffe Medical Press Inc., New York.

Rampant Horse Ltd
140 Whitehall Road, Norwich, Norfolk NR2 3EW
☎01603 665843   Fax 01603 661589
Managing Director *Susan Curran*

FOUNDED 1993. Independent publishing house founded by a group of East Anglian writers. *Publishes* literary and historical fiction mostly by already-published authors. 8–12 titles a year planned. TITLES *Coromandel* Pat Barr; *Voices* Jeremy Leland; *Communion With Death* Susan Curran; *The Opal Diviner* Alan Martin; *Silver's Way* Michael Pollard. Unsolicited synopses and sample chapters (not full mss) welcome.
Royalties paid twice yearly.

The Ramsay Head Press
15 Gloucester Place, Edinburgh EH3 6EE
☎0131 225 5646
Managing Directors *Conrad Wilson, Mrs Christine Wilson*

FOUNDED 1968 by Norman Wilson OBE. A small independent family publisher. *Publishes* biography, cookery, Scottish fiction and non-fiction, plus the quarterly literary magazine *Books in Scotland*. About 3–4 titles a year. TITLES *Medusa Dozen* Tessa Ransford; *The Happy Land* Howard Denton & Jim C. Wilson. Synopses and ideas for books of Scottish interest welcome.
Royalties paid twice yearly.

Random House UK Ltd
Random House, 20 Vauxhall Bridge Road, London SW1V 2SA
☎0171 973 9000   Fax 0171 233 6058
Chief Executive *Gail Rebuck*
Executive Chairman *Simon Master*

Random's increasing focus on trade publishing, both here and in the US, has been well rewarded, with sales continuing to grow over the last year. Random House UK Ltd is the parent company of three separate publishing divisions following the Group's reorganisation under Gail Rebuck. These are: General Books Division, the Group's largest publishing division; Children's Books & Enterprises; and Ebury Press Special Books Division.

DIVISIONS
General Books Publishing director: *Simon King* (Trade). Divided into two operating groups,

allowing hardcover editors to see their books through to publication in paperback. The literary imprints Jonathan Cape and Chatto & Windus work side by side with paperback imprints Vintage and Pimlico to form one group; trade imprints Century and Hutchinson go hand-in-hand with Arrow and Legend to form the other group.

IMPRINTS
Jonathan Cape Ltd Tel: 0171 973 9730 Fax: 0171 233 6117 Publishing Director: *Dan Franklin* Archaeology, biography and memoirs, current affairs, economics, fiction, history, philosophy, photography, poetry, politics, sociology and travel.

Chatto & Windus Ltd Tel: 0171 973 9740 Fax: 0171 233 6123 Managing Director: *Jonathan Burnham* Archaeology, art, belles-lettres, biography and memoirs, cookery, crime, current affairs, essays, fiction, history, illustrated and fine editions, poetry, politics, psychoanalysis, translations and travel.

Century (including **Business Books**) Tel: 0171 973 9670 Fax: 0171 233 6127 Publishing Director: *Kate Parkin* General fiction and non-fiction, plus business management, advertising, communication, marketing, selling, investment and financial titles.

Hutchinson Books Ltd Tel: 0171 973 9680 Fax: 0171 233 6129 Publishing Director: *Sue Freestone* General fiction and non-fiction including notably belles-lettres, current affairs, politics, travel and history.

Arrow Tel: 0171 973 9700 Fax: 0171 233 6127 Publishing Director: *Andy McKillop* Mass-market paperback fiction and non-fiction.

Legend Tel: 0171 973 9700 Fax: 0171 233 6127 Editorial Director: *John Jarrold* Science fiction and fantasy (hardback and paperback).

Pimlico Tel: 0171 973 9680 Fax: 0171 233 6129 Publishing Director: *Will Sulkin* Large-format quality paperbacks in the fields of history, biography, autobiography and literature.

Vintage Tel: 0171 973 9700 Fax: 0171 233 6127 Publisher: *Will Sulkin* Quality paperback fiction and non-fiction. Vintage was founded in 1989 by Frances Coady and has been described as one of the 'greatest literary success stories in recent British publishing'.

Children's Books & Enterprises Tel: 0171 973 9750 Fax: 0171 233 6058 Publishing Directors: *Piet Snyman, Clare Conville, Caroline Roberts, Margaret Conroy, Julia MacRae, Tom Maschler.* IMPRINTS **Bodley Head; Jonathan Cape; Hutchinson; Random House; Tell-a-**

Story; **Julia MacRae Books; Porpoise** and the paperback imprint **Red Fox**. Picture books, fiction, non-fiction and books on audio cassette (see **Audio Books**). Launched the **Safeway Superbooks** series in 1993 under the management of Julia MacRae, with nationwide marketing through the supermarket chain.

Enterprises IMPRINTS **Fodor's**; **Audio Books; TRS** (audio books also).

Ebury Press Special Books Tel: 0171 973 9690 Fax: 0171 233 6057 Publishing Director: *Amelia Thorpe.* IMPRINTS **Ebury Press** *Fiona McIntyre*; **Barrie & Jenkins** *Julian Shuckburgh*; **Stanley Paul; Ebury Press Stationery** and the paperback imprints **Rider** and **Vermilion** *Sarah Sutton.* Art, architecture, antiques and collection under the Barrie & Jenkins umbrella, plus cookery, health and beauty, photography, travel, transport, humour, crafts, antiques, hobbies, gardening, natural history, DIY, diaries, gift stationery. Ebury is the publishing vehicle too for National Magazine Co. book tie-ins. About 150 titles a year. Unsolicited mss, synopses and ideas for books welcome.

Royalties paid twice yearly for the most part.

Authors' Rating A collection of famous names, all of which seem to be thriving under the Random umbrella. Restructuring has led to a sharp cutback in title output. The two paperback imprints, Arrow (mass market) and Vintage (literary), are leaders in their fields. Open to ideas with money to back their judgement. Strong on marketing and publicity.

Reader's Digest Association Ltd
Berkeley Square House, Berkeley Square, London W1X 6AB
☎0171 629 8144   Fax 0171 236 5956
Managing Director *Neil McRae*
Editorial Head *Robin Hosie*
Approx. Annual Turnover £160 million

Publishes gardening, natural history, cookery, history, DIY, travel and word books. About 10 titles a year. TITLES *Family Medical Adviser; The Gardening Year; Nature Lover's Library; New DIY Manual; When, Where, Why and How it Happened.* Unsolicited mss, synopses and ideas for books welcome.

Reardon Publishing
56 Upper Norwood Street, Leckhampton, Cheltenham, Gloucestershire GL53 0DU
☎01242 231800
Managing Editor *Nicholas Reardon*
FOUNDED in the mid 1970s. Family-run pub-

lishing house specialising in local interest and tourism in the Cotswold area. Member of the **Outdoor Writers Guild**. *Publishes* walking and driving guides, and family history for societies. 10 titles a year. TITLES *Cotswold Walkabout; Cotswold Driveabout; The Donnington Way; The Haunted Cotswolds; The Cotswold Way.* Unsolicited mss, synopses and ideas welcome with return postage only.

Royalties paid twice yearly.

Recollections
See **George Mann Books**

Red Fox
See **Random House UK Ltd**

William Reed Directories
Merchant House, 4A Reading Road, Pangbourne, Berkshire RG8 7LL
☎01734 844111   Fax 01734 841579
Publishing Director *Ray Hurst*

FOUNDED 1978. Formerly Elvendon Press. *Specialises* in information books, magazines and booklets for government departments, national organisations, media/PR agencies and blue-chip companies. Database facility for publishing directories, yearbooks and exhibition programmes. No unsolicited mss. Preliminary letter essential.

Reed International Books
Michelin House, 81 Fulham Road, London SW3 6RB
☎0171 581 9393   Fax 0171 225 9424
Chairman *Paul Hamlyn*
Chief Executive, Consumer Division
   Richard Charkin
Approx. Annual Turnover £350 million

Reed International Books is the holding company for the three branches of parent company Reed Elsevier: **Reed Consumer Books, Butterworth-Heinemann** academic books, and **Heinemann/Ginn** educational books.

REED CONSUMER BOOKS DIVISIONS
This division has several different offices: addresses and telephone numbers have been given if different from that above.

FICTION AND GENERAL NON-FICTION:
William Heinemann (hardback) Fax: 0171 225 9095 Publisher: *Tom Weldon*, Editorial Director: *Louise Moore*. TITLES *Free to Trade* Michael Ridpath; *A Simple Life* Rosie Thomas; **Mandarin** (paperback) TITLES *Charity* Leslie Pearse; *Running Away* Leslie Thomas; *Kolymsky Heights* Lionel Davidson. No unsolicited mss.

Secker & Warburg (hardback) Fax: 0171 225 9095 Publisher: *Max Eilenberg*, Editorial Director: *Geoff Mulligan* Literary fiction and general non-fiction TITLES *The Island of the Day Before* Umberto Eco; *Therapy* David Lodge; *Athena* John Banville; **Minerva** (paperback) TITLES *Paddy Clarke Ha Ha Ha* Roddy Doyle; *Made in America* Bill Bryson; *How Late It Was, How Late* James Kelman.

Methuen Fax: 0171 589 9095 Publisher: *Geoffrey Strachan* Plays, drama, humour, fiction, music, arts TITLES *Letters* John Betjeman; *Running Away* Leslie Thomas; *Joan's Book* Joan Littlewood. Plays by Brecht, Bond, Churchill, Mamet, Miller, Orton, Soyinka. Please write with synopsis before submitting mss.

Sinclair-Stevenson Tel: 0171 225 9095 Fiction and general non-fiction TITLES *Evelyn Waugh* Selina Hastings; *Dan Leno and the Limehouse Golem* Peter Ackroyd; *The History Puzzle* Cherry Denman.

ILLUSTRATED NON-FICTION:
Hamlyn Fax: 0171 225 9458 Publisher: *Laura Bamford* Popular non-fiction, particularly cookery, gardening, craft, sport, film tie-ins, rock 'n' roll, road atlases TITLES *Larousse Gastronomique; Variety Movie Guide; Sunday Times Chronicle of Sport; Jean Moss Designer Knits Collection.*

Mitchell Beazley Fax: 0171 225 9458 Publisher: *Jane Aspden* Illustrated encyclopedias and other quality illustrated books, including wine TITLES *Hugh Johnson's Pocket Wine Book; The New Joy of Sex; Miller's Antiques Price Guide.*

Osprey Militaria, aviation, automotive, natural history TITLES *Jaguar XJ220; Midway 1942; Jet Bombers; Waterloo, The 100 Days.*

Conran Octopus 37 Shelton Street, London WC2H 9HN. Tel: 0171 240 6961 Fax: 0171 836 9951 Publisher: *John Wallace* Quality illustrated books, particularly lifestyle, cookery, gardening TITLES *Terence Conran's New House Book; The Complete Mothercare Manual; Creating Small Gardens; 10 Minute Cuisine.*

George Philip Fax: 0171 225 9477 Publisher: *John Gaisford* Atlases, maps, astronomy TITLES *Philip's Atlas of the World; Philip's Road Atlas of Modern Britain; Philip's Guide to the Night Sky; Philip's School Atlas.*

Pitkin Pictorials Healey House, Dene Road, Andover, Hampshire SP10 2AA. Tel: 01264 334303 Fax: 01264 334110 Publisher: *Ian Corsie* Illustrated souvenir guides.

REED CHILDREN'S BOOKS:
Offices: 38 Hans Crescent, London SW1X

0LZ. Tel: 0171 225 9713 Fax: 0171 225 9731 Managing Director: *Jane Winterbotham*.

Heinemann Young Books Quality picture books, novels, anthologies and TV tie-ins TITLES *Thomas The Tank Engine; Animals of Farthing Wood; The Jolly Postman*; **Mammoth Paperbacks** TITLES *Winnie the Pooh; The Trouble with Mum; Frog and Toad*; **Methuen Children's Books** Quality picture books and fiction for babies to early teens TITLES *Babar; Tintin; The Wind in the Willows*; **Hamlyn** Illustrated non-fiction and reference books for children TITLES *History of Britain* series; *See Through History* series. No unsolicited mss.

Brimax Books Units 4/5, Studlands Park Industrial Estate, Exning Road, Newmarket, Suffolk CB8 7AU. Tel: 01638 664611 Fax: 01638 665220 Managing Director: *Patricia Gillette* Mass-market board and picture books for children age groups 1–10.

REED ACADEMIC
Butterworth-Heinemann Linacre House, Jordan Hill, Oxford OX2 8DP. Tel: 01865 310366 Fax: 01865 310898 Managing Director: *Philip Shaw*. **Engineering & Technology** *Peter Dixon*; **Business** *Kathryn Grant*; **Medical** *Geoff Smaldon* Scientific, technical, medical and business books.

REED EDUCATIONAL PUBLISHING:
Incorporating Heinemann Educational, Heinemann English Language Teaching and Ginn in the UK; Heinemann Inc. and Rigby Inc. in the USA, and Rigby Heinemann in Australia.

Heinemann Educational Halley Court, Jordan Hill, Oxford OX2 8EJ. Tel: 01865 311366 Fax: 01865 310043 Managing Director: *Bob Osborne*. **Primary** *Paul Shuter*; **Secondary** *Kay Symons* Textbooks, literature and other educational resources for primary and secondary school and further education. Mss, synopses and ideas welcome.

Heinemann English Language Teaching For address, see Heinemann Educational. Managing Director: *Mike Esplen*. Publishing Directors: *Chris Hartley* (Adult); *Sue Bale* (Schools) English-language teaching books and materials.

Ginn Prebendal House, Parson's Fee, Aylesbury, Bucks. HP20 2QY. Tel: 01296 394442 Fax: 01296 393433 Managing Director: *Nigel Hall*; Editorial Director: *Ann Foster* Textbooks and other educational resources for primary schools.
    Royalties paid twice yearly/annually, according to contract in all divisions.

Authors' Rating Judged to be the world's most profitable publishing group, Reed's merger with Elsevier has made the company '*the* blue chip stock of European publishing' according to one analyst, and opens up the prospect of expansion into the European market. A pointer to the future is the decision to sell off more than a billion pounds of print publishing to concentrate exclusively on the new technology, in particular the online distribution of academic and professional publications. At the time of writing, potential purchasers are still jockeying for position.

Reed Reference Publishing
See **Bowker-Saur Ltd**

Reinhardt Books Ltd
Flat 2, 43 Onslow Square, London
SW7 3LR
☎0171 589 3751
Chairman/Managing Director *Max Reinhardt*
Directors *Joan Reinhardt, John Hews*
FOUNDED 1887 as H. F. L. (Publishers) and was acquired by Max Reinhardt in 1947. Changed its name to the present one in 1987. First publication under the new name was Graham Greene's *The Captain and the Enemy*. Also publishes under the **Nonesuch Press** imprint. AUTHORS include Mitsumasa Anno, Alistair Cooke and Maurice Sendak. Unsolicited mss are not welcome.
    Royalties paid according to contract.

Religious & Moral Educational Press
See **The Canterbury Press Norwich/Chansitor Publications**

Richmond House Publishing Company
9/11 Richmond Buildings, London
W1V 5AF
☎0171 437 9556   Fax 0171 287 3463
Managing Director *Gloria Gordon*
Editorial Head *Samantha Blair*
Publishes directories for the theatre and entertainment industries. Synopses and ideas welcome.

Rider
See **Random House UK Ltd**

Right Way
See **Elliot Right Way Books**

Robson Books Ltd

Bolsover House, 5–6 Clipstone Street,
London W1P 7EB
☎0171 323 1223   Fax 0171 636 0798
Managing Director *Jeremy Robson*
Editorial Head *Louise Dixon*

FOUNDED 1973. *Publishes* mainly general non-fiction, including biography, cinema, cookery, gardening, guidebooks, health and beauty, humour, sports and games, theatre and drama and travel. About 60 titles a year. Unsolicited mss, synopses and ideas for books welcome (s.a.e. essential).
Royalties paid twice yearly.

Authors' Rating The hard-pressed gift buyers' favourite publisher. A Robson book is always good for a laugh.

ROC

See **Penguin Books Ltd**

Rosendale Press Ltd

Premier House, 10 Greycoat Place, London
SW1P 1SB
☎0171 222 8866   Fax 0171 799 1416
Chairman *Timothy S. Green*
Editorial Director *Maureen P. Green*

FOUNDED 1985. Independent publisher of non-fiction and illustrated books, namely food and drink, travel, business entertainment and family health. About 10 titles a year. TITLES *The Top 100 Pasta Sauces; Favourite Indian Food; The Vegetable Market Cookbook; The World of Gold; Eating Out in Barcelona and Catalunya; Understanding Your Baby.* Synopses and ideas for books considered within their specialist fields only.
Payment varies according to contract.

Roundhouse Publishing Ltd

PO Box 140, Oxford OX2 7FF
☎01865 512682   Fax 01865 59594
Managing Director/Publisher *Alan T. Goodworth*

Publisher of cinema, theatre and other media-related titles, and general-interest non-fiction. TITLES *Hitchcock: The First Forty Four Films; Shoot the Piano Player: Director, Francois Truffaut; Animating Culture: Movie Cartoons from the Sound Era; Toms, Coons, Mulattoes, Mammies and Bucks; Encyclopedia of World Geography.*

Represents **Facts on File, Inc.** (see under **US Publishers**) information and reference titles across an endless list of subjects for children aged 8 and over; Breakwater Books; Continuum

Publishing; Crossroad Publishing counselling titles; Chatham House Publishers; Douglas & McIntyre; MapEasy; **University Press of Mississippi; Paragon House**; Self-Counsel Press.
Royalties paid twice yearly.

Routledge

11 New Fetter Lane, London EC4P 4EE
☎0171 583 9855   Fax 0171 583 0701
Managing Director *Janice Price*
Publishing Director *Peter Sowden*
Publishers *Gordon Smith, Claire L'Enfant*
Approx. Annual Turnover £20 million (Group)

The new Routledge company was formed in 1987 through an amalgamation of Routledge & Kegan Paul, Methuen & Co., Tavistock Publications, and Croom Helm. The **HarperCollins** academic list acquired in 1991 added a substantial new list, bringing in textbooks and monographs in social sciences. *Publishes* access, addiction, anthropology, archaeology, Asian studies, business and management, classical heritage and studies, counselling, criminology, development and environment, dictionaries, economics, education, geography, health, history, Japanese studies, linguistics, literary criticism, media and culture, Middle East, philosophy, politics, political economy, psychiatry, psychology, reference, social administration, social studies and sociology, women's studies and journals. No poetry, fiction, travel or astrology. About 750 titles a year.

Send synopses with sample chapter and c.v. rather than complete mss.
Royalties paid annually.

Saga

See **Barracuda Books Ltd/Quotes Ltd**

St Paul's Bibliographies

1 Step Terrace, Winchester, Hampshire
SO22 5BW
☎01962 860524   Fax 01962 842409
Chairman/Managing Director *Robert Cross*
Approx. Annual Turnover £50,000

FOUNDED 1982. *Publishes* bibliographical reference books and works on the history of the book. 2–3 titles a year. TITLES *A Millenium of the Book 900–1900* ed. Robin Myers and Michael Harris; *An Introduction to Bibliography for Litany Students* R. B. McKerrow; *Anthony Powell: A Bibliography* George Lilley. Unsolicited mss, synopses and ideas welcome if relevant to subjects covered.
Royalties paid twice yearly.

St Pauls

St Paul's House, Middlegreen, Slough,
Berkshire SL3 6BT
☎01753 520621   Fax 01753 574240
Managing Director *Karamvelil Sebastian*

Publishing division of the Society of St Paul.
Began publishing in 1914 but activities were
fairly limited until around 1948. *Publishes* religious material only: theology, scripture, cate-
chetics, prayer books, children's material and
biography. Unsolicited mss, synopses and ideas
welcome. About 50 titles a year.

Salamander Books Ltd

129–137 York Way, London N7 9LG
☎0171 267 4447   Fax 0171 267 5112
Managing Director *Ray Bonds*

FOUNDED 1973. Independent publishing
house. *Publishes* collecting, cookery and wine,
crafts, military and aviation, pet care, sport,
transport, technical and children's non-fiction.
About 55 titles a year. Unsolicited synopses and
ideas for books welcome.
Royalties outright fee paid instead of royalties.

Sangam Books Ltd

57 London Fruit Exchange, Brushfield Street,
London E1 6EP
☎0171 377 6399   Fax 0171 375 1230
Executive Director *Anthony de Souza*

Traditionally an educational publisher of
school and college level textbooks. Also *publishes* art, India, medicine, science, technology,
social sciences, religion, plus some fiction in
paperback.

W. B. Saunders & Co. Ltd/Saunders Scientific Publications

See **Harcourt Brace and Company Ltd**

SAUS Publications

University of Bristol, School for Advanced
Urban Studies, Rodney Lodge, Grange Road,
Bristol, Avon BS8 4EA
☎0117 9741117   Fax 0117 9737308
Managing Director *Alison Shaw*
Approx. Annual Turnover £150,000

FOUNDED in 1978 to publish research findings
from SAUS. It has since developed into a substantial small academic publisher producing
paperback books on a wide range of social science topics. Due to relaunch as a new press and
planning to become more commercially orientated, increasing the number of books produced

and range of topics covered, but still focusing
on social sciences. 20 titles in 1994. No unsolicited mss; brief synopses and ideas welcome.

SB Publications

c/o 19 Grove Road, Seaford, East Sussex
BN25 1TP
☎01323 893498
Managing Director *Steve Benz*
Approx. Annual Turnover £200,000

FOUNDED 1987. *Specialises* in local history,
including themes illustrated by old picture post-
cards and photographs; also travel, maritime
history and railways. 20 titles a year. IMPRINTS
Brampton Publications *Steve Benz*; **Ship
Pictorial Publications** *A. S. Mallett*. TITLES
Potteries Picture Postcards; *The Cunard Line*.
Royalties paid annually.

Scarlet Press

5 Montague Road, London E8 2HN
☎0171 241 3702   Fax 0171 275 0031
Directors *Christine Considine, Avis Lewallen,
Ann Treneman*

FOUNDED 1989. Independent publishing
house. *Publishes* feminist non-fiction covering
politics, autobiography, social policy, arts,
leisure, history, lesbian and gay studies. No fic-
tion or any 'non-woman-centred' material.
About 6 titles a year. TITLES *Within Me,
Without Me, Adoption: An Open and Shut Case?*
Sue Wells; *Women and Film* Pam Cook and
Philip Dodds (eds); *Passions Between Women,
British Lesbian Culture 1668–1801* Emma
Donoghue. Unsolicited mss, synopses and ideas
welcome.
Royalties paid twice yearly.

Sceptre

See **Hodder Headline plc**

Scholastic Publications Ltd

Villiers House, Clarendon Avenue,
Leamington Spa, Warwickshire CV32 5PR
☎01926 887799   Fax 01926 883331
Chairman *M. R. Robinson*
Managing Director *David Kewley*
Approx. Annual Turnover £23 million

FOUNDED 1964. Owned by US parent company. *Publishes* education for primary school
teachers, children's fiction and non-fiction.

DIVISIONS
Scholastic Children's Books *David Fickling*
7–9 Pratt Street, London NW1 0AE. Tel: 0171
284 4474. Fax: 0171 284 4234. IMPRINTS **André**

Deutsch Children's Books (hardbacks); **Adlib** (12+ fiction); **Hippo** (paperbacks); **Point** (paperbacks). TITLES *Postman Pat; Rosie & Jim; Tots TV; Goosebumps; Point Horror.*

Educational Publishing *Anne Peel, Regina Nuttall* Professional books and classroom materials for primary teachers, plus magazines such as *Child Education, Junior Education, Art & Craft, Junior Focus, Infant Projects.*

Direct Marketing to Schools The largest school-based book club operator in the UK, selling to children via their schools through four book clubs: *See-Saw, Lucky, Chip* and *Scene,* covering ages 5–13, and to teachers through *Criterion.* Also operates *Scholastic Book Fairs,* a complementary school marketing operation which sells books to children in schools.
Royalties paid twice yearly.

SCM Press Ltd
26–30 Tottenham Road, London N1 4BZ
☎0171 249 7262   Fax 0171 249 3776
Managing Director *Rev. Dr John Bowden*
Approx. Annual Turnover £1 million

Publishes religion and theology, with some ethics and philosophy. About 40 titles a year. Unsolicited mss and synopses considered if sent with s.a.e.
Royalties paid annually.

Authors' Rating Leading publisher of religious ideas with well-deserved reputation for fresh thinking. At SCM, 'questioning theology is the norm'. The deal with Trinity Press of New York, requiring both to work as a single organisation, publishing under both imprints, means that SCM authors can now be published worldwide.

Scolar Press
See **Ashgate Publishing Co. Ltd**

Scope International Ltd/ Milestone Publications
Forestside House, Forestside, Rowlands Castle, Hampshire PO9 6EE
☎01705 631468   Fax 01705 631777
Managing Director/Editorial Director
  Nicholas J. Pine

Publishes business, economics, finance, privacy, tax haven and tax planning, antique porcelain.
IMPRINTS **Milestone Publications, Scope.** No unsolicited mss. Approach in writing with ideas/proposals.
Royalties paid twice yearly.

Scottish Academic Press
56 Hanover Street, Edinburgh EH2 2DX
☎0131 225 7483   Fax 0131 225 7662
Managing Editor *Dr Douglas Grant*

FOUNDED 1969. *Publishes* academic: architecture, education, geology, history, literature, poetry, social sciences, theology.
Royalties paid annually.

Seafarer Books
See **Merlin Press Ltd**

Seagull Books
See **The Book Guild Ltd**

Search Press Ltd/Burns & Oates
Wellwood, North Farm Road, Tunbridge Wells, Kent TN2 3DR
☎01892 510850   Fax 01892 515903
Managing Director *Countess de la Bédoyère*

FOUNDED 1847. Publishers to the Holy See. *Publishes* (Search Press) full-colour art, craft, cookery, needlecrafts and organic gardening; (Burns & Oates) philosophy, theology, history, spirituality, educational, reference.
  DIVISIONS **Academic** *Paul Burns* TITLES include the *Liberation & Theology* series, currently ten volumes. **Craft** *John Dalton, Clare Turner* Books on papermaking and papercrafts, painting flowers on silk, calligraphy and embroidery, and the *Organic Handbooks* series. Unsolicited mss, synopses and ideas for books welcome.
Royalties paid annually.

Secker & Warburg
See **Reed International Books**

Senate
See **Studio Editions Ltd**

Sensation
See **Harlequin Mills & Boon Ltd**

Serpent's Tail
4 Blackstock Mews, London N4 2BT
☎0171 354 1949   Fax 0171 704 6467
Contact *Pete Ayrton*
Approx. Annual Turnover £650,000

FOUNDED 1986. Won the *Sunday Times* Small Publisher of the Year Award (1989) and the Ralph Lewis Award for new fiction (1992). Serpent's Tail has introduced to British audiences a number of major internationally known writers. Noted for its strong emphasis on design – including flaps on paperback covers in the continental style – and an eye for the unusual.

In 1994, launched a new series imprint **High Risk Books**. *Publishes* contemporary fiction, including works in translation, crime, popular culture and biography. No poetry, science fiction, horror, romance or fantasy. About 40 titles a year.

IMPRINTS **Masks** TITLES *One Night Stands* Rosa Likson; *Makbara* Juan Goytisolo; **Mask Noir** TITLES *White Butterfly; A Red Death; Black Betty* all by Walter Mosley; **High Risk Books** *Rent Boy* Gary Indiana; *Stripping* Pagan Kennedy; *Bombay Talkie* Armeena Meer. Send preliminary letter outlining proposal (include s.a.e. for reply). No unsolicited mss. Prospective authors who are not familiar with Serpent's Tail are advised to study the list before submitting anything.

Royalties normally paid yearly.

Authors' Rating A small publisher with a reputation for way-out and original subject matter.

Settle Press
10 Boyne Terrace Mews, London W11 3LR
☎0171 243 0695

Chairman/Managing Director *D. Settle*

FOUNDED 1981. *Publishes* travel, guidebooks, general non-fiction. About 12 titles a year. **Travel/Tourist Guides/General** *D. Settle* TITLES *City Break Series* (Paris, Rome, Vienna, etc.); *Where to Go Series* (Romania, Turkey, Greece, etc.); *Key To Series* (Far East, Africa, Caribbean, etc). Unsolicited synopses accepted but no mss.

Royalties paid by arrangement.

Severn House Publishers Ltd
9–15 High Street, Sutton, Surrey SM1 1DF
☎0181 770 3930   Fax 0181 770 3850

Chairman *Edwin Buckhalter*
Editorial *Deborah Smith*

FOUNDED 1974. A leader in library fiction publishing. *Publishes* hardback fiction: romance, science fiction, horror, fantasy, crime. About 120 titles a year. No unsolicited material. Synopses/proposals preferred through bona fide literary agents only.

Royalties paid twice yearly. *Overseas associates* Severn House Publishers Inc., New York.

Shakespeare Head Press
See **Blackwell Publishers Ltd**

Sheffield Academic Press
Mansion House, 19 Kingfield Road, Sheffield S11 9AS
☎0114 2554433   Fax 0114 2554626

Managing Director *Mrs Jean R.K. Allen*

Approx. Annual Turnover £1.1 million

FOUNDED in 1976. Originally known as JSOT Press. Now the leading academic publisher of biblical titles. Recently expanded its list to include archaeology, literary studies, history and culture, languages. 80 titles in 1994. Unsolicited mss, synopses and ideas welcome. No fiction.

IMPRINTS **Sheffield Academic Press** *Andrew Kirk*; **Subis** *Duncan Chambers*.

Royalties paid annually

Sheldon Press
See **Society for Promoting Christian Knowledge**

Shepheard–Walwyn (Publishers) Ltd
Suite 34, 26 Charing Cross Road, London WC2H 0DH
☎0171 240 5992   Fax 0171 379 5770

Managing Director *Anthony Werner*
Approx. Annual Turnover £140,000

FOUNDED 1972. 'We regard books as food for the mind and want to offer a wholesome diet of original ideas and fresh approaches to old subjects.' *Publishes* general non-fiction in three main areas: Scottish interest; gift books in calligraphy and/or illustrated; history, political economy, philosophy and religion. About 4 titles a year. Synopses and ideas for books welcome.

Royalties paid twice yearly.

Ship Pictorial Publications
See **SB Publications**

Shire Publications Ltd
Cromwell House, Church Street, Princes Risborough, Buckinghamshire HP27 9AJ
☎01844 344301   Fax 01844 347080

Commissioning Editor *Jackie Fearn*

FOUNDED 1967. *Publishes* original non-fiction paperbacks. About 25 titles a year. No unsolicited material; send introductory letter with detailed outline of idea.

Royalties paid annually.

Sidgwick & Jackson
See **Macmillan Publishers Ltd**

Sigma Press
1 South Oak Lane, Wilmslow, Cheshire SK9 6AR
☎01625 531035   Fax 01625 536800

Chairman/Managing Director *Graham Beech*

FOUNDED in 1980 as a publisher of technical books. Sigma Press grew rapidly with popular computer books which are still a major part of the list. *Publishes* outdoor, leisure, local heritage, myths and legends, sports, computing. Recently launched a popular science series. Approx. 55 titles in 1994. No unsolicited mss; synopses and ideas welcome.

DIVISIONS **Sigma Leisure** TITLES *50 Classic Walks in the Pennines; Cycling in Scotland; Lakeland Rocky Rambles*; **Sigma Press** TITLES *Communications & Networks; PC Engineer's Reference Book; Alice in Quantumland.*

Royalties paid twice yearly.

Signet
See **Penguin Books Ltd**

Silhouette Desire
See **Harlequin Mills & Boon Ltd**

Simon & Schuster
West Garden Place, Kendal Street, London W2 2AQ
☎0171 724 7577   Fax 0171 402 0639
Managing Director *Nick Webb*
Editorial Directors *Joanna Frank, Martin Fletcher, Helen Gummer*

FOUNDED 1986. Offshoot of the leading US publisher. *Publishes* general fiction and non-fiction in hardback and paperback. The company's academic division is based in Hemel Hempstead. No academic or technical material.
Royalties paid twice yearly.

Authors' Rating Best known in the States for its technology list, Simon & Schuster has made its British reputation with new fiction and children's books. Expansion into school publishing which started with the purchase of Blackwell's education list has continued with the takeover of Cassell's ELT list. But the company's single biggest advantage is being able to take in books from the American side of Simon & Schuster, an economic bonus that nonetheless makes it harder for British authors to gain a foothold.

Sinclair-Stevenson
See **Reed International Books**

Skoob Books Publishing Ltd
11A–17 Sicilian Avenue, Southampton Row, London WC1A 2QH
☎0171 404 3063   Fax 0171 404 4398
Editorial office: 25 Lowman Road, London N7 6DD. Tel/Fax 0171 609 0699.
Managing Director *I.K. Ong*

Publishes three series: **Skoob Seriph** literature, lost classics and poetry; **Skoob Esoterica**

occult and esoterica; **Skoob Pacifica** new writing from the countries of the Pacific Rim. Recent interest in contemporary gay fiction and 'cultural studies'. **Literary & Esoteric** *Christopher Johnson* TITLES *Collected Poems* George Eliot; *Personae* Peter Abbs; *Outer Gateways* Kenneth Grant; *Qabalah* John Bonner; *Sensuous Horizons* K.S. Maniam.

Smith Gryphon Ltd
Swallow House, 11–21 Northdown Street, London N1 9BN
☎0171 278 2444   Fax 0171 833 5680
Chairman/Managing Director *Robert Smith*

FOUNDED 1990. Family-owned company. *Publishes* biography, autobiography, music (mostly rock), cinema, true crime, topical issues, finance and business, personality-led fiction, wine, food and cookery, and illustrated. 20 titles in 1995. TITLES *Diana in Private* Lady Colin Campbell; *The Quest for Anastasia* John Klier; *The Diary of Jack the Ripper* Shirley Harrison; *Harry's Bar Cookbook* Arrigo Cipriani; *Young Marilyn* James Haspiel. No unsolicited mss; ideas and synopses welcome.
Royalties paid twice yearly.

Authors' Rating Living up to its early promise, Smith Gryphon favours concentration on a select group of strong sellers.

Colin Smythe Ltd
PO Box 6, Gerrards Cross, Buckinghamshire SL9 8XA
☎01753 886000   Fax 01753 886469
Managing Director *Colin Smythe*
Approx. Annual Turnover £950,000

FOUNDED 1966. *Publishes* Anglo-Irish literature, drama, and criticism, history. About 15 titles a year. No unsolicited mss; send synopses and ideas for books in first instance.
Royalties paid annually/twice yearly.

Society for Promoting Christian Knowledge (SPCK)
Holy Trinity Church, Marylebone Road, London NW1 4DU
☎0171 387 5282   Fax 0171 388 1921
Publishing Director *Simon Kingston*
Approx. Annual Turnover £2 million

FOUNDED 1698, SPCK is the third oldest publisher in the country. *Publishes* academic theology, general religious and pastoral titles, with popular self-help, and business books under the Sheldon general trade imprint. About 95 titles a year.

IMPRINTS **SPCK** *Philip Law* TITLES *Who Was Jesus?*; *Understanding the Dead Sea Scrolls; Christianity and Child Sexual Abuse;* **Triangle** *Naomi Starkey* TITLES *Facing Anxiety; The Voice from the Cross;* **Sheldon Press** *Joanna Moriarty* TITLES *Coping with Panic Attacks; Self-Defence for Every Day; Taking the Macho Out of Management.* No unsolicited material. Enquiries only.

Royalties paid annually.

Authors' Rating Religion with a strong social edge.

SoftbABCks
See **ABC – All Books for Children**

Solo Books Ltd
49–53 Kensington High Street, London
W8 5ED
☎0171 376 2166   Fax 0171 938 3165
Chairman/Managing Director *Don Short*
Approx. Annual Turnover £1.3 million
(Group)

Publishing arm of **Solo Literary Agency** (see under **UK Agents**). *Publishes* biography and autobiography and celebrity books, some non-fiction and business titles. About 15 titles a year. No fiction. Unsolicited mss not welcome; approach in writing with synopses or ideas.

Royalties paid quarterly.

Souvenir Press Ltd
43 Great Russell Street, London WC1B 3PA
☎0171 580 9307/8 & 637 5711/2/3
Fax 0171 580 5064
Chairman/Managing Director *Ernest Hecht*
Senior Editor *Tessa Harrow*

Independent publishing house. FOUNDED 1952. *Publishes* academic and scholarly, animal care and breeding, antiques and collecting, archaeology, autobiography and biography, business and industry, children's, cookery, crafts and hobbies, crime, educational, fiction, gardening, health and beauty, history and anti-quarian, humour, illustrated and fine editions, magic and the occult, medical, military, music, natural history, philosophy, poetry, psychology, religious, sociology, sports, theatre and women's studies. About 60 titles a year. Souvenir's Human Horizons series for the dis-abled and their carers is one of the most pre-eminent in its field and recently celebrated fif-teen years of publishing for the disabled.

IMPRINTS **Condor; Pictorial; Presentations; Pop Universal; Human Horizons.** TITLES *The Descent of the Child, Human Evolution From a New Perspective* Elaine Morgan; *The Artists'*

Way, A Spiritual Path to Higher Creativity Julia Cameron; *Great Irish Tales of the Unimaginable* ed. Peter Haining; *Politically Correct Bedtime Stories* James Finn Garner; *The Specialist* Charles Sale; *How to Live with a Neurotic Cat Owner* Stephen Baker; *The Food Medicine Bible* Earl Mindell; *Singing From the Soul* José Carreras. Unsolicited mss considered but initial letter of enquiry preferred.

Royalties paid twice yearly.

Authors' Rating After 40 years as an inde-pendent publisher, Ernest Hecht is fondly regarded as one of the great characters of the book business. His widely eclectic list ranges from novels of **Nobel Prize** winner Knut Hamson to an illustrated history of knickers. Souvenir claims to the be the 'most successful cat book publisher in Europe'. An apparently chaotic office is a cover for a highly efficient operation.

SPCK
See **Society for Promoting Christian Knowledge**

Special Edition
See **Harlequin Mills & Boon Ltd**

Spellmount Ltd
The Old Rectory, Staplehurst, Kent
TN12 0AZ
☎01580 893730   Fax 01580 893731
Managing Director *Jamie Wilson*
Approx. Annual Turnover £150,000

FOUNDED 1983. *Publishes* non-fiction in hard-cover; primarily history and military history, biography. About 20 titles a year. Synopses/ideas for books welcome in above specialist fields only.

Royalties six-monthly for two years, then annually.

Spindlewood
70 Lynhurst Avenue, Barnstaple, Devon
EX31 2HY
☎01271 71612   Fax 01271 25906
Managing Director *Michael Holloway*

FOUNDED 1980. *Publishes* children's books. 6 titles in 1995. No unsolicited mss; send synop-sis with sample chapter or two.

Royalties paid according to contract.

E & F N Spon
2–6 Boundary Row, London SE1 8HN
☎0171 865 0066   Fax 0171 522 9623
Managing Director *D. Inglis*

Publishing Director *Phillip Read*

FOUNDED 1834 by the son and grandson of Baron de Spon, a refugee from the French Revolution, the company has always specialised in science and technology. In the 1950s, it became an imprint of Chapman & Hall and since 1987 has concentrated solely on construction-related titles. About 70 titles a year. *Publishes* architecture, building, civil and environmental engineering, landscape, planning & property (all built-environment), sports science, leisure & recreation management. TITLES *The Channel Tunnel Story; The Buildings Around Us; Building Services Engineering; European Cities: Planning Systems and Property Markets; Coaching Children in Sport, Science and Golf.* Unsolicited mss, synopses and ideas welcome.
Royalties paid annually.

Sporting & Leisure Press
See **The Barracuda Collection**

Springfield Books Ltd
Norman Road, Denby Dale, Huddersfield, West Yorkshire HD8 8TH
☎01484 864955   Fax 01484 865443
Chairman/Managing Director *Brian Lewis*
Approx. Annual Turnover £1.2 million

FOUNDED 1984. *Publishes* sport and leisure titles only. About 8 titles a year. TITLES *Cycle Repair: Step by Step; Mountain Bike Maintenance; Left-handed Golfer.* Unsolicited mss, synopses and ideas welcome if they fall within range of subject areas above.
Royalties paid twice yearly.

Stainer & Bell Ltd
PO Box 110, 23 Gruneisen Road, London N3 1DZ
☎0181 343 3303   Fax 0181 343 3024
Chairman *Bernard A. Braley*
Managing Directors *Carol Y. Wakefield, Keith M. Wakefield*
Publishing Manager *Nicholas Williams*
Approx. Annual Turnover £575,000

FOUNDED 1907 to publish sheet music. *Publishes* music and religious subjects related to hymnody. Unsolicited synopses/ideas for books welcome. Send letter enclosing brief précis.
Royalties paid annually.

Stam Press
See **Stanley Thornes (Publishers) Ltd**

Stanley Paul
See **Random House UK Ltd**

Harold Starke Publishers Ltd
Pixey Green, Stradbroke, Near Eye, Suffolk IP21 5NG
☎01379 388334   Fax 01379 388335
Directors *Harold K. Starke, Naomi Galinski*
Publishes adult non-fiction, medical and reference. No unsolicited mss.
Royalties paid annually.

Patrick Stephens Ltd
See **Haynes Publishing**

Stevens
See **Sweet & Maxwell Ltd**

STL Ltd
PO Box 300, Carlisle, Cumbria CA3 0QS
☎01228 512512   Fax 01228 514949
Publishing Director *Pieter Kwant*
Publishing Manager *Jeremy H. L. Mudditt*
Approx. Annual Turnover £1,200,000

Owns two publishing subsidiaries, the Paternoster Press and OM Publishing:

The Paternoster Press FOUNDED 1935. *Publishes* religion and learned/church/life-related journals. About 50 titles a year. TITLES *The New International Dictionary of New Testament Theology* (4 vols) ed. Colin Brown; *Acts in its 1st Century Setting* ed. Bruce Winter; *Calvin's Old Testament Commentaries.*

OM Publishing FOUNDED 1978. *Publishes* Christian books on evangelism, discipleship and mission. About 30 titles a year. TITLES *Operation World* Patrick Johnstone; *You Can Change the World* Jill Johnstone.

Unsolicited mss, synopses and ideas for books welcome.
Royalties paid twice yearly.

Studio Editions Ltd
Princess House, 50 Eastcastle Street, London W1N 7AP
☎0171 636 5070   Fax 0171 580 3001
Executive Chairman *Sonia Land*
Managing Director *Kenneth Webb*
Publishing Director *Ruth Binney*
Approx. Annual Turnover £8 million

FOUNDED 1982. Acquired its present identity in 1990. *Publishes* illustrated non-fiction: fine and decorative art, music and photography, military history, natural history and the plant world, travel and topography, children's books, social stationery. Over 85 titles a year.
IMPRINTS **Studio Editions** Trade publishing imprint; **Bracken Books** Promotional reprints;

Senate Facsimilie paperbacks; **Studio Designs** Social stationery. TITLES *Post Impressionism; Master Painter Series; The Map-Makers' Art.*
Royalties paid according to contract.

Studio Vista
See **Cassell**

Subis
See **Sheffield Academic Press**

Summersdale Publishers
PO Box 49, Chichester, West Sussex PO19 2FJ
☎01850 303119/110414   Fax 01243 786930
Manager *Alastair Williams*
Editor *Stewart Ferris*
FOUNDED 1990. *Publishes* non-fiction: cookery, biography, gardening, sport (including martial arts/self defence), humour, self-improvement, travel, local interest, arts/entertainment. TITLES *The Student Grub Guide; Man About the Kitchen; Real Self Defence; How to Chat-up Women; 101 Ways to Become a Millionaire By the End of the Century; How to Save Money.* Unsolicited mss welcome (with return postage). Keen to work with new authors with strong, marketable ideas.
Royalties paid.

Susquehanna University Press
See **Golden Cockerel Press**

Alan Sutton Publishing Ltd
Phoenix Mill, Far Thrupp, Stroud,
Gloucestershire GL5 2BU
☎01453 731114   Fax 01453 731117
Managing Director *David Hogg*
Publishing Director *Peter Clifford*
Approx. Annual Turnover £3 million
FOUNDED 1978. Owned by Guernsey Press. *Publishes* academic, archaeology, biography, countryside, history, regional interest, local history, pocket classics (lesser known novels by classic authors), topography, transport, travel. About 240 titles a year. Send synopses rather than complete mss.
Royalties paid twice yearly.

Authors' Rating Some confusion was caused when Alan Sutton departed the company he had founded and set up a rival Alan Sutton Ltd. As a result of court action, this latest venture was renamed The Chalford Publishing Company. Meanwhile, the original Alan Sutton Publishing, the subject of this rating, continues on a path of steady development providing for growth in the local history market, in particular, books of old photographs.

Swan Hill Press
See **Airlife Publishing Ltd**

Sweet & Maxwell Ltd
South Quay Plaza, 183 Marsh Wall, London
E14 9FT
☎0171 538 8686   Fax 0171 538 8625
Chairman *Robert Kiernan*
Managing Director *Stephen White*
Deputy Managing Director *Chris White*
Publishing Director *Carol Tullo*
FOUNDED 1799. Part of The Thomson Corporation. *Publishes* legal and professional materials in all media, looseleaf works, journals and law reports. About 150 book titles a year, with live backlist of over 400 titles, 67 looseleaf services and more than 60 legal periodicals. Not interested in material which is non-legal. The legal and professional list is varied and contains many academic titles, as well as treatises and reference works in the legal and related professional fields.
IMPRINTS **Sweet & Maxwell**; **Stevens**; **Sweet & Maxwell/ESC** *Carol Tullo, W. Green, Anthony Kinahan* (Managing Director). Ideas welcome. Writers with legal/professional projects in mind are advised to contact the company at the earliest possible stage in order to lay the groundwork for best design, production and marketing of a project.
Royalties and fees vary according to contract.

Take That Ltd
PO Box 200, Harrogate, North Yorkshire
HG1 4XB
☎01423 507545   Fax 01423 507545
Chairman/Managing Director *C. Brown*
FOUNDED 1986. Independent publisher of business, humour, how-to and recreation titles (books and magazines). TITLES *The Hangover Handbook; Playing Lotteries For the Big Money; Tax Loopholes.* About 10 titles a year. Unsolicited mss for books welcome – any humour titles should be heavily illustrated.
Royalties paid twice yearly.

Tango Books
See **Sadie Fields Productions Ltd** under **(UK Packagers)**

Tarragon Press
Moss Park, Ravenstone, Whithorn DG8 8DR
☎01988 850368   Fax 01988 850304
Director/Editorial Head *David Sumner*
FOUNDED 1987. *Publishes* medical and scientific for the layperson. About 3 titles a year.

Unsolicited mss, synopses and ideas for books welcome.
Royalties paid annually.

I. B. Tauris & Co. Ltd
45 Bloomsbury Square, London WC1A 2HY
☎0171 916 1069   Fax 0171 916 1068
Chairman/Publisher *Iradj Bagherzade*
Editorial Director *Anna Enayat*

FOUNDED 1984. Independent publisher. *Publishes* general non-fiction and academic in the fields of international relations, current affairs, history, cultural studies, Middle East, East-West relations, Russia and East European studies. Joint projects with Cambridge University Centre for Middle Eastern Studies and Institute for Latin American Studies.
Distributes The New Press (New York) outside North America. IMPRINTS **Tauris Parke Books** Illustrated books on architecture, travel, design and culture. **British Academic Press** Academic monographs. TITLES *Beginning with My Street* Czeslaw Milosz; *Who's Who in Russia and the New States* ed. Alex Pravda. Unsolicited mss, synopses and ideas for books welcome.
Royalties paid twice yearly.

Tavistock Publications
See **Routledge**

Taxation Publishing
See **Tolley Publishing Co. Ltd**

Taylor & Francis
4 John Street, London WC1N 2ET
☎0171 400 3500   Fax 0171 831 2035
Chairman *Prof. Bryan Coles*
Managing Director *Anthony Selvey*
Approx. Annual Turnover £17 million

FOUNDED 1798 with the launch of *Philosophical Magazine* which has been in publication ever since (now a solid state physics journal). The company is privately owned with strong academic connections among the major shareholders. **Falmer Press** joined the group in 1979 and it doubled its size in the late '80s with the acquisition of Crane Russak in 1986 and Hemisphere Publishing Co in 1988. *Publishes* scientific, technical, education titles at university, research and professional levels. About 120 titles a year. Unsolicited mss, synopses and ideas welcome.
Royalties paid yearly. *Overseas office* Taylor & Francis Inc., Washington DC.

Authors' Rating After several years of cost cutting and having set itself against the time-honoured publishing formula of pricing itself out of a crisis, Taylor & Francis is in buoyant health as it comes up to its 200th anniversary. An expansion into electronic publishing is promised. Last year, Taylor & Francis was the only publisher to earn a Queen's Award for Export Achievement, acknowledgement of the remarkable fact that 85 per cent of its turnover comes from overseas.

Teach Yourself
See **Hodder Headline plc**

Tell-a-Story
See **Random House UK Ltd**

Temple House Books
See **The Book Guild Ltd**

Test Your Child
See **Hodder Headline plc**

Thames and Hudson Ltd
30–34 Bloomsbury Street, London WC1B 3QP
☎0171 636 5488   Fax 0171 636 4799
Managing Director *Thomas Neurath*
Editorial Head *Jamie Camplin*

Publishes art, archaeology, architecture and design, biography, crafts, fashion, garden and landscape design, graphics, history, illustrated and fine editions, mythology, music, photography, popular culture, travel and topography. Over 150 titles a year. SERIES *World of Art; New Horizons; Chic Simple; Celtic Design.* TITLES *Claude Monet 1840–1926; Colour and Culture; The Shock of the New; Chronicle of the Pharaohs; Streetstyle; Kilim: The Complete Guide; The Most Beautiful Villages of Provence; David Bailey: The Lady is a Tramp; The Graphic Language of Neville Brody 1 & 2; The Body: Photoworks of the Human Form; The French Café.* Send preliminary letter and outline before mss.
Royalties paid twice yearly.

Authors' Rating A long-running battle between Thames & Hudson and the Design and Artists Copyright Society culminated in a criminal prosecution brought by DACS' accusing Thames & Hudson of breach of copyright in a jacket illustration. What might have been a far-reaching test case was called off at the last moment with both sides claiming vindication and the Bow Street magistrate saying the case should never have been started. Who exactly holds copyright on fine art reproductions is likely to trouble publishers for some time to come. Meanwhile, Thames & Hudson thrives with its wonderfully accessible *World of Art* series accumulating sales of over 23 million copies.

Thames Head
See **BLA Publishing Ltd** under **UK Packagers**

Thames Publishing
14 Barlby Road, London W10 6AR
☎0181 969 3579   Fax 0181 969 1465
Managing Director *John Bishop*

FOUNDED 1970. *Publishes* music, and books about English music and musicians. About 4 titles a year. No unsolicited mss; send synopses and ideas in first instance.

Stanley Thornes (Publishers) Ltd
Ellenborough House, Wellington Street, Cheltenham, Gloucestershire GL50 1YD
☎01242 228888   Fax 01242 221914
Managing Director *David Smith*
Approx. Annual Turnover £17 million

FOUNDED 1972. Part of the Wolters-Kluwer Group. Merged with Mary Glasgow Publications in 1992. *Publishes* secondary school and college curriculum textbooks and primary school resources. About 200 titles a year. Unsolicited mss, synopses and ideas for books welcome if appropriate to specialised list.
IMPRINTS **Stam Press** technical books; **Mary Glasgow Publications** foreign-language teaching materials and teacher support.
Royalties paid annually.

Thornhill Press Ltd
Castlemain, Parkend, Near Lydney, Gloucestershire GL15 4HH
☎01594 564984   Fax 01594 564984
Directors *John Pemberthy, Bryan Robinson*
Editorial Head *John Pemberthy*
Approx. Annual Turnover £80,000

FOUNDED 1972. *Publishes* walking and touring guides, English heritage, activity and general titles. No fiction or poetry. About 8 titles a year. TITLES *Hallowed Ground* Hilary Lees; *Walks for All Seasons* David Hunter; *Cotswold Way* Mark Richards; *Golden Guide to Wye Valley and Forest of Dean* (series). Unsolicited mss, synopses and ideas for books welcome.
Royalties paid yearly.

Thorsons
See **HarperCollins Publishers Ltd**

Threshold Books
See **Kenilworth Press Ltd**

Times Books
See **HarperCollins Publishers Ltd**

Times Mirror International Publishers Ltd
Lynton House, 7–12 Tavistock Square, London WC1H 9LB
☎0171 388 7676   Fax 0171 391 6555
President *Timothy Hailstone*
Managing Director *John Hirst*
Vice-President of Publishing *Fiona Foley*
Approx. Annual Turnover £15 million

Part of Times Mirror Co., Los Angeles. Acquired Wolfe Publishing at the beginning of the 90s, broadening its horizon from the core list of books and journals for nurses to a list which now includes colour atlases and texts in medicine, dentistry and veterinary science. Approx. 88 titles in 1985.
IMPRINTS **Richard D. Irwin**; **Irwin Professional Publishing**; **Mosby**; **Mosby Wolfe Publishing**; **CRC Press**; **WCB Brown** TITLES *Handbook of Chemistry & Physics; A Colour Atlas & Text of Clinical Medicine; A Colour Atlas of Human Anatomy; 1995 Nursing Drug Reference; Guy's Hospital.* Synopses and ideas for books welcome.
Royalties paid twice yearly.

Titan Books
42–44 Dolben Street, London SE1 0UP
☎0171 620 0200   Fax 0171 620 0032
Managing Director *Nick Landau*
Editorial Director *Katy Wild*

FOUNDED 1981. Now a leader in the publication of graphic novels and in film and television tie-ins. *Publishes* comic books/graphic novels, cartoon strips, film and television titles, science fiction and fantasy, true crime. About 70–80 titles a year.
IMPRINTS **Titan Books**; **Mondo** True crime and the bizarre extremes of human behaviour; **Eros Plus** Erotic fiction. TITLES *Batman; Superman; Star Trek; Dr Who; Beginners Guide to Japanese Animation; Star Wars; Guide to Monster Make-up.* No unsolicited fiction or children's books please. Ideas considered; send synopsis/outline with sample chapter. Author guidelines available.
Royalties paid twice yearly.

Tolkein
See **HarperCollins Publishers Ltd**

Tolley Publishing Co. Ltd
Tolley House, 2 Addiscombe Road, Croydon, Surrey CR9 5AF
☎0181 686 9141   Fax 0181 686 3155
Chairman *G. J. S. Wilson*

Managing Director *Harry L. King*

Owned by United Newspapers plc, publishers of the *Daily Express, Sunday Express* and *Daily Star. Publishes* taxation, accounting, legal, business, technical and professional books.

DIVISIONS **Tolley Publishing; Charles Knight Publishing; Benn Technical Books; Taxation Publishing; Fourmat Publishing; Finborough Services**. Unsolicited mss, synopses and ideas welcome.

Tracks
See **HarperCollins Publishers Ltd**

Transworld Publishers Ltd
61–63 Uxbridge Road, London W5 5SA
☎0181 579 2652   Fax 0181 579 5479
Managing Director *Mark Barty-King*

FOUNDED 1950. A subsidiary of **Bantam, Doubleday, Dell Publishing Group Inc.**, New York, which is a wholly-owned subsidiary of Bertelsmann, Germany. *Publishes* general fiction and non-fiction, children's books, sports and leisure.

DIVISIONS
Adult Trade *Patrick Janson-Smith* IMPRINTS **Bantam** *Tony Mott*; **Bantam Press** *Ursula Mackenzie*; **Black Swan** *Tony Mott*; **Corgi** *Tony Mott*; **Doubleday** *Ursula Mackenzie*; **Partridge Press** *Ursula Mackenzie*. AUTHORS Brian Clough, Jilly Cooper, Frederick Forsyth, Elizabeth George, Stephen Hawking, Anthony Holden, Frank Keating, Frank Muir, Terry Pratchett, Joanna Trollope, Mary Wesley.

Children's & Young Adult Books *Philippa Dickinson* IMPRINTS **Doubleday** (hardcover); **Picture Corgi; Young Corgi; Yearling; Corgi; Corgi Freeway** (paperback imprints); **Bantam** (paperback). AUTHORS Malorie Blackman, Peter Dickinson, Francine Pascal, K.M. Peyton, Terry Prachett, Robert Swindells, Jacqueline Wilson. Unsolicited mss welcome only if preceded by preliminary letter.

Royalties paid twice yearly. *Overseas associates* Transworld Australia/New Zealand, Trans-South Africa Book Distributors.

Authors' Rating Much loved by its best-selling authors and admired by insiders for its ability to shift books in large numbers, Transworld seems curiously reluctant to sign the Minimum Terms Agreement. An agreement is said to be close but the minor sticking points suggest an unwillingness to take too many chances with untried talent. Tried talent is another matter, however. Transworld had 17 titles in the 1994 Guardian Top 100 Fastseller list.

Trentham Books Ltd
Westview House, 734 London Road, Stoke on Trent, Staffordshire ST4 5NP
☎01782 745567   Fax 01782 745553
Chairman/Managing Director *Dr John Eggleston*
Editorial Head *Gillian Klein*
Approx. Annual Turnover £500,000

Publishes education (nursery, school and higher), social sciences, intercultural studies, design and technology education for professional readers *not* for children and parents. About 25 titles a year. Unsolicited mss, synopses and ideas welcome if relevant to their interests.
Royalties paid annually.

Triangle
See **Society for Promoting Christian Knowledge**

Trotman & Co. Ltd
12 Hill Rise, Richmond, Surrey TW10 6UA
☎0181 940 5668   Fax 0181 948 9267
Managing Director *Andrew Fiennes Trotman*
Publishing Director *Morfydd Jones*
Approx. Annual Turnover £2.5 million

Publishes general careers books, higher education guides, teaching support material, education. About 50 titles a year. TITLES *Complete Degree Course Offers* (book and CD-ROM); *How to Complete Your UCAS Form; Students' Money Matters*. Unsolicited material welcome. Also active in the educational resources market, producing recruitment brochures.
Royalties paid twice yearly.

Two-Can Publishing Ltd
346 Old Street, London EC1V 9NQ
☎0171 613 3376   Fax 0171 613 3371
Chairman *Andrew Jarvis*
Marketing Director *Ian Grant*
Creative Director *Sara Lynn*
Approx. Annual Turnover £4 million

FOUNDED 1987 to publish innovative, high-quality material for children. *Publishes* books and magazines, including *Young Telegraph* (weekend supplement for 9–12-year-olds).
DIVISIONS **Books** *Ian Grant*; **Magazines** *Andrew Jarvis*. No unsolicited mss; send synopses and ideas in the first instance.
Royalties paid twice yearly.

UCL Press Ltd
University College London, Gower Street, London WC1E 6BT
☎0171 380 7707   Fax 0171 413 8392

Chairman *D. H. Roberts*
Publisher/Chief Executive *R. F. J. Jones*

FOUNDED 1991. *Publishes* academic books only. About 40 titles a year. No unsolicited mss; synopses and ideas welcome.
Royalties paid annually.

The Umberleigh Press
See **Headstart History**

University Presses of California, Columbia & Princeton Ltd
1 Oldlands Way, Bognor Regis, West Sussex PO22 9SA
☎01243 842165   Fax 01243 842167

Publishes academic titles only. US-based editorial offices. Over 200 titles a year. Enquiries only.

Unwin Hyman
See **HarperCollins Publishers Ltd**

Usborne Publishing Ltd
83–85 Saffron Hill, London EC1N 8RT
☎0171 430 2800   Fax 0171 430 1562
Managing Director *Peter Usborne*
Editorial Director *Jenny Tyler*
Approx. Annual Turnover £14 million

FOUNDED 1973. *Publishes* non-fiction, fiction, puzzle books, and music for children and young adults. Some titles for parents. Up to 100 titles a year. Also, **Usborne Books at Home** imprint. Based at Oasis Park, Eynsham, Oxford OX8 1TU. Books are written in-house to a specific format and therefore unsolicited mss are not normally welcome. Ideas which may be developed in-house are considered. Keen to hear from new illustrators and designers.
Royalties paid twice yearly.

Authors' Rating One of the best publishers of information books for children. Potential authors must believe that knowledge can be fun.

Vallentine Mitchell
See **Frank Cass & Co Ltd**

Variorum
See **Ashgate Publishing Co. Ltd**

Ventura
See **Penguin Books Ltd**

Vermilion
See **Random House UK Ltd**

Verso
6 Meard Street, London W1V 3HR
☎0171 434 1704/437 3546
Fax 0171 734 0059
Chairman *Robin Blackburn*
Managing Director *Colin Robinson*
Approx. Annual Turnover £1.7 million

Formerly New Left Books which grew out of the *New Left Review*. *Publishes* politics, history, sociology, economics, philosophy, cultural studies, feminism. No memoirs. TITLES *Theatres of Memory* Raphael Samuel; *For the Sake of Argument* Christopher Hitchens; *City of Quartz* Mike Davis; *The Enemy Within* Seumas Milne; *Lord Gnome's Literary Companion* Francis Wheen; *Anyone but England* Mike Marqusee; *Dialectic* Roy Bhaskar; *Year 501* Noam Chomsky; *Ideology* Terry Eagleton. No unsolicited mss; synopses and ideas for books welcome.
Royalties paid annually. *Overseas office* in New York.

Authors' Rating Dubbed by *The Bookseller* as 'one of the most successful small independent publishers'.

Viking
See **Penguin Books Ltd**

Vintage
See **Random House UK Ltd**

Virago Press Ltd
20 Vauxhall Bridge Road, London SW1V 2SA
☎0171 973 9750   Fax 0171 233 6123
Managing Director *Harriet Spicer*
Editorial Director *Lenore Goodings*
Approx. Annual Turnover £2.75 million

FOUNDED 1973 by Carmen Callil, with the aim of publishing a wide range of books which illuminate and celebrate all aspects of women's lives. Most titles are published in paperback; a distinguished reprint list makes up one third of these, with two thirds original titles commissioned across a wide range of interest: autobiography, biography, crime, fiction, history, social issues, politics, psychology, women's studies. About 60 titles a year. TITLES *Flesh and Blood* Michèle Roberts; *Talking From 9 to 5* Deborah Tannen. Telephone before sending unsolicited material.
Royalties paid twice yearly.

Authors' Rating A giant step towards sex equality was achieved by Virago's decision to publish male writers in its non-fiction list. The risk is Virago losing its identity as the leading feminist publisher. But Harriet Spicer insists that the company will still be 'run and controlled by women, publishing books about and for women'. Changes at the top – chairman and founder Carmen Callil resigned last February – suggest a painful struggle between ideology and economic reality.

Virgin Publishing
332 Ladbroke Grove, London W10 5AH
☎0181 968 7554   Fax 0181 968 0929
Chairman *Robert Devereux*
Managing Director *Robert Shreeve*
Approx. Annual Turnover £10 million

Virgin group's own imprint. *Publishes* popular culture, particularly film, TV, showbiz, music, biography, autobiography, popular reference and humour.
IMPRINTS **Virgin** *Mal Peachey*; **Virgin Illustrated** *Philip Dodd*; **Nexus, Black Lace** *Peter Darvill-Evans* erotic fiction; **True Crime** *Lorna Russell* mass-market imprint; **Doctor Who** *Peter Darvill-Evans*. Unsolicited mss, synopses and ideas for books welcome.
Royalties paid twice yearly.

Authors' Rating A much revitalised operation is making a bid for the popular market with series such as Black Lace erotic fiction aimed at women readers.

Volcano Press Ltd
PO Box 139, Leicester LE2 2YH
☎0116 2706714   Fax 0116 2706714
Chairman *F. Hussain*
Managing Director *A. Hussain*

FOUNDED 1992. *Publishes* academic non-fiction in the following areas: Islam, women's studies, human rights, Middle East, strategic studies and cultural studies. About 15 titles a year. TITLES *Beyond Islamic Fundamentalism: the Sociology of Faith and Action; Islamic Fundamentalism in Britain; Islam: Faith in a Global Perspective; Muslim Women in the Western World*. No unsolicited mss; synopses and ideas welcome. No fiction, poetry or plays.
Royalties paid twice yearly.

University of Wales Press
6 Gwennyth Street, Cathays,
Cardiff CF2 4YD
☎01222 231919   Fax 01222 230908
Director *E. M. Thomas*
Approx. Annual Turnover £350,000

FOUNDED 1922. *Publishes* academic and scholarly books in English and Welsh, particularly humanities, modern languages and social sciences, and scholarly Celtic works. 60 titles in 1995.
IMPRINTS **GPC Books**; **Gwasg Prifysgol Cymru**; **University of Wales Press**. TITLES *The Literature of Wales – A Pocket Guide* Dafydd Johnston; *A History of Money: From Ancient Times to the Present Day* Glyn Davies; *The Anglo-Irish Agreement* Arwel Ellis Owen. Unsolicited mss considered.
Royalties paid annually; more frequently by negotiation.

Walker Books Ltd
87 Vauxhall Walk, London SE11 5HJ
☎0171 793 0909   Fax 0171 587 1123
Editors *Wendy Boase, David Lloyd, Caroline Royds, Sally Christie, Jacqui Bailey, Lucy Ingrams, Sally Foord-Kelcey*
Approx. Annual Turnover £23 million

FOUNDED 1979. *Publishes* illustrated children's books and children's fiction. About 300 titles a year. TITLES *Where's Wally?* Martin Handford; *Five Minutes' Peace* Jill Murphy; *Can't You Sleep, Little Bear?* Martin Waddell & Barbara Firth. Unsolicited mss welcome.
Royalties paid twice yearly.

Authors' Rating Having won over the US market Walker is in expansionist mood, promising a new non-fiction list within a year and up to a third increase in title output. Much praised for author care, Walker has a profit share scheme which benefits staff, illustrators and writers.

Ward Lock
See **Cassell**

Ward Lock Educational Co. Ltd
1 Christopher Road, East Grinstead,
West Sussex RH19 3BT
☎01342 318980   Fax 01342 410980
Owner *Ling Kee (UK Ltd)*
Director *Vincent Winter*
Publishing Manager *Andrew Thraves*

FOUNDED 1952. *Publishes* educational books (primary, middle, secondary, teaching manuals) for all subjects, specialising in maths, science, geography, reading and English.
Royalties paid annually.

Frederick Warne
See **Penguin Books Ltd**

Warner Chappell Plays Ltd
See under **UK Agents**

Warner/Warner-Futura
See **Little, Brown & Co. (UK)**

Waterline Books
See **Airlife Publishing Ltd**

The Watts Publishing Group
96 Leonard Street, London EC2A 4RH
☎0171 739 2929   Fax 0171 739 2318
Managing Director *Marlene Johnson*
Part of Hachette SA. *Publishes* general non-fiction, reference, information and children's (fiction, picture and novelty). About 300 titles a year.
IMPRINTS **Watts Books** *Chester Fisher* Non-fiction and information; **Orchard Books** *Francesca Dow* children's fiction, picture and novelty books. Unsolicited mss, synopses and ideas for books welcome.
Royalties paid twice yearly. *Overseas associates* in Australia and New Zealand, US and Canada

Wayland Publishers Ltd
61 Western Road, Hove, East Sussex
BN3 1JD
☎01273 722561   Fax 01273 329314
Managing Director *John Lewis*
Editorial Director *Stephen White-Thomson*
Approx. Annual Turnover £6 million
Part of the Wolters Kluwer Group. FOUNDED 1969. *Publishes* a broad range of subjects particularly colour-illustrated non-fiction for children of 5 years and upwards. About 300 titles a year. No unsolicited mss or synopses as all books are commissioned.
Royalties paid annually. *Overseas associates* Thomson Learning Inc., USA.

Weidenfeld & Nicolson Ltd
See **Orion Publishing Group**

Wharncliffe Publishing Ltd
47 Church Street, Barnsley, South Yorkshire
S70 2AS
☎01226 734222   Fax 01226 734437
Chairman *Sir Nicholas Hewitt*
Managing Director *T. G. Hewitt*
Part of Barnsley Chronicle Holdings Ltd. Wharncliffe is the book and magazine publishing arm of an old-established, independently owned newspaper publishing and printing house. *Publishes* local and regional interest and activities, field sports and related material. Unsolicited mss, synopses and ideas welcome

but return postage must be included with all submissions.
Royalties paid twice yearly. *Associated company* **Leo Cooper/Pen & Sword Books Ltd**.

Which? Books/Consumers' Association
2 Marylebone Road, London NW1 4DF
☎0171 830 6000   Fax 0171 830 7660
Director *Sheila McKechnie*
Head of Publishing *Gill Rowley*
FOUNDED 1957. Publishing arm of the consumer research organisation, a registered charity. *Publishes* non-fiction: information, reference and how-to books on travel, gardening, health, personal finance, consumer law, food, education, crafts, DIY. Titles must offer direct value or utility to the UK consumer. 25–30 titles a year.
IMPRINT **Which? Books** *Gill Rowley* TITLES *Good Food Guide; Good Skiing Guide; Good Walks Guide; Which? Travel Guides; Which? Consumer Guides*. No unsolicited mss; send synopses and ideas only.
Royalties paid twice yearly; but owing to in-house editorial development of many titles, royalties are not always applicable.

Whittet Books Ltd
18 Anley Road, London W14 0BY
☎0171 603 1139   Fax 0171 603 8154
Managing Director *Annabel Whittet*
Publishes natural history, horses, rural interest and transport. Unsolicited mss, synopses and ideas for books welcome.
Royalties paid twice yearly.

John Wiley & Sons Ltd
Baffins Lane, Chichester, West Sussex
PO19 1UD
☎01243 779777   Fax 01243 775878
Chairman *The Duke of Richmond*
Managing Director *Dr John Jarvis*
Publishing Director, STM Division
  Dr Michael Dixon
Publishing Director, Professional
  Division *Steven Mair*
Approx. Annual Turnover £34 million
FOUNDED 1807. US parent company. *Publishes* professional, reference trade and text books, scientific, technical and biomedical.
DIVISIONS **Behavioural & Professional Sciences** *Richard Baggaley*; **Physical Sciences** *Dr Ernest Kirkwood*; **Biomedical & Natural Sciences** *Mike Davis*; **Technology** *Rosemary Altoft, Ian McIntosh*; **Wiley Chancery Law**

David Wilson. Unsolicited mss welcome, as are synopses and ideas for books.
Royalties paid annually.

Authors' Rating Best known for its scientific and technical books, Wiley is now making substantial inroads into the professional market with law, finance and management promising to increase the list by up to 100 titles a year. A deal with Gallup should see a development into electronic publishing.

Willow
See **HarperCollins Publishers Ltd**

Neil Wilson Publishing Ltd
Suite 303, The Pentagon Centre, 36 Washington Street, Glasgow G3 8AZ
☎0141 221 1117   Fax 0141 221 5363
Chairman *Gordon Campbell*
Managing Director/Editorial Director
   Neil Wilson
Approx. Annual Turnover £200,000

FOUNDED 1992. *Publishes* Scottish interest and history, biography, humour and hillwalking, whisky and beer; also cookery and Irish interest. About 10 titles a year. Unsolicited mss, synopses and ideas welcome. No fiction, politics, academic or technical.
Royalties paid twice yearly.

Windrow & Greene Ltd
19a Floral Street, London WC2E 9DS
☎0171 240 2318   Fax 0171 240 2341
Managing Director *Alan Greene*
Editorial Director *Martin Windrow*

FOUNDED 1990 by ex-conglomerate refugees wanting to publish quality books in close consultation with authors. *Publishes* military history and hobbies, cars and motorcycling, aviation and transport, directories and specialist journals. About 28 titles a year. Unsolicited mss considered but synopses and ideas preferred in the first instance.
Royalties paid twice yearly.

The Windrush Press
Little Window, High Street, Moreton in Marsh, Gloucestershire GL56 0LL
☎01608 652012/652025   Fax 01608 652125
Managing Director *Geoffrey Smith*
Editorial Head *Victoria Huxley*

FOUNDED 1987. Independent company. *Publishes* travel, biography, history, general, local interest. About 10 titles a year. TITLES *The*

Letters of Private Wheeler; Lanzarote: A Windrush Island Guide; A Traveller's History of India. Send synopsis and letter with s.a.e.
Royalties paid twice yearly.

Windsor Large Print
See **Chivers Press Ltd**

Wise
See **Omnibus Press**

Woburn Press
See **Frank Cass & Co Ltd**

Wolfe Publishing
See **Times Mirror International Publishers Ltd**

Oswald Wolff Books
See **Berg Publishers Ltd**

The Women's Press
34 Great Sutton Street, London EC1V 0DX
☎0171 251 3007   Fax 0171 608 1938
Publishing Director *Kathy Gale*
Approx. Annual Turnover £1 million

Part of the Namara Group. First title 1978. *Publishes* women only: quality fiction and non-fiction. Fiction usually has a female protagonist and a woman-centred theme. International writers and subject matter encouraged. Non-fiction: subjects of general interest, both practical and theoretical, to women generally; art books, feminist theory, health and psychology, literary criticism. About 50 titles a year.

IMPRINTS **Women's Press Handbooks Series**; **Women's Press Crime**; **Livewire Books for Teenagers** *Carole Spedding* fiction and non-fiction series for young adults. Synopses and ideas for books welcome. No mss without previous letter, synopsis and sample material.
Royalties paid twice yearly.

Woodhead Publishing Ltd
Abington Hall, Abington, Cambridge CB1 6AH
☎01223 891358   Fax 01223 893694
Chairman *Alan Jessup*
Managing Director *Martin Woodhead*
Approx. Annual Turnover £800,000

FOUNDED 1989. *Publishes* engineering, materials technology, finance and investment. TITLES *The TWI Journal* (welding research); *Advanced Composites Letters; The International Grain/ Nickel/Zinc/Tin/Silver Trade* series; *Base Metals*

Handbook; Foreign Exchange Options. About 30 titles a year.

DIVISIONS **Woodhead Publishing** (in association with the Welding Institute) *Martin Woodhead;* **Abington Publishing** *Patricia Morrison;* **Gresham Books** (in association with the Charter Institute of Bankers). Unsolicited material welcome.

Royalties paid annually.

Woodstock Books

Spelsbury House, Spelsbury, Oxford OX7 3JR
☎01608 810635   Fax 01608 811401

Chairman/Managing Director *James Price*
Approx. Annual Turnover £100,000

FOUNDED 1989. *Publishes* literary reprints only. Main series: *Revolution and Romanticism, 1789–1874; Decadents, Symbolists, Anti-Decadents: Poetry of the 1890s.* No unsolicited mss.

Wordsworth Editions Ltd

Cumberland House, Crib Street, Ware, Hertfordshire SG12 9ET
☎01920 465167   Fax 01920 462267

Editorial Office: 6 London Street, London W2 1HR. ☎0171 706 8822 Fax 0171 706 8833
Directors *M. C. W. Traylor, E. G. Traylor*
Director/Editorial Head *C. M. Clapham*
Approx. Annual Turnover £7 million

FOUNDED 1987. *Publishes* reprints of English literature, paperback reference books, poetry, children's classics, women writers, classic erotica and American classics. About 150 titles a year. No unsolicited mss.

Authors' Rating A non-starter for living writers, Wordsworth is dedicated to high run, low cost editions of books everyone has heard of. The formula has proved a winner, particularly with young people, who don't mind paying a pound for required reading but resent the fiver charged by up-market publishers for essentially the same product.

World International

Egmont House, PO Box 111, 61 Great Ducie Street, Manchester M60 3BL
☎0161 834 3110   Fax 0161 834 0059

Chairman/Managing Director *Ian Findlay*
Publishing Manager *Nina Filipek*

Part of the Egmont Group, Denmark. *Specialises* in children's books for home and international markets: activity, sticker, board, bath, cloth, novelty/sound books, character books and annuals. Over 200 titles a year. SERIES *Fun to Learn; I Can Learn; Mr Men.* Unsolicited material rarely used.

Titles tend to be commissioned once programme has been finalised.

X Libris

See **Little, Brown & Co (UK)**

Y Lolfa Cyf

Talybont, Ceredigion SY24 5HE
☎01970 832304   Fax 01970 832782

Managing Directors *Robat and Enid Gruffudd*
Editor *Eiry Jones*
Approx. Annual Turnover £400,000

FOUNDED 1967. Small company which publishes mainly in Welsh. It handles all its own typesetting and printing too. *Publishes* Welsh language publications; Celtic language tutors; English language books about Wales for the visitor; nationalism and sociology (English language). 30 titles in 1994. Expanding slowly. Not interested in any English language books except political and Celtic. Write first with synopses or ideas.

Royalties paid twice yearly.

Yale University Press (London)

23 Pond Street, London NW3 2PN
☎0171 431 4422   Fax 0171 431 3755

Managing Director/Editorial Director
John Nicoll

FOUNDED 1961. Owned by US parent company. *Publishes* academic and humanities. About 160 titles (worldwide) a year. Unsolicited mss and synopses welcome if within specialised subject areas.

Royalties paid annually.

Roy Yates Books

Smallfields Cottage, Cox Green, Rudgwick, Horsham, West Sussex RH12 3DE
☎01403 822299   Fax 01403 823012

Chairman/Managing Director *Roy Yates*
Approx. Annual Turnover £120,000

FOUNDED 1990. *Publishes* children's books only. No unsolicited material as books are adaptations of existing popular classics suitable for translation into dual-language format.

Royalties paid quarterly.

Yearling

See **Transworld Publishers Ltd**

Young Library Ltd

3 The Old Brushworks, 56 Pickwick Road, Corsham, Wiltshire SN13 9BX
☎01249 712025   Fax 01249 715558

Managing Director *Roger Bonnett*

FOUNDED 1982. *Publishes* children's information

books. About 12 titles a year. No unsolicited mss; send synopsis/ideas in the first instance.
Royalties paid annually.

Young Lions
See **HarperCollins Publishers Ltd**

Zed Books Ltd
7 Cynthia Street, London N1 9JF
☎0171 837 4014   Fax 0171 833 3960
Approx. Annual Turnover £850,000
FOUNDED 1976. *Publishes* international and Third World affairs, development studies, women's studies and specific area studies, namely the Middle East, Africa and Asia. No fiction, children's or poetry. About 40 titles a year.

DIVISIONS **Development & Environment** *Robert Molteno;* **Women's Studies** *Louise Murray;* **Asia** *Carol Bois.* TITLES *The Development Dictionary* ed. Wolfgang Sachs; *Staying Alive* Vandana Shiva; *An A–Z of the Middle East.* No unsolicited mss; synopses and ideas welcome though.
Royalties paid annually.

Zomba
See **Omnibus Press**

As we go to press . . .

Ringpull
Albion Wharf, Albion Street, Manchester M1 5LN
☎0161 236 4186   Fax 0161 236 0734
Editorial Director *Stephen Powell*

New Manchester-based imprint of **Fourth Estate**. Young, modern, British fiction only.

Selling Words

Frank Herrmann of Bloomsbury Book Auctions
explains how authors can bequeath more than their royalties

For us, it all began with John Braine. He wrote to ask if we would sell his diaries. I went to see him in his flat in Hampstead. The background seemed all wrong for the man who had written *Room at the Top*: neat modern furniture, carefully selected to blend, lacking lustre. John seemed out of character in the place. I had known him at the height of his success. Is this what success did to authors? But John needed money. A sale of the diaries offered the hope of a capital sum. I explained that we were a new auction house and though I had never heard of anyone selling an author's diaries while he was still alive, we would be prepared to give it a try.

The diaries had been collected from John's former house by his son and a friend. They filled a large cabin trunk. Driving up to London, the son's car caught fire and was destroyed. By a Herculaean effort, the two lads dragged the trunk out of the car and saved the diaries. John regarded this as divine intervention.

We got John Bright-Holmes, Braine's former editor at Eyre and Spottiswoode, to sort the many dozens of cheap exercise books into a chronological sequence and then to write us a long catalogue description. We publicised the sale widely. The press lapped it up. On the day of the auction, the sale room was crowded and filled further with television cameras and lights. We had printed an estimate of £25,000–£35,000 in the catalogue. The bidding started slowly, went up to £16,000 and stopped. We had spectacularly failed to sell the diaries. But after the sale, John faced the cameras with equanimity and said 'No doubt the diaries will sell much better when I am dead'. It was a major item on the BBC News at 5, 6, 7 and 10 o'clock. it did much to revive John's reputation and the repeated mention of Bloomsbury Book Auction's name certainly did us no harm.

John, who was of course already a sick man, died shortly afterwards. And we did indeed then sell the diaries to a major Northern library at exactly the price he had wanted. It was much welcomed by his estate. As so often happens, a further large bundle of his notebooks came to light later and with the family's blessing they were presented to the same institution.

By now we were being asked quite frequently if we were prepared to sell literary archives as an entity by private treaty, that is not by auction, but by direct negotiation. It is an activity which requires a good deal of patience. Contrary to common belief, there are still quite a number of British institutions that buy this sort of material as well as a multitude of American ones. But it is not easy to find one which is interested and has funds available at the same time. Often it is a case of a budget being exhausted early in the year.

A literary archive can be wonderfully useful raw material to show how an author worked. A particularly interesting example of this was the case of H. A. Manhood, a very talented short-story writer and novelist who had been extremely active and popular in the twenty years from the late twenties to just after the war. He had kept everything: his notebooks filled with ideas; his first drafts; his revised, handwritten drafts; and finally his corrected typescripts after they came back (in his case from Jonathan Cape) after publication. He had even had these exquisitely bound in vellum by the distinguished Cambridge binder, Sandy Cockerell. He also kept every review of every one of his many books, and several copies of the UK and American editions.

In the case of his short stories, Manhood kept his entire correspondence with editors: the first approaches, negotiations of fees, requests for changes, cheques received, hand-written manuscripts, typescripts, cuttings of the actual published stories and even occasional subsequent comments and letters. It was as complete a record of an author's work as one could hope for and was bought for this very reason by the British Library, to the great joy of his widow.

The archive of Christopher Hassall was, again, huge but quite different. Throughout his life Hassall had carried on a vast correspondence with a multitude of intellectual friends. When researching his life of Eddie Marsh, who had been Winston Churchill's secretary and a great patron of the arts, ever more correspondents were drawn into his network. Each recorded a small slice of interesting, often unique information. It all added up to a very sizeable cake. In addition Hassall had written poetry and provided the lyrics for Noel Coward's musicals. This revealed another fascinating world, very much of its own time. The whole had been meticulously ordered and catalogued by Hassall's one-time secretary, which made it a joy to deal with. It was bought by Cambridge University Library.

Quite different again was a tiny archive retained by someone who as a young man had had ambitions of becoming a poet. He wrote to T.S. Eliot in the early thirties and the two men met. Eliot was clearly impressed and must have seen in the young man the possibility of development which in many ways mirrored his own. The result was that they corresponded over a long period and Eliot's letters expounded views on the contemporary literary scene with a candour which he hardly ever expressed elsewhere. Interestingly enough, this cycle of letters was rejected by a number of American university libraries, but bought with alacrity by the British Library when we offered it to them. The young man in question, in fact, forsook poetry as a career and became a BBC producer specialising in rural affairs.

Very often when we sell an author's personal library we are also asked to deal with his or her working papers. This happened in the case of Margery Fisher who for nearly forty years had owned, published and edited the magazine *Growing Point*, which concerned itself exclusively with the reviewing of new children's books and the occasional re-assessment of an established author in that field. There was a vast correspondence, a huge quantity of back numbers of the magazine, but above all a wonderful card index of every book which had ever passed through Margery Fisher's hands, often with detailed critical comments. There were approximately 100,000 cards: an amazing conspectus of four decades of children's book publishing at a time when it went through a particularly creative period. With the help of a famous American bookseller specialising in children's books, we sold the archive to a Californian university who, unlike most of the other institutions to whom we had offered this material, were delighted to have the mass of back numbers as a teaching tool.

Mrs Fisher had been married to James Fisher, one of the earliest popularisers of natural history and animal programmes on radio and television after the war. His working papers, films, photographs and records (of bird song) were sold to the Natural History Museum with the assistance of a generous admirer of Fisher's pioneering work.

Probably the most interesting archive of the many we have now handled at Bloomsbury Book Auctions, was that of Graham Greene last year. It came to us via Nicholas Dennys, the author's nephew and himself a bookseller. A few years before Greene's death, Dennys had been given the author's personal library and his entire extant correspondence, as well as a number of his manuscripts. They were to be sold for the express purpose of raising money sufficient to look after Greene's sister, Elizabeth Dennys, who had acted as his secretary for twenty-five years and had then become totally incapacitated.

It is not generally known that despite his substantial output, Greene actually had great difficulty in the physical act of writing because he suffered from carpal tunnel syndrome. Yet he conducted a vastly extensive correspondence from his home in France. He did this by dictating all his letters and sending the tapes and the letters to which he was replying to England several times a week. There Elizabeth typed them out on notepaper he had pre-signed. She filed her carbons and the letters meticulously and thus there was preserved the complete two-sided correspondence: a great rarity where authors are concerned. We took over some 60,000 documents. They threw a wonderfully clear light on Greene's own personality, his attitudes, his irrepressible sense of humour and his loyalty to his friends. They also showed, incidentally, how much trouble he took over his answers to fan letters. A particularly revealing part of the archive was Greene's entire professional correspondence with his publishers, agents, lawyers, film producers and a complete record of all the interviews he had given during his lifetime.

Greene's library complemented his papers most unusually in that he frequently annotated his books with comments, criticism, ideas for future work, even drafts for novels and short stories. Sometime she used them as files for relevant cuttings, photographs and letters. In this way the 3,000 volumes provided clear examples of the relationship between Greene's source material and his creative work, which often was illuminated further by items in the documentary archive.

Nicholas Dennys and Jean McNeil had earlier compiled a very detailed catalogue of Greene's library. We proceeded to compile at breakneck speed a separate catalogue of the working papers. Because it was known that all this material was to be sold, there had been a large number of enquiries for its purchase. What we therefore did was to work out a suggested guide price both for the library and the archive, sent the two catalogues to all enquirers and expressed the hope that the library and archive could be sold together.

The detailed study of the material by interested buyers took some months, and in the end there was fierce competition for it from three American universities. The negotiations with them kept us on tenterhooks for many weeks. Happily in the end both the library and the papers were sold together. They went to Boston College in Massachusetts.

While all this private treaty work is going on we also hold some 25 auctions every year, which involves the work of five or six full-time cataloguers. Each sale will probably contain over 400 lots of books: the more valuable ones are sold on their own; the others in groups, as far as possible relating to the same subject. To a large extent our buyers are members of the antiquarian book trade not only from the UK but from all over the world; to a lesser extent they are private collectors with special interests. Five or six times a year we include manuscript material in the sales: letters, notebooks, scrapbooks, recipe books, old deeds and records from the seventeenth century onwards to the present day. When they are of particular local interest we often advise the relevant record offices that they are coming up for sale. Perhaps I should add that while we seem to be able to sell scripts produced by word processors, computer-generated material is not yet finding favour with the people who buy archives. Similarly, photostats, even of interesting documents, rarely have any commercial value.

Why then do we sell collections of such material by private treaty, that is direct to a buyer and not by auction? The answer is that in such cases it is important to keep all the material together, as a single entity, because therein lies its interest to future students and scholars. The essential criterion is that such archives should have an element of the unique in a social, historical or literary context; that they should provide information that is not available in another form. As I have tried to show, the diversity of material that comes to us is what makes it challenging. If you have something similar, please let us know about it.

The author spent many years in publishing before becoming a director of Sotheby's.
In 1983 he founded Bloomsbury Book Auctions, now one of the leading auctioneers of
books and literary property. They are at 3/4 Hardwick Street, London EC1R 4RY.
Tel: 0171 636 1945.

Irish Publishers

An Gúm
44 Sráid Uí Chonaill, Uacht, Dublin 1,
Republic of Ireland
☎00 353 1 873 4700   Fax 00 353 1 873 1140
Senior Editor *Caoimhín ó Marcaigh*
FOUNDED 1926. Publications branch of the
Department of Arts, Culture and the Gaellacht.
Established to provide general reading, textbooks and dictionaries in the Irish language.
Publishes educational, children's, music, lexi-
cography and general. No fiction or poetry.
About 50 titles a year. Unsolicited mss, synopses and ideas for books welcome. Also wel-
come reading copies of first and second level
school textbooks with a view to translating
them into the Irish language.
Royalties paid annually.

Anvil Books
45 Palmerston Road, Dublin 6,
Republic of Ireland
☎00 353 1 497 3628
Managing Director *Rena Dardis*
FOUNDED 1964 with the emphasis on Irish history and biography. Expansion of the list followed to include more general interest Irish
material and in 1982 The Children's Press was
established, making Anvil the first Irish publisher
of mass-market children's books of Irish interest.
Publishes illustrated books, history, biography
(particularly 1916–22), folklore, children's fiction (for ages 6–14) and quiz books. No adult
fiction or illustrated books for children under 5.
About 7 titles a year. Unsolicited mss, synopses
and ideas for books welcome.

DIVISIONS
General TITLES *Guerilla Days in Ireland* Tom
Barry; *My Fight For Irish Freedom* Dan Breen; *I
Heard the Wild Birds Sing* Patrick O'Sullivan;
On Another Man's Wound Ernie O'Malley. **The
Children's Press** TITLES *Urban Heroes* Peter
Regan; *The Secret of the Ruby Ring* Yvonne
MacGrory; *In Search of the Liberty Tree* Tom
McCaughren; *Best Friends* Pauline Devine.
Royalties paid annually.

Attic Press Ltd
29 Upper Mount Street, Dublin 2,
Republic of Ireland
☎00 353 1 661 6128   Fax 00 353 1 661 6176
Publisher *Róisín Conroy*
Editor *Ríona MacNamara*
FOUNDED 1988. Began life in 1984 as a forum
for information on the Irish feminist movement. *Publishes* adult and teenage fiction, and
non-fiction. About 22 titles a year. A second
imprint, **Basement Press**, was launched in
1994 to publish popular fiction and non-fiction
(politics, entertainment and information) by
men and women. Unsolicited mss, synopses
and ideas for books welcome. Not interested in
poetry or short stories.
Royalties paid twice yearly.

Basement Press
See **Attic Press**

Beacon
See **Poolbeg Press Ltd**

Blackwater Press
c/o Folens Publishers, Broomhill Business
Park, Broomhill Road, Tallaght, Dublin 24,
Republic of Ireland
☎00 353 1 451 5311   Fax 00 353 1 451 5308
Chairman *Dirk Folens*
Managing Director *John O'Connor*

Part of Folens Publishers. *Publishes* political,
sports, fiction (*Anna O'Donovan*) and children's
(*Deidre Whelan*). 22 titles in 1994.

Boole Press
26 Temple Lane, Temple Bar, Dublin 2,
Republic of Ireland
☎00 353 1 679 7655   Fax 00 353 1 679 2469
Managing Director *Paulene McKeever*

A division of AIC Ltd, Dublin. *Publishes* scientific and technical, medical, and conference
proceedings. About 2 titles a year.
Royalties paid every two years.

Brandon Book Publishers Ltd

Dingle, Co. Kerry, Republic of Ireland
☎00 353 66 51463 Fax 00 353 66 51234
Chairman *Steve MacDonogh*
Managing Director *Bernie Goggin*
Approx. Annual Turnover £450,000

FOUNDED 1982 and in the 13 years since its inception Brandon has earned itself something of a reputation for new fiction authors and for challenging, often controversial, non-fiction. *Publishes* politics, biography, local history, children's, commercial and literary fiction. About 15 titles a year. Not interested in educational, scientific and technical or instruction material. Submit outlines with sample mss in the first instance. Ideas welcome.
Royalties paid annually.

Edmund Burke Publisher

Cloonagashel, 27 Priory Drive, Blackrock,
Co. Dublin, Republic of Ireland
☎00 353 1 288 2159 Fax 00 353 1 283 4080
Chairman *Eamonn De Búrca*
Approx. Annual Turnover £100,000

Small family-run business publishing historical and topographical and fine limited edition books relating to Ireland. TITLES *The History of the County of Mayo; Burke, Bourke and De Burgh People and Places; The Annals of the Kingdom of Ireland by the Four Masters; Maamtrasna: The Murders and The Mystery; Flowers of Mayo; The Admiral from Mayo.* Unsolicited mss welcome. No synopses or ideas.
Royalties paid twice yearly.

Butterworth Ireland Limited

26 Upper Ormond Quay, Dublin 7,
Republic of Ireland
☎00 353 1 873 1555 Fax 00 353 1 873 1876
Chairman *D. L. Summers*
General Manager *Gerard Coakley*

Subsidiary of Butterworth & Co. Publishers, London, (Reed Elsevier is the holding company). *Publishes* solely law and tax books. **Tax Editor** *Susan Keegan*, **Legal Editor** *Louise Leavy.*
17 titles in 1994. Leading publisher of Irish law and tax titles. Unsolicited mss, synopses and ideas welcome for titles within the broadest parameters of tax and law.
Royalties paid twice yearly.

The Children's Press

See **Anvil Books**

Cló Iar-Chonnachta

Indreabhán, Connemara, Galway,
Republic of Ireland
☎00 353 91 93307 Fax 00 353 91 93362
Chairman/Managing Director *Micheál Ó Conghaile*
Editor *Nóirín Ní Ghrádaigh*
Approx. Annual Turnover £250,000

FOUNDED 1985. *Publishes* fiction, poetry, plays and children's, mostly in Irish but not exclusively. Also publishes cassettes of writers reading from their own works. 25 titles in 1994. Unsolicited mss, synopses and ideas for books welcome.
Royalties paid annually.

The Columba Press

93 The Rise, Mount Merrion, Blackrock,
Co. Dublin, Republic of Ireland
☎00 353 1 283 2954 Fax 00 353 1 288 3770
Chairman *Neil Kluepfel*
Managing Director *Seán O'Boyle*
Approx. Annual Turnover £750,000

FOUNDED 1985. Small company committed to growth. *Publishes* only religious titles. 30 titles in 1994. (Backlist of 225 titles.) TITLES *Nine Faces of God* Pat Collins; *Through the Year with George Otto Simms* Lesley Whiteside. Unsolicited ideas and synopses rather than full mss preferred.
Royalties paid twice yearly.

Cork University Press

University College, Cork, Co. Cork,
Republic of Ireland
☎00 353 21 276871 Fax 00 353 21 273553
Managing Director *Sara Wilbourne*
Production Editor *Eileen O'Carroll*

FOUNDED 1925. Relaunched in 1992 the Press *publishes* academic and some trade titles. In 1994 it published 15 titles and plans to publish 25 in 1995. Unsolicited synopses and ideas welcome for textbooks, academic monographs, belles lettres and illustrated histories.
Royalties paid annually.

Flyleaf Press

4 Spencer Villas, Glenageary, Co. Dublin,
Republic of Ireland
☎00 353 1 280 6228 Fax 00 353 1 283 0670
Managing Director *Dr James Ryan*

FOUNDED 1981 to publish natural history titles. Now concentrating on family history and Irish history as a background to family history. No fiction. TITLES *Irish Records; Longford and its*

People; Tracing Kerry Ancestors; Tracing Dublin's Ancestors. Unsolicited mss, synopses and ideas for books welcome.
Royalties paid twice yearly.

Four Courts Press Ltd

Kill Lane, Blackrock, Co. Dublin,
Republic of Ireland
☎00 353 1 289 2922   Fax 00 353 1 289 3072
Chairman/Managing Director *Michael Adams*
Approx. Annual Turnover £150,000
FOUNDED 1972. *Publishes* theology, philosophy, Celtic and medieval studies. 16 titles in 1994. Unsolicited mss, synopses and ideas for books welcome.
Royalties paid annually.

Gill & Macmillan

Goldenbridge, Inchicore, Dublin 8,
Republic of Ireland
☎00 353 1 453 1005   Fax 00 353 1 454 1688
Managing Director *M. H. Gill*
Approx. Annual Turnover £4.5 million
FOUNDED 1968 when M. H. Gill & Son Ltd and Macmillan Ltd formed a jointly owned publishing company. *Publishes* biography/autobiography, history, current affairs, literary criticism (all mainly of Irish interest), guidebooks, cookery, religion, theology, counselling/psychology. Also professional books in law and accountancy, and educational textbooks for secondary and tertiary levels. About 100 titles a year. Contacts: *Hubert Mahony* (educational); *Fergal Tobin* (general); *Finola O'Sullivan* (professional); *Ailbhe O'Reilly* (tertiary textbooks). Unsolicited synopses and ideas welcome. Not interested in fiction or poetry.
Royalties paid subject to contract.

Impact Publications Ltd

9 Victoria Terrace, Dundrum, Dublin 14,
Republic of Ireland
☎00 353 1 298 0310   Fax 00 353 1 298 6237
Chairman *Brian McCarthy*
Approx. Annual Turnover £30,000
Publishes religious and paramedical titles – 2 in 1993.

Institute of Public Administration

57–61 Lansdowne Road, Dublin 4,
Republic of Ireland
☎00 353 1 269 7011   Fax 00 353 1 269 8644
Chairman *Denis Lucey*
Director General *John Gallagher*
Publisher *Jim O'Donnell*

Approx. Annual Turnover £450,000
FOUNDED 1957 by a group of public servants, the Institute of Public Administration is the Irish public sector management development agency. The publishing arm of the organisation is one of its major activities. *Publishes* academic and professional books and periodicals: history, law, politics, economics and Irish public administration for students and practitioners. 8 titles in 1994. TITLES *Administration Yearbook & Diary; Personnel & Industrial Relations Directory; Your Rights at Work; Decentralisation.* No unsolicited mss; synopses and ideas welcome. No fiction or children's publishing.
Royalties paid annually.

Irish Academic Press

Kill Lane, Blackrock, Co. Dublin,
Republic of Ireland
☎00 353 1 289 2922   Fax 00 353 1 289 3072
Chairman *Gilbert Raff*
Managing Editor *Michael Adams*
Approx. Annual Turnover £200,000
FOUNDED 1974. *Publishes* academic monographs and humanities. 14 titles in 1994. Unsolicited mss, synopses and ideas welcome.
Royalties paid annually.

Irish Management Institute

Sandyford Road, Dublin 16,
Republic of Ireland
☎00 353 1 295 6911   Fax 00 353 1 295 5150
Director General *Barry Kenny*
Manager, Book Publishing *Alex Miller*
Approx. Annual Turnover £8 million
FOUNDED 1952. The Institute is owned by its members (individual and corporate) and its major activities involve management education, training and development. The book publishing arm of the organisation was established in 1970. *Publishes* management practice, interpersonal skills and aspects of national macroeconomics. 5 titles in 1992. TITLES *The Economy of Ireland; Practical Finance; Pricing For Results; Personnel Management.* Unsolicited mss welcome provided that any case material is relevant to Irish management practice. Synopses and ideas also welcome.
Royalties paid annually.

The Lilliput Press

4 Rosemount Terrace, Arbour Hill, Dublin 7,
Republic of Ireland
☎00 353 1 671 1647   Fax 00 353 1 671 1647
Chairman *Ms Vivienne Guinness*

Managing Director *Antony Farrell*
Approx. Annual Turnover £150,000
FOUNDED 1984. *Publishes* non-fiction: literary, history, autobiography and biography, ecology, essays; fiction and poetry. About 20 titles a year. TITLES *Beckett in Dublin* (essays); *Seventy Years Young* (memoir); *The Growth Illusion* (ecology); *The Great Famine* (history); *Trees of Ireland; North of Naples, South of Rome.* Unsolicited mss, synopses and ideas welcome. No children's or sport titles.
Royalties paid annually.

Marino Books
See **Mercier Press Ltd**

Mercier Press Ltd
PO Box No 5, 5 French Church Street, Cork, Republic of Ireland
☎00 353 021 275040 Fax 00 353 021 274969
Chairman *George Eaton*
Managing Director *John F. Spillane*
FOUNDED 1944. One of Ireland's lagest publishers with a list of approx 250 Irish interest titles and a smaller range of religious titles. *Publishes* alternative lifestyle, folklore, women's interest, popular psychology, dual language, children's, cookery, history, politics, poetry and fiction. No academic books. IMPRINTS **Mercier Press** *Mary Feehan* **Marino Books** *Jo O'Donoghue.* 25 titles in 1994. TITLES *The Course of Irish History; The Field; Irish High Crosses; Irish Myths & Legends; Alternative Loves; Born to Die; Whose Housework Is It Anyway?.* Unsolicited mss, synopses and ideas welcome.
Royalties paid annually.

The O'Brien Press Ltd
20 Victoria Road, Rathgar, Dublin 6, Republic of Ireland
☎00 353 1 492 3333 Fax 00 353 1 492 2777
Chairman/Managing Director *Michael O'Brien*
Editorial Director *Íde Ní Laoghaire*
FOUNDED 1974 to publish biography and books on the environment. In recent years the company has become a substantial force in children's publishing, concentrating mainly on juvenile novels and non-fiction in the craft and history areas. Also *publishes* business, adult fiction, popular biography, music and travel. No poetry or academic. About 30 new titles a year.

Unsolicited mss (with return postage enclosed), synopses and ideas for books welcome.
Royalties paid annually.

Oak Tree Press
4 Arran Quay, Dublin 7, Republic of Ireland
☎00 351 1 872 3923 Fax 00 351 1 872 3902
Managing Director *Brian O'Kane*
FOUNDED 1992. Part of Cork Publishing. Specialist publisher of business and professional books: accounting, finance, management and law, aimed at students and practitioners in Ireland and the UK. About 25 titles a year. TITLES *Accounting Standards; Winning Business Proposals; Economics for an Open Economy; Personal Finance; Understanding Services Management.* Unsolicited mss and synopses welcome.
Royalties paid twice in the first year and annually thereafter.

On Stream Publications Ltd
Cloghroe, Blarney, Co. Cork, Republic of Ireland
☎00 353 21 385798   Fax 00 353 21 385798
Chairman/Managing Director *Roz Crowley*
Approx. Annual Turnover £50,000
FOUNDED 1992. Formerly Forum Publications. *Publishes* cookery, wine, general health and fitness, local history, railways, photography and practical guides. About 3 titles a year. TITLES *The Tackling Series of Practical Books: Tackling Men's Health; The Man From The Railway.* Unsolicited mss, synopses and ideas welcome. No children's books.
Royalties paid twice yearly.

Poolbeg Press Ltd
Knocksedan House, 123 Baldoyle Industrial Estate, Baldoyle, Dublin 13, Republic of Ireland
☎00 353 1 832 1477 Fax 00 353 1 832 1430
Managing Director *Philip MacDermott*
Approx. Annual Turnover £1,000,000
FOUNDED 1976 to publish the Irish short story and has since diversified to include all areas of fiction (literary and popular), children's fiction and non-fiction, and adult non-fiction: history, biography and topics of public interest. About 100 titles a year. Unsolicited mss, synopses and ideas welcome (mss preferred). No drama.
IMPRINTS **Poolbeg** (paperback and hardback); **Children's Poolbeg**; **Torc**; **Salmon**; **Beacon**.
Royalties paid bi-annually.

Real Ireland Design Ltd
27 Beechwood Close, Boghall Road, Bray,
Co. Wicklow, Republic of Ireland
☎00 353 1 286 0799   Fax 00 353 1 282 9962
Managing Director *Desmond Leonard*

Producers of calendars, diaries, posters, greeting cards and books, servicing the Irish tourist industry. *Publishes* photography, cookery and tourism. About 2 titles a year. No fiction. Unsolicited mss, synopses and ideas welcome.
Royalties paid twice yearly.

Relay Publications
Tyone, Nenagh, Co. Tipperary,
Republic of Ireland
☎00 353 67 31734
Managing Director *Donal A. Murphy*

FOUNDED 1980; in abeyance 1985–92. *Publishes* regional history. 3 titles in 1994. Welcomes unsolicited mss, ideas and synopses. Not interested in adult fiction.
Royalties paid twice yearly.

Roberts Rinehart Publishers
Trinity House, Charleston Road, Dublin 6,
Republic of Ireland
☎00 353 1 497 6860   Fax 00 353 1 497 6861
Chairman *Rick Rinehart*
Managing Director *Jack Van Zandt*
Approx. Annual Turnover £2 million

European branch of a US company first established in 1983. Particularly active in the Irish-American market. *Publishes* general non-fiction, particularly arts, environment, nature, Irish interest, photography, history and biography; and colour illustrated children's books, fiction and non-fiction. About 40 titles a year. TITLES *Ireland: The Living Landscape; Festive Foods of Ireland; The IRA; Under the Black Flag; The People Who Hugged Trees.* No adult fiction. Unsolicited mss, synopses and ideas for books welcome (include s.a.e. with mss for return).
Royalties paid twice yearly.

Royal Dublin Society
Science Section, Ballsbridge, Dublin 4,
Republic of Ireland
☎00 353 1 668 0866   Fax 00 353 1 660 4014
President *Sean Tinney*
Approx. Annual Turnover £3000

FOUNDED 1731 for the promotion of agriculture, science and the arts, and throughout its history has published books and journals towards this end. Publishers hired on contract basis. *Publishes* conference proceedings, biology and the history of Irish science. TITLES *Water of Life* proceedings of a conference on Ireland's inland waterways; *Vulgar & Mechanick: The Scientific Instrument Trade in Ireland 1650–1921; The Right Trees in the Right Places.*
Royalties not generally paid.

Royal Irish Academy
19 Dawson Street, Dublin 2,
Republic of Ireland
☎00 353 1 676 2570   Fax 00 353 1 676 2346
Executive Secretary *Patrick Buckley*
Approx. Annual Turnover £50,000

FOUNDED in 1785, the Academy, has been publishing since 1787. Core publications are journals but more books published in last 10 years. *Publishes* academic, Irish interest and Irish language. 7 titles in 1994. Welcomes mss, synopses and ideas of an academic standard.
Royalties paid once yearly, where applicable.

Salmon
See **Poolbeg Press Ltd**

Tír Eolas
Newtownlynch, Doorus, Kinvara,
Co. Galway, Republic of Ireland
☎00 353 91 37452
Publishers *Anne Korff, Jeff O'Connell*
Managing Director *Anne Korff*
Approx. Annual Turnover £50,000

FOUNDED 1987. *Publishes* books and guides on ecology, archaeology, folklore and culture. TITLES *The Book of the Burren; The Shannon Floodlands; Not a Word of a Lie; The Book of Aran.* Unsolicited mss, synopses and ideas for books welcome. No specialist scientific and technical, fiction, plays, school textbooks or philosophy.
Royalties paid annually.

Torc
See **Poolbeg Press Ltd**

Town House and Country House
Trinity House, Charleston Road, Ranelagh,
Dublin 6, Republic of Ireland
☎00 353 1 497 2399   Fax 00 353 1 497 0927
Managing Director *Treasa Coady*

FOUNDED 1980. *Publishes* commercial fiction, art and archaeology, biography and environment. About 20 titles a year. TITLES *A Place of Stones; Irish Painting; The Illustrated Archaeology of Ireland; Lifelines.* Good production and design standards. Unsolicited mss, synopses and ideas welcome. No children's books.
Royalties paid twice yearly.

Veritas Publications

7–8 Lower Abbey Street, Dublin 1,
Republic of Ireland
☎00 353 1 878 8177
Fax 00 353 1 878 6507

Chairman *James Lenehan*
Managing Director *Fr Sean Melody*

FOUNDED 1969 to supply religious textbooks to schools and later introduced a more general religious list. Part of the Catholic Communications Institute. *Publishes* religious books only. About 20 titles a year. Unsolicited mss, synopses and ideas for books welcome.

Royalties paid annually.

Wolfhound Press

68 Mountjoy Square, Dublin 1,
Republic of Ireland
☎00 353 1 874 0354   Fax 00 353 1 872 0207

Managing Director *Seamus Cashman*

FOUNDED 1974. Member of **Clé** - the Irish Book Publishers Association. *Publishes* art, biography, children's, drama, fiction, general non-fiction, history, law, literature, literary studies, poetry and gift books. About 30 titles a year. TITLES *Famine; Run With the Wind; Transitions.* Unsolicited mss (with synopses and s.a.e.) and ideas welcome.

Royalties paid annually.

Talking Books

If I was starting again as a book writer I would extend my education to take in a year at drama school. The purpose would be to learn the craft of presentation; how to hold a live audience, to put up a creditable front on radio and television and, more especially, to read aloud my own work as I would want to hear it. The skills that come easily to a trained actor are a mystery to the typical author whose public utterances are liable to bore for Britain. Just listen to poets mangle their creativity when they are tempted out of their garrets to give public readings. Or, to certain famous novelists whose appearance in front of a microphone or television camera is their signal for an immediate descent into mindless inanities.

So what, you might say. Let the writer write and the actor speak. Each to his own. But there is a financial consideration that cannot be ignored. An increasing proportion of the money that is generated by literary effort goes to those who speak the words that others compose. Talking Books are a prime example. After years of muddling along on story tapes for children and vintage radio comedy, this market is at last taking off. Its total value is anyone's guess - figures from £25 million to £50 million are bandied about. The best evidence of increasing buoyancy is the range of titles on offer – romance, thrillers, travel, biographies, even political memoirs, they are all there on cassette, read, invariably, not by their authors but by well known actors who have cornered that profitable sector of the business known as 'voice overs'. Naturally, there are star turns such as Martin Jarvis and Miriam Margoyles whose talent for creating images by voice alone is unlikely ever to be matched by the authors they serve. But judging by results there are many in this game who treat it as an optional extra to their main living. Their performances are competent but hardly inspiring. The authors might do no better and could do a lot worse but if it is too late to reform those who are set in their prosaic ways, it is surely reasonable to encourage the younger generation to nurture whatever dramatic skills they may possess. Even a short course of voice training can do wonders.

The alternative is to risk being marginalised. It is already happening. While a Talking Books publisher will offer a modest advance to an author – £2000 on a cassette forecast to sell 5000 copies a year is considered generous – he will not blink at paying a reader £1000 for a day or two's work not to mention a similar sum to an editor for cutting a text to the required length. The author does get a royalty, anything from four per cent of receipts to 15 per cent of the published price, but Equity, the actors' union, has caught on to what it sees as a discrepancy that must be corrected. In other words, the author will get less, and the actor more. The publishers say they have no room to manoeuvre. The production costs including recording, duplicating and packaging are higher than for the average printed book while profit margins are correspondingly thinner, which begs the question as to why so many are keen to get into the business but hey ho, that's free enterprise.

The best literary agents, primed on the knowledge that in the States the Talking Books market is roaring ahead and audio rights secure million dollar deals, are beginning to fight back on behalf of their clients. Speaking to a conference organised by the Society of Authors, Anthea Morton-Saner of Curtis Brown urged resistance to any publisher who presses for world rights (the US should not be so lightly discarded) and recommended a five-year limit on the granting of options. Moreover, the right of consultation on production values and distribution deals, should be enshrined in the contract.

In the end it comes back to the question of what the author is prepared to do to promote his own interest. Getting in on the performance circuit, whether it is talking books, lectures, chat show appearances or one-man shows, can be a nice little double earner – attracting fees for appearances and royalties from increased sales of titles. But no one wants to listen to a dull speaker. To judge the competition and to set a standard to aim for, listen to Dirk Bogarde reading his latest volume of autobiography, *A Short Walk from Harrods* (Penguin) or to Alan Clark's *Diaries* (Polygram). In their different ways, the two old charmers are totally compelling. But, then, they have had to work hard to make it look easy.

Barry Turner

Audio Books

Abbey Home Entertainment
Warwick House, 106 Harrow Road,
London W2 1XD
☎0171 262 1012   Fax 0171 262 6020
Managing Director *Anne Miles*

Abbey were the instigators (previously as MSD Holdings) in the development of the spoken word. With over 20 years' experience in recording, marketing and distribution of audio, book and cassette, their catalogue includes major children's story characters such as *Thomas the Tank Engine, Rosie and Jim, Postman Pat, Rupert Bear* and *Winnie the Pooh. Specialises* in adult fiction and children's book/cassette packs. 60 titles in 1994. Ideas from authors and agents welcome.

BBC Radio Collection
Woodlands, 80 Wood Lane,
London W12 0TT
☎0181 576 2600   Fax 0181 749 8766
Owner *BBC Worldwide Publishing*
Director of Books & Spoken Word
  Publishing *Chris Weller*

ESTABLISHED in 1988 to release material from BBC Radio. Recently launched a new label **BBC Classic Collection** – classic readings and dramatisations from BBC Radio and Television – which includes works by authors such as Charles Dickens, Jane Austen and Thomas Hardy. *Publishes* comedy, children's, science fiction, fiction, non-fiction and sound effects. TITLES *Hancock's Half Hour, Round the Horne; Alan Bennett's Diaries; Knowing Me, Knowing You; Spiderman; Animals of Farthing Wood.* Ideas for cassettes welcome.

Canongate Audio
14 High Street, Edinburgh EH1 1TE
☎0131 557 5111   Fax 0131 557 5211
Managing Director *Jamie Byng*

Part of **Canongate Books.** Purchased the Schiltron and Whigmaleerie lists in 1993. *Publishes* fiction, children's, humour, poetry, historical and Scottish titles. 13 in 1994, with a large backlist. TITLES *Sweet Peas* read by Judi Dench; *Parahandy* Neil Munro; *Scots Quair* Lewis Grassic Gibbon; Robert Louis Stevenson titles.

Cavalcade Story Cassettes
See **Chivers Audio Books**

Champs Elysées
See under **Magazines**

Chivers Audio Books
Windsor Bridge Road, Bath, Avon BA2 3AX
☎01225 335336   Fax 01225 448005
Managing Director *Simon D. Gibbs*

Part of **Chivers Press Ltd.** *Publishes* a wide range of titles, mainly for library consumption. Fiction, autobiography, children's and crime. 216 titles in 1994. TITLES *Taken on Trust* Terry Waite; *Brideshead Revisited* Evelyn Waugh; *If Only They Could Talk* James Herriot; *The Power and the Glory* Graham Greene; *Goggle-Eyes* Anne Fine; *The Incredible Journey* Sheila Burnford.
  IMPRINTS **Chivers Audio Books, Chivers Children's Audio, Cavalcade Story Cassettes, Word-for-Word Audio Books, Sterling Audio Books.**

Cover To Cover Cassettes Ltd
PO Box 112, Marlborough, Wiltshire
SN8 3UG
☎01264 337725   Fax 01264 337742
Managing Director *Helen Nicoll*

Publishes classic 19th century fiction – Jane Austen, Charles Dickens, Anthony Trollope, plus children's titles – *Fantastic Mr Fox* Roald Dahl; *Worst Witch* Jill Murphy; *Sheep-Pig* Dick King-Smith. 8 titles in 1994.

Dove Audio
See **Redback Audiobooks**

Faber & Faber Audiobooks
3 Queen Square, London WC1N 3AU
☎0171 465 0045
Marketing Development Manager *Jonathan Tilston*

Part of **Faber & Faber** publishers. First cassettes were issued in 1994 to coincide with Poetry Day on October 6th. TITLES *Two Cures For Love – A Collection of Poems Introduced and Read by the Poet* Wendy Cope; *Readings – A Collection of Poems Introduced and Read by the Poets* Douglas Dunn,

Thom Gunn, Seamus Heaney, Ted Hughes, Philip Larkin, Paul Muldoon and Tom Paulin; *The Thought-Fox and Other Poems* Ted Hughes.

Golden Days of Radio
See **Hodder Headline Audio Books**

HarperCollins AudioBooks
77–85 Fulham Palace Road, London W6 8JB
☎0181 741 7070   Fax 0181 307 4813(adult)/ 307 4440(child.)

The Collins audio and video company was acquired in the mid-eighties but the video section was later sold. In 1990/91 HarperCollins overhauled the audio company, dividing the adult and children's tapes into two separate divisions.

ADULT
Managing Director *Robert Williams*
Publisher *Rosalie George*
Publishes a wide range including popular and classic fiction, non-fiction, Shakespeare and poetry. 50 titles in 1994. TITLES *Honour Among Thieves* Jeffrey Archer; *The Rector's Wife* Joanna Trollope; *The Final Cut* Michael Dobbs; *Neither Here Nor There* Bill Bryson; *Heart of Danger* Gerald Seymour; *Simisola* Ruth Rendell.

CHILDREN'S
Managing Director *Roy Davey*
Senior Editor *Stella Paskins*
Publishes picture books/cassettes and story books/cassettes as well as single and double tapes for children aged 2–13 years. Fiction, songs, early learning, poetry etc. 61 titles in 1994. AUTHORS Roald Dahl, C. S. Lewis, Enid Blyton, Michael Rosen, Robert Westall, Jean Ure, Nick Butterworth, Colin and Jacqui Hawkins, Judith Kerr, Jonathan Langley. Welcomes ideas for titles.

Hodder Headline Audio Books
338 Euston Road, London NW1 3BH
☎0171 873 6000   Fax 0171 873 6027
Managing Director *Rupert Lancaster*
LAUNCHED in 1994 with 50 titles. A strong list, especially for theatre, vintage radio, poety plus fiction, non-fiction, children's, religious. 120 titles in 1995. AUTHORS Enid Blyton, Edwina Currie, Mick Inkpen (*Kipper* books), Stephen King, Rosamunde Pilcher, Emma Tennant, Joanna Trollope, Terry Waite, Mary Wesley
   IMPRINT **Golden Days of Radio** series of classic vintage radio broadcasts. Welcome ideas for cassettes.

Isis Audio Books
7 Centremead, Osney Mead, Oxford OX2 0ES
☎01865 250333   Fax 01865 790358
Managing Director *John Durrant*
Editorial Head *Veronica Babington Smith*
Part of **Isis Publishing Ltd.** *Publishes* fiction and a few non-fiction titles. AUTHORS Virginia Andrews, Barbara Taylor Bradford, Edwina Currie, Leslie Thomas, Douglas Adams, Terry Pratchett.

Laughing Stock
PO Box 408, London SW11 5TA
☎0171 498 0102   Fax 0171 498 1460
Managing Director *Colin Collino*
FOUNDED 1991. Issues a wide range of comedy cassettes from family humour to alternative comedy. 12–16 titles per year. TITLES *Red Dwarf; Shirley Valentine* (read by Willy Russell); *Rory Bremner; Peter Cook Anthology; Sean Hughes*.

Life Stories
See **PolyGram Spoken Word**

Listen for Pleasure
113 Uxbridge Road, Hayes, Middlesex UB4 0SY
☎0181 561 8722   Fax 0181 569 2163
Managing Director *Roger Woodhead*
Part of E.M.I. Records, the Listen for Pleasure label started in 1977 as part of Music for Pleasure. Also covers Virgin, E.M.I. and Corgi Audio. *Publishes* fiction and non-fiction, children's, humour, poetry, comedy classics. 28 titles in 1994. Planning to issue more titles on CD as well as cassette. TITLES *Morecambe & Wise; The Goon Shows; The Railway Children; The Borrowers; The Silence of the Lambs; The Beiderbecke Affair; All Creatures Great and Small; Under Milk Wood*. Welcome ideas for cassettes.

MCI Spoken Word
36-38 Caxton Way, Watford, Hertfordshire WD1 8UF
☎01923 255558   Fax 01923 816880
Owner VCI Plc
Managing Director *Peter Stack*
Established in 1993 and now a rapidly expanding publisher of a wide range of audiobooks: comedy, children's, classics, thrillers & chillers, true crime, TV programmes. 35 titles in 1994. TITLES *Inspector Morse; Barbie; Max Miller; Sherlock Holmes* (Granada TV); *The Dubliners; The Last of the Mohicans*. Open to ideas for cassettes.

Naxos AudioBooks

55 Long Lane, London N3 2HY
☎0181 346 6816   Fax 0181 346 6816
Owner *HNH International, Hong Kong*
Managing Director *Nicolas Soames*

FOUNDED 1994. Part of Naxos, the classical budget CD company. *Publishes* classic and modern fiction, non-fiction, children's and junior classics, drama and poetry. 50 titles planned for 1995. TITLES *Paradise Lost* Milton; *Ulysses* Joyce; *Kim* Kipling; *Travels With a Donky* R.L. Stevenson. Ideas for cassettes welcome.

Penguin Audiobooks

27 Wrights Lane, London W8 5TZ
☎0171 416 3000   Fax 0171 416 3289
Owner *Penguin Books Ltd*
Publishing Manager *Jan Paterson*

Launched in November 1993 and has rapidly expanded since then to reflect the diversity of **Penguin Books'** list. *Publishes* mostly fiction, both classical and contemporary, non-fiction and autobiography. Approx. 65–70 titles a year. TITLES *The Iliad; The Prophet; Middlemarch; Martin Chuzzlewit; Wild Horses* Dick Francis; *A Short Walk From Harrods* Dirk Bogarde.

PolyGram Spoken Word

1 Sussex Place, Hammersmith,
London W6 9XS
☎0181 910 5000   Fax 0181 910 5400
Owner *PolyGram*
Managing Director *Gary Richards*

Part of PolyGram, the Spoken Word division has been in operation for two years, publishing under the **Speaking Volumes** and **Life Stories** labels. *Publishes* comedy, biography, fiction and children's titles. Approx. 50 titles in 1994. TITLES *Diaries* Alan Clark; *A Suitable Boy* Vikram Seth. Ideas for cassettes welcome.

Random House Audiobooks

20 Vauxhall Bridge Road,
London SW1V 2SA
☎0171 973 9000   Fax 0171 233 6127
Owner *Random House UK Ltd*
Managing Director *Simon King*

The audiobooks division of Random House started early in 1991 and *publishes* fiction, non-fiction, self help and children's. 32 titles in 1994. AUTHORS include John Grisham, Stephen Fry, P.G. Wodehouse, Frederick Forsythe, Michael Caine, Michael Crichton and Anne Rice.

Redback Audiobooks

Pickwick House, The Waterfront, Elstree
Road, Elstree, Hertfordshire WD6 3BS
☎0181 236 0532   Fax 0181 207 3706
Owner *Pickwick Group Ltd*
Managing Director *Jonathan Hayden*

Redback Audiobooks is a newly formed division of Pickwick Group. Established for nearly 30 years, Pickwick is now part of Carlton Communications, one of Europe's leading media corporations. Redback launched into the market place in 1995 with a strong catalogue comprising licensed product from Dove Audio and new acquisitions. *Publishes* action, thrillers, classics, non-fiction and children's. TITLES *The Shocking Story of Murder Victim Nicole Brown Simpson and Her Life with O. J.* Faye D. Resnick with Mike Walker; *Nothing Lasts Forever* Sidney Sheldon; *Grace* Robert Lacey; *The Prince of Wales, A Biography* Jonathan Dimbleby; *Storming Heaven* Dale Brown. Welcomes ideas for cassettes.

Reed Audio

Michelin House, 81 Fulham Road,
London SW3 6RB
☎0171 581 9393   Fax 0171 589 8419
Owner *Reed Consumer Books*
Managing Director *John Potter*

Publishes fiction, humour and non-fiction. 48 titles planned for 1995. *Paddy Clarke Ha Ha Ha* Roddy Doyle; *Mind Over Matter* Ranulph Fiennes; *Free to Trade* Michael Ridpath.

Simon & Schuster Audio

West Garden Place, Kendal Street,
London W2 2AG
☎0171 724 7555   Fax 0171 402 0639
Managing Director *Nick Webb*

Simon & Schuster Audio began by distributing their American parent company's audio products. Moved on to repackaging products specifically for the UK market and in 1994 became more firmly established in this market with a huge rise in turnover. *Publishes* adult fiction, self help, business, Star Trek titles. 4–5 titles per month. TITLES *The Body Farm* Patricia Cornwell; *Forrest Gump* Winston Groom; *Closing Time* Joseph Heller; *Giant Steps* Anthony Robbins.

Speaking Volumes

See **PolyGram Spoken Word**

Sterling Audio Books

See **Chivers Audio Books**

Word-for-Word Audio Books

See **Chivers Audio Books**

Poetry Has to be Easier than Working

Peter Finch

It is liked. It glitters. Poetry today has high street cred. Its practitioners have been photographed by *Vogue* decked out in Armani shirts, Versace jackets and Zegna suits. Faber have put Larkin and even the venerable Auden on t-shirts. The profile of poetry could not be higher. For the few, it has certainly been a good time. Sudden fame and fortune, more media attention than they could hope for in a life-time. £10,000 to be won for a single volume; £800 for a half-hour reading. Poetry has to be easier than working.

But the danger is to get caught by its surface. Where are you if, like the vast majority of poets, you do not have a hyped name and a pushy publisher. The chances are that the 90's boom will have done little more for you than pass by at high speed on TV. Your work is good too, so why aren't you famous? No one wants to know. It's the nature of the beast, I'm afraid.

The bubble of the past few years has certainly raised poetry's profile, everyone agrees on that. National Poetry Day was a media success which got everyone talking. The New Generation push earned a thousand column inches and glorious colour snaps of the poets looking artily creative in the Sunday supplements. But did any of this actually increase general sales? The answer drifting in from the publishers – ever defensive of their turnover targets – turns out to be no. 'Tapped a well of enthusiasm,' said William Seighart of Forward Publishing. 'Whether there is a real poetry boom is questionable,' admitted Faber. 'Poetry is now much more a part of people's lives but the sales are still to come through,' reported Martha Smart from the **Poetry Book Society**. Stephen Stuart-Smith at Enitharmon was more definite, 'It did not assist,' he said.

Still, some things have gone well. Penguin paid Craig Raine £60,000 for his novel-length poem *History: The Home Movie*. Judith Chernaik's highly successful **Poetry on the Underground** scheme reported sales in excess of 100,000 units fcr their Cassell anthology. Pam Ayres, still touring strongly with the doggerel roadshow, reckons to have moved more than 30,000 of her collection *The Works*. **Poetry International**, the annual grand gala of global greats which brings the likes of John Ashbery, Marin Sorescu, Kamau Braithwaite and Les Murray to the UK, has been revived. Commendable stuff. And with the poetry slam and contest activities of Phil Dirtbox, Nuyorican Mike Tyler ('the most dangerous poet in America') and our own legendary British bruiser, Adrian Mitchell, poetry has been turned into a martial art as well.

You can get it on your PC (mail poetry@poetry.demon.co.uk asking <send poetry details><firstname><lastname>), in your daily newspaper and all over the place on radio and TV. John Hegley slots in with the pop records, Ian Macmillan teaches the youth of Britain how on Radio One. On Radio Four contemporary poets whack it amid reruns of old favourites, Radio Three plays Poet of the Month, on BBC2 poets appear as latenight fillers and in documentaries devoted to their mysterious arts. Poets are everywhere.

The problem is that while they may write wonderfully well and have such enticing images, they are never actually read or bought enough to alter the fundamental shape of the world in which they write. 'Most people ignore most poetry because most poetry ignores most people,' – Adrian Mitchell. Bookstores agree. When asked by the trade journal, *The Bookseller*, to recommend bestselling poetry titles, a panel of representative buyers came up once again with those traditional, ancient warhorses *Palgrave's Treasury* and *The Oxford Book of English Verse*.

Despite the blitz of attention most poetry activities are actually largely invisible. Writing is a private, silent art. New slim collections appear in editions of a few hundred copies. Audiences at readings can be embarrassingly small. The whole business is spread too thin, for we all want to take part and few of us are content simply to consume.

Ian and Tracy Walton at the Forward Press in Peterborough, depressed with 'twenty years of not being able to enjoy poetry' because it was invariably obscure, have exploited the tendency well. Identifying nearly 85,000 active British verse scribblers, they and their £1 million turnover *Poetry Now* empire currently receive in excess of 100,000 submissions each year. Perpetuating a poetry world's Home and Away image, the Waltons jam more than two hundred poems into each of their anthologies. These are sold not to the public but back to the contributors. 'It's a bit like amateur dramatics,' Ian told me, 'anyone can take part'.

So how do you get ahead? You join in at whatever level you want: at the *PN Review* with its insistence on the 'centrality of poetry in cultural life and on the necessity of critical engagement'; with National Poetry Day's verse to be read in supermarkets, distributed by taxi drivers or delivered by Interflora; or even with Steve Turner's enormously well circulated Christian poetry circus which, if anything, proves that good messages can still sell. Very little in the UK is excluded. Stuffiness may well be a natural way of life (try Auberon Waugh's *The Literary Review* for more of that – poets are 'unpleasant people who dress badly and don't pay for their drinks') but it is not the only one. If your poems are post-modernist smears then try *Object Permanence* or Bob Cobbing's long-lived *Writer's Forum*. Keep looking and you'll find a slot. And don't complain that nothing rhymes anymore. It does. That revival has been rolling now for years.

Are you up to this?

Check that you are ready first. Are you personally convinced that your work is up to it? If you are uncertain, then most likely that will also be the view of everyone else. Check your text for glips and blips. Rework it. Root out any clichés or the odd appearance of what Peter Sansom calls 'spirit of the age' poetry words. Do without shards, lozenges, lambent patina, stippled seagulls. If by this time your writing still sounds realistic, then go ahead.

Commercial publishers

Where they make real money from books, a small number of imprints keep up an interest in verse. If you are a sure seller like Wendy Cope, Roger McGough or Simon Armitage, you'll be here in the thick of it – sought after, considered, possibly even offered reasonable advances on your work. But if you are simply a decent poet; then you'll be on the list, if you are there at all, simply to enhance the imprint. Slim volumes are not money spinners. Commercial poetry editors are rarely allowed to publish everyone they would like.

Long-term market leader, the envy of the whole business and still streets ahead of anyone else is **Faber & Faber**. Since the great days of T.S. Eliot, as editor, this is the imprint most poets would like to join. 'Put some poetry into your life' ran their recent promotion. Faber with their distinctive jackets and their enormous backlist have twentieth-century verse sewn up. Eliot, Pound, Hughes, Heaney and Plath are all with them. Faber competitors do not have this pedigree. Promotions and marketing ploys may help to increase public awareness of verse but editor Christopher Reid will continue to publish good poetry regardless. Faber are aware of their leading role and intend to maintain it. Sales can be enormous – Auden's *Tell Me the Truth About Love* passing 100,000 copies and Wendy Cope's *Serious Concerns* shifting 60,000. Big contemporary names include Tom Paulin, Douglas Dunn, Simon Armitage and Paul Muldoon. Faber will look at work from new poets for both new volumes and their *Poetry Introduction* series. Send 20 poems plus s.a.e. if this is where you think you'll fit in.

Robin Robertson's move from **Secker & Warburg** to **Jonathan Cape**, one of Random House's many divisions, has seen that imprint revive its 60s and 70s glory days as one of the UK's great poetry outlets. Robertson expects to bring out between four and six titles annually, no anthologies, no reprints. New stuff only. 'Originality and excellence are the requirements.' Already David Dabydeen and John Burnside have met high sales targets. New titles are in hand from Michael Longley, James Lasdun, Sharon Olds, Adam Thorpe, Sarah Maguire and Matthew Sweeney. Worth trying? 'Yes. Look at the books on the list first. Then submit at least 40 pages of poems with a covering letter and return postage.' At **Chatto & Windus**, where Simon Armitage has taken over as poetry editor, things continue to move on slowly. Alan Jenkins, Blake Morrison, Peter Reading and Gerard Woodward form the backbone. No signs of non-male voices yet and not much room for rank beginners.

At **Oxford University Press**, the traditional centre of English verse, poetry editor Jacqueline Simms maintains her aim to publish about ten titles annually. Thick in the mix of Keats, Milton and Pope will be found contemporary voices:

Jo Shapcott, Moniza Alvi, Jamie McKendrick and Michael Donaghy. Loyalty to the 24 active writers on the list comes first but the press is 'always looking for distinct, original new poets.' Are total newcomers welcome? Yes but 'we suggest new poets get experience of seeing their poems in print first among the literary magazines. We like to see a full collection, say 30–50 poems, worked out in a book order.'

Reed International's only outlet for new poetry was Christopher Sinclair-Stevenson's eponymous **Sinclair-Stevenson** but it was announced in the Spring of 1995 that their poetry list would close.

The **Harvill Press** still try to publish the occasional poetry title annually. Under poetry editor Christopher MacLehose, they've managed Paul Durcan, Alan Ross, Raymond Carver and Gjertrud Schnackenburg. They'll look at new manuscripts so long as the poet has 'taken note of who is publishing what (and how much) and acted accordingly'.

Elsewhere the lists appear to have closed down. **Hutchinson** stick with Dannie Abse, **Methuen** recycle their Bertolt Brecht. **Dent**, once the bolt hole for Dylan Thomas and more recently home of R.S.Thomas's selected verse claim no longer to publish anything other than classics. Secker & Warburg, without Robin Robertson, report they are 'not taking on any poetry for the indefinite future'. In commercial terms the poetry market has a definite size.

The smaller operators

Not all commercial publishing is vast and conglomerate. The innovative **Serpent's Tail** have recently tested the field with an exciting, avant garde set by American John Giorno. The Scottish family firm **Ramsay Head Press** publish Tessa Ransford. In Wales **Gwasg Gomer** do Jon Dressel, Nigel Jenkins, Chris Bendon and Harri Webb. The **Edinburgh University Press** imprint of **Polygon**, under poetry editor Robert Crawford, has steadily moved ahead with a policy of Scottish 'poetry for the new generation'. The press has at least a dozen poets on its lists including Thomas Clark, W. N. Herbert and Liz Lochhead, and is keen to see more. Northern Ireland's general publisher, **The Blackstaff Press**, brings out between two and three poetry titles annually, mainly of Irish interest. Paul Durcan and Frank Ormsby are typical.

Other dabblers

Poetry in the shape of single titles dot the lists of many UK publishers but this is hardly a declaration of interest or a desire to see more. **Robert Hale** publish Raymond Tong, **Marion Boyers** do Robert Creeley, **Robson Books** make money out of former boxer Vernon Scannell. Generic anthologies are always popular. **J. A. Allen** do the poetry of horses, **Headline** poetry of the countryside, **Frontier** green poetry, **Bloomsbury** do the war poets, while **Pavilion** publish love poems. It is no good sending in single poems. These presses will not wish to know. **Macmillan, Deutsch, Michael Joseph**, and others have the occasional title but it is all tokenism. American University Presses such as **Yale, Ohio, Duke, Iowa** and **California** along with **W.W. Norton** do some poetry, but exclusively by Americans, so no chances there. Some specialist interests are dealt with at **Lion** (Christian verse), **Peepal Tree** (Caribbean) and **Oscars** (gay) but it isn't a lot.

Women

It would be good to report that Britain's major feminist publishing house, **Virago**, had decided to run a major poetry list but according to editor Melanie Silgardo most of the little they do anyway is now on hold. Work by poets with established reputations such as Merle Collins, Michèle Roberts and Margaret Atwood will continue to appear as will prints of new volumes by American poets such as Janice Mirikitani. But for the average UK woman poet? Not very much. 'We're not keen to see new volumes,' said Melanie, 'send them to **Bloodaxe**'. Virago's competitor, **The Women's Press**, have little interest in poetry other than the occasional black American title and the continued success of the work of Alice Walker.

The paperbackers

The cheap and popular end is where many poets imagine is the best starting place. Mass-market paperback houses were founded to publish inexpensive reprints of cloth-covered originals and to a large extent they still fulfil this role. But being neither cheap nor popular, poetry does not really fit in. Check the empires of **Pan, Minerva, Arrow, Headline** and **Transworld**. If you discount the inspirational, there is not a book of verse between them. At **Penguin**, however, things have always been different. Ever innovative, the company has correctly assessed the market for both traditional and contemporary verse and has systematically and successfully filled it. Reprinting important volumes pioneered by poetry presses such as **Anvil, Carcanet** and Bloodaxe, originating historic and thematic anthologies, reviving classic authors and producing a multitude of translations en route, Penguin continues to provide an almost unrivalled introduction to the world of verse. But, despite appearances, Penguin is definitely not the place for the untried. So flooded have they become with unsolicited manuscripts that they simply do not want to see any more. 'We don't need to provide this kind of service,' poetry editor Paul Kegan told me, 'the smaller poetry presses do it well enough already.' He contents himself with repackaged topsellers such as James Fenton, Dannie Abse and Carol Ann Duffy in selected form, and a programme of modern poets in translation along with larger sets from the likes of Allen Ginsberg, John Ashbery and Hugh MacDiarmid. His big news this year is the revival, after a number of decades, of the ground breaking *Penguin Modern Poets* series, again to contain three poets per volume but no longer linked by stylistic or geographical considerations. 'We have adopted a non-doctrinaire approach,' said Kegan, 'no ghettos this time'. Poets to be packaged include Mick Imlah, Carol Ann Duffy, Samuel Menashe, Allen Curnow, Kit Wright, Donald Davie, Edwin Morgan, and James Fenton. A wide ranging, catholic selection but, again, only poets who have already succeeded elsewhere before. For the future, Penguin would like to explore the gap left by the much-missed Paladin and look at the likes of Tom Raworth, Denise Riley and J.H. Pryne. There could be some quite good times ahead.

The specialists

The real poetry presses of the UK and Ireland are the specialists. These semi-commercial independents are run by genuine poetry enthusiasts whose prime concern is not so much money as the furtherance of their art. They all began as classic small presses in the late 70s and early 80s but soon outgrew the restraints of back-bedroom offices and under-the-stairs warehousing. All now have national representation of some sort, with a number using *Password*, the subsidised poetry specialists (23 New Mount Street, Manchester M4 4DE), who issue a very useful catalogue. These presses have learned well how to do it. You can find them in Waterstones. Most (but not all) receive substantial grant aid, without which their publishing programmes would be sunk. They are models of what poetry publishing should be – active, involving, alert, and exciting. The problem is that they are too few.

For many years leader of the pack, Carcanet is by now almost indistinguishable from its trade competitors. Although no longer exclusively a publisher of verse, it still maintains a substantial interest in poetry, and has over 500 titles in print and reps in 42 countries. Managing director Michael Schmidt agrees with Auden's observation that most people who read poetry read it for some reason other than the poetry. No guidance comes from our national press who offer serious criticism far less frequently than they used to. Sales of individual titles have sunk to three figures. He fights the tide with his own serious journal, *PN Review*, whose fat 100th issue provides a splendid overview of Carcanet's style. The press concentrates on producing substantial editions which make a poet's whole *oeuvre* available alongside cheap selected poems and new titles from both the untried and the famous. Typical of their list are Eavan Boland, Sophie Hannah, Les Murray, Vicki Raymond and bestseller, Elizabeth Jennings. New poets are welcome to send in material, so long as they have at least read carefully a selection of Carcanet's output and enclose the all important s.a.e. Carcanet has an air of studied seriousness about it. 'We avoid the Technicolour and pyrotechnic media razzmatazz", says Schmidt. In an increasingly frivolous world, this can be no bad thing.

Tony Ward's stylish **Arc Publications**, which successfully incorporates the former poetry imprint of Littlewood Arc, uses two associate editors, Michael Hulse and David Morley, to promote a contemporary list which increases at the rate of around ten titles annually. Arc look for innovation and diversity ignoring fashion and the 'philistine camp of market forces'. The unacknowledged but worthy have a real chance here. Bestsellers include the ever popular Ivor Cutler, E.A. Markham, Tom Rawling and Jacqueline Brown. Ward is quite sniffy about bookshops who won't stock his product. Arc poetry gets there by other routes. Advice to contributors: 'Unsolicited material is welcome from writers whose work has appeared in poetry magazines and is compatible with the current list". Send a large s.a.e. for a catalogue.

Enitharmon Press represents quality, cares about presentation and, rare among poetry presses, has a real concern for internal design. Its books, poet/artist editions and pamphlets are produced to the highest of standards. Enitharmon has little interest in fashion, preferring 'poetry of the human spirit', which exhibits 'moral imagination'. Owner Stephen Stuart-Smith continues a policy of publishing poetry by new, established and unjustly neglected poets not only from Britain and Ireland but from many other parts of the world. David Gascoyne's *Selected Poems* sells alongside Jane Duran's *Breathe Now, Breathe*. Unique among UK presses, Enitharmon publish collaborations between distinguished artists and writers. Ted Hughes and Thom Gunn appear with artists Christopher Le Brun, Shinro Ohtake and Howard Hodgkin. Typical Enitharmon poets include Jeremy Reed, Hilary Davies and Ruth Pitter. Prospective conteributors should write before sending.

Peterloo Poets, run by the redoubtable Harry Chambers, represents poetry without frills, without fuss and most definitely without the avant-garde. The press aims to publish quality work by new or neglected poets (many of them late-starters), to co-publish with reputable presses in the USA and in Canada and to establish a Peterloo list of succeeding volumes by a core of poets of proven excellence. Chambers avoids anthologies and has finished with magazines and newsletters. The press does books and does them well. Bestsellers include U.A. Fanthorpe, John Whitworth and Dana Gioia. Ann Drysdale, Gary Geddes, Anna Crowe and Diana Hendry are recent additions to the list. Chambers runs his own poetry competition (1st prize £2000) and insists that prospective contributors to his press have had at least five poems in the magazines. If you are unpublished, do not try here. Send submissions with a stamped envelope large enough to carry your mss back to you and avoid, at all costs, folders, ring files and plastic grippers.

Peter Jay's **Anvil Press** was founded in 1968 and for a long time ran as a classic alternative publisher, set up in formal opposition to the Fabers and OUPs of the poetry scene. He still sticks to an original small coterie of poets and makes what personality cult he can of Harry Guest, Peter Levi, Anthony Howell and

Heather Buck, although by now the emphasis has shifted to work in translation, much of it from Europe. The press has quiet style and pays much attention to presentation both inside the book and out. Anvil's runaway bestseller is Carol Ann Duffy who also edits their useful *Anvil New Poets* anthology. Check this for a sample of the press's work. Typical poets include Dennis O'Driscoll, Vasko Popa, Yannis Ritsos, and Bei Dao.

Seren Books (the Welsh for 'star') was an offshoot of the magazine *Poetry Wales* until 1988, when founder Cary Archard correctly perceived that poetry alone would never keep them afloat and diversified into novels, short fiction, biographies and critical texts. In receipt of significant Arts Council finance, their commitment to poetry still remains central with at least half a dozen new titles annually. Leslie Norris, Tony Curtis, Robert Minhinick, R.S. Thomas, Sheenagh Pugh and Duncan Bush are among their topsellers. Poetry editor Amy Wack is always on the look out for new voices and advises potential contributors to 'send your best work, not what you think the editor might want to see'. A good press sampler is their anthology *Poetry Wales 25 Years*. They have also published their own guide to the scene, *The Poetry Business*.

If poets once went to the commercial operators for wide distribution, they now cluster around Neil Astley's **Bloodaxe Books** for the concern, company and intelligent promotion that the imprint provides. Based in Newcastle-upon-Tyne and begun little over a decade ago, the press is unhindered by a past catalogue of classical greats or an overly regional concern. It relentlessly pursues the new. Regarded by some as garish and fast, Bloodaxe are now the UK's only real rival to the otherwise unassailable Faber. Poetry is absolutely central with a vast list as exciting, innovative and varied as anyone could wish. Astley presents the complete service from thematic anthologies, world greats, and 'selecteds' to individual slim volumes by total newcomers. The press have their own range of excellent handbooks to the scene, including Paul Hyland's *Getting Into Poetry* and Peter Sansom's *Writing Poems*, along with an increasing range of critical volumes. Astley agrees totally with the current view that serious verse criticism is fast vanishing from our national press. Teachers and academics complain that students are at sea without appropriate critical texts. The general reader stands no chance. Bloodaxe will step in to fill the gap. Sean O'Brien's survey of contemporary British and Irish poetry, *The Deregulated Muse*, is the first of many. Bestsellers include Helen Dunmore, Tony Harrison, R. S. Thomas and their Lorca translations, along with Linda France's anthology *Sixty Women Poets* and Jenni Couzyn's *Contemporary Women Poets*. Way out front, as expected, is their controversial, decade-framing anthology *The New Poetry*. Mainstream poets continue to desert their metropolitan commercial imprints for Newcastle – Selima Hill, Peter Reading and James Berry are typical catches. But it is not all one way – Simon Armitage was a Bloodaxe find well before Faber made him famous. Bloodaxe welcome newcomers but since they receive at least 100 new collections a week, you can increase your chance of an early answer by restricting yourself to sending a dozen of your best. If Bloodaxe want to see more, they'll ask. A simple way to taste the imprint's range is to try their anthology *Poetry With An Edge.*

There are other publishers who show strong signs of outgrowing their hobbyist regional status. In Dublin, John F. Deane's **Dedalus Press** is a decade-old, exclusively-poetry operator with almost 60 titles on its list, mostly Irish but not exclusively. Typical poets include Thomas Kinsella, Denis Delvin, John Jordan and Pat Boran. Peter Fallon's County Meath-based **Gallery Press** has been around since 1970, publishing pamphlets and volumes by young Irish poets. In Newcastle, Peter Elfed Lewis's **Flambard Press** produces books to rival Bloodaxe as does the flared-trouser **Iron Press** which despite its claim to 'remain in spirit a small press' has had a number of runaway commercial successes. There are others: Rupert Loydell's eccentric, high energy **Stride,** whose volumes once held more typos than the *Guardian,* is now certainly commercially acceptable. **Smith/Doorstop**, the book imprint of Peter Sansom and Janet Fisher's **The Poetry Business** and run in parallel with poetry journal *The North,* produces volumes indistinguishable from trade standard. Just where these publishers end and classic small presses start is getting harder and harder to tell.

The traditional outlets

There exists a small, traditional market for new poetry, enlarged in the face of hype-driven booms, but nonetheless still a very minor component of the total scene. Poetry has a place in the national press. *The Independent* runs a daily poem (for which no one gets paid, the poets apparently doing it for prestige alone), *The Guardian* regularly features verse, as do the Sunday heavies. Nothing yet in *The Daily Star* or *The Sun. The Times Literary Supplement* gives over considerable space on a regular basis; whole double page spreads devoted to the work of one poet or to a long single poem are not unusual. *The London Review of Books* shows a similar interest. Mostly though, the traditional market centres around *The London Magazine,* which has the reputation for being the fastest responder in the business (you walk to the post box, mail your poems, then return home to find them rejected and waiting for you on the mat); *The Spectator, New Statesman and Society* (where Adrian Mitchell is poetry editor); Auberon Waugh's *The Literary Review;* plus the occasional spot in magazines like *The Lady* and *The Countryman* – all paying outlets, which sounds quite reassuring. Some local newspapers also consider poetry, although the chances of earning much in this market are much slighter. Try sending your work in the form of a letter to Postbag. For those interested, the magazine *Poetry Now* has published a list. But the truth is that were poetry to cease to exist overnight, then these publications would continue to publish without a flicker. Who, other than the poets, would notice?

The small press and the little magazine

Amateur publishing ventures have been with us for quite a long time. Virginia Woolf began the Hogarth Press this way, quite literally on the kitchen table. But it was not until well after the Second World War and the rise of what the Americans called the mimeo revolution that poetry magazine and pamphlet publishing really took off. Recent advances in technology have seen that revolution moved on to a considerable degree. Computer literate poets are everywhere. Publishing has been stripped of its mystery. Access to photocopiers, laser printers and desktop publishing packages are commonplace. Disposable income has gone up. Poets in growing number are able and willing to set up competent one-person publishing operations, turning out neat professional-looking titles on a considerable scale.

These are the small presses and the little magazines. They sell to new and often non-traditional markets, rarely finding space on bookshop shelves, where they are regarded as unshiftable nuisances. Instead they go hand to hand among friends at poetry readings, creative writing classes, literary functions, via subscriptions, and are liberally exchanged among all those concerned. The question remains: is anyone out there not directly concerned with the business of poetry actually reading it? But that is another story.

Numerically, the small presses and the little magazines are the largest publishers of new poetry both in terms of range and total sales. They operate in a variety of shapes and sizes everywhere from Cardiff to Caithness and Lewes to Llandudno. The present wave of enthusiasm has thrown up a variety of support organisations to whom new poets may well direct their initial enquiries. Both the **Association Of Little Presses** and the **Small Press Group** produce catalogues as well as running bookfairs and events around the country (see **Professional Associations**).

This country's best poetry magazines all began as classic littles. Between them *PN Review*, *Ambit*, *Agenda*, *Outposts*, *Orbis*, *Poetry Review*, *Rialto*, *Verse* and *Stand* do not come up to even half the circulation of journals like *Shooting Times* and *Camping and Caravanning* – which says a lot about the way in which we value our poetry. Nonetheless between them they will get to almost everyone who matters. In the second division in terms of kudos lie the regional or genre specialists such as *Poetry Wales*, *Lines Review*, *Poetry Ireland*, *New Welsh Review*, *Poetry Nottingham*, *Poetry Durham*, *Pomes* (performance poetry's only tabloid), *Psycopoetica* (psychologically based poetry), *Ostinato* (jazz poetry), *Haiku Quarterly*, *Hjok Finnie's Sanguines* (the native poetry broadsheet from the highlands) and *Krax* (humorous verse). All these magazines are well produced, often with the help of grants, and all representative of a specific point of view. In Wales there is *Barddas* for poets using the strict meters and in Scotland *Lallans* for poets writing in Lowland Scots. The vast majority of small magazines, however, owe no allegiance. They range from fat irregulars like *Bête Noire* and *Global Tapestry Journal*, quality general round-ups like *Scratch* and *Iron* (Why Iron?

Because we hate poetry competitions, because we've never been in the *TLS*), to fleeting pamphlets like *The Yellow Crane* (interesting new poems), *Reflections* (by and for men and women of goodwill), *The People's Poetry* (poetry and lyrics of all kinds), *Fat Chance* and *Rustic Rub*. Some, such as *Sepia* insist on poetry without cliché and without rhyme; *Living Poets* you get only if you have an on-line computer; while *Poetry Now* from Peterborough is run like a verse tabloid awash with stuff from totally new names.

Among the presses there is a similar range. **Hippopotamus Press** publish first collections and work by the neglected; Bob Cobbing's **Writers Forum** sticks to mainstream experimental; **Forest Books**, run with panache by Brenda Walker and bringing out just as many new titles as the specialists, concentrates on English translations of foreign, often East European, texts; **Direction Poetry** publishes cassettes; **Dangaroo** and **Peepal Tree Press** have third world and ethnic concerns; **Katabasis** is interested in Latin American poetry and is now expanding its English list; **Scratch**, **Staple First Editions** and **Rockingham Press** work at the edge of the mainstream; **KQBX** handles quality; **The Black Gate Press** has an interest in the byzantine; **Honno** supports Welsh women; **The Daft Lad Press** specialises in the work of Chris Challis; **Oscars Press** covers gay poetry; **On The Wire Press** does Christian verse; **Y Lolfa** publish unofficial bards; **Envoi** and the **National Poetry Foundation** brings out the accessible; **The Red Sharks Press** deals in anti-sheepist verse. For the new writer, these kinds of presses are the obvious places to try first. Indeed, it is where many have. Who put out T.S. Eliot first? A small publisher. Dannie Abse, Peter Redgrove, James Fenton and Dylan Thomas, the same. R. S. Thomas, Ezra Pound, and Edgar Allen Poe didn't even go that far – they published themselves.

Cash

A lot of writers new to the business are surprised to learn that their poetry will not make them much money. Being a poet is not really much of an occupation. You get better wages delivering papers. There will be the odd pound from the better heeled magazine, perhaps even as much as £40 or so from those periodicals lucky enough to be in receipt of a grant, but generally it will be free copies of the issues concerned, thank you letters and little more. Those with collections published by a subsidised, specialist publisher can expect a couple of hundred as an advance on royalties. Those using the small presses can look forward to a few dozen complimentary copies. The truth is that poetry itself is undervalued. You can earn money writing about it, reviewing it, lecturing on it or certainly by giving public recitations (£100 standard here, £500 if you are Tony Harrison, more if you are Ted Hughes). In fact, most things in the poetry business will earn better money than the verse itself. Expect to spend a lot on stamps and a fair bit on sample copies. Most of the time all you'll get in return is used envelopes.

Readings

Since the great Beat Generation Albert Hall reading of 1964, there has been an ever-expanding phenomenon of poets on platforms, reading or reciting their stuff to an audience that can be anywhere between raptly attentive and fast asleep. There is a magic in the spoken poem. The music lives, the images echo. For some writers, the reading has devolved so far as to become a branch of the entertainment industry; for others, it is an essential aspect of what they do. Whichever way you view it, it is certainly an integral part of the business and one in which the beginner is going to need to engage sooner or later. Begin by attending and see how others manage. Watch out for local events advertised at your library or ring your local arts board. Poets with heavy reputations can often turn out to be lousy performers while many an amateur can really shake it down. Don't expect to catch every image as you listen. Readings do not go in for total comprehension but more for glancing blows. Treat it as fun and it will be. If you are trying things yourself for the first time, make sure you've brought your books along to sell, stand upright, drop the shoulders, gaze at a spot at the back of the hall and blow.

Competitions

Poetry competitions have been the vogue for more than a decade now with the most unlikely organisations sponsoring them. The notion here is that anonymity ensures fairness. Entries are made under pseudonyms so that if your name does happen to be Miroslav Holub, then this won't help you much. Results seem to bear this out too. The big competitions such as the one run biennially by the **Arvon Foundation** with the help of commercial sponsors, or the Poetry Society's National attract an enormous entry and usually throw up quite a number of complete unknowns among the winners. And why do people bother? Cash prizes can be large – thousands of pounds – but it costs at least a pound a poem to enter, and often much more than that. If it is cash you want, then horses are a better bet. And there has been a trend for winners to come from places like Cape Girardeau, Missouri and Tibooburra, Australia. The odds are getting longer. Who won the last Arvon? I don't remember. But if you do fancy a try, then it is a pretty innocent activity. You tie up a poem for a few months and you spend a couple of pounds. Winners' tips include reading the work of the judges to see how they do it, submitting non-controversial middle-of-the-road smiling things, and doing this just before the closing date so you won't have to wait too long. Try two or three of your best. Huge wodges are costly and will only convince the judges of your insecurity. Watch the small mags for details, write to your regional arts board, check out *Quartos*, *Writer's News* or the listings in *Orbis* magazine, look on the notice board at your local library, or write for the regularly updated list from **The Poetry Library** in London (see **Poetry Organisations**).

Radio and TV

The regular slots are all on radio, naturally enough. It is so hard to make verse visually appealing. Some TV producers have tried, notably Peter Symes who produced both *Poet's News* and *Words On Film* for BBC2. The former ran commissioned poems which commented on the day's news while the latter showcased a section of our better known contemporary poets suffering visual interpretations of their work. On Radio Four, the unstinting Sue Roberts produces two regular programmes: *Poetry Please*, presented by Simon Rae and running listeners' requests (everything from John Donne to Carol Ann Duffy) and *Stanza*, a late night poetry news and views presented by Andrew McAllister. Variations have included *Stanza on Stage*, which presents live readings, and *Talking Poetry,* an occasional series of readings for youngsters. Newcomers can try their hands at sending in but most of the slots go to the better knowns. On Radio Three, Fiona McLean produces a series of poets on earlier poets, *Poetry In Action*, where contemporary poets plug into the real world, along with an irregular series of specially commissioned works including pieces by Les Murray, Simon Armitage, Kenneth Fearing, W.N. Herbert, Lavinia Greenlaw, Adam Johnson and others. In addition there is *Best Words*, a monthly magazine of reviews and new work presented by Michael Roson. An enlarging but difficult market. If you are determined to put your verse on air, then local radio offers better possibilities. Try sending in self-produced readings on cassette (if you are any good at it) or topical poetry which regional magazine programmes could readily use. Don't expect to be paid much.

Starting up

Probaby the best place will be locally. Find out through the library or the nearest arts board which writers groups gather in your area and attend. There you will meet others of a like mind, encounter whatever locally produced magazines there might be and get a little direct feedback on your work. 'How am I doing?' is a big question for the emerging poet and although criticism is not all that hard to come by, do not expect it from all sources. Magazine editors, for example, will rarely have the time to offer advice. It is also reasonable to be suspicious of that offered by friends and relations - they will no doubt be trying only to please. Writers groups present the best chance for poets to engage in honest, mutual criticism. But if you'd prefer a more detached, written analysis of your efforts and are willing to pay a small sum, then you could apply to the service operated nationally by the Poetry Society (22 Betterton Street, London WC2H 9BU), or The Arts Council of Wales (see under **Professional Associations and Socities**) or to one of those run on an area basis by your local arts board. There are also a number of non-subsidised critical services which you will find advertised in writers magazines.

If you have made the decison to publish your work – and I don't suppose you'd be reading this if you hadn't – then the first thing to do is a little market research. I've already indicated how overstocked the business is with periodicals and publications, yet surprisingly you will not find many of these in your local W.H. Smith. Most poetry still reaches its public via the specialist. Begin, though, by reading a few newly published mainstream books. Ask at your bookseller for their recommendations. Most shops these days carry a basic stock, especially the Waterstones chain who have taken to advertising their interest. But if you need a specialist, then get hold of the Poetry Library's current list of shops with a specific interest in poetry. Enquire at the library. Try selecting a recent anthology of contemporary verse. To get a broad view of what's going on, not only should you read Hulse, Kennedy and Morley's Bloodaxe *The New Poetry*; the annual *Forward Book of Poetry* (Faber); Mike Horovitz's *Grandchildren of Albion* (New Departures); Paul Beasley's *Popular Front of Contemporary Poetry* (Apples and Snakes); Bob Cobbing's *Verbi Visi Voco* (Writer's Forum); Edward Lucie-Smith's Penguin *British Poetry Since 1945*; and perhaps Seamus Heaney and Ted Hughes' *The Rattle Bag* (Faber); Jeni Couzyn's *The Bloodaxe Book of Contemparary Women Poets*; Linda France's *Sixty Women Poets* (Bloodaxe); Paula Burnett's *Penguin Book of Caribbean Verse in English*; Helen Vendler's *Faber Book of Contemporary American Poetry*; Donald Allen and George F. Butterick's *The Postmoderns; The New American Poetry Revised* (Grove); and *Postmodern American Poetry*, a really splendid selection edited by Paul Hoover (Norton). These last two might be harder to find but will be worth the effort. Progress to the literary magazine. Write off to a number of the magazine addresses which follow this article and ask the price of sample copies. Enquire about subscriptions. Expect to pay a little but inevitably it will not be a lot. It is important that poets read not only to familiarise themselves with what is currently fashionable and to increase their own facility for self-criticism, but to help support the activity in which they wish to participate. Buy – this is vital for little mags, it is the only way in which they are going to survive. Read; if it's all a mystery to you, try Tony Curtis's *How to Study Modern Poetry* (Macmillan); Peter Sansom's excellent *Writing Poems* (Bloodaxe); my own *How To Publish Your Poetry* (Allison and Busby); or even The Writers College (7 Dale Street, Manchester M1 1JB) *Art of Writing Poetry* correspondence course – expensive but, for real beginners, not a bad idea. How real poets actually work can be discovered by reading C.B. McCully's *The Poet's Voice and Craft* (Carcanet). After all this, if you still think it's appropriate, try sending in.

How to do it

Increase your chances of acceptance by following simple, standard procedure:

● Type, on a single side of the paper, A4 size, single-spacing with double between stanzas *exactly* as you'd wish your poem to appear when printed.

- Give the poem a title, clip multi-page works together, include your name and address at the foot of the final sheet. Avoid files, plastic covers, stiffeners and fancy clips of any sort.
- Keep a copy, make a record of what you send where and when, leave a space to note reaction.
- Send in small batches – six is a good number – with a brief covering letter saying who you are. Leave any justification, apology and explanation for your writers circle.
- Include a self addressed, stamped envelope of sufficient size for reply and/or return of your work
- Be prepared to wait some weeks for a response. Don't pester. Be patient. Most magazines will reply in the end.
- Never send the same poem to two places at the same time.
- Send your best. Work which fails to fully satisfy even the author is unlikely to impress anyone else.

Where?

Try the list which follows, sending for samples as suggested. The total market is vast – 200 or so addresses here – hundreds more in *Small Presses and Little Magazines of the UK and Ireland* (Oriel, The Friary, Cardiff – £4.00 including postage for the latest edition) and in *Light's List of Literary Magazines* which contains both UK and US addresses (John Light, The Lighthouse, 29 Longfield Road, Tring, Herts HP23 4DG). There are literally thousands and thousands worldwide in *Poet's Market* (Writer's Digest Books) and Len Fulton's *Directory of Poetry Publishers* (Dustbooks) – the two main American directories. The British Council have also published *British Literary Periodicals – A Selected Bibliography* which covers some littles along with scholarly journals. Up to the minute information can be found in *Zene*, the small press guide, published quarterly by Andy Cox and Mark Rose at 5 Martin's Lane, Witcham, Ely, Cambs CB6 2LB.

The next step

Once you have placed a few poems, you may like to consider publishing a booklet. There are as many small presses around as there are magazines. Start with the upmarket professionals by all means – Oxford University Press, Chatto & Windus, Jonathan Cape, Faber and Faber – but be prepared for compromise. The specialists and the small presses are swifter and more open to new work.

If all else fails, you could do it yourself. Blake did, so did Walt Whitman. Modern technology puts the process within the reach of us all and if you can put up a shelf, there is fair chance you will be able to produce a book to go on it.

Read my *How To Publish Yourself* (Allison & Busby) and Jonathan Zeitlyn's *Print: How You Can Do It Yourself* (Journeyman). Remember that publishing the book may be as hard as writing it but marketing and selling it is quite something else. If you are determined, have a look at Bill Godber, Robert Webb and Keith Smith's excellent *Marketing For Small Publishers* (Journeyman).

What to avoid – the vanity press

Requests which should make you suspicious: 'Poems wanted for new anthology – Publisher seeks new authors and poets for well established list'; 'Authors Wanted – Publisher seeks new material. Special interest in autobiography, war memoirs and poetry'. You'll find these small ads scattered throughout the classifieds of Sunday papers and in the Personal sections of large circulation magazines. You can tell that something is wrong by the fact that they are there at all. No reputable publisher ever has to advertise a need for poetry. The natural state of things is that there is always too much.

Vanity Presses are shady businesses run by sharks interested in fleecing the unsuspecting. There are no considerations of literary worth here. The system works by making the amateur writer feel significant. You send in your work and receive a glowing response by return. 'The editor has read your poems with interest and is pleased to report that they show considerable talent. We would like to include them in our forthcoming anthology *Pageant of the British Muse*. This important anthology of new verse will be circulated among the editors of national newspapers such as *The Daily Mirror*, *The Daily Express* and *The Daily Mail* as well as being put on the shelves of the libraries of Oxford University, Cambridge University, Trinity College Dublin, The National Library of Wales at Aberystwyth and the British Library in London. Leading critics use our anthologies as touchstones. Inclusion is a considerable achievement.' It sounds terrific. You are dancing round the room. There follows a lot of hoo-hah about copyright, assignment of author's rights, royalties, etc., all bound up in the form of a legal sounding document with bits marked 'upon this day...... the..... of.......... witnessed the undersigned.......' and so forth. The importance of the deal is made abundantly clear. The sting is in the small print at the bottom. 'In order to help defray publisher's overheads in this period of increasing printing costs we are asking you for a small contribution of £40 per poem printed. . .' But by the time you get to this you are so enraptured with the success of your obvious talent that you pay up without a murmur.

It is a deception, of course. Hundreds of others have received the same letter. The anthology will be badly set, poems crammed in like sardines, and it will not be sold in bookshops (no shop owners will stock it), nor bought by libraries (those mentioned are copyright libraries and by law need to receive a copy of everything printed); it will be ignored by newspapers (those listed never review poetry anyway); and, in fact, bought and read by no one bar the contributors themselves. My personal collection of such volumes were rescued from a skip I came across in a Cardiff side street.

Criticise the presses for this piece of bamboozlery and they will tell you that they are doing no more than providing a service. People want their names in print and are willing to pay to see that happen. The establishment of vanity presses is the inevitable consequence. The immorality is that those who participate are always the inexperienced – often the young and the very old – generally those least able to pay. It is not that the vanity presses provide any value judgement on work submitted either. There is no discrimination – they print everything they receive. As a test, one press was sent a poem by Gerard Manley Hopkins, a cut-up of *The Daily Star*, jottings by a 7-year-old and a piece assembled from overheard conversations in a launderette. They accepted the lot.

Variations and embellishments on the vanity press theme include offers to put your poetry to music setting you off on the road to stardom, readings of your verse by actors with deep voices to help you break into the local radio market (there isn't one) and further requests for cash to help pay for your collected poems to appear in book form, preferably bound in expensive leather with your name gold-blocked on the front. Do not pay one penny. If a publisher asks you for money, forget them. It is not the way things should be done.

Subsidy publishing

This is the half-legitimate brother of the vanity press. Here, authors of completed books, often poets, help out the publisher by providing some (or all) of the initiation costs with the idea that they will subsequently share any profits. The system has a long history. Dickens did it, as did Jane Austen, and so too did poets T.S. Eliot and R.S. Thomas. In the world of small presses, it is a common practice but potential participants should take care. Genuine self-publishing is almost always a cheaper alternative.

If you are approached for money in this context, it is imperative to check the publisher's credentials carefully. Look at their list and get in touch with one or more of their authors. Find out how the deal worked for them. Ask about reputations at your local library and bookshop. The kind of money involved can run into thousands. Further information on the whole rolling scam can be found in Johnathon Clifford's *The Vanity Press & The Proper Poetry Publishers* (27 Mill Road, Fareham, Hampshire). In the wake of this investigation, a number of newspapers have suspended vanity press advertisements and the Advertising Standards Institute have issued guidelines.

Regional anthologies

A recent innovation has been the regional or thematic poetry anthology to which contributors are attracted by either classified advertising or, more commonly, features in local newspapers. *County Durham In Poetry*, *Wah Hey Nottinghamshire* and *Poetry Now West Midlands* are typical titles. Progress in printing technology has considerably reduced the price of typeset, short-run paperbacks and made it possible now for bulky anthologies to be produced with ease. Contributors to these books do not pay for inclusion and indeed may even be vaguely offered some sort of future share in royalties 'should the title sell well enough'. They are not, however, offered complimentary contributors' copies and this is the fulcrum on which the operation turns. If your poetry appears in print, possibly for the first time, then the chances are you will buy, and usually more than one copy. Naturally publishers exploit this tendency by cramming in as many contributors as possible, always opting for the shorter poem. This is not a vanity operation by any means. No one is actually being ripped off nor are the publishers raking in exorbitant profits. But the literary achievement of appearing in one of these books is questionable. In mitigation it must be said, though, that for some people this will be a much needed beginning and for others the only success they are ever going to get.

The listings

None of the lists of addresses which follow are exhaustive. Publishers come and go with amazing frequency. There will always be the brand new press on the look out for talent and the projected magazine desperate for contributions. For up to the minute information, check some of the **Organisations of Interest To Poets** in the lists which follow. Poetry has a huge market. It pays to keep your ear to the ground.

Commercial publishers carrying contemporary poetry

See main article. For addresses, see **UK Publishers**

The specialists

See main article. For addresses, see **UK Publishers** and **Poetry Presses**

Poetry Presses

Active in Airtime See also **Active in Airtime** magazine, *Ralph Hawkins*, 24 Regent Road, Brightlingsea, Essex CO7 0NL.

Acumen Publications See also **Acumen** magazine, *Patricia Oxley*, 6 The Mount, High Furzeham, Brixham, Devon TQ5 8QY

Agenda Editions See also **Agenda** magazine, *William Cookson & others*, 5 Cranbourne Court, Albert Bridge Road, London SW11 4PE

Aireings Press See also **Aireings** magazine, *Jean Barker*, 24 Brudenell Road, Leeds, West Yorks LS6 1BD

Akros Publications *Duncan Glen*, 18 Warrender Park Terrace, Edinburgh EH9 1EF

Allardyce, Barnett, Publishers *Anthony Barnett*, 14 Mount Street, Lewes, East Sussex BN7 1HL

Aloes Books *Jim Pennington & others*, 110 Mountview Road, London N4 4JH

Alun Books (includes **Goldleaf & Barn Owl Press**) *Sally Jones*, 3 Crown Street, Port Talbot, West Glamorgan SA13 1BG

Amazing Colossal Press *Maureen Richardson*, 4 Gretton Road, Mapperley, Nottingham NG3 5JT

Amra Imprint *Bill Griffiths*, 21 Alfred Street, Seaham, Co. Durham SR7 7LH

Anarcho Press *Stan Trevor*, 30 Greenhill, Hampstead High Street, London NW3 5UA

Anchor Press See also **Poetry Now** and **Rhyme Arrival** magazines, *Ian Walton*, 1–2 Wainman Road, Woodston, Peterborough, Cambs PE2 7BU

Ankle Books 153 Gwydir Street, Cambridge CB1 2LJ

Anvil Press Poetry See under **UK Publishers**

Appliance Books *Tabitha Webb*, 1 Bolton Lane, Ipswich, Suffolk 1PX 2BX

Arc Publications See under **UK Publishers**

Arrival Press Also **Poetry Now** magazine, 1–2 Wainman Road, Woolston, Peterborough, Cambs PE2 7BU

Astrapost Press *Eric Ratcliffe*, 7 The Towers, Stevenage, Herts SG1 1HE

Atlas Press *Alastair Brotchie*, BCM Atlas Press, London WC1N 3XX

Aural Images *Alan White*, 5 Hamilton Street, Astley Bridge, Bolton, Greater Manchester BL1 6RT

Avalanche Books *Deborah Gaye*, 125 Derricke Road, Stockwood, Bristol

Aylesford Press *D. A. Ashton*, 158 Moreton Road, Upton, Wirral, Cheshire LA9 4NZ

Bander-Snatch Books *Graham Holter*, 6 Highgrove, 63 Carlisle Road, Eastbourne, East Sussex BN20 7BN

BB Books See also **Global Tapestry Journal**, *Dave Cunliffe*, Springbank, Longsight Road, Copster Green, Blackburn, Lancs BB1 9EU

Bedlam Press *David Moody*, Church Green House, Old Church Lane, Pateley Bridge, Harrogate, North Yorks HG3 5LZ

Benjamin Press, The *Douglas Clark*, 69 Hillcrest Drive, Bath, Avon BA2 1HD

Beyond the Cloister *Hugh Hellicar*, Flat 1, 14 Lewes Crescent, Brighton, East Sussex

Big Little Poem Books *Robert Richardson*, 3 Park Avenue, Melton Mowbray, Leics LE13 0JB

Black Cygnet Press *A. D. Burnett*, 33 Hastings Avenue, Merry Oaks, Durham DH1 3QG

Black Gate Press, The *John Spence*, 25 York Close, Cramlington, Northumberland NE23 9TN

Blackstaff Press 3 Galway Park, Dundonald BT16 0AN, N. Ireland

Blaxland Family Press *John Jarrett*, 12 Matthews Road, Taunton, Somerset TA1 4NH

Bloodaxe Books Ltd See under **UK Publishers**

Blue Cage See also **Blue Cage** magazine, 98 Bedford Road, Birkdale, Southport, Merseyside PR8 4HL

Blue Nose Press 32 Northolme Road, London N5

Bogle-l'ouverture Press Ltd *Valerie Bloom*, PO Box 2186, London W13 9ZQ

Bradgate Press See also **Poetry Digest** magazine *Maureen Forrest*, 28 Stainsdale Green, Whitwick, Leics LE67 5PW

Brentham Press *Margaret Tims*, 40 Oswald Road, St Albans, Herts AL1 3AQ

Carcanet Press See also **PN Review**, and under **UK Publishers**

Carnival Press *Jill Franklin*, 32 Somerset Road, Erdington, Birmingham B23 6NG

Carnivorous Arpeggio (Press) *George Messo*, 329 Beverley Road, Hull, Humberside HU5 1LD

Chapman Press See also **Chapman** magazine, *Joy M Hendry*, 4 Broughton Place, Edinburgh EH1 3RX

The Chrysalis Press 11 Convent Close, Kenilworth, Warwickshire CV8 2FQ

Clocktower Press 27 Alfred Street, Stromness, Orkney KW16 3DF

Cloud *Michael Thorp*, 48 Biddleston Road, Heaton, Newcastle-upon-Tyne NE6 5SL

Coelecanth Press *Maurice Scully*, 21 Corrovorrin Grove, Ennis, Co Claire, Eire

The Collective *John Jones*, Penlanlas Farm, Llantilio Pertholey, Y-Fenni, Gwent NP7 7HN

Commonword See also **Crocus** *Cathy Bolton*, Cheetwood House, 21 Newton Street, Manchester M1 1FZ

Community of Poets Press 147 Old Dover Road, Canterbury, Kent CT1 3NX

Company of Poets Books Oversteps, Froude Road, Salcombe, S. Devon TQ8 8LH

Crabflower Pamphlets See also **Frogmore Papers** magazine and press, *Jeremy Page*, 42 Morehall Avenue, Folkstone, Kent CT19 4EF

Credo Publishing *Annie Manning*, 45 Melstead Road, Boxmoor, Hemel Hempstead, Herts HP1 1SX

Crescent Moon Publishing and **Joe's Press** See under **Small Presses**

Crocus *Cathy Bolton*, Cheetwood House, 21 Newton Street, Manchester M1 1FZ

Curlew Press See also **Curlew** magazine, *P. J. Precious*, Hare Cottage, Kettlesing, Harrogate, North Yorks HG3 2LB

Cwm Nedd Press *Robert King*, 16 Rhydhir, Neath Abbey, Neath, West Glamorgan SA10 7HP

Dangaroo Press See also **Kunapipi** magazine, PO Box 20, Hebden Bridge, West Yorks HX7 5UZ

Christopher Davies (Publishers) Ltd See under **UK Publishers**

Day Dream Press See also **Haiku Quarterly**, *Kevin Bailey*, 39 Exmouth Street, Swindon, Wilts SN1 3PU

Dedalus Press/Peppercanister Books *John F. Deane*, 24 The Heath, Cypress Downs, Dublin 6, Eire

Diamond Press *G. Godbert*, 5 Berners Mansions, 34–36 Berners Street, London W1P 3DA

Diehard Publishers *Ian King & others*, Grindles Bookshop, 3 Spittal Street, Edinburgh EH3 9DY

Direction Poetry Companion label to **Direction Music**, *Peter Harrison*, 28 Nant y Felin, Pentraeth, Anglesey LL75 8UY

Dissident Editions *Frederik Wolff*, 71 Ballyculter Road, Loughkeelan, Downpatrick, County Down BT30 7BD

Dog and Bone Publishers 175 Queen Victoria Drive, Scotstown, Glasgow G12 9BP

Dragonheart Press See also **Living Poets** magazine, *Sean Woodward*, 11 Menin Road, Allestree, Derby DE22 2NL

Enitharmon Press See under **UK Publishers**

Equinox Press Sinodun House, Shalford, Braintree, Essex CM7 5MW

Eros Press See also **Interactions** magazine, *Andrew Yardwell*, PO Box 250, St Helier, Jersey JE4 8TZ, Channel Islands

Farrago Collective Press 106 High Street, West Wickham, Kent BR4 0ND

Feather Books See under **Small Presses**

57 Productions *Paul Besley*, 57 Effingham Road, Lee Green, London SE12 8NT

Fire River Poets 19 Green Close, Holford, Bridgwater, Somerset TA5 1SB

First Time Publications See also **First Time** magazine, *Josephine Austin*, 4 Burdett Place, George Street, Hastings TN34 3ED

Flambard Press *Peter Elfed Lewis*, 4 Mitchell Avenue, Jesmond, Newcastle-upon-Tyne NE2 3LA

Forest Books See under **UK Publishers**

Form Books *Harry Gilonis*, 42a Lowden Road, London SE24 0BH

Forward Press/New Fiction/Arrival Press See also **Poetry Now** and **Rhyme Arrival** magazines, *Ian Walton*, 1–2 Wainman Road, Woolston, Peterborough PE2 7BU

Fox Press/Winter Sweet Press *Beryl Bron*, Oak Tree, Main Road, Colden Common, Nr Winchester, Hants SO21 1TL

The Frogmore Press See also **The Frogmore Papers** magazine, *Jeremy Page*, 42 Morehall Avenue, Folkestone, Kent CT19 4EF

Gallery Press *Peter Fallon*, Loughcrew, Oldcastle, County Meath, Eire

Gill's Verse Publications *Gillian Rose Peace*, 25 Braden Road, Penn, Wolverhampton WV4 4JR

Golgonooza Press *Brian Keeble*, 3 Cambridge Drive, Ipswich, Suffolk IP2 9EP

Gomer Press/Gwasg Gomer See under **UK Publishers**

Green Lantern Press 9 Milner Road, Wisbech, Cambs PE12 2LR

Greylag Press *Jim Vollmar*, 2 Grove Street, Higham Ferrars, Rushden, Northants NN10 8HX

Gruffyground Press *Anthony Baker*, Ladram, Sidcot, Winscombe, Somerset BS25 1PW

Hangman Books *Jack Ketch*, 2 May Road, Rochester, Kent ME1 2HY

Hard Pressed Poetry *Billy Mills*, 1st Floor, 80 Ashford Road, Eastbourne, East Sussex BN21 3TE

Hastings Arts Pocket Press/Pickpockets *Margaret Rose*, 25 St Mary's Terrace, Hastings, East Sussex TN34 3LS

Headland Publications *Gladys Mary Coles*, Ty Coch, Galltegfa, Ruthin, Clwyd LL15 2AR

Hearing Eye *John Rety*, Box 1, 99 Torriano Avenue, London NW5 2RX

Here Now *Tom Kelly*, 69 Wood Terrace, Jarrow, Tyne & Wear NE32 5LU

Hillside Books See also **Linear A** magazine, *Johan de Wit*, Flat 1, Sylva Court, 81 Putney Hill, London SW15 3NX

Hippopotamus Press See also **Outposts Poetry Quarterly** *Roland John*, 22 Whitewell Road, Frome, Somerset BA11 4EL

Honno *Elin Ap Hywel* Alisa Craig, Heol y Cawl, Dinas Powys, S. Glamorgan CF6 4AH

Hub Editions 11 The Ridgway, Flitwick, Beds MK45 1DH

Hunter House – Anachoresis *J. E. Rutherford* 36 Lisburn Street, Hillsborough, Co Down BT26 4AH

I★D Books *Clive Hopwood*, Connah's Quay Library, High Street, Connah's Quay, Deside, Clwyd

Iron Press See also **Iron** magazine, *Peter Mortimer*, 5 Marden Terrace, Cullercoats, North Shields, Tyne & Wear NE30 4PD

Jackson's Arm Press See also **Sunk Island Review** (see under **Magazines**) *Michael Blackburn*, PO Box 74, Lincoln LN1 1QG

Joe's Press See also **Passion** magazine & **Crescent Moon Publishing** See under **Small Presses**

Jugglers Fingers Press See also **Uncompromising Positions** magazine, *Cheryl Wilkinson*, 92 Staneway, Leam Lane, Gateshead, Tyne & Wear NE10 8LS

K. T. Publications *Kevin Troop*, 16 Fane Close, Stamford, Lincs PE9 1HG

Katabasis *Dinah Livingstone*, 10 St Martin's Close, London NW1 0HR

Kerin Publishers *Irene & Keith Thomas*, 29 Glan yr Afon, Ebbw Vale, Gwent NP3 5NR

Kernow Poets Press *Bill Headdon*, 41 Harries Road, Tunbridge Wells, Kent TN2 3TW

King of Hearts *Aude Gotto*, 13–15 Fye Bridge Street, Norwich, Norfolk NR3 1LJ

Klinker Zoundz, *Ian Metcalf*, 10 Malvern House, Stamford Hill Esate, London N16 6RR

The KQBX Press *James Sale & others*, 16 Scotter Road, Poverstown, Bournemouth, Dorset BH7 6LY

The Lansdowne Press 33 Lansdowne Place, Hove, East Sussex BN3 1HF

Lapwing Publications *Dennis & Rene Greig*, 1 Ballysillan Drive, Belfast BT14 8HQ

Ligden Publishers *Jill Meredith*, 34 Lineacre Close, Grange Park, Swindon, Wilts SN5 6DA

Lobby Press *Richard Tabor*, Simonburn Cottage, Sutton Montis, Yeovil, Somerset BA22 7HF

Lomond Press *R. L. Cook*, Whitecraigs, Kinnesswood, Kinross KY13 7JN

Luath Press Ltd See under **Small Presses**

Lymes Press, The *Alex Crossley*, Greenfields, Agger Hill, Finney Green, Newcastle-under-Lyme, Staffs ST5 6AA

Magenta *Maggie O'Sullivan*, Middle Fold Farm, Colden, Heptonstall, Hebden Bridge, West Yorks HX7 7PG

Making Waves *Anthony Selbourne* PO Box 226, Guildford, Surrey GU3 1EW

Malfunction Press See also **Bardonni/Stopgap** magazine, *Peter E Presford*, Rose Cottage, 3 Tram Lane, Buckley, Clwyd

Mammon Press *Fred Beake*, 12 Dartmouth Avenue, Bath, Avon BA2 1AT

Mandeville Press *Peter Scupham & others*, Old Hall, Norwich Road, South Burlingham, Norfolk NR13 4EY

Many Press, The *John Welch*, 15 Norcott Road, London N16 7BJ

Mariscat Press *Hamish White & others*, 3 Mariscat Road, Glasgow G41 4ND

Marvell Press c/o 2 Kelly Gardens, Calstock, Cornwall PL18 9SA

Menard Press *Anthony Rudolf*, 8 The Oaks, Woodside Avenue, London N12 8AR

Moschatel Press *Thomas A Clarke,* Iverna Cottage, Rockness Hill, Nailsworth, Gloucester

Mr Pillow's Press See also **Apostrophe** magazine, *Diana Andersson*, 41 Canute Road, Faversham, Kent ME13 8SH

Mudflat Press *M.U. Fiorillo*, 176 Clive Stret, Grangetown, Cardiff CF1 7JG

MidNAG Publications Leisure Department, Wansbeck Square, Ashington, Northumberland NE63 9XL

National Poetry Foundation See also
Pause magazine, *Johnathon Clifford & others*,
27 Mill Road, Fareham, Hants PO16 0TH

New Albion Press *David Geall*, 42 Overhill
Road, London SE22 0PH

New Departures *Michael Horovitz*, Piedmont,
Bisley, Glos GL6 7BU

New Hope International *Gerald England*,
20 Werneth Avenue, Gee Cross, Hyde,
Cheshire SK14 5NL

New River Project See also **Writers Forum**
& And magazines, *Bob Cobbing & others*,
89a Petherton Road, London N5 2QT

Next Step See also **Wits End** magazine, *Jean
Turner*, 27 Pheasant Close, Winnersh,
Wokingham, Berks RG11 5LS

North and South *Peterjon & Yasmin Skelt*,
23 Egerton Road, Twickenham, Middx
TW2 7SL

Northern House Poets See also **Stand**
magazine, 19 Haldane Terrace, Newcastle-
upon-Tyne NE2 3AN

Oasis Books See also **Oasis** magazine, *Ian
Robinson*, 12 Stevenage Road, London
SW6 6ES

Odyssey Poets See also **Odyssey** magazine
Derrick Woolf, Coleridge Cottage, Nether
Stowey, Somerset TA5 1NQ

Old Style Press *Frances and Nicholas
McDowell*, Catchmays Court, Llandogo,
Nr Monmouth, Gwent NP45 4TN

Oleander Press, The *Philip Ward*,
17 Stansgate Avenue, Cambridge CB2 2QZ

Oscars Press *Peter Daniels*, BM Oscars,
London WC1N 3XX

Other Press, The *Frances Presley*,
19b Marriott Road, London N4 3QN

Peepal Tree Press See under **Small Presses**

Pennine Pens *Chris Ratcliffe*, 32 Windsor
Road, Hebden Bridge, West Yorkshire
HX7 8LF

Pennyworth Press *Douglas Evans*,
64 Rosehill Park, Emmer Green, Reading,
Berks RG4 8XF

Permanent Press *Robert & Vas Dias*,
5B Compton Avenue, London N1 2XD

Peterloo Poets *Harry Chambers*, 2 Kelly
Gardens, Calstock, Cornwall PL18 9SA

Pig Press *Richard Caddel*, 7 Cross View
Terrace, Durham DH1 4JY

Pocket Prints *Florence Williams*, 425 Footscray
Road, New Eltham, London SE9 3UL

Poet and Printer *Alan Tarling*, 30 Grimsdyke
Road, Hatch End, Pinner, Middlesex
HA5 4PW

Poetical Histories *Peter Riley*, 27 Sturton
Street, Cambridge CB1 2QG

Poetry Wales Press See also **Seren Books**
and **Poetry Wales** magazine, *Mick Felton*,
First Floor, 2 Wyndham Street, Bridgend
CF31 1EF

Polygon Books See **Edinburgh University
Press** under **UK Publishers**

Polyptoton – Sea Dream Music *Keith
Dixon*, 236 Sebert Road, Forest Gate,
London E7 0NP

Precious Pearl Press See also **The People's
Poetry** magazine, *Peter Thompson*,
71 Harrow Crescent, Romford, Essex
RM3 7BJ

Press Upstairs, The *Giles Goodland*, 360
Cowley Road, Oxford OX4 2AG

Prest Roots Press *P. E. Larkin*, 34 Alpine
Court, Lower Ladyes Hills, Kenilworth ,
Warwickshire CV8 2GP

Pretani Press *Harris Adamson*, 78 Abbey
Street, Bangor, Co Down BT20 4JB,
N. Ireland

Priapus Press *John Cotton*, 37 Lombardy
Drive, Berkhamstead, Herts HP4 2LQ

Prospero Illustrated Poets Clarion
Publishing, Neatham Mill, Holybourne,
Alton, Hampshire GU24 4NP

Providence Press (Whitstable) *John &
Lesley Dench*, 22 Plough Lane, Swalecliffe,
Whitstable, Kent CT5 2NZ

Psychopoetica Publications See also
Psychopoetica magazine, *Geoff Lowe*,
Dept of Psychology, University of Hull,
Hull HU6 7RX

Queenscourt Publishing *David E. Cox*
1 Queens Court, Kenton Lane, Harrow,
Middlesex HA3 8RN

Ram Press *Catherine Dawson*, 42 Bradmore
Park Road, London W6 0DT

Raunchland Publications *John Mingay*,
2 Henderson Street, Kingseat, by
Dunfermline, Fife KY12 0TP

Raven Arts Press PO Box 1430, Finglass,
Dublin 11, Eire

Reality Street Editions *Ken Edwards &
others*, 4 Howard Court, Peckham Rye,
London SE15 3PH

Rebec Press 79 Bronwydd Road,
Carmarthen SA31 2AP

Red Sharks Press *Topher Mills*, 122 Clive
Street, Grangetown, Cardiff CF1 7JE

Redbeck Press *David Tipton*, 24 Aireville
Road, Frizinghall, Bradford, West Yorks
BD9 4HH

River Publishing Company, 39 Cumberland
Street, London SW1V 4LU

Road Books *Judy Kravis & others*, Garravagh,
Inniscarra, Co Cork, Eire

Rockingham Press *David Penman*, 11 Musley Lane, Ware, Herts SG12 7EN

Rump Books See also **Krax** magazine, *Andy Robson*, 63 Dixon Lane, Wortley, Leeds, West Yorks LS12 4RR

Satis *Matthew Mead*, Knoll Hill House, Ampleforth, West End, York YO6 4DU

Scratch Publications See also **Scratch** magazine, *Mark Robinson*, 9 Chestnut Road, Eaglescliffe, Stockton-on-Tees TS16 0BA

Seren Books See also **Poetry Wales Press** and **Poetry Wales** magazine, *Mick Felton*, First Floor, 2 Wyndham Street, Bridgend, Mid Glamorgan CF31 1EF

Shearsman Books See also **Shearsman** magazine, *Tony Frazer*, 47 Dayton Close, Plymouth, Devon PL6 5DX

Shell Press See also **Unicorn** magazine, *Alex Warner*, 12 Milton Avenue, Millbrook, Stalybridge, Cheshire SK15 3HB

Ship of Fools See also **Pages** magazine, *Robert Sheppard*, 239 Lessingham Avenue, London SW17 8NQ

Shoestring Press 19 Devonshire Avenue, Beeston, Nottingham NG9 1BS

Skoob Books Publishing Ltd See under **UK Publishers**

Slow Dancer Press *John Harvey*, Flat 2, 59 Parliament Hill, London NW3 2TB

Smith/Doorstop Books See also **The North** magazine, *Peter Sansom & others*, The Studio, Byram Arcade, Westgate, Huddersfield, West Yorks HD1 1ND

Sol Publications See also **Sol Poetry Magazine**, *Malcolm E. Wright*, 58 Malvern, Coleman Street, Southend on Sea, Essex SS2 5AD

South Manchester Poets *Dave Tarrant*, 122 Peterburgh Road, Edgeley Park, Stockport SK3 9RB

Spanner Press See also **Spanner** magazine, *Allen Fisher*, 14 Hopton Road, Hereford HR1 1BE

Spectacular Diseases See also **Spectacular Diseases** magazine, *Paul Green*, 83b London Road, Peterborough, Cambridgeshire PE2 9BS

Spike Press 57 Spencer Avenue, Earlsdon, Coventry CV5 6NQ

Staple First Editions See also **Staple** magazine, Tor Cottage, 387 Beverley Road, Hull, N. Humbs HU5 1LS

Stingy Artist Book Co. *Bernard Hemensley*, 85 Goldcroft Road, Weymouth, Dorset DT4 0EA

Street Editions See **Reality Street Editions**

Stride Publications See also **Taxus Press** *Rupert Loydell*, 11 Sylvan Road, Exeter, Devon EX4 6EW

Swansea Poetry Workshop *Nigel Jenkins*, 124 Overland Road, Mumbles, Swansea SA3 4EU

Talus Editions See also **Talus** magazine, *Hanne Bramness & others*, Dept of English, King's College, Strand, London WC2R 2LS

Taranis Books See also **West Coast Magazine** *Kenny MacKenzie*, 2 Hugh Miller Place, Edinburgh EH3 5JG

Taurus Press of Willow Dene *Paul Peter Piech*, 11 Limetree Way, Danygraig, Porthcawl, Mid Glam CF36 5AU

Taxus Press See also **Stride Publications** 11 Sylvan Road, Exeter, Devon EX4 6EW

Tenormen Press, The See also **Ostinato** magazine, *Stephen C. Middleton*, PO Box 552, London N8 7SZ

Triple Cat Publishing *R. E. Field*, 3 Back Lane Cottages, Bucks Horn Oak, Farnham, Surrey GU10 4LN

Triumph House *Ian Walton*, 1–2 Wainman Road, Woodston, Peterborough PE2 7BU

Tuba Press See also **Tuba** magazine, *Peter Ellison*, Tunley Cottage, Tunley, Nr Cirencester, Glos GL7 6LW

Twist In The Tail, A *Paul Cookson*, PO Box 25, Retford, Nottinghamshire DN22 7ER

Ulsterman Pamphlets See also **The Honest Ulsterman** magazine, *Tom Clyde*, 14 Shaw Street, Belfast BT4 1PT

Underground Press *John Evans*, 9 Laneley Terrace, Maesycoed, Pontypridd, Mid Glamorgan CF37 1ER

Ure Group Press *Gary Boswell & others*, 22 Moss Lane, Parr, St Helens, Lancs WA9 3SB

Vennel Press See also **Gairfish** magazine, *Richard Price*, 8 Richmond Road, Staines, Middlesex TW18 2AB

Ver Poets *May Badman*, Haycroft, 61/63 Chiswell Green Lane, St Albans, Herts AL2 3AL. See also under **Professional Associations**

Vigil Publications See also **Vigil** magazine, *John Howard-Greaves*, 12 Priory Mead, Bruton, Somerset BA10 0DZ

Wanda Publications See also **Doors** and **South** magazines, Word and Action, 61 West Borough, Wimborne, Dorset BH21 1LX

Weatherlight Press *David Keefe*, 34 Cornwallis Crescent, Clifton, Bristol, Avon BS8 4PH

Wellsweep Press *John Cayley*, 1 Grove End House, 150 Highgate Road, London NW5 1PD

Westwords See also **Westwords** magazine, *Dave Woolley*, 15 Trelawney Road, Peverall, Plymouth, Devon PL3 4JS

White Box Publications *James Turner*, 114 Monks Road, Exeter EX4 7BQ

Windows Publications See also **Windows Poetry Broadsheet** *Heather Brett*, Nature Haven, Legaginney, Ballinagh, Cavan, Eire

Wolfskin Press *Laura Barnes*, Flat 2, 52 Tresillian Road, Brockley, London SE4 1YB

Writers Forum See also **And** magazine & **New River Project** *Bob Cobbing*, 89a Petherton Road, London N5 2QT

Wysiwyg Chapbooks *Ric Hool*, 89 Abertillery Road, Blaina, Gwent

Yorkshire Art Circus Ltd School Lane, Glass Houghton, Castleford, W. Yorks WF10 4QH

Poetry magazines

Many poetry magazines have links with or are produced by companies listed in **Poetry Presses**.

Active in Airtime *Ralph Hawkins & others*, 24 Regent Road, Brightlingsea, Essex CO7 0Nl

Acumen See also **Acumen Publications**, *Patricia Oxley*, 6 The Mount, Higher Furzeham, Brixham, Devon TQ5 8QY

Agenda See also **Agenda Editions** *William Cookson*, 5 Cranbourne Court, Albert Bridge Road, London SW11 4PE

Aireings See also **Aireings Press** *Jean Barker*, 3/24 Brudenell Road, Leeds, West Yorks LS6 1BD

Ambit *Martin Bax*, 17 Priory Gardens, London N6 5QY

And See also **Writers Forum** *Bob Cobbing & others*, 89a Petherton Road, London N5 2QT

Angel Exhaust *Andrew Duncan & others*, 27 Sturton Street, Cambridge, Cambridgeshire CB1 2QG

Anthem *Howard Roake*, 36 Cyril Avenue, Bobbers Mill, Nottingham NG8 5BA

Apostrophe See also **Mr Pillows Press** *Diana Andersson*, Orton House, 41 Canute Road, Faversham, Kent ME13 8SH

Aquarius *Eddie S. Linden*, Flat 10, Room A, 116 Sutherland Avenue, Maida Vale, London W9

Arcadian, The *Mike Boland*, 30 Byron Court, Byron Road, Harrow, Middlesex HA1 1JT

Avon Literary Intelligencer 20 Byron Place, Clifton, Bristol, Avon BS8 1JT

Banshee, The *Rachel Fones*, 16 Rigby Close, Waddon Road, Croydon CR0 4JU

Bardonni/Stopgap/Songs See also **Malfunction Press** *Peter E. Presford*, Rose Cottage, 3 Tram Lane, Buckley, Clwyd

Bare Bones *Brian Tasker*, 16 Wren Close, Frome, Somerset

Bete Noire *John Osbourne*, American Studies Dept., The University of Hull, Cottingham Road, Hull, Humberside HU6 7RX

Blithe Spirit *Jackie Hardy*, Farnley Gate Farmhouse, Riding Mill, Northumberland NE44 6AA

Blue Cage *Paul Donnelly*, 98 Bedford Road, Birkdale, Southport, Merseyside PR8 4HL

Bogg *George Cairncross*, 31 Bellevue Street, Filey, N. Yorks YO14 9HU

Borderlines *Dave Bingham*, 20 Hodgebower, Ironbridge, Shropshire TF8 7QG

Bound Spiral *M. Petrucci*, Open Poetry Conventricle, 72 First Avenue, Bush Hill Park, Enfield EN1 1BW

Braquemard *David Allenby*, 20 Terry Street, Hull HU3 1UD

Bridge, The *James Mawer*, 112 Rutland Street, Grimsby DN32 7NF

Brimstone Signatures *Isabel Gillard*, St Lawrence Cottage, Sellman Street, Gnosall, Stafford ST20 0EP

Brink.e.journal *Alexis Kirke*, Alexis@zeus.sc.plym.ac.uk

Candelabrum Poetry Magazine *M. L. McCarthy*, 9 Milner Road, Wisbech, Cambridgeshire PE13 2LR

Carnival *Jill Franklin*, 693 Chester Road, Erdington, Birmingham B23 5TH

Cascando *Lisa Boardman*, PO Box 1499, London SW10 9TZ

Celtic Pen *Diarmuid O'Breaslain*, 36 Fruithill Park, Belfast B11 8GE

Cencrastus – The Curly Snake *Raymond Ross & others*, Unit 1, Abbeymount Techbase, 8 Easter Road, Edinburgh EH8 8EJ

Chapman See under **Magazines**

City Writings *David Wright*, 47 Thornbury Avenue, Shirley, Southampton SO1 5BZ

Cobweb *Peter Kenny* 7 Isis Court, Grove Park Road, London W4 3SA

Critical Quarterly *Brian Cox & others*, University of Strathclyde, Glasgow G1 1XH

Curlew See also **Curlew Press** *P. J. Precious*, Hare Cottage, Kettlesing, Harrogate, North Yorks HG3 2LR

D.A.M. (Disability Arts Magazine) *Roland Humphrey*, 10 Wood Lane, Great Coates, Grimsby DN37 9NH

Dandelion Arts Magazine *Jacqueline Gonzalez-Marina*, 24 Frosty Hollow, East Hunsbury, Northants NN4 0SY

Dial 174 *Joseph Hemmings*, 8 Higham Green, King's Lynn, Norfolk PE30 4RX

Distaff *J. Brice*, London Women's Centre, Wesley House, 4 Wild Court, Kingsway, London WC2

Dog *David Crystal*, 32b Breakspears Road, London SE4 1UW

Doors See also **Wanda Publications**, Word and Action, 61 West Borough, Wimborne, Dorset BH21 1LX

The Echo Room *Brendan Cleary*, 45 Bewick Court, Princess Square, Newcastle-upon-Tyne NE1 8HG

Eco-runes *D. O'Ruie*, 68b Fivey Road, Ballymoney BT53 8JH, N. Ireland

Edible Society 10 Lincoln Street, Brighton, East Sussex BN2 2UH

Edinburgh Review See under **Magazines**

Envoi *Roger Elkin*, 44 Rudyard Road, Biddulph Moor, Stoke-on Trent, Staffs ST8 7JN

Exile *Herbert Marr*, 8 Snow Hill, Clare, Suffolk CO10 8QF

Fatchance *Louise Hudson and others*, Lake Cottage, South Street, Sheepwash, Beaworthy, Devon EX21 5ND

Fire *Chris Ozzard & others*, 3 Holywell Mews, Holywell, Malvern, Worcs WR14 1LF

First Offense *T. Fletcher*, Syringa, The Street, Stodmarsh, Canterbury, Kent CT3 4BA

First Time See also **First Time Publications** *Josephine Austin*, 4 Burdett Place, George Street, Hastings, East Sussex TN34 3ED

Flaming Arrows *Leo Regan*, County Sligo V.E.C., Riverside, Sligo, Eire

Foolscap *Judi Benson*, 78 Friars Road, East Ham, London E6 1LL

Fragmente *Andrew Lawson & others*, 8 Hertford Street, Oxford OX4 3AJ

Freedom Rock *Mike Coleman*, 18 Sunningdale Avenue, Sale, Cheshire M33 2PH

Frogmore Papers, The See also **The Frogmore Press** *Jeremy Page*, 42 Morehall Avenue, Folkestone, Kent CT19 4EF

Full Moon *Barbara Parkinson*, Church Road, Killybegs, Co Donegal, Eire

Gairfish See also **Vennel Press**, *W. N. Herbert*, 34 Gillies Place, Dundee DD5 3LE

Gairm *Derek Thomson*, 29 Waterloo Street, Glasgow G2 6BZ

Global Tapestry Journal See also **BB Books** *Dave Cunliffe*, Spring Bank, Longsight Road, Copster Green, Blackburn, Lancs BB1 9EU

Good Society Review, The *Mary MacGregor*, Holman's Place, Butleigh, Glastonbury BA6 8SZ

Granite – new verse from Cornwall *Alan M. Kent*, South View, Wheal Bull, Foxhole, St Austell, Cornwall PL26 7UA

Grille *Simon Smith*, 53 Ormonde Court, Upper Richmond Road, Putney, London SW15 5TP

Haiku Quarterly See also **Daydream Press** *Kevin Bailey*, 39 Exmouth Street, Swindon, Wilts SN1 3PU

Handshake *John Francis Haines*, 5 Cross Farm, Station Road, Padgate, Warrington WA2 0QC

Headlock *Tony Charles*, The Old Zion Chapel, The Triangle, Somerton, Somerset TA11 6QP

Heart Throb Formerly **People to People** *Mike Palmer*, 95 Spencer Street, Birmingham B18 6DA

Honest Ulsterman, The See also **Ulsterman Pamphlets** *Tom Clyde*, 14 Shaw Street, Belfast BT4 1PT

Hjok Finnies Sanguines *Jim Inglis*, 8 Knockbain Road, Dingwall IV15 9NR

Interactions See also **Eros Press** *Diane M. Moore*, PO Box 250, St Helier, Jersey JE4 8TZ

Iota *David Holliday*, 67 Hady Crescent, Chesterfield, Derbys S41 0EB

Iron See also **Iron Press** *Peter Mortimer*, 5 Marden Terrace, Cullercoats, North Shields, Tyne & Wear NE30 4PD

Issue One/The Bridge See also **Eon Publications** *Ian Brocklebank*, 2 Tewkesbury Drive, Grimsby, South Humberside DN34 4TL

Krax See also **Rump Books** *Andy Robson*, 63 Dixon Lane, Wortley, Leeds, West Yorks LS12 4RR

Krino – the review *Gerald Dawe & others*, PO Box 65, Dun Laoghaire, Co. Dublin, Eire

Kunapipi See also **Dangaroo Press** *Anna Rutherford*, PO Box 20, Hebden Bridge, West Yorks HX7 5UZ

Lallans *David Purves*, 8 Strathalmond Road, Edinburgh EH4 8AD

Linear A *Johan de Wit*, Flat 1, Sylva Court, 81 Putney Hill, London SW15 3NX

Lines Review *Tessa Ransford*, Macdonald Publishing, Edgefield Street, Loanhead, Mid Lothian EH20 9SY

Link, The *David Pollard*, Brumus Management, PO Box 317, Hounslow, Middx TW3 2SD

Lit Up *Jeremy Rogers*, 8a Mill Street, Torrington, Devon EX38 8HQ

Living Poets – online ezine see also **Dragonheart Press** *Sean Woodward*, 11 Menin Road, Allestree, Derby DE22 2NL

London Magazine See under **Magazines**

Magpie's Nest *Bal Saini*, 176 Stoney Lane, Sparkhill, Birmingham B12 8AN

Mosaic *L Williamson* 16 Vale Close, Eastwood, Nottingham

Narvis *Robert Bush & others*, 211 Bedford Hill, London SW12 9HQ

Never Bury Poetry *Bettina Jones*, 30 Beryl Avenue, Tottington, Bury, Lancs BL8 3NF

New Departures/Poetry Olympics See also **New Departures** press, *Mike Horowitz*, Piedmont, Bisley, Stroud, Glos GL6 7BU

New Hope International *Gerald England*, 20 Werneth Avenue, Gee Cross, Hyde, Cheshire SK14 5NL

New Journal Time 95 *K. K. Facey*, 105 Kings Head Hill, London E4 7JG

New Poetry Quarterly *Simon Brittan*, 5 Stockwell, Colchester, Essex CO1 1HP

New Scottish Epoch *Neil Mathers*, 57 Murray Street, Montrose, Angus DD10 8JZ

New Welsh Review *Robin Reeves*, Chapter Arts Centre, Market Road, Canton, Cardiff CF5 1QE

Nineties Poetry *Graham Ackroyd*, 33 Lansdowne Place, Hove, E. Suusex BN3 1HF

North, The See **Smith/Doorstop Books** *Peter Sansom & Janet Fisher*, The Studio, Byram Arcade, Westgate, Huddersfield, West Yorks HD1 1ND

Northlight *Anne Thomson*, 136 Byres Road, Glasgow G12 8TD

Northwords *Tom Bryan*, 68 Strathkanaird, Ullapool, Rosshire IV26 2TN

Novocaine (Zdhu010@uk.ac.kd.cc.bay) 22 Wilderness Road, Mannamead, Plymouth, Devon PL3 4RN

Oasis See also **Oasis Books**, *Ian Robinson*, 12 Stevenage Road, Fulham, London SW6 6ES

Object Permanence *Robin Purves & others*, 121 Menock Road, Kingspark, Glasgow G44 5SD

Odyssey See also **Odyssey Poets** *D. Woolf*, Coleridge Cottage, Nether Stowey, Somerset TA5 1NQ

One *Wendy B Cardy*, 48 South Street, Colchester, Essex CO2 7BJ

Orbis *Mike Shields*, 199 The Long Shoot, Nuneaton, Warwickshire CV11 6JQ

Ostinato – Jazz and Jazz Poetry See also **Tenormen Press** *Stephen C. Middleton*, PO Box 522, London N8 7SZ

Otter *R. Skinner*, Little Byspock, Richmond Road, Exeter, Devon

Outposts See also **Hippopotamus Press** *Roland John*, 22 Whitewell Road, Frome, Somerset BA11 4EL

Oxford Poetry *Ian Sansom & others*, Magdalen College, Oxford OX1 4AU

Pages See also **Ship of Fools Press**, *Robert Sheppard*, 239 Lessingham Avenue, London SW17 8NQ

Paladin *Ken Morgan*, 66 Heywood Court, Tenby, Dyfed SA70 8BS

Parataxis: Modernism & Modern Writing *Drew Milne*, School of English Studies, Arts Building, University of Sussex, Falmer, Brighton BN1 9NQ

Passion See also **Crescent Moon Publishing** and **Joe's Press** *Jeremy Robinson*, 18 Chaddesley Road, Kidderminster, Worcs DY10 3AD

Pause See also **National Poetry Foundation** *Helen Robinson*, 27 Mill Road, Fareham, Hants PO16 0TH

Peace and Freedom *Paul Rance*, 17 Farrow Road, Whaplode Drove, Spalding, Lincs PE12 0TS

Pen Magazine, The *Pam Probert*, 15 Berwyn Place, Penlan, Swansea, West Glamorgan SA5 5AX

Pennine Platform *Brian Merrikin Hill*, Ingmanthorpe Hall, Farm Cottage, Wetherby, West Yorkshire LS22 5EQ

People's Poetry, The See also **Precious Pearl Press** *P. G. P. Thompson*, 71 Harrow Crescent, Romford, Essex RM3 7BJ

Planet – the Welsh Internationalist *John Barnie*, PO Box 44, Aberystwyth, Dyfed

PN Review See also **Carcanet Press** *Michael Schmidt*, 402–406 Corn Exchange Buildings, Manchester M4 3BQ

Poetry and Audience *Anthony Rowland*, School of English, University of Leeds, Leeds, West Yorks LS2 9JT

Poetry Digest See also **Bradgate Press** *Alan Forrest*, Bradgate Press, 28 Stainsdale Green, Whitwick, Leics LE67 5PW

Poetry Durham *David Hartnett & others* Dept of English Studies, University of Durham, Elvet Riverside, Durham DH1 3JT

Poetry Ireland Review Bermingham Tower, Upper Yard, Dublin Castle, Dublin, Eire

Poetry Life Magazine *Adrian Bishop*, 14 Pennington Oval, Lymington, Hampshire SO41 8BQ

Poetry London Newsletter *Leon Cych*, Box 4LF, London W1A 4LF

Poetry Manchester *Sean Boustead*, 13 Napier Street, Swinton, Manchester M27 0JQ

Poetry Nottingham *Martin Holroyd*, 39 Cavendish Road, Long Eaton, Nottingham NG10 4HY

Poetry Now See also **Arrival** and **Forward Presses** *Ian Walton*, 1–2 Wainman Road, Woolston, Peterborough, Cambs PE2 7BU

Poetry Review *Peter Forbes,* Poetry Society, 22 Betterton Street, London WC2H 9BU

Poetry Wales See also **Seren Books** *Richard Poole*, Glan-y-Werydd, Llandanwg, Harlech LL46 2SD

Poet's Voice, The Published with Univ Salzburg *Fred Beake*, 12 Dartmouth Avenue, Bath, Avon BA2 1AT

Pomes *Adrian Spendlow*, 23 Bright Street, York YO2 4XS

Premonitions *Tony Lee*, 13 Hazely Combe, Arreton, Isle of Wight PO30 3 AJ

Printer's Devil, The *Sean O'Brien & others*, Top Offices, 13a Western Road, Hove, East Sussex BN3 1AE

Psychopoetica See also **Psychopoetica Publications** *Geoff Lowe*, Dept. of Psychology, University of Hull, Hull HU6 7RX

Purge *Robert Hampson*, 88 Ashburnham Road, London NW10 5SE

Purple Patch *Geoff Stevens*, 8 Beaconview House, Charlemont Farm, West Bromwich B71 3PL

Quartos See under **Magazines**

Ramraid Extraordinaire *Kerry Sowerby*, 17 King's Avenue, Leeds LS6 1QS

Reflections PO Box 70, Sunderland SR1 1DU

Rhyme Arrival See also **Poetry Now** and **Forward Press** *Trudi Ramm*, 1–2 Wainman Road Woolston, Peterborough, Cambs PE2 7BU

Rialto, The *John Wakeman & others*, 32 Grosvenor Road, Norwich, Norfolk NR2 2PZ

Riot of Emotions, A *Andrew Cocker*, Dark Diamonds Pubs, PO Box HK 31, Leeds, West Yorks LS11 9XN

Rivet 74 Walton Drive, High Wycombe, Buckinghamshire HP13 6TT

Rustic Rub (formerly **And What Of Tomorrow**) *Jay Woodman*, 14 Hillfield, Selby, N. Yorkshire YO8 0ND

Scratch See also **Scratch Publications** *Mark Robinson*, 9 Chestnut Road, Eaglescliffe, Stockton-on-Tees TS16 0BA

Sepia *Colin David Webb*, Knill Cross House, Nr Anderton Road, Millbrook, Torpoint, Cornwall PL10 1DX

Shearsman See also **Shearsman Books** *Tony Frazer*, 47 Dayton Close, Plymouth, Devon PL6 5DX

Sheffield Thursday *E. A. Markham,* School of Cultural Studies, Sheffield Hallam University, 36 Collegiate Crescent, Sheffield S10 2BP

Smiths Knoll *Roy Blackman & others* 49 Church Road, Little Glemham, Woodbridge, Suffolk 1P13 0BJ

Smoke *Dave Ward*, The Windows Project, 40 Canning Street, Liverpool L8 7NP

Sol Poetry Magazine See also **Sol Publications** *Malcolm E. Wright*, 58 Malvern, Coleman Street, Southend-on-Sea, Essex SS2 5AD

South See also **Wanda Publications** Word and Action, 61 West Borough, Wimborne, Dorset BH21 1LX

Southfields *Raymond Friel & others*, 98 Gresenhall Road, Southfields, London SW18 5QJ

Spanner *Allen Fisher*, 14 Hopton Road, Hereford HR1 1BE

Spear *Jacqueline Jones* 2 Fforest Road, Lampeter, Dyfed

Spectacular Diseases See also **Spectacular Diseases** press *Paul Green*, 83b London Road, Peterborough, Cambs PE2 9BS

Spokes *Alister & Gine Wisker*, 319a Hills Road, Cambridge CB2 2QT

Stand See also **Northern House Publications** *Jon Silkin & others*, 179 Wingrove Road, Newcastle-upon-Tyne NE4 9DA

Staple See also **Staple First Editions** *Bob Windsor*, Tor Cottage, 81 Cavendish Road, Matlock, Derbys DE4 3HD

Steeple, The *Patrick Cotter*, Three Spires Press, Killeen, Blackrock Village, Cork City, Eire

Sunk Island Review See also **Jackson's Arm Press** *Michael Blackburn*, PO Box 74, Lincoln LN1 1QG

Super-Trouper *Andrew Savage*, 81 Castlerigg Drive, Burnley, Lancs BB12 8AT

Superreal – Reflexes of the Future *Patricia Scanlan*, 34 Waldemar Avenue, Fulham, London SW6 5NA

Swansea Review, The *Glyn Pursglove*, Dept of English, University College Swansea, Singleton Park, Swansea SA2 8PP

Symphony Bemerton Press, 9 Hamilton Gardens, London NW8 9PU

Tabla *S. J. Ellis & others*, PO Box 93, Lancaster, Lancs LA1 3HB

Talus See also **Talus Editions** *Marzia Balzani & others*, Dept of English, King's College, Strand, London WC2R 2LS

Tandem *Michael J. Woods*, 13 Stephenson Road, Barbourne, Worcester WR1 3EB

Tears In The Fence *David Caddy*, 38 Hod View, Stourpaine, Nr Blandford Forum, Dorset DT11 8TN

Tees Valley Writer *Derek Gregory*, 57 The Avenue, Linthorpe, Middlesborough, Cleveland TS5 6QU

10th Muse *Andrew Jordan*, 33 Hartington Road, Southampton SO2 OEW

Terrible Work *Tim Allen*, 21 Overston Gardens, Mannamead, Plymouth PL3 5BX

Third Alternative, The *Andy Cox*, 5 St Martin's Lane, Witcham, Ely, Cambs CB4 2LB

Threads *Geoff Lynas*, 32 Irvin Avenue, Saltburn, Cleveland TS12 1QH

Thumbscrew PO Box 657, Oxford OX2 6PH

Tops *Anthony Cooney*, Rose Cottage, 17 Hadassah Grove, Liverpool L17 8XH

Tuba See also **Tuba Press** *Charles Graham*, Tunley Cottage, Tunley, Nr Cirencester, Glos GL7 6LW

Uncompromising Positions See also **Jugglers Fingers Press** *Cheryl Wilkinson* 92 Staneway, Leam Lane, Gateshead, Tyne & Wear NE10 8LS

Under Surveillance *Eddie Harriman* 60 Arnold Street, Brighton BN2 2XT

Unicorn See also **Shell Press** *Alex Warner*, 12 Milton Avenue, Millbrook, Stalybridge, Cheshire SK15 3HB

Various Artists *Tony Lewis Jones*, 65 Springfield Avenue, Horfield, Bristol, Avon BS7 9QS

Verse *Robert Crawford & others*, School of English, University of St Andrews, St Andrews, Fife KY16 9AL

Vigil *John Howard-Greaves*, 12 Priory Mean, Bruton, Somerset BA10 0DZ

West Coast Magazine See also **Taranis Books** *Joe Murray*, EM-DEE Productions, Unit 7, 29 Brand Street, Glasgow G51 1DN

Westwords *Dave Wooley*, 15 Trelawney Road, Peverall, Plymouth, Devon PL3 4JS

Weyfarers *Margaret Palin*, Guildford Poets Press, Hilltop Cottage, 9 White Rose Lane, Woking, Surrey GU22 7JA

Wide Skirt, The *Geoff & Jeanette Hattersley*, 28 St Helen's Street, Elsecar, Barnsley, South Yorks, S74 8BH

Windows Poetry Broadsheet See also **Windows Publications** *Heather Brett & others*, Nature Haven, Legaginney, Ballinagh, Cavan, Eire

Wits End See also **Next Step** press, *Jean Turner*, 27 Pheasants Close, Winnersh, Wokingham, Berks RG11 5LS

Wordsworth *Alaric Sumner*, Simonsbury Cottage, Sutton Montis, Yeovil, Somerset BA22 7HF

Working Titles *Rachel Bentham & others*, The Hollies, 29 St Martin's Road, Knowle, Bristol, Avon BS4 2NQ

Writer's Viewpoint PO Box 514, Eastbourne, E. Sussex BN23 6RE

Writing Women *Linda Anderson & others*, Unit 14, Hawthorn House, Forth Banks, Newcastle-upon-Tyne NE1 3SG

Yellow Crane, The Flat 6, 23 Richmond Crescent, Roath, Cardiff CF2 3AH

Zimmerframe Pileup *Stephen Jessener*, Loose Hand Press, 54 Hillcrest Road, Walthamstow, London E17 4AP

Zone – The last word in sf, The *Tony Lee*, 13 Hazely Combe, Arreton, Isle of Wight PO30 3AJ

Organisations of interest to poets

A survey of some of the societies, groups and other bodies in the UK which may be of interest to practising poets. Organisations not listed should send details of themselves to the editor, 45 Islington Park Street, London N1 1QB to facilitate inclusion in future editions.

Apples & Snakes

Unit A11, Hatcham Mews Business Centre, Hatcham Mews Park, London SE14 5QA
☎0171 639 9656

Contact *Steve Tasane, Ruth Harrison, Andrea Smith, Ben Raikes*

A unique, independent promotional organisation for poetry and poets – promoting poetry as an innovative and popular medium and cross-cultural activity. A&S organises an annual programme of over 150 events (including their London season that actively pushes new voices), tours, residencies and festivals, and operates a Poets-in-Education Scheme and a non-profit booking agency for poets.

The Arvon Foundation

See under **Professional Associations**.

The Association of Little Presses

See under **Professional Associations**.

The British Haiku Society

Sinodun, Shalford, Braintree, Essex CM7 5HN
☎01371 851097

Secretary *David Cobb*

Formed in 1990. Promotes the appreciation and writing within the British Isles of haiku, senryu, tanka and renga, by way of tutorials, workshops, exchange of poems, critical comment and information. It publishes a quarterly journal, *Blithe Spirit*, and administers the annual James W. Hackett Award for haiku.

The Eight Hand Gang

5 Cross Farm, Station Road, Padgate, Warrington WA2 0QG

Secretary *John F. Hanes*

An association of SF poets. Publishes *Handshake*, a newsletter of poetry and information, available free in exchange for a s.a.e.

The Little Magazine Collection and Poetry Store

Housed at University College London Library, these are the fruits of Geoffrey Soar and David Miller's interest in UK alternative publishing, with a strong emphasis on poetry. The Little Magazines Collection runs to over 3500 titles mainly in the more experimental and avant-garde areas. The Poetry Store consists of over 11,000 small press items, mainly from the '60s onwards, again with some stress on experimental work. In addition, there are reprints of classic earlier little magazines, from Symbolism through to the present. Anyone who is interested can consult the collections, and it helps if you have some idea of what you want to see. Bring evidence of identity for a smooth ride. The collections can be accessed by visiting the Manuscripts and Rare Books Room at University College in Gower Street, London WC1E 6BT, between 10.00 a.m. and 5.00 p.m. on weekdays. (Tel: 0171–380 7796). Most items are available on inter-library loans.

The Living Poets Society

Dragonheart Press, 11 Menin Road, Allestree, Derby DE22 2NL

Secretary *Sean Woodward*

Established to encourage poets of any age and location to share their work through the medium of electronic mail. Membership benefits include access to the electronic journal *Living Poets* and the right to submit material for inclusion, free entry in the *Living Poets Directory* and access to various e-mail poetry work in progress and comment portfolios. Membership costs £10 (free to secondary schools and poets under 16).

The National Convention Of Poets And Small Presses

Kirklees Cultural Services, Red Doles Lane, Huddersfield HD2 1YF
☎01484 513808   Fax 01484 513901

Literature   Development   Coordinator *David Morley*

An accessible, some might say disorganised, weekend jamboree of writers and poetry publishers, held at a different venue each year. The amateur status of the event is undisputed but it can be good fun for those with enough stamina to last out the marathon readings. There is no central organising committee – bids to host future conventions being made in person at the event itself. So far it has visited Liverpool, Hastings, Corby, Dartford, Stamford, Norwich, North Shields, Exeter, Stockton-on-Tees and Middlesborough. Write for information on the next convention.

National Poetry Foundation
27 Mill Road, Fareham, Hants PO16 0TH
☎01329 822218

The rather grand-sounding title for the charitable poetry organisation (Registered Charity No: 283032) founded by Johnathon Clifford and administered by a board of trustees from the address above. With the financial assistance of Rosemary Arthur, who has so far put over £20,000 into the kitty, the NPF attempts to encourage new writers through a criticism scheme and a series of rather well produced poetry books. Subscription costs £20 which, in addition, gives members access to *Pause*, the organisation's internal magazine. The NPF has a strong interest in the professional poetry recital as a fund raising device for the furtherance of its work. Eight small mags and a number of individual poets have to date benefited from NPF financial aid. Grants are small, unrenewable and directed at that sector of the poetry community traditionally ignored by other bodies. A good history of the NPF, together with information on poetry and the poetry scene can be found in Johnathon Clifford's self-published *Metric Feet & Other Gang Members* available from the same address.

Northern Poetry Library
Central Library, The Willows, Morpeth, Northumberland NE61 1TA
☎01670 511156/512385   Fax 01670 518012

Membership available to everyone in Cleveland, Cumbria, Durham, Northumberland and Tyne & Wear. Associate membership available for all outside the region. Over 13,000 books and magazines for loan including virtually all poetry published in the UK since 1968. Access to English Poetry, the full text database of all English Poetry from 600–1900. Postal lending available too.

Open University Poets
9 Monks Close, Farnborough, Hants GU14 7DB
☎01252 548823

A society open to anyone who has a connection with the OU. Membership includes a workshop magazine produced five times a year, an anthology, poetry competition, guest redaings at the AGM and a poetry weekend with a tutor (charged extra). Fees are £12.

Oriel Bookshop
The Friary, Cardiff CF1 9BU
☎01222 395548

Publishes at regular intervals *Small Presses and Little Magazines of The UK and Ireland – An Address List* (currently into its eleventh edition – £4.00 including p&p), specialises in twentieth-century poetry, operates a mail-order service, hosts poetry readings and provides information on local competitions, workshops, groups and literary activities.

The Poetry Association of Scotland
38 Dovecot Road, Edinburgh EH12 7LE
President *Norman MacCaig*
Secretary *Robin Bell*

Formerly the Scottish Association for the Speaking of Verse, founded in 1924 by John Masefield. Promotes poetry through readings and related activities.

The Poetry Bookshop
Westhouse, Broad Street, Hay-on-Wye, HR3 5DB
☎01497 820305
Contact *Alan Halsey*

Holds a large stock of modern and contemporary poetry – British, Irish, American, translations, concrete, etc. – mostly secondhand but including some new small press material and poetry magazines. Deals extensively by post and produces a regular catalogue.

The Poetry Book Society
PBS Freepost, Book House, 45 East Hill, London SW18 2BR
☎0181 870 8403   Fax 0181 877 1615
Secretary *Martha Smart*

Can't choose? This is one way to increase your reading of mainstream poetry. For an annual fee of £27.50 members receive quarterly a new volume of verse selected by experts and a quarterly bulletin. Members are also able to buy from a vast selection of PBS recommendations, all at 25% discount, free tickets to PBS readings and a right to an advisory vote in any poetry prizes organised by the society. If that's not enough, Charter Membership, costing £112, will bring you 20 new books annually, while the new

Associate form of membership, at £10, offers just the four bulletins and the discount offers on books. The PBS also administer the annual **T. S. Eliot Prize** for the best new collection of poetry.

The Poetry Business

The Studio, Byram Arcade, Westgate, Huddersfield HD1 1ND
☎01484 434840   Fax 01484 426566

Contact *Peter Sansom, Janet Fisher*

The Business runs an annual competition and organises monthly writing Saturdays. It publishes *The North* magazine and books, pamphlets and cassettes under the Smith/Doorstop imprint. Send s.a.e. for their catalogues.

Poetry Ireland

Bermingham Tower, Upper Yard, Dublin Castle, Dublin
☎00 353 1 6714632   Fax 00 353 1 6714634
Director *Theo Dorgan*
Administrator *Niamh Morris*

The national poetry organisation for Ireland, supported by Arts Councils both sides of the border. It publishes a quarterly magazine, *Poetry Ireland Review*, and a bi-monthly newsletter of upcoming events and competitions, as well as organising tours and readings by Irish and foreign poets and the National Poetry Competition of the Year, open to poets working in both Irish and English. Administers the Austin Clarke Library, a collection of over 6000 volumes.

The Poetry Library

South Bank Centre, Royal Festival Hall (Level 5, Red Side), London SE1 8XX
☎0171 921 0943/0664/0940
Fax 0171 921 0939

FOUNDED by the Arts Council in 1953. A collection of 45,000 titles of modern poetry since 1912, from Georgian poetry to Rap, representing all English-speaking countries and including translations into English by contemporary poets. Two copies of each title are kept, one for loan and one for reference. A wide range of poetry magazines and periodicals from all over the world are kept; also cassettes, records and videos for consultation, with some available for loan. Plus children's poetry section – school visits welcome. An information service compiles lists of poetry magazines, competitions, publishers, groups and workshops, which are available from the library on receipt of a large s.a.e. It also has a noticeboard for lost quotations, through which it tries to identify lines or fragments of poetry which have been sent in by other readers. General enquiry service also available. Open 11.00 a.m. to 8.00 p.m. seven days a week.

Poetry London Newsletter

26 Clacton Road, London E17 8AR
e-mail: leon@easynet.co.uk
Contact *Leon Cych, Pascale Petit, Katherine Gallagher, Peter Daniels*

The UK's first online poetry magazine, it is for and about poetry activity in the capital. Published both as hard copy and electronically at the beginning of every academic term, it has three parts: new poetry by emergent and established writers, reviews, and an encyclopaedic listings section of virtually everything to do with poetry in London and fairly extensive coverage of events up and down the country too. Invaluable at £12 annually.

In conjunction with the **Poetry Society** and the BBC, PLN is also responsible for the establishment of a web site that lists all UK poetry groups along with other useful poetry information. For further details e-mail: poetry@poetry.demon.co.uk. However, Editor Leon Cych warns not to send in poetry – you may get a gigabyte of data files by return!

The Poetry Society

22 Betterton Street, London WC2H 9BU
☎0171 240 4810   Fax 0171 240 4818
Chairman *Bill Swainson*
General Secretary *Chris Meade*

FOUNDED in 1909, which ought to make it venerable, the Society exists to help poets and poetry thrive in Britain. At one time notoriously strife-ridden, it has been undergoing a renaissance lately, reaching out from its Covent Garden base to promote the national health of poetry in a range of imaginative ways. Membership costs £24 for individuals and there are a range of different options available to libraries, schools, European Union members, students etc. Current activities include:

● A quarterly magazine of new verse, views and criticism, *Poetry Review*, edited by Peter Forbes.
● A quarterly newsletter, *Poetry News*, edited by Rachel Bourke.
● Promotions, events and cooperation with Britain's many literature festivals, poetry venues and poetry publishers.
● Competitions and awards including the annual **National Poetry Competition** with a substantial first prize.

● A questionnaire and mss diagnosis service, *The Script*, which gives detailed reports on submissions. Reduced rates for members.
● Seminars, fact sheets, training courses, ideas packs, t-shirts.
● An education service, run in conjunction with W.H. Smith, which annually puts over 1500 children in direct contact with poets. It also publishes the excellent *Poetry Society Resources* files for primary and secondary levels, and provides specialist information and advice on all aspects of poetry in education. This special 'education' membership (schools £30) offers an additional quarterly bulletin which is a teacher's guide to the current issue of *The Poetry Review*.
● A library service which assists participating libraries to become poetry friendly. A resources pack is available along with special arrangements for book purchase through library suppliers T. C. Farries. Library membership costs £40.

Current developments at the Society include Maura Dooley's Commission for Poetic Justice which is producing guidelines for good practice on all aspects of poetic activity; the ground floor Imagination Centre which contains DTP computer equipment; and *Poetry Map*, a new resource disseminated on the Internet.

Point

Apdo 119, E-03590 Altea, Spain
☎00 34 966 5842350
Fax 00 34 9666 5842350
Director *Germain Droogenbroodt*

FOUNDED as Poetry International in 1994, Point has offices in Spain and Belgium. A multilingual publisher of contemporary verse from both established and new poets, the organisation has brought out more than 50 titles in at least 8 languages, including English. Editions run the original work alongside a verse translation into Dutch made in cooperation with the poet. Point also organises an annual international poetry festival in Althea, Spain.

Quartos

BCM Writer, London WC1N 3XX
'Bi-monthly magazine for creative writers'. Subscription £14. Best single source of information on poetry competitions (see under **Magazines**). Runs an inexpensive critical service for poets, currently £1.50 per poem or £5 for six. Send s.a.e.

Regional Arts Boards

For full list of addresses see **Arts Councils** and **Regional Arts Boards**. Most are of invaluable interest to poets as a source of information on local activities, poetry groups, competitions, publications, readings and creative writing weekends. Many publish a magazine of their own, a number run critical services for writers. Some provide fellowships for poets, paying for school visits or for poet's workshops to be established. Service varies from region to region depending on demand and the influence and interest of the local literature officer.

Scottish Poetry Library

Tweeddale Court, 14 High Street,
Edinburgh EH1 1TE
☎0131 557 2876
Librarian *Penny Duce*

Freely open to the public; membership scheme £10 p.a. A comprehensive collection of work by Scottish poets in Gaelic, Scots and English, plus the work of international poets, including books, tapes, videos and magazines. Borrowing is free to all. Services include: a postal lending scheme, for which there is a small fee (catalogue of the lending collection available for fee); and a mobile library which can visit schools and other centres by arrangement. Members receive a newsletter and support the library, whose work includes exhibitions, bibliographies, information and promotion in the field of poetry. Also available is an online catalogue and computer index to poetry and poetry periodicals.

Small Press Group of Britain

See under **Professional Associations**

Survivors' Poetry

Diorama Arts Centre, 34 Osnaburgh Street,
London NW1 3ND
☎0171 916 5317
Coordinators *Anna M. Neeter, Debbie McNamara*

Arts Council funded support organisation for disabled poets who have survived the mental health system. Organises workshops, performances and readings throughout the UK. Runs performance workshops to help new writers and publishes anthologies of Survivors' work. Through its Outreach project, it is currently engaged in establishing centres nationwide, with groups already operating in London, Leeds, Liverpool, Manchester, Wolverhampton, Exeter, Bradford and Swindon.

Ty Newydd

Llanystumdwy, Cricieth, Gwynedd
LL52 0LW

Director *Sally Baker*

Run by the Taliesin Trust, an independent, Arvon-style residential writers centre in North Wales. Programme has a strong poetry content. Fees start at £100 for weekends and £245 for week courses. Tutors to date have included Beryl Bainbridge, Gillian Clarke, Wendy Cope, Jan Mark, Carol Ann Duffy, Bernice Rubens and Liz Lochead. See under **Writers' Courses, Circles and Workshops**.

Small Presses

Aard Press
c/o Aardverx, 31 Mountearl Gardens,
London SW16 2NL
Managing Editor D. *Jarvis, Dawn Redwood*
FOUNDED 1971. *Publishes* artists' bookworks,
experimental/visual poetry, 'zines, eonist liter-
ature, topographics ephemera and international
mail-art documentation. TITLES: *Eos- The Arts
& Letters of Transkind* (TG & M-A 'zine); *I, Jade
Green, Jade's Ladies, Jade AntiJade* (thrillers) by
A. K. Ashe. AUTHORS/ARTISTS: Petal Jeffery,
Dawn Redwood, Phaedra Kelly, Barry Edgar
Pilcher (Eire), D. Jarvis, Y. Kumykov (Russia).
No unsolicited material or proposals.
Royalties not paid. No sale-or-return deals.

ABCD
See **Allardyce, Barnett, Publishers**

Agneau 2
See **Allardyce, Barnett, Publishers**

AK Press/AKA Books
22 Lutton Place, Edinburgh EH8 9PE
☎0131 667 1507   Fax 0131 667 1507
Managing Editor *Alexis McKay*

AK Press grew out of the activities of AK
Distribution which distributes a wide range of
radical (anarchist, feminist, etc.) literature (books,
pamphlets, periodicals, magazines), both fiction
and non-fiction. Long-term goal is to have
some sort of high-street retail outlet for radical
material. *Publishes* politics, history, situationist
work, occasional fiction and poetry in both
book and pamphlet form. About 12 titles
a year. TITLES *Pen and the Sword* Edward W.
Said; *Chronicles of Dissent* Noam Chomsky; *Some
Recent Attacks* James Kelman; *Ecstatic Incisions:
The Collage Art of Freddie Baer.* Unsolicited mss,
proposals and synopses welcome if they fall
within AK's specific areas of interest.
Royalties paid.

The Alembic Press
Hyde Farm House, Marcham, Abingdon,
Oxon OX13 6NX
☎01865 391391   Fax 01865 391322
Owner *Claire Bolton*
FOUNDED 1976. Publisher of hand-produced
books by traditional letterpress methods. Short
print-runs. *Publishes* bibliography, book arts
and printing, miniatures and occasional poetry.
3 titles in 1994. Book production service to
like-minded authors wishing to publish in this
manner. No unsolicited mss.

Allardyce, Barnett, Publishers
14 Mount Street, Lewes, East Sussex
BN7 1HL
☎01273 479393   Fax 01273 479393
Publisher *Fiona Allardyce*
Managing Editor *Anthony Barnett*

FOUNDED 1981. *Publishes* art, literature and
music, with some emphasis on contemporary
English poets. About 5 titles a year.
IMPRINTS **Agneau 2, ABCD, Allardyce
Book**. TITLES *Poems* Andrea Zanzotto; *Desert
Sands: The Recordings and Performances of Stuff
Smith* Anthony Barnett; *The Black Heralds*
César Vallejo. Unsolicited mss and synopses
discouraged.

Amate Press
See **IKON Productions Ltd**

Anglo-Saxon Books
Frithgarth, Thetford Forest Park, Hockwold
cum Wilton, Norfolk IP26 4NQ
☎01842 828430   Fax 01842 828430
Managing Editor *Tony Linsell*
FOUNDED 1990 to promote a greater awareness
of early English society and history. Originally
concentrated on translations of Old English
texts but has now moved on to include less academic, more popular titles. *Publishes* English
history, culture, language and society before
1066. About 5 titles a year. TITLES *A Handbook
of Anglo-Saxon Food; Alfred's Metres of Boethius;
Spellcraft: Old English Heroic Legends.* Unsolicited
mss, synopses and ideas welcome but return
postage essential if material is to be returned.
Royalties paid.

Atlas Press
BCM Atlas Press, London WC1N 3XX
Fax 0171 831 9489
Managing Editor *Alastair Brotchie*
FOUNDED 1983. *Publishes* prose translations
from French and German and the international

avant-garde. TITLES include works by authors associated with surrealism, expressionism, etc. About 15 titles a year. Interested in translations of 19th- and 20th-century writers only. Do not send unsolicited mss; write first.
Royalties paid.

Aurora Publishing

Unit 9, Bradley Fold Trading Estate, Radcliffe Moor Road, Bradley Fold, Bolton, Lancashire BL2 6RT
☎01204 370752   Fax 01204 370751
Managing Editor *Dawn Robinson*

FOUNDED 1993 as part of Aurora Enterprises Ltd. *Publishes* general and local interest titles, especially oral history and personal experience. No poetry. About 10 titles a year. Looking to expand range and list. TITLES *Labours of Love: Personal Experiences of Childbirth; Land Army Days; 100 Years of the Manchester Ship Canal; Cotton Everywhere; A Dales Odyssey; War Memories.* Unsolicited mss, synopses and ideas welcome.
Royalties Payment Royalties or fixed fee.

Aussteiger Publications

8 Back Skipton Road, Barnoldswick, Lancashire BB8 5NE
☎01282 812741
Managing Editor *John Leonard Dixon*

FOUNDED 1990. *Publishes* historical and archaeological field guides and historical town/area guides. Through the medium of walking, Aussteiger aims to bring the neglected economic and social (Celtic) history of the North of England to the fore in its 'journeys of exploration'. 1–2 titles a year. TITLES *Historic Walks around the Pendle Way; Journeys through Brigantia* (vols 1–11); *The Pendle Witches* (novel). All work is commissioned. Synopses and ideas welcome.
Royalties 10% of trade sales.

Avant-Garde Publishing Ltd

Private Box BCM 6137, London WC1N 3XX
☎01734 420688 (24 hrs)
Managing Director *Jurgen Schwartz*

FOUNDED 1994 to publish intellectual theory, literature, propaganda and ideology, both modernist and traditional, intellectual rather than academic. 5 titles in 1995. TITLES *Jonathan Bowden – Collected Works (Vols 1–5)* ed. Jurgen Schwartz. No unsolicited mss, synopses or ideas.
Royalties not paid.

AVERT

AIDS Education and Research Trust, 11 Denne Parade, Horsham, West Sussex RH12 1JD
☎01403 210202   Fax 01403 211001
Managing Editor *Annabel Kanabus*

Publishing arm of the AIDS Education and Research Trust, a national registered charity established 1986. *Publishes* books and leaflets about HIV infection and AIDS. About 3 titles a year. TITLES *AIDS: The Secondary Scene; Guidelines for Management of Children with HIV Infection.* Unsolicited mss, synopses and ideas welcome.
Royalties paid accordingly.

M. & M. Baldwin

24 High Street, Cleobury Mortimer, Near Kidderminster, Worcestershire DY14 8BY
☎01299 270110   Fax 01299 271154
Managing Editor *Dr Mark Baldwin*

FOUNDED 1978. *Publishes* local interest/history and inland waterways books. Up to 5 titles a year. TITLES *Idle Women; Tom Rolt & the Cressy Years; Canal Coins.* Unsolicited mss, synopses and ideas for books welcome.
Royalties paid.

BB Books

Spring Bank, Longsight Road, Copster Green, Blackburn, Lancashire BB1 9EU
☎01254 249128
Managing Editor *Dave Cunliffe*

FOUNDED 1962. A non-commercial literary press publishing mainly post-Beat-orientated writing. Now specialising in poetry pamphlets and anarchic psycho-cultural tracts. Projected 1996 publications include a series of poetry pamphlets by contemporary UK Beat and post-Beat poets. Unsolicited mss, synopses and ideas for books welcome.
Royalties not paid (authors get 10% of print-run).

Bellevue Books

Unit E4, Sunbury International Business Centre, Brooklands Close, Sunbury on Thames, Middlesex TW16 7DX
☎01932 765119   Fax 01932 765429
Chairman *Howard Barkway*
Approx. Annual Turnover £20,000

FOUNDED 1991 to publish a book on the unsolved mystery of Rennes-le-Chateau. *Publishes* unsolved natural and scientific mysteries, both ancient and modern. Also distributes books on these subjects from the USA.

Black Ace Books

Ellemford Farmhouse, Duns, Berwickshire
TD11 3SG
☎01361 890370   Fax 01361 890287

Managing Director *Hunter Steele*

FOUNDED 1991. *Publishes* new fiction, Scottish
and general; some non-fiction including history
and philosophy. 4 titles in 1994 with 6–8 titles
planned for 1995. IMPRINTS **Black Ace Books**,
Black Ace Paperbacks TITLES *Kintalloch*
Mercedes Clarasó; *On My Way Weeping* Steve
McGiffen; *The Sound of My Voice* Ron Butlin;
The Lords of Montplaisir Hunter Steele; *The Song
of the Forest* Colin Mackay. No unsolicited mss.
Preliminary letter essential with large s.a.e. for
details of current requirements. Will respond to
ideas (with s.a.e.) but does not commission
books on the basis of synopses. No poetry,
children's, cookery, DIY, religion.
Royalties paid twice yearly.

Bois Books

Argyle House, 1a All Saints Passage,
London SW18 1EP
☎01580 241021   Fax 01580 241022

Managing Editor *Richard Maybe*
General Manager *Richard Capstick*

FOUNDED 1994. *Publishes* popular gay fiction.
TITLE *What You Cannot Finish* Derek Taylor. 6
titles in 1995. Synopsis with sample chapters
welcome with s.a.e.
Royalties paid.

The Book Castle

12 Church Street, Dunstable, Bedfordshire
LU5 4RU
☎01582 605670   Fax 01582 662431

Managing Editor *Paul Bowes*

FOUNDED 1986. *Publishes* non-fiction of local
interest (Bedfordshire, Hertfordshire, Buckinghamshire, Northamptonshire, the Chilterns).
6+ titles a year. About 40 titles in print. TITLES
Chiltern Walks series; *The Hill of the Martyr;
Journeys into Bedfordshire/Hertfordshire.* Unsolicited
mss, synopses and ideas for books welcome.
Royalties paid.

The Book Gallery

Bedford Road, St. Ives, Cornwall TR26 1SP
☎01736 793545

Directors *David & Tina Wilkinson*

FOUNDED 1991. *Publishes* limited edition monographs by and about writers/painters associated
with the so-called Newlyn and St Ives schools
of painting. AUTHORS in the *Book Gallery*

Monographs series include Sven Berlin, Ilse
Barker and Diana Calvert. Ideas welcome.
Royalties not paid; flat fee.

Book-in-Hand Ltd

20 Shepherds Hill, London N6 5AH
☎0181 341 7650

Contact *Ann Kritzinger*

Print production service to self-publishers.
Includes design and editing advice to give customers a greater chance of selling in the open
market. Also runs an editing and reading service called **Scriptmate** which held the *Guinness
Book of Records* world title for fastest publisher
in 1989.

Bookmarque Publishing

26 Cotswold Close, Minster Lovell,
Oxfordshire OX8 5SX
☎01993 775179

Managing Editor *John Rose*

FOUNDED 1987. Publishing business with aim of
filling gaps in motoring history of which it is said
'there are many!' Publishes motoring history
and biography and general titles. About 8 titles a
year (increasing). All design and phototypeset-
ting of books done in-house. TITLES *Microcar
Mania; Ginetta – The Inside Story; The History of
Oxford Airport.* Unsolicited mss, synopses and
ideas welcome on transport (motoring, although
some aircraft/WW2 titles considered if not too
large in extent). S.a.e. required for reply or
return of material. No novels or similar.
Royalties paid.

Bozo

BM Bozo, London WC1N 3XX
☎01234 211606

Managing Editors *John & Cecilia Nicholson*

FOUNDED 1981. Began by producing tiny pamphlets (*Patriotic English Tracts*) and has gained a
reputation for itself as one of England's foremost
pamphleteers. *Publishes* historical analyses, apoc-
alyptic rants, wry/savage humour and political
'filth'. Considerable expansion of titles is under-
way. No unsolicited mss, synopses or ideas.
Royalties not paid.

Brentham Press

See under **Poetry Presses**

Business Innovations Research

Tregeraint House, Zennor, St Ives, Cornwall
TR26 3DB
☎01736 797061   Fax 01736 797061

Managing Director *John T. Wilson*

Publishes business books and newsletters, home study courses, and guidebooks. Production service available to self-publishers.

Businesslike Publishing
Burnside, Station Road, Beauly, Inverness-shire IV4 7EQ
☎01463 782258
Managing Editor *Iain R. McIntyre*

FOUNDED 1989. Provides a printing and publishing service for members of the **Society of Civil Service Authors**. *Publishes* poetry, short stories and magazines. About 6 titles a year. TITLES *Focus* (poetry anthology series); *Of Unicorns and Kings* (Inverness writers' anthology); *Tales of a Glasgow Childhood; Closet Collection; To Freedom Born* (Doric Scots poetry); *Wee Glasgow Gems; Whitby Writers' Anthology; Never Goodbye*. Ideas/synopses accepted. No unsolicited mss.

Royalties generally not paid but negotiable in some circumstances for non-fiction material.

Cakebreads Publications
5a The High Street, Saffron Walden, Essex CB10 1AT
☎01799 524131
Managing Editor *Mrs Brenda Fuller*

Publishes history and Second World War nursing books. 1 title in 1993. TITLES *A Nurse's War; Quiet Heroines*. No unsolicited mss.
Royalties not paid.

Canterbury Press Norwich
See **Hymns Ancient & Modern Ltd** under **UK Publishers**

Chapter Two
13 Plum Lane, Plumstead Common, London SE18 3AF
☎0181 316 5389   Fax 0181 854 5963
Managing Editor *E. N. Cross*

FOUNDED 1976. Chief activity is the propagation of the Christian faith through the printed page. *Publishes* exclusively on Plymouth Brethren. About 12 titles a year. No unsolicited mss, synopses or ideas. Enquiries only.
Royalties not paid.

Charlewood Press
7 Weavers Place, Chandlers Ford, Eastleigh, Hampshire SO53 1TU
☎01703 261192
Managing Editor *Gerald Ponting, Anthony Light*

FOUNDED 1987. Publishes local history book-

lets on the Fordingbridge area, researched and written by the two partners and leaflets on local walks. 1 title in 1994. TITLES: *Breamore - A Short History & Guide; Tudor Fordingbridge; The Tragedies of the Dodingtons*. No unsolicited mss.
Royalties not paid.

The Cheverell Press
Manor Studios, Manningford Abbots, Pewsey, Wiltshire SN9 6HS
☎01672 63163   Fax 01672 64301
Managing Editor *Sarah de Larrinaga*

Publishes careers, media and performing arts. No fiction. IMPRINTS **The Cheverell Press, First Hand Books**. TITLES *The Guide to Drama Training in the UK 1995/6; The Guide to Careers and Training in the Performing Arts; I Want to be an Actor; I Want to be a Journalist*. Currently using researchers/writers on a fee basis, rather than royalties. No unsolicited mss. Started as a self-publisher and has produced a self-publishers information pack. Write for details.

Chrysalis Press
11 Convent Close, Kenilworth, Warwickshire CV8 2FQ
☎01926 55223   Fax 01926 56116
Managing Editor *Brian Buckley*

FOUNDED 1994. *Publishes* fiction, literary criticism and biography. 3 titles in 1994. TITLES *Two Tales; Challenge and Renewal: D.H. Lawrence and the Thematic Novel*. Unsolicited mss, synopses and ideas welcome.
Royalties paid.

Nigel J. Clarke Publications
Unit 2, Russell House, Lym Close, Lyme Regis, Dorset DT7 3DE
☎01297 442513/3699   Fax 01297 442513
Managing Editor *Penny Hall*

FOUNDED 1982. *Publishes* walking guides, maps and local interest (Wiltshire, West Country). About 4 titles a year. TITLES *The Unusual Guide to Bath/Salisbury; The Rude Man of Cerne Abbas and Other Wessex Landscape Oddities*. No fiction or poetry. Unsolicited mss, synopses and ideas welcome.
Royalties paid.

CNP Publications
Roseland, Gorran, St Austell, Cornwall
☎01726 843501   Fax 01726 843501
Managing Editor *Dr James Whetter*

FOUNDED 1975. *Publishes* poetry, political essays, local Cornish interest/biography and

Celtic design. 1–2 titles a year. TITLES *An Baner Kernewek (The Cornish Banner)* – quarterly local-interest magazine; Cornish history published under the **Lyfrow Trelyspen** imprint: *Cornish Weather and Cornish People in the 17th Century.* Unsolicited mss, synopses and ideas welcome.

Royalties not paid.

The Cosmic Elk
68 Elsham Crescent, Lincoln LN6 3YZ
☎01522 691146
Managing Editor *Heather Hobden*
FOUNDED 1988 to publish books, booklets, leaflets and posters on science, history and the history of science. New authors and commissions welcome (phone or write in the first instance). TITLES: *John Harrison and the Problem of Longitude; The Telescope Revolution: First Scientific Ideas on the Universe; Newton's Cosmos: The Universe at the End of the 17th Century; The Land Where Time Began: The History of Yakutia; Window on the Universe; Time, Space and Aliens.*

Crescent Moon Publishing and Joe's Press
18 Chaddesley Road, Kidderminster, Worcestershire DY10 3AD
Managing Editor *Jeremy Robinson*
FOUNDED 1988 to publish critical studies of figures such as D. H. Lawrence, Thomas Hardy, André Gide, Powys, Rilke, Piero, Bellini, Beckett, Cavafy and Robert Graves. *Publishes* literature, criticism, media, art, feminism, painting, poetry, travel, guidebooks, cinema and some fiction. New literary magazine, *Passion*, launched Feb. 1994. Quarterly. Twice-yearly anthology of American poetry, *Pagan America*. Expansion into fiction planned over the next couple of years. About 15–20 titles per year. TITLES *Samuel Beckett Goes into the Silence; Pagan America: An Anthology of New American Poetry; Jackie Collins and the Blockbuster Novel; Vincent van Gogh; The Poetry of Cinema; Wild Zones: Pornography, Art and Feminism; Andrea Dworkin.* Unsolicited mss, synopses and ideas welcome. Approach in writing only.

Royalties negotiable.

Crocus
See **Poetry Presses**

Daniels Publishing
38 Cambridge Place, Cambridge CB2 1NS
☎01223 467144   Fax 01223 467145
Publisher *Dr Victor G. Daniels*
Educational press specialising in A4 photocopiable resource packs on health and social educa-

tion, study and work skills, and self development for schools, colleges and health authorities. Also photocopiable resources for the training market. Also educational materials for the pharmaceutical industry. Unsolicited mss, synopses and ideas welcome.

Dark Diamonds Publications
PO Box HK 31, Leeds, West Yorkshire
LS11 9XN
☎0113 2453868
Managing Editor *Andrew Cocker*
FOUNDED 1987. Member of the **Small Press Group of Britain**. *Publishes* 2–3 titles a year. Print runs average 1000 copies. Limited funds. Current titles: *Dark Diamonds* magazine: journal covering social and political subjects. Mainly concerned with environmental development and human rights issues. Unsolicited articles and illustrations on the above subject matter welcome. *A Riot of Emotions* magazine features art and poetry, and carries reviews of small press publications and independent music releases. Unsolicited poetry/short story mss welcome (2000 words max.). Also unsolicited art (b/w illustrations only) welcome. Return postage must be included with all unsolicited contributions. Unsolicited material for review also welcome. Free copy to all contributors. Contributors guidelines and current catalogue available (send s.a.e.).

Royalties not paid.

Diamond Press
See under **Poetry Presses**

Doghouse Publications
18 Marlow Avenue, Eastbourne, East Sussex
BN22 8SJ
☎01323 729214
Managing Editor *Catherine Langridge*
FOUNDED 1990. Publishes books and booklets on dog behaviour and related subjects. 5 titles in 1993. Unsolicited mss, synopses and ideas welcome but must be relative. TITLES: *Rescue Dog, Separation Anxiety, Your Dog and Your Baby, Take the Class, The Harmony Programme.* Branching out into other doggie subjects, e.g. health and general new age dog care and training.

Royalties paid.

The Dragonby Press
15 High Street, Dragonby, Scunthorpe
DN15 0BE
☎01724 840645
Managing Editor *Richard Williams*
FOUNDED 1987 to publish affordable bibliogra-

phy for reader, collector and dealer. About 3 titles a year. TITLES *Collins Crime Club: A Checklist.* Unsolicited mss, synopses and ideas welcome for bibliographical projects only.
Royalties paid.

Dragonfly Press
Courtyard Mews, Southover, Burwash,
East Sussex TN19 7JB
☎01435 882580
Managing Editor *C. Bell*

FOUNDED 1989. Owned by Words & Images. *Publishes* local history, literary fiction, poetry and how-to titles. 1–2 titles a year. TITLES *The Writer's Guide to Self-Publishing; Ask a Silly Question About Your IBM Computer; Saheli Kitchen* (ethnic cookery book). No unsolicited material accepted. Commissions only.
Royalties paid where applicable.

Education Now Publishing Cooperative Ltd
113 Arundel Drive, Bramcote Hills,
Nottingham NG9 3FQ
☎0115 9257261   Fax 0115 9257261
Managing Editors *Dr Roland Meighan,*
  Philip Toogood

A non-profit research and writing group set up in reaction to 'the totalitarian tendencies of the 1988 Education Act'. Its aim is to widen the terms of the debate about education and its choices. *Publishes* reports on positive educational initiatives such as flexi-schooling, mini-schooling, small schooling, home-based education and democratic schooling. 4–5 titles a year. TITLES *Praxis Makes Perfect* Iram Siraj–Blatchford; *Skills for Self–Managed Learning* Mike Roberts; *Beyond Authoritarian School Management* Lynn Davies. No unsolicited mss or ideas. Enquiries only.
Royalties generally not paid.

Educational Heretics Press
113 Arundel Drive, Bramcote Hills,
Nottingham NG9 3FQ
☎0115 9257261   Fax 0115 9257261
Directors *Janet & Roland Meighan*

Non-profit venture which aims to question the dogmas of schooling in particular and education in general. TITLES *Alice Miller: The Unkind Society, Parenting and Schooling* Chris Shute; *The Freethinkers' Guide to the Educational Universe* Roland Meighan; *Compulsory Schooling Disease* Chris Shute; *Theory and Practice of Regressive Education* Roland Meighan. No unsolicited material. Enquiries only.
Royalties not paid but under review.

Enable Communications
PO Box 86, Coventry CV6 5ZS
☎01203 682706
Contact *Simon Stevens*

Established to provide information processing and opportunity, primarily in the field of equal opportunities and Dysability ('an enhancement of the term Disability') meaning 'difficulty to perform a task imposed by society due to the physical, learning, sensory, behavioural, cultural or medical characteristics of a person'. TITLES *Dysability Handbook; Dysability Pages 1995.* Unsolicited material welcome, especially in the field of information on organisations in this field as well as personal experiences of discrimination.

estamp
204 St Albans Avenue, London W4 5JU
☎0181 994 2379   Fax 0181 994 2379
Contact *Silvie Turner*

Independent publisher of fine art books on printmaking, papermaking and artists' bookmaking. Books are designed and written for artists, craftspeople and designers. TITLES *British Printmaking Studios; About Prints; Europe for Printmakers; British Artists Books; Which Paper?.* Approach in writing in first instance.

Feather Books
Fair View, Old Coppice, Lyth Bank,
Shrewsbury, Shropshire SY3 0BW
☎01743 872177
Managing Editor *Rev. John Waddington-Feather*

FOUNDED 1980 to publish writers' group work and has since expanded into children's fiction. All material has a strong Christian ethos. *Publishes* children's environmental fiction, good poetry (mainly, but not exclusively, religious), biography, local history. 2–3 titles a year. TITLES *The Quill Hedgehog Series; Feather Poets Series; Feather's Little Birthday Book Series.* No unsolicited mss, synopses or ideas. All correspondence to include s.a.e. please.

Ferry Publications
12 Millfields Close, Pentlepoir, Kilgetty,
Pembrokeshire SA68 0SA
☎01834 813991   Fax 01834 814484
Managing Editor *Miles Cowsill*

FOUNDED 1987 to publish ferry and shipping books. 3–4 titles a year. TITLES *Only Britanny Ferries, Harwich – Hoek van Holland – A 100 Years of Service.* Unsolicited mss, synopses and ideas welcome.
Royalties paid.

Field Day Publications

Foyle Arts Centre, Old Foyle College,
Lawrence Hill, Derry BT48 7NJ
☎01504 360196   Fax 01504 365419

Specialises in work of Irish interest. Pamphlets,
essays, playscripts. Usually commissioned. TITLES
*Revising the Rising; Field Day Anthology of Irish
Writing.*

First Hand Books

See **The Cheverell Press**

Fitzgerald Publishing

PO Box 804, London SE13 5JJ
☎0181 690 0597

Managing Editor *Tim Fitzgerald*
General Editor *Andrew Smith*

FOUNDED 1974. *Specialises* in scientific studies
of insects and spiders. 1–2 titles a year. TITLES
*Tarantulas of the USA & Mexico; Stick Insects of
Europe & The Mediterranean; How To Keep
Tarantulas/Scorpions; Tarantula Classification and
Identification Guide.* Unsolicited mss, synopses
and ideas for books welcome. Also considers
video scripts for video documentaries.
Royalties paid.

Forth Naturalist & Historian

University of Stirling, Stirling,
Clackmannanshire FK9 4LA
☎01259 215091   Fax 01786 464994

Also at: 30 Dunmar Drive, Alloa,
Clackmannanshire FK10 2EH
Honorary Editor *Lindsay Corbett*

FOUNDED 1975 by the collaboration of Stirling
University members and the Central Regional
Council to promote interests and publications
on central Scotland. Aims to provide a 'valuable local studies educational resource for mid-
Scotland schools, libraries and people.' *Publishes*
naturalist, historical and environmental studies
and maps. TITLES *The Forth Naturalist &
Historian from 1976; Doune, Historical Notes;
Doune, Postcards of the Past; Central Scotland:
Land, Wildlife, People* (a new survey); *The Ochil
Hills: Landscapes, Wildlife, Heritage, Walks*; In
preparation: *Lure of Loch Lomond; Alloa in Days
of Prosperity 1830–1914*; 1890s maps 25" to the
mile – 24 of Central Scotland areas/places with
historical notes. Welcomes papers, mss and
ideas relevant to central Scotland. Promotes
annual environment/heritage symposia – 1995
is the 21st year.
Royalties not paid.

Fox Press

Oak Tree, Main Road, Colden Common,
Near Winchester, Hampshire SO21 1TL
☎01703 694650   Fax 01703 694650

Managing Editor *Beryl Bron*

FOUNDED 1986. *Publishes* poetry, local/country
interest and animal welfare. No fiction. 1–2
titles a year. TITLES *As the Months Go By* Donald
Christie; *Fettered Kingdoms* John Bryant; *Poetry
My Pleasure; Cat Calls* Jeannette Arnold anthologies; *No Bitter Springs,* (animal welfare) Jeannette
Arnold. **Winter Sweet Press** IMPRINT
launched 1993. Country matters and poetry
titles: *Where Trees Stand Tall* Jeannette Arnold;
Winter Jasmine Joan Howes. Mss considered but
the list of possible productions is already long;
send return postage.
Royalties are only paid to poets when sales
have covered cost of production.

The Frogmore Press

See under **Poetry Presses**

Frontier Publishing

Windetts, Kirstead, Norfolk NR15 1BR
☎01508 558174   Fax 01508 550194

Managing Editor *John Black*

FOUNDED 1983. *Publishes* travel, photography
and literature. 2–3 titles a year. TITLES *Eye on
the Hill: Horse Travels in Britain; Euphonics: A
Poet's Dictionary of Sounds; Broken China; The
Green Book of Poetry.* No unsolicited mss; synopses and ideas welcome.
Royalties paid.

Full House Productions

12 Sunfield gardens, Bayston Hill,
Shrewsbury, Shropshire SY3 0LA
☎01743 872914

Managing Editor *Judith A. Shone*

FOUNDED 1993 by writer/producer Judith
Shone in order to supply professionally written
pantomime scripts to small production companies such as operatic societies, amateur dramatic societies and other performing groups –
village halls etc. *Publishes* a complete low-cost
'panto-pack' consisting of scripts, posters and
tickets. Future plans are to expand into publication of plays and sketches. All titles are written and published in-house. 3 titles in 1995.

Galactic Central Publications

Imladris, 25A Copgrove Road, Leeds, West
Yorkshire LS8 2SP

Managing Editor *Phil Stephensen-Payne*

FOUNDED 1982 in the US. *Publishes* science fiction bibliographies. About 4 titles a year. TITLES *Gene Wolfe: Urth-Man Extraordinary; Andre Norton: Grand Master of Witch World.* All new publications originate in the UK. Unsolicited mss, synopses and ideas welcome. *Royalties* paid.

Geological Society Publishing House

Unit 7, Brassmill Enterprise Centre, Brassmill Lane, Bath, Avon BA1 3JN
☎01225 445046   Fax 01225 442836
Managing Editor *Mike Collins*

Publishing arm of the Geological Society which was founded in 1807. *Publishes* undergraduate and postgraduate texts in the earth sciences. 10 titles a year. Unsolicited mss, synopses and ideas welcome.
Royalties not paid.

Global Publishing Ltd

788–790 Finchley Road, Temple Fortune, London NW11 7UR
☎0181 209 1151   Fax 0181 905 5344
Chief Executive *Dr I. O. Azuonye*

FOUNDED 1993. *Publishes* contemporary issues, politics, economics, personal development, general fiction, education and humour. TITLE *If We Elect Her President in November of the Year 2000* Ikechukwu O. Azuonye. Welcomes synopses and sample chapters with return postage. Reading fee charged.
Royalties paid twice yearly.

Glosa

PO Box 18, Richmond, Surrey TW9 2AU
☎0181 948 8417
Managing Editors *Wendy Ashby, Ronald Clark*

FOUNDED 1981. *Publishes* textbooks, dictionaries and translations for the teaching, speaking and promotion of Glosa (an international, auxiliary language); also a newsletter and journal. Rapid growth in the last couple of years. TITLES *Glosa 6000 Dictionary; Introducing Euro-Glosa; Eduka-Glosa; Central Glosa; Glosa 1000 – Chinese; Glosa 1000 – Swahili Dictionary.* Spring 1994 launched *Sko-Glosa,* a new publication for and by younger students of Glosa to be distributed to schools in different countries. Also in 1994 published several fairy stories and activity pages for school children who are learning Glosa in school. Unsolicited mss and ideas for Glosa books welcome.

Gothic Press

PO Box 542, Highgate, London N6 6BG
Managing Editor *Robin Crisp*

Specialist publisher of gothic titles in quality, case editions. Non-fiction only at present. *Publishes* mysticism, supernatural, history, biography. TITLES *The Highgate Vampire; Mad, Bad and Dangerous to Know; From Satan to Christ; The Grail Church.* No unsolicited mss; synopses and ideas may be welcome.
Royalties not paid.

The Gothic Society

Chatham House, Gosshill Road, Chislehurst, Kent BR7 5NS
☎0181 467 8475   Fax 0181 295 1967
Managing Editor *Jennie Gray*

FOUNDED 1990. *Publishes* a quarterly magazine, books and supplements on Gothic and macabre subjects. History, literary criticism, reprints of forgotten texts, biography, architecture, art etc., all with a gloomy and black-hued flavour. About 8 titles a year. Synopses and ideas welcome. (Also see **Literary Societies**).
Royalties flat fee.

Grant Books

The Coach House, New Road, Cutnall Green, Droitwich, Worcestershire WR9 0PQ
☎01299 851588   Fax 01299 851446
Managing Editor *H. R. J. Grant*

FOUNDED 1978. *Publishes* golf-related titles only: course architecture, history, biography, some essays on golf course architecture, hazards etc., but no instructional material. New titles and old, plus limited editions. About 4 titles a year. TITLES *Harold H. Hilton: His Golfing Life and Times; St Andrews Night and Other Golfing Stories; Denham Described: A History of Denham Golf Club; Royal Cinque Ports Golf Club: A Personal Record; The Whitcombes: A Golfing Legend; The Murdoch Golf Library; Wirral Ladies Golf Club – A Centenary Portrait; A Lively Octogenarian – Hillside Golf Club.* Unsolicited mss, synopses and ideas welcome.
Royalties paid.

Grevatt & Grevatt

9 Rectory Drive, Newcastle upon Tyne NE3 1XT
Chairman/Editorial Head *Dr S. Y. Killingley*

FOUNDED 1981. Alternative publisher of works not normally commercially viable. Three books have appeared with financial backing from professional bodies. *Publishes* academic titles and conference reports, particularly language, linguistics and religious studies. Some poetry also. Dr Killingley is editor of the Linguistic Association's *British Linguistic Newsletter*. TITLES *The Sanskrit Tradition in the Modern World*, a series of rewritten conference/lecture proceedings launched 1988. New title: *Rammohun Roy in Hindu and Christian Tradition: The Teape Lectures 1990*. No unsolicited mss. Synopses and ideas should be accompanied by s.a.e.

Royalties paid annually (after first 500 copies).

Guildhall Press
41 Great James Street, Derry,
Northern Ireland BT48 7DF
☎01504 364413   Fax 01504 372949
Managing Editor *Paul Hippsley*

FOUNDED 1979 by a local schoolteacher to produce local history material for schools. Government funding has helped establish the press as a community publishing house with increased output across a wider range of subjects. Interested in joint ventures with similar organisations throughout Europe to increase output and gain commercial experience. About 6 titles a year. TITLES *Memory of Memories of Derry* Roy Clements; *Thinking Green* Dan McAllister; *Derry's Walls* Paul Hippsley; *Parade of Phantoms* Peter McCartney; *Talk of the Town* Seamus McConnell; *Derry Jail* Colm Cavanagh. Unsolicited mss, synopses and ideas welcome.
Royalties negotiable.

Happy House
3b Castledown Avenue, Hastings, East Sussex TN34 3RJ
☎01424 434778

FOUNDED 1992 as a self-publishing venture for Dave Arnold/Martin Honeysett collaboration of poetry and cartoons. TITLES *Out to Lunch; Under the Wallpaper; Before and After the Shrink*

Haunted Library
Flat 1, 36 Hamilton Street, Hoole, Chester, Cheshire CH2 3JQ
☎01244 313685
Managing Editor *Rosemary Pardoe*

FOUNDED 1979. *Publishes* a twice-yearly ghost story magazine, and booklets, mostly in the antiquarian tradition of M. R. James. The magazine publishes stories and articles; booklets tend to be single-author collections. 3–4 titles a year. TITLES *Ghosts & Scholars* (magazine); *The James Gang; The Reluctant Ghost-Hunter; Spirits of Another Sort*. No unsolicited mss.
Royalties not paid.

Heart of Albion Press
2 Cross Hill Close, Wymeswold,
Loughborough, Leicestershire LE12 6UJ
☎01509 880725
Managing Editor *R. N. Trubshaw*

FOUNDED 1990 to publish books and booklets on the East Midlands area. *Publishes* local history and earth mysteries. About 6–8 titles a year. TITLES *Cinema in Leicester 1896–1931; User-Friendly Dictionary of Old English*. No unsolicited mss but synopses and ideas welcome.
Royalties negotiable.

Hedgerow Publishing Ltd
325 Abbeydale Road, Sheffield, South Yorkshire S7 1FS
☎0114 2554873   Fax 0114 2509400
Managing Editor *T. Hale*

FOUNDED 1988. Publisher of local interest postcards and greeting cards. Expanded into book publishing in 1990 with the emphasis on tourist-orientated material. Ideas for books relevant to the South Yorkshire and Northern Peak District areas will be considered. Interested in photographic submissions of colour transparencies of local views. Outright purchase only. Telephone *before* sending.
Royalties negotiable.

Highcliff Press
23 Avon Drive, Guisborough TS14 8AX
☎01287 637274
Managing Editor *Robert Sampson*

FOUNDED 1994 to publish *Possible Worlds* (a short prose sequence). Publication of *Possible Writings* planned for 1995. Self-publisher only at present.

Hilmarton Manor Press
Calne, Wiltshire SN11 8SB
☎01249 760208   Fax 01249 760379
Chairman/Managing Director *Charles Baile de Laperriere*

Publishes fine art reference only. No unsolicited material. Enquiries only.
Royalties paid.

Hisarlik Press
4 Catisfield Road, Enfield Lock, Middlesex EN3 6BD
☎01992 700898   Fax 0181 292 6118
Managing Editors *Dr Jeffrey Mazo, Georgina Clark-Mazo*

FOUNDED 1991. *Publishes* academic books and journals on folklore, local history and medieval

Scandinavia. 4 titles in 1995. TITLES *With Disastrous Consequences: London Disasters 1830–1917; The Maiden Who Rose From The Sea and Other Finnish Folktales; From Sagas to Society: Comparative Approaches to Early Iceland*. No unsolicited mss; synopses and ideas welcome.
  Royalties paid.

Horseshoe Publications
PO Box 37, Kingsley, Warrington, Cheshire WA6 8DR
☎01928 787477 (Afternoons and evenings)
Managing Editor *John C. Hibbert*
FOUNDED 1994. Initially to publish work of Cheshire writers. Poetry, short stories and own writing. Shared cost publishing considered in certain circumstances. Reading fee on full mss £10. Unsolicited mss, synopses and ideas in the realm of commercial fiction welcome. S.a.e. for return.

IKON Productions Ltd
Manor Farm House, Manor Farm Road, Wantage, Oxfordshire OX12 8NE
☎01235 767467   Fax 01235 767467
Publisher *Clare Goodrick-Clarke*
FOUNDED 1988. *Publishes* religion and history, some poetry, heritage and countryside. 2 titles a year. Also, under **Amate Press** imprint, publish non-commercially viable books on profit-sharing basis and can offer book production service to authors. No unsolicited mss. Please write with ideas and synopses first.

Indelible Inc
BCM 1698, London WC1N 3XX
Managing Editor *Roberta McKeown*
FOUNDED 1988. *Publishes* experimental neglected literature, including Renaissance poetry and literary pamphlets. TITLES *The Overthrow of the Gout* (a 16th-century scientific poem); *Monstrous Births* (an illustrated introduction to early English teratology); *Massacre* (annual magazine of new anti-naturalist fiction and literary criticism, e.g. Dada and surrealism). Unsolicited material, synopses and ideas welcome in areas previously neglected, e.g. criticism of avant-garde literature. Also experimental fiction (up to 5000 words).
  Royalties nominal.

Intellect Books
108–110 London Road, Headington, Oxford OX3 9AW
☎01392 475110   Fax 01392 475110
Publisher *Masoud Yazdani*

Assistant Publisher *Robin Beecroft*
FOUNDED 1984. *Publishes* books and journals on social implications of computing, language learning and European studies. 12 titles in 1994. TITLES *The Art and Science of Handwriting; Regionalism in Europe; Computers and Law; Computers and Creativity*. Unsolicited mss, synopses and ideas welcome.
  Royalties paid.

Iolo
38 Chaucer Road, Bedford MK40 2AJ
☎01234 270175   Fax 01234 270175
Managing Director *Dedwydd Jones*
Publishes Welsh theatre related material and campaigns for a Welsh National Theatre. SERIES *Black Books on the Welsh Theatre*. Ideas on Welsh themes welcome; approach in writing.

Ironside Books
27A Crescent Road, Rowley Park, Stafford ST17 9AL
☎01785 52625
Managing Editor *Roger Butters*
FOUNDED 1994. First publications July 1995 with plans to publish at least 6 books per year, mostly genre fiction. TITLES *All Wind and Pistol; Murder in a Cathedral City*. Unsolicited mss and synopses (with s.a.e. for return) welcome.
  Royalties paid.

JAC Publications
28 Bellomonte Crescent, Drayton, Norwich, Norfolk NR8 6EJ
☎01603 861339
Managing Editor *John James Vasco*
Publishes World War II Luftwaffe history only. TITLES *Zerstörer: The Messerschmitt 110 and its Units in 1940* John J. Vasco and Peter D. Cornwell; *Bombsights Over England* John James Vasco; *Defending the Reich* Eric Mombeak. Unsolicited mss welcome. No synopses or ideas.
  Royalties paid.

Jackson's Arm Press
See under **Poetry Presses**

John Jones Publishing Ltd
Borthwen, Wrexham Road, Ruthin, Clwyd LL15 1DA
☎01824 707255
Managing Editor *John Idris Jones*
FOUNDED 1989. *Publishes* inexpensive books and booklets in English with a Welsh background. Interested in short, illustrated texts for

the tourist and schools market. Approach in writing with s.a.e.
Royalties paid.

Katabasis
See under **Poetry Presses**

Kittiwake Press
3 Glantwymyn Village Workshops,
Nr. Machynlleth, Montgomeryshire
SY20 8LD
☎01650 511314   Fax 01650 511602
Managing Editor *David Perrott*

FOUNDED 1986. Owned by Perrott Cartographics. *Publishes* guidebooks only, with an emphasis on good design/production. TITLES *Western Islands Handbook; Outer Hebrides Handbook*. Unsolicited mss, synopses and ideas welcome. Specialist cartographic and electronic publishing services available.
Royalties paid.

Lily Publications
12 Millfields Close, Kilgetty, Pembrokeshire
SA68 0SA
☎01834 811895   Fax 01834 814484
Managing Editor *Miles Cowsill*

FOUNDED 1991. *Publishes* holiday guides and specialist books. 5 titles in 1994. TITLES *Pembrokeshire 1995; Cardiganshire 1995/6; Brecon Beacons and Heart of Wales Guide 1995; Cardiff Guide 1995/6; Isle of Man 1994/5*, tourist guide to the island; *Isle of Man – A Photographic Journey*. Unsolicited mss, synopses and ideas welcome. Sister company **Lily Publications (Isle of Man) Ltd.**, PO Box 1, Portland House, Ballasalla, Isle of Man. Tel/fax 01624 823848.
Royalties paid.

Logaston Press
Logaston, Woonton, Almeley, Herefordshire
HR3 6QH
☎01544 327344
Managing Editors *Andy Johnson, Ron Shoesmith*

FOUNDED 1985. *Publishes* walking guides, social history, rural issues and local history for Wales and West Midlands. 3–4 titles a year. TITLES *The Folklore of Hereford & Worcester; James Wathen's Herefordshire 1770–1820; The Prehistoric Sites of Herefordshire; Owain Glyndwr in the Marches*. Unsolicited mss, synopses and ideas welcome. Return postage appreciated.
Royalties paid.

Luath Press Ltd
Barr, Ayrshire KA26 9TN
☎0146 586636   Fax 0146 586625
Managing Editor *T. W. Atkinson*

FOUNDED 1980 to publish books of Scottish interest. *Publishes* guidebooks and books with a Scottish connection. About 6 titles a year. TITLES *Seven Steps in the Dark* (autobiography of a Scottish miner); *Mountain Days and Bothy Nights*. Unsolicited mss, synopses and ideas welcome.
Royalties paid.

Lyfrow Trelyspen
See **CNP Publications**

Mandrake of Oxford
PO Box 250, Oxford OX1 1AP
☎01865 243671
Managing Editor *Kris Morgan*

Publishes occult, surreal, magical art, sexology, heretical and radically new ideas. 3–5 titles a year. TITLES *Shadow Matter and Psychic Phenomena* Gerhard Wassermann; *Rune Magician Trilogy* Jan Fries. No mss; send synopsis first with return postage. There are plans to expand the list into specialist fiction and new science.
Royalties paid.

Marine Day Publishers
64 Cotterill Road, Surbiton, Surrey
KT6 7UN
☎0181 399 7625   Fax 0181 399 1592
Managing Editor *Stephen H. Day*

FOUNDED 1990. Part of The Marine Press Ltd. *Publishes* local history. 1 title a year. TITLES *Malden Old & New; Malden Old & New Revisited; Kingston and Surbiton Old & New; All Change*. Unsolicited synopses and ideas welcome; no mss.
Royalties not paid.

Maypole Editions
22 Mayfair Avenue, Ilford, Essex IG1 3DQ
☎0181 252 0354
Contact *Barry Taylor*

Publisher of fiction and poetry in the main. About 3 titles a year. TITLES *A Crusty Tome; Metallum Damnantorum; Love Sonnets; X and the Glawkoid Party; Laurel Trireme; Frog; Battle Beach*. Unsolicited mss welcome provided return postage is included. Poetry welcome for forthcoming collection. Poems should be approximately 30 lines long, broadly covering social concerns, ethnic minorities, feminist issues, romance, lyric. No politics. The annual collected anthology is designed as a small press platform for first-time poets and a permanent showcase for those already published.

Meadow Books
22 Church Meadow, Milton under Wychwood, Chipping Norton, Oxfordshire OX7 6JG
☎01993 831338
Managing Director C. O'Neill
FOUNDED 1990. *Publishes* a social history of hospitals. TITLES *A Picture of Health; More Pictures of Health* Cynthia O'Neill.

Mercia Cinema Society
19 Pinder's Grove, Wakefield, West Yorkshire WF1 4AH
☎01924 372748
Managing Editor Brian Hornsey
FOUNDED 1980 to foster research into the history of picture houses. *Publishes* books and booklets on the subject, including cinema circuits and chains. Books are often tied in with specific geographical areas. TITLES *Cinemas of Lincoln; The Cinemas of South Tyneside; How to Research the History of Cinemas; Cinemas of York; Cinemas of Southampton; Cinemas of Exeter.* Unsolicited mss, synopses and ideas.
Royalties not paid.

Meridian Books
40 Hadzor Road, Oldbury, Warley, West Midlands B68 9LA
☎0121 429 4397
Managing Editor Peter Groves
FOUNDED 1985 as a small home-based enterprise following the acquisition of titles from Tetradon Publications Ltd. *Publishes* local history, walking and regional guides. 5–6 titles a year. TITLES *Ridges & Valleys II: More Walks in the Midlands* Trevor Antill; *The Navigation Way: A Hundred Mile Towpath Walk* Peter Groves & Trevor Antill; New titles 1994: *Out For the Day in the East Midlands* Ron Wilson; *Favourite Walks in the West Midlands* Tom Birch and Mary Wall; *In the Footsteps of the Gunpowder Plotters* Conall Boyle; *And the Road Below* John Westley; *Wanderers in Northamptonshire: The Second Journey* John & Vera Worledge; *Ridges & Valleys III: A Third Collection of Walks in the Midlands* Trevor Antill. Unsolicited mss, synopses and ideas welcome if relevant. Send s.a.e. if mss is to be returned.
Royalties paid.

Miller Publications
Mount Cottage, Grange Road, Saint Michael's, Tenterden, Kent TN30 6EE
Managing Editor Neil Miller
FOUNDED 1994. *Publishes* short stories – horror and mystery, comedy and romance. IMPRINT **Black Cat Books**. Unsolicited mss, synopses and ideas welcome; will consider any subject provided the story is well-written, i.e. crime, ghost, esoteric. (S.a.e. essential).
Royalties paid.

Minimax Books Ltd
Broadgate House, Church Street, Deeping St James, Peterborough PE6 8HD
☎01778 347609   Fax 01778 341198
Chairman Bob Lavender
Managing Director Lynn Green
Approx. Annual Turnover £40,000
FOUNDED in the early 1980s. *Publishes* books of local interest, children's and history. 3 titles in 1994. Planning to double the size of the list. Unsolicited mss, synopses and ideas welcome. No academic or technical.
Royalties paid twice yearly.

Minority Rights Group Publishing
379 Brixton Road, London SW9 7DE
☎0171 978 9498   Fax 0171 738 6265
Head of Publications Brian Morrison
FOUNDED in the late 1960s, MRG has offices in many other countries and through its publications and the United Nations, works to raise awareness of minority issues worldwide. *Publishes* books, reports and educational material on minority rights. 6–8 titles a year. TITLES *Cutting the Rose - Female Genital Mutilation; The Kurds: A Nation Denied; Somalia: A Nation in Turmoil.* Unsolicited mss, synopses/ideas welcome.
Royalties not paid.

New Arcadian Press
13 Graham Grove, Burley, Leeds, West Yorkshire LS4 2NF
☎0113 2304608
Managing Editor Patrick Eyres
FOUNDED 1981 to publish artist-writer collaborations on landscape and garden themes through *The New Arcadian Journal* (limited edition collector's items). TITLES 1990–95: *Castle Howard; The Wentworths; A Cajun Chapbook; Hearts of Oak; Sons of the Sea; Bushy Topped Trees.* No unsolicited mss, synopses or ideas.
Royalties not paid.

Norvik Press Ltd

School of Modern Languages & European History, University of East Anglia, Norwich, Norfolk NR4 7TJ
☎01603 593356   Fax 01603 250599
Managing Editors *James McFarlane, Janet Garton*

Small academic press. *Publishes* the journal *Scandinavica* and books related to Scandinavian literature. About 4 titles a year. TITLES *Literary History and Criticism* (series); *English Translations of Works of Scandinavian Literature* (series); *A Sudden Liberating Thought* Kjell Askildsen; *From Baltic Shores* ed Christopher Moseley; *Days with Diam* Svend Åge Madsen; *My Son on the Galley* Jacob Wallenberg; *A Century of Swedish Narrative* eds Sarah Death & Helena Forsås-Scott. Interested in synopses and ideas for books within its *Literary History and Criticism* series. No unsolicited mss. *Royalties* paid.

Oriflamme Publishing

60 Charteris Road, London N4 3AB
☎0171 281 8501   Fax 0171 281 8501
Managing Editor *Tony Allen*

FOUNDED 1982, originally to publish science fiction and fantasy but now concentrating on a range of educational textbooks, mainly English and mathematics. Some fiction and special interest also. About 7 titles a year. SERIES *The Rules of Maths; Help Yourself to English; The Rules of English.* No unsolicited mss; synopses/ideas welcome but must be brief. *Royalties* paid.

Owl Press

PO Box 315, Downton, Salisbury, Wiltshire SP5 3YE
☎01243 572988   Fax 01243 572988
Managing Editors *Annie & Paul Musgrove*

FOUNDED 1990. *Publishes* humour, thrillers and books of military interest. No poetry or children's. About 10 titles a year. TITLES *David, We're Pregnant!; 101 Cartoons* Lynn Johnston; *Jungle Campaign, A Regimental Mess.* Unsolicited mss welcome if accompanied by s.a.e. *Royalties* paid.

Palladour Books

Hirwaun House, Aberporth, Nr. Cardigan, Dyfed SA43 2EU
☎01239 811658   Fax 01239 811658
Managing Editors *Jeremy Powell/Anne Powell*

FOUNDED 1986. Started with a twice-yearly issue of catalogues on the literature and poetry of the First World War. Occasional catalogues on Second World War poetry have also been issued. TITLES *A Deep Cry*, a literary pilgrimage to the battlefields and cemeteries of First World War British soldier–poets killed in Northern France and Flanders. No unsolicited mss. *Royalties* not paid.

Partizan Press

816–818 London Road, Leigh on Sea, Essex SS9 3NH
☎01702 73986   Fax 01702 73986
Managing Editor *David Ryan*

Caters for the growing re-enactment and wargaming market. *Publishes* military history and local history, with particular regard to the 17th and 18th centuries. About 30 titles a year. TITLES *Winchester in the Civil War; Eye & Eye Witnesses; Discovery of Witchcraft.* Unsolicited mss welcome. *Royalties* paid.

Paupers' Press

27 Melbourne Road, West Bridgford, Nottingham NG2 5DJ
☎0115 9815063   Fax 0115 9815063
Managing Editor *Colin Stanley*

FOUNDED 1983. *Publishes* extended essays in booklet form (about 15,000 words) on literary criticism and philosophy. About 6 titles a year. TITLES *Becoming Mr Nobody: The Philosophy and Poetry of John Cowper Powys* Paul Roberts; *A Report on the Violent Male* A. E. van Vogt; *Mozart's Journey to Prague: A Playscript* Colin Wilson; *More on the Word Hoard: The Poetry of Seamus Heaney* Stephen Wade; *Proportional Representation: A Debate on the Pitfalls of our Electoral System* Gregory K. Vincent. Limited hardback editions of bestselling titles. No unsolicited mss but synopses and ideas for books welcome. *Royalties* paid.

Peepal Tree Books

17 King's Avenue, Leeds, West Yorkshire LS6 1QS
☎0113 2451703   Fax 0113 2300345
Managing Editor *Jeremy Poynting*

FOUNDED 1985. *Publishes* fiction, poetry, drama and academic studies. *Specialises* in Caribbean, Black British and South Asian Writing. About 18 titles a year. In-house printing and finishing facilities. AUTHORS Kamau Brathwaite, Cyril Dabydeen, Beryl Gilroy, Velma Pollard, Jan Shinebourne and **Forward Poetry Prize** winner Kwame Dawes.

Approach by letter with synopsis and sample chapters/poems in the first instance. Synopses and ideas for books welcome. Write or telephone for a free catalogue.
Royalties paid.

Penny Press
176 Greendale Road, Coventry,
Warwickshire CV5 8AY
☎01203 717275
Publisher *Philip J. Brown*
FOUNDED 1988. *Publishes* science and technology, computer-user manuals and integrated science, against a background of the history of the universe. No unsolicited mss; synopses and ideas welcome especially for science and technology subjects. Currently developing titles for its *History of Natural Creation* series. TITLES *Global Vision: A History of the Universe; Introduction to Basic Science; Review of Current World Problems; Thoughts About the Future.*
Royalties paid twice yearly.

Phoenix Publications
PO Box 255, London SW16 6HA
☎0181 677 1813   Fax 0181 769 6692
Managing Editor *Dennis Sofocleous*
FOUNDED 1993. Publishes fiction, psychological dramas, horror, fantasy and New Age. Some romance considered. TITLE *Spiral Terra.* Unsolicited mss, synopses and ideas welcome.
Royalties not paid.

Playwrights Publishing Co.
70 Nottingham Road, Burton Joyce,
Nottinghamshire NG14 5AL
☎0115 9313356
Managing Editors *Liz Breeze, Tony Breeze*
FOUNDED 1990. *Publishes* one-act and full-length plays. TITLES *Birthmarks* Mark Jenkins; *Lifestyles* Silvia Vaughan; *Undercoats* Roger Pinkham. Unsolicited scripts welcome. No synopses or ideas. Reading fee £10 one act; £20 full length.
Royalties paid.

Polymath Publishing
The Old School House, Streatley Hill,
Streatley-on-Thames, Berkshire RG8 9RD
☎01491 875032   Fax 01491 875035
Owner *Charles Knevitt*
FOUNDED 1989. *Publishes* general interest and technical architecture and construction industry books, postcard books, calendars, etc., also cartoon anthologies. TITLES *From Pecksniff to The*

Prince of Wales: 150 Years of Punch Cartoons on Architecture, Planning and Development 1851–1991; The Responsive Office: People and Change; Seven Ages of the Architect: The Very Best of Louis Hellman 1967–92; Shelter: Human Habitats From Around the World; re-issue of *Community Architecture* (Penguin 1987). Synopses and ideas welcome.
Royalties negotiable.

Power Publications
1 Clayford Avenue, Ferndown, Dorset
BH22 9PQ
☎01202 875223
Contact *Mike Power*
FOUNDED 1989. *Publishes* local interest, pub walk guides and mountain bike guides. 2–3 titles a year. TITLES *Pub Walks in Cornwall/Hampshire* etc (series); *Ferndown: A Look Back; Dorset Coast Path; Famous Women in Dorset.* Unsolicited mss, synopses and ideas welcome.
Royalties paid.

Praxis Books
Sheridan, Broomers Hill Lane, Pulborough,
West Sussex RH20 2DU
☎01798 873504
Proprietor *Rebecca Smith*
FOUNDED 1992. *Publishes* philosophy, theology, reissues of Victorian fiction, travel, general interest. 9 titles to date. TITLES *In Search of Life's Meaning* R. Matley and R. Smith; *The Poet's Kit* Katherine Knight; *A Book of Folklore* Sabine Baring-Gould; *A Bulgarian Diary* Becky Smith. Unsolicited mss accepted with s.a.e. Shared funding, shared profits.

Previous Parrot Press
The Foundry, Church Hanborough,
Nr. Witney, Oxford OX8 8AB
☎01993 881260
Managing Editor *Dennis Hall*
Publishes limited illustrated editions of poetry and prose, and books on book illustration. About 3 titles a year. TITLES *A School for Life* Fiona Pitt Kethley; *The Illustrated Editions of Candide* Peter Tucker.

QED Books
1 Straylands Grove, York YO3 0EB
☎01904 424381   Fax 01904 424381
Managing Editor *John Bibby*
Publishes and *distributes* resource guides and learning aids, including laminated posters, for mathematics and science. TITLES *Fun Maths*

Calendar; Maths Resource Guides; Maths and Art; Joy of Maths. Synopses (3pp) and ideas for books welcome. QED arranges publicity for other small presses and has many contacts overseas. *Royalties* by agreement.

Quay Books Exeter
Tuck Mill Cottage, Payhembury, Near Honiton, Devon EX14 0HF
☎01404 84376

Managing Editor *Chris Smith*

FOUNDED 1990 to publish *Village Profiles*, a down-your-way type series broadcast on **BBC Radio Devon**. *Publishes* local history and general fiction by Devon authors. There are plans to expand the list. No unsolicited mss; synopses and ideas welcome but opportunities are limited at present. S.a.e. essential with submissions. *Royalties* paid.

QueenSpark Books
Brighton Media Centre, 11 Jew Street, Brighton, East Sussex BN1 1UT
☎01273 748348

A community writing and publishing group run mainly by volunteers who work together to write and produce books. Since the early 1970s they have published 40 titles: local autobiographies, humour, poetry, history and politics. Free writing workshops and groups held on a regular basis. New members welcome.

Redstone Press
7A St Lawrence Terrace, London W10 5SU
☎0171 352 1594   Fax 0171 352 8749

Managing Editor *Julian Rothenstein*

FOUNDED 1987. *Publishes* art and literature. About 5 titles a year. No unsolicited mss; synopses and ideas welcome but familiarity with Redstone's list advised in the first instance. *Royalties* paid.

Rivers Oram Press
144 Hemingford Road, London N1 1DE
☎0171 607 0823   Fax 0171 609 2776

Managing Director *Elizabeth Fidlon*

FOUNDED 1990. *Publishes* radical political and social sciences. No fiction, children's or cookery. *Royalties* paid annually.

The Robinswood Press
30 South Avenue, Stourbridge, West Midlands DY8 3XY
☎01384 397475   Fax 01384 440443

Managing Editor *Christopher J. Marshall*

FOUNDED 1985. *Publishes* education, particularly remedial and Steiner-based. About 3–5 titles a year. TITLES *Waldorf Education, An Introduction; Take Time; Phonic Rhyme Time; The Extra Lesson* (exercises for children with learning difficulties); *Stories for the Festivals; Spotlight on Words.* Unsolicited mss, synopses and ideas welcome. *Royalties* paid.

Romer Publications
170 Brick Lane, London E1 6RU
☎0171 247 3581   Fax 0171 247 3581

Also at: PO Box 10120, NL–1001 EC Amsterdam, The Netherlands
☎/fax 00 31 20 6769442

Managing Editor *Hubert de Brouwer*

FOUNDED 1986. Recent expansion into children's books (*Dominic Dormouse Goes to Town* by Anthony Wall) but main tenet remains critical reflection on origins and legitimacy of established institutions. Specialises in history, education and law. TITLES *The Children's Kosher Funbook* Rabbi L. Book; *The Decline of the House of Herod; Fascism Down the Ages: From Caesar to Hitler* Frank Ridley; *The Rise and Fall of the English Empire* Frank Ridley; *Marquis de Sade, Monster or Martyr* Robert Laws; *African Mythology for Children* Impendoh Dan Iyan. Sound, coherent and quality mss, synopses or ideas appropriate to the publisher's list will be seriously considered. *Royalties* paid.

Sawd Books
Plackett's Hole, Bicknor, Sittingbourne, Kent ME9 8BA
☎01795 472262   Fax 01795 422633

Managing Editor *Susannah Wainman*

FOUNDED 1989 to supply the local interests of the people of Kent. *Publishes* local interest, cookery, gardening and general non-fiction. About 3 titles a year. No unsolicited mss; synopses and ideas welcome (include s.a.e.). No fiction. *Royalties* paid.

Scottish Cultural Press
PO Box 106, Aberdeen AB9 8ZE
☎01224 583777   Fax 01224 583777

Chair/Managing Editor *Jill Dick*

FOUNDED 1992. Began publishing in 1993. *Publishes* Scottish interest titles, including cultural, local history and children's non-fiction. Pre-publication consultancy. Subscription journal management. Distribution for individual publishers provided subject in general SCP interest bands.

IMPRINTS
Scottish Cultural Press, Scottish Children's Press. TITLES *Teach Yourself Doric; Moray Firth Ships and Trade; A–Z Scots Words for Younger Children*. Unsolicited mss, synopses and ideas welcome provided return postage is included.

Royalties paid. Trade Counter and office: 13 Millburn Street, Aberdeen AB1 2SS

Serif
47 Strahan Road, London E3 5DA
☎0181 981 3990   Fax 0181 981 3990
Managing Editor *Stephen Hayward*

FOUNDED 1994. *Publishes* fiction, cookery, Irish studies and modern history. 9 titles in 1994. TITLES *Gifts* Nuruddin Farah; *The Crowd in History* George Rudé; *The Alice B. Toklas Cookbook; The Crime Studio* Steve Aylett. Ideas and synopses welcome; no unsolicited mss.

Royalties paid.

The Sharkti Laureate
104 Argyle Gardens, Upminster, Essex RM14 3EU
Managing Editor *Pamela Constantine*

FOUNDED 1976 to produce books and journals heralding the Renaissance Movement which is now international. TITLES: *The Celtic Collection* (poetry) by The Pleiades; *Valley of Wings*, a miscellany of poetry, prose and songs; *Orfeo's Tale*, a verse re-telling of the Orphic Legend; *New English Renaissance* by the SL Writing Group; *The Cornerstone* (poetry) by Pamela Constantine. Unsolicited mss welcome, but only those in line with the Renaissance, which is 'an inclusive medium for the revival of the human spirit, reflecting and respecting the many ways of being, through the world of ideas and the imagination'. Only prose mss (fiction/articles/essays) up to 1500 words, poems up to 32 lines. Aim to provide good writing at accessible prices.

Royalties not paid; complimentary copies only.

Sherlock Publications
6 Bramham Moor, Hill Head, Fareham, Hampshire PO14 3RU
☎01329 667325
Managing Editor *Philip Weller*

FOUNDED to supply publishing support to a number of Sherlock Holmes societies. *Publishes* Sherlock Holmes studies only. About 14 titles a year. TITLES *Elementary Holmes; Alphabetically,* *My Dear Watson; Anonymously, My Dear Lestrade; The Annotated Sherlock Holmes Cases*. No unsolicited mss; synopses and ideas welcome.

Royalties not paid.

Silent Books Ltd
10 Market Street, Swavesey, Cambridge CB4 5QG
☎01954 232199/231000   Fax 01954 232199
Managing Director *Carole A. Green*

FOUNDED 1985. *Publishes* general art titles, gardening, cookery, community care and books for the gift market, all high quality productions. No fiction. About 12 titles a year. Unsolicited mss, synopses and ideas welcome.

Silver Link Publishing Ltd
Unit 5, Home Farm Close, Church Street, Wadenhoe, Peterborough PE8 5TE
☎01832 720440   Fax 01832 720440
Managing Editor *William Adams*

FOUNDED 1985 in Lancashire, changed hands in 1990 and now based in Northamptonshire. Small independent company specialising in top quality illustrated books on railways, trams, ships and other transport subjects, also, under the Past and Present Publishing imprint, postwar nostalgia on all aspects of social history. 20 titles in 1994. TITLES: *British Railways Past and Present* series; *British Roads Past and Present* series; *British Counties, Towns and Cities Past and Present* series; *Daily Life In Britain Past and Present* series; *Classic Steam; Railway Heritage; A Nostalgic Look at ...* photographic collections: *Silver Link Library of Railway Modelling*. Unsolicited synopses and ideas welcome.

Royalties and fees paid.

Spacelink Books
115 Hollybush Lane, Hampton, Middlesex TW12 2QY
☎0181 979 3148
Managing Director *Lionel Beer*

FOUNDED 1986. Named after a UFO magazine published in the 1960/70s. *Publishes* titles connected with UFOs, Fortean phenomena and paranormal events. TITLES *The Moving Statue of Ballinspittle and Related Phenomena*. No unsolicited mss; send synopses and ideas. Publishers of *TEMS News* for the Travel and Earth Mysteries Society.

Royalties and fees paid according to contract.

Springboard
See **Yorkshire Art Circus Ltd**

Stepney Books Publications
19 Tomlins Grove, Bow, London E3 4NX
Contact *Jenny Smith*

FOUNDED 1976. A community publishing project run on a part-time basis. Heavily reliant on fundraising and grants for each new publication of which there is one about every 18 months. *Publishes* history and autobiography of Tower Hamlets in London. TITLES *Memories of Old Poplar; Children of the Green.* Unsolicited material considered but 'any publication we undertake to do can take years to get to press whilst we raise the money to fund it'.

Stone Flower Ltd
2 Horder Road, London SW6 5EE
☎0171 736 0477

Chairman *J. Norman*
Managing Director *L. G. Norman*

Publishes biography, fiction, humour and legal. 'No anthropomorphism. No hype. Some indication of literacy, please.' Unsolicited synopses and ideas welcome with return postage, *otherwise* mss only with return postage and £100 reading fee.

Royalties paid twice yearly.

Stride
See under **Poetry Presses**

Sunk Island Publishing
PO Box 74, Lincoln LN1 1QG
☎01522 575660   Fax 01522 568353
Managing Editor *Michael Blackburn*

FOUNDED 1989. Publishes paperback fiction and the literary magazine, *Sunk Island Review.* TITLES *Hallowed Ground* Robert Edric; *Radio Activity* John Murray. Also publishes poetry under the **Jackson's Arm** imprint. TITLES *Harvest* Pat Winslow; *The Constructed Space – A Celebration of W.S. Graham* ed Duncan & Davidson. Now publishing books on disk. TITLES *The Electronic Poetry Pack.*

Royalties by arrangement, on publication.

Tamarind Ltd
PO Box 296, Camberley, Surrey GU15 1QW
☎01276 683979   Fax 01276 685365
Managing Editor *Verna Wilkins*

FOUNDED 1987 to publish material in which Black children are given an unselfconscious, positive profile. Publishes a series of picture books and other educational material (puzzles, recipes, maps) with the emphasis on a balance between education and fun. Titles include 4

tie-ins with BBC Education. No unsolicited mss. Approach in writing.

Tarquin Publications
Stradbroke, Diss, Norfolk IP21 5JP
☎01379 384218   Fax 01379 384289
Managing Editor *Gerald Jenkins*

FOUNDED 1970 as a hobby which gradually grew and now *publishes* mathematical, cut-out models, teaching and pop-up books. Other topics covered if they involve some kind of paper cutting or pop-up scenes. 7 titles in 1994. TITLES *Make Shapes – Mathematical Models; DNA – The Marvellous Molecule; Dragon Mobiles.* No unsolicited mss; letter with 1–2 page synopses welcome.

Royalties paid.

Terminus Publications
15 Woodbridge Rise, Walton, Chesterfield, Derbyshire S40 3LL
☎01246 278486
Managing Editor *A. R. Kaye*

FOUNDED 1981. Formerly known as Lowlander Publications. *Publishes* general transport titles and 'then & now' type illustrated books. TITLES *Great Central Railway North of Nottingham; Cromford & High Peak Railway, Final Years; Chesterfield Through the Years; North Midland Railways in the Steam Age.* Also video publishing – about 15 titles a year – railways and buses (lists sent on receipt of s.a.e.). Unsolicited mss, synopses and ideas can't always be considered, but are sometimes welcome.

Royalties paid.

Two Heads Publishing
9 Whitehall Park, London N19 3TS
☎0171 561 1606   Fax 0171 561 1607
Contact *Charles Frewin*

Independent publisher of sport, humour and guides with a London focus. Also publishes a range of cycling guides under the *Two Wheels* imprint. Synopses and ideas welcome; write in the first instance.

Royalties paid quarterly.

Tyrannosaurus Rex Press
BM Box 1129, London WC1N 3XX
☎01923 229784
Managing Editor *Dr Keith H. Seddon*

FOUNDED 1993. *Publishes* gothic, literary fiction, philosophy and religion. 1–2 titles a year. TITLES *Grim Fairy Tales; The Faceless Tarot; The*

Agonies of Time. No unsolicited mss; synopses and ideas welcome with s.a.e.

Royalties paid.

Underhill Press

6 St James Court, Piper Lane, Thirsk, North Yorkshire YO7 1FN
☎01845 526749   Fax 01845 524347

Managing Editor *Peter Pack*

Publishing arm of the Learning Resources Development Group. Began by publishing conference and seminar proceedings but has since expanded. *Publishes* further and higher education material with particular reference to the management of learning resources; alternative systems of delivering learning; information strategy and IT in colleges; independent and distance learning; new developments in college management. 2–3 titles a year. TITLES *Product & Performance; Citing Your References; Bridging the Gap; Funding and Performance; College Learning Resources: Are They Really Worth It?*. Ideas and synopses welcome. No unsolicited mss.

Payment negotiable.

Wakefield Historical Publications

19 Pinder's Grove, Wakefield, West Yorkshire WF1 4AH
☎01924 372748

Managing Editor *Kate Taylor*

FOUNDED 1977 by the Wakefield Historical Society to publish well-researched, scholarly works of regional (namely West Riding) historical significance. 1–2 titles a year. TITLES *Aspects of Medieval Wakefield; Landscape Gardens in West Yorkshire 1680–1880; Coal Kings of Yorkshire; The Aire and Calder Navigation; Right Royal, a History of Wakefield's Westgate Theatres*. Unsolicited mss, synopses and ideas for books welcome.

Royalties not paid.

Westwood Press

44 Boldmere Road, Sutton Coldfield, West Midlands B73 5TD
☎0121 354 5913   Fax 0121 355 6920

Managing Editor *Reg Hollins*

FOUNDED 1955 as a general printer and commenced local publication in the 1970s. *Publishes* local history of the Birmingham area only and specialised printing 'Know How' publications. 2 titles in 1994. TITLES *A History of Boldmere; The Book of Brum; Up the Terrace – Down Aston and Lozells*. No unsolicited mss; synopses and ideas welcome.

Royalties paid.

Whyld Publishing Co-op

Moorland House, Kelsey Road, Caistor, Lincolnshire LN7 6SF
☎01472 851374   Fax 01472 851374

Managing Editor *Janie Whyld*

Having taken over former ILEA titles on anti-sexist work with boys which would otherwise have vanished, Janie Whyld has gone on to publish a specialist list of educational materials for teachers, trainers and students, with an emphasis on equal opportunities and interpersonal skills. About 2 titles a year. Now moving into 'paperless publishing'. TITLES *Anti-Sexist Work with Boys and Young Men; NVQs and the Assessment of Interpersonal Skills; The Essence of Yin and Yang; Multicultural Stories; Countering Objections to Anti-Sexist Work; Teaching Assertiveness in Schools and Colleges; Equal Opportunities in Training and Groupwork; Using Counselling Skills to Help People Learn*. Mss, synopses/ideas which meet these requirements welcome.

Royalties nominal.

Winter Sweet Press

See **Fox Press**

Working Books Ltd

23–24 George Street, Richmond, Surrey TW9 1HY
☎0181 332 0746   Fax 0181 332 9300

Directors *E. Ephraums, G. Jones*

FOUNDED in 1983. *Publishes* highly illustrated and informative practical photography books covering conventional processes and digital imaging techniques. Also new technology books covering areas such as CD-ROM, Photo CD, etc. About 5 titles a year. Unsolicited mss, synopsis and ideas for books welcome.

Royalties paid quarterly.

Works Publishing

12 Blakestones Road, Slaithwaite, Huddersfield, West Yorkshire HD7 5UQ
☎01484 842324

Managing Editor *Dave W. Hughes*

One-man operation publishing two magazines: *Works* (science fiction) and *The Modern Dance* (music review). Stories and poems welcome for *Works* but no submissions for *Modern Dance*. Unsolicited mss (with s.a.e.) welcome; no synopses/ideas. Advertising rates, single issue rates, guidelines and subscription rates are all available for an s.a.e.

Royalties not paid.

Yoffoy Publications

7 Upper Dumpton Park Road, Ramsgate,
Kent CT11 7PE
☎01843 851419

Managing Editor *Frank Foy*

FOUNDED 1988. *Publishes* non-fiction and educational, plus information packs in various subject areas, including music and games. 1–2 titles a year. TITLES *Employment in Europe, A Guide; Music Network Guide* (to the music industry); *Play it Now!* (electric guitar tutor manual). Unsolicited mss, synopses and ideas welcome. Educational game material of interest.

Royalties paid depending on contract.

Yorkshire Art Circus Ltd

School Lane, Glass Houghton, Castleford,
West Yorkshire WF10 4QH
☎01977 550401   Fax 01977 512819

Approx. Annual Turnover £180,000

FOUNDED 1987. *Specialises* in new writing by first-time authors. *Publishes* autobiography, community books, fiction and local interest (Yorkshire, Humberside). No local history, children's, reference or nostalgia. TITLES *When Push Comes to Shove* ed. Ian Clayton; *Chapati and Chips* Almas Khan. Unsolicited mss discouraged; authors should send for fact sheet in first instance. **Springboard** fiction imprint launched 1993.

UK Packagers

The Albion Press Ltd
Spring Hill, Idbury, Oxfordshire OX7 6RU
☎01993 831094   Fax 01993 831982
Chairman/Managing Director *Emma Bradford*

FOUNDED 1984 to produce high-quality illustrated titles. *Commissions* illustrated trade titles, particularly children's, English literature, social history and art. About 10 titles a year. TITLES *The Darling Buds of May Book of the Seasons* H. E. Bates; *A Child's Book of Prayers* Linda Yeatman; *A New Treasury of Poetry* Neil Philip. Unsolicited synopses and ideas for books not generally welcome.

Royalties paid; fees paid for introductions and partial contributions.

Alphabet & Image Ltd
See **Marston House** under **UK Publishers**

Andromeda Oxford Ltd
11–15 The Vineyard, Abingdon, Oxfordshire OX14 3PX
☎01235 550296   Fax 01235 550330
Managing Director *Mark Ritchie*
Approx. Annual Turnover £7 million

FOUNDED 1986. *Commissions* adult and junior international illustrated reference, both single volume and series. About 30 titles a year.

DIVISIONS
Adult Books *Graham Bateman* (Editorial Director); **Children's Books** *Derek Hall* (Editorial Director); **Transedition Books** *Ed Glover* (Publishing Director); **Andromeda Interactive** *Jonathan Taylor* (Managing Director). TITLES *Encyclopedia of World Geography; Cultural Atlases; Junior Science Encyclopedia; Encyclopedia of World History; Pointers; Spotlights, Interactive Space Encyclopedia; Complete Shakespeare; Classic Library* on CD ROM. Approach by letter in the first instance.

Anness Publishing Ltd
See under **UK Publishers**

Archival Facsimiles Ltd
The Old Bakery, 52 Crown Street, Banham, Norwich, Norfolk NR16 2HW
☎01953 887277   Fax 01953 888361
Contact *Cris de Boos*

FOUNDED 1986. Produces scholarly reprints for the **British Library** among others, plus high-quality limited edition publications for academic/business organisations in Europe and the USA, ranging from leather-bound folios of period print reproductions to small illustrated booklets. *Publishes* Antarctic exploration titles (about 2 a year) under the **Erskine Press** imprint. No unsolicited mss. Ideas welcome.

Payment usually fees.

AS Publishing
73 Montpelier Rise, London NW11 9DU
☎0181 458 3552   Fax 0181 458 0618
Managing Director *Angela Sheehan*

FOUNDED 1987. *Commissions* children's illustrated non-fiction. No unsolicited synopses or ideas for books, but approaches welcome from experienced authors, editors and illustrators in this field.

Fees paid.

Autumn Publishing Ltd
See under **UK Publishers**

BCS Publishing Ltd
1 Bignell Park Barns, Kirtlington Road, Chesterton, Bicester, Oxon OX6 8TD
☎01869 324423   Fax 01869 324385
Managing Director *Steve McCurdy*
Approx. Annual Turnover £350,000

Commissions general interest non-fiction for international co-edition market.

Belitha Press Ltd
31 Newington Green, London N16 9PU
☎0171 241 5566   Fax 0171 254 5325
Editorial Director *Mary-Jane Wilkins*

FOUNDED 1980. *Commissions* children's non-fiction in all curriculum areas. About 50 titles a year. Strong on international co-edition packaging. All titles are expected to sell in at least four co-editions. TITLES *The Satellite Atlas; The Children's First Atlas; Exploration Into . . .* (8 titles exploring the history and culture of different regions); *History's Big Mistakes; History's Heroes and Villains; Science Horizons; CLICK! Fun with Photography; Magic in Art; Introducing Composers.* No unsolicited mss. Synopses and ideas for books welcome from experienced children's writers.

Bellew Publishing Co. Ltd
See under **UK Publishers**

David Bennett Books Ltd
94 Victoria Street, St Albans, Hertfordshire
AL1 3TG
☎01727 855878   Fax 01727 864085
Managing Director *David Bennett*
FOUNDED 1989. Producer of children's books:
picture and novelty books, baby gifts and non-
fiction. Synopses and ideas for books welcome.
No fiction or poetry.
Payment both fees and royalties.

Bison Books Ltd
Kimbolton House, 117A Fulham Road,
London SW3 6RL
☎0171 823 9222   Fax 0171 823 8863
Managing Director *Sydney L. Mayer*
Editorial Head *Ian Westwell*
Part of the Bison Group, one of the world's
largest book packagers. *Commissions* large-format illustrated books on art, history, aviation,
militaria, transport, travel, entertainment, sport
and wildlife. About 100 new titles and 200
reprint and foreign editions a year. TITLES
*Ukiyo-e; Art Deco in Europe; Harley Davidson;
History of the World*. No unsolicited mss. The
vast majority of titles originate by commission;
synopses/ideas will be considered.
Royalties by arrangement.

BLA Publishing Ltd
1 Christopher Road, East Grinstead, West
Sussex RH19 3BT
☎01342 318980   Fax 01342 410980
Owner *Ling Kee (UK) Ltd*
Director *Vincent Winter*
Packagers of multi-volume encyclopedias for
younger readers, and information book series
on various topics. *Publishes* illustrated general
non-fiction under the **Thames Head** imprint.
Payment varies according to contract (reference books tend to be flat fees; royalties for single author or illustrator).

Book Packaging and Marketing
3 Murswell Lane, Silverstone, Towcester,
Northamptonshire NN12 8UT
☎01327 858380   Fax 01327 858380
Contact *Martin F. Marix Evans*
FOUNDED 1989. Essentially a project management service, handling books demanding close
designer/editor teamwork or complicated multi-
contributor administration, for publishers, business 'or anyone who needs one'. Mainly illustrated adult non-fiction including travel, historical, home reference and coffee-table books. No
fiction or poetry. 3–5 titles a year. Proposals considered. Writers are often required for projects in
development. TITLES *Royal College of Nursing
Manual of Family Health; The Golfers Diary; D-
Day and the Battle of Normandy; Canals of England;
Contemporary Photographers, 3rd ed.; World War II;
Nelles Guide to London, England and Wales.*
Payment Authors contract direct with client
publishers. Usually, fees paid on first print, royalties on reprint – but depends on publisher.

Breslich & Foss Ltd
20 Wells Mews, London W1P 3FJ
☎0171 580 8774   Fax 0171 580 8784
Director *Paula Breslich*
Approx. Annual Turnover £1.5 million
Packagers of non-fiction titles only, including
art, children's, crafts, gardening and health.
Unsolicited mss welcome but synopses pre-
ferred. Include s.a.e. with all submissions.
Royalties paid twice yearly.

Brown Wells and Jacobs Ltd
Forresters Hall, 25–27 Westow Street, London
SE19 3RY
☎0181 771 5115   Fax 0181 771 9994
Managing Director *Graham Brown*
FOUNDED 1979. *Commissions* non-fiction, nov-
elty, pre-school and first readers, natural history
and science. About 40 titles a year. Unsolicited
synopses and ideas for books welcome.
Fees paid.

Calmann & King Ltd
71 Great Russell Street, London WC1B 3BN
☎0171 831 6351   Fax 0171 831 8356
Chairman *Robin Hyman*
Managing Director *Laurence King*
Approx. Annual Turnover £2.8 million
FOUNDED 1976. *Commissions* books on art, the
decorative arts, design and nature. About 20
titles a year. Unsolicited synopses and ideas for
books welcome.
Royalties paid twice yearly.

Cameron Books (Production) Ltd
PO Box 1, Moffat, Dumfriesshire DG10 9SU
☎01683 220808   Fax 01683 220012
Directors *Ian A. Cameron, Jill Hollis*
Approx. Annual Turnover £350,000
Commissions natural history, social history, dec-
orative arts, fine arts, collectors' reference, edu-

cational reference, gardening, cookery, conservation, countryside, film and design. About 6 titles a year. Unsolicited synopses and ideas for books welcome.

Payment varies with each contract.

Chancerel International Publishers Ltd
40 Tavistock Street, London WC2E 7PB
☎0171 240 2811   Fax 0171 836 4186
Managing Director *W. D. B. Prowse*

FOUNDED 1976. *Commissions* educational books, and *publishes* language-teaching materials in most languages. Language teachers/writers often required as authors/consultants, especially native speakers other than English.

Payment generally by flat fee but royalties sometimes.

Philip Clark Ltd
53 Calton Avenue, Dulwich, London SE21 7DF
☎0181 693 5605   Fax 0181 299 4647
Managing Director *Philip Clark*

Founder member of the **Book Packagers Association**. *Commissions* heavily illustrated titles on a variety of subjects. TITLES include *The Complete Guide to Windsurfing* and the *Travellers Wine Guides* series (both projects have sold over 100,000 copies in several languages). Unsolicited synopses and ideas for books, particularly on international subjects, are welcome.

Fees paid.

Diagram Visual Information Ltd
195 Kentish Town Road, London NW5 8SY
☎0171 482 3633   Fax 0171 482 4932
Managing Director *Bruce Robertson*

FOUNDED 1967. Producer of library, school, academic and trade reference books. About 10 titles a year. Unsolicited synopses and ideas welcome.

Fees paid; no payment for sample material/submissions for consideration.

Dorling Kindersley Ltd
See under **UK Publishers**

Eddison Sadd Editions
St Chad's Court, 146B King's Cross Road, London WC1X 9DH
☎0171 837 1968   Fax 0171 837 2025
Managing Director *Nick Eddison*
Editorial Director *Ian Jackson*
Approx. Annual Turnover £3 million
FOUNDED 1982. Produces a wide range of popu-

lar illustrated non-fiction, with books published in 25 countries. Ideas and synopses are welcome but titles must have international appeal.

Royalties paid twice yearly; flat fees paid when appropriate.

Erskine Press
See **Archival Facsimiles Ltd**

Greenpeace Books
5 Baker's Row, London EC1R 3DB
☎0171 833 0600   Fax 0171 837 6606
Executive Director *Richard Titchen*

FOUNDED 1987. *Commissions* books across the entire area of environmental concerns and *publishes* titles for Greenpeace. TITLES *The Greenpeace Book of Coral Reefs; The Greenpeace Global Warming Report.* No unsolicited mss; synopses and ideas for books considered.

Hessayon Books Ltd
Britannica House, Waltham Cross, Hertfordshire EN8 7DY
☎01992 641144   Fax 01992 641225
Chairman *Dr. D. G. Hessayon*

FOUNDED 1993. Produces the Expert series of books by Dr. D. G. Hessayon. TITLES *The Flowering Shrub Expert; The Greenhouse Expert; The Flower Arranging Expert; The Container Expert; The Bulb Expert.* No unsolicited material.

Labyrinth Publishing (UK) Ltd
32 Leighton Road, London NW5 2QE
☎0171 284 4783   Fax 0171 284 3038
Publisher *Philip Dunn*
Managing Director *Yashen Jones*

Packagers of illustrated non-fiction across a range of subjects from religion and mythology to psychology and self-help. Books are sold in high volume to major international publishing houses. About 10 titles a year. Synopses and ideas welcome. Authors are offered a high degree of involvement in the design and production stages. Expansion planned in the areas of reference, children's non-fiction, youth lifestyle guides and sponsored books.

Royalties Fees paid to authors on ideas generated in-house; otherwise twice yearly.

Leading Edge Press & Publishing Ltd
Old Chapel, Burtersett, Hawes, North Yorkshire DL8 3PB
☎01969 667566   Fax 01969 667788
Chairman/Managing Director *Stan Abbott*

Approx. Annual Turnover £300,000

FOUNDED 1984. Primarily a commercial magazine/brochure/newsletter design and production house. Book production accounts for about a quarter of the company's activities. *Commissions* transport and outdoor leisure, including walking. 8–10 titles a year. Synopses and ideas for books welcome subject to prior contact by phone. The publisher encourages joint financial ventures, or sponsorship, in appropriate cases.

Royalties paid thrice yearly and/or fees.

Lennard Associates Ltd
Windmill Cottage, Mackerye End,
Harpenden, Hertfordshire AL5 5DR
☎01582 715866   Fax 01582 715121

Chairman/Managing Director *Adrian Stephenson*

FOUNDED 1979. Packager and publisher of sport, humour and personality books, plus television associated titles. TITLES include *Arthur's World of Cats; Mike Tyson – The Release of Power* Reg Gutteridge & Norman Giller; *Dark Places* James Herbert; *The Cricketers' Who's Who* ed. Iain Sproat; *The Whitbread Rugby World*. No unsolicited mss. IMPRINTS **Lennard Publishing, Queen Anne Press**. Acquired the latter and most of its assets in 1992.

Payment both fees and royalties by arrangement.

Lexus Ltd
205 Bath Street, Glasgow G2 4HZ
☎0141 221 5266   Fax 0141 226 3139

Managing/Editorial Director *P. M. Terrell*

FOUNDED 1980. *Commissions* bilingual reference, language and phrase books. About 20 titles a year. TITLES *Chambers Travelmate Series; Collins Italian Concise Dictionary; Harrap Study Aids; Hugo's Phrase Books; Harrap Shorter French Dictionary* (revised); *Impact Specialist Bilingual Glossaries; Oxford Student's Japanese Learner*. No unsolicited material. Books are mostly commissioned. Freelance contributors employed for a wide range of languages.

Payment generally flat fee.

Lionheart Books
10 Chelmsford Square, London NW10 3AR
☎0181 459 0453   Fax 0181 451 3681

Senior Partner *Lionel Bender*
Partner *Madeleine Samuel*
Designer *Ben White*
Approx. Annual Turnover £250,000

A design/editorial packaging team. Titles are either conceived by the partnership or commissioned from publishers. Highly illustrated non-fiction for children aged 8–14, mostly natural history, history and general science. About 20 titles a year.

Payment generally flat fee.

Market House Books Ltd
2 Market House, Market Square, Aylesbury,
Buckinghamshire HP20 1TN
☎01296 84911   Fax 01296 437073

Directors *Dr Alan Isaacs/Dr John Daintith*

FOUNDED 1970. Formerly Laurence Urdang Associates. *Commissions* dictionaries, encyclopedias and reference. About 15 titles a year. TITLES *European Culture; Concise Medical Dictionary; Brewer's 20th Century Phrase and Fable; Oxford Dictionary for Science Writers and Editors; Concise Dictionary of Business; Concise Dictionary of Finance; Bloomsbury Thesaurus; Collins English Dictionary; The Macmillan Encyclopedia*. Unsolicited material not welcome – most books compiled in-house.

Fees paid.

Marshall Cavendish Books
119 Wardour Street, London W1V 3TD
☎0171 734 6710   Fax 0171 439 1423

Head of Editorial *Martin Annable*
Approx. Annual Turnover £3 million

A division of Marshall Cavendish Partworks Ltd. FOUNDED 1968. Primarily partwork material in book form but also originates its own material. Freelance editorial services sought on occasions.

Fees paid, not royalties.

Marshall Editions Ltd
170 Piccadilly, London W1V 9DD
☎0171 629 0079   Fax 0171 834 0785

Publisher *Bruce Marshall*
Editorial Director *Sophie Collins*

FOUNDED 1977. *Commissions* non-fiction, including thematic atlases, leisure, self-improvement and visual information for children. TITLES *The Human Body Explained; Revelations: The Medieval World; The Robot Zoo; The Natural History of Evolution; Your Personal Trainer*.

MM Productions Ltd
16–20 High Street, Ware, Hertfordshire
SG12 9BX
☎01920 466003   Fax 01920 466003

Chairman/Managing Director *Mike Moran*

Packager and publisher. TITLES *MM Publisher Database; MM Printer Database* (available in UK, European and international editions).

Neil & Ting Morris
27 Riverview Grove, London W4 3QL
☎0181 994 1874   Fax 0181 742 8643

Partners *Neil Morris, Ting Morris*

FOUNDED 1979. Mainly children's fiction and non-fiction including information books, activity books and dictionaries. About 20 titles a year. No unsolicited mss but interested in seeing examples of illustrators' work.
Royalties usually paid.

Oyster Books Ltd
Unit 4B, Kirklea Farm, Badgworth, Axbridge, Somerset BS26 2QH
☎01934 732251   Fax 01934 732514

Managing Director *Jenny Wood*

FOUNDED 1985. Packagers of quality books and book/toy/gift items for children of pre-school age to ten years. About 20 titles a year. Most material is created in-house.
Payment usually fees.

Parke Sutton Ltd
The Old Bakery, 52 Crown Street, Banham, Norwich, Norfolk NR16 2HW
☎01953 887277   Fax 01953 888361

Director *Crispin De Boos*

FOUNDED 1982. Produces newspapers, magazines and reference books for organisations and training offices; and packages books for publishers. About 10 titles a year. Unsolicited synopses and ideas for books welcome. S.a.e. essential.
Royalties paid twice yearly; fees sometimes paid rather than royalties.

Playne Books
Trefin, Haverfordwest, Dyfed SA62 5AU
☎01348 837073   Fax 01348 837063

Director *David Playne*
Editor *Gill Davies*

FOUNDED 1987. *Commissions* highly illustrated and practical books on any subject. Currently developing a new list for young children. Unsolicited synopses and ideas for books welcome.
Royalties paid 'on payment from publishers'. Fees sometimes paid instead of royalties.

Mathew Price Ltd
The Old Glove Factory, Bristol Road, Sherborne, Dorset DT9 4HP
☎01935 816010   Fax 01935 816310

Chairman/Managing Director *Mathew Price*
Approx. Annual Turnover £1 million

Commissions high-quality, full-colour picture books and fiction for young children; also nov-

elty and non-fiction. Unsolicited synopses and ideas for books welcome.
Fees sometimes paid instead of royalties.

Quarto Publishing
The Old Brewery, 6 Blundell Street, London N7 9BH
☎0171 700 6700/333 0000
Fax 0171 700 4191/700 0077

Chairman *Laurence Orbach*
Approx. Annual Turnover £18 million

FOUNDED 1976. Britain's largest book packager. *Commissions* illustrated non-fiction, including painting, graphic design, visual arts, history, cookery, gardening, crafts. *Publishes* under the Apple imprint. Unsolicited synopses/ideas for books welcome.
Payment flat fees paid.

Queen Anne Press
See **Lennard Associates**

Sadie Fields Productions Ltd
3D West Point, 36–37 Warple Way, London W3 0RG
☎0181 746 1171   Fax 0181 746 1170

Directors *David Fielder/Sheri Safran*

FOUNDED 1981. Quality children's books with international co-edition potential: pop-ups, three-dimensional, novelty, picture and board books. About 20 titles a year. Approach with preliminary letter and sample material in the first instance. *Publishes* under the **Tango Books** imprint.
Royalties based on a per copy sold rate and paid in stages.

Salariya Book Company Ltd
25 Marlborough Place, Brighton, East Sussex BN1 1UB
☎01273 603306   Fax 01273 693857

Managing Director *David Salariya*

FOUNDED 1989. Children's information books – fiction, history, art, music, science, architecture, education and picture books. No unsolicited material.
Payment by arrangement.

Savitri Books Ltd
115J Cleveland Street, London W1P 5PN
☎0171 436 9932   Fax 0171 580 6330

Managing Director *Mrinalini S. Srivastava*
Approx. Annual Turnover £200,000

FOUNDED 1983. Keen to work 'very closely with authors/illustrators and try to establish long-term relationships with them, doing more books with the same team of people'. *Commissions* high-quality, illustrated non-fiction, mainly nature, natural history and craft. About 4 titles a year. Unsolicited synopses and ideas for books 'very welcome'.

Royalties 10–15% of the total price paid by the publisher.

Sheldrake Press
188 Cavendish Road, London SW12 0DA
☎0181 675 1767   Fax 0181 675 7736
Publisher *Simon Rigge*
Approx. Annual Turnover £250,000

Commissions illustrated non-fiction: history, travel, style, cookery and stationery. TITLES *The Victorian House Book; The Shorter Mrs Beeton; The Power of Steam; The Railway Heritage of Britain; Wild Britain; Wild France; Wild Spain; Wild Italy; Wild Ireland; The Kate Greenaway Baby Book.* Synopses and ideas for books welcome, but not interested in fiction.

Fees or royalties paid.

Templar Publishing
Pippbrook Mill, London Road, Dorking, Surrey RH4 1JE
☎01306 876361   Fax 01306 889097
Managing Director/Editorial Head
    Amanda Wood
Approx. Annual Turnover £4 million

FOUNDED 1981. A division of The Templar Company plc. *Commissions* novelty and gift books, children's illustrated non-fiction, educational and story books, children's illustrated non-fiction. 100–175 titles a year. Synopses and ideas for books welcome.

Royalties by arrangement.

Toucan Books Ltd
Albion Courtyard, Greenhills Rents, London EC1M 6BN
☎0171 251 3921   Fax 0171 251 1692
Managing Director *Robert Sackville-West*
Approx. Annual Turnover £900,000

FOUNDED 1985. Originally specialised in international co-editions, now focusing on fee-based editorial, design and production services to film. *Commissions* illustrated non-fiction only. About 20 titles a year. TITLES *The Earth, It's Wonders, It's Secrets; Leith's Cookery Bible; Charles II; The Complete Photography Course; Journeys into the Past* series; *People and Places.* Unsolicited synopses and ideas for books welcome. No fiction or non-illustrated titles.

Royalties twice yearly; fees paid in addition to or instead of royalties.

Touchstone Publishing Ltd
68 Florence Road, Brighton, East Sussex BN1 6DJ
☎01273 884179   Fax 01273 550415
Chairman/Managing Director *Roger Goddard-Coote*

FOUNDED 1989. Packager of children's non-fiction for trade, school and library markets. About 8 titles a year. No fiction, textbooks or adult material. Synopses and ideas welcome. Include s.a.e. for return.

Fees paid; no royalties.

Transedition Books
See **Andromeda Oxford Ltd**

Twin Books Ltd
Kimbolton House, 117A Fulham Road, London SW3 6RL
☎0171 823 9222   Fax 0171 244 7139
Managing Director *Sydney L. Mayer*

FOUNDED 1986. *Specialises* in children's books: picture books, leisure and fiction. TITLES include *The Little Mermaid; Beauty and the Beast; Babar* (TV series); *Babar and His Friends.* No unsolicited material.

Payment both fees and royalties.

Victoria House Publishing Ltd
4 North Parade, Bath, Avon BA1 1LF
☎01225 463401   Fax 01225 460942
Managing Director *Mrs M. F. Challis*
Approx. Annual Turnover £6 million

Part of the Reader's Digest Group. Trade imprint: Joshua Morris. *Commissions* children's novelty, pop-up, jigsaw books and acetate board books and religious titles. About 50 titles a year.

Royalties or flat fee according to contract.

Wordwright Books
25 Oakford Road, London NW5 1AJ
☎0171 284 0056   Fax 0171 284 0041
Contact *Charles Perkins*

FOUNDED by ex-editorial people 'so good writing always has a chance with us'. *Commissions* illustrated non-fiction: social history and comment, military history, women's issues, sport. *Specialises* in military and social history, natural history, science, art, cookery, and gardening. About 6–7 titles a year. Unsolicited synopses/ideas (a paragraph or so) welcome for illustrated non-fiction. *Payment* usually fees but royalties (twice-yearly) paid over a certain agreed number of copies.

Zöe Books Ltd
15 Worthy Lane, Winchester, Hampshire
SO23 7AB
☎01962 851318   Fax 01962 843015
Managing Director *Imogen Dawson*
Director *Bob Davidson*

FOUNDED 1990. *Specialises* in full-colour information and reference books for schools and libraries. *Publishes* about 20 titles a year. Tends to generate own ideas but happy to hear from freelance writers and editors.
Fees paid.

UK Agents

Aitken, Stone & Wylie Ltd★
29 Fernshaw Road, London SW10 0TG
☎0171 351 7561   Fax 0171 376 3594
Contact *Gillon Aitken, Brian Stone, David Godwin*

FOUNDED 1984. *Handles* fiction and non-fiction. No plays or scripts unless by existing clients. Send preliminary letter, with synopsis and return postage, in the first instance. No reading fee. CLIENTS include Martin Amis, Agatha Christie, Germaine Greer, Susan Howatch, V. S. Naipaul, Piers Paul Read, Salman Rushdie, Paul Theroux. *Commission* Home 10%; US 15%; Translation 20%. *Overseas office* Wylie, Aitken & Stone Inc., 250 West 57th Street, New York, NY 10107, USA.

Jacintha Alexander Associates★
47 Emperor's Gate, London SW7 4HJ
☎0171 373 9258   Fax 0171 373 4374
Contact *Julian Alexander, Kirstan Romano*

FOUNDED 1981. *Handles* full-length general and literary fiction and non-fiction of all kinds. No plays, poetry, textbooks or science fiction. Film and TV scripts handled for established clients only. Preliminary letter with s.a.e. essential. *Commission* Home 10–15%; US & Translation 20%. *Overseas associates* in New York, Los Angeles, Japan, and throughout Europe.

Darley Anderson Literary, TV & Film Agency★
Estelle House, 11 Eustace Road, London SW6 1JB
☎0171 385 6652   Fax 0171 386 5571
Contact *Darley Anderson, Tara Lawrence (Crime/Foreign Rights), Pippa Dyson (Film/TV scripts), Elizabeth Wright (Fantasy/Erotica)*

Run by an ex-publisher with a sympathetic touch and a knack for spotting and encouraging talent who is known to have negotiated a £150,000 UK advance and a TV mini-series deal for a first-time novelist. *Handles* commercial fiction & non-fiction; also scripts for film, TV and radio. No academic books or poetry. *Special interests* Fiction: all types of thrillers and women's fiction including contemporary, 20th century romantic sagas, erotica, women in jeopardy; also crime (cosy/hard-boiled/historical), horror, fantasy, comedy and Irish novels; Non-fiction: celebrity autobiographies, biographies, 'true life' women in jeopardy, popular psychology, self-improvement, diet, health, beauty and fashion, gardening, cookery, inspirational and religious. Send letter and outline with 1–3 chapters; return postage/s.a.e. essential. CLIENTS Beryl Kingston, Tessa Barclay, Martina Cole, Joseph Corvo, Debbie Frank, Martica Heaner, Frank Lean, Deborah McKinlay, Lesley Pearse, Allan Pease, Adrian Plass, Jean Saunders, Fred Secombe, Jane Walmsley. *Commission* Home 15%; US & Translation 20%; TV/Film/Radio 20%, *Overseas associates* Mitchell Rose Agency (New York), Renaissance-Swanson Film Agency (LA/Hollywood); and leading foreign agents throughout the world.

Anubis Literary Agency
79 Charles Gardner Road, Leamington Spa, Warwickshire CV31 3BG
☎01926 832644
Contact *Steve Calcutt, Val Bissell, Maggie Heavey, Carol Sclepari*

FOUNDED 1994. Aims to target new and unpublished writers. *Handles* mainstream adult fiction, especially historical, horror, crime and women's. Also TV/film. Especially interested in westerns. No children's books, poetry, short stories, journalism, academic or non-fiction. No unsolicited scripts; send synopsis/outline and first two chapters (s.a.e. essential). No reading fee. *Commission* Home 15%; USA & Translation 20%.

Yvonne Baker Associates
8 Temple Fortune Lane, London NW11 7UD
☎0181 455 8687   Fax 0181 458 3143
Contact *Yvonne Baker*

FOUNDED 1987. *Handles* scripts for TV, theatre, film and radio. Books extremely rarely. No poetry. Approach by letter giving as much detail as possible, including s.a.e. No reading fee. *Commission* Home 10%; US & Translation 20%.

Blake Friedmann Literary Agency Ltd★
37–41 Gower Street, London WC1E 6HH
☎0171 631 4331   Fax 0171 323 1274

Contact *Carole Blake* (books), *Julian Friedmann* (film/TV), *Conrad Williams* (original scripts/radio)

FOUNDED 1977. *Handles* all kinds of fiction from genre to literary; a varied range of specialised and general non-fiction, plus scripts for TV, radio and film. No poetry, juvenile or science fiction unless from existing clients. *Special interests* commercial women's fiction, literate thrillers. Unsolicited mss welcome but initial letter with synopsis and first two chapters preferred. Letters should contain as much information as possible on previous writing experience, aims for the future, etc. No reading fee. CLIENTS include Gilbert Adair, Ted Allbeury, Jane Asher, Teresa Crane, Daniel Easterman, Barbara Erskine, Maeve Haran, John Harvey, Ken Hom, Lawrence Norfolk, Joseph O'Connor, Michael Ridpath, John Trenhaile. *Commission* Books: Home 15%; US & Translation 20%. Radio/TV/Film: 15%. *Overseas associates* throughout Europe, Asia and the US.

David Bolt Associates
12 Heath Drive, Send, Surrey GU23 7EP
☎01483 721118   Fax 01483 222878

Contact *David Bolt*

FOUNDED 1983. *Handles* fiction and general non-fiction. No books for small children or verse (except in special circumstances). No scripts. *Special interests* fiction, African writers, biography, history, military, theology. Preliminary letter with s.a.e. essential. Reading fee for unpublished writers. Terms on application. CLIENTS include Chinua Achebe, David Bret, Eilis Dillon, Arthur Jacobs, James Purdy, Joseph Rhymer, Colin Wilson. *Commission* Home 10%; US & Translation 19%.

Rosemary Bromley Literary Agency
Avington, Near Winchester, Hampshire SO21 1DB
☎01962 779656   Fax 01962 779656

Contact *Rosemary Bromley*

FOUNDED 1981. *Handles* non-fiction. Also scripts for TV and radio. No poetry or short stories.

Special interests natural history, leisure, biography and cookery. No unsolicited mss. Send preliminary letter with full details. Enquiries unaccompanied by return postage will not be answered. CLIENTS include Elisabeth Beresford, Gwen Cherrell, Teresa Collard, estate of Fanny Cradock, Cécile Curtis, Jacynth Hope-Simpson, David Rees, Judy Strafford, Keith West, Ron Wilson, John Wingate, John Wood. *Commission* Home 10%; US 15%; Translation 20%; Illustration 20%.

Felicity Bryan★
2A North Parade, Banbury Road, Oxford OX2 6PE
☎01865 513816   Fax 01865 310055

Contact *Felicity Bryan*

FOUNDED 1988. *Handles* fiction of various types and non-fiction with emphasis on history, biography, science and current affairs. No scripts for TV, radio or theatre. No crafts, how-to, science fiction or light romance. No unsolicited mss. Best approach by letter. No reading fee. CLIENTS include John Julius Norwich, Roy Strong, Miriam Stoppard, Rosamunde Pilcher, John Charmley, Barbara Trapido, Liza Cody. *Commission* Home 10%; US & Translation 20%. *Overseas associates* Lennart Sane, Scandinavia; Andrew Nurnberg, Europe; **Curtis Brown Ltd**, US.

Peter Bryant (Writers)
94 Adelaide Avenue, London SE4 1YR
☎0181 691 9085   Fax 0181 692 9107

Contact *Peter Bryant*

FOUNDED 1980. *Special interests* children's fiction and TV sitcoms. Also *handles* drama scripts for theatre, radio, film and TV. No reading fee for these categories but return postage essential for all submissions. CLIENTS include Isabelle Amyes, Roy Apps, Joe Boyle, Lucy Daniel, Jimmy Hibbert, Ruth Silvestre, Peter Symonds, Bernard Taylor. *Commission* 10%. *Overseas associates* Hartmann & Stauffacher, Germany.

Diane Burston Literary Agency
46 Cromwell Avenue, London N6 5HL
☎0181 340 6130

FOUNDED 1984. *Handles* fiction, namely women's (not romance); also crime, general fiction and non-fiction, and short stories for women's magazines. Not interested in horror, fantasy, thriller or children's. No unsolicited mss, except for short stories. Send letter with synopsis and opening chapter if possible.

Reading fee charged for full reading and report. CLIENTS include Margaret James, Paula Lawrence, Richard Lazarus, Gillian Nelson, L. D. Tetlow. *Commission* Home 10%; US 15%; Elsewhere 20%.

Bycornute Books

76A Ashford Road, Eastbourne, East Sussex BN21 3TE
☎01323 726819   Fax 01323 649053
Contact *Ayeshah Haleem*

FOUNDED 1987. *Handles* illustrated books on art, archaeology, cosmology, symbolism and metaphysics, both ancient and modern. No scripts. No unsolicited mss. Send introductory letter outlining proposal. No reading fee. *Commission* 10%.

Campbell Thomson & McLaughlin Ltd★

1 King's Mews, London WC1N 2JA
☎0171 242 0958   Fax 0171 242 2408
Contact *John McLaughlin, Charlotte Bruton*

FOUNDED 1931. *Handles* book-length mss (excluding children's, science fiction and fantasy). No plays, film scripts, articles, short stories or poetry. No unsolicited mss. Send preliminary letter with s.a.e. in the first instance. No reading fee. *Overseas associates* Fox Chase Agency, Philadelphia; Raines & Raines, New York.

Carnell Literary Agency★

Danescroft, Goose Lane, Little Hallingbury, Hertfordshire CM22 7RG
☎01279 723626
Contact *Pamela Buckmaster*

FOUNDED 1951. *Handles* fiction and general non-fiction, specialising in science fiction and fantasy. No poetry. No scripts except from published authors. No unsolicited mss. Send preliminary letter with brief synopsis and first two chapters (include s.a.e. for acknowledgement and postage for return of material). No phone calls. *Commission* Home 10%; US & Translation 19%. Works in conjunction with agencies worldwide.

Casarotto Ramsay Ltd

National House, 60–66 Wardour Street, London W1V 3HP
☎0171 287 4450   Fax 0171 287 9128
Film/TV/Radio *Jenne Casarotto, Greg Hunt, Tracey Smith, Rachel Swann*
Stage *Tom Erhardt, Mel Kenyon*
(Books *Handled by* **Lutyens and Rubinstein)**

Took over the agency responsibilities of Margaret Ramsay Ltd in 1992, incorporating a strong client list, with names like Alan Ayckbourn, Caryl Churchill, Willy Russell and Muriel Spark. *Handles* scripts for TV, theatre, film and radio, plus general fiction and non-fiction. No poetry or books for children. No unsolicited material without preliminary letter. CLIENTS include J. G. Ballard, Robert Bolt, Edward Bond, Simon Callow, David Hare, Terry Jones, Neil Jordan, Willy Russell, David Yallop. *Commission* Home 10%; US & Translation 20%. *Overseas associates* worldwide.

Mic Cheetham Literary Agency

138 Buckingham Palace Road, London SW1W 9SA
☎0171 730 3027   Fax 0171 730 0037
Contact *Mic Cheetham*

ESTABLISHED 1994. *Handles* general and literary fiction, crime and science fiction, and non-fiction. No scripts apart from existing clients. No children's, illustrated books or poetry. No unsolicited mss. Approach in writing or by phone in the first instance. No reading fee. CLIENTS Iain Banks, Janette Turner Hospital, Glyn Hughes, Kathy Lette, Martin Millar, Antony Sher. *Commission* Home 10%; USA & Translation 20%. Works with **The Marsh Agency** for all translation rights.

Judith Chilcote Agency★

8 Wentworth Mansions, Keats Grove, London NW3 2RL
☎0171 794 3717   Fax 0171 794 7431
Contact *Judith Chilcote*

FOUNDED 1990. *Handles* commercial fiction, royal books, TV tie-ins, health, beauty and fitness, cinema, self-help, popular psychology, biography and autobiography, cookery and current affairs. No academic, science fiction, children's, short stories or poetry. No unsolicited mss. Send letter with c.v., synopsis, three chapters and s.a.e. for return. No reading fee. CLIENTS include Jane Alexander, Ann Chubb, Vanessa Feltz, Jane Gordon, Lesley-Ann Jones, Philippa Kennedy, Ingrid Millar, Douglas Thompson, Stuart White. *Commission* Home 15%; Overseas 25%. *Overseas associate* in the US, plus overseas agents.

Teresa Chris Literary Agency

16 Castellain Mansions, Castellain Road, London W9 1HA
☎0171 289 0653
Contact *Teresa Chris*

FOUNDED 1989. *Handles* general, commercial and literary fiction, and non-fiction: health, business, travel, cookery, sport and fitness, gardening etc. *Specialises* in crime fiction and commercial women's fiction. No scripts. Film and TV rights handled by co-agent. No poetry, short stories, fantasy, science fiction or horror. Unsolicited mss welcome. Send query letter with sample material (s.a.e. essential) in first instance. No reading fee. CLIENTS include Prof. Eysenck, John Malcolm, Marguerite Patten. *Commission* Home 10%; US 15%; Translation 20%. *Overseas associates* Thompson & Chris Literary Agency, California; representatives in most other countries.

Serafina Clarke★
98 Tunis Road, London W12 7EY
☎0181 749 6979   Fax 0181 740 6862
Contact *Serafina Clarke, Amanda White*

FOUNDED 1980. *Handles* fiction: romance, horror, thrillers, literary; and non-fiction: travel, cookery, gardening and biography. Only deals in scripts by authors already on its books. *Special interests* gardening, history, country pursuits. No unsolicited mss. Introductory letter with synopsis (and return postage) essential. No reading fee. *Commission* Home 15%; US & Translation 20%. *Represents* Permanent Press, US; Second Chance Press, US.

Robert Clarson-Leach
'Downlands', Jevington Road, Wannock, East Sussex BN26 5NX
☎and fax: accepted clients only
Contact *Robert Clarson-Leach, Daphne Adams*

FOUNDED 1985. *Handles* biography, finance and law, adventure; full-length fiction occasionally. Will suggest revision where appropriate. Modest reading fee charged. Film/TV rights negotiated. Preliminary letter with s.a.e. in first instance. Correct postage required for return of mss. CLIENTS Elizabeth James, Tom Jones, Robert Leach, Molly Lillis, Bob Maraschino, Ross Maynard, Bill Mercer, Robert Nemes, Lt.-Col. Walter Rowley, Abigail Saunders, Bronwen Vickers. *Commission* Home 12½%; Overseas 25%. *Overseas associates* various.

Mary Clemmey Literary Agent
6 Dunollie Road, London NW5 2XP
☎0171 267 1290   Fax 0171 267 1290
Contact *Mary Clemmey*

FOUNDED 1992. *Handles* fiction and non-fiction – high quality work with an international market. No science fiction, fantasy or children's books. TV, film, radio and theatre scripts from existing clients only. No unsolicited mss.

Approach by letter giving a description of the work in the first instance. S.a.e. essential. No reading fee. CLIENTS Paul Gilroy, Sheila Kitzinger, Ray Shell. *Commission* Home 10%; USA & Translation 20%. *Overseas Associate*: Elaine Markson Literary Agency, New York.

Jonathan Clowes Ltd★
10 Iron Bridge House, Bridge Approach, London NW1 8BD
☎0171 722 7674   Fax 0171 722 7677
Contact *Brie Burkeman*

FOUNDED 1960. Pronounced 'clewes'. Now one of the biggest fish in the pond, and not really for the untried unless they are true highflyers. Fiction and non-fiction, plus scripts. No textbooks or children's. *Special interests* situation comedy, film and television rights. No unsolicited mss; authors come by recommendation or by successful follow-ups to preliminary letters. CLIENTS include Kingsley Amis, David Bellamy, Len Deighton, Carla Lane, Doris Lessing, David Nobbs. *Commission* Home 10%; US 15%; Translation 19%. *Overseas associates* **Andrew Nurnberg Associates**; Lennart Sane Agency.

Elspeth Cochrane Agency
11–13 Orlando Road, London SW4 0LE
☎0171 622 0314   Fax 0171 622 0314
Contact *Elspeth Cochrane*

FOUNDED 1960. *Handles* fiction, biography and autobiography. Subjects have included Dame Peggy Ashcroft, Dirk Bogarde, Marlon Brando, Sir John Gielgud, Sir Alec Guinness, Lord Olivier, Sir Ralph Richardson, Leonard Rossiter, Shakespeare. Also scripts for all media, with special interest in drama. No unsolicited mss. Preliminary letter with a description of the work, a brief outline, and s.a.e., is essential in the first instance. No reading fee. CLIENTS include David Pinner, Royce Ryton, Robert Tanitch. *Commission* 12½% ('but this can change; the percentage is negotiable, as is the sum paid to the writer').

Dianne Coles Agency
The Old Forge House, Sulgrave, Banbury, Oxfordshire OX17 2RP
☎01295 760692   Fax 01295 760170
Contact *Dianne Coles, Philip Gosling*

FOUNDED 1980. *Handles* non-fiction, including investigative journalism, craft and leisure, biography, travel and human interest. Preliminary letter and return postage essential. *Commission* Home 15%; Radio/TV/Film 15%; Journalism/

Short stories 25%; Translation 20%; Overseas 20%. *Overseas office* in the US.

Rosica Colin Ltd
1 Clareville Grove Mews, London SW7 5AH
☎0171 370 1080   Fax 0171 244 6441
Contact *Joanna Marston*

FOUNDED 1949. *Handles* all full-length mss, plus theatre, film, television and sound broadcasting. Preliminary letter with return postage essential; writers should outline their writing credits and whether their mss have previously been submitted elsewhere. May take 3–4 months to consider full mss; synopsis preferred in the first instance. No reading fee. *Commission* Home 10%; US 15%; Translation 20%.

Collins & Collins (incorporating Edward England Books) Literary Agency
Broadway House, The Broadway, Crowborough, East Sussex TN6 1HQ
☎01892 652364   Fax 01892 663329
Contact *Tony Collins, Mrs Carol Lewry*

FOUNDED 1980. *Handles* Christian: devotional, autobiography, biography, apologetics. No fiction, poetry or children's books. No scripts for TV, film, radio or theatre. CLIENTS include Archbishop George Carey, Richard Foster, Jennifer Rees Larcombe, Colin Urquhart. Unsolicited mss welcome; approach in writing with s.a.e. No reading fee. *Commission* Home 10%; US 15%; Translation 19%.

Combrógos Literary Agency
10 Heol Don, Whitchurch, Cardiff CF4 2AU
☎01222 623359
Contact *Meic Stephens*

FOUNDED 1990. *Specialises* in books about Wales or by Welsh authors, including novels, short stories, poetry, biography and general. Good contacts in Wales and London. Also editorial services, arts and media research. No unsolicited manuscripts; preliminary letter (s.a.e. essential). *Commission* 10%.

Vernon Conway Ltd
5 Spring Street, London W2 3RA
☎0171 262 5506/7   Fax 0171 402 4834
Contact *Vernon Conway*

FOUNDED 1977. *Special interests* novels, biographies, plays. No textbooks or academic. Send introductory letter with return postage in the first instance. No reading fee. CLIENTS include Brian Blessed, Anne Born, Leslie Glazer, Ian

Grimble, Max Hafler, David Halliwell, Angela Meyer, Elizabeth Morgan, Aled Vaughan. *Commission* 10% on all sales.

Jane Conway-Gordon★
1 Old Compton Street, London W1V 5PH
☎0171 494 0148   Fax 0171 287 9264
Contact *Jane Conway-Gordon*

FOUNDED 1982. Works in association with **Andrew Mann Ltd**. *Handles* fiction and general non-fiction, plus occasional scripts for TV/radio/theatre. No poetry or science fiction. Unsolicited mss welcome; preliminary letter and return postage preferred. No reading fee. *Commission* Home 10%; US & Translation 20%. *Overseas associates* **McIntosh & Otis, Inc.**, New York; plus agencies throughout Europe and Japan.

Rupert Crew Ltd★
1A King's Mews, London WC1N 2JA
☎0171 242 8586   Fax 0171 831 7914
Contact *Doreen Montgomery, Caroline Montgomery*

FOUNDED 1927. International representation, handling volume and subsidiary rights in fiction and non-fiction properties. No plays or poetry, journalism or short stories. Preliminary letter essential. No reading fee. *Commission* Home 10–15%; Elsewhere 20%.

Cruickshank Cazenove Ltd
97 Old South Lambeth Road, London SW8 1XU
☎0171 735 2933   Fax 0171 820 1081
Contact *Harriet Cruickshank*

FOUNDED 1983. *Specialises* in scripts for TV/radio/film. No unsolicited mss. Preliminary letter with synopsis and s.a.e. essential. *Commission* Home 10%; US & Translation varies according to contract. *Overseas associates* Various.

Curtis Brown Group Ltd
4th Floor, Haymarket House, 28/29 Haymarket, London SW1Y 4SP
☎0171 396 6600   Fax 0171 396 0110

Long-established literary agency, whose first sales were made in 1899. Merged with John Farquharson, forming the Curtis Brown Group Ltd in 1989. *Handles* a wide range of subjects including fiction, general non-fiction, children's and specialist, scripts for film, TV, theatre and radio. Send synopsis with covering letter and c.v. rather than complete mss. No reading fee. *Commission* Home 10%; US 15%; Translation

20%. *Overseas associates* in Australia, Canada and the US.

Judy Daish Associates Ltd

2 St Charles Place, London W10 6EG
☎0181 964 8811   Fax 0181 964 8966
Contact *Judy Daish, Sara Stroud, Deborah Harwood*

FOUNDED 1978. Theatrical literary agent. *Handles* scripts for film, TV, theatre and radio. No books. Preliminary letter essential. No unsolicited mss.

Caroline Davidson & Robert Ducas Literary Agency

5 Queen Anne's Gardens, London W4 1TU
☎0181 995 5768   Fax 0181 994 2770
Contact *Caroline Davidson, Stephanie Cabot, Robert Ducas*

FOUNDED 1988. Caroline Davidson and Stephanie Cabot work in London; Robert Ducas works in New York. *Handles* fiction and non-fiction, including architecture, art, biography, cookery, crafts, design, gardening, history, investigative journalism, music, natural history, photography, reference, science, travel. Many highly illustrated books. No occult, plays or poetry. Writers should telephone or send an initial letter giving details of the project together with c.v. and s.a.e. CLIENTS Robert Baldock, Philip Beresford, Elizabeth Bradley, Lynda Brown, Lesley Chamberlain, Emma Donoghue, Willi Elsener, Hazel Evans, Anissa Helou, Paul Hillyard, Mary Hollingsworth, Tom Jaine, Bernard Lavery, Huon Mallalieu, Gemma Nesbitt, Sri Owen, Rena Salaman, Jehanne Wake, Helena Whitbread, Roland Vernon. *Commission* US, Home/Commonwealth Translation 12½%; occasionally more (20%) if sub-agents have to be used.

Merric Davidson Literary Agency

Oakwood, Ashley Park, Tunbridge Wells, Kent TN4 8UA
☎01892 514282   Fax 01892 514282
Contact *Merric Davidson*

FOUNDED 1990. *Handles* fiction and general non-fiction. No scripts. No children's, academic, short stories or articles. Particularly keen on contemporary fiction and popular music titles. No unsolicited mss. Send preliminary letter with synopsis and biographical details. S.a.e. essential for response. No reading fee. CLIENTS include Simon Campbell, Susan

Compo, Louise Doughty, Elizabeth Harris, Alison Habens, Nick Hamlyn, Alison MacLeod. *Commission* Home 10%; US 15%; Translation 20%.

Felix de Wolfe

Manfield House, 376–378 The Strand, London WC2R 0LR
☎0171 379 5767   Fax 0171 836 0337
Contact *Felix de Wolfe*

FOUNDED 1938. *Handles* quality fiction only, and scripts. No non-fiction or children's. No unsolicited mss. No reading fee. CLIENTS include Robert Cogo-Fawcett, Brian Glover, Sheila Goff, Derek Hoddinott, Jennifer Johnston, John Kershaw, Bill MacIlwraith, Angus Mackay, Gerard McLarnon, Braham Murray, Charles Savage, Alan Sievewright, Julian Slade, Malcolm Taylor, David Thompson, Paul Todd, Dolores Walshe. *Commission* Home 12½%; US 20%.

Dorian Literary Agency

Upper Thornehill, 27 Church Street, St Marychurch, Torquay, Devon TQ1 4QY
☎01803 312095
Contact *Dorothy Lumley*

FOUNDED 1986. *Handles* mainstream and commercial full-length adult fiction; specialties are women's (including contemporary and sagas), crime and thrillers; horror, science fiction and fantasy. Also limited non-fiction: primarily environmental issues and media-related subjects; plus scripts for TV and radio. No poetry, children's, theatrical scripts, short stories, academic or technical. Introductory letter with synopsis/outline and first chapter (with return postage) only please. No reading fee. CLIENTS include Brian Lumley, Amy Myers, Dee Williams. *Commission* Home 10%; US 15%; Translation 20–25%. Works with agents in most countries for translation.

Anne Drexl

8 Roland Gardens, London SW7 3PH
☎0171 244 9645
Contact *Anne Drexl*

FOUNDED 1988. *Handles* commercially orientated full-length mss for women's fiction, general, family sagas and crime. Ideas welcome for business-related books, how-to, DIY, hobbies and collecting. Strong interest too in juvenile fiction, including children's games, puzzles and activity books. Writers should approach with preliminary letter and synopsis (including s.a.e.). No reading fee but may ask for a contribution to admin. costs. *Commission* Home 12½%; US & Translation 20% (but varies depending on agent used).

Toby Eady Associates Ltd

9 Orme Court, London W2 4RL
☎0171 792 0092   Fax 0171 792 0879

Contact *Toby Eady, Alexandra Pringle, Victoria Hobbs, Xandra Hardie*

In association with Xandra Hardie. *Handles* books on Africa, the Middle East, India and China; plus fishing, fiction, and non-fiction. No scripts. No unsolicited mss. Approach by letter first. No reading fee. CLIENTS include Nuha Al-Radi, Elspeth Barker, Sister Wendy Beckett, Ronan Bennett, Julia Blackburn, Jung Chang, Bernard Cornwell, Lucy Ellmann, Esther Freud, Kuki Gallmann, Sean Hardie, Michael Hofmann, Tim Jeal, Rana Kabbani, Susan Lewis, Que Lei Lei, Matthew Parris, Tim Pears, Shona Ramaya, Sun Shuyun, Amir Taheri. *Commission* Home 10%; US & Translation 20%. *Overseas associates* La Nouvelle Agence; Mohr Books; The English Agency, Tokyo; Jan Michael; Rosemarie Buckman.

Edward England Books

See **Collins & Collins Literary Agency**

Faith Evans Associates★

Clerkenwell House, 45 Clerkenwell Green, London EC1R 0EB
☎0171 490 2535   Fax 0171 490 4958

Contact *Faith Evans, Anne McGonigle*

FOUNDED 1987. Small, selective agency. *Handles* fiction and non-fiction. No scripts, unsolicited mss or phone enquiries. CLIENTS include Melissa Benn, Eleanor Bron, Helena Kennedy, Seumas Milne, Sheila Rowbotham. *Commission* Home 15%; US & Translation 20%. *Overseas associates* worldwide.

John Farquharson★

See **Curtis Brown Group Ltd**

Film Rights Ltd

See **Laurence Fitch Ltd**

Laurence Fitch Ltd

483 Southbank House, Black Prince Road, Albert Embankment, London SE1 7ST
☎0171 735 8171

Contact *Laurence Fitch, Brendan Davis*

In association with Film Rights Ltd. FOUNDED 1952 (incorporating the London Play Company,

FOUNDED 1922). *Handles* scripts for theatre, film, TV and radio only. No unsolicited mss. Send synopsis with sample scene(s) in the first instance. No reading fee. CLIENTS include Judy Allen, Hindi Brooks, John Chapman & Ray Cooney, John Graham, Glyn Robbins, Gene Stone, and the estate of Dodie Smith. *Commission* 10%. *Overseas associates* worldwide.

Jill Foster Ltd

3 Lonsdale Road, London SW13 9ED
☎0181 741 9410   Fax 0181 741 2916

Contact *Jill Foster, Alison Finch, Ann Foster*

FOUNDED 1976. *Handles* scripts for TV, drama and comedy. No fiction, short stories or poetry. No unsolicited mss; approach by letter in the first instance. No reading fee. CLIENTS include Colin Bostock-Smith, Jan Etherington and Gavin Petrie, Rob Gittins, Paul Hines, Julia Jones, Chris Ralling, Peter Tilbury, Susan Wilkins. *Commission* Home 12½%; US & Translation 15%.

Fox & Howard Literary Agency

4 Bramerton Street, London SW3 5JX
☎0171 352 8691   Fax 0171 352 8691

Contact *Chelsey Fox, Charlotte Howard*

FOUNDED 1992. *Handles* general non-fiction: biography, naval, military and popular history, current affairs, business, self-help, health and mind, body and spirit; educational and reference: GCSE and A-level texts. No scripts. No poetry, plays, short stories, children's, science fiction, fantasy and horror. No unsolicited mss; send letter, synopsis and sample chapter with s.a.e. for response. No reading fee. CLIENTS Sir Rhodes Boyson, Dr Graham Handley, Anthony Kemp, Bruce King, Betty Parsons, Geoffrey Regan. *Commission* Home 10%; US & Translation 20%.

French's

9 Elgin Mews South, London W9 1JZ
☎0171 266 3321   Fax 0171 286 6716

Contact *John French*

FOUNDED 1973. *Handles* fiction and non-fiction; and scripts for all media. No religious or medical books. No unsolicited mss. 'For unpublished authors we offer a reading service at £40 per mss, exclusive of VAT and postage.' Interested authors should write in the first instance. CLIENTS include James Duke, Gillian Hanna, Barry Heath, Susanna Hughes, Mal Middleton, Shaun Prendergast. *Commission* Home 10%.

Vernon Futerman Associates★

159a Goldhurst Terrace, London NW6 3EU
☎0171 625 9601
Fax 0171 625 9601(direct)/372 1282

Academic/Politics/Current Affairs/Show Business/Art *Vernon Futerman*
Educational *Alexandra Groom*
Fiction/TV, Film & Theatre Scripts
  Guy Rose

FOUNDED 1984. *Handles* fiction and non-fiction, including academic, art, educational, politics, history, current affairs, show business, travel, business and medicine; also scripts for film, TV and theatre. No short stories, science fiction, crafts or hobbies. No unsolicited mss; send preliminary letter with detailed synopsis and s.a.e. to Submissions Dept. 100, Richmond Hill, Richmond, Surrey TW10 6RJ. No reading fee. CLIENTS Dr Juliet Barker, Sally Becker, Prof. Wu Ningkun, Russell Warren Howe, Ernie Wise. *Commission* Home 12½–17½%; USA 17½–22½%; Translation 17½–25%. *Overseas associates* Brigitte Axster, Germany/Scandinavia; Lora Fountain, France.

Jüri Gabriel

35 Camberwell Grove, London SE5 8JA
☎0171 703 6186   Fax 0171 703 6186
Contact *Jüri Gabriel*

Handles fiction, non-fiction and scripts for TV/radio. Jüri Gabriel worked in television, wrote books for 20 years and is chairman of **Dedalus** publishers. No short stories, articles, verse or books for children. Unsolicited mss welcome if accompanied by return postage and letter giving sufficient information about author's writing experience, aims etc. CLIENTS include Nigel Cawthorne, Diana Constance, Alf Draper, Robert Irwin, Mark Lloyd, David Miller, John Outram, Dr Margaret Pollak, Ewen Southby-Tailyour, Adisakdi Tantimedh, Dr Terence White, Herbert Williams, John Wyatt, Dr. Robert Youngson. *Commission* Home 10%; US & Translation 20%.

Eric Glass Ltd

28 Berkeley Square, London W1X 6HD
☎0171 629 7162   Fax 0171 499 6780
Contact *Eric Glass, Janet Glass*

FOUNDED 1934. *Handles* fiction, non-fiction and scripts for publication or production in all media. No poetry. No unsolicited mss. No reading fee. CLIENTS include Philip King, Wolf Mankowitz and the estates of Jean Cocteau, Robin Maugham, Jean-Paul Sartre. *Commission* Home 10%; US 15%; Translation 20% (to

include sub-agent's fee). *Overseas associates* in the US, Australia, France, Germany, Greece, Holland, Italy, Japan, Poland, Scandinavia, South Africa, Spain.

Christine Green Authors' Agent★

2 Barbon Close, London WC1N 3JX
☎0171 831 4956   Fax 0171 831 4840
Contact *Christine Green*

FOUNDED 1984. *Handles* fiction (general and literary) and general non-fiction. No scripts, poetry or children's. No unsolicited mss; initial letter and synopsis preferred. No reading fee but return postage essential. *Commission* Home 10%; US & Translation 20%.

Greene & Heaton Ltd★

37 Goldhawk Road, London W12 8QQ
☎0181 749 0315   Fax 0181 749 0318
Contact *Carol Heaton*

A small agency that likes to involve itself with its authors. *Handles* fiction, general non-fiction and children's books. No original scripts for theatre, film or TV. No unsolicited mss without preliminary letter. CLIENTS include Sybille Bedford, Bill Bryson, Kate Charles, Jan Dalley, Colin Forbes, P. D. James, Mary Morrissy, Conor Cruise O'Brien, William Shawcross. *Commission* Home 10%; US & Translation 20%.

Gregory & Radice Authors' Agents★

3 Barb Mews, London W6 7PA
☎0171 610 4676   Fax 0171 610 4686
Contact *Jane Gregory, Dr Lisanne Radice*(Editorial), *Pippa Dyson*(Film/TV)

FORMED 1986, incorporating the former Jane Gregory Agency established 1982. *Handles* fiction and non-fiction. *Special interest* crime, thrillers, literary fiction, politics. No plays, film or TV scripts, science fiction, poetry, academic or children's. No unsolicited mss, but preliminary letter with synopsis and first three chapters (plus return postage) welcome. No reading fee. *Commission* Home 15%; Newspapers 20%; US & Translation 20%. *Represents* three American companies, and is itself represented in most countries.

David Grossman Literary Agency Ltd

118b Holland Park Avenue, London W11 4UA
☎0171 221 2770   Fax 0171 221 1445
Contact *Material should be addressed to the Company*

FOUNDED 1976. *Handles* full-length fiction and general non-fiction – good writing of all kinds and anything controversial. No verse or technical books for students. No original screenplays or teleplays (only works existing in volume form are sold for performance rights). Generally works with published writers of fiction only but 'truly original, well-written novels from beginners' will be considered. Best approach by preliminary letter giving full description of the work. All material must be accompanied by return postage. No approaches or submissions by fax. No unsolicited mss. No reading fee. *Commission* Rates vary for different markets. *Overseas associates* throughout Europe, Asia, Brazil and the US.

The Guidelines Partnership, Publishing Consultants & Agents

18 Pretoria Road, Cambridge CB4 1HE
☎01223 314668   Fax 01223 64619
Contact *Mr G. Black, Mrs L. Black*

FOUNDED 1986. Strong links with major publishing houses throughout the Far East. *Handles* educational materials, particularly study guides, for most age groups and across all subject areas, e.g. Longman GCSE and A Level Revise Guides. No fiction. Unsolicited mss welcome subject to prior letter enclosing c.v. and s.a.e. Approach by phone, fax or letter. No reading fee. *Commission* Home 10–15%; USA & Translation by negotiation.

Margaret Hanbury

27 Walcot Square, London SE11 4UB
☎0171 735 7680   Fax 0171 793 0316

Represents general fiction and non-fiction. No plays, scripts, poetry, children's books, fantasy, horror. No unsolicited mss; preliminary letter with s.a.e. essential. *Commission* Home 15%; Overseas 20%.

Roger Hancock Ltd

4 Water Lane, London NW1 8NZ
☎0171 267 4418   Fax 0171 267 0705
Contact *Material should be addressed to the Company*

FOUNDED 1961. *Special interests* drama and light entertainment. Scripts only. No books. Unsolicited mss not welcome. Initial phone call required. No reading fee. *Commission* 10%.

Xandra Hardie Literary Agency

See **Toby Eady Associates Ltd**

A. M. Heath & Co. Ltd★

79 St Martin's Lane, London WC2N 4AA
☎0171 836 4271   Fax 0171 497 2561
Contact *Michael Thomas, Bill Hamilton, Sara Fisher, Sarah Molloy*

FOUNDED 1919. *Handles* fiction and general non-fiction. No scripts or poetry. Preliminary letter and synopsis essential. No reading fee. CLIENTS include Christopher Andrew, Anita Brookner, Marika Cobbold, Lesley Glaister, Graham Hancock, Hilary Mantel, Hilary Norman, Adam Thorpe, Elizabeth Walker. *Commission* Home 10–15%; US & Translation 20%; Film & TV 15%. *Overseas associates* in the US, Europe, South America, Japan.

David Higham Associates Ltd★

5–8 Lower John Street, Golden Square, London W1R 4HA
☎0171 437 7888   Fax 0171 437 1072
Scripts *Elizabeth Cree, Nicky Lund*
Books *Anthony Goff*

FOUNDED 1935. *Handles* fiction and general non-fiction: biography, history, current affairs, art, music, etc. Also scripts. Preliminary letter with synopsis essential in first instance. No reading fee. CLIENTS include John le Carré, Stephen Fry, James Herbert, Alice Walker. *Commission* Home 10%; US & Translation 20%.

Vanessa Holt Ltd★

59 Crescent Road, Leigh-on-Sea, Essex SS9 2PF
☎01702 73787/714698   Fax 01702 471890
Contact *Vanessa Holt*

FOUNDED 1989. *Handles* general adult fiction and non-fiction. No scripts, poetry, academic or technical. *Specialises* in commercial and crime fiction; social issues in non-fiction. No unsolicited mss. Approach by letter in first instance; s.a.e. essential. No reading fee. *Commission* Home 10%; US & Translation 20%. *Overseas associates* in the US, Europe, South America and Japan.

Valerie Hoskins

20 Charlotte Street, London W1P 1HJ
☎0171 637 4490   Fax 0171 637 4493
Contact *Valerie Hoskins*

FOUNDED 1983. *Handles* scripts for film, theatre, TV and radio. *Special interests* feature films and TV. No unsolicited scripts; preliminary letter of introduction essential. No reading fee. CLIENTS include David Ashton, Daniel Boyle, Bryan Elsley, Matthew Graham, Kit Hesketh-

Harvey, Jeff Povey, Stephen Wyatt. *Commission* Home 12½%; US 20% (maximum).

Tanja Howarth Literary Agency★
19 New Row, London WC2N 4LA
☎0171 240 5553/836 4142
Fax 0171 379 0969

Contact *Tanja Howarth*

FOUNDED 1970. Interested in taking on both fiction and non-fiction from British writers. No children's books, plays or poetry, but all other subjects considered providing the treatment is intelligent. No unsolicited mss. Preliminary letter preferred. No reading fee. Also an established agent for foreign literature, particularly from the German language. *Commission* Home 10%; Translation 15%.

ICM
Oxford House, 76 Oxford Street, London W1N 0AX
☎0171 636 6565   Fax 0171 323 0101

Contact *Alan Brodie*

FOUNDED 1973. *Handles* film, TV and theatre scripts. No books. No unsolicited mss. Preliminary letter essential. No reading fee. *Commission* 10%. *Overseas associates* ICM, New York/Los Angeles.

Imagination
The Old Forge, 72 The Street, Ash, Kent CT3 2AA
☎01304 813378   Fax 01304 813378

Contact *Janine Gregory*

FOUNDED 1995. Television and film scripts. Full-length fiction and non-fiction. *Special interests*: drama, comedy drama, sitcom, women's fiction, historical fiction, science fiction, fantasy, horror, new age, non-fiction. No poetry or children's. No reading fee. Send synopsis, first three chapters and s.a.e. in the first instance with letter outlining career history, publishing details etc. *Commission* Home 15%; Film & TV 20%; US & Translation 20%.

Michael Imison Playwrights Ltd
28 Almeida Street, London N1 1TD
☎0171 354 3174   Fax 0171 359 6273

Contact *Michael Imison, Sarah McNair*

FOUNDED 1944. Michael Imison is an ex-TV director and script editor for the BBC. *Handles* plays and books based on scripts, e.g. *Yes Minister*; also film, TV, radio and theatre. No fiction or general books. *Special interest* in writers motivated primarily by writing for the the-atre, and in translations, particularly from Russian and Italian. No unsolicited mss. Initial letter (plus s.a.e.) with recommendation from a known theatre professional essential. No reading fee. CLIENTS David Edgar, Dario Fo, Timberlake Wertenbaker, the Nöel Coward estate. *Commission* Home 10%; US & Translation 15%.

International Copyright Bureau Ltd
22A Aubrey House, Maida Avenue, London W2 1TQ
☎0171 724 8034   Fax 0171 724 7662

Contact *Joy Westendarp*

FOUNDED 1905. *Handles* scripts for TV, theatre, film and radio. No books. Preliminary letter for unsolicited material essential. *Commission* Home 10%; US & Translation 19%. *Overseas agents* in New York and most foreign countries.

International Management Group
Pier House, Strand on the Green, Chiswick, London W4 3NN
☎0181 233 5000   Fax 0181 233 5001

Contact *Jean Sewell (London), Julian Bach, Trish Lande (New York)*

FOUNDED 1960. Overseas offices in New York. *Handles* commercial fiction, non-fiction, celebrity books, sports-related books, how-to business books. No TV, film, radio or theatre. Not interested in children's books, poetry or academic books. Unsolicited mss welcome; send letter with c.v., synopsis, three chapters and samples of previously published work with s.a.e. No reading fee. CLIENTS include Ross Benson, Tony Buzan, Pat Conroy, Mark McCormack, professional sports stars, classical musicians, broadcasting personalities. *Commission* Home & USA 15%; Translation 25%.

International Scripts
1 Norland Square, London W11 4PX
☎0171 229 0736   Fax 0171 792 3287

Contact *Bob Tanner, Pat Hornsey, Jill Lawson*

FOUNDED 1979 by Bob Tanner. *Handles* all types of books and scripts for all media. No poetry or short stories. Preliminary letter required. CLIENTS include Masquerade (USA), Barricade Books (USA), Barrons (USA), Ed Gorman, Peter Haining, Julie Harris, Robert A. Heinlein, Anna Jacobs, Dean R. Koontz, Richard Laymon, Jean Moss, Mary Ryan, John Spencer. *Commission* Home 15%; US & Translation 20–25%. *Overseas associates* include Ralph Vicinanza, Spectrum, USA; Thomas

Schluck, Germany; Irina Reylander, Italy; Eliane Benisti, France.

Heather Jeeves Literary Agency*
9 Dryden Place, Edinburgh EH9 1RP
☎0131 668 3859   Fax 0131 668 3859
Contact *Heather Jeeves*

FOUNDED 1989. *Handles* general trade fiction and non-fiction, specialising in crime and cookery. Also handles historians, biographers and entertainers. Scripts for TV, film, and theatre are handled through **Casarotto Ramsay Ltd.** Not interested in academic, fantasy, science fiction, Mills & Boon romances, poetry, short stories, sports, military history or freelance journalism. No unsolicited mss. Approach in the first instance in writing describing the project and professional experience. Return postage essential. No reading fee. CLIENTS include Debbie Bliss, Lindsey Davis, Elspeth Huxley, Susan Kay, Sue Lawrence, Claire Macdonald, Mark Timlin. *Commission* Home 10%; US 15–20%; Translation 20%. *Overseas associates* throughout Europe and in the US.

JJK Scenarios
21 Metropole Towers, Argyle Road, West Cliff, Whitby, North Yorkshire YO21 3HU
☎01947 602475   Fax 01947 602475
Contact *Joseph John Kopel*

FOUNDED 1994. *Handles* all types of fiction, TV and radio scripts, TV documentaries, non-fiction. *Special interests*: well constructed drama scripts and comedy sketches. No racist, obscene or political material. No unsolicited mss. In first instance approach with a brief synopsis and s.a.e. for acknowledgement and/or return of mss. No reading fee. *Commission* Home 10%; US 15%.

Harry Joyce Literary and Talent Agency
16 Castle Road, Grays, Essex RM17 5YR
☎01375 390127
Contact *Ian Sales (Television), Simon Bashan (Theatre), Neil Sales (Films)*

FOUNDED 1990. *Handles* scripts for TV, film, radio and theatre. Not interested in books. *Specialises* in comedy scripts, good film drama. Approach first in writing with synopsis, s.a.e. essential. No reading fee. *Commission* Home 10%; US 15%; Translation 10%.

Jane Judd Literary Agency*
18 Belitha Villas, London N1 1PD
☎0171 607 0273   Fax 0171 607 0623
Contact *Jane Judd*

FOUNDED 1986. *Handles* general fiction and non-fiction: women's fiction, crime, fantasy, thrillers, literary fiction, cookery, humour, pop/rock, biography/autobiography, investigative journalism, health, women's interests and travel. 'Looking for good sagas/women's read but not Mills & Boon-type'. No scripts, academic, gardening or DIY. Approach with letter, including synopsis, first chapter and return postage. Initial telephone call helpful in the case of non-fiction. CLIENTS include Patrick Anthony, John Brunner, Jillie Collings, John Grant, Jill Mansell, Jeremy Pascall, Lester Piggott, Jonathon Porritt. *Commission* Home 10%; US & Translation 20%.

Juvenilia
Avington, Near Winchester, Hampshire SO21 1DB
☎01962 779656   Fax 01962 779656
Contact *Rosemary Bromley*

FOUNDED 1973. *Handles* young/teen fiction and picture books; non-fiction and scripts for TV and radio. No poetry or short stories unless part of a collection or picture book material. No unsolicited mss. Send preliminary letter with full details of work and biographical outline in first instance. Preliminary letters unaccompanied by return postage will not be answered. Phone calls not advised. CLIENTS include Stephanie Baudet, Elisabeth Beresford, Linda Birch, Denis Bond, Nicola Davies, Linda Dearsley, Terry Deary, Steve Donald, Gaye Hicyilmaz, Chris Masters, Phil McMylor, Saviour Pirotta, Kelvin Reynolds, Enid Richemont, Cathy Simpson, Margaret Stuart Barry, Keith West, Kay Widdowson, Jennifer Zabel. *Commission* Home 10%; US 15%; Translation 20%; Illustration 20%.

Michelle Kass Associates
12 Moor Street, London W1V 5LH
☎0171 439 1624   Fax 0171 734 3394
Contact *Michelle Kass*

FOUNDED 1991. *Handles* fiction, TV, film, radio and theatre scripts. Approach by phone or explanatory letter in the first instance. No reading fee. *Commission* Home 10%; US & Translation 15–20%.

Frances Kelly*
111 Clifton Road, Kingston upon Thames, Surrey KT2 6PL
☎0181 549 7830   Fax 0181 547 0051
Contact *Frances Kelly*

FOUNDED 1978. *Handles* non-fiction, including illustrated: biography, history, art, self-help, food & wine, complementary medicine and therapies, New Age; and academic non-fiction in all disciplines. No scripts except for existing clients. No unsolicited mss. Approach by letter with brief description of work or synopsis, together with c.v. and return postage. *Commission* Home 10%; US & Translation 20%.

Paul Kiernan
13 Embankment Gardens, London SW3 4LW
☎0171 352 5562   Fax 0171 351 5986
Contact *Paul Kiernan*

FOUNDED 1990. *Handles* fiction and non-fiction, including autobiography and biography, plus specialist writers like cookery or gardening. Also scripts for TV, film, radio and theatre (TV and film scripts from book-writing clients only). No unsolicited mss. Preferred approach is by letter or personal introduction. Letters should include synopsis and brief biography. No reading fee. CLIENTS include K. Banta, Lord Chalfont, Sir Paul Fox. *Commission* Home 15%; US 20%.

Knight Features
20 Crescent Grove, London SW4 7AH
☎0171 622 1467   Fax 0171 622 1522
Contact *Peter Knight, Gaby Martin, Ann King-Hall, Carolinie Figini, Tony Phillips, Andrew Knight*

FOUNDED 1985. *Handles* motor sports, cartoon books for both adults and children, puzzles, factual and biographical material, and scripts (on a very selective basis). No poetry, science fiction or cookery. No unsolicited mss. Send letter accompanied by c.v. and s.a.e. with synopsis of proposed work. Reading fee charged. CLIENTS include Michael Crozier, Frank Dickens, Christopher Hilton, Frederic Mullally. *Commission* dependent upon authors and territories. *Overseas associates* United Media, US; Auspac Media, Australia.

Lemon, Unna & Durbridge Ltd★
24 Pottery Lane, London W11 4LZ
☎0171 727 1346   Fax 0171 727 9037
Contact *Bethan Evans, Sheila Lemon, Stephen Durbridge, Wendy Gresser, Hilary Delamere, Girsha Reid*

Specialises in representation of writers for theatre, TV, film and radio drama, and in publishing for existing clients. Hilary Delamere represents children's writers and illustrators for book publication and exploitation in film, TV and merchandising. No unsolicited mss; preliminary letter and outline essential. No reading fee. *Commission* Home 10%; US, Translation and

merchandising by arrangement. *Overseas associates* worldwide.

Barbara Levy Literary Agency★
16 Jeffrey's Place, London NW1 9PP
☎0171 485 6037   Fax 0171 267 3024
Contact *Barbara Levy, John Selby*

FOUNDED 1986. *Handles* general fiction, non-fiction and scripts for TV and radio. No unsolicited mss. Send detailed preliminary letter in the first instance. No reading fee. *Commission* Home 10%; US 20%; Translation by arrangement, in conjunction with **The Marsh Agency**. *US associates* Arcadia Ltd, New York.

Limelight Management
9 Coptic Street, London WC1A 1NH
☎0171 436 6949   Fax 0171 323 6791
Contact *Fiona Lindsay, Linda Shanks*

FOUNDED 1991. *Handles* general non-fiction and fiction books; cookery, gardening, wine, art and crafts, health, historical and romantic. No TV, film, radio or theatre. Not interested in science fiction, short stories, plays, children's. *Specialises* in illustrated books. Unsolicited mss welcome; send preliminary letter (s.a.e. essential). No reading fee. *Commission* Home 12½%; USA & Translation 20%.

The Christopher Little Literary Agency★
48 Walham Grove, London SW6 1QR
☎0171 386 1800   Fax 0171 381 2248
Fiction/Non-fiction *Christopher Little, Patrick Walsh*
Office Manager *Bryony Evens*

FOUNDED 1979. *Handles* commercial and literary full-length fiction, non-fiction, and film/TV scripts. *Special interests* crime, thrillers, celebrities and narrative plus investigative non-fiction. Also makes a particular speciality out of packaging celebrities for the book market and representing book projects for many Fleet Street journalists. Rights representative in the UK for six American literary agencies. No reading fee. Send detailed letter ('giving a summary of present and future intentions together with track record, if any'), synopsis, first two chapters and s.a.e. in first instance. CLIENTS include Simon Beckett, Marcus Berkmann, Linford Christie, Simon Gandolfi, Damon Hill, Tom Holland, Clare Latimer, Ginny Leng, Alastair MacNeill, Anna Pasternak, A. J. Quinnell, Candace Robb, Peter Rosenberg, John Spurling, David Thomas, James Whitaker, Wilbur Wright.

London Independent Books Ltd

1A Montagu Mews North, London W1H 1AJ
☎0171 706 0486   Fax 0171 724 3122
Contact *Mrs C. Whitaker*

FOUNDED 1971. A self-styled 'small and idio-syncratic' agency. *Handles* fiction and non-fiction reflecting the tastes of the proprietors. All subjects considered (except computer books and young children's), providing the treatment is strong and saleable. Scripts handled only if by existing clients. *Special interests* boats, travel, travelogues, commercial fiction. No unsolicited mss; letter, synopsis and first two chapters with return postage the best approach. No reading fee. *Commission* Home 15%; US & Translation 20%.

Clive Luhrs Publishing Services

PO Box 151, Leeds, West Yorkshire LS5 3TD
☎0113 2746701
Contact *Clive B. Luhrs*

FOUNDED 1990. *Handles* and *specialises* in railway history (British and foreign subjects), local history utilising old photographs, Russian émigré autobiography. No TV, film, radio or theatre. No unsolicited mss. Approach by letter enclosing detailed synopsis of proposed book/finished mss. S.a.e. required for initial response. Reading fee charged. *Commission* negotiable.

Lutyens and Rubinstein

231 Westbourne Park Road, London W11 1EB
☎0171 792 4855   Fax 0171 792 4833
Contact *Sarah Lutyens, Felicity Rubinstein*

FOUNDED 1993. *Handles* adult fiction and non-fiction books. No TV, film, radio or theatre scripts. Unsolicited mss accepted; send introductory letter, c.v., two chapters and return postage for material submitted. No reading fee. *Commission* Home 10%; USA & Translation 20%.

Maclean Dubois (Writers & Agents)

Hillend House, Hillend, Edinburgh EH10 7DX
☎0131 445 5885   Fax 0131 445 5898
Contact *Charles MacLean*

FOUNDED 1977. *Handles* fiction and general non-fiction. No scripts. *Specialises* in Scottish fiction and non-fiction, food and drink, historical fiction, literary fiction. Unsolicited mss will be considered. Approach by phone or in writing in the first instance for explanation of terms. Reading fee of £60 per 1000 words. *Commission* Home 10%; US 15%; Translation 20%. *Overseas associates* Deedes-Vincke Associates, 2 Impasse Dechêne, 37290 Boussay, France.

Andrew Mann Ltd★

1 Old Compton Street, London W1V 5PH
☎0171 734 4751   Fax 0171 287 9264
Contact *Anne Dewe, Tina Betts*

In association with **Jane Conway-Gordon**. FOUNDED 1975. *Handles* fiction, general non-fiction and film, TV, theatre, radio scripts. No unsolicited mss. Preliminary letter, synopsis and s.a.e. essential. No reading fee. *Commission* Home 10%; US & Translation 19%. *Overseas associates* various.

Manuscript ReSearch

PO Box 33, Bicester, Oxfordshire
OX6 7PP
☎01869 323447   Fax 01869 324096
Contact *Graham Jenkins*

FOUNDED 1988. *Handles* fiction: thrillers, literary novels, crime and general; biographies, children's books and scripts for TV and radio. No technical, religious, science fiction, poetry or short stories unless from established clients. *Special interests* revision/rewriting scripts for selected clients. Optional criticism service available, including professional line-by-line editing and laser printing. Approach by letter with s.a.e. in first instance. No reading fee. CLIENTS include Tom Barrat, Margaritte Bell, Richard Butler, Nicholai Kollantoy, Roscoe Howells, Val Manning, Peter Pook, Kev Shannon. *Commission* Home 10%; US 20%.

Marsh & Sheil Ltd

19 John Street, London WC1N 2DL
☎0171 405 7473   Fax 0171 405 5239
Contact *Benita Edzard*

FOUNDED 1985. Deals only in translation rights. No unsolicited mss, ideas or synopses. CLIENTS include **Sheil Land Associates Ltd**. *Commission* Translation 10%.

The Marsh Agency★

138 Buckingham Palace Road, London
SW1W 9SA
☎0171 730 1124   Fax 0171 730 0037
Contact *Paul Marsh*

FOUNDED 1994. *Handles* translation rights only. No TV, film, radio or theatre. Not interested in anything to be sold to English language publishers. No unsolicited mss. CLIENTS include The Judith Murdoch Agency, Scott Ferris Associates, Barbara Levy Agency, **Serpent's Tail**, publishers, and several US companies. *Commission* 10%.

Judy Martin Literary Agency
138 Buckingham Palace Road,
London SW1W 9SA
☎0171 730 3779   Fax 0171 730 3801

FOUNDED 1990. *Handles* fiction and non-fiction, including humour (no gardening, cookery or children's books); plus scripts for film and TV. No plays, poetry or photography. Unsolicited mss will be considered. Include letter giving past publishing history and details of rejections, together with s.a.e. for reply or return of mss. No reading fee. *Commission* Home 15%; US & Translation 20%.

M. C. Martinez Literary Agency
60 Oakwood Avenue, Southgate,
London N14 6QL
☎0181 886 5829

Contact *Mary Caroline Martinez, Francoise Budd*

FOUNDED 1988. *Handles* high-quality fiction, children's books, arts and crafts, interior design, DIY, cookery, travel and business. Also scripts for TV, radio and theatre. *Specialises* in fiction, children's and travel. No unsolicited mss. Phone call in the first instance before sending letter with synopsis; s.a.e. is advised. (Possible change of address; telephone first before sending submissions.) No reading fee but may charge an admin. fee where appropriate. DTP service available. *Commission* Home 15%; US & Translation 20%. *Overseas associates* various.

MBA Literary Agents Ltd★
45 Fitzroy Street, London W1P 5HR
☎0171 387 2076/4785   Fax 0171 387 2042

Contact *Diana Tyler, John Richard Parker, Meg Davis, Ruth Needham*

FOUNDED 1971. *Handles* fiction and non-fiction. No poetry or children's fiction. Also scripts for film, television, radio and theatre. CLIENTS include Jeffrey Caine, Glenn Chandler, Neil Clarke, Valerie Georgeson, Andrew Hodges, Roy Lancaster, Paul J. McAuley, Anne McCaffrey, Anne Perry, Iain Sinclair, Tom Vernon, Douglas Watkinson, Freda Warrington, Patrick Wright, Valerie Windsor and the estate of B. S. Johnson. No unsolicited mss. No reading fee. Preliminary letter with outline and s.a.e. essential. *Commission* Home 10%; US & Translation 20%; Theatre/TV/Radio 10%; Film 10–15%. *Overseas associates* in the US, Japan and throughout Europe. Also rights representative in the UK for the Donald Maass Agency and **Susan Schulman Agency**, New York.

Duncan McAra
30 Craighall Crescent, Edinburgh EH6 4RZ
☎0131 552 1558   Fax 0131 552 1558

Contact *Duncan McAra*

FOUNDED 1988. *Handles* fiction (thrillers and literary fiction) and non-fiction, including art, architecture, archaeology, biography, film, military, travel. Preliminary letter, synopsis and sample chapter (including return postage) essential. No reading fee. *Commission* Home 10%; Overseas by arrangement.

Bill McLean Personal Management
23B Deodar Road, London SW15 2NP
☎0181 789 8191

Contact *Bill McLean*

FOUNDED 1972. *Handles* scripts for all media. No books. No unsolicited mss. Phone call or introductory letter essential. No reading fee. CLIENTS include Dwynwen Berry, Jane Galletly, Tony Jordan, Bill Lyons, John Maynard, Glen McCoy, Michael McStay, Les Miller, Jeffrey Segal, Frank Vickery, Mark Wheatley. *Commission* Home 10%.

Eunice McMullen Children's Literary Agent Ltd
38 Clewer Hill Road, Windsor, Berkshire SL4 4BW
☎01753 830348   Fax 01753 833459

Contact *Eunice McMullen*

FOUNDED 1992. *Handles* all types of children's material from picture books to teenage fiction. Particularly interested in younger children's fiction and illustrated texts. Has a strong list of picture book author/illustrators. Send preliminary letter with s.a.e., outline and biographical details in the first instance. No unsolicited scripts. CLIENTS include Wayne Anderson, Reg Cartwright, Mark Foreman, Simon James, Sue Porter, James Riordan, Susan Winter, David Wood. *Commission* Home 10%; US 15%; Translation 20%.

Media House Literary Agents
179 King's Cross Road, London WC1X 9BZ
☎0171 833 9111   Fax 0171 833 8211

Contacts *Jennifer Chapman, Gilly Vincent*

A new, small agency not at present actively seeking clients but handling a few selected writers of original non-fiction (in particular, with film, TV and audio potential), and quality literary fiction including novellas. No poetry, children's, romantic fiction, science fiction or avant-garde works. Approach in the first instance for non-fiction with fully developed idea and at least half the complete mss. For fiction approach with full synopsis and two sample chapters. S.a.e. essential. No phone calls. *Commission* Home 15%; US & Europe 20%.

Millstone Lit
27–28 Lion Chambers, John Williams Street, Huddersfield, West Yorkshire HD1 1ES
☎01484 512817   Fax 01484 512817
Contact *Anne Kershaw, David Stern*
FOUNDED 1991. *Handles* fiction, non-fiction and children's. No unsolicited mss. Approach by letter or phone; synopses (with s.a.e.) considered. Reading fee may be asked. CLIENTS include Hope Dubé, Sylvia Duncan and James Lansbury. *Commission* Home 10%; US 15%.

Richard Milne Ltd
15 Summerlee Gardens, London N2 9QN
☎0181 883 3987   Fax 0181 883 3987
Contact *R. M. Sharples, K. N. Sharples*
FOUNDED 1956. *Specialises* in drama and comedy scripts for radio, film and television. Not presently in the market for new clients as 'fully committed handling work by authors we already represent'. No unsolicited mss. *Commission* Home 10%; US 15%; Translation 25%.

William Morris Agency UK Ltd★
31–32 Soho Square, London W1V 6HH
☎0171 434 2191   Fax 0171 437 0238
Films *Stephen M. Kenis*
Television/Theatre *Jane Annakin*
Books *Sappho Clissitt*
FOUNDED 1965. Worldwide theatrical and literary agency with offices in New York, Beverly Hills and Nashville; associates in Rome, Munich and Sydney. *Handles* theatre, TV, film and radio scripts; fiction and general non-fiction. No unsolicited material. *Commission* Film/TV/Theatre/UK Books 10%; US & Translation 20%.

Michael Motley Ltd★
42 Craven Hill Gardens, London W2 3EA
☎0171 723 2973   Fax 0171 262 4566
Contact *Michael Motley*
FOUNDED 1973. *Handles* all subjects, except short mss (e.g. journalism), poetry and original dramatic material. *Special interest* literary fiction and crime novels. Mss will be considered but

must be preceded by a preliminary letter with specimen chapters and s.a.e. No reading fee. CLIENTS include Simon Brett, Doug Nye, K. M. Peyton, Annette Roome, Barry Turner. *Commission* Home 10%; US 15%; Translation 20%. *Overseas associates* in all publishing centres.

The Maggie Noach Literary Agency★
21 Redan Street, London W14 0AB
☎0171 602 2451   Fax 0171 603 4712
Contact *Maggie Noach*
FOUNDED 1982. Pronounced 'no-ack'. *Handles* a wide range of books including commercial, well-written fiction, general non-fiction and some children's. No scientific, academic or specialist non-fiction. No romantic fiction, poetry, plays, short stories or books for the very young. Recommended for promising young writers but *very* few new clients taken on as it is considered vital to give individual attention to each author's work. Unsolicited mss not welcome. Approach by letter (*not by telephone*), giving a brief description of the book and enclosing a few sample pages. Return postage essential. No reading fee. *Commission* Home 15%; US & Translation 20%.

Andrew Nurnberg Associates Ltd★
Clerkenwell House, 45–47 Clerkenwell Green, London EC1R 0HT
☎0171 417 8800   Fax 0171 417 8812
Directors *Andrew Nurnberg, Klaasje Mul, Sarah Nundy*
FOUNDED in the mid-1970s. *Specialises* in foreign rights, representing leading authors and agents. Recently opened a branch in Moscow to provide representation for western writers in Russia and the republics of the CIS. *Commission* Home 15%; US & Translation 20%.

Alexandra Nye
45 Blackheath Road, Greenwich, London SE10 8PE
☎0181 691 9532
Contact *Alexandra Nye*
FOUNDED 1991. *Handles* fiction and topical non-fiction. *Special interests* literary fiction, historicals, thrillers. No children's, horror or crime. No scripts, poetry or plays. Preliminary approach by letter, with synopsis and sample chapter, preferred (s.a.e. essential for return). Reading fee for supply of detailed report on mss. CLIENTS include Dr Tom Gallagher,

Robin Jenkins. *Commission* Home 10%; US 20%; Translation 15%.

David O'Leary Literary Agents

10 Lansdowne Court, Lansdowne Rise,
London W11 2NR
☎0171 229 1623   Fax 0171 727 9624
Contact *David O'Leary*

FOUNDED 1988. *Handles* fiction, both popular and literary, and non-fiction. Areas of interest include thrillers, history, popular science, Russia and Ireland (history and fiction), TV drama and documentaries. No poetry or children's. No unsolicited mss but happy to discuss a proposal. Ring or write in the first instance. No reading fee. CLIENTS include James Barwick, Alexander Keegan, Jim Lusby, Roy MacGregor-Hastie, Charles Mosley, Edward Toman. *Commission* Home 10%; US 10%. *Overseas associates* Lennart Sane, Scandinavia/Spain/South America; Tuttle Mori, Japan.

Deborah Owen Ltd★

78 Narrow Street, Limehouse,
London E14 8BP
☎0171 987 5119/5441   Fax 0171 538 4004
Contact *Deborah Owen, Gemma Hirst*

FOUNDED 1971. Small agency specialising in representing authors direct around the world. *Handles* international fiction and non-fiction (books which can be translated into a number of languages). No scripts, poetry, science fiction, children's or short stories. No unsolicited mss. No new authors at present. CLIENTS include Amos Oz, Ellis Peters, Delia Smith, Murray Smith. *Commission* Home 10%; US & Translation 15%.

Mark Paterson & Associates★

10 Brook Street, Wivenhoe, Colchester, Essex CO7 9DS
☎01206 825433   Fax 01206 822990
Contact *Mark Paterson, Mary Swinney*

FOUNDED 1961. World rights representatives of authors and publishers handling many subjects, with specialisation in psychoanalysis and psychotherapy. CLIENTS range from Balint, Bion, Casement and Ferenczi, through to Freud and Winnicott; plus Hugh Brogan, Peter Moss and the estates of Sir Arthur Evans and Dorothy Richardson. No scripts, poetry, children's, articles, short stories or 'unsaleable mediocrity'. No unsolicited mss, but preliminary letter and synopsis with s.a.e. welcome. Reading fee may be charged. *Commission* 20% (including sub-agent's commission).

John Pawsey

60 High Street, Tarring, Worthing, West Sussex BN14 7NR
☎01903 205167   Fax 01903 205167
Contact *John Pawsey*

FOUNDED 1981. Experience in the publishing business has helped to attract some top names here. *Handles* non-fiction: biography, politics, current affairs, show business, gardening, travel, sport, business and music; and fiction; will consider any well written novel. *Special interests* sport, politics, current affairs and popular fiction. No scripts, poetry, short stories, journalism or academic. Preliminary letter with s.a.e. essential. No reading fee. CLIENTS include Jonathan Agnew, Simon Barnes, Dr David Lewis, David Rayvern Allen, Caroline Fabre, Peter Hobday, Ben Bova, Orson Scott Card. *Commission* Home 10–15%; US & Translation 19%. *Overseas associates* in the US, Japan, South America and throughout Europe.

Maggie Pearlstine★

31 Ashley Gardens, Ambrosden Avenue,
London SW1P 1QE
☎0171 828 4212   Fax 0171 834 5546
Contact *Maggie Pearlstine*

FOUNDED 1989. Small, selective agency. *Handles* commercial fiction, general and illustrated non-fiction: home and leisure, health, biography, history and politics. No children's or poetry. Deals only with scripts and short stories by existing clients. No unsolicited mss. Best approach first by letter with synopsis, sample material and s.a.e. for response. No reading fee. CLIENTS James Cox, John Drews, Mary Evans Young, Glorafilia, Prof Roger Gosden, Roy Hattersley, Prof Lisa Jardine, Charles Kennedy, Prof Nicholas Lowe, Sara Morrison, Lesley Regan MD,MRCOG, Jack Straw, Dr Thomas Stuttaford, Brian Wilson, Prof Robert Winston, Tony Wright. Translation rights handled by **Aitken, Stone & Wylie Ltd**. *Commission* Home 12½% (fiction), 10% (non-fiction); US & Translation 20%; TV, Film & Journalism 20%.

Penman Literary Agency

185 Daws Heath Road, Benfleet,
Essex SS7 2TF
☎01702 557431
Contact *Mark Sorrell*

FOUNDED 1950. Under new management since October 1993. *Handles* all types of fiction and non-fiction. No plays. Send preliminary letter, synopsis and sample chapters with s.a.e.

No reading fee. *Commission* Home 10%; Overseas 15–20%.

Peters Fraser & Dunlop Group Ltd★
503–504 The Chambers, Chelsea Harbour, Lots Road, London SW10 0XF
☎0171 344 1000Fax 0171 352 7356/351 1756
Managing Director *Anthony Baring*
Books *Michael Sissons, Pat Kavanagh, Caroline Dawnay, Araminta Whitley, Mark Lucas, Charles Walker, Rosemary Canter*
Serial *Pat Kavanagh*
Film/TV *Anthony Jones, Tim Corrie, Norman North, Charles Walker, Louisa Stevenson, Vanessa Jones, St. John Donald, Gavin Knight, Rosemary Scoular*
Actors *Maureen Vincent, Ginette Chalmers, Dallas Smith*
Theatre *Kenneth Ewing, St John Donald, Nicki Stoddart*
Children's *Rosemary Canter*

FOUNDED 1988 as a result of the merger of A. D. Peters & Co. Ltd and Fraser & Dunlop, and was later joined by the June Hall Literary Agency. *Handles* all sorts of books including fiction and children's, plus scripts for film, theatre, radio and TV material. No third-rate DIY. No unsolicited mss. Prospective clients should write 'a full letter, with an account of what he/she has done and wants to do'. No reading fee. CLIENTS include Martin Amis, Julian Barnes, Alan Bennett, A. S. Byatt, Alan Clark, Margaret Drabble, Clive James, Robert McCrum, John Mortimer, Douglas Reeman, Ruth Rendell, Anthony Sampson, Gerald Seymour, Tom Stoppard, Joanna Trollope Evelyn Waugh. *Commission* Home 10%; US & Translation 20%.

Laurence Pollinger Ltd
18 Maddox Street, London W1R 0EU
☎0171 629 9761   Fax 0171 629 9765
Contacts *Gerald J. Pollinger, Margaret Pepper*
Negotiating Editor *Juliet Burton*
Children's Books *Lesley Hadcroft*

FOUNDED 1958. A successor of Pearn, Pollinger & Higham. *Handles* all types of books including children's. No pure science, academic or technological. Good for crime and romantic fiction. No plays. CLIENTS include the estates of H. E. Bates, W. Heath Robinson, William Saroyan, John Cowper Powys, D. H. Lawrence and other notables. Unsolicited mss welcome if preceded by letter. No phone calls. A contribution of £10 is requested towards editorial costs. *Commission* Home & US 15%; Translation 20%.

Murray Pollinger★
222 Old Brompton Road, London SW5 0BZ
☎0171 373 4711   Fax 0171 373 3775
Contact *Murray Pollinger, Gina Pollinger, Sara Menguc*

FOUNDED 1969. Part of the Pollinger dynasty (Murray is the youngest son of Laurence), with a particularly strong name for new writers. Securely based on serious fiction and nature and science non-fiction. *Handles* all types of general fiction, non-fiction and children's fiction. No poetry, plays or travel; no drama scripts. No unsolicited mss; writers should send a letter with synopsis and names of other agents and publishers previously approached. CLIENTS include J. M. Coetzee, Anne Fine, John Gribbin, Molly Keane, Penelope Lively, Lyall Watson, and the estate of Roald Dahl. *Commission* Home 10%; Elsewhere 20%. *Overseas associates* in all major cultural centres.

Shelley Power Literary Agency Ltd★
Le Montaud, 24220 Berbiguières, France
☎00 33 5329 6252   Fax 00 33 5329 6254
Contact *Shelley Power*

FOUNDED 1976. Shelley Power works between London and France. This is an English agency with London-based administration/accounts office and the editorial office in France. *Handles* general commercial fiction, quality fiction, business books, self-help, true crime, investigative exposés, film and entertainment. No scripts, short stories, children's or poetry. Preliminary letter with brief outline of project (plus s.a.e.) essential. No reading fee. CLIENTS Michael Beer, Paul Fifield, Stephen Gray, Sutherland Lyall, Shirley McLaughlin, Clive Reading, Richard Stern, Madge Swindells, Roger Wilkes. *Commission* Home 10%; US & Translation 19%.

PVA Management Ltd
Hallow Park, Worcester WR2 6PG
☎01905 640663   Fax 01905 640633
Contact *Laraine King*

FOUNDED 1978. *Handles* mainly non-fiction, plus some fiction and scripts. Send preliminary letter with synopsis and return postage. *Commission* 15%.

Radala & Associates
17 Avenue Mansions, Finchley Road, London NW3 7AX
☎0171 794 4495   Fax 0171 431 7636
Contact *Richard Gollner, Neil Hornick, Anna Swan, Andy Marino*

FOUNDED 1970. *Handles* quality fiction, non-fiction, drama, performing and popular arts, psychotherapy, writing from Eastern Europe. Also provides editorial services, initiates in-house projects and can recommend independent professional readers if unable to read or comment on submissions. No poetry or screenplays. Prospective clients should send a shortish letter plus synopsis (maximum 2pp), first two chapters (double-spaced, numbered pages) and s.a.e. for return. *Commission* Home 10%; US 15–20%; Translation 20%. *Overseas associates* **Writers House, Inc.** (Al Zuckermann), New York; plus agents throughout Europe.

Margaret Ramsay Ltd
See **Casarotto Ramsay Ltd**

Rogers, Coleridge & White Ltd★
20 Powis Mews, London W11 1JN
☎0171 221 3717   Fax 0171 229 9084
Contacts *Deborah Rogers, Gill Coleridge, Patricia White*
Foreign Rights *Ann Warnford-Davis, Clare Loeffler, Rosalind Ramsay*

FOUNDED 1967. *Handles* fiction, non-fiction and children's books. No poetry, plays or technical books. Rights representative in UK and translation for several New York agents. *Commission* Home 10%; US 15%; Translation 20%. *Overseas associates* ICM, New York.

Hilary Rubinstein Books
61 Clarendon Road, London W11 4JE
☎0171 792 4282   Fax 0171 221 5291
Contact *Hilary Rubinstein*

FOUNDED 1992. *Handles* fiction and non-fiction, also occasional scripts for TV, film, radio and theatre. No poetry or drama. Approach in writing in the first instance. No reading fee. CLIENTS include Monique Charlesworth, Elisabeth Maxwell, Donna Williams. *Commission* Home 10%; US & Translation 20%. *Overseas associates* **Ellen Levine Literary Agency** New York; **Andrew Nurnberg Associates** (European rights).

Uli Rushby-Smith and Shirley Stewart
72 Plimsoll Road, London N4 2EE
☎0171 354 2718   Fax 0171 354 2718
Contacts *Ulie Rushby-Smith, Shirley Stewart*

FOUNDED 1993. *Handles* fiction and non-fiction, commercial and literary, both adult and children's. Scripts handled in conjunction with

a sub-agent. No plays, poetry or science fiction. Approach with an outline, two or three sample chapters and explanatory letter in the first instance (s.a.e. essential). No reading fee. *Commission* Home 10%; US & Translation 20%. Represents UK rights for **Curtis Brown (New York)** and Henry Holt & Co. Inc.

Herta Ryder
c/o Toby Eady Associates Ltd, 9 Orme Court, London W2 4RL
☎0181 948 1010
Contact *Herta Ryder*

FOUNDED 1984. *Handles* fiction and non-fiction, including children's (particularly older children's), music (lives rather than specialist), military history and German books of quality (Herta Ryder is London representative for Liepman AG, Zurich). No scripts, poetry, individual short stories, technical, textbooks or articles. No unsolicited mss without initial letter of enquiry. CLIENTS include Judy Blume, Gwyneth Jones (Ann Halam), Adrienne Kennaway, Jean Morris, Farley Mowat, David Henry Wilson. *Commission* Home 10%; US 15%; Translation 20%. *Overseas associates* Harold Ober Associates, New York; plus associates in most other countries.

Rosemary Sandberg Ltd
6 Bayley Street, London WC1B 3HB
☎0171 304 4110   Fax 0171 304 4109
Contact *Rosemary Sandberg*

FOUNDED 1991. In association with **Ed Victor Ltd.** *Handles* children's picture books and novels; women's fiction (although not exclusively women's); women's interests e.g. cookery. *Specialises* in children's writers and illustrators and women's fiction. No unsolicited mss. *Commission* Home 10–15%; US 15%; Translation 15–20%.

Tessa Sayle Agency★
11 Jubilee Place, London SW3 3TE
☎0171 823 3883   Fax 0171 823 3363
Books *Rachel Calder*
Film/TV *Jane Villiers*

FOUNDED 1976 by Tessa Sayle who retired shortly before her death in 1993. *Handles* fiction: literary novels rather than category fiction; non-fiction: current affairs, social issues, travel, biographies, historical; and drama (TV, film and theatre): contemporary social issues or drama with comedy, rather than broad comedy. No poetry, children's, textbooks, science fiction, fantasy, horror or musicals. No unsolicited mss.

Preliminary letter essential, including a brief biographical note and a synopsis. No reading fee. CLIENTS Books: Stephen Amidon, Peter Benson, Rose Boyt, Pete Davies, Margaret Forster, Georgina Hammick, Paul Hogarth, Mark Illis, Andy Kershaw, Phillip Knightley, Rory MacLean, Ann Oakley, Kate Pullinger, Ronald Searle, Gitta Sereny, William Styron, Mary Wesley. Drama: William Corlett, Shelagh Delaney, Marc Evans, Stuart Hepburn, Kathy Lette, Geoff McQueen, Chris Monger, Don Shaw, Sue Townsend. *Commission* Home 10%; US & Translation 20%. *Overseas associates* in the US, Japan and throughout Europe.

Howard Seddon Associates
BM Box 1129, London WC1N 3XX
☎01923 229784   Fax 01923 229784
Contact *Dr Keith H. Seddon*

FOUNDED 1988. *Handles* full-length general and literary fiction, general non-fiction and academic. No scripts. No poetry, crime, glitzy women's, short stories, gardening, cooking or children's. *Specialises* in fantasy, gothic, horror and literary fiction; folklore, New Age, occult, philosophy, religion, social issues. No unsolicited mss. Authors come via recommendation or follow-ups to preliminary letter. Full reading and report service available. Return postage/s.a.e. essential with all enquiries. CLIENTS include Jocelyn Almond, Ravan Christchild, G.E. Vane. *Commission* Home 15%; US & Translation 20–25%.

Seifert Dench Associates
24 D'Arblay Street, London W1V 3FH
☎0171 437 4551   Fax 0171 439 1355
Contact *Linda Seifert, Elizabeth Dench*

FOUNDED 1972. *Handles* scripts for TV and film. Unsolicited mss will be read, but a letter with sample of work and c.v. (plus s.a.e.) is preferred. CLIENTS include Peter Chelsom, Tony Grisoni, Michael Radford, Stephen Volk. *Commission* Home 12½–15%. *Overseas associates* William Morris/Sanford Skouras Gross and C.A.A., Los Angeles.

James Sharkey Associates Ltd★
21 Golden Square, London W1R 3PA
☎0171 434 3801   Fax 0171 494 1547
Contact *Cat Ledger*

FOUNDED 1983. Actors' and literary agency. *Handles* adult fiction and non-fiction. No scripts. Preliminary letter and synopsis with s.a.e. essential in the first instance. No reading fee. *Commission* 10%.

The Sharland Organisation Ltd
9 Marlborough Crescent, London W4 1HE
☎0181 742 1919   Fax 0181 995 7688
Contact *Mike Sharland, Alice Sharland*

FOUNDED 1988. *Specialises* in national and international film and TV negotiations. Also negotiates multimedia, interactive TV deals and computer game contracts. *Handles* scripts for film, TV, radio and theatre; also fiction and non-fiction. Markets books for film and handles stage, radio, film and TV rights for authors. No scientific, technical or poetry. No unsolicited mss. Preliminary enquiry by letter or phone essential. *Commission* Home 15%; US & Translation 20%. *Overseas associates* various.

Vincent Shaw Associates
20 Jay Mews, Kensington Gore,
London SW7 2EP
☎0171 581 8215   Fax 0171 225 1079
Contact *Vincent Shaw*

FOUNDED 1954. *Handles* TV, radio, film and theatre scripts. Unsolicited mss welcome. Approach in writing enclosing s.a.e. No phone calls. *Commission* Home 10%; US & Translation by negotiation. *Overseas associates* Herman Chessid, New York.

Sheil Land Associates Ltd★
43 Doughty Street, London WC1N 2LF
☎0171 405 9351   Fax 0171 831 2127
Contact *Anthony Sheil, Sonia Land, Giles Gordon, Vivien Green, Robert Kirby, Simon Trewin, John Rush (film/drama/TV)*
Consultant, Film/Drama/TV *Lynda Myles*
Foreign *Benita Edzard*

FOUNDED 1962. Incorporates the Richard Scott Simon Agency. *Handles* full-length general and literary fiction, biography, travel, cookery and humour. Also theatre, film, radio and TV scripts. One of the UK's more dynamic agencies, Sheil Land represents over 270 established clients and welcomes approaches from new clients looking either to start or to develop their careers. Known to negotiate sophisticated contracts with publishers. Preliminary letter with s.a.e. essential. No reading fee. CLIENTS include Peter Ackroyd, Melvyn Bragg, John Banville, Catherine Cookson, Josephine Cox, Nick Fisher, John Fowles, Susan Hill, HRH The Prince of Wales, Michael Ignatieff, John Keegan, Graham King, Bernard Kops, Richard Mabey, Michael Moorcock, James Roose-Evans, Eddy Shah, Tom Sharpe, Sue Townsend, Rose Tremain, John Wilsher. *Commission* Home 10%; US & Translation 20%. *Overseas associates* Georges

Borchardt, Inc. (Richard Scott Simon); **Sanford J. Greenburger Associates**, Scovil Chichak Galen (Sheil Land Associates). UK representatives for **Farrar, Straus & Giroux, Inc.** US Film and TV representation: CAA, **H.N. Swanson**, and others.

Caroline Sheldon Literary Agency*

71 Hillgate Place, London W8 7SS
☎0171 727 9102
Contact *Caroline Sheldon*

FOUNDED 1985. *Handles* adult fiction, in particular women's, both commercial sagas and literary novels. Also full-length children's fiction. No TV/film scripts unless by book-writing clients. Send letter with all relevant details of ambitions and four chapters of proposed book (enclose large s.a.e.). No reading fee. *Commission* Home 10%; US & Translation 20%.

Jeffrey Simmons

10 Lowndes Square, London SW1X 9HA
☎0171 235 8852   Fax 0171 235 9733
Contact *Jeffrey Simmons*

FOUNDED 1978. *Handles* biography and autobiography, cinema and theatre, fiction (both quality and commercial), history, law and crime, politics and world affairs, parapsychology, sport and travel (but not exclusively). No science fiction/fantasy, children's books, cookery, crafts, hobbies or gardening. Film scripts handled only if by book-writing clients. *Special interests* personality books of all sorts and fiction from young writers (i.e. under 40) with a future. Writers become clients by personal introduction or by letter, enclosing a synopsis if possible, a brief biography, a note of any previously published books, plus a list of any publishers and agents who have already seen the mss. CLIENTS include Michael Bentine, Billy Boy, Clive Collins, Doris Collins, Euphrosyne Doxiadis, Fred Lawrence Guiles, Jim Haskins, Sanda Miller, Keith Wright. *Commission* Home 10–15%; US 15-20%; Translation 20%.

Simpson Fox Associates

52 Shaftesbury Avenue,
London W1V 7DE
☎0171 434 9167   Fax 0171 494 2887
Contact *Georgina Capel*

ESTABLISHED 1973. *Handles* literary and commercial fiction, general non-fiction, and film/play scripts. No children's books. Approach with synopsis and sample chapter, with s.a.e., in the first instance. CLIENTS Niall

Ferguson, Deborah Levy, Andrew Roberts, Peter York. *Commission* Home, US & Translation 15%.

Carol Smith Literary Agency

25 Hornton Court, Kensington High Street,
London W8 7RT
☎0171 937 4874   Fax 0171 938 5323
Contact *Carol Smith*

FOUNDED 1976. *Handles* general fiction of all sorts and general non-fiction. No technical material of any kind. Submissions by invitation only. CLIENTS include John Cornwell, Alexander Frater, Sarah Harrison, Katie Stewart, Mike Wilks. *Commission* Home 10%; US & Translation 20%.

Solo Literary Agency Ltd

49–53 Kensington High Street,
London W8 5ED
☎0171 376 2166   Fax 0171 938 3165
Chairman *Don Short*
Senior Executive/Accounts *John Appleton*

FOUNDED 1978. *Handles* non-fiction. *Special interests* celebrity autobiographies, unauthorised biographies, sports and adventure stories, wildlife, nature & ecology, crime, fashion, beauty & health. Also some fiction but only from established authors. No unsolicited mss. Preliminary letter essential. CLIENTS include Nicholas Davies, Peter Essex, Uri Geller, James Oram, Betty Palko, Rick Sky. Also *specialises* in worldwide newspaper syndication of photos, features and cartoons. Professional contributors only. *Commission* Books: Home 15%; US 20%; Translation 20–30%; Journalism 50%.

Elaine Steel

110 Gloucester Avenue,
London NW1 8JA
☎0171 483 2681   Fax 0171 483 4541
Contact *Elaine Steel*

FOUNDED 1986. *Handles* scripts and screenplays. No technical or academic. Initial phone call preferred. CLIENTS include Les Blair, Michael Eaton, Brian Keenan, Troy Kennedy Martin, G. F. Newman, Rob Ritchie, Snoo Wilson. *Commission* Home 10%; US & Translation 20%.

Abner Stein*

10 Roland Gardens, London SW7 3PH
☎0171 373 0456   Fax 0171 370 6316
Contact *Abner Stein*

FOUNDED 1971. *Handles* full-length fiction and general non-fiction. No scientific, technical, etc. No scripts. Send letter and outline in the first instance rather than unsolicited mss. *Commission* Home 10%; US & Translation 20%.

Micheline Steinberg Playwrights' Agent

110 Frognal, London NW3 6XU
☎0171 433 3980   Fax 0171 794 8355

Contact *Micheline Steinberg*

FOUNDED 1988. *Specialises* in plays for stage, TV, radio and film. Best approach by preliminary letter (with s.a.e.). Dramatic associate for **Laurence Pollinger Ltd**. *Commission* Home 10%; Elsewhere 15%.

Peter Tauber Press Agency

94 East End Road, London N3 2SX
☎0181 346 4165

Directors *Peter Tauber, Robert Tauber*

FOUNDED 1950. *Handles* women's fiction, especially sagas and glitz; thrillers, crime, horror and fantasy. Also non-fiction primarily celebrity auto/biographies. No poetry, short stories, plays, children or foreign books. Please send synopsis, first three chapters, copies of all previous rejections, a non-returnable submission fee of £50 and fully stamped addressed envelope. Failure to comply with these exact terms will result in no reply. *Commission* 20%.

J. M. Thurley

213 Linen Hall, 162–168 Regent Street, London W1R 5TA
☎0171 437 9545/6   Fax 0171 287 9208

Contact *Jon Thurley, Patricia Preece*

FOUNDED 1976. *Handles* all types of fiction, non-fiction, coffee-table books, etc. Also scripts for TV, film, radio and theatre. No short stories or children's illustrated books. No unsolicited mss; approach by letter in the first instance. No reading fee. *Commission* Home 10% (15% where substantial editorial/creative input involved); US & Translation 15%.

Lavinia Trevor Agency★

6 The Glasshouse, 49A Goldhawk Road, London W12 8QP
☎0181 749 8481   Fax 0181 749 7377

Contact *Lavinia Trevor*

FOUNDED 1993. *Handles* general fiction and non-fiction. No poetry, academic or technical work. No TV, film, radio, theatre scripts. Approach with a preliminary letter and first 50–100 typewritten pages, including s.a.e. No reading fee. *Commission* Rate by agreement with author.

Jane Turnbull

13 Wendell Road, London W12 9RS
☎0181 743 9580   Fax 0181 749 6079

Contact *Jane Turnbull*

FOUNDED 1986. *Handles* fiction and non-fiction. No science fiction, sagas or women's sagas. No scripts. *Specialises* in literary fiction, history, current affairs, health and diet. No unsolicited mss. Approach with letter in the first instance. No reading fee. CLIENTS include Kirsty Gunn, James Long, Judith Wills. Translation rights handled by **Aitken, Stone & Wylie Ltd**. *Commission* Home 10%; USA & Translation 20%.

Vardey & Brunton Associates★

6 The Glasshouse, 49A Goldhawk Road, London W12 8QP
☎0181 749 9956   Fax 0181 749 7377

Contact *Carolyn Brunton, Lucinda Vardey*

FOUNDED 1985. *Specialises* in representation for US & Canadian publishers and agents. No unsolicited mss.

Ed Victor Ltd★

6 Bayley Street, Bedford Square, London WC1B 3HB
☎0171 304 4100   Fax 0171 304 4111

Contact *Ed Victor, Graham Greene, Maggie Phillips, Sophie Hicks*

FOUNDED 1977. *Handles* a broad range of material from Iris Murdoch to Jack Higgins, Erich Segal to Stephen Spender. Leans towards the more commercial ends of the fiction and non-fiction spectrums. No scripts, no academic. Takes on very few new writers. After trying his hand at book publishing and literary magazines, Ed Victor, an ebullient American, found his true vocation. Strong opinions, very pushy and works hard for those whose intelligence he respects. Loves nothing more than a good title auction. Preliminary letter essential, setting out very concisely and clearly what the book aims to do. No unsolicited mss. CLIENTS include Douglas Adams, Josephine Hart, Jack Higgins, Erica Jong, Iris Murdoch, Erich Segal, Will Self, Stephen Spender, Fay Weldon and the estates of Raymond Chandler and Irving Wallace. *Commission* Home 15%; US 15%; Translation 20%.

Cecily Ware Literary Agents

19C John Spencer Square, London N1 2LZ
☎0171 359 3787   Fax 0171 226 9828

Contact *Cecily Ware, Gilly Schuster, Ben Holland*

FOUNDED 1972. Primarily a film and TV script

agency representing work in all areas: drama, children's, series/serials, adaptations, comedies, etc. Also radio and occasional general fiction. No unsolicited mss or phone calls. Approach in writing only. No reading fee. *Commission* Home 10%; US 10–20% by arrangement.

Warner Chappell Plays Ltd
129 Park Street, London W1Y 3FA
☎0171 514 5236   Fax 0171 514 5201
Contact *Michael Callahan*

Formerly the English Theatre Guild, Warner Chappell are now both agents and publishers of scripts for the theatre. No unsolicited mss; introductory letter essential. No reading fee. CLIENTS include Ray Cooney, John Godber, Peter Gordon, Debbie Isitt, Arthur Miller, Sam Shepard, John Steinbeck. *Overseas representatives* in the US, Canada, Australia, New Zealand, India, South Africa and Zimbabwe.

Watson, Little Ltd★
12 Egbert Street, London NW1 8LJ
☎0171 722 9514   Fax 0171 586 7649
Contact *Sheila Watson, Mandy Little*

Handles fiction and non-fiction. *Special interests* popular science, psychology, self-help, military history and business books. No scripts. Not interested in authors who wish to be purely academic writers. Send preliminary ('intelligent') letter rather than unsolicited synopsis. *Commission* Home 10%; US & Translation 19%. *Overseas associates* worldwide.

A. P. Watt Ltd★
20 John Street, London WC1N 2DR
☎0171 405 6774   Fax 0171 831 2154
Directors *Caradoc King, Linda Shaughnessy, Rod Hall, Lisa Eveleigh, Nick Marston, Derek Johns*

FOUNDED 1875. The oldest-established literary agency in the world. *Handles* full-length typescripts, including children's books, screenplays for film and TV, and plays. No poetry, academic or specialist works. Unsolicited mss and outlines welcome but must be preceded by introductory letter, plus return postage. No reading fee. CLIENTS include Evelyn Anthony, Quentin Blake, Martin Gilbert, Nadine Gordimer, Michael Holroyd, Garrison Keillor, Alison Lurie, Timothy Mo, Jan Morris, Michael Ondaatje, Graham Swift, and the estates of Wodehouse, Graves and Maugham. *Commission* Home 10%; US & Translation

20%. *Overseas associates* Ellen Levine Literary Agency, Inc., US.

John Welch, Literary Consultant & Agent
Milton House, Milton,
Cambridge CB4 6AD
☎01223 860641   Fax 01223 440575
Contact *John Welch*

FOUNDED 1992. *Handles* military history, children's books, history, art, biography and some sport. No scripts for radio, TV, film or theatre. No unsolicited mss. Send letter with synopsis, two chapters and s.a.e. for return. Consultancy fees may apply, especially to unpublished authors. CLIENTS include Lynda Britnell, Michael Calvert, Paul Clifford, Patrick Delaforce, Norman Scarfe, David Wragg. *Commission* Home 10%; US & Translation 15%.

Dinah Wiener Ltd★
27 Arlington Road,
London NW1 7ER
☎0171 388 2577   Fax 0171 388 7559
Contact *Dinah Wiener*

FOUNDED 1985. *Handles* fiction and general non-fiction: auto/biography, popular science, cookery. No scripts, children's or poetry. In first instance approach with preliminary letter, giving full but brief c.v. of past work and future plans. Mss submitted must include s.a.e. and be typed in double-spacing. CLIENTS include Catherine Alliott, T. J. Armstrong, Joy Berthoud, Malcolm Billings, Guy Burt, David Deutsch, Tania Kindersley, Dalene Matthee, Daniel Snowman, Peta Taylor, Michael Thornton, Lailan Young. *Commission* Home 15%; US & Translation 20%.

Michael Woodward Creations Ltd
Parlington Hall, Aberford, West Yorkshire
LS25 3EG
☎0113 2813913   Fax 0113 2813911
Contact *Michael Woodward, Janet Becker*

FOUNDED 1979. International Licensing company with own in-house studio. Worldwide representation. Current properties include *Teddy Tum Tum, Railway Children, Oddbods, Angel Babies, Kit 'n' Kin*. New artists should forward full concept synopses with sample illustrations. Scripts or stories not accepted without illustration/design or concept mock-ups. No standard commission rate; varies according to contract.

THE GOOD ENGLISH GUIDE

English Usage in the 1990s

Compiled and written by

Godfrey Howard

Three years' research and thousands of consultations make this book *the writer's guide* to the use of English.

Keep it alongside your dictionary: its 6000 entries give quick, balanced, up-to-date answers to every question of grammar and the use of words. And enjoy it as a celebration of English in all its complexity, beauty, wit and poetry.

'What an achievement! Amazing what you can find out from this book.'
Fay Weldon

'Splendidly up-to-date. The Good English Guide *will certainly be at my bedside!'*
Sue MacGregor

'A Fowler for the age.'
Keith Waterhouse *Daily Mail*

'The entries are splendid . . . I salute Godfrey Howard who knows the way the language works.'
Philip Howard *The Times*

'It seems so indispensable when you open it, that you wonder why it has not been written before.'
The Observer

Published by Macmillan, £18.99 hardback, £12.99 paperback

The State of the Language

Godfrey Howard

At the beginning of this century the English language seemed as steady as a rock. The Union Jack fluttered over it. An Englishman's word was his bond, all the more so because that word was in English. The Fowler brothers declared, 'Americanisms are foreign words, and should be so treated.' Their book, published in 1906, was called *The King's English,* as if Edward VII's standard of using the language was unimpeachable. An eminent philologist of the time, Henry Wyld, defined *Standard English* as 'the best type' of English, with *Modified Standard* as 'the various vulgar forms of this, heard among the inferior ranks of the population'. Good English was élitist, the birthright of caste and privilege.

When the BBC (the British Broadcasting Company, as it was then) went on the air in 1922, announcers wore dinner jackets to mark the formality of the occasion and of the language they used. Henry Watson Fowler's *Modern English Usage* was published in 1926, and his linguistic edicts were delivered in such magisterial tones, that for generations, long after he died in 1933, disputes over grammar and the use of words were settled by, 'But Fowler says...'.

Sometime after World War II, all that changed. The doors of British English were forced wide open, and the trickle of American words became a flood. Words, such as *gatecrasher, debunk, teenager, bulldoze, crank, boom, slump, bestseller, paperback, blurb,* lost all taint of foreignness, as we found we couldn't live without them.

The existence of two predominant forms of English no longer means there are two standards, one below the other. British dictionaries are now expected to include American usage, spelling and pronunciation. An Israeli diplomat or a Japanese industrialist is as likely as not to use American English, having learnt their English from an American. There are, after all, at least four times as many people using English in North America as there are in Britain.

Lexicographers have long since come out of their ivory towers, to plunge into the rough and tumble of the real linguistic world of Aboriginal, Zimbabwean, Caribbean and many other forms of English. No one can now define *Standard English* in a way that all users of the language would accept. For English has become a world language, taking many different forms. There are so many expected and unexpected places where people use English, from the Australian outback to the road to Katmandu, although it may be very different from the language of Stoke-on-Trent and Stoke Newington, of Old Sodbury and the Old Kent Road, forms of English which in turn are different from the language of Oxford dons, Wiltshire farmers, the Archbishop of Canterbury, John Lennon, or the language you hear on the New York subway or the Mississippi River.

There was worse to come. Writers using such outlandish forms of our language began to win the top literary prizes. A reviewer, commenting on *How Late It Was, How Late,* the novel that won the 1994 Booker Prize, said you need subtitles to read it.

Inevitably there is a backlash against so much linguistic permissiveness, with 19th-century grammatical orthodoxy fighting for survival. Norman Tebbit is alleged to have blamed football hooliganism on the cut-back in grammar lessons. The Prince of Wales has lamented a 30-year decline in standards of English, Katharine Whitehorn reports that 'The changing nature of words brings out more protesters than an eight-lane motorway.' Even a headline in a Paris newspaper, *Le Figaro,* proclaimed, 'Le bon anglais en chute libre', as the paper's London correspondent reported that the English language is in a state of free fall, without a parachute.

Never before has English usage registered so much violent passion and outrage. The middle-aged in power bang the drum ever more loudly about 'traditional values'. What they are doing is remembering the rules they were taught at school twenty, thirty, forty or more years ago. But the language has moved on. William Safire, who writes a famous column on language for *The New York Times,* warns that '. . . if sticking grimly to the rules of grammar makes you sound like a pompous pedant, you *are* a pompous pedant'. Philip Howard, former literary editor of *The Times*, rejoices that 'the language does not run along railway lines of rules, but along the rolling English roads, and through bogs and well-ploughed fields'.

So much about language is convention. And conventions change. Good standards of literacy do not require English to be in the arthritic grip of Colonel Blimps, out of date and out of touch. A living language has to be all things to all people in their never-ending drive to express what they think and feel. English cannot be contained in a straitjacket of logic since it holds up a mirror to life itself, which constantly confounds logic. Language is at the same time as basic as mother's milk, and as infinitely complex and perverse as the human situation.

We cannot imagine Shakespeare staying awake at night worrying about grammar. For him there was no proper dictionary, so he could twist words to make them do what he wanted, even spell them as he fancied, without anyone challenging him by 'looking it up'. The English language basked and stretched in the warmth and glory of Elizabethan England, as Shakespeare and other writers made the language as they used it.

In the mid-1990s writers are experiencing some of that freedom. Because of films, radio and television, spoken English is lubricating the wheels of the written language, leaving it more easygoing. The permissiveness in our morals and manners, the breaking down of rigid authoritarian dogma offer greater freedom to explore human experience, which demands greater freedom in the way we use language. Depending upon how you see it, or perhaps how old you are, this linguistic permissiveness is 'the final descent into darkness for the English language', as one grammarian despairs, or a transfusion of rich vigorous lifeblood that makes English the most lively and adaptable of all languages in the long history of lexical communication.

We can no longer claim territorial rights over English. Of course, the language had its origin here, in the 5th century AD as a modest dialect brought to the country by Germanic tribes. But in our time, English is the property of everyone who uses it, not of the literati, the great and the good, nor of the Secretary of State for Education. *The Times Literary Supplement* has observed, 'West African writers regard English . . . as a language which is theirs to use and which they are entitled to mould and pound and batter into any shape they please.'

Our ability as writers depends on ideas and imagination, and on the way we choose words and put them together, as I am doing at this moment. That, after all, is the meaning of *style*. It is style in this sense that sets Graham Greene apart from, say Jeffrey Archer. David Lodge maintains, 'That the authority of great writers is an authority of style.' Attitudes towards grammar are part of our style. Even experienced writers these days hesitate over when to follow traditional rules, and what are the new rules. For the goalposts are moving. You can sometimes tell how old a writer is by punctiliousness over *who* and *whom,* or concern over using the subjunctive ('If he *were* to arrive late...'). On the teaching side of the counter, 552 university professors and lecturers signed a letter in *The Times Higher Education Supplement* maintaining that 'the teaching of grammar and spelling is not all that important'.

If grammar, as a form of moral compulsion as once taught by a Mr Chips or a Miss Trump, is no longer sustainable, an awareness of the structure and organisation of language (which is another way of saying grammar) is part of being literate. Brian Friel, a playwright hardly hemmed in by convention, considers '. . . the entire social order depends . . . on words mutually agreed, and mutually understood'.

The balance for writers is uneasy. Bernice Rubens, the first woman writer to win the Booker Prize, has expressed her ambivalence: 'If I start thinking about grammar, I get caught up in the *how* instead of the *what*. . . Grammar is a stranglehold on passion! But before a writer discards grammar, he must know it intimately. . . Only then is its irrelevance clear and logical.' For the rest of us, how can we find our way through the contradictions and conflicting advice on English usage? We cannot prescribe for others, for we have to find our own way. We each have our own idiolect, an individual personal way of using language, preferences or hobby-horses about certain words or grammatical forms. But we can take comfort: there is hardly a writer, from the translators of the Bible to Dickens, E. M. Forster and Agatha Christie, who has not been picked on for making mistakes.

The best we can do is respond to and respect the way the language is changing, without opening the floodgates. There is much more freedom now in the way we can use English, but there is also order. As writers, we have to walk the tightrope between personal choice in English usage, and what is obscure or out of touch with the language on the brink of the 21st century.

The usage dilemma of the decade is the lack in the English language of a third-person *unisex* singular pronoun. For centuries *he* in certain contexts was taken to include *she*. The 1975 Sex Discrimination Act makes that less comfortable, and in some situations a possible breach of the law. Some leases and other legal documents still say coyly that 'words importing the masculine gender shall be deemed to embrace females'.

The awkward alternative that sometimes appears is *s/he*. We can wear ourselves and our readers out writing *he or she* (varying that out of fairness with *she or he*). Some of us see the way ahead as using *they, them, their* as unisex singular pronouns ('Nobody has taken *their* seat yet.'). There is nothing new in this: long ago Bernard Shaw grumbled, 'Nobody would ever marry if they thought it over.'

In this present article, *they, them, their,* are freely used as singular unisex pronouns, and I have to live with the regret that some readers will shake their heads over this elastic attitude towards singular and plural. But even purists have to accept that at times there is no other way out, as Thackeray found when he wrote, 'Nobody prevents you, do they?' Just as Kazuo Ishiguro, in *The Remains of the Day,* settled for 'some fellow professional . . . would be accompanying their employer'. And in a conversation on the BBC, Antonia Byatt and Bryan Magee agreed this is the best resolution of the problem. So I am in good company.

The *who* or *whom* dilemma has become almost as sociolinguistic as grammatical. Many people try to use *who* and *whom* strictly according to the copybook rules, in case it is thought they don't know any better. Conservative MPs seem particularly on guard, as if they might lose the party whip if they get it wrong. Nor are diehards reassured to be told that good authorities, from Eric Partridge to, over a century earlier, Noah Webster, were prepared to abandon *whom* altogether.

The *who* and *whom* distinction preserves a grammatical museum piece, and does nothing to avoid ambiguity. At least one Oxford lexicographer has ruled that *whomever is* stilted, and recommends that *whoever* should be used right across the board. Many writers remain ambivalent, slipping in *whom* after prepositions ('to whom', 'for whom' . . .), perhaps because this is enshrined in Hemingway's title (taken from John Donne's poem), *For Whom the Bell Tolls,* but using *who* in all other contexts. If that's your style, expect to be rebuked for it occasionally, but the tide is going your way. Philip Howard, for one, believes that by the end of the century *whom* will be 'as old-fashioned as wing-collars and corsets'. But for a long time to come, there will be people who sustain the old grammatical principle, or dare not give it up for fear of what people might think.

Political correctness is another tightrope we have to walk in the mid-1990s, as we hover between Orwellian newspeak and linguistic racism, sexism and homophobia. Can we change underlying attitudes by changing the language that reflects them? It seems a step in the right direction to avoid words that sneer, even unintentionally, at women, blacks, Jews, gays. . . Our language is loaded with prejudices, and Stuart Hall has summed up our dilemma: '. . . challenging the assumptions built into our ordinary use of language is one thing, policing language is another'. We have to decide our own principles and take our own responsibility, standing up to any publisher or editor who insists that we avoid all risks, offending no one by saying nothing, or by blunting the edge of the truth as we see it.

We should be lost without dictionaries. They chart the vast wilderness of words in which we wander all our lives. A survey has shown that when people are asked, 'Would you buy a dictionary?', the majority answer, 'We've already got one.' But things are getting better. English dictionaries have become big publishing business, as users discover that, like railway timetables, dictionaries have a limited bookshelf-life. Elizabeth Barrett Browning wrote in a letter, when she was on honeymoon in 1846, 'After two months of uninterrupted intercourse he loves me better every day . . . and my health improves too.' She would hardly write that now. It is surprising how many writers still treat dictionaries like their favourite armchairs. They go on using them until the pages become brittle and yellow with age. In the linguistic fast-lanes of the 1990s, five years is a generous lifespan for a dictionary.

Where do writers stand over that deep-rooted linguistic fetish, *four-letter words?* It was 30 years ago, 13 November 1965, that Kenneth Tynan made broadcasting history by saying *fuck* for the first time on British television. Twenty years later, *The Concise Oxford Dictionary* still solemnly declared that four-letter words are 'used only by those who have no wish to be thought either polite or educated'. That is a slap in the face for the BBC, a parade of poets and novelists (a slap on both cheeks, and then some, for James Kelman and the judges who awarded his novel the 1994 Booker Prize), me and very likely most of the readers of *The Writer's Handbook*.

There is a descending scale of supposed degradation. 'Piss' and 'shit', while not commonly heard at royal garden parties, hardly shock anymore. 'Fuck' can still cause a tightening of the lips for many people. 'Cunt' seems to give the greatest offence of all. The whole subject is loaded with double standards, and the genteel game still goes on of placing a typographical veil over the last three letters of offending words (f..., c...). Bernard Levin is right to scorn the notion that 'a handful of dots leave the most obscene and licentious words robbed of their dreadful power'.

Here again, writers have to decide for themselves whether to toe the socio-linguistic line, which is not all that clearly defined these days, or use the language that belongs to us in ways that seem natural and appropriate to a particular situation. The alternative is pussyfooting. (Is it all right to say 'pussy', which dictionaries label as *coarse* or *taboo?*). I agree with Stephen Fry, who finds this whole business 'a coitus of a worry. In fact, it scares the faecal solids out of me!'

Godfrey Howard read linguistics at Oxford during a remarkable period for English studies, under scholars who included C T Onions (the last surviving editor of the original Oxford English Dictionary*), David Cecil, C S Lewis and J R R Tolkien. He devoted over three years to researching, compiling and writing* The Good English Guide, *published by Macmillan. The BBC has commissioned for Radio 4 his series of programmes called* The State of the Language.

National Newspapers

Daily Express
Ludgate House, 245 Blackfriars Road,
London SE1 9UX
☎0171 928 8000   Fax 0171 620 1654

Owner *United Newspapers*
Editor *Sir Nicholas Lloyd*
Circulation 1.28 million

The general rule of thumb is to approach in writing with an idea; all departments are prepared to look at an outline without commitment. Ideas welcome but already receives many which are 'too numerous to count'.

News Editor *Ian Walker*
Diary Editor *Ross Benson*
Features Editor *Nikki Chessworth*
Literary Editor *Peter Grosvenor*
Sports Editor *David Emery*
Women's Page *Julia Finch*
Planning Editor (News Desk) should be circulated with copies of official reports, press releases, etc., to ensure news desk cover at all times.

This Week magazine **Editor** *Heather McGlone* **Payment** depends on the nature of the article accepted.

Daily Mail
Northcliffe House, 2 Derry Street,
Kensington, London W8 5TT
☎0171 938 6000   Fax 0171 937 4463

Owner *Lord Rothermere*
Editor *Paul Dacre*
Circulation 1.81 million

In-house feature writers and regular columnists provide much of the material. Photo-stories and crusading features often appear; it's essential to hit the right note to be a successful *Mail* writer. Close scrutiny of the paper is strongly advised. Not a good bet for the unseasoned. Accepts news on savings, building societies, insurance, unit trusts, legal rights, tax and small businesses.

News Editor *John Steafel*
Diary Editor *Nigel Dempster*
Features Editor *Richard Addis*
Sports Editor *Vic Robbie*
Women's Page *Alistair Sinclair*

Weekend: Saturday supplement **Editor** *Aileen Doherty*

Daily Mirror
1 Canada Square, Canary Wharf,
London E14 5AP
☎0171 293 3000   Fax 0171 293 3409

Owner *Mirror Group Newspapers*
Editor *Colin Myler*
Circulation 2.48 million

No freelance opportunities for the inexperienced but strong writers who understand what the tabloid market demands are always needed.

News Editor *Martin Clark*
Diary Editor *Garth Gibbs*
Features Editor *Richard Holledge*
Political Editor *John Williams*
Sports Editor *David Balmforth*
Women's Page *Fiona McIntosh*

Daily Record
Anderston Quay, Glasgow G3 8DA
☎0141 248 7000   Fax 0141 242 3145/6

Owner *Mirror Group Newspapers*
Editor *Terry Quinn*
Circulation 742,543

Mass-market Scottish tabloid. Freelance material is generally welcome.

News Editor *Murray Morse*
Features Editor *John McGorty*
Education *Mike Ritchie*
Political Editor *Nicholas Comfort*
Women's Page *Julia Clarke*

Daily Sport
19 Great Ancoats Street, Manchester M60 4BT
☎0161 236 4466   Fax 0161 236 4535

Owner *Sport Newspapers Ltd*
Editor *Jeff McGowan*
Circulation 300,000

Tabloid catering for young male readership. Unsolicited material welcome; send to News Editor.

News/Feature Editor *Neil MacKay*
Sports Editor *Kevin Kelly*

Daily Star
Ludgate House, 245 Blackfriars Road,
London SE1 9UX
☎0171 928 8000   Fax 0171 922 7960

Owner *United Newspapers*
Editor *Philip Walker*
Circulation 732,397

In competition with *The Sun* for off-the-wall

news and features. Freelance opportunities almost non-existent. Most material is written in-house or by regular outsiders.

News Editor *Hugh Whittow*
Features Editor *Mike Parker*
Entertainments *Pat Codd*
Sports Editor *Phil Rostron*
Women's Page *Fiona Webster*

The Daily Telegraph
1 Canada Square, Canary Wharf,
London E14 5DT
☎0171 538 5000   Fax 0171 538 6242

Owner *Conrad Black*
Editor *Max Hastings*
Circulation 1.06 million

Unsolicited mss not generally welcome – 'all are carefully read and considered, but only about one in a thousand is accepted for publication'. As they receive about 20 weekly, this means about one a year. Contenders should approach the paper in writing, making clear their authority for writing on that subject. No fiction.

News Editor *Sue Ryan* Tip-offs or news reports from *bona fide* journalists. Must phone the news desk in first instance. Maximum 200 words. *Payment* minimum £10 (tip).

Arts Editor *Sarah Crompton*
Business Editor *Roland Gribben*
Diary Editor *Quentin Letts* Always interested in diary pieces; contact *Peterborough* (Diary column).

Education *John Clare*
Environment *Charles Clover*
Features Editor/Women's Page *Corinna Honan* Most material supplied by commission from established contributors. New writers are tried out by arrangement with the features editor. Approach in writing. Max. 1500 words.

Literary Editor *John Coldstream*
Political Editor *George Jones*
Sports Editor *David Welch* Occasional opportunities for specialised items.
Women's Page *Veronica Wadley*
Payment by arrangement.

Telegraph Magazine: Saturday colour supplement. **Editor** *Emma Soames*. **Young Telegrapah** (see under **Magazines**).

The European
200 Gray's Inn Road, London WC1X 8NE
☎0171 418 7777   Fax 0171 353 4386

Owner *The Barclay Brothers*
Editor *Charles Garside*
Circulation 160,511 (excl. US sales)

LAUNCHED May 1990. Three-section colour weekly aimed at a European weekend market. News and current affairs, business, sport, European affairs, society and politics, plus European arts and lifestyle section, *The European Magazine*. Freelance contributions from recognised experts in their field will be considered. First approach in writing.

News *David Meilton*
Features *Peter Taylor*
Business *Tim Castle*

The European Magazine *Sebastian O'Kelly*
Payment by arrangement.

Financial Times
1 Southwark Bridge, London SE1 9HL
☎0171 873 3000   Fax 0171 873 3076

Owner *Pearson*
Editor *Richard Lambert*
Circulation 290,954

FOUNDED 1888. Business and finance-orientated certainly, but by no means as featureless as some suppose. All feature ideas must be discussed with the department's editor in advance. Not snowed under with unsolicited contributions – they get less than any other national newspaper. Approach in writing with ideas in the first instance.

News Editor *Julia Cuthbertson*
Features Editor *John Willman*
Arts/Literary Editor *Annalena McAfee*
City Editor *Jane Fuller*
Business/Financial Editor *Peter Martin*
Diary Editor *Bill Hall*
Education *John Authers*
Environment *Haig Simonian*
Political Editor *Philip Stephens*
Small Businesses *Richard Gourlay*
Sports Editor *Peter Berlin*
Women's Page *Lucia van der Post*

The Guardian
119 Farringdon Road, London EC1R 3ER
☎0171 278 2332Fax 0171 837 2114/833 8342

Owner *The Scott Trust*
Editor *Alan Rusbridger*
Circulation 397,139

Of all the nationals *The Guardian* probably offers the greatest opportunities for freelance writers, if only because it has the greatest number of specialised pages which use freelance work. But mss must be directed at a specific slot.

News Editor *Paul Webster* No opportunities except in those regions where there is presently no local contact for news stories.

Arts Editor *Claire Armitstead*
City/Financial Editor *Alex Brummer*

On Line Science, computing and technology. A major part of Thursday's paper, almost all written by freelancers. Expertise essential – but not a trade page; written for 'the interested man in the street' and from the user's point of view. Computing/communications (Internet) articles should be addressed to *Jack Schofield*; science articles to *Tim Radford*. Mss on disk or by e-mail (online@guardian.co.uk).

Diary Editor *Matthew Norman*

Education Editor *John Carvel* Expert pieces on modern education welcome. Maximum 1000 words.

Environment *John Vidal*

Features Editor *Roger Alton* Receives up to 30 unsolicited mss a day; these are passed on to relevant page editors.

Guardian Society *Malcolm Dean* Focuses on social change in the 90s – the forces affecting us, from environment to government policies. Top journalists and outside commentators on nine editorial pages.

Literary Editor *Liz Jobey*

Media Editor *John Mulholland* Approximately 6 pieces a week, plus diary. Outside contributions considered. All aspects of modern media, advertising, PR, consumer trends in arts/entertainments. Background insight important. Best approach is a note, followed by phone call.

Political Editor *Mike White*

Sports Editor *Mike Averis*

Women's Page *Clare Longrigg* Now runs three days a week. Unsolicited ideas used if they show an appreciation of the page in question. Maximum 800–1000 words.

Guardian Weekend Saturday issue. **Editor** *Deborah Orr*.

The Herald (Glasgow)
195 Albion Street, Glasgow G1 1QP
☎0141 552 6255   Fax 0141 552 2288
Owner *Caledonian Newspaper Publishing*
Editor *George McKechnie*
Circulation 113,342

The oldest national newspaper in the English-speaking world, The Herald, which dropped its 'Glasgow' prefix in February 1992, returned to Scottish hands in mid-1992 following a management buy-out and the establishment of the newly created company, Caledonian Newspaper Publishing. Lively, quality Scottish daily which is expanding into a national Scottish broadsheet. Approach with idea in writing or by phone in first instance.

News Editor *Colin McDiarmid*

Arts Editor *Keith Bruce*

Business Editor *Ronald Dundas*

Diary *Tom Shields*

Education *Barclay McBain*

Environment *Liz Buie*

Sports Editor *Iain Scott*

Women's Page *Jackie McGlone*

Independent
1 Canada Square, Canary Wharf, London E14 5AP
☎0171 293 2000   Fax 0171 293 2435
Owner *Mirror Group Newspapers*
Editor *Ian Hargreaves*
Circulation 291,369

FOUNDED October 1986. The first new quality national in over 130 years. Particularly strong on its arts/media coverage, with a high proportion of feature material. Theoretically, opportunities for freelancers are good. However, unsolicited mss are not welcome; most pieces originate in-house or from known and trusted outsiders. Ideas should be submitted in writing. The newspaper runs annual travel writing awards. Details, which vary from year to year, are advertised in the paper.

News Editor *David Felton*

Arts Editor *Tristan Davies*

Business Editor *Jeremy Warner*

City/Financial Editor *Peter Rodgers*

Education *Judith Judd*

Environment *Nicholas Schoon*

Features Editor *Charles Leadbeater*

Literary Editor *John Walsh*

Political Editor *Donald MacIntyre*

Sports Editor *Paul Newman*

The Independent Magazine: Saturday colour supplement. **Editor** *David Robson*

Independent on Sunday
1 Canada Square, Canary Wharf, London E14 5AP
☎0171 293 2000   Fax 0171 293 2435
Owner *Mirror Group Newspapers*
Editor *Peter Wilby*
Circulation 334,242

FOUNDED 1986. Regular columnists contribute most material but feature opportunites exist. Approach with idea in first instance.

News Editor *Stephen Davis*

Arts Editor *Nigel Reynolds*

Commissioning Editor, Features *Isabel O'Keeffe*

City/Financial Editor *Jeremy Warner*

Environment *Geoffrey Lean*

Political Editor *Steven Castle*

Sports Editor *Simon Kelner*

International Herald Tribune

181 avenue Charles de Gaulle,
92200 Neuilly-sur-Seine, France
☎0033 1 4143 9300   Fax 0033 1 4143 9338

Editor *John Vinocur*
Circulation 174,200

Published in France, Monday to Saturday, and circulated in Europe, the Middle East, North Africa, the Far East and the USA. General news, business and financial, arts and leisure. Use regular freelance contributors. Query letter to features editor in first instance.

> **Features Editor** *Katherine Knorr*
> **News Editor** *Walter Wells*

The Mail on Sunday

Northcliffe House, 2 Derry Street,
Kensington, London W8 5TS
☎0171 938 6000   Fax 0171 937 3829

Owner *Lord Rothermere*
Editor *Jonathon Holborrow*
Circulation 1.94 million

Sunday paper with a high proportion of newsy features and articles. Experience and judgement required to break into its band of regular feature writers.

> **News Editor** *Jon Ryan*
> **City/Financial Editor** *Bill Kay*
> **Diary Editor** *Nigel Dempster*
> **Features Editor** *Andy Bull*
> **Literary Editor** *Paula Johnson*
> **Political Editor** *Peter Dobbie*
> **Sports Editor** *Roger Kelly*

Night & Day: review supplement. **Editor** *Jocelyn Targett*

You — The Mail on Sunday Magazine: colour supplement. Many feature articles, supplied entirely by freelance writers.

> **Editor** *Dee Nolan*
> **Features Editor** *Martin Townsend*
> **Arts Editor** *Liz Galbraith*

Morning Star

1–3 Ardleigh Road, London N1 4HS
☎0171 254 0033   Fax 0171 254 5950

Owner *Peoples Press Printing Society*
Editor *John Haylett*
Circulation 9,000

Not to be confused with the *Daily Star*, the *Morning Star* is the farthest left national daily. Those with a penchant for a Marxist reading of events and ideas can try their luck, though feature space is as competitive here as in the other nationals.

News/Arts/Features/Women's Page
Paul Corry
> **Political Editor** *Mike Ambrose*
> **Sports Editor** *Tony Braisby*

The News of the World

1 Virginia Street, London E1 9XR
☎0171 782 4000
Fax 0171 488 3262 (features)

Owner *Rupert Murdoch*
Editor *Piers Morgan*
Circulation 4.74 million

Highest circulation Sunday paper. Freelance contributions welcome. Features Department welcomes tips and ideas. Approach by fax in first instance with follow-up phone call.

> **News Editor** *Alex Marunchak*
> **Features Editor** *Rebecca Wade*
> **Literary Editor** *Roy Stockdill*
> **Sports Editor** *Mike Dunn*
> **Women's Page** *Jane Butterworth*

Sunday Magazine: colour supplement. **Editor** *Tony Harris*. Showbiz interviews and strong human-interest features make up most of the content, but there are no strict rules about what is 'interesting'. Unsolicited mss and ideas welcome.

The Observer

119 Farringdon Road,
London EC1R 3ER
☎0171 278 2332   Fax 0171 713 4250

Owner *Guardian Newspapers Ltd*
Editor *Andrew Jaspan*
Circulation 455,268

FOUNDED 1791. Acquired by Guardian Newspapers from Lonrho in May 1993. Occupies the middle ground of Sunday newspaper politics. Unsolicited material is not generally welcome, 'except from distinguished, established writers'. Receives far too many unsolicited offerings already. No news, fiction or special page opportunities. The newspaper runs annual competitions which change from year to year. Details are advertised in the newspaper.

> **News Editor** *Paul Dunn*
> **Arts Editor** *Nigel Billen*
> **Business Editor** *Michael Smith*
> **City Editor** *Nick Goodway*
> **Diary Editor** *Julia Langdon*
> **Education** *Barry Hugill*
> **Features Editor** *Lisa O'Kelly*
> **Literary Editor** *Michael Ratcliffe*

Life: arts and lifestyle supplement. **Editor** *Mike Pilgrim.*

The People

1 Canada Square, Canary Wharf,
London E14 5AP
☎0171 293 3000   Fax 0171 293 3810
Owner *Mirror Group Newspapers*
Editor *Bridget Rowe*
Circulation 2.06 million

Slightly up-market version of *The News of the World*. Keen on exposés and big-name gossip. Interested in ideas for investigative articles. Phone in first instance.

News Editor *Tom Petrie*
City/Financial Editor *Cathy Gunn*
Arts Editor *Maurice Krais*
Features Editor *Geri Hosier*
Political Editor *Nigel Nelson*
Sports Editor *Ed Barry*
Women's Page *Geri Hosier*

Yes! Magazine **Editor** *Bridget Rowe*. Approach by phone with ideas in first instance.

Scotland on Sunday

20 North Bridge, Edinburgh EH1 1YT
☎0131 225 2468   Fax 0131 220 2443
Owner *Thomson Regional Newspapers Ltd*
Editor *Brian Groom*
Circulation 87,936

Scotland's top-selling quality broadsheet. Welcomes ideas rather than finished articles.

News Editor *William Paul*
Features Editor *Euan Ferguson*
Political *John Forsyth*

Scotland on Sunday Magazine: colour supplement. **Editor** *Fiona Macleod*. Features on personalities, etc.

The Scotsman

20 North Bridge, Edinburgh EH1 1YT
☎0131 225 2468   Fax 0131 226 7420
Owner *The Scotsman Publications Ltd*
Editor *Jim Seaton*
Circulation 80,603

Scotland's national newspaper. Unsolicited material stands a good chance of being read, although a small army of regulars supply much of the feature material not written in-house.

News Editor *Ian Stewart*
City/Financial Editor *Clifford German*
Education *Graeme Wilson*
Environment *Auslan Cramb*
Features Editor *Alan Taylor*
Literary Editor *Catherine Lockerbie*
Women's Page *Gillian Glover*
Weekend **Editor** *Maggie Lennon*. Includes book reviews, travel articles, etc.

The Sun

1 Virginia Street, London E1 9XP
☎0171 782 4000   Fax 0171 488 3253
Owner *Rupert Murdoch*
Editor *Stuart Higgins*
Circulation 4.08 million

Highest circulation daily. Right-wing, populist outlook; very keen on gossip, pop stars, TV soap, scandals and exposés of all kinds. Not much room for feature writers but 'investigative journalism' of a certain hue is always in demand.

News Editor *Robin Bowman*
Features Editor *Mike Ridley*
Sports Editor *Paul Ridley*
Women's Page *Jane Moore*

Sunday Express

Ludgate House, 245 Blackfriars Road,
London SE1 9UX
☎0171 928 8000   Fax 0171 620 1656
Owner *United Newspapers*
Editor *Brian Hitchen*
Circulation 1.39 million

FOUNDED 1918. Unsolicited mss are generally welcome. Approach in writing with ideas.

News Editor *Shan Lancaster* Occasional news features by experienced journalists only. All submissions must be preceded by ideas. 750 words.

Features Editor *Peter Birkett* General features (1000 words); profiles of personalities (900 words); showbiz features (1000–1500 words).

Literary Editor *Jim Anderson*
Sports Editor *Peter Watson*
Women's Page/Fashion *Serena Marler*

Sunday Express Magazine: colour supplement. **Editor** *Jean Carr*. No unsolicited mss. All contributions are commissioned. Ideas in writing only. *Payment* negotiable.

Sunday Life

124–144 Royal Avenue, Belfast BT1 1EB
☎01232 331133   Fax 01232 248968
Owner *Thomson Regional Newspapers Ltd*
Editor *Martin Lindsay*
Circulation 94,415

Deputy Editor *Jim Flanagan*
Sports Editor *Jim Gracey*

Sunday Mail

Anderston Quay, Glasgow G3 8DA
☎0141 248 7000   Fax 0141 242 3145/6
Owner *Mirror Group Newspapers*
Editor *James Cassidy*
Circulation 880,470

Popular Scottish Sunday paper.
News Editor *Brian Steel*
Features Editor *Jeanette Harkess*
Political Editor *Angus McLeod*
Women's Page *Melanie Reid*

Sunday Mail Magazine: monthly colour supplement. **Editor** *Jeanette Harkess.*

Sunday Mirror

1 Canada Square, Canary Wharf,
London E14 5AP
☎0171 293 3000   Fax 0171 293 3939
Owner *Mirror Group Newspapers*
Editor *Tessa Hilton*
Circulation 2.53 million

Receives anything up to 100 unsolicited mss weekly. In general terms, these are welcome, though the paper patiently points out it has more time for contributors who have taken the trouble to study the market. Initial contact in writing preferred, except for live news situations. No fiction.
News Editor *Chris Boffey* The news desk is very much in the market for tip-offs and inside information. Contributors would be expected to work with staff writers on news stories.
City/Financial Editor *Diane Boliver*
Features Editor *Clive Nelson* 'Anyone who has obviously studied the market will be dealt with constructively and courteously.' Cherishes its record as a breeding ground for new talent.
Sports Editor *Keith Fisher*

Sunday Mirror Magazine: colour supplement. **Editor** *Kate Bravery.*

Sunday Post

2 Albert Square, Dundee DD1 9QJ
☎01382 223131   Fax 01382 201064
Owner *D. C. Thomson & Co. Ltd*
Editor *Russell Reid*
Circulation 965,171

The highest circulation Scottish Sunday paper. Contributions should be addressed to the editor.
News Editor *Iain MacKinnon*

Sunday Post Magazine: monthly colour supplement. **Editor** *Maggie Dun.*

Sunday Sport

19 Great Ancoats Street, Manchester M60 4BT
☎0161 236 4466   Fax 0161 236 4535
Owner *David Sullivan*
Editor *Tony Livesey*
Circulation 300,135

FOUNDED 1986. Sunday tabloid catering for a particular sector of the male 18–35 readership.

As concerned with 'glamour' (for which, read: 'page 3') as with human interest, news, features and sport. Regular short story competition (maximum 1000 words). Unsolicited mss are welcome; receives about 90 a week. Approach should be made by phone in the case of news and sports items, by letter for features. All material should be addressed to the news editor.
News Editor *Nick Cracknall* Off-beat news, human interest, preferably with photographs.
Features Editor *John Wise* Regular items: glamour, showbiz and television, as well as general interest.
Sports Editor *Kevin Kelly* Hard-hitting sports stories on major soccer clubs and their personalities, plus leading clubs/people in other sports. Strong quotations to back up the news angle essential.
Payment negotiable and on publication.

Sunday Telegraph

1 Canada Square, Canary Wharf,
London E14 5DT
☎0171 538 5000   Fax 0171 513 2504
Owner *Conrad Black*
Editor *Charles Moore*
Circulation 706,300

Right-of-centre quality Sunday paper (meaning it has the least tendency to bend its ear to the scandals of the hour). Traditionally formal, it has pepped up its image to attract a younger readership and sales over the last year have increased and as a result the magazine supplement will be revived in autumn 1995. Unsolicited material from untried writers is rarely ever used. Contact with idea and details of track record.
News Editor *Mark Palmer*
City/Financial Editor *John Jay*
Features Editor *Lisa Freedman*
Arts Editor *John Preston*
Literary Editor *Miriam Gross*
Diary Editor *Kenneth Rose*
Sports Editor *Colin Gibson*
Women's Page *Alice Hart-Davis*

Sunday Telegraph Magazine *Alexander Chancellor*

The Sunday Times

1 Pennington Street, London E1 9XW
☎0171 782 5000   Fax 0171 782 5658
Owner *Rupert Murdoch*
Editor *John Witherow*
Circulation 1.23 million

FOUNDED 1820. Tendency to be anti-establishment, with a strong crusading investigative tradition. Approach the relevant editor with an idea in writing. Close scrutiny of the style of each section of the paper is strongly advised before sending mss. No fiction. All fees by negotiation.

News Editor *Mark Skipworth* Opportunities are very rare.

News Review Editor *Ian Birrell* Submissions are always welcome, but the paper commissions its own, uses staff writers or works with literary agents, by and large. The features sections where most opportunities exist are *Style & Travel* and *The Culture*.

Arts Editor *David Mills*
Economics Editor *David Smith*
Education *Cathy Scott-Clark*
Environment *Sean Ryan*
Literary Editor *Geordie Greig*
Sports Editor *Nick Pitt*
Style Editor *To be appointed*

Sunday Times Magazine: colour supplement. **Editor** *Kate Carr*. No unsolicited material. Write with ideas in first instance.

The Times

1 Pennington Street,
London E1 9XN
☎0171 782 5000   Fax 0171 488 3242

Owner *Rupert Murdoch*
Editor *Peter Stothard*
Circulation 630,277

Generally right (though columns/features can range in tone from diehard to libertarian). *The Times* receives a great many unsolicited offerings. Writers with feature ideas should approach by letter in the first instance. No fiction.

News Editor *James McManus*
Arts Editor *Richard Morrison*
Business/City/Financial Editor *Lindsay Cook*
Diary Editor *Andrew Yates*
Education *John O'Leary*
Environment *Michael Hornsby*

Executive Features Editor *Brian MacArthur*
Literary Editor *Daniel Johnson*
Political Editor *Phil Webster*
Sports Editor *David Chappell*
Women's Page *Graham Paterson*

Weekend Times **Editor** *Jane Owen*

The Times Magazine: Saturday supplement. **Editor** *Nicholas Wapshott*

Today

1 Virginia Street, Wapping,
London E1 9BS
☎0171 782 4600   Fax 0171 782 4822

Owner *Rupert Murdoch*
Editor *Richard Stott*
Circulation 563,565

The first of the new technology papers. According to Richard Stott, *Today* is 'aggressive, left of centre but queries the Labour Party'. Accepts news on tax, insurance, unit trusts, building societies, small businesses, legal rights and investments.

News Editor *Geoff Sutton*
Business/City/Financial Editor *George Campbell*
Features Editor *Tina Weaver*
Political Editor *Paul Wilenius*
Sports Editor *Mike Crouch*

Wales on Sunday

Thomson House, Havelock Street, Cardiff CF1 1WR
☎01222 223333   Fax 01222 342462

Owner *Thomson Regional Newspapers Ltd*
Editor *Peter Hollinson*
Circulation 60,923

LAUNCHED 1989. Tabloid with sports supplement. Does not welcome unsolicited mss.

News Editor *Richard Williams*
Features Editor *Mike Smith*
Sports Editor *Nick Rippington*
Women's Page *Mike Smith*

Freelance Rates – Newspapers

Freelance rates vary enormously. The following minimum rates, negotiated by the **National Union of Journalists**, should be treated as guidelines. Most work can command higher fees from employers whether or not they have NUJ agreements. It is up to freelancers to negotiate the best deal they can.

National Newspapers and News Agencies

Words
(A premium of 50% should be added to all the rates listed below for exclusive coverage.)

Home news: £20+ per 200 words or part thereof
Foreign news: £20+ per 100 words
City and business news: £20+ per 100 words
Sports match reports: Minimum £60.

National Daily Papers
Features: £160–200+ per 1000 words
Reviews: £150–175+ per 1000 words
Listings: £125–150+ per 1000 words
Gazette: £190+ per 1000 words

Sunday Papers
Features: £200–300+ per 1000 words
Reviews: £150–200+ per 1000 words

Diary paragraphs: Gossip column items, art reviews and notices: these attract a higher fee than the minimum per word since they are of restricted length. Lead items – about £100, others £45.

Photographic Fees
National papers day rate: £130, half-day: £80 (some papers may work on an assignment rate rather than half-day rates).
Studio or location work or commissions requiring special equipment/techniques (e.g. aerial): £650 per day.
Black and White reproduction fees for one British use only in a national newspaper:

Up to (sq in)	20	20–30	30–50	50–80	Over 80
Minimum	£68	£77	£87	£100	by negotiation

Colour reproduction fees: by negotiation.
Cover and front page: 50% extra.
Photographs ordered and accepted but not used: at least £68.
Print fee: at least £6.

Cartoons and Illustrations
Cartoon size: 1 column £90, thereafter subject to individual negotiation.
Colour: Double the above rate. (All rates quoted are for one-time British use.)

Colour Supplements

Words
Rates are high. Commissioning editors will pay by 1000 words or by the page.
A fee should not be less than £250+ for up to 1000 words.

Photographic Fees
Commissioned work : about £280 a day plus expenses; £160 per half-day.
Studio work: £650
Colour reproduction fees:

Up to:	¼ page	½ page	¾ page	full page
Minimum	£170	£233	£275	£330

Cartoons, Illustrations, Crosswords
Should be at least double the national newspaper rate.

Crosswords
Under 15x15: at least £92; 15x15 and upwards: at least £106.

Provincial Newspapers (England & Wales)

Words
Minimum News Lineage Rate Weekly newspapers: £1.52 for up to and including
10 lines; 15.2p per line thereafter. Daily, evening and Sunday newspapers:
£2.66 for up to and including 10 lines; 24p per line thereafter.

Minimum Feature Rate (for features submitted on spec.) Weekly newspapers:
£1.68 for up to and including 10 lines; 16.8p per line thereafter. Daily,
evening and Sunday newspapers: £2.94 for up to and including 10 lines; 24p
per line thereafter.

Commissioned features Vary from paper to paper, taking into account, when
negotiating, circulation (including the area), plus advertising revenue per page.

Photographic Reproduction Fees

Black and White	Daily/Evening/Sunday	Freesheet/Weekly
Up to 10 sq in	£18.50	£13
Over 10 and up to 50 sq in	£24	£15.50
Over 50 and up to 80 sq in	£36.50	£24
Over 80 and up to 150 sq in	by negotiation	by negotiation

Colour: Daily newspapers minimum rate of £25.50 for colour pictures of less
than 8 sq in which do not exceed single column width. For other colour pictures, minimum fees will be as for black and white above, plus 25% subject to a
minimum rate of £28.75 for daily and Sunday papers, £19.25 for weeklies.

Cartoons
Single Frame: at least £47.50
Feature Strip (up to 4 frames): £87
Crosswords: at least £54.

Provincial Newspapers (Scotland)

Words
Minimum News and Sport Lineage Rate At least 20.7p per line, subject to a minimum payment of £2.45 for each contribution. Copy used as a front page lead: at least 41.5p a line.
Minimum Feature Rate At least £73.20 per 1000 words.

Photography
Black and White Commissioned: £21.25; submitted: £20.25
Colour By negotiation.

Regional Newspapers

Regional newspapers are listed in alphabetical order under town. Thus the *Evening Standard* appears under 'L' for London; the *Lancashire Evening Post* under 'P' for Preston.

Northcliffe Newspapers Group Ltd
31–32 John Street, London WC1N 2QB
☎0171 242 7070

Central office of the regional papers belonging to the group: *The Citizen* (Gloucester); *Hull Daily Mail*; *Derby Evening Telegraph*; *Evening Sentinel* (Stoke); *Gloucestershire Echo* (Cheltenham); *Grimsby Evening Telegraph*; *Herald Express* (Torquay); *Leicester Mercury*; *Lincolnshire Echo*; *Evening Herald* (Plymouth); *Western Morning News* (Plymouth); *Scunthorpe Evening Telegraph*; *South Wales Evening Post*. See separate listings for details.

Thomson Regional Newspapers Ltd
100 Avenue Road, Swiss Cottage, London NW3 3HF
☎0171 393 7000   Fax 0171 393 7465

Central office of the group which owns the following regional daily papers: *Belfast Telegraph*; *Evening News* (Edinburgh); *Evening Chronicle* (Newcastle); *Evening Express* (Aberdeen); *Evening Gazette* (Middlesbrough); *The Journal* (Newcastle); *Chester Chronicle*; *The Press & Journal* (Aberdeen); *South Wales Echo* (Cardiff); *Sunday Life* (Belfast); *Sunday Sun* (Newcastle); *Western Mail* (Cardiff). Also the following national Sunday papers: *Scotland on Sunday* and *Wales on Sunday*. See separate listings for details. City editors of *The Press & Journal* (Aberdeen) and *The Journal* (Newcastle) are based at 52 St John Street, Smithfield, London EC1M 4DT (Tel: 0171 490 5581. Fax: 0171 490 8765).

Aberdeen
Evening Express (Aberdeen)
PO Box 43, Lang Stracht, Mastrick, Aberdeen AB9 8AF
☎01224 690222   Fax 01224 699575
Owner *Thomson Regional Newspapers Ltd*
Editor *Richard J. Williamson*
Circulation 69,562

Circulates in Aberdeen and the Grampian region. Local, national and international news and pictures, family finance and property news. Unsolicited mss welcome 'on a controlled basis'.

News Editor *Robert McAllister* Freelance news contributors welcome.

Features Editor *Raymond Anderson* Women, fashion, showbiz, health, hobbies, property – anything will be considered on its merits.

Sports Editor *Jim Strachan*
Women's Page *Judy Mackie*
Payment £30–60.

The Press and Journal
PO Box 43, Lang Stracht, Mastrick, Aberdeen AB9 8AF
☎01224 690222   Fax 01224 663575
Owner *Thomson Regional Newspapers Ltd*
Editor *Derek Tucker*
Circulation 107,965

Circulates in Aberdeen, Grampians, Highlands, Tayside, Orkney, Shetland and the Western Isles. A well-established regional daily which is said to receive more unsolicited mss a week than the *Sunday Mirror*. Unsolicited mss are nevertheless welcome; approach in writing with ideas. No fiction.

News Editor *David Knight* Wide variety of hard or off-beat news and features relating especially, but not exclusively, to the North of Scotland.

Sports Editor *Jim Dolan*
Women's Page *Moreen Simpson*
Payment by arrangement.

Aylesford
Kent Today
Messenger House, New Hythe Lane, Larkfield, Aylesford, Kent ME20 6SG
☎01622 717880   Fax 01622 719637
Owner *Kent Messenger Group*
Editor *C. Stewart*
Circulation 26,552
Assistant Editor (News) *Peter Erlam*
Sports Editor *Neil Webber*
Women's Page *Jane Millington*
Business Editor *Trevor Sturgess*

Barrow in Furness
North West Evening Mail
Abbey Road, Barrow in Furness, Cumbria
LA14 5QS
☎01229 821835   Fax 01229 840164

Owner CN Group Ltd
Editor Donald Martin
Circulation 21,382

All editorial material should be addressed to the editor.
  Features Editor Mike Gardner.
  Sports Editor Leo Clarke.

Basildon
Evening Echo
Newspaper House, Chester Hall Lane,
Basildon, Essex SS14 3BL
☎01268 522792   Fax 01268 282884

Owner Westminster Press
Editor Bob Dimond
Circulation 56,000

Relies almost entirely on staff and regular outside contributors, but will consider material sent on spec. Approach the editor in writing with ideas. Although the paper is Basildon-based, its largest circulation is in the Southend area.

Bath
The Bath Chronicle
33/34 Westgate Street, Bath, Avon BA1 1EW
☎01225 444044   Fax 01225 445969

Owner Westminster Press (Media in Wessex)
Editor David Gledhill
Circulation 19,286

  Deputy Editor John McCready
  News Editor Anne Harrison
  Features Editor Andrew Knight
  Sports Editor Alex Murphy
  Local news and features especially welcomed.

Belfast
Belfast Telegraph
Royal Avenue, Belfast BT1 1EB
☎01232 264000   Fax 01232 554506

Owner Thomson Regional Newspapers Ltd
Editor Edmund Curran
Circulation 133,436

Weekly business supplement.
  Deputy Editor Nick Garbutt
  News Desk David Neely
  Features Editor Janet Devlin
  Sports Editor Sammy Hamill
  Business Editor Martina Purdy

The Irish News
113/117 Donegall Street, Belfast BT1 2GE
☎01232 322226   Fax 01232 337505

Owner Irish News Ltd
Editor Tom Collins
Circulation 44,126

All material to appropriate editor (phone to check), or to the news desk.
  News Editor Pauline Reynolds
  Features Editor Noel Doran
  Sports Editor P. J. McKeefry
  Women's Page Ann Molloy

Sunday Life (Belfast)
See **National Newspapers**

Ulster News Letter
46–56 Boucher Crescent, Belfast BT12 6QY
☎01232 680000   Fax 01232 664412

Owner Century Newspapers Ltd
Editor Geoff Martin
Circulation 33,214

Supplements: Farming Life (weekly); Shopping News; Belfast Newsletter.
  Deputy Editor Mike Chapman
  Assistant Editor Billy Kennedy
  News Editor Harry Robinson
  Features Editor Geoff Hill
  Sports Editor Brian Millar
  Women's Page Sandra Chapman

Birmingham
Birmingham Evening Mail
28 Colmore Circus, Queensway, Birmingham
B4 6AX
☎0121 236 3366   Fax 0121 233 0271

Owner Midland Independent Newspapers plc
Editor Ian Dowell
Circulation 201,007

Freelance contributions are welcome, particularly topics of interest to the West Midlands and Women's Page pieces offering original and lively comment.
  News Editor Norman Stinchcombe
  Features Editor Paul Cole
  Women's Page Briony Jones

Birmingham Post
28 Colmore Circus, Queensway, Birmingham
B4 6AX
☎0121 236 3366   Fax 0121 233 0271

Owner Midland Independent Newspapers plc
Editor Nigel Hastilow
Circulation 26,071

One of the country's leading regional newspapers. Freelance contributions are welcome. Topics of interest to the West Midlands and pieces offering lively, original comment are particularly welcome.

News Editor *Chris Russon*
Features Editor *Peter Bacon*
Women's Page *Ros Dodd*

Sunday Mercury (Birmingham)
28 Colmore Circus, Birmingham B4 6AZ
☎0121 236 3366   Fax 0121 625 1105
Owner *Birmingham Post & Mail Ltd*
Editor *Peter Whitehouse*
Circulation 145,565

News Editor *Bob Haywood*
Features Editor *Stefan Bartlett*
Sports Editor *Roger Skidmore*

Blackburn
Lancashire Evening Telegraph
Newspaper House, High Street, Blackburn, Lancashire BB1 1HT
☎01254 678678   Fax 01254 680429
Owner *Reed Northern Newspapers Ltd*
Editor *Peter Butterfield*
Circulation 47,059

News stories and feature material with an East Lancashire flavour (a local angle, or written by local people) welcome. Approach in writing with an idea in the first instance. No fiction.

News/Features/Women's Page Editor *Nick Nunn*

Blackpool
Evening Gazette (Blackpool)
PO Box 20, Preston New Road, Blackpool, Lancashire FY4 4AU
☎01253 839999   Fax 01253 766799
Owner *United Newspapers*
Editor *Robin Fletcher*
Circulation 44,578

Unsolicited mss welcome in theory. Approach in writing with an idea. Supplements: *Monday Green* (sport); *Eve* (women, Tuesday); *Wheels* (motoring, Wednesday); *Property* (Thursday); *Sevendays* (entertainment & leisure, Saturday).

Head of Content *Tom Ainge*
Sports Editor *Tony Durkin*

Bolton
Bolton Evening News
Newspaper House, Churchgate, Bolton, Lancashire BL3 4SQ
☎01204 22345   Fax 01204 365068

Owner *Northern Counties Newspapers*
Editor *Andrew Smith*
Circulation 44,451

Business, children's page, travel, local services, motoring, fashion and cookery.

News Editor *Melvyn Horrocks*
Features Editor *Derrick Grocock*
Women's Page *Angela Kelly*

Bournemouth
Evening Echo
Richmond Hill, Bournemouth, Dorset BH2 6HH
☎01202 554601   Fax 01202 292115
Owner *Southern Newspapers plc*
Editor *Gareth Weekes*
Circulation 49,979

FOUNDED 1900. Has a strong features content and invites specialist articles, particularly on unusual and contemporary subjects with a local angle. Supplements: business, gardening, motoring. Regular features on weddings, property, books, local history, green issues, the Channel coast. All editorial material should be addressed to the **News Editor** *Andy Bissell*.

Payment on publication.

Bradford
Telegraph & Argus (Bradford)
Hall Ings, Bradford, West Yorkshire BD1 1JR
☎01274 729511   Fax 01274 723634
Owner *Bradford & District Newspapers*
Editor *Perry Austin-Clarke*
Circulation 60,090

No unsolicited mss – approach in writing with samples of work. No fiction.

News Editor *Rob Irvine*
Features Editor *John Walton* Local features and general interest. Showbiz pieces. 600–1000 words (maximum 1500).

Sports Editor *Peter Rowe*
Women's Page *Steven Teale*

Yorkshire on Sunday
PO Box 470, Drake Street, Bradford, West Yorkshire BD1 1JG
☎01274 732244   Fax 01274 726633
Owner *Bradford & District Newspapers*
Editor *Mike Glover*
Circulation 53,832

FOUNDED August 1992.

Features Editor *Stephanie Smith*
Sports Editor *Stephen Joyce*
Women's Page *Sharon Dale*

Brighton
Evening Argus
Argus House, Crowhurst Road, Hollingbury,
Brighton, East Sussex BN1 8AR
☎01273 544544   Fax 01273 505703
Owner *Southern Publishing (Westminster Press) Ltd*
Editor *Chris Fowler*
Circulation 64,264

  News Editor *John Sage*
  Features Editor *Mike Bacon*
  Sports Editor *Chris Giles*
  Women's Page *Winifred Blackmore*

Bristol
Evening Post
Temple Way, Bristol, Avon BS99 7HD
☎0117 9260080   Fax 0117 9279568
Owner *Bristol Evening Post plc*
Editor *Adrian Faber*
Circulation 89,219

Unsolicited mss welcome; receives about a dozen a week. Approach in writing with ideas.
  News Editor *Rob Stokes*
  Features Editor *Brian Feeney*
  Sports Editor *Chris Bartlett*

Western Daily Press
Temple Way, Bristol, Avon BS99 7HD
☎0117 9260080   Fax 0117 9279568
Owner *Bristol United Press Ltd*
Editor *Ian Beales*
Circulation 63,293

  News Editor *Steve Hughes*
  Features Editor *Norrie Drummond*
  Sports Editor *Bill Beckett*
  Women's Page *Lynda Cleasby*

Burton upon Trent
Burton Mail
65–68 High Street, Burton upon Trent,
Staffordshire DE14 1LE
☎01283 512345   Fax 01283 510075/515351
Owner *Burton Daily Mail Ltd*
Editor *Brian Vertigen*
Circulation 20,352

Fashion, health, wildlife, environment, nostalgia, financial/money (Monday); consumer, motoring (Tuesday); women's world, rock (Wednesday); property (Thursday); motoring, farming, what's on (Friday); what's on, leisure (Saturday).
  News/Features Editor *Andrew Parker*
  Sports Editor *Rex Page*
  Women's Page *Corry Adger*

Cambridge
Cambridge Evening News
51 Newmarket Road, Cambridge CB5 8EJ
☎01223 358877   Fax 01223 460846
Owner *Cambridge Newspapers Ltd*
Editor *Robert Satchwell*
Circulation 41,770

  News Editor *Peter Wells*
  Sports Editor *Mike Finnis*
  Women's Page *Angela Singer*

Cardiff
South Wales Echo
Thomson House, Cardiff CF1 1WR
☎01222 223333   Fax 01222 583624
Owner *Thomson Regional Newspapers Ltd*
Editor *Keith Perch*
Circulation 79,844

Circulates in South and Mid Glamorgan.
  News Editor *Jeremy Clifford*
  Features Editor *John Scantlebury*
  Sports Editor *Terry Phillips*

Western Mail
Thomson House, Cardiff CF1 1WR
☎01222 223333   Fax 01222 583652
Owner *Thomson Regional Newspapers Ltd*
Editor *Neil Fowler*
Circulation 64,570

Circulates in Cardiff, Merthyr Tydfil, Newport, Swansea and towns and villages throughout Wales. Mss welcome if of a topical nature, and preferably of Welsh interest. No short stories or travel. Approach in writing to the editor. 'Usual subjects already well covered, e.g. motoring, travel, books, gardening. We look for the unusual.' Maximum 1000 words. Opportunities also on women's page. Supplement: *TV Wales*.
  Head of News & Features *Alan Edmunds*
  Sports Editor *Mark Tattersall*

Carlisle
News & Star
Newspaper House, Dalston Road, Carlisle,
Cumbria CA2 5UA
☎01228 23488   Fax 01228 512828
Owner *Cumbrian Newspaper Group Ltd*
Editor *Keith Sutton*
Circulation 27,549

  News Editor *Mark Brown*
  Features Editor *John Reynolds*
  Sports Editor *Jeff Connor*
  Women's Page *Jane Loughran*

Cheltenham
Gloucestershire Echo
1 Clarence Parade, Cheltenham,
Gloucestershire GL50 3NZ
☎01242 526261   Fax 01242 578395
Owner *Northcliffe Newspapers Group Ltd*
Editor *Anita Syvret*
Circulation 27,056

All material, other than news, should be
addressed to the editor.
    News Editor *John Flint*

Chester
Chester Chronicle
Chronicle House, Commonhall Street,
Chester CH1 2BJ
☎01244 340151   Fax 01244 340165
Owner *Thomson Regional Newspapers Ltd*
Editor-in-Chief *Bob Adams*

All unsolicited feature material will be considered.

Colchester
Evening Gazette (Colchester)
Oriel House, 43–44 North Hill, Colchester,
Essex CO1 1TZ
☎01206 761212   Fax 01206 769523
Owner *Essex County Newspapers*
Editor *Martin McNeill*
Circulation 28,676

Unsolicited mss not generally used. Relies
heavily on regular contributors.
    News Editor *Irene Kettle*
    Features Editor *Iris Clapp*

Coventry
Coventry Evening Telegraph
Corporation Street, Coventry CV1 1FP
☎01203 633633   Fax 01203 550869
Owner *Midland Independent Newspapers*
Editor *Dan Mason*
Circulation 83,087

Unsolicited mss are read, but few are published. Approach in writing with an idea. No
fiction. All unsolicited material should be
addressed to the editor. Maximum 600 words
for features.
    News Editor *Peter Mitchell*
    Features Editor *Paul Simoniti*
    Sports Editor *Roger Draper*
    Women's Page *Barbara Argument*
    Payment negotiable.

Darlington
The Northern Echo
Priestgate, Darlington, Co. Durham
DL1 1NF
☎01325 381313   Fax 01325 380539
Owner *North of England Newspapers*
Editor *David Flintham*
Circulation 77,750

FOUNDED 1870. Freelance pieces welcome but
telephone first to discuss submission.
    Zone Page Editor *John Dean* Interested in
reports involving the North-east or North
Yorkshire. Preferably phoned in.
    Women's Editor *Adrienne Hunter* Back-
ground pieces to topical news stories relevant
to the area. Must be arranged with the features
editor before submission of any material.
    Head of Content *Liz Page*
    Local Industrial Reports *Paul Stokes*
    Sports Editor *Kevin Dinsdale*
    Payment and length by arrangement.

Derby
Derby Evening Telegraph
Northcliffe House, Meadow Road, Derby
DE1 2DW
☎01332 291111   Fax 01332 253027
Owner *Northcliffe Newspapers Group Ltd*
Editor *Mike Lowe*
Circulation 65,163

Weekly business supplement.
    News Editor *Kevin Booth*
    Features Editor *Ross Bravo*
    Sports Editor *Steve Nicholson*
    Women's Page *Marion Gleave*

Devon
Herald Express
See under *Torquay*

Doncaster
The Doncaster Star
40 Duke Street, Doncaster, South Yorkshire
DN1 3EA
☎01302 344001   Fax 01302 329072
Owner *Sheffield Newspapers Ltd*
Editor *Lynne Fletcher*
Circulation 14,000

All other editorial material to be addressed to
the editor.
    Sports Editor *Steve Hossack*
    Women's Page *Janet Makinson*

Dundee

The Courier and Advertiser

80 Kingsway East, Dundee DD4 8SL
☎01382 223131 Fax 01382 454590

Owner *D. C. Thomson & Co. Ltd*
Editor *Adrian Arthur*
Circulation 105,957

Circulates in Dundee, Tayside, Fife and parts of Central and Grampian. Features welcome on a wide variety of subjects, not solely of local/Scottish interest. Two pages devoted to features each weekend, supplied by freelancers and in-house. Finance, insurance, agriculture, EC topics, motoring, women, modern homes. Only rule of thumb is to keep it short. Maximum 500 words.

News Editor *Steve Bargeton*
Features Editor/Women's Page *Shona Lorimer*
Sports Editor *Graham Dey*

Evening Telegraph & Post

80 Kingsway East, Dundee DD4 8SL
☎01382 223131 Fax 01382 454590

Owner *D. C. Thomson & Co. Ltd*
Editor *Harold Pirie*
Circulation 37,170

Circulates in Tayside, Dundee and Fife. All material should be addressed to the editor.

East Anglia

East Anglian Daily Times

See under ***Ipswich***

Eastern Daily Press

See under ***Norwich***

Edinburgh

Evening News

20 North Bridge, Edinburgh EH1 1YT
☎0131 225 2468 Fax 0131 225 7302

Owner *Thomson Regional Newspapers Ltd*
Editor *Harry Roulston*
Circulation 96,412

FOUNDED 1873. Circulates in Edinburgh, Fife, Central and Lothian. Coverage includes: lifestyle and entertainments (daily); motoring column (Friday); gardening, computers, book reviews, DIY, historical memories, shopping, fashion, nature, show business, and *The Doctor* (health). Unsolicited feature material welcome. Approach the appropriate editor by telephone.

News Editor *Simon Reynolds*
Features Editor *Helen Martin* Weekender magazine supplement of broad general/historical interest. Occasional Platform pieces (i.e. sounding off, topical or opinion pieces). Maximum 1000 words.
Sports Editor *Paul Greaves*
Payment NUJ/house rates.

Exeter

Express & Echo

Heron Road, Sowton, Exeter, Devon
EX2 7NF
☎01392 442211
Fax 01392 442294/442287 (editorial)

Owner *Express & Echo Publications Ltd*
Editor *Rachael Campey*
Circulation 27,830

Weekly supplements: *Business Week; Property Echo; Wheels; Weekend Echo.*

News Editor *Mike Beard*
Features Editor/Women's Page *Sue Kemp*
Sports Editor *Jerry Charge*

Glasgow

Evening Times

195 Albion Street, Glasgow G1 1QP
☎0141 552 6255 Fax 0141 553 1355

Owner *Caledonian Publishing*
Editor *John D. Scott*
Circulation 139,463

Circulates in the Strathclyde region. Supplement: *Evening Times Sport.*

News Editor *Robbie Wallace*
Features Editor *Russell Kyle*
Sports Editor *Iain Scott*
Women's Page *Marian Pallister*

The Herald (Glasgow)

See **National Newspapers**

Gloucester

The Citizen

St John's Lane, Gloucester GL1 2AY
☎01452 424442 Fax 01452 307238

Owner *Northcliffe Newspapers Group Ltd*
Editor *Graham Glen*
Circulation 37,556

All editorial material to be addressed to the **Head of Content** *Jon Grubb.*

Gloucestershire Echo

See under ***Cheltenham***

Greenock
Greenock Telegraph
2 Crawfurd Street, Greenock PA15 1LH
☎01475 726511   Fax 01475 783734

Owner *Clyde & Forth Press Ltd*
Editor *Ian Wilson*
Circulation 20,450

Circulates in Greenock, Port Glasgow, Gourock, Kilmacolm, Langbank, Bridge of Weir, Inverkip, Wemyss Bay, Skelmorlie, Largs. Unsolicited mss considered 'if they relate to the newspaper's general interests'. No fiction.
All material to be addressed to the editor or the **News Editor** *David Carnduff.*

Grimsby
Grimsby Evening Telegraph
80 Cleethorpe Road, Grimsby, South Humberside DN31 3EH
☎01472 359232   Fax 01472 358859

Owner *Northcliffe Newspapers Group Ltd*
Editor *Peter Moore*
Circulation 72,703

Sister paper of the *Scunthorpe Evening Telegraph.* Unsolicited mss generally welcome. Approach in writing. No fiction. Monthly supplement: *Business Telegraph.* All material to be addressed to the **News Editor** *S. P. Richards.* Particularly welcome hard news stories – approach in haste by telephone.
Special Publications Editor *B. Farnsworth*

Guernsey
Guernsey Evening Press & Star
Braye Road, Vale, Guernsey, Channel Islands GY1 3BW
☎01481 45866   Fax 01481 48972

Owner *Guernsey Press Co. Ltd*
Editor *Graham Ingrouille*
Circulation 15,764

Special pages include children's and women's interest, gardening and fashion.
News Editor *Dave Edmonds*
Features Editor *Nick Le Messurier*
Sports Editor *John Le Poidevin*
Women's Page *Jo Porter*

Halifax
Evening Courier
PO Box 19, Halifax, West Yorkshire HX1 2SF
☎01422 365711   Fax 01422 330021

Owner *Johnston Press Plc*
Editor *Edward Riley*
Circulation 32,051

News Editor *John Kenealy*
Features Editor *William Marshall*
Sports Editor *Ian Rushworth*
Women's Page *Diane Crabtree*

Hartlepool
Mail (Hartlepool)
Clarence Road, Hartlepool, Cleveland TS24 8BU
☎01429 274441   Fax 01429 869024

Owner *Northeast Press Ltd*
Editor *Christopher Cox*
Circulation 26,730

Deputy Editor *Harry Blackwood*
News Editor *Phillip Hickey*
Features Editor *Bernice Saltzer*
Sports Editor *Neil Watson*
Women's Page *Margaret O'Rourke*

Huddersfield
Huddersfield Daily Examiner
Queen Street South, Huddersfield, West Yorkshire HD1 2TD
☎01484 430000   Fax 01484 423722

Owner *Trinity International plc*
Editor *Richard Mallinson*
Circulation 38,480

Home improvement, home heating, weddings, dining out, motoring, fashion, services to trade and industry.
News Editor *Peter D. Hinchcliffe*
Features Editor *Malcolm Cruise*
Sports Editor *John Gledhill*
Women's Page *Hilarie Stelfox*

Hull
Hull Daily Mail
Blundell's Corner, Beverley Road, Hull, North Humberside HU3 1XS
☎01482 327111   Fax 01482 584353

Owner *Northcliffe Newspapers Group Ltd*
Editor *Michael Wood*
Circulation 92,263

News/Features Editor *Michelle Lalor*
Sports Editor *Chris Harvey*
Women's Page *Jo Davison*

Ipswich
East Anglian Daily Times
30 Lower Brook Street, Ipswich, Suffolk IP4 1AN
☎01473 230023   Fax 01473 225296

Owner *East Anglian Daily Times Co. Ltd*
Editor *Malcolm Pheby*

Circulation 48,354

FOUNDED 1874. Unsolicited mss generally not welcome; three or four received a week and almost none are used. Approach in writing in the first instance. No fiction. Supplement: *Anglia Business Scene*; plus specials: Property and industry in East Anglia; and Look at the Land.

News Editor *Robyn Bechelet* Hard news stories involving East Anglia (Suffolk, Essex particularly) or individuals resident in the area are always of interest.

Features Editor *Derek Clements* Mostly in-house, but will occasionally buy in when the subject is of strong Suffolk/East Anglian interest. Photo features preferred (extra payment). Special advertisement features are regularly run. Some opportunities here. Maximum 1000 words.

> **Sports Editor** *Tony Garnett*
> **Women's Page** *Cathy Brown*

Evening Star

30 Lower Brook Street, Ipswich, Suffolk IP4 1AN
☎01473 230023   Fax 01473 225296

Owner *East Anglian Daily Times Co. Ltd*
Editor *Terry Hunt*
Circulation 30,628

> **Deputy Editor** *Nigel Pickover*
> **Sports Editor** *Mike Horne*

Jersey
Jersey Evening Post

PO Box 582, Five Oaks, St Saviour, Jersey, Channel Islands JE4 8XQ
☎01534 873333   Fax 01534 879681

Owner *Jersey Evening Post Ltd*
Editor *Chris Bright*
Circulation 23,861

Special pages: gardening, motoring, farmers and growers, property, boating, computer and office, young person's (16–25), women, food and drink, personal finance, rock and classical reviews.

> **News Editor** *Sue Le Ruez*
> **Features Editor** *Rob Shipley*
> **Sports Editor** *Ron Felton*

Kent
Kent Messenger

See under *Maidstone*

Kent Today

See under *Aylesford*

Kettering
Evening Telegraph

Northfield Avenue, Kettering, Northamptonshire NN16 9TT
☎01536 81111   Fax 01536 85983

Owner *EMAP*
Editor *Colin Grant*
Circulation 35,980

Business Telegraph (weekly); *Weekender* supplement (Saturday), featuring TV, gardening, videos, films, eating out; two monthly supplements, *Home & Garden* and *Car Driver*; quarterly women's magazine, *Telegraph Woman*.

> **News Editor** *Paul Napier*
> **Business Editor** *Tony Bacon*
> **Sports Editor** *Ian Davidson*

Lancashire
Lancashire Evening Post

See under *Preston*

Lancashire Evening Telegraph

See under *Blackburn*

Leamington Spa
Leamington Spa Courier

32 Hamilton Terrace, Leamington Spa, Warwickshire CV32 4LY
☎01926 888222   Fax 01926 451690

Owner *Central Counties Newspapers*
Editor *Martin Lawson*
Circulation 19,232

One of the Leamington Spa Courier Series which also includes the *Warwick Courier* and *Kenilworth Weekly News*. Unsolicited feature articles considered, particularly matter with a local angle. Telephone with idea first.

> **News Editor** *John Hunter*

Leeds
Yorkshire Evening Post

Wellington Street, Leeds, West Yorkshire LS1 1RF
☎0113 2432701   Fax 0113 2388536

Owner *Yorkshire Post Newspapers Ltd*
Editor *Christopher Bye*
Circulation 108,587

Evening sister of the *Yorkshire Post*.

> **News Editor** *Richard Spencer*
> **Features Editor** *Anne Pickles*
> **Sports Editor** *Ian Ward*
> **Women's Page** *Carmen Bruegmann*

Yorkshire Post
Wellington Street, Leeds, West Yorkshire
LS1 1RF
☎0113 2432701   Fax 0113 2388537
Owner *Yorkshire Post Newspapers Ltd*
Editor *Tony Watson*
Circulation 78,049

A serious-minded, quality regional daily with a
generally conservative outlook. Three or four
unsolicited mss arrive each day; all will be considered but initial approach in writing preferred. All submissions should be addressed to
the editor. No fiction.
  News Editor *Richard Clark*
  Features Editor *Mick Hickling* Open to suggestions in all fields (though ordinarily commissioned from specialist writers).
  Sports Editor *Bill Bridge*
  Women's Page *Jill Armstrong*

Leicester
Leicester Mercury
St George Street, Leicester LE1 9FQ
☎0116 2512512   Fax 0116 2530645
Owner *Northcliffe Newspapers Group Ltd*
Editor *Nick Carter*
Circulation 117,877

Monthly supplement: *The Merc.*
  News Editor *Simon Orrell*
  Features Editor *Mark Clayton*

Lincoln
Lincolnshire Echo
Brayford Wharf East, Lincoln LN5 7AT
☎01522 525252   Fax 01522 545759
Owner *Northcliffe Newspapers Group Ltd*
Editor *Cliff Smith*
Circulation 30,662

Best buys, holidays, motoring, dial-a-service,
restaurants, sport, leisure, home improvement,
women's page, record review, gardening corner, stars. All editorial material to be addressed
to the **Assistant Editor** *Mike Gubbins.*

Liverpool
Daily Post
PO Box 48, Old Hall Street, Liverpool
L69 3EB
☎0151 227 2000   Fax 0151 236 4682
Owner *Liverpool Daily Post & Echo Ltd*
Editor *Alastair Machray*
Circulation 73,691

Unsolicited mss welcome. Receives about six a

day. Approach in writing with an idea. No fiction. Local, national/international news, current affairs, profiles – with pictures. Maximum
800–1000 words.
  Features Editor *David Jones*
  Sports Editor *Len Capeling*
  Women's Page *Margaret Kitchen*

Liverpool Echo
PO Box 48, Old Hall Street, Liverpool
L69 3EB
☎0151 227 2000   Fax 0151 236 4682
Owner *Liverpool Daily Post & Echo Ltd*
Editor *John Griffith*
Circulation 167,459

One of the country's major regional dailies.
Unsolicited mss welcome; initial approach
with ideas in writing preferred.
  News Editor *Tony Storey*
  Features Editor *Paul Burnell* Maximum
1000 words.
  Sports Editor *Ken Rogers*
  Women's Editor *Janet Tansley*

London
Evening Standard
Northcliffe House, 2 Derry Street,
London W8 5EE
☎0171 938 6000   Fax 0171 937 3193
Owner *Lord Rothermere*
Editor *Stewart Steven*
Circulation 534,066

Long-established evening paper, serving
Londoners with both news and feature mater-
ial. Genuine opportunities for London-based
features. Produces a weekly colour supple-
ment, *ES The Evening Standard Magazine.*
  Deputy Editor *Peter Boyer*
  Associate Editor *Sarah Sands*
  News Editor *Stephen Clackson*
  Features Editor *Alex Renton*
  Sports Editor *Brian Alexander*
  **Editor, *ES* ** *Adam Edwards*

Maidstone
Kent Messenger
6 & 7 Middle Row, Maidstone, Kent
ME14 1TG
☎01622 695666   Fax 01622 757227
Owner *Kent Messenger Group*
Editor *Jill Stevens*
Circulation 42,000

For economic reasons, very little freelance
work is being commissioned.

Manchester
Manchester Evening News
164 Deansgate, Manchester M60 2RD
☎0161 832 7200   Fax 0161 834 3814
Owner *Manchester Evening News Ltd*
Editor *Michael Unger*
Circulation 193,952

One of the country's major regional dailies. Initial approach in writing preferred. No fiction. *Property* (Tuesday); holiday feature (Saturday); *Lifestyle* (Friday).

News Editor *Paul Horrocks*
Features Editor *Diane Robinson* Regional news features, personality pieces and showbiz profiles considered. Maximum 1000 words.
Sports Editor *Neville Bolton*
Women's Page *Nicolette Webster*
Payment based on house agreement rates.

Middlesbrough
Evening Gazette
Borough Road, Middlesbrough, Cleveland TS1 3AZ
☎01642 245401   Fax 01642 232014
Owner *Thomson Regional Newspapers Ltd*
Editor *Ranald Allan*
Circulation 77,000

Special pages: business, motoring, home, computing.

News Editor *Tony Beck*
Features Editor *Alan Sims*
Sports Editor *Allan Boughey*
Women's Page *Kathryn Armstrong*
Crime *Damian Bates*
Environment *Iain Laing*
Consumer *Julia Paul*
Health *Amanda Todd*
Councils *Sandy McKenzie*

Mold
Evening Leader
Mold Business Park, Wrexham Road, Mold, Clwyd CH7 1XY
☎01352 700022   Fax 01352 752180
Owner *North Wales Newspapers*
Editor *Reg Herbert*
Circulation 32,178

Circulates in Wrexham, Clwyd, Deeside and Chester. Special pages/features: motoring, travel, arts, women's, children's, photography, local housing, information and news for the disabled, music and entertainment.

Features Page *Jeremy Smith*
News Editor *David Metcalf*

Women's Page *Gail Cooper*
Sports Editor *Doug Mortimer*

Newcastle upon Tyne
Evening Chronicle
Thomson House, Groat Market, Newcastle upon Tyne, Tyne & Wear NE1 1ED
☎0191 232 7500   Fax 0191 232 2256
Owner *Thomson Regional Newspapers Ltd*
Editor *Neil Benson*
Circulation 118,492

Receives a lot of unsolicited material, much of which is not used. 'Motors Mart', 'Print Out' (computers), women's page, amateur photography, gardening, pop, fashion, cooking, consumer, films and entertainment guide, home improvements, motoring, property, angling, sport and holidays. Approach in writing with ideas.

News Editor *David Bourn*
Features Editor *Jane Pickett* Limited opportunities due to full-time feature staff. Maximum 1000 words.
Sports Editor *Paul New*
Women's Page *Kay Jordan*

The Journal
Thomson House, Groat Market, Newcastle upon Tyne, Tyne & Wear NE1 1ED
☎0191 232 7500   Fax 0191 232 2256
Owner *Thomson Regional Newspapers Ltd*
Editor *Bill Bradshaw*
Circulation 56,032

Daily platforms include farming and business. Monthly full-colour business supplement: *The Journal Northern Business Magazine*.

News/Features Editor *Paul Robertson*
Sports Editor *To be appointed*
Women's Page *Jennifer Wilson*
Agricultural Editor *David Leach*
Arts & Entertainment Editor *David Whetstone*
Environmental Editor *Tony Henderson*

Sunday Sun
Thomson House, Groat Market, Newcastle upon Tyne, Tyne & Wear NE1 1ED
☎0191 232 7500   Fax 0191 230 0238
Owner *Thomson Regional Newspapers Ltd*
Editor *Chris Rushton*
Circulation 127,702

All material should be addressed to the appropriate editor (phone to check), or to the editor.

Head of Content *Mike McGiffen*
Sports Editor *David Lamont*

Newport
South Wales Argus
Cardiff Road, Maesglas, Newport, Gwent
NP9 1QW
☎01633 810000   Fax 01633 810195
Owner South Wales Argus Ltd
Editor Gerry Keighley
Circulation 36,744

Circulates in Newport, Gwent and surrounding areas.
  News Editor Jeremy Flye
  Features Editor/Women's Page Lesley Williams
  Sports Editor Carl Difford

North of England
The Northern Echo
See under **Darlington**

Northampton
Chronicle and Echo
Upper Mounts, Northampton NN1 3HR
☎01604 231122   Fax 01604 233000
Owner Northampton Mercury Co. Ltd
Editor-in-Chief David Rowell
Circulation 30,267

Unsolicited mss are 'not necessarily unwelcome but opportunities to use them are rare'. Some three or four arrive weekly. Approach in writing with an idea. No fiction. Supplements: Sports Chronicle (Monday); Business Chronicle (Tuesday); Property Chronicle (Wednesday); women's page, pop page (Thursday); motoring (Friday).
  Head of Content Peter Clarke
  Features Editor/Women's Page Ruth Supple
  Sports Editor Mark Beesley

Norwich
Eastern Daily Press
Prospect House, Rouen Road, Norwich,
Norfolk NR1 1RE
☎01603 628311   Fax 01603 612930
Owner Eastern Counties Newspapers
Editor Peter Franzen
Circulation 79,192

Unsolicited mss welcome. Approach in writing with ideas. News (if relevant to Norfolk), and features up to 900 words. Other pieces by commission only. Supplements: what's on (daily); employment (twice-weekly); motoring (weekly); business (weekly); property pages (weekly); industrial property (monthly); plus motoring, agriculture, and arts focus.
  News Editor Paul Durrant
  Features Editor Colin Chinery
  Sports Editor David Thorpe
  Women's Page Sarah Hardy

Evening News
Prospect House, Rouen Road, Norwich,
Norfolk NR1 1RE
☎01603 628311   Fax 01603 612930
Owner Eastern Counties Newspapers
Editor Claire Gillingwater
Circulation 41,563

Includes special pages on local property, motoring, children's page, pop, fashion, arts, heavy entertainments and TV, gardening, local music scene, home and family.
  Assistant Editor Roy Stronger
  Deputy Editor Celia Sutton
  Features Editor Derek James

Nottingham
Evening Post Nottingham
Forman Street, Nottingham NG1 4AB
☎0115 9482000   Fax 0115 9484116
Owner Northcliffe Newspapers Group Ltd
Editor Graham Glen
Circulation 110,000

Unsolicited mss welcome. Send ideas in writing. Supplements: Car Buyer (thirteen issues a year); Citizens Guide (annual); Business Directory (annual); business, holidays and travel supplements; financial, employment and consumer pages.
  News Editor Gordon Boreland
  Features Editor Jeremy Lewis Good local interest only. Maximum 800 words. No fiction.
  Sports Editor Duncan Hamilton
  Fashion Page Lynne Dixon

Nuneaton
Evening Telegraph
1 New Century Way, Nuneaton,
Warwickshire CV11 5NE
☎01203 382664   Fax 01203 353184
Owner Coventry Newspapers Ltd
Editor Andy Turner
Circulation 11,000

Oldham
Evening Chronicle
PO Box 47, Union Street, Oldham,
Lancashire OL1 1EQ
☎0161 633 2121   Fax 0161 627 0905

Owner *Hirst Kidd & Rennie Ltd*
Editor *Philip Hirst*
Circulation 36,009

'We welcome the good but not the bad.'
Motoring, food and wine, women's page, business page.

News Editor *Mike Attenborough*
Women's Page *Ron Fletcher*

Oxford
Oxford Mail

Osney Mead, Oxford OX2 0EJ
☎01865 244988   Fax 01865 243382
Owner *Oxford & County Newspapers*
Editor *Tim Blott*
Circulation 34,383

Unsolicited mss are considered but a great many unsuitable offerings are received. Approach in writing with an idea, rather than by phone. No fiction. All fees negotiable.

News Editor *John Chipperfield*
Features Editor *Annette Nix* Any features of topical or historical significance. Maximum 800 words.

Sports Editor *Stuart Earp*
Women's Page *Fiona Tarrant*

Paisley
Paisley Daily Express

14 New Street, Paisley PA1 1YA
☎0141 887 7911   Fax 0141 887 6254
Owner *Scottish & Universal Newspapers Ltd*
Acting Editor *Jackie Linton*
Circulation 8,464

Circulates in Paisley, Linwood, Renfrew, Johnstone, Elderslie, Raiston and Barrhead. Unsolicited mss welcome only if of genuine local (Paisley) interest. The paper does not commission work, and will consider submitted material. Maximum 1000–1500 words. All submissions to the editor.

Features Editor/Women's Page *Anne Dalrymple*
Sports Editor *Ken MacDonald*

Peterborough
Evening Telegraph

New Priestgate House, 57 Priestgate,
Peterborough, Cambridgeshire
PE1 1JW
☎01733 555111   Fax 01733 313147
Owner *EMAP*
Editor *Bob Crawley*

Circulation 28,354

Unsolicited mss not welcome. Approach in writing with ideas. Special pages include fashion, farming, motoring, property, women, gardening, pop, travel, television, books and film. Plus weekly lifestyle supplement.

Features Editor *Alex Gordon*
Sports Editor *Bob French*
Women's Page *Rosie Sandall*

Plymouth
Evening Herald

17 Brest Road, Derriford Business Park,
Derriford, Plymouth, Devon PL6 5AA
☎01752 765500   Fax 01752 765527
Owner *Northcliffe Newspapers Group Ltd*
Editor *Alan Cooper*
Circulation 56,147

All editorial material to be addressed to the editor or the **News Editor** *Mike Bramhall*.

Sunday Independent

Burrington Way, Plymouth,
Devon PL5 3LN
☎01752 777151   Fax 01752 780680
Owner *West of England Newspapers Ltd*
Editor *Anna Jenkins*
Circulation 41,195

Fashion, what's on, gardening, computers, DIY, business, motors and motorcycles, furniture, food and wine, out and about property, photography, hobbies, health and beauty, kitchens.

All editorial should be addressed to the **Assistant Editor** *Ken Sheldon*

Western Morning News

17 Brest Road, Derriford Business Park,
Derriford, Plymouth, Devon PL6 5AA
☎01752 765500   Fax 01752 765535
Owner *Northcliffe Newspapers Group Ltd*
Editor *Barrie Williams*
Circulation 53,767

Unsolicited mss welcome, but best to telephone features editor first. Special pages include a motoring supplement, West country matters, books, antiques, lifestyle and arts.

News Editor *Philip Bowern*
Features Editor *Janet Wooster* Mostly local interest, 600–800 words. Must be topical.
Sports Editor *Rick Cowdery*
All other editorial material to be addressed to the editor.

Portsmouth
The News
The News Centre, Hilsea, Portsmouth,
Hampshire PO2 9SX
☎01705 664488   Fax 01705 673363
Owner *Portsmouth Printing & Publishing Ltd*
Editor *Geoffrey Elliott*
Circulation 78,633

Unsolicited mss not generally welcome.
Approach by letter.
   News Editor *Mark Acheson*
   Features Editor *Paul Bithell* General sub-
jects of SE Hants interest. Maximum 600
words. No fiction.
   Sports Editor *Colin Channon* Sports back-
ground features. Maximum 600 words.
   Women's Page *Anne King*

Preston
Lancashire Evening Post
Olivers Place, Eastway, Fulwood, Preston,
Lancashire PR2 4ZA
☎01772 254841   Fax 01772 880173
Owner *United Newspapers Publications Ltd*
Editor *Philip Welsh*
Circulation 67,195

Unsolicited mss are not generally welcome;
many are received and not used. All ideas in
writing to the editor.

Reading
Evening Post
PO Box 22, Tessa Road, Reading, Berkshire
RG1 8NS
☎01734 575833   Fax 01734 599363
Owner *Guardian Media Group*
Editor *Kim Chapman*
Circulation 23,257

Unsolicited mss welcome; one or two received
every day. Fiction rarely used. Interested in
local news features, human interest, well-
researched investigations. Special sections
include women's page (Monday & Thursday);
motoring and motorcycling (Tuesday); business (Wednesday); gardening (Friday); rock
music (Friday); children's page (Friday); travel
(Friday).
   Features Editor *Brian Sansome*
   News Editor *Chris Bishop* Topical subjects,
particularly of Thames Valley interest.
Maximum 800 words.
   Women's Page *Helen Riley*

Scarborough
Scarborough Evening News
17–23 Aberdeen Walk, Scarborough, North
Yorkshire YO11 1BB
☎01723 363636   Fax 01723 354092
Owner *Yorkshire Regional Newspapers Ltd*
Editor *David Penman*
Circulation 17,320

Special pages include women (Tuesday); prop-
erty (Wednesday); motoring (Tuesday/Friday);
pop (Thursday).
   News Editor *Chris Nixon*
   Motoring *Dennis Sissons*
   Sports Editor *Charles Place*
All other material should be addressed to the
editor.

Scotland
Daily Record (Glasgow)
See **National Newspapers**

Scotland on Sunday
See **National Newspapers**

The Scotsman
See **National Newspapers**

Sunday Mail (Glasgow)
See **National Newspapers**

Sunday Post (Dundee)
See **National Newspapers**

Scunthorpe
Scunthorpe Evening Telegraph
Doncaster Road, Scunthorpe, South
Humberside DN15 7RE
☎01724 843421   Fax 01724 853495
Owner *Northcliffe Newspapers Group Ltd*
Editor *P. L. Moore*
Circulation 25,182

All correspondence should go to the news edi-
tor.
   Assistant Editor *D. H. Stephens*
   News Editor *Simon Drury*

Sheffield
The Star
York Street, Sheffield, South Yorkshire S1 1PU
☎0114 2767676   Fax 0114 2725978
Owner *Sheffield Newspapers Ltd*
Editor *Peter Charlton*
Circulation 100,370

Unsolicited mss not welcome, unless topical and local.

News Editor *Paul License* Contributions only accepted from freelance news reporters if they relate to the area.

Features Editor *Jim Collins* Very rarely require outside features, unless on specialised subject.

Sports Editor *Derek Fish*
Women's Page *Fiona Firth*
Payment negotiable.

Shropshire
Shropshire Star
See under *Telford*

South Shields
Gazette
Chapter Row, South Shields, Tyne & Wear
NE33 1BL
☎0191 455 4661   Fax 0191 456 8270
Owner *Northeast Press Ltd*
Editor *Ian Holland*
Circulation 24,780
  News Editor *Chris Storey*
  Sports Editor *John Cornforth*
  Women's Page *Joy Yates*

Southampton
The Southern Daily Echo
45 Above Bar, Southampton, Hampshire
SO9 7BA
☎01703 634134   Fax 01703 630289
Owner *Southern Newspapers Ltd*
Editor *Patrick Fleming*
Circulation 62,535

Unsolicited mss 'tolerated'. Approach the editor in writing with strong ideas; staff supply almost all the material.

Stoke on Trent
Evening Sentinel
Sentinel House, Etruria, Stoke on Trent,
Staffordshire ST1 5SS
☎01782 289800   Fax 01782 280781
Owner *Staffordshire Sentinel Newspapers Ltd*
Editor *Sean Dooley*
Circulation 96,589

Weekly sports final supplement. All material should be sent to the **News Editor** *Michael Wood*.

Sunderland
Sunderland Echo
Echo House, Pennywell, Sunderland, Tyne & Wear SR4 9ER
☎0191 534 3011   Fax 0191 534 5975
Owner *North East Press Ltd*
Editor *Andrew Hughes*
Circulation 63,342

All editorial material to be addressed to the news editor.

Swansea
South Wales Evening Post
Adelaide Street, Swansea, West Glamorgan
SA1 1QT
☎01792 650841   Fax 01792 469665
Owner *Northcliffe Newspapers Group Ltd*
Editor *Hugh Berlyn*
Circulation 71,155

Circulates throughout South West Wales.
  News Editor *Jonathan Isaacs*
  Sports Editor *David Evans*
  Women's Page *Betty Hughes*

Swindon
Evening Advertiser
100 Victoria Road, Swindon, Wiltshire
SN1 3BE
☎01793 528144   Fax 01793 542434
Owner *Media in Wessex*
Editor *Geoff Teather*
Circulation 27,831

Copy and ideas invited. 'All material must be strongly related or relevant to the town of Swindon, borough of Thamesdown or the county of Wiltshire.' Little scope for freelance work. Fees vary depending on material.
  Head of Content *Pauline Leighton*
  Sports Editor *Alan Johnson*
  Women's Page *Shirley Mathias*

Telford
Shropshire Star
Ketley, Telford, Shropshire TF1 4HU
☎01952 242424   Fax 01952 254605
Owner *Shropshire Newspapers Ltd*
Editor *Andy Wright*
Circulation 95,047

No unsolicited mss; approach the editor with ideas in writing in the first instance. No news or fiction.
  News Editor *Kim Bennett*
  Features Editor *Roy Williams* Limited

opportunities; uses mostly in-house or syndi-
cated material. Maximum 1200 words.
   Sports Editor *Peter Byram*
   Women's Page *Shirley Tart*

Torquay
Herald Express
Harmsworth House, Barton Hill Road,
Torquay, Devon TQ2 8JN
☎01803 213213   Fax 01803 313093
Owner *Northcliffe Newspapers Group Ltd*
Editor *J. C. Mitchell*
Circulation 30,531

Drive scene, property guide, Monday sports,
special pages, rail trail, Saturday surgery, nature
and conservation column, Saturday children's
page. Supplements: *Curriculum, Gardening,
Healthcare News* (all quarterly); *Visitors Guide* and
Antiques & Collectables (fortnightly); *Devon Days
Out* (every Saturday in summer and at Easter and
May Bank Holidays). Unsolicited mss generally
not welcome. All editorial material should be
addressed to the editor in writing.

Wales
South Wales Argus
See under *Newport*

South Wales Echo
See under *Cardiff*

South Wales Evening Post
See under *Swansea*

Wales on Sunday
See **National Newspapers**

Western Mail
See under *Cardiff*

West of England

Express & Echo
See under *Exeter*

Western Daily Press
See under *Bristol*

Western Morning News
See under *Plymouth*

Weymouth
Dorset Evening Echo
57 St Thomas Street, Weymouth, Dorset
DT4 8EU
☎01305 784804   Fax 01305 760387
Owner *Southern Newspapers plc*
Editor *Michael Woods*
Circulation 22,188

Farming, by-gone days, films, arts, showbiz,
brides, teens page, children's page, and video.
   News Editor *Paul Thomas*
   Sports Editor *Jack Wyllie*

Wolverhampton
Express & Star
Queen Street, Wolverhampton, West
Midlands WV1 3BU
☎01902 313131   Fax 01902 21467
Owner *Midlands News Association*
Editor *Warren Wilson*
Circulation 209,819

   Deputy Editor *Richard Ewels*
   News Editor *David Evans*
   Features Editor *Garry Copeland*
   Sports Editor *Brian Clifford*
   Women's Page *Julia Cooper*

Worcester
Evening News
Berrow's House, Hylton Road, Worcester
WR2 5JX
☎01905 748200   Fax 01905 429605
Owner *Reed Midland Newspapers Ltd*
Editor *Malcolm Ward*
Circulation 23,886

Pulse pop page (Thursday/Friday/Saturday);
leisure (Wednesday); property (Thursday).
Weekly Supplements: *Midweek News; Motoring
News; Weekend News and Entertainment.*
   News Editor *John Murphy*
   Features Editor/Women's Page *Chris
   Lloyd*
   Sports Editor *Paul Ricketts*

York
Yorkshire Evening Press
PO Box 29, 76–86 Walmgate, York YO1 1YN
☎01904 653051   Fax 01904 612853
Owner *York & County Press*
Editor *David Nicholson*
Circulation 48,629

Unsolicited mss not generally welcome, unless submitted by journalists of proven ability. *Business Press Pages* (Monday); *Women's Press Extra* (monthly section); *Property Press* (Thursday); *Preview* leisure and entertainments supplement (Friday); *Weekender* supplement (Saturday)

News Editor *Claire Timms*
Picture Editor *Martin Oates*
Sports Editor *Martin Jarred*
Payment negotiable.

Yorkshire
Yorkshire Evening Post
See under *Leeds*

Yorkshire on Sunday
See under *Bradford*

Yorkshire Post
See under *Leeds*

Blood from a Stone

*Hilary Townsend spells out the problems freelancers have
in getting paid and suggests some remedies*

If an editor buys a pint of beer or a pair of socks he expects to pay for them at the market rate. The same holds true in the literary marketplace. An editor has no business to assume that my goods are free or that I am having a sudden clearance sale. If my work is of a sufficiently high standard for a going commercial concern to wish to publish it, then I want to be suitably rewarded for delivering my part of the contract.

So why is getting paid so often fraught with difficulties and time-consuming arguments? One of the principal reasons relates to the attitude of freelancers themselves – the way they see themselves and their low opinion of their own worth. Novice writers often don't expect to get paid or – good grief – they cannot bring themselves to mention anything so vulgar as money, let alone send an invoice. This lack of self-esteem is reflected in a writers' magazine to which I subscribe. It bears the patronising legend, 'You may not be paid by your local paper but at least you will have the thrill of seeing your work in print'. Don't you believe it. By the same token, writing classes which encourage their pupils to write for nothing do their students and the profession a disservice. Meek, grovelling attitudes are reinforced and novices' confidence is bludgeoned.

Unscrupulous editors know this and are likely to target the novice knowing that if they pay peanuts for prose and nothing for illustrations, the grateful writing class pupil will respond with an effusive letter of thanks and more free or sweatshop rate features. Not only meekness but vanity in writers can be targeted by advertisements for features on specialist topics placed by editors who blithely admit that they have little or no money to pay for them.

The biggest single obstacle to being paid comes from two sorts of editors – muddlers and rogues. Muddlers are a particularly serious threat because they are usually so charming. They are always going to use the features, they are 'delighted with the transparencies you sent with them, which are here somewhere', and as for the features they have already published, the invoice and related correspondence have sunk to the bottom of the in-tray, never to re-emerge. Freelancers should not waste time on incorrigible muddlers – they are going to be fired eventually.

Rogues present a much greater difficulty. The fact that novice writers may be prepared to work for nothing encourages them to try it on with anyone they do not know first-hand. The most flagrant attempt to avoid paying me came about when I responded to a magazine request for material about property. I sent in a piece about a campaign to right a particular wrong related to listed buildings, a subject on which I write extensively. The editor accepted the material and asked for a series of transparencies and black and white photographs. When I rang up to enquire about my invoice his blithe comment was 'But we were helping you with your campaign'. Fortunately, the threat of legal proceedings brought a change of heart and a cheque.

Interestingly, editors in the USA and Canada issue full guidelines at the outset of negotiations. These clearly set out not only rates of payment but the length of time a decision and publication will take, and when payment can be expected. The reason for this polite treatment relates to a cultural difference in attitude – writers are held in much more respect over there.

Positive Action

To be accepted as a serious writer and be paid like one means being thoroughly professional in your targeting of outlets and the presentation of work. Make it very clear in your first query letter to a new editor that you expect payment – 'If this subject is of interest I look forward to hearing from you with details of length, slant and rates of payment'. A professional looking invoice should either accompany the finished feature or go off very soon afterwards. I always send the invoice to the editor to whom I addressed the feature, so that the invoice can be matched to the feature before they reach the accounts department.

A bring forward system for chasing invoices is essential. I chase up work after six months with editors I know, three months if they are unknown. The third invoice is sent by recorded delivery and if there is no response to that I consider the next move.

Don't be put off by people who tell you that if you complain about not being paid you won't get any more work. If the editor isn't inclined to pay you without a great deal of expensive, time-consuming fuss, then you have nothing to lose by complaining. In any case, making a fuss can bring positive results. It did for me when, after years of sending in news items and odd weekend supplement pieces to my local daily, and being paid meticulously every month, the cheques suddenly stopped coming. Nobody could tell me why. Finally, after six months, I wrote to the editor with a complete list of work outstanding and a polite letter regretting that after a long and happy association I was now obliged to pursue my grievances against him through the Small Claims Court. The astonished editor took the matter up with his Accounts Department and found the complaint to be justified. The clerk who used to deal with my claims had left and his replacement, not sure what they related to, put them in a file and hoped they would go away. The result, a rocket for an accountant, a grovelling letter to me from the editor, a name higher up the chain to whom I should address myself in future, and a very happy and profitable relationship with that newspaper ever since.

Cancellation fees and compensation

Sometimes an editor asks me to do work for him but is then quite unable to use it for reasons he cannot control. Pages may be cut back or a change of circumstances may relegate an article to yesterday's news. The responsible editor will offer a kill fee to compensate the freelancer for work put in, time lost and expenses involved. If it is not offered, the freelancer should ask for compensation. I know a journalist who, having offered a specialised piece to a well-known glossy magazine, was asked for more information which she meticulously researched and sent in. The editor then regretted that she could not use it after all and the writer did not get round to asking for a kill fee – until, that is, a year later when she read her work, staff written, in the dentist's waiting room. I have sticky labels printed saying 'Terms NUJ: Kill Fee 2/3' which I attach to relevant letters to editors. This does not mean I automatically get the kill fee rate demanded, any more than I get NUJ terms, but to spell out a rate from the outset is a useful basis for subsequent negotiations.

You can only expect a kill fee if the editor specifically asked you to do the work, not if you just lobbed it off. If you incurred expenses on an unsolicited piece compensation might be payable (a) if the editor intended to publish it before events overtook him and (b) if there is any money left. I once profited unexpectedly when an upmarket publishing house decided to fold a glossy, well-presented magazine it had brought out in the housing boom of the late 1980s. The publishing house, both prestigious and affluent, felt its image had been dented by deciding to discontinue the magazine and the embarrassed editor paid me in full.

On another occasion a magazine that had taken my work but not published it went bankrupt. The editor suggested to me at once that I submit a claim as a creditor and eventually – after the hearing and many months – I was paid a percentage like all the other creditors. I probably should not have thought of claiming if the editor had not suggested it.

Incidentally, compensation is payable by the Post Office when either a manuscript sent with a certificate of posting fails to arrive or a Royal Mail machine has chewed up envelope and script. After one of my own articles suffered in this way, I sent the Post Office a bill to cover time put in and loss of goodwill. Royal Mail sent me a cheque in full settlement.

There are times when the freelancer has simply got to write off a loss. In recent years, fall of advertising revenue has resulted all too often in the sudden folding of an established magazine or the collapse of a publishing house. If you can stake a claim you may rank with the creditors and get something eventually – but you may not. If you have kept a copy of your work and negatives of black and white pictures, and taken a second copy of transparencies when they were developed – as you should – it is usually best to call it quits. Why spend good money chasing after bad?

The small claims court

A small claim is for £1000 or less made through a County Court. Most are made to recover debt owed, though they can be for other things such as bad workmanship or faulty goods. The Citizens' Advice Bureau (CAB) can provide you with an excellent set of leaflets about making small claims, all bearing the 'Crystal Mark' for clarity approved by the Plain English Campaign, so that's a good start. The CAB will also tell you where to apply for County Court Summons forms on which to make your claim. It is all very simple.

Such is the effect of threatening a small claim in the County Court that I have never had to pursue it. It is generally well known among persons who owe money that the County Court will recover the sum owing and make the defendant pay the court fee as well.

Membership of a professional association

Freelancers should investigate early the advantages of joining a professional association such as **The Society of Authors**, the **National Union of Journalists** or **The Writers' Guild**. While acceptance by some requires a body of published work, others will accept novice writers into a probationary category and encourage them towards full membership.

Membership of a professional association helps enormously in overcoming obstacles to being paid. After I was accepted by the **Society of Women Writers and Journalists** as a full member I had this fact printed on my letterhead and found at once that I was pushed around far less.

As a last resort, a highly original, if unconventional idea for putting the squeeze on recalcitrant editors comes from Buzz Rodwell, a contributor to *Writers' Newsletter*. His success came when, 'confronted with the usual interminable baloney about failure to receive my invoice', he decided to resort to the Yardlong Fax. This is how it works. 'Take one yard, or thereabouts, of continuous stationery, a thick black felt pen and a dose of wry vitriol, and scrawl a clear and unmistakable message sideways along paper (something like PAY UP NOW OR THIS WILL GET EVEN LONGER!) in 6-inch high letters. Insert into fax machine and transmit to errant publisher. It'll probably screw up after the first foot or so, but they are starting to get the idea. After five minutes an agonised voice on the other end of the telephone promised payment within a week.'

Writing for peanuts

If you are writing for peanuts you may be writing for the wrong markets unless, that is, you wish to support peanut paying magazines. You are quite free to do this without letting the side down. I do it regularly for small presses and struggling magazines I like when I know that they cannot pay very much. I've also been known to work for nothing for a charity I support.

But if you were a plumber who worked only for the sheer love of plumbing and flatly refused to be paid for it, would you really expect to be called on to tackle complicated plumbing disasters? Unlikely. You'd only be considered fit for little jobs.

So, mindful of Townsend's Law – that good editors who pay promptly and well tend to edit the most worthwhile publications – the serious freelancer would do well to target honest, worthwhile editors; the sort that always intended to pay you as a matter of course. Then you're more likely to find yourself working for good publications.

And when you find good editors stay with them. The rewards you get from such a partnership extend far beyond being paid.

Magazines

Abraxas
57 Eastbourne Road, St Austell, Cornwall
PL25 4SU
☎01726 64975

Owner *Paul Newman*
Editor *Paul Newman, Geoffrey Lee Cooper*

FOUNDED 1991. QUARTERLY (Incorporating the *Colin Wilson Newsletter*). Aims at being a periodical, but sometimes turns out to be a spasmodical. Unsolicited mss welcome after a study of the magazine – initial approach by phone or letter preferred.

Features essays, translations and reviews. Recent issues have had Colin Wilson surveying the work and career of the psychologist R.D. Laing and the philosopher Jacques Derrida, Stefan Ball introducing the 'madman from Loja' or the Ecuadorian genius Pablo Palacio, Gordon Rumson reviewing the magian composer Sorabji, Paul Newman on *Creepers* or British Horror Fiction and philosopher Joe Felser tracing the genealogy of 'Angels' in response to the craze sweeping across the States. *Abraxas* also welcomes provocative, lively articles on little-known literary figures (e.g. David Lindsay/E. H. Visiak/Laura Del Rivo/P. D. Ouspensky/Brocard Sewell) and new slants on psychology, existentialism and ideas. Maximum length 2000 words. *Payment* nominal if at all.

Fiction one story per issue. Favours compact, obsessional stories – think of writers like Kafka, Borges or Wolfgang Borchert – of not more than 2000 words.

Poetry double-page spread – has published D. M. Thomas, Zofia Ilinksa, A. R. Lamb and J. B. Pick.

Payment free copy of magazine.

Acclaim
PO Box 101, Tunbridge Wells, Kent
TN4 8YD
☎01892 511322   Fax 01892 514282

Owner *Merric Davidson*
Editor *Barbara Large*

FOUNDED 1992. BI-MONTHLY. Short story digest, with emphasis on shortlisted entries from the annual **Ian St James Award**. Not interested in poetry, plays, sketches or children's material; the magazine is devoted solely to the short story. No unsolicited mss. Approach with ideas only, by phone or in writing.

News *Merric Davidson* Anything at all that is solely connected with the writing of short stories.

Features *Barbara Large/Merric Davidson* As above for news, plus articles by writers on tricks of the trade, etc. Maximum 2000 words.

Reviews Of short story collections only.

Payment negotiable/nothing for news items.

Accountancy
40 Bernard Street, London WC1N 1LD
☎0171 833 3291   Fax 0171 833 2085

Owner *Institute of Chartered Accountants in England and Wales*
Editor *Brian Singleton-Green*
Circulation 72,757

FOUNDED 1889. MONTHLY. Written ideas welcome.

Features *Brian Singleton-Green* Accounting/tax/business-related articles of high technical content aimed at professional/managerial readers. Maximum 2000 words.

Payment by arrangement.

Accountancy Age
32–34 Broadwick Street, London W1A 2HG
☎0171 439 4242   Fax 0171 437 7001

Owner *VNU Business Publications*
Editor *Robert Outram*
Circulation 70,000

FOUNDED 1969. WEEKLY. Unsolicited mss welcome. Ideas may be suggested in writing provided they are clearly thought out.

Features Topics right across the accountancy, business and financial world. Maximum 2000 words.

Payment negotiable.

Active Life
Aspen Specialist Media, Christ Church, Cosway Street, London NW1 5NJ
☎0171 262 2622   Fax 0171 706 4811

Owner *Aspen Specialist Media*
Editor *Helene Hodge*

FOUNDED 1990. BI-MONTHLY magazine aimed at over 50s. General consumer interests including travel, finance, property and leisure.

Opportunities for freelancers in all departments, including fiction. Approach in writing with synopsis of ideas. Authors' notes available on receipt of s.a.e.

Active Lifestyle Magazine
Centre – The Fitness, 41 Overstone Road, Hammersmith, London W6 0AD
☎0181 741 0215   Fax 0181 748 7812
Owner *Active Lifestyle*
Editor *Lydia Campbell*
Circulation 50,000

FOUNDED 1992. BI-MONTHLY for people who lead an active life. Unsolicited mss, synopses and ideas welcome. Approach in writing with ideas. No fiction or any material not related to fitness, health and an active lifestyle.
    Features Across a wide range of interests: health, nutrition, fitness, beauty, activities (active ones such as hiking, biking or scuba diving!), etc. Maximum 1000 words.
    News Club reviews and developments of interest to those engaged in an active lifestyle.
    Special Pages Items relating to personal improvement towards an active lifestyle.
    Payment £150 per 1000 words.

Acumen
See under **Poetry, Little Magazines**

adviser
Hamilton Web (a division of Bernard Kaymar Ltd), Trout Street, Preston, Lancashire PR1 4AL
☎01772 562211   Fax 01772 257813
Owner *British Dietetic Association*
Editor *Neil Donnelly*
Circulation 3500

FOUNDED 1981. QUARTERLY. Unsolicited mss welcome from dietitians and nutritionists. Make initial approach in writing. All pieces should be appropriate to dietitians. Maximum 1200 words. *Payment* £40–50.

African Affairs
Dept of Politics, University of Reading, Whiteknights, PO Box 218, Reading, Berkshire RG6 2AA
☎01734 318501   Fax 01734 753833
Owner *Royal African Society*
Editors *Peter Woodward, David Killingray*
Circulation 2250

FOUNDED 1901. QUARTERLY learned journal publishing articles on contemporary developments on the African continent. Unsolicited mss welcome.
    Features Should be well researched and written in a style that is immediately accessible to the intelligent lay reader. Max. 8000 words.
    Payment up to £40 per 1000 words for non-academics; no payment for academics.

Air International
PO Box 100, Stamford, Lincolnshire PE9 1XQ
☎01780 55131   Fax 01780 57261
Owner *Key Publishing Ltd*
Editor *Malcolm English*

FOUNDED 1971. MONTHLY. Civil and military aircraft magazine. Unsolicited mss welcome but initial approach by phone or in writing preferred.

Airforces Monthly
PO Box 100, Stamford, Lincolnshire PE9 1XQ
☎01780 55131   Fax 01780 57261
Owner *Key Publishing Ltd*
Editor *David Oliver*
Circulation 33,000

FOUNDED 1988. MONTHLY. Modern military aircraft magazine. Unsolicited mss welcome but initial approach by phone or in writing preferred.

All About Cats
40 Gray's Inn Road, London WC1X 8LR
☎0171 404 2604   Fax 0171 831 5426
Owner *Gong Publishing*
Editor-in-Chief *Grace McHatty*

FOUNDED 1994. MONTHLY covering everything about cats – wildcats, celebrities, pedigree and non-pedigree information, veterinary features, quizzes, book reviews, photo features, poetry and stories. Welcome unsolicited material. No 'twee or cutesy' pieces. All preliminary approaches should be made in writing.
    Features Bright and original pieces. No Egyptian cat gods, mummies, cat proverbs and sayings. Maximum 1000 words.
    Fiction Only opening is a monthly short story competition. *Prizes* £50+ for each finalist; overall winner receives a valuable prize (currently a fax machine).
    Letters *Payment* £25 for letter of the month/£5 for all others printed.

Amateur Film and Video Maker
24c West Street, Epsom, Surrey KT18 7RJ
☎01372 739672
Owner *Film Maker Publications*
Editor *Mrs Liz Donlan*
Circulation 3000

FOUNDED in the 1930s. BI-MONTHLY magazine of the Institute of Amateur Cinematographers.

Reports news and views of the Institute. Unsolicited mss welcome but all contributions are unpaid.

Amateur Gardening

Westover House, West Quay Road, Poole, Dorset BH15 1JG

☎01202 680586   Fax 01202 674335

Owner *IPC Magazines Ltd*
Editor *Graham Clarke*
Circulation 81,520

FOUNDED 1884. WEEKLY. New contributions are welcome provided that they have a professional approach. Of the twenty unsolicited mss received each week, 90% are returned as unsuitable. All articles/news items are supported by colour pictures (which may or may not be supplied by the author).

Features Topical and practical gardening articles. Maximum 800 words.

News Compiled/edited in-house generally.

Payment negotiable.

Amateur Golf

129A High Street, Dovercourt, Harwich, Essex CO12 3AX

☎01255 507526   Fax 01255 508483

Editor *Paul Baxter*
Publisher *Park View Publications Ltd*
Circulation 13,000

MONTHLY journal of the English Golf Union. UK coverage of amateur golf interests, club events and international matches. Unsolicited mss considered. Approach with ideas in writing or by phone.

Features *John Lelean* Golf course management, new developments and equipment, golf holidays, profiles and general amateur golf concerns. Maximum 2000 words.

Amateur Photographer

King's Reach Tower, Stamford Street, London SE1 9LS

☎0171 261 5100   Fax 0171 261 5404

Owner *IPC Magazines Ltd*
Editor *Keith Wilson*
Circulation 39,169

WEEKLY. For the competent amateur with a technical interest. Freelancers are used but writers should be aware that there is ordinarily no use for words without pictures.

Amateur Stage

83 George Street, London W1H 5PL

☎0171 486 1732   Fax 0171 224 2215

Owner *Platform Publications Ltd*

Editor *Charles Vance*

Some opportunity here for outside contributions. Topics of interest include amateur premières, technical developments within the amateur forum and items relating to landmarks or anniversaries in the history of amateur societies. Approach in writing only (include s.a.e for return of mss).

No payment.

Ambit

See under **Poetry, Little Magazines**

The American

114–115 West Street, Farnham, Surrey GU9 7HL

☎01252 713366   Fax 01252 716792

Owner *British American Newspapers Ltd*
Editor *David J. Williams*
Circulation 15,000

FOUNDED 1976. FORTNIGHTLY community newspaper for US citizens resident in the UK and as such requires a strong American angle in every story. 'We are on the look-out for items on business and commerce, diplomacy and international relations, defence and 'people' stories.' Maximum length 'five minutes read'. First approach in writing with samples of previous work.

Payment 'modest but negotiable'.

Amiga Format

30 Monmouth Street, Bath, Avon BA1 2AP

☎01225 442244   Fax 01225 318740

Owner *Future Publishing*
Editor *Nick Veitch*
Circulation 132,137

FOUNDED 1988. MONTHLY. Specialist computer magazine dedicated to Commodore Amiga home computers, offering reviews, features and product information of specific interest to Amiga users. Unsolicited material welcome. Contact by phone with ideas.

News *Steve McGill* Amiga-specific exclusives and product information – 500–1000 words.

Features *Nick Veitch* Computer-related features (i.e. CD, games, virtual reality) with Amiga-specific value. Maximum 10,000.

Special Pages *Jason Holborn* Hardware and software reviews. Maximum 3000 words.

Payment £100 per 1000 words.

Animal Action

Causeway, Horsham, West Sussex RH12 1HG

☎01403 264181   Fax 01403 241048

Owner *RSPCA*

Editor *Michaela Miller*
Circulation 70,000

BI-MONTHLY. RSPCA youth membership magazine. Articles (pet care, etc.) are written in-house. Good-quality animal photographs welcome.

Antique and New Art
10–11 Lower John Street,
London W1R 3PE
☎0171 434 9180   Fax 0171 287 5488
Owner *Antique Publications*
Editor *Alistair Hicks*
Circulation 22,000

FOUNDED 1986. QUARTERLY. Amusing coverage of antiques and art. Unsolicited mss not welcome. Approach by phone or in writing in the first instance. Interested in freelance contributions on international art news items.

The Antique Collector
7 St John's Road, Harrow, Middlesex
HA1 2EE
☎0181 863 2020   Fax 0181 863 2444
Owner *Orpheus Publications*
Editor *Susan Morris*
Circulation 15,000

FOUNDED 1930. TEN ISSUES YEARLY. Opportunities for freelance features. Submit ideas in writing. Acceptance depends primarily on how authoritative and informative they are. Topical and controversial material is always welcome. Maximum 2000 words with illustrations in colour and/or black and white.

Payment £250 for a major feature (1500 words).

The Antique Dealer and Collectors' Guide
PO Box 805, Greenwich, London SE10 8TD
☎0181 318 5868   Fax 0181 691 2489
Owner *Statuscourt Ltd*
Publisher *Philip Bartlam*
Circulation 13,500

FOUNDED 1946. MONTHLY. Covers all aspects of the antiques and fine art worlds. Unsolicited mss welcome.

Features Practical but readable articles on the history, design, authenticity, restoration and market aspects of antiques and fine art. Maximum 2000 words. *Payment* £76 per 1000 words.

News *Philip Bartlam* Items on events, sales, museums, exhibitions, antique fairs and markets. Maximum 300 words.

Apollo Magazine
24 Chesham Place, London SW1X 8HB
☎0171 235 1676   Fax 0171 235 1673
Owner *Paul Z. Josefowitz*
Editor *Robin Simon*

FOUNDED 1925. MONTHLY. Specialist articles on art and antiques, exhibition and book reviews, exhibition diary, information on dealers and auction houses. Unsolicited mss welcome. Interested in specialist, usually new research in fine arts, architecture and antiques. Approach in writing. Not interested in crafts or practical art or photography.

Aquarist & Pondkeeper
9 Tufton Street, Ashford, Kent TN23 1QN
☎01233 621877   Fax 01233 645669
Owner *Dog World Ltd*
Editor *John Dawes*
Circulation *c.* 20,000

FOUNDED 1924. MONTHLY. Covers all aspects of aquarium and pondkeeping: conservation, herpetology (study of reptiles and amphibians), news, reviews and aquatic plant culture. Unsolicited mss welcome. Ideas should be submitted in writing first.

Features *John Dawes* Good opportunities for writers on any of the above topics or related areas. 1500 words (maximum 2500), plus illustrations. 'We have stocks in hand for up to two years, but new material and commissioned features will be published as and when relevant.' Average lead-in 4–6 months.

News *John Dawes* Very few opportunities.

Architects' Journal/ The Architectural Review
33–39 Bowling Green Lane,
London EC1R 0DA
☎0171 837 1212   Fax 0171 278 4003
Owner *EMAP Architecture*
Editor *Paul Finch* (AJ)
Editor *Peter Davey* (AR)
Circulation 20,000 (AJ); 18,000 (AR)

WEEKLY (*Architects' Journal*) and MONTHLY (*The Architectural Review*) trade magazines dealing with all aspects of the industry. No unsolicited mss. Approach in writing with ideas.

Architectural Design
42 Leinster Gardens, London W2 3AN
☎0171 402 2141   Fax 0171 723 9540
Owner *Academy Group Ltd*
Editor *Maggie Toy*
Circulation 12,000

FOUNDED 1930. BI-MONTHLY. Theoretical architectural magazine. Unsolicited mss not generally welcome. Copy tends to come from experts in the field.

Arena

Block A, Exmouth House, Pine Street,
London EC1R 0JL
☎0171 837 7270   Fax 0171 837 3906
Owner *Wagadon Ltd/Condé Nast Publications*
Editor *Kathryn Flett*

Style and general interest magazine for men. Intelligent feature articles and profiles, plus occasional fiction.
Features Fashion, lifestyle, film, television, politics, business, music, media, design, art, architecture and theatre.
Payment £150 per 1000 words.

Art & Craft

Villiers House, Clarendon Avenue,
Leamington Spa, Warwickshire CV32 5PR
☎01926 887799   Fax 01926 883331
Owner *Scholastic Publications Ltd*
Editor *Sian Morgan*
Circulation 23,000

FOUNDED 1936. MONTHLY aimed at a specialist market – the needs of primary school teachers and pupils. Ideas and synopses considered for commission.
Features The majority of contributors are primary school teachers with good art and craft skills and familiar with the curriculum.
News Handled by in-house staff. No opportunities.

Art Monthly

Suite 17, 26 Charing Cross Road, London
WC2H 0DG
☎0171 240 0389   Fax 0171 240 0389
Owner *Britannia Art Publications*
Editor *Patricia Bickers*
Circulation 4000

FOUNDED 1976. TEN ISSUES YEARLY. News and features of relevance to those interested in modern and contemporary visual art. Unsolicited mss welcome. Contributions should be addressed to the editor, accompanied by an s.a.e.
Features Alongside exhibition reviews: usually 750–1000 words and almost always commissioned. Interviews and articles of up to 1500 words on art theory, individual artists, contemporary art history and issues affecting the arts (e.g. funding and arts education). Book reviews of 750–1000 words.

News Brief reports (250–300 words) on art issues.
Payment negotiable.

The Art Newspaper

27-29 Vauxhall Grove,
London SW8 1SY
☎0171 735 3331   Fax 0171 735 3332
Owner *Umberto Allemandi & Co. Publishing*
Editor *Laura Suffield*
Circulation 30,000

FOUNDED 1990. MONTHLY. Broadsheet format with up-to-date information on the international art market, news, museums, exhibitions, archaeology, conservation, books and current debate topics. Length 250 – 2000 words No unsolicited mss. Approach with ideas in writing. Commissions only. *Payment* £120 per 1000 words.

The Artist

Caxton House, 63–65 High Street,
Tenterden, Kent TN30 6BD
☎0158076 3673   Fax 0158076 5411
Owner *Irene Briers*
Editor *Sally Bulgin*
Circulation 17,500

FOUNDED 1931. MONTHLY.
Features *Sally Bulgin* Art journalists, artists, art tutors and writers with a good knowledge of art materials are invited to write to the editor with ideas for practical and informative features about art, materials, techniques and artists.

Artscene

Dean Clough Industrial Park, Halifax,
West Yorkshire HX3 5AX
☎01422 322527   Fax 01422 322518
Owner *Yorkshire and Humberside Arts*
Editor *Victor Allen*
Circulation 25,000

FOUNDED 1973. MONTHLY. Listings magazine for Yorksire and Humberside. No unsolicited mss. Approach by phone with ideas.
Features Profiles of artists (all media) and associated venues/organisers events of interest. Topical relevance vital. Maximum length 1500 words. *Payment* £100 per 1000 words.
News Artscene strives to bring journalistic values to arts coverage – all arts 'scoops' in the region are of interest. Maximum length 500 words. *Payment* £100 per 1000 words.

Asian Times

See **Caribbean Times/Asian Times**

Audit

19 Rutland Street, Cork, Republic of Ireland
☎00 353 21313 855   Fax 00 353 21313 496
Editor *Ken Ebbage* (0438 840770)
Circulation 700

MONTHLY with a specialist, professional readership and world-wide circulation. Features tend to be commissioned. Approach in writing with ideas. Maximum 3000 words. No unsolicited mss. *Payment* £250.

The Author

84 Drayton Gardens, London SW10 9SB
☎0171 373 6642
Owner *The Society of Authors*
Editor *Derek Parker*
Manager *Kate Pool*
Circulation 6000

FOUNDED 1890. QUARTERLY journal of **The Society of Authors**. Unsolicited mss not welcome.

Autocar

38–42 Hampton Road, Teddington,
Middlesex TW11 0JE
☎0181 943 5013   Fax 0181 943 5653
Owner *Haymarket Magazines Ltd*
Editor *Michael Harvey*
Circulation 84,159

FOUNDED 1895. WEEKLY. All news stories, features, interviews, scoops, ideas, tip-offs and photographs welcome.

    Features *Gavin Conway*
    News *Julian Rendell*
    Payment from £175 per 1000 words/negotiable.

Baby Magazine

The Publishing House, Highbury Station Road, Islington, London N1 1SE
☎0171 226 2222   Fax 0171 359 5225
Owner *Harrington Kilbride Plc*
Editor *Lorna Pettipher*

BI-MONTHLY for parents-to-be and parents of children up to five years old. No unsolicited mss.

    Features Send synopsis of feature with covering letter in the first instance. Unsolicited material is not returned.

Back Brain Recluse (BBR)

PO Box 625, Sheffield S1 3GY
Owner *Chris Reed*
Editor *Chris Reed*
Circulation *c.* 3000

International speculative fiction magazine providing opportunity for new writers. 'We strongly recommend familiarity with our guidelines for contributors, and with recent issues of *BBR*, before any material is submitted.' All correspondence must be accompanied by s.a.e. or international reply coupons.
    Payment £5 per 1000 words.

Badminton

Connect Sports, 14 Woking Road, Cheadle Hulme, Cheshire SK8 6NZ
☎0161 486 6159/0171 938 7399 (editorial)
Fax 0161 486 6159
Owner *Mrs S. Ashton*
Editor *William Kings*

BI-MONTHLY. Specialist badminton magazine, with news, views, product information, equipment reviews, etc. Unsolicited material will be considered. Approach the editor by phone with an idea.

    Features *William Kings* Open to approaches and likes to discuss ideas in the first instance. Interested in badminton-related articles on health, fitness, psychology, clothing, accessories, etc.
    Payment £60.

Balance

British Diabetic Association, 10 Queen Anne Street, London W1M 0BD
☎0171 323 1531   Fax 0171 637 3644
Owner *British Diabetic Association*
Editor *Lesley Hallett*
Circulation 150,000

FOUNDED 1935. BI-MONTHLY. Unsolicited mss are not accepted. Writers may submit a brief proposal in writing. Only topics relevant to diabetes will be considered.

    Features *Lesley Hallett* Medical, diet and lifestyle features written by people with diabetes or with an interest and expert knowledge in the field. General features are mostly based on experience or personal observation. Maximum 1500 words. *Payment* £75 per 1000 words.
    News *Lesley Hallett* Short pieces about activities relating to diabetes and the lifestyle of diabetics. Maximum 150 words.
    Young Balance *Maggie Gibbons* Any kind of article written by those under 18 and with personal experience of diabetes. *Payment* varies.

The Banker

Greystoke Place, Fetter Lane,
London EC4A 1ND
☎0171 405 6969   Fax 0171 831 9136
Owner *Pearson Professional*
Editor *Stephen Timewell*

Circulation 14,376

FOUNDED 1926. MONTHLY. News and features on banking, finance and capital markets worldwide.

BBC Gardeners' World Magazine

101 Bayham Street, London NW1 0AG
☎0171 331 8204   Fax 0171 331 8162
Owner *BBC Worldwide Publishing Ltd*
Editor *Adam Pasco*
Circulation 275,185

FOUNDED 1991. MONTHLY. Gardening advice, ideas and inspiration. No unsolicited mss. Approach by phone or in writing with ideas.

BBC Good Food

101 Bayham Street, London NW1 0AG
☎0171 331 8041   Fax 0171 331 8161
Owner *BBC Worldwide Publishing Ltd*
Editor *Mitzie Wilson*
Circulation 446,000

FOUNDED 1989. MONTHLY food and drink magazine with television and radio links. No unsolicited mss.

BBC Holiday Magazine

101 Bayham Street, London NW1 0AG
☎0171 331 8000   Fax 0171 331 8030
Owner *BBC Worldwide Publishing Ltd*
Editor *Alison Rice*
Circulation 450,000

FOUNDED 1992. MONTHLY. Unbiased, informative features on all aspects of holidays and time off. Unsolicited mss not welcome. Approach in writing enclosing examples of published or written work.
    Features All commissioned work. Nothing bought on spec. Maximum length 800–3000 words.
    Payment average £350 per 1000 words.

BBC Homes & Antiques

110 Bayham Street, London NW1 0AG
☎0171 331 3939   Fax 0171 331 8001
Owner *BBC Worldwide Publishing Ltd*
Editor *Judith Hall*
Circulation 105,000

FOUNDED 1993. MONTHLY traditional home interest magazine with a strong bias towards antiques and collectables. Welcome unsolicited material, although most features are commissioned. No fiction, health and beauty, fashion or general showbusiness. Approach with ideas by phone or in writing.
    Features *Judith Hall* At-home features:

inspirational houses – people-led items. Pieces commissioned on recce shots and cuttings. Guidelines available on request. Celebrity features: 'at homes or favourite things' – send cuttings of relevant work published. Maximum 1500 words. General items on antiques or collecting.
    Special Pages Single pages on nostalgia, in particular, memories of childhood homes. Maximum 850 words.
    Payment negotiable.

BBC Music Magazine

Room A1130, Woodlands, 80 Wood Lane, London W12 0TT
☎0181 576 3283   Fax 0181 576 3292
Owner *BBC Worldwide Publishing Ltd*
Editor *Fiona Maddocks*
Circulation 275,910 (worldwide)

FOUNDED 1992. MONTHLY. All areas of classical music. Not interested in unsolicited material. Approach with ideas only, by phone or in writing.

BBC Vegetarian Good Food

101 Bayham Street, London NW1 0AG
☎0171 331 8281   Fax 0171 331 8161
Owner *BBC Worldwide Publishing Ltd*
Editor *Mary Gwynn*

FOUNDED 1992. MONTHLY magazine containing recipes, health and environment features. Unsolicited mss not welcome. Approach in writing with ideas.

BBC Wildlife Magazine

Broadcasting House, Whiteladies Road, Bristol, Avon BS8 2LR
☎0117 973 2211   Fax 0117 946 7075
Owner *BBC Worldwide Publishing Ltd*
Editor *Rosamund Kidman Cox*
Circulation 132,717

FOUNDED 1963 (formerly *Wildlife*, née *Animals*). MONTHLY. Unsolicited mss not welcome.
    Competition The magazine runs an annual competition for professional and amateur writers with a first prize of £1000 (see entry under **Prizes**).
    Features Most features commissioned from writers with expert knowledge of wildlife or conservation subjects. Unsolicited mss are usually rejected. Maximum 3500 words. *Payment* £120–350.
    News Most news stories commissioned from known freelancers. Maximum 800 words. *Payment* £40–100.

Bedfordshire Magazine
50 Shefford Road, Meppershall, Bedfordshire
SG17 5LL
☎01462 813363
Owner *White Crescent Press*
Editor *Betty Chambers*
Circulation 2400

FOUNDED 1947. QUARTERLY. Unsolicited material welcome on Bedfordshire. No general interest articles. Approach by phone or in writing in the first instance.
Features History, biography, natural history and arts. Nothing in the way of consumer features.
News Very little.
Fiction Occasional stories and poems of county interest only.
Special Pages Primarily historical material on Bedfordshire. Maximum 1500 words.
Payment nominal.

Bee World
18 North Road, Cardiff CF1 3DY
☎01222 372409   Fax 01222 665522
Owner *International Bee Research Association*
Editor *Dr P. A. Munn*
Circulation 1700

FOUNDED 1919. QUARTERLY. High-quality factual journal with international readership. Features on apicultural science and technology. Unsolicited mss welcome. It is recommended that authors write to the Editor for guidelines before submitting mss.

Bella
H. Bauer Publishing, Shirley House,
25–27 Camden Road, London NW1 9LL
☎0171 284 0909   Fax 0171 485 3774
Owner *H. Bauer Publishing*
Editor-in-Chief *Jackie Highe*
Circulation 1.2 million

FOUNDED 1987. WEEKLY. General interest women's magazine. Contributions welcome.
Features *Jacky Hyams* Maximum 1200–1300 words.
Fiction *Linda O'Byrne* Maximum 1200–3000 words. Send s.a.e. for guidelines.
Payment about £300 per 1000 words/varies.

Best
Portland House, Stag Place,
London SW1E 5AU
☎0171 245 8700   Fax 0171 245 8825
Owner *G & J (UK)*
Editor *Maire Fahey*
Circulation 664,972

FOUNDED 1987. WEEKLY women's magazine and stablemate of the magazine *Prima*. Multiple features, news, short stories on all topics of interest to women. Important for would-be contributors to study the magazine's style which differs from many other women's weeklies. Approach in writing with s.a.e.
Features Maximum 1500 words. No unsolicited mss.
Fiction 'Five-Minute Story' slot; mss accepted. Maximum 1400 words.
Payment £100.

Best of British
Apex House, Oundle Road, Peterborough,
Cambridgeshire PE2 9NP
☎01733 555123   Fax 01733 898487
Owner *Choice Publications (EMAP)*
Editor *Neil Patrick*

FOUNDED 1994. BI-MONTHLY magazine celebrating all things British, both past and present. Study of the magazine is advised in the first instance. All preliminary approaches should be made in writing.

The Big Issue
Fleet House, 57–61 Clerkenwell Road,
London EC1M 5NP
☎0171 418 0418   Fax 0171 418 0428
Owner *The Big Issue*
Editor *A. John Bird*
Deputy Editor *Joanne Mallabar*
Circulation 102,142

FOUNDED 1991. WEEKLY. A campaigning and general interest magazine with a bias towards social issues such as homelessness.
Features On London life and getting the most out of the Capital on little money; street-life human-interest features and social issues. Only one or two freelance features carried in each issue usually, so it is best to approach the deputy editor with an idea in the first instance, either by phone or in writing. Maximum 1400 words. *Payment* £100 for main feature, but the majority of work is donated to help the homeless (a percentage of the proceeds from sales goes directly to the homeless).
News *Lucy Johnston* Hard-hitting social injustice orientated stories, with the emphasis on London. *No payment.*
Fiction Must be written by homeless people. Not interested otherwise.
Special Pages Finance, sport, arts, etc. Reviews and news. Maximum 300 words. *No payment.*

the Bike mag

Link House, 9 Dingwall Avenue, Croydon,
Surrey CR9 2TA
☎0181 686 2599

Owner *United Leisure Magazines*
Editor *Gerard Brown*

MONTHLY. Aimed at anyone who rides a bike.
Looks at all facets of cycling from the Tour de
France to BMX street action to a weekend
away in the Cotswolds, to a mountain bike
tour over the Himalayas. No unsolicited material. Phone with details first. 'Freelance potential very good.' *Payment* by negotiation.

Birds

The Lodge, Sandy, Bedfordshire SG19 2DL
☎01767 680551   Fax 01767 692365

Owner *Royal Society for the Protection of Birds*
Editor *R. A. Hume*
Circulation 501,000

QUARTERLY magazine which covers not only
wild birds but also wildlife and related conservation topics. No interest in features on pet
birds or 'rescued' sick/injured/orphaned ones.
Mss or ideas welcome. On the look-out for
photo features (colour transparencies) from
photographers. Especially interested in unusual
bird behaviour. 'No captive birds, please.'

Birdwatch

310 Bow House, 153 – 159 Bow Road,
London E3 2SE
☎0181 983 1855   Fax 0181 983 0246

Owner *Solo Publishing*
Editor *Dominic Mitchell*
Circulation 20,000

FOUNDED 1991. MONTHLY high quality magazine featuring illustrated articles on all aspects
of birds and birdwatching, especially in Britain.
No unsolicited mss. Approach in writing with
synopsis of 100 words maximum.

Features *Dominic Mitchell* Unusual angles/
personal accounts, if well-written. Articles of an
educative or practical nature suited to the readership. Maximum 2000–3000 words.

Fiction *Dominic Mitchell* Very little opportunity although occasional short story published.
Maximum 15000 words.

News *Tim Harris* Rarely use external material.
Payment £40 per 1000 words.

Black Beauty & Hair

Hawker Consumer Publications Ltd,
13 Park House, 140 Battersea Park Road,
London SW11 4NB
☎0171 720 2108   Fax 0171 498 3023

Owner *Hawker Consumer Publications Ltd*
Editor *Irene Shelley*
Circulation 21,006

QUARTERLY with two annual specials: Bridal
issue in March, hairstyle book in October.
Black beauty and fashion magazine with
emphasis on humorous but authoritative articles relating to clothes, hair, lifestyle, sexual
politics, women's interests, etc. Unsolicited
contributions welcome.

Features Beauty and fashion pieces welcome from writers with a sound knowledge of
the Afro-Caribbean beauty scene plus bridal
features. Minimum 1000 words.
Payment £85 per 1000 words.

Boat International

5–7 Kingston Hill, Kingston upon Thames,
Surrey KT2 7PW
☎0181 547 2662   Fax 0181 547 1201

Owner *Edisea Ltd*
Editor *Jason Holtom*
Circulation 24,000

FOUNDED 1983. MONTHLY. Unsolicited mss
welcome. Approach with ideas in writing.

Features Maximum 2500 words.
News Maximum 300 words.
Payment £100 per 1000 words.

Book and Magazine Collector

45 St. Mary's Road, London W5 5RQ
☎0181 579 1082   Fax 0181 566 2024

Owner *John Dean*
Editor *Crispin Jackson*
Circulation 12,000

FOUNDED 1984. MONTHLY. Contains articles
about collectable authors/publications/sub-
jects. Unsolicited mss welcome – but write
first. Must be bibliographical and include a full
bibliography and price guide. Not interested in
purely biographical features. Approach in writing with ideas.

Features Maximum length 4000 words.
Payment £30 per 1000 words.

The Book Collector

20 Maple Grove, London NW9 8QY
☎0181 200 5004   Fax 0181 200 5004

Owner *The Collector Ltd*
Editor *Nicolas J. Barker*

FOUNDED 1950. QUARTERLY magazine containing matters of bibliographical interest.

Bookdealer

Suite 34, 26 Charing Cross Road,
London WC2H 0DH
☎0171 240 5890   Fax 0171 379 5770
Editor *Barry Shaw*

WEEKLY trade paper which acts almost exclusively as a platform for people wishing to buy or sell rare/out-of-print books. Eight-page editorial only; occasional articles and book reviews by regular freelance writers.

Books

43 Museum Street, London WC1A 1LY
☎0171 404 0304   Fax 0171 242 0762
Editor *Richard Mabb*
Circulation *c.* 120,000

Formerly *Books and Bookmen*. Consumer magazine dealing chiefly with features about authors and reviews of books. *Payment* negotiable.

Books in Wales

See **Llais Llyfrau**

The Bookseller

12 Dyott Street, London WC1A 1DF
☎0171 836 8911   Fax 0171 836 6381
Owner *J. Whitaker & Sons Ltd*
Editor *Louis Baum*

Trade journal of the publishing and book trade – the essential guide to what is being done to whom. Trade news and features, including special features, company news, publishing trends, etc. Unsolicited mss rarely used as most writing is either done in-house or commissioned from experts within the trade. Approach in writing first.
Features *Penny Mountain, Helen Paddock*
News *Jason Cowley*

Brides and Setting Up Home

Vogue House, Hanover Square, London
W1R 0AD
☎0171 499 9080   Fax 0171 493 1345
Owner *Condé Nast Publications Ltd*
Editor *Sandra Boler*
Circulation 63,161

BI-MONTHLY. Much of the magazine is produced in-house, but a good, relevant feature on cakes, jewellery, music, flowers, etc. is always welcome. Maximum 1000 words. Prospective contributors should telephone with an idea in the first instance.

British Birds

Fountains, Park Lane, Blunham, Bedford
MK44 3NJ
☎01767 640025   Fax 01767 640025
Owner *British Birds Ltd*
Editor *Dr J. T. R. Sharrock*
Circulation 10,000

FOUNDED 1907. MONTHLY ornithological magazine published by non-profit-making company. Features annual *Reports on Rare Birds in Great Britain*, bird news from official national correspondents throughout Europe and sponsored competitions for Bird Photograph of the Year, Bird Illustrator of the Year and Young Ornithologists of the Year. Unsolicited mss welcome from ornithologists only.
Features Well-researched, original material relating to Western Palearctic birds welcome. Maximum 6000 words.
News *Bob Scott/Wendy Dickson* Items ranging from conservation to humour. Max. 200 words.
Payment only for photographs, drawings and paintings.

British Chess Magazine

The Chess Shop, 69 Masbro Road, London
W14 0LS
☎0171 603 2877   Fax 0171 371 1477
Owner *Murray Chandler*
Editor *Murray Chandler*

FOUNDED 1881. MONTHLY. Emphasis on tournaments, the history of chess and chess-related literature. Approach in writing with ideas. Unsolicited mss not welcome unless from qualified chess experts and players.

British Journalism Review

John Libbey & Co. Ltd., 13 Smiths Yard,
Summerley Street, London SW18 4HR
☎0181 947 2777   Fax 0181 947 2664
Owner *British Journalism Review Ltd*
Editor *Geoffrey Goodman*
Circulation *c.* 800

FOUNDED 1989. QUARTERLY. Aims to create a vehicle for professional and academic consideration of British journalism, establishing a critical forum for media matters. Best approach by writing. Unsolicited material welcome.
News/Features *Geoffrey Goodman* Any article about journalism, journalists or broadcasting considered. Specific areas of interest include ethics, censorship and training.
Book Reviews *Mark Hollingsworth* On issues specified above, and usually by commission only.
Payment negotiable.

British Medical Journal

BMA House, Tavistock Square,
London WC1H 9JR
☎0171 387 4499   Fax 0171 383 6418

Owner *British Medical Association*
Editor *Professor Richard Smith*

No market for freelance writers.

British Philatelic Bulletin

Royal Mail, Royal London House, Finsbury
Square, London EC2A 1NL
Owner *Royal Mail*
Editor *J. R. Holman*
Circulation 40,000

FOUNDED 1963. MONTHLY. News and features
on British stamps, postmarks, postal stationery
and services. Unsolicited mss considered.

Features On British stamps or postal history.
Non-British stamps are only mentioned in articles on stamp design or thematic collecting.
Maximum 2000 words but longer articles may
be serialised. *Payment £30 per 1000 words.*

News Short items on British philatelic
events. *No payment.*

British Railway Modelling

The Maltings, West Street, Bourne,
Lincolnshire PE10 9PH
☎01778 393313   Fax 01778 394748

Owner *Warners Group Holdings Plc*
Editor *David Brown*
Circulation 18,224

FOUNDED 1993. MONTHLY. A general magazine for the practising modeller. Unsolicited
mss welcome. Interested in features on quality
models, from individual items to complete lay-
outs. Approach in writing.

Features articles on practical elements of
the hobby, e.g. locomotive construction, kit
conversions etc. Layout features and articles on
individual items which represent high standards
of the railway modelling art. Maximum length
6000 words (single feature). *Payment* up to £35
per published page.

News news and reviews containing the
model railway trade, new products etc. Maximum length 1000 words. *Payment* up to £35
per published page.

Broadcast

33-39 Bowling Green Lane,
London EC1R 0DA
☎0171 837 1212   Fax 0171 837 8250

Owner *EMAP Business Publications*
Editor *Mike Jones*

Circulation 11,200

FOUNDED 1960. WEEKLY. Opportunities for
freelance contributions. Write to the relevant
editor in the first instance.

Features Any broadcasting issue. Maximum
1500 words.

News *Matt Baker* Broadcasting news. Maximum 400 words.

Payment £160 per 1000 words.

Brownie

17–19 Buckingham Palace Road, London
SW1W 0PT
☎0171 834 6242   Fax 0171 828 8317

Owner *The Guide Association*
Editor *Marion Thompson*
Circulation 30,000

FOUNDED 1962. MONTHLY. Aimed at Brownie
members aged 7–10.

Articles Crafts and simple make-it-yourself
items using inexpensive or scrap materials.

Features Of general interest (500–600 words).

Fiction Brownie content an advantage. No
adventures involving unaccompanied children
in dangerous situations – day or night. Maximum 1000 words.

Payment £40 per 1000 words pro rata.

Building

Builder House, 1 Millharbour,
London E14 9RA
☎0171 537 6070   Fax 0171 537 6004

Owner *The Builder Group*
Editor *Peter Bill*
Circulation 24,000

FOUNDED 1842, WEEKLY. Features articles on
aspects of the modern building industry. Unsolicited mss are not welcome but freelancers
with specialist knowledge of the industry are
often used.

Features Focus on the modern industry. No
building history required. Max. 1500 words.

News Max. 500 words.

Payment by arrangement.

The Burlington Magazine

14–16 Duke's Road, London WC1H 9AD
☎0171 388 1228   Fax 0171 388 1230

Owner *The Burlington Magazine Publications Ltd*
Editor *Caroline Elam*

FOUNDED 1903. MONTHLY. Unsolicited contributions welcome on the subject of art history
provided they are previously unpublished. All
preliminary approaches should be made in
writing.

Exhibition Reviews Usually commissioned, but occasionally unsolicited reviews are published if appropriate. Maximum 1000 words.
Features Maximum 4500 words. *Payment £100* (maximum).
Shorter Notices Maximum 2000 words. *Payment £50* (maximum).

Business Life
Haymarket House, 1 Oxendon Street, London SW1Y 4EE
☎0171 925 2544   Fax 0171 839 4508
Owner *Premier Magazines*
Editor *Sandra Harris*
Circulation 193,000

MONTHLY. Glossy business travel magazine with few opportunities for freelancers. Distributed on BA European routes, TAT and Deutsche BA only. Unsolicited mss not welcome. Approach with ideas in writing only.

Business Traveller
Compass House, 22 Redan Place, London W2 4SZ
☎0171 229 7799   Fax 0171 229 9441
Owner *Perry Publications*
Editor *Gillian Upton*
Circulation 41,500

MONTHLY. Consumer publication. Opportunities exist for freelance writers but unsolicited contributions tend to be 'irrelevant to our market'. Would-be contributors advised to study the magazine first. Approach in writing with ideas.
Payment varies.

Camcorder User
57–59 Rochester Place, London NW1 9JU
☎0171 485 0011   Fax 0171 482 6269
Owner *W. V. Publications*
Editor *Robert Uhlig*
Circulation 35,061

FOUNDED 1988. MONTHLY magazine dedicated to camcorders, with features on creative technique, shooting advice, new equipment, accessory round-ups and interesting applications on location. Unsolicited mss, illustrations and pictures welcome. *Payment negotiable.*

Campaign
22 Lancaster Gate, London W2 3LY
☎0171 413 4036   Fax 0171 413 4507
Owner *Haymarket Publishing Ltd*
Editor *Dominic Mills*
Circulation 16,004

FOUNDED 1968. WEEKLY. Lively magazine serving the advertising and related industries. Freelance contributors are best advised to write in the first instance.
Features Articles of 1500–2000 words.
News *Belinda Archer* Relevant news stories of up to 300 words.
Payment negotiable/£35–50 for news.

Camping and Caravanning
Greenfields House, Westwood Way, Coventry, Warwickshire CV4 8JH
☎01203 694995   Fax 01203 694886
Owner *Camping and Caravanning Club*
Editor *Peter Frost*
Circulation 109,569

FOUNDED 1901. MONTHLY. Interested in journalists with camping and caravanning knowledge. Write with ideas for features in the first instance.
Features Outdoor pieces in general, plus items on specific regions of Britain. Maximum 1200 words. Illustrations to support text essential.

Camping Magazine
Link House, Dingwall Avenue, Croydon, Surrey CR9 2TA
☎0181 686 2599   Fax 0181 781 6044
Owner *Link House Magazines Ltd*
Editor *John Lloyd*

FOUNDED 1961. MONTHLY magazine with features on walking and camping. Aims to reflect this enjoyment by encouraging readers to appreciate the outdoors and to pursue an active camping holiday, whether as a family in a frame tent or as a lightweight backpacker. Articles that have the flavour of the camping lifestyle without being necessarily expeditionary or arduous are always welcome. Study of the magazine is advised in the first instance. Ideas welcome. Contact editor by phone before sending mss. *Payment negotiable.*

Canal and Riverboat
Stanley House, 9 West Street, Epsom, Surrey KT18 7RL
☎01372 741411   Fax 01372 744493
Owner *A. E. Morgan Publications Ltd*
Editor *Norman Alborough*
Circulation 26,000

Covers all aspects of waterways, narrow boats and cruisers. Contributions welcome. Make initial approach in writing.
Features *Norman Alborough* Waterways, narrow boats and motor cruisers, cruising reports, practical advice, etc. Unusual ideas and personal comments are particularly welcome.

Maximum 2000 words. *Payment* around £50 per page.

Fiction Considered only if subject matter is relevant. Maximum 1500 words. *Payment* around £40 per page.

News *Norman Alborough* Items of up to 300 words welcome on the Inland Waterways System, plus photographs if possible. *Payment* £15.

Capital Gay
1 Tavistock Chambers, Bloomsbury Way, London WC1A 2SE
☎0171 242 2750   Fax 0171 242 3334

Owner *Stonewall Press Ltd*
Editor *Simon Edge*
Circulation 21,468

FOUNDED 1981. WEEKLY newspaper for London's gay community, with an emphasis on social and political news, plus features and general interest. Some opportunities for freelance work. Approach in writing first.

Arts & Entertainments *Pas Paschali* Maximum 250 words.
Features *Simon Edge* Maximum 1000 words.
News Maximum 400 words.
Payment by arrangement.

Car Mechanics
Kelsey Publishing, 77 High Street, Beckenham, Kent BR3 1AN
☎0181 658 3531   Fax 0181 650 8035

Owner *Kelsey Publishing*
Editor *Peter Simpson*
Circulation 35,000

MONTHLY. Practical guide to DIY, maintenance and repair. Unsolicited mss welcome 'at sender's risk'. Ideas preferred. Approach by phone.

Features Good, technical, entertaining and well-researched material welcome.
Payment by arrangement.

Caravan Life
Suite 2, 1st Floor, Northburgh House, Northburgh Street, Clerkenwell, London EC1V 0AY
☎0171 490 8141   Fax 0171 336 7193

Editor *Stuart Craig*

FOUNDED 1987. Magazine for experienced caravanners and enthusiasts providing practical and useful information and product evaluation. Opportunities for caravanning, relevant touring and travel material with good quality colour photographs.

Caravan Magazine
Link House, Dingwall Avenue, Croydon, Surrey CR9 2TA
☎0181 686 2599Fax 0181 760 0973/781 6044

Owner *Link House Magazines Ltd*
Editor *Barry Williams*
Circulation 25,786

FOUNDED 1933. MONTHLY. Unsolicited mss welcome. Approach in writing with ideas. All correspondence should go direct to the editor.
Features Touring with strong caravan bias and technical/DIY features. Maximum 1500 words. *Payment* by arrangement.

Caress Newsletter
'The Write Solution', Flat 1, 11 Holland Road, Hove, East Sussex BN3 1JF
☎01273 726281   Fax 01273 726281

Owner *David Weldon*
Editor *David Weldon*

FOUNDED 1993. Gives information on markets, resources, reviews and products for writers of erotica. No unsolicited mss but will consider reviews of books, videos and clubs; 400 words maximum. Initial approach in writing. *Payment* negotiable.

Caribbean Times/Asian Times
3rd Floor, Tower House, 141–149 Fonthill Road, London N4 3HF
☎0171 281 1191   Fax 0171 263 9656

Owner *Arif Ali*
Editor *Arif Ali*

Two WEEKLY community papers for the Asian, African and Caribbean communities in Britain. *Caribbean Times* has a circulation of 23,000 and was founded in 1981; *Asian Times* was founded two years later and has a circulation of 25,000. Interested in general, local and international issues relevant to these communities. Approach in writing with ideas for submission.

Cars and Car Conversions Magazine
Link House, Dingwall Avenue, Croydon, Surrey CR9 2TA
☎0181 686 2599   Fax 0181 760 0973

Owner *Link House Magazines Ltd*
Editor *Nigel Fryatt*
Circulation 70,000

FOUNDED 1965. MONTHLY. Unsolicited mss welcome but prospective contributors are advised to make initial contact by telephone.
Features *Nigel Fryatt* Technical articles on

current motorsport and unusual sport-orientated road cars. Length by arrangement.

Payment negotiable.

Cat World

10 Western Road, Shoreham by Sea, West Sussex BN43 5WD

☎01273 462000   Fax 01273 455994

Owner *D. M. & J. H. Colchester*
Editor *Joan Moore*
Circulation 19,000

FOUNDED 1981. MONTHLY. Unsolicited mss welcome but initial approach in writing preferred.

Features Lively, first-hand experience features on every aspect of the cat. Breeding features and veterinary articles by acknowledged experts only. Maximum 1000 words. *Payment* £35 per 1000 words.

News Short, concise, factual or humorous items concerning cats. Maximum 100 words. *Payment* £5.

Poems Maximum 50 words. *Payment* £7.50.

Catch

Albert Square, Dundee DD1 9QJ

☎01382 223131   Fax 01382 200880

Owner *D. C. Thomson & Co. Ltd*
Editor *Jacquie Fraser*
Assistant Editor *Nicola Gilray Scott*
  General Features *Michelle Simpson*
  Fashion *Paula Moore*
  Beauty *Felicity Donohoe*
  Health *Paula Moore*

FOUNDED 1990. MONTHLY magazine for young women aged 16–19; typical reader viewed as 17 and single. Works towards a much broader editorial base than *Looks*, going beyond the beauty and personality profile pages, and aims to bridge the gap between magazines like *Just Seventeen* and titles for the older woman.

Catholic Herald

Lamb's Passage, Bunhill Row, London EC1Y 8TQ

☎0171 588 3101   Fax 0171 256 9728

Editor *Cristina Odone*
Deputy Editor *Murray White*
Literary Editor *Lucy Lethbridge*
Circulation 22,000

Interested not only in straight Catholic issues but also in general humanitarian matters, social policies, the Third World, the arts and books. *Payment* by arrangement.

Certified Accountant

19 Rutland Street, Cork, Republic of Ireland

☎00 353 21313 855   Fax 00 353 21313 496

Editor *Brian O'Kane*
Circulation 56,000

MONTHLY. Specialist, professional readership with world-wide circulation. No unsolicited mss. Most features tend to be commissioned. Make initial contact in writing. No fiction.

Features Maximum 3000 words. *Payment* £150.

Challenge

Revenue Buildings, Chapel Road, Worthing, West Sussex BN11 1BQ

☎01903 214198   Fax 01903 217663

Owner *Challenge Publishing*
Editor *Donald Banks*
Circulation 80,000

FOUNDED 1958. MONTHLY Christian newspaper which welcomes contributions. Send for sample copy of writers' guidelines in the first instance.

Fiction Short children's stories. Maximum 600 words.

News Items of up to 500 words (preferably with pictures) 'showing God at work', and human interest photo stories. 'Churchy' items not wanted.

Women's Page Relevant items of interest welcome.

Payment negotiable.

Champs-Elysées

119 Altenburg Gardens, 16 The Bakehouse, Bakery Place, London SW11 1JQ

☎0171 738 9324   Fax 0171 738 0707

Owner *Wes Green*
European Editor *David Ralston*

FOUNDED 1984. MONTHLY audio magazine for advanced speakers of French, German, Italian and Spanish issued in two parts: Part One is an hour-long programme (original stories, interviews and songs) in one of the above languages on cassette; Part Two is a booklet comprising a complete transcript with a glossary of difficult words plus features in English relating to topics covered on the tape. Interested in receiving ideas for unusual, well-researched stories for a sophisticated and well-educated readership.

News 500 words maximum. *Payment* £180 per 1000 words.

Features European culture and travel. 1500 words maximum. *Payment* £150 per 1000 words. Approach in writing in the first instance.

Chapman

4 Broughton Place, Edinburgh EH1 3RX
☎0131 557 2207   Fax 0131 556 9565

Owner *Joy M. Hendry*
Editor *Joy M. Hendry*
Circulation 2000

FOUNDED 1970. QUARTERLY. Scotland's quality literary magazine. Features poetry, short works of fiction, criticism, reviews and articles on theatre, politics, language and the arts. Unsolicited material welcome if accompanied by s.a.e. Approach in writing unless discussion is needed.

Features *Joy Hendry* Topics of literary interest, especially Scottish literature, theatre, culture or politics. Maximum 5000 words.

Fiction *Joy Hendry* Short stories, occasionally novel extracts if self-contained. Maximum 6000 words. *Payment* £15 per 1000 words.

Special Pages *Joy Hendry* Poetry, both UK and non-UK in translation (mainly, but not necessarily, European). *Payment* £8 per published page.

Chapter One

See **Alliance of Literary Societies**

Chat

King's Reach Tower, Stamford Street,
London SE1 9LS
☎0171 261 6565   Fax 0171 261 6534

Owner *IPC Magazines Ltd*
Editor *Ms Terry Tavner*
Circulation 520,000

FOUNDED 1985. WEEKLY general interest women's magazine. Unsolicited mss considered (about 100 received each week). Approach in writing with ideas. Not interested in contributors 'who have never bothered to read *Chat* and don't therefore know what type of magazine it is'.

Features *Karen Swayne* Human interest and humour. Maximum 1000 words. *Payment* up to £250 maximum.

Fiction *Shelley Silas* Maximum 1,000 words.

Cheshire Life

2nd Floor, Oyston Mill, Strand Road,
Preston, Lancashire PR1 8UR
☎01772 722022   Fax 01772 736496

Owner *Life Magazines*
Editor *Peter Williams*
Circulation 11,000

FOUNDED 1934. MONTHLY. Homes, gardens, personalities, business, farming, conservation, heritage, books, fashion, arts, science – anything which has a Cheshire connection somewhere.

Child Education

Villiers House, Clarendon Avenue,
Leamington Spa, Warwickshire CV32 5PR
☎01926 887799   Fax 01926 883331

Owner *Scholastic Publications Ltd*
Editor *Gill Moore*
Circulation 65,000

FOUNDED 1923. MONTHLY magazine aimed at nursery, pre-school playgroup, infant and first teachers. Articles from teachers, relating to education for 4–7-year age group, are welcome. Maximum 1700 words. Approach in writing with synopsis. No unsolicited mss.

Choice

Apex House, Oundle Road, Peterborough,
Cambridgeshire PE2 9NP
☎01733 555123   Fax 01733 898487

Owner *EMAP/Bayard Presse*
Editor *Sue Dobson*
Circulation 130,000

MONTHLY full-colour, lively and informative magazine for people aged 50–69 which celebrates all that's good about life after full-time work.

Features Real-life stories, hobbies, interesting (older) people, British heritage and countryside, involving activities for active bodies and minds, health, competitions. Unsolicited mss read (s.a.e. for return of material); write with ideas and copies of cuttings if new contributor. No phone calls.

Rights/News All items affecting the magazine's readership are written by experts. Areas of interest include pensions, state benefits, health, money, property, legal, and caring for elderly relatives.

Payment by arrangement.

Christian Herald

Herald House, 96 Dominion Road,
Worthing, West Sussex BN14 8JP
☎01903 821082   Fax 01903 821081

Owner *Herald House Ltd*
Editor *Bruce Hardy*
Circulation 20,000

FOUNDED 1867. WEEKLY. Evangelical Christian newspaper intended for adults with families. Articles on theological, spiritual and practical matters tend to be commissioned. *Payment* Herald House rates.

Church Music Quarterly
151 Mount View Road, London N4 4JT
☎0181 341 6408   Fax 0181 340 0021
Owner *Royal School of Church Music*
Editor *Trevor Ford*
Associate Editor *Marianne Barton*
Circulation 13,700

QUARTERLY. Contributions welcome. Telephone in the first instance.

Features *Trevor Ford* Articles on Church music or related subjects considered. Maximum 2000 words. *Payment* £60 per page.

Church of England Newspaper
10 Little College Street, London SW1P 3SH
☎0171 976 0783   Fax 0171 976 7760
Owner *Parliamentary Communications Ltd*
Editor *John K. Martin*
Circulation 12,000

FOUNDED 1828. WEEKLY. Almost all material is commissioned but unsolicited mss are considered. Some fiction and poetry, but rarely.

Features *Penny Dale* Preliminary enquiry essential. Maximum 1200 words.

News *James Lindsay* Items must be sent promptly and should have a church/Christian relevance. Maximum 200–400 words.
Payment by negotiation.

Church Times
33 Upper Street, London N1 0PN
☎0171 359 4570   Fax 0171 226 3073
Owner *Hymns Ancient & Modern*
Editor *Paul Handley*
Circulation 38,847

FOUNDED 1863. WEEKLY. Unsolicited mss considered.

Features *Paul Handley* Religious topics. Maximum 1600 words. *Payment* £100 per 1000 words.

News *Paul Handley* Occasional reports (commissions only) on out-of-London events. *Payment* by arrangement.

Classic Boat
Link House, Dingwall Avenue, Croydon, Surrey CR9 2TA
☎0181 686 2599   Fax 0181 781 6535
Owner *Boating Publications Ltd*
Editor *Robin Gates*
Circulation 17,043

FOUNDED 1987. MONTHLY. Traditional boats and classic yachts old and new; maritime history. Unsolicited mss, particularly if supported by good photos, are welcome. Sail and power boat pieces considered. Approach in writing with ideas. Interested in well-researched stories on all nautical matters. Cruising articles welcome. No fiction or poetry. Contributor's notes available (s.a.e.).

Features Boatbuilding, boat history and design, events, yachts and working boats. Material must be well-informed and supported where possible by good-quality or historic photos. Maximum 3000 words. Classic is defined by excellence of design and construction – the boat need not be old and wooden! *Payment* £75-100 per published page.

News Discarded famous classic boats, events, boatbuilders, etc. Maximum 500 words. *Payment* according to merit.

Classic Cars
Kings Reach Tower, Stamford Street, London SE1 9LS
☎0171 261 5858   Fax 0171 261 6731
Owner *IPC Magazines Ltd*
Editor *Robert Coucher*
Circulation 78,894

FOUNDED 1973. MONTHLY magazine containing entertaining and informative articles about old cars and associated personalities.

Classical Guitar
Olsover House, 43 Sackville Road, Newcastle upon Tyne NE6 5TA
☎0191 276 0448   Fax 0191 276 1623
Owner *Ashley Mark Publishing Co.*
Editor *Colin Cooper*

FOUNDED 1982. MONTHLY.

Features *Colin Cooper* Usually written by staff writers. Maximum 1500 words. *Payment* by arrangement.

News *Thérèse Wassily Saba* Small paragraphs and festival concert reports welcome. *No payment.*

Reviews *Chris Kilvington* Concert reviews of up to 250 words. Approach in writing.

Classical Music
241 Shaftesbury Avenue, London WC2H 8EH
☎0171 333 1742   Fax 0171 333 1769
Owner *Rhinegold Publishing Ltd*
Editor *Keith Clarke*

FOUNDED 1976. FORTNIGHTLY. A specialist magazine using precisely targeted news and feature articles aimed at the music business. Most material is commissioned but professionally written unsolicited mss are occasionally published. Freelance contributors may approach in writing with an idea but should familiarise themselves beforehand with the style and market of the magazine. *Payment negotiable.*

Classical Piano
241 Shaftesbury Avenue,
London WC2H 8EH
☎0171 333 1724   Fax 0171 333 1769
Owner *Rhinegold Publishing*
Editor *Jessica Duchen*
Circulation 11,000

FOUNDED 1993. BI-MONTHLY magazine containing features, profiles, technical information, news, reviews of interest to those with a serious amateur or professional concern with pianos or their playing. Unsolicited mss occasionally accepted but no unsolicited reviews, artist profiles or musical analysis. Freelance material should be well-written, legible and pertain to the piano at a high level. Approach with ideas in writing.

Climber
The Plaza Tower, East Kilbride,
Glasgow G74 1LW
☎013552 46444   Fax 013552 63013
Owner *Caledonian Magazines Ltd*
Editor *Tom Prentice*
Circulation 16,000

FOUNDED 1962. MONTHLY. Unsolicited mss welcome (they receive about ten a day). Ideas welcome.
   Features Freelance features are accepted on climbing, mountaineering and hillwalking in the UK and abroad, but the standard of writing must be extremely high. Maximum 2000 words. *Payment negotiable.*
   News No freelance opportunities as all items are handled in-house.

Clothing World Magazine
578 Kingston Road, Raynes Park,
London SW20 8DR
☎0181 540 8381   Fax 0181 540 8388
Owner *Company Clothing Information Services Ltd*
Editor *Carole Bull*
Circulation 6000

A leading source of technical and business information for the UK's sophisticated clothing industry. Unsolicited mss welcome on any aspect of the design, manufacture and distribution of clothing.

Club International
2 Archer Street, London W1V 7HE
☎0171 734 9191   Fax 0171 734 5030
Owner *Paul Raymond*
Editor *Robert Swift*
Circulation 180,000

FOUNDED 1972. MONTHLY. Features and short humorous items in the style of *Viz, Private Eye,* etc.
   Features Maximum 1000 words.
   Shorts 200–750 words.
   Payment negotiable.

Coin News
Token Publishing Ltd, 105 High Street,
Honiton, Devon EX14 8PE
☎01404 45414   Fax 01404 45313
Owner *J. W. Mussell*
Editor *J. W. Mussell*
Circulation 10,000

FOUNDED 1964. MONTHLY. Contributions welcome. Approach by phone in the first instance.
   Features Opportunity exists for well-informed authors 'who know the subject and do their homework'. Maximum 2500 words.
   Payment £20 per 1000 words.

Combat and Militaria
Castle House, 97 High Street, Colchester,
Essex CO1 1TH
☎01206 540621   Fax 01206 564214
Owner *Aceville Publications Ltd*
Editor *James Marchington*

MONTHLY publication about military affairs. Unsolicited mss welcome on any military matters. *Payment by agreement.*

Commerce Magazine
Station House, Station Road, Newport Pagnell, Milton Keynes MK16 0AG
☎01908 614477   Fax 01908 616441
Owner *Holcot Press Group*
Group Editor *Steve Brennan*
Circulation 35,000

MONTHLY. Ideas welcome. Approach by phone or in writing first.
   Features *Isabelle Morgan* By-lined articles frequently used. Generally 750–800 words with photos.
   News Handled in-house.
   Special Pages Throughout the year – media and marketing; building and construction; finance and professional; office update.
   No payment.

Company

National Magazine House, 72 Broadwick
Street, London W1V 2BP
☎0171 439 5000   Fax 0171 439 5117
Owner *National Magazine Co. Ltd*
Editor *Mandi Norwood*
Circulation 268,022

MONTHLY. Glossy women's magazine appealing to the independent and intelligent young
woman. A good market for freelancers: 'we've
got more space for them, as we have fewer staff
feature writers'. Keen to encourage bright,
new, young talent, but uncommissioned material is rarely accepted. Feature outlines are the
only sensible approach in the first instance.
Maximum 1500–2000 words. Features to *Tara
Barker.*
    Payment £180 per 1000 words.

Company Clothing Magazine

Willowbrook House, The Green, Leire,
Lutterworth, Leicestershire LE17 5HL
☎010455 202088   Fax 010455 202692
Owner *Company Clothing Information
    Services Ltd*
Editor *Carole Bull*
Circulation 12,000

Only UK magazine dedicated to the corporate
clothing industry. Unsolicited mss welcome on
any aspect of business clothing and workwear.

Complete Car

Compass House, 22 Redan Place,
London W2 4SZ
☎0171 229 7799   Fax 0171 229 7846
Owner *Perry Motorpress Ltd*
Editor-in-Chief *John Blauth*
Circulation 100,000 plus

FOUNDED 1994. MONTHLY car magazine. Unsolicited mss are rarely, if ever, used. Prospective contributors are advised to make initial
approach in writing 'once they have read the
magazine from cover to cover at least once'.

Computer Weekly

Quadrant House, The Quadrant, Sutton,
Surrey SM2 5AS
☎0181 652 3122   Fax 0181 652 8979
Owner *Reed Business Publishing*
Editor *John Lamb*
Circulation 112,000

FOUNDED 1966. Freelance contributions welcome.
    Features *David Evans* Always looking for
good new writers with specialised industry

knowledge. Previews and show features on
industry events welcome. Maximum 2000
words.
    News *David Bicknell* Some openings for
regional or foreign news items. Maximum 300
words.
    Payment Up to £50 for stories/tips.

Computing, The IT Weekly

32–34 Broadwick Street, London W1A 2HG
☎0171 439 4242   Fax 0171 437 3516
Owner *VNU Business Publications Ltd*
Editor *Dr Jerry Sanders*
Circulation 114,000

WEEKLY newspaper.
    Features *Janine Milne*
    News *Stuart Lauchlan*
    Unsolicited mss *Linda Leung*
    Unsolicited technical articles welcome.
Please enclose s.a.e. for return.
    Payment Technical notes: £60; book reviews:
£30; feature articles: £160 per 1000 words;
news leads (leading to story) £30; fully
researched story: £60 per 350 words.

Contemporary Review

Cheam Business Centre, 14 Upper Mulgrave
Road, Cheam, Surrey SM2 7AZ
☎0181 643 4846
Owner *Contemporary Review Co. Ltd*
Editor *Dr Richard Mullen*

FOUNDED 1866. MONTHLY. One of the first
periodicals to devote considerable space to the
arts. Covers a wide spectrum of interests,
including home affairs and politics, literature
and the arts, history, travel and religion. No
fiction.
    Literary Editor *Betty Abel* Monthly book
section with reviews which are generally commissioned. Maximum 3000 words.
    Payment £5 per page.

Cosmopolitan

National Magazine House, 72 Broadwick
Street, London W1V 2BP
☎0171 439 5000   Fax 0171 439 5016
Owner *National Magazine Co. Ltd*
Editor *Marcelle D'Argy Smith*
Circulation 417,014

MONTHLY. Designed to appeal to the mid-
twenties, modern-minded female. Popular mix
of articles, with some emphasis on relationships
and careers, and strong fiction. Known to have
a policy of not considering unsolicited mss but
always on the look-out for 'new writers with
original and relevant ideas and a strong voice'.

Send short synopsis of idea. All would-be writers should be familiar with the magazine.

Payment about £200 per 1000 words.

Cotswold Life
West One House, 23 St George's Road,
Cheltenham, Gloucestershire GL50 3DT
☎01242 226367/226373   Fax 01242 222665
Owner *Beshara Press*
Editor *John Drinkwater*
Circulation *c.* 10,000

FOUNDED 1968. MONTHLY. News and features on life in the Cotswolds. Most news written in-house but contributions welcome for features.

Features Interesting places and people, reminiscences of Cotswold life in years gone by, and historical features on any aspect of Cotswold life. Approach in writing in the first instance. Maximum 1500–2000 words.

Payment by negotiation after publication.

Country Garden
Broad Leys Publishing Company, Buriton House, Station Road, Newport, Saffron Walden, Essex CB11 3PL
☎01799 540922   Fax 01799 541367
Owner *D. and K. Thear*
Editor *Helen Sears*
Circulation 28,000

FOUNDED 1975. MONTHLY journal dealing with practical country living. Unsolicited mss welcome; around 30 are received each week. Articles should be detailed and practical, based on first-hand knowledge about aspects of small farming and country living.

Country Homes and Interiors
King's Reach Tower, Stamford Street,
London SE1 9LS
☎0171 261 5000   Fax 0171 261 6895
Owner *Home Interest Group/IPC Magazines Ltd*
Editor *Julia Watson*
Circulation 128,348

FOUNDED 1986. MONTHLY. The best approach for prospective contributors is with an idea in writing as unsolicited mss are not welcome.

Features *Dominic Bradbury* Monthly personality interviews of interest to an intelligent, affluent readership (women and men), aged 25–44. Maximum 1200 words.

Travel *Caroline Suter* Articles 1200 words. Also hotel reviews, leisure pursuits and weekending pieces in England and abroad. Length 750 words.

Houses *Rebecca Duke* Country style homes with excellent design ideas. Length 1000 words. *Payment* negotiable.

Country Life
King's Reach Tower, Stamford Street,
London SE1 9LS
☎0171 261 7058   Fax 0171 261 5139
Owner *IPC Magazines Ltd*
Editor *Clive Aslet*
Circulation 42,066

Features which relate to the countryside, wildlife, rural events, sports and pursuits, and are of interest to well-heeled country dwellers, are welcome. Strong informed material rather than amateur enthusiasm. *Payment* from £120 per 1000 words.

Country Living
National Magazine House, 72 Broadwick Street, London W1V 2BP
☎0171 439 5000   Fax 0171 439 5093
Owner *National Magazine Co. Ltd*
Editor *Francine Lawrence*
Circulation 193,000

Magazine aimed at country dwellers and town dwellers who love the countryside. Covers people, conservation, wildlife, houses (gardens and interiors) and country businesses. No unsolicited mss. *Payment* negotiable.

Country Quest
P.O. Box 658, Mold, Clwyd CH7 1X4
☎01352 700022   Fax 01352 700048
Editor *Brian Barrett*

FOUNDED 1960. MONTHLY. Welsh interest magazine dealing with countryside, nature and environmental concerns in Wales and the Welsh border country. Also interested in Welsh history and personality items. Unsolicited material or ideas in writing welcome. Maximum 750–1000 words, with photos and illustrations. No fiction. *Payment* negotiable.

Country Sports
59 Kennington Road, London SE1 7PZ
☎0171 928 4742   Fax 0171 620 1401
Owner *British Field Sports Society*
Editor *Graham Downing*
Circulation 84,000

FOUNDED 1983. BI-MONTHLY magazine on matters relating to field sports. No unsolicited mss.

Country Walking
Bretton Court, Bretton, Peterborough,
Cambridgeshire PE3 8DZ
☎01733 264666   Fax 01733 261984
Owner *EMAP Plc*
Editor *Lynne Maxwell*
Circulation 40,065

FOUNDED 1987. MONTHLY magazine containing walks, features related to walking and things you see, country crafts, history, nature, photography etc, plus pull-out walks guide containing 28 routes every month. Unsolicited mss welcome. Interested in articles appropriate to style of magazine with good-quality landscape slides. Not interested in book or gear reviews, news cuttings or poor-quality pictures. Approach by phone with ideas.

Features *Lynne Maxwell* reader's story (maximum 1000 words). Features on specific areas of country, perhaps to include walks (maximum 1500 words). Walking trips abroad and fact file on how to get there etc. (maximum 1500 words). *Payment* negotiable.

Special Pages *Gill Page* 'Down your way' section walks. Accurately and recently researched walk and fact file. Points of interest along the way and pictures to illustrate. Please contact for guidelines (unsolicited submissions not often accepted for this section). *Payment* not negotiable.

Country-Side
BNA, 48 Russell Way, Higham Ferrers,
Northamptonshire NN10 8EJ
☎01933 314672   Fax 01933 314672
Owner *British Naturalists' Association*
Editor *Dr D. Applin*
Circulation *c.* 15,000

FOUNDED 1905. BI-MONTHLY. Conservation and natural history magazine. Unsolicited mss and ideas for features welcome on conservation, environmental and natural history topics. Approach in writing with ideas. Maximum 1400 words. *Payment* £50 (with pictures).

The Countryman
Sheep Street, Burford, Oxon OX18 4LH
☎01993 822258   Fax 01993 822703
Owner *Link House Magazines Limited*
Editor *Christopher Hall*
Circulation 50,000

FOUNDED 1927. SIX ISSUES YEARLY. Unsolicited mss with s.a.e. welcome; about 120 received each week. Contributors are strongly advised to study the magazine's content and character in the first instance. Approach in writing with ideas.

The Countryman's Weekly
Yelverton, Devon PL20 7PE
☎01822 855281   Fax 01822 855372
Owner *Vic Gardner*
Editor *Jayne Willcocks*

FOUNDED 1982. WEEKLY. Unsolicited material welcome. A list of special editions and subjects covered by the magazine is available on request. No fiction.

Features On any field sport topic. Maximum 1500 words.

News Items considered.

Payment rates available on request.

County
70–72 St Mark's Road, Maidenhead,
Berkshire SL6 6DW
☎01628 789444   Fax 01628 789396
Owner *Mr and Mrs Watts*
Editor *Mrs Ashlyn Watts*
Circulation 50,000

FOUNDED 1986. QUARTERLY lifestyle magazine featuring homes, interiors, gardening, fashion and beauty, motoring, leisure and dining. Welcome unsolicited mss. All initial approaches should be made in writing.

The Cricketer International
Third Street, Langton Green, Tunbridge
Wells, Kent TN3 0EN
☎01892 862551   Fax 01892 863755
Owner *Ben G. Brocklehurst*
Editor *Peter Perchard*
Circulation 40,000

FOUNDED 1921. MONTHLY. Unsolicited mss considered. Ideas in writing only. No initial discussions by phone. All correspondence should be addressed to the editor.

Cumbria
Dalesman Publishing Co. Ltd, Stable
Courtyard, Broughton Hall, Skipton, North
Yorkshire BD23 3AE
☎01756 701381   Fax 01756 701326
Owner *Dalesman Publishing Co. Ltd*
Editor *Terry Fletcher*
Circulation 15,300

FOUNDED 1951. MONTHLY. County magazine of strong regional and countryside interest only. Unsolicited mss welcome. Maximum 1000 words. Approach in writing or by phone with feature ideas.

Cycle Sport

King's Reach Tower, Stamford Street,
London SE1 9LS
☎0171 261 5588   Fax 0171 261 5758

Owner *IPC Magazines Ltd*
Editor *Andrew Sutcliffe*
Circulation 22,956

Magazine dedicated to professional cycle racing.

Cycling Today

67 Goswell Road, London EC1V 7EN
☎0171 410 9410   Fax 0171 410 9440

Owner *Stonehart Group*
Editor *David Ramsden*
Circulation 30,845

Previously *New Cyclist*. MONTHLY general
interest cycling magazine. Unsolicited feature
proposals welcome. Not interested in personal
accounts such as how you began cycling.

Features Almost any cycling subject. Touring pieces with high-quality transparencies.
Submissions welcomed from writers and illustrators with specialist knowledge: e.g. sports medicine, bike mechanics. NB it may take them
some time to reply. Maximum 2000 words.

Cycling Weekly

King's Reach Tower, Stamford Street,
London SE1 9LS
☎0171 261 5588   Fax 0171 261 5758

Owner *IPC Magazines Ltd*
Editor *Andrew Sutcliffe*
Circulation 38,134

FOUNDED 1891. WEEKLY. All aspects of cycle
sport covered. Unsolicited mss and ideas for
features welcome. Approach in writing with
ideas. Fiction rarely used.

Features Cycle racing, technical material
and related areas. Maximum 2000 words. Most
work commissioned but interested in seeing
new work. *Payment* £60–100 per 1000 words
(quality permitting).

News Short news pieces, local news, etc.
Maximum 300 words. *Payment* £15 per story.

The Dalesman

Stable Courtyard, Broughton Hall, Skipton,
North Yorkshire BD23 3AE
☎01756 701381   Fax 01756 701326

Owner *Dalesman Publishing Co. Ltd*
Editor *Terry Fletcher*
Circulation 57,000

FOUNDED 1939. Now the biggest-selling
regional publication of its kind in the country.
MONTHLY magazine with articles of specific
Yorkshire interest. Unsolicited mss welcome;
receive approximately ten per day. Initial
approach in writing preferred. Maximum 2000
words. *Payment* negotiable.

Dance & Dancers

214 Panther House, 38 Mount Pleasant,
London WC1X 0AP
☎0171 837 2711   Fax 0171 837 2711

Owner *Dance & Dancers Ltd*
Editor *John Percival*

FOUNDED 1950. MONTHLY magazine covering
ballet and modern dance throughout the
world. Some opportunity here for 'good writers with good knowledge of dance', but preliminary discussion is strongly advised. *Payment*
nominal.

Dance Theatre Journal

Laban Centre for Movement & Dance, Laurie
Grove, London SE14 6NH
☎0181 694 9620   Fax 0181 694 8749

Owner *Laban Centre for Movement & Dance*
Editor *Fiona Burnside*

FOUNDED 1983. QUARTERLY. Interested in
features on every aspect of the contemporary
dance scene, particularly issues such as the
funding policy for dance, critical assessments of
choreographers' work and the latest developments in the various schools of contemporary
dance. Unsolicited mss welcome. Length
1000–3000 words. *Payment* varies 'according to
age and experience'.

The Dancing Times

Clerkenwell House, 45–47 Clerkenwell
Green, London EC1R 0EB
☎0171 250 3006   Fax 0171 253 6679

Owner *The Dancing Times Ltd*
Editor *Mary Clarke*

FOUNDED 1910. MONTHLY. Freelance suggestions welcome from specialist dance writers
and photographers only. Approach in writing.

Darts World

9 Kelsey Park Road, Beckenham, Kent
BR3 2LH
☎0181 650 6580   Fax 0181 650 2534

Owner *World Magazines Ltd*
Editor *A. J. Wood*
Circulation 24,500

Features Single articles or series on technique
and instruction. Maximum 1200 words.

Fiction Short stories with darts theme of no
more than 1000 words.

News Tournament reports and general or personality news required. Max. 800 words.
Payment negotiable.

Dateline Magazine
23 Abingdon Road, London W8 6AL
☎0171 938 1011   Fax 0171 937 3146
Owner *John Patterson*
Editor *Peter Bennett/Nicky Boult*
Circulation 23,000

FOUNDED 1976. MONTHLY magazine for single people. Unsolicited mss welcome.

Features Anything of interest to, or directly concerning, single people. Max. 2500 words.

News Items required at least six weeks ahead. Maximum 2500 words.

Payment from £45 per 1000 words; £10 per illustration/picture used (black & white preferred at present).

David Hall's Coarse Fishing Magazine
69 Temple Street, Rugby, Warwickshire CV21 3TB
☎01788 535218   Fax 01788 541845
Owner *Chrisreel Ltd*
Editor *Alan Barnes*
Publisher *David Hall*
Circulation 50,000

FOUNDED 1985. MONTHLY. Unsolicited mss welcome but initial approach by phone or in writing preferred.

Features Any general coarse angling interest accepted. Length 1000–2000 words.

Reviews Product reviews welcome.

Payment variable.

Day by Day
Woolacombe House, 141 Woolacombe Road, Blackheath, London SE3 8QP
☎0181 856 6249
Owner *Loverseed Press*
Editor *Patrick Richards*
Circulation 24,000

FOUNDED 1963. MONTHLY. News commentary and digest of national and international affairs, with reviews of the arts (books, plays, films, opera, musicals) and county cricket reports among regular slots. Unsolicited mss welcome (s.a.e. essential). Approach in writing with ideas. Contributors are advised to study the magazine in the first instance.

News *Ronald Mallone* Interested in themes connected with non-violence and social justice only. Maximum 600 words.

Features No scope for freelance contributions here.

Fiction *Michael Gibson* Very rarely published.

Poems *Michael Gibson* Short poems in line with editorial principles considered. Maximum 20 lines.

Payment negotiable.

Decanter
Priory House, 8 Battersea Park Road, London SW8 4BG
☎0171 627 8181   Fax 0171 738 8688
Editor *Giles Kime*
Circulation 32,000

FOUNDED 1975. Glossy wines and spirits magazine. Unsolicited material welcome but an advance telephone call is appreciated. No fiction.

News/Features All items and articles should concern wines, spirits, food and related subjects.

Derbyshire Life and Countryside
Lodge Lane, Derby DE1 3HE
☎01332 347087   Fax 01332 290688
Owner *B. C. Wood*
Editor *Vivienne Irish*
Circulation 11,719

FOUNDED 1931. MONTHLY county magazine for Derbyshire. Unsolicited mss and photographs of Derbyshire welcome, but written approach with ideas preferred.

Descent
51 Timbers Square, Roath, Cardiff, South Glamorgan CF2 3SH
☎01222 486557   Fax 01222 486557
Owner *Ambit Publications*
Editor *Chris Howes*
Assistant Editor *Judith Calford*

FOUNDED 1969. BI-MONTHLY magazine for cavers and mine enthusiasts. Submissions welcome from freelance contributors who can write accurately and knowledgeably on any aspect of caves, mines or underground structures.

Features General interest articles of under 1000 words welcome, as well as short foreign news reports, especially if supported by photographs/illustrations. Suitable topics include exploration (particularly British, both historical and modern), expeditions, equipment, techniques and regional British news. Maximum 2000 words.

Payment on publication according to page area filled.

Director

Mountbarrow House, Elizabeth Street,
London SW1W 9RB
☎0171 730 8320   Fax 0171 235 5627
Editor *Stuart Rock*
Circulation 40,000

1991 Business Magazine of the Year. Published by The Director Publications Ltd. for the members of the Institute of Directors. Wide range of features from political and business profiles and management thinking to employment and financial issues. Also book reviews. Regular contributors used. Send letter with synopsis/published samples rather than unsolicited mss. Strictly no 'lifestyle' writing. *Payment* negotiable.

Dirt Bike Rider (DBR)

PO Box 100, Stamford, Lincolnshire
PE9 1XQ
☎01780 55131   Fax 01780 57261
Owner *Key Publishing Ltd*
Editor *Mike Greenough*
Circulation 33,000

FOUNDED 1981. MONTHLY. Off-road dirt bikes (motor-cross, endurance, trial and trail). Interested in personality features.

Disability Now

12 Park Crescent, London W1N 4EQ
☎0171 636 5020   Fax 0171 436 4582
Editor *Mary Wilkinson*
Publisher *SCOPE* (Formerly The Spastics Society)
Circulation 25,000

FOUNDED 1984. MONTHLY. Leading publication for disabled people in the UK, reaching those with a wide range of physical disabilities, as well as their families, carers and relevant professionals. No unsolicited material but freelance contributions welcome. Approach in writing.

Features Covering new initiatives and services, personal experiences and general issues of interest to a wide national readership. Maximum 1200 words. Disabled contributors welcomed.

News Maximum 500 words.

Special Pages Possible openings for cartoonists.

Payment by arrangement.

Disabled Driver

DDMC, Cottingham Way, Thrapston,
Northamptonshire NN14 4PL
☎01832 734724   Fax 01832 733816
Owner *Disabled Drivers' Motor Club*
Circulation 14,500 plus

BI-MONTHLY publication of the Disabled Drivers' Motor Club. Includes information for members, members' letters. Approach in writing with ideas. Unsolicited mss welcome.

Dog World

9 Tufton Street, Ashford,
Kent TN23 1QN
☎01233 621877   Fax 01233 645669
Owner *Dog World Ltd*
Editor *Simon Parsons*
Circulation 30,210

FOUNDED 1902. WEEKLY newspaper for people who are seriously interested in pedigree dogs. Unsolicited mss occasionally considered but initial approach in writing preferred.

Features Well-researched historical items or items of unusual interest concerning dogs. Maximum 1000 words. Photographs of unusual 'doggy' situations often of interest. *Payment* up to £50.

News Freelance reports welcome on court cases and local government issues involving dogs.

Fiction Very occasionally.

The Ecologist

Agriculture House, Bath Road, Sturminster Newton, Dorset DT10 1DU
☎01258 473476   Fax 01258 473795
Owner *Ecosystems Ltd*
Co-Editors *Nicholas Hildyard, Sarah Sexton*
Circulation 9000

FOUNDED 1970. BI-MONTHLY. Unsolicited mss welcome but initial approach in writing preferred.

Features Contents tend to be academic, but accessible to the general reader, looking at the social, political, economic and gender aspects of environmental and related issues. Writers are advised to study the magazine for style. Maximum 5000 words.

Payment £20 per 1000 words.

The Economist

25 St James's Street,
London SW1A 1HG
☎0171 830 7000   Fax 0171 839 2968
Owner *Financial Times/individual shareholders*
Editor *Bill Emmott*
Circulation 570,000

FOUNDED 1843. WEEKLY. Worldwide circulation. Approaches should be made in writing to the editor. No unsolicited mss.

Edinburgh Review
22 George Square, Edinburgh EH8 9LF
☎0131 650 4218   Fax 0131 662 0053
Owner *Polygon Books*
Editors *Gavin Wallace, Robert Alan Jamieson*
Circulation 1500

FOUNDED 1969. TWICE YEARLY. Articles and fiction on Scottish and international literary, cultural and philosophical themes. Unsolicited contributions are welcome (1600 are received each year), but prospective contributors are strongly advised to study the magazine first. Allow up to three months for a reply.

Features Interest will be shown in accessible articles on philosophy and its relationship to literature or visual art.

Fiction Scottish and international. Maximum 6000 words.

Education
5 Bentinck Street, London W1M 5RN
☎0171 242 2548   Fax 0171 935 0121
Owner *Pitman Publishing*
Editor *George Low*
Circulation 31,000

WEEKLY journal read by educational administrators and professionals. Interested solely in articles which appeal to these groups. Areas of interest include practical administration and how schools are run, plus comment on the state of administration at the present time. Freelancers used but they tend to be regulars. *Payment* by arrangement.

Electrical Times
Quadrant House, The Quadrant, Sutton, Surrey SM2 5AS
☎0181 652 3115   Fax 0181 652 8972
Owner *Reed Business Publishing*
Editor *Steve Hobson*
Circulation 15,000

FOUNDED 1891. MONTHLY. Aimed at electrical contractors, designers and installers. Unsolicited mss welcome but initial approach preferred.

Elle
20 Orange Street, London WC2H 7ED
☎0171 957 8383   Fax 0171 930 0184
Owner *Hachette/EMAP Consumer Publications*
Editor *Nicola Jeal*
Circulation 220,000

FOUNDED 1985. MONTHLY glossy. Prospective contributors should approach the relevant editor in writing in the first instance, including cuttings.

Features *Sasha Miller* Maximum 2000 words.

News/Insight Short articles on current/cultural events with an emphasis on national, not London-based, readership. Maximum 500 words.

Fashion *Nicola Jeal*
Payment about £350 per 1000 words.

Embroidery
PO Box 42B, East Molesley, Surrey KT8 9BB
☎0181 943 1229   Fax 0181 977 9882
Owner *Embroiderers' Guild*
Editor *Valerie Campbell-Harding*
Circulation 14,500

FOUNDED 1933. QUARTERLY. Features articles on embroidery techniques, historical and foreign embroidery, and specific artists' work with illustrations. Also reviews. Unsolicited mss welcome. Maximum 1000 words. *Payment* negotiable.

Empire
Mappin House, 4 Winsley Street, London W1N 7AR
☎0171 436 1515   Fax 0171 637 7031
Owner *EMAP Metro Publications*
Editor *Philip Thomas*

FOUNDED 1989. Launched at the Cannes Film Festival. MONTHLY guide to the movies which aims to cover the world of films in a 'comprehensive, adult, intelligent and witty package'. Although most of *Empire* is devoted to films and the people behind them, it also looks at the developments and technology behind television and video. Wide selection of in-depth features and stories on all the main releases of the month, and reviews of over 100 films and videos. Contributions welcome but must approach in writing first.

Features Short, behind-the-scenes features on films.
Payment £125 per 1000 words.

The Engineer
30 Calderwood Street, London SE18 6QH
☎0181 855 7777   Fax 0181 316 3040
Owner *Morgan Grampian Ltd*
Editor *Richard Northcote*
Circulation 38,000

FOUNDED 1856. News magazine for engineers and their managers.

Features Most outside contributions are commissioned but good ideas are always welcome. Maximum 2000 words.

News Some scope for specialist regional freelancers, and for tip-offs. Maximum 500 words.

Techscan Technology news from specialists, and tip-offs. Maximum 500 words.
Payment by arrangement.

ES (Evening Standard magazine)
See under **Regional Newspapers**

Escape: The Career and Lifestyle Magazine
113 Abbotts Ann Down, Andover, Hampshire SP11 7BX
☎0126 4710701
Owner *Weavers Press Publishing Ltd*
Editor *Allan Travell*
Circulation 2000

SIX ISSUES YEARLY. Articles, news, features, reviews, personal experience and information for anyone who wants to change jobs and get into a new career or self-employment. Also articles on how to improve one's Quality of Life. Send letter outlining proposal in the first instance. Length 700–1700 words. No work considered unless accompanied by s.a.e. *Payment* £20 per 1000 words.

Esquire
National Magazine House, 72 Broadwick Street, London W1V 2BP
☎0171 439 5000   Fax 0171 439 5067
Owner *National Magazine Co. Ltd*
Editor *Rosie Boycott*
Circulation 96,405

FOUNDED 1991. MONTHLY. Quality men's general interest magazine aimed at readers aged 25–44. No unsolicited mss.

Essentials
King's Reach Tower, Stamford Street, London SE1 9LS
☎0171 261 6970   Fax 0171 261 5262
Owner *IPC Magazines*
Editor *Sue James*
Circulation 421,112

FOUNDED 1988. MONTHLY women's interest magazine. Unsolicited mss (not originals) welcome if accompanied by s.a.e. Initial approach in writing preferred. Prospective contributors should study the magazine thoroughly before submitting anything.
Features *Sarah Barbour* Maximum 2000 words (double-spaced on A4).
Fiction *Carrie Taylor* 'We are looking for something outside the mainstream of romantic fiction, which reflects life in the '90s for busy women in their twenties and thirties. The subject matter should preferably reflect the features

in the rest of the magazine, which could be about credit-card debts, the ozone layer or how to tell if your wardrobe is out of date!' Length 1800–2500 words (double-spaced on A4).
Payment negotiable, but minimum £100 per 1000 words.

Essex Countryside
Griggs Farm, West Street, Coggeshall, Essex CO6 1NT
☎01376 562578   Fax 01376 562578
Owner *Market Link Publishing Ltd*
Editor *Andy Tilbrook*
Circulation 15,000

FOUNDED 1952. MONTHLY. Unsolicited material of Essex interest welcome. No general interest material.
Features Countryside, culture and crafts in Essex. Maximum 1500 words.
Payment £40.

European Medical Journal
PO Box 30, Barnstaple, Devon EX32 9YU
Owner *Dr Vernon Coleman*
Editor *Dr Vernon Coleman*
Circulation 21,000

FOUNDED 1991. OCCASIONAL critical medical review published simultaneously in English and German. Approach in writing after careful study of journal.

Eventing
King's Reach Tower, Stamford Street, London SE1 9LS
☎0171 261 5388   Fax 0171 261 5429
Owner *IPC Magazines Ltd*
Editor *Kate Green*

FOUNDED 1984. MONTHLY. Specialist horse trials magazine. Opportunities for freelance contributions. *Payment* NUJ rates.

Evergreen
PO Box 52, Cheltenham, Gloucestershire GL50 1YQ
☎01242 577775   Fax 01242 222034
Editor *R. Faiers*
Circulation 75,000

FOUNDED 1985. QUARTERLY magazine featuring articles and poems about Britain. Unsolicited contributions welcome.
Features Britain's natural beauty, towns and villages, nostalgia, wildlife, traditions, odd customs, legends, folklore, crafts, etc. Length 250–2000 words.
Payment £20 per 1000 words; poems £5.

Everywoman

9 St Alban's Place, London N1 0NX
☎0171 704 8440/359 5496 Fax 0171 226 9448
Editor *Louisa Saunders*
Circulation 15,000

Feminist magazine providing general news and features geared towards women's interests in current affairs and practical concerns, such as health, employment and relationships, rather than traditional consumer lifestyle pursuits. No short stories please. Contributors must study the magazine, show an understanding of its point of view, and indicate which section submissions are intended for. Approach in writing with a synopsis, not by phone.

Executive Travel

Reed Travel Group, 6 Chesterfield Gardens, London W1Y 8DN
☎0171 355 1600   Fax 0171 355 9630
Owner *Reed Travel Group*
Editor *Mike Toynbee*
Circulation 41,444

FOUNDED 1979. MONTHLY. Aimed specifically at frequent corporate travellers.

The Expatriate

175 Vauxhall Bridge Road, London SW1V 1ER
☎0171 233 8595   Fax 0171 233 8718
Owner *FMI Publishers*
Editor *Vera Madan*
Circulation c. 2000

FOUNDED 1977. MONTHLY. Serves the expatriate community. Unsolicited mss welcome.

Features Special features on working in particular countries, and international travel. Also psychological problems for spouses, education difficulties, pensions, investment and taxation features, health matters.

News Information on special facilities for expatriates, e.g. mail-order presents, financial services, relocation agents, etc.

The Face

3rd Floor, Block A, Exmouth House, Pine Street, London EC1R 0JL
☎0171 837 7270   Fax 0171 837 3906
Owner *Wagadon Ltd*
Editor *Sheryl Garratt*
Fashion Editor *Ashley Heath*
Circulation 100,000

FOUNDED 1980. Magazine of the style generation, concerned with who's what and what's cool. Profiles, interviews and stories. No fiction. Acquaintance with the 'voice' of *The Face* is essential before sending mss on spec.

Features *Richard Benson* New contributors should write to the features editor with their ideas. Maximum 3000 words.
Payment £150 per 1000 words.
Diary No news stories.

Family Circle

King's Reach Tower, Stamford Street, London SE1 9LS
☎0171 261 5000   Fax 0171 261 5929
Owner *IPC Magazines Ltd*
Editor *Gilly Batterbee*
Circulation 310,000

FOUNDED 1964. THIRTEEN ISSUES YEARLY. Little scope for freelancers as most material is produced in-house. Unsolicited material is rarely used, but it is considered. Prospective contributors are best advised to send written ideas to the relevant editor.

Fashion and Beauty *Janine Steggles*
Food and Drink *Sally Mansfield*
Features *Deborah Murdoch* Very little outside work commissioned. Max. 2500–3000 words.
Fiction *Dee Remmington* Short stories of 1000–1500 words. 'No fiction for the moment.'
Home *Caroline Rodriguez*
Payment not less than £100 per 1000 words.

Family Tree Magazine

61 Great Whyte, Ramsey, Huntingdon, Cambridgeshire PE17 1HL
☎01487 814050
Owner *J.M. & M. Armstrong & Partners*
Editorial Director J.M. Armstrong
Circulation 38,000

FOUNDED 1984. MONTHLY. News and features on matters of genealogy. Unsolicited mss considered. Keen to receive articles about unusual sources of genealogical research. Not interested in own family histories. Approach in writing with ideas. All material should be addressed to *Michael Armstrong*.

Features Any genealogically related subject. Maximum 3000 words. No puzzles or fictional articles.
Payment £20 per 1000 words (news/features).

Fancy Fowl & Turkeys

Andover Road, Highclere, Newbury, Berkshire RG15 9PH
☎01635 253239   Fax 01635 254146
Owner *Fancy Fowl Publications Ltd*
Editor *Shirley Murdoch*
Circulation 3000

FOUNDED 1981. Two BI-MONTHLY publications, one specialising in rare poultry and waterfowl, the other in commercial turkey production. *Fancy Fowl* caters for those interested in keeping and exhibiting rare and pure breeds of poultry and waterfowl. Interested in news (maximum 300 words) and features (maximum 800 words) in line with the magazine's content. *Payment* £30 per 1000 words. *Turkeys* aims to deal with all aspects of turkey breeding, growing, processing and marketing at an international level. Specialist technical information from qualified contributors will always be considered. Length by arrangement. No unsolicited mss. Approach in writing with ideas, or by phone. *Payment* £70 per 1000 words.

Farmers Weekly

Quadrant House, Sutton, Surrey SM2 5AS
☎0181 652 4911   Fax 0181 652 4005
Owner *Reed Business Publishing*
Editor *Stephen Howe*
Circulation 97,000

WEEKLY. For practising farmers. Unsolicited mss considered.

Features A wide range of material relating to farmers' problems and interests: specific sections on arable and/or livestock farming, farm life, practical and general interest, machinery and business.
News General interest farming news.
Payment negotiable.

Farming News

Morgan Grampian House, 30 Calderwood Street, London SE18 6QH
☎0181 855 7777   Fax 0181 854 6795
Owner *Morgan Grampian Farming Press Ltd*
Editor *Donald Taylor*
Circulation 74,000

News and features of direct concern to the industry. Freelance writers used occasionally.

Fast Car

Argosy House, 161A-163A High Street, Orpington, Kent BR6 0LW
☎01689 874025   Fax 01689 896847
Owner *Security Publications*
Editor *Danny Morris*
Circulation 60,000

FOUNDED 1987. MONTHLY. Concerned with the modification of road and race vehicles, with technical data and testing results. Unsolicited mss welcome. Approach in writing with ideas. No kit-car features, race reports or road-test reports of standard cars.

Features Innovative ideas in line with the magazine's title – about five pages in length.
News Any item in line with magazine's title. Copy should be as concise as possible.
Payment negotiable.

The Field

King's Reach Tower, Stamford Street, London SE1 9LS
☎0171 261 5198   Fax 0171 261 5358
Owner *IPC Magazines*
Editor *J. Young*
FOUNDED 1853. MONTHLY magazine for those who are serious about the British countryside and its pleasures. Unsolicited mss (and transparencies) welcome but initial approach should be made in writing.

Features Exceptional work on any subject concerning the countryside. Most work tends to be commissioned.
Payment varies.

Film Review

Visual Imagination Ltd, 9 Blades Court, Deodar Road, London SW15 2NU
☎0181 875 1520   Fax 0181 875 1588
Owner *Visual Imagination Ltd*
Editor *David Richardson*
Circulation 50,000

MONTHLY. Reviews, profiles, interviews and special reports on films. Unsolicited material considered.

First Down

The Spendlove Centre, Enstone Road, Charlbury, Chipping Norton, Oxon OX7 3PQ
☎01608 811266   Fax 01608 811380
Owner *UK Sporting Publications*
Editor *Stephen Anglesey*
Circulation 25,000

FOUNDED 1986. WEEKLY American football tabloid paper. Features and news.

Fishkeeping Answers

Bretton Court, Bretton, Peterborough, Cambridgeshire PE3 8DZ
☎01733 264666   Fax 01733 265515
Owner *EMAP Pursuit Publications*
Managing Editor *Steve Windsor*
Circulation 20,000

FOUNDED 1992. MONTHLY. Concerned with all aspects of keeping fish. Unsolicited mss, synopses and ideas welcome. Approach by phone or in writing with ideas. No fiction.

Features Specialist answers to specific fishkeeping problems, breeding, plants, health, etc; aquatic plants and ponds; plus coldwater fish, marine and tropical. 1500 words. Quality fish photographs welcome.

Flight International
Quadrant House, The Quadrant, Sutton, Surrey SM2 5AS
☎0181 652 3882   Fax 0181 652 3840
Owner *Reed Business Publishing*
Editor *Allan Winn*
Circulation 60,000

FOUNDED 1909. WEEKLY. International trade magazine of the aerospace industry, including civil, military and space. Unsolicited mss considered. Commissions preferred – phone with ideas and follow up with letter. E-mail, modem and disc submissions encouraged.
Features *Forbes Mutch* Technically informed articles and pieces on specific geographical areas with international appeal. Analytical, in-depth coverage required, preferably supported by interviews. Maximum 1800 words.
News *Andrew Chuter* Opportunities exist for news pieces from particular geographical areas on specific technical developments. Maximum 350 words.
Payment NUJ rates.

Flora International
46 Merlin Grove, Eden Park, Beckenham, Kent BR3 3HU
☎0181 658 1080
Owner *Maureen Foster*
Editor *Russell Bennett*
Circulation 15,000

FOUNDED 1974. BI-MONTHLY magazine for flower arrangers and florists. Unsolicited mss welcome. Approach in writing with ideas. Not interested in general gardening articles.
Features Fully illustrated, preferably with b&w photos or illustrations/colour transparencies. Flower arranging, flower gardens and flowers. Floristry items written with practical knowledge and well illustrated are particularly welcome. Maximum 2000 words.
Profiles/Reviews Personality profiles and book reviews.
Payment £40 per 1000 words.

FlyPast
PO Box 100, Stamford, Lincolnshire PE9 1XQ
☎01780 55131   Fax 01780 57261
Owner *Key Publishing Ltd*
Editor *Ken Delve*
Circulation 41,742

FOUNDED 1981. MONTHLY. Historic aviation, mainly military and Second World War. Unsolicited mss welcome but initial approach by phone or in writing preferred.

Folk Roots
PO Box 337, London N4 1TW
☎0181 340 9651   Fax 0181 348 5626
Owner *Southern Rag Ltd*
Editor *Ian A. Anderson*
Circulation 14,000

FOUNDED 1979. MONTHLY. Features on folk and roots music, and musicians. Maximum 3000 words.

Football Monthly
15 Mill View Close, Bourne Place, off Kingston Road, Ewell, Surrey KT17 2DW
☎0181 546 0048   Fax 0181 393 2113
Owner *Football Monthly Ltd*
Editor *Tony Flood*
Circulation 28,000

FOUNDED 1951. MONTHLY football magazine. Features, interviews and historical items.

For Women
Portland Publishing, 4 Selsdon Way, London E14 9EL
☎0181 538 8969   Fax 0181 987 0756
Circulation 60,000

FOUNDED 1992. MONTHLY magazine of women's general interest – celebrity interviews, beauty, health and sex, erotic fiction and erotic photography. No homes and gardens articles. Approach in writing in the first instance.
Features Relationships and sex. Maximum 2500 words. *Payment* £150 per 1000 words.
Fiction Erotic short stories. Maximum 2000 words. *Payment* £125 total.

Fortean Times: The Journal of Strange Phenomena
PO Box 2409, London NW5 4NP
☎0171 485 5002   Fax 0171 485 5002
Owners/Editors *Bob Rickard/Paul Sieveking*
Circulation 30,000

FOUNDED 1973. BI-MONTHLY. Accounts of strange phenomena and experiences, curiosities, mysteries, prodigies and portents. Unsolicited mss welcome. Approach in writing with ideas. No fiction, poetry, rehashes or politics.
Features Well-researched and referenced material on current or historical mysteries, or first-hand accounts of oddities. Maximum

3000 words, preferably with good relevant photos/illustrations.

News Concise copy with full source references essential.

Payment negotiable.

Foundation: The Review of Science Fiction

c/o University of York, The King's Manor, York YO1 2EP

☎01904 433915   Fax 01904 433918

Owner *Science Fiction Foundation*
Editor *Dr Edward James*

THRICE-YEARLY publication devoted to the critical study of science fiction.

Payment None.

France Magazine

France House, Digbeth Street, Stow-on-the-Wold, Gloucestershire GL54 1BN

☎01451 831398   Fax 01451 830869

Owner *France Magazine Ltd*
Editor *Philip Faiers*
Circulation 60,000

FOUNDED 1989. QUARTERLY magazine containing all things of interest to Francophiles – in English. No unsolicited mss. Approach with ideas in writing.

Freelance Market News

Cumberland House, Lissadell Street, Salford, Manchester M6 6GG

☎0161 745 8850   Fax 0161 745 8865

Owner *Arthur Waite*
Editor *Saundrea Williams*
Circulation 2200

MONTHLY. News and information on the freelance writers' market, both inland and overseas. Includes market information on competitions, seminars, courses, overseas openings, etc. Unsolicited contributions welcome.

Freelance Writing & Photography

113 Abbotts Ann Down, Andover, Hampshire SP11 7BX

☎0126 4710701

Owner *Weavers Press Publishing Ltd*
Editor *Allan Travell*

Articles, features, reviews, interviews, competitions, tips, hints, market news for the freelance writer and photographer. 250–1000 words. No work considered unless accompanied by s.a.e. Ideas in writing preferred in first instance.

Payment £20 per 1000 words.

The Freelance

NUJ, Acorn House, 314 Gray's Inn Road, London WC1X 8DP

☎0171 278 7916   Fax 0171 837 8143

BI-MONTHLY published by the **National Union of Journalists**. Contributions welcome.

Garden Answers

Apex House, Oundle Road, Peterborough, Cambridgeshire PE2 9NP

☎01733 898100   Fax 01733 898433

Owner *EMAP Apex Publications Ltd*
Editor *Adrienne Wild*
Circulation 186,889

FOUNDED 1982. MONTHLY. 'It is unlikely that unsolicited manuscripts will be used, as writers rarely consider the style and format of the magazine before writing.' Prospective contributors should approach the editor in writing. Interested in hearing from gardening writers on any subject, whether flowers, fruit, vegetables, houseplants or greenhouse gardening.

Garden News

Apex House, Oundle Road, Peterborough, Cambridgeshire PE2 9NP

☎01733 898100   Fax 01733 898433

Owner *EMAP Apex Publications Ltd*
Editor *Andrew Blackford*
Circulation 100,838

FOUNDED 1958. Britain's biggest-selling gardening WEEKLY. News and advice on growing flowers, fruit and vegetables, plus colourful features on all aspects of gardening for the committed gardener. News and features welcome, especially if accompanied by photos or illustrations. Contact the editor before submitting material.

The Gardener Magazine

IPC Magazines Ltd, Westover House, West Quay Road, Poole, Dorset BH15 1JG

☎01202 687418   Fax 01202 674335

Owner *IPC Magazines Ltd*
Editor *Graham Clarke*
Circulation 67,146

FOUNDED 1987. MONTHLY full-colour magazine for those interested in garden design. No unsolicited mss; all articles are commissioned. 'Always approach in writing.'

Gay Times

Worldwide House, 116–134 Bayham Street, London NW1 0BA

☎0171 482 2576   Fax 0171 284 0329

Owner *Millivres Ltd*

Editor *David Smith*
Circulation 40,000

Covers all aspects of gay life, plus general interest likely to appeal to the gay community, art reviews and news. Regular freelance writers used. Unsolicited contributions welcome. Some fiction. *Payment* negotiable.

Gibbons Stamp Monthly

Stanley Gibbons, 5 Parkside, Ringwood, Hampshire BH24 3SH
☎01425 472363   Fax 01425 470247

Owner *Stanley Gibbons Holdings plc*
Editor *Hugh Jefferies*
Circulation 22,000

FOUNDED 1890. MONTHLY. News and features. Unsolicited mss welcome. Make initial approach in writing or by telephone to avoid disappointment.
    Features *Hugh Jefferies* Unsolicited material of specialised nature and general stamp features welcome. Maximum 3000 words but longer pieces can be serialised. *Payment* £20–50 per 1000 words.
    News *Michael Briggs* Any philatelic news item. Maximum 500 words. *No payment.*

Girl About Town

9 Rathbone Street, London W1P 1AF
☎0171 636 6651   Fax 0171 255 2352

Owner *Commuter Publishing Partnership*
Editor *Angela Cooke*
Circulation 100,000

FOUNDED 1972. Free WEEKLY magazine for women aged 16 to 26. Unsolicited mss may be considered. No fiction.
    Features Standards are 'exacting'. Commissions only. Some chance of unknown writers being commissioned and unsolicited material is considered. Maximum 1200 words.
    News Some, including film, music, fashion and beauty. Maximum 200 words.
    Payment negotiable.

Golf Monthly

King's Reach Tower, Stamford Street, London SE1 9LS
☎0171 261 7237   Fax 0171 261 7240

Owner *IPC Magazines Ltd*
Editor *Colin Callander*
Circulation 87,021

FOUNDED 1911. MONTHLY. Player profiles, golf instruction, general golf features and columns. Not interested in instruction material from out-side contributors. Unsolicited mss welcome. Approach in writing with ideas.
    Features Maximum 1500–2000 words. *Payment* by arrangement.

Golf Weekly

Advance House, 37 Millharbour, London E14 9TX
☎0171 538 1031   Fax 0171 537 2053

Owner *EMAP Pursuit Ltd*
Editor *Paul Trow*
Circulation 20,000

FOUNDED 1890. WEEKLY. Unsolicited material welcome from full-time journalists only. For features, approach in writing in first instance; for news, fax or phone.
    Features Maximum 1500 words.
    News Maximum 300 words.
    Payment negotiable.

Golf World

Advance House, 37 Millharbour, London E14 9TX
☎0171 538 1031   Fax 0171 538 4106

Owner *EMAP Pursuit Ltd*
Editor *Robert Green*
Circulation 92,122

FOUNDED 1962. MONTHLY. No unsolicited mss. Approach in writing with ideas.

Good Food Retailing

Stanstead Publications, Edwards House, 2 Alric Avenue, New Malden, Surrey KT3 4JN
☎0181 336 0558   Fax 0181 336 0672

Owner *Robert Farrand*
Editor *Jennifer Muir*
Circulation 8500

FOUNDED 1980. TEN ISSUES YEARLY. Serves the food retailing industry. No budget for freelance material.

Good Holiday Magazine

91 High Street, Esher, Surrey KT10 9QD
☎01372 468140   Fax 01372 470765

Editor *John Hill*
Circulation 100,000

FOUNDED 1985. QUARTERLY. aimed at better-off holiday-makers rather than travellers. Worldwide destinations including Europe and domestic. Any queries regarding work/commissioning must be in writing. Copy must be precise and well-researched – the price of everything from coffee and tea to major purchases are included along with exchange rates, etc. *Payment* negotiable.

Good Housekeeping

National Magazine House, 72 Broadwick Street, London W1V 2BP
☎0171 439 5000   Fax 0171 439 5591
Owner *National Magazine Co. Ltd*
Editor-in-Chief *Sally O'Sullivan*
Circulation 518,435

FOUNDED 1922. MONTHLY glossy. No unsolicited mss. Write with ideas in the first instance to the appropriate editor.

Features *Hilary Robinson* Most work is commissioned but original ideas are always welcome. Send short synopsis, plus relevant cuttings, showing previous examples of work published. No unsolicited mss.

Fiction *Hilary Robinson* No unsolicited mss.

Entertainment *Alison Pylkkänen* Three pages of reviews and previews on film, television, theatre and art.

Good Ski Guide

91 High Street, Esher, Surrey KT10 9QD
☎01372 468140   Fax 01372 470765
Owner *Paula Hill*
Editor *John Hill*
Circulation 350,000

FOUNDED 1976. QUARTERLY. Unsolicited mss welcome from writers with a knowledge of skiing and ski resorts. Prospective contributors are best advised to make initial contact in writing as ideas and work need to be seen before any discussion can take place. *Payment* negotiable.

Good Stories

23 Mill Crescent, Kingsbury, Warwickshire B78 2LX
☎01827 873435
Owner *Oakwood Publications*
Editor *Andrew Jenns*
Circulation 5000

FOUNDED 1990. QUARTERLY of A5 format featuring up to 20 short stories in each issue, plus crossword, letters and various filler columns. Mss welcome but have to be accompanied by a coupon from the magazine at certain times if there is a backlog of unpublished stories. Contributors are advised to study the magazine's style in the first instance. No poetry.

Fiction Short stories of any kind. Maximum 2500 words but shorter (1000 words or less) always preferred. *Payment* up to about £30 per story.

Genuine Mystery Articles Short articles on any unexplained mystery, up to 1000 words.

Special Pages Readers' Letters: preferably humorous. Maximum 100 words. Crosswords: not too complex and suitable for use as Prize Crosswords; also other word puzzle games from time to time. Fillers: short and humorous, based on true-life incidents. Maximum 250 words; plus cartoons. *Payment* up to £10 for genuine mystery articles; up to £5 for readers' letters; £5-10 for crosswords depending on complexity; up to £10 for fillers (small non-cash prizes sometimes awarded instead of cash payment for letters and short fillers).

GQ

Vogue House, Hanover Square, London W1R 0AD
☎0171 499 9080   Fax 0171 495 1679
Owner *Condé Nast Publications Ltd*
Editor *Michael VerMeulen*
Circulation 109,235

FOUNDED 1988. MONTHLY. No unsolicited material. Phone or write with an idea in the first instance.

Commissioning   Editors   *Jessany Calkin/Philip Watson*

Special Pages *John Morgan* Small news, grooming and style items.

Gramophone

177-179 Kenton Road, Harrow, Middlesex HA3 0HA
☎0181 907 4476   Fax 0181 907 0073
Owner *General Gramophone Publications Ltd*
Editor *James Jolly*
Circulation 65,941

Classical music magazine, of which 95% is reviews. At any time they are using around 50 regular freelance writers, who provide classical music reviews and, on occasion, features or interviews. Reviewing is the starting place on the magazine, however. Submit samples of published work to the editor.

Granta

2–3 Hanover Yard, Noel Road, London N1 8BE
☎0171 704 9776   Fax 0171 704 0474
Editor *Ian Jack*
Managing Director *Catherine Eccles*

QUARTERLY. Literature and politics magazine published in paperback book form in association with **Penguin**. Highbrow, diverse and contemporary, with a thematic approach. Unsolicited mss (including fiction) considered. A lot of material is commissioned. Important to read the magazine first to appreciate its very particular fusion of cultural and political interests. No reviews. *Payment* negotiable.

The Great Outdoors
See **TGO**

Guardian Weekend
See under **National Newspapers (The Guardian)**

Guiding
17–19 Buckingham Palace Road,
London SW1W 0PT
☎0171 834 6242   Fax 0171 828 8317
Owner *The Guide Association*
Editor *Nora Warner*
Circulation 31,000

FOUNDED 1914. MONTHLY. Unsolicited mss welcome provided topics relate to the movement and/or women's role in society. Ideas in writing appreciated in first instance.

Features Topics that can be useful in the Guide programme, or special interest features with Guide link. Maximum 1300 words.

News Guide activities. Max. 100–150 words.

Special Pages Outdoor activity, information pieces, Green issues. Max. 1400 words.

Payment £70 per 1000 words.

Hair
King's Reach Tower, Stamford Street,
London SE1 9LS
☎0171 261 6975   Fax 0171 261 7382
Owner *IPC Magazines Ltd*
Editor *Annette Dennis*
Circulation 154,957

FOUNDED 1980. BI-MONTHLY hair and beauty magazine. No unsolicited mss, but always interested in good photographs. Approach with ideas in writing.

Features *Jacki Wadeson/Sharon Christal* Fashion pieces on hair trends. Maximum 1000 words. *Payment* £150.

Hairflair
4th Floor, 27 Maddox Street,
London W1R 9LE
☎0171 493 1081   Fax 0171 499 6686
Owner *Hairflair Publishing Ltd*
Editor *Hellena Barnes*
Circulation 47,756

FOUNDED 1982. MONTHLY. Original and interesting hair-related features written in a young, lively style to appeal to a readership aged 16–35 years. Unsolicited mss not wel-

come, but as the magazine is expanding new ideas are encouraged. Write to the editor.

Features Hair and beauty. Maximum 1000 words. *Payment* £150 per 1000 words.

Harpers & Queen
National Magazine House, 72 Broadwick Street, London W1V 2BP
☎0171 439 5000   Fax 0171 439 5506
Owner *National Magazine Co. Ltd*
Editor *Fiona Macpherson*
Circulation 85,000

MONTHLY. Up-market glossy combining the Sloaney and the streetwise. Approach in writing (not phone) with ideas.

Features *Anthony Gardner/Carey Sedgwick* Ideas only in the first instance.

Fiction *Selina Hastings* Literary fiction only welcome. Maximum 3000 words.

News Snippets welcome if very original. *Payment* negotiable.

Health & Fitness Magazine
50 Doughty Street, London WC1N 2LP
☎0171 405 2055   Fax 0171 405 6528
Owner *HHL Publishing Group Ltd*
Editor *Sharon Walker*
Circulation 65,000

FOUNDED 1983. MONTHLY. Will consider ideas; approach in writing in the first instance.

Health and Efficiency
1st Floor, 64 Great Eastern Street,
London EC2A 3QR
☎0171 739 5052   Fax 0171 729 8053
Owner *Peenhill Publishers Ltd*
Editor *Kate Sturdy*
Circulation 120,000

FOUNDED 1900. MONTHLY, QUARTERLY and BI-ANNUAL editions in three languages. Preliminary letter advised for prospective contributors.

Features Naturist travel, preferably accompanied by photos; human and sexual relationships; personal experiences of nudity, naturism or relationship problems; plus occasional food, health and fitness features. Maximum 2000 words (1000 preferred). *Payment* negotiable.

Health Education
MCB University Press, 60–62 Toller Lane, Bradford, West Yorkshire 6DB 9BY
☎01274 499821   Fax 01274 547143
Owner *MCB University Press*
Editor *Sharon Kingman*
Circulation 2000

FOUNDED 1992. SIX ISSUES YEARLY. Health education magazine with a strong emphasis on schools and young people. Professional readership. Most copy commissioned; ideas considered.

Health Shopper/Now
The Old Auction Mart, Station Approach, Godalming, Surrey GU7 1EU
☎01483 860116   Fax 01483 860938
Owner *Nigel Cross*
Editor *Nigel Cross*
Circulation 250,000

FOUNDED 1977. BI-MONTHLY. Unsolicited mss welcome only if related to the specialised interests of the magazine in encouraging a healthy lifestyle and increased awareness of alternative therapies. Prospective contributors are advised to make their first approach in writing.

Hello!
Wellington House, 69–71 Upper Ground, London SE1 9PQ
☎0171 334 7404   Fax 0171 334 7412
Owner *Hola!* (Spain)
Editor *Maggie Koumi*
Circulation 453,746

WEEKLY. Owned by a Madrid-based publishing family, Hello! has grown faster than any other British magazine since its launch here in 1988 and continues to grow despite the recession. The magazine is printed in Madrid, with editorial offices both there and in London. Major colour features plus regular b&w news and local interest pages. Although much of the material is provided by regulars, good proposals do stand a chance. Approach with ideas in the first instance. No unsolicited mss.

Features Interested in personality-based features, often with a newsy angle, and exclusive interviews from generally unapproachable personalities.
Payment by arrangement.

Here's Health
EMAP Elan, 20 Orange Street, London WC2H 7ED
☎0171 957 8383   Fax 0171 930 4637
Owner *EMAP Consumer Magazines Ltd*
Editor *Erika Harvey*
Circulation 36,235

FOUNDED 1956. MONTHLY. Full-colour magazine dealing with alternative medicine, nutrition, natural health, wholefoods, supplements, organics and the environment. Prospective contributors should bear in mind that this is a specialist magazine with a pronounced bias towards alternative/complementary medicine, using expert contributors on the whole.
Features Length varies.
Payment negotiable.

Heritage
4 The Courtyard, Denmark Street, Wokingham, Berkshire RG11 2AZ
☎01734 771677   Fax 01734 772903
Owner *Bulldog Magazines*
Editor *Sian Ellis*
Circulation 70,000

FOUNDED 1984. BI-MONTHLY. Unsolicited mss welcome. Interested in complete packages of written features with high-quality transparencies – words or pictures on their own also accepted. Not interested in poetry, fiction or non-British themes. Approach in writing with ideas.

Features on British villages, tours, towns, castles, gardens, traditions, crafts, historical themes and people. Maximum length 1200–1500 words. *Payment* approx. £100 per 1000 words.

News Small pieces – usually picture stories in Diary section. Limited use. Maximum length 200–250 words. *Payment* £20–£30.

Heritage Scotland
5 Charlotte Square, Edinburgh EH2 4DU
☎0131 243 9510   Fax 0131 243 9501
Owner *National Trust for Scotland*
Editor *Peter Reekie*
Circulation 141,214

FOUNDED 1983. QUARTERLY magazine containing heritage/conservation features. No unsolicited mss.

Hi-Fi News & Record Review
Link House, Dingwall Avenue, Croydon, Surrey CR9 2TA
☎0181 686 2599   Fax 0181 781 6046
Owner *Link House Magazines Ltd*
Editor *Steve Harris*
Circulation 30,012

FOUNDED 1956. MONTHLY. Write in the first instance with suggestions based on knowledge of the magazine's style and subject. All articles must be written from an informed technical or enthusiast viewpoint.
Music *Christopher Breunig*
Payment negotiable, according to technical content.

High Life
Haymarket House, 1 Oxendon Street, London SW1Y 4EE
☎0171 925 2544   Fax 0171 839 4508

Owner *Premier Magazines*
Editor *William Davis*
Circulation *c.* 275,000

FOUNDED 1973. MONTHLY glossy. British Airways in-flight magazine. Almost all the content is commissioned. No unsolicited mss. Few opportunities for freelancers.

Home & Country
104 New Kings Road, London SW6 4LY
☎0171 731 5777   Fax 0171 736 4061
Owner *National Federation of Women's Institutes*
Editor *Penny Kitchen*
Circulation 90,000

FOUNDED 1919. MONTHLY. Official full-colour journal of the Federation of Women's Institutes, containing articles on a wide range of subjects of interest to women. Strong environmental country slant with crafts and cookery plus gardening appearing every month. Unsolicited mss, photos and illustrations welcome. *Payment* by arrangement.

Home & Family
Mary Sumner House, 24 Tufton Street, London SW1P 3RB
☎0171 222 5533   Fax 0171 222 5533
Owner *The Mothers' Union*
Editor *Margaret Duggan*
Circulation 90,000

FOUNDED 1976. QUARTERLY. Unsolicited mss considered. No fiction or poetry.
    Features Family life, social problems, marriage, Christian faith, etc. Maximum 1000 words. *Payment* modest.

Homebrew Supplier
304 Northridge Way, Hemel Hempstead, Hertfordshire HP1 2AB
☎01442 67228   Fax 01442 67228
Owner *Homebrew Publications*
Editor *Evelyn Barrett*
Circulation 2100

FOUNDED 1960. QUARTERLY trade magazine. Unsolicited mss welcome.

Homebrew Today
304 Northridge Way, Hemel Hempstead, Hertfordshire HP1 2AB
☎01442 67228   Fax 01442 67228
Owner *Homebrew Publications*
Editor *Evelyn Barrett*
Circulation 150,000

FOUNDED 1986. QUARTERLY. Articles on all aspects of home brewing and the use of home-made wine in cooking, etc. Unsolicited mss welcome.

Homes & Gardens
King's Reach Tower, Stamford Street, London SE1 9LS
☎0171 261 5678   Fax 0171 261 6247
Owner *IPC Magazines Ltd/Reed Publishing*
Editor *Amanda Evans*
Circulation 180,100

FOUNDED 1919. MONTHLY. Almost all published articles are specially commissioned. No fiction or poetry. Best to approach in writing with an idea.

Horse & Pony Magazine
Bretton Court, Bretton, Peterborough, Cambridgeshire PE3 8DZ
☎01733 264666   Fax 01733 261984
Owner *EMAP Pursuit Publications*
Editor *Andrea Oakes*
Circulation 60,562

Magazine for young (aged 10–16) owners and 'addicts' of the horse. Features include pony care, riding articles and celebrity pieces. Some interest in freelancers but most feature material is produced by staff writers.

Horse and Hound
King's Reach Tower, Stamford Street, London SE1 9LS
☎0171 261 6315   Fax 0171 261 5429
Owner *IPC Magazines Ltd*
Editor-in-Chief *Michael Clayton*
Circulation 78,803

WEEKLY. The oldest equestrian magazine on the market, now re-launched with modern make-up and colour pictures throughout. Contains regular veterinary advice and instructional articles, as well as authoritative news and comment on fox hunting, international showjumping, horse trials, dressage, driving and cross-country riding. Also weekly racing and point-to-points, breeding reports and articles. The magazine includes a monthly pull-out section called *Pony Club*. Regular books and art reviews, and humorous articles and cartoons are frequently published. Plenty of opportunities for freelancers. Unsolicited contributions welcome.
    Now also publishes a sister monthly publication, *Eventing*, which covers the sport of horse trials comprehensively.
    Payment NUJ rates.

Horse and Rider

296 Ewell Road, Surbiton, Surrey KT6 7AQ
☎0181 390 8547   Fax 0181 390 8696
Owner *D. J. Murphy (Publishers) Ltd*
Editor *Alison Bridge*
Circulation 39,000

FOUNDED 1949. MONTHLY. Adult readership, largely horse-owning. News and instructional features, which make up the bulk of the magazine, are almost all commissioned. New contributors and unsolicited mss are occasionally used. Approach the editor in writing with ideas.

Horticulture Week

38–42 Hampton Road, Teddington,
Middlesex TW11 0JE
☎0181 943 5000   Fax 0181 943 5673
Owner *Haymarket Magazines Ltd*
Editor *Stovin Hayter*
Circulation 11,000

FOUNDED 1841. WEEKLY. Specialist magazine involved in the supply of business-type information. No unsolicited mss. Approach in writing in first instance.
Features No submissions without prior discussion. *Payment* negotiable.
News *Hooman Bassirian* Information about horticultural businesses – nurseries, garden centres, landscapers and parks departments in the various regions of the UK. No gardening stories.

House & Garden

Vogue House, Hanover Square,
London W1R 0AD
☎0171 499 9080   Fax 0171 629 2907
Owner *Condé Nast Publications Ltd*
Editor *Susan Crewe*
Circulation 150,000

Most feature material is produced in-house but occasional specialist features are commissioned from qualified freelancers, mainly for the architectural or wine and food sections.
Features *Leonie Highton* Suggestions for features, preferably in the form of brief outlines of proposed subjects, will be considered.

House Beautiful

National Magazine House, 72 Broadwick Street, London W1V 2BP
☎0171 439 5000   Fax 0171 439 5595
Owner *National Magazine Co. Ltd*
Editor *Pat Roberts Cairns*
Circulation 320,396

FOUNDED 1989. MONTHLY. Lively magazine offering sound, practical information and plenty of inspiration for those who want to make the most of where they live. Over 100 pages of easy reading editorial. Regular features about decoration, DIY and home finance. Contact the editor with ideas.

House Buyer

137 George Lane, South Woodford,
London E18 1AJ
☎0181 532 9299   Fax 0181 532 9329
Owner *Brittain Publications*
Editor *Con Crowley*
Circulation 18,000

FOUNDED 1955. MONTHLY magazine with features and articles for house buyers, including retirement homes, mortgage information, etc. A 32-page section includes details of over 200,000 new homes throughout the UK. Unsolicited mss will neither be read nor returned.

ID Magazine

Universal House, 251–255 Tottenham Court Road, London W1P 0AE
☎0171 813 6170   Fax 0171 813 6179
Owner *Levelprint*
Editor *Avril Mair*
Circulation *c.* 45,000

FOUNDED 1980. MONTHLY lifestyle magazine for both sexes aged 16–24. Very hip. 'We are always looking for freelance writers with new or unusual ideas.' A different theme each issue – past themes include Green politics, taste, films, sex, love and loud dance music – means it is advisable to discuss feature ideas in the first instance.

Ideal Home

King's Reach Tower, Stamford Street,
London SE1 9LS
☎0171 261 6474   Fax 0171 261 6697
Owner *IPC Magazines Ltd*
Editor *Terence Whelan*
Circulation 226,316

FOUNDED 1920. MONTHLY glossy. Unsolicited feature articles are welcome if appropriate to the magazine (one or two are received each week). Prospective contributors wishing to submit ideas should do so in writing to the editor. No fiction.
Features Furnishing and decoration of houses, kitchens or bathrooms; interior design, soft furnishings, furniture and home improvements, etc. Length to be discussed with editor. *Payment* negotiable.

The Illustrated London News
20 Upper Ground, London SE1 9PF
☎0171 928 2111   Fax 0171 620 1594
Owner *James Sherwood*
Editor-in-Chief *James Bishop*
Circulation 47,547

FOUNDED 1842. Although the *ILN* covers issues concerning the whole of the UK, its emphasis remains on the capital and its life. Travel, wine, restaurants, events, cultural and current affairs are all covered but the magazine now only publishes the occasional special issue. There are few opportunities for freelancers but all unsolicited mss are read (receives about 20 a week). The best approach is with an idea in writing. Particularly interested in articles relating to events and developments in contemporary London, and about people working in the capital. All features are illustrated, so ideas with picture opportunities are particularly welcome.

Impact Journal
10 Victoria Terrace, Dundrum, Dublin 14, Republic of Ireland
☎00 353 1 2980310   Fax 00 353 1 2986237
Publisher *The Brothers of Charity*
Editor *Brian McCarthy*

FOUNDED 1968. QUARTERLY. Articles of interest to parents of children with learning disability and professionals in the field of learning disability formerly referred to as 'mental handicap'.

In Britain
Haymarket House, 1 Oxendon Street, London SW1Y 4EE
☎0717 976 1515   Fax 0171 976 1088
Owner *HHL Publishing*
Editor *Andrea Spain*
Circulation 29,853

MONTHLY. Travel and leisure magazine. No unsolicited mss. Approach in writing with ideas. Articles vary from 800–1500 words in length.

The Independent Magazine
See under **National Newspapers (The Independent)**

Infusion
16 Trinity Churchyard, Guildford, Surrey GU1 3RR
☎01483 62888   Fax 01483 302732
Publisher *Bond Clarkson Russell*
Editor *Lorna Swainson*
Circulation 800,000

FOUNDED 1986. THREE ISSUES YEARLY. Sponsored by the Tea Council. Features women's general interest, health, leisure and all subjects related to tea. All editorial features are commissioned. Approach with ideas only in writing.

InterCity
Redwood Publishing, 12–26 Lexington Street, London W1R 4HQ
☎0171 312 2600   Fax 0171 312 2601
Owner *Abbott Mead Vickers/BBDO*
Editor *Sophie Hanscombe*
Deputy Editor *Victoria Saer*
Circulation 70,000

FOUNDED 1985. TEN ISSUES YEARLY. Complimentary business magazine distributed to first-class passengers on InterCity rail routes. Contributions welcome on management, the executive lifestyle and leisure (sport, shopping, etc). Approach by phone with idea and follow up by letter, enclosing cuttings if work unknown to the editor.

Interzone: Science Fiction & Fantasy
217 Preston Drive, Brighton, East Sussex BN1 6FL
☎01273 504710
Owner *David Pringle*
Editor *David Pringle*
Circulation 10,000

FOUNDED 1982. MONTHLY magazine of science fiction and fantasy. Unsolicited mss are welcome 'only from writers who have a knowledge of the magazine and its contents'. S.a.e. essential for return.
    Fiction 2000–6000 words. *Payment* £30 per 1000 words.
    Features Book/film reviews, interviews with writers and occasional short articles. Length by arrangement. *Payment* negotiable.

Investors Chronicle
Greystoke Place, Fetter Lane, London EC4A 1ND
☎0171 405 6969   Fax 0171 405 5276
Owner *Financial Times*
Editor *Ceri Jones*
Surveys Editor *Christina Nordenstahl*
Circulation 64,000

FOUNDED 1861. WEEKLY. Opportunities for freelance contributors in the survey section only. All approaches should be made in writing. Over forty surveys are published each year on a wide variety of subjects, generally with a financial, business or investment emphasis.

Copies of survey list and synopses of individual surveys are obtainable from the surveys editor. *Payment* from £100.

Irish Optician
9 Victoria Terrace, Dundrum, Dublin 14, Republic of Ireland
☎00 353 1 2980310   Fax 00 353 1 2986237
Publisher *Irish Optician Ltd*
Editor *Brian McCarthy*

FOUNDED 1990. QUARTERLY. Full-colour journal on optometry. Particular articles and papers on contact lens work. Reports on optometrists and dispensing conventions, nationally and internationally. *Payment* £50 per 1000 words.

Jane's Defence Weekly
Sentinel House, 163 Brighton Road, Coulsdon, Surrey CR5 2NH
☎0181 763 1030   Fax 0181 763 1007
Owner *Jane's Information Group*
Publishing Director *Simon Kay*
Editor *Peter Howard*
Circulation 25,827

FOUNDED 1984. WEEKLY. No unsolicited mss. Approach in writing with ideas in the first instance.

Features Current defence topics (politics, strategy, equipment, industry) of worldwide interest. No history pieces. Max. 2000 words. *Payment* minimum £100 per 1000 words.

Jazz Journal International
1–5 Clerkenwell Road, London EC1M 5PA
☎0171 608 1348   Fax 0171 608 1292
Owner *Jazz Journal Ltd*
Editor-in-Chief *Eddie Cook*
Circulation 12,000

FOUNDED 1948. MONTHLY. A specialised jazz magazine, mainly for record collectors, principally using expert contributors whose work is known to the editor. Unsolicited mss not welcome, with the exception of news material (for which no payment is made). It is not a gig guide, nor a free reference source for students.

Jewish Chronicle
25 Furnival Street, London EC4A 1JT
☎0171 405 9252   Fax 0171 405 9040
Owner *Kessler Foundation*
Editor *Edward J. Temko*
Circulation 50,000

Unsolicited mss welcome if 'the specific interests of our readership are borne in mind by writers'. Approach in writing, except for urgent current news items. No fiction. Maximum 2000 words for all material. Same policy applies for colour supplement.
  Features *Gerald Jacobs*
  Leisure/Lifestyle *Alan Montague*
  Home News *Barry Toberman*
  Foreign News *Joseph Millis*
  Supplements *Angela Kiverstein*
  Payment negotiable.

Jewish Quarterly
PO Box 1148, London NW5 2AZ
☎0171 485 4062(admin)/0181 361 6372(edit)
Owner *Jewish Literary Trust Ltd*
Editor *Elena Lappin*

FOUNDED 1953. QUARTERLY. Featuring Jewish literature and fiction, politics, art, music, film, poetry, history, dance, community, autobiography, Hebrew, Yiddish, Israel and the Middle East, Judaism, interviews, Zionism, philosophy and holocaust studies. Also book reviews. Unsolicited mss welcome but letter or phone call preferred in first instance.

Johnny Miller 96 Not Out
9 Whitehall Park, Highgate, London N19 3TS
☎0171 561 1606   Fax 0171 561 1607
Owner *Two Heads Publishing*
Editor *David Cotton*
Circulation 9000

MONTHLY cricket magazine styled as 'the essential word on cricket today'. Welcome approaches from potential contributors who have something new and, preferably, humorous to say about cricket today.

Just Seventeen
20 Orange Street, London WC2H 7ED
☎0171 957 8383   Fax 0171 930 5728
Owner *EMAP Metro Publications*
Editor *Toni Rodgers*
Circulation 265,000

FOUNDED 1983. WEEKLY. Top of the mid-teen market, with news, articles and fiction of interest to girls aged 12–18. Ideas are sought in all areas. Prospective contributors should send ideas to the relevant editorial department, then follow up with a phone call.
  Beauty *Maria Deevoy*
  Features *Sarah Bailey/Harvey Marcus*
  Fiction *Joanna Briscoe* Maximum 2000 words.
  Music *Piers Wenger*
  News *Sophie Wilson*
  Payment by arrangement.

Kennel Gazette

Kennel Club, 1–5 Clarges Street, Piccadilly,
London W1Y 8AB
☎0171 493 6651   Fax 0171 495 6162

Owner *Kennel Club*
Editor *Charles Colborn*
Circulation 10,000

FOUNDED 1873. MONTHLY concerning dogs
and their breeding. Unsolicited mss welcome.
   Features Maximum 2500 words.
   News Maximum 500 words.
   Payment £70 per 1000 words.

Kent Life

Datateam House, Tovil Hill, Maidstone, Kent
ME15 6QS
☎01622 687031   Fax 01622 757646

Editor *Roderick Cooper*
Publisher *Datateam Publishing*
Circulation 10,000

FOUNDED 1962. MONTHLY. Strong Kent interest plus fashion, food, books, wildlife, motoring, property, sport, interiors with local links.
Unsolicited mss welcome. Interested in anything with a genuine Kent connection. No fiction or non-Kentish subjects. Approach in
writing with ideas. Maximum length 1500
words. *Payment* negotiable.

Keyboard Review

Alexander House, Forehill, Ely,
Cambridgeshire CB7 4AF
☎01353 665577   Fax 01353 662489

Owner *Music Maker Publications*
Editor *Sam Molineaux*
Circulation 18,000

FOUNDED 1985. MONTHLY. Broad-based keyboard magazine, covering organs, pianos, key-
boards, synthesisers, MIDI keyboard, add-ons
such as samplers and modules, and their players. Approach by phone or in writing with
ideas.
   Features *Sally Frances* Interviews with keyboard players and instrument reviews.
Maximum 3000 words.
   News *Beck Laxton* Brief items on keyboard
world. Maximum 400 words.
   Payment negotiable.

The Lady

39–40 Bedford Street, Strand,
London WC2E 9ER
☎0171 379 4717   Fax 0171 497 2137

Owner *T. G. A. Bowles*
Editor *Arline Usden*

Circulation 66,000

FOUNDED 1885. WEEKLY. Unsolicited mss are
accepted provided they are not on the subject
of politics or religion, or on topics covered by
staff writers, i.e. fashion and beauty, health,
cookery, household, gardening, finance and
shopping.
   Features Well-researched pieces on British
and foreign travel, historical subjects or events;
interviews and profiles and other general interest topics. Maximum 1000 words for illustrated
articles; 900 words for one-page features; 450
words for first-person 'Viewpoint' pieces. All
material should be addressed to the editor.
Payment £60 per 1000 words printed.
   Photographs supporting features may be
supplied as colour transparencies or b&w
prints. *Payment* £14–18 per picture used.

Land Rover World Magazine

Link House, Dingwall Road, Croydon, Surrey
CR9 2TA
☎0181 686 2599   Fax 0181 781 6042

Owner *Link House Magazines Ltd*
Editor *Alan Kidd*
Circulation 30,000

FOUNDED 1993. MONTHLY. Unsolicited mss
welcome, especially if supported by high-quality illustrations. Best, however, to make initial
contact by letter or telephone.
   Features *Alan Kidd* All articles with a Land
Rover theme of interest. Potential contributors
are strongly advised to examine previous issues
before starting work.
   Payment negotiable.

Learning Resources Journal

11 Malford Grove, Gilwern, Abergavenny,
Gwent NP7 0RN
☎01873 830872

Owner *Learning Resources Development Group*
Editor *David P. Bosworth*
Circulation 600

THRICE-YEARLY publication on the organisation of resources in schools and colleges, which
aims to enhance learning in general.
Unsolicited mss welcome. Interested in
descriptions of classroom/lab/workshop practice and in new resource sources such as
telelink/satellite communication; the application of educational technology to the learning
situation; European outlooks, etc. Maximum
2500 words (news pieces 100 words). Ideas
should be discussed with the editor – sample
copy available. *No payment.*

Liberal Democrat News

4 Cowley Street, London SW1P 3NB
☎0171 222 7999   Fax 0171 222 7904

Owner *Liberal Democrats*
Editor *David Boyle*

FOUNDED 1988. WEEKLY. As with the political parties, this is the result of the merger of *Liberal News* (1946) and *The Social Democrat* (1981). Political and social topics of interest to party members and their supporters. Unsolicited contributions welcome.

Features Maximum 800 words.
News Maximum 350 words.
No payment.

Lincolnshire Life

County Life Ltd, PO Box 81, Lincoln LN1 1HD
☎01522 527127   Fax 01522 560035

Publisher *A.L. Robinson*
Executive Editor *Jez Ashberry*
Circulation 10,000

FOUNDED 1962. MONTHLY county magazine featuring geographically relevant articles. Max. 1000–1500 words. Contributions supported by 3 or 4 good-quality photographs are always welcome. Approach in writing. *Payment varies.*

The List

14 High Street, Edinburgh EH1 1TE
☎0131 558 1191   Fax 0131 557 8500

Owner *The List Ltd*
Publisher *Robin Hodge*
Editor *Lila Rawlings*
Circulation 12,000

FOUNDED 1985. FORTNIGHTLY. Arts and events guide covering Glasgow and Edinburgh. Interviews and profiles of people working in film, theatre, music and the arts. Maximum 1200 words. Not interested in anything not related to the arts or to life in Central Scotland. No unsolicited mss. Phone with ideas. News material tends to be handled in-house. *Payment £70.*

Literary Review

51 Beak Street, London W1R 3LF
☎0171 437 9392   Fax 0171 734 1844

Owner *Namara Group*
Editor *Auberon Waugh*
Circulation 15,000

FOUNDED 1979. MONTHLY. Publishes book reviews (commissioned), features and articles on literary subjects. Prospective contributors should contact the editor in writing. Unsolicited mss not welcome. Runs a monthly competition, the Literary Review Grand Poetry Competition, on a given theme. Open to subscribers only. Details published in the magazine. *Payment varies.*

Living

King's Reach Tower, Stamford Street, London SE1 9LS
☎0171 261 5000   Fax 0171 261 6892

Owner *IPC Magazines Ltd*
Editor *Sharon Brown*
Circulation 142,616

FOUNDED 1968. MONTHLY. Women's and family interest glossy magazine sold at supermarket checkouts and newsagents. Features are commissioned from freelance writers. Wide-ranging feature needs include real life stories, medical issues, successful women in small business-type one-offs, and major issues (divorce, drugs, etc.). *Payment by arrangement.*

Living France

Gairnside House, Gate End, Northwood, Middlesex HA6 3QG
☎01923 828100   Fax 01923 836572

Editor *Trevor Yorke*

FOUNDED 1989. MONTHLY. For francophiles and people wishing to buy property in France. No unsolicited mss except perhaps for readers' page material. Approach in writing with an idea.

Llais Llyfrau/Books in Wales

Cyngor Llyfrau Cymraeg/Welsh Books Council, Castell Brychan, Aberystwyth, Dyfed SY23 2JB
☎01970 624151   Fax 01970 625385

Owner *Cyngor Llyfrau Cymraeg/Welsh Books Council*
Editors *R. Gerallt Jones, Katie Gramich, D. Geraint Lewis*

FOUNDED 1961. QUARTERLY bilingual magazine containing articles of relevance to the book trade in Wales plus reviews of new books and comprehensive lists of recent titles. A complete section devoted to children's books appears every quarter. No unsolicited mss. All initial approaches should be made in writing.

Features *R. Geraint Jones* (Welsh)/*Katie Gramich* (English) Each edition features a writer's diary in Welsh and English, plus articles on books, publishing, the media etc. Most items commissioned. Articles on the literature of Wales are welcome, in either language.

Special pages *D. Geraint Lewis* Children's Books section – latest Welsh-language and Welsh-interest books reviewed.
Payment £30 maximum.

Logos

5 Beechwood Drive, Marlow,
Buckinghamshire SL7 2DH
☎01628 477577   Fax 01628 477577
Owner *Whurr Publishers Ltd*
Editor *Gordon Graham*
Associate Editor *Betty Cottrell Graham*

FOUNDED 1990. QUARTERLY. Aims to 'deal in depth with issues which unite, divide, excite and concern the world of books,' with an international perspective. Each issue contains 6–8 articles of between 3500–7000 words. Hopes to establish itself as a forum for contrasting views. Suggestions and ideas for contributions are welcome, and should be addressed to the editor. 'Guidelines for Contributors' available. Contributors write from their experience as authors, publishers, booksellers, librarians, etc. A share of the royalties goes to a trust fund for causes connected with the book.
No payment.

London Magazine

30 Thurloe Place, London SW7 2HQ
☎0171 589 0618
Owner *Alan Ross*
Editor *Alan Ross*
Deputy Editor *Jane Rye*
Circulation *c.* 4500

FOUNDED 1954. BI-MONTHLY paperback journal providing an eclectic forum for literary talent, thanks to the dedication of Alan Ross. *The Times* once said that '*London Magazine* is far and away the most readable and level-headed, not to mention best value for money, of the literary magazines'. Today it boasts the publication of early works by the likes of William Boyd, Graham Swift and Ben Okri among others. The broad spectrum of interests includes art, memoirs, travel, poetry, criticism, theatre, music, cinema, short stories and essays, and book reviews. Unsolicited mss welcome; s.a.e. essential. About 150–200 unsolicited mss are received weekly.
    Fiction Maximum 5000 words.
    Payment £100 maximum.
    Annual Subscription £28.50 or $67.

London Review of Books

28 Little Russell Street, London WC1A 2HN
☎0171 404 3336   Fax 0171 404 3337
Owner *LRB Ltd*
Editor *Mary-Kay Wilmers*
Circulation 20,000

FOUNDED 1979. FORTNIGHTLY. Reviews, essays and articles on political, literary, cultural and scientific subjects. Also poetry. Unsolicited contributions welcome (approximately 35 received each week). No pieces under 2000 words. Contact the editor in writing. *Payment* £100 per 1000 words; poems £50.

Looking Good

7 Cheyne Walk, Northampton NN1 5PT
☎01604 602345   Fax 01604 602249
Owner *Herald Group Newspapers Ltd*
Editor *Graham Punter*
Circulation 12,500

FOUNDED 1984. MONTHLY county lifestyle magazine of Northamptonshire. Contributions are not required as all work is done in-house.

Looks

20 Orange Street, London WC2H 7ED
☎0171 957 8383   Fax 0171 930 4091
Owner *EMAP Women's Group Magazines*
Editor *Annabel Goldstaub*
Circulation 231,000

MONTHLY magazine for young women aged 15–22, with emphasis on fashion, beauty and hair, as well as general interest features, including celebrity news and interviews, giveaways, etc. Freelance writers are occasionally used in all areas of the magazine. Contact the editor with ideas. *Payment* varies.

Loving

King's Reach Tower, Stamford Street,
London SE1 9LS
Owner *IPC Magazines Ltd*
Editor *Jo Pink*
Circulation 22,813

MONTHLY. Unusual love stories for women under 30. Story lengths 1000–4000 words. Write for a style guide before putting pen to paper. At the time of going to press, *Loving* had been suspended, but expected to appear again in autumn 1995.

Machine Knitting Monthly

17 Grove Park, Waltham Road,
White Waltham, Maidenhead,
Berkshire SL6 3LW
☎01628 829815   Fax 01628 829816
Owner *Anne Smith*
Editor *Sheila Berriff*
Circulation 55,000

FOUNDED 1986. MONTHLY. Unsolicited mss considered 'as long as they are applicable to this specialist publication. We have our own regular contributors each month but we're always willing to look at new ideas from other writers.' Approach in writing in first instance.

Management Today
22 Lancaster Gate, London W2 3LY
☎0171 413 4566   Fax 0171 413 4138
Owner *Management Publications Ltd*
Editor *Charles Skinner*
Circulation 103,000

General business topics and features. Ideas welcome. Send brief synopsis to the editor.
Payment about £300 per 1000 words.

Map Collector
48 High Street, Tring, Hertfordshire HP23 5BH
☎01442 891004   Fax 01442 827712
Owner *Valerie G. Scott*
Editor *Valerie G. Scott*
Circulation 2500

FOUNDED 1977. QUARTERLY magazine dedicated to the history of cartography and study of early maps. Articles, book reviews, news items and guide to prices. Not interested in modern mapping.
Features Articles on early maps particularly welcome. Maximum 2500 words.
News Events and exhibitions of early maps. Maximum 300 words.
Payment NUJ rates.

marie claire
2 Hatfields, London SE1 9PG
☎0171 261 5240   Fax 0171 261 5277
Owner *European Magazines Ltd*
Editor *Glenda Bailey*
Circulation 398,019

FOUNDED 1988. MONTHLY. An intelligent glossy magazine for women, with strong international features and fashion. No unsolicited mss. Approach with ideas in writing. No fiction.
Features *Michele Lavery* Detailed proposals for feature ideas should be accompanied by samples of previous work.

Marketing Week
St Giles House, 50 Poland Street, London W1V 4AX
☎0171 439 4222   Fax 0171 439 9669
Owner *Centaur Communications*
Editor *Stuart Smith*
Circulation 35,960

WEEKLY trade magazine of the marketing industry. Features on all aspects of the business,

written in a newsy and up-to-the-minute style. Approach with ideas in the first instance.
Features *Helen Jones*
Payment negotiable.

Match
Bretton Court, Bretton, Peterborough, Cambridgeshire PE3 8DZ
☎01733 260333   Fax 01733 267198
Owner *EMAP Pursuit Publications*
Editor *Chris Hunt*
Circulation 140,296

FOUNDED 1979. Popular WEEKLY football magazine aimed at 10–15-year-olds. Most material is generated in-house by a strong news and features team. Some freelance material used if suitable, apart from photographs. No submissions without prior consultation with editor, either by phone or in writing.
Features/News Good and original material is always considered. Maximum 500 words.
Payment negotiable.

Matrix
See **British Science Fiction Association** under **Professional Associations**

Mayfair
2 Archer Street, Piccadilly Circus, London W1V 7HE
☎0171 734 9191   Fax 0171 734 5030
Owner *Paul Raymond Publications*
Editor *Robert Swift*
Circulation 331,760

FOUNDED 1966. THIRTEEN ISSUES YEARLY. Unsolicited material accepted if suitable to the magazine. Interested in features and humour aimed at men aged 20–30. For style, length, etc., writers are advised to study the magazine.

Mayfair Times
102 Mount Street, London W1X 5HF
☎0171 629 3378   Fax 0171 629 9303
Owner *Mayfair Times Ltd*
Editor *Stephen Goringe*
Circulation 20,000

FOUNDED 1985. MONTHLY. Features on Mayfair of interest to both residential and commercial readers. Unsolicited mss welcome.

Medal News
Token Publishing Ltd, 105 High Street, Honiton, Devon EX14 8PE
☎01404 45414   Fax 01404 45313
Owner *J. W. Mussell*

Editor *Diana Birch*
Circulation 2500

FOUNDED 1989. MONTHLY. Unsolicited material welcome but initial approach by phone or in writing preferred.

Features Only interested in articles from well-informed authors 'who know the subject and do their homework'. Max. 2500 words. *Payment* £20 per 1000 words.

Media Week

33–39 Bowling Green Lane, London
EC1R 0DA
☎0171 837 1212   Fax 0171 837 3285
Owner *EMAP Business Publishing*
Editor *Mark Street*
Circulation 16,486

FOUNDED 1986. WEEKLY trade magazine. UK and international coverage on all aspects of the media. No unsolicited mss. Approach in writing with ideas.

Melody Maker

King's Reach Tower, Stamford Street,
London SE1 9LS
☎0171 261 6229   Fax 0171 261 6706
Owner *IPC Magazines Ltd*
Editor *Allan Jones*
Circulation 61,781

WEEKLY. Freelance contributors used on this tabloid magazine competitor of the *NME*. Opportunities exist in reviewing and features.

Features *Paul Lester* A large in-house team, plus around six regulars, produce most feature material.

Reviews *Simon Price* Sample reviews, whether published or not, welcome on pop, rock, soul, funk, etc.

Payment negotiable.

Metropolitan

19 Victoria Avenue, Didsbury,
Manchester M20 2GY
☎0161 434 6290
Publishers *John Ashbrook, Elizabeth Baines,
Ailsa Cox*
Editors *Elizabeth Baines, Ailsa Cox*
Circulation 1500

FOUNDED 1993. BI-ANNUAL magazine devoted to the short story, with the occasional novel extract (usually of a forthcoming novel), author interview or cultural commentary. In its first year recognised by *The Sunday Times* as one of 'the livelier literary magazines'. A platform for new talent alongside names such as Colum McCann, Carl Tighe, Moy McCrory and Livi Michael.

Features Usually commissioned, but open to proposals. Approach in writing with idea, c.v. and s.a.e.

Fiction Stories of high literary standard engaging with contemporary issues. Unsolicited mss welcome. S.a.e. essential. Maximum length 6000 words (2,500 ideal).

No poetry please.

Payment negotiable (depending on grants). Annual subscription £6.

MiniWorld Magazine

Link House, Dingwall Road, Croydon,
Surrey CR9 2TA
☎0181 686 2599   Fax 0181 781 6042
Owner *Link House Magazines Ltd*
Editor *Mike Askew*
Circulation 45,000

FOUNDED 1992. MONTHLY car magazine devoted to the Mini. Unsolicited material welcome but prospective contributors are advised to make initial contact by phone.

Features Restoration, tuning tips, technical advice and sporting events. Readers' cars and product news. Length by arrangement. *Payment* negotiable.

Mizz

King's Reach Tower, Stamford Street,
London SE1 9LS
☎0171 261 6319   Fax 0171 261 6032
Owner *IPC Magazines Ltd*
Editor *Jeanette Baker*
Circulation 193,700

FOUNDED 1985. FORTNIGHTLY magazine for the 14–19-year-old girl: 'a useful rule of thumb is to write for a 16-year-old'. Freelance articles welcome on real life, human interest stories and emotional issues. All material should be addressed to the features editor.

Features *Julie Burniston* Approach in writing, with synopsis, for feature copy; send sample writing with letter for general approach. No fiction.

The Modern Dance

See under **Small Presses (Works Publishing)**

Modern Machine Knitting

17 Grove Park, Waltham Road, White
Waltham, Maidenhead, Berkshire SL6 3LW
☎01628 829815   Fax 01628 829816

Owner *Modern Knitting Ltd*
Editor *Anne Smith*
Circulation 35,000

FOUNDED 1951. MONTHLY. Any article related
to machine knitting considered. The magazine
has its own specialist writers each month but
unsolicited mss or ideas in writing are welcome.

Features Around thirty pages of magazine
including illustrations, diagrams, etc.

Payment negotiable.

The Modern Review

As we went to press, it was announced that the
magazine had folded.

Moneywise

Berkeley Magazines Ltd, 10 Old Bailey,
London EC4M 7NB
☎0171 629 8144   Fax 0171 409 5261

Owner *Reader's Digest Association*
Editor *Christine Michael*
Circulation 124,250

FOUNDED 1990. MONTHLY. Unsolicited mss
with s.a.e. welcome but initial approach in
writing preferred.

More!

20 Orange Street, London WC2H 7ED
☎0171 957 8383   Fax 0171 930 4637

Owner *EMAP Elan Publications*
Editor *Marie O'Riordan*
Circulation 393,707

FOUNDED 1988. FORTNIGHTLY women's magazine aimed at the working woman aged
18–24. Features on sex and relationships plus
news. Most items are commissioned; approach
features editor with idea. Prospective contributors are strongly advised to study the magazine's style before submitting anything.

Mother and Baby

Victory House, Leicester Place,
London WC2H 7BP
☎0171 437 9011   Fax 0171 434 0656

Owner *EMAP Elan Publications*
Editor *Sharon Parsons*
Circulation 110,000

FOUNDED 1956. MONTHLY. Unsolicited mss
welcome, about practical baby and childcare.
Personal 'viewpoint' pieces are considered.
Approach by telephone or in writing.

Motor Boat and Yachting

King's Reach Tower, Stamford Street,
London SE1 9LS
☎0171 261 5333   Fax 0171 261 5419

Owner *IPC Magazines Ltd*
Editor *Alan Harper*
Circulation 25,094

FOUNDED 1904. MONTHLY for those interested
in motor boats and motor cruising.

Features *Alan Harper* Cruising features and
practical features especially welcome. Illustrations (mostly colour) are just as important as
text. Maximum 3000 words. *Payment* £100
per 1000 words or by arrangement.

News *Alan Harper* Factual pieces. Maximum
200 words. *Payment* up to £50 per item.

Motorcaravan & Motorhome Monthly (MMM)

14 Eastfield Close, Andover,
Hampshire SP10 2QP
☎01264 324794   Fax 01264 324794

Owner *Sanglier Publications Ltd*
Editor *Penny Smith*
Circulation 22,000

FOUNDED 1966. MONTHLY. 'There's no money
in motorcaravan journalism but for those wishing to cut their first teeth...' Unsolicited mss
welcome if relevant, but ideas in writing preferred in first instance.

Features Caravan site reports – contact the
editor for questionnaire. Max. 600 words.

Travel Motorcaravanning trips (home and
overseas). Max. 3000 words.

News Short news items for miscellaneous
pages. Max. 200 words.

Fiction Must be motorcaravan-related and
include artwork/photos if possible. Max. 2000
words.

Special pages DIY – modifications to
motorcaravans. Max. 1500 words.

Owner Reports Contributions welcome
from motorcaravan owners. Max. 3000 words.

Payment varies.

Ms London

7–9 Rathbone Street,
London W1V 1AF
☎0171 636 6651   Fax 0171 872 0806

Owner *Employment Publications*
Editor-in-Chief *Bill Williamson*
Editor *Cathy Howes*
Circulation 120,000

FOUNDED 1968. WEEKLY. Aimed at working
women in London, aged 18–35. Unsolicited

mss must be accompanied by s.a.e. Because the magazine is purely London-orientated, there is a real bias towards London-based writers who are in touch with the constantly changing trends and attitudes of the capital.

Features Content is varied and ambitious, ranging from stage and film interviews to fashion, careers, relationships, homebuying and furnishing. Approach with ideas first and sample of published writing. Material should be London-angled, sharp and fairly sophisticated in content. Maximum 1500 words. *Payment* about £125 per 1000 words.

News Handled in-house but follow-up feature ideas welcome.

Music Week
Spotlight Publications, Ludgate House, 245 Blackfriars Road, London SE1 9UR
☎0171 620 3636   Fax 0171 401 8035
Owner *Morgan-Grampian Ltd*
Editor-in-Chief *Steve Redmond*
Managing Editor *Selina Webb*
Circulation 13,900

WEEKLY. Britain's only weekly music business magazine also includes dance industry title *Record Mirror*. No unsolicited mss. Approach in writing with ideas.

Features *Selina Webb* Analysis of specific music business events and trends. Maximum 2000 words.

News Music industry news only. Maximum 350 words.

Musical Option
2 Princes Road, St Leonards on Sea, East Sussex TN37 6EL
☎01424 715167   Fax 01424 712214
Owner *Musical Option Ltd*
Editor *Denby Richards*
Circulation 5000

FOUNDED 1877. QUARTERLY with free supplement in intervening months. Classical music content, with topical features on music, musicians, festivals, etc., and reviews (concerts, festivals, opera, ballet, jazz, CDs, CD-Roms, videos, books and music). International readership. No unsolicited mss; commissions only. Ideas always welcome though; approach by phone. It should be noted that topical material has to be submitted six months prior to events. Not interested in review material, which is already handled by the magazine's own regular team of contributors.
Payment Negotiable.

Musical Times
63B Jamestown Road, London NW1 7DB
☎0171 627 3688(admin)
Fax 0171 482 5697(editorial)
Owner *The Musical Times Publications Ltd*
Editor *Antony Bye*

FOUNDED 1844. Scholarly journal with a practical approach to its subject. Ideas in writing welcome. Unsolicited mss will occasionally be considered. *Payment* negotiable.

My Guy Magazine
27th Floor, King's Reach Tower, Stamford Street, London SE1 9LS
☎0171 261 5000   Fax 0171 261 6032
Owner *IPC Magazines Ltd*
Editor *Frank Hopkinson*
Circulation 47,675

FOUNDED 1977. WEEKLY teen magazine for girls and boys. No freelance contributions.

My Weekly
80 Kingsway East, Dundee DD4 8SL
☎01382 464276   Fax 01382 452491
Owner *D. C. Thomson & Co. Ltd*
Editor *Sandra Monks*
Circulation 434,031

A traditional women's WEEKLY. D.C. Thomson has long had a policy of encouragement and help to new writers of promise. Ideas welcome. Approach in writing.

Features Particularly interested in human interest pieces (1000–1500 words) which by their very nature appeal to all age groups.

Fiction Three stories a week, ranging in content from the emotional to the off-beat and unexpected. 2000–4000 words. Also serials. *Payment* negotiable.

The National Trust Magazine
36 Queen Anne's Gate, London SW1H 9AS
☎0171 222 9251   Fax 0171 222 5097
Owner *The National Trust*
Editor *Sarah-Jane Forder*
Circulation 2.2 million

FOUNDED 1968. THRICE-YEARLY. Conservation of historic houses, coast and countryside in the UK. No unsolicited mss. Approach in writing with ideas.

Natural World
20 Upper Ground, London SE1 9PF
☎0171 928 2111   Fax 0171 620 1594
Publishers *Illustrated London News Group on behalf of The Wildlife Trusts*

Editor *Linda Bennett*
Circulation 143,600

FOUNDED 1981. THRICE-YEARLY. Unsolicited mss welcome if of high quality and relevant to ideals of the magazine. Ideas in writing preferred. No poetry.

Features Popular but accurate articles on British wildlife and the countryside, particularly projects associated with the local Wildlife Trusts. Maximum 1500 words. *Payment* £150 per 1000 words.

News Interested in national wildlife conservation issues, particularly those involving local nature conservation or wildlife trusts. Maximum 300 words.

The Naturalist

c/o University of Bradford, Bradford, West Yorkshire BD7 1DP
☎01274 384212   Fax 01274 384231
Owner *Yorkshire Naturalists' Union*
Editor *Prof. M. R. D. Seaward*
Circulation 5000

FOUNDED 1875. QUARTERLY. Natural history, biological and environmental sciences for a professional and amateur readership. Unsolicited mss welcome. Approach with ideas in writing. Particularly interested in material – scientific papers – relating to the north of England. *No payment.*

Nature

Porters South, 4–6 Crinan Street, London N1 9SQ
☎0171 833 4000
Owner *Macmillan Magazines Ltd*
Editor *John Maddox*
Circulation 54,152

Covers all fields of science, with articles and news on science policy only. No features. Little scope for freelance writers.

Needlecraft

30 Monmouth Street, Bath, Avon BA1 6LH
☎01225 442244   Fax 01225 462986
Owner *Future Publishing*
Editor *Rebecca Bradshaw*
Circulation 74,095

FOUNDED 1991. MONTHLY. Needlework projects with full instructions covering cross-stitch, needlepoint, embroidery, patchwork quilting and lace. Will consider ideas or sketches for projects covering any of the magazine's topics. Initial approaches should be made in writing.

Features on the needlecraft theme. Discuss ideas before sending complete mss. Maximum 1000 words.

Technical pages on 'how to' stitch, use different threads, etc. Only suitable for experienced writers.
Payment negotiable.

Netball

Netball House, 9 Paynes Park, Hitchin, Hertfordshire SG5 1EH
☎01462 442344   Fax 01462 442343
Owner *All England Netball Association Ltd*
Editor *Geoff Harrold*
Circulation 6000

FOUNDED 1940. QUARTERLY. No unsolicited mss. No freelance opportunities.

New Beacon

224 Great Portland Street, London W1N 6AA
☎0171 388 1266   Fax 0171 388 0945
Owner *Royal National Institute for the Blind*
Editor *Ann Lee*
Circulation 6000

FOUNDED 1917. MONTHLY. Published in print, braille and on tape. Unsolicited mss welcome. Approach with ideas in writing. Personal experiences by writers who have a visual impairment (partial sight or blindness), and authoritative items by professionals or volunteers working in the field of visual impairment welcome. Maximum 1500 words.
Payment £30 per 1000 words.

New Humanist

Bradlaugh House, 47 Theobald's Road, London WC1X 8SP
☎0171 430 1371   Fax 0171 430 1271
Owner *Rationalist Press Association*
Editor *Jim Herrick*
Circulation 3000

FOUNDED 1885. QUARTERLY. Unsolicited mss welcome. No fiction.

Features Articles with a humanist perspective welcome in the following fields: religion (critical), humanism, human rights, philosophy, current events, literature, history and science. 2000–4000 words. *Payment* nominal, but negotiable.

Book reviews 750–1000 words, by arrangement with the editor.

New Impact

Anser House, PO Box 1448, Marlow, Bucks SL7 3HD
☎01628 481581   Fax 01628 481581
Owner *Mrs B. Bernard, D. E. Sihera*

Editor *Elaine Sihera*
Circulation 10,000

FOUNDED 1993. BI-MONTHLY. Promotes training enterprise and initiative from a minority ethnic perspective. Unsolicited mss welcome. Interested in training, arts, features, personal achievement, small business features, profiles or personalities especially for a multicultural audience. Not interested in anything unconnected to training or business. Approach in writing with ideas.

News local training/business features – some opportunities. Maximum length 250 words. *Payment* negotiable.

Features original, interesting pieces with a deliberate multicultural/equal opportunity focus. Personal/professional successes and achievements welcome. Maximum length 1500 words. *Payment* negotiable.

Fiction Short stories, poems – especially from minority writers. Maximum length 1500 words. *Payment* negotiable.

Special Pages Interviews with personalities – especially Asian, Afro-Caribbean. Maximum length 1200 words. *Payment* negotiable.

New Internationalist

55 Rectory Road, Oxford OX4 1BW
☎01865 728181   Fax 01865 793152
Owner *New Internationalist Trust*
Co-Editors *Vanessa Baird, Chris Brazier, David Ransom, Nikki van der Gaag*
Circulation 70,000

Radical and broadly leftist in approach, but unaligned. Concerned with world poverty and global issues of peace and politics, feminism and environmentalism, with emphasis on the Third World. Difficult to use unsolicited material as they work to a theme each month and features are commissioned by the editor on that basis. The way in is to send examples of published or unpublished work; writers of interest are taken up. Unsolicited material for shorter articles and relevant fiction (up to 1500 words) could be used in the magazine's regular *Update, Endpiece* and *Interview* sections.

New Musical Express

Floor 25, King's Reach Tower, Stamford Street, London SE1 9LS
☎0171 261 5000   Fax 0171 261 5185
Owner *IPC Magazines Ltd*
Editor *Steve Sutherland*
Circulation 118,755

Britain's best-selling musical WEEKLY. Freelancers used, but always for reviews in the first instance. Specialisation in areas of music (or film, which is also covered) is a help.

Reviews: Books *Gavin Martin* **Film** *Gavin Martin* **LPs** *Keith Cameron* **Live** *Jestyn George, Ted Kessler.* Send in examples of work, either published or specially written samples.

New Scientist

King's Reach Tower, Stamford Street, London SE1 9LS
☎0171 261 5000   Fax 0171 261 6464
Owner *IPC Magazines Ltd*
Editor *Alun Anderson*
Circulation 111,000

FOUNDED 1956. WEEKLY. No unsolicited mss. Approach in writing or by phone with an idea.

Features *Bill O'Neill* Commissions only, but good ideas welcome. Maximum 3500 words.

News *Stephanie Pain* Mostly commissions, but ideas for specialist news, particularly from academics and specialist writers, are welcome. Maximum 1000 words.

Reviews *Maggie McDonald* Reviews are commissioned.

Forum *Richard Fifield* Unsolicited material welcome if of general/humorous interest and related to science. Maximum 1000 words.

Payment £170–190 per 1000 words.

New Statesman and Society

Foundation House, Perseverance Works, 38 Kingsland Road, London E2 8DQ
☎0171 739 3211   Fax 0171 739 9307
Owner *Statesman and Nation Publishing Co.*
Editor *Steve Platt*
Deputy Editor *Paul Anderson*
Circulation 25,000

WEEKLY magazine, the result of a merger (May 1988) of *New Statesman* and *New Society*. Coverage of news, book reviews, arts, current affairs, politics and social reportage. Unsolicited contributions with s.a.e. will be considered.

Literary *Boyd Tonkin*
Arts *Marina Benjamin*

New Welsh Review

Chapter Arts Centre, Market Road, Cardiff CF5 1QE
☎01222 665529   Fax 01222 665529
Owner *New Welsh Review Ltd*
Editor *Robin Reeves*
Circulation 1000

FOUNDED 1988. QUARTERLY Welsh literary magazine, published in English. Welcomes material of literary interest to Welsh readers and those with an interest in Wales. Approach in writing in the first instance.

Features Maximum 3000 words. *Payment* £15 per 1000 words.

Fiction Maximum 5000 words. *Payment* £50 average.

News Maximum 400 words. *Payment* £5 – £15.

New Woman
20 Orange Street, London WC2H 7ED
☎0171 957 8383   Fax 0171 930 7246

Owner *Hachette/EMAP Magazines Ltd*
Editor *Eleni Kyriacou*

MONTHLY women's interest magazine – a 'self-indulgent, informative and intelligent' read. Main topics of interest include men, sex, love, health, careers, beauty and fashion. Uses mainly established freelancers but unsolicited ideas submitted in synopsis form will be considered.

Features/News *Sam Baker* Articles must be original and look at subjects or issues from a new or unusual perspective.

Beauty *Jan Marsters*
Fashion *Deborah Bee*

News From the Centre (NFC)
The National Small Press Centre, Middlesex University, All Saints Site, White Hart Lane, London N17 8HR
☎0181 362 6058

Editor *John Nicholson*

BI-MONTHLY 8-page magazine containing information about the activities of the many organisations catering for small presses, both in Britain and abroad. Features and a letters column. 'Provides a unique way of keeping up-to-date and in touch with what is going on in the world of independent publishing.'

Next Magazine
Russell House, 28 Little Russell Street,,
London WC1A 2HN
☎0171 404 0123   Fax 0171 404 1670

Owner *ICG Baronage Publishing*
Editor *Joani Walsh*
Circulation 300,000

SEASONAL general interest/consumer magazine. No unsolicited material. All preliminary approaches should be made by phone.

Features Celebrity interviews, fashion, history/nostalgia, travel, real-life stories, pets. Maximum length 1500 words. *Payment* up to £250.

Special pages Health, fitness, beauty, hair, wine, coffee/tea and food.

19
King's Reach Tower, Stamford Street,
London SE1 9LS
☎0171 261 6410   Fax 0171 261 7634

Owner *IPC Magazines Ltd*
Editor *April Joyce*
Circulation 200,648

MONTHLY women's magazine aimed at 17–22-year-olds. A little different from the usual teen magazine mix: *19* are now aiming for a 50/50 balance between fashion/lifestyle aspects and newsier, meatier material, e.g. women in prison, boys, abortion, etc. 40% of the magazine's feature material is commissioned, ordinarily from established freelancers. 'But we're always keen to see bold, original, vigorous writing from people just starting out.'

Features *Lee Kynaston* Approach in writing with ideas.

Norfolk Life
See **Suffolk Life**

North East Times
Tattler House, Beech Avenue, Fawdon, Newcastle upon Tyne NE3 4LA
☎0191 284 4495   Fax 0191 285 9606

Owner *Chris Robinson (Publishing) Ltd*
Editor *Chris Robinson*
Circulation 10,000

MONTHLY county magazine incorporating *Newcastle Life*. No unsolicited mss. Approach with ideas in writing.

The North
See **Poetry, Little Magazines**

Northamptonshire Image
Upper Mounts, Northampton NN1 3HR
☎01604 231122   Fax 01604 233000

Owner *Northampton Mercury Co.*
Editor *Peter Hall*
Circulation 20,000

FOUNDED 1905. MONTHLY general interest county magazine. No unsolicited mss. Approach by phone or in writing with ideas. No fiction.

Features Local issues, personalities, businesses, etc., of Northamptonshire interest only. Maximum 500 words. *Payment* £60.

News No hard news as such, just monthly diary column.

Other Regulars on motoring, fashion, lifestyle, sport, travel, history, country walks, and picture files. Maximum 500 words. *Payment* £60.

Nottinghamshire Topic

1st Floor, Maychalk House, 8 Musters Road,
West Bridgford, Nottingham NG2 7PL
☎0115 9810101   Fax 0115 9826565

Owner *Lionel Pickering*
Editor *Cheryl Albery*
Circulation 10,000

FOUNDED 1964. MONTHLY. Features, news
stories, celebrity interviews, local history, historic houses, motoring, gardening, eating out,
what's on listings, theatre, and travel. Freelance
opportunities for features on local history and
unusual homes and interiors in Nottinghamshire. No motoring, gardening or travel items.
Initial approaches should be made in writing.
Payment negotiable.

Nursing Times

Porters South, 4–6 Crinan Street,
London N1 9SQ
☎0171 833 4000

Owner *Macmillan Magazines Ltd*
Editor *John Gilbert*
Circulation 81,117

A large proportion of *Nursing Times* feature
content is from unsolicited contributions sent
on spec. Pieces on all aspects of nursing and
health care, both practical and theoretical,
written in a lively and contemporary way, are
welcome. Commissions also.
Payment varies/NUJ rates apply to commissioned material from union members only.

Office Secretary

Brookmead House, Thorney Leys Business
Park, Witney, Oxfordshire OX8 7GE
☎01993 775545

Owner *Trade Media Ltd*
Editor *Jayne Belcher*
Circulation 60,000

FOUNDED 1986. QUARTERLY. Features articles
of interest to secretaries and personal assistants
aged 25–60. No unsolicited mss.
     Features Informative pieces on current
affairs, health, food, fashion, hotel, travel,
motoring, office and employment-related topics. Length 1000 words.
Payment by negotiation.

The Oldie

45 Poland Street, London W1V 4AU
☎0171 734 2225   Fax 0171 734 2226

Owner *Oldie Publications Ltd*
Editor *Richard Ingrams*
Circulation 20,000

FOUNDED 1992. MONTHLY general interest
magazine with a strong humorous slant for the
older person.

OLS (Open Learning Systems) News

11 Malford Grove, Gilwern, Abergavenny,
Gwent NP7 0RN
☎01873 830872   Fax 01873 830872

Owner *David P. Bosworth*
Editor *David P. Bosworth*
Circulation 800

FOUNDED 1980. QUARTERLY dealing with the
application of open, flexible, distance learning
and supported self-study at all educational/
training levels. Interested in open access learning and the application of educational technology to learning situations. Case studies particularly welcome. Not interested in theory of
education alone, the emphasis is strictly on
applied policies and trends.
     Features Learning programmes (how they
are organised); student/learner-eye views of
educational and training programmes with an
open access approach. Approach the editor by
phone or in writing.
No payment for 'news' items. Focus items
will negotiate.

Opera

1A Mountgrove Road, London N5 2LU
☎0171 359 1037   Fax 0171 354 2700

Owner *Opera Magazine Ltd*
Editor *Rodney Milnes*
Circulation 11,500

FOUNDED 1950. MONTHLY review of the current opera scene. Almost all articles are commissioned and unsolicited mss are not welcome.
All approaches should be made in writing.

Opera Now

241 Shaftesbury Avenue, London WC2H 8EH
☎0171 333 1740   Fax 0171 333 1769

Owner *Rhinegold Publishing Ltd*
Editor *Graeme Kay*

FOUNDED 1989. MONTHLY. News, features
and reviews for those interested in opera. No
unsolicited mss. All work is commissioned.
Approach with ideas in writing.

Options

King's Reach Tower, Stamford Street,
London SE1 9LS
☎0171 261 5000   Fax 0171 261 7344

Owner *IPC Magazines Ltd*

Editor *Maureen Rice*
Circulation 162,000

Aims to entertain the modern renaissance woman, worker, mother and wife. Almost all material is written by a regular team of free-lancers, but new writers are encouraged.
Payment about £250 per 1000 words.

Orbis

See under **Poetry, Little Magazines**

Panurge

Crooked Holme Farm Cottage, Brampton, Cumbria CA8 2AT
☎016977 41087

Editor *John Murray*
Circulation 2000

FOUNDED 1984. BI-ANNUAL (April/October). 'New writing by new writers' is the logo of this magazine dedicated exclusively to prose. Primarily short stories, plus special features of interest to fiction writers, e.g. minority publishing. All fiction is unsolicited; features are commissioned.

Fiction 'We are looking for very good stories, especially those by new and up-and-coming writers. The standard is high and our work is frequently anthologised.' No restrictions on length. 'We have printed 12,000-word stories by unknown writers.'
Payment £10 per three printed pages.

Parents

Victory House, Leicester Place, London WC2H 7BP
☎0171 437 9011   Fax 0171 434 0656

Owner *EMAP Elan Publications*
Editor *Julia Goodwin*
Circulation 70,000

FOUNDED 1976. MONTHLY. Features commissioned from outside contributors. Approach with ideas. Age span: from pregnancy to six years.

Paris Transcontinental

Institut des Pays Anglophones, Sorbonne Nouvelle, 5 rue de l'Ecole de Médicine, Paris, France 75006
☎00 33 1 69018635

Owner *Claire Larrière*
Editor-in-chief *Claire Larrière*
Editors *Devorah Goldberg, Albert Russo*
Circulation 550

FOUNDED 1990. BI-ANNUAL. French magazine which publishes original short stories in English from around the world. No poetry, non-fiction or artwork. All themes. A good style, originality and strength. The magazine purports to be a forum for writers of excellent stories whose link is the English language and the short story. Length 2500–4500 words. Original short stories only. No translations: stories must be written in English. Stories should be submitted along with a few lines about yourself and your work (about 100 words only) and must be accompanied by International Reply Coupons (sufficient for response and subsequent return of mss). *Payment* two copies of the magazine.

PCW Plus

30 Monmouth Street, Bath, Avon BA1 2BW
☎01225 442244   Fax 01225 446019

Owner *Nick Alexander*
Editor *Andrew Chapman*
Circulation 14,012

FOUNDED 1986. MONTHLY. Unsolicited contributions welcome but initial approach in writing preferred.

Features *Martin Le Poidevin* 'We will welcome any interesting feature-length articles on writing but must involve reference to PCW. Good illustrations preferred as well.' Maximum 2000 words.

Case in Point Regular feature on original uses to which people have put their Amstrad PCWs. Good illustrations important. Maximum 1600 words.
Payment negotiable.

Penthouse

Northern & Shell Tower, 4 Selsdon Way, City Harbour, London E14 9GL
☎0171 987 5090   Fax 0171 987 2160

Owner *Northern & Shell plc*
Editor *Derek Botham*
Editorial Director *Paul Ashford*
Managing Editor *Jonathan Richards*
Circulation *c.*102,421

FOUNDED 1965. THIRTEEN ISSUES YEARLY. No fiction.

Features *Stewart Meagher* Unsolicited mss welcome, 'but most of those we do receive are unsuitable because the authors haven't looked at the magazine'. First approach by phone or in writing with ideas. Maximum 3500 words. Must have a fairly long-term appeal. *Payment* negotiable 'but generally pretty good'.

News *Stewart Meagher* Limited opportunities for unsolicited material.

The People's Friend

80 Kingsway East, Dundee DD4 8SL
☎01382 462276/223131   Fax 01382 452491
Owner *D. C. Thomson & Co. Ltd*
Editor *Sinclair Matheson*
Circulation 520,000

The *Friend* is basically a fiction magazine, with two serials and several short stories each week. FOUNDED in 1869, it has always prided itself on providing 'a good read for all the family'. All stories should be about ordinary, identifiable characters with the kind of problems the average reader can understand and sympathise with. 'We look for the romantic and emotional developments of characters, rather than an over-complicated or contrived plot. From time to time we can also use a romantic/mystery/adventure/period-type story.'

Short Stories Can vary in length from 1000 words or less to as many as 4000.

Serials Long-run serials of 10–15 instalments or more preferred. Occasionally shorter.

Articles Short fillers welcome.

Payment on acceptance.

Period House and Its Garden

7 St Johns Road, Harrow, Middlesex
HA1 2EE
☎0181 863 2020   Fax 0181 863 2444
Owner *Cornelius Bohane*
Editor *Richard Porter*
Circulation *c*.25,000–35,000

FOUNDED 1991. MONTHLY on the pleasures and perils of period house ownership. Freelance opportunities for articles on relevant renovation and period topics. Approach by phone or in writing in the first instance.

Features 'Lots of opportunities for competent writers well-versed in the period house and garden world.' Case study ideas on renovated houses always welcome. Maximum 2000 words. *Payment* variable.

Period Living & Traditional Homes

Victory House, 14 Leicester Place, London
WC2H 7BP
☎0171 437 9011   Fax 0171 434 0656
Owner *EMAP Elan Publications*
Editor *Clare Weatherall*
Circulation *c*. 50,014

FOUNDED 1992. Formed from the merger of *Period Living* and *Traditional Homes*. The new magazine covers interior decoration in a period style, period house profiles, traditional crafts, traditional cookery, renovation of period properties, antiques and profiles of collectors.

Features *Dominique Coughlin*

Payment varies according to length/type of article.

The Philosopher

BM Box 1129, London WC1N 3XX
☎01923 229784   Fax 01923 229784
Owner *The Philosophical Society of Great Britain*
Editor *Dr Keith H. Seddon*

FOUNDED 1913. BI-ANNUAL journal of the Philosophical Society of Great Britain. Analytical philosophy in the Anglo-American tradition. Wide range of interests, but leaning towards articles that present philosophical investigation which is relevant to the individual and to society in our modern era. Accessible to the non-specialist. Will consider articles and book reviews. No 'new age' philosophy, pseudo-science, amateur essays on 'philosophy of life'. Notes for Contributors available; send s.a.e.

News about lectures, conventions, philosophy groups. Activities of members (e.g. new publications). Ethical issues in the news. Maximum 3000 words.

Reviews of philosophy books (maximum 600 words); discussion articles of individual philosophers and their published works (maximum 2000 words)

Payment free copies.

Picture Postcard Monthly

15 Debdale Lane, Keyworth, Nottingham
NG12 5HT
☎0115 9374079   Fax 0115 9376197
Owners *Brian & Mary Lund*
Editor *Brian Lund*
Circulation 4300

FOUNDED 1978. MONTHLY. News, views, clubs, diary of fairs, sales, auctions, and well-researched postcard-related articles. Might be interested in general articles supported by postcards. Unsolicited mss welcome. Approach by phone or in writing with ideas.

Pilot

The Clock House, 28 Old Town, Clapham, London SW4 0LB
☎0171 498 2506   Fax 0171 498 6920
Owner *James Gilbert*
Editor *James Gilbert*
Circulation 30,000

FOUNDED 1968. MONTHLY magazine for private plane pilots. No staff writers; the entire magazine is written by freelancers – mostly regulars. Unsolicited mss welcome but ideas in writing preferred. Perusal of any issue of the magazine will reveal the type of material bought.

Features *James Gilbert* Many articles are unsolicited personal experiences/travel accounts from pilots of private planes; good photo coverage is very important. Maximum 5000 words. *Payment* £100–700 (first rights). Photos £25 each.

News *Mike Jerram* Contributions need to be as short as possible. See *Pilot Notes* in the magazine.

The Pink Paper
13 Hercules Street, London N7 6AT
☎0171 272 2155   Fax 0171 263 2572
Owner *Mindmaster Ltd*
Editor *Andrew Saxton*
Circulation 40,160

FOUNDED 1987. WEEKLY. National newspaper for lesbians and gay men covering politics, social issues, health, the arts and all areas of concern to the lesbian/gay community. Incorporates *Boyz* and *Shebang*. Unsolicited mss welcome. Initial approach by phone with an idea preferred. Interested in profiles, reviews, in-depth features and short news pieces.

News *Andrew Saxton* Maximum 300 words.
Listings *Mark C. O'Flaherty*
Arts & Reviews *Mark C. O'Flaherty* Maximum 200 words.
Books *James Cary Parkes*

Boyz **Editor** *Simon Gage*
Listings, Bars & Clubs *David Hudson*
Editorial Assistant *Murray Healey*

Shebang **Editor** *Lisa Sabbage*
Album & Single Reviews should be sent to *Mark C. O'Flaherty* (Pink Paper at Hercules Street address) and *Mark Turner* (Boyz), c/o James Alexander, 77 City Garden Row, London N1 8EZ Tel 0171 608 2566, Fax 0171 608 2544.
Payment by arrangement.

Plays and Players
Northway House, 1379 High Road, London N20 9LP
☎0181 343 8515   Fax 0181 343 9540
Owner *Mineco Design*
Editor *Sandra Rennie*
Circulation 9500

Theatre MONTHLY which publishes a mixture of reviews, festival reports and features on all aspects of the theatre. Rarely uses unsolicited material but writers of talent are taken up. Almost all material is commissioned.

PN Review
See under **Poetry, Little Magazines**

Poetry Ireland Review
See under **Poetry, Little Magazines**

Poetry Review
See under **Poetry, Little Magazines**

Poetry Wales
See under **Poetry, Little Magazines**

Pony
296 Ewell Road, Surbiton, Surrey KT6 7AQ
☎0181 390 8547   Fax 0181 390 8696
Owner *D. J. Murphy (Publishers) Ltd*
Editor *Janet Rising*
Circulation 38,000

FOUNDED 1948. Lively MONTHLY aimed at 10–16-year-olds. News, instruction on riding, stable management, veterinary care, interviews. Approach in writing with an idea.

Features welcome. Maximum 900 words.
News Written in-house. Photographs and illustrations (serious/cartoon) welcome.
Short Story Regular slots of no more than 1000 words.
Payment £65 per 1000 words.

Popular Crafts
Nexus House, Boundary Way, Hemel Hempstead, Hertfordshire HP2 7ST
☎01442 66551   Fax 01442 66998
Owner *Nexus Special Interests*
Editor *Charlotte Collis*
Circulation 32,000

FOUNDED 1980. MONTHLY. Covers crafts of all kinds. Freelance contributions welcome – copy needs to be lively and interesting. Approach in writing with an outline of idea.

Features Project-based under the following headings: Homecraft; Needlecraft; Popular Craft; Kidscraft; News and Columns. Any craft-related material including projects to make, with full instructions/patterns supplied in all cases; profiles of crafts people and news of craft group activities or successes by individual persons; articles on collecting crafts; personal experiences and anecdotes.
Payment on publication.

PR Week

22 Lancaster Gate, London W2 3LP
☎0171 413 4520   Fax 0171 413 4509
Owner *Haymarket Business Publications Ltd*
Editor *Stephen Farish*
Circulation 20,000

FOUNDED 1984. WEEKLY. Contributions are accepted from experienced journalists. Approach in writing with an idea.

Features *Ed Charles*
News *Amanda Hall*
Payment £175 per 1000 words.

Practical Caravan

38–42 Hampton Road, Teddington,
Middlesex TW11 0JE
☎0181 943 5021   Fax 0181 943 5098
Owner *Haymarket Magazines Ltd*
Editor *Ally Watson*
Circulation 53,633

FOUNDED 1964. MONTHLY. Contains caravan reviews, travel features, investigations, products, park reviews. Unsolicited mss welcome on travel relevant only to caravanning/touring vans. No beginner caravanning, motorcaravan or static van stories. Approach with ideas by phone.

Features must refer to caravanning, towing. Written in friendly, chatty manner. Max. length 2000 words. *Payment* £100 per 1000 words.

Special Pages Caravan park reviews, geared towards touring facilities and use. Should be accompanied by photos. Max. length 700 words per park. *Payment* £80 per 1000 words.

Practical Fishkeeping

Bretton Court, Bretton, Peterborough,
Cambridgeshire PE3 8DZ
☎01733 264666   Fax 01733 265515
Owner *EMAP Pursuit Publishing Ltd*
Managing Editor *Steve Windsor*
Circulation 39,000

MONTHLY. Practical articles on all aspects of fishkeeping. Unsolicited mss welcome. Approach in writing with ideas. Quality photographs of fish always welcome. No fiction or verse.

Practical Gardening

Apex House, Oundle Road, Peterborough,
Cambridgeshire PE2 9NP
☎01733 898100   Fax 01733 898433
Owner *EMAP Apex Publications Ltd*
Editor *Susie Johns*
Circulation 111,181

FOUNDED 1960. MONTHLY aimed at broad-based readership of relatively knowledgeable gardeners and enthusiasts. Unsolicited mss will be considered but there are few acceptances out of the 200 or so received each year. Careful study of the magazine's content and market is essential.

Features *Nicola Williams* Pieces on real-life gardens, particularly those with an unusal angle, welcome, provided they are in keeping with the magazine's style. Emphasis on creative planting schemes and features – but also on the people *behind* the gardens. Maximum 1200 words. *Practical Gardening* is not a how-to publication, but aims to offer creative ideas and inspiration.

Payment from £120 per 1000 words.

Practical Motorist

Arrowsmith Court, Station Approach,
Broadstone, Dorset BH18 8PW
☎01202 659910
Owner *PW Publishing Ltd*
Editor *Rodney Jacques*
Circulation 26,000

FOUNDED 1934. MONTHLY. Unsolicited mss welcome. All approaches should be made to the editor. Maximum 1500 words. *Payment* 'on merit'. 'Ours is a very specialised field and not many can hope to match our established contributors.'

Practical Parenting

King's Reach Tower, Stamford Street,
London SE1 9LS
☎0171 261 5058   Fax 0171 261 5366
Owner *IPC Magazines Ltd*
Editor *Helen Gill*
Circulation 125,000

FOUNDED 1987. MONTHLY. Practical advice on pregnancy, birth, babycare and childcare up to five years. Submit ideas in writing with synopsis or send mss on spec. Interested in feature articles of up to 3000 words in length, and in readers' experiences/personal viewpoint pieces of between 750–1000 words. Humorous articles on some aspect of parenthood may also stand a chance. All material must be written for the magazine's specifically targeted audience and in-house style. *Payment* negotiable.

Practical Photography

Apex House, Oundle Road, Peterborough,
Cambridgeshire PE2 9NP
☎01733 898100   Fax 01733 894472
Owner *EMAP Apex Publications Ltd*
Editor *William Cheung*
Circulation 85,000

MONTHLY. All types of photography, particularly technique-orientated pictures. No unsolicited mss. Preliminary approach may be made by telephone. Always interested in new ideas.

Features Anything relevant to the world of photography, but not 'the sort of feature produced by staff writers'. Features on technology and humour are two areas worth exploring. Bear in mind that there is a three-month lead-in time. Maximum 2000 words.

News Only 'hot' news applicable to a monthly magazine. Maximum 400 words.

Payment varies.

Practical Wireless
Arrowsmith Court, Station Approach, Broadstone, Dorset BH18 8PW
☎01202 659910   Fax 01202 659950
Owner *P.W. Publishing*
Editor *Rob Mannion*
Circulation 27,000

FOUNDED 1932. MONTHLY. News and features relating to amateur radio, radio construction and radio communications. Unsolicited mss welcome. Guidelines available (send s.a.e.) Approach by phone with ideas in the first instance. Copy should be supported where possible by artwork, either illustrations, diagrams or photographs. *Payment* £54-70 per page.

Practical Woodworking
Kings Reach Tower, Stamford Street, London SE1 9LS
☎0171 261 6689   Fax 0171 261 7555
Owner *IPC Magazines Ltd*
Editor *A. R. Mitchell*
Circulation 41,000

FOUNDED 1965. MONTHLY. Contains articles relating to woodworking – projects, techniques, new products, tips, letters etc. Unsolicited mss welcome. No fiction. Approach with ideas in writing or by phone.

News anything related to woodworking. *Payment* £60 per published page.

Features projects, techniques etc. *Payment* £60 per published page.

Prediction
Link House, Dingwall Avenue, Croydon, Surrey CR9 2TA
☎0181 686 2599   Fax 0181 781 1164
Owner *Link House Magazines Ltd*
Editor *Jo Logan*
Circulation 35,000

FOUNDED 1936. MONTHLY. Covering astrology and occult-related topics. Unsolicited

material in these areas welcome (about 200–300 mss received every year).

Astrology Pieces, ranging from 800–2000 words, should be practical and of general interest. Charts and astro data should accompany them, especially if profiles.

Features *Jo Logan* Articles on mysteries of the earth, alternative medicine, psychical/occult experiences and phenomena are considered. Maximum 2000 words. *Payment* £25–75.

News *Jon Taylor* Items of interest to readership welcome. Maximum 300 words. *No payment.*

Prima
Portland House, Stag Place, London SW1E 5AU
☎0171 245 8700   Fax 0171 630 5509
Owner *Gruner & Jahr (UK)*
Editor *Lynn Cardy*
Circulation 565,048

FOUNDED 1986. MONTHLY women's magazine.

Features *Jenny Campbell* Mostly practical and written by specialists, or commissioned from known freelancers. Unsolicited mss not welcome.

Private Eye
6 Carlisle Street, London W1V 5RG
☎0171 437 4017   Fax 0171 437 0705
Owner *Pressdram*
Editor *Ian Hislop*
Circulation 190,000

FOUNDED 1961. FORTNIGHTLY satirical and investigative magazine. Prospective contributors are best advised to approach the editor in writing. News stories and feature ideas are always welcome, as are cartoons. All jokes written in-house.

Payment in all cases is 'not great', and length of piece varies as appropriate.

Psychic News
2 Tavistock Chambers, Bloomsbury Way, London WC1A 2SE
☎0171 405 3340/3345   Fax 0171 430 0535
Owner *Psychic Press Ltd*
Editor *Tim Haigh*
Circulation 15,000

FOUNDED 1932. *Psychic News* is the world's only WEEKLY spiritualist newspaper. It covers subjects such as psychic research, hauntings, ghosts, poltergeists, spiritual healing, survival after death, and paranormal gifts.

Publishing News

43 Museum Street, London WC1A 1LY
☎0171 404 0304   Fax 0171 242 0762
Editor *Fred Newman*

WEEKLY newspaper of the book trade. Hardback and paperback reviews and extensive listings of new paperbacks and hardbacks. Interviews with leading personalities in the trade, authors, agents and features on specialist book areas.

Q

Mappin House, 4 Winsley Street, London W1N 7AR
☎0171 436 1515   Fax 0171 323 0680
Owner *EMAP Metro Publications*
Editor *Danny Kelly*
Circulation 187,000

FOUNDED 1986. MONTHLY. Glossy aimed at educated rock music enthusiasts of all ages. Few opportunities for freelance writers. Unsolicited mss are strongly discouraged. Prospective contributors should approach in writing only.

Quartos Magazine

BCM Writer, 27 Old Gloucester Street, London WC1N 3XX
☎01559 371108
Owner *Suzanne Riley*
Editor *Suzanne Riley*
Circulation 1500

FOUNDED 1987. BI-MONTHLY. Contains practical 'nuts and bolts' advice on creative writing. Unsolicited mss welcome on non-fiction. Interested in lively, original articles on writing in its broadest sense. Approach with ideas in writing. No material returned unless accompanied by s.a.e.

News Writers' workshops, courses, circles etc. Competitions, new writing books. Maximum length 200 words. *Payment* none.

Features Any interesting writing features including interviews with writers. Maximum 1000 words. *Payment* £20 per 1000 words.

Poetry Both short and long unpublished poems, provided they are original and interesting. No 'therapeutic/confessional poems and those which meander without rhyme or reason'. Short critique service offered: £1.50 per poem or £5 for a collection of six poems, plus s.a.e. Material should be addressed to The Poetry Editor.

Fiction None – although a regular readers' competition provides the fiction in each issue.

Maximum length 1000 words. *Payment* £10 prize and publication.

Special Pages: *Vellum* indulges the literary-minded by featuring old favourites from Marlowe and Johnson to Machen and Orwell. Maximum 1000 words. *Payment* £20 per 1000 words.

Raconteur

44 Gray's Inn Road, London WC1X 8LR
☎0171 242 3595   Fax 0171 242 3598
Owner *Mr D.J. Jenkins*
Editor *Graham Lord*
Circulation 25,000

FOUNDED 1944. QUARTERLY publication of prize-winning short stories by new authors and commissioned new stories by established authors. Stories only accepted if entered under the rules of the short story competition (length 1200 – 5000 words). All stories submitted must be sent with completed entry form and fee. Send s.a.e. for details and entry form.

Prizes £200–£1000; £10,000; gold medal.

Radio Times

Woodlands, 80 Wood Lane, London W12 0TT
☎0181 576 2000   Fax 0181 576 3160
Owner *BBC Enterprises Ltd*
Editor *Nicholas Brett*
Executive Editor *Sue Robinson*
Features Editor *Michelle Dickson*
Circulation 1,441,280

WEEKLY. UK's leading broadcast listings magazine. The majority of material is provided by freelance and retained writers, but the topicality of the pieces means close consultation with editors is essential. Very unlikely to use unsolicited material. Detailed BBC, ITV, Channel 4 and satellite television and radio listings are accompanied by feature material relevant to the week's output. *Payment* by arrangement.

RAIL

Apex House, Oundle Road, Peterborough, Cambridgeshire PE2 9NP
☎01733 898100 ext. 6949 Fax 01733 894472
Owner *EMAP Apex Publications*
Editor *Peter Kelly*
Circulation 36,018

FOUNDED 1981. FORTNIGHTLY magazine dedicated to modern railway. News and features, and topical newsworthy events. Unsolicited mss welcome. Approach by phone with ideas. Not interested in personal journey reminiscences. No fiction.

Features By arrangement with the editor. Traction-related subjects of interest. Maximum 2000 words. *Payment* varies/negotiable.

News Any news item welcomed. Maximum 500 words. *Payment* varies (up to £100 per 1000 words).

The Railway Magazine

King's Reach Tower, Stamford Street, London SE1 9LS
☎0171 261 5533/5821   Fax 0171 261 5269

Owner *IPC Magazines Ltd*
Editor *Nick Pigott*
Circulation 33,803

FOUNDED 1897. MONTHLY. Articles, photos and short news stories of a topical nature, covering modern railways, steam preservation and railway history, welcome. Maximum 2000 words, with sketch maps of routes, etc., where appropriate. Unsolicited mss welcome. Maximum 2000 words.

Payment negotiable.

Rambling Today

1–5 Wandsworth Road, London SW8 2XX
☎0171 582 6878   Fax 0171 587 3799

Owner *Ramblers' Association*
Editor *Annabelle Birchall*
Circulation 95,000

QUARTERLY. Official magazine of the Ramblers' Association, available to members only. Unsolicited mss welcome. S.a.e. required for return.

Features Freelance features are invited on any aspect of walking in Britain and abroad. Length 900–1300 words, preferably with good photographs. No general travel articles.

Reader's Digest

Berkeley Square House, Berkeley Square, London W1X 6AB
☎0171 629 8144   Fax 0171 408 0748

Owner *Reader's Digest Association Ltd*
Editor *Russell Twisk*
Circulation 1.6 million

In theory, a good market for general interest features of around 2500 words. However, 'a tiny proportion' comes from freelance writers, all of which are specially commissioned. Currently trying to toughen up its image with a move into investigative journalism. Opportunities exist for short humorous contributions to regular features – 'Life's Like That', 'Humour in Uniform'. Issue a helpful booklet called 'Writing for Reader's Digest' available by post at £2.50. *Payment* £150.

Record Collector

43–45 St Mary's Road, Ealing, London W5 5RQ
☎0181 579 1082   Fax 0181 566 2024

Owner *Johnny Dean*
Editor *Peter Doggett*

FOUNDED 1979. MONTHLY. Detailed, well-researched articles welcome on any aspect of record collecting or any collectable artist in the field of popular music (1950s–1990s), with complete discographies where appropriate. Unsolicited mss welcome. Approach with ideas by phone. *Payment* negotiable.

Reed

Reed Magazine, Philippa's Bookshop, C/Nuestra Señora de Gracia, 24, 29600 Marbella (Málaga) Spain
☎00 34 52 2862619   Fax 00 34 52 2863410

Owner *Philippa Bach and F. Manasseer*
Editor *F. Manasseer*
Circulation 7000

FOUNDED 1991. QUARTERLY literary magazine containing short stories, humour, art, memoirs anecdotes. Unsolicited mss welcome. Interested in anything which has an international rather than a regional character. Chiefly aimed at readers who speak English as their lingua franca, i.e. a European magazine in English. Not interested in politics, sex, controversial subjects, sport, five-syllable words, slangy English. Approach in writing with ideas. Only commissioned work is paid and the fee is always minimal.

Reincarnation International

Phoenix Research Publications, PO Box 26, London WC2H 9LP
☎0171 240 3956   Fax 0171 379 0620

Publisher *Reincarnation International Ltd*
Editor *Roy Stemman*
Circulation 3000

QUARTERLY. The only publication in the world dealing with all aspects of reincarnation – from people who claim to recall their past lives spontaneously to the many thousands who have done so through hypnotic regressions. It also examines reincarnation in the light of various religious beliefs and the latest discoveries about the mind and how it works.

Report

ATL, 7 Northumberland Street, London WC2N 5DA
☎0171 930 6441   Fax 0171 930 1359

Owner *Association of Teachers and Lecturers*
Editor *Richard Margrave*

Circulation 150,000

FOUNDED 1978. EIGHT ISSUES YEARLY during academic terms. Contributions welcome. All submissions should go directly to the editor. Articles should be no more than 800 words and must be of practical interest to the classroom teacher and F.E. lecturers.

Resident Abroad

Greystoke Place, Fetter Lane,
London EC4A 1ND
☎0171 405 6969   Fax 0171 242 0263
Owner *Financial Times*
Editor *William Essex*
Circulation 17,919

FOUNDED 1979. MONTHLY magazine aimed at British expatriates. Unsolicited mss considered, if suitable to the interests of the readership.
Features Up to 1200 words on finance, property, employment opportunities and other topics likely to appeal to readership, such as living conditions in countries with substantial expatriate population.
Fiction Rarely published, but exceptional, relevant stories (no longer than 1000 words) might be considered.
Payment £150 per 1000 words for good pieces from expatriate or former expatriate writers.

Riding

Corner House, Foston, Grantham,
Lincolnshire NG32 2JU
☎01400 282032   Fax 01400 282275
Owner *Riding Magazine Ltd*
Editor *Helen Scott*
Circulation 30,000

Aimed at an adult, horse-owning audience. Most of the writers on *Riding* are freelance but feature opportunities are limited as regular columnists take up much of the magazine. New and authoritative writers always welcome. *Payment* negotiable.

Right Now!

PO Box 3561, London E1 5LU
Owner *Right Now!*
Editor *Derek Turner*
Circulation 1000

FOUNDED 1993. QUARTERLY right-wing conservative commentary. Welcome well-documented disputations, news stories and elegiac features about British heritage ('the more politically incorrect, the better!'). No fiction and poems, although exceptions may be made. Approach in writing in the first instance.
No payment.

Risqué

2 Caversham Street, London SW3 4AH
☎0171 351 4995   Fax 0171 351 4995
Owner *Rockzone Ltd*
Editor *Leonard Holdsworth*
Circulation 85,000

FOUNDED 1991. MONTHLY. Elegant international magazine for men, covering all men's interests. Unsolicited ideas welcome, but not complete mss at first. Maximum 3500 words. *Payment* negotiable.

Rouge

46 Frostic Walk, London E1 5LT
☎0171 377 9426   Fax 0171 377 9426
Owner *Breakaway Publications Ltd.*
Editor *Roger Evans*

FOUNDED 1989. QUARTERLY. News, features and reviews for lesbians, gay men and bisexuals, with a focus on sexual politics, HIV and AIDS and safer sex. Politics rather than lifestyle. Unsolicited features of up to 1700 words welcome. *Payment* by arrangement.

Rugby News & Monthly

113 Stephendale Road, London SW6 2PS
☎0171 371 9909   Fax 0171 371 9877
Owner *Rugby Magazines Limited*
Editor *Richard Bath*
Circulation 25,000

FOUNDED 1987 and incorporated *Rugby Monthly* magazine in July 1994. Contains news, views and features on the UK and the world rugby scene, with special emphasis on clubs, schools, fitness and coaching.

Rugby World

25th Floor, King's Reach Tower, Stamford Street, London SE1 9LS
☎0171 261 6830   Fax 0171 261 7183
Owner *IPC Magazines Ltd*
Editor *Peter Bills*
Circulation 42,135

MONTHLY. Features of special rugby interest only. Unsolicited contributions welcome but s.a.e. essential for return of material. Prior approach by phone or in writing preferred.

Saga Magazine

The Saga Building, Middelburg Square, Folkestone, Kent CT20 1AZ
☎01303 711523   Fax 01303 220391
Owner *Saga Publishing Ltd*
Editor *Paul Bach*
Circulation 600,000

FOUNDED 1984. TEN ISSUES YEARLY. 'Saga Magazine sets out to celebrate the role of older people in society. It reflects their achievements, promotes their skills, protects their interests, and campaigns on their behalf. A warm personal approach, addressing the readership in an upbeat and positive manner, required.' It has a hard core of celebrated commentators/writers (e.g. Clement Freud) as regular contributors and there is limited scope for well-written features – good-quality, colour transparencies enhance acceptance chances. Subjects of interest include achievement, hobbies, finance, food, wine, social comment, motoring, fitness, diet, etc. Length 1000–1200 words (maximum 1600).

Sailplane and Gliding
281 Queen Edith's Way, Cambridge CB1 4NH
☎01223 247725   Fax 01223 413793
Owner *British Gliding Association*
Editor *Gillian Bryce-Smith*
Circulation 8400

FOUNDED 1930. BI-MONTHLY for gliding enthusiasts. A specialist magazine with very few opportunities for freelancers. *No payment.*

Sainsbury's The Magazine
20 Upper Ground, London SE1 9PD
☎0171 633 0266   Fax 0171 401 9423
Owner *New Crane Publishing*
Editor *Michael Wynn Jones*
Circulation 325,000

FOUNDED 1993. MONTHLY featuring a main core of food and cookery, health, beauty, fashion, home, gardening, travel and news. No unsolicited mss. Approach in writing with ideas only in the first instance.

The Salisbury Review
33 Canonbury Park South, London N1 2JW
☎0171 226 7791   Fax 0171 354 0383
Owner *Claridge Press*
Editor *Roger Scruton*
Managing Editor *Merrie Cave*
Circulation 1700

FOUNDED 1982. QUARTERLY magazine of conservative thought. Editorials and features from a right-wing viewpoint. Unsolicited material welcome.
Features Maximum 4000 words.
Reviews Maximum 1000 words.
No payment.

Scotland on Sunday Magazine
See under **National Newspapers (Scotland on Sunday)**

The Scots Magazine
2 Albert Square, Dundee DD1 9QJ
☎01382 223131   Fax 01382 322214
Owner *D. C. Thomson & Co. Ltd*
Editor *Alan Halley*
Circulation 82,000

FOUNDED 1739. MONTHLY. Covers a wide field of Scottish interests ranging from personalities to wildlife, climbing, reminiscence, history and folklore. Outside contributions welcome; 'staff delighted to discuss in advance by letter or phone'.

The Scottish Farmer
The Plaza Tower, The Plaza, East Kilbride G74 1LW
☎013552 46444   Fax 013552 63013
Owner *Caledonian Magazines Ltd*
Editor *Alasdair Fletcher*
Circulation 23,086

FOUNDED 1893. WEEKLY. Farmer's magazine covering most aspects of Scottish agriculture. Unsolicited mss welcome. Approach with ideas in writing.
Features *Alasdair Fletcher* Technical articles on agriculture or farming units. 1000–2000 words.
News *John Duckworth* Factual news about farming developments, political, personal and technological. Maximum 800 words.
Weekend Family Pages Rural and craft topics.
Payment £8 per 100 words; £23 per photo.

Scottish Field
Special Publications, Royston House, Caroline Park, Edinburgh EH5 1QJ
☎0131 551 2942   Fax 0131 551 2938
Owner *Oban Times*
Editor *Archie Mackenzie*

FOUNDED 1903. MONTHLY. Scotland's quality lifestyle magazine. Unsolicited mss welcome but writers should study the magazine first.
Features Articles of general interest on Scotland and Scots abroad with good photographs or, preferably, colour slides. Approx 1000 words.
Payment negotiable.

Scottish Golfer
The Cottage, 181A Whitehouse Road, Edinburgh EH14 6BY
☎0131 339 7546   Fax 0131 339 1169
Owner *Scottish Golf Union*
Editor *Martin Dempster*
Circulation 30,000

FOUNDED MID-1980S. MONTHLY. Features and results, in particular the men's events. No unsolicited mss. Approach in writing with ideas.

Scottish Home & Country
42A Heriot Row, Edinburgh EH3 6ES
☎0131 225 1934   Fax 0131 225 8129
Owner *Scottish Women's Rural Institutes*
Editor *Stella Roberts*
Circulation 16,000

FOUNDED 1924. MONTHLY. Scottish or rural-related issues. Unsolicited mss welcome but reading time may be from 2–3 months. Commissions are rare and tend to go to established contributors only.

Scottish Rugby Magazine
11 Dock Place, Leith, Edinburgh EH6 6LU
☎0131 554 0540   Fax 0131 554 0482
Owner *Hiscan Ltd*
Editor *Kevin Ferrie*
Circulation 19,200

FOUNDED 1990. MONTHLY. Features, club profiles, etc. Approach in writing with ideas.

Scouting Magazine
Baden Powell House, Queen's Gate, London SW7 5JS
☎0171 584 7030   Fax 0171 581 9953
Owner *The Scout Association*
Editor *David Easton*
Circulation 33,000

MONTHLY magazine for adults connected to or interested in the Scouting movement. Interested in Scouting-related features only. No fiction. *Payment* by negotiation.

Screen
The John Logie Baird Centre, University of Glasgow, Glasgow G12 8QQ
☎0141 330 5035   Fax 0141 307 8010
Owner *The John Logie Baird Centre*
Editors *Annette Kuhn, John Caughie, Simon Frith, Norman King, Sandra Kemp, Karen Lury, Jackie Stacey*
Editorial Assistant *Caroline Beven*
Circulation 2500

QUARTERLY academic journal of film and television studies for a readership ranging from undergraduates to media professionals. There are no specific qualifications for acceptance of articles. Straightforward film reviews are not normally published. Check the magazine's style and market in the first instance.

Screen International
33–39 Bowling Green Lane, London EC1R 0DA
☎0171 837 1212   Fax 0171 837 8305
Owner *EMAP Business Publishers*
Editor *Boyd Farrow*

Trade paper of the film, video and television industries. Expert freelance writers are occasionally used in all areas. No unsolicited mss. Approach with ideas in writing.
    Features *Benedict Carver*
    Payment negotiable on NUJ basis.

Sea Breezes
202 Cotton Exchange Building, Old Hall Street, Liverpool L3 9LA
☎0151 236 3935
Owner *Kinglish Ltd*
Editor *Mr C. H. Milsom*
Circulation 17,000

FOUNDED 1919. MONTHLY. Covering virtually everything relating to ships and seamen. Unsolicited mss welcome; they should be thoroughly researched and accompanied by relevant photographs. No fiction, poetry, or anything which 'smacks of the romance of the sea'.
    Features Factual tales of ships, seamen and the sea, Royal or Merchant Navy, sail or power, nautical history, shipping company histories, epic voyages, etc. Length 1000–4000 words. 'The most readily acceptable work will be that which shows it is clearly the result of first-hand experience or the product of extensive and accurate research.'
    Payment £6 per page (about 640 words).

She Magazine
National Magazine House, 72 Broadwick Street, London W1V 2BP
☎0171 439 5000   Fax 0171 439 5350
Owner *National Magazine Co. Ltd*
Editor *Linda Kelsey*
Circulation 256,689

Glossy MONTHLY for the thirtysomething woman and modern mother, addressing her needs as an individual, a partner and a parent. Talks to its readers in an intelligent, humorous and sympathetic way. Features should be about 1500 words long. Approach with ideas in writing. No unsolicited material. *Payment* NUJ rates.

Shoot Magazine
King's Reach Tower, Stamford Street, London SE1 9LS
☎0171 261 6287   Fax 0171 261 6019

Owner *IPC Magazines Ltd*
Editor *David C. Smith*
Circulation 147,000

FOUNDED 1969. WEEKLY football magazine. No unsolicited mss. Present ideas for news, features or colour photo-features to the editor by telephone.

Features Hard-hitting, topical and off-beat. Length 400–1000 words.

News Items welcome, especially exclusive gossip and transfer speculation. Max. 150 words.

Payment NUJ rates (negotiable for exclusive material).

Shooting and Conservation (BASC)

Marford Mill, Rossett, Wrexham, Clwyd LL12 0HL
☎01244 570881   Fax 01244 571678

Owner *The British Association for Shooting and Conservation (BASC)*
Editor *Mike Barnes*
Circulation 111,000

QUARTERLY Unsolicited mss welcome.

Features/Fiction Good articles and stories on shooting, conservation and related areas are always sought. Maximum 1500 words. *Payment* negotiable.

Shooting Times & Country Magazine

King's Reach Tower, Stamford Street, London SE1 9LS
☎0171 261 6180   Fax 0171 261 7179

Owner *IPC Magazines*
Editor *John Gregson*
Circulation 36,108

FOUNDED 1882. WEEKLY. Covers shooting, fishing and related countryside topics. Unsolicited mss considered. Maximum 1100 words. *Payment* negotiable.

Shropshire Magazine

77 Wyle Cop, Shrewsbury, Shropshire SY1 1UT
☎01743 362175

Owner *Leopard Press Ltd*
Editor *Pam Green*

FOUNDED 1950. MONTHLY. Unsolicited mss welcome but ideas in writing preferred.

Features Personalities, topical items, historical (e.g. family) of Shropshire; also general interest: homes, weddings, antiques, food, holidays, etc. Maximum 2000 words.

Payment negotiable but modest.

Sight & Sound

British Film Institute, 21 Stephen Street, London W1P 1PL
☎0171 255 1444   Fax 0171 436 2327

Owner *British Film Institute*
Editor *Philip Dodd*

FOUNDED 1932. MONTHLY. Topical and critical articles on international cinema, with regular columns from the USA and Europe. Length 1000–5000 words. Relevant photographs appreciated. Also book, film and video release reviews. Unsolicited material welcome. Approach in writing with ideas. *Payment* by arrangement.

The Sign

See under **(The Canterbury Press Norwich/Chansitor Publications Ltd)**

Ski Survey

118 Eaton Square, London SW1W 9AF
☎0171 245 1033   Fax 0171 245 1258

Owner *Ski Club of Great Britain*
Editor *Gill Williams*
Circulation 22,195

FOUNDED 1903. FIVE ISSUES YEARLY. Features from established ski writers only.

The Skier and The Snowboarder Magazine

48 London Road, Sevenoaks, Kent TN13 1AP
☎01732 743644   Fax 01732 743647

Owner *Hollander Publishing Ltd*
Editor *Frank Baldwin*
Circulation 30,000

SEASONAL From September to May. SIX ISSUES YEARLY. Outside contributions welcome.

Features Various topics covered, including race reports, resort reports, fashion, equipment update, dry slope, school news, new products, health and safety. Crisp, tight, informative copy of 1000 words or less preferred.

News All aspects of skiing news covered. *Payment* negotiable.

Slimming

Victory House, 14 Leicester Place, London WC2H 7BP
☎0171 437 9011   Fax 0171 434 0656

Owner *EMAP Elan Publications*
Editor *Christine Michael*
Circulation 191,000

FOUNDED 1969. TEN ISSUES YEARLY. Basically a scientific magazine with most of its material written by staff. Freelance opportunities are very few indeed. There is some scope for first-person experiences of weight control/loss, but only a small number of those received prove suitable. It is best to approach with an idea in writing. *Payment* negotiable.

Small Press Listings

The National Small Press Centre, Middlesex University, All Saints Site, White Hart Lane, London N17 8HR
☎0181 362 6058

Editor *John Nicholson*

QUARTERLY 8-page record of small presses and their publications. Companion publication of *News From the Centre*.

Smallholder

Hook House, Wimblington March, Cambridgeshire PE15 0QL
☎01354 740719   Fax 01354 741182

Owner *Smallholder Publications*
Editor *Liz Wright*
Circulation 18,000

FOUNDED 1982. MONTHLY. Outside contributions welcome. Send for sample magazine and editorial schedule before submitting anything. Follow up with samples of work to the editor so that style can be assessed for suitability. No poetry or humorous but unfocused personal tales.

Features New writers always welcome, but must have high level of technical expertise – 'not textbook stuff'. Length 750–1500 words.

News All agricultural and rural news welcome. Length 200–500 words.

Payment negotiable ('but modest').

Smash Hits

Mappin House, Winsley Street, London W1N 7AR
☎0171 436 1515   Fax 0171 636 5792

Owner *EMAP Metro Publications*
Editor *Mark Frith*
Circulation 350,000

FOUNDED 1979. FORTNIGHTLY. Top of the mid-teen market. Unsolicited mss are not accepted, but prospective contributors may approach in writing with ideas.

Snooker Scene

Cavalier House, 202 Hagley Road, Edgbaston, Birmingham B16 9PQ
☎0121 454 2931   Fax 0121 452 1822

Owner *Everton's News Agency*
Editor *Clive Everton*
Circulation 16,000

FOUNDED 1971. MONTHLY. No unsolicited mss. Approach in writing with an idea.

Somerset Magazine

23 Market Street, Crewkerne, Somerset TA18 7JU
☎01460 78000   Fax 01460 76718

Owner *Smart Print Publications Ltd*
Editor *Roy Smart*
Circulation 6000

FOUNDED 1990. MONTHLY magazine with features on any subject of interest (historical, geographical, arts, crafts) to people living in Somerset. Length 1000–1500 words, preferably with illustrations. Unsolicited mss welcome but initial approach in writing preferred. *Payment* negotiable.

The Spectator

56 Doughty Street, London WC1N 2LL
☎0171 405 1706   Fax 0171 242 0603

Owner *The Spectator (1828) Ltd*
Editor *Dominic Lawson*
Circulation 48,672

FOUNDED 1828. WEEKLY political and literary magazine. Prospective contributors should write in the first instance to the relevant editor. Unsolicited mss welcome, but over twenty are received every week and few are used.

Arts *Rebecca Nicolson*
Books *Mark Amory*
Payment nominal.

Sport Magazine

The Sports Council, 16 Upper Woburn Place, London WC1H 0QP
☎0171 388 1277   Fax 0171 383 5740

Owner *The Sports Council*
Editor *Louise Fyfe*
Circulation 15000

FOUNDED 1949. BI-MONTHLY. Covering sports development, policies and politics, plus new ideas and innovations in the world of sport. Approach by phone with ideas.

News/Features On any of the areas mentioned above. Features should be 750–1000 words. *Payment* £100 per 1000 words.

The Sporting Life

1 Canada Square, Canary Wharf, London E14 5AP
☎0171 293 3000   Fax 0171 293 3758

Owner *Mirror Group Newspapers Ltd*
Editor *Tom Clarke*
Circulation 95,181

DAILY newspaper of the horse-racing world. Always on the look-out for specialised, well-informed racing writers – not necessarily estab-

lished sports writers. No unsolicited mss. Phone or write with an idea in first instance. 'The talented will be taken up and used again.'
Associate Editor/Features *Alastair Down*

Springboard – Writing To Succeed
30 Orange Hill Road, Prestwich, Manchester M25 1LS
☎0161 773 5911
Owner *Leo Brooks*
Editor *Leo Brooks*
Circulation *c.* 200

FOUNDED 1990. QUARTERLY. *Springboard* is not a market for writers but a forum from which they can find encouragement and help. Interested in articles, news, market information, competition/folio news directed at helping writers to achieve success.

Staffordshire Life
Hourds Publishing Centre, Derby Street, Stafford ST16 2DT
☎01785 57700   Fax 01785 53287
Owner *Hourds Publications Ltd*
Editor *Philip Thurlow-Craig*
Circulation 16,000

FOUNDED 1982. BI-MONTHLY county magazine devoted to Staffordshire, its surroundings and people. Contributions welcome. Approach in writing with ideas.
Features Maximum 1500 words.
Fashion Copy must be supported by photographs.
Payment NUJ rates.

Stage and Television Today
47 Bermondsey Street, London SE1 3XT
☎0171 403 1818   Fax 0171 403 1418
Owner *The Stage Newspaper Ltd*
Editor *Brian Attwood*
Circulation 42,000

FOUNDED 1880. WEEKLY. No unsolicited mss. Prospective contributors should write with ideas in the first instance. Occasional feature suggestions from freelancers are considered.
Features Preference for middle-market, tabloid style articles. 'Puff pieces', PR plugs and extended production notes will not be considered. Maximum 800 words.
News News stories from outside London are always welcome. Maximum 300 words.
Payment £100 per 1000 words.

Stand Magazine
See under **Poetry, Little Magazines**

Staple Magazine
See under **Poetry, Little Magazines**

Stone Soup
37 Chesterfield Road, London W4 3HQ
☎0181 742 7554   Fax 0181 742 7554
Editor *Igor Klikovac, Ken Smith*
Associate Editor *Srdja Pavlović*
Circulation 2000

International literary magazine for new writing. Edited by English poet Ken Smith and Bosnian poet Igor Klikovac, the magazine is printed in English and languages of former Yugoslavia. Also interested in publishing writing in all European languages. Issued three times a year, the editors actively encourage correspondence. Mss should be sent in duplicate, preferably on disc; s.a.e. essential for return of material.

Storm
120 Clarendon Road, London W11 1SA
Editor *Joanna Labon*

FOUNDED 1990. *Storm: New Writing from East and West* . FOUNDED in response to the fall of the Berlin Wall, 1989, to publish prose fiction (short stories and extracts from novels) from Eastern Europe which has not been available to British readers. While the magazine quickly expanded to include writers from Mexico, France and Germany, it remains a catalyst bringing work into the lingua franca, English, for the first time. British, Irish, American and Canadian writers have also published here, but they tend to be well established at home. *Storm* is not somewhere for new writers to send their work, and unsolicited mss are not welcome. If you are a translator or have ideas of an excellent foreign writer whom you feel should be published, please read some back numbers of *Storm* before writing a brief letter to the editors outlining your proposal. *Storm* is supported by the Arts Council.

The Strad
7 St. John's Road, Harrow, Middlesex HA12 2EE
☎0181 863 2020   Fax 0181 863 2444
Owner *Orpheus Publications*
Editor *Brian Yule*
Circulation 11,500

FOUNDED 1890. MONTHLY for classical string musicians, makers and enthusiasts. Unsolicited mss welcome.
Features Profiles of string players, composers and musical instruments. Max. 3000 words.
News/Reviews *Brian Yule.*
Payment £100 per 1000 words.

Student Outlook

87 Kirkstall Road, London SW2 4HE
☎0181 671 7920

Owner *I.J. Hensall*
Editor *D. Patton*
Circulation 80,000

FOUNDED 1990. THRICE-YEARLY (one for each academic term). Student-related topics across a broad range of interests, including music, film, books 'Campus News' and 'Planet News' (politics from a green perspective). Unsolicited mss welcome from both students and ex-students who are not long out of student life.

Payment £50 per two-page feature. Shorter pieces by negotiation.

Studies in Accounting & Finance

19 Rutland Street, Cork, Republic of Ireland
☎00 353 21 313 855   Fax 00 353 21 313 496

Editor *Conal O'Boyle*
Circulation 1000

QUARTERLY. Specialist, professional readership. Features tend to be commissioned. No unsolicited mss. Approach in writing with ideas. Maximum 3000 words. *Payment* £200.

Suffolk Countryside

Griggs Farm, West Street, Coggeshall, Essex CO6 1NT
☎01376 562578   Fax 01376 562578

Owner *Market Link Publishing*
Editor *Andy Tilbrook*

FOUNDED 1995. MONTHLY. Unsolicited material of Suffolk interest welcome. No general interest material.

Features Countryside, culture and crafts in Suffolk. Maximum 1500.

Payment £40.

Suffolk Life

Barn Acre House, Saxtead Green, Suffolk IP13 9QJ
☎01728 685832   Fax 01728 685842

Owner *Today Magazines Ltd*
Editor *Kevin Davis*
Circulation 17,000

FOUNDED 1989. MONTHLY. General interest, local stories, historical, personalities, wine, travel, food. Unsolicited mss welcome. Approach by phone or in writing with ideas. Not interested in anything which does not relate specifically to East Anglia. Sister publications run jointly include *Norfolk Life* circ. 13,000.

Features *Kevin Davis* Maximum 1700 words, with photos.

News *Kevin Davis* Maximum 1000 words, with photos.

Special Pages *Sue Wright* Study the magazine for guidelines. Maximum 1700 words.

Payment £20 (news); £25 (other).

Sunday Express Magazine

See under **National Newspapers (Sunday Express)**

Sunday Magazine

See under **National Newspapers (News of the World)**

Sunday Mail Magazine

See under **National Newspapers (Sunday Mail, Glasgow)**

Sunday Mirror Magazine

See under **National Newspapers (Sunday Mirror)**

Sunday Post Magazine

See under **National Newspapers (Sunday Post, Glasgow)**

Sunday Times Magazine

See under **National Newspapers (The Sunday Times)**

Sunk Island Review

Sunk Island Publishing, PO Box 74, Lincoln LN1 1QG
☎01522 575660   Fax 01522 568353

Owner *Sunk Island Publishing*
Editor *Michael Blackburn*
Circulation 1000

FOUNDED 1989. BI-ANNUAL magazine containing new short stories, novel extracts, poetry, some articles and reviews, also translations. Unsolicited mss welcome. Seeking new creative writing. No horror, romance, religious writing. No maximum length. Approach with ideas in writing. *Payment* on publication by arrangement.

Superbike Magazine

Link House, Dingwall Avenue, Croydon, Surrey CR9 2TA
☎0181 686 2599   Fax 0181 760 0973

Editor *Grant Leonard*
Circulation 40,000

FOUNDED 1977. MONTHLY. Dedicated to all that is best and most exciting in the world of high-performance motorcycling. Unsolicited mss, synopses and ideas welcome.

Surrey County Magazine
PO Box 154, South Croydon, Surrey
CR2 0XA
☎0181 657 8568   Fax 0181 657 8568
Owner *Datateam Publishing*
Editor *Theo Spring*
Circulation 8500

FOUNDED 1970. MONTHLY. County matters for Surrey dwellers. News, views, history and comment. Interested in product information for an A/AB readership. Unsolicited mss welcome. Approach by phone or in writing with ideas.

Sussex Life
30–32 Teville Road, Worthing, West Sussex
BN11 1UG
☎01903 204628   Fax 01903 820193
Owner *Sussex Life Ltd*
Editor *Trudi Linscer*
Circulation 17,500

FOUNDED 1965. MONTHLY. Sussex and general women's interest magazine. Interested in investigative, journalistic pieces relevant to the area and celebrity profiles. No historical pieces. Unsolicited mss, synopses and ideas in writing welcome. Maximum 500 words. *Payment* £15 per 500 words.

Swimming Times
Harold Fern House, Derby Square,
Loughborough, Leicestershire LE11 0AL
☎01509 234433   Fax 01509 235049
Owner *Amateur Swimming Association*
Editor *P. Hassall*
Circulation 18,600

FOUNDED 1923. MONTHLY about competitive swimming and associated subjects. Unsolicited mss welcome.

Features Technical articles on swimming, water polo, diving or synchronised swimming. Length and payment negotiable.

The Tablet
1 King Street Cloisters, Clifton Walk, London
W6 0QZ
☎0181 748 8484   Fax 0181 748 1550
Owner *The Tablet Publishing Co Ltd*
Editor *John Wilkins*
Circulation 18,313

FOUNDED 1840. WEEKLY. Quality international Roman Catholic magazine featuring articles of interest to concerned laity and clergy. Unsolicited material welcome (1500 words) if relevant to magazine's style and mar-

ket. All approaches should be made in writing. *Payment* from about £50.

Take a Break
Shirley House, 25–27 Camden Road, London
NW1 9LL
☎0171 284 0909   Fax 0171 284 3778
Owner *H. Bauer*
Editor *John Dale*
Circulation 1.3 million

FOUNDED 1990. WEEKLY. True-life feature magazine. Approach with ideas in writing.

News/Features Always on the look-out for good, true-life stories. Maximum 1200 words. *Payment* negotiable.

Fiction Sharp, succinct stories which are well told and often with a twist at the end. All categories, provided it is relevant to the magazine's style and market. Maximum 1000 words. *Payment* negotiable.

Talking Business
237 Kennington Lane, London SE11 5QY
☎0171 582 0536   Fax 0171 582 4917
Owner *Square One Publishing Ltd*
Editor *Sue Sillitoe*
Circulation 6,500

FOUNDED 1994. MONTHLY. News, reviews, features and charts covering the expanding audiobooks market. Interested in considering business-oriented material and personality profiles. Approach in writing in the first instance.

The Tatler
Vogue House, Hanover Square, London
W1R 0AD
☎0171 499 9080   Fax 0171 409 0451
Owner *Condé Nast Publications Ltd*
Editor *Jane Procter*
Circulation 80,373

Up-market glossy from the Condé Nast stable. New writers should send in copies of either published work or unpublished material; writers of promise will be taken up. The magazine works largely on a commission basis: they are unlikely to publish unsolicited features, but will ask writers to work to specific projects.

Features *Rebecca Tyrrel*

The Tea Club Magazine
PO Box 221, Guildford, Surrey GU1 3YT
☎01483 62888   Fax 01483 302732
Publisher *Bond Clarkson Russell*
Editor *Lorna Swainson*

FOUNDED 1992 by The Tea Council. THRICE

YEARLY. Specialist focus on tea and tea-related topics. All editorial features are commissioned. Approach with ideas only.

Tees Valley Writer

See under **Poetry, Little Magazines**

Telegraph Magazine

See under **National Newspapers (The Daily Telegraph)**

TGO (The Great Outdoors)

The Plaza Tower, East Kilbride, Glasgow G74 1LW
☎013552 46444   Fax 013552 63013
Owner *Caledonian Magazines Ltd*
Editor *Cameron McNeish*
Circulation 22,000

FOUNDED 1978. MONTHLY. Deals with walking, backpacking and countryside topics. Unsolicited mss are welcome.

Features Well-written and illustrated items on relevant topics. Maximum 2000 words. Colour photographs only please.

News Short topical items (or photographs). Maximum 300 words.

Payment £100–200 for features; £10–20 for news.

Theologia Cambrensis

Church in Wales Centre, Woodland Place, Penarth, South Glamorgan CF64 2EX
☎01222 705278   Fax 01222 712413
Owner *The Church in Wales*
Editor *John Herbert*

FOUNDED 1988. THRICE YEARLY. Concerned exclusively with theology and news of theological interest. Includes religious poetry, letters and book reviews (provided they have a scholarly bias). No secular material. Unsolicited mss welcome. Approach in writing with ideas.

The Third Alternative

5 Martins Lane, Witcham, Ely, Cambridgeshire CB6 2LB
☎01353 777931
Owner *Andy Cox*
Editor *Andy Cox*

FOUNDED 1993. Quarterly magazine of horror, fantasy, science fiction and slipstream fiction, plus poetry, features and art. Publishes talented newcomers alongside award-winning authors. Unsolicited mss welcome if accompanied by s.a.e. or International Reply Coupons. Guidelines are available but potential contributors are also advised to study the magazine.

This England

PO Box 52, Cheltenham, Gloucestershire GL50 1YQ
☎01242 577775   Fax 01242 222034
Owner *This England Ltd*
Editor *Roy Faiers*
Circulation 180,000

FOUNDED 1968. QUARTERLY, with a strong overseas readership. Celebration of England and all things English: famous people, natural beauty, towns and villages, history, traditions, customs and legends, crafts, etc. Generally a rural basis, with the 'Forgetmenots' section publishing readers' recollections and nostalgia. Up to one hundred unsolicited pieces received each week. Unsolicited mss/ideas welcome. Length 250–2000 words. *Payment* £25 per 1000 words.

Time

Brettenham House, Lancaster Place, London WC2E 7TL
☎0171 499 4080   Fax 0171 322 1230
Owner *Time Warner, Inc.*
Editor *Barry Hillenbrand* (London Bureau Chief)
Circulation 5.46 million

FOUNDED 1923. WEEKLY current affairs and news magazine. There are no opportunities for freelancers on *Time* as almost all the magazine's content is written by staff members from various bureaux around the world. No unsolicited mss.

Time Out

Universal House, 251 Tottenham Court Road, London W1A 1BZ
☎0171 813 3000   Fax 0171 813 6001
Editor *Dominic Wells*
Publisher *Tony Elliott*
Circulation 90,000

FOUNDED 1968. WEEKLY magazine of news and entertainment in London.

Features *Elaine Paterson* 'Usually written by staff writers or commissioned, but it's always worth submitting an idea by phone if particularly apt to the magazine.' Maximum 2500 words.

News *Tony Thompson* Despite having a permanent team of staff news writers, sometimes willing to accept contributions from new journalists 'should their material be relevant to the issue'.

Payment £164 per 1000 words.

The Times Educational Supplement Scotland

37 George Street, Edinburgh EH2 2HN
☎0131 220 1100 Fax 0131 220 1616
Owner *Times Supplements Ltd*
Editor *Willis Pickard*
Circulation 6000
FOUNDED 1965. WEEKLY. Unsolicited mss welcome.
Features Articles on education in Scotland. Maximum 1200 words.
News Items on education in Scotland. Maximum 600 words.
Payment NUJ rates for NUJ members.

The Times Educational Supplement

Admiral House, 66–68 East Smithfield, London E1 9XY
☎0171 782 3000 Fax 0171 782 3200
Owner *News International*
Editor *Patricia Rowan*
Circulation 137,287
FOUNDED 1910. WEEKLY. New contributors are welcome and should phone with ideas for news or features; write for reviews.
Arts and Books *Heather Neill*
Media & Resources *Gillian Macdonald* Unsolicited reviews are not accepted. Anyone wanting to review should write, sending examples of their work and full details of their academic and professional background to either the literary editor or the media and resources editor. Maximum 1200 words.
Opinion *Patricia Rowan* 'Platform': a weekly slot for a well-informed and cogently argued viewpoint. Maximum 1200 words. 'Second Opinion': a shorter comment on an issue of the day by somebody well placed to write on the subject. Maximum 700 words.
Further Education *Ian Nash* Includes college management.
Primary *Diane Hofkins*
School Management *Bob Doe* Weekly pages on practical issues for school governors and managers. Maximum 1000 words.
Features *Sarah Bayliss* Longer articles on contemporary practical subjects of general interest to the *TES* reader. Maximum 1000–1500 words; longer or multi-part features are rarely accepted.
Extra *Joyce Arnold* Subjects covered include: science, travel, music, modern languages, home economics, school visits, primary education, history, geography, mathematics, health, life skills, environmental education, technology, special needs. Articles should relate to current educational practice. Age-range covered is primary to sixth form. Maximum 1000–1300 words. *Payment* by arrangement.
Update a monthly magazine section devoted to Primary (*Diane Hofkins*); Computers/IT (*Merlin John*); School management (*Bob Doe*); or FE (*Ian Nash*).

The Times Higher Education Supplement

Admiral House, 66–68 East Smithfield, London E1 9XY
☎0171 782 3000 Fax 0171 782 3300/1
Owner *News International*
Editor *Auriol Stevens*
Circulation 22,000
FOUNDED 1971. WEEKLY. Unsolicited mss are welcome but most articles and *all* book reviews are commissioned. 'In most cases it is better to write, but in the case of news stories it is all right to phone.'
Books *Andrew Robinson*
Features *Sian Griffiths* Most articles are commissioned from academics in higher education.
News *Martin Ince* Freelance opportunities very occasionally.
Science *Kam Patel / Aisling Irwin*
Science Books *Andrew Robinson*
Foreign *David Jobbins*
Payment NUJ rates.

The Times Literary Supplement

Admiral House, 66–68 Smithfield, London E1 9XY
☎0171 782 3000 Fax 0171 782 3100
Owner *News International*
Editor *Ferdinand Mount*
Circulation 30,000
FOUNDED 1902. WEEKLY review of literature. Contributors should approach in writing and be familiar with the general level of writing in the *TLS*.
Literary Discoveries *Alan Jenkins*
Poems *Alan Hollinghurst*
News *Ferdinand Mount* News stories and general articles concerned with literature, publishing and new intellectual developments anywhere in the world. Length by arrangement.
Payment by arrangement.

Titbits

2 Caversham Street, London SW3 4AH
☎0171 351 4995 Fax 0171 351 4995
Owner *Sport Newspapers Ltd*

Editor *Leonard Holdsworth*
Circulation 150,000

FOUNDED 1895. MONTHLY. Consumer magazine for men covering show business and general interests. Unsolicited mss and ideas in writing welcome. Maximum 3000 words. News, features, particularly photofeatures (colour), and fiction.
Payment negotiable.

To & Fro
17 Grove Park, Waltham Road, White Waltham, Maidenhead, Berkshire SL6 3LW
☎01628 829815   Fax 01628 829816
Owner *Anne Smith*
Editor *Anne Smith*
Circulation 35,000

FOUNDED 1978. BI-MONTHLY. Specialist machine knitting magazine. Interested in material related to machine knitting only. Unsolicited mss and ideas welcome. Contact the editor in writing in the first instance.

Today's Golfer
Bretton Court, Bretton, Peterborough, Cambridgeshire PE3 8DZ
☎01733 264666   Fax 01733 267198
Owner *EMAP Pursuit Publishing*
Editor *David Clarke*

FOUNDED 1988. MONTHLY. Golf instruction, features, player profiles and news. Unsolicited mss welcome. Approach in writing with ideas. Not interested in instruction material from outside contributors.
Features/News *Scott MacCallum* Opinion, player profiles and general golf-related features. Maximum 3000 words. Small interesting news items, oddities and fillers. Max. 250 words.
Payment £100 per 1000 words.

Today's Runner
Bretton Court, Bretton, Peterborough, Cambridgeshire PE3 8DZ
☎01733 264666   Fax 01733 267198
Owner *EMAP Pursuit Publishing Ltd*
Editor *Allan Haines*
Circulation 30,000

FOUNDED 1985. MONTHLY. Instructional articles on running and fitness, plus running-related activities and health.
Features Specialist knowledge an advantage. Opportunities are wide, but approach with idea in first instance.
News Opportunities for people stories, especially if backed up by photographs.

Top Santé Health and Beauty
Presse Publishing, 17 Radley Mews, Kensington, London W8 6JP
☎0171 938 3033   Fax 0171 938 5464
Owner *Presse Publishing*
Editor *Jane Garton*
Circulation 152,269

FOUNDED 1993. MONTHLY magazine covering all aspects of health and beauty. Unsolicited mss not generally accepted. Not interested in anything except health and beauty. Approach in writing with ideas.

Townswoman
Media Associates, 8 Capitol House, Heigham Street, Norwich, Norfolk NR2 4TE
☎01603 616005   Fax 01603 767397
Owner *Townswomen's Guilds*
Editor *Moira Eagling*
Circulation 32,000

FOUNDED 1933. MONTHLY. No unsolicited mss. Few opportunities as in-house editorial staff are strong.

Traditional Homes
See **Period Living & Traditional Homes**

Trail Walker
Bretton Court, Bretton, Peterborough, Cambridgeshire PE3 8DZ
☎01733 264666   Fax 01733 261984
Owner *EMAP Pursuit Publishing Ltd*
Editor *David Ogle*
Circulation 30,099

FOUNDED 1990. MONTHLY. Gear reports, where to walk and practical advice for the hillwalker and long distance walker. Approach by phone or in writing in the first instance.
Features *David Ogle* Very limited requirement for overseas articles, 'written to our style'. Ask for guidelines. Max. 2000 words.
Special pages *Alec Jiggins* (News/sub-editor) Big requirement for guided walks articles. Specialist writers only. Ask for guidelines. Max. 750 – 2000 words (depending on subject).
Payment £60 per 1000 words.

Traveller
45–49 Brompton Road, London SW3 1DE
☎0171 581 4130   Fax 0171 581 1357
Owner *I. M. Wilson*
Editor *Caroline Brandenburger*
Circulation 35,359

FOUNDED 1970. QUARTERLY. Unsolicited mss/ideas welcome.

Features Six colour features per issue – copy must be accompanied by good-quality colour transparencies. Articles welcome on off-beat cultural or anthropological subjects. Western Europe rarely covered. No general travel accounts. Maximum 2000 words.
Payment £125 per 1000 words.

Trout Fisherman

Bretton Court, Bretton, Peterborough, Cambridgeshire PE3 8DZ
☎01733 264666   Fax 01733 263294
Owner *EMAP Pursuit Publications*
Editor *Chris Dawn*
Circulation 46,032

FOUNDED 1977. MONTHLY instructive magazine on trout fishing. Most of the articles are commissioned, but unsolicited mss and quality colour transparencies welcome.
Features Maximum 2500 words.
Payment varies.

Turkeys
See **Fancy Fowl**

TV Times

King's Reach Tower, Stamford Street, London SE1 9LS
☎0171 261 5000   Fax 0171 261 7777
Owner *IPC Magazines*
Editor *Liz Murphy*
Circulation 998,378

FOUNDED 1968. WEEKLY magazine of listings and features serving the viewers of independent television, BBC, satellite and radio. Almost no freelance contributions used, except where the writer is known and trusted by the magazine. No unsolicited contributions.

UK Press Gazette

Maclean Hunter House, Cockfosters Lane, Barnet, Hertfordshire EN4 0BU
☎0181 242 3081   Fax 0181 242 3088
Owner *EMAP*
Editor *Tony Loynes*
Circulation 10,000

WEEKLY magazine containing news, features and analysis of all areas of journalism, print and broadcasting. Unsolicited mss welcome, interested in personality profiles, technical and current affairs relating to the world of journalism. No vague, trite and ill-directed pieces; we serve a professional market which requires professional reading. Approach with ideas by phone or in writing.

Ulster Tatler

39 Boucher Road, Belfast BT12 6UT
☎01232 681371   Fax 01232 381915
Owner *Richard Sherry*
Editor *Richard Sherry*
Circulation 10,000

FOUNDED 1965. MONTHLY. Articles of local interest and social functions appealing to Northern Ireland's ABC1 population. Welcome unsolicited material; approach by phone or in writing in the first instance.
Features *Noreen Dorman* Maximum 1500 words. *Payment* £50.
Fiction *Richard Sherry* Maximum 3000 words. *Payment* £150.

The Universe

St James's Buildings, Oxford Street, Manchester M1 6FP
☎0161 236 8856   Fax 0161 236 8530
Owner *Gabriel Communications Ltd*
Editor *To be appointed*
Circulation 90,000

Occasional use of new writers, but a substantial network of regular contributors already exists. Interested in a very wide range of material: all subjects which might bear on Christian life. Fiction not usually accepted. *Payment* negotiable.

Vector
See **British Science Fiction Association** under **Professional Associations**

The Vegan

Donald Watson House, 7 Battle Road, St Leonards on Sea, East Sussex TN37 7AA
☎01424 427393   Fax 01424 717064
Owner *Vegan Society*
Editor *Richard Farhall*
Circulation 5000

FOUNDED 1944. QUARTERLY. Deals with the ecological, ethical and health aspects of veganism. Unsolicited mss welcome. Maximum 2000 words. *Payment* negotiable.

Verbatim, The Language Quarterly

PO Box 199, Aylesbury, Buckinghamshire HP20 2HY
☎01296 395880
Editor *Laurence Urdang*
Circulation 25,000

FOUNDED 1974. QUARTERLY. Authors are urged to review a copy of the periodical before submitting anything. Sample copy and writers' guidelines available on request. Unsolicited mss welcome. Approach in writing with ideas. No phone calls.

Features Any aspect of language. Maximum 1500 words.

Payment negotiable/up to £200 for full-length article.

Veteran Car

Jessamine Court, High Street, Ashwell, Hertfordshire SG7 5NL
☎01462 742818   Fax 01462 742997

Owner *The Veteran Car Club of Great Britain*
Editor *Elizabeth Bennett*
Circulation 1500

FOUNDED 1938. BI-MONTHLY magazine which exists primarily for the benefit of members of The Veteran Car Club of Great Britain. It is concerned with all aspects of the old vehicle hobby – events, restoration, history, current world news, legislation, etc., relating to pre-1919 motor cars. Most professional writers who contribute to the magazine are Club members. No budget for paid contributions.

Vintage Times/Vintage Homes

PhD Publishing, Navestock Hill, Navestock, Essex RM4 1HA
☎01708 370380/370053

Owner *PhD Publishing*
Editor *David Hoppit*
Circulation 48,000

FOUNDED 1994. QUARTERLY lifestyle magazine 'for over-40s who have not quite given up hope of winning Wimbledon'. Preliminary approach by phone or in writing with ideas.

Vogue

Vogue House, Hanover Square, London W1R 0AD
☎0171 499 9080   Fax 0171 408 0559

Owner *Condé Nast Publications Ltd*
Editor *Alexandra Shulman*
Circulation 186,162

Condé Nast Magazines tend to use known writers and commission what's needed, rather than using unsolicited mss. Contacts are useful.

Features *Eve MacSweeney* Upmarket general interest rather than 'women's'. Good proportion of highbrow art and literary articles, as well as travel, gardens, food, home interest and reviews. No fiction.

The Voice

370 Coldharbour Lane, London SW9 8PL
☎0171 737 7377   Fax 0171 274 8994

Owner *Vee Tee Ay Media Resources*
Editor *Winsome Cornish*
Circulation 50,060

FOUNDED 1982. WEEKLY newspaper, particularly aimed at the black British community. Copy for consideration welcome but 'publication is not guaranteed'. Initial approach in writing preferred. Few opportunities except in features.

Payment from £100 per 1000 words/negotiable.

The War Cry

101 Queen Victoria Street, London EC4P 4EP
☎0171 236 5222   Fax 0171 236 3491

Owner *The Salvation Army*
Editor *Captain Charles King*
Circulation 90,000

FOUNDED 1879. WEEKLY magazine containing Christian comments on current issues. Unsolicited mss welcome if appropriate to contents. No fiction or poetry. Approach by phone with ideas.

News relating to Christian Church or social issues. Maximum length 500 words. *Payment* £20 per article.

Features Magazine-style articles of interest to the 'man/woman-in-the-street'. Maximum length 500 words. *Payment* £20 per article.

The Water Gardener

9 Tufton Street, Ashford, Kent TN23 1QN
☎01233 621877   Fax 01233 645669

Owner *Dog World Publishing*
Editor *David Papworth*

FOUNDED 1944. Nine issues per year. Everything relevant to water gardening. Will consider in-depth features on aspects of the subject; write with idea in the first instance. Maximum 2000 words. *Payment* £100–£200.

Waterways World

Kottingham House, Dale Street, Burton on Trent, Staffordshire DE14 3TD
☎01283 564290   Fax 01283 561077

Owner *Waterway Productions Ltd*
Editor *Hugh Potter*
Circulation 21,963

FOUNDED 1972. MONTHLY magazine for inland waterway enthusiasts. Unsolicited mss welcome, provided the writer has a good knowledge of the subject. No fiction.

Features *Hugh Potter* Articles (preferably illustrated) are published on all aspects of inland waterways in Britain and abroad, including recreational and commercial boating on rivers and canals.

News *Regan Milnes* Maximum 500 words. *Payment* £35 per 1000 words.

Wedding and Home

King's Reach Tower, Stamford Street, London SE1 9LS
☎0171 261 7471   Fax 0171 261 7459

Owner *IPC Magazines Ltd*
Editor *Debbie Djordjević*
Circulation 48,000

BI-MONTHLY for women planning their wedding, honeymoon and first home. Most features are written in-house or commissioned from known freelancers. Unsolicited mss are not welcome, but approaches may be made in writing.

Weekly News

Albert Square, Dundee DD1 9QJ
☎01382 23131   Fax 01382 201390

Owner *D. C. Thomson & Co. Ltd*
Editor *David Hishmurgh*
Circulation 365,000

WEEKLY. Newsy, family-orientated magazine designed to appeal to the busy housewife. 'We get a lot of unsolicited stuff and there is great loss of life among them.' Usually commissions, but writers of promise will be taken up. Series include showbiz, royals and television. No fiction. *Payment* negotiable.

West Lothian Life

Ballencrieff Cottage, Ballencrieff Toll, Bathgate, West Lothian EH48 4LD
☎01506 632728   Fax 01506 632728

Owner *Pages Editorial & Publishing Services*
Editor *Susan Coon*

QUARTERLY for people who live, work or have an interest in West Lothian. Includes three major features (1500 words) on successful people, businesses or initiatives. A local walk takes up the centre spread. Regular articles by experts on collectables, property, photography, cookery and local gardening, plus news items, letters and a competition. Freelance writers used exclusively for main features. Phone first to discuss content and timing.

Payment by arrangement.

What Car?

38–42 Hampton Road, Teddington, Middlesex TW11 0JE
☎0181 943 5637   Fax 0181 943 5659

Owner *Haymarket Motoring Publications Ltd*
Editor *Mark Payton*
Circulation 133,129

MONTHLY. The car buyer's bible, *What Car?* concentrates on road test comparisons of new cars, news and buying advice on used cars, as well as a strong consumer section. Some scope for freelancers. Testing is only offered to the few, and general articles on aspects of driving are only accepted from writers known and trusted by the magazine as conclusions arrived at can be controversial and need to be scrupulously researched. No unsolicited mss. *Payment* negotiable.

What Hi-Fi?

38–42 Hampton Road, Teddington, Middlesex TW11 0JE
☎0181 943 5000   Fax 0181 943 5098

Owner *Haymarket Magazines Ltd*
Editor *Rahiel Nasir*
Circulation 71,330

FOUNDED 1976. MONTHLY. Features on hi-fi and new technology. No unsolicited contributions. Prior consultation with the editor essential.

Features General or more specific on hi-fi and new technology pertinent to the consumer electronics market. Length 2500–3000 words. *Payment* £90 per page.

Reviews Specific product reviews. Generally from an established pool of reviewers but 'willing to look at material from hi-fi enthusiasts who also happen to be journalists'.

What Investment

3rd Floor, 4–8 Tabernacle Street, London EC2A 4LU
☎0171 638 1916   Fax 0171 638 3128

Owner *Charterhouse Communications*
Editor *Keiron Root*
Circulation 37,000

FOUNDED 1983. MONTHLY. Features articles on a variety of savings and investment matters. Unsolicited mss welcome. All approaches should be made in writing.

Features Length 1200–1500 words (maximum 2000).
Payment NUJ rates minimum.

What Mortgage

4–8 Tabernacle Street, London EC2A 4LU
☎0171 638 1916   Fax 0171 638 3128
Owner *Charterhouse Communications*
Editor *Nia Williams*
Circulation 30,000

FOUNDED 1982. MONTHLY magazine on property purchase, choice and finance. Unsolicited mss welcome; prospective contributors may make initial contact either by telephone or in writing.
Features Up to 1500 words on related topics are considered. Particularly welcome are new angles, new ideas or specialities relevant to mortgages.
Payment £140 per 1000 words.

What's New in Building

Morgan-Grampian House, 30 Calderwood Street, London SE18 6QH
☎0181 855 7777   Fax 0181 316 3169
Owner *Morgan-Grampian Ltd*
Editor *Janice Purath*
Assistant Editor *Mark Pennington*
Circulation 31,496

MONTHLY. Specialist magazine covering new products for building. Unsolicited mss not generally welcome. The only freelance work available is rewriting press release material. This is offered on a monthly basis of 25–50 items of about 150 words each. *Payment* £5.25 per item.

What's new in Farming

Morgan-Grampian House, 30 Calderwood Street, London SE18 6QH
☎0181 855 7777 ext. 5070Fax 0181 854 6795
Owner *United Newspapers*
Managing Editor *Don Taylor*
Circulation 48,500

FOUNDED 1977. Published eight times a year. The magazine is primarily a guide to new agricultural products, with features covering the application of new technology. All copy is written in-house or by established freelance contributors.
Features Articles on relevant agricultural topics. Maximum 2000 words.
Payment negotiable.

What's New in Interiors

Morgan-Grampian House, 30 Calderwood Street, London SE18 6QH
☎0181 855 7777   Fax 0181 855 2342
Owner *Morgan-Grampian Ltd*
Editorial Contact *Janice Purath*

Circulation 22,000

FOUNDED 1981. QUARTERLY. Aimed at interior designers, architects and specifiers. Make initial contact in writing or by telephone.
Features New product information only. Maximum 150 words for each product item.

What's On in London

180–182 Pentonville Road, London N1 9LB
☎0171 278 4393   Fax 0171 837 5838
Owner *E. G. Shaw*
Editor *Michael Darvell*
Circulation 40,000

FOUNDED 1935. WEEKLY entertainment-based guide and information magazine. Features, listings and reviews. Always interested in well-thought-out and well-presented mss. Articles should have London/Home Counties connection, except during the summer when they can be of much wider tourist/historic interest, relating to unusual traditions and events. Approach the editor by telephone in the first instance.
Features *Graham Hassell*
Art *Ria Higgins*
Cinema *Marshall Julius*
Pop Music *Danny Scott*
Classical Music *Michael Darvell*
Theatre *Neil Smith*
Events *David Clark*
Payment by arrangement.

J. D. Williams Magazine

Russell House, 28 Little Russell Street, London WC1A 2HN
☎0171 404 0123   Fax 0171 404 1670
Owner *ICG Baronage Publishing*
Editor *Joani Walsh*
Circulation 300,000

SEASONAL general interest/consumer magazine. No unsolicited material. All preliminary approaches should be made by phone.
Features Celebrity interviews, fashion, history/nostalgia, travel, real-life stories, pets. Max. length 1500 words. *Payment* up to £250.
Special pages Health, fitness, beauty, hair, wine, coffee/tea and food.

Wine

Quest Magazines Ltd., 652 Victoria Road, South Ruislip, Middlesex HA4 0SXG
☎0181 842 1010   Fax 0181 841 2557
Owner *Wilmington Publishing*
Editor *To be appointed*
Circulation 35,000

FOUNDED 1983. MONTHLY. No unsolicited mss.

News/Features Wine, food and food/wine-related travel stories. Prospective contributors should approach in writing.

Wisden Cricket Monthly
6 Beech Lane, Guildford, Surrey GU2 5ES
☎01483 32573/570358   Fax 01483 33153
Owner *Wisden Cricket Magazines Ltd*
Editor *David Frith*
Circulation *c.*42,000

FOUNDED 1979. MONTHLY. Very few uncommissioned articles are used, but would-be contributors are not discouraged. Approach in writing. *Payment* varies.

Woman
King's Reach Tower, Stamford Street,
London SE1 9LS
☎0171 261 5000   Fax 0171 261 5997
Owner *IPC Magazines Ltd*
Editor *Carole Russell*
Circulation 750,000

Long-running, popular women's magazine which boasts a readership of over 2.5 million. No unsolicited mss. Most work commissioned. Approach with ideas in writing.
    Features *Keith Kendrick* Maximum 1250 words.
    Books *Sally Pearce*

Woman and Home
King's Reach Tower, Stamford Street,
London SE1 9LS
☎0171 261 5000   Fax 0171 261 7346
Owner *IPC Magazines Ltd*
Editor *Orlando Murrin*
Circulation 395,000

FOUNDED 1926. MONTHLY. Prospective contributors are advised to write with ideas, including photocopies of other published work or details of magazines to which they have contributed. S.a.e. essential for return of material. Most freelance work is specially commissioned.
    Features *Jackie Hatton*
    Fiction *Kati Nicholl* (tel: 0171 261 6475) Short stories are usually submitted by agents; serials are always submitted by agents or publishers. No poetry.
    Homes and Gardens *Carolyn Bailey* (tel: 0171 261 5257) Suitable locations should be submitted with brief description and general photographs.
    Other Fashion, knitting, beauty, health, cookery and travel, all covered by staff writers and specially commissioned freelancers.
    Payment negotiable.

Woman's Journal
King's Reach Tower, Stamford Street,
London SE1 9LS
☎0171 261 6220   Fax 0171 261 7061
Owner *IPC Magazines Ltd*
Editor *Deirdre Vine*
Circulation 166,412

MONTHLY. Feature ideas welcome, with samples of previous work.
    Features *Jane Dowdeswell* Major features are generally commissioned, but new fresh ideas on all subjects welcome. Maximum 2000 words. *Payment* negotiable.
        Design and Homes *Sue Price*
        Fashion *Alex Parnell*
        Food *Katie Stewart*
        Beauty *Kate Shapland*
        Health *Cherry Maslen*

Woman's Own
King's Reach Tower, Stamford Street,
London SE1 9LS
☎0171 261 5474   Fax 0171 261 5346
Owner *IPC Magazines Ltd*
Editor *Keith McNeill*
Circulation 700,178

WEEKLY. Prospective contributors should contact the features editor *in writing* in the first instance before making a submission.
    Features *Keith Richmond*
    Fiction No unsolicited fiction. Annual short story competition. Max. 3500 words.

Woman's Realm
King's Reach Tower, Stamford Street,
London SE1 9LS
☎0171 261 5000   Fax 0171 261 5326
Owner *IPC Magazines Ltd*
Editor *Sue Reid*
Deputy Editor *Kathy Watson*
Circulation 390,548

FOUNDED 1958. WEEKLY. Some scope here for freelancers. Write to the appropriate editor in the first instance.
    Features Interested in human-interest ideas/articles, dramatic emotional stories, strong adventure and chilling ghost/supernatural stories. Plus real-life love stories with a difference. *Payment* NUJ rates.
    Fiction Two short stories used every week, a one-pager (up to 1200 words), plus a longer one (2500 words). Unsolicited mss no longer accepted.

Woman's Weekly

King's Reach Tower, Stamford Street,
London SE1 9LS
☎0171 261 5000   Fax 0171 261 6322
Owner *IPC Magazines Ltd*
Editor *Olwen Rice*
Circulation 785,604

Mass-market women's WEEKLY.

Features *Frances Quinn* Focus on strong
human interest and inspirational, stories, film
and television personalities, as well as light,
entertaining stories and family features of interest to women of 35 upwards. Freelancers used
regularly, but tend to be experienced magazine
journalists.

Fiction *Gaynor Davies* Short stories 1500–
5000 words; serials 12,000–30,000 words.
Guidelines for serials: 'a strong romantic emotional theme with a conflict not resolved until
the end'; short stories allow for more variety.

Woodworker

Argus House, Boundary Way, Hemel
Hempstead, Hertfordshire HP2 7ST
☎01442 66551   Fax 01442 66998
Owner *Argus Specialist Publications*
Managing Editor *Stuart Cooke*
Circulation 45,000

FOUNDED 1901. MONTHLY. Contributions
welcome; approach with ideas in writing.

Features *Zachary Taylor* Articles on woodworking with good photo support appreciated.
Maximum 2000 words. *Payment* £40–60 per
page.

News Stories and photos (black and white)
welcome. Maximum 300 words. *Payment*
£10–25 per story.

Workbox

Upcott Hall, Bishop's Hull, Taunton,
Somerset TA4 1AQ
☎01823 326561
Owner *Audrey Babington*
Editor *Audrey Babington*
Circulation 26,000

FOUNDED 1984. QUARTERLY. The magazine
caters for enthusiasts of textiles and all branches
of handicrafts.

Features All aspects of embroidery, design
and related subjects.

News New products, processes, etc., and
events.

Telephone before sending submissions.
Payment by arrangement.

Working Titles

See under **Poetry, Little Magazines**

Works Magazine

See under **Small Presses (Works Publishing)**

World Fishing

Royston House, Caroline Park, Edinburgh
EH5 1QJ
☎0131 551 2942   Fax 0131 551 2938
Owner *The Oban Times Ltd*
Editor *Martin Gill*
Circulation 6500

FOUNDED 1952. MONTHLY. Unsolicited mss
welcome; approach by phone or in writing
with an idea.

News/Features Technical or commercial
nature relating to commercial fishing industry
worldwide. Maximum 1000 words.

Payment by arrangement.

World of Bowls

48 London Road, Sevenoaks, Kent TN13 1AS
☎01732 743644   Fax 01732 743647
Owner *HBP Ltd*
Editor *Frank Baldwin*
Circulation 50,000

MONTHLY on all aspects of flat green bowling.
Welcome personality pieces. No tuition articles. Approach in writing in the first instance.

Features Unusual, off-the-wall bowling
features. Maximum 1000 words. *Payment* £50.

News Hard news stories. Maximum 200
words. *Payment* £20.

The World of Interiors

Condé Nast Publications, Vogue House,
Hanover Square, London W1R 0AD
☎0171 499 9080   Fax 0171 493 4013
Owner *Condé Nast Publications Ltd*
Editor *Min Hogg*
Circulation 71,407

FOUNDED 1981. MONTHLY. Best approach by
phone or letter with an idea, preferably with
reference snaps or guidebooks.

Features *Sarah Howell* Most feature material
is commissioned. 'Subjects tend to be found by
us, but we are delighted to receive suggestions
of houses unpublished elsewhere, and would
love to find new writers.'

World Soccer

King's Reach Tower, Stamford Street,
London SE1 9LS
☎0171 261 5737   Fax 0171 261 7474

Owner *IPC Magazines Ltd*
Editor *Keir Radnedge*
Circulation 55,000

FOUNDED 1960. MONTHLY. Unsolicited material welcome but initial approach by phone or in writing preferred. News and features on world soccer.

Writers' Monthly
29 Turnpike Lane, London N8 0EP
☎0181 342 8879   Fax 0181 347 8847
Owner *The Writer Ltd*
Editor *Alan Williams*

FOUNDED 1984. MONTHLY. For writers and aspiring writers. 'Publishers and agents use the magazine to find new writers and help them publish their works.' Articles on writing for television, theatre, radio, newspapers and magazines. Regular features include publisher/ agency profile, poets press, author interviews, regular short story and poetry competitions. Unsolicited mss from new and established writers welcome

Features On any aspect of writing, max. 2200 words.
Payment negotiable.

Xenos
29 Prebend Street, Bedford MK40 1QN
☎01234 349067
Editor *Stephen Copestake*

FOUNDED 1990. BI-MONTHLY. Science fiction, fantasy, horror, occult, humour, mystery and suspense short story digest. Devoted to a very wide definition of 'fantasy'. 'We favour an optimistic emphasis.' No purely romantic stories, blood and gore, or prurient material. Length 2000–10,000 words. All stories printed are evaluated by readers and their comments are printed in the 'Evaluations' section of the subsequent issue. All submissions receive free and prompt analysis by the editor, plus suggestions for revision if appropriate. Annual competition with cash prizes (closing date May 31st). Single issue £3.45; annual subscription £16.50.

Yachting Monthly
King's Reach Tower, Stamford Street, London SE1 9LS
☎0171 261 6040   Fax 0171 261 7555
Owner *IPC Magazines Ltd*
Editor *Geoff Pack*
Circulation 43,202

FOUNDED 1906. MONTHLY magazine for yachting enthusiasts. Unsolicited mss welcome, but many are received and not used. Prospective contributors should make initial contact in writing.

Features *Paul Gelder* A wide range of features concerned with maritime subjects and cruising under sail; well-researched and innovative material always welcome, especially if accompanied by colour transparencies. Maximum 2750 words.
Payment up to £113.40 per 1000 words.

Yachting World
King's Reach Tower, Stamford Street, London SE1 9LS
☎0171 261 6800   Fax 0171 261 6818
Owner *IPC Magazines Ltd*
Editor *Andrew Bray*
Circulation 32,500

FOUNDED 1894. MONTHLY with international coverage of yacht racing, cruising and yachting events. Will consider well researched and written sailing stories. Preliminary approaches should be by phone for news stories and in writing for features.
Payment by arrangement.

Yes Magazine
See under **National Newspapers (The People)**

You – The Mail on Sunday Magazine
See under **National Newspapers (The Mail on Sunday)**

You and Your Wedding
Silver House, 31–35 Beak Street, London W1R 3LD
☎0171 437 2998 (editorial)Fax 0171 287 8655
Owner *AIM Publications Ltd*
Editor *Carole Hamilton*
Circulation *c.* 50,000

FOUNDED 1985. QUARTERLY. Anything relating to weddings, setting up home, and honeymoons. No unsolicited mss. Ideas may be submitted in writing only. No phone calls.

Young Telegraph
346 Old Street, London EC1V 9NQ
☎0171 613 3376   Fax 0171 613 3372
Editor *Damian Kelleher*
Circulation 1.25 million

FOUNDED 1990. WEEKLY colour supplement for 8–12-year-olds. Unsolicited mss and ideas in writing welcome.

Features *Jason Page* Usually commissioned.

Any youth-orientated material. Maximum 500 words.

News *Rupert Mellor* Short, picture-led articles always welcome. Maximum 80 words.

Payment by arrangement.

Your Garden Magazine

IPC Magazines Ltd., Westover House, West Quay Road, Poole, Dorset BH15 1JG
☎01202 680603   Fax 01202 674335

Owner *IPC Magazines Ltd*
Editor *Graham Clarke*
Circulation 122,267

FOUNDED 1993. MONTHLY full colour glossy for all gardeners. Welcome good, solid gardening advice that is well written. No garden history or humour. Receive approx 50 mss per month but only five per cent are accepted. Always approach in writing in the first instance.

Features *Graham Clarke* Good gardening features, preferably with a new slant. Small gardens only. Maximum 1000 words.

Payment negotiable.

Yours Magazine

Apex House, Oundle Road, Peterborough, Cambridgeshire PE2 9NP
☎01733 555123   Fax 01733 898487

Owner *Choice Publications*
Editor *Neil Patrick*
Circulation 181,819

FOUNDED 1973. MONTHLY. Aimed at a readership aged 55 and over.

Features Best approach by letter with outline in first instance. Maximum 1000 words.

News Short, newsy items of interest to readership welcome. Length 300–500 words.

Fiction One or two short stories used in each issue.

Payment negotiable.

Zene

5 Martins Lane, Witcham, Ely, Cambridgeshire CB6 2LB
☎01353 777931

Owner *Andy Cox and Mark Rose*
Editor *Andy Cox*

FOUNDED 1994. Features detailed contributors' guidelines of international small press and semi-professional publications, plus varied articles, news, views and reviews.

Features Unsolicited articles, maximum 2000 words, welcome on any aspect of small press publishing: market information, writing, editing, illustrating, interviews and reviews. All genres.

Freelance Rates – Magazines

Freelance rates vary enormously. The following guidelines are minimum rates negotiated by the **National Union of Journalists**. Most work can command higher fees from employers whether or not they have NUJ agreements. It is up to freelancers to negotiate the best deal they can.

The following NUJ grouping is according to the prosperity of the publication (i.e. based on advertising rates per page):

Group A (over £5000 per page of advertising)
Accountancy Age, Bella, Best, Chat, Company, Cosmopolitan, Country Living, Elle, GQ, Hello!, Harpers & Queen, Ideal Home, Just Seventeen, LOOKS, More!, Meloday Maker, Next, Options, Prima, Q, Reader's Digest, Radio Times, Woman, Woman's Own, Woman's Realm, Woman's Weekly, Woman and Home, Vogue.

Group B (£3000 to £5000 per page of advertising)
Arena, Business Life, Computer Weekly, Choice, Computing, Director, Essentials, The Economist, marie claire, Marketing Week, New Scientist, Mother and Baby, Time Out, Yours.

Group C (£1500 to £3000 per page of advertising)
Accountancy, Country Life, Executive Travel, Home & County, Living, Mizz, New Statesman & Society, Parents, Tatler, TES, The Universe, Wedding and Home.

Group D (£500 to £1500 per page of advertising)
Everywoman, Gay Times, Nursing Times, The Lady, Practical Photography.

Group E (no advertising or less than £500 per page)
Ethnic newspapers and magazines, The Pink Paper, The Big Issue.

Words
These figures (rounded off to the nearest £) are the minimum rates which should be paid by magazines in these groups.

	Features (per 1000 words)	News (per 100 words)	Research/production/ reporting/sub-editing/ picture research (per day)
Group A	negotiable	negotiable	£120
Group B	£235	£23	£110
Group C	£201	£20	£105
Group D	£145	£15	£100
Group E	£120	£14	£ 90

The fee for working as an editor should be at least £125 per day.

Photographic Fees

Commission fees are based on day rates (over 4 hours) and half-day rates (up to 4 hours). Rates are for one use only. Most companies recognise that commission fees are payment for time and will therefore pay reproduction fees on top. Where freelancers are paid over and above the minimum commission fees outlined below this may not apply. Reproduction fees are based on A4 pages, black and white, one British use only. The fees listed are intended as a minimum.

Commission fees

	day	half-day
Group A	£245	£144
Group B	£205	£122
Group C	£180	£111
Group D	£165	£ 95
Group E	£155	£ 85

Reproduction fees

Up to:	¼ page	½ page	¾ page	full page
Group A	£85	£122	£153	£250+
Group B	£75	£104	£138	£190
Group C	£60	£ 87	£122	£170
Group D	£55	£ 75	£104	£140
Group E	£45	£ 51	£ 80	£108

Colour: By negotiation
Cover: 50% extra.
Studio/location work and specialist assignments: £650 per day.

Cartoons

	Group A	Group B & C	Group D & E
Minimum fee	£ 85	£69	£55
Feature strip	£105	£92	£85

Illustrations

Payment at not less than the appropriate rate for photographs. Colour and cover rates should be agreed by negotiation but should not be less than double the above rates. All rates quoted are for one British use only.

News Agencies

AP Dow Jones
10 Fleet Place, London EC4M 7RB
☎0171 832 9105   Fax 0171 832 9101

Everything is generated in-house. No unsolicited material.

Associated Press News Agency
12 Norwich Street, London EC4A 1BP
☎0171 353 1515/353 6323 (News)/353 4731
Fax (Photos) 071 353 8118

Material is either generated in-house or by regulars. Hires the occasional stringer. No unsolicited mss.

Central Office of Information
Hercules Road, London SE1 7DU
☎0171 261 8484   Fax 0171 928 7652

Material generally commissioned or produced in-house. No unsolicited mss.

Financial Times Extel Group
Fitzroy House, 13–17 Epworth Street,
London EC2A 4DL
☎0171 251 3333   Fax 0171 251 2725

Specialist financial agency. No unsolicited mss.

National News Agency
30 St John's Lane, London EC1M 4BJ
☎0171 417 7707   Fax 0171 250 1204

No unsolicited material. Most work is generated in-house or commissioned. Proposals occasionally considered after consultation by phone with the relevant editor.

PA News Ltd
292 Vauxhall Bridge Road,
London SW1V 1AE
☎0171 963 7000

No unsolicited mss. They will be returned unread with an apology. Most material is produced in-house though occasional outsiders may be used. A phone call to discuss specific material may lead somewhere 'but this is rare'.

Reuters Ltd
85 Fleet Street, London EC4P 4AJ
☎0171 250 1122

No unsolicited mss.

Solo Syndication Ltd
49-53 Kensington High Street,
London W8 5ED
☎0171 376 2166   Fax 0171 938 3165

FOUNDED 1978. *Specialises* in world-wide newspaper syndication of photos, features and cartoons. Professional contributors only.

From Book to Box

Mark Bell, a books researcher for Music and Arts at the BBC, lays bare the uneasy relationship between books and television

Books and television have always had an uncomfortable relationship. Sir Maurice Bowra's paradox, 'All television corrupts and absolute television corrupts absolutely', reveals the pervasive fear in high-brow circles of the medium's low level intellect. Publishers have been traditionally suspicious of their juvenile and popularising competitor in the race to disseminate information. Thirty-five years ago the Pilkington Committee reported that 'trivialisation is the natural vice of television'; on 28 October 1994 the *Independent* commented that, 'put simply, television is the enemy of print'.

Writers and publishers sneer at their peril. Television may once have depended on the written word for all its ideas, but the market has turned the tables, and publishing relies increasingly on the small screen for its daily bread. Traditionally, a tie-in (a spin-off from a series) looks like a children's annual, sells well before Christmas and is in the bargain bookshops shortly after the final episode. These are still published in large numbers (the book of the last series of *Have I Got News for You!* was one of the best-selling books of last year) but they are now a part of an increasing market.

Novelisations of drama serials also have a short shelf-life, but they are a growing part of the market, particularly for teenagers. Dramatisations of the classics tend to have one or more accompanying editions with a luvvie gracing the cover. The quality end of the non-fiction market is occupied by cookery, history and science, where the presenter tends to be both author and personality. A number of channels (notably the BBC) have their own imprints, which take the pick from the schedules. For independent publishers, profits from tie-ins tend to be spread further, as the production company might well be looking for some reward, without having contributed to the initiation costs. Moreover, if a series fails to find an airing overseas, then the book is not going to find a market there either.

How does an author who hasn't written the book of the series get his or her work featured on TV? The criteria are similar for TV and radio. News and current affairs take up an increasing proportion of air-time; producers are hungry for any non-fiction that is newsworthy in some way – a book might either be politically contentious, deal with a subject that is topical (perhaps a financial or natural disaster) or break new ground in science. (The book is unlikely to be the main feature, but researchers are always on the lookout for expert commentators.) Prime-time talk shows are interested mainly in celebrities, but will also look at anything that is scandalous, off-beat or attention-grabbing, such as death-defying travelogues, unauthorised biographies or self-help manuals.

The most crucial thing to bear in mind when putting a book forward for television is to target the right programme and, if possible, the right producer. There is little point in submitting cookbooks or gardening manuals to a late-night documentary slot. Watch a programme before considering whether your book might be suitable for it. If the subject of the book is outside a programme's normal territory, try to think of an angle that might be of interest. A books feature on TV never gives a straight rendition of what occurs in a book, but has to offer something more than the experience of reading a narrative. A film or feature has to have its own narrative; a books feature might work if it tells the story behind the story, or an author's life, or if it reflects on an issue raised in a book.

It is important to consider how a film will work visually – dramatisations of an author's life are expensive and notoriously difficult to pull off. A prospective producer will be interested in how eloquent an author is in front of a camera, as well as in locations that might have provided the inspiration for a piece of fiction. For a dead author or biographical subject it is useful to know about archive footage, living interviewees who knew the character in question as well as relevant personal effects. (It is also worth thinking about what could be used to illustrate readings from a book.)

James Runcie, a producer of literary documentaries for BBC TV is influenced first by the track record of the person recommending the book. Publicists should be selective: 'If a publicist offers me thirty books, saying that they are each perfect for an arts documentary, it is simply a waste of my time to look at the ones that are inappropriate.'

Long documentaries require a large amount of raw material, his rule is that an author needs to have written at least five books before a fifty-minute film will be commissioned about him. Authors should try to talk about a proposal for at least twenty minutes without hesitation – it is a useful way of realising how quickly material is used up.

Arts review programmes, the main forum for discussion of new publications, make the same kinds of demands as other productions. A feature normally centres around a subject or issue rather than a book on its own, and will tend to deal with more than one book in an item.

Daisy Goodwin, series editor of *The Bookworm* on BBC1, is responsive to a personal approach from a published author: 'Authors should not rely solely on their PR company or publicity department to get their book on TV. In many cases the authors themselves have a better idea of how their book might be featured, and a direct approach to a production office is well worth the effort.'

There are no arts programmes that are on air all year round. Production offices grow and shrink, and many staff do not work on the same show two seasons running. Check who is working on a programme before sending in a book or feature idea, and address all submissions personally. Above all, it is important to be familiar with the range and style of the programme, and provide an outline of possible angles which a feature might take. Competition for air-time is fierce, but books are what arts programmes survive on. In Gore Vidal's memorable phrase, 'television is now so desperately hungry for material that it's scraping the top of the barrel'.

National and Regional Television

BBC Television

Television Centre, Wood Lane,
London W12 7RJ
☎0181 743 8000

Managing Director, Network TV *Will Wyatt*
**Managing Director, Regional
   Broadcasting** *Ronald Neil*
Controller, BBC1 *Alan Yentob*
Controller, BBC2 *Michael Jackson*
Head of Features *Anne Morrison*
Head of Purchased Programmes *June
   Dromgoole*

The principal divisions within BBC TV (excluding News and Current Affairs, Education,
and Religious Broadcasting, which operate as
separate directorates within the BBC) are:
Children's Programmes; Documentaries; Drama
Group; Entertainment Group; Music & Arts;
Science & Features; Sport & Events Group.

CHILDREN'S PROGRAMMES
Head of Children's Programmes *Anna Home*
Executive Producer, Drama *Richard
   Callanan*
Executive Producer, Entertainment *Chris
   Pilkington*
Executive Producer, Factual Programmes
   Eric Rowan
Editor, Blue Peter *Lewis Bronze*
Producer, Grange Hill *Christine Secombe*
Producer, Jackanory *Nel Romano*
Editor, Live & Kicking *Christopher Bellinger*
Editor, Newsround *Nick Heathcote*

DOCUMENTARIES
Head of Documentaries *Paul Hamann*
Editor, Inside Story *Olivia Lichtenstein*
Producer, Rough Justice *Edward Brayman*
Editor, Timewatch *Laurence Rees*

DRAMA GROUP
Head of Drama Group *Charles Denton*
Head of Film *Mark Shivas*
Head of Serials *Michael Wearing*
**Head of Singles/Executive Producer,
   Screen Two** *George Faber*
Executive Producer, Screen One
   Margaret Matheson
Executive Producer, Performance
   Simon Curtis
Development Executive, Independents
   Jenny Killick

ENTERTAINMENT GROUP
Head of Entertainment Group & Variety
   David Liddiment
Head of Comedy *Martin Fisher*
Head of Light Entertainment *Michael Leggo*
Head of Comedy Entertainment
   Jon Plowman
**Commissioning Executive, Independent
   Productions** *Chris Pye*
Editor, Comedy Development *Rosie Bunting*
Head of Development, Entertainment
   Kevin Lygo

MUSIC AND ARTS
Head of Music & Arts *Kim Evans*
Head of Music Programmes *Avril MacRory*
Editor, Arts Features *Keith Alexander*
Editor, Omnibus *Nigel Williams*
Editors, Arena *Anthony Wall*
Editor, Bookmark/One Foot in the Past
   Roly Keating

SCIENCE AND FEATURES
Head of Science & Features *Jana Bennett*
Editor, Tomorrow's World *Edward Briffa*
Editor, Horizon *John Lynch*
Editor, QED *Lorraine Heggess*

SPORT AND EVENTS GROUP
Head of Sport & Events Group
   Jonathan Martin
Editor, Match of the Day/Sportsnight
   Brian Barwick
Editor, Grandstand *David Gordon*

BBC News and Current Affairs

BBC Television Centre, Wood Lane,
London W12 7RJ
☎0181 743 8000

News and current affairs broadcasting across
television and radio were unified as a single
operation under the new directorate estab-
lished 1987.
**Managing Director, News and Current
   Affairs** *Tony Hall*
Head of Weekly Programmes *Tim Gardam*
Managing Editor, Weekly Programmes
   Tim Suter
Head of News Programmes *Peter Bell*
Managing Editor, News Programmes
   Christopher Graham
Head of Political Programmes *Samir Shah*

Head of News Gathering *Chris Cramer*
Editor, Foreign Affairs Unit *John Simpson*
Editor, Business & Economics Unit
Peter Jay
News Editor, Breakfast News *Tim Orchard*
News Editor, One O'Clock News
Jon Barton
News Editor, Six O'Clock News
John Morrison
News Editor, Nine O'Clock News
Malcolm Balen
News Editor, Newsnight *Peter Horrocks*
Editor, Public Eye *Mark Wakefield*
Editor, Panorama *Steve Hewlett*
Editor, The Money Programme *Jane Ellison*
Editor, On the Record *Nelson Mews*
News Editor, Ceefax *Graham Norwood*
Head of Subtitling *Ruth Griffiths*

Ceefax
Room 7013, Television Centre, Wood Lane,
London W12 7RJ
☎0181 576 1801

The BBC's main news and information service, broadcasting hundreds of pages on both BBC1 and BBC2. It is on the air at all times when transmitters are broadcasting.

Subtitling
Room 1460, BBC White City, Wood Lane,
London W12 7RJ
☎0181 752 7054/0141 330 2345 ext. 2128

A rapidly expanding service (approx 35% of total BBC output is subtitled including all news bulletins) available via Ceefax page 888. Units based in both London and Glasgow.

BBC Educational Directorate
BBC White City, 201 Wood Lane,
London W12 7TS
☎0181 752 5252

Director of Education *Jane Drabble*
Head of Educational Policy & Services
Lucia Jones
Head of Publishing Division *David Mortimer*
Head of Schools Programmes *Terry Marsh*
Head of Continuing Education and Training *Glenwyn Benson*
Head of Open University Production Centre (Walton Hall, Milton Keynes, MK7 6BH. Tel 01908 655544 Fax 01908 376324) *Colin Robinson*
Managing Editor, BBC Select *Paul Gerhardt*

The educational programme-making and publishing activities of the BBC were brought together in 1993 under the aegis of the education directorate. This incorporates radio and television broadcasting of school programmes, continuing education and training, Open University and the multimedia publishing service (books, videos, etc.) in the main. The BBC produces audio and visual material on behalf of and in partnership with the Open University. BBC Select (Woodlands, 80 Wood Lane, W12 0TT. Tel 0181–743 5588) is a mixed subscription and open access service, broadcasting specialist education, training and information programmes during the night.

BBC Religious Broadcasting
New Broadcasting House, PO Box 27,
Oxford Road, Manchester M60 1SJ
☎0161 955 3600   Fax 0161 955 3677
Head of Religious Broadcasting *Rev. Ernest Rea*

Regular programmes for television include *This is the Day; Songs of Praise; Everyman; Heart of the Matter*. Radio output includes *Good Morning Sunday; Sunday Half-hour; Choral Even Song; Thought for the Day; Morning Has Broken; Seeds of Faith*.

BBC Regional Broadcasting
The BBC Regional Broadcasting Directorate consists of BBC Northern Ireland, BBC Scotland, BBC Wales, Midlands & East Region, North Region, South Region, all with an autonomous management structure, making local, regional and network programmes.

BBC Northern Ireland
Broadcasting House, 25–27 Ormeau Avenue,
Belfast BT2 8HQ
☎01232 338000

Controller *Patrick Loughrey*
Head of Programmes *Anna Carragher*
Head of News & Current Affairs *Keith Baker*
Editor, Current Affairs *Andrew Colman*
Editor, News *Tom Kelly*
Managing Editor, General Programmes
Paul Evans
Managing Editor, Specialist Programmes
Maureen Gallagher
Producer, Drama *Robert Cooper*
Political Editor *Jim Dougal*
Chief Producer, Features *Charlie Warmington*
Chief Producer, Current Affairs *Michael Cairns*

Chief Producer, Sport *Terry Smith*
Chief Producer, Agriculture *Veronica Hughes*
Chief Producer, Music & Arts *Ian Kirk-Smith*
Chief Producer, Youth & Community
  Fedelma Harkin
Chief Producer, Education *Michael McGowan*
Chief Producer, Religion *Bert Tosh*

Regular programmes include *In Performance; Ulster in Focus; The Back Page; 29 Bedford Street; Country Times* and *Anderson on the Box.* Religious, educational, news & current affairs programming across both TV and radio come under the aegis of separate directorates within the BBC. See individual entries this section for each.

BBC Scotland

Broadcasting House, Queen Margaret Drive, Glasgow G12 8DG
☎0141 330 8844

Controller *John McCormick*
Head of Television *Colin Cameron*
Head of News & Current Affairs *Kenneth Cargill*
Head of Music & Arts *John Archer*
Head of Drama *Andrea Calderwood*
Head of Gaelic & Features *Ken MacQuarrie*
Head of Comedy Unit *Colin Gilbert*
Head of Education & Religious
  Broadcasting *Andrew Barr*
Scottish Political Editor *Brian Taylor*

Headquarters of BBC Scotland with opt-out stations based in Aberdeen, Dundee, Edinburgh and Inverness. Regular programmes include the nightly *Reporting Scotland* plus *Friday Sportscene; Frontline Scotland* and *Landward* (bi-monthly farming news).

Aberdeen
Broadcasting House, Beechgrove Terrace, Aberdeen AB9 2ZT.
☎01224 625233

News, plus some features, but most programmes are made in Glasgow.

Dundee
Nethergate Centre, 66 Nethergate, Dundee DD1 4ER
☎01382 202481
News only.

Edinburgh
Broadcasting House, Queen Street, Edinburgh EH2 1JF
☎0131–469 4200
All programmes made in Glasgow.

Inverness
7 Culduthel Road, Inverness 1V2 4AD
☎01463 221711
News only.

BBC Wales

Broadcasting House, Llandaff, Cardiff CF5 2YQ
☎01222 572888   Fax 01222 552973

Controller *Geraint Talfan Davies*
Head of Programmes (Welsh Language)
  Gwynn Pritchard
Head of Programmes (English Language)
  Dai Smith
Head of News & Current Affairs *Aled Eirug*
Head of Drama *Ruth Caleb*
Head of Sport *Arthur Emyr*
Head of Factual Programmes *John Geraint*

Headquarters of BBC Wales, with regional television centres in Bangor and Swansea. All Welsh language programmes are transmitted by S4C and produced in Cardiff or Swansea. Regular programmes include *Wales Today; Wales on Saturday;* and *Pobol y Cwm* (Welsh-language drama series).

Bangor
Broadcasting House, Meirion Road, Bangor, Gwynedd LL57 2BY
☎01248 370880 Fax 01248 351443
Head of Production *R. Alun Evans*
News only.

Swansea
Broadcasting House, Alexandra Road, Swansea, West Glamorgan SA1 5DZ
☎01792 654986 Fax 01792 468194
Production Manager *Daniel Jones*

BBC Midlands & East

Broadcasting Centre, Pebble Mill Road, Birmingham B5 7QQ
☎0121 414 8888   Fax 0121 414 8634

Head of Broadcasting *Nigel Chapman*
Head of Network Television *Rod Natkiel*
Head of Television Drama *Chris Parr*
Head of Local Programmes *Adrian Van Klaveren*
Editor, News & Current Affairs *Peter Lowe*
Managing Editor, Network Television, Daytime and Lifestyle Programmes
  Stephanie Silk
Managing Editor, Network Television Leisure & Countryside Programmes
  John King

Managing Editor, Network Television Multicultural Programmes *Narendhra Morar*

Home of the Pebble Mill Studio. Regular programmes include *Midlands Today* and *The Midlands Report*. Output for the network includes: *The Clothes Show; Good Morning Anne and Nick; Gardener's World; Kilroy*. Openings exist for well-researched topical or local material.

BBC Midlands & East serves opt-out stations in Nottingham and Norwich.

BBC East Midlands (Nottingham)
East Midlands Broadcasting Centre,
York House, Mansfield Road,
Nottingham, NG1 3JB.
☎0115 9472395

Head of Local Programmes *Richard Lucas*

Local news programmes such as *East Midlands Today*

BBC East (Norwich)
St Catherine's Close, All Saint's Green,
Norwich, Norfolk, NR1 3ND.
☎01603 619331. Fax: 01603 667865.

Head of Centre *Arnold Miller*
Editor, News & Current Affairs *David Holdsworth*

Regular slots include *Look East* (regional magazine) and *Matter of Fact*.

BBC North

New Broadcasting House, Oxford Road,
Manchester M60 1SJ
☎0161 200 2020

Head of Broadcasting *Colin Adams*
Head of Youth & Entertainment Features *John Whiston*
Head of Local Programmes, Manchester *Roy Saatchi*
Editor, News & Current Affairs *Richard Porter*

Headquarters of BBC North, incorporating the former North East and North West divisions. Leeds and Newcastle continue to make their own programmes, each having its own head of centre.

Leeds
Broadcasting Centre, Woodhouse Lane,
Leeds, West Yorkshire, LS2 9PX.
☎01132 441188

Head of Centre *Martin Brooks*
Editor, News & Current Affairs *Russell Peasgood*

Regional Political Editor *Geoff Talbott*
Producer, Close Up North *Patrick Hargreaves*

Newcastle upon Tyne
Broadcasting Centre, Barrack Road,
Newcastle Upon Tyne, NE99 2NE.
☎0191–232 1313

Acting Head of Centre/News and Current Affairs Editor/News Editor, Look North *Ian Cameron*
Producers, Look North *Iain Williams, Brid Fitzpatrick, Andrew Lambert, Fiona MacBeth*
Producer, North of Westminster *Michael Wild*

BBC South

Broadcasting House, Whiteladies Road,
Bristol, Avon BS8 2LR
☎0117 9732211

Head of Broadcasting *John Shearer*
Head of Television Features *Jeremy Gibson*
Head of Natural History Unit *Alastair Fothergill*
Editor, The Natural World *John Sparks*

BBC South incorporates BBC West (Bristol), BBC South (Southampton), BBC South West (Plymouth), and BBC South East (Elstree), each with its own head of centre. Bristol is the home of the BBC's Natural History Unit, producing programmes like *Wildlife on One; The Natural World* and *The Really Wild Guide to Britain*. BBC South produces a wide range of television features for regional programming across its four centres, such as *999; Lifesavers; Great Journeys; Antiques Roadshow; 10x10*.

BBC West (Bristol)
(address/telephone number as above)

Head of Local Programmes *John Conway*
Editor, West Political Unit *Paul Cannon*

BBC South (Southampton)
Broadcasting House, Havelock Road,
Southampton, Hampshire SO1 1XQ
☎01703 226201

Head of Centre *Nigel Kay*
Editor, News & Current Affairs *Andy Griffee*

BBC South West (Plymouth)
Broadcasting House, Seymour Road,
Plymouth, Devon PL3 5BD
☎01752 229201

Head of Centre *Roy Roberts*
Editor, News & Current Affairs *Tony Maddox*

BBC South East (Elstree)

Elstree Centre, Clarendon Road,
Borehamwood, Hertfordshire WD6 1JF
☎0181 953 6100

Head of Centre *Michele Romaine*
Editor, Newsroom South East *Guy Pelham*
Editor, First Sight *Alison Rooper*

The regional broadcasting centres produce little more than news, being supplied with programmes from BBC West at Bristol.

Independent Television

Anglia Television

Anglia House, Norwich, Norfolk NR1 3JG
☎01603 615151   Fax 01603 631032

London office: 48 Leicester Square, London WC2H 7FB
☎0171 321 0101   Fax 0171 930 8499

Managing Director *Malcolm Wall*
Controller of News *Mike Read*
Director of Programmes *Graham Creelman*

Anglia Television is a major producer of programmes for the ITV network and Channel 4. These include *Gardens Without Borders, Go Fishing,* and the *Survival* wildlife documentaries, Britain's best-selling programme export. A wide range of peak-time drama includes *The Chief* and the P.D. James murder mysteries.

Border Television plc

Television Centre, Durranhill, Carlisle, Cumbria CA1 3NT
☎01228 25101   Fax 01228 41384

Managing Director *James Graham OBE*
Head of Production *Neil Robinson*

Border's programming includes children's television with features and documentaries rather than drama. Most scripts are supplied in-house but occasionally there are commissions. Apart from notes, writers should not submit written work until their ideas have been fully discussed.

Carlton UK Television

101 St Martin's Lane, London WC2N 4AZ
☎0171 240 4000   Fax 0171 240 4171

Chairman *Nigel Walmsley*
Chief Executive *Andy Allan*
Managing Director, Carlton Broadcasting
Paul Corley

Carlton UK Television comprises four separate entities: Carlton Broadcasting, which is responsible for the ITV licence for London and the South East, with programmes produced by independent companies; **Central Broadcasting** (see entry); **Carlton UK Productions** (see under **Film, TV and Video Producers**); Carlton UK Sales which sells airtime and sponsorship for both broadcasters. Also runs two facilities operations: The Television House in Nottingham, supplying studios and related services and Carlton 021, the largest commercial operator of Outside Broadcast Services in Europe.

Central Broadcasting

Central House, Broad Street,
Birmingham B1 2JP
☎0121 643 9898   Fax 0121 643 4897

Chairman *Leslie Hill*
Managing Director *Rod Henwood*

Part of **Carlton UK Television**. Responsible for the ITV licence for East, West and South Midlands. Regular programmes include *Central Weekend; Gardening Time; Crime Stalker.*

Channel 4

124 Horseferry Road, London SW1P 2TX
☎0171 396 4444   Fax 0171 306 8350

Chief Executive *Michael Grade*
Director of Programmes *John Willis*
Head of Drama *David Aukin*

Commissioning editors:
Independent Film & Video *Stuart Cosgrove*
Documentaries *Peter Moore*
News & Current Affairs *David Lloyd*
Entertainment *Seamus Cassidy*
Arts & Music *Waldemar Januszczak*
Sport *Mike Miller*
Education *Karen Brown*
Youth *David Stevenson*
Multicultural Programmes *Farrukh Dhondy*
Religion & Features *Peter Grimsdale*
Head of Purchased Programmes *Mairi MacDonald*

When Channel 4 started broadcasting as a national TV channel in November 1982, it was the first new TV service to be launched in Britain for 18 years. Under the 1981 Broadcasting Act it was required to cater for tastes and audiences not previously served by the other broadcast channels, and to provide a suitable proportion of educational programmes. Channel 4 does not make any of its own programmes; they are commissioned from the independent production companies, from the ITV sector, or co-produced with other organisations. The role of the commissioning editors is to sift through proposals for programmes and see interesting projects through to broadcast. Regulated by the **ITC**.

Channel 5

Channel 5 will be Britain's third commercial terrestrial television station. At the time of going to press, the Independent Television Commission had received four bids for the 10-year franchise. The highest, £36 million, came from UKTV; the other bidders were Channel 5 Broadcasting, Virgin TV and New Century Television. The winner is due to be announced in the autumn of 1995 and will be on air by January 1997.

Channel Television

The Television Centre, La Pouquelaye, St Helier, Jersey, Channel Isles JE2 3ZD
☎01534 868999   Fax 01534 859446

Also at: The TV Centre, St George's Place, St Peter Port, Guernsey
☎01481 723451

Managing Director *John Henwood*
Director of Television *Michael Lucas*

News, current affairs and documentaries provide the bulk of programmes. Ideas are assessed but only commissioned after sale is made to the network.

GMTV

The London Television Centre, Upper Ground, London SE1 9TT
☎0171 827 7000   Fax 0171 827 7001

Managing Director *Christopher Stoddart*
Director of Programmes *Peter McHugh*
Managing Editor *John Scammell*

Winner of the national breakfast television franchise with a bid of £34.6 million a year, compared to TV-AM's £14.5 million a year. Jointly owned by LWT, Scottish Television, Carlton Television, The Guardian and Manchester Evening News, and Disney. GMTV took over from TV-AM on 1 January 1993, with live programming from 6 am to 9.25 am. Regular news headlines, current affairs, topical features, showbiz and lifestyle, sports and business, quizzes and competitions, travel and weather reports. More family-orientated than its predecessor, with a softer approach altogether to news and less time given over to City news.

Grampian Television plc

Queen's Cross, Aberdeen AB9 2XJ
☎01224 646464   Fax 01224 635127

Director of Programmes *George W. Mitchell, MA*
Head of News & Current Affairs *Alistair Gracie*
Head of Documentaries & Features *Edward Brocklebank*
Head of Gaelic *Robert Kenyon*

Extensive regional news and reports including farming, fishing and sports, interviews and leisure features, various light entertainment, Gaelic and religious programmes, and live coverage of the Scottish political, economic and industrial scene. Serves the area stretching from Fife to Shetland. Regular programmes include *Gaelic News; Criomagan* (Gaelic Diary); and *Reflections*.

Granada Television

Granada TV Centre, Quay Street, Manchester M60 9EA
☎0161 832 7211   Fax 0161 953 0283

London office: 36 Golden Square, London W1R 4AH
☎0171 734 8080   Fax 0171 439 6084

Joint Managing Directors *Jules Barnes, Andrea Wonfor*
Director of Production *Max Graesser*
Controller of Factual Programming *Ian McBride*
Head of Features *James Hunt*
Controller of Drama *Gub Neal*
Head of Drama Serials *Carolyn Reynolds*
Head of Current Affairs & Documentaries *Charles Tremayme*
Head of Comedy *Antony Wood*
Head of Music *Iain Rousham*

Opportunities for freelance writers are not great but mss from professional writers will be considered. All mss should be addressed to the head of scripts. Regular programmes include *Coronation Street; World in Action* and *This Morning*.

HTV Group plc

Television Centre, Culverhouse Cross, Cardiff CF5 6XJ
☎01222 590590   Fax 01222 599108

Chief Executive *Christopher Rowlands*
Group Director of Broadcasting *Ted George*
Controller of Children's & Family Programmes (Wales & West) *Dan Maddicott*

HTV (Wales)
(address/telephone number as above)
Director of Programmes *Menna Richards*

HTV (West)
Television Centre, Bath Road, Bristol,
Avon BS4 3HG
☎0117 9778366

Director of Programmes *Stephen Matthews*
Head of Features & Commissions *Tony Holmes*

Strong local programming in all departments. HTV (West) would be interested in scripts with a West Country flavour or written by people who live and work in the West Country region. Scripts of Welsh interest should be sent to the Cardiff office: news and current affairs, parliamentary coverage, the arts, sports, farming, business, education and the community, reflections on local life, its history and traditions. Regular programmes include *Soccer Sunday; Fair's Fair* (consumer programme); *The Really Helpful Programme; Good Health!; Wales This Week* and *West This Week.*

ITN (Independent Television News Ltd)

200 Gray's Inn Road, London WC1X 8XZ
☎0171 833 3000

Editor-in-Chief *Richard Tait*
Editor, ITN Programmes for ITV *To be appointed*
Editor, ITN Programmes for Channel 4 *To be appointed*

Regulated by the **ITC**, ITN provides the main national and international news for ITV and Channel 4. Programmes on ITV: *Lunchtime News; Early Evening News; News at Ten; ITN Morning News,* plus regular news summaries. There are also three programmes a day at weekends. Programmes on Channel 4: in-depth news analysis programmes, including *Channel 4 News* and *The Big Breakfast News.* ITN also provides the news, sport and business news for *ITN's World News,* the first international English-language news programme.

LWT (London Weekend Television)

The London Television Centre, Upper Ground, London SE1 9LT
☎0171 620 1620

Chief Executive *Charles Allen*
Managing Director *Steve Morrison*
Controller of Entertainment *John Kaye-Cooper*

Controller of Drama *Sally Head*
Controller of Arts *Melvyn Bragg*
Controller of Factual and Regional Programmes *Simon Shaps*

Makers of current affairs, entertainment and drama series such as *Blind Date, Surprise Surprise, The Knock, London's Burning;* also *The South Bank Show* and *Jonathan Dimbleby.* Provides a large proportion of the network's drama and light entertainment, and is a major supplier to Channel 4. Joint ventures with Carlton TV and Granada have established the London News Network and Granada LWT International respectively.

Meridian Broadcasting

Television Centre, Southampton, Hampshire SO4 0PZ
☎01703 222555   Fax 01703 335050

London office: 48 Leicester Square, London WC2H 7LY
☎0171 839 2255

Chief Executive *Roger Laughton*
Director of Broadcasting *Richard Platt*
Director of Programmes *Mary McAnally*
Controller of Drama *Colin Rogers*
Controller of Children's Programmes *Janie Grace*
Controller of News, Sport & Current Affairs *Jim Raven*

All network and most regional output is usually commissioned from independent producers and programming is bound by the **ITC** guidelines which insist upon news, current affairs, children's and religious programming across a wide range of tastes. Regular programmes include: *Meridian Tonight; The Pier* (arts/entertainment); *Countryways.*

S4C

Parc Ty Glas, Llanishen, Cardiff CF4 5GG
☎01222 747444   Fax 01222 754444

Chief Executive *Huw Jones*
Director of Programmes *Deryk Williams*

The Welsh 4th Channel was established by the Broadcasting Act 1980 with responsibility for a schedule of Welsh and English programmes on the Fourth Channel in Wales. The service, known as S4C, consists of about 30 hours per week of Welsh language programmes and more than 85 hours of English language output from Channel 4. Ten hours a week of the Welsh programmes are provided by the BBC; the remainder are purchased from HTV and independent producers. Drama, comedy and documentary are all part of S4C's programming.

Scottish Television

Cowcaddens, Glasgow G2 3PR
☎0141 332 9999   Fax 0141 332 4868

London office: 200 Gray's Inn Road,
London WC1X 8XZ
☎0171 843 8350 Fax 0171 843 8367

Director of Broadcasting *Blair Jenkins*
Controller of Drama *Robert Love*
Controller of Entertainment *Sandy Ross*
Controller of Factual Entertainment
  Eamonn O'Neil
Head of News, Sport & Current Affairs
  Scott Ferguson

An increasing number of STV programmes such
as *Taggart* and *Doctor Finlay* are now networked
nationally. Programme coverage includes drama,
religion, news, sport, outside broadcasts, special
features, entertainment and the arts, education
and Gaelic programmes. Produces many one-
offs for ITV and Channel 4.

Teletext Ltd

101 Farm Lane, Fulham, London SW6 1QJ
☎0171 386 5000   Fax 0171 386 5002

Managing Director *Peter Van Gelder*
Editor *Graham Lovelace*

On 1 January 1993 Teletext Ltd took over the
electronic publishing service, previously the
domain of Oracle, servicing both ITV and
Channel 4. Transmits a wide range of news
pages and features, including current affairs,
sport, TV listings, weather, travel, holidays,
finance, games, competitions, etc. Provides a
regional service to each of the ITV regions.

Tyne Tees Television

Television Centre, Newcastle upon Tyne
NE1 2AL
☎0191 261 0181   Fax 0191 261 2302

London office: 15 Bloomsbury Square,
London WC1A 2LJ
☎0171 405 8474 Fax 0171 242 2441

Managing Director *John Calvert*
Director of Broadcasting *Peter Moth*
Head of Young People's Programmes
  Lesley Oakden
Head of Entertainment *Christine Williams*
Head of Community Affairs *Sheila Browne*
Head of Sport *Roger Tames*

Programming covers religion, farming, politics,
news and current affairs, regional documen-
taries, business, entertainment, sport and arts.
Regular programmes include *The Dales Diary;
Northern Eye; Earthmovers* (gardening); *Tyne
Tees Today* and *Lives in Focus* (religion).

UTV (Ulster Television)

Havelock House, Ormeau Road,
Belfast BT7 1EB
☎01232 328122   Fax 01232 246695

Controller of Programming *A. Bremner*
Head of Factual Programmes *Michael Beattie*
News Editor *Colm McWilliams*
Director of Arts *Bob Brien*
Director of Outside Broadcasts *Alan Hailes*
Directors of Gardening/Heritage *Ruth
  Johnston, Robert Lamrock*

Regular programmes on news and current
affairs, sport, farming, education, music, light
entertainment, arts, politics and industry.

Westcountry Television Ltd

Western Wood Way, Langage Science Park,
Plymouth, Devon PL7 5BG
☎01752 333333   Fax 01752 333444

Managing Director *John Prescott-Thomas*
Controller of News & Current Affairs
  Richard Myers
Controller of Features *Jane Clarke*

Came on air in 1 January 1993. News, current
affairs, documentary and religious programming.
Regular programmes include *Westcountry Live;
Westcountry Focus; Westcountry Showcase; Anybody
Out There?; My Story.*

Yorkshire Television

The Television Centre, Leeds,
West Yorkshire LS3 1JS
☎0113 2438283   Fax 0113 2445107

London office: 15 Bloomsbury Square,
London WC1A 2LJ
☎0171 312 3700

Managing Director *Bruce Gyngell*
Controller, Drama *Keith Richardson*
**Controller, Documentaries & Current
  Affairs** *Chris Bryer*
Controller, Entertainment *David Reynolds*
Head of Sport *Robert Charles*
**Head of Education, Children's &
  Religious Programmes** *Chris Jelley*

Drama series, film productions, studio plays and
long-running series like *Emmerdale* and
Heartbeat. Always looking for strong writing in
these areas, but prefers to find it through an
agent. Documentary/current affairs material
tends to be supplied by producers; opportunities
in these areas are rare but adaptations of published work as a documentary subject are considered. Light entertainment comes from an
already well-established circle of professionals in
this area which is difficult to infiltrate. In theory

opportunity exists within series, episode material. Best approach is through a good agent.

Cable and Satellite Television

Channel One Television Ltd
60 Charlotte Street, London W1P 2AX
☎0171 209 1234   Fax 0171 209 1235
Managing Director *Julian Aston*

Owned by Associated Newspapers. 24-hour, news-led channel broadcasting. Based in London, Channel One focuses on news and views of Londoners plus city issues.

CNN International (CNNI)
CNN House, 19–22 Rathbone Place, London W1P 1DF
☎0171 637 6700   Fax 0171 637 6768
Managing Director *Mark Rudolph*

Owned by Turner Broadcasting System Inc. The world's only international 24-hour television news network, transmitted from the USA and adapted for a European audience. Live coverage of world events, global business reports, sport, in-depth features, weather, etc. via satellite.

European Business News (EBN)
10 Fleet Place, London EC4M 7RB
☎0171 653 9300   Fax 0171 653 9333
Managing Director *Michael Connor*

24-hour European financial and corporate news broadcasting.

Live TV
24th Floor, One Canada Square, Canary Wharf, London E14 5AP
☎0171 293 3900   Fax 0171 293 3820
Managing Director *Janet Street-Porter*

At the time of going to press, no detailed information was available.

Maxat Ltd
200 Gray's Inn Road, London WC1X 8XZ
☎0171 430 4400   Fax 0171 430 4321
Chief Executive *Julian Costley*

European satellite providing sports, news-gathering and uplink services to, for example, the BBC, ITN, ABC, NBC, MTV and UK Gold.

MTV Europe (Music Television)
Hawley Crescent, London NW1 8TT
☎0171 284 7777   Fax 0171 284 7788

President, International *William Roedy*

ESTABLISHED 1987. Europe's 24-hour music and youth entertainment channel, available on cable and via satellite. Transmitted from London in English across Europe.

Sky Television plc (BSkyB)
6 Centaurs Business Park, Grant Way, Isleworth, Middlesex TW7 5QD
☎0171 705 3000   Fax 0171 705 3030
Managing Director *Sam Chisholm*

The nine-channel British Sky Broadcasting group (owned by News International, Chargeurs, Granada and Pearson) broadcasts via Astra satellite, cable TV operators and SMATV in the UK and Ireland.

Sky Movies
24-hours of blockbuster action, comedy, horror and adventure films.

The Movie Channel
24-hours of motion pictures with a film première every day.

Sky Sports and **Sky Sports 2**
Dedicated to a UK audience with an emphasis on live coverage of major sports events, British and international football, Test cricket, boxing, tennis and snooker.

Sky Movies Gold
Described as a film treasure-trove of some of the best-loved films of all time.

SKY MULTI-CHANNELS PACKAGE:
Sky One (general family entertainment channel); **Sky News** (24-hour news); **Sky Travel** (holiday information); **Sky Soap** (American soaps); **TLC** (home and family interests, DIY, cookery, etc); **Nickelodeon** (children's channel); **Bravo** (classic television); **The Discovery Channel** (adventure, travel, nature, history and technology explored); **CMT Europe** (country music); **The Children's Channel** (children's television from around the world); **The Family Channel** (family entertainment); **UK Gold** (vintage BBC and Thames TV programmes); **QVC** (24-hour shopping channel); **UK Living** (women's channel); **MTV** (music television); **VH1** (classic hit music).

NBC Super Channel
NBC Superchannel, Melrose House, 14 Lanark Square, Limeharbour, London E14 9QD
☎0171 418 9418   Fax 0171 418 9419/20/21
Managing Director *Ruud Hendriks*

Head of Programming *Suzette Knittl*

Launched in January 1987 and relaunched under NBC ownership in December 1993. 24-hour European broad-based news, information and entertainment service in English (with occasional programmes and advertisements in Dutch and German).

UK Living

The Quadrangle, 180 Wardour Street, London W1V 4AE

☎0171 306 6170   Fax 0171 306 6101

Chief Executive *Bruce Steinberg*

Broadcasts from 6.00 am to midnight daily. Magazine programmes, gameshows, soaps and films.

Wire TV

United Artists Programming, Twymann House, 16 Bonny Street, London NW1 9PG

☎0171 813 5000   Fax 0171 284 2042

General Manager *Nigel Haunch*
Head of Programmes *Derek Wyatt*

Britain's only national cable exclusive lifestyle channel. Broadcasts ten hours a day between 1.00 pm and 11.00 pm.

National and Regional Radio

BBC and Independent

BBC Radio

Broadcasting House, London W1A 1AA
☎0171 580 4468   Fax 0171 636 9786

Managing Director, Network Radio *Liz Forgan*
Controller, Radio 1 *Matthew Bannister*
Controller, Radio 2 *To be appointed*
Controller, Radio 3 *Nicholas Kenyon*
Controller, Radio 4 *Michael Green*
Controller, Radio 5 Live *Jenny Abramsky*

Radio output for religious and educational broadcasting comes under the aegis of separate directorates established to handle both TV and radio output in these areas. See entries **BBC Religious Broadcasting** and **BBC Educational Directorate** (incorporating Schools Programmes and Continuing Education and Training) under **BBC Television**. Continuing Education and Training has amongst its programmes *Writers Weekly* produced by Clare Sunka. Radio 1 is the popular-music-based station. Radio 2, traditionally popular light entertainment with celebrity presenters, won the 1995 Sony Radio Award for UK Station of the Year, beating Radio 5 Live into second place. Radio 3 is devoted mainly to classical and contemporary music, while Radio 4 is the main news and current affairs station. It broadcasts a wide range of other programmes such as consumer matters, wildlife, science, gardening, etc., and produces the bulk of drama, comedy, serials and readings. Radio 5 Live is the 24-hour news and sport station which replaced Radio 5 in March 1994.

DRAMA

Head of Drama *Caroline Raphael*
Editor, Single Plays & Readings *Jeremy Mortimer*
Editor, Series & Serials *Marilyn Imrie*

Caroline Raphael, Head of Drama reports that they are 'keen to commission more comedy, more women and more work from writers from ethnic minorities in both the play and serial slots.' Writers interested in dramatising extant work should always check with the Chief Producer of Series and Serials to ensure that it has not already been done, or is not already being considered. All mss should be sent to the appropriate Chief Producer of three areas: Single Plays, Series & Serials, or Readings and Short Stories. The response time is approximately 3–4 months. Plays are commissioned twice a year as part of a commissioning cycle. Drama slots include: *Classic Serial; Playhouse; The Monday Play; Thirty Minute Play; Thursday Afternoon Play; Book at Bedtime; The Archers*. Plays for Radio 4 take about two years to reach production due to current backlog though the schedules remain flexible enough to allow for adjustments. Radio 3 is mainly committed to established classics.

LIGHT ENTERTAINMENT & COMEDY

Head of Light Entertainment *Jonathan James-Moore*
Script Editor *Paul Schlesinger*

Alternative comedy was not embraced by BBC Radio, which considered much of The Comedy Store material unbroadcastable. Yet, virtually every comic talent in Britain got their first break writing one-liners for topical comedy weeklies like Radio 4's *Week Ending* and Radio 2's *The News Huddlines* (currently paying about £8 for a 'quickie' – one- or two-liners – and £20 per minute for a sketch – but these are usually commissioned). Comedy writers say it is easier to get a radio pilot launched than a TV pilot, but then TV pays ten times as much as radio. Ideas welcome. Regular programmes include *The News Quiz; Just a Minute; I'm Sorry I Haven't a Clue; The Movie Quiz; Brain of Britain; King Street Junior* (comedy drama); *Quote ... Unquote*.

SPORT & OUTSIDE BROADCASTS

Head of Sport & Outside Broadcasts *Bob Shennan*
Editor, Sports *Andy Gilles*

Sports news and commentaries across Radio 1, 4 and 5 Live, with the majority of output on Radio 5 Live (regular programmes include *Sports Report* and *6-0-6* (presented by David Mellor).

MAGAZINE PROGRAMMES

Head of Magazine Programmes *Dave Stanford*
Editor, Factual Entertainment *Ian Gardhouse*
Editor, Face the Facts *Graham Ellis*
Editor, You and Yours *Ken Vass*
Joint Editors, Woman's Hour *Clare Selerie, Sally Feldman*

Regular programmes include *Midweek; You and Yours; Face the Facts; Call Nick Ross; The Food Programme; Desert Island Discs; Any Questions.* There are also programmes for the handicapped: *Does He Take Sugar?*; and for the blind: *In Touch.* Contributions to existing series considered.

ARTS, SCIENCE & FEATURES
Head of Arts, Science & Features *Anne Winder*
Editor, Arts *John Boundy*
Editor, Documentary Features *Richard Bannerman*
Editor, Topical Features *Sharon Banoff*
Editor, Science *Deborah Cohen*

Incorporates Radio 3's *Nightwaves; Blue Skies*; Radio 4's *Pick of the Week; Kaleidoscope* (arts review and features); *Medicine Now; Science Now,* and Radio 5 Live's *Gut Reaction; Chain Reaction* and *Acid Test.* Written ideas for 20-minute talks or 45-minute documentaries welcome.

MUSIC
Head of Radio 3 Music *Dr John Evans*
Head of Radio 2 Music *Bill Morris*
Head of Radio 1 Music *Chris Lycett*
Editor, Music Talks & Documentaries *Tony Cheevers*

Regular programmes include *Music in Mind; Composer of the Week; In Tune* (music, arts, interviews); *Impressions* (jazz magazine).

BBC News and Current Affairs (Radio)

Broadcasting House, London W1A 1AA
☎0171 580 4468

Managing Director, Radio & Television *Tony Hall*
Head of Weekly Programmes *Tim Gardam*
Head of News Programmes *Peter Bell*
Head of Political Programmes *Samir Shah*
Head of News Gathering *Chris Crener*
Editor, Radio News Programmes *Steve Mitchell*
Editor, General News Service *Dave Dunford*
Foreign Editors *Chris Wyld, Vin Ray*
Home Editors *Nikki Clarke, Peter Mayne*

BBC Radio news and current affairs broadcasting comes under the aegis of BBC News & Current Affairs, a directorate established in 1987 to unify news and current affairs across both radio and television.

Programme Editors
Today *Roger Mosey*
The World at One/The World This Weekend *Kevin Marsh*

PM *Margaret Budy*
The World Tonight *Anne Koch*
Radio 1 News *Bob Doran*
Business Programmes *Alan Griffiths*
Deputy Head of Weekly Programmes *Anne Sloman*

Contributions from outside writers to existing series welcome.

BBC World Service

PO Box 76, Bush House, Strand, London WC2B 4PH
☎0171 240 3456   Fax 0171 379 6841

Managing Director *Sam Younger*
Editor, Radio Features *Mary Raine*
Head, English Programmes *Alastair Lack*
Editor, World Service News & Current Affairs *Bob Jobbins*

The World Service broadcasts in English and 40 other languages. The English service is round-the-clock, with news and current affairs as the main component. The BBC World Service is financed by a grant-in-aid voted by Parliament and by Foreign and Commonwealth Office contracts for services, amounting to around £178 million for 1995/96. With 130 million regular listeners, excluding any estimate for countries such as China where research has not been possible, it reaches a bigger audience than its five closest competitors combined. Coverage includes world business, politics, people/events/opinions, topical and development issues, the international scene, developments in science, technology and medicine, health matters, farming, sport, religion, music, the media, the arts. Regular Sunday programmes include *Play of the Week* (classic/ contemporary drama) and *Short Story* (unpublished stories by listeners living outside Britain).

The Radio Features Department produces a wide range of programme material for broadcast in English and for translation by the 40 foreign language services. Covers three main areas: analysis of international current affairs; cultural, social and economic affairs in Britain; science, technology and export promotion. Contributors should bear in mind that the target audience cannot be taken to have a ready familiarity with life in this country or with British institutions. Translation skills are not necessary; this is done exclusively by their own professionals.

BBC Radio Nan Gaidheal

See **BBC Radio Scotland**

BBC Radio Northern Ireland

Broadcasting House, 25–27 Ormeau Avenue, Belfast BT2 8HQ
☎01232 338000

Controller, Northern Ireland *Patrick Loughrey*
Senior Producer, Drama *Pam Brighton*
Editor, Current Affairs *Andrew Colman*
Editor, News *Tom Kelly*

Local stations: Radios Foyle and Ulster (see **Local Radio**).

BBC Radio Scotland

Broadcasting House, Queen Margaret Drive, Glasgow G12 8DG
☎0141 338 2345   Fax 0141 334 0614

Broadcasting House, 5 Queen Street, Edinburgh EH2 1JF.
☎0131–469 4200

Broadcasting House, Beechgrove Terrace, Aberdeen AB9 2ZT.
☎01224 625233 Fax 01224 642931

Broadcasting House, 7 Culduthel Road, Inverness IV2 4AD.
☎01463 720720 Fax: 01463 236125

Controller, Scotland *John McCormick*
Head of Radio *James Boyle*
Head of News & Current Affairs *Ken Cargil*
Managing Editor *Caroline Adam*
Editor, Glasgow *Neil Fraser*
Editor, Edinburgh *Allan Jack*
Executive Producer, Aberdeen *Andrew Jones*
Editor, Radio Nan Gaidheal *Maggie Cunningham*
Editor, Programme Development *Mike Shaw*

Produces a full range of news and current affairs programmes, plus comedy, documentaries, drama, short stories, talks and features. The emphasis is on speech-based programmes, reflecting Scottish culture. BBC Radio Scotland provides a national radio service, primarily from its centres in Glasgow, Edinburgh, Inverness and Aberdeen, and represents Scottish culture in the UK. Radio Nan Gaidheal, the Gaelic radio service, broadcasts about 32 hours per week and is used at both national and regional levels. The main production centre is in Stornoway on the Isle of Lewis (general and youth programmes). Regular programmes broadcast by BBC Radio Scotland include *Good Morning Scotland; Speaking Out* (topical); *Travel Time* and *Macgregor's Folk*. Community stations: Highland, Borders, Dumfries, Orkney and Shetland (see **Local Radio**).

BBC Wales

Broadcasting House, Llandaff, Cardiff CF5 2YQ
☎01222 572888   Fax 01222 552973

Broadcasting House, 32 Alexandra Road, Swansea, West Glamorgan SA1 5DZ
☎01792 654986   Fax 01792 468194

Broadcasting House, Meirion Road, Bangor, Gwynedd LL57 2BY.
☎01248 370880   Fax: 01248 351443

Controller, Wales *Geraint Talfan Davies*
Head of Programmes (English) *Dai Smith*
Head of Programmes (Welsh) *Gwynn Pritchard*
Editor, Radio Wales *Nick Evans*
Editor, Radio Cymru *Aled Glynne Davies*
Head of News/Current Affairs (TV & Radio) *Aled Eirug*
Head of Production, Bangor *R. Alun Evans*

Two national radio services now account for nearly 200 hours of programmes per week. Radio Wales transmits a wide mix of output in the English language, whilst Radio Cymru broadcasts a comprehensive range of programmes in Welsh. Regular programmes include *Wake Up; Weekday Wales* and *Street Life*.

BFBS (British Forces Broadcasting Service)

Bridge House, North Wharf Road, London W2 1LA
☎0171 724 1234

Controller of Programmes *Charly Lowndes*

Classic FM

Academic House, 24–28 Oval Road, London NW1 7DQ
☎0171 284 3000   Fax 0171 713 2680

Chief Executive *John Spearman*
Programme Controller *Michael Bukht*
Head of News *Clare Carson*

Classic FM, on the air from autumn 1992, is Britain's first independent national commercial radio station. It plays accessible classical music 24 hours a day and broadcasts news, weather, travel, business information, charts, music and book event guides, political/celebrity/general interest talks, features and interviews. Classic has gone well beyond its expectations, attracting 4.7 million listeners a week.

Talk Radio UK

76 Oxford Street, London W1N 0TR
☎0171 636 1089   Fax 0171 636 1053

Director of Programmes *Jerry Thomas*
LAUNCHED in February 1995, Talk Radio UK won the third national commercial radio licence with a bid of £3.8 million. Broadcasts 24 hours a day. Up-front, irreverent and controversial, programmes are aimed at the 25–45 age group, 'to plug the gap' between Classic FM and Virgin audiences. Presenters include Jeremy Beadle, Terry Christian, Tommy Boyd and Anna Raeburn.

Virgin Radio
1 Golden Square, London W1 3AB
☎0171 434 1215   Fax 0171 434 1197
Chief Executive *David Campbell*
Programme Director *Suzy Moyzel*
Britain's second national commercial station launched April 1993. Solid gold rock and classic pop from the last 25 years, targeting an older audience than its main rival BBC Radio 1.

BBC Local Radio
BBC Regional Broadcasting
White City, 201 Wood Lane, London W12 7TS
☎0181 752 5252   Fax 0181 752 4131
Managing Director *Ronald Neil*
Deputy Managing Director *Mark Byford*
There are 38 local BBC radio stations in England transmitting on FM and medium wave. These present local news, information and entertainment to local audiences and reflect the life of the communities they serve. They have their own newsroom which supplies local bulletins and national news service. Many have specialist producers. A comprehensive list of programmes for each is unavailable and would soon be out of date. For general information on programming, contact the relevant station direct.

BBC Radio Aberdeen
See **BBC Radio Scotland**

BBC Radio Bedfordshire
See **BBC Three Counties Radio**

BBC Radio Berkshire
42A Portman Road, Reading, Berkshire RG3 1NB
☎01734 567056   Fax 01734 503393
Managing Editor *Henry Yelf*
On the air since January 1992. Arts and enter-

tainment feature in the afternoon programme, produced and presented by Elizabeth Funning.

BBC Radio Bristol
PO Box 194, Bristol, Avon BS99 7QT
☎0117 9741111   Fax 0117 9732549
Managing Editor *Michael Hapgood*
Wide range of feature material used. Broadcasts up to half a dozen original radio plays each year – usually in collaboration with **South West Arts** and/or **Bristol Old Vic**.

BBC Radio Cambridgeshire
104 Hills Road, Cambridge CB2 1LD
☎01223 259696   Fax 01223 460832
Managing Editor *Margaret Hyde*
Assistant Editors *Gerald Main, Alison Sargent*
Short stories are broadcast occasionally. Scripts from listeners within the county of Cambridgeshire are considered but there is no payment.

BBC Radio Cleveland
Broadcasting House, PO Box 95FM, Middlesbrough, Cleveland TS1 5DG
☎01642 225211   Fax 01642 211356
Assistant Editor *John Ogden*
Material used is almost exclusively local to Cleveland, Co. Durham and North Yorkshire, and written by local writers. Contributions welcome for *House Call* (Saturdays 1.05–2 pm, presented by Bill Hunter). Poetry and the occasional short story are included.

BBC Radio Cornwall
Phoenix Wharf, Truro, Cornwall TR1 1UA
☎01872 75421   Fax 01872 75045
News Editor *Pauline Causey*
Arts/Literary Producer *Daphne Skinnard*
On air from 1983 serving Cornwall and the Isles of Scilly. The station broadcasts a news/talk format 18 hours a day on 103.9/95.2 FM. Daphne Skinnard's afternoon programme features interviews with local authors and previews of the arts scene.

BBC Radio Coventry
See **BBC CWR**

BBC Radio Cumbria
Annetwell Street, Carlisle, Cumbria CA3 8BB
☎01228 592444   Fax 01228 511195
Managing Editor *John Watson*
Few opportunities for writers apart from *Write Now*, a weekly half-hour regional local writing

programme, shared with Radios Merseyside, Manchester and Lancashire. Contact *Jenny Collins* on 0151–708 5500.

BBC CWR

25 Warwick Road, Coventry CV1 2WR
☎01203 559911   Fax 01203 520080
Managing Editor *Andy Wright*
Assistant Editors *Andy Conroy, Caroline Wilson*

Commenced broadcasting in January 1990. News, current affairs, public service information and community involvement, relevant to its broadcast area: Coventry and Warwickshire. Occasionally uses the work of local writers, though cannot handle large volumes of unsolicited material. Any material commissioned will need to be strong in local interest and properly geared to broadcasting.

BBC Radio Derby

PO Box 269, Derby DE1 3HL
☎01332 361111   Fax 01332 290794
Station Manager *Alex Trelinski*

News and information (the backbone of the station's output), local sports coverage, daily magazine and phone-ins, minority interest, Asian and West Indian weekly programmes.

BBC Radio Devon

PO Box 5, Broadcasting House, Seymour Road, Plymouth, Devon PL1 1XT
☎01752 260323   Fax 01752 234599
Managing Editor *Bob Bufton*

Short stories – up to 1000 words from local authors only – used weekly on the Sunday afternoon show (2.05–3.30 pm) and on Friday's late-night *Sou' West* (10.05 pm–midnight). Contact *Debbie Peters*.

BBC Essex

198 New London Road, Chelmsford, Essex CM2 9XB
☎01245 262393   Fax 01245 492983
Acting Managing Editor *Mark Wray*

Provides no regular outlets for writers but mounts special projects from time to time; these are well publicised on the air.

BBC Radio Foyle

8 Northland Road, Londonderry BT48 7JT
☎01504 262244   Fax 01504 260067
Station Manager *Jim Sheridan*
News Editor *Poilin Ni Chiarain*

Arts/Book Reviews *Frank Galligan, Stephen Price, Marie-Louise Kerr*
Features *Michael Bradley*

Radio Foyle broadcasts about seven hours of original material a day, seven days a week to the north west of Northern Ireland. Other programmes are transmitted simultaneously with Radio Ulster. The output ranges from news, sport, and current affairs to live music recordings and arts reviews. Provides programmes as required for Radio Ulster and the national networks and also provides television input to nightly BBC NI News Magazine programme.

BBC Radio Gloucestershire

London Road, Gloucester GL1 1SW
☎01452 308585   Fax 01452 306541
Managing Editor *Steve Egginton*
Assistant Editor *Keith Beech*

News and information covering the large variety of interests and concerns in Gloucestershire. Leisure, sport and music, plus Afro-Caribbean and Asian interests. Unsolicited material is not generally welcome. Competition and twice-yearly short story series encourage local authors. Mss should last 5–6 minutes on air and should be sent to the programme editor. Weekly short stories from local writers are also broadcast as well as a short local play (weekdays, with repeats at weekends).

BBC GLR

PO Box 94.9, 35c Marylebone High Street, London W1A 4LG
☎0171 224 2424   Fax 0171 487 2908
Managing Editor *Steve Panton*
Assistant Editor (News) *Sandy Smith*
Assistant Editor (General Programmes) *Jude Howells*

Greater London Radio was launched in 1988. It broadcasts news, information, travel bulletins, sport and rock music to Greater London and the Home Counties.

BBC GMR

New Broadcasting House, PO Box 951, Oxford Road, Manchester M60 1SD
☎0161 200 2000   Fax 0161 228 6110
Managing Editor *Colin Philpott*
Contacts *Ev Draper, Phil Korbel*

Programmes of particular interest to writers are: *GM Arts*, a weekly arts programme, Thursdays at 6.05 pm; and Caroline Woodruff's afternoon programme, Monday to Friday 1.30 pm to 4.00 pm, includes coverage of leisure, entertainment and arts. Very few opportunities for writers apart from *Write Now*, a weekly half-hour regional local writing programme, shared with Radios Merseyside and Lancashire. Contact *Jenny Collins* on 0151–708 5500.

BBC Radio Guernsey
Commerce House, Les Banques, St Peter Port, Guernsey, Channel Isles GY1 2HS
☎01481 728977   Fax 01481 713557
Managing Editor *Bob Lloyd-Smith*

BBC Hereford & Worcester
Hylton Road, Worcester WR2 5WW
☎01905 748485   Fax 01905 748006
Also at: 43 Broad Street, Hereford HR4 9HH
Tel 01432 355252 Fax 01432 356446
Managing Editor *Eve Turner*
Senior Producer (Programme) *Denzil Dudley*

Interested in short stories, plays or dramatised documentaries with a local flavour.

BBC Radio Highland
Broadcasting House, 7 Culduthel Road, Inverness IV2 4AD
☎01463 720720   Fax 01463 236125

Station Manager *Maggie Cunningham*

BBC Radio Humberside
9 Chapel Street, Hull, North Humberside HU1 3NU
☎01482 323232   Fax 01482 226409
Station Manager *John Lilley*

Broadcasts short stories by local writers each morning. Occasional competitions for local amateur authors and playwrights.

BBC Radio Jersey
18 Parade Road, St Helier, Jersey, Channel Isles JE2 3PL
☎01534 870000   Fax 01534 832569
Station Manager *Bob Lloyd-Smith*
News Editor *Mike Vibert*

Local news, current affairs and community items.

BBC Radio Kent
Sun Pier, Chatham, Kent ME4 4EZ
☎01634 830505   Fax 01634 830573
Managing Editor *To be appointed*
Assistant Editor *Graham Majin*

Opportunities exist for writers on the specialist arts programme, *Scene and Heard*. Features need

to be of strong local interest, as do drama/fiction, for which there are few openings. Occasional commissions are made for local interest documentaries and other one-off programmes.

BBC Radio Lancashire
Darwen Street, Blackburn, Lancashire BB2 2EA
☎01254 262411   Fax 01254 680821
Managing Editor *Steve Taylor*

Journalism-based radio station, interested in interviews with local writers. Also *Write Now*, a weekly half-hour regional local writing programme, shared with Radios Merseyside and GMR. Contact *Jenny Collins* on 0151–708 5500.

BBC Radio Leeds
Broadcasting House, Woodhouse Lane, Leeds, West Yorkshire LS2 9PN
☎0113 2442131   Fax 0113 2420652
Station Manager *John Jefferson*

One of the country's biggest local radio stations, BBC Radio Leeds was also one of the first, coming on air in the 1960s as something of an experimental venture. The accent here is on speech, with a comprehensive news, sport and information service as the backbone of its daily output.

BBC Radio Leicester
Epic House, Charles Street, Leicester LE1 3SH
☎0116 2516688   Fax 0116 2511463 (News)/ 2513632 (Management)
Station Manager *Jeremy Robinson*

The first local station in Britain. Concentrates on speech-based programmes in the morning and on a music/speech mix in the afternoon. Leicester runs a second station (on AM) for the large Asian community.

BBC Radio Lincolnshire
PO Box 219, Newport, Lincoln LN1 3XY
☎01522 511411   Fax 01522 511726
Managing Editor *David Wilkinson*
Assistant Editor *Malcolm Swire*

Unsolicited material considered only if locally relevant. Maximum 1000 words: straight narrative preferred, ideally with a topical content.

BBC Radio Manchester
See **BBC GMR**

BBC Radio Merseyside

55 Paradise Street, Liverpool L1 3BP
☎0151 708 5500   Fax 0151 708 5356
Station Manager *Richard Duckenfield*

Write Now, a weekly 25-minute regional writers' programme, is produced at Radio Merseyside and also broadcast on BBC Radios GMR and Lancashire. Short stories (maximum 1200 words), plus poetry and features on writing. Contact *Jenny Collins* on 0151–708 5500. A regular weekly short story is broadcast in the lunchtime programme (max. 1000 words). Local writers only. Contact Angela Heslop on 0151–708 5500.

BBC Radio Newcastle

Broadcasting Centre, Newcastle upon Tyne
NE99 1RN
☎0191 232 4141   Fax 0191 232 5082
Station Manager *Tony Fish*
Assistant Editor *Andrew Hartley*

'We welcome short stories of about 10 minutes duration for consideration for broadcast in our afternoon programme. We are *only* interested in stories by local writers.' Afternoon programme producer: *Sarah Miller.*

BBC Radio Norfolk

Norfolk Tower, Surrey Street, Norwich,
Norfolk NR1 3PA
☎01603 617411   Fax 01603 622229
Assistant Editors *Jill Bennett, David Clayton*

Good local material welcome for features/documentaries, but must relate directly to Norfolk.

BBC Radio Northampton

Broadcasting House, Abington Street,
Northampton NN1 2BH
☎01604 239100   Fax 01604 230709
Assistant Editors *Mike Day, Steve Taschini*

Literary outlets limited, but they do occur occasionally in the form of short story competitions/poetry week, and are trailed accordingly.

BBC Radio Nottingham

PO Box 222, Nottingham NG1 3HZ
☎0115 9550500   Fax 0115 9550501
Deputy Manager *Nick Brunger*

Rarely broadcasts scripted pieces of any kind but interviews with authors form a regular part of the station's output. Some cooperation with **East Midland Arts** towards assisting and promoting local writers through seminars advertised on air.

BBC Radio Orkney

Castle Street, Kirkwall KW15 1DF
☎01856 873939   Fax 01856 872908
Senior Producer *John Fergusson*

Regular programmes include *Around Orkney; Sing Gospel; Moot Point.*

BBC Radio Oxford

269 Banbury Road, Oxford OX2 7DW
☎01865 311444   Fax 01865 311996
Assistant Editor *David Campbell*

No opportunities at present as the outlet for short stories has been discontinued for the time being.

BBC Radio Peterborough

PO Box 957, Peterborough, Cambridgeshire
PE1 1YT
☎01733 312832   Fax 01733 343768
Managing Editor *Margaret Hyde*
Assistant Editor *Gerald Main*
Senior Producer (Peterborough) *Steve Somers*

Sister service to **BBC Radio Cambridgeshire**. Steve Somers' new afternoon programme (1.30–4.00 pm) deals with topics such as arts, entertainment, leisure, sport, etc.

BBC Radio Scotland (Borders)

Municipal Buildings, High Street, Selkirk
TD7 4BU
☎01750 21884   Fax 01750 22400
Editor *Bob Burgess*

Formerly broadcast as Radio Tweed.

BBC Radio Scotland (Dumfries)

Elmbank, Lover's Walk, Dumfries DG1 1NZ
☎01387 268008   Fax 01387 252568
News Editor *Willie Johnston*
Senior Producer *Glenn Cooksley*

Previously Radio Solway. The station mainly outputs news bulletins (four daily). Recent changes have seen the station become more of a production centre with programmes being made for the local radio network as well as BBC Radio 4 and 5 Live. Freelancers of a high standard, familiar with Radio Scotland, should contact the producer.

BBC Radio Sheffield

60 Westbourne Road, Sheffield S10 2QU
☎0114 2686185   Fax 0114 2664375
Managing Editor *Barry Stockdale*
Assistant Editor *Everard Davy*

During the early part of 1995, Radio Sheffield

broadcast a series of short stories by writers in Yorkshire and Humberside.

BBC Radio Shetland
Brentham House, Lerwick, Shetland ZE1 0LR
☎01595 694747   Fax 01595 694307
Senior Producer *Mary Blance*

Regular programmes include *Good Evening Shetland.*

BBC Radio Shropshire
2–4 Boscobel Drive, Shrewsbury, Shropshire SY1 3TT
☎01743 248484   Fax 01743 271702
Managing Editor *Barbara Taylor*
Assistant Editor *Eric Smith*

Unsolicited literary material very rarely used, and then only if locally relevant.

BBC Radio Solent
Broadcasting House, Havelock Road, Southampton, Hampshire SO1 0XR
☎01703 631311   Fax 01703 339648

Managing Editor *Chris Van Schaick*

BBC Radio Solway
See **BBC Radio Scotland (Dumfries)**

BBC (Radio) Somerset Sound
14–15 Paul Street, Taunton, Somerset TA1 3PF
☎01823 252437   Fax 01823 332539
Senior Producer *Norman Rickard*

Informal, speech-based programming, with strong news and current affairs output and regular local-interest features, including local writing.

BBC Southern Counties Radio
Broadcasting Centre, Guildford, Surrey GU2 5AP
☎01483 306306   Fax 01483 304952
Managing Editor *Mark Thomas*
Assistant Editor *Neil Pringle*

Formerly known as BBC Radio Sussex and Surrey.

BBC Radio Stoke
Cheapside, Hanley, Stoke on Trent, Staffordshire ST1 1JJ
☎01782 208080   Fax 01782 289115
Managing Editor *John Collard*
Assistant Editors *Mervyn Gamage, Chris Ramsden*

Emphasis on news, current affairs and local

topics. Music represents one third of total output. Unsolicited material of local interest is welcome – send to an assistant editor.

BBC Radio Suffolk
Broadcasting House, St Matthews Street, Ipswich, Suffolk IP1 3EP
☎01473 250000   Fax 01473 210887
Managing Editor *Ivan Howlett*
Assistant Editors *Jim Ensom, Kevin Burch*

Strongly speech-based, dealing with news, current affairs, community issues, the arts, agriculture, commerce, travel, sport and leisure. Programmes frequently carry interviews with writers.

BBC Radio Sussex and Surrey
See **BBC Southern Counties Radio**

BBC Three Counties Radio
PO Box 3CR, Hastings Street, Luton, Bedfordshire LU1 5XL
☎01582 441000   Fax 01582 401467
Managing Editor *Mike Gibbons*
Assistant Editor *Jeff Winston*

Formerly BBC Radio Bedfordshire. Encourages freelance contributions from the community across a wide range of radio output, including interview and feature material. The station very occasionally broadcasts drama. Stringent local criteria are applied in selection. Particularly interested in historical topics (five minutes max.).

BBC Radio Tweed
See **BBC Radio Scotland (Borders)**

BBC Radio Ulster
Broadcasting House, Ormeau Avenue, Belfast BT2 8HQ
☎01232 338000   Fax 01232 338800
Controller, Northern Ireland *Pat Loughrey*
Head of Programmes *Anne Carragher*

Programmes now broadcast from 6.30 am–midnight weekdays and from 8.00 am–midnight at weekends. Radio Ulster has won six Sony awards in the last two years. Main programmes: *Good Morning Ulster, Gerry Anderson, Talkback, All Arts and Parts, Inside Politics.*

BBC Radio Wales in Clwyd
The Old School House, Glanrafon Road, Mold, Clwyd CH7 1PA
☎01352 700367   Fax 01352 759821
Chief News Assistant *Tracy Cardwell*

Broadcasts regular news bulletins Monday to

Friday and until lunchtime on Saturday, and *Revolution*, produced by Jane Morris, a network youth music programme on Tuesday and Thursday evenings (10.30 pm–midnight).

BBC Radio WCR
See **BBC Radio WM/WCR**

BBC Wiltshire Sound
Broadcasting House, Prospect Place, Swindon, Wiltshire SN1 3RW
☎01793 513626   Fax 01793 513650
Managing Editor *Sandy Milne*

BBC Radio WM/WCR
PO Box 206, Birmingham B5 7SD
☎0121 414 8484   Fax 0121 472 3174

Managing Editor *Peter Davies*
Senior Producer, Programmes *Tony Wadsworth*

This is a news and current affairs station with no interest in short stories or plays.

BBC Radio York
20 Bootham Row, York YO3 7BR
☎01904 641351   Fax 01904 610937
Managing Editor *Geoff Sargieson*
Assistant Editor *Dan Farthing*

A limited outlet for short stories and features, provided they are either set locally (i.e. North Yorkshire) or have some other local relevance.

Independent Local Radio

Aire FM/Magic 828
PO Box 2000, 51 Burley Road, Leeds, West Yorkshire LS3 1LR
☎0113 2452299   Fax 0113 2421830
Programme Controller *Paul Fairburn*

Beacon Radio/WABC
267 Tettenhall Road, Wolverhampton, West Midlands WV6 0DQ
☎01902 757211   Fax 01902 745456
Programme Director *Peter Wagstaff*
No outlets for unsolicited literary material at present.

Radio Borders
Tweedside Park, Tweedbank, Galashiels TD1 3TD
☎01896 759444   Fax 01896 759494
Programme Controller *Rod Webster*
Head of News *Leslie Railton*

Breeze
See **Essex FM**

96.4 FM BRMB FM/XTRA am
Radio House, Aston Road North, Birmingham B6 4BX
☎0121 359 4481   Fax 0121 359 1117

Head of Programmes *Clive Dickens, Steve Marsh*
Head of News *Nicole Pullman*

Some demand for comedy material. Opportunities for writers in the various feature series which the station puts out.

Broadland 102
St Georges Plain, 47–49 Colegate, Norwich, Norfolk NR3 1DB
☎01603 630621   Fax 01603 666252

Programme Director *Mike Stewart*
Head of Features *Dick Hutchinson*
Head of News *Julian Smith*

Brunel Classic Gold
See **GWR FM (West)**

Capital FM/Capital Gold
Euston Tower, London NW1 3DR
☎0171 608 6080   Fax 0171 387 2345

Head of News & Talks *David Harvey*

Britain's largest commercial radio station. Main outlet is news and showbiz programme each weekday evening at 7 pm called *The Way It Is*. This covers current affairs, showbiz, features and pop news, aimed at a young audience. The vast majority of material is generated in-house.

Century Radio
Century House, PO Box 100, Church Street, Gateshead NE8 2YY
☎0191 477 6666   Fax 0191 477 4660

Programme Controller *John Simons*
Music, talk, news and interviews, 24 hours a day.

CFM
PO Box 964, Carlisle, Cumbria CA1 3NG
☎01228 818964   Fax 01228 819444
Programme Controller *Alex Rowland*
News Editor *Gill Garston*
Music, news and information station.

Chiltern Radio
Chiltern Road, Dunstable, Bedfordshire LU6 1HQ
☎01582 666001   Fax 01582 661725
Programme Controller *Paul Chantler*
Part of the Chiltern Radio Network. Oppor-

tunities for radio drama only, but these are rare. If a script is of exceptional local interest, it has a fair chance of being considered.

Radio City/City FM/ Radio City Gold
PO Box 194, 8–10 Stanley Street, Liverpool L1 6AF
☎0151 227 5100   Fax 0151 471 0330
Managing Director *Lynne Wood*
Programme Controller, City FM *Tony McKenzie*
Programme Controller, City Gold *Richard Duncan*

Opportunities for writers are very few and far between as this is predominantly a music station.

Radio Clyde/Clyde 1 FM/Clyde 2
Clydebank Business Park, Clydebank G81 2RX
☎0141 306 2272   Fax 0141 306 2265
Programme Director *Alex Dickson*

Radio Clyde and the IBA, together with the **Society of Authors** and **The Writers' Guild**, launched a major new commissioning scheme for radio drama in 1989. The aim was to create a regular strand of specially produced plays for independent radio stations. Members of the Society or Guild were asked to submit outlines for previously unsubmitted work towards a one-hour production for radio – preference for contemporary themes, and no special emphasis on Scottish works. Accepted outlines led to full-length script commissions for production at Radio Clyde's drama department. Few opportunities outside of this now as programmes usually originate in-house or by commission. All documentary material is made in-house. Good local news items always considered.

Cool FM
See **Downtown Radio**

DevonAir Radio
See **Gemini Radio FM/AM**

Downtown Radio/Cool FM
Newtownards, Co. Down, Northern Ireland BT23 4ES
☎01247 815555   Fax 01247 815252
Programme Head *John Rosborough*

Downtown Radio first ran a highly successful short story competition in 1988, attracting over 400 stories. The competition is now an annual event and writers living within the station's transmission area are asked to submit material during the winter and early spring. The competition is promoted in association with Eason Shops. For further information, write to *Derek Ray* at the station.

Essex FM/Breeze
Radio House, Clifftown Road, Southend on Sea, Essex SS1 1SX
☎01702 333711   Fax 01702 345224
Programme Controller, Essex FM *Peter Holmes*
Programme Controller, Breeze *Keith Rogers*

No real opportunities for writers' work as such, but will often interview local authors of published books. Contact *Heather Bridge* (Programming Secretary) in the first instance.

Forth FM/Max AM
Forth House, Forth Street, Edinburgh EH1 3LF
☎0131 556 9255   Fax 0131 558 3277
Director of Programming *Tom Steele*
News Editor *David Johnston*

News stories welcome from freelancers. Max AM, launched 1990, is aimed at the 35+ age group. Although music-based, it includes a wide range of specialist general interest programmes.

Fortune 1458
PO Box 1458, Quay West, Trafford Park, Manchester M17 1FL
☎0161 872 1458   Fax 0161 872 0206
Programme Management *Colin Slade*

Music, news and regional features, focusing on lifestyle, travel, food and drink, business and entertainment.

Fox FM
Brush House, Pony Road, Cowley, Oxford OX4 2XR
☎01865 748787
Fax 01865 748721/748736 (news)
Programme Controller *Mark Flanagan*
Head of News *Fiona Leslie*

Backed by an impressive list of shareholders including the Blackwell Group of Companies. No outlet for creative writing; however, authors soliciting book reviews should contact *David Freeman* at the station.

GEM-AM
29–31 Castle Gate, Nottingham NG1 7AP
☎0115 9581731   Fax 0115 9588614
Station Director *Chris Hughes*
Part of the GWR Group.

Gemini Radio FM/AM

Hawthorn House, Exeter Business Park,
Exeter, Devon EX1 3QS
☎01392 444444   Fax 01392 444433
Programme Controller (FM) *Kevin Kane*
Programme Controller (AM) *Mike Allen*

Took over the franchise previously held by
DevonAir Radio in January 1995. Part of West
Country Broadcasting. Occasional outlets for
poetry and short stories on the AM wave-
length. Contact *Mike Allen*.

Great North Radio (GNR)

See **Metro FM**

Great Yorkshire Gold

See **The Pulse**

GWR FM (West)/ Brunel Classic Gold

PO Box 2000 (Brunel: PO Box 2020), Bristol,
Avon BS99 7SN
☎0117 9843200   Fax 0117 9843202
Station Director, Brunel (Bristol) *Chris Scott*
Station Director, GWR (Swindon) *Neil
    Cooper*

Very few opportunities. Almost all material
originates in-house. GWR is targeted at the
under 40s; Brunel at a slightly older audience.
Part of the GWR Group.

Hallam FM

Radio House, 900 Herries Road,
Sheffield S6 1RH
☎0114 2853333   Fax 0114 2853159
Programme Director *Steve King*

Heart FM

1 The Square, 111 Broad Street, Birmingham
B15 1AS
☎0121 626 1007   Fax 0121 696 1007
Managing Director *Phil Riley*
Programme Director *Paul Fairburn*

Commenced broadcasting in September 1994.
Music, regional news and information.

Hereward FM

PO Box 225, Queensgate Centre,
Peterborough, Cambridgeshire PE1 1XJ
☎01733 460460   Fax 01733 281444 (news)
Programme Controller *Adrian Cookes*

Few openings offered to writers as all material is
compiled and presented by in-house staff.

Horizon Radio

Broadcast Centre, Crownhill, Milton Keynes,
Buckinghamshire MK8 0AB
☎01908 269111   Fax 01908 564893
Programme Director *Paul Chantler*

Part of the Chiltern Radio Network.

Invicta FM/Invicta Supergold

PO Box 100, Whitstable, Kent CT5 3QX
☎01227 772004   Fax 01227 771558
Programme Controller *Francis Currie*

Music-based station, serving listeners in the
South East. 'Always on the look-out for creative,
innovative programming ideas of any kind.'

Isle of Wight Radio

Dodnor Park, Newport, Isle of Wight
☎01983 822557   Fax 01983 821690
Programme Controller *Andy Shier*

Part of the GWR Group, Isle of Wight Radio
is the island's only radio station broadcasting
local news, music and general entertainment.

Key 103

See **Piccadilly Gold**

Leicester Sound FM

Granville House, Granville Road, Leicester
LE1 7RW
☎0116 2561300   Fax 0116 2561305
Station Director *Carlton Dale*
Programme Controller *Colin Wilsher*
News Editor *Julie Langtry-Langton*

Predominantly a music station. Very occasionally, unsolicited material of local interest – 'targeted at our particular audience' – may be
broadcast.

London News 97.3 FM/London News Talk 1152 AM

72 Hammersmith Road, London W14 8YE
☎0171 973 1152   Fax 0171 371 2199
**Programme Controller, London News
    97.3 FM** *Stephen Gardiner*
**Programme Controller, London News
    Talk 1152 AM** *Robin Malcolm*
News Information Editor *Charles Rose*

Took over from LBC early in October 1994.
London News 97.3 FM – 24-hour rolling
news station; London News talk 1152 AM –
phone-in and conversation station.

Magic 828

See **Aire FM**

Marcher Sound

The Studios, Mold Road, Wrexham, Clwyd
LL11 4AF
☎01978 752202   Fax 01978 759701

Programme Controller *Kevin Howard*

Occasional features and advisory programmes.
Welsh language broadcasts weekdays at 6.00
pm.

Max AM

See **Radio Forth RFM**

Mercia FM/Mercia Classic Gold

Mercia Sound Ltd., Hertford Place, Coventry,
Warwickshire CV1 3TT
☎01203 868200   Fax 01203 868202

Station Director *Stuart Linnell*
Programme Controller *Steve Dawson*

Mercury FM/
Mercury Extra AM

Broadfield House, Brighton Road, Crawley,
West Sussex RH11 9TT
☎01293 519161   Fax 01293 560927

Also at: PO Box 964, Guildford, Surrey GU1
4XX. Tel 01483 32903 Fax 01483 31612
Programme Controller *Martin Campbell*

Mercury FM is predominantly music. Mercury
Extra AM broadcasts 50% music, 50% speech.
Contact Jane Wickens.

Metro FM/Great North Radio
(GNR)

Swalwell, Newcastle upon Tyne NE99 1BB
☎0191 488 3131/496 0337
Fax 0191 488 9222

Programme Director, Metro *Giles Squire*
Programme Controller, GNR *Jim Brown*

Very few opportunities for writers, but phone-
in programmes may interview relevant authors.
Some interest in short comedy for the Metro
FM station.

Moray Firth Radio

PO Box 271, Scorgvie Place, Inverness
IV3 6SF
☎01463 224433   Fax 01463 243224

Programme Controller *Thomas Prag*
Book Reviews *May Marshall*

Book reviews every Monday afternoon at 2.20
pm. Also fortnightly arts programme called *The
North Bank Show* which features interviews
with authors, etc.

NorthSound Radio

45 King's Gate, Aberdeen AB2 6BL
☎01224 632234   Fax 01224 633282

Station Manager *John Martin*
Programme Controller *John Trousdale*

Ocean FM/South Coast Radio

Whittle Avenue, Segensworth West, Fareham,
Hampshire PO15 5PA
☎01489 589911   Fax 01489 589453

Programme Controller *Nick Martin*
News Editor *Karen Woods*

South Coast Radio ran a very successful short
story competition in the autumn of 1994 and
hoped to repeat the exercise in 1995.

Orchard FM

Haygrove House, Shoreditch, Taunton,
Somerset TA3 7BT
☎01823 338448   Fax 01823 321044

Programme Controller *Phil Easton*
News Room Manager *Lyndsey Ashwood.*

Summaries for music programming welcome.
Send ideas in the first instance.

Piccadilly Gold/Key 103

127–131 The Piazza, Piccadilly Plaza,
Manchester M1 4AW
☎0161 236 9913   Fax 0161 228 1503

Programme Director *John Dash*

Music-based programming only.

Plymouth Sound FM/AM

Earl's Acre, Alma Road, Plymouth, Devon
PL3 4HX
☎01752 227272   Fax 01752 670730

Programme Controllers *Simon Willis*(FM),
Peter Greig (AM)

Music-based station. No outlets for writers.

The Pulse/Great Yorkshire Gold

Forster Square, Bradford, West Yorkshire
BD1 5NE
☎01274 731521   Fax 01274 392031

Also at: Great Yorkshire Gold, PO Box 777,
Sheffield, South Yorkshire S6 1RH. Tel 0114
853333 Fax 0114 853159.

Programme Director (The Pulse)
Steve Martin
Programme Controller (GYG)
Steven Parkinson

The Pulse broadcasts news on the hour and a
late night phone-in, but is principally a music-

based station. Provides the GYG service on its AM transmitters, featuring oldies, news, features and competitions.

Q103.FM
PO Box 103, Vision Park, Chivers Way, Histon, Cambridge CB4 4WW
☎01223 235255   Fax 01223 235161
Station Director *Alistair Wayne*

Part of GWR Commercial Radio Group.

Red Dragon FM/Touch AM
Radio House, West Canal Wharf, Cardiff CF1 5XJ
☎01222 384041/237878   Fax 01222 384014
Programme Controller *Phil Roberts*
News Editor *Andrew Jones*

Red Rose Gold/Rock FM
PO Box 301, St Paul's Square, Preston, Lancashire PR1 1YE
☎01772 556301   Fax 01772 201917
Programme Director *Mark Matthews*

Music-based stations. No outlets for writers.

Scot FM
Number 1 Shed, Albert Quay, Leith, Edinburgh EH6 7DN
☎0131 554 6677   Fax 0131 554 2266
Also at: Anderston Quay, Glasgow G3 8DA
Tel 0141 204 1003 Fax 0141 204 1067
Managing Director *Tom Hunter*
Programme Controller *Jason Bryant*

Commenced broadcasting in September 1994 to the central Scottish region. Music and talk shows, sport and phone-ins.

Severn Sound/Severn Sound Supergold
67 Southgate Street, Gloucester GL1 2DQ
☎01452 423791
Fax 01452 529446/423008 (news)
Station Manager *Gordon McRae*

Part of the Chiltern Radio Network.

SGR FM 97.1/96.4
Alpha Business Park, Whitehouse Road, Ipswich, Suffolk IP1 5LT
☎01473 461000   Fax 01473 741200
Programme Director *Mike Stewart*
Head of Presentation *Mark Pryke*
Features Producer *Nigel Rennie*

Few openings here and 'even fewer' in drama and light entertainment.

Signal Cheshire
Regent House, Heaton Lane, Stockport, Cheshire SK4 1BX
☎0161 480 5445   Fax 0161 474 1806
Programme Director *John Evington*
Programme Co-ordinator *Neil Cossar*

Music-based station. No outlets for writers. Part of the Signal Network.

Signal One/Signal Gold/ Signal Stafford
Studio 257, Stoke Road, Stoke on Trent, Staffordshire ST4 2SR
☎01782 747047   Fax 01782 744110
Programme Director *John Evington*
Head of News *Paul Sheldon*

Part of the Signal Network.

South Coast Radio
See **Ocean FM**

South West Sound FM
See **West Sound Radio**

Southern FM
PO Box 2000, Brighton, East Sussex BN41 2SS
☎01273 430111   Fax 01273 430098
Programme Manager *Chris Copsey*
News Manager *Phil Bell*

Spectrum Radio
Endeavour House, Brent Cross, London NW2 1JT
☎0181 905 5000   Fax 0181 209 1029
Managing Director *Wolfgang Bucci*

Minority community programmes across a broad spectrum of groups: Afro-Caribbean, Asian, Arabic, Chinese, Greek, Irish, Italian, Jewish, Persian, Spanish. Appropriately targeted news/ magazine items and book reviews will receive consideration.

Spire FM
City Hall Studios, Malthouse Lane, Salisbury, Wiltshire SP2 7QQ
☎01722 416644   Fax 01722 415102
Managing Director *Chris Carnegy*

Music, news current affairs, quizzes and sport. Holds the Sony Award for the best local radio station.

Swansea Sound
Victoria Road, Gowerton, Swansea, West Glamorgan SA4 3AB
☎01792 893751   Fax 01792 898841
Head of Programmes *Rob Pendry*
Head of News *Lynn Courtney*

Interested in a wide variety of material, though news items must be of local relevance. An explanatory letter, in the first instance, is advisable.

Radio Tay
PO Box 123, Dundee DD1 9UF
☎01382 200800   Fax 01382 224549
Station Manager/Director *Sandy Wilkie*
Programme Controller *Ally Ballingall*

Wholly-owned subsidiary of **Radio Forth**. Unsolicited material is assessed. Short stories and book reviews of local interest are welcome. Send to the programme controller.

Touch AM
See **Red Dragon FM**

Trent FM
29–31 Castlegate, Nottingham NG1 7AP
☎0115 9581731   Fax 0115 9588614
Station Director *Chris Hughes*

Part of the GWR Group. Few opportunities: in documentaries some locally orientated material discussed up-front may stand a chance; Christmas material only in light entertainment.

2CR (Two Counties Radio)
5–7 Southcote Road, Bournemouth, Dorset BH1 3LR
☎01202 294881   Fax 01202 299314
Programme Controller *Paul Allen*

Wholly-owned subsidiary of the GWR Group. Serves Dorset and Hampshire.

2-Ten FM/Classic Gold 1431
PO Box 210, Reading, Berkshire RG3 5RZ
☎01734 254400   Fax 01734 254448
Programme Controller *Andrew Phillips*

Simon Marlow produces and presents a weekly 3-hour entertainment programme, *Entertainment 95*. Authors are interviewed, and there is particular emphasis on music/film/video-related books. A subsidiary of the GWR Group.

Viking FM
Commercial Road, Hull, North Humberside HU1 2SA
☎01482 325141   Fax 01482 218650/587067

Programme Controller *Phil White*
News Co-ordinator *Stephen Edwards*
Features Producer *Paul Bromley*

WABC (Nice 'n' Easy Radio)
See **Beacon Radio**

Wear FM, 103.4
Foster Building, Chester Road, Sunderland, Tyne & Wear SR1 3SD
☎0191 515 2103   Fax 0191 515 2270
Programme Controller *Roy Leonard*

Came on the air towards the end of 1990 and was named 'Station of the Year' for its 'life, verve, style and wit' in the Sony Radio Awards 1992 . Music, community-based programmes, talks, etc. 24 hours a day, seven days a week.

Wessex FM
Radio House, Trinity Street, Dorchester, Dorset DT1 1DJ
☎01305 250333   Fax 01205 250052
Programme Manager *Roger Kennedy*

Music, local news, information and features.

West Sound Radio/South West Sound FM
Radio House, 54 Holmston Road, Ayr KA7 3BE
☎01292 283662
Fax 01292 283665/262607 (news)
Programme Controller, News Editor
   Gordon McArthur

1332 WGMS
PO Box 225, Queensgate Centre, Peterborough, Cambridgeshire PE1 1XJ
☎01733 460460   Fax 01733 281445
Programme Controller *Robert Jones*

Golden oldies, news and sport.

Radio Wyvern
PO Box 22, 5–6 Barbourne Terrace, Worcester WR1 3JZ
☎01905 612212
Managing Director *Norman Bilton*
Programme Controller *Stephanie Denham*

Independent company, not part of any larger group. *Very* occasionally, a local writer may be commissioned to produce something of interest to the Wyvern audience.

XTRA AM
See **BRMB FM**

Freelance Rates – Broadcasting

Freelance rates vary enormously. The following guidelines are minimum rates negotiated by the **National Union of Journalists**. Most work can command higher fees from employers whether or not they have NUJ agreements. It is up to freelancers to negotiate the best deal they can.

BBC

Radio News Reports (excluding local radio, including External Services): £36.20 for up to two minutes (domestic news broadcasts) and up to three minutes; £8.10 for each minute thereafter.

Television News Reports (including regional): £44.50 for up to two minutes; £11 for each minute thereafter.

Radio (excluding local): £67 for up to two minutes; £14 for each minute thereafter.

Radio (local): £18 for up to two minutes; £6.60 for each minute thereafter.

News Copy: £10.90 (network); £8.10 non-network.

Commissioned Sports Results: £3 per result.

Still Photographers (commission rates): £47.50 (half-day); £95 (full day).

Still Fees (black and white or colour): £35.40 for a single picture or first picture in a series: second use £17.70; third or subsequent use £11.80. Where a series is provided on the same event: £17.70 for first use of the second picture; £11.80 for first use of third and subsequent use.

Day and half-day rates Category one (reporters in network regional television and radio): £102 a day; £51 half-day. Category two (experienced broadcast journalists): £80.50 a day; £40.25 half-day. Category three (junior reporters in local radio): £69.50 a day; £34.75 half-day.

Radio talks and features

Interviews

Up to five minutes:	£47
Five to ten minutes:	negotiable
Ten to fifteen minutes:	£62
Fifteen minutes and over:	negotiable
Script and read:	£18 per minute
Script only:	£14 per minute

Illustrated talks: £14.40 per minute

Linked interviews: one interview £77; two interviews: £100

Features/documentaries

Up to seven minutes: £166.60; £23.80 per minute thereafter.

Talks

Contributions for one national region (Scotland, Wales or Northern Ireland) may be contracted at two-thirds of the rates above.

Independent radio

News Copy Ordered or submitted, and broadcast by the station: £7.28 per item.

News Reports (Voice) For a report or talk on tape or broadcast by a freelancer: £19.64 for first two minutes; £6.54 per minute thereafer. *Day Rates* £68.39 a day (over 4 hours and up to 8); £34.20 half-day (up to 4 hours).

Sports Ordered match coverage, including previews, flashes and summaries: £34.96; ordered calls for running reports and additional telephone fee: £13.21; result only service: £2.85.

Tip offs £7.49 for each tip off supplied and used.

Travelling and out-of-pocket expenses are generally paid.

ITV Association

News

Report or *Talk* Recorded on tape/film, or broadcast: not less than £49.22

Sports Copy Not recorded or broadcast by the freelancer: not less than £11.50, with payment for results only £5.11.

News Copy Not recorded or broadcast by the freelancer: not less than £9.95.

Ordered Assignments Ordered reports or talks shall be paid for even if not used; in such cases the minimum rate shall be paid.

Daily engagements Day rate: £103; half-day: £57.

Commission fee for photographers to take still photographs For an assignment taking up to a day: £103. For an assignment taking up to half a day: £57.

The above items do not include travelling and out-of-pocket expenses.

Stills

Black and white and colour: First use: £31.85; second use: £15.35; third and subsequent use: £9.25.

For a series of pictures First use: £66.69; second use: £30.75; third and subsequent use: £20.50. Travel and out-of-pocket expenses shall be paid in addition.
Tip offs £17.40 for each tip off supplied and used.

Research
TV organisations which hire freelancers to research programme items should pay on a day rate which reflects the value of the work and the importance of the programme concerned.

Presentation
In all broadcast media, presenters command higher fees than news journalists. There is considerable variation in what is paid for presenting programmes and videos, according to their audience and importance. Day rates with television companies are usually about £154 a day.

Radio drama

A beginner in radio drama should receive at least £36.72 per minute for a sixty-minute script. For an established writer – one who has three or more plays to his credit – the minimum rate per minute is £55.90.
Fees for dramatisations range from 65–85% of the full drama rate, depending on the degree of original material and dialogue.
An attendance payment of £32.88 per production is paid to established writers.

Television drama

For a sixty-minute teleplay, the BBC will pay an established writer £6790 and a beginner £4310. The corresponding figures for ITV are £8168 for the established writer, £5803 for a writer new to television but with a solid reputation in other literary areas.
Day rates for attendance at read-throughs and rehearsals is £61.57 for the BBC and £65.75 for ITV.

Feature films

An agreement between **The Writers' Guild** and **PACT** allows for a minimum guaranteed payment to the writer of £31,200 on a feature film with a budget in excess of £2 million; £19,000 on a budget from £750,000 to £2 million; £14,000 on a budget below £750,000.

Film, TV and Video Producers

Absolutely Productions Ltd
6–7 Fareham Street, London W1V 3AH
☎0171 734 9824   Fax 0171 734 8284

Executive Producer *Miles Bullough*

TV and radio production company specialising in comedy and entertainment. OUTPUT *Absolutely* Series 1–4 (Ch4); *mr don and mr george* (Ch4); *Squawkietalkie* (comedy wildlife programme for Ch4); *In Montreal Just for Laughs* (Radio 1 documentary).

Acrobat Television
The Media Playground, 19 Lind Street, Manchester M40 7ES
☎0161 274 3000   Fax 0161 273 3122

Contact *David Hill, Graeme Oxby*

Film, video and TV: drama, documentary, commercials and corporate. OUTPUT includes sport and features, commercials and promotional material. CLIENTS Thomas Cook, North West Water. Scripts welcome.

Action Time Ltd
Wrendal House, 2 Whitworth Street West, Manchester M1 5WX
☎0161 236 8999   Fax 0161 236 8845

Chairman *Stephen Leahy*
Director of Programming *Trish Kinane*

Major producers and licensers of TV quiz, game and entertainment shows such as *You've Been Framed; Catchphrase; Cluedo; Runway; Joker in the Pack; Love at First Sight*. Action Time has a production base in Germany and co-production partners in France, Ireland, Canada, Russia, Spain, Norway, Sweden, Belgium, Wales and Finland. All original material is processed through the UK office. Format ideas should be sent to the Chairman.

The Actual Production Company
71 Lower Bank Road, Fulwood, Preston, Lancashire PR2 4NU
☎01772 715999   Fax 01772 715999

Contact *Terence Charnley*

Film, video and TV producers: documentary and corporate. OUTPUT *Little America Burtonwood; Finney the Perfect Player*. CLIENTS BBC, Granada TV, Pilkington, Tarmac, Optical Fibres, GEC, etc.

Alomo
See **SelecTV plc**

Amy International Productions Ltd
2A Park Avenue, Wraysbury, Middlesex TW19 5ET
☎01784 483131   Fax 01784 483812

Contact *Simon MacCorkindale, Susan George*

Makers of drama for film and TV. OUTPUT *Stealing Heaven; That Summer of White Roses; The House that Mary Bought*. In development: *Manimal; Lucan; The Liaison; Such a Long Journey; Dragon Under the Hill*. Scripts welcome subject to workload. 'Always happy to find good writers – experience isn't necessarily a testimony of ability.'

Anglia TV Entertainment (Part of Anglia Television Plc)
48 Leicester Square, London WC2H 7FB
☎0171 389 8555   Fax 0171 930 8499

Managing Director *Sarah Lawson*
Contact *Anna Dickie (Script Executive)*

Television drama. OUTPUT 1993: *Unnatural Causes* P. D. James (TV movie); *Riders* Jilly Cooper (3-part drama); *The Chief* Series 3 (6-part drama series). 1994: *The Chief* Series 5 (7-part drama series); *A Mind to Murder* (P.D. James TV movie). No unsolicited scripts, but as from January 1993 Anglia Television Ltd in Norwich in a joint venture with **Eastern Arts** runs a scheme for new writers/directors *First Take*. Entry and details from *First Take*, Anglia TV, Norwich NR1 3JG.

Apex Television Production & Facilities Ltd
Button End Studios, Harston, Cambridge CB2 5NX
☎01223 872900   Fax 01223 873092

Contact *Bernard Mulhern*

Video producer: drama, documentary, commercials and corporate. Largely corporate production for a wide range of international companies. Many drama-based training programmes and current affairs orientated TV work. No scripts. All work is commissioned against a particular project.

Arcadia Films

45 Lowndes Square, London SW1X 9JF
☎0171 235 5935   Fax 0171 235 2537

Contact *Marina Gratsos*

Documentaries, features and television films.
No unsolicited scripts.

Arena Films Ltd

16 Woodlands Road, London SW13 0JZ
☎0181 392 9161   Fax 0181 392 1189

Producer *David Conroy*
Production Assistant *Cathy Tyler*

Film and TV drama. OUTPUT *Vincent and Theo*
(directed by Robert Altman); *Coup de Foudre*
(half-hour love stories for PPI-Telecip/
Reteitalia). Scripts with some sort of European
connection or tie-in particularly welcome.
Open-minded with regard to new writing.

AVC Group Ltd

Walters Farm Road, Tonbridge, Kent
TN9 1QT
☎01732 365107   Fax 01732 362600

Contact *Brian Adams*

Practitioners in audio and visual communications. *Specialises* in corporate videos, conferences, PR events and award ceremonies, safety,
sales and marketing, and training.

Azur Film & Video Productions Ltd

26 Woodsford Square, London W14 8DP
☎0171 602 0657   Fax 0171 602 0657

Contact *Max Morgan-Witts*

Film, video and TV: drama, documentary, corporate and sell-through videos. OUTPUT
Corporate: short comedy for Unilever's copyright division; location-based documentaries for
Loctite. Television: Space documentary shot in
Russia for Quanta; major 'soap opera' in development. Sell-through: *The Satellite Video* (instructional documentary). Literary: Joint-author
10 non-fiction books including re-published
Voyage of the Damned; Enola Gay; Guernica.

Humphrey Barclay Productions

5 Anglers Lane, London NW5 3DG
☎0171 482 1992   Fax 0171 485 4287

Development Consultant *Christopher Skala*

TV situation comedy and drama. OUTPUT
Surgical Spirit (Granada).

Barony Film and Television Productions Ltd

1 Abercorn Place, Edinburgh EH8 7HP
☎0131 661 8803

Contact *Murdoch Rodgers*

Broadcast and non-broadcast documentary,
drama and current affairs.

Michael Barratt Ltd

Profile House, 5–7 Forlease Road,
Maidenhead, Berkshire SL6 1RP
☎01628 770800   Fax 01628 770144

Contact *Michael Barratt*

Corporate and educational video, and TV programmes. Also a wide range of publishing
work including company newspapers, brochures
and training manuals. Unsolicited scripts and
ideas welcome 'if they are backed by commercial realism – like sources of funding for development. However, straightforward notification
of availability, special writing skills, contact
addresses, etc, will find a place in the company
records.' Also trades as MBL Publishing Ltd.

Bazal Productions

See **Broadcast Communications**

Beckmann Communications Ltd

Britannia House, 1 Glenthorne Road,
London W6 0LF
☎0181 748 9898   Fax 0181 748 4250

Contact *David Willoughby*

London office of Isle of Man based company.
Video and television documentary. OUTPUT
Festival Europe (travel series); *Maestro* (12-part
series on classical composers); *Wars in Peace* (co-
production with ITN). One-page proposals
considered. No scripts.

beejay Productions

12 Beech Grove, Whitley Bay,
Northumberland NE26 3PJ
☎0191 252 7354/0370 418926(mobile)

Contact *Brian Jenkinson*

Commercials, documentary and corporate.
Freelance scriptwriting used in all categories.

Behr Cinematography

22 Redington Road, London NW3 7RG
☎0171 794 2535   Fax 0171 794 2535

Contact *Arnold Behr, Betty Burghes*

Documentary, educational, corporate film and/
or video, often for voluntary organisations. No
actors, except for voice-overs. No unsolicited
mss.

Paul Berriff Productions Ltd

The Chestnuts, Woodfield Lane, Hessle,
North Humberside HU13 0EW
☎01482 641158   Fax 01482 649692

Contact *Paul Berriff, Janice Kearns*

Television documentary. OUTPUT *Rescue* (13-part documentary for ITV); *M25: The Magic Roundabout* ('First Tuesday'); *Animal Squad Undercover* (Ch4); *Evidence of Abuse* (BBC1 'Inside Story'); *Lessons of Darkness* (BBC2 'Fine Cut'); *The Nick* (Ch4 series).

BFI Production
29 Rathbone Street, London W1P 1AG
☎0171 636 5587   Fax 0171 580 9456
Head of Production *Ben Gibson*

Part of the **British Film Institute**. Produces a range of projects from short films and videos to feature-length films, acting as producer and co-investor. Low-budget, short scripts accepted in January for consideration; feature treatments or screenplays throughout the year, generally low-budget and innovative. Unsolicited mss have a two-month turnaround period. OUTPUT includes *Long Day Closes; Wittgenstein, Anchoress.* Runs a New Directors Scheme (advertised annually).

Martin Bird Productions
Saucelands Barn, Coolham, Horsham, West Sussex RH13 8QG
☎01403 741620   Fax 01403 741647
Contact *Alastair Martin-Bird*

Makers of film and video specialising in programmes covering equestrianism and the countryside. No unsolicited scripts, but always looking for new writers who are fully acquainted with the subject.

Blackrod
See **First Information Group**

Blue Heaven Productions Ltd
45 Leather Lane, London EC1N 7TJ
☎0171 404 4222   Fax 0171 404 4266
Contact *Graham Benson, Christine Benson*

Television drama and documentary. OUTPUT *The Ruth Rendell Mysteries; Crime Story: Dear Roy, Love Gillian; Ready When You Are* (2 series for Meridian Regional). Scripts considered but treatments or ideas preferred in the first instance. New writing encouraged.

Bond Clarkson Russell Ltd
16 Trinity Churchyard, Guildford, Surrey GU1 3RR
☎01483 62888   Fax 01483 302732
Contact *Peter Bond, Chris Russell, Nigel Mengham*

Corporate literature, film, video and multi-media producer of a wide variety of material, including conference videos, for blue-chip companies in the main. No scripts. All work is commissioned.

Matt Boney Associates
Woodside, Holdfast Lane, Grayswood, Haslemere, Surrey GU27 2EU
☎01428 656178
Contact *Matt Boney*

Writer/director for video and television: commercials, documentaries, skiing and travel. No unsolicited mss.

Box Clever Productions
25 Bewdley Street, London N1 1HB
☎0171 607 5766   Fax 0171 700 2248
Contact *Claire Walmsley*

Broadcast TV, film and video documentaries, specialising in social and current affairs. Sister company of Boxclever Communication Training, specialising in media interview skills. OUTPUT documentaries for BBC and Channel 4; corporate videos for the European Commission, public sector and voluntary organisations. No unsolicited scripts; outlines and proposals only.

British Lion Screen Entertainment Ltd
Pinewood Studios, Iver, Buckinghamshire SL0 0NH
☎01753 651700   Fax 01753 656391
Chief Executive *Peter R. E. Snell*

Film production. OUTPUT has included *A Man for All Seasons; Treasure Island; Turtle Diary; Lady Jane; The Crucifer of Blood; Death Train.* No unsolicited mss. Send synopses only.

Broadcast Communications
14 King Street, London WC2E 8HN
☎0171 240 6941   Fax 0171 379 5808
Contact *Michael Braham*

Television division of *The Guardian Media Group*. One of Britain's largest independent producers, responsible for more than 700 hours of programmes a year, for the BBC, ITV, Channel 4 and BSkyB. It has six programme production companies, all wholly owned. These are: Initial Film and Television; Bazal Productions; Connaught Films; Business Television; Lomond Television; and Hawkshead. OUTPUT spans drama, music, entertainment and factual programmes.

Clive Brooks

23 Sylvan Avenue, Bitterne, Southampton,
Hampshire SO2 5JW
☎01703 432579   Fax 01703 432579
Contact *Clive Brooks*

Specialises in video productions for cultural and
leisure industries. Currently developing Internet-
based educational and publishing strategies.
Interested in Cyberspace proposals along these
lines. Ideas with guaranteed market potential
welcome. In the first instance, write in with a
detailed proposal and s.a.e.

Business Television
See **Broadcast Communications**

Business Video Communications Ltd

2 Dixwell Close, Parkwood, Rainham, Kent
ME8 9TB
☎01634 262606   Fax 01634 263606
Contact *David Neale*

Commercials and business communications
programming. CLIENTS include Saudi American
Bank, L'Oréal, Food Giant, Britain's Petite,
Lombard Banking, Metropole Hotels. No need
for outside writers. No scripts.

Caledonian Television Ltd

Caledonian House, Phoenix Crescent,
Strathclyde Business Park, Strathclyde
ML4 3UJ
☎01698 845522   Fax 01698 845811
Contact *Russell Galbraith, Jock Brown*

Film, video and TV: documentary and corpor-
ate. OUTPUT includes studio-based TV discus-
sion/magazine programmes and sell-through
videos: *Sport in Question* (STV); *Return to Paradise
– The Tommy Burns Celtic Story; Dancing in the
Streets* (how Raith Rovers won the Coca-Cola
Cup); *The Winning Way* (profile of Cardinal
Thomas J. Winning); *First Pony* (video); *Abair
Spors! Series 2* (Grampian); Scottish football cov-
erage and Tartan Extra football magazine for
Sky. Send preliminary letter in the first instance.

Camerson a.v.

8A, Intec 2, Wade Road, Basingstoke,
Hampshire RG24 8NE
☎01256 460457   Fax 01256 817378
Contact *Paul Friend*

Broadcast and corporate television production
company. Scripts and ideas for development
welcome, including treatments for interactive
television and multimedia.

Caravel Film Techniques Ltd

The Great Barn Studios, Cippenham Lane,
Slough, Berkshire SL1 5AU
☎01753 534828   Fax 01753 571383
Contact *Nick See*

Film, video and TV: documentary, commericals and corporate. OUTPUT Promos for commercial TV, documentaries BBC & ITV, sales
and training material for corporate blue chip
companies. No unsolicited scripts. Prepared to
review mostly serious new writing.

Carlton UK Productions

35–38 Portman Square, London W1H 9FH
☎0171 486 6688   Fax 0171 486 1132
Managing Director *Paul Jackson*
Director of Drama *Jonathan Powell*
Executive Producer *Ted Childs*
Executive Producer *Jane Tranter*

Makers of independently-produced TV drama
for ITV. OUTPUT *Morse; Boon; Gone to the
Dogs; The Guilty; Tanamera; Soldier, Soldier;
Seekers; Sharpe; Peak Practice, Cadfael, Faith.*
'We try to use new writers on established long-
running series.' Scripts welcome from experienced writers and agents only.

Carnival (Films & Theatre) Ltd

12 Raddington Road, Ladbroke Grove,
London W10 5TG
☎0181 968 0968/1818/1717
Fax 0181 968 0155/0177
Film *Brian Eastman*
Theatre *Andrew Welch*

Film, TV and theatre producers. OUTPUT Film:
Shadowlands (Savoy/Spelling); *In Hitler's Shadow*
(Home Box Office); *Under Suspicion* (Columbia/
Rank/LWT); *Wilt* (Rank/LWT); *Whoops
Apocalypse* (ITC). Television: *Poirot* I–VI (LWT);
Bugs (BBC); *Anna Lee* (LWT); *All or Nothing At
All* (LWT); *Head Over Heels* (Carlton); *The Big
Battalions* (Ch4); *Jeeves & Wooster* I–IV (Granada);
Traffik (Ch4); *Forever Green* (LWT); *Porterhouse
Blue* (Ch4); *Blott on the Landscape* (BBC).
Theatre: *What a Performance; Juno & the Paycock;
Murder is Easy; Misery; Ghost Train; Map of the
Heart; Shadowlands; Up on the Roof.*

Cartwn Cymru

Screen Centre, Llantrisant Road,
Cardiff CF5 2PH
☎01222 575999   Fax 01222 575919
Contact *Naomi Jones*

Animation production company. OUTPUT
Toucan 'Tecs (YTV/S4C) for ITV children's

network; *Funnybones* (S4C/BBC); *Turandot: the Animated Opera*, operavox series (S4C/BBC). In production: *Moses, Elijah, David* and *Saul* in *The Old Testament* – *the animated version*.

Pearl Catlin Associates

Production Centre, The Clock House, Summersbury Drive, Shalford, Guildford, Surrey GU4 8JQ

☎01483 67932   Fax 01483 302646

Contact *Pearl Catlin, Peter Yolland, Paul Bernard*

Film and video: drama, documentary, children's, factual, feature film, corporate and commercials. Interested in creative ideas for all kinds of programmes.

Causeway Video

425 Holywood Road, Belfast BT4 2PL

☎01232 761007   Fax 01232 761012

Contact *Brenda Boal*

Video: corporate and training. OUTPUT Corporate videos for health trusts, industrial development; housing, fashion, government bodies; training videos for private sector companies – industry. No unsolicited scripts. Scripting tends to be undertaken by in-house writers or known freelancers.

CCC Wadlow Productions Ltd

47 Dean Street, London W1V 5HL

☎0171 287 0833   Fax 0171 434 4278

Head of Productions *Sarah Dent*

Film and video, multimedia and graphic design: corporate and commercials. CLIENTS include BBC; Bovis; Camelot; Del Monte Foods International; East Midlands Electricity; Hill & Norton; Lloyds of London; P&O; Saatchi & Saatchi; Samaritans. 'We are very keen to hear from new writers, but please send c.v.s rather than scripts.'

Celador Productions Ltd

39 Long Acre, London WC2E 9JT

☎0171 240 8101   Fax 0171 836 1117

Contact *Paul Smith, Nic Phillips*

Primarily light entertainment programming for all broadcast channels, including game shows, variety, factual and documentary projects and sitcoms. OUTPUT *Everybody's Equal; Crazy Comparisons; Wild Oats; The Hypnotic World of Paul McKenna; The South Bank Show – Cliff Richard; Schofield's Christmas TV Gold* (all for ITV); *Canned Carrott; Carrott's Commercial Breakdown; The Detectives; Auntie's Bloomers;*

Gibberish; Digging The Dancing Queens (all for BBC); *Classic Country* (BSB) and Sky TV's London link for the Oscar Awards.

Central Office of Information Productions

Hercules Road, London SE1 7DU

☎0171 261 8667   Fax 0171 261 8776

Contact *Geoff Raison*

Film, video and TV: drama, documentary, commercials, corporate and public information films. OUTPUT includes government commercials and corporate information, plus a monthly magazine for overseas use. No scripts. New writing commissioned as required.

Channel X

Middlesex House, 34–42 Cleveland Street, London W1P 5FB

☎0171 436 2200   Fax 0171 436 1475

Contact *Alan Marke, Mike Bolland*

FOUNDED 1986 by Jonathan Ross and Alan Marke to develop Ross's first series *The Last Resort*. Now producing comedy series and documentary. Actively developing narrative comedy and game shows. OUTPUT *Unpleasant World of Penn & Teller; XYZ; Jo Brand – Through the Cakehole; Sean's Show; The Smell of Reeves & Mortimer; Fantastic Facts; One for the Road.*

Charisma Films Ltd

14–15 Vernon Street, London W14 0RJ

☎0171 603 1164   Fax 0171 603 1175

Contact *Alex Farquhar (Production Assistant)*

Film and TV (limited). Unsolicited scripts welcome. New writing also welcome but only in 'screenplay form'.

Chatsworth Television Ltd

97–99 Dean Street, London W1V 5RA

☎0171 734 4302   Fax 0171 437 3301

Head of Drama Development *Stephen Jeffrey-Poulter*

Drama and light entertainment TV producers. All unsolicited drama scripts will be considered. Mainly interested in contemporary, factually-based or comedy drama material, but *not* sitcoms.

Childsplay Productions Ltd

8 Lonsdale Road, London NW6 6RD

☎0171 328 1429   Fax 0171 328 1416

Contact *Kim Burke*

Television: drama, children's (not pre-school)

and educational. OUTPUT includes *Streetwise; All Change; Picture Box; Miles Better; Eye of the Storm; Pirates.* Some unsolicited work accepted but telephone to discuss first.

Cinecosse Video
Riversfield, Castle Road, Ellon, Aberdeenshire AB41 9EY
☎01358 722150   Fax 01358 720053
Contact *Michael Marshall*

Video and TV production for corporate and documentary material, plus promotional, sales and training presentations. OUTPUT *Scotland's Larder* (documentary series for GTV). CLIENTS InterCity, IBM, BP Exploration, Total Oil. No unsolicited mss. 'We commission scripts from specialist writers according to type of production in hand.'

Cinexsa Film Productions Ltd
209 Manygate Lane, Shepperton, Middlesex TW17 9ER
☎01932 225950   Fax 01932 225950
Contact *Mrs J. Wright*

Film, video and TV production for drama, documentary, commercials and corporate. CLIENTS BMA, British Telecom, Charity. Solicited scripts welcome. Interested in new writing.

Circus Films
See **Elstree (Production) Co. Ltd.**

The Clear Picture Co.
Folds Head Farm, Calver, Nr Sheffield S30 1XJ
☎01433 631086   Fax 01433 631050
Contact *Shaun Gilmartin, Judy Laybourn*

Television documentaries, multimedia and corporate programmes. OUTPUT includes programmes for 'First Tuesday' (ITV), Central Television, YTV and Channel 4 News. Consultants and filmmakers to the Army Presentation Team. No drama. 'We use in-house writers on most projects. However, we do occasionally use freelance talent from across a range of skills.'

Cleveland Productions
5 Rainbow Court, Oxhey, Near Watford, Hertfordshire WD1 4RP
☎01923 254000   Fax 01923 254000
Contact *Michael Gosling*

Film and video production for documentary and commercials. Tape slide and multi-track recording facilities available. Also stills photography.

Collingwood Productions Ltd
See **Convergence**

Compass Film Productions Ltd
175 Wardour Street, London W1V 3FB
☎0171 734 8115   Fax 0171 439 6456
Contact *Simon Heaven, Heather Simms*

Specialists since 1974 in documentary, educational and promotional programmes for TV and corporate clients. OUTPUT *Violent Lives; A Door to Understanding; Cardboard Citizens* (all for Ch4); *Last Chance Hotel* (BBC); *Behind the Mask* (BBC 40 Minutes); *Loneliness Week* (BBC Wales).

Complete Communications
Communications House, Garsington Road, Cowley, Oxford OX4 2NG
☎01865 383073/384004   Fax 01865 749854
Contact *A. M. Black, Ms C. Richman, Ms V. Andrews*

Video production for corporate, commercial and documentary work, plus satellite/business production. No unsolicited mss. Samples of work are kept on file. Freelancers used.

Component TV Productions Ltd
31 Barrowgate Road, London W4 4QX
☎0181 747 0069
Contact *Piers Bedford*

Film and video production for documentary, commercials and corporate material. OUTPUT includes computer documentaries, farming programmes, IBA, memorex, documentaries/corporate video cassette releases, yoga etc.

Connaught Films
See **Broadcast Communications**

Convergence Productions Ltd/ Tony Collingwood Productions Ltd
Unit 10, The Chandlery, 50 Westminster Bridge Road, London SE1 7QY
☎0171 721 7531   Fax 0171 721 7533
Producers *Christopher O'Hare, Terence Clegg*
Development Director *Helen Stroud*

Film and TV: drama, documentary, popular entertainment and animated series. OUTPUT *Coral Browne: Caviar to the General* (Ch4 documentary); *On the Road Again* (8-part documentary series for BBC and Discovery Channel UK); *RARG* (award-winning animated film); two series of *Captain Zed and the Zee Zone* (ITV); *Daisy-Head Mayzie* (Dr Seuss animated series for Turner Network and Hanna-Barbera). Currently producing *Oscar's Orchestra*

(13-part animated series for BBC and Time Warner). Programmes in development include a documentary on Harry S. Truman; *The Last Executioner* (feature film developed with the support of the European Script Fund); *Dennis and Gnasher* (13-episode animated series for HIT Entertainment and D.C. Thomson).

Courtyard Productions

Little Postlings Farmhouse, Four Elms, Kent TN8 6NA
☎01732 700324   Fax 01732 700543
Contacts *Toni Yardley, David Yardley*

Film, video and TV production for drama, documentary and corporate material. OUTPUT *If Wishes were Horses* Children's TV series (Ch4); *The Borrowers* BBC series; *Jewel of the Curzons* National Trust/Ch4 documentary. Music videos/programmes. Unsolicited scripts welcome. New writing encouraged and used where possible, though often difficult to market.

Creative Channel Ltd

Channel TV, Television Centre,
La Pouquelaye, St Helier, Jersey,
Channel Islands JE2 3ZD
☎01534 868999   Fax 01534 859446
Managing Director *Gordon de Ste Croix*

Part of the Channel Television Group. Producers of TV commercials and corporate material: information, promotional, sales, training and events coverage. OUTPUT *Exploring Guernsey* and *This is Jersey* (video souvenir travel guides); *Hold Tight* (magazine programme screened on UK buses); promotional videos for all types of businesses in the Channel Islands and throughout Europe; plus over 300 commercials a year. No unsolicited mss; new writing/scripts commissioned as required. Interested in hearing from local writers resident in the Channel Islands.

Creative Film Makers Ltd

Pottery Lane House, 34A Pottery Lane,
London W11 4LZ
☎0171 229 5131   Fax 0171 229 4999
Contact *Michael Seligman, Nicholas Seligman*

Corporate and sports documentaries, commercials and television programmes. OUTPUT *The World's Greatest Golfers*, plus various corporate and sports programmes for clients like Nestlé, Benson & Hedges, Wimpey, Bouygues. 'Always open to suggestions but have hardly ever received unsolicited material of any value.' Keen nevertheless to encourage new writers.

Creative Film Productions

68 Conway Road, London N14 7BE
☎0181 447 8187   Fax 0181 886 3054
Contact *Phil Davies*

OUTPUT Animation: *Joey* in production (Ch4). Drama: *Billy* (ITV); *Baby Love* (feature). Documentary: short series about food (BBC). Corporate: *A little Time* in post-production for Parkinson's Disease Soc. Pop Promotions: two in production at present. Unsolicited scripts welcome, no outlines or synopsis.

The Creative Partnership

13 Bateman Street, London W1V 5TB
☎0171 439 7762   Fax 0171 437 1467
Contact *Christopher Fowler, Jim Sturgeon*

Producers of film commercials and marketing campaigns. OUTPUT includes campaigns for *Pulp Fiction; The Lion King; Goldeneye; Star Trek: Generations.* No scripts. 'We train new writers in-house, and find them from submitted c.v.s. All applicants must have previous commercial writing experience.'

Cricket Ltd

1 Lower James Street, London W1R 3PN
☎0171 287 4848   Fax 0171 413 0654
Creative Director *Andrew Davies*
Head of Production (Film & Video)
Jonathan Freer
Production Director *Robert Hollingsworth*

Communications solutions for business clients wishing to influence targeted external and internal audiences. Film and video, live events and conferences, print and design, and business television.

Croft Television and Graphics Ltd

Croft House, Progress Business Centre,
Whittle Parkway, Slough SL1 6DQ
☎01628 668735   Fax 01628 668791
Contact *Keith Jones, Terry Adlam*

Producers of video and TV for drama, documentary, commercials, corporate, training and children's educational programmes. Also any form of visual communication and entertainment. Unsolicited scripts welcome but write first with synopsis, reading fee also charged. Fresh and creative new writing encouraged.

Cromdale Films Ltd

12 St Paul's Road, London N1 2QN
☎0171 226 0178   Fax 0181 871 2158
Contact *Ian Lloyd*

Film, video and TV: drama and documentary.

OUTPUT *The Face of Darkness* (feature film); *Drift to Dawn* (rock music drama); *The Overdue Treatment* (documentary); *Russia, The Last Red Summer* (documentary). Initial phone call advised before submission of scripts.

Crown Business Communications Ltd

United House, 9 Pembridge Road, London W11 3JY
☎0171 727 7272   Fax 0171 727 9940
Contact *Nicky Havelaar*

Leading producers of videos and conferences for business. Interested in talented scriptwriters who understand that business can be exciting and rewarding.

CTR Productions

12A St Andrew's Road, Stogursey, Bridgwater, Somerset
☎01278 732848   Fax 01278 548475
Contact *Ian Cunningham, Roseanna Coils*

Radio: children's, specialist music programmes and commercials; also television documentary, game shows, children's and music programmes.

CVG Television

1 Sutton Street, Birmingham B1 1PE
☎0121 622 1337   Fax 0121 622 3080
Contact *Sally Murcutt*

Video and TV: drama, documentary and corporate, predominantly for charity organisations. Programmes target the whole age spectrum, and cover topical and moral issues from a Christian perspective. Unsolicited scripts welcome as assessment for commissions. All work must be sympathetic to Christian beliefs.

Dareks Production House

58 Wickham Road, Beckenham, Kent BR3 2RQ
☎0181 658 2012   Fax 0181 658 2012
Contact *David Crossman*

Independent producers of corporate and broadcast television.

DBA Television

7 Lower Crescent, Belfast BT7 1NR
☎01232 231197   Fax 01232 333302
Contact *David Barker*

Long-established makers of documentary. OUTPUT includes *Heart on the Line* for Ch4; *Drink Talking* a series on alcoholism; *Because of the Sun* directed by Carlo Gebler; *New York Law* a BBC Inside Story. In production: *Plain Tales from Northern Ireland*; *A Little Local Difficulty* a three-part series for BBC2. Freelancers are encouraged to present written summaries in the first instance.

DBI Communication

21 Congreve Close, Warwick CV34 5RQ
☎01926 497695   Fax 01926 490512
Contact *David B. Impey*

Video: corporate, promotional, safety, training and sales. No unsolicited mss as most programmes are 'customised'. OUTPUT has included *Play Safe* with Keith Chegwin about the dangers of children entering quarries, shown in schools nationwide; *Guide Dog Training* (series); *Restoration of Wellesbourne Watermill*; *Professional Make-Up* (series); *Dog Breeding*; *Transport Kills*, a safety training package for Mobile Plant.

Dibgate Productions Ltd

Studio 4, Parkstead Lodge, 31 Upper Park Road, London NW3 2UL
☎0171 722 5634
Contact *Nicholas Parsons*

Documentary and travel films; plus comedy shorts for cinema and television. OUTPUT has included *A Fair Way to Play*; *Mad Dogs and Cricketers*; *Relatively Greek*; *Viva Menorca*; *Terribly British*.

Directors Video Company

89A Victoria Road, Aldershot, Hampshire GU11 1JE
☎01252 316429   Fax 01252 344362
Contact *Sarah Beardsmoore*

Corporate video; drama and documentary. OUTPUT Mostly corporate identity programmes, recruitment and new product launches. Writers 'with new ideas and showreels of video scripts' are particularly welcome.

Diverse Productions Limited

Gorleston Street, London W14 8XS
☎0171 603 4567   Fax 0171 603 2148
Contact *Rita Shamia*

Broadcast television production with experience in news, current affairs, documentaries, training and education, religion, consumer and graphics-based programming. Now also developing drama, children's and entertainment series. OUTPUT *The Pulse*; *Checkout*; *Europe Express*; *African Footsteps*; *Mind Field*; *The Experimenter* and many single documentaries.

Drake A-V Video Ltd
89 St Fagans Road, Fairwater, Cardiff CF5 3AE
☎01222 560333   Fax 01222 554909

Contact *Ian Lewis*

Corporate A-V film and video, mostly promotional, training or educational. Scripts in these fields welcome.

The Drama House Ltd
1 Hertford Place, London W1P 5RS
☎0171 388 9140   Fax 0171 388 3511

Contact *Gwynneth Lloyd, Jack Emery*

Television drama and documentary. OUTPUT *The Gospels* (drama); *Call to Prayer* (documentary), both for BBC1. Scripts welcome. Interested in developing contacts with new and established writers.

Charles Dunstan Communications Ltd
42 Wolseley Gardens, London W4 3LS
☎0181 994 2328   Fax 0181 994 2328

Contact *Charles Dunstan*

Producers of film, video and TV for documentary and corporate material. OUTPUT *Renewable Energy* for broadcast worldwide in *Inside Britain* series; National Power Annual Report Video *The Electric Environment.* No unsolicited scripts.

Eagle and Eagle Ltd
15 Marlborough Road, London W4 4EU
☎0181 995 1884   Fax 0181 995 5648

Contact *Robert Eagle, Catharine Alen-Buckley*

Film, video and TV: drama, documentary and children's programmes. Broadcast work includes programmes on aviation, psychology, medicine, education and arts. No unsolicited scripts.

Eagle Vision
3 Hanson Street, London W1P 7LJ
☎0171 436 2707   Fax 0171 436 7167

Contact *John Court*

Video production for documentary and corporate material includes training, sales/marketing, staff information and public relations videos. CLIENTS Barclays, Marks and Spencer, IBM etc. No unsolicited scripts.

East Anglian Productions
Studio House, 21–23 Walton Road, Frinton on Sea, Essex CO13 0AA
☎01255 676252   Fax 01255 850528

Contact *Ray Anderson*

Film, video and TV: drama and documentary, commercials and corporate. Interested in comedy too. Scripts welcome. Keen to encourage new writing.

Edinburgh Film & Video Productions
Nine Mile Burn, by Penicuik, Midlothian EH26 9LT
☎01968 672131   Fax 01968 672685

Contact *R. Crichton*

Film, TV drama and documentary. OUTPUT *Moonacre; Torch; Silent Mouse; The Curious Case of Santa Claus; The Stamp of Greatness.* No unsolicited scripts at present.

Elstree (Production) Co. Ltd
Shepperton Studios, Studios Road, Shepperton, Middx TW17 0QD
☎01932 572680/1   Fax 01932 572682

Produces feature films and TV drama/situation comedy. OUTPUT *Prospects* (Euston Films/Ch4); *Rude Health* (Ch4); *Othello* (BBC); *Porgy & Bess* (with Trevor Nunn); *Great Expectations* (Disney Channel); *Old Curiosity Shop* (Disney Channel/RHI). Currently established Circus Films with Trevor Nunn for feature film projects.

Enigma Productions Ltd
13–15 Queen's Gate Place Mews, London SW7 5BG
☎0171 581 0238   Fax 0171 584 1799

Contact *Steve Norris*

Backed by Warner Bros. OUTPUT *Memphis Belle* (true story of an American B-17 bomber crew in Second World War); *Meeting Venus* (a comedy about a multinational opera company). In post-production: Bill Forsyth's *Being Human; War of the Buttons* (children's film). In development: *Fade Out* (drama set in Prague in the 1940s); *Shackleton* (true story of the Antarctic explorer); *Serenade* (musical romantic comedy); *The Scarlet Pimpernel.* Unsolicited submissions accepted only from a recognised agent or motion picture lawyer.

The Entertainment Partnership
(incorporating Entertainment Productions & People)
305 Gray's Inn Road, London WC1X 8QF
☎0171 713 1234   Fax 0171 713 1741

Chief Executive *Tony Fitzpatrick*

Video and TV productions for documentary, corporate and factual entertainment. OUTPUT *Take That and Party; Pop Goes Summer; Music from the Bridge/Music from the Circus; Dance into Fitness; The Common Sense Guide to Pregnancy.* Unsolicited scripts welcome. Information on and work from new writers welcome in any field.

Farnham Film Company Ltd
34 Burnt Hill Road, Lower Bourne, Farnham, Surrey GU10 3LZ
☎01252 710313   Fax 01252 725855
Contact *Ian Lewis*

Television and film: children's drama and documentaries. Unsolicited mss welcome. 'Always looking for new material which is commercially viable.'

Farrant Partnership
91 Knatchbull Road, London SE5 9QU
☎0171 733 0711   Fax 0171 738 5224
Contact *James Farrant*

Corporate video productions.

Ffilmiau'r Bont
Uned 2, Cibyn, Caernarfon, Gwynedd LL55 2BD
☎01286 675766   Fax 01286 671131
Contact *Vaughan Hughes, Angharad Anwyl*

Factual, current affairs, entertainment and the arts.

Filmit Productions
2 Tunstall Road, London SW9 8BN
☎0171 738 4175   Fax 0171 738 3787
Contact *John Samson*

Television documentaries and corporate work. OUTPUT *A Polite Enquiry; The Gulf Between Us; Loyalty on the Line; Who Let Our Children Die* (all documentaries for Ch4); *Free for All; Speak Out* (Ch4 series). Unsolicited scripts welcome. Keen to discover and nurture new writing talent.

First Creative Group Ltd
The Stables, Mellings Farm, Benson Lane, Catforth, Preston, Lancashire PR4 0HY
☎01772 690450   Fax 01772 690964
Contact *M. Mulvihill*

Film, video and TV productions for documentary and corporate material. Unsolicited scripts welcome. Open to new writing.

First Information Group
Knightsbridge House, 197 Knightsbridge, London SW7 1RB
☎0171 393 3000   Fax 0171 393 3033
Contact *Michael Rodd*

Corporate TV: drama and documentary. One of the biggest corporate video makers, with a number of awards for excellence in the field. 'Since we make bespoke programmes for corporate clients, we have no use for unsolicited material.'

Fitting Images Ltd
Alfred House, 127A Oatlands Drive, Weybridge, Surrey KT13 9LB
☎01932 840056   Fax 01932 858075
Managing Director *Sue Fleetwood*

Promotional, training, medical/pharmaceutical; contacts from experienced writers of drama and comedy welcome. We are also interested in broadcast projects.

Flashback Communication Ltd
25 Greenhead Street, Glasgow G40 1ES
☎0141 554 6868   Fax 0141 554 6869
Contact *Chris Attkins, John Rocchiccioli*

Video and TV producers: drama, documentary, corporate, training and education, and sell-throughs. OUTPUT includes dramatised training videos and TV programmes or inserts for the ITV network, BBC and stations worldwide. Proposals considered; no scripts. New talent encouraged. Interested in fresh ideas and effective style.

Flicks Films Ltd
101 Wardour Street, London W1V 3TD
☎0171 734 4892   Fax 0171 287 2307
Managing Director/Producer *Terry Ward*

Film and video: children's animated series and specials. OUTPUT *The Mr Men; Little Miss; Bananaman; The Pondles; Junglies; Nellie the Elephant; See How They Work With Dig and Dug.* Scripts specific to their needs will be considered. 'Always willing to read relevant material.'

Flying Pig Productions Ltd
CVA House, 2 Cooper Road, Thornbury, Bristol, Avon BS12 2UP
☎01454 281898   Fax 01454 281868
Contact *Anthony Boyle*

TV: documentary and drama. Video: promotional, training and educational. CLIENTS include Royal Mail, British Rail and The Burton Group. Projects in development for Ch4, ITV and the BBC. No unsolicited mss; send treatments, synopses or script sample if possible. No animation; interested in new writing. Likes film scripts, TV drama series and comedy. Unusual perspectives and ideas welcome.

Focus Films Ltd

The Rotunda Studios, Rear of 116–118
Finchley Road, London NW3 5HT
☎0171 435 9004/5   Fax 0171 431 3562

Contact *David Pupkewitz, Lisa Disler*

Film and TV producers. Drama OUTPUT *CrimeTime* (European Script Fund Award, medium-budget feature thriller); *Diary of a Sane Man* (experimental feature for Ch4); *Othello* (Ch4 drama). Projects in development include *Sweet Banana* (Feature – European Script Fund Award) and *Lethal ID* (Feature – European Script Fund Award). No unsolicited scripts.

Folio Productions

141–143 Drury Lane, London WC2B 5TB
☎0171 240 5389   Fax 0171 240 5391

Contact *Charles Thompson*

Film, TV and video: documentary and corporate work. OUTPUT includes programmes for *Dispatches, Cutting Edge, Secret History* and *Black Bag* (Ch4); plus a 7-part commando series for ITV. Scripts and ideas welcome, including work from new writers.

Forge Productions Ltd

14 Ceylon Road, London W14 0PY
☎0171 602 1867   Fax 0171 602 1867

Contact *Ralph Rolls*

Video and TV: documentary and promotions for campaigns. OUTPUT includes *Everyman: Celtic Britain* for BBC1; religious programmes for the BBC, including four programmes on Islamic communities in the UK. Radio work under development. New writers encouraged but no unsolicited scripts.

Mark Forstater Productions Ltd

Suite 66, 124–128 Barlby Road,
London W10 6BL
☎0181 964 1888   Fax 0181 960 9819

Production *Doug Manuel*

Active in the selection, development and production of material for film and TV. OUTPUT *Monty Python and the Holy Grail; The Odd Job; The Grass is Singing; Xtro; Forbidden; Separation; The Fantasist; Shalom Joan Collins; The Silent Touch; Grushko.* No unsolicited mss.

Friday Productions Ltd

23a St. Leonards Terrace, London SW3 4QG
☎0171 730 0608   Fax 0171 730 0608

Contact *Georgina Abrahams*

Film and TV productions for drama material.

OUTPUT *Goggle Eyes; Harnessing Peacocks; The December Rose.* No unsolicited scripts. New writing encouraged especially from under-represented groups.

Gala International Ltd

222 Kensal Road, London W10 5BN
☎0181 969 4502   Fax 0181 969 5337

Producer *David Lindsay*

Corporate videos, including product documentaries and sales promotion material. Unsolicited scripts welcome. New writing encouraged.

Gateway Audio Visual and Video

472 Green Lanes, London N13 5XF
☎0181 882 0177   Fax 0181 882 4161

Contact *Graham L. Smart*

Producers of video and film for sponsors. OUTPUT has included marketing, training and corporate programmes for various clients; also TV commercials. No unsolicited mss but 'always on the look-out for new scriptwriters'.

John Gau Productions

Burston House, 1 Burston Road, Putney,
London SW15 6AR
☎0181 788 8811   Fax 0181 789 0903

Contact *John Gau*

Documentaries and series for TV, plus corporate video. OUTPUT includes *Assignment Adventure* (Ch4); *Korea* series (BBC1); *Reaching for the Skies* (BBC2); *Voyager* (Central); *The Power and The Glory* (BBC2); *The Team – A Season With McLaren* (BBC2); *The Great Outdoors* (Ch4).

Noel Gay Television

6th Floor, 76 Oxford Street, London
W1N 0AT
☎0171 412 0400   Fax 0171 412 0300

Contact *Charles Armitage*

The association with Noel Gay (agency/management and music publishing) makes this one of the most securely financed independents in the business. Recent OUTPUT includes *Searching* (Series I – Carlton/ITV); *Dave Allen Boxing Day Special* (Carlton/ITV); *Dave Allen* (Series I – Carlton/ITV); *Frank Stubbs* (Series I & II, Carlton/ITV); *Red Dwarf* (Series VI & VII); *10%ers* (Series I & II, Carlton/ITV); *Smegs Ups* (BBC Video); *Blossom* (NBC/Ch4) and *Aids Is a Way of Life* (Carlton). Current development and co-production deals with leading Indian commercials, corporate film and documentary maker, Odyssey Video Communications, and Reed Consumer Books to develop book and magazine ideas for television, video and film. Associate NGTV companies are Grant Naylor Productions, Rose Bay Films & Television, Picture That, Addictive Television and the Noel Gay Motion Picture Company.

GCP
5 Drayton Gardens, London W13 0LG
☎0181 997 3513   Fax 0181 997 3513
Contact *Geoff Cotton*

Video and TV: comedy, drama and corporate work. OUTPUT includes sitcom and drama for broadcast stations and corporate videos. No unsolicited scripts. Not interested in new writing except by recommendation.

Geofilms Ltd
12 Thame Lane, Culham, Oxford OX14 3DS
☎01235 555422   Fax 01235 530581
Contact *Ms. Martine Benoit*

Film, video and TV productions for documentary, corporate and education material. OUTPUT *Equinox: The Bermuda Triangle* (Ch4); *Antenna: Hot Ice* (BBC2); also training programmes for the Resource Industry. Unsolicited scripts welcome relating to earth sciences and the environment.

Goldcrest Films and Television Ltd
65–66 Dean Street, London W1V 6PL
☎0171 437 8696   Fax 0171 437 4448
Chief Executive Officer *John Quested*

FOUNDED in the late 70s. Formerly part of the Brent Walker Leisure Group but independent since 1990 following management buy-out led by John Quested. The company's core activities are film production and worldwide distribution. Scripts via agents only.

The Good Film Company
2nd Floor, 14–15 D'Arblay Street, London W1V 3FP
☎0171 734 1331   Fax 0171 734 2997
Contact *Yanina Barry*

Commercials, pop videos and corporate. OUTPUT has included *Water Safety; Hypothermia in the Elderly* (for the COI). CLIENTS include National Express Coaches, Camel Cigarettes, Tunisian Tourist Board. Unsolicited mss welcome.

Carol Gould Productions Plc
9 Cedric Chambers, Northwick Close, London NW8 8JH
☎0171 266 1953   Fax 0171 266 1954
Contact *Carol Gould*

Up and running since late 1993, Carol Gould Productions is a new company producing television/film documentary and drama. Projects in development include a feature film *A Twig From the Cherry Orchard*; and two drama series: *Spitfire Girls* (published as a novel September, 1995); and *Hot Shots*. No unsolicited mss. Write or call with ideas in the first instance.

Granada Film
36 Golden Square, London W1R 4AH
☎0171 494 6388   Fax 0171 494 6360
Contact *Pippa Cross*

Films and TV films. OUTPUT *My Left Foot; Jack & Sarah* and *August* (both feature films in post-production). No unsolicited scripts. Supportive of new writing but often hard to offer real help as Granada are developing mainstream commercial projects which usually require some status in talent areas.

John Grant Programme Developments
37 Ladywell Way, Ponteland, Newcastle upon Tyne NE20 9TE
☎01661 825186   Fax 0191 232 9823
Contact *John Grant*

Film and video development, broadcast and non-broadcast.

Grasshopper Productions Ltd
50 Peel Street, London W8 7PD
☎0171 229 1181   Fax 0171 229 2070
Contact *Joy Whitby*

Children's programmes and adult drama. No unsolicited mss.

Green Umbrella Ltd
The Production House, 147A St Michaels Hill, Bristol, Avon BS2 8DB
☎0117 9731729   Fax 0117 9467432

Television documentary makers. OUTPUT includes episodes for *The Natural World* and *Wildlife on One*. Unsolicited scripts relating to natural history subjects are welcome.

Greenpoint Films
5A Noel Street, London W1V 3RB
☎0171 437 6492   Fax 0171 437 0644
Contact *Ann Scott, Patrick Cassavetti*

A small company whose members act as individual producers and directors. Check before sending unsolicited material.

Reg Grundy Productions (GB) Ltd

Grundy House, 1 Bargehouse Crescent, 34 Upper Ground, London SE1 9PD
☎0171 928 8942   Fax 0171 928 8417

Television: drama and light entertainment. OUTPUT Game shows: *Celebrity Squares; Going for Gold; Small Talk; Pot of Gold*. Factual: *How Do They Do That?*

Halas and Batchelor Animation Ltd

6 Holford Road, London NW3 1AD
☎0171 435 8674   Fax 0171 431 6835

Contact *Andi Mindel*

Film, video and TV productions for documentary and animation material. OUTPUT *Animal Farm* (feature length animated film); *Masters of Animation* (13-part documentary series); *Classic Fairy Tales* (children's animation series).

Howard Hall

6 Foster Road, Abingdon, Oxfordshire OX14 1YN
☎01235 533981/0860 775438
Fax 01235 533981

Contact *Howard Hall*

Film, video and TV: drama, documentary, commercials and corporate programmes. OUTPUT includes drama training programmes, satellite programmes, commercials, and programmes for broadcast channels. Scripts welcome. 'Always looking for new writers. We need a store of good writers in different fields of work.' Howard Hall has published his own book, *Directing Corporate Video* (Focal Press).

Hammer Film Productions Ltd

Millennium Studios, Elstree Way, Borehamwood, Hertfordshire WD6 1SF
☎0181 207 4011   Fax 0181 905 1127

Contact *Roy Skeggs, Jane Herd*

Film production company. No unsolicited scripts.

Hammerwood Film Productions

110 Trafalgar Road, Portslade, East Sussex BN41 1GS
☎01273 748353   Fax 01273 822247

Contact *Ralph Harvey, Karen King*

Film, video and TV drama. In development: *Sacre Bleu* and *Operation Pandora*. 1996 projects: *Sawney Beane* and *The Last of the Hapsburgs* – 52-part TV series (co-production with Imperial Productions). Most material is written in-house. 'We do not have the time to read scripts but will always read 2–3-page synopses/plot outlines. Anything of interest will be followed up.' Hammerwood are also distributors with a stock of 5000 movies and TV programmes.

Hand Pict Independent Productions

4 Picardy Place, Edinburgh EH1 3JT
☎0131 558 1543   Fax 0131 556 0792

Contact *George Cathro*

Television production for drama and documentary material. OUTPUT *The Ken Fine Show* (6-part series for Scottish Television); *Face Value* (Ch4); *Et in Stadia Ego* ('Without Walls', Ch4); *Blood Ties* (arts documentary for BBC Wales); *Blackfish* (current affairs for Ch4). Unsolicited scripts welcome but pressure of work and programmes in production can lead to delays in response. Encourages new writing.

HandMade Films Ltd

15 Golden Square, London W1R 3AG
☎0171 434 3132   Fax 0171 434 3143

Feature films. OUTPUT has included *Mona Lisa; The Missionary; Time Bandits; Withnail and I; The Lonely Passion of Judith Hearne; The Raggedy Rawney; Checking Out; How To Get Ahead in Advertising; Nuns on the Run*. No unsolicited mss at present.

Hartswood Films Ltd

Shepperton Studios, Shepperton, Middlesex TW17 0QD
☎01932 572294   Fax 01932 572299

Contact *Beryl Vertue, Elaine Cameron*

Film and TV production for drama and light entertainment. OUTPUT *Men Behaving Badly* BBC (previously Thames); *Is It Legal?* (Carlton); *The English Wife* (Meridian); *A Woman's Guide to Adultery* (Carlton); *My Good Friend* (ITV); *Code Name Kyril* (HTV). No unsolicited scripts. New writing read if recommended by agents.

Hat Trick Productions Ltd

10 Livonia Street, London W1V 3PH
☎0171 434 2451   Fax 0171 287 9791

Contact *Denise O'Donoghue*

Television programmes. OUTPUT includes *Confessions; A Very Open Prison; Room 101; Whose Line is it Anyway?; Drop the Dead Donkey; Harry Enfield's Television Programme; Have I Got News For You; Clive Anderson Talks Back; S & M; Paul Merton Series*.

Hawkshead Ltd
48 Bedford Square, London WC1B 3DP
☎0171 255 2551   Fax 0171 580 8101
Chief Executive *Tom Barnicoat*
Head of Broadcasting *Frances Whitaker*
Head of Corporate *Angela Law*

Owned by **Broadcast Communications**.
Film and video. Broadcast: documentary,
lifestyle, educational and factual entertainment.
Corporate: training, promotional and employee
communications. OUTPUT includes *Delia
Smith's Summer Collection* (BBC2); *Sunday Best*
(GMTV); *Roots Schmoots* (Ch4/WNET); *Grass
Roots* (Meridian); *Metroland* (Carlton); *Advice
Shop* (BBC2). CLIENTS include Brittany Ferries,
Department of Employment, Equitable Life,
London Underground, Metropolitan Police,
PowerGen, Learning International.

Hawthornden Films
Cambridge Court, Cambridge Road, Frinton
on Sea, Essex CO13 9HN
☎01255 676381   Fax 01255 851825
Contact *Timothy Foster*

Active in European film co-production in the
Netherlands, France and Italy. Mainstream
connections in the USA. Also documentaries.

Head to Head Communication Ltd
The Hook, Fiveways Business Centre, Plane
Tree Crescent, Feltham, Middlesex TW13 7AQ
☎0181 893 7766   Fax 0181 893 2777
Contact *Bob Carson*

Makers of business and corporate communication programmes.

Jim Henson Productions Ltd
30 Oval Road, Camden, London NW1 7DE
☎0171 428 4000   Fax 0171 428 4001
Contact *Angus Fletcher*

Feature films and TV: family entertainment and
children's. OUTPUT *The Muppet Christmas
Carol; Labyrinth; The Witches* (films); *The Muppet
Show* (ITV); *The Storyteller* (Ch4); *Mother Goose
Stories* (ITV); *Jim Henson's Greek Myths* (Ch4);
The Secret Life of Toys (BBC); *The Animal Show*
(BBC). Scripts via agents only.

Hightimes Productions Ltd
5 Anglers Lane, London NW5 3DG
☎0171 482 5202   Fax 0171 485 4254
Contact *A. C. Mitchell, A. Humphreys*

Television comedies. OUTPUT *Trouble in Mind*
situation comedy, 9 episodes LWT; *Me & My
Girl* situation comedy, 5 series, LWT (package);

The Zodiac Game game show, 2 series, Anglia
(package); *Guys 'n' Dolls* (L.E.) 13 episodes,
BSB. Unsolicited scripts welcome. New writing
encouraged where possible.

Philip Hindin
66 Melbourne Way, Bush Hill Park, Enfield,
Middlesex EN1 1XQ
☎0181 366 2978   Fax 0181 363 7523
Contact *P. Hindin*

Producer of quiz-panel game shows for TV and
theatre. No unsolicited material but always interested in new ideas/writing. Comedy material –
revue style, blackout sketches in vaudeville style
considered.

Gerard Holdsworth Productions Ltd
140 Buckingham Palace Road, London
SW1W 9SA
☎0171 824 8770   Fax 0171 824 8762
Contact *P. Filmer-Sankey, A. Brunker*

Corporate video producers. OUTPUT training,
public relations and industrial processes. No
unsolicited scripts. Have done work with new
writers.

Holmes Associates
17 Rathbone Street, London W1P 1AF
☎0171 637 8251   Fax 0171 637 9024
Contact *Andrew Holmes, Alison Carter*

Prolific originators, producers and packagers of
documentary, drama and music television.
OUTPUT has included *The House of Bernarda
Alba* (Ch4/WNET/Amaya); *Piece of Cake*
(drama mini-series for LWT); *Well Being* and
Signals (Ch4); *The Cormorant* (BBC/Screen 2);
John Gielgud Looks Back (Ch4); *Four Up Two
Down* and *Rock Steady* (Ch4); *Timeline* (with
MPT, TVE Spain & TRT Turkey).

Horntvedt Television
100 New Kings Road, London SW6 4LX
☎0171 731 8199   Fax 0171 731 8312
Managing Director *Kit Horntvedt*

Produces and creates a wide range of film and
video products for the corporate, national and
international television markets, particularly
interactive media. Each project is conceived,
written and produced by in-house staff.

Hourglass Pictures Ltd
117 Merton Road, Wimbledon, London
SW19 1ED
☎0181 540 8786   Fax 0181 542 6598

Director *Martin Chilcott*

Film and video: documentary, drama and commercials. OUTPUT includes television science documentaries; public relations material for government and industrial bodies; health and social issues for the World Health Organisation; product promotion for pharmaceutical companies. Open to new writing.

Hubner Films Ltd

14a Princes Mews, London W2 4NX
☎0171 229 3140/229 9158 Fax 0171 792 1029

Contact *Martin Hubner, Christine Fontaine*

Film commercials, corporate videos and documentaries, and feature film scripts. CLIENTS Associated Newspapers, Gateway Supermarkets, De Beers Diamonds, Bentalls, British Gas, IBM, Nat West, Audi, Parkfield/Ford (USA). Unsolicited scripts or outlines for feature films and documentaries welcome. Material is read and discussed before being forwarded if promising to TV/film companies or agents for production packaging.

Alan Hydes Associates

East Royd House, Woodlands Drive,
Apperley Bridge, West Yorkshire BD10 0PA
☎0113 2503467   Fax 0113 2503467

Contact *Alan Hydes*

Film, video and TV: drama and corporate work, including children's TV programmes, promotional, recruitment and security films for the Halifax Building Society. No unsolicited scripts. Interested in new ideas for conversion to drama.

Icon Films

56 Kingsdown Parade, Bristol, Avon BS6 5UQ
☎0117 9248535   Fax 0117 9240386

Contact *Harry Marshall*

Film and TV documentaries. OUTPUT *The Royal Collection* (6-part series for Ch4); *Elephant Walk* (Discovery Channel special); *Lost Civilisations – Tibet* (Time Life for NBC). Open-minded to new writing. Scripts welcome.

Ideal Image Ltd

Cherrywood House, Crawley Down Road,
Felbridge, Surrey RH19 2PP
☎01342 312566   Fax 01342 312566

Contact *Alan Frost*

Producer of documentary and drama for film, video, TV and corporate clients. OUTPUT *The Devils' Year* (documentary on the Red Devils); *Just Another Friday* (corporate drama). Scripts welcome.

In Video Productions Ltd

16 York Place, Edinburgh EH1 3EP
☎0131 557 2151   Fax 0131 557 5465

Contact *Jamie Swinton*

Film, video and TV production for documentary, commercials, corporate and title sequences material. Unsolicited scripts welcome.

INCA (Independent Communications Associates) Ltd

20–28 Dalling Road, London W6 0JB
☎0181 748 0160   Fax 0181 748 3114

Managing Director *William Woollard*

Television documentary and corporate work. OUTPUT includes science, technology and medical documentaries for programmes such as *Equinox* and *Horizon*; also educational, current affairs, music, arts and light entertainment. Proposals for documentary programmes or series welcome. Positive policy towards new writing.

Independent Image Ltd

33–34 Soho Square, London W1V 6DP
☎0171 292 4300   Fax 0171 292 4299

Joint Managing Directors *Tom Kinninmont,*
David Wickham

Film, video and TV productions for drama, documentary, commercials and corporate material. OUTPUT *Hostage* (TV/feature film); *More Than a Game* (8-part documentary series on sport). Unsolicited scripts welcome but write first. Positive view on new writing: 'good track record of using new writers'. Has some involvement with The Annual Young Playwrights Course run by the Scottish Youth Theatre.

Initial Film and Television
See **Broadcast Communications**

Interesting Television Ltd

Oakslade Studios, Station Road, Hatton,
Warwickshire CV35 7LH
☎01926 843777

Senior Producer *John Pluck*

Producers of broadcast television documentaries and feature series on film and video for ITV and BBC TV. Currently looking towards cable, satellite and home video to broaden its output. Ideas for television documentaries particularly welcome. Send a treatment in the first instance, particularly if the subject is 'outside our area of current interest'. OUTPUT has included television programmes on heritage, antiques, gardening, science and industry; also projects on heritage, health and sports for the home video front.

ISIS Productions Ltd

14–15 Vernon Street, London W14 0RG
☎0171 602 0959   Fax 0171 603 0644
Contact *Nick De Grunwald*

Film, video and TV productions for drama, documentary, music, educational and children's material. OUTPUT *The Making of Sgt Pepper* ('South Bank Show' 1992 – BAFTA nominated); *Mine Eyes Have Seen the Glory* (3-part series on American Evangelicalism for Ch4); *Teenage Health Freak* (two series of cult comedy drama for Ch4). Short outlines and treatments of unsolicited scripts welcome. Would like to see new writing.

Michael Kann Associates Ltd

53A Brewer Street, London W1R 3FD
☎0171 439 9882   Fax 0171 287 2289
Contact *Michael Kann*

Corporate films, including documentary and drama. CLIENTS include Ford Motor Co., British Council, Bank of England, Post Office, Foreign & Commonwealth Office. No unsolicited mss but always looking for fresh new writing.

Kay Communications Ltd

Gauntley Court Studios, Gauntley Court, Nottingham NG7 5HD
☎0115 9781333   Fax 0115 9783734
Contact *John Alexander*

Makers of industrial video programmes and training programmes. Scripts written in-house. No unsolicited mss.

King Rollo Films Ltd

Dolphin Court, High Street, Honiton, Devon EX14 8LS
☎01404 45218   Fax 01404 45328
Contact *Clive Juster*

Film, video and TV: children's animated series. OUTPUT *Mr Benn; King Rollo; Victor & Maria; Towser; Play-It-Again; The Adventures of Spot; Not Now, Bernard; The Hill and the Rock; Two Can Toucan; The Sad Story of Veronica Who Played the Violin; Elmer; I Want a Cat; Oscar Got the Blame; Super Dooper Jezebel; I'm Coming to Get You; I Want My Potty; The Adventures of Ric; It's Fun to Learn With Spot; Art; Budds & Pip; Spot's Magical Christmas.* Generally work from existing published material 'although there will always be the odd exception'. Proposals or phone calls in the first instance. No scripts.

Kingfisher Television Productions Ltd

The Television House, Lenton Lane, Nottingham NG7 2NA
☎0115 9645262   Fax 0115 9645263
Contact *Tony Francis*

Broadcast television production.

Koninck

175 Wardour Street, London W1V 3AB
☎0171 734 4943   Fax 0171 494 0405
Contact *Keith Griffiths*

Film and TV: drama and documentary. OUTPUT includes projects with directors like Jan Svankmajer, the Brothers Quay, G. F. Newman, Chris Petit and Patrick Keiller. Unsolicited scripts welcome. 'We try to promote new talent and develop work by young writers new to the screen and experienced writers looking for new and imaginative ways to express their ideas.'

Ladbroke Productions (Films) Ltd

28 Narrow Street, London E14 8DQ
☎0171 702 8700   Fax 0171 702 8701
Contact *Mike Bluett*

Film and TV: drama and documentary. OUTPUT *Menuhin; Maria Callas; Testimony; In From the Cold; Pushkin; Purcell* (by John Osborne). Unsolicited material is read, but please send a written outline first.

Lagan Pictures Ltd

7 Rugby Court, Agincourt Avenue, Belfast BT7 1PN
☎01232 326125
Producer/Director *Stephen Butcher*
Producer *Alison Grundle*

Film, video and TV: drama, documentary and corporate. OUTPUT *A Force Under Fire* (Ulster TV). In development: one-off and series drama, documentaries and dramatised documentaries. 'We welcome unsolicited manuscripts from writers based in or originating from Northern Ireland and from any writer on subjects relevant to Northern Ireland.' Scripts welcome.

Landseer Film and Television Productions Ltd

140 Royal College Street, London NW1 0TA
☎0171 485 7333   Fax 0171 485 7573
Contact *Derek Bailey*

Film and video production: documentary, drama, music and arts, children's and current affairs. OUTPUT *Winter Dreams* (BBC2); *Sunny*

Stories – Enid Blyton (Arena); J. R. R. Tolkien (Tolkien Partnership); Kenneth MacMillan at 60 (BBC); Discovering Delius (Delius Trust); Should Accidentally Fall (BBC/Arts Council); Nobody's Fool ('South Bank Show' on Danny Kaye for LWT); Mister Abbott's Broadway ('Omnibus' BBC).

Helen Langridge Associates
75 Kenton Street, London WC1N 1NN
☎0171 833 2955   Fax 0171 837 2836
Managing Directors Helen Langridge, Mike Wells

Film, video and TV: drama, music videos and commercials.

Lawson Productions Ltd
4th Floor, 48 Leicester Square,
London WC2H 7FB
☎0171 389 8555   Fax 0171 930 6024
Contact Sarah Lawson

Film and TV: drama and comedy. OUTPUT has included That's Love (UK and US); Home to Roost (US version); The Dawning with Anthony Hopkins; Life After Life (ITV) with George Cole; Natural Lies (BBC); Seekers (ITV). No unsolicited mss unless via agents, but always interested in new talent.

Lightarama Ltd
12a Wellfield Avenue,
London N10 2EA
☎0181 444 8315   Fax 0181 444 8315
Contact Alexis Key

Video and TV production for commercials and corporate material and also special effects (lighting). OUTPUT Mercedes Benz training programme; Renault UK training programme; British Gas special effects; Discovery Channel, new idents, lighting effects; Video London Sound Studios Ltd; French to English translation of French Natural History series; IPSEN International Ltd, brochure and communication consultancy. No unsolicited scripts but c.v.s welcome. Interested in new and creative ideas.

Lilyville Productions Ltd
7 Lilyville Road, London SW6 5DP
☎0171 371 5940   Fax 0171 736 9431
Contact Tony Cash

Drama and documentaries for TV. OUTPUT Poetry in Motion (series for Ch4); South Bank Show: Ben Elton & Vanessa Redgrave; Musique Enquè te (drama-based French language series,

Ch4); Landscape and Memory arts documentary series for the BBC; Jonathan Miller's production of the St Matthew Passion for the BBC. Scripts with an obvious application to TV may be considered. Interested in new writing for documentary programmes.

Limelight
3 Bromley Place (off Conway Street),
London W1P 5HB
☎0171 255 3939   Fax 0171 436 4334
Head of Television Sally Woodward
Managing Director Adam Whittaker

Film, music video and TV drama and commercials. OUTPUT Hear My Song; Teenage Mutant Ninja Turtles I (feature films); Teenage Health Freak I & II (TV series); ReBoot (animated TV series). New writing encouraged. Scripts welcome.

Little Dancer Ltd
Avonway, Naseby Road,
London SE19 3JJ
☎0181 653 9343   Fax 0181 653 9343
Contact Robert Smith, Sue Townsend

Television and cinema, both shorts and full-length features.

Little King Productions
Greek Court, 14A Old Compton Street,
London W1V 5PE
☎0171 437 1772   Fax 0171 437 1782
Contact Dr Simon Nicholas

Film and video: documentary and corporate, concentrating on the health education market.

Living Tape Productions
See **Videotel Productions**

Lomond Television
See **Broadcast Communications**

Lucida Productions
1st Floor, 53 Greek Street,
London W1V 5LR
☎0171 437 1140   Fax 0171 287 5335
Contact Paul Joyce

Television and cinema: arts, adventure, current affairs, documentary, drama and music. OUTPUT has included Motion and Emotion: The Films of Wim Wenders 1989; Dirk Bogarde – By Myself; Sam Peckinpah – Man of Iron; The Making of Naked Lunch; Kris Kristofferson – Pilgrim; Wild One: Marlon Brando; Reel Women. Unsolicited scripts welcome.

Magnetic Image Productions Ltd

6 Grand Union Centre, West Row,
London W10 5AX
☎0181 964 5000   Fax 0181 964 4110
Contact *Mike Bailey*

Video and TV producers: corporate and documentary material. No unsolicited scripts.

Maiden Films

Quarry Bank, Quarry Wood, Marlow,
Buckinghamshire SL7 1RF
☎01628 890999
Contact *Brian Jonson*

Film and video production for documentary, commercials and corporate material. OUTPUT includes TV commercials, sales promotions, product launches – many varied programmes normally with something to sell. CLIENTS World of Leather, Wyns Oil, Eastern Elec. Unlikely to be able to use unsolicited scripts as most productions are pre-commissioned. Have 'from time to time' used new writers.

Main Communications

City House, 16 City Road, Winchester,
Hampshire SO23 8SD
☎01962 870680   Fax 01962 870699
Contact *Eben Wilson*

Multimedia marketing, communications, electronic and publishing company for film, video and TV: drama, documentary and commercials. OUTPUT includes marketing communications, educational, professional and managerial distance learning, documentary programmes for broadcast TV and children's material. Interested in proposals for television programmes, and in ideas for video sell-throughs, interactive multimedia and business information texts and programming.

Malone Gill Productions Ltd

Canaletto House, 39 Beak Street, London
W1R 3LD
☎0171 287 3970   Fax 0171 287 8146
Contact *Georgina Denison*

Mainly documentary, some drama. OUTPUT *Highlanders* (ITV); *Storm Chasers* (Ch4); *Nature Perfected* (Ch4); *The Feast of Christmas* (Ch4); *The Buried Mirror: Reflections on Spain and the New World* by Carlos Fuentes (BBC2/Discovery Channel); *Nomads* (Ch4/ITEL), Bronze medal winner, New York Film Festival 1991. First at 11th Rencontres Internationales de l'Environnement et de la Nature, Paris 1992. Approach by letter with proposal.

Mike Mansfield Television Ltd

5–7 Carnaby Street, London W1V 1PG
☎0171 494 3061   Fax 0171 494 3057
Contact *Hilary Stewart*

Television for BBC, ITV network and Ch4. OUTPUT includes *Animal Country; Just a Minute; The James Whale Show; The Exchange; The Entertainers; HRH the Princess of Wales Concert of Hope; Cue the Music.*

Bill Mason Films Ltd

Orchard House, Dell Quay, Chichester,
West Sussex PO20 7EE
☎01243 783558
Contact *Bill Mason*

Film and video: documentaries only. OUTPUT *The Daimler Benz Story; The Sound and the Fury* (historic motor-racing film). No need for outside writing; all material is written in-house. The emphasis is on automotive history.

Maya Vision Ltd

43 New Oxford Street, London WC1A 1BH
☎0171 836 1113   Fax 0171 836 5169
Contact *Rebecca Dobbs*

Film and TV: drama and documentary. OUTPUT *Saddam's Killing Fields* (for 'Viewpoint', Central TV); *3 Steps to Heaven* (feature film for BFI/Ch4); *A Place in the Sun* (drama for Ch4/Arts Council); *Barcelona* (for 'Omnibus', BBC1); *North of Vortex* (drama for Ch4/Arts Council); *Out* (several pieces for Ch4's lesbian and gay series). Scripts welcome.

Medical & Scientific Productions

Stoke Grange, Fir Tree Avenue, Stoke Poges,
Buckinghamshire SL2 4NN
☎01753 516644   Fax 01753 516965
Contact *Peter Fogarty, Caroline Witts*

Corporate: medical programmes and training packages for health care professionals. Health care ideas welcome. No unsolicited mss.

Meditel Productions Ltd

Bedford Chambers, The Piazza, Covent
Garden, London WC2E 8HA
☎0171 836 9216   Fax 0171 240 3818
Contact *Joan Shenton*

Investigative documentaries: science, medicine and health, education and social issues; daytime magazine programmes factually based with an element of fun; drama and animation. OUTPUT *Dispatches: AIDS & Africa; AZT – Cause for Concern; The Power to Change* (education project for deprived children in Colombia). No unsolicited mss; writers should submit programme ideas on factual/drama/documentary ideas. Either previous experience is essential or new writers will work closely with a producer appointed by the company.

Melendez Films
33 Gresse Street, London W1P 2AH
☎0171 323 2311   Fax 0171 323 2331
Contact *Steven Melendez, Graeme Spurway*

Independent producers working with TV stations. Animated films aimed mainly at a family audience, produced largely for the American market, and prime-time network broadcasting. Also develops and produces feature films (eight so far). OUTPUT has included *Peanuts* (half-hour TV specials); *The Lion, the Witch and the Wardrobe; Babar the Elephant* (TV specials); *Dick Deadeye or Duty Done*, a rock musical based on Gilbert & Sullivan operettas; and a video of fairytales *Happily Ever After, Jules Feiffer Series.* Always interested in new ideas. 'Three of the above walked in through the door.' No scripts. Typed outlines/treatments welcome. Enclose s.a.e. for return.

Melrose Film Productions
16 Bromells Road, London SW4 0BL
☎0171 627 8404   Fax 0171 622 0421
Contact *Alison Roux*

Producers of generic management and staff training films, and interactive programmes.

Mentorn Films
138–140 Wardour Street,
London W1V 3AV
☎0171 287 4545   Fax 0171 287 3728
Contact *Tom Gutteridge, Tom Needham*

FOUNDED in 1985 by ex-BBC arts producer Tom Gutteridge. Producer of successful peaktime show *Challenge Anneka* and Emmy award-winning drama *The Bullion Boys.* Co-producing Gerry Anderson's *Space Precinct.* Film, video and television: cinema, documentary, drama, music and arts.

Mersey Television Company Ltd
Campus Manor, Childwall Abbey Road,
Liverpool L16 0JP
☎0151 722 9122   Fax 0151 722 1969
Contact *Donna Smith*

The best known of the independents in the North of England. Makers of television programmes: drama and fiction serials for popular consumption. OUTPUT *Brookside* (Channel 4).

MITV Ltd
15 Trent Way, West End, Southampton,
Hampshire SO3 3FW
☎01703 473320   Fax 01703 470485
Contact *Chris Harnett, Sue Knight*
Video and television documentary. No scripts.

MJW Productions
13 Carlisle Road, London NW6 6TL
☎0181 968 6542   Fax 0181 968 0038
Contact *Margaret Williams*

Film, video and TV: music and arts documentaries, including opera and dance. Also drama. OUTPUT *Different Trains; Tights Camera Action!,* Series 1&2; *Blond Eckbert; Small Forces, Big Noises; Quartet* (all for Ch4); *Cross Channel* (BBC2). No scripts but interested in new writers.

MNV
4 Barrack Row, Little Ellingham,
Attleborough, Norfolk NR17 1JJ
☎01953 851067   Fax 01953 851067
Contact *Michael Norman*

Video production: corporate, training and communications. Also video publishing and conference television. No unsolicited mss but interested in new writers.

Monaco Films Ltd
56 Queens Court, Queens Road, Richmond,
Surrey TW10 6LB
☎0181 332 7379   Fax 0181 332 7275
Contact *Ingrid Pitt*

Monaco originates scripts, formats and concepts, and sells the rights and franchises to production companies. Projects include drama, documentary and light entertainment for film and television. No scripts.

Alan More Films
Suite 205–206, Pinewood Studios, Pinewood
Road, Iver, Buckinghamshire SL0 0NH
☎01753 656789   Fax 01753 656844
Contact *Alan More, Judith More*

Film, video and TV: documentary, commercials and corporate. No scripts. No need of outside writers.

The Morrison Company
302 Clive Court, Maida Vale, London W9 1SF
☎0171 289 7976   Fax 0171 289 7976
Contact *Don Morrison*

Film and video: drama, documentary and commercials. Unsolicited mss welcome.

Mosaic Pictures Ltd

2nd Floor, 8–12 Broadwick Street,
London W1V 1FH
☎0171 437 6514/3769   Fax 0171 494 0595

Contact *Colin Luke*

Makers of film for television.

Mother Films

3 Pulborough Road, London SW18 5UN
☎0181 870 8189   Fax 0181 877 1173

Contact *Nick O'Hagan, Terry O'Hagan*

Film and TV: drama, comedy and documentary. Keen to work with new writers. Approach by letter for update on current interest. No unsolicited scripts.

Mott Productions

4 Childs Place, London SW5 9RX
☎0171 370 0668   Fax 0171 244 8890

Contact *John Mott*

Film, video and TV: drama, documentary and corporate. 'Always willing to read strong, well-written material with a unique central idea and universal appeal, but please write first, with idea.'

Navigator Films Ltd

99 Henderson Row, Edinburgh EH3 5BB
☎0131 558 3275

Contact *Barbara McKissack*

Broadcast drama and documentary. Developing short and feature-length drama.

New Century Films Ltd

41B Hornsey Lane Gardens, Milton Park,
London N6 5NY
☎0181 348 7298

Artistic Director *Peter Bloore*

Feature films only, no TV drama or sitcoms. 'Keen to see well thought out and commercially viable feature film storylines/synopses/screenplays (preferably intelligent thrillers). Plot-driven storytelling is very poor in most of the material we receive.' *No unsolicited faxes.*

Newgate Company

13 Dafford Street, Larkhall, Bath,
Avon BA1 6SW
☎01225 318335

Contact *Jo Anderson*

A commonwealth of established actors, directors and playwrights, Newgate originally concerned itself solely with theatre writing (at the Bush, Stratford, Roundhouse, etc.) However, in the course of development, several productions have fed into a list of ongoing drama for BBC TV/Ch4. Now looking to develop this co-production strand for film and television projects with other 'Indies'.

Northlight Productions Ltd

Commerce Street Public School, Castle
Terrace, Aberdeen AB2 1BN
☎01224 210007   Fax 01224 211700

Contact *Robert Sproul-Cran*

Film, video and TV: drama, documentary and corporate work. OUTPUT ranges from high-end corporate fundraising videos for the National Museum of Scotland to *Anything But Temptation*, a feature film currently in development, and *Calcutta Chronicles* (5-part documentary series for Ch4). Scripts welcome. Has links with EAVE (European Audio-Visual Entrepreneurs) and Media 95.

Open Media

Ground Floor, 9 Leamington Road Villas,
London W11 1HS
☎0171 229 5416   Fax 0171 221 4842

Contact *Alice Kramers, Sebastian Cody*

Broadcast television: OUTPUT *After Dark; The Secret Cabaret; James Randi Psychic Investigator; Opinions; Is This Your Life?; Don't Quote Me; Brave New World; The Talking Show.*

Open Mind Productions

6 Newburgh Street, London W1V 1LH
☎0171 437 0624   Fax 0171 434 9256

Directors *Chris Ellis, Roland Tongue*

Video and TV production, including documentary and educational. OUTPUT *The Geography Programme: Images of the Earth* (for BBC Schools TV); *Eureka: The Earth in Space; Geography, Start Here: The Local Network; Rat-a-tat-tat; One Last Lie* (for Ch4 Schools). No unsolicited material. Currently developing children's drama series. 'We are a small company interested in programmes that reflect our name. We want to produce more drama and multimedia resources.' Chris Ellis, a writer himself, is a guest lecturer on scriptwriting with BBC TV Training and the London Media Workshop.

Optomen Television

8 Graphite Square, Vauxhall Walk, London
SE11 5EE
☎0171 820 8280   Fax 0171 820 8281

Contact *Peter Gillbe*

Television and video: documentary and corporate, plus animation. OUTPUT *Fire in the Blood* (documentary for BBC2); *Double the Trouble, Twice the Fun* (Ch4 'Out'); *To Kill & Kill Again* (Ch4 'Equinox'); *Old Bear Stories* (ITV – children's animation); *Marcus the Mole* (children's language teaching video).

Original Film & Video Productions Ltd

Greek Court, 14A Old Compton Street, London W1V 5PE
☎0171 734 9721/9804   Fax 0171 437 1782

Contact *Boyd Catling*

Corporate film and video: commercials, broadcast TV and video publishing. Unsolicited mss welcome. Most writing is commissioned by clients themselves and some is originated in-house.

Orpheus Productions

6 Amyand Park Gardens, Twickenham, Middlesex TW1 3HS
☎0181 892 3172   Fax 0181 892 4821

Contact *Richard Taylor*

Television documentaries and corporate work. OUTPUT has included programmes for BBC Current Affairs, Music and Arts, and the African-Caribbean Unit as well as documentaries for the Shell Film Unit and Video Arts. Unsolicited scripts are welcomed with caution. 'We have a preference for visually stirring documentaries with quality writing of the more personal and idiosyncratic kind, not straight reportage.'

Ovation Productions

Osprey House, 10 Little Portland Street, London W1N 5DF
☎0171 637 8575   Fax 0171 580 5686

Contact *John Plews*

Corporate video and conference scripts. Unsolicited mss not welcome. 'We talk to new writers from time to time.'

Oxford Scientific Films Ltd

Lower Road, Longer Hanborough, Oxfordshire OX8 8LL
☎01993 881881   Fax 01993 882808
10 Poland Street, London W1V 3DE
☎0171 494 0720   Fax 0171 287 9125

Managing Director *Karen Goldie-Morrison*

Established production company with specialist knowledge and expertise in natural history films and science-based programmes, many of which have won awards. Film, video and TV: documentaries, TV commercials, multimedia, and educational films. Scripts welcome. Operates an extensive stills and film footage library specialising in wildlife and special effects (see **Picture Libraries**).

Pace Productions Ltd

12 The Green, Newport Pagnell, Buckinghamshire MK16 0JW
☎01908 618767   Fax 01908 617641

Contact *Chris Pettit*

Film and video: drama, documentary, corporate and commercials.

Pacesetter Productions Ltd

New Barn House, Leith Hill Lane, Ockley, Surrey RH5 5PH
☎01306 621433   Fax 0171 732 5911

Contact *Adele Spencer, Ronnie Spencer*

Film and video producers of drama, documentary and corporate work. OUTPUT *History of the Telephone; Pictures from the Past; The Wheatfield; Merchant of Wood Street* (the latter two feature films in development). CLIENTS include British Telecom, British Gas, Midland Bank, Lloyds Bank. No unsolicited scripts.

Barry Palin Associates Ltd

143 Charing Cross Road, London WC2H 0EE
☎0171 439 0039   Fax 0171 494 1305

Contact *Barry Palin*

Film, video and TV production for drama, documentary, commercials and corporate material. OUTPUT *Harmfulness of Tobacco* Anton Chekhov short story – BAFTA Best Short Film Award-winner (Ch4); Corporate: Kraft Jacobs Suchard. Unsolicited scripts welcome. New writing encouraged.

Paper Moon Productions

Wychwood House, Burchetts Green Lane, Littlewick Green, Nr. Maidenhead, Berkshire SL6 3QW
☎01628 829819   Fax 01628 822428

Contact *David Haggas*

Television and video: medical and health education documentaries. OUTPUT includes *Shamans and Science*, a medical documentary examining the balance between drugs discovered in nature and those synthesised in laboratories. Unsolicited scripts welcome. Interested in new writing 'from people who really understand television programme-making'.

Parallax Pictures Ltd
7 Denmark Street, London WC2H 8LS
☎0171 836 1478   Fax 0171 497 8062
Contact *Sally Hibbin*

Feature films/television drama. OUTPUT *I.D.; Riff-Raff; Bad Behaviour; Raining Stones; Ladybird, Ladybird; Land and Freedom; The Englishman Who Went up a Hill But Came Down a Mountain; Bliss.*

Philip Partridge Productions Ltd
The High Street, South Woodchester,
Nr Stroud, Glos. GL5 5EL
☎01453 872743   Fax 01453 872743
Contact *Phil Partridge*

Film and TV producers for drama and comedy material. OUTPUT *Once Upon a Time in the North* Tim Firth six 30-minute comedies on film (BBC1). Unsolicited scripts welcome 'providing writers are patient while they're read'. Particularly interested in developing new writing with writers who are totally committed.

PBF Motion Pictures
The Little Pickenhanger, Tuckey Grove,
Ripley, Surrey GU23 6JG
☎01483 225179   Fax 01483 224118
Contact *Peter B. Fairbrass*

Film, video and TV: drama, documentary, commercials and corporate. Also televised chess series and chess videos. OUTPUT *Grandmaster Chess* (in association with Thames TV); *Glue Sniffing; RN Special Services; Nightfrights* (night-time TV chiller series). CLIENTS include GEC-Marconi, Coca Cola, MoD, Marks & Spencer, various government departments, British Consulate. No scripts; send one-page synopsis only in the first instance. Good scripts which relate to current projects will be followed up, otherwise not as PBF have no time to reply to proposals which do not interest them. Only good writing stands a chance.

PCP (The Producers Creative Partnership Ltd)
48a Goodge Street, London W1P 1FJ
☎0171 636 1918   Fax 0171 580 4982
Contact *Michael Darlow, Christina Burnett*

Television drama and documentary makers. OUTPUT *Decisions, Decisions; The Boy Who Sang O' for the Wings of a Dove.* Scripts welcome. New writing encouraged.

Peake Productions
141 Victor Road, London SE20 7JU
☎0181 659 4122
Contact *Andrew Peake*

TV news and documentary; drama and comedy; also scripting and producing promotional and training videos for foreign markets.

Pelicula Films
7 Queen Margaret Road, Glasgow G20 6DP
☎0141 945 3333   Fax 0141 946 8345
Contact *Mike Alexander*

Television producers. Makers of drama documentaries and music programmes for Ch4 and the BBC. OUTPUT *As an Eilean (From the Island); Gramsci; Down Home; Scapa Flow 1919; The Jazz Apple; The Land of Europe.*

Pentagon Communications
Anchor House, The Maltings, Hull,
Humberside HU1 3HA
☎01482 226298   Fax 01482 226245
Contact *Jon Levy*

Mainly corporate; also TV documentary, drama and commercials. Unsolicited mss welcome.

Penumbra Productions Ltd
21A Brondesbury Villas, London NW6 6AH
☎0171 328 4550   Fax 0171 328 3844
Contact *H. O. Nazareth*

Film, video and TV: drama, documentary and information videos on health, housing, arts and political documentaries. OUTPUT includes *Repomen* (Cutting Edge, Ch4); *Doctors and Torture* (Inside Story, BBC); *Bombay & Jazz* (BBC2); *Awaaz* (information video in eight languages for Kings Fund/Manchester Council for Community Relations). In development: *Slave Brides* (for TV/cinema). Film treatments, drama proposals and documentary synopses welcome. Keen to assist in the development of new writing.

PHI Television Ltd
106 Cheyne Walk, London SW10 0DG
☎0171 351 4160   Fax 0171 376 7051
Contact *P. Holmans*

Television drama, games and light entertainment. OUTPUT *Operation Julie; Treasure Hunt; Bullseye; Jangles.* New writing encouraged, but no scripts in the first instance: send one-page outlines only.

Picture Palace Films Ltd
53A Brewer Street, London W1R 3FD
☎0171 734 6630   Fax 0171 734 8574
Contact *Malcolm Craddock*

Leading independent producer of TV drama. OUTPUT *Sharpe's Rifles* (8 x 2-hour films for Central TV); *Little Napoleons* (4-part comedy drama for Ch4; *The Orchid House* (4-part drama series for Ch4); numerous episodes for *Eurocops; Tandoori Nights; 4 Minutes; When Love Dies; Ping Pong* (feature film).

Picture This Productions
23 Newman Street, London W1P 3HB
☎0171 636 3663   Fax 0171 436 3989
Contact *Paul Bates*

Film, video and TV production for documentary, commercials, music and corporate material. Also the record industry EPKs, promotions. Unsolicited scripts and new writing welcome.

Phil Pilley Productions
Ferryside, Felix Lane, Shepperton, Middlesex TW17 8NG
☎01932 246455   Fax 01932 246455
Contact *Phil Pilley*

Programmes for TV and video, mainly sports, including documentaries for the BBC, ITV, Ch4 and the US. Also books, newspapers and magazine features, mainly sports. Unsolicited ideas and synopses welcome.

Planet 24 Ltd
The Planet Building, Thames Quay, 195 Marsh Wall, London E14 9SG
☎0171 345 2424   Fax 0171 345 9400
Executive Producer/Managing Director
  Charles Parsons

Television producers of light entertainment, comedy and music programmes. OUTPUT *The Big Breakfast; The Word; The Messiah* (live recording). Unsolicited scripts welcome.

Platinum Film & TV Production Ltd
79 Islip Street, London NW5 2DL
☎0171 916 9091   Fax 0171 916 5238
Contact *Terry Kelleher*

Television documentaries, including dramadocumentary. OUTPUT *South Africa's Black Economy* (Ch4); *Murder at the Farm* (Thames TV); *The Biggest Robbery in the World* (major investigative true crime drama-documentary for Carlton TV). Scripts and treatments welcome.

Portman Entertainment
43–45 Dorset Street, London W1H 4AB
☎0171 224 3344   Fax 0171 224 1057
Head of Development *Steve Matthews*

Screenplays for cinema and television drama.

Premiere Productions Ltd
16 Castello Avenue, London SW15 6EA
☎0181 785 2933   Fax 0181 780 1684
Contact *Peter Fudakowski*

Film and video: drama and corporate, including dramatised training videos. Currently looking for feature film scripts, with Anglo/American/East European themes. Preference for stories with humour. No horror or sci-fi.

Pretty Clever Pictures Ltd
Post 59, Shepperton Studios, Studios Road, Shepperton, Middlesex TW17 0QD
☎01932 572047/562611   Fax 01932 568989
Contact *Geraldine Morgan*

Broadcast programmes, commercials, corporate communication, promos, special projects and titles, and media training. Unsolicited mss welcome.

Primetime Television Ltd
Seymour Mews House, Seymour Mews, Wigmore Street, London W1H 9PE
☎0171 935 9000   Fax 0171 935 1992
Contact *Richard Price*

Television production, distribution and packaging, plus international co-productions. OUTPUT *Porgy and Bess* (BBC, Homevale, Greg Smith); *Re:Joyce* (BBC); *The CIA* (BBC/A&E/NRK); José Carreras – A Life (LWT); *Othello* (BBC); *Ustinov on the Orient Express* (A&E/CBC/NOB/JMP); *Ethan Frome* (American Playhouse). Works closely with international sister distribution company PTA and associated US company, Primetime Entertainment. No unsolicited scripts.

Prometheus Productions
Maughanby Farm, Little Salkeld, Penrith, Cumbria CA10 1NP
☎01768 898334   Fax 01768 897084
Contact *Clem Shaw*

Film and TV: drama and documentary. OUTPUT Documentaries: *Cutting Edge; Encounters* (Ch4); *Secret History;* Drama: *Batman Can't Fly* (BBC Screen 2); *Conchies; State Control.* Keen to seek out, encourage and promote new writing. Scripts welcome.

PTA (Peter Thierry Associates)
15 Kingsmere Road, Wimbledon Common, London SW19 6PY
☎0181 788 9795   Fax 0181 788 0266
Contact *Peter Thierry, Carol Thierry*

Film, video and TV: drama, commercials and

corporate work. OUTPUT includes game shows, drama series and training films.

Richard Purdum Productions

Kings Court, 2–16 Goodge Street,
London W1P 1FF
☎0171 636 5162   Fax 0171 436 5628
Contact *Jill Thomas*

Producer of animated television commercials in the main. No unsolicited scripts.

Purkis Neale Productions Ltd

4 Dunstable Mews, London W1N 1RQ
☎0171 486 8166   Fax 0171 487 2620
Producer *David Neale*
Writer/Director *Chris Purkis*

Video producers: commercials and corporate material. CLIENTS Britain's Petite, Crown & Andrews, ScreenSport, Yorkshire Bank, Varig Airlines, London Metropole Hotel, Saudi Bank. No unsolicited scripts. 'We write all our own work.' Scripts via agents may occasionally be considered.

Ragdoll Productions (UK) Ltd

11 Chapel Street, Stratford on Avon,
Warwickshire CV37 6EP
☎01789 262772   Fax 01789 262773
Contact *Anne Wood*

Young children's productions. OUTPUT *Brum, the Big Adventures of a Little Car; Rosie & Jim; Tots TV.* No unsolicited scripts. Seek collaborators rather than writers.

Alvin Rakoff Productions Ltd

1 The Orchard, Chiswick,
London W4 1JZ
☎0181 994 1269   Fax 0181 995 3191
Contact *Alvin Rakoff*

TV and film. OUTPUT *Paradise Postponed* (TV mini-series); *A Voyage Round My Father; The First Olympics 1896; Dirty Tricks.* No unsolicited mss.

Red Lion Communications Ltd

76 Cleveland Street, London W1P 5DS
☎0171 323 4540   Fax 0171 323 0263
Contact *Mike Kilcooley*

Video producers: commercials, training and corporate work, including product launch videos, in-house training, open learning, multimedia programmes, etc. 'We are always on the look-out for new, well thought through ideas for broadcast.'

Red Rooster Film and Television Entertainment

29 Floral Street, London WC2E 9DP
☎0171 379 7727   Fax 0171 379 5756
Contact *Linda James*

Film and TV drama. OUTPUT *Crocodile Shoes; Body & Soul; The Life and Times of Henry Pratt; Smokescreen.* No unsolicited scripts. Encourages new writers; 'recommend that they find an agent'.

Renaissance Vision

15 Capitol House, Heigham Street, Norwich,
Norfolk NR2 4TE
☎01603 767272   Fax 01603 768163
Contact *B. Gardner*

Video: full range of corporate work (training, sales, promotional, etc.). Production of educational and special interest video publications. Willing to consider good ideas and proposals.

Richmond Films & Television Ltd

5 Dean Street, London W1V 5RN
☎0171 734 9313   Fax 0171 287 2058
Contact *Sandra Hastie*

Film and TV: drama, comedy and children's. OUTPUT *Press Gang; The Lodge.* Scripts welcome provided they are accompanied by explanatory note with regard to where they have been submitted previously and the response they received. A treatment or synopsis must be included. 'We are quite prepared to use new writers if they are good.'

Roberts & Wykeham Films

7 Barb Mews, Hammersmith,
London W6 7PA
☎0171 602 4897   Fax 0171 602 3016
Contact *S. Wykeham*

Television documentaries and packaging. OUTPUT *The Late Late Show* 1988–1994 (post-production package for Ch4); Ch4 Dispatches: *Trail of Red Mercury; Kurdistan: The Dream Betrayed;* BBC Everyman *Road Back to Hell.* No unsolicited scripts.

Rose Bay Film Productions

6th Floor, 76 Oxford Street,
London W1N 0AT
☎0171 412 0400   Fax 0171 412 0300
Contact *Matthew Steiner, Simon Usiskin*

Film and TV production for drama, entertainment and documentary. Unsolicited scripts welcome.

Saffron Productions Ltd

Craigs End, Stambourne, Halstead,
Essex CO9 4NQ
☎01440 785200   Fax 01440 785775
Contact *Victor Pemberton, David Spenser*

Film and TV production for drama and documentary. OUTPUT *Omnibus* Arts documentaries (BBC) (Emmy Award Winners); *Keys of the Kingdom* 4 x 60 mins drama series (BBC); *Our Family* 3 x 90 mins drama series (BBC); *The Animated Dickens* 6 x 30 mins series. Also a variety of other programmes. Unsolicited scripts welcome. Keen to promote new writers and experienced writers of any age.

Sam Entertainment Limited

12 Moylan Road, London W6 8QB
☎0171 385 7053
Contact *Ian Sales, Peter Moore*

FOUNDED 1994. Production company with 'big plans for the coming year'. Prefers scripts to be sent via an agent but will consider unsolicited synopses with covering letter and s.a.e.

Sands Films Ltd

119 Rotherhithe Street, London SE16 4NF
☎0171 231 2209   Fax 0171 231 2119
Contact *Richard Goodwin, Christine Edzard*

Film and TV drama. OUTPUT *Little Dorrit; The Fool; As You Like It; A Dangerous Man; The Long Day Closes; A Passage to India.* No unsolicited scripts.

Scala Productions

39–43 Brewer Street, London W1R 3FD
☎0171 734 7060   Fax 0171 437 3248
Contact *Stephen Woolley, Nik Powell, Elisabeth Karlsen*

Production company set up by ex-Palace Productions Nik Powell and Steve Woolley, who have an impressive list of credits including *Company of Wolves, Absolute Beginners* and *Mona Lisa.* Projects in development: *Hollow Reed; Galatea; Jonathan Wild.*

Schonfeld Productions International (SPI 1980 Ltd)

27 Old Gloucester Street, London WC1N 3XX
☎0171 435 1007
Contact *Victor Schonfeld*

Drama, arts, current affairs, documentary, films for TV and cinema. OUTPUT includes *Snip of a Lad; Money Love; Shattered Dreams; The Animals Film; Courage Along the Divide; And I Don't*

Have to Do the Dishes. Send a brief letter prior to submission of unsolicited material.

Schwops Productions

34 Ashton Road, Luton, Bedfordshire LU1 3QE
☎01582 412622   Fax 01582 412095
Contact *Maureen Brown*

Video producer of drama, documentary and corporate material. Areas of interest include music, travel, ballet, medical and training material. Also distribution, facilities, duplication, and sell-through videos. Open-minded to new writing. Scripts welcome.

Scope Picture Productions Ltd

Keppie House, 147 Blythswood Street, Glasgow G2 4EN
☎0141 332 7720   Fax 0141 332 1049
TV Commercials *Alison Bye*
Corporate *Bill Gordon*

Corporate film and video; broadcast documentaries and sport; TV commercials. Unsolicited mss, realistic scripts/ideas welcome.

Screen First Ltd

The Studios, Funnells Farm, Down Street, Nutley, East Sussex TN22 3LG
☎01825 712034/5   Fax 01825 713511
Contact *M. Thomas*

Television dramas, documentaries, arts and animation programmes. OUTPUT *Secret Passions* series I, II, III (presenting new animation for Ch4); *Elidor* (children's drama series for BBC). No scripts.

Screen Ventures Ltd

49 Goodge Street, London W1P 1FB
☎0171 580 7448   Fax 0171 631 1265
Contact *Christopher Mould, David Chambers*

Film, video and TV: documentary, music videos and drama. OUTPUT *Woodstock Diary; Vanessa Redgrave* (LWT 'South Bank Show'); *Mojo Working; Burma: Dying for Democracy* (Ch4); *Genet* (LWT 'South Bank Show').

Securicor Communication & Media Services

15 Carshalton Road, Sutton, Surrey SM1 4LE
☎0181 770 7000   Fax 0181 722 2672
Contact *Paul Fahey, Gill Arney*

Television producers of drama, documentary and corporate material. OUTPUT includes promotional, information and training videos for the Securicor Group and selected clients. Also audio, print design and production. Unsolicited scripts are sometimes welcome.

SelecTV plc
6 Derby Street, London W1Y 7HD
☎0171 355 2868   Fax 0171 629 1604

Comprising Alomo, Clement/La Frenais and WitzEnd Productions. Producers of television drama and comedy. OUTPUT *Pie In the Sky; Goodnight Sweetheart; Birds of a Feather; Love Hurts; Lovejoy; The New Statesman; Tracey Ullman: A Class Act; Over the Rainbow*. Scripts not welcome unless via agents but new writing is encouraged.

Seventh House Films
1 Hall Farm Place, Bawburgh, Norwich, Norfolk NR9 3LW
☎01603 749068   Fax 01603 749069
Contact *Clive Dunn, Angela Rule*

Documentary for film, video and TV. OUTPUT *Rockin' the Boat* (memories of pirate radio); *White Knuckles* (on the road with a travelling funfair); *King Romance* (life of Henry Rider Haggard); *A Drift of Angels* (three women and the price of art); *Bare Heaven* (the life and fiction of L. P. Hartley); *A Swell of the Soil* (life of Alfred Munnings); *Light Out of the Sky* (the art and life of Edward Seago). 'We welcome programme proposals with a view to collaborative co-production. Always interested in original and refreshing expressions for visual media.'

Sianco
Uned 2, Cibyn, Caernarfon, Gwynedd LL55 2BD
☎01286 675766   Fax 01286 671131
Contact *Siân Teifi*

Children's programmes including drama.

Signals, Essex Media Centre
21 St Peter's Street, Colchester, Essex CO1 1EW
☎01206 560255   Fax 01206 369086
Coordinator *Caroline Norbury*

Promotion and documentary work for the voluntary and arts sectors. Specialists in media education projects. No unsolicited mss.

Siriol Productions
3 Mount Stuart Square, Butetown, Cardiff CF1 6RW
☎01222 488400   Fax 01222 485962
Contact *Andrew Offiler*

Animated series, mainly for children. OUTPUT includes *The Hurricanes; Tales of the Toothfairies; Billy the Cat*, as well as the feature films, *Under Milkwood* and *The Princess and the Goblin*. Write with ideas and sample script in the first instance.

Skyline Film & TV Productions Ltd
126 Rusthall Avenue, London W4 1BS
☎0171 631 4649   Fax 0171 637 3376
Contact *Mairi Bett*

Television programmes, educational, drama and feature films. Supplier of programmes to all major broadcasters. Always interested in new ideas/talent, but a preliminary phone call is advisable.

Sleeping Giant Films
56–58 Clerkenwell Road, London EC1M 5PX
☎0171 490 5060   Fax 0171 490 5060
Contact *Harriet Pacaud*

Documentary film producer. OUTPUT includes *Kirkby's Kingdom*, the story of a Yorkshire smallholder whose land is threatened by property developers. Interested in original ideas with strong visual potential on environmental, natural history, arts and cultural themes. No fiction-based material. Happy to look at documentary ideas. Commentary writers used.

Smith & Watson Productions
The Gothic House, Fore Street, Totnes, South Devon TQ9 5EH
☎01803 863033   Fax 01803 864219
Contact *Chris Watson, Nick Smith*

Film, video and TV: documentaries, drama, party political broadcasts (for the Liberal Democrats), and commercials. Unsolicited mss welcome. Interested in new writing.

Solo Vision Ltd
49–53 Kensington High Street, London W8 5ED
☎0171 376 2166   Fax 0171 938 3165
Contact *Don Short*

Video and TV: documentary, game shows, and corporate work. OUTPUT *Starmate* (the astrology game); *Surrogate Grandmother* (documentary, LWT/Cable USA); plus video packaging.

Specific Ltd
25 Rathbone Street, London W1P 1AG
☎0171 580 7476   Fax 0171 494 2676
Contact *Michael Hamlyn*

FOUNDED 1976. Currently working on a six-picture development deal with PolyGram

International to develop and produce comedy feature scripts with the Comedy Committee. OUTPUT includes *The Adventures of Priscilla, Queen of the Desert* a full-length feature film co-produced with Latent Image (Australia) and financed by PolyGram and AFFC; *U2 Rattle and Hum* (full-length feature film – part concert film/part cinema verité documentary); and numerous pop promos for major international artists.

Spectel Productions Ltd
184 Alcester Road South, Kings Heath, Birmingham B14 6DE
☎0121 443 5958   Fax 0121 443 5958
Contact *David Webster*

Film and video: documentary and corporate; also video publishing. No unsolicited scripts.

Spellbound Productions Ltd
90 Cowdenbeath Path, Twyford Street, London N1 0LG
☎0171 278 0052   Fax 0171 278 0052
Contact *Paul Harris*

Film and television drama. OUTPUT includes *Leave to Remain* for 'Film on 4'. Unsolicited scripts welcome. Keen to support and encourage new writing.

'Spoken' Image Ltd
The Design Centre, 44 Canal Street, Manchester M1 3WD
☎0161 236 7522   Fax 0161 236 0020
Contact *Geoff Allman, Murray Carden, Steve Foster*

Film, video and TV production for documentary and corporate material. Specialising in high quality brochures and reports, exhibitions, conferences, film and video production for broadcast, industry and commerce. Unsolicited scripts welcome. Interested in educational, and historical new writing, mainly for broadcast programmes.

Stephens Kerr Ltd
Braycrest House, 8–12 Camden High Street, London NW1 0JH
☎0171 916 2124   Fax 0171 916 2125
Contact *Eleanor Stephens*

Film, video and TV: drama and documentary. OUTPUT *Sex Talk; Love Talk; Men Talk; The Love Weekend* (all for Ch4); *Nights; Food File.* Unsolicited scripts welcome. Keen to support new writing.

Straight Forward Film & Television Productions Ltd
Crescent Studios, 18 High Street, Holywood, Co. Down BT18 9AD
☎01232 427697   Fax 01232 422289
Contact *Moya Neeson, John Nicholson, Ian Kennedy*

Video and TV: documentary and corporate work. OUTPUT *Close to Home* (Ch4 documentary); *Greenfingers* (BBC/RTE gardening series); *Places Apart* (BBC Northern Ireland); plus various corporates for local industry which are handled by the sister company Morrow Communications. Unsolicited scripts welcome. New work in drama and documentary fields welcome, particulary if with a strong Irish theme, contemporary or historical.

Strawberry Productions Ltd
36 Priory Avenue, London W4 1TY
☎0181 994 4494   Fax 0181 742 7675
Contact *John Black*

Film, video and TV: drama and documentary; corporate and video publishing.

Supervision (West) Ltd
26–27 West Street, Horsham, West Sussex RH12 1PB
☎01403 274488   Fax 01403 269264
Contact *Charles Marriott, Teresa Reed*

Film, video and TV: drama, documentary, corporate, sell-through videos, and commercials, including radio. Unsolicited scripts welcome. New writing supported if good.

Swanlind Communication
The Wharf, Bridge Street, Birmingham B1 2JR
☎0121 616 1701   Fax 0121 616 1520
Contact *Mike Davies*

Producer of business television and internal communication strategies.

Tabard Productions
Savoy Hill House, Savoy Hill, London WC2R 0BL
☎0171 497 0830   Fax 0171 497 0850
Contacts *Vance Chapman, John Herbert*

Film and video: corporate and commercials. Unsolicited mss welcome.

Talisman Films Ltd
5 Addison Place, London W11 4RJ
☎0171 603 7474   Fax 0171 602 7422
Contact *Alan Shallcross*

Drama for film and TV: developing the full range of drama – TV series, serials and single films, as well as theatric features. 'We will only consider material submitted via literary agents.' Interested in supporting and encouraging new writing.

TalkBack Productions

36 Percy Street, London W1P 0LN
☎0171 323 9777   Fax 0171 637 5105
Contact *Peter Fincham, Sally Macdougall*

Independent TV production company set up in 1981 by comedians Mel Smith and Griff Rhys Jones. Specialises in comedy, comedy drama and drama; also corporate and training films. OUTPUT *Smith and Jones; Murder Most Horrid; Bonjour la Classe; Demob; The Day Today; Paris; Knowing Me Knowing You with Alan Patridge; Milner; Loose Talk.*

Tandem TV & Film Ltd

10 Bargrove Avenue, Hemel Hempstead, Hertfordshire HP1 1QP
☎01442 61576   Fax 01442 219250
Contact *Barbara Page*

Film and video production for drama, documentary and corporate material, including dramatised health and safety programmes for training; series of five-minute programmes for television, corporate programmes for various companies. Specialise in construction and civil engineering films, and Christian programming. Writers are usually commissioned. Welcomes new writing.

Teamwork Productions

Gate House, Walderton, Chichester, West Sussex PO18 9ED
☎01705 631384   Fax 01705 631399
Contact *Rob Widdows*

Video and TV producer of documentary, corporate and commercial work. OUTPUT includes motor racing coverage, motor sport productions and corporate motor sport videos. Good ideas will always be considered. No scripts.

Telemagination Ltd

41 Buckingham Palace Road, London SW1W 0PP
☎0171 828 5331   Fax 0171 828 7631
Contact *John M. Mills*

Producers of television animation. OUTPUT *The Animals of Farthing Wood* 39 half-hour episodes, for children's television. Original animated adult and comedy sitcoms for TV.

Unsolicited scripts welcome, but outline must be submitted either in writing or by phone. New writings considered after discussing the outline.

Televideo Productions

Sovereign House, 3–7 Sidney Street, Sheffield, South Yorkshire S1 4RG
☎0114 2491500   Fax 0114 2491505
Contact *Graham King*

Video and television: TV news and sports coverage, documentary and corporate work; sell-through videos (distributed on own label). OUTPUT includes *The Premier Collection* (football club videos); live coverage of Vauxhall conference football for cable; *Ice Wars GB* (ice hockey) for 'Sportswire'; *World Special Olympic Games* for BBC; plus a wide range of corporate work from drama-based material to documentary.

Teliesyn

Helwick House, 19 David Street, Cardiff CF1 2EH
☎01222 667556   Fax 01222 667546
Director of Productions *Carmel Gahan*

Film and video: produces drama, documentary, music and social action in English and Welsh. Celtic Film Festival, BAFTA Cymru, Grierson and Indie award winner. OUTPUT *Branwen* (90 minute feature film for S4C); *Wales Playhouse 3* (a series of six drama shorts for BBC Wales – new writing initiative); *Excalibur – The Search for Arthur* (drama-documentary series for BBC2); *A Generation Arises* (arts programme for BBC Wales' 'The Slate' on young writers in Wales); *Codi Clawr Hanes* (drama-documentary series on women's history for S4C); *Flying High* (documentary for Ch4's 'Short Stories' strand). Will consider unsolicited mss only if accompanied by synopsis and c.v. Encourages new writing wherever possible, in close association with a producer.

Tern Television Productions Ltd

73 Crown Street, Aberdeen AB1 2EX
☎01224 211123   Fax 01224 211199
74 Victoria Crescent Road, Glasgow G12 9JN
☎0141 337 2892
Contact *David Strachan, Gwyneth Hardy, Nick Ibbotson*

Broadcast, video, corporate and training. Specialises in religious and factual entertainment. Currently developing drama. Unsolicited mss welcome.

Thames Television International Ltd

Broom Road, Teddington Lock, Middlesex
TW11 9NT
☎0181 614 2800

Managing Director *Mike Phillips*
Controller of Production *Keith Mosedale*
Head of Drama *Antony Root*
Executive Producer, Variety *John Fisher*

UK's largest independent and distribution company. OUTPUT includes *The Bill; This is Your Life; Strike it Lucky; Take Your Pick; Wish You Were Here?*

Theatre of Comedy Co.

See **Theatre Producers**

Huw Thomas & Associates

17 Brunswick Gardens, London W8 4AS
☎0171 727 9953   Fax 0171 727 9931

Contact *Anne E. Thomas*

Video and TV: documentary and corporate; also media training. CLIENTS include Lloyd's of London, Nestlé, Morgan Crucible. No unsolicited scripts.

Tiger Aspect Productions

5 Soho Square, London W1V 5DE
☎0171 434 0672   Fax 0171 287 1448

Contact *Charles Brand*

Television producers for documentary programmes and comedy – variety, sitcom and comedy drama. OUTPUT *Mr Bean; The Vicar of Dibley; Enfield and Chums; Just for Laughs; Paul Merton's Life of Comedy; Our Man In; Heroes and Villains.* Unsolicited mss read but a higher priority is given to work submitted through agents. Writers submitting work on spec. should bear in mind that when the volume of material is heavy, it can take up to three months to respond. Writers are advised to submit a brief c.v. with scripts.

Tonfedd

Uned 33, Cibyn, Caernarfon, Gwynedd
LL55 2BD
☎01286 676800   Fax 01286 676466

Contact *Hefin Elis*

Light entertainment, music.

Alan Torjussen Productions Ltd

17 Heol Wen, Cardiff CF4 6EG
☎01222 624669   Fax 01222 624669

Contact *Alan Torjussen*

Film, video and TV production for drama, documentary, commercials and corporate material. Particular interested in all types of documentary, education, schools and drama. Background includes work in the Welsh language. Unsolicited scripts welcome, particularly if about Wales by Welsh writers (includes Welsh language scripts). 'Positively welcome new writing, on all subjects. Brief ideas and outlines always welcome'.

Touch Productions Ltd

3rd Floor, 14–18 Haddon Street, London
W1R 8DP
☎0171 287 5520   Fax 0171 437 3675

Contact *Will Aslett*

Main output consists of human–interest documentaries. OUTPUT network documentaries including programmes for *Inside Story, Cutting Edge, 40 Minutes, QED, Dispatches,* and *Short Stories.* In addition, they are currently developing a new strand of drama–documentaries and drama shorts: 'We would particularly like to hear from writers with an interest in this area.'

Transatlantic Films Production and Distribution Company

100 Blythe Road, London W14 0HE
☎0171 727 0132   Fax 0171 603 5049

Contact *Revel Guest*

Producers of TV documentaries. OUTPUT *Greek Fire* 10 x 30 mins on Greek culture (Ch4); *Four American Composers* 4 x 1 hour (Ch4); *The Horse in Sport* 8 x 1 hour (Ch4); *A Year in the Life of Placido Domingo.* No unsolicited scripts. Interested in new writers to write 'the book of the series', e.g. for *Greek Fire* and *The Horse in Sport,* but not usually drama script writers.

Turning Point Productions

Pinewood Studios, Pinewood Road, Iver
Heath, Buckinghamshire SL0 0NH
☎01753 630666   Fax 01753 650855

Contact *Adrian Bate*

Television drama producer. OUTPUT includes *Red Fox* (mini-series for LWT). No unsolicited scripts. Very keen to nurture new writing talent though. The company is involved with the Edinburgh Television Festival.

TurnOver Titles

Quoin House, High Street, Bray, Berkshire
SL6 2AH
☎01628 22560

Contact *Paul Friend*

A television and film production company.

Looking to produce and develop original scripts and ideas for big and small screen. Mainly interested in sitcoms and drama series, also radical and cult ideas for low budget programming. Write in the first instance, please.

Twentieth Century Fox Productions Ltd

Twentieth Century House, 31–32 Soho Square, London W1V 6AP
☎0171 437 7766   Fax 0171 434 2170
Contact *Company Secretary*

London office of the American giant.

Two Four Productions Ltd

Quay Studios West, Old Newnham, Plymouth, Devon PL7 5BH
☎01752 345424   Fax 01752 344244
Joint Managing Directors *Charles Wace, Christopher Slade*
Senior Producer *Charles Boydell*

Video and television: drama, documentary, commercials and corporate. OUTPUT includes *Close to Home: Journey for Life* (current affairs for Ch4); *The West at Work* (business magazine for Westcountry Television); *Great Westerners* (documentary for HTV) and *The Church in Crisis* (current affairs programme for BBC2 South West). Currently in production are *The Big House* (a 6-part documentary filmed inside Dartmoor Prison); *Soul Mates* and *The Right Thing* (two 13-part series for satellite television); and *Westcountry Focus* (a series of weekly business programmes for Westcountry Television). Ideas welcome.

Two Plus Two Videographics

6 Lake End Court, Bath Road, Taplow, Maidenhead, Berkshire SL6 0JQ
☎01628 668099/77   Fax 01628 668055
Contact *Barry Tyler*

Producers of corporate, training, and promotional videos. Most work is done for blue chip companies. Unsolicited scripts welcome 'but we don't want to be swamped especially with "follow up" phone calls'.

UBA Ltd

32 Porchester Terrace, London W2 3TP
☎0171 402 6313   Fax 0171 724 5825
Contact *Peter Shaw*

Quality feature films and TV for an international market. OUTPUT *Windprints; The Lonely Passion of Judith Hearne* (co-production with **Hand-Made Films Ltd**); *Taffin; Castaway; Turtle*

Diary. In development: *Hunting the Devil; A Witch in New York; Sweeney Todd; Leo, The Magnificent; The Honeytrap; The Kitchen Garden; Wind in the Willows*. Prepared to commission new writing whether adapted from another medium or based on a short outline/treatment. Concerned with the quality of the script (*Turtle Diary* was written by Harold Pinter) and breadth of appeal. 'Exploitation material' not welcome.

United International Pictures (UK)

Mortimer House, 37–41 Mortimer Street, London W1A 2JL
☎0171 636 1655   Fax 0171 636 4118

UK office of American giant; distributes for Paramount.

United Media Ltd

1 Northumberland Avenue, London WC2N 5BW
☎0171 925 2105   Fax 0171 930 6788
Contact *Mr N. Mackie*

Film, video and TV: drama. OUTPUT *To the Lighthouse* (TV movie with BBC); *Jamaica Inn* (HTV mini-series); *The Krays* (feature film with Fugitive/Rank). Unsolicited scripts welcome but synopses preferred in the first instance. 'We encourage new writing if we see commercially orientated talent.'

Upstream Presentation Ltd

Ridings House, 66 Alma Road, Windsor, Berkshire SL4 3EZ
☎01753 858895   Fax 01753 864123
Contact *Peter Wrigglesworth, Nick Woollard*

Film, video and TV: documentary and corporate, plus conferences and live events. Upstream provides a broad range of business communication services for major European clients, covering employee communications, sales promotion, corporate image and video news releases. Also sell-through video production. Unsolicited scripts welcome in the area of broadcast programmes which can attract corporate sponsorship. 'We welcome writers from advertising and broadcast who seek opportunities in the corporate sector.'

Vanson Wardle Productions

72 Chatham Road, London SW11 6HG
☎0171 223 1919   Fax 0171 924 4072
Contact *Yvette Vanson*

Film, video and TV: drama, documentary and educational material. OUTPUT *Making Advances* (BBC1) a 5-part series on sexual harassment at work presented by Emma Freud; *How Low Can You Go?* (Ch4 'Critical Eye'); *Presumed Guilty* (BBC1 'Inside Story'); *Law Matters* (Granada 'This Morning'). Supportive of new writing.

Vera Productions
30–38 Dock Street, Leeds, West Yorkshire LS10 1JF
☎0113 2428646   Fax 0113 2451238
Contact *Alison Garthwaite, Catherine Mitchell*

Video: drama, documentary, corporate, promotional, training and campaigning material. OUTPUT *Children Who Foster; I Want to be an Astronaut; Video 28* (celebration and record of lesbians' response to Section 28 of the Local Government Bill); *International Women's Day; Gender on the Timetable.* Unsolicited mss welcome from women only. New writers welcome.

Video Arts (Production) Ltd
Dumbarton House, 68 Oxford Street, London W1N 0LH
☎0171 637 7288   Fax 0171 580 8103
Contact *Margaret Tree*

Film and video, CDI and CD-ROM: training, corporate and educational.

Video Enterprises
12 Barbers Wood Road, High Wycombe, Buckinghamshire HP12 4EP
☎01494 534144 (mobile: 0831 875216)   Fax 01494 534144
Contact *Maurice R. Fleisher*

Video and TV, mainly corporate: business and industrial training, promotional material and conferences. No unsolicited material 'but always ready to try out good new writers'.

Video Newsreels
Church Cottage, Ruscombe, Nr Twyford, Berkshire RG10 9UB
☎01734 321123   Fax 01734 321333
Contact *Gerry Clarke*

Corporate video production: sales and training. OUTPUT has included staff training videos for British Airways and Midland Bank. Unsolicited mss welcome.

Video Presentations
PO Box 281, Wimbledon, London SW19 3DD
☎0181 542 7721   Fax 0181 542 7721
Contact *John Holloway*

Corporate video. CLIENTS include the Post Office, IBM, British Gas, Freemans, Eastern Electricity.

Videoplus Communications
3 Braunfels Walk, Craven Road, Newbury, Berkshire RG14 5NQ
☎01635 37653
Contact *Mike Spencer*

Video: corporate, sales, training, promotional and documentary. CLIENTS include the Reader's Digest Association, Radio Rentals, Hewlett Packard, Safeway, GE Capital and Black & Decker.

Videotel Productions/ Living Tape Productions
Ramillies House, 1–2 Ramillies Street, London W1V 1DF
☎0171 439 6301   Fax 0171 437 0731
Contact *Robert Wallace*

Film, video and TV of a broadly educational nature but not exclusively so. Unsolicited mss welcome in the education and training fields only. 'We would like to support new writers who can put up with the ego-bashing they are likely to get from industrial and commercial sponsors.' OUTPUT has included *Oceans of Wealth* (British Gas, DTI & Channel 4); *Response to Marine Chemical Spills* (for industrial consortium); *Dealing with Violence and Aggression at Work* (NHS, THF); *Defence against Drug Traffickers* (SKULD); *Alcohol, Beware!* (Mobil); *Responsible Chemical Manufacturing* (consortium of chemical companies); *Hospital Security* (NAHAT); *The Office* (BBC/EBS Trust); *More than Meets the Eye* (DOH, EBS Trust).

Visionventures International Ltd
7 Morland Drive, Lamberhurst, Tunbridge Wells, Kent TN3 8HZ
☎01892 890097   Fax 01892 890097
Contact *Joe McCann*

Distributors and producers of film and TV. Unsolicited mss welcome but 80% of those received are usually rejected on financial grounds alone.

Brian Waddell Productions Ltd
Strand Studios, 5/7 Shore Road, Holywood, Co. Down BT18 9HX
☎01232 427646   Fax 01232 427922
Contacts *Brian Waddell, Stephen Stewart*

Producers of a wide range of television programmes in leisure activities, the arts, music, children's, comedy, travel/adventure and documentaries. Currently developing several drama projects. Interested in encouraging new writers, particularly within Ireland.

Wadlow Grosvenor Ltd
18 Grosvenor Street,
London W1X 9FD
☎0171 409 1225   Fax 0171 491 1631
Contact *Gerard Hargreaves*

Presentation and media skills training.

Wall to Wall Television
8–9 Spring Place, London NW5 3ER
☎0171 485 7424   Fax 0171 267 5292
Contact *Jane Root, Alex Graham*

Documentary series, features and drama. OUTPUT includes *Big City; Statement of Affairs* (for Carlton TV); *You, Me and It* (BBC); *For Love or Money* (Ch4). Material is produced in-house; occasional outside ideas accepted, but unusual. Intended expansion means 'there should be more opportunities for writers'.

The Walnut Partnership
Crown House, Armley Road, Leeds,
West Yorkshire LS12 2EJ
☎0113 2456913   Fax 0113 2439614
Contact *Geoff Penn*

A film and video production company specialising in business communication.

Warner Sisters
21 Russell Street,
London WC2B 5HP
☎0171 836 0134   Fax 0171 836 6559
Chief Executives *Lavinia Warner, Jane Wellesley, Anne-Marie Casey, Dorothy Viljoen*

FOUNDED 1984. Film and video: drama, documentary, TV and feature films. OUTPUT includes *GI Brides; Selling Hitler; Rides; Life's a Gas; She-Play; That's Entertaining;* documentaries about Tristan da Cunha, Madagascar and Sarawak. Developing dramas and documentaries with various companies including Carlton, CTE and ITEL.

Christopher P. Warren Television & Video Production
108 Debden Road, Saffron Walden, Essex
CB11 4AL
☎01799 500542   Fax 01799 500542
Contact *Christopher Warren*

Video and TV: documentary and corporate work. OUTPUT *Road to War* (BBC2); *Soldiers* (BBC1); ideas and one-page treatments for factual programmes, particularly any with a 20th-century historical angle, are welcome. No full-length scripts.

Waterfront Productions
17–21 Dean Street, Newcastle upon Tyne,
Tyne & Wear NE1 1PQ
☎0191 261 0162   Fax 0191 261 0160
Contact *Chris Potter*

Wildlife and countryside, environmental, travel, current affairs – documentary and TV series. OUTPUT *Wild West Country* (WestCountry TV); *Lambs Tales* (Ch4); *Wind Beneath My Wings* (BBC); *Commercial Break* (Tyne Tees Television).

Watershed Television
11 Regent Street, Bristol, Avon BS8 4HW
☎0117 9733833   Fax 0117 9733722
Contact *Chris James*

Film and video: broadcast, corporate, training and educational programmes. No unsolicited mss. 'We know that we only produce good programmes on the basis of good scripts. Can you work to tight deadlines, tight budgets and still be good?'

Wave Communication Group
Wave Studios, 12 Park Street, Lytham,
Lancashire FY8 5LU
☎01253 796399   Fax 01253 796399
Contact *Roy Turner*

Corporate film and video, including sell-throughs, sponsored, tourism-based programmes, and technical and specialist videograms. OUTPUT *England's North Country; Why Thermal Storage; Just Two Drops; Safe Isolation of Chemical Plant.* Unsolicited scripts not normally welcome. Keen to support new writing talent. 'We welcome contact with new writers whom we assess on track record or sample writing.'

Western Eye Business Television
Easton Business Centre, Felix Road, Easton,
Bristol, Avon BS5 0HE
☎0117 9415854   Fax 0117 9415899
Contact *Steve Spencer*

Corporate video production for Royal Mail, Motorola, HNE Healthcare, British Airways, and various charities. Use freelance writers. Unsolicited scripts not usually accepted.

Camilla Whitby Films
Deerfield House, Dunsfold Road, Plaistow,
West Sussex RH14 0PJ
☎01403 871406   Fax 01403 871403
Contact *Camilla Whitby, Roger Whitby*

Film, video and TV production for documentary and corporate material. OUTPUT *Horizon*

(BBC); *Equinox; High Interest* (Ch4). CLIENTS Nuclear Electric, IBM, ICI, Kenwood – Corporate.

Michael White Productions Ltd
13 Duke Street, St James's,
London SW1Y 6DB
☎0171 839 3971   Fax 0171 839 3836
Contact *Michael White*
High-output company whose credits include *Widow's Peak; White Mischief; Nuns on the Run* (co-production with **HandMade Films Ltd**); *The Comic Strip Series*. Also theatre projects, including *Fame; Me and Mamie O'Rourke; She Loves Me; Crazy for You*. Contributions are passed by Michael White to a script reader for consideration.

White City Films
79 Sutton Court Road, Chiswick, London W4 3EQ
☎0181 994 6795/4856   Fax 0181 995 9379
Contact *Aubrey Singer*
Film producers. OUTPUT has included *The Restoration of the Sistine Chapel* (NTV); *The Witness of the Long March* (Ch4); *Return to Saigon; Return to Peking; Joseph Needham, FRS FBA*. No unsolicited scripts.

David Wickes Productions Ltd
169 Queen's Gate, London SW7 5HE
☎0171 225 1382   Fax 0171 589 8847
Contact *David Wickes, Heide Wilsher*
Film and television drama.

Maurice Winnick Associates Ltd
66 Melbourne Way, Bush Hill Park, Enfield, Middlesex EN1 1XQ
☎0181 366 2978   Fax 0181 363 7523

Producer of quiz panel game shows for TV and theatre. No unsolicited material but always interested in new ideas/writing.

WLS On Line
Suite 6, Camelot Court, Alverton Street, Penzance, Cornwall TR18 2QN
☎01736 331833   Fax 01736 331822
Contact *Claire Welsh, Philip Morris*
Film and TV production for dramas and commercials. OUTPUT ranging from Korean commercials to features, both national and international. Have a growing list of overseas clients. Unsolicited scripts welcome. New writing 'always welcome'.

Wolfhouse Productions Ltd
13–15 Northgate, Heptonstall, West Yorkshire HX7 7ND
☎01422 844595
Contact *Jay Jones*
Formerly Flying Tiger Film & TV Productions. Corporate programmes, sell-throughs and sponsored, documentaries, commercials and experimental. Scripts, ideas and proposals welcome provided they are accompanied by s.a.e.

The Word Business
56 Leyborne Park, Kew, Richmond, Surrey TW9 3HA
☎0181 948 8346   Fax 0181 948 8346
Contact *John Mabbett*
Copywriter, scriptwriter, producer of corporate video material, generally low-budget projects. No unsolicited scripts. Writing is handled in-house.

Wordsmith TV
Cowburn House, Latchley Plain, Cornwall PL18 9AY
☎01822 833627   Fax 01822 834493
Contact *Kanthi Ford*
Video and TV: drama, documentary, corporate and commercials. OUTPUT *People Games; Home from Home*; and news coverage. Unsolicited scripts and ideas welcome. Keen to support new writing.

Workhouse Television
Granville House, St Peter Street, Winchester, Hampshire SO23 9AF
☎01962 863449   Fax 01962 841026
Television Coordinator *Carol Wade*
Video and TV: documentary, light entertainment, magazine programmes and corporate work. OUTPUT *Lifeschool A–Z* (BBC); *Big Day Out* (BBC); *Parents Talking; DIY; Cash in Hand* (The Learning Channel); *Up Front* (Meridian/ HTV); *Time Off; Tale of Four Sea Ports* (Meridian); *Mastercraft* (WestCountry TV); *Wiza Dora* (network). Corporate clients include BZW, Barclays, Price Waterhouse, Nuclear Electric. Programme briefs, outlines and treatments welcome. 'We hope to encourage new writing.'

Working Title Films Ltd
Oxford House, 76 Oxford Street, London W1N 9FD
☎0171 307 3000   Fax 0171 307 3001
Films *Tim Bevan, Eric Fellner, Alison Owen, Debra Hayward*

Television *Simon Wright*

Production arm of **PolyGram International**. Mostly feature films and TV drama; also family/children'sentertainment and TV comedy. OUTPUT Films: *My Beautiful Laundrette; Caravaggio* (with BFI); *The Tall Guy; For Queen & Country; Romeo is Bleeding; Posse; The Young Americans; The Hudsucker Proxy; Four Weddings and a Funeral.* Television: *TV Squash; The Borrowers; Tales of the City; Echoes; Smack and Thistle; News Hounds.* No unsolicited mss at present, but keen to encourage new writing nevertheless.

Worldview Pictures

35 Inkerman Road, London NW5 3BT
☎0171 916 4696   Fax 0171 916 1091

Contact *Stephen Trombley, Bruce Eadie*

Documentaries and series for television, plus theatrical. OUTPUT *Raising Hell: The Stories of A.J. Bannister; The Execution Protocol* (both for Discovery/BBC/France 2); *The Lynchburg Story; Drancy: A Concentration Camp in Paris;* (both for Discovery/Ch4/France 2). Synopses welcome from writers.

Worldwide Television News

The Interchange, Oval Road,
London NW1 7EP
☎0171 410 5200   Fax 0171 413 8302

Contact *Gerry O'Reilly*

Video and TV: documentary, news, features, sport and entertainment. OUTPUT *Roving Report* (weekly current affairs series); *Earthfile* (weekly environment series); *Earth Works* (children's environmental series); *Crime International* (reality-based crime show); plus many one-off specials. Unsolicited material welcome.

Wortman Productions UK

48 Chiswick Staithe, London W4 3TP
☎0181 994 8886

Producer *Neville Wortman*

Film, video and TV production for drama, documentary, commercials and corporate material. OUTPUT *House in the Country* John Julius Norwich (ITV series); *Ellington* (Jazz series); *'C'm on to My House* (TV feature series); *Florence Nightingale* (feature film in development); *Go West* (series in development for CCTV – China). Numerous major corporate videos. Send outline treatments 2–3 pages and s.a.e. and a couple of pages of dialogue if appropriate. Open to new writing.

ZED Ltd

2nd Floor, 29 Heddon Street,
London W1R 7LL
☎0171 494 3181   Fax 0171 434 1203

Contact *Glenn Wilhide, Sophie Balhetchet, Ruth Walsh*

Television drama. OUTPUT includes *The Manageress; The Camomile Lawn; The Missing Reel* (co-production), all for Channel 4.

Zenith Productions Ltd

43–45 Dorset Street, London W1H 4AB
☎0171 224 2440   Fax 0171 224 3194

Script Executive *Ming Ho*

Feature films and TV. OUTPUT Films: *Prick Up Your Ears; Deadly Advice; Just Like A Woman,* and Hal Hartley's *Simple Men* and *Amateur.* Television: *Inspector Morse; Paradise Club; Shoot to Kill; Firm Friends; 99–1; Hamish MacBeth.* No unsolicited scripts.

The Zoom Production Company

102 Dean Street, London W1V 5RA
☎0171 434 3895   Fax 0171 734 2751

Managing Director *Mark Bergin*

Film and video production for corporate clients. Full spectrum of corporate communications in both public and private sectors.

Theatre Producers

Aba Daba

30 Upper Park Road, London NW3 2UT
☎0171 722 5395

Contact *Aline Waites, Robin Hunter*

Plays and satirical pantomimes performed at venues like the Water Rats, Underneath the Arches and the Canal Café in London. The company writes all its own material but would be happy to consider some of the great piles of unsolicited mss they receive, were it not for the fact that there is absolutely no money available for outsiders.

Actors Touring Company

Alford House, Aveline Street,
London SE11 5DQ
☎0171 735 8311Fax 0171 735 1031 attn ATC

Artistic Director *Nick Philippou*

'Actors Touring Company turn European classics into modern masterpieces.' ATC produces new versions of either lesser-known plays by well-known writers (eg *The Modern Husband* by Henry Fielding) or seminal plays by writers unknown in the UK (eg *Celestina* by Ferdinand de Rojas). Collaborations with writers are based on adaptation and/or translation work and unsolicited mss will only considered in this category. 'We endeavour to read mss but do not have the resources to do so quickly.' As a small-scale company, all plays must have a cast of eight or less.

Almeida Theatre Company

Almeida Street, Islington, London N1 1TA
☎0171 226 7432   Fax 0171 704 9581

Artistic Directors *Ian McDiarmid, Jonathan Kent*

FOUNDED 1980. Now in its seventh year as a full-time producing theatre, presenting a year-round theatre and music programme in which international writers, composers, performers, directors and designers are invited to work with British artists on challenging new and classical works. Previous productions: *Butterfly Kiss; The Rules of the Game; Medea; No Man's Land; The Rehearsal; Bajazet; Galileo; Moonlight; The School for Wives; Hamlet.* No unsolicited mss: 'our producing programme is very limited and linked to individual directors and actors'.

Alternative Theatre Company Ltd

Bush Theatre, Shepherds Bush Green,
London W12 8QD
☎0171 602 3703   Fax 0171 602 7614

Literary Manager *Joanne Reardon*

FOUNDED 1972. Trading as The Bush Theatre. Produces about six new plays a year (principally British) and hosts up to four visiting companies also producing new work: 'we are a writer's theatre.' Previous productions: *Kiss of the Spiderwoman* Manuel Puig; *More Light* Snoo Wilson; *Raping the Gold* Lucy Gannon; *Handful of Stars* Billy Roche; *Boys Mean Business* Catherine Johnson; *The Pitchfork Disney* Philip Ridley; *Phoenix* Roy MacGregor; *Democracy* John Murrell; *Beautiful Thing* Jonathan Harvey. Scripts are read by a team of associates, then discussed with the management, a process which takes three months. The theatre offers a small number of commissions, recommissions to ensure further drafts on promising plays, and a guarantee against royalties so writers are not financially penalised even though the plays are produced in a small house.

Yvonne Arnaud Theatre

Millbrook, Guildford, Surrey GU1 3UX
☎01483 440077   Fax 01483 64071

Contact *James Barber*

New work always considered. Credits include: *Otherwise Engaged* Simon Gray; *Time of My Life* Alan Ayckbourn; *The Weekend* Michael Palin; *Glyn and It* Ken Hoare; *Home* David Storey; *Cellmates* Simon Gray.

Belgrade Theatre, Coventry

Belgrade Square, Coventry CV1 1GS
☎01203 256431   Fax 01203 550680

Chief Executive *To be appointed*

Main-house productions include a significant number of first and second productions with most new plays commissioned by the theatre. The studio theatre is dedicated to new writing, first and second productions. Is part of the *Stagecoach* Initiative – a creative partnership between playwrights and theatre companies to find and develop new plays through producing an annual festival that workshops selected plays. The Coventry Playwrights Group based at the theatre also runs a script reading service for unsolicited scripts.

Birmingham Repertory Theatre
Broad Street, Birmingham B1 2EP
☎0121 236 6771   Fax 0121 236 7883
Artistic Director *Bill Alexander*

Main-house and studio forum. In the main theatre plays are chosen because they fully exploit the epic size of the stage (with its 60-foot proscenium) and auditorium (900 seats in a single curved rake). This applies to new plays as much as to established ones. In the studio theatre, the Rep presents a mix of touring and in-house productions throughout the year, and priority is given to the work of local writers. 'We have a panel of readers who assess all new plays sent in to us. We run a writers' group in association with our local theatre writers' union, for writers based in the West Midlands, who meet to read and discuss scripts and work in progress.'

Black Theatre Co-op
8 Bradbury Street, London N16 8JN
☎0171 249 9150   Fax 0171 275 9440
Artistic Director *Joan-Ann Maynard*
Administrator *Donna Munday*

FOUNDED 1978. Plays to a mixed audience, approximately 65% female. Usually tour nationally twice a year. 'Committed in the first instance to new writing by Black British writers and work which relates to the Black culture and experience throughout the Diaspora, although anything considered.' Unsolicited mss welcome.

Bootleg Theatre Company
Sherborne House, 20 Greyfriars Close, Salisbury, Wiltshire SP1 2LR
☎01722 421476
Contact *Colin Burden*

FOUNDED 1984. Tries to encompass as wide an audience as possible and has a tendency towards plays with socially relevant themes. A good bet for new writing since unsolicited mss are very welcome. 'Our policy is to produce new and/or rarely seen plays and anything received is given the most serious consideration.' Actively seeks to obtain grants to commission new writers for the company. Playwrights whose work has been performed include Tony Marchant, Barrie Keeffe, Sam Snape and Mike Harris. Future productions include a revised version of Philip Goulding's *Different Animal, Strange Weather* by Susie Campbell and starring Honey Bane, plus new work by Peter Merron, Robert Hamilton and Tony Marchant.

Borderline Theatre Company
Darlington New Church, North Harbour Street, Ayr KA8 8AA
☎01292 281010   Fax 01292 263825
Artistic Director *John Murtagh*

FOUNDED 1974. A touring company taking shows to main-house theatres in city centres and small venues in outlying districts, plus the Edinburgh Festival, Mayfest and, occasionally, London. Mainly new and contemporary work, plus revivals: *George's Marvellous Medicine* Roald Dahl (a spectacular children's show); *Misterio Buffo* Dario Fo (one-man show with Robbie Coltrane); *A Night in the Ukraine* Voxburgh & Laxarus; *Four in a Million* Les Blair; *Shanghied* Liz Lochhead; plus pantomime and children's plays. Synopsis with cast size preferred in the first instance. Borderline try to include one new work every season. 'We are looking for writing which is stimulating, relevant and, above all, entertaining, which will lend itself to dynamic physical presentation.'

Bristol Express Theatre Company
16 Frederick Street, Totterdown, Bristol, Avon BS4 3AZ
☎0117 9717279
Director *Andy Jordan*

A non-funded, professional, middle-scale national touring company which has a continuing commitment to the discovery, development and encouragement of new writing, principally through its research and development programme *The Play's The Thing!* This consists of public/private staged and rehearsed readings; workshops and full-scale productions. Previous productions: *Child's Play* Jonathan Wolfman; *Winter Darkness* Allan Cubitt; *Prophets in the Black Sky* John Matshikiza; *Lunatic & Lover* Michael Meyer; *Heaven* Sarah Aicher; *Syme* Michael Bourdages; *Gangster Apparel* Richard Vetere. 'We look for plays that are socially/emotionally/theatrically/politically significant, analytical and challenging. The company is keen to produce work which attempts to mix genres (and create new ones!), is eloquent and honest, while remaining accessible and entertaining.'

Bristol Old Vic Company
Theatre Royal, King Street, Bristol, Avon BS1 4ED
☎0117 9493993   Fax 0117 9493996

The Bristol Old Vic has a serious commitment to new writing, however, 'we are unable to accept unsolicited scripts at the present time. Having achieved "Writer Friendly" status, we have a great many scripts to look at, and a number we would like to produce. Rather than offer false hope we ask writers to "watch this space". We hope to offer a much warmer welcome soon.'

Bush Theatre
See **Alternative Theatre Company**

Cambridge Theatre Company
25 Short Street, London SE1 8LJ
☎0171 401 9797   Fax 0171 401 9777
Artistic Director *Mike Alfreds*

Limited script reading facilities. Unsolicited mss may not be read. Letters and synopses welcome; scripts only returned with s.a.e.

Carnival (Films & Theatre) Ltd
See **Film, TV and Video Producers**

Chester Gateway Theatre Trust Ltd
Hamilton Place, Chester,
Cheshire CH1 2BH
☎01244 344238   Fax 01244 317277
Artistic Director *Jeremy Raison*

FOUNDED 1968. Plays to a broad audience across a wide range of work, classical to contemporary, including Shakespeare, John Godber, Ira Levin, Alan Ayckbourn, Arthur Miller, Ibsen, etc. Current season has an emphasis on new writing. 'We are in the process of developing new writing and have a resident playwright's group.' Writer-in-Residence is Lavinia Murray. Small-cast material, children's and young people, large-scale youth theatre, people with learning difficulties, plays by women and adaptations of novels. Anything with a cast of over eight is unlikely to reach production. The smaller the cast the better. Scripts welcome but reading will take some time.

Churchill Theatre
High Street, Bromley, Kent BR1 1HA
☎0181 464 7131   Fax 0181 290 6968
Contact *John Wallbank*

Produces a broad variety of popular plays, both new and revivals. Previous productions: *Phantom of the Opera* Ken Hill; *Some Like It Hot; Don't Dress for Dinner* Marc Camoletti (adap. Robin Hawdon); *High Flyers* Paul Kember; *A Slight Hangover* Ian Ogilvy; *Intent to Kill* Ted Willis; *The Heiress* Henry James. Most productions go on either to tour or into the West End.

Citizens Theatre
Gorbals, Glasgow G5 9DS
☎0141 429 5561   Fax 0141 429 7374
Artistic Director *Giles Havergal*

No formal new play policy. The theatre has a play reader but opportunities to do new work are limited.

Michael Codron Ltd
Aldwych Theatre Offices, Aldwych, London WC2B 4DF
☎0171 240 8291   Fax 0171 240 8467
General Manager *Gareth Johnson*

Michael Codron Ltd manages the Aldwych and owns the Vaudeville Theatre in London's West End. The plays it produces don't necessarily go into these theatres, but always tend to be big-time West End fare. Previous productions: *Hapgood; Look Look; Uncle Vanya; The Sneeze; Rise and Fall of Little Voice; Arcadia; Dead Funny*. No particular rule of thumb on subject matter or treatment. The acid test is whether 'something appeals to Michael'. Straight plays rather than musicals.

The Coliseum, Oldham
Fairbottom Street, Oldham,
Lancashire OL1 3SW
☎0161 624 1731   Fax 0161 624 5318
Artistic Director *Warren Hooper*

Considered a good bet for new playwrights, the Coliseum is besieged by more scripts than it can read. 'We like to do new writing that's popular and relevant to our audience.' Previous productions: *A Night on the Tiles* Frank Vickery; *Girlfriends* Howard Goodall; *Stage Fright* Peter Fieldson; *The Steamie* Tony Roper; *Clowns on a School Outing* Ken Campbell; *Hotstuff*. The Coliseum has recently opened up its rehearsal room as a studio theatre (max. capacity audience of 60), and the theatre is therefore looking for new, small-cast plays with simple staging requirements. Plays often come by way of contacts or commissions but good unsolicited scripts still stand a chance. Enclose a large s.a.e. Response time about eight weeks. Ideas in writing preferred to unsolicited scripts.

Communicado Theatre Company
12A Castle Terrace, Edinburgh EH1 2DP
☎0131 228 5465   Fax 0131 221 9003
Artistic Director *Gerard Mulgrew*

FOUNDED 1982. Scottish touring company which aims to present dynamic and challenging theatre to the widest range of audience in

Scotland and internationally. 'We encourage new writing, especially, but not exclusively, of Scots origin. Unfortunately there are no facilities for dealing with unsolicited scripts'. Productions have included: *The House with the Green Shutters* adapt. Gerard Mulgrew; *Carmen 1936* Stephen Jeffreys; *The Hunchback of Notre Dame* adapt. Andrew Dallmeyer; *Mary Queen of Scots Got Her Head Chopped Off* Liz Lochhead; *Blood Wedding* trans. David Johnston; *Cyrano de Bergerac* trans. Edwin Morgan; *Crying Wolf* Gerald Mangan; *Sacred Hearts* Sue Glover.

Contact Theatre Company
Oxford Road, Manchester M15 6JA
☎0161 274 3434   Fax 0161 273 6286
Artistic Director *Benjamin Twist*

FOUNDED 1972. Plays predominantly to a young audience (15–30), with an interest in contemporary work, especially from the North-West, and in highly theatrical writing. Limited opportunities for new plays without a specific marketing 'hook' for young people. Recent new productions: *Criminals in Love* George F. Walker (British première). Work by black, female and young writers, and work which creates opportunities for black and female performers, is particularly welcome. Commissions up to two plays a year.

Crucible Theatre
55 Norfolk Street, Sheffield S1 1DA
☎0114 2760621   Fax 0114 2701532
Contact *Director's Secretary*

Unsolicited scripts are seen by a reader and a small number may go on to a rehearsed reading/workshop. Finished scripts are always preferred to synopses or ideas. Scripts sent by a recognised theatre agent, director or actor are given more attention.

Cwmni Theatr Gwynedd
Deiniol Road, Bangor, Gwynedd LL57 2TL
☎01248 351707   Fax 01248 351915
Artistic Director *Graham Laker*

FOUNDED 1984. A mainstream company, performing in major theatres on the Welsh circuit. Welsh-language work only at present. Classic Welsh plays, translations of European repertoire and new work, including adaptations from novels. New Welsh work always welcome; work in English considered if appropriate for translation (i.e. dealing with issues relevant to Wales). 'We are keen to discuss projects with established writers and offer commissions where possible.' Other activities include the hosting of an annual new writing festival in March.

Derby Playhouse
Eagle Centre, Derby DE1 2NF
☎01332 363271   Fax 01332 294412
Artistic Director *Mark Clements*

FOUNDED 1948. Plays to a mixed audience. Currently developing a younger audience so particularly interested in work suitable for them. Previous productions: *Richard III* ; *Happy Families* John Godber; *Assassins* Stephen Sondheim. Studio theatre: *Ham* Mark Chatterton (première). Unsolicited mss welcome. 'We read all plays submitted, and have a small budget for commissioning.'

Dramatis Personae Ltd
19 Regency Street, London SW1P 4BY
☎0171 834 9300
Contacts *Nathan Silver*

Run by Nathan Silver and Nicolas Kent, the company turns its hand to a variety of production projects and is currently co-producing with the BBC on arts documentary subjects. No unsolicited scripts. Approach by letter in the first instance.

Druid Theatre Company
Chapel Lane, Galway, Republic of Ireland
☎00 353 91 68660   Fax 00 353 91 63109
Literary Managers *Garry Hynes, Jane Daly*

FOUNDED 1975. Plays to a wide-ranging audience, urban and rural, from young adults to the elderly. National and international theatre with an emphasis on new Irish work, though contemporary European theatre is commonplace in the repertoire. At least one new Irish work a year, however, is commissioned and the company is keen for more. No large-scale work as finances are prohibitive. Enclose s.a.e. for return of scripts. Runs workshops.

The Dukes
Moor Lane, Lancaster LA1 1QE
☎01524 67461   Fax 01524 846817
Artistic Director *Han Duijvendak*

FOUNDED 1971. Plays to a mixed audience which is difficult to target. Previous productions: *Romeo and Juliet; The Hobbit* (outdoor promenades); *Forty Years On* Alan Bennett; *Death and the Maiden* Ariel Dorfman; *A Christmas Carol* Dickens; *Fishy Tales* Chris Speyer. Developing work with music and for young children. No unsolicited mss.

Dundee Repertory Theatre

Tay Square, Dundee DD1 1PB
☎01382 227684   Fax 01382 228609
Artistic Director *Hamish Glen*

FOUNDED 1939. Plays to a varied audience. Translations and adaptations of classics, and new local plays. Most new work is commissioned. Interested in contemporary plays in translation and in new Scottish writing. No scripts except by prior arrangement.

Eastern Angles Theatre Company

Sir John Mills Theatre, Gatacre Road, Ipswich, Suffolk IP1 2LQ
☎01473 218202   Fax 01473 250954
Contact *Ivan Cutting*

FOUNDED 1982. Plays to a rural audience for the most part. New work only: some commissioned, some devised by the company, some researched documentaries. Unsolicited mss welcome. 'We are always keen to develop and produce new writing, especially that which is germane to a rural area.' Involved in **Eastern Arts'** Write Lines project.

English Stage Company Ltd
See **Royal Court Theatre**

English Touring Theatre

New Century Building, Hill Street, Crewe CW1 1BX
☎01270 501800   Fax 01270 501888
Artistic Director *Stephen Unwin*

FOUNDED 1993. National touring company visiting middle-scale receiving houses and arts centres throughout England. Mostly mainstream. Largely classical programme, but with increasing interest to tour one modern English play per year. Strong commitment to Education and Community Outreach work.

Everyman Theatre

5–9 Hope Street, Liverpool L1 9BH
☎0151 708 0338   Fax 0151 709 0398
Artistic Director *Peter Rowe*

After re-opening in February 1994, the Everyman is on course to once again be a major producer of new work. By 1996 they expect to have a policy in place committed to developing local and national writing talent.

Everyman Theatre (Cheltenham)
See **Gloucestershire Everyman Theatre Company Ltd**

Farnham Repertory Company Ltd

Redgrave Theatre, Brightwells, Farnham, Surrey GU9 7SB
☎01252 727000   Fax 01252 712350
Artistic Director *Roland Jacquarello*

Plays to a middle-class, middle-aged audience in the main, but there is a growing younger audience. Classics, new plays, 20th-century dramas, comedies, thrillers. Unsolicited scripts welcome. New writing produced 'as often as we can'. Not interested in plays with large casts.

Field Day Theatre Company

Foyle Arts Centre, Old Foyle College, Lawrence Hill, Derry BT48 7NJ
☎01504 360196   Fax 01504 365419

ESTABLISHED 1980, Field Day is a touring company which tends to commission plays from Irish writers. Their 1994 production was a version by Frank McGuinness of Chekhov's *Uncle Vanya*.

Finborough Theatre
See **The Steam Industry**

Vanessa Ford Productions

Upper House Farm, Upper House Lane, Shamley Green, Guildford, Surrey GU5 0SX
☎01483 278203/268530   Fax 01483 278203
Contact *Vanessa Ford*

Touring and West End. Previous productions: *Treasure Island; A Christmas Carol; The Magician's Nephew; The Wind in the Willows; Winnie the Pooh; The Voyage of Dawn Treader; The Horse and His Boy*. Also classical seasons touring and in London. Keen to see new work. Finished scripts, ideas or synopses welcome, but the company tends to do a lot of its own writing in-house.

Robert Fox Ltd

6 Beauchamp Place, London SW3 1NG
☎0171 584 6855   Fax 0171 225 1638
Contact *Robert Fox*

Producers and co-producers of work suitable for West End production. Previous productions: *Another Country; Chess; Lettice and Lovage; Madhouse in Goa; Burn This; When She Danced; The Ride Down Mount Morgan; Me & Mamie O'Rouke; The Importance of Being Earnest; The Seagull; Goosepimples; Vita & Virginia; The Weekend; Three Tall Women*. Scripts, while usually by established playwrights, are always read.

Gate Theatre Company Ltd
11 Pembridge Road, London W11 3HQ
☎0171 229 5387   Fax 0171 221 6055

Literary Manager *Gaynor MacFarlane*

FOUNDED 1979. Plays to a mixed, London-wide audience, depending on production. Aims to produce British premières of plays which originate from abroad and translations of neglected classics. Most work is with translators. Previous productions: *Damned For Despair* Tirso de Molina (tr. Laurence Boswell); *Flamingo* Bode Sowande; *The Television Programme* Michel Vinaver (tr. David & Hannah Bradby); *Seven Doors* Botho Strauss (tr. Antony Meech); *Hecuba* Euripides (tr. Kenneth McLeish); *Elisabeth II* Thomas Bernhard (tr. Meredith Oakes); *Madness in Valencia* Lope de Vega (tr. David Johnston); *Bohemian Lights* Ramòn Maria del Valle-Inclàn (tr. David Johnston); *The Great Highway* Strindberg (tr. Kenneth McLeish). Unsolicited scripts welcome. Enclose s.a.e.

Gay Sweatshop
The Holborn Centre, Three Cups Yard, Sandland Street, London WC1R 4PZ
☎0171 242 1168   Fax 0171 242 3143

Artistic Directors *James Neale-Kennerley, Lois Weaver*

FOUNDED 1975. Plays to a wide audience, particularly one interested in lesbian/gay theatre and sexual politics. Previous productions: *Threesome* Claire Dowie, David Greenspan & Phyllis Wagg; *Kitchen Matters* Bryony Lavery; *Raising the Wreck* Sue Frumin; *Compromised Immunity* Andy Kirby; *This Island's Mine* Philip Osment; *Stupid Cupid* Phil Willmott; *Fucking Martin* adapted by Malcolm Sutherland from the novel by Dale Peck. Also experimental performance club *One Night Stands*, annual *Queerschool* for gay and lesbian theatre practitioners; also festivals of new work presented as staged rehearsed readings: *Gay Sweatshop x 10; GS x 12*. Committed to encouraging new work by gay, lesbian, black and disabled playwrights. Work submitted generally includes representation of those sections of the community which are under-represented in mainstream theatre. Unsolicited scripts welcome.

Geese Theatre Company
See **MAC – The Centre for Birmingham**

Gloucestershire Everyman Theatre Company Ltd
Regent Street, Cheltenham, Gloucestershire GL50 1HQ
☎01242 512515   Fax 01242 224305

Artistic Director *Martin Houghton*
New Writing Co-ordinator *Sebastian Baczkiewicz*

FOUNDED 1891. Describes its audience as broad, and is in the process of developing a younger audience. Revivals of both classic and contemporary plays; musicals, new plays with particular emphasis on the life of the region; Christmas shows for children and families. Unsolicited mss welcome but approach in writing with brief synopsis in the first instance is preferred. Priority is given to local writers and plays need to be relevant to the region.

Derek Glynne
17 Wilton Place, London SW1X 8RL
☎0171 245 6912   Fax 0171 245 6468

Derek Glynne is a producer in partnership with American and Australian producers. Plays are largely for Australian and American audiences. Most of these originate abroad so there is little hope for playwrights here.

Graeae Theatre Company
Interchange Studios, Dalby Street, London NW5 3NQ
☎0171 267 1959   Fax 0171 267 2703
Minicom 0171 267 3164

Artistic Director *Ewan Marshall*
Administrative Director *Steve Mannix*
Administrator *Alison Barker*

Europe's premier theatre company of disabled people. The company tours nationally and internationally with innovative theatre productions highlighting both historical and contemporary disabled experience. Graeae also runs T.I.E. and educational programmes available to schools, youth clubs and day centres nationally, provides vocational training in theatre arts (including playwriting) and runs London's only fully accessible Young People's Theatre Programme for the disabled community. Unsolicited scripts – particularly from disabled writers – welcome. New work examining disability issues is commissioned.

Greenwich Theatre Ltd
Crooms Hill, London SE10 8ES
☎0181 858 4447   Fax 0181 858 8042

Artistic Director *Matthew Francis*

Strong policy of encouraging new writing, which must by necessity be two, maybe three, productions per year. 'We do positively encourage writers to send in scripts; we are always on the look-out for new writing which is accessible to our mixed audience.' Less keen on initial approach with ideas, preferring to read a finished script, but write in the first instance and do not send scripts until requested.

Hampstead Theatre

Swiss Cottage Centre, Avenue Road,
London NW3 3EX
☎0171 722 9224   Fax 0171 722 3860
Literary Manager *Ben Jancovich*

Produces new plays and the occasional modern classic. Scripts are initially assessed by a team of script readers and their responses are shared with management in monthly script meetings. The literary manager and/or artistic director then read and consider many submissions in more detail. It can therefore take 2–3 months to reach a decision. Writers produced in the past ten years include Marguerite Duras, Terry Eagleton, Brad Fraser, Brian Friel, Beth Henley, Stephen Jeffreys, Terry Johnson, Tom Kempinski, Hanif Kureishi, Tony Kushner, Mike Leigh, Doug Lucie, Frank McGuinness, Mustapha Matura, Anthony Minghella, Rona Munro, Jennifer Phillips, Dennis Potter, Philip Ridley, Martin Sherman and Michael Wall.

Harrogate Theatre Company

Oxford Street, Harrogate, North Yorkshire
HG1 1QF
☎01423 502710   Fax 01423 563205
Artistic Director *Andrew Manley*

FOUNDED 1950. Describes its audience as 'eclectic, all ages and looking for innovation'. Previous productions: *The Marriage of Figaro* (commissioned adaptation of Beaumarchais, Mozart, Da Ponte); *Barber of Seville* (commissioned translation and adaptation of Beaumarchais, Rossini and Sterbini); *School for Wives*; *A Man with Connections*; *Don Juan*; *The Baltimore Waltz* Paula Vogel (European première); *Hot 'n' Throbbing* Paula Vogel (European première); *My Children! My Africa!*; *Wings* (Kopit, Lunden & Perlman European première); new adaptations of *The Government Inspector* and *The Turn of the Screw*; European premières of adaptations/translations by David Mamet of *The Cherry Orchard* and *Uncle Vanya*; *Marisol* Jose Rivera. Always struggling to produce new work.

Haymarket Theatre Company

Haymarket Theatre, Wote Street, Basingstoke, Hampshire RG21 1NW
☎01256 55844   Fax 01256 57130
Artistic Director *Adrian Reynolds*

Main house and studio. Programme in 1994, main house: *The Rise and Fall of Little Voice* Jim Cartwright; *Dangerous Obsession* N. J. Crisp; *One Good Turn* Francis Verber/Ray Cooney. Studio: *Impatience* Pete Lawson (world première). In 1995: *The Innocents*; William Archibald; *The Trouble With Old Lovers* Angela Huth (world première); *Dancing at Lughnasa* Brian Friel; *The Diary of Anne Frank* Frances Goodrich and Albert Hackett; *Stepping Out* Richard Harris. The Haymarket Theatre has recently re-opened after a £3.2 million refurbishment funded by Basingstoke and Deane Borough Council.

The Hiss & Boo Company

24 West Grove, Walton on Thames, Surrey
KT12 5NX
☎01932 248931   Fax 01932 248946
Contact *Ian Liston*

Particularly interested in new thrillers, comedy thrillers, comedy and melodrama – must be commercial full-length plays. Also interested in plays/plays with music for children. No one-acts. Previous productions: *Sleigh Ride; Beauty and the Beast; An Ideal Husband; Mr Men's Magical Island; Mr Men and the Space Pirates; Nunsense; Corpse!; Groucho: A Life in Revue; See How They Run; Christmas Cat and the Pudding Pirates; Pinocchio*. No unsolicited scripts. Send synopsis and introductory letter in the first instance.

Hull Truck Theatre Company

Spring Street, Hull HU2 8RW
☎01482 224800   Fax 01482 581182
Executive Producer *Barry Nettleton*

John Godber, of *Teechers, Bouncers, Up 'n' Under* fame, the artistic director of this high-profile Northern company since 1984, has very much dominated the scene in the past with his own successful plays. The emphasis is still on new writing but Godber's work continues to be toured extensively. Most new plays are commissioned. Previous productions: *Dead Fish* Gordon Steel; *Off Out* Gill Adams; *Fish and Leather* Gill Adams; *Happy Families* John Godber. The company now reads all unsolicited scripts and aims to respond within two months. Bear in mind the artistic policy of Hull Truck, which is 'accessibility and popularity'. In general they are not interested in musicals, or in plays with casts of more than eight.

Humberside Theatre in Education

Humberside Cultural Enterprise Centre,
Middleton Street, Springbank, Hull HU3 1NB
☎01482 324256   Fax 01482 326190
Artistic Director *John Hazlett*

FOUNDED 1983. Full-time company playing to

Humberside schools, with a strong tradition of devising its own work. Previous productions: *Natural Forces* (for 13–14-year-olds); *The Wrong Side of the River* by Mary Cooper (for 15–18-year-olds); *Whose Voices?* by John Hazlett, Linda Taylor and Carol Bush (for 10–12-year-olds); *Festival* devised by the company for rural schools and communities. Interested in developments in new writing and in working with new writers.

Inner City Theatre Company
26 Stodart Road, London SE20 8ET
☎0181 659 2930   Fax 0181 659 2930
Artistic Director *Les Miller*

FOUNDED 1982. London and national small-scale touring. Also co-productions with repertory theatres. New plays on topical themes of particular interest to urban multi-cultural audiences. Works for both young (12–18 years) and adult audiences. OUTPUT *Single Sex* Dave Simpson; *Hitting Home* James Woolf. No unsolicited scripts but treatments welcome. Tries to commission one script annually and seeks to find or develop at least two others. Interested in sharp, witty material, preferably 'entertaining, up-front and fast-moving'.

Richard Jackson
59 Knightsbridge, London SW1X 7RA
☎0171 235 3671   Fax 0171 235 6126

Independent-minded producer who only does 'plays which appeal to me'. Besieged by mss, he tends to go out for what he wants (particularly European material). Works mainly in smaller-scale London fringe theatres taking risks the West End can no longer afford. Credits include bringing *Quentin Crisp* to a theatre audience. Previous productions: *Don't Play with Love* Alfred de Musset; *Pasolini* Michel Azama; *I Ought to Be in Pictures* Neil Simon; *Eden Cinema* and *Suzanna Andler* Marguerite Duras; *Noonbreak* Paul Claudel; *The Eagle Has Two Heads* Jean Cocteau; *Happy Days* Samuel Beckett.

Pola Jones Associates Ltd
14 Dean Street, London W1V 5AH
☎0171 439 1165   Fax 0171 437 3994
Contact *Andre Ptaszynski, Andrew Fell*

FOUNDED 1982. Comedy and musicals preferred. Previous productions have included: *Neville's Island*; *The Nerd*, with Rowan Atkinson; *Progress* Doug Lucie; *The Gambler*, with Mel Smith. Currently touring musicals including *Return to the Forbidden Planet* and *Me and My Girl*. Also produces comedy for TV: *Tygo Road*; *Joking Apart*. Unsolicited scripts welcome.

Stephen Joseph Theatre
Valley Bridge Parade, Scarborough,
North Yorkshire YO11 2PL
☎01723 370540   Fax 01723 360506
Artistic Director *Alan Ayckbourn*

A small theatre-in-the-round seating 307 people, with additional studio theatre seating 75–90. Move into a new and permanent home in 1996 when the theatre's programme will expand. Positive policy on new work. For obvious reasons, Alan Ayckbourn's work is featured heavily in the repertoire, but plays from other sources are encouraged. Previous productions: *Neville's Island* Tim Firth; *Woman in Black* (adap. Stephen Mallatratt); *The Ballroom* Peter King; *The End of the Food Chain* Tim Firth; *Penny Blue* Vanessa Brooks; *White Lies* Robert Shearman. Plays should have a strong narrative and be accessible. Minimum three-month reading period 'but, sadly, it can take longer'. S.a.e. required for return of mss.

Bill Kenwright Ltd
55–59 Shaftesbury Avenue,
London W1V 8JA
☎0171 439 4466   Fax 0171 437 8370
Contact *Bill Kenwright*

Presents both revivals and new shows for West End and touring theatres. Although new work tends to be by established playwrights, this does not preclude or prejudice new plays from new playwrights. Scripts should be addressed to Bill Kenwright with a covering letter. 'We have enormous amounts of scripts sent to us. They are read systematically. Please do not phone; the return of your script or contact with you will take place in time.'

King's Head Theatre
115 Upper Street, London N1 1QN
☎0171 226 8561   Fax 0171 226 8507

The first pub theatre since Shakespearean times and the first venue in the UK for dinner theatre, the King's Head produces some strong work, including previously neglected work by playwrights such as Terence Rattigan, Geatrix Newman and Vivian Ellis. Noël Coward's work also has a strong presence; the company is committed to its contribution to the reappraisal of Coward's work. Previous productions: *Philadelphia, Here I Come!* Brian Friel; *Accapulco* Steven Berkoff; *Elegies for Angels, Punks and Raging Queens* Bill Russell; *A Day in the Death of Joe Egg* Peter Nichols. Unsolicited submissions are not encouraged.

Knightsbridge Theatrical Productions Ltd

21 New Fetter Lane, London EC4A 1JJ
☎0171 583 8687   Fax 0171 583 1040

Contact *Mr S. H. Gray*

Straight plays and musicals suitable for production in the West End only.

Komedia

14–17 Manchester Street, Brighton,
East Sussex BN2 1TF
☎01273 694583   Fax 01273 563515

Contact *David Lavender*

Komedia is a new theatre venue which promotes the innovative and international. It combines theatre and cabaret performance spaces and presents its own productions as well as the work of top small-scale touring companies and performers. Mss of new plays welcome.

Leeds Playhouse

See **West Yorkshire Playhouse**

Leicester Haymarket Theatre

Belgrave Gate, Leicester LE1 3YQ
☎0116 2530021   Fax 0116 2513310

Artistic Director *Paul Kerryson*

'We aim for a balanced programme of original and established works.' Recent productions include: *Safar* (première); *Through the Leaves*; *Queen & I* (première); *Destiny of Me* (British première); *Lives and Loves* (première); *Pacific Overtures; Follies; Calamity Jane*. A script reading panel has been established, and new writing is welcome.

Library Theatre Company

St Peter's Square, Manchester M2 5PD
☎0161 234 1913   Fax 0161 228 6481

Artistic Director *Christopher Honer*

Produces new and contemporary work, as well as occasional classics. No unsolicited mss. Send outline of the nature of the script first. Encourages new writing through the commissioning of new plays and through a programme of staged readings to help writers' development.

Live Theatre Company

7–8 Trinity Chare, Newcastle upon Tyne
NE1 3DF
☎0191 261 2694

Artistic Director *Max Roberts*

FOUNDED 1973. The company has recently won a revenue funding franchise from Northern Arts to continue to produce work at both its newly refurbished and fully developed 200-seat venue, The Live Theatre, and to tour extensively regionally and nationally. Company policy is to produce high quality accessible theatrical productions primarily for the Northern Region: particularly for those audiences currently alienated from traditional arts and theatre venues. The company produces new and existing plays by established and new writers who share the above interests. As well as full-scale productions, workshops, rehearsed readings and other new writing, activities are initiated intending to foster and develop new writing. The company also enjoys a close relationship with Northern Playwrights Society. Recent plays include *Close the Coalhouse Door* Alan Plater; *Only Joking* Steve Chambers; *Blow Your House Down* Sarah Daniels; *The Grass House* Pauline Hadaway (writer in residence), *Your Home in the West* Rod Wooden, *Seafarers* Tom Hadaway, *Up and Running* Phil Woods, *Buffalo Girls* by Karin Young.

Liverpool Everyman

See **Everyman Theatre**

Liverpool Playhouse

Williamson Square, Liverpool L1 1EL
☎0151 709 8478   Fax 0151 709 7113

Chief Executive and Artistic Director *Ian Kellgren*

Regional theatre very active in promoting new writing, with an impressive record of first plays. Previous productions: *Self-Catering: A Short History of the World* Andrew Cullen; *Weldon Rising* Phyllis Nagy; *At Fifty She Discovered the Sea* Denise Chalem; *Boy* Shaun Duggan; *The Dark Side* Liam Lloyd; *Home for the Holidays* Cheryl Martin; *A Message for the Broken Hearted* Gregory Motton; *Somewhere* Judith Johnson. Scripts welcome.

London Bubble Theatre Company

3–5 Elephant Lane, London SE16 4JD
☎0171 237 4434   Fax 0171 231 2366

Artistic Director *Jonathan Petherbridge*

Produces workshops, plays and events for a mixed audience of theatregoers and non-theatregoers, wide-ranging in terms of age, culture and class. Previous productions: *Measure for Measure; The Good Person of Sezuan; Brainpower*. Unsolicited mss welcome but 'our reading service is extremely limited and there can be a considerable wait before we can give a response'. Produces at least one new show a year which is invariably commissioned.

Lyric Theatre Hammersmith

King Street, London W6 0QL
☎0181 741 0824   Fax 0181 741 7694
Chief Executive *Sue Storr*
Artistic Director *Neil Bartlett*
Administrative Producer *Simon Mellor*

Theatre with a long tradition of putting on new work: *State of Affairs* Graham Swannell (tr. Duchess); *Mumbo Jumbo* Robin Glendinning (Mobil prizewinner); *Atonement* Barry Collins; *Asylum* Paul Kember; *Madhouse in Goa* Martin Sherman; *Prin* Andrew Davies (trans. Lyric); *La Bête* David Hirson. Interested in developing projects with writers, translators and adaptors. Treatments, synopses and c.v.s only. No longer able to produce in its 110-seat studio owing to reduced funding but the studio continues to host work, including new, by some of the best touring companies in the country.

MAC – The Centre for Birmingham

Cannon Hill Park, Birmingham B12 9QH
☎0121 440 4221   Fax 0121 446 4372
Programme Director *Dorothy Wilson*

Home of the Geese Theatre Company and a host of other arts/performance-related organisations based in Birmingham. Details on Geese available from the Centre.

Cameron Mackintosh

1 Bedford Square, London WC1B 3RA
☎0171 637 8866   Fax 0171 436 2683

Successful West End producer of musicals. Credits include *Cats; Les Misérables; Phantom of the Opera; The Card; Putting it Together; Miss Saigon; Oliver!*. Unsolicited scripts are read and considered (there is no literary manager, however) but chances of success are slim.

The Made In Wales Stage Company

Mount Stuart House, Mount Stuart Square, Cardiff CF1 6DQ
☎01222 484017   Fax 01222 492930
Artistic Director *Gilly Adams*
Administrator *Donna Gower*

Varied audience. Works with Welsh and Wales-based writers and actors to create new and exciting plays which reflect the authentic Anglo-Welsh voice, whilst not being parochially Welsh. Formed in 1982, since when it has premièred and toured 27 new plays. Previous productions: *The Search for Odysseus* Charles Way; *Ted's Creatures* Tim Rhys; *Facing Up* Ieuan Watkins; *Wanting* Jane Buckler; *On the Black Hill* Charles

Way (adap. from Bruce Chatwin's novel); *Branwen* Tony Conran; *The Scam* Peter Lloyd. In addition, the company mounts a festival of new writing called *Write On*, and runs a programme of development work for playwrights at different levels of experience throughout the year. This includes workshops, rehearsed readings and a free script reading service.

Major Road Theatre Company

29 Queens Road, Bradford, West Yorkshire BD8 7BS
☎01274 480251   Fax 01274 548528
Artistic Director *Graham Devlin*
General Manager *Sue Cullen*

FOUNDED 1973. Each show has a very specific target audience which varies considerably from show to show. Previous productions include: *The Bottle Imp* Robert Louis Stevenson (middle-scale tour, commissioned by the Warwick Arts Centre); *Final Cargo* Noel Greig (small scale touring theatre); *Four Note Opera* Tom Johnson (small scale contemporary opera); *Leaves of Life* Mick Eaton (community show – cast of 100); *Bow Down* Harrison Birtwistle (music theatre tour); *Wonderland* Mick Martin (young people's touring show). Would prefer a synopsis of unsolicited mss first. Regularly commissions new work, interested in innovative, non-naturalistic work.

Manchester Library Theatre

See **Library Theatre Company**

Midland Arts Centre

See **MAC – The Centre for Birmingham**

Midnight Theatre Company

103 Redston Road, London N8 7HG
☎0181 341 6607   Fax 0181 341 6607
Artistic Director *Derek Wax*

FOUNDED 1990. New or neglected plays from Britain and the world. Search for plays which are ambitious in scope and explore relationships and ideas in an original and imaginative way. Productions to date include: the British premières of *Games* (Gate, Notting Hill); *The True Story of AH Q* (Soho Theatre); *No Remission* (Lyric Hammersmith and Arts Council supported UK Tour), nominated Best Production in 1993 London Fringe Awards; *Return to the Desert* (Traverse Theatre); *The Life of the World to Come* (Almeida); *Disappeared* (Leicester Haymarket co-production and Arts Council-supported UK tour). Send synopsis with s.a.e. in first instance.

N.T.C. Touring Theatre Company

The Playhouse, Bondgate Without, Alnwick,
Northumberland NE66 1PQ
☎01665 602586

Contact *Gillian Hambleton*

FOUNDED 1978. Formerly Northumberland
Theatre Company. Recent winner of one of
only two drama production franchises in the
Northern region. Predominantly rural, small-
scale touring company, playing to village halls
and community centres throughout the Northern region, the Scottish Borders and country-
wide. Recently expanded into touring middle-
scale theatre venues throughout the North.
Productions range from established classics to
new work and popular comedies, but must be
appropriate to their audience. Unsolicited scripts
welcome provided they are suitable for touring.
The company encourages new writing and commissions when possible. Financial constraints
restrict casting to a *maximum* of seven.

New Shakespeare Company

Open Air Theatre, Regent's Park,
London NW1 4NP
☎0171 935 5884   Fax 0171 487 4562

Artistic Director *Ian Talbot*

Mainly Shakespeare and revivals except for summer lunchtime children's theatre, usually specially commissioned. Very occasional new work.

New Victoria Theatre

Etruria Road, Newcastle under Lyme,
Staffordshire ST5 0JG
☎01782 717954   Fax 01782 712885

Theatre Director *Peter Cheeseman*

FOUNDED 1962. Plays to a fairly broad-based
audience which tends to vary from one production to another. A high proportion are not regular theatregoers and new writing is one of the
theatre's main ways of contacting new audiences.
Commissions about four new plays each year
and is determined to increase the number.
Recent new plays: *Nice Girls*, documentary; *The
Sleeping Beauty* Berlie Doherty; *Come on Stan*
Rony Robinson; *David Copperfield* Chris Martin;
The Tinderbox Peter Whelan. Unsolicited scripts
welcome provided they are accompanied by
s.a.e. for return.

Newpalm Productions

26 Cavendish Avenue, London N3 3QN
☎0181 349 0802   Fax 0181 346 8257

Contact *Phil Compton*

Rarely produces new plays (*As Is* by William M.

Hoffman, which came from Broadway to the
Half Moon Theatre, was an exception to this).
National tours of productions such as *Noises Off*,
Seven Brides for Seven Brothers and *Rebecca*, at
regional repertory theatres, are more typical
examples of Newpalm's work. Unsolicited mss,
both plays and musicals, are, however, welcome; scripts are preferable to synopses.

Northampton Royal Theatre

See **Royal Theatre**

Northcott Theatre

Stocker Road, Exeter, Devon EX4 4QB
☎01392 56182   Fax 01392 263108 attn
Northcott Theatre

Artistic Director *John Durnin*

FOUNDED 1967. The Northcott is the South-
west's principal subsidised repertory theatre, situated on the University of Exeter campus.
Describes its audience as 'geographically diverse,
financially comfortable, conservative in taste,
with a core audience of AB1s (40–60 age range)'.
Currently looking to broaden the base of its
audience profile, targeting younger and/or non-
mainstream theatregoers in the 16–35 age range.
Aims to develop, promote and produce quality
new writing which reflects the life of the region
and addresses the audience it serves. Previous
productions: *Taking Steps* Alan Ayckbourn;
Breaking Bread Together Robert Shearman; *The
Last Yankee* Arthur Miller; *Amadeus* Peter
Shaffer; *Great Expectations* adapt. Robert
Shearman. Unsolicited mss welcome but turnaround is necessarily slow and the script reading
service tends to be locally orientated. Not interested in 'pastiche drawing-room comedy, imita-
tion Ayckbourn, farce from the Ray Cooney
school of theatre, murder-mysteries or thrillers,
or anything that employs TV naturalism'. It is
hoped that the company will be able to return to
its previous target of a minimum of two new
pieces each season, one for the main house, the
other for the studio theatre in Emmanuel Hall.
The Northcott is a founder-member of the
South West Theatre Consortium, which actively
supports and participates in a variety of new writing projects, showcases, workshops, rehearsed
readings and competitions.

Northern Stage Company

Newcastle Playhouse, Barras Bridge,
Newcastle upon Tyne NE1 7RH
☎0191 232 3366   Fax 0191 261 8093

Artistic Director *Alan Lyddiard*

A young company which plans to involve itself

in the production of new work, including co-productions with other local companies. Writers' workshops arc likely to be arranged. Before submitting unsolicited scripts, please contact Brenda Gray.

Norwich Puppet Theatre
St James, Whitefriars, Norwich,
Norfolk NR3 1TN
☎01603 615564   Fax 01603 617578
Artistic Director *Luis Boy*
General Manager *R. W. Skinner*

Plays to a young audience (aged 3–12), with occasional shows for adult audiences interested in puppetry. Christmas/summer season shows, plus school tours. Unsolicited mss welcome if relevant.

Nottingham Playhouse
Nottingham Theatre Trust, Wellington Circus, Nottingham NG1 5AF
☎0115 9474361   Fax 0115 9475759
Artistic Director *Martin Duncan*

Aims to make innovation popular, and present the best of world theatre, working closely with the communities in the county. Unsolicited mss will be read. It normally takes about six months, however, and 'we have never yet produced an unsolicited script. All our plays have to achieve a minimum of sixty per cent audiences in a 732-seat theatre. We have no studio.' Also see **Roundabout** – the Nottingham Playhouse's theatre-in-education company.

Nuffield Theatre
University Road, Southampton, Hampshire SO2 1TR
☎01703 315500   Fax 01703 315511
Artistic Director *Patrick Sandford*
Script Executive *Penny Gold*

Well known as a good bet for new playwrights, the Nuffield gets an awful lot of scripts. They do a couple of new plays every season. Previous productions: *Exchange* by Yri Trifonov (trans. Michael Frayn) which transferred to the Vaudeville Theatre; *The Floating Light Bulb* Woody Allen (British première); new plays by Claire Luckham: *Dogspot; The Dramatic Attitudes of Miss Fanny Kemble;* and by Claire Tomalin: *The Winter Wife.* Open-minded about subject and style, producing musicals as well as straight plays. Scripts preferred to synopses in the case of writers new to theatre. All will, eventually, be read 'but please be patient. We do not have a large team of paid readers. We read everything ourselves.'

Octagon Theatre Trust Ltd
Howell Croft South, Bolton,
Lancashire BL1 1SB
☎01204 529407   Fax 01204 380110
Artistic Director *Lawrence Till*
Administrative Director *Amanda Belcham*

FOUNDED 1967. Attracts a wide age range of audience. Productions range from Shakespeare, 'Northern' plays, European plays, new plays, 1960s plays. Unsolicited mss considered, but may take up to six months for reply. Commission and present at least two new plays or translations/adaptations a year. Interested in good theatrical pieces that connect with the audience – socially, politically, emotionally and often geographically with casts of about six. No thin comedies or epic plays with casts over eight.

The Old Vic
Waterloo Road, London SE1 8NB
☎0171 928 2651   Fax 0171 261 9161
General Manager *Andrew Leigh*

The Old Vic now operates as a West End theatre. There are intentions to return to producing three or four plays a year with star casts. No unsolicited scripts at present.

Orange Tree Theatre
1 Clarence Street, Richmond, Surrey TW9 2SA
☎0181 940 0141   Fax 0181 332 0369
Artistic Director *Sam Walters*

One of those theatre venues just out of London which are good for new writing, both full-scale productions and rehearsed readings (although these usually take place in The Room, above the Orange Tree pub). Productions, from August 1994: *The Case of Rebellious Susan* Henry Arthur Jones; *Dr. Knock* Jules Romains; *Flora, the Red Menace* musical by Kander and Ebb; *Portrait of a Woman* Michel Vinaver; *The Memorandum* Vaclav Havel; *Retreat* James Saunders; *Each Day Dies With Sleep* José Rivera. The Room: *Rosencrantz & Guildenstern* W.S. Gilbert; *Dummy Run* Caroline Graham; *Out in the Open* (devised piece); *Roma's Song* Caroline Graham; *The Gift* Nicholas McInerny; plus six rehearsed readings and two workshops. Unsolicited mss are read, but patience (and s.a.e.) required.

Orchard Theatre
108 Newport Road, Barnstaple,
Devon EX32 9BA
☎01271 71475   Fax 01271 71825
Artistic Director *Bill Buffery*

FOUNDED 1969. Plays appealing to a wide age

range, which tour some 60 or 70 cities, towns and villages throughout Devon, Cornwall, Dorset, Somerset, Avon and Gloucestershire. Programme includes classics, new adaptations, outstanding modern work and newly commissioned plays. OUTPUT *Uncle Vanya; Talking Heads; Hansel & Gretel; Plantation.* Unsolicited mss are usually unsuccessful simply because the theatre is committed to several commissioned new plays at any one time.

Oxford Stage Company
3rd Floor, 15–19 George Street,
Oxford OX1 2AU
☎01865 723238   Fax 01865 790625

Artistic Director *John Retallack*

A middle-scale touring company producing established and new plays. At least one new play or new adaptation a year. Special interest in new writing for young people aged 13–18.

Paines Plough – New Writing New Theatre
4th Floor, 43 Aldwych, London NW5 3NQ
☎0171 240 5433   Fax 0171 240 4534

Literary Manager *Tony Dinner*
Artistic Director *Penny Ciniewicz*

Produces new writing. Previous productions: *Wild Things* Anna Reynolds (co-production with Salisbury Playhouse); *Wax* Lavinia Murray; *Down and Out in Paris and London* adap. Nigel Gearing; *Augustine (Big Hysteria)* Anna Furse; *Crossfire* Michael Azama. Receives around five unsolicited scripts a week and reports are made on most plays received. Enclose s.a.e. for response/return.

Palace Theatre, Watford
Clarendon Road, Watford, Hertfordshire
WD1 1JZ
☎01923 235455   Fax 01923 819664

Artistic Director *Giles Croft*

An important point of policy is the active commissioning of new plays. Previous productions: Lou Stein's adaptation of *The Adventures of Pinocchio; Woman Overboard* Adrian Mitchell; *Diplomatic Wives* Louise Page; *Over A Barrel* Stephen Bill; *The Marriage of Figaro* (adap. Ranjit Bolt). Recently produced an entire season of new and commissioned work, including Bolt's *The Barber of Seville*; Jon Canter's *The Baby*; Lou Stein's musical adaptation of *La Celestina* by Fernando de Rojas, entitled *Salsa Celestina* and *Borders of Paradise* by Sharman Macdonald.

Perth Repertory Theatre Ltd
185 High Street, Perth PH1 5UW
☎01738 638123   Fax 01738 624576

Artistic Director *Andrew McKinnon*
General Manager *Paul McLennan*

FOUNDED 1935. A wide range of productions, including musicals, classics, new plays, comedy, etc. for a loyal audience. Unsolicited mss are read when time permits, but the timetable for return of scripts is lengthy. New plays staged by the company are invariably commissioned under the SAC scheme.

Plymouth Theatre Royal
See **Theatre Royal**

Polka Children's Theatre
240 The Broadway, London SW19 1SB
☎0181 542 4258   Fax 0181 542 7723

Contact *Artistic Director*

This Wimbledon theatre is interested in receiving scripts suitable for children of all ages, but principally 3–5, 5–8 and 9–12. 'Our overall writing policy is to present excellent theatre for children which is both educational and entertaining.' Main-house productions include original plays connected to school project work, Christmas plays, summer musical-plays, adaptations of classic stories, novels, folk tales and puppet plays. Particularly interested in plays that need a cast of no more than five to seven people.

Queen's Theatre, Hornchurch
Billet Lane, Hornchurch, Essex RM11 1QT
☎0078 456118   Fax 01708 452348

Artistic Director *Marina Caldarone*

FOUNDED 1953. Nothing too adventurous for this mainly white, middle-class audience. Modern work, translations or classics are difficult to sell without a household name in the production. Marina Caldarone, however, wishes to broaden the company's repertoire. Committed to producing at least one new work per season (two a year), and keen to set up a complementary studio company which would develop new work. 'We try to offer as broad a repertoire as we can within our economic limitations.' Eight shows a year, including one musical and one Christmas/panto slot. Always interested in 'the well-made play' and now encouraging the submission of more experimental work as well as translations, adaptations, and classics. Has an established tradition of successful comedies and musicals which have transferred to the West End, e.g. *Blood Brothers*. Unsolicited mss welcome; all are assessed but this can take some considerable time.

The Questors Theatre
12 Mattock Lane, Ealing, London W5 5BQ
☎0181 567 0011   Fax 0181 567 8736
Artistic Director *David Emmet*
Theatre Manager *Elaine Orchard*
New Plays Secretary *Christine Greening*

FOUNDED 1929. Attracts an intelligent, discerning, wide age range audience looking for something different, innovative, daring. Recent productions include: *The Surgeon of Honour* Calderon; *The Summer of the Seventeenth Doll* Ray Lawler; *Julius Caesar* Shakespeare; *Uncle Vanya* Chekhov; *Judgement Day* Odon von Horvath; *The Beaux' Stratagem* Farquhar; *The Horse Among the Stars* Michel Tremblay; *Dracula* Liz Lochhead; *Sketches in the Dark* Scott Perry (new play). Unsolicited mss welcome. All new plays are carefully assessed. All scripts received are acknowledged and all writers receive a written response to their work. Some unsolicited plays receive productions, others rehearsed readings. Runs annual **Questors Theatre Student Playwright Competition**.

Quill Theatre Productions
247 Norwood Road, London SE24 9AG
☎0181 674 1050
Artistic Director *Ann Parnell McGarry*

Quill exists to produce new work and suffers enormous gaps in its production schedule when, as is often the case, decent new work can't be found. Writing can be set in any time or dimension imaginable, as long as it offers a fresh insight. 'Originality of approach is the most important thing.' In the market for serious work and fast witty comedies. Finished scripts are preferred unless someone wants to try out 'a truly brilliant idea which we can develop together. We have no preconceptions on size of cast. It is a lengthy process.'

The Really Useful Group Ltd
20 Tower Street, London WC2H 9NS
☎0171 240 0880   Fax 0171 240 1204
Contact *Tania Slayter*

Commercial/West End theatre producers whose output has included *Sunset Boulevard; Joseph and the Amazing Technicolor Dreamcoat; Cats; Phantom of the Opera; Starlight Express; Daisy Pulls It Off; Lend Me a Tenor; Arturo Ui* and *Aspects of Love*.

Red Ladder Theatre Company
Cobden Avenue, Lower Wortley, Leeds, West Yorkshire LS12 5PB
☎0113 2792228   Fax 0113 2310660
Artistic Director/Literary Manager *Kully Thiarai*
Administrator *Susie Hargreaves*

FOUNDED 1968. Commissioning company touring 2–3 shows a year with a strong commitment to new work and new writers. Aimed at an audience of young people aged between 14–25 years who have little or no access to theatre. Performances held in youth clubs and similar venues (not schools) where young people choose to meet. Recent productions: *Sleeping Dogs* Philip Osment, originally toured to youth clubs in 1993 but re-toured to Arts Centres in Autumn 1994. Other youth club tours included *Mixed Blessings* by Mary Cooper and *The Wound* by Gilly Fraser. 'The company is currently developing its writing policy which will be available to writers interested in working for the company. Whilst unsolicited scripts are not discouraged, the company is particularly keen to enter into a dialogue with writers with regard to creating new work for young people.'

Michael Redington
10 Maunsel Street, London SW1P 2QL
☎0171 834 5119   Fax 0171 828 6947
Contact *Michael Redington*

Interested only in new work but unsolicited mss are not welcome; new plays generally come by way of contacts in the business. Plays for the West End.

Roundabout Theatre in Education
College Street Centre for Performing Arts, College Street, Nottingham NG1 5AQ
☎0115 9476202   Fax 0115 9411073
Contact *Kitty Parker*

FOUNDED 1973. Theatre-in-Education company of the Nottingham Playhouse. Plays to a young audience aged 5–18 years of age. Some programmes are devised or adapted in-house, some are commissioned. Unable to resource the adequate response required for unsolicited scripts. 'We are committed to the encouragement of new writing as and when resources permit.'

Royal Court Theatre/English Stage Company Ltd
Sloane Square, London SW1W 8AS
☎0171 730 5174   Fax 0171 730 4705
Literary Manager *Graham Whybrow*

The English Stage Company was founded by George Devine in 1956 to put on new plays. John Osborne, John Arden, Arnold Wesker, Edward Bond, Caryl Churchill, Howard Barker and Michael Hastings are all writers this theatre has discovered. Christopher Hampton and David Hare have worked here in the literary department. The aim of the Royal Court is to develop and perform the best in new writing for the theatre, encouraging writers from all sections of society to address the problems and possibilities of our times.

Royal Exchange Theatre Company

St Ann's Square, Manchester M2 7DH
☎0161 833 9333   Fax 0161 832 0881
Literary Manager *Alan Pollock*

FOUNDED 1976. The Royal Exchange has developed a new writing policy, which they find is attracting a younger audience to the theatre. The company produces plays by young dramatists like Iain Heggie, Michael Wall, Alex Finlayson, Rod Wooden, Simon Burke and Randhi McWilliams; also English and foreign classics, modern classics, adaptations and new musicals. The Royal Exchange receives 500–2000 scripts a year. These are read by Alan Pollock and a team of readers. Only a tiny percentage is suitable, but a number of plays are commissioned each year. Runs the **Mobil Playwriting Competition**.

Royal National Theatre

South Bank, London SE1 9PX
☎0171 928 2033   Fax 0171 620 1197
Script Adviser *Jack Bradley*

The majority of the National's new plays come about as a result of direct commission or from existing contacts with playwrights. There is no quota for new work, though so far more than a third of plays presented have been the work of living playwrights. Writers new to the theatre would need to be of exceptional talent to be successful with a script here, though the NT Studio acts as a bridge between the theatre and a limited number of playwrights, through readings, workshops and discussion. In some cases a new play is presented for a shorter-than-usual run in the Cottesloe Theatre. Scripts considered (send s.a.e).

Royal Shakespeare Company

Barbican Centre, London EC2Y 8BQ
☎0171 628 3351   Fax 0171 374 0818
Literary Manager *Colin Chambers*

The literary department, receives around 500 unsolicited mss a year of which ninety-eight per cent are totally unsuitable for the RSC. But the RSC is committed to new plays and roughly a third of the company's total output is new work. This is generally commissioned and unsolicited offerings from unknowns are rarely successful. Bear in mind that the RSC is *not* interested in straightforwardly biographical plays (they get an awful lot of Lives of Elizabeth I) or singlemindedly topical writing, and have no use for reworkings of Shakespeare. Musicals, particularly rewritings of *Kiss Me Kate* or *Les Misérables* ('these used to arrive by the sackful') are not generally welcome. 'There is a tendency among playwrights to assume that because the RSC have done a play once, they're in the market for more of the same. Usually the reverse is true, and it's wise to check whether a subject has been covered previously before submitting mss.' RSC actors organise festivals in which new work is often a prominent feature but the company has little, if any, involvement with rehearsed readings and workshops.

Royal Theatre

15 Guildhall Road, Northampton NN1 1EA
☎01604 38343   Fax 01604 602408
Artistic Director *Michael Napier Brown*

FOUNDED 1927. Describes its audience as 'wide-ranging in terms of taste; 50% middle-class, of all ages; and fairly conservative, but a growing population'. Produces at least three new works each year. The studio theatre, theatre-in-education, community touring and youth theatre tend to produce the majority of new work, but there are normally two main-house premières each year. Previous productions: *Below the Belt; To Serve Them All My Days; Mrs Klein; Martin Chuzzlewit; The Go-Between; A Doll's House.* Unsolicited scripts welcome and always read.

Salisbury Playhouse

Malthouse Lane, Salisbury, Wiltshire SP2 7RA
☎01722 320117   Fax 01722 421991
Contact *Artistic Director*

At the time of going to press, a new artistic director had still to be appointed and no policy statement was available. In 1995, the Playhouse was closed from January to September.

Shared Experience Theatre

Soho Laundry, 9 Dufours Place,
London W1V 1FE
☎0171 434 9248   Fax 0171 287 8763
Artistic Director *Nancy Meckler*

FOUNDED 1975. Varied audience depending on venue, since this is a touring company. Recent productions have included: *The Birthday Party* Harold Pinter; *The Closing Number* (devised by the company); *Sweet Sessions* Paul Godfrey; *Anna Karenina* (adap. Helen Edmundson); *Trilby & Svengali* (adap. David Fielder); *Mill on the Floss* (adap. Helen Edmundson); *The Danube* Maria Irene Fornes. No unsolicited mss. Primarily not a new writing company but 'we are interested in innovative new scripts'.

Sherman Theatre Company
Senghennydd Road, Cardiff CF2 4YE
☎01222 396844   Fax 01222 665581
Artistic Director *Phil Clark*

FOUNDED 1973. Theatre for Young People, with main house and studio. Encourages new writing. Previous productions: *Erogenous Zones, Loose Ends* Frank Vickery; *Fern Hill, A Long Time Ago* Mike Kenny. In 1994, five half-hour plays by new Welsh writers and in 1995, six half-hour plays by young writers under 25 years were produced. Priority will be given to Wales-based writers.

Snap People's Theatre Trust
Unit A, Causeway Business Centre, Bishop's Stortford, Hertfordshire CM23 2UB
☎01279 504095/503066   Fax 01279 501472
Contact *Andy Graham, Mike Wood*

FOUNDED 1979. Plays to young people in four age groups (5–7, 7–11, 11–14, 15–21), and to the thirty-something age group. Classic adaptations and new writing. Writers should make an appointment to discuss possibilities rather than submit unsolicited material. New writing encouraged. 'Projects should reflect the writer's own beliefs, be thought-provoking, challenging and accessible.'

Soho Theatre Company
The Cockpit Theatre, Gateforth Street, London NW8 8EH
☎0171 262 7907   Fax 0171 723 8146
Artistic Director *Abigail Morris*
Literary Manager *Paul Sirett*

A new writing theatre company. The company produces around four new shows a year. Previous productions: *Kindertransporte* Diane Samuels; *The Yiddish Trojan Women* Carol Braverman; *Rock Station* Ger FitzGibbon. The system for dealing with unsolicited mss is as follows: scripts go out to a team of readers; those they find interesting are passed on to the artistic director, who invites writers of promise to join the workshop series. Presents the **Verity Bargate Award** annually. (At the time of going

to press, the Soho Theatre Company was fighting Westminster College's decision to terminate their tenancy of the College's Cockpit Theatre.)

The Sphinx
Sadler's Wells, Rosebery Avenue, London EC1R 4TN
☎0171 713 0991/2
Artistic Director *Sue Parrish*

FOUNDED 1973. Formerly Women's Theatre Group. Tours new plays nationally to studio theatres and arts centres.

Barrie Stacey Productions
9 Denmark Street, London WC2
☎0171 836 4128   Fax 0171 836 2949
Contact *Barrie Stacey*

Touring company, much of the work being Barrie Stacey's own but not exclusively so. Previous productions: *Adventures of Pinocchio; Snow White and the Seven Dwarfs; West End to Broadway Songbook* Barrie Stacey; *Two in Tandem* Andrew Wallace. Always interested in two/three-handers for production, and in film synopses. Fast, experienced scriptwriters in-house.

The Steam Industry
Finborough Theatre, 118 Finborough Road, London SW10 9ED
☎0171 244 7439   Fax 0171 835 1853
Artistic Director *Phil Willmott*
Contact *The Literary Manager*

Since June 1944, the venue has been a base for The Steam Industry who produce in and out of the building. Their output is diverse and prolific and includes a high percentage of new writing alongside radical adaptations of classics and musicals. The space is also available for a number of hires per year and the hire fee is sometimes waived to encourage innovative work. Unsolicited scripts are welcome but due to minimal resources it can take up to six months to respond. Send s.a.e. with material. The company regularly workshops new scripts at Monday night play readings. Previous productions include: *Born Bad; The Oedipus Table; Succulence; Mermaid Sandwich; Illyria.* The venue has presented new works by Anthony Neilson, Jack Bradley, Clare Bayley, Philip Kingston, Mark Ravenhill and Kate Dean.

Stoll Moss Theatres Ltd
Manor House, 21 Soho Square, London W1V 5FD
☎0171 494 5200   Fax 0171 434 1217
Contact *Nica Burns, Richard Johnston*

Influential theatrical empire, with eleven theatres under its umbrella: Apollo; Cambridge; Duchess; Garrick; Gielgud; Her Majesty's; London Palladium; Lyric Shaftesbury Avenue; Queen's; Royalty and Theatre Royal Drury Lane.

Swan Theatre
The Moors, Worcester WR1 3EF
☎01905 726969   Fax 01905 723738
Artistic Director *Jenny Stephens*

Repertory company producing a wide range of plays to a mixed audience coming largely from the City of Worcester and the county of Hereford and Worcester. A writing group meets at the theatre and unsolicited scripts will be read eventually, although, due to under-staffing, it could take as long as a year.

Swansea Little Theatre Ltd
Dylan Thomas Theatre, Maritime Quarter, 7 Gloucester Place, Swansea, West Glamorgan SA1 1TY
☎01792 473238
Contact *The Secretary*

A wide variety of plays, from pantomime to the classics. New writing encouraged. New plays considered by the Artistic Committee.

Tabard Theatre Company
2 Bath Road, London W4 1LW
☎0181 995 6035
Artistic Director *Kate Bone*

FOUNDED 1985. Interested in new good writing for a mixed audience, no sagas or epics. No unsolicited mss. Previous productions include: Shakespeare (*Henry V, Richard III*); new writing – *Hungry Ghosts* P. Kingston; *Theodora* Clare L. Price.

Talawa Theatre Company Ltd
The Cochrane Theatre, Southampton Road, London WC2B 4AP
☎0171 404 5662   Fax 0171 831 2407
Artistic Director *Yvonne Brewster*
Administrator *Angela McSherry*

FOUNDED 1985. Plays to an ABC audience of 60% black, 40% white across a wide age range depending upon the nature of productions and targeting. Previous productions include all-black performances of *The Importance of Being Earnest* and *Antony and Cleopatra*; plus Jamaican pantomime *Arawak Gold; The Gods Are Not to Blame; The Road* Wole Soyinka; *O! Babylon* Derek Walcott. Restricted to new work from Black writers only. Occasional commissions,

though these tend to go to established writers. Interested in the epic, ritualistic and boundary breaking stuff. No domestic comedy material. Runs a Black Women's Writers' project funded by **London Arts Board** for three years.

Theatr Clwyd
County Civic Centre, Mold, Clwyd CH7 1YA
☎01352 756331   Fax 01352 758323
Dramaturg *Lloyd Trott*

Repertory company with a lively programming policy attracting audiences of all ages. The company has touring commitments within Wales and tours across Britain. Productions of classics and revivals have predominated but an international interest in contemporary drama is being developed. Previous productions: *India Song* Marguerite Duras; *The Choice* Claire Luckham; *Barnaby and the Old Boys* Keith Baxter; *Self Portrait* Sheila Yeger; *HRH* Snoo Wilson; *Full Moon* by Caradog Prichard, adapt. Helena Kaut-Howson and John Owen. Unsolicited material is unlikely to be considered for production, but special consideration is given to Welsh writers and scripts with Welsh themes. Scripts are read by the Dramaturg who then writes a full report for the Artistic Director.

Theatre of Comedy Company
210 Shaftesbury Avenue, London WC2H 8DP
☎0171 379 3345   Fax 0171 836 0466
Artistic Director *Alan Strachan*

FOUNDED 1983 to produce new work. Interested in strong comedy in the widest sense – Chekhov comes under the definition as does farce. Also has a light entertainment division, developing new scripts for television, namely situation comedy and series. A good bet for new work.

Theatre Royal, Plymouth
Royal Parade, Plymouth, Devon PL1 2TR
☎01752 668282   Fax 01752 671179
Contact *Liz Turgeon*

Stages small, middle and large-scale drama with an emphasis on musicals and music theatre. Commissions and produces new plays. Unsolicited scripts are read and reported on.

Theatre Royal Stratford East
Gerry Raffles Square, London E15 1BN
☎0181 534 7374   Fax 0181 534 8381
Associate Director *Jeff Teare*

Lively East London theatre, catering for a very mixed audience, both local and London-wide.

Produces plays, musicals, youth theatre and local community plays/events, all of which is new work. Special interest in Asian and Black British work. Unsolicited scripts are welcome: 'we do read them eventually!'

Theatre Royal Windsor
Windsor, Berkshire SL4 1PS
☎01753 863444   Fax 01753 831673
Artistic Director *Mark Piper*
FOUNDED 1938. Plays to a middle-class, West End-type audience. Produces thirteen plays a year and 'would be disappointed to do fewer than two new plays in a year; always hope to do half a dozen'. Modern classics, thrillers, comedy and farce. Only interested in scripts along these lines.

Theatre Workshop Edinburgh
34 Hamilton Place, Edinburgh EH3 5AX
☎0131 225 7942   Fax 0131 220 0112
Artistic Director *Adrian Harris*
Plays to a young, broad-based audience with much of the work targeted towards particular groups or communities. OUTPUT has included adaptations of Gogol's *The Nose* and Aharon Appelfeld's *Badenheim 1939* – two community performance projects – and *Breaking Free*, a Theatre-in-Education programme touring to secondary schools in Scotland. Particularly interested in new work for children and young people. Frequently engages writers for collaborative/devised projects. Commissions a significant amount of new writing for a wide range of contexts, from large-cast community plays to small-scale professional tours. Favours writers based in Scotland, producing material relevant to a contemporary Scottish audience. Member of Scottish Script Centre to whom it refers senders of unsolicited manuscripts.

Thorndike Theatre (Leatherhead) Ltd
Church Street, Leatherhead, Surrey KT22 8DF
☎01372 376211   Fax 01372 362595
Artistic Director *Bill Kenwright*
West End and touring for an audience described as fairly conservative. 70% of the company's work goes out on tour; children's and family plays. Out of a total of ten in-house productions each year, five new plays are sought. Previous productions: *Travels With My Aunt* Graham Greene; *She Stoops to Conquer* Goldsmith; *Piaf* Pam Gems; *An Absolute Turkey* Feydeau, trans. Peter Hall and Nicki Frei; *September Tide* Daphne Du Maurier.

Tiebreak Touring Theatre
George White Middle School, Silver Road, Norwich, Norfolk NR3 4RG
☎01603 426374   Fax 01603 418524
Artistic Director *David Farmer*
FOUNDED 1981. Specialises in high quality theatre for children and young people, touring schools, youth centres, museums and festivals. Previous productions: *Love Bites; Singing in the Rainforest; Boadicea – The Movie; Dinosaurs on Ice; Touch Wood*. New writing encouraged. Interested in low-budget, small-cast material only. School, educational and socially relevant material of special interest. Scripts welcome.

Torch Theatre
St Peter's Road, Milford Haven, Pembrokeshire, Dyfed SA73 2BU
☎01646 694192   Fax 01646 690718
Contact *Artistic Director*
FOUNDED 1976. Plays to a mixed audience hard to attract to new work on the whole. Committed to new work but financing has become somewhat prohibitive. Small-cast pieces with broad appeal welcome. Previous productions: *Frankie and Tommy; School for Wives; Tess of the d'Urbervilles*. The repertoire runs from Ayckbourn to Friel. Scripts sometimes welcome.

Traverse Theatre
Cambridge Street, Edinburgh EH1 2ED
☎0131 228 3223   Fax 0131 229 8443
Contact *Jane Ellis*
The Traverse is the best known theatre in Scotland for new writing; indeed it has a policy of putting on nothing but new work by new writers. Also has a strong international programme of work in translation and visiting companies. Previous productions: *Unidentified Human Remains* and *Poor Superman* both by Brad Fraser; *Moscow Stations* (adap. Stephen Mulrine). No unsolicited scripts. Writers welcome to make contact by phone or in writing.

Trestle Theatre Company
47–49 Wood Street, Barnet, Hertfordshire EN5 4BS
☎0181 441 0349   Fax 0181 449 7036
Artistic Directors *Joff Chafer, Toby Wilsher*
FOUNDED 1981. Physical, mask theatre for mostly student-based audiences (18–36 years). All work is devised by the company. Scripts which have the company's special brand of

theatre in mind will be considered. No non-physical-based material. New writing welcome.

Tricycle Theatre
269 Kilburn High Road,
London NW6 7JR
☎0171 372 6611   Fax 0171 328 0795
Artistic Director *Nicolas Kent*

FOUNDED 1980. Plays to a very mixed audience, in terms of both culture and class. Previous productions: *The Day the Bronx Died* Michael Henry Brown; *Half the Picture* Richard Norton-Taylor and John McGrath; *Nativity* Nigel Williams; *Playboy of the West Indies* Mustapha Matura; *Boots for the Footless* Brian Behan; *Joe Turner's Come and Gone* and *The Piano Lesson* August Wilson; *A Long Way From Home* Yemi Ajibade; *Pecong* Steve Carter; *A Love Song for Ulster* Bill Morrison; *Three Hotels* Jon Robin Baitz. New writing welcome from women and ethnic minorities (particularly Black and Irish). Looks for a strong narrative drive with popular appeal, not 'studio' plays. Also runs workshops for writers.

Tron Theatre Company
63 Trongate, Glasgow G1 5HB
☎0141 552 3748   Fax 0141 552 6657
Artistic Director *Michael Boyd*

FOUNDED 1981. Plays to a very broad cross-section of Glasgow and beyond, including international tours (Toronto 1990; New York 1991; Montreal 1992). Previous productions: *Hosanna* Michel Tremblay (trans. Bowman & Findlay); *Cinzano* Petrushevskaya (trans. Mulrine); *The Offski Variations* Marcella Evaristi; *Crow* Hughes & Boyd; *Macbeth* (dir. Michael Boyd); *Dumbstruck* David Kane; *The Trick is to Keep Breathing* Janice Galloway/Boyd. Interested in premières of ambitious plays by experienced Scottish writers, and in new Irish and international work. No unsolicited mss.

Umoja Theatre Company
The Base, 59 Bethwin Road,
London SE5 0XY
☎0171 701 6396   Fax 0171 703 3796
Artistic Director *Gloria Hamilton*

FOUNDED 1983. Plays to a predominantly Black audience with two productions each year. New writers encouraged. The company's own venue, The Base, houses incoming shows, workshops and training. Unsolicited mss welcome.

Unicorn Arts Theatre for Children
Arts Theatre, 6–7 Great Newport Street,
London WC2H 7JB
☎0171 379 3280   Fax 0171 836 5366
Contact *Dorothy Wooder*

FOUNDED 1947 as a touring company, and took up residence in the Arts Theatre in 1967. Plays mainly to children between the ages of 4–12. Previous productions: *Chalk Circle* Diane Samuels, and *Hans Christian Anderstories* – a recreation by Ken Campbell, Charles Causley, Claire Luckham, Adrian Mitchell and Fay Weldon of some of the famous tales. Unsolicited scripts welcome. Runs the **Unicorn Theatre Young Playwrights' Competition** annually (for children between the ages of 4 and 12).

Charles Vance Productions
83 George Street, London W1H 5PL
☎0171 486 1732   Fax 0171 224 2215
Contact *Charles Vance, Jill Streatfield*

In the market for medium-scale touring productions and summer season plays. Hardly any new work and no commissions but writing of promise stands a good chance of being passed on to someone who might be interested in it. Occasional try-outs for new work in the Sidmouth repertory theatre. Send s.a.e. for return of mss.

Michael Ward Theatre Productions
Radnors, 39 Thames Street, Windsor,
Berkshire SL4 1PR
☎01753 863982
Contact *Michael Ward*

FOUNDED 1984. New writing encouraged (non-political preferred). Interested in quality new work that could be used for touring or London. Send synopsis with script, including s.a.e. for return. Close association with leading literary agent and with two West End management companies. Allow six months for return of scripts.

Warehouse Theatre, Croydon
Dingwall Road, Croydon CR0 2NF
☎0181 681 1257   Fax 0181 688 6699
Artistic Director *Ted Craig*
Writers' Workshop Manager *Sheila Dewey*

South London's new writing theatre, seating 100. Produces six new plays a year and co-produces with companies who share a commitment to new work. Continually building upon a tradition of discovering and nurturing new writers, with activities including a monthly writers' workshop and the annual **South London International Playwriting Festival**. Previous productions: *Don Quixote* Vince Foxall; *Fat Souls* James Martin Charlton; *Playing Sinatra* Bernard Kops; *Fighting for the Dunghill* Guy Jenkins; *Eva and the Cabin Boy* Sheila Dewey; *The Court Jester* Roy Smiles. Unsolicited scripts welcome but writers should bear in mind that the theatre is committed to productions at least nine months in advance.

Watermill Theatre
Bagnor, Newbury, Berkshire RG16 8AE
☎01635 45834   Fax 01635 45834
Contact *Jill Fraser*

The Watermill tries to put on one new piece of work each year. Previous productions: *Just So* George Stiles & Anthony Drewe; *Hindsight* Richard Everett; *The Great Big Radio Show* Philip Glassboron and David Rhind-Tutt; *The Ugly Duckling* George Stiles & Anthony Drene; *Goodbye Mr Chips* adapt. Norman Coaler; *Laura* (musical) Michael Heath.

Watford Palace Theatre
See **Palace Theatre**

West Yorkshire Playhouse
Quarry Hill Mount, Leeds, West Yorkshire LS9 8AW
☎0113 2442141   Fax 0113 2448252
Literary Co-ordinator *Claire Malcolm*

Committed to programming new writing as part of its overall policy. Before sending an unsolicited script please phone or write. The Playhouse does readings, workshops and script surgeries on new plays with writers from all over Britain and also has strong links with local writers and Yorkshire playwrights. The theatre has writers-in-residence. Previous productions: *The Gulf Between Us* Trevor Griffiths; *A Passionate Woman* Kay Mellor; *Fathers Day* Maureen Lawrence; *Postcards from Rome* Adam Pernak; *The Winter Guest* Sharman Macdonald. Launched the first W. H. Smith Plays for Children in 1992 and produced the winning play *Burning Everest* by Adrian Flynn in 1993.

Whirligig Theatre
14 Belvedere Drive, Wimbledon, London SW19 7BY
☎0181 947 1732   Fax 0181 879 7648
Contact *David Wood*

One play a year in major theatre venues, usu-ally a musical for primary school audiences and weekend family groups. Interested in scripts which exploit the theatrical nature of children's tastes. Previous productions: *The See-Saw Tree; The Selfish Shellfish; The Gingerbread Man; The Old Man of Lochnagar; The Ideal Gnome Expedition; Save the Human; Dreams of Anne Frank.*

Windsor Theatre Royal
See **Theatre Royal**

Wolsey Theatre Company
Civic Drive, Ipswich, Suffolk IP1 2AS
☎01473 218911   Fax 01473 212946
Artistic Director *Antony Tuckey*
Contact *Eileen Kidd*

FOUNDED 1979. Tries to do one new play a year in the main house and studio (which opened in October 1992). New writing encouraged. Unsolicited mss welcome. Previous productions: *Hamlet; What I Did in the Holidays* (new play, co-produced with Cambridge Theatre Company); *Keyboard Skills* Lesley Bruce; *The Apple Cart* G.B. Shaw; *Olenna* David Mamet; *Summer Lightning* P.G. Wodehouse.

Women's Theatre Group
See **The Sphinx**

York Theatre Royal
St Leonard's Place, York YO1 2HD
☎01904 658162   Fax 01904 611534
Artistic Director *John Doyle*

Not a new writing theatre in the main. Previous productions: *The Wars of the Roses; The Madness of George III; The Rivals; Dracula* (adapt. John Doyle). No scripts.

The Young Vic
66 The Cut, London SE1 8LZ
☎0171 633 0133   Fax 0171 928 1585
Artistic Director *Tim Supple*

FOUNDED 1970. The Young Vic produces adventurous and demanding work for an audi-ence with a youthful spirit. The main house is one of London's most exciting spaces and seats up to 500. In addition, a smaller, entirely flexi-ble space, The Cut, seats 100 and is used for experiment, performance, rehearsals and instal-lations. 'We are not able to produce many new scripts at the moment; nor are we able to develop or read unsolicited scripts with the care they deserve. However, we are always happy to receive work.'

Festivals

Aldeburgh Poetry Festival
Goldings, Goldings Lane, Leiston, Suffolk
IP16 4EB
☎01728 830631   Fax 01728 832029
Contact *Michael Laskey*

Now in its eighth year, an annual international festival of contemporary poetry held over one weekend each November in Aldeburgh and attracting large audiences. Regular features include a two-week residency leading up to the festival, poetry readings, a children's event, workshops, a public masterclass, a lecture, a performance spot and the festival prize for the year's best first collection (see entry **Prizes**).

Arundel Festival
The Arundel Festival Society Ltd, The Mary Gate, Arundel, West Sussex BN18 9AT
☎01903 883690   Fax 01903 884243
Contact *Mrs R. J. Buckland*

Annual festival held at the end of August/beginning of September for eleven days. Events include poetry, prose readings and lectures, open-air Shakespeare in Arundel Castle, concerts with internationally known artists, jazz, visual arts and active fringe.

Bath Fringe Festival
The Bell, 103 Walcot Street, Bath BA1 5BW
☎01225 480079   Fax 01225 427441
Chair/Coordinator *Wendy Matthews*

FOUNDED 1981. Complementing the international music festival, they present theatre, poetry, jazz, blues, comedy, cabaret, storytelling, carnival and more in venues, parks and streets of Bath during late May and early June.

BBC Radio Young Playwrights' Festival
See **First Bite**

Belfast Festival at Queen's
Festival House, 25 College Gardens, Belfast
BT9 6BS
☎01232 667687   Fax 01232 663733
Acting Director *Robert Agnew*

FOUNDED 1964. Annual three-week festival held in November. Organised by Queen's University in association with the **Arts Council of Northern Ireland**, the festival covers a wide variety of events, including literature. Programme available in September.

Berkshire Literary Festival
See **Writers Live**

Birmingham Readers and Writers Festival
Festival Office, Central Library, Chamberlain Square, Birmingham B3 3HQ
☎0121 235 4244/3146   Fax 0121 233 9702
Festival Director *Jonathan Davidson*
Festival Coordinator *Bernadette Bogan*

FOUNDED 1983. Annual two-week festival held in May. Concerned with all aspects of contemporary reading and writing, with visiting authors, workshops, performances, cabaret, conferences and special programmes for young people.

Book Now!
Langholm Lodge, 146 Petersham Road, Richmond, Surrey TW10 6UX
☎0181 332 0534   Fax 0181 940 7568
Director *Nigel Cutting*

FOUNDED 1992. Annual festival which runs throughout the month of November, administered by the Arts Section of Richmond Council. Principal focus is on poetry and serious fiction, but events also cover biography, writing for theatre, children's writing. Programme includes readings, discussions, workshops, debates, exhibitions, schools events. Writers to appear at past festivals include A.S. Byatt, Penelope Lively, Benjamin Zephaniah, Sir Dirk Bogarde, Roger McGough, Rose Tremain, John Mortimer and Sean Hughes.

Bournemouth International Festival
Suite 2, Digby Chambers, Bournemouth, Dorset BH1 1BA
☎01202 297327   Fax 01202 552510
Contact *Julian Robbins, Marketing & Publicity*

FOUNDED 1991 and now under the new artistic direction of Gavin Henderson. Features opera, jazz, comedy, literature, theatre, visual arts, concerts (both classical and rock).

Brighton Festival

Festival Office, 21–22 Old Steine, Brighton,
East Sussex BN1 1EL
☎01273 713875   Fax 01273 622453

Contact *General Administrator*

FOUNDED 1967. For 24 days every May,
Brighton hosts England's largest mixed arts fes-
tival. Music, dance, theatre, film, opera, litera-
ture, comedy and exhibitions. In 1993 the
Observer declared, 'The broad minded Brighton
Festival is a cultural feast'.

Literary enquiries will be passed to the literature officer. Deadline October for the following May.

Buxton Opera Festival

1 Crescent View, Hall Bank, Buxton,
Derbyshire SK17 6EN
☎01298 70395   Fax 01298 72289

Contact *General Manager*

FOUNDED 1979. Annual two-and-a-half-week
festival held in July. Rarely performed operas
are staged in Buxton Opera House in collaboration with Opera North, and the programme
is complemented by a wide variety of other
musical events, including the Buxton Jazz
Festival, 30 July.

Canterbury Festival

Christ Church Gate, The Precincts,
Canterbury, Kent CT1 2EE
☎01227 452853   Fax 01227 781830

Festival Director *Mark Deller*

FOUNDED 1984. Annual two-week festival
held in October. A mixed programme of
events including talks by visiting authors, readings and storytelling, walks, concerts in the
cathedral, jazz, master classes, drama, visual
arts, opera, film, cabaret and dance.

Cardiff Literature Festival

The Welsh Academy, 3rd Floor,
Mount Stuart House, Mount Stuart Square,
Cardiff CF1 6DQ
☎01222 492025   Fax 01222 492930

Director *Kevin Thomas*

FOUNDED 1986. Annual week-long festival
held in the autumn. Readings, workshops, discussions, children's events, science fiction and
fantasy conventions and prize-givings.

Cheltenham Festival

See **The Daily Telegraph Cheltenham
Festival of Literature**

Chester Literature Festival

c/o Bookland & Co. Ltd., 1 Stanley Street,
Chester CH1 2NJ
☎01244 324394   Fax 01244 344780

Chairman *John Elsley*

FOUNDED 1989. Annual festival during October, organised by local bookshops, writers'
groups and Chester Arts Association. Major
events sponsored by publishers.

Cleveland Festival

See **Write Around — A Celebration of
Cleveland Writing**

Colchester–Essex Arts Festival

Department of Literature, University of Essex,
Colchester, Essex CO4 3SQ
☎01206 872636   Fax 01206 873130

Contact *Joseph Allard*

Began life as a literature festival but later
expanded to include a variety of other events.
Held annually, around November. (Cancelled
in 1995 but the festival is expected to take
place in 1996.) Check for precise details.

Contact Young Playwrights' Festival

Oxford Road, Manchester M15 6JA
☎0161 274 3434

Contact *Lisa Renowden*

FOUNDED 1986. Annual summer festival open
to young people aged between 11 and 25 living in the North-west of England. From the
entries, which need to be in by the January of
the festival year, twenty are selected for workshops and from these, a number are produced
by a professional company before a two-week
tour to schools in the region. All of the finalists
are taken on a residential writing course in the
Lake District with professional writers and
directors who help them to develop their
work. All scripts submitted to the festival
receive a critical analysis.

The Daily Telegraph Cheltenham Festival of Literature

Town Hall, Imperial Square, Cheltenham,
Gloucestershire GL50 1QA
☎01242 521621   Fax 01242 573902

Festival Organiser *Nicola Bennett*

FOUNDED 1949. Sponsored by *The Daily
Telegraph*. Annual festival held in October. The
first purely literary festival of its kind, it has
developed over the past decade into the largest
and most popular in Europe. A wide range of

events including talks and lectures, poetry readings, novelists in conversation, exhibitions, discussions, cabaret and a large bookfair.

Dartington Literary Festival
See **Ways With Words**

Doncaster Library Festival
Doncaster Central Library, Waterdale, Doncaster, South Yorkshire DN1 3JE
☎01302 734305 Fax 01302 369749
Contact *Festival Organiser*

FOUNDED 1988. Annual festival (4–5 days) in October/November, covering a wide range of events for adults and children. Readings, cabaret, drama, music and creative writing workshops. Visiting authors have included Andrea Newman, Stan Barstow, Michael Hardcastle, Carol Ann Duffy, Simon Armitage, Pete Morgan, Adrian Henri, Matt Simpson, Sarah Harrison, Ian McMillan, Martyn Wiley, Margaret Drabble, Berlie Doherty. Features the Doncaster Writers' Stakes Race held at the town's racecourse.

The Festival of Dover
Dover District Council, White Cliffs Business Park, Dover, Kent CT16 3PD
☎01304 821199 Fax 01304 827269
Festival Organiser *Sarah Pascoe*

Two-week festival held in May, including a wide variety of arts activities. The programme encompasses exhibitions, concerts, dance, drama, walks and literary talks/workshops. 1995 guests included Michelle Magorian and Jan Mark.

Dublin International Writers' Festival
An Chomhairle Ealaíon (The Arts Council), 70 Merrion Square, Dublin 2
☎00 353 1 6611840 Fax 00 353 1 6761302
Festival Director *Laurence Cassidy*

Biennial festival held in September. Features conference sessions, public interviews, debates, readings and exhibitions, with some of the world's leading authors in attendance.

Durham Literary Festival
Durham City Arts, Byland Lodge, Hawthorn Terrace, Durham City DH1 4TD
☎0191 386 6111 ext. 338 Fax 0191 386 0625
Secretary *Paul Rubinstein*

FOUNDED 1989. Annual 2–3-week event, end May–June, held at various locations in the city. Workshops, plus performances, cabaret, and other events.

Edinburgh Book Festival
Scottish Book Centre, 137 Dundee Street, Edinburgh EH11 1BG
☎0131 228 5444 Fax 0131 228 4333
Director *Shona Munro*

FOUNDED 1983. Biennial book festival held during the first fortnight of the Edinburgh International Festival. Now established as Britain's biggest book event, the programme includes discussions, readings and lectures by writers of national and international reputation. The next festival dates are 9–25 August, 1997.

Exeter Festival
Festival Office, Civic Centre, Exeter, Devon EX1 1JN
☎01392 265200 Fax 01392 265265
Festival Organiser *Lesley Maynard*
Artistic Director *Paul Patterson*

FOUNDED 1980. Annual two-week festival with a variety of events including concerts, theatre, dance and exhibitions.

First Bite – BBC Radio Young Writers' Festival
Room 620, Broadcasting House, London W1A 1AA
Contact *Anne Edyvean*

FOUNDED 1988 – formerly the Young Play-wright's Festival. Takes place every 2/3 years. Open to writers aged 16 – 30 (inclusive) who are new to radio. Plays and stories in five categories. For more details contact the above.

Glasgow Mayfest
See **Mayfest**

Greenwich Festival
6 College Approach, London SE10 9HY
☎0181 305 1818 Fax 0181 305 1188
Director *Bradley Hemmings*

FOUNDED 1970. Annual festival in June. Features a wide variety of events, including world music, theatre, dance, classical music, jazz, comedy, art.

Guildford Book Festival
Arts Office, University of Surrey, Guildford, Surrey GU2 5XH
☎01483 259167
Book Festival Organiser *Camilla Dinkel*

FOUNDED 1989. A ten-day celebration of books and writing held annually, during the autumn half term, throughout the town. The programme includes literary lunches; poetry readings; a writer-in-residence; children's events; the Annual University Poetry Lecture; writing workshops and bookshop events.

The Hay Festival
Festival Office, Hay-on-Wye, Powys HR3 5BX
☎01497 821217   Fax 01497 821066
Festival Director *Peter Florence*
FOUNDED 1988. Annual May festival sponsored by *The Independent*. Guests have included Salman Rushdie, Toni Morrison, Stephen Fry, Joseph Heller, Carlos Fuentes, Maya Angelou, Amos Oz, Arthur Miller.

Huddersfield Poetry Festival
c/o The Word Hoard, 46/47 Byram Arcade, Westgate, Huddersfield, West Yorkshire HD1 1ND
☎01484 452070   Fax 01484 455049
Contact *Dianne Darby*
Thrice-yearly event consisting of a spring season of around six events over as many weeks, a one-day open-air poetry marathon in June, and one or more weekend writing courses sometime in the autumn. Also occasional one-off events. Though very interested in local writers, the festival has a cosmopolitan outlook and features related performance arts within the curriculum.

Hull Literature Festival
Festival Office, 79 Ferensway, Hull HU2 8LE
☎01482 595673   Fax 01482 595656
Director *David Porter*
FOUNDED 1992. Annual festival running in November.

Ilkley Literature Festival
Festival Office, Manor House Museum, Ilkley, West Yorkshire LS29 9DT
☎01943 601210
Director *David Porter*
FOUNDED 1973. Three festivals a year of 4–5 days' duration. Previous guests have included Tony Harrison, Sarah Dunant, Irina Ratushinskaya, Colin Thubron. Also presents children's events, storytellers, theatre and music, and creative writing workshops. Runs the **Yorkshire Open Poetry Competition**. Telephone to join free mailing list.

Kent Literature Festival
The Metropole Arts Centre, The Leas, Folkestone, Kent CT20 2LS
☎01303 255070
Festival Director *David Stone*

Festival Administrator *Ann Fearey*
FOUNDED 1980. Annual week-long festival held at the end of September which aims to bring the best in modern writing to a large audience. Visiting authors and dramatic presentations are a regular feature along with creative writing workshops, seminars, discussions and children's/family events. Also runs the **Kent Young Writers of the Year Award** and **Short Story Competition**. Brochure for the 1996 festival available from the end of July.

King's Lynn, The Fiction Festival
19 Tuesday Market Place, King's Lynn, Norfolk PE30 1JW
☎01553 691661 (office hours) or 761919
Fax 01553 691779
Contact *Anthony Ellis*
FOUNDED 1989. Annual weekend festival held in March. Over the weekend there are readings and discussions, attended by guest writers of which there are usually eight. Previous guests have included Beryl Bainbridge, Malcolm Bradbury, Marina Warner, William Golding, Hilary Mantel, Elizabeth Jane Howard.

King's Lynn, The Poetry Festival
19 Tuesday Market Place, King's Lynn, Norfolk PE30 1JW
☎01553 691661 (office hours) or 761919
Fax 01553 691779
Contact *Anthony Ellis*
FOUNDED 1985. Annual weekend festival held at the end of September, with guest poets (usually eight). Previous guests have included Carol Ann Duffy, Paul Durcan, Gavin Ewart, Peter Porter, Stephen Spender. Events include readings and discussion panels.

Lancaster LitFest
67 Church Street, Lancaster LA1 1ET
☎01524 62166   Fax 01524 841216
Director *John Freeman*
FOUNDED 1978. Annual festival in October which focuses on contemporary writing and includes performance poetry, readings, theatre, film, dance, music and workshops. Plus a year-round programme of regular writers' and readers' events and development projects.

City of London Festival
230 Bishopsgate, London EC2M 4QD
☎0171 377 0540   Fax 0171 377 1972
FOUNDED 1962. Annual three-week festival held in June and July. Features over forty classical

and popular music events alongside poetry and prose readings, street theatre and open-air jazz extravaganzas, in some of the most outstanding performance spaces in the world.

London Radio Playwrights' Festival

Independent Radio Drama Productions Ltd, Manningtree, Essex CO11 1XD
Directors *Tim Crook, Richard Shannon*

FOUNDED 1990 for writers working, studying or living in Greater London and attracts over 300 scripts every year. The festival, which falls into two parts (workshops and script competition) offers an opportunity to learn about radio writing. Part one (workshop) begins with an open discussion on radio drama led by **London Radio**'s resident drama directors at various venues throughout London. There is also a programme of workshops and masterclasses with well-known playwrights such as Alan Plater, Olwen Wymark and Wally K. Daly. Phase two of the festival invites anyone living, working or studying in London to submit scripts to the competition. Five plays will be chosen to go into production and will be broadcast on London Radio the following year. Scripts should be no more than 60 minutes in length and should be sent to the address above. Sponsored by the **London Arts Board**. **Writer's Guild** rates paid for transmission. Festival brochure available from address above.

Ludlow Festival

Castle Square, Ludlow, Shropshire SY8 1AY
☎01584 875070   Fax 01584 877673
Contact *Festival Administrator*

FOUNDED 1959. Annual two-week festival held in the last week of June and first week of July with an open-air Shakespeare production held at Ludlow Castle and a varied programme of events including recitals, opera, dance, popular and classical concerts, literary and historical lectures.

Manchester Festival of Writing

Manchester Central Library, St Peter's Square, Manchester M2 5PD
☎0161 234 1901
Contact *Tang Lin*

FOUNDED 1990. An annual event organised by Manchester Libraries and Commonword community publishers as part of the Boddington's Manchester Festival in September/October. It consists of a programme of practical writing workshops on specific themes/genres run by well-known writers. Attendance at all workshops is free to Manchester residents.

Mayfest

18 Albion Street, Glasgow G1 1LH
☎0141 552 8000   Fax 0141 552 6612
Director *Paul Bassett*

FOUNDED 1982. Annual three-week festival in May of arts and entertainments for both the people of Glasgow and visitors from all over the world. Encompasses all art forms and in 1995 included three large open-air celebrations and explorations of new technology.

Royal Court Young Writers' Festival

Royal Court Young People's Theatre, 309 Portobello Road, London W10 5TD
☎0181 960 4641   Fax 0181 960 1434
Contact *Festival Organiser*

Open to young people up to the age of 23 in targeted regions. Focuses on the process of playwriting: writers and directors from the Royal Court visit a number of selected parts of Britain with five centres in each area, leading a workshop on playwriting. A second visit extends this process to the point at which young people attending are invited to submit work for the festival. Intensive work on the final draft of plays precedes production at the Royal Court Theatre Upstairs, before going on tour in the participating areas.

Salisbury Festival

Festival Office, The King's House, 65 The Close, Salisbury, Wiltshire SP1 2EN
☎01722 323883   Fax 01722 410552
Director *Helen Marriage*

FOUNDED 1972. Annual festival held in the last two weeks of May. Previous participants have included Max Hastings, Victoria Glendinning, Joanna Trollope, Colin Thubron, Bernice Rubens, Howard Jacobson, Jo Shapcott, Andrew Motion, Leslie Thomas and John Julius Norwich.

Scottish Young Playwrights Festival

Scottish Youth Theatre, Old Athenaeum Theatre, 179 Buchanan Street, Glasgow G1 2JZ
☎0141 332 5127   Fax 0141 332 2333
Aritistic Director *Mary McCluskey*

The Scottish Young Playwrights project operates throughout Scotland. In every region an experienced theatre practitioner runs regular young writers' workshops aimed at developing the best possible scripts from initial ideas. A representative selection of scripts is then selected to form a showcase. The festival is mounted at the Old Athenaeum in December, in conjunction with the Royal Scottish Academy of Music and Drama. Scripts will be workshopped, revised and developed culminating in an evening presentation. Scripts are welcome throughout the year from young people aged 15–25 who are native Scots and/or resident in Scotland. Scripts should last no less than 15 minutes and no more than 45; synopses of unfinished scripts also considered. No restriction on style, content or intended media, but work must be original and unperformed. Further details from above.

South London International Playwriting Festival

Warehouse Theatre, Dingwall Road, Croydon CR0 2NF
☎0181 681 1257   Fax 0181 688 6699

FOUNDED 1985. Annual autumn competition of full-length and unperformed plays, judged by a panel of theatre professionals. Finalists given rehearsed readings during the festival in November. Entries welcomed from all parts of the world. Scripts, plus two stamped addressed envelopes (one script-sized), should reach the **Warehouse Theatre** by the beginning of July. Previous winners produced at the theatre include: Kevin Hood *Beached;* Anne Aylor *Children of the Dust;* Mark Bunyan *Dinner;* Ellen Fox *Conversations with George Sandburgh After a Solo Flight Across the Atlantic;* Guy Jenkin *Fighting for the Dunghill;* James Martin Charlton *Fat Souls*; Douglas Esson *Nervous Breakdown*; Dino Mahoney *Yo Yo.*

Stratford-upon-Avon Poetry Festival

The Shakespeare Centre, Henley Street, Stratford-upon-Avon, Warwickshire CV37 6QW
☎01789 204016   Fax 01789 296083
Festival Director *Roger Pringle*

FOUNDED 1953. Annual festival held on Sunday evenings during July and August. Readings by poets and professional actors.

Warwick & Leamington Festival

Warwick Arts Society, Northgate, Warwick CV34 4JL
☎01926 410747   Fax 01926 407606
Festival Director *Richard Phillips*

FOUNDED 1980. Annual festival lasting 12 days in the first half of July. Basically a chamber music festival, with some open-air, large-scale concerts in Warwick Castle, the festival also promotes plays by Shakespeare in historical settings. Large-

scale education programme. Interested in increasing its literary content, organised in conjunction with Pauline Prior-Pitt.

Ways with Words

Droridge Farm, Dartington, Totnes, Devon TQ9 6JQ
☎01803 867311   Fax 01803 863688
Contact *Kay Dunbar*

FOUNDED 1992. Ways with Words is a literature festival held in South Devon at Dartington Hall, a setting of exceptional beauty. Features lectures, readings, interviews, discussions, performances, master classes and workshops. Guest participants have included Melvyn Bragg, Mavis Cheek, Lucy Ellman, Penelope Lively, Brian Patten, Alan Plater, Ruth Rendell, Sue Townsend, Robin Skynner and Mary Wesley. The festival organisers offer a package deal (seven nights board with admission to all events except classes and workshops) but tickets are available to individual events with B&B accommodation on-site if required. Ways with Words also arranges winter literary weekends around the country plus writing and watercolour courses in Tuscany.

Write Around, A Celebration of Cleveland Writing

Berwick Hills Library, Ormesby Road, Berwick Hills, Middlesbrough, Cleveland TS3 7RP
☎01642 246947
Contact *Alyson Perry*

FOUNDED 1989. Annual two-week festival with a commitment to local writers. Held during the last two weeks of October, featuring workshops and readings, plus guest writers and opportunities for new writers. Publishes anthologies of poetry and short stories compiled from submissions by Cleveland writers. Contact above for further information. Programmes available in August.

Writers Live

Cultural Services, Shire Hall, Shinfield Park, Reading, Berkshire RG2 9XD
☎01734 233255   Fax 01734 233203
Contact *Festival Director*

This annual autumn book festival in Berkshire is held in October over four consecutive weekends. The festival aims to celebrate new writing of high quality in all its forms, as well as the oral traditions and literary heritage.

The Translator
as a Creative Artist

Literary translation is not confined to the translation of great literature. When the 1988 Copyright Act refers to 'literary works' it places no limitations on their style or quality. All kinds of books, plays, poems, short stories and other writings are covered, including a collection of jokes, the script of a documentary, a travel guide and an encyclopedia.

Who qualifies?

It is possible to be a translator without holding any formal qualifications. Some translators develop their skills from a bilingual family or having lived for long periods in two countries. However, a formal university education in Modern Languages is helpful, especially if it includes classes in translation. Courses and workshops designed to improve translation techniques may be useful though there is no guarantee of subsequent commissions. The value of language diplomas can be enhanced by specialist qualifications. For example, a publisher who wants a book on genetic engineering translated may be keen to commission a translator with a degree in biology.

A degree is not enough

The translator needs to have a feeling and fascination for language, an intimate knowledge of the source language of a particular project and of its regional culture and literature as well as a reasonable knowledge of any relevant special subject. But more than this, the translator must be a skilled and creative writer in the target language. The aim always should be to convey the meaning of the original work, as opposed to producing a mere accurate rendering of the words. The text must read well, while echoing the style and tone of the original – as if the original author were writing in the target language.

Making a living

Almost without exception, translators of books and plays work on a freelance basis. As in all freelance occupations, it is not easy for the beginner to ensure a constant flow of commissions. Only a few translators can earn a full salary and may well have other sources of income such as language teaching or lecturing. Equally, they may write books themselves as well as translating other authors' work; or be registered with a translation agency and accept shorter (and possibly more lucrative) commercial items between longer stretches of literary translation.

Ground rules

Under the Copyright Act, a translation is an adaptation of the original foreign language work, so the translator must ensure that the owner's permission has been obtained before starting work.

There is a popular misconception that translating a text from one language into another is a mechanical exercise – a matter of straight conversion or even copying. Yet if two translators are given the same source text, the result may be two quite different but equally valid versions in the target language. In the theatre too, we are used to seeing a succession of new translations of classic plays, proving that each translator creates something original that is specially made to 'speak' to a particular audience. The law recognises this 'original' nature of a translation and affords copyright protection to the translation, separate from the copyright protection to which the original foreign work is entitled and also separate from the protection of someone else's translation of the same work. In European countries, protection generally lasts until the end of the seventieth year after the death of the translator.

It is a golden rule that unless the author has given permission for changes to be made in the text, the translation must be faithful to the original work.

Rate for the job

When a translation is made in the course of employment, the employer is the owner of the copyright. A self-employed translator, on the other hand, is not simply 'doing a job' but according to copyright law, creating an original literary work. Anyone who wants to publish the translation or reproduce it in any way must obtain a licence from the translator for the relevant rights, in return for suitable remuneration. Like the original author, the translator should expect remuneration to reflect the amount of use that is made of the translation. If payment is in the form of a fee: i.e. a lump sum, it should not be 'for the translation' but for a specified use of the translator's work, e.g. for the right to print 5,000 copies for sale in the UK. Such an arrangement makes fair allowance for additional fees to be paid, for example if further copies are sold or if the licence is extended to include America. For the translation of a book, the Model Contract issued by the Translators Association recommends that there should be an advance payment on account of a royalty on each copy sold and a share of the proceeds from uses such as serialisation. In the case of a play, the translator should receive a percentage of the gross box office receipts. The translator should be able to obtain additional payment if asked to edit a literary work as well as translate it: and there should be an additional fee for the preparation of an index for the translated edition. When translations are borrowed from public libraries, the translator receives a 30% share of the full Public Lending Right payment.

Finding work

For the beginner, the usual method of obtaining commissions is to send a letter and a short sample translation to selected publishers, letting them know that the translator is seeking commissions.

Only a fraction of all the works published in their original language are published subsequently in translation but a translator who knows the market may spot a likely candidate for translation. The first step is to contact the owner of the translation rights who may be the original author or a foreign publisher. The translator needs to know if translation rights are available; and, if so, whether the owner is willing to authorise an approach to potential publishers.

It is no easy task to obtain commissions. Opportunities are likely to arise after trade gatherings such as the Frankfurt Book Fair and the Bologna Children's Book Fair where publishers and literary agents are busily engaged in buying and selling translation rights.

Author and translator: a joint venture?

Usually the rights owner, either author or publisher, accepts lower royalties on the translated edition, say, a 7½% royalty on sales of a translated book compared with 10% on sales in its original language. On a theatre production the original author might receive 6% instead of 10%. The author may also forego a share of secondary rights, e.g. of the proceeds from the sale of American rights. This means that some or all of the payment received by the translator is money that would otherwise have been paid to the original author. To that extent, the *author* is the person who is paying the translator.

Sometimes the foreign author of a work is so keen to see it translated that he will offer to pay the translation costs directly. But translating the text is not a guarantee that the translation will be published. A written contract between author and translator should clarify the rights of each party and specify how any proceeds from publication or production are to be divided.

Grants, bursaries and prizes

There are very few grants for translators but a limited number of residential bursaries are offered from time to time by The British Centre for Literary Translation, Department of Modern Languages and European History. The University of East Anglia, Norwich NR4 1TJ. For up-to-date information about similar bursaries abroad, it may be worth contacting the Cultural Attaché of the relevant embassy or bodies such as the French Institute, the Goethe Institut and the Italian Institute. The Arts Council of England offers bursaries to theatre translators under its Theatre Translation Schemes. The Translators Association administers several prizes for already published translations and the Arts Council sometimes contributes towards the cost of producing translations.

The Translators Association

The Translators Association is a subsidiary group within the Society of Authors. Published translators can apply for full membership. Translators in the making may apply for Associate Membership either when they have received an offer for a full length translation or if they have had occasional translations of shorter material, e.g. articles, short stories and poems, published or performed commercially.

For translators of books, the Association's Model Contract, with explanatory Notes, is available free to members; and the Association also issues Guidelines for translators of dramatic works. The Association's journal, *In Other Words*, contains a wide variety of articles, reviews and information.

Information about translation courses may be obtained from educational services and the cultural institutes of relevant countries; and the Institute of Linguists and the Institute of Translation and Interpreting may also be willing to help. The Translators Association does not usually organise training courses although it holds seminars that are helpful to working translators.

European Publishers

Austria

Paul Neff, Verlag
Hackingerstrasse 52, A-1140 Vienna
☎00 43 222 9406115
Fax 00 43 222 947641288
FOUNDED 1829. *Publishes* art, biography, general fiction, music and dance.

Springer-Verlag
Mölkerbastei 5, Postfach 367, 1D11 Vienna
☎00 43 222 3302415 Fax 00 43 222 3302426
FOUNDED 1924. *Publishes* engineering (general), medicine and textbooks (university), science (general).

Verlag Carl Ueberreuter
Alserstrasse 24, Postfach 306, A-1090 Vienna
☎00 43 222 404440 Fax 00 43 222 404445
FOUNDED 1548. *Publishes* fiction and general non-fiction: history, politics, economics, general and political science, science fiction, fantasy, music and art.

Paul Zsolnay Verlag GmbH
Prinz Eugenstrasse 30, Postfach 142,
A-1041 Vienna
☎00 43 222 50576610
Fax 00 43 222 505766110
FOUNDED 1923. *Publishes* biography, fiction, general non-fiction, history, poetry.

Belgium

Facet NV
Wetstraat 63, 2008 Antwerp
☎00 32 3 235 8183 Fax 00 32 3 236 6146
FOUNDED 1976. *Publishes* miscellaneous subjects, specialising in children's books.

Uitgeverij Lannoo NV
Kasteelstrasse 97, B-8700 Tielt
☎00 32 51 424211 Fax 00 32 51 401152
FOUNDED 1909. *Publishes* art, biography, economics, general non-fiction, guide books, history, management, photography, poetry, politics, religion.

Standaard Uitgeverij
Belgiëlei 147a, B-2018 Antwerp
☎00 32 3 2395900 Fax 00 32 3 2308550
FOUNDED 1919. *Publishes* fiction, humour, education.

Forlaget Apostrof ApS
Berggreensgade 24, Postboks 2580, DK-2100
Copenhagen Ø
☎00 45 31 208420 Fax 00 45 31 208453
FOUNDED 1980. *Publishes* fiction, literature, humour, general non-fiction, psychology.

Denmark

Aschehoug Fakta
7 Vognmagergade, PO Box 2179, DK-1017
Copenhagen 0
☎00 45 31 919222 Fax 00 45 31 918218
FOUNDED 1877. *Publishes* popular reference.

Borgens Forlag A/S
Valbygaardsvej 33, DK-2500 Valby
☎00 45 36 462100 Fax 00 45 36 441488
FOUNDED 1948. *Publishes* art, computers, crafts and leisure, education, general fiction and non-fiction, health and social science, nutrition, religion.

Forum Publishers
Snaregade 4, DK-1205 Copenhagen K
☎00 45 33 147714 Fax 00 45 33 147791
FOUNDED 1940. *Publishes* fiction and mysteries.

G.E.C. Gads Publishers
Vimmelskaftet 32, DK-1161 Copenhagen K
☎00 45 33 150558 Fax 00 45 33 123825
FOUNDED 1855. *Publishes* biological sciences, cookery, crafts, hobbies, economics, education, English as a second language, environmental studies, gardening, plants, law, mathematics, natural history, non-fiction (general), physics, travel.

Gyldendalske Boghandel-Nordisk Forlag A/S
Klareboderne 3, DK-1001 Copenhagen K
☎00 45 33 110775 Fax 00 45 33 110323
FOUNDED 1770. *Publishes* general fiction,

poetry, biography, history, how-to, music, art, philosophy, medicine, psychology, general and social sciences.

Hekla Forlag
Valbygaardsvej 33, DK-2500 Valby
☎00 45 36 462100   Fax 00 45 36 441488
FOUNDED 1979. *Publishes* general fiction and non-fiction.

Høst & Søns Publishers Ltd
Norre Sogade 35, PO Box 2212, DK-1018 Copenhagen K
☎00 45 33 153031   Fax 00 45 33 155155
FOUNDED 1836. *Publishes* environmental studies, hobbies and crafts, language arts and linguistics, travel, reference.

Det Ny Lademann A/S
Gerdasgade 37, DK-2500 Valby
☎00 45 36 441120   Fax 00 45 36 442236
FOUNDED 1954. *Publishes* general non-fiction.

Lindhardt and Ringhof
Kristianiagade 14, DK-2100 Copenhagen K
☎00 45 35 434455   Fax 00 45 35 436520
FOUNDED 1971. *Publishes* general fiction and non-fiction.

Nyt Nordisk Forlag
Arnold Busck A/S
Købmagergade 49, DK-1150 Copenhagen K
☎00 45 33 111103   Fax 00 45 33 934490
FOUNDED 1896. *Publishes* general fiction, biography, history, how-to, music, art, philosophy, reference, religion, medicine, psychology, general and social sciences.

Politikens Forlag A/S
Vestergade 26, DK-1456 Copenhagen K
☎00 45 33 112122   Fax 00 45 33 932152
FOUNDED 1946. *Publishes* art, general non-fiction, how-to, history, hobbies, music, natural history, sports, travel.

Samlerens Forlag A/S
Snaregade 4, DK-1205 Copenhagen K
☎00 45 33 131023   Fax 00 45 33 144314
FOUNDED 1942. *Publishes* biography, history, politics, general fiction.

Det Schönbergske Forlag A/S
Landemaerket 5, DK-1119 Copenhagen K
☎00 45 33 113066   Fax 00 45 33 330045
FOUNDED 1857. *Publishes* art, poetry, biography,

general fiction and non-fiction, history, philosophy, travel

Spektrum Forlagsaktieselskab
4 Snaregade, DK-1205 Copenhagen K
☎00 45 33 147714   Fax 00 45 33 147791
FOUNDED 1990. *Publishes* general non-fiction only.

Tiderne Skifter Forlag A/S
51 Pilestrade, DK-1159 Copenhagen K
☎00 45 33 325772   Fax 00 45 33 144205
FOUNDED 1979. *Publishes* fiction, literature and literary criticism, photography.

Wangels Forlag AS
Gerdasgade 37, DK-2500 Valby
☎00 45 36 441120   Fax 00 45 36 441162
FOUNDED 1946. *Publishes* general fiction.

Finland

Gummerus Publishers
Erottajankatu 5C, PO Box 2, SF-00130 Helsinki
☎00 358 0 644301   Fax 00 358 0 604998
FOUNDED 1872. *Publishes* general fiction, non-fiction, reference.

Karisto Oy
Paroistentie 2, PO Box 102, SF-13100 Hämeenlinna
☎00 358 17 6161551   Fax 00 358 17 6161555
FOUNDED 1900. *Publishes* general fiction and non-fiction.

Kirjayhtymä Oy
Eerikinkatu 28, PO Box 207, SF-00180 Helsinki
☎00 358 0 6944522   Fax 00 358 0 6947265
FOUNDED 1958. *Publishes* fiction, non-fiction, textbooks.

Otava Kustannusosakeyhtiö
Undenmaankatu 8–12, PO Box 134, SF-00120 Helsinki
☎00 358 0 19961   Fax 00 358 0 643136
FOUNDED 1890. *Publishes* general fiction, biography, history, how-to, music, art, philosophy, reference, religion, children's, textbooks.

Werner Söderström Osakeyhtiö (WSOY)
Bulevardi 12, PO Box 222, SF-00121 Helsinki
☎00 358 0 161681   Fax 00 358 0 6168405

FOUNDED 1878. *Publishes* fiction, general non-fiction, children's, textbooks, encyclopedias.

Tammi Kustannusosakeyhtiö
Eerikinkatu 28, SF-00180 Helsinki
☎00 358 0 6942700   Fax 00 358 0 6942711
FOUNDED 1943. *Publishes* fiction, general non-fiction, children's.

France

Alyscamps Press
35 rue de l'Esperance, 75013 Paris
☎00 33 1 4581 1524   Fax 00 33 1 4581 1524
FOUNDED 1993. Small independent literary publisher specialising in literary translation into English and reprints of neglected classics. *Publishes* literary criticism, bibliography, belles lettres, poetry, biography, regional studies, translations. No unsolicited mss; synopses welcome for non-fiction only. S.a.e. required for reply.

Editions Arthaud SA
20 rue Monsieur le Prince, F-75006 Paris
☎00 33 1 4329 1220   Fax 00 33 1 4329 2148
FOUNDED 1890. *Publishes* art, history, literature, sport, travel.

Editions Pierre Belfond
216 blvd St-Germain, F-75243 Paris 07
☎00 33 1 4544 3823   Fax 00 33 1 4544 9804
FOUNDED 1963. *Publishes* art, belles lettres, bibliography, biography, general fiction and non-fiction, history, music, mysteries and poetry.

Editions Bordas
17 rue Rémy Dumoncel, BP50, F-75661 Paris
☎00 33 1 4279 6200   Fax 00 33 1 4322 8518
FOUNDED 1946. *Publishes* dictionaries, encyclopedias, education, general non-fiction and reference.

Editions Calmann-Lévy SA
3 rue Auber, F-75009 Paris
☎00 33 1 4742 3833   Fax 00 33 1 4742 7781
FOUNDED 1836. *Publishes* biography, general fiction, history, humour, philosophy, psychology, science fiction, social sciences, sports.

Editions Denoël Sàrl
73–74 rue Pascal, F-75013 Paris
☎00 33 1 4336 2728   Fax 00 33 1 4336 6396
Publishes art, deluxe editions, documents, economics, general and science fiction, history, philosophy, political science, psychology, reference, sports, thrillers.

Librairie Arthème Fayard
75 rue des Sts-Pères, F-75006 Paris
☎00 33 1 4544 3845   Fax 00 33 1 4222 4017
FOUNDED 1854. *Publishes* biography, general fiction, history, human and social sciences, music, religion, reference, technology.

Librairie Ernest Flammarion
26 rue de Racine, F-75278 Paris 06
☎00 33 1 4051 3100
Fax 00 33 1 4329 2148
FOUNDED 1875. *Publishes* general fiction and non-fiction, belles lettres, poetry, biography, history, how-to, photography, art, philosophy, reference, economics, general and social science, textbooks (university), education, medicine, children's.

Editions Gallimard
5 rue Sébastien-Bottin, F-75007 Paris
☎00 33 1 4954 4200   Fax 00 33 1 4286 8388
FOUNDED 1911. *Publishes* art, belles lettres, poetry, biography, general fiction, history, music, philosophy.

Société des Editions Grasset et Fasquelle
61 rue des Sts-Pères, F-75006 Paris
☎00 33 1 4544 3814   Fax 00 33 1 4222 6418
FOUNDED 1907. *Publishes* general fiction and non-fiction, philosophy.

Hachette
24 blvd St-Michel, F-75288 Paris 06
☎00 33 1 4634 8634   Fax 00 33 1 4634 6545
FOUNDED 1826. *Publishes* general fiction and non-fiction, history, architecture, art, travel, reference, education, science, textbooks, engineering, politics, economics, social science, philosophy, sports, languages.

Editions Robert Laffont
31 rue Falguière, F-75279 Paris 15
☎00 33 1 4329 1233   Fax 00 33 1 4327 1412
FOUNDED 1941. *Publishes* general fiction, history, philosophy, religion, art, music, biography, medicine, general and social sciences, psychology, textbooks.

Librairie Larousse
17 rue du Montparnasse, F-75298 Paris 06
☎00 33 1 4439 4400   Fax 00 33 1 4439 4343
FOUNDED 1852. *Publishes* dictionaries, encyclo-

pedias, general and social sciences, linguistics, reference, technical, textbooks, children's.

Editions Jean–Claude Lattès
17 rue Jacob, F-75006 Paris
☎00 33 1 4441 7400   Fax 00 33 1 4325 3047
FOUNDED 1968. *Publishes* biography, documents, general fiction and non-fiction, Jewish religion, music.

Les Editions Magnard Sàrl
91 blvd St-Germain, BP 265, F-75279 Paris 06
☎00 33 1 4326 3952   Fax 00 33 1 4633 9604
FOUNDED 1933. *Publishes* textbooks, educational, international series in basic French, and children's.

Michelin et Cie (Services de Tourisme)
46 ave de Breteuil, F-75324 Paris 07
☎00 33 1 4566 1234   Fax 00 33 1 4566 1163
FOUNDED 1900. *Publishes* atlases, maps, travel and tourist guides in various languages.

Les Editions de Minuit SA
7 rue Bernard-Palissy, F-75006 Paris
☎00 33 1 4439 3920
FOUNDED 1942. *Publishes* general fiction, literature, philosophy, social science.

Fernand Nathan
9 rue Méchain, F-75014 Paris
☎00 33 1 4587 5000   Fax 00 33 1 4331 2169
FOUNDED 1881. *Publishes* reference, dictionaries, art, philosophy, textbooks, psychology, general and social sciences, guidebooks, nature, history, education and children's paperbacks.

Les Presses de la Cité
12 Ave d'Italie, F-75627 Paris 13
☎00 33 1 4416 0500   Fax 00 33 1 4416 0511
FOUNDED 1947. *Publishes* French and foreign literature, history, biography, anthropology, essays, science fiction, fiction, war, how-to, travel, children's.

Presses Universitaires de France (PUF)
108 blvd St-Germain, F-75279 Paris 06
☎00 33 1 4634 1201   Fax 00 33 1 4634 6541
FOUNDED 1921. *Publishes* biography, history, geography, music, art, philosophy, reference, religion, engineering, psychology, medicine, general, social and political science, textbooks (university).

Editions du Seuil
27 rue Jacob, F-75261 Paris 06
☎00 33 1 4046 5050   Fax 00 33 1 4329 0829
FOUNDED 1935. *Publishes* general fiction, literature, poetry, biography, history, how-to, music, art, philosophy, religion, psychology, general and social sciences, textbooks (university), politics.

Les Editions de la Table Ronde
7 rue Corneille, F-75006 Paris
☎00 33 1 4326 0395   Fax 00 33 1 4407 0930
FOUNDED 1944. *Publishes* belles lettres, biography, general fiction and non-fiction, history, psychology, religion.

Librairie Vuibert SA
63 blvd St-Germain, F-75005 Paris
☎00 33 1 4325 6100   Fax 00 33 1 4325 7586
FOUNDED 1877. *Publishes* sciences, economics, law, mathematics, physics and schoolbooks.

Germany

Verlag C. H. Beck (OHG)
Wilhelmstr. 9, Postfach 400340,
80703 Munich
☎00 49 89 381890   Fax 00 49 89 38189398
FOUNDED 1763. *Publishes* archaeology, history, social sciences, philosophy, theology, economics, law, art, music, linguistics, general non-fiction, anthropology.

Bertelsmann AG
Carl-Bertelsmann-Str 270, Postfach 111,
33311 Gütersloh
☎00 49 5241 801   Fax 00 49 5241 75166
FOUNDED 1835. *Publishes* fiction and non-fiction, anthropology, current affairs, art, biography, business, economics, film, how-to, law, medicine, travel, foreign works in translation.

Carlsen Verlag GmbH
Völckersstrasse 14–20, Postfach 500380,
22703 Hamburg
☎00 49 40 3910090   Fax 00 49 40 39100962
FOUNDED 1953. *Publishes* humour and general non-fiction.

Droemersche Verlagsanstalt Th. Knaur Nachfolger
Rauchstr. 9–11, Postfach 800480,
81664 Munich
☎00 49 89 92710   Fax 00 49 89 9271168

FOUNDED 1901. *Publishes* general fiction, non-fiction, cookery, travel and general science.

DTV Deutscher Taschenbuch Verlag GmbH & Co. KG

Friedrichstr. 1a, Postfach 400422, 80704 Munich
☎00 49 89 3817060   Fax 00 49 89 346428
FOUNDED 1961. *Publishes* general fiction, biography, art, music, poetry, history, how-to, psychiatry, philosophy, religion, medicine, social sciences, literature, maps and travel guides.

Econ-Verlag GmbH

Kaiserswerthe Strasse 282, Postfach 300321, 40403 Düsseldorf
☎00 49 211 439596 Fax 00 49 211 43959786
Publishes general science, economics and fiction.

Falken-Verlag GmbH

Schöne Aussicht 21, Postfach 1120, 65521 Niedernhausen
☎00 49 6127 7020   Fax 00 49 6127 702133
FOUNDED 1923. *Publishes* health, cookery, nutrition, gardening, how-to, photography, computer science, crafts and hobbies, sports, motorcycles, travel, videos.

S Fischer Verlag GmbH

Hedderichstr. 114, Postfach 700355, 60596 Frankfurt am Main
☎00 49 69 60620   Fax 00 49 69 6062319
FOUNDED 1952. *Publishes* general fiction, non-fiction, essays and literature.

Carl Hanser Verlag

Kolbergerstrasse 22, Postfach 860420, 81631 Munich
☎00 49 89 926940   Fax 00 49 89 984809
FOUNDED 1928. *Publishes* fiction and general non-fiction, poetry, general science, philosophy, mathematics, medicine, chemistry, chemical, electrical and mechanical engineering, computer science, physics, biotechnology, dentistry, business management.

Wilhelm Heyne Verlag

Türkenstr. 5–7, Postfach 201204, 80333 Munich
☎00 49 89 2317170   Fax 00 49 89 2800943
FOUNDED 1934. *Publishes* general fiction, mystery, romance, humour, science fiction, biography, history, occult, psychology, how-to, film, cookery, cartoons, poetry.

Hoffmann und Campe Verlag

Harvestehuder Weg 4, Postfach 13044, 220149 Hamburg
☎00 49 40 441880   Fax 00 49 40 44188310
FOUNDED 1781. *Publishes* fiction and general non-fiction, biography, poetry, history, art, philosophy, psychology, music, social sciences.

Klett-Cotta Verlag

Rotebühlstr. 77, Postfach 106016, 70049 Stuttgart
☎00 49 711 66720   Fax 00 49 711 28053
FOUNDED 1977. *Publishes* fiction, history, art, environmental studies, education, policial science, psychology and related fields, linguistics and sociology.

Gustav Lübbe Verlag GmbH

Scheidtbachstrasse 23–25, Postfach 200127, 51469 Bergisch Gladbach 2
☎00 49 2202 1210   Fax 00 49 2202 36727
FOUNDED 1963. *Publishes* general fiction and non-fiction, biography, archaeology, history and how-to.

Mosaik Verlag GmbH

Neumarkter Str. 18, Postfach 800360, 81673 Munich
☎00 49 89 43189577   Fax 00 49 89 4312837
Publishes cookery, gardening, crafts, health, nutrition, pets, sports, women's studies, antiques, architecture and design, economics, film, self-help.

Pestalozzi Verlag Graphische GmbH

Am Pestalozziring 14, Postfach 2829, 91058 Erlangen
☎00 49 9131 60600   Fax 00 49 9131 773090
FOUNDED 1844. *Publishes* children's books.

Rowohlt Taschenbuch Verlag GmbH

Hamburger Strasse 17, Postfach 1349, 21465 Reinbeck
☎00 49 40 72720   Fax 00 49 40 7272319
FOUNDED 1953. *Publishes* fiction and general non-fiction, general science, history, archaeology, art, political science, psychology, philosophy, religion, social sciences, crafts and hobbies.

Springer-Verlag GmbH & Co KG

Heidelberger Platz 3, 14197 Berlin 33
☎00 49 30 820710   Fax 00 49 30 8214091
FOUNDED 1842. *Publishes* biology, chemistry,

psychology, physics, mathematics, computer science, technology, engineering, economics, philosophy, law, reference, scientific periodicals (German and English).

Suhrkamp Verlag
Lindenstr. 29–35, Postfach 101945,
60019 Frankfurt am Main
☎00 49 69 756010   Fax 00 49 69 75601522
FOUNDED 1950. *Publishes* general fiction, biography, poetry, general science, philosophy and psychology.

K. Thienemanns Verlag
Blumenstrasse 36, 70182 Stuttgart
☎00 49 711 210550   Fax 00 49 711 2105539
FOUNDED 1849. *Publishes* fiction and general non-fiction.

Verlag Ullstein GmbH
Lindenstr. 76, Postfach 110303, 10969 Berlin
☎00 49 30 25913570 Fax 00 49 30 25913590
FOUNDED 1903. *Publishes* fiction, biography, poetry, music, art, history, ethnology, politics, militaria, travel, general science, social sciences.

Italy
Adelphi Edizioni SpA
Via S. Giovanni sul Muro 14, I-20121 Milan
☎00 39 2 72000975   Fax 00 39 2 89010337
FOUNDED 1962. *Publishes* general fiction, biography, art, philosophy, religion, psychology, general science, music.

Bompiana
Via Mecenate 91, I-20138 Milan, Italy
☎00 39 2 50951   Fax 00 39 2 5065361
FOUNDED 1929. *Publishes* fiction, children's, non-fiction, art, theatre and general science.

Bulzoni Editore SRL (Le Edizioni Universitarie d'Italia)
Via De Liburni 14, I-00185 Rome
☎00 39 6 4455207   Fax 00 39 6 4450355
FOUNDED 1969. *Publishes* fiction, literature, essays, philosophy, arts, theatre, cinema, social sciences, sociology, engineering, law, linguistics.

Nuova Casa Editrice Licinio Cappelli SRL GEM
Via Farini 14, I-40124 Bologna
☎00 39 51 239060   Fax 00 39 51 239286
FOUNDED 1851. *Publishes* fiction, political sci-

ence, poetry, biography, history, art, philosophy, religion, medicine, psychology, general science, social sciences and sociology, film, drama, theatre, music and dance.

Gruppo Editoriale Fabbri SpA
Via Mecenate 91, I-20138 Milan
☎00 39 2 50951   Fax 00 39 2 5065361
FOUNDED 1945. *Publishes* art, music, dance, medicine, general science, history, nature, crafts and hobbies, children's.

Garzanti Editore
Via Senato 25, PO Box 971, I-20121 Milan
☎00 39 2 77871   Fax 00 39 2 76009233
FOUNDED 1861. *Publishes* general fiction, literature, biography, poetry, art, history and political science.

Giunti Publishing Group
Via Bolognese 165, I-50139 Florence
☎00 39 55 66791   Fax 00 39 55 6679298
FOUNDED 1840. *Publishes* fiction, essays, art, history, handbooks, mathematics, psychology, chemistry, linguistics. Italian publishers of National Geographical Society books.

Gremese Editore SRL
Via Agnelli 88, I-00151 Rome
☎00 39 6 65740507   Fax 00 39 6 65740509
FOUNDED 1978. *Publishes* theatre, music, dance, art, photography, fashion, cookery, travel, literature, sport, hobbies.

Istituto Geografico de Agostini SpA
Via Giovanni da Verrazano 15, I-28100 Novara
☎00 39 321 4241   Fax 00 39 321 471286
FOUNDED 1901. *Publishes* art, literature, history, religion, geology and geography.

Longanesi & C.
Corso Italia 13, I-20122 Milan
☎00 39 2 8692640   Fax 00 39 2 72000306
FOUNDED 1946. *Publishes* general fiction, biograhy, art, music, history, philosophy, religion, psychology, general and social sciences, medicine and how-to.

Arnoldo Mondadori Editore SpA
Via Arnoldo Mondadori, I-20090 Segrate (Milan)
☎00 39 2 75421   Fax 00 39 2 75422302
FOUNDED 1907. *Publishes* general fiction, mystery, biography, art, music, poetry, philosophy,

religion, history, how-to, reference, medicine, psychology, general science, educational materials and children's.

Società Editrice Il Mulino
Str Maggiore 37, I-40125 Bologna
☎00 39 51 256011 Fax 00 39 51 256034
FOUNDED 1954. *Publishes* linguistics, music, theatre, history, philosophy, law, political science, economics, social science, psychology, textbooks.

Gruppo Ugo Mursia Editore SpA
Via Tadino 29, I-20124 Milan
☎00 39 2 29403030 Fax 00 39 2 29525557
FOUNDED 1922. *Publishes* general fiction, poetry, art, history, biography, maritime, philosophy, religion, reference, textbooks, educational material, general and social science.

RCS Rizzoli Libri SpA
Via Mecenate 91, 1-20138 Milan
☎00 39 2 50950 Fax 00 39 2 508012131
FOUNDED 1909. *Publishes* art, biography, hobbies, medicine, music, religion, social science, economics, textbooks and reference.

SEI (Società Editrice Internationale)
Corso Regina Margherita 176, I-10152 Turin
☎00 39 11 52271 Fax 00 39 11 5211320
FOUNDED 1908. *Publishes* literature, history, philosophy, religion, psychology, educational materials (textbooks and software for PCs/language laboratories).

Sonzogno
Via Mecenate 91, I-20138 Milan
☎00 39 2 50951 Fax 00 39 2 5065361
FOUNDED 1818. *Publishes* fiction, mysteries, and general non-fiction.

Sperling e Kupfer Editori SpA
Via Borgonuovo 24, I-20121 Milan
☎00 39 2 290341 Fax 00 39 2 6590290
FOUNDED 1899. *Publishes* general fiction and non-fiction, general science, biography, health, travel, sport, how-to, management, economics.

Sugarco Edizioni SRL
Via Fermi 9, 1-21040 Carnago (Varese)
☎00 39 2 331 985511Fax 00 39 2 331 985385
FOUNDED 1956. *Publishes* general fiction, biography, history, philosophy, how-to.

Todariana Editrice
Via Gardone 29, I-20139 Milan
☎00 39 2 55213405 Fax 00 39 2 55213405
FOUNDED 1967. *Publishes* fiction, poetry, fantasy and science fiction, essays, sociology, psychology.

The Netherlands
De Boekerij BV
Herengracht 540, 1017 CG Amsterdam
☎00 31 20 6261655 Fax 00 31 20 6237675
FOUNDED 1986. *Publishes* fiction and general non-fiction, film, mysteries, romance, science fiction and fantasy.

A.W. Bruna Uitgevers
Postbus 8411, 3503 RK Utrecht
☎00 31 30 470411 Fax 00 31 30 410018
FOUNDED 1868. *Publishes* general fiction, belles lettres, history, philosophy, psychology, general and social science, computer books.

Uitgeverij BZZTÔH
Laan van Meerdervoort 10, 2517 AJ The Hague
☎00 31 70 3632934 Fax 00 31 70 3631932
FOUNDED 1970. *Publishes* fiction, mysteries, travel, cookery.

Elsevier Science BV
Sara Burgerhartstr. 25, PO Box 2400, 1000 CK Amsterdam
☎00 31 20 5862911 Fax 00 31 20 5863843
FOUNDED 1946. Parent company: Reed Elsevier. *Publishes* sciences (all fields), management and professional, medicine, engineering, economics, law, trade journals, newspapers, periodicals, electronic databases.

Uitgeverij Hollandia BV
Beukenlaan 20, Postbus 70, 3740 AB Baarn
☎00 31 2154 18941 Fax 00 31 2154 21917
FOUNDED 1899. *Publishes* general fiction, nautical, travel.

Uitgeversmaatschappij J. H. Kok BV
Gildestr. 5, PO Box 130, 8260 AH Kampen
☎00 31 5202 92555 Fax 00 31 5202 27331
FOUNDED 1894. *Publishes* general fiction, poetry, biography, history, art, psychology, religion, general and social sciences, medicine, crafts, how-to, textbooks and educational material.

M & P Publishing House
Schoutlaan 4, 6002 EA Weert
☎00 31 4950 36880   Fax 00 31 4950 21145
FOUNDED 1974. *Publishes* general non-fiction.

Meulenhoff International
Herengracht 507, PO Box 100, 1000 AC
Amsterdam
☎00 31 20 6267555   Fax 00 31 20 6205516
Publishes international co-productions, art and
general non-fiction. Specialises in Dutch and
translated literature, science fiction, non-fiction
and children's.

Uitgeverij Het Spectrum BV
Montalbaendreef 2, Postbus 2073, 3500 GB
Utrecht
☎00 31 30 650650   Fax 00 31 30 620850
FOUNDED 1935. *Publishes* science fiction, mystery, crime, general non-fiction, encyclopedias,
computer science, history, travel, management.

Time-Life Books BV
Ottho Heldringstr 5, 1066 AZ Amsterdam
☎00 31 20 5104911   Fax 00 31 20 6175077
Publishes art, cookery, gardening, how-to, general science and history.

Unieboek BV
Outendoor 7, 3995 DB Houten
☎00 31 3403 77660   Fax 00 31 3403 77600
FOUNDED 1891. *Publishes* fiction, children's,
literature, cookery, design, archaeology, politics, multi-volume reference.

Uniepers BV
Postbus 69, 1390 AB Abcoude
☎00 31 2946 5111   Fax 00 31 2946 3013
FOUNDED 1961. *Publishes* (mostly in co-editions) art, music, gardening, history, cookery
and wine.

Veen Uitgevers Group
Vinkenburgstr. 2a, PO Box 14095,
3508 SC Utrecht
☎00 31 30 349211   Fax 00 31 20 349208
FOUNDED 1887. A member of the Wolters
Kluwer Group. *Publishes* general non-fiction,
fiction, Dutch and foreign literature, business,

Wolters Kluwer NV
Stadhouderskade 1, PO Box 818,
1000 AV Amsterdam
☎00 31 20 6070400   Fax 00 31 20 6070490
FOUNDED 1889. *Publishes* education, technical

encyclopedias, trade books and journals, law
and taxation, newspapers and periodicals.

Norway

H. Aschehoug & Co
(W. Nygaard) A/S
Sehestedsgate 3, PO Box 363 Sentrum,
0102 Oslo 1
☎00 47 22400400   Fax 00 47 22206395
FOUNDED 1872. *Publishes* general fiction and
non-fiction, general and social science.

J. W. Cappelens Forlag A/S
Maribosgaten 13, Postboks 350, Sentrum,
0101 Oslo 1
☎00 47 22365000   Fax 00 47 22365040
FOUNDED 1829. *Publishes* fiction, general non-
fiction, religion.

N. W. Damm & Søn A/S
Kristian Augustsgt. 3, Postboks 1755,
N-0122 Oslo 1
☎00 47 22941500   Fax 00 47 22360874
FOUNDED 1845. *Publishes* fiction and general
non-fiction.

Ex Libris Forlag A/S
Nordregt 22, PO Box 2130 Grünerløkka,
0505 Oslo 5
☎00 47 22384450   Fax 00 47 22385160
FOUNDED 1982. *Publishes* general fiction and
non-fiction, art, children's, biography and philosophy.

Gyldendal Norsk Forlag A/S
Sehestedsgt. 4, Postboks 6860, St Olavs Plass,
0130 Oslo
☎00 47 22034100   Fax 00 47 22034105
FOUNDED 1925. *Publishes* fiction and non-fiction, science fiction, social sciences, poetry, art,
music, dance, biography, history, how-to,
political science, philosophy, psychology, religion, children's.

Hjemmets Bokforlag AS
Kristian Augustsgt 10, Postboks 1755 Vika,
N-0122 Oslo 1
☎00 47 22941500   Fax 00 47 22322054
FOUNDED 1969. *Publishes* general fiction, non-
fiction, reference, children's, young adult.

NKS-Forlaget
PO Box 5853 Majorstuna, Industrigata 41/45,
N-0308 Oslo
☎00 47 22568500   Fax 00 47 22566820

FOUNDED 1971. *Publishes* health, nutrition and mathematics.

Tiden Norsk Forlag
PO Box 8813, Youngstorget, 0028 Oslo
☎00 47 22429520   Fax 00 47 22426458
FOUNDED 1933. *Publishes* general fiction and non-fiction, plus children's.

Portugal
Bertrand Editora Lda
Rua Anchieta 29 – 1, 1200 Lisbon
☎00 351 1 3420084   Fax 00 351 1 3468286
FOUNDED 1727. *Publishes* literature (Portuguese and foreign), art, essays, children's social sciences.

Editorial Caminho SARL
Rua S. Bernardo 14–3 Esq, 1200 Lisbon
☎00 351 1 3952193   Fax 00 351 1 3968793
FOUNDED 1977. *Publishes* general fiction, children's and politics.

Livraria Civilizacão (Américo Fraga Lamares & Ca Lda)
Rua Alberto Aires de Gouveia 27,
4000 Porto
☎00 351 2 2002286   Fax 00 351 2 312382
FOUNDED 1921. *Publishes* fiction, children's, history, social and political science, economics and art.

Publicações Dom Quixote Lda
Rua Luciano Cordeiro 116-2, 1000 Lisbon
☎00 351 1 538079   Fax 00 351 1 574595
FOUNDED 1965. *Publishes* general fiction, poetry, philosophy, general and social science, history, education, reference, children's.

Publicações Europa-America Lda
Apdo 8, Estrada Lisbon-Sintra Km 14,
2726 Mem Martins
☎00 351 1 9211461   Fax 00 351 1 9217940
FOUNDED 1945. *Publishes* general fiction, belles lettres, poetry, biography, art, music, history, philosophy, general and social science, how-to, medicine, psychology, children's, textbooks (university), technical, engineering.

Gradiva – Publicações Lda
Rua Almeida e Sousa 21 r/c Esq, 1300 Lisbon
☎00 351 1 3974067   Fax 00 351 1 3953471
FOUNDED 1981. *Publishes* science, human sciences), philosophy, history, education, fiction, science fiction, illustrated books, children's.

Livros Horizonte Lda
Rua das Chagas 17 – 1 Dto, 1121 Lisbon
☎00 351 1 3466917   Fax 00 351 1 3426921
FOUNDED 1953. *Publishes* sociology, psychology, textbooks (university), art, history, children's.

Edições 70
Rua Luciano Cordeiro No 123–2 Esq,
1000 Lisbon
☎00 351 1 3158752   Fax 00 351 1 3158429
FOUNDED 1970. *Publishes* anthropology, architecture, art, general science, philosophy, history, literature, essays, health and nutrition.

Editorial Verbo SA
Rua Carlos Testa 1–2, 1000 Lisbon
☎00 351 1 562131   Fax 00 351 1 562139
FOUNDED 1959. *Publishes* educational material, general science, history, children's.

Spain
Editorial Alhambra SA
Fernandez de la Hoz 9, 28013 Madrid
☎00 34 1 5940020   Fax 00 34 1 5921220
FOUNDED 1942. *Publishes* medicine and nursing, general science, psychology, philosophy, history, literature, children's, languages, textbooks (all levels), audiovisual aids.

Alianza Editorial SA
Milan 38, 28043 Madrid
☎00 34 1 3000045   Fax 00 34 1 3811810
FOUNDED 1965. *Publishes* general fiction, poetry, belles lettres, art, music, philosophy, political and social sciences, history, mathematics and general science.

Ediciones Anaya SA
Telémaco 43, E, 28027 Madrid
☎00 34 1 3200119   Fax 00 34 1 7426631
FOUNDED 1959. *Publishes* textbooks (all levels) and educational materials.

Editorial Don Quijote
Compãs del Porvenir 6, 41013 Seville
☎00 34 58 4235080
FOUNDED 1981. *Publishes* fiction, literature, poetry, essays, theatre, history.

EDHASA (Editora y Distribuidora Hispano – Americana SA)
Av Diagonal 519, 08029 Barcelona
☎00 34 3 2395105   Fax 00 34 3 4194584
FOUNDED 1946. *Publishes* historical and general fiction, literature and essays.

Editorial Espasa-Calpe SA
Apdo 547, Carretera de Irún Km 12,200,
28049 Madrid
☎00 34 1 3589689   Fax 00 34 1 3589505
FOUNDED 1925. *Publishes* general fiction, belles
lettres, biography, history, how-to, music, art,
philosophy, religion.

Ediciones Grijalbo SA
Aragò 385 Apdo 5675, 08013 Barcelona
☎00 34 3 4587000   Fax 00 34 3 4580495
FOUNDED 1942. *Publishes* general fiction and
non-fiction, biography, history, politics, philosophy, religion, psychology, social sciences,
technology, reference, art.

Ediciones Hiperión SL
Salustiano Olózaga 14, 28001 Madrid
☎00 34 1 5776015/6
FOUNDED 1976. *Publishes* fiction, poetry, literary criticism, essays, philosophy, history, medicine, Islamic studies.

Editorial Laia SA
Guitard 43-5, 08014 Barcelona
☎00 34 3 3215562   Fax 00 34 3 3217975
FOUNDED 1972. *Publishes* literature, essays, education, social sciences, psychology, general non-
fiction.

LaSal (Edicions de les Dones)
Riereta 13, 08001 Barcelona
☎00 34 3 3298450
FOUNDED 1978. *Publishes* women studies only.

Editorial Molino
Calabria 166, 08015 Barcelona
☎00 34 3 2260625   Fax 00 34 3 2266998
FOUNDED 1933. *Publishes* education and fiction.

Mondadori España SA
Aragó 385, 08013 Barcelona
☎00 34 1 4587000   Fax 00 34 1 4159033
FOUNDED 1987. *Publishes* fiction, essays, biography, illustrated books, history, science and
general non-fiction.

Editorial Planeta SA
Córcega 273-277, 08008 Barcelona
☎00 34 3 2179050   Fax 00 34 3 2177140
FOUNDED 1952. *Publishes* fiction and general
non-fiction.

Plaza y Janés SA
Enrique Granados 86–88, 08008 Barcelona
☎00 34 3 4151100   Fax 00 34 3 4156976

FOUNDED 1959. *Publishes* fiction and general
non-fiction.

Santillana SA
Elfo 32, 28027 Madrid
☎00 34 1 3265400   Fax 00 34 1 4049465
FOUNDED 1964. Formerly Ediciones Alfaguara.
Publishes general fiction, world classics and
children's books.

Editorial Seix Barral SA
Córcega 270-4, Apdo, 08008 Barcelona
☎00 34 3 2186400   Fax 00 34 3 2184773
FOUNDED 1945. *Publishes* fiction (including
classics) from Europe, the Americas and the Far
East, plus poetry and drama.

Editorial Timun Mas SA
Castillejus 294, 08025 Barcelona
☎00 34 3 3077233   Fax 00 34 3 2357470
Publishes teaching handbooks and children's.

Tusquets Editores
Calle Iradier 24 bajos, E-08017 Barcelona
☎00 34 3 4174170   Fax 00 34 3 4176703
FOUNDED 1969. *Publishes* fiction, biography,
art, literature, erotica, history, social sciences.

Ediciones Versal SA
Calabria 108, 08015 Barcelona
☎00 34 3 3257404   Fax 00 34 3 4236898
FOUNDED 1984. *Publishes* general non-fiction,
and biography.

Editorial Luis Vives (Edelvives)
Avda Dr Frederico Rubio y Gali 1,
28039 Madrid
☎00 34 1 2347000   Fax 00 34 1 5531919
FOUNDED 1932. *Publishes* textbooks (all levels),
educational material and children's.

Sweden

Bokförlaget Bonnier Alba AB
Box 3159 Sveavägen 56, S-103 63 Stockholm
☎00 46 8 6968660   Fax 00 46 8 6968361
FOUNDED 1981. *Publishes* general non-fiction,
fiction and textbooks (university level).

Albert Bonniers Förlag AB
Box 3159, Sveavägen 56, S-103 63 Stockholm
☎00 46 8 229120   Fax 00 46 8 208451
FOUNDED 1837. *Publishes* general fiction, teenage, reference, general non-fiction, periodicals.

Bokförlaget Bra Böcker AB

Humlegardsgatan 8, 41274 Goteborg
☎00 46 42 831276   Fax 00 46 42 358314
FOUNDED 1965. *Publishes* general fiction, illustrated books, history, geography and geology.

Brombergs Bokförlag AB

Industrigaton 4A, Box 12886,
11298 Stockholm
☎00 46 8 6503390   Fax 00 46 8 6500160
FOUNDED 1973. *Publishes* general fiction and non-fiction, general and political science.

Bokförlaget Forum AB

Riddargatan 23A, Box 14115,
S-104 41 Stockholm
☎00 46 8 6968440   Fax 00 46 8 6968368
FOUNDED 1944. *Publishes* fiction and general non-fiction.

Bokförlaget Natur och Kultur

Karlavägen 31, Box 27323,
S-102 54 Stockholm
☎00 46 8 4538600   Fax 00 46 8 4538790
FOUNDED 1922. *Publishes* fiction and general non-fiction, general science, biography, history, psychology, textbooks and audiovisual material (primary and secondary), and children's.

Norstedts Förlag AB

Box 2052, S-103 12 Stockholm
☎00 46 8 7893000   Fax 00 46 8 7893010
FOUNDED 1823. *Publishes* general fiction and non-fiction, dictionaries and children's.

AB Rabén och Sjögren Bokförlag

Tegnérgatan 28, Box 45022,
S-104 30 Stockholm
☎00 46 8 349960   Fax 00 46 8 302899
FOUNDED 1942. *Publishes* general fiction and non-fiction, children's, how-to, nature, outdoor pursuits, music, art, history and social science, economics and psychology.

Richters Förlag AB

Ostra Förstadsgatan 46, S-205 75 Malmö
☎00 46 40 380600   Fax 00 46 40 933708
FOUNDED 1942. *Publishes* fiction.

Bokförlags AB Tiden

Box 30184, S-104 25 Stockholm
☎00 46 8 6198520   Fax 00 46 8 6198540
FOUNDED 1912. *Publishes* general fiction, non-fiction, children's, illustrated, memoirs, history, poetry, politics, social sciences, psychology.

B Wählströms Bokförlag AB

Box 30022, S-104 25 Stockholm
☎00 46 8 6198600   Fax 00 46 8 6189761
FOUNDED 1911. *Publishes* general fiction and non-fiction, and children's.

Switzerland

Arche Verlag AG, Raabe und Vitali

Hoelderlinstr. 14, CH-8030 Zurich
☎00 41 1 2522410   Fax 00 41 1 2611115
FOUNDED 1944. *Publishes* belles lettres and modern literature.

Artemis Verlags AG

Munstergasse 9, CH-8024 Zurich
☎00 41 1 2521100   Fax 00 41 1 2624792
FOUNDED 1943. *Publishes* art, architecture, travel guides, philosophy, history and current affairs, biography, politics, textbooks and children's.

Diogenes Verlag AG

Sprecherstr. 8, CH-8032 Zurich
☎00 41 1 2548511   Fax 00 41 1 2528407
FOUNDED 1952. *Publishes* fiction, mysteries, essays, children's, drama, theatre, literature, philosophy and art.

Langenscheidt AG Zürich-Zug

Gubelstr. 11, CH-6301 Zug
☎00 41 42 232300   Fax 00 41 42 232325
Publishes linguistics and languages.

Larousse (Suisse) SA

3 Route du Grand-Mont, CH-1052 Le Mont-sur-Lausanne
☎00 41 22 369140
Publishes dictionaries, reference and textbooks.

Neptun-Verlag

Fidlerstrasse 6, Postfach 8, CH-8272 Ermatingen
☎00 41 72 642020   Fax 00 41 72 62023
FOUNDED 1946. *Publishes* modern history, travel and children's.

Orell Füssli Verlag

Dietzingerstrasse 3, CH-8036 Zurich
☎00 41 1 2113630   Fax 00 41 1 2113411
FOUNDED 1519. *Publishes* children's, educational material, art, how-to, history, geography, geology, economics, biography.

Editions Payot Lausanne
33 ave de la Gare, CH-1006 Lausanne
☎00 41 21 3495015   Fax 00 41 21 3495029
FOUNDED 1875. *Publishes* art, music, belles lettres, history, general science, law, business, psychology, philosophy, agriculture, sport, environment.

Verlag Rot-Weiss AG
Baelliz 56, Postfach 1308,
CH-3601 Thun
☎00 41 33 229803   Fax 00 41 33 229810
FOUNDED 1988. *Publishes* restaurant, hotel and general tourist guides, in German and English.

Sauerländer AG
Postfach Laurenzenvorstadt 89,
CH-5001 Aarau
☎00 41 64 268626   Fax 00 41 64 245780
FOUNDED 1807. *Publishes* children's, textbooks and educational materials (all levels), belles lettres, poetry, biography, social sciences, medicine, history.

Scherz Verlag AG
Theaterplatz 4–6, CH-3000 Berne 7
☎00 41 31 3116831   Fax 00 41 31 3120375
FOUNDED 1939. *Publishes* general fiction, biography, history, psychology, philosophy, parapsychology; general non-fiction.

US Publishers

International Reply Coupons

For return postage, send International Reply Coupons (IRCs), available from the Post Office. Letters 60 pence; mss according to weight.

William Abrahams
See **Penguin USA**

ABC–Clio, Inc.
Suite 805, 50 South Steele Street, Denver CO 80209
☎001 303 333 3003   Fax 001 303 333 4037
President *Heather Cameron*
Editorial Director *Jeff Serena*

FOUNDED 1955. *Publishes* non-fiction: reference, including mythology, native American studies, government and politics, history, military and war, women's studies/issues, current world issues. About 35–40 titles a year. No unsolicited mss; synopses and ideas welcome.
Royalties paid annually. *UK subsidiary* **ABC-Clio Ltd**, Oxford.

Abingdon Press
201 Eighth Avenue South, Box 801, Nashville TN 37202–0801
☎001 615 749 6404   Fax 001 615 749 6512
Editorial Director *Neil M. Alexander*

Publishes non-fiction: religious (lay and professional), children's religious and academic texts. About 100 titles a year. Approach in writing only with synopsis and samples. IRCs essential.

Harry N. Abrams, Inc.
100 Fifth Avenue, New York NY 10011
☎001 212 206 7715   Fax 001 212 645 8437
Publisher/Editor-in-chief *Paul Gottlieb*

Subsidiary of Times Mirror Co. *Publishes* illustrated books: art, design, nature, entertainment. No fiction. About 90 titles a year. Submit completed mss (no dot matrix), together with sample illustrations.

Academy Chicago Publishers
363 W. Erie Street, Chicago IL 60610
☎001 312 751 7300   Fax 001 312 751 7306
Editorial Director *Anita Miller*

FOUNDED 1975. *Publishes* fiction: mystery and mainstream; and non-fiction: biography, sociology, travel, true crime and historical. No romance, children's, young adult, religious, sexist or avant-garde. About 30 titles a year.
IMPRINT **Cassandra Editions** ('Lost' Women Writers) TITLES *Murder on the Thirteenth* A. E. Eddenden; *Memoirs of an Ex-Prom Queen* Alix Kates Shulman; *A Mirror for Witches* Esther Forbes. Send first three chapters only, accompanied by IRCs; no synopses or ideas.
Royalties paid twice yearly. *Distributed* in the UK and Europe by Gazelle, Lancaster.

Ace Science Fiction
See **Berkley Publishing Group**

Adams Publishing
260 Center Street, Holbrook MA 02343
☎001 617 767 8100   Fax 001 617 767 0994
President *Robert L. Adams*

FOUNDED 1980. *Publishes* general non-fiction: careers, business, personal finance, relationships, parenting and maternity, self-improvement, reference, cooking, sports, games and humour. TITLES *101 Reasons Why a Cat is Better Than a Man; I Go To Pieces: The Biography of Patsy Cline; Kids Explore Boston; 100 Best Mutual Funds You Can Buy.* Ideas welcome.

Addison-Wesley Publishing Co., Inc.
General Publishing Group, Jacob Way, Reading MA 01867
☎001 617 944 3700   Fax 001 617 944 8243
Publisher *David Goehring*

Publishes general non-fiction, biography, business/economics, health, history, how-to, parenting, politics, psychology, children's multimedia, computers and science. No fiction. About 125 titles a year. Approach in writing or by phone in first instance, then submit synopsis and one sample chapter.
Royalties paid.

University of Alabama Press
Box 870380, Tuscaloosa AL 35487
☎001 205 348 5180   Fax 001 205 348 9201
Director *Malcolm MacDonald*

Publishes academic books in the fields of American history, American and British literature, history of science and technology, linguistics, archaeology, rhetoric and speech communication. About 40 titles a year.

Aladdin Books
See **Simon & Schuster Children's Publishing Division**

University of Alaska Press
1st Floor, Gruening Building, PO Box 756240, University of Alaska, Fairbanks AK 99775-6240
☎001 907 474 6389   Fax 001 907 474 5502
Manager *Debbie Van Stone*
Managing Editor *Carla Helfferich*
Acquisitions *Pam Odom*

Traces its origins back to 1927 but was relatively dormant until the early 1980s. *Publishes* scholarly works about Alaska and the North Pacific rim, with a special emphasis on circumpolar regions. 5–10 titles a year. No fiction or poetry.

DIVISIONS
Ramuson Library Historical Translation Series *Marvin Falk* TITLES *Bering's Voyages: The Reports from Russia; Tlingit Indians of Alaska* **Oral Biography Series** *William Schneider* TITLES *The Life I've Been Living; Kusiq: An Eskimo Life History from the Arctic Coast of Alaska* **Monograph Series** *Carla Helfferich* TITLES *Intertidal Bivalves: A Guide to the Common Marine Bivalves of Alaska* **Classic Reprint Series** *Terrence Cole* TITLES *Arctic Village: A 1930s Portrait of Wiseman, Alaska* **Lanternlight Library** informal non-fiction covering Northern interest. TITLES *Aleutian Echoes*. Unsolicited mss, synopses and ideas welcome.

AMACOM
135 West 50th Avenue, New York NY 10020
☎001 212 903 8081   Fax 001 212 903 8083
Director/Submissions *Weldon P. Rackley*

Owned by American Management Association. *Publishes* business books only, including general management, business communications, sales and marketing, small business, finance, computers and information systems, human resource management and training, career/personal growth skills, research development, project manage-

ment and manufacturing, quality/customer service titles. 65–70 titles a year. TITLES *Crossing the Minefield; Voices of Diversity; Career Power!; The Reengineering Handbook; Up Against the Wal-Marts*. Proposals welcome.
Royalties paid twice yearly.

University Press of America, Inc.
4720 Boston Way, Lanham MD 20706
☎001 301 459 3366   Fax 001 301 459 2118
Publisher *James E. Lyons*

FOUNDED 1975. *Publishes* scholarly monographs, college and graduate level textbooks. No children's, elementary or high school. About 450 titles a year. Submit outline or request proposal questionnaire.
Royalties paid annually. *Distributed* by Eurospan Ltd, London.

Anvil
See **Krieger Publishing Co., Inc.**

Ann Arbor Paperbacks
See **University of Michigan Press**

Archway
See **Pocket Books**

University of Arizona Press
1230 North Park Avenue, Suite 102, Tucson AZ 85719–4140
☎001 520 621 1441   Fax 001 520 621 8899
Director *Stephen Cox*
Senior Editor *Joanne O'Hare*

FOUNDED 1959. *Publishes* academic non-fiction, particularly with a regional/cultural link, plus Native-American and Hispanic literature. About 50 titles a year.

Arkana
See **Penguin USA**

University of Arkansas Press
McIlroy House, 201 Ozark Avenue, Fayetteville AR 72701
☎001 501 575 3246   Fax 001 501 575 6044
Director *Miller Williams*

FOUNDED 1980. *Publishes* scholarly monographs, short fiction, poetry and general trade including essays, biography, etc. Particularly interested at present in scholarly works in history, politics, sociology and literary criticism. About 30 titles a year. TITLES *Rugged and Sublime: The Civil War in Arkansas* ed. Mark Christ; *Fierce Solitude: The Life of John Gould*

Fletcher Ben Johnson; *Black Charlestonians: A Social History, 1822–1885* Bernard Powers. *Royalties* paid annually.

Aspect
See **Warner Books Inc.**

Athaneum Publishers
See **Simon & Schuster Trade Division**

Atheneum Books for Young Readers
See **Simon & Schuster Children's Publishing Division**

Atlantic Disk Publishers, Inc.
1153 Alabama Road, Suite 104, Acworth GA 30102–2506
☎001 404 591 2051   Fax 001 404 591 0369
Exec. Editor/Publisher *Dorothy Deering*
Editor-in-Chief/Publisher *Charles Deering*
Publishes mass market fiction as well as non-fiction on DOS, IBM compatible/readable disks and CD ROM. Send query/synopsis/mss disk. Reports in 4–6 weeks. 256 titles in 1994. *Royalties* Pays 35%. No advances.

Atlantic Monthly Press
See **Grove/Atlantic Inc**

AUP (Associated University Presses)
AUP New Jersey titles are handled in the UK by **Golden Cockerel Press** (see **UK Publishers**).

Avery Publishing Group, Inc.
120 Old Broadway, Garden City Park, New York NY 11040
☎001 516 741 2155   Fax 001 516 742 1892
Managing Editor *Rudy Shur*
FOUNDED 1976. *Publishes* adult trade non-fiction, specialising in childbirth, childcare, alternative health, self-help, New Age, military history and natural cooking. About 30 titles a year. TITLES *To Save A Child* Audrey Talkington; *Sharks Don't Get Cancer* Dr William Lane; *Cooking For Good Health* Gloria Rose; . No unsolicited mss; synopses and ideas welcome if accompanied by s.a.e. *Royalties* paid twice yearly.

Avon Books
1350 Avenue of the Americas, New York NY 10019
☎001 212 261 6800   Fax 001 212 261 6895
Vice President/Editor-in-Chief *Robert Mecoy*
FOUNDED 1941. A division of the Hearst Corporation. *Publishes* mass-market and trade paperbacks, adult, young adult and children's. Fiction: contemporary and historical romance, science fiction and fantasy, action and adventure, suspense and thrillers, mystery and westerns. Non-fiction (all types): how-to, popular psychology, self-help, health, history, war, sports, business and economics, biography and politics. No textbooks. 375 titles in 1994.

DIVISIONS **Avon Books** Adult mass-market paperbacks and trade paperbacks **Avon Camelot Books** Children's books **Avon Flare** Young adult readers. Submit query letter only in the first instance.

Back Bay Books
See **Little, Brown & Co. Inc.**

Baker Book House
PO Box 6287, Grand Rapids MI 49516-6287
☎001 616 676 9185   Fax 001 616 676 9573
President *Richard Baker*
Director of Publications *Allan Fisher*
FOUNDED 1939. Began life as a used-book store and began publishing in earnest in the 1950s, primarily serving the evangelical Christian market. *Publishes* religious non-fiction and fiction; children's books; college/seminary textbooks and academic; Bible reference and professional (pastors and church leaders) books. About 190 titles a year.

DIVISIONS/IMPRINTS
Trade *Allan Fisher* TITLES *The Hope at Hand* David Bryant; *Real Presence* Leanne Payne **Children's** *Betty De Vries* **Academic & Reference** *Jim Weaver* TITLES *God in Three Persons* Millard Erickson; *20th Century Dictionary of Christian Biography* **Professional Books** *Paul Engle* TITLES *Marketplace Preaching* Calvin Miller. No unsolicited mss. Send for proposal outlines specifying whether you will be proposing a trade, professional or academic book. **Chosen Books** *Jane Campbell* FOUNDED 1971. *Publishes* charismatic adult non-fiction for a Christian market. TITLES *Healing Evangelism* Don Dunkerley; *Angels All Around* Sarah Hornsby. About 10 titles a year. Synopses or ideas welcome. **Fleming H. Revell, Spire Books** *William J. Petersen* Adult fiction and non-fiction for evangelical Christians. A family-owned business until 1978, Fleming H. Revell was one of the first Christian publishers to take the step into secular publishing. TITLES *The Dual-Earner Marriage* Jack and Judy Balswick; *The Search for Lost Fathering* James Schaller. About 40 titles a year. Synopses or ideas welcome. *Royalties* paid twice yearly.

Balch Institute Press
See **Golden Cockerel Press** under **UK Publishers**

Ballantine/Del Rey/Fawcett/ Ivy Books
201 East 50th Street, New York NY 10022
☎001 212 572 2713   Fax 001 212 572 4912
Group President/Publisher *Linda Grey*
FOUNDED 1952. Division of **Random House, Inc.** *Publishes* fiction and non-fiction, science fiction. 497 titles in 1994.

IMPRINTS **Ballantine Books; Ballantine Available Press; Del Rey; Fawcett Columbine; Fawcett Crest; Fawcett Gold Medal; Fawcett Juniper; House of Collectibles; Moorings; One World.**

Banner Books
See **University Press of Mississippi**

Bantam Doubleday Dell Publishing Group Inc
1540 Broadway, New York NY 10036
☎001 212 354 6500   Fax 001 212 302 7985
Group President *Jack Hoeft*
President/Publisher, Bantam Books *Irwyn Applebaum*
President/Publisher, Doubleday *Stephen Rubin*
President/Publisher, Dell Publishing *Carole Baron*
Group Senior Vice President/Publisher International Division *Alun Davies*
Publishes general commercial fiction: mysteries, westerns, romance, war, science fiction and fantasy, crime and thrillers, adventure; non-fiction, including New Age, computers, crime and adventure; young readers and children's.

DIVISIONS/IMPRINTS **Bantam Books; Doubleday; Dell Publishing** (incorporating **Bantam Doubleday Dell Books for Young Readers**); **International Division; Golden Apple; Loveswept; New Age Books; New Sciences; Peacock Press; Perigord Press; Spectra; Sweet Dreams.** Most work comes through agents. No unsolicited mss.

Barron's Educational Series
250 Wireless Boulevard, Hauppauge NY 11788
☎001 516 434 3311   Fax 001 516 434 3723
Chairman/President *Manuel H. Barron*
Managing Editor *Grace Freedson*
FOUNDED 1942. *Publishes* adult non-fiction, children's fiction and non-fiction, test preparation materials and language materials/tapes. No adult fiction. 200 titles a year. Unsolicited mss, synopses and ideas for books welcome.
Royalties paid twice yearly.

Basic Books
See **HarperCollins Publishers, Inc.**

Beacon Press
25 Beacon Street, Boston MA 02108
☎001 617 742 2110   Fax 001 617 723 3097
Director *Wendy J. Strothman*
Publishes general non-fiction. About 50 titles a year. Approach in writing, or submit synopsis and sample chapters (with IRCs) to the editorial department.

Bedford Books
See **St Martin's Press, Inc.**

Beech Tree Books
See **William Morrow & Co., Inc.**

Berkley Publishing Group
200 Madison Avenue, New York NY 10016
☎001 212 951 8800   Fax 001 212 213 6706
Editorial Heads *Leslie Gelbman, John Duff*
FOUNDED 1954. Subsidiary of **The Putnam Berkley Group.** *Publishes* paperbacks: general interest fiction and non-fiction. About 500 titles a year. IMPRINTS **Ace Science Fiction & Fantasy** submit synopsis and first three chapters; **Berkley Books; Berkley Trade Paperbacks; Boulevard; Jove.**
Royalties paid twice yearly.

Blackie
See **Penguin USA**

H. & R. Block
See **Simon & Schuster Trade Division**

The Blue Sky Press
See **Scholastic, Inc.**

Boulevard
See **Berkley Publishing Group**

Bowling Green State University Popular Press
Bowling Green OH 43403
☎001 419 372 7867   Fax 001 419 372 8095
Managing Director *Pat Browne*
FOUNDED 1970. *Publishes* non-fiction for libraries as reference or textbooks. 25 titles a year.

Unsolicited mss, synopses and ideas welcome.
No fiction.
Royalties paid twice yearly.

Boyds Mills Press
815 Church Street, Honesdale PA 18431
☎001 717 253 1164   Fax 001 717 253 0179
Publisher *Kent Brown Jr*
Managing Editor *Janet L. Keen*

A subsidiary of Highlights for Children, Inc.
FOUNDED 1990 as a publisher of children's
trade books. *Publishes* children's fiction, non-
fiction and poetry. About 50 titles a year.
TITLES *Bitter Bananas* Isaac Olaleye; *Bingleman's
Midway* Barry Moser; *The Always Prayer Shawl*
Sheldon Oberman; *Miss Violet's Shining Day*
Jane Breskin Zalben. Unsolicited mss, synopses
and ideas for books welcome. No romance.
Royalties paid twice yearly.

Bradford Books
See **The MIT Press**

Brassey's Inc.
1313 Dolley Madison Boulevard, Suite 401,
McLean VA 22101
☎001 703 442 4535   Fax 001 703 442 9848
President and Publisher *Franklin D.*
Margiotta, Ph.D.

FOUNDED 1983. Associated with **Brassey's** of
London. *Publishes* primarily non-fiction titles on
defence and military affairs – national and international, current affairs and foreign policy, history, biography and intelligence. About 30 titles
a year. TITLES *The Court of Blue Shadows*
Maynard Allington; *Blood in Zion* Saul Zadka;
Brassey's Defence Yearbook 1995 ed. Michael
Clarke; *One of the President's Men: Twenty Years
with Eisenhower and Nixon* Maurice H. Stans. No
unsolicited mss; synopses and ideas welcome.
Royalties paid twice annually.

Browndeer Press
See **Harcourt Brace Children's Books
Division**

Bulfinch Press
See **Little, Brown & Co., Inc.**

University of California Press
2120 Berkeley Way, Berkeley CA 94720
☎001 510 642 4247   Fax 001 510 643 7127
Director *James H. Clark*

Publishes academic non-fiction, fiction and
poetry in translation. About 275 titles a year.
Preliminary letter with outline preferred.

Carol Publishing
600 Madison Avenue, New York NY 10022
☎001 212 486 2200   Fax 001 212 486 2231
Publisher *Steven Schragis*

FOUNDED 1989. *Publishes* some fiction but
mostly non-fiction: biography and autobiography, history, science, humour, how-to, illustrated and self-help. About 150 titles a year.

Carolrhoda Books, Inc.
241 First Avenue North, Minneapolis
MN 55401
☎001 612 332 3344   Fax 001 612 332 7615
Editorial Director *Emily Kelley*

Publishes children's: nature, biography, history,
beginners' readers, world cultures, photo essays
and historical fiction. Please send s.a.e. for
author guidelines.

Carroll & Graf Publishers, Inc.
260 Fifth Avenue, New York NY 10001
☎001 212 889 8772   Fax 001 212 545 7909
Publisher/Exec. Editor *Kent Carroll*

FOUNDED 1983. General trade publisher.
Publishes fiction: literary, mainstream, mystery,
science fiction, erotica, fantasy and suspense.
No genre romance. Also non-fiction: history,
biography, psychology and current affairs. 130
titles in 1994. Query with synopsis in the first
instance. IRCs essential.
Royalties paid twice yearly.

Cassandra Editions
See **Academy Chicago Publishers**

Charlesbridge Publishing
85 Main Street, Watertown MA 02172–4411
☎001 617 926 0329   Fax 001 617 926 5720
Chairman *Brent Farmer*
Managing Editor *Elena Wright*

FOUNDED 1980 as an educational publisher
focusing on teaching thinking processes. *Publishes*
children's educational programmes (pre-kinder-
garten through to grade 8), non-fiction picture
books and multicultural fiction for 3- to 12-year-
olds. TITLES include *In My Own Backyard* Judi
Kurjian; *A Walk in the Wild* Lorraine Ward; *The
M&M's® Chocolate Candies Counting Book*
Barbara Barbieri McGrath; *Albertina anda
arriba/Albertina Goes Up*, an alphabet book in
Spanish and English by Nancy Maria Grande
Tabor. Complete mss or proposal welcome with
self-addressed envelope and IRCs. Mss should be
paged, with suggested illustrations described for
each page. No talking animals.
Royalties paid yearly.

University of Chicago Press
5801 South Ellis Avenue, Chicago
IL 60637–1496
☎001 312 702 7700   Fax 001 312 702 9756

FOUNDED 1891. *Publishes* academic non-fiction
only.

Children's Press
See **Grolier, Inc.**

Chosen Books
See **Baker Book House**

Chronicle Books
275 Fifth Street, San Francisco CA 94103
☎001 415 777 7240   Fax 001 415 777 8887

Publisher *Jack Jensen*
Executive Editor *Christine Carswell*

FOUNDED 1966. Division of Chronicle Publishing. *Publishes* art and design, food and cookery,
gardening, nature, photography, leisure and
travel, adult fiction and short stories, children's,
and stationery/gift items. About 200 titles a year.

DIVISIONS **Art** *Annie Barrows* **Children's**
Victoria Rock **Cooking/Gardening** *Bill LeBond*
Fiction *Jay Schaefer* **Giftworks** *Caroline Herter/
Debra Lande* **Multimedia** *Nion McEvoy* **Nature/
Humour** *Charlotte Stone* **Nature/Novelty**
Leslie Bruynesteyn. Query or submit outline/syn-
opsis and sample chapters and artwork.

Royalties paid twice yearly.

Clarion Books
215 Park Avenue South, New York NY 10003
☎001 212 420 5800

Publisher *Dorothy Briley*
Executive Editor *Dinah Stevenson*

Clarion Books began in 1965 as an imprint of
Seabury Press. The Clarion name was inaugu-
rated in 1974 and acquired by **Houghton
Mifflin Co.** in 1979. *Publishes* children's
books. TITLES *Tuesday* David Wiesner; *Red Fox
Running* Eve Bunting; *It Goes Eeeeeeeeeeeee!*
Jamie Gilson; *Across America on an Emigrant
Train* Jim Murphy. About 50 titles a year. No
novelty, series or genre fiction. Unsolicited
mss, synopses and ideas welcome. Synopses
should be accompanied by sample chapter(s).

Royalties paid twice yearly.

Clarkson Potter
See **Crown Publishing Group**

Classic Reprint
See **University of Alaska Press**

Cobblehill Books
See **Penguin USA**

Contemporary Books, Inc.
Two Prudential Plaza, Suite 1200, Chicago
IL 60601
☎001 312 540 4500   Fax 001 312 540 4657

Publisher *Christine Albritton*
Managing Editor *Kathy Willhoite*

FOUNDED 1947. *Publishes* general adult non-fiction and adult education books. 60 titles in 1994.

DIVISIONS **Trade** *Nancy Crossman* Editorial
Director; **Adult Education** *Mark Boone* Editorial Director.

Coward-McCann
See **Putnam Berkley Publishing Group**

Crown Publishing Group
201 East 50th Street, New York NY 10022
☎001 212 572 6117   Fax 001 212 572 6161

President/Publisher *Michelle Sidrane*

FOUNDED 1933. Division of **Random House,
Inc.** *Publishes* popular trade fiction and non-
fiction. 259 titles in 1994.

IMPRINTS **Clarkson Potter** *Lauren Shakely*;
Crown Arts and Letters, **Harmony** *Peter
Guzzardi*; **Living Language**; **Carol Southern
Books** *Carol Southern*.

DAW Books, Inc.
375 Hudson Street, 3rd Floor, New York
NY 10014-3658
☎001 212 366 2096/Submissions 366 2095
Fax 001 212 366 2090

Publishers *Elizabeth R. Wollheim, Sheila E.
Gilbert*
Submissions Editor *Peter Stampfel*

FOUNDED 1971 by Donald and Elsie Wollheim
as the first mass-market publisher devoted to
science fiction and fantasy. *Publishes* science
fiction/fantasy, and some horror. No short
stories, anthology ideas or non-fiction. Unsolicited mss, synopses and ideas for books
welcome. About 36 titles a year.

Royalties paid twice yearly.

Dearborn Financial Publishing, Inc.
155 N. Wacker Drive, Chicago IL 60606-1719
☎001 312 836 4400   Fax 001 312 836 1021

President *Robert C. Kyle*
Senior Vice Presidents *Anita A. Constant,
Dennis Blitz, Tim Honaker*

A niche publisher serving the financial services
industries. Formerly part of **Longman**. *Publishes*

real estate, insurance, financial planning, securities, commodities, investments, banking, professional education, motivation and reference titles, investment reference and how-to books for the consumer (individual investor) and small business owner. About 150 titles a year.

DIVISIONS/IMPRINTS
Trade/Professional *Caroline Carney* TITLES *Dive Right In – The Sharks Won't Bite; Benjamin Graham on Value Investing.* **Textbook: Real Estate Education Company** *Carol Luitjens* TITLES *Modern Real Estate Practice* (13th ed.); *Realty Blue Book* (30th ed.). **COURSE: Dearborn/R&R Newkirk** *Marjorie Sher* Insurance titles. TITLES *Property & Casualty Insurance* (3rd ed.); *ACCESS AUS (Advanced Underwriting Service)* on CD-ROM. **Training-Securities** *Mark Emmons* TITLES *PassTrak Series 6 Principles & Practices; OnTrak Professional Sales Assistant.* **Upstart Publishing Co., Inc.** *Jere Calmes* TITLES *Strategic Planning for the New and Small Business; Problems and Solutions in Small Business Management.* **Commodity Trend Service** *Dennis Blitz* TITLES *Futures Charts.* **Vernon Publishing, Inc.** *Gary Schulte* TITLES *Personal Financial Plan; Financial Need Analysis II.* **Enterprise** *Kevin Shanley* TITLES *The Complete Book of Corporate Forms; The Executive's Business Letter Book.* Unsolicited mss, synopses and ideas welcome.
Royalties paid twice yearly.

Del Rey
See **Ballantine/Del Rey/Fawcett/Ivy Books**

Dell Books
See **Bantam Doubleday Dell Publishing Group**

Michael di Capua Books
See **HarperCollins Publishers**

Dial Books for Young Readers
375 Hudson Street, New York NY 10014
☎001 212 366 2800   Fax 001 212 366 2020
Queries *Manuscript Reader*
FOUNDED 1961. Part of **Penguin USA**. *Publishes* children's books, including picture books, beginners' readers, fiction and non-fiction for junior and young adults. 70 titles a year.
IMPRINTS **Dial Easy-to-Read** Hardback and softcover editions; **Puffin Pied Piper/ Puffin Pied Piper Giant** Softcover only. No unsolicited mss; queries only.
Royalties paid twice yearly.

Dimensions for Living
201 Eighth Avenue South, Box 801, Nashville TN 37202
☎001 615 749 6404   Fax 001 615 749 6512
Acquisitions Editor *Sally Sharpe*
Publishes non-fiction books for laity (inspirational, Christian living and self-help).

Doubleday
See **Bantam Doubleday Dell Publishing Group**

Lisa Drew
See **Simon & Schuster Trade Division**

Thomas Dunne Books
See **St Martin's Press, Inc.**

Sanford J. Durst Publications
11 Clinton Avenue, Rockville Centre, New York NY 11570
☎001 516 766 4444   Fax 001 516 766 4520
Owner *Sanford J. Durst*
FOUNDED 1975. *Publishes* non-fiction: numismatic and related, philatelic, legal and art. Also children's books. About 12 titles a year.
Royalties twice yearly.

Dutton Children's Books
See **Penguin USA**

Dutton/Signet
See **Penguin USA**

East Woods Books
See **The Globe Pequot Press**

William B. Eerdmans Publishing Co.
255 Jefferson Avenue SE, Grand Rapids MI 49503
☎001 616 459 4591   Fax 001 616 459 6540
President *William B. Eerdmans Jr*
Vice President/Editor-in-Chief *Jon Pott*
FOUNDED 1911 as a theological and reference publisher. Gradually began publishing in other genres with authors like C. S. Lewis, Dorothy Sayers and Malcolm Muggeridge on its lists. *Publishes* religious: theology, biblical studies, ethical and social concern, social criticism and children's. 116 titles in 1994.
DIVISIONS **Children's** *Amy Eerdmans* **Other** *Charles van Hof* TITLES *Dictionary of Biblical Tradition in English Literature; Systematic Theology; The Divine Dramatist: George Whitfield and the Rise*

of Modern Evangelicalism. Unsolicited mss, synopses and ideas welcome.
Royalties paid twice yearly.

Enterprise
See **Dearborn Financial Publishing, Inc.**

M. Evans & Co., Inc.
216 East 49th Street, New York NY 10017
☎001 212 688 2810   Fax 001 212 486 4544
Chairman *George C. de Kay*

FOUNDED 1954 as a packager. Began publishing in 1962. Best known for its popular psychology and medicine books, with titles like *Body Language, Open Marriage, Pain Erasure* and *Aerobics. Publishes* general non-fiction and western fiction. TITLES *The Arthritis Breakthrough* Henry Scammell; *Total Concentration* Harold Levinson; *Born in Blood* and *Dungeon, Fire and Sword* John J. Robinson; *Dr Atkins' Diet Revolution* Robert Atkins. About 40 titles a year. No unsolicited mss; query first. Synopses and ideas welcome.
Royalties paid twice yearly.

Everyman's Library
See **Alfred A. Knopf, Inc.**

Faber & Faber, Inc.
50 Cross Street, Winchester MA 08190
☎001 617 721 1427   Fax 001 617 729 2783
Chairman *Tom Kelleher*
Approx. Annual Turnover $4.5 million

Part of the UK-based company. *Publishes* fiction and non-fiction for adults. About 100 titles a year. No unsolicited mss. Send brief synopsis, chapter outlines, etc, together with IRCs for response or return.
Royalties paid twice yearly.

Facts On File, Inc.
460 Park Avenue South, New York NY 10016
☎001 212 683 2244   Fax 001 212 683 3633
President *Thomas C. Conoscenti*
Publisher *Remmel Nunn*

Started life in the early 1940s with News Digest subscription series to libraries. Began publishing on specific subjects with the Checkmark Books series and developed its current reference and trade book programme in the 1970s. *Publishes* general trade and academic reference only. *Specialises* in single subject encyclopedias. About 135 titles a year. No fiction, cookery or popular non-fiction.

DIVISIONS **General Reference** *Susan Schwartz* TITLES *Shakespeare A–Z; Eyewitness History Series* **Academic Reference** *Eleanora Von Dehsen* TITLES *Maps on File; Encyclopedia of the Third World* **Young Adult** *James Warren* TITLES *Straight Talk Series; Discovering Science Series; Fashions of the Decade Series* **Electronic Publishing** *Thomas Hitchings* TITLES *Facts On File News Digest CD-ROM; The American Indian Multimedia CD-ROM.* Unsolicited synopses and ideas welcome; no mss. Send query letter in the first instance.
Royalties paid twice yearly.

Farrar, Straus & Giroux, Inc.
19 Union Square West, New York NY 10003
☎001 212 741 6900   Fax 001 212 633 9385
President/Chief Executive *Roger W. Straus III*
Snr Vice-President/Editor-in-Chief *Jonathan Galassi*

FOUNDED 1946. *Publishes* general fiction, non-fiction, juveniles. About 190 titles a year.

DIVISIONS **Children's Books** *Margaret Ferguson.* Publishes fiction and non-fiction, books and novels for children and young adults. Approximately 100 titles a year. Submit synopsis and sample chapters (copies of artwork/photographs as part of package). **Hill & Wang** *Sara Bershtel*
IMPRINTS **MIRASOL Libros Juveniles**; **Noonday Press** *Elisabeth Dyssegaard*; **North Point Press**; **Sunburst Books**.

Fawcett
See **Ballantine/Del Rey/Fawcett/Ivy Books**

Fireside
See **Simon & Schuster Trade Division**

Fodor's Travel Publications
See **Random House, Inc.**

Forge
See **St Martin's Press, Inc.**

Samuel French, Inc.
45 West 25th Street, New York NY 10010
☎001 212 206 8990   Fax 001 212 206 1429
Editor *Lawrence Harbison*

FOUNDED 1830. *Publishes* plays in paperback: Broadway and off-Broadway hits, light comedies, mysteries, one-act plays and plays for young audiences. Unsolicited mss welcome. No synopses. About 80 titles a year.
Royalties paid annually (books); twice yearly

(amateur productions); monthly (professional productions). *Overseas associates* in London, Toronto and Sydney.

The Globe Pequot Press

PO Box 833, 6 Business Park Road,
Old Saybrook CT 06475
☎001 203 395 0440   Fax 001 203 395 0312
President *Linda Kennedy*
Editorial Director *Michael K. Urban*

Publishes regional and international travel, cooking, gardening, how-to, personal finance, and outdoor recreation. About 100 titles a year.

IMPRINTS **East Woods Books; Voyager Books**. TITLES include the *Off The Beaten Path* series, of which there are currently 40 titles, e.g. *Ohio: Off the Beaten Path*. Also publishes the *Recommended Country Inns* guides. Unsolicited mss, synopses and ideas welcome, particularly for travel and outdoor recreation books.

Royalties paid.

Golden Apple

See **Bantam Doubleday Dell Publishing Group Inc**

Greenwillow Books

See **William Morrow and Co., Inc.**

Grolier, Inc.

Sherman Turnpike, Danbury CT 06816
☎001 203 797 3500   Fax 001 203 797 3197
Chief Executive Officer *William C. Johnson*

FOUNDED 1895. *Publishes* juvenile non-fiction, encyclopedias, speciality reference sets, children's fiction and picture books, professional and scholarly.

DIVISIONS **Children's Press; Grolier Educational Corp.; Grolier Reference; Orchard Books; Scarecrow Press, Inc.** (see entry); **Franklin Watts** (see entry).

Grosset & Dunlap

See **Putnam Berkley Publishing Group**

Grove/Atlantic Inc.

841 Broadway, New York
NY 10003–4793
☎001 212 614 7850   Fax 001 212 614 7886
President/Publisher *Morgan Entrekin*
Senior Editor *Anton Mueller*

FOUNDED 1952. *Publishes* general fiction and non-fiction. 70 titles in 1994.

IMPRINTS **Atlantic Monthly Press; Grove Press**.

Gulliver Books

See **Harcourt Brace Children's Books Division**

Harcourt Brace Children's Books Division

525 B Street, Suite 1900, San Diego
CA 92101–4495
☎001 619 699 6810   Fax 001 619 699 6777
Vice President/Director *Louise Howton*

A division of Harcourt Brace & Company. *Publishes* fiction, poetry and non-fiction covering a wide range of subjects: biography, environment and ecology, history, travel, science and current affairs for children and young adults. About 120 titles a year.

IMPRINTS **Browndeer Press; Gulliver Books; Gulliver Green® Books** ecology and environment; **Harcourt Brace Children's Books; Harcourt Brace Paperbacks; Odyssey Paperbacks** novels; **Red Wagon Books** for ages 6 months to 3 years; **Voyager Paperbacks** picture books; **Jane Yolen Books**. No unsolicited mss.

Harlequin Historicals

See **Silhouette Books**

Harmony

See **Crown Publishing Group**

HarperCollins Publishers, Inc.

10 East 53rd Street, New York NY 10022
☎001 212 207 7000   Fax 001 212 207 7797
President/Chief Executive *George Craig*

FOUNDED 1817. Owned by News Corporation. *Publishes* general fiction, non-fiction and college textbooks in hardcover, trade paperback and mass-market formats.

DIVISIONS/IMPRINTS
Adult Trade *Gladys Justin Carr* Vice President/Assoc. Publisher; **Harper Business** *Virginia Smith* Executive Editor; **Harper Reference** *Linda Cunningham* Vice President/Publisher/Editorial Director; **HarperCollins Children's Books** *Marilyn Kriney* Senior Vice President/Publisher; **Harper Paperbacks & Audio** *Geoff Hannell* Senior Vice President/Publisher; **Basic Books** *Mike Mueller* Managing Editor; **Michael di Capua Books** *Michael di Capua* Vice President/Publisher.

SUBSIDIARIES **Scott, Foresman & Co** (see entry); **Zondervan Publishing House** (see entry).

Harvard University Press
79 Garden Street, Cambridge MA 02138
☎001 617 495 2611   Fax 001 617 496 4677
Editor-in-Chief *Aida D. Donald*

Publishes scholarly non-fiction only: general interest, science and behaviour, social science, history, humanities, psychology, political science, sociology, economics, business. 120 new titles a year and 60–70 paperbacks. Free book catalogue available.

Harvest House Publishers
1075 Arrowsmith, Eugene OR 97402
☎001 503 343 0123   Fax 001 503 342 6410
President *R. C. Hawkins Jr*
Vice President, Editorial *Eileen L. Mason*

Publishes Christian living, fiction, children's and contemporary issues. TITLES *Beloved* Kay Arthur. Unsolicited mss, synopses and ideas for books welcome, with IRCs.
Royalties paid annually.

Hearst Books/
Hearst Marine Books
See **William Morrow & Co., Inc.**

Hill & Wang
See **Farrar, Straus & Giroux, Inc**

Hippocrene Books, Inc.
171 Madison Avenue, New York NY 10016
☎001 212 685 4371   Fax 001 212 779 9338
President/Editorial Director *George Blagowidow*

FOUNDED 1971. *Publishes* general non-fiction and reference books. Particularly strong on dictionaries, language studies and military history. No fiction. Send brief summary, table of contents and one chapter for appraisal. S.a.e. essential for response. For manuscript return include sufficient postage cover (IRCs).

Holiday House, Inc.
425 Madison Avenue, New York NY 10017
☎001 212 688 0085   Fax 001 212 421 6134
Vice President/Editor-in-Chief *Margery Cuyler*

Publishes children's general fiction and non-fiction (pre-school to secondary). About 50 titles a year. TITLES *The Miracle of the Potato Latkes* Malka Penn/illus. Giora Carmi; *Peeping Beauty* Mary Jane Auch. Submit synopsis and three sample chapters for novels and chapter books; complete mss (without artwork) for picture books.

Henry Holt and Company, Inc.
115 West 18th Street, New York,
NY 10011
☎001 212 886 9200   Fax 001 212 633 0748
President *Bruno A. Quinson*

FOUNDED 1866. Henry Holt is one of the oldest publishers in the United States. *Publishes* fiction, by both American and international authors, biographies, and books on history and politics, ecology and psychology. AUTHORS include: Sue Grafton, Norman Mailer, Toni Morrison, Thomas Pynchon and Kurt Vonnegut.

Houghton Mifflin Co.
222 Berkeley Street, Boston MA 02116
☎001 617 351 5000   Fax 001 617 227 5409
Contact *Submissions Editor*

FOUNDED 1832. *Publishes* literary fiction and general non-fiction, including autobiography, biography and history. Also school and college textbooks; children's fiction and non-fiction. Average 100 titles a year. Queries only for adult material; synopses, outline and sample chapters for children's non-fiction; complete mss for children's fiction. IRCs required with all submissions/queries.

DIVISIONS **Riverside Publishing Co.; Ticknor & Fields Books for Young Readers; Clarion Books** (see entry).

House of Collectibles
See **Ballantine/Del Rey/Fawcett/Ivy Books**

Hudson River Editions
See **Simon & Schuster Trade Division**

University of Illinois Press
1325 South Oak Street, Champaign
IL 61820-6903
☎001 217 333 0950   Fax 001 217 244 8082
Editorial Director *Richard L. Wentworth*

Publishes: non-fiction, scholarly and general, with special interest in Americana, women's studies and African–American studies; poetry, three volumes a year; short fiction, two or three volumes a year. 110–120 titles a year.

Indiana University Press
601 North Morton Street, Bloomington
IN 42404-3797
☎001 812 855 4203   Fax 001 812 855 7931
Director *John Gallman*

Publishes scholarly non-fiction in the following subject areas: African studies, anthropology,

Asian studies, Black studies, criminal justice, environment and ecology, film, folklore, history, Jewish studies, literary criticism, medical ethics, Middle East studies, military, music, philanthropy, philosophy, politics, religion, semiotics, Russian and East European studies, Victorian studies, women's studies. Query in writing in first instance.

University of Iowa Press
Kuhl House, 119 West Park Road, Iowa City IA 52242
☎001 319 335 2000   Fax 001 319 335 2055
Director *Paul Zimmer*
FOUNDED 1969 as a small scholarly press publishing about five books a year. Now publishing about 35 a year in a variety of scholarly fields, plus local interest, short stories, autobiography and poetry. No unsolicited mss; query first. Unsolicited ideas and synopses welcome.
Royalties paid annually.

Iowa State University Press
2121 South State Avenue, Ames IA 50010
☎001 515 292 0140   Fax 001 515 292 3348
Director *Linda Speth*
FOUNDED 1934 as an offshoot of the university's journalism department. *Publishes* agriculture, aviation, economics, engineering, history, home economics, journalism, veterinary, education, philosophy, biography, ethnic studies, music and film.
Royalties paid annually; sometimes twice yearly.

Ivy Books
See **Ballantine/Del Rey/Fawcett/Ivy Books**

Jove
See **Berkley Publishing Group**

Joy Street Books
See **Little, Brown & Co., Inc.**

University Press of Kansas
2501 West 15th Street, Lawrence KS 66049
☎001 913 864 4154   Fax 001 913 864 4586
Director *Fred M. Woodward*
FOUNDED 1946. Became the publishing arm for all six state universities in Kansas in 1976. *Publishes* scholarly books in American history, women's studies, presidential studies, social and political philosophy, political science, military history, environmental and rural studies. About 45 titles a year. Proposals welcome.
Royalties paid annually.

Kent State University Press
Kent OH 44242-0001
☎001 216 672 7913   Fax 001 216 672 3104
Director *John T. Hubbell*
Editor *Julia Morton*
FOUNDED 1965. *Publishes* scholarly works in history and biography, literary studies, archaeological research, arts and general non-fiction. 20–25 titles a year. Queries welcome; no mss.
Royalties paid twice yearly.

Alfred A. Knopf Inc.
201 East 50th Street, New York NY 10022
☎001 212 751 2600   Fax 001 212 572 2593
President/Editor-in-Chief *Sonny Mehta*
FOUNDED 1915. Division of **Random House, Inc.** *Publishes* fiction and non-fiction, poetry, juvenile. 208 titles in 1994. IMPRINT **Everyman's Library**

Krieger Publishing Co., Inc.
PO Box 9542, Melbourne FL 32902
☎001 407 724 9542   Fax 001 407 951 3671
Chairman *Robert E. Krieger*
President *Donald E. Krieger*
Editorial Head *Mary Roberts*
FOUNDED 1970. *Publishes* business science and economics, education and communication, history, mathematics and computer science, medical science, psychology, chemistry, physical and natural sciences, reference, technology and engineering.
IMPRINTS **Anvil; Exploring Community History Series; Open Forum; Orbit; Professional Practices in Adult Education and Human Resource Development; Public History**. Unsolicited mss welcome. Not interested in synopses/ideas.
Royalties paid yearly.

Lanternlight Library
See **University of Alaska Press**

Lehigh University Press
See **Golden Cockerel Press** under **UK Publishers**

Lerner Publications Co.
241 First Avenue North, Minneapolis MN 55401
☎001 612 332 3344   Fax 001 612 332 7615
Editorial Director *Nancy Campbell*
Publishes children's and young adults: nature, biography, history, world cultures, world and US geography, sports, fiction, mysteries, physi-

cal science. Please send IRCs for author guidelines

Little Simon
See **Simon & Schuster Children's Publishing Division**

Little, Brown & Co., Inc.
1271 Avenue of the Americas, New York NY 10020
☎001 212 522 8700

Children's & Bulfinch editorial at: 34 Beacon Street, Boston, MA 02108
☎001 617 227 0730

President *Charles E. Hayward*

Division of Time Warner, Inc. FOUNDED 1837. *Publishes* contemporary popular fiction and literary fiction. Also non-fiction: distinctive cookbooks, biographies, history, poetry, art, photography, science, sport, and children's. About 100 titles a year.
    IMPRINTS **Back Bay Books; Bulfinch Press; Joy Street Books**. No unsolicited mss. Query letter in the first instance.

Living Language
See **Crown Publishing Group**

Llewellyn Publications
PO Box 64383, St Paul MN 55164
☎001 612 291 1970   Fax 001 612 291 1908

President/Publisher *Carl L. Weschcke*
Acquisitions Manager *Nancy J. Mostad*

Division of Llewellyn Worldwide Ltd. FOUNDED 1902. *Publishes* self-help and how-to: astrology, alternative health, tantra, Fortean studies, tarot, yoga, santeria, dream studies, metaphysics, magic, witchcraft, herbalism, Shamanism (religion of Siberian origin), organic gardening, women's spirituality, graphology, palmistry, parapsychology. Also fiction with a dominant magical or metaphysical theme. About 72 titles a year. Unsolicited mss welcome; proposals preferred. IRCs essential in all cases. Books are distributed in the UK by Foulsham.

Lodestar Books
See **Penguin USA**

Lothrop, Lee & Shepard
See **William Morrow and Co., Inc.**

Louisiana State University Press
Baton Rouge LA 70893
☎001 504 388 6294   Fax 001 504 388 6461

Director *L. E. Phillabaum*

Publishes non-fiction: Southern history, American history, French history, Southern literary criticism, American literary criticism, biography, political science, music (jazz) and Latin American studies. About 70 titles a year. Send IRCs for mss guidelines.

Loveswept
See **Bantam Doubleday Dell Publishing Group Inc**

Lyons & Burford, Publishers
31 West 21st Street, New York NY 10010
☎001 212 620 9580   Fax 001 212 929 1836

Chairman *Nick Lyons*
Managing Director *Peter Burford*

Publishes outdoor, nature, sports, gardening and angling titles, plus cookery and art. About 75 titles a year. No unsolicited mss; synopses and ideas welcome.
    Royalties paid twice yearly.

Macmillan Children's Book Group
See **Simon & Schuster Children's Publishing Division**

Macmillan/McGraw-Hill School Publishing Group
See **McGraw-Hill, Inc.**

University of Massachusetts Press
PO Box 429, Amherst MA 01004–0429
☎001 413 545 2217   Fax 001 413 545 1226

Managing Director *Bruce Wilcox*

FOUNDED 1964. *Publishes* scholarly, general interest, Black, ethnic, women's studies, cultural criticism, architecture and environmental design, literary criticism, poetry, philosophy, political science, sociology. Unsolicited mss considered; prefer query letter in the first instance. Synopses and ideas welcome. About 40 titles a year.
    Royalties paid annually.

Margaret K. McElderry Books
See **Simon & Schuster Children's Publishing Division**

McFarland & Company, Inc., Publishers
PO Box 611, Jefferson NC 28640
☎001 910 246 4460   Fax 001 910 246 5018

President/Editor-in-Chief *Robert Franklin*
Vice President *Rhonda Herman*
Editors *Lisa Camp, Steve Wilson*

FOUNDED 1979. A library-orientated press, pub-

lishing reference books and scholarly monographs in many fields: International studies, performing arts, popular culture, sports, women's studies, music and fine arts, business, history, war memoirs and librarianship. *Specialises* in general reference. No fiction, poetry, children's, New Age, inspirational or autobiographical works. About 130 titles a year. TITLES *Heads of States and Governments*; *International Holidays*; *African Placenames*; *Opera Companies and Houses*; *Christopher Lee and Peter Cushing*; *The Sexual Harassment of Women*; *The Recreation Handbook*. No unsolicited mss; send query letter first. Synopses and ideas welcome.
Royalties paid annually.

McGraw-Hill, Inc.
1221 Avenue of the Americas, New York NY 10020
☎001 212 512 2000
Contact *Submissions Editor*
FOUNDED 1873. US parent of the UK-based **McGraw-Hill Book Co. Europe**. *Publishes* a wide range of business and computing books.

DIVISIONS **Legal Information Group**; **Macmillan/McGraw-Hill School Publishing Group**; **Osborne/McGraw-Hill**; **Professional Publishing Group**.

Mentor
See **Penguin USA**

Meridian
See **Penguin USA**

The University of Michigan Press
839 Greene Street, PO Box 1104, Ann Arbor MI 48106
☎001 313 764 4394   Fax 001 313 936 0456
Managing Director *Colin Day*
FOUNDED 1930. *Publishes* non-fiction, textbooks, literary criticism, theatre, economics, political science, history, classics, anthropology, law studies, women's studies, and English as a Second Language textbooks. 130 titles in 1994.

IMPRINTS
University of Michigan Press *LeAnn Fields* Specialises in monographs in anthropology, economics, classics, women's studies, theatre, political science. **Ann Arbor Paperbacks** TITLES *Castle of My Skin* George Lamming; *Roots* Kamau Braithwaite; *Galileo* James Langford. No unsolicited mss. Synopses and ideas welcome.
Royalties paid twice yearly.

The Millbrook Press, Inc.
2 Old New Milford Road, PO Box 335, Brookfield CT 06804
☎001 203 740 2220   Fax 001 203 740 2526
President *Jean Reynolds*
Editorial Director *Elaine Pascoe*
Managing Editor *Marilyn Smith*
FOUNDED 1989. *Publishes* mainly non-fiction, children's and young adult, for trade, school and public library. About 120 titles a year.
Royalties paid twice yearly.

Minstrel Books
See **Pocket Books**

MIRASOL Libros Juveniles
See **Farrar, Straus & Giroux, Inc**

University Press of Mississippi
3825 Ridgewood Road, Jackson MS 39211-6492
☎001 601 982 6205   Fax 001 601 982 6217
Chairman *Dr O. Finley Graves*
Managing Director *Dr Richard Abel*
Associate Director/Editor-in-Chief *Seetha A-Srinivasan*
Approx. Annual Turnover $1.5 million
FOUNDED 1970. The non-profit book publisher of the eight State universities. *Publishes* scholarly and trade titles in literature, history, American culture, Southern culture, African-American, women's studies, popular culture, folklife, ethnic, performance, art and photography, and other liberal arts. About 50 titles a year. TITLES *Anabasis* Ellen Gilchrist; *Country Music Culture; Punk and Neo-Tribal Body Art*.
IMPRINTS **Muscadine Books** *JoAnne Prichard* Regional trade titles. TITLES *The New Orleans Garden; The Crawfish Book; The Catfish Book*. **Banner Books** paperback reprints of significant fiction and non-fiction. TITLES *Savage Holiday* Richard Wright; *Dark Princess* W.E.B. DuBois. Send letter of enquiry, prospectus, table of contents and sample chapter prior to submission of full mss.
Royalties paid annually. *Represented* worldwide. UK representatives: **Roundhouse Publishing Ltd**, PO Box 140, Oxford OX2 7FF; tel: 01865 512682/fax: 01865 59594.

University of Missouri Press
2910 LeMone Boulevard, Columbia MO 65201-8227
☎001 314 882 7641   Fax 001 314 884 4498
Director/Editor-in-Chief *Beverly Jarrett*
Publishes academic: history, literary criticism,

intellectual history and related humanities disciplines and short stories – usually four volumes a year. Best approach is by letter. Send one short story for consideration, and synopses for academic work. About 50 titles a year.

The MIT Press
55 Hayward Street, Cambridge MA 02142
☎001 617 253 5646   Fax 001 617 258 6779
Managing Editor *Michael Sims*

Publishes non-fiction: technologically sophisticated books, including computer science and artificial intelligence, economics, architecture, cognitive science, neuroscience, environmental studies, linguistics and philosophy. 214 titles in 1994. IMPRINT **Bradford Books**.

Monograph Series
See **University of Alaska Press**

Moorings
See **Ballantine/Del Rey/Fawcett/Ivy Books**

William Morrow & Co., Inc.
1350 Avenue of the Americas, New York NY 10019
☎001 212 261 6500   Fax 001 212 261 6595
Editorial Director *William Schwalbe*

FOUNDED 1926. *Publishes* fiction, poetry and general non-fiction. Approach in writing only. No unsolicited mss or proposals. Proposals read only if submitted through a literary agent (50,000–100,000 words). About 600 titles a year.
IMPRINTS **Hearst Books/Hearst Marine Books** *Ann Bramson*; **Quill Trade Paperbacks** *Toni Sciarra*; **Morrow Junior Books** *David Reuther*; **Lothrop, Lee & Shepard** *Susan Pearson*; **Greenwillow Books** *Susan Hirschman*; **Tambourine Books** *Paulette Kaufmann*; **Mulberry Books/Beech Tree Books** (trade paperbacks) *Paulette Kaufmann*.

Mulberry Books
See **William Morrow and Co., Inc.**

Muscadine Books
See **University Press of Mississippi**

Mysterious Press
See **Warner Books Inc.**

University of Nevada Press
MS 166, Reno NV 89557-0076
☎001 702 784 6573   Fax 001 702 784 6200
Director *Thomas Radko*
Editor-in-Chief *Margaret Dalrymple*

FOUNDED 1960. *Publishes* serious fiction, Native American studies, natural history, Western Americana, Basque studies and regional studies. About 40 titles a year including reprints. Unsolicited material welcome if it fits in with areas published, or offers a 'new and exciting' direction.
Royalties paid twice yearly.

New Age Books
See **Bantam Doubleday Dell Publishing Group Inc**

University Press of New England
23 South Main, Hanover NH 03755-2048
☎001 603 643 7100   Fax 001 603 643 1540
Chair/Director *Thomas L. McFarland*
Editorial Director *Philip Pochoda*

FOUNDED 1970. A scholarly book publisher sponsored by ten institutions of higher education in the region: Brandeis, Brown, Dartmouth, Middlebury, Tufts, Wesleyan and the universities of New Hampshire, Rhode Island, Vermont and the Salzburg Seminar. *Publishes* general and scholarly non-fiction: American and European history, literature and literary criticism, cultural theory, art history, philosophy, psychology, environmental studies, regional interest and natural sciences. Plus poetry, essays and short stories through the Wesleyan Poetry Series, Bread Loaf Writers Conference and Hardscrabble Books, contemporary and classic fiction from New England. Lead titles for 1994–95: *Double Vision* Alexandra Todd; *American Identities* Robert Pack & Jay Parini. Also publishers of various journals: *Jewish History; International Environmental Affairs; New England Review: Middlebury Series.* About 65 titles a year.
IMPRINTS **Wesleyan University Press** Interdisciplinary studies, history, literature, women's studies, government and public issues, biography, poetry, social and natural sciences. Unsolicited material welcome.
Royalties paid annually. *Overseas associates:* UK – University Presses Marketing; Europe – Trevor Brown Associates.

University of New Mexico Press
1720 Lomas NE, Albuquerque NM 87131-1591
☎001 505 277 2346   Fax 001 505 277 9270
Editor *Larry Durwood Ball*

Publishes scholarly non-fiction across a wide range of fields, plus illustrated and biography. No fiction, how-to, children's, humour, self-help, technical or textbooks. About 70 titles a year.

New Sciences
See **Bantam Doubleday Dell Publishing Group Inc**

Noonday Press
See **Farrar, Straus & Giroux, Inc**

North Point Press
See **Farrar, Straus & Giroux, Inc**

University of North Texas Press
PO Box 13856, Denton TX 76203
☎001 817 565 2142   Fax 001 817 565 4590

Director *Frances B. Vick*
Editor *Charlotte M. Wright*
FOUNDED 1987. *Publishes* folklore, ecology, regional interest, contemporary, social issues, history, military, women's issues, writing and publishing reference, and Western literature. About 14 titles a year. No unsolicited mss. Approach by letter in the first instance. Synopses and ideas welcome.
Royalties paid annually.

W. W. Norton & Company
500 Fifth Avenue, New York NY 10110
☎001 212 354 5500   Fax 001 212 869 0856

Editor *Liz Malcolm*
FOUNDED 1923. *Publishes* quality fiction and non-fiction, college textbooks, professional and medical books. No occult, paranormal, religious, arts and crafts, genre fiction (formula romances, science fiction or westerns), children's books or young adult. About 300 titles a year. Query letters should include brief description of submission, writing credentials and experience relevant to submissions. Submissions should consist of 2 or 3 sample chapters including the first; non-fiction submissions should also include a detailed outline of content. Return postage essential for response.

Odyssey Paperbacks
See **Harcourt Brace Children's Books Division**

University of Oklahoma Press
1005 Asp Avenue, Norman OK 73019-0445
☎001 405 325 5111   Fax 001 405 325 4000

Editor-in-Chief *John N. Drayton*
Publishes general scholarly non-fiction only: American Indian studies, history of American West, classical studies, literary theory and criticism, anthropology, archaeology, natural history, political science and women's studies. About 80 titles a year.

One World
See **Ballantine/Del Rey/Fawcett/Ivy Books**

Onyx
See **Penguin USA**

Open Forum
See **Krieger Publishing Co., Inc.**

Orb
See **St Martin's Press, Inc.**

Orbit
See **Krieger Publishing Co., Inc.**

Orchard Books
See **Grolier, Inc.**

Osborne/McGraw Hill
2600 Tenth Street, Berkeley CA 94710
☎001 510 549 6600   Fax 001 510 549 6603

Publisher *Larry Levitsky*
FOUNDED 1970. Osborne has been publishing computer books for almost twenty years and has grown to become a leader in its field. *Publishes* computer software and microcomputer titles. About 85 titles a year. TITLES *DOS Made Easy; WordPerfect: The Complete Reference.*
Royalties paid twice yearly.

Paladin Press
PO Box 1307, Boulder CO 80306
☎001 303 443 7250   Fax 001 303 442 8741

Chairman *Peder C. Lund*
Editorial Director *Jon Ford*
FOUNDED 1970 as Panther Publications and changed its name in the mid 1970s. Claims to be the largest publisher in the world of 'unconventional action-oriented' books. *Publishes* non-fiction: how-to books and videos on weapons, police and military science, explosives and demolitions, self-defence and martial arts, personal freedom, espionage, investigation, knives, terrorism, action careers and related topics. About 40 titles a year. TITLES *The Ultimate Sniper: An Advanced Training Manual for Military & Police Snipers; Zips, Pipes and Pens: Arsenal of Improvised Weapons; Get Even: The Complete Book of Dirty Tricks.* Unsolicited mss, synopses and ideas welcome. Write or call for free copy of author style guide, newsletter and catalogue.
Royalties paid twice yearly. *UK subsidiary.*
CEP Europe, Birmingham.

Pantheon Books/Schocken Books

201 East 50th Street, New York NY 10022
☎001 212 572 2404   Fax 001 212 572 6030

Senior Editor (Pantheon) *Shelley Wanger*
Editor Director (Shocken) *Arthur Samuelson*

FOUNDED 1942. Division of **Random House, Inc.** *Publishes* Fiction and non-fiction, Jewish interest (Shocken Books). 74 titles in 1994.

Paragon House

401 Fifth Avenue, New York NY 10016
☎001 212 725 3380   Fax 001 212 725 3617

Director/Vice-President *Mike Giampaoli*

FOUNDED 1982. *Publishes* non-fiction: reference and academic. Subjects include history, religion, philosophy, New Age, Jewish interest. 21 titles in 1994.
Royalties paid twice yearly.

Peacock Press

See **Bantam Doubleday Dell Publishing Group Inc**

Pelican Publishing Company

1101 Monroe Street, Box 3110, Gretna LA 70053
☎001 504 368 1175

Editor *Nina Kooij*

Publishes general non-fiction: popular history, cookbooks, travel, art, business, architecture and motivational. About 45 titles a year. Initial enquiries required for all submissions.

Pelion Press

See **Rosen Publishing Group, Inc.**

Penguin USA

375 Hudson Street, New York NY 10014
☎001 212 366 2000   Fax 001 212 366 2666

Chairman *Peter Mayer*

Owned by Pearson. *Publishes* fiction and non-fiction in paperback; adult and children's. About 1000 titles a year. IMPRINTS: **Arkana**; **Blackie**; **Mentor**; **Meridian**; **Onyx**; **Penguin Classics**; **Plume** *Arnold Dolin*; **Puffin** *Tracy Tang*; **ROC Books** *Amy Stout*; **Seafarer** *Christopher Franceschelli*; **Signet**; **Signet Classics**; **Topaz**; **Viking** *Barbara Grossman*; **Viking Studio** *Michael Fragnito*; **Frederick Warne**.

DIVISIONS
Dutton/Signet *Donna Cullen* FOUNDED 1852.
IMPRINTS **William Abrahams**; **Dutton**; **Truman M. Talley**.
Dial Books for Young Readers *Phyllis J.*

Fogelman (see entry); **Dutton Children's Books** *Christopher Franceschelli/Lucia Monfried* FOUNDED 1852. *Publishes* picture books, fiction and non-fiction, board and novelty books.
IMPRINTS **Cobblehill Books** *Rosanne Lauer*; **Lodestar Books** *Rosemary Brosnan*; **Viking Children's Books** *Regina Hayes*.
Viking/Penguin *Cynthia Achar* Non-fiction and fiction.
Royalties paid twice yearly.

University of Pennsylvania Press

418 Service Drive, Philadelphia PA 19104
☎001 215 898 1671   Fax 001 215 898 0404

Managing Director *Thomas M. Rotell*

FOUNDED 1896. *Publishes* scholarly, reference, professional, textbooks and trade. No fiction or poetry. TITLES include *Dearest Wilding: A Memoir With Love; Letters from Theodore Dreiser; Television Culture and Women's Lives.* About 70 titles a year. No unsolicited mss but synopses and ideas for books welcome.
Royalties paid annually.

Perigord Press

See **Bantam Doubleday Dell Publishing Group Inc**

Perigree Books

See **Putnam Berkley Group**

Philomel Books

See **Putnam Berkley Group**

Platt & Munk

See **Putnam Berkley Publishing Group**

Players Press

PO Box 1132, Studio City CA 91614–0132
☎001 818 789 4980

Chairman *William-Alan Landes*
Managing Director *Sharon Gorrell*
Editorial Head *Robert W. Gordon*

FOUNDED 1965 as a publisher of plays; now publishes across the entire range of performing arts: plays, musicals, theatre, film, cinema, television, costume, puppetry, plus technical theatre and cinema material. 55–65 titles a year. TITLES *Corrugated Cardboard Scenery*; *Historic American Costume*; *Tangled Garden*; *Prometheus Bound*; *Try A Little Shakespeare*; *Rapunzel 'n' the Witch*. No unsolicited mss; synopses/ideas welcome. Send query letter.
Royalties paid twice yearly. *Overseas subsidiaries* in Canada, Australia and the UK.

Plenum Publishing

233 Spring Street, New York NY 10013
☎001 212 620 8000   Fax 001 212 463 0742

Senior Editor, Trade Books *Linda Greenspan Regan*

FOUNDED 1946. *Publishes* quality non-fiction for the intelligent layman and the professional: trade science, social sciences, health, psychology, anthropology and criminology. About 350 titles a year. Queries only.

Plume

See **Penguin USA**

Pocket Books

1230 Avenue of the Americas, New York NY 10020
☎001 212 698 7000

President/Publisher *Gina Centrello*
Senior Editors *Jane Chelius, Paul McCarthy, Linda Marrow, Thomas W. Miller*

FOUNDED 1939. A division of Simon & Schuster Consumer Group. *Publishes* trade paperbacks and hardcovers; mass market, reprints and originals. IMPRINTS **Archway; Minstrel Books; Pocket Star Books; Washington Square Press**.

Clarkson Potter

See **Crown Publishing Group**

Princeton University Press

41 William Street, Princeton NJ 08540
☎001 609 258 4900   Fax 001 609 258 6305

Editor-in-Chief *Emily Wilkinson*

Publishes scholarly non-fiction: art and architecture, anthropology, history, philosophy, religion, political science, music, biological and physical sciences, biography, computer science, language and literature, translation and women's studies. About 180 titles a year. Queries only.

Public History

See **Krieger Publishing Co., Inc.**

Puffin

See **Penguin USA**

Puffin Pied Piper

See **Dial Books for Young Readers**

Putnam Berkley Publishing Group

200 Madison Avenue, New York NY 10016
☎001 212 951 8400   Fax 001 212 213 6706

Editorial Heads, Putnam *Nancy Paulsen, Neil Nyren, Margaret Frith*

Editorial Heads, Berkley *Leslie Gelbman, John Duff*
Editorial Director, Philomel Books *Patricia Lee Gauch*

FOUNDED 1838. *Publishes* general fiction and non-fiction, including children's. Also business, how-to, nutrition and general fiction under the **Berkley** imprints. **The Putnam & Grosset Group** includes **G. P. Putnam's Sons, Philomel Books** and **Grosset & Dunlap** *publishes* children's picture books, young adult fiction, children's fiction and non-fiction. Over 1000 titles a year.

DIVISIONS **Berkley** Mass market paperback division (see entry). **Perigree Books** *John Duff/Steve Ross* Trade paperback division. Non-fiction: cookbooks, crafts, humour, music & dance, health, nutrition, psychology, self-help, social sciences and sociology, biography, child care and development, behavioural sciences, business, human relations, education. **Putnam & Grosset Book & Activity Group** (Tel: 951 8700 Fax: 213 6706): **G.P. Putnam's Sons** *Neil Nyren/Faith Sale*; **Coward-McCann, Grosset & Dunlap** *Jane O'Connor*; **Philomel Books** *Patricia Lee Gauch* IMPRINTS **Sandcastle** paperback reissues; **Platt & Munk; Tuffy Books** fiction and general non-fiction.

Royalties paid twice yearly.

Questar

See **Warner Books Inc.**

Quill Trade Paperbacks

See **William Morrow and Co., Inc.**

Rabbit Ears

See **Simon & Schuster Children's Publishing Division**

Rand McNally & Co.

8255 North Central Park Avenue, Skokie IL 60076
☎001 708 329 6772   Fax 001 708 329 1985

Editor *Jon Leverenz*

Publishes world atlases and maps, road atlases of North America and Europe, city and state maps of the United States and Canada, educational wall maps, atlases and globes. Includes electronic publications.

Random House, Inc.

201 East 50th Street, New York NY 10022
☎001 212 751 2600   Fax 001 212 572 8700

Chairman/President & CEO *Alberto Vitale*

FOUNDED 1925. *Publishes* trade fiction: adventure, confessional, experimental, fantasy, historical, horror, humour, mainstream, mystery and suspense; and non-fiction: biography, history, economics, politics, health, business, sports, humour, food and cookery, self-help, Americana, nature and environment, psychology, religion, sociology. Plus children's fiction: adventure, confessional (young adult), fantasy, historical, horror, humour, mystery, picture books, science fiction, suspense, young adult; and children's non-fiction: biography, humour, illustrated, nature and the environment, leisure, science and sport. 3444 titles in 1994. Submissions via agents preferred.

DIVISIONS
Juvenile & Merchandise Group (☎940 7682. Fax: 940 7640) IMPRINTS **Random House Juvenile** *Jennifer Fanelli* Senior Editor; **Knopf Juvenile** *Ruth Katcher* Editor; **Crown Juvenile** *Simon Boughton* VP/Editor-in-Chief; **Bullseye Books** *Lisa Banim* Executive Editor. **Crown Publishing Group** (see entry). **Ballantine/Del Rey/Fawcett/Ivy Books** (see entry). **Alfred A. Knopf, Inc.** (see entry). **Pantheon Books/Shocken Books** (see entry) **Random House Adult Trade Books** (Tel: 572 2120. Fax: 572 4949) *Harold Evans* President/Publisher. **Times Books** (see entry); **Villard Books** Fiction and non-fiction; **Vintage Books** Trade paperbacks. Other divisions: **Random House Reference and Electronic Publishing**; **Fodor's Travel Publications, Inc.**
Royalties paid twice yearly.

Rawson Associates
See **Simon & Schuster Trade Division**

Red Wagon Books
See **Harcourt Brace Children's Books Division**

Fleming H. Revell
See **Baker Book House**

Riverside Publishing Co.
See **Houghton Mifflin Co.**

ROC Books
See **Penguin USA**

The Rosen Publishing Group, Inc.
29 East 21st Street, New York NY 10010
☎001 212 777 3017   Fax 001 212 777 0277
President *Roger Rosen*
Editors *Patra McSharry Sevastiades, Gina Strazzabosco, Jennifer Croft*

Publishes non-fiction books (reference, self-help and textbooks) for a young adult audience

on careers and personal guidance, and high-lo books for reluctant readers. Areas of interest include art, health (coping), music, biography, geography, self-esteem, drug abuse prevention, African studies. About 100 titles a year.
IMPRINT **Pelion Press** Music titles. Write with outline and sample chapters.

Rutgers University Press
109 Church Street, New Brunswick NJ 08901
☎001 908 932 7762   Fax 001 908 932 7039
Editor-in-Chief *Leslie Mitchner*
FOUNDED 1936. *Publishes* scholarly books, regional and social sciences. Unsolicited mss, synopses and ideas for books welcome. No original fiction or poetry. About 70 titles a year.
Royalties paid annually.

Sandcastle
See **Putnam Berkley Group**

Scarecrow Press, Inc.
52 Liberty Street, PO Box 4167, Metuchen NJ 08840
☎001 908 548 8600   Fax 001 908 548 5767
President *Albert W. Daub*
Vice President *Norman Horrocks*
FOUNDED 1950 as a short-run publisher of library reference books. Acquired by **Grolier, Inc.**, Connecticut, in 1970. *Publishes* reference, scholarly and monographs (all levels) for libraries. Reference books in all areas except sciences, specialising in the performing arts, music, cinema and library science. About 130 titles a year. Publisher for the Medical Library Association, Society of American Archivists, Children's Literature Association, Institute of Jazz Studies of Rutgers – the State University of New Jersey, the American Theological Library Association. Also publisher of of *VOYA* (Voice of Youth Advocates); six issues a year. Unsolicited mss welcome but material will not be returned unless requested and accompanied by return postage. Unsolicited synopses and ideas for books welcome.
Royalties paid annually.

Schocken Books
See **Pantheon Books**

Scholastic, Inc.
555 Broadway, New York NY 10012
☎001 212 343 6100   Fax 001 212 343 4535
Editorial Director *Bonnie Verburg*
Executive Editor (picture books) *Dianne Hess*
Executive Editor (middle grade, young adult, non-fiction) *Ann Reit*

Executive Editor (middle grade, young adult, fiction) *Regina Griffin*

FOUNDED 1920. *Publishes* picture books and fiction for middle grade (8–12-year-olds) and young adults: family stories, friendship, humour, fantasy, mysteries and school. Also non-fiction: biography and multicultural subjects. Mss with outlines and three sample chapters welcome. IMPRINT **The Blue Sky Press**.

Scott, Foresman & Co

1900 E Lake Avenue, Glenview IL 60025
☎001 708 729 3000   Fax 001 708 486 3968

President/Chief Executive *Kate Nyquist*

FOUNDED 1896. Subsidiary of **HarperCollins Publishers**. *Publishes* elementary and secondary education books. 1300 titles in 1994.

Charles Scribner's Sons

See **Simon & Schuster Trade Division**

Signet/Signet Classics

See **Penguin USA**

Silhouette Books

300 East 42nd Street, New York NY 10017
☎001 212 682 6080   Fax 001 212 682 4539

Editorial Director *Isabel Swift*

FOUNDED 1979 as an imprint of **Simon & Schuster** and was acquired by a wholly owned subsidiary of Toronto-based Harlequin Enterprises Ltd in 1984. *Publishes* category, contemporary romance fiction and historical romance fiction only. Over 360 titles a year across a number of imprints.

IMPRINTS **Silhouette Romance** *Anne Canadeo*; **Silhouette Desire** *Lucia Macro;* **Silhouette Special Edition** *Tara Gavin*; **Silhouette Intimate Moments** *Leslie Wainger;* **Silhouette Shadows** *Leslie Wainger,* **Silhouette Yours Truly** *Melissa Senate*; **Harlequin Historicals** *Tracy Farrell.* No unsolicited mss. Submit query letter in the first instance or write for detailed submission guidelines/tip sheets.

Royalties paid twice yearly. *Overseas associates* worldwide.

Royalties paid twice yearly. *Overseas associates* worldwide.

Simon & Schuster Children's Publishing Division

866 Third Avenue, New York NY 10022
☎001 212 698 7200   Fax 001 212 605 3068

President and Publisher *Willa Perlman*

A division of the Simon & Schuster Consumer Group. *Publishes* pre-school to young adult, picture books, hardcover and paperback fiction, non-fiction, trade, library and mass market titles. Purchased Macmillan Children's Book Group in 1994.

IMPRINTS

Aladdin Books *Ellen Krieger* picture books, paperback fiction and non-fiction reprints and originals and limited series for ages pre-school to young adult; **Atheneum Books for Young Readers** *Jonathan Lanman* picture books, hardcover fiction and non-fiction books across all genres for ages 3 to young adult; **Little Simon** *Robin Corey* mass-market novelty books and merchandise (book and audio cassette) for ages birth through 8; **Margaret K. McElderry Books** *Margaret K. McElderry* picture books, hardcover fiction and non-fiction trade books for children aged 3 to young adult; **Rabbit Ears** *Robin Corey* children's audiocassettes, packaged with companion books in hardcover, paperback, and mini-book formats. Entire programme derived from the videos produced by the entertainment company, Rabbit Ears; **Simon & Schuster Books for Young Readers** *Stephanie Owens Lurie* picture books, hardcover fiction and non-fiction for children aged 3 to young adult.

Send envelope (US size 10) for guidelines, attention: *Manuscript Submissions Guidelines.*

Simon & Schuster Trade Division

1230 Avenue of the Americas, New York NY 10020
☎001 212 698 7000   Fax 001 212 698 7007

President/Publisher *Carolyn K. Reidy*
Executive Vice President *Michael Jacobs*
Snr Vice President/Editor-in-Chief *Michael V. Korda*

A division of the Simon & Schuster Consumer Group. *Publishes* fiction and non-fiction.

IMPRINTS **Fireside/Touchstone** *Mark Gompertz, Marilyn Abraham;* **Charles Scribner's Sons/Scribner** *Susan Moldow, Nan Graham*; **Simon and Schuster** *Alice Mayhew,* **Hudson River Editions; H. & R. Block; Lisa Drew Books; Rawson Associates; Atheneum Publishers**. No unsolicited mss.

Royalties paid twice yearly.

Carol Southern Books

See **Crown Publishing Group**

Southern Illinois University Press

PO Box 3697, Carbondale IL 62902
☎001 618 453 2281   Fax 001 618 453 1221

Associate Director, Editorial *Curtis L. Clark*

FOUNDED 1953. *Publishes* scholarly non-fiction

books and educational materials. 62 titles a year.
Royalties paid annually.

Spectra
See **Bantam Doubleday Dell Publishing Group Inc**

Spire Books
See **Baker Book House**

St Martin's Press, Inc.
175 Fifth Avenue, New York NY 10010
☎001 212 674 5151   Fax 001 212 420 9314

Chairman/Chief Executive *Thomas J. McCormack*
President/Publisher (Trade Division) *Sally Richardson*

FOUNDED 1952. A subsidiary of **Macmillan Publishers** (UK), St Martin's Press made its name and fortune by importing raw talent from the UK to the States and has continued to buy heavily in the UK. *Publishes* general fiction, especially mysteries and crime; and adult non-fiction: history, self-help, political science, travel, biography, scholarly, popular reference, college textbooks. 1500 titles in 1994.
IMPRINTS **Bedford Books**; **Thomas Dunne Books**; **Forge**; **Orb**; **Tor Books**; **A. Wyatt Books**.

Stackpole Books
5067 Ritter Road, Mechanicsburg PA 17055
☎001 717 796 0411   Fax 001 717 796 0412

President *M. David Detweiler*
Vice President/Editorial Director *Judith Schnell*

FOUNDED 1933. *Publishes* outdoors, nature, gardening, crafts and hobbies, adventure, military reference, history, fishing, hunting, woodworking and carving. 70 titles in 1994.
Royalties paid twice yearly.

Stanford University Press
Stanford CA 94305-2235
☎001 415 723 9598   Fax 001 415 725 3457

Editor *Norris Pope*
Publishes non-fiction: scholarly works in all areas of the humanities, social sciences and natural sciences, plus a few general interest titles. About 75 titles a year. No unsolicited mss; query in writing first.

Sterling Publishing Co. Inc.
387 Park Avenue South, 5th Floor, New York NY 10016–8810
☎001 212 532 7160   Fax 001 212 213 2495

President/Editor *Burton Hobson*
Contact *Sheila Barry*

FOUNDED 1949. *Publishes* non-fiction: reference and information books, science, nature, arts and crafts, architecture, home improvement, history, photography, humour, careers, health, self-help, wine and food, social sciences, sports, drama, music, psychology, occult, woodworking, dance, pets, hobbies, business, military science, gardening. Also juvenile and young adult fiction. 441 titles in 1994.

Gareth Stevens Children's Books
1555 North River Center Drive, Suite 201, Milwaukee WI 53212
☎001 414 225 0333   Fax 001 414 225 0377

President *Gareth Stevens*
Publishes children's books only. About 100 titles a year. No unsolicited material at present as schedule is full for some time to come.
Royalties paid annually.

Stonehenge Press
See **Time-Life Inc.**

Sunburst Books
See **Farrar, Straus & Giroux, Inc**

Susquehanna University Press
See **Golden Cockerel Press** under **UK Publishers**

Sweet Dreams
See **Bantam Doubleday Dell Publishing Group Inc**

Syracuse University Press
1600 Jamesville Avenue, Syracuse NY 13244
☎001 315 443 5541   Fax 001 315 443 5545

Director *Robert Mandel*
FOUNDED 1943. *Publishes* scholarly books in the following areas: contemporary Middle East studies, international affairs, Irish studies, medieval and Renaissance studies – especially the role of women, New York State and the region, Iroquois studies, American history, special education, peace studies and conflict resolution, utopian and communal societies. About 30 titles a year. TITLES *Intellectual Life in Arab East* M. Buheiry; *Middle Eastern Lives* M. Kramer. SERIES TITLES *Irish Studies; New York Classics; Syracuse Studies on Peace and Conflict Resolution; Utopianism and Communitarianism.* Also co-publishes with a number of organisations such as the American University of Beirut. No unsolicited mss. Send query letter with IRCs.
Royalties paid annually.

Truman M. Talley
See **Penguin USA**

Tambourine Books
See **William Morrow and Co., Inc.**

Temple University Press
Broad and Oxford Streets, Philadelphia
PA 19122
☎001 215 204 8787   Fax 001 215 204 4719
Editor-in-Chief *Michael Ames*

Publishes scholarly non-fiction: American history, Latin American studies, gay and lesbian studies, ethnic studies, psychology, Asian American studies, anthropology, law, cultural studies, sociology, women's studies, health care, philosophy, public policy, labour studies, urban and environmental studies, photography and Black studies. About 70 titles a year. Authors generally academics. Write in first instance.

University of Tennessee Press
293 Communications Building, Knoxville
TN 37996-0325
☎001 615 974 3321   Fax 001 615 974 3724

FOUNDED in the late 1800s. Began full-time publication of scholarly works in 1947. *Publishes* non-fiction: anthropology, folklore, literature, American history, Southern studies, feminist literary criticism, women's studies, American religious history and African-American studies. Unsolicited material/outlines welcome in these areas. About 28–32 titles a year.
Royalties paid twice yearly.

University of Texas Press
PO Box 7819, Austin TX 78713-7819
☎001 512 471 7233/Editorial: 471 4278
Fax 001 512 320 0668
Director *Joanna Hitchcock*
Assistant Director/Executive Editor
Theresa J. May

Publishes scholarly non-fiction: anthropology, archaeology, cultural geography, Latin/ Mexican/native American studies, politics, biology and earth sciences, environmental, American/Texan urban studies, Texana, women's, film, cultural, media, literary studies, Middle Eastern studies, regional cookbooks, natural history, Latin American/Middle Eastern literature in translation, art and architecture, classics. Unsolicited material welcome in above subject areas only. About 70 titles a year.
Royalties paid annually.

Ticknor & Fields Books for Young Readers
See **Houghton Mifflin Co.**

Time-Life Inc.
777 Duke Street, Alexandria VA 22314
☎001 703 838 7000   Fax 001 703 838 7225
President/Chief Executive *John M. Fahey Jr*

FOUNDED 1961. *Publishes* non-fiction: art, cooking, crafts, food, gardening, health, history, home maintenance, nature, photography, science. No unsolicited mss. 300 titles in 1994.
DIVISIONS/IMPRINTS **Time-Life Books; Time-Life Education; Time-Life Music; Time-Life International; Time-Life Video & Television; Stonehenge Press**.

Times Books
201 East 50th Street, New York NY 10022
☎001 212 572 8104   Fax 001 212 572 4949
Editorial Director *Steve Wasserman*

FOUNDED 1959. A division of **Random House**. *Publishes* general non-fiction only. 90 titles in 1994. Unsolicited mss not considered. Letter essential.

Topaz
See **Penguin USA**

Tor Books
See **St Martin's Press, Inc.**

Touchstone
See **Simon & Schuster Trade Division**

Tuffy Books
See **Putnam Berkley Publishing Group**

Tyndale House Publishers, Inc.
351 Executive Drive, PO Box 80, Wheaton
IL 60189
☎001 708 668 8300   Fax 001 708 668 6885
Chairman *Kenneth N. Taylor*
President *Mark D. Taylor*

FOUNDED 1962 by Kenneth Taylor. Non-denominational religious publisher of around 100–150 titles a year for the evangelical Christian market. Books cover a wide range of categories from home and family to inspirational, theology, doctrine, Bibles and general reference. Also produces video material, calendars and audio books for the same market. No poetry. No unsolicited mss; they will be returned unread. Synopses and ideas considered. Send query letter summarising contents of books and length. Include a brief biography, detailed outline and sample chapters. IRCs essential for response or return of material. No audio cassettes, disks or video tapes in lieu of mss. Response time around 6–12 weeks. No phone calls. Send s.a.e. for free catalogue and full submission guidelines.

Royalties paid annually, sometimes twice yearly.

Upstart Publishing Co., Inc.
See **Dearborn Financial Publishing, Inc.**

Van Nostrand Reinhold
115 Fifth Avenue, New York NY 10003
☎001 212 254 3232   Fax 001 212 477 2719
President/CEO *Marianne J. Russell*

FOUNDED 1848. *Publishes* professional, technical, scientific reference and texts in the following fields: technology management; environmental/occupational health and safety; electrical engineering; computer science and data processing; architecture, graphic arts and interior design; culinary arts and hospitality; and science reference. Approximately 150 titles a year.

Vernon Publishing Inc.
See **Dearborn Financial Publishing, Inc.**

Viking/Viking Penguin/Viking Studio
See **Penguin USA**

Villard Books
See **Random House, Inc.**

Vintage Books
See **Random House, Inc.**

Voyager Books
See **The Globe Pequot Press**

Voyager Paperbacks
See **Harcourt Brace Children's Books Division**

Walker & Co.
435 Hudson Street, New York NY 10014
☎001 212 727 8300   Fax 001 212 727 0984
Contact *Submissions Editor*

FOUNDED 1959. *Publishes* fiction: mystery and suspense, westerns and children's; and non-fiction. Unsolicited submissions are welcome as follows:

Mystery/suspense *Michael Seidman* 60,000–70,000 words. Send first three chapters and 3-5 page synopsis. **Westerns** *Jacqueline Johnson* 65,000 words, strong plot and character development. 50–75 pages plus short synopsis, or complete mss.

Trade non-fiction Permissions and documentation must be available with mss. Submit prospectus first, with sample chapters and marketing analysis.

Books for Young Readers *Emily Easton/ Mary Rich* Fiction and non-fiction. Query before sending non-fiction proposals. Especially interested in young science, photoessays, historical fiction for middle grades, biographies, current affairs, and YA non-fiction.

Frederick Warne
See **Penguin USA**

Warner Books Inc.
1271 Avenue of the Americas, New York NY 10020
☎001 212 522 7200   Fax 001 212 522 7991
Executive Vice President/Publisher
Nancy Neiman

FOUNDED 1961. *Publishes* fiction and non-fiction, audio books, gift books, electronic and multimedia products. 330 titles in 1994.

IMPRINTS **Aspect** *Betsy Mitchell*; **Mysterious Press** *William Malloy*; **Questar**. Query or submit outline with sample chapters and letter.

Washington Square Press
See **Pocket Books**

Washington State University Press
Cooper Publications Building, Pullman WA 99164-5910
☎001 509 335 3518   Fax 001 509 335 8568
Director *Thomas H. Sanders*

FOUNDED 1928. Revitalised in 1984 to publish hardcover originals, trade paperbacks and reprints. *Publishes* mainly on the history, prehistory and culture of the Northwest United States (Washington, Idaho, Oregon, Montana) and British Columbia, but works that focus on national topics or other regions may also be considered. 8–10 titles a year. TITLES *Fighting the Odds: The Life of Senator Frank Church*; *Fields of Toil: A Migrant Family's Journey*; *Backwoods Railroads: Branchlines and Shortlines of Western Oregon*; *Women and the Journey: The Female Travel Experience*; *Bearing Dreams, Shaping Visions: Asian Pacific American Perspectives*. Unsolicited mss welcome. No synopses or ideas.

Royalties paid annually.

Franklin Watts

95 Madison Avenue, 11th Floor, New York
NY 10016
☎001 212 951 2650   Fax 001 212 689 7803
Vice President/Publisher *John W. Selfridge*

Part of **Grolier, Inc.**, Connecticut. FOUNDED
1942 and acquired by Grolier in 1975. *Publishes*
non-fiction: curriculum-based material for ages
5–18 across a wide range of subjects, including
history, social sciences, natural and physical sciences, health and medicine, biography. Over
100 titles a year. No unsolicited mss. Synopses
and ideas considered. Address samples to 'Submissions' and include IRCs if response required.
Be prepared for a three-month turnaround.

Royalties paid twice yearly.

Wesleyan University Press

See **University Press of New England**

J. Weston Walch, Publisher

321 Valley Street, PO Box 658, Portland
ME 04104-0658
☎001 207 772 2846   Fax 001 207 772 3105
President *Suzanne Austin*
Editor-in-Chief *Richard Kimball*

FOUNDED 1927. *Publishes* supplementary educational materials for secondary schools across a
wide range of subjects, including art, business,
computer education, languages, careers, health
and fitness, home economics, literacy, mathematics, science, music, social studies, special
needs, etc. Always interested in ideas from secondary school teachers who develop materials
in the classroom. About 70 titles a year. Unsolicited mss, synopses and ideas welcome.

Royalties paid twice yearly.

A. Wyatt Books

See **St Martin's Press, Inc.**

Jane Yolen Books

See **Harcourt Brace Children's Books
Division**

Zondervan Publishing House

5300 Patterson Avenue SE, Grand Rapids
MI 49530
☎001 616 698 6900   Fax 001 616 698 3439
President/Chief Executive *Bruce E.
Ryskamp*
Senior Editor *Bob Hudson*

FOUNDED 1931. Subsidiary of **HarperCollins
Publishers, Inc.** *Publishes* Protestant religion,
Bibles, mini-books, audio & video, computer
software, calendars and speciality items.

US Agents

International Reply Coupons (IRCs) are necessary for return postage. They are available from the Post Office: letters 60 pence, mss according to weight.

Adler & Robin Books, Inc.
3409 29th Street NW,
Washington DC 20008
☎001 202 363 7410   Fax 001 202 686 1804
President/Agent *Bill Adler Jr*
Agent *Lisa Swayne*

FOUNDED 1988. *Handles* popular adult fiction and non-fiction, specialising in how-to. Represents illustrators. Occasionally represents children's books. Unsolicited mss, synopses and queries welcome. Send letter with outline or proposal and sample chapters if possible. Electronic submissions accepted. No reading fee or any other charges. CLIENTS Laura Bergheim, Michael Leccese, Peggy Robin, Jennifer Toth. *Commission* Home 15%; UK 20%.

The Ahearn Agency, Inc.
2021 Pine Street, New Orleans LA 70118
☎001 504 861 8395   Fax 001 504 866 6434
President *Pamela G. Ahearn*

FOUNDED 1992. *Handles* general and genre fiction, and non-fiction. Particularly interested in women's fiction, suspense fiction and historical romance. No children's books, poetry, autobiography, plays, screenplays or short fiction. Reading fee charged to unpublished authors. Send brief query letter with s.a.e. for reply in the first instance. CLIENTS include John Ames, Meagan McKinney, Marc Vargo. *Commission* Home 15%; Translation and UK 20%. *Overseas associates* in Europe and Latin America.

Marcia Amsterdam Agency
Suite 9A, 41 West 82nd Street, New York NY 10024
☎001 212 873 4945
Contact *Marcia Amsterdam*

FOUNDED 1969. *Specialises* in mainstream fiction, horror, suspense, humour, young adult, TV and film scripts. No poetry, books for the 8–10 age group or how-to. No unsolicited mss. First approach by letter only and enclose IRCs. No reading fee for outlines and synopses. CLIENTS include Kristopher Franklin, Ruby Jean Jensen, Robert Leininger, William H. Lovejoy, Patricia Rowe, Joyce Sweeney.

Commission Home 15%; Dramatic 10%; Foreign 20%.

Bart Andrews & Associates
7510 Sunset Boulevard 100, Los Angeles CA 90046
☎001 213 851 8158
Contact *Bart Andrews*

FOUNDED 1982. General non-fiction: show business, biography, autobiography, film books, trivia, TV and nostalgia. No scripts, no fiction, poetry, children's or science – no books of less than major commercial potential. *Specialises* in working with celebrities on autobiographies. No unsolicited mss. 'Send a brilliant letter (with IRCs for response) extolling your manuscript's virtues. Sell me!' CLIENTS J. Randy Taraborrelli, Wayne Newton, Bart Andrews, Bill Givens. No reading fee. *Commission* Home & Translation 15%. *Overseas associates* **Abner Stein**, London.

Joseph Anthony Agency
15 Locust Court Road, 20 Mays Landing, New Jersey NJ 08330
☎001 609 625 7608
Contact *Joseph Anthony*

FOUNEDD 1964. *Handles* all types of novel and scripts for TV: 2-hour mini-series, screenplays and ½-hour sitcoms. No poetry, short stories or pornography. *Specialises* in action, romance and detective novels. Unsolicited mss welcome. Return postage essential. Reading fee charged to new writers: novels $85; screenplays $100. CLIENTS include Ed Adair, Robert Long, Joseph McCullough, Sandi Wether. Signatory of the Writer's Guild of America. *Commission* Home 15%; Dramatic & Translation 20%.

The Artists Group
10100 Santa Monica Boulevard, Suite 2490, Los Angeles CA 90067
☎001 213 552 1100   Fax 001 213 277 9513
Contact *Robert Malcolm, Hal Stalmaster, Nancy Moon-Broadstreet, Art Rutter*

FOUNDED 1978. Screenplays and plays for film/TV/theatre and radio. No unsolicited mss. Write with list of credits, if any. No reading fee. *Commission* 10%.

Author Aid Associates

340 East 52nd Street, New York NY 10022
☎001 212 758 4213/980 9179

Editorial Director *Arthur Ormont*

FOUNDED 1967. *Handles* fiction and non-fiction, both children's and adult, scripts for film, TV and theatre. No cookbooks, computing. *Specialises* in war, aviation, New Age, occult, history, literary/commercial fiction, biography and autobiography. TITLES include *A Guide to Literary Agents of North America* (5th ed.). No unsolicited mss. Advance query essential. Reading fee charged to new/unpublished authors. Short queries answered by return mail. CLIENTS include Eddie Ensley, Maurice Rowdon, John S. Snydet. *Commission* Home 15%; Dramatic & Translation 20%.

Julian Bach Literary Agency

See **IMG**

Malaga Baldi Literary Agency

PO Box 591, Radio City Station, New York NY 10101
☎001 212 222 1221

Contact *Malaga Baldi*

FOUNDED 1986. *Handles* quality fiction and non-fiction. No scripts. No westerns, men's adventure, science fiction/fantasy, romance, how-to, young adult or children's. Writers of fiction should send mss with covering letter, including IRCs for return of mss and stamped addressed postcard for notification of receipt. Allow ten weeks minimum for response. For non-fiction, approach in writing with a proposal, table of contents and two sample chapters. No reading fee. CLIENTS include Margaret Erhart, Maud Farrell, Heather Lewis, David J. Skal. *Commission* 15%. *Overseas associates* **Abner Stein, Marsh & Sheil Ltd**, London; Japan Uni.

The Balkin Agency, Inc.

PO Box 222, Amherst MA 01004
☎001 413 548 9835   Fax 001 413 548 9836

Contact *Richard Balkin*

FOUNDED 1973. *Handles* adult non-fiction only. No reading fee for outlines and synopses. *Commission* Home 15%; Foreign 20%.

Maximilian Becker Agency

See **Aleta M. Daley**

Lois Berman

21 West 26th Street, New York NY 10010
☎001 212 684 1835   Fax 001 212 684 6563

Contact *Lois Berman, Judy Boals*

FOUNDED 1972. Dramatic writing only, by referral.

Meredith Bernstein Literary Agency, Inc.

2112 Broadway, Suite 503A, New York NY 10023
☎001 212 799 1007   Fax 001 212 799 1145

Contact *Meredith Bernstein, Elizabeth Cavanaugh*

FOUNDED 1981. Fiction and non-fiction of all types. Send query letter first; unpublished authors welcome. IRCs essential for response. Nominal reading fee for unpublished writers. CLIENTS include Georgina Gentry, Shirl Henke, David Jacobs, Nancy Pickard. *Commission* Home & Dramatic 15%; Translation 20%. *Overseas associates* **Abner Stein**, London; Lennart Sane; Thomas Schluck, Germany; Bardon Chinese Media Agency; William Miller, Japan; Frederique Porretta, France.

Reid Boates Literary Agency

PO Box 328, 274 Cooks Crossroad, Pittstown NJ 08867-0328
☎001 908 730 8523   Fax 001 908 730 8931

Contact *Reid Boates*

FOUNDED 1985. *Handles* general fiction and non-fiction. *Specialises* in journalism and media, serious self-help, biography and autobiography, true crime and adventure, popular science, current affairs, trade reference and quality fiction. No scripts. No science fiction, fantasy, romance, western, gothic, children's or young adult. Enquire by letter with IRCs in first instance. No reading fee. CLIENTS include James Sterngold, Dr Donald Johanson, Jon Winokur and the estate of Ava Gardner. *Commission* Home & Dramatic 15%; Translation 20%. *Overseas associates* **David Grossman Literary Agency Ltd, The Marsh Agency** (Paul Marsh), London; Japan Uni.

Georges Borchardt, Inc.

136 East 57th Street, New York NY 10022
☎001 212 753 5785   Fax 001 212 838 6518

FOUNDED 1967. Works mostly with established/published authors. *Specialises* in fiction, biography, and general non-fiction of unusual interest. Unsolicited mss not read. *Commission* Dramatic 10%; UK 15%; Translation 20%. *UK associates* **Sheil Land Associates Ltd** (Richard Scott Simon), London.

Brandenburgh & Associates Literary Agency

24555 Corte Jaramillo, Murrieta CA 92562
☎001 909 698 5200

Contact *Don Brandenburgh*

FOUNDED 1986. *Specialises* in non-fiction for the evangelical Christian market, including Christian living and education, social issues, Christian ministry and missions, theology and doctrine, evangelism, marriage and family, fiction (limited), devotional (limited). No poetry, children's, young adult, occult or metaphysical. No unsolicited mss; send query letter with IRCs. No reading fee. CLIENTS Evelyn Minshull, Thomas Naylor, Barbara Scott, Carrie Younce, Will Willimon. *Commission* Home 10%; Dramatic & Translation 20%.

Brandt & Brandt Literary Agents, Inc.

1501 Broadway, New York NY 10036
☎001 212 840 5760   Fax 001 212 840 5776

Contact *Carl D. Brandt, Gail Hochman, Charles Schlessiger*

FOUNDED 1914. *Handles* non-fiction and fiction. No poetry or children's books. No unsolicited mss. Approach by letter describing background and ambitions. No reading fee. *Commission* Home & Dramatic 15%; Foreign 20%. *UK associates* **A. M. Heath & Co. Ltd.**

Pema Browne Ltd

Pine Road, HCR Box 104B, Neversink
NY 12765
☎001 914 985 2936   Fax 001 914 985 7635

Contact *Pema Browne, Perry Browne*

FOUNDED 1966. *Handles* mass-market mainstream and hardcover fiction: romance, men's adventure, horror, humour, westerns, children's picture books and young adult; non-fiction: how-to, politics, religion and reference; also scripts for film. No unsolicited mss; send query letter with IRCs. Selected reading fee charged according to length of mss. Also handles illustrators' work. CLIENTS include Joanne Goodman, Eilene Hehl, Valerie Mangrum, Catherine Toothman. *Commission* Home & Translation 15%; Dramatic 10%; Overseas authors 20%.

Sheree Bykofsky Associates, Inc.

211 East 51st Street, 11D, New York
NY 10022
☎001 212 308 1253

Contact *Sheree Bykofsky*

FOUNDED 1985. *Handles* adult fiction and non-fiction. No scripts. No children's, young adult, horror, science fiction, romance, westerns, occult or supernatural. *Specialises* in popular reference, biography and highly commercial or highly literary fiction. No unsolicited mss. Send query letter first with brief synopsis or outline and writing sample (1–3 pp) for fiction. IRCs essential for reply or return of material. No phone calls. No reading fee. CLIENTS include Ken & Lois Anderson, Glenn Ellenbogen, Merrill Furman, Ed Morrow. *Commission* Home 15%; UK (including sub-agent's fee) 25%. Member A.A.R.

Maria Carvainis Agency, Inc.

235 West End Avenue, New York NY 10023
☎001 212 580 1559   Fax 001 212 877 3486

Contact *Maria Carvainis*

FOUNDED 1977. *Handles* fiction: literary and mainstream, contemporary women's, mystery, suspense, fantasy, historical, children's and young adult novels; non-fiction: business, finance, women's issues, political and film biography, medicine, psychology and popular science. No film scripts unless from writers with established credits. No science fiction. No unsolicited mss; they will be returned unread. Queries only, with IRCs for response. No reading fee. *Commission* Home & Dramatic 15%; Translation 20%.

Martha Casselman, Literary Agent

PO Box 342, Calistoga CA 94515-0342
☎001 707 942 4341

Contact *Martha Casselman, Judith Armenta*

FOUNDED 1979. *Handles* all types of non-fiction. No fiction at present. Main interests: food/cookery, biography, current affairs, popular sociology. No scripts, textbooks, poetry, coming-of-age fiction or science fiction. Especially interested in cookery with an appeal to the American market for possible co-publication in UK. Send queries and brief summary, with return postage. No mss. If you do not wish return of material, please state so. Also include, where applicable, any material on previous publications, reviews, brief biography. No proposals via fax. No reading fee. *Commission* Home 15%.

The Catalog Literary Agency

PO Box 2964, Vancouver WA 98668
☎001 206 694 8531

Contact *Douglas Storey*

FOUNDED 1986. *Handles* popular, professional and textbook material in all subjects, especially business, health, money, science, technology, computers, electronics and women's interests; also how-to, self-help, mainstream fiction and children's non-fiction. No genre fiction. No scripts, articles, screenplays, plays, poetry or short stories. No reading fee. No unsolicited mss. Query with an outline and sample chapters and include IRCs. CLIENTS include Malcolm S. Foster, Isaac O. Olaleye, Deborah Wallace. *Commission* Home 15%; Dramatic & Translation 20%.

The Linda Chester Literary Agency
666 Fifth Avenue, 37th Floor, New York
NY 10103
☎001 219 439 0881   Fax 001 212 439 9858
Contact *Billie Fitzpatrick*
FOUNDED 1978. *Handles* literary and commercial fiction and non-fiction in all subjects. No scripts, children's or textbooks. No unsolicited mss; send query letter with IRCs for reply. No reading fee for solicited material. *Commission* Home & Dramatic 15%; Translation 25%.

Connie Clausen Associates
250 East 87th Street, Suite 16H, New York
NY 10128
☎001 212 427 6135   Fax 001 212 996 7111
Contact *Connie Clausen, Lisa Kaiser, Elyse Cheney*
Handles non-fiction work such as self-help, psychology, spirituality, health, fashion and beauty, women's issues, entertainment, humour, cookbooks etc. Books include Quentin Crisp's *How to Go to the Movies*, the Pulitzer Prize-winning Jackson Pollack's biography, Robert Haas' *Eat to Win*, Sonya Hamlin's *How to Talk So People Listen*. Send query letter and/or proposal, outline and sample chapter. Include IRCs. Do not send complete mss. *Commission* 15%. *UK associates* **David Grossman Literary Agency Ltd**.

Diane Cleaver, Inc.
55 Fifth Avenue, New York NY 10003
☎001 212 206 5606   Fax 001 212 463 8718
President *Diane Cleaver*
Associate *Daniel Mandel*
FOUNDED 1983. Fiction and non-fiction. No scripts. No how-to, science fiction or illustrated. No unsolicited mss. Query first. No reading fee. *Commission* Home 15%; Translation 19%. *Overseas associates* **Abner Stein**, London.

Hy Cohen Literary Agency Ltd
111 West 57th Street, New York
NY 10019·
☎001 212 757 5237   Fax 001 212 397 1580
President *Hy Cohen*
FOUNDED 1975. Fiction and non-fiction. No scripts. Unsolicited mss welcome, but synopsis with sample 100 pp preferred. IRCs essential. No reading fee. *Commission* Home & Dramatic 10%; Foreign 20%. *Overseas associates* **Abner Stein**, London.

Ruth Cohen, Inc.
Box 7626, Menlo Park CA 94025
☎001 415 854 2054
President *Ruth Cohen*
FOUNDED 1982. Works mostly with established/published authors but will consider new writers. *Specialises* in high-quality children's, young adult and women's fiction, plus genre fiction: mystery and historical romance. No poetry, short stories or film scripts. No unsolicited mss. Send opening 10 pp with synopsis. Include enough IRCs for return postage or materials will not be returned. No reading fee. *Commission* Home & Dramatic 15%; Foreign 20%.

Frances Collin Literary Agent
PO Box 33, Wayne PA 19087–9998
☎001 610 254 0555   Fax 001 610 254 5029
Contact *Frances Collin*
FOUNDED 1948. Successor to Marie Rodell. *Handles* general fiction and non-fiction. No scripts. No unsolicited mss. Send query letter only, with IRCs for reply. No reading fee. Rarely accepts non-professional writers or writers not represented in the UK. *Overseas associates* worldwide.

Don Congdon Associates, Inc.
156 Fifth Avenue, Suite 625, New York
NY 10010–7002
☎001 212 645 1229   Fax 001 212 727 2688
Contact *Don Congdon, Michael Congdon, Susan Ramer*
FOUNDED 1983. *Handles* fiction and non-fiction. No academic, technical, romantic fiction, or scripts. No unsolicited mss. Approach by letter in the first instance. No reading fee. *Commission* Home 10%; UK & Translation 19%. *Overseas associates* **The Marsh Agency** (Europe), **Abner Stein** (UK), Michelle Lapautre (France), Tuttle Mori Agency (Japan).

The Connor Literary Agency
640 West 153rd Street, D2, New York
NY 10031
☎001 212 491 5233
7333 Gallagher Drive, Edina, MN 55435
☎001 612 835 7251

Contact *Marlene Connor, John Lynch*

FOUNDED 1985. *Handles* general non-fiction,
contemporary women's fiction, popular fiction,
Black fiction and non-fiction, how-to, mysteries
and crafts. Particularly interested in illustrated
books. No unsolicited mss; send query letter in
the first instance. Reading fee charged when
necessary ($100 full mss, with reader's report).
CLIENTS include Simplicity Pattern Company,
Essence Magazine, Bonnie Allen, Lenore Carroll,
Sindiwe Magona, Nadezda Obradovic, Randy
Russell. *Commission* Home 15%; UK & Translation 25%. *Overseas associates* in England, Spain,
Japan, France and Germany.

The Content Company
See **Richard Curtis Associates, Inc.**

Richard Curtis Associates, Inc./ The Content Company
171 East 74th Street, Second Floor,
New York NY 10021
☎001 212 772 7363   Fax 001 212 772 7393

Contact *Richard Curtis*

FOUNDED 1969. Works in association with
Robert P. Mills. *Handles* genre and mainstream
fiction, plus some commercial non-fiction.
Scripts rarely. *Specialises* in electronic rights and
multimedia.

Curtis Brown Ltd
10 Astor Place, New York NY 10003
☎001 212 473 5400

Book Rights *Laura Blake, Emilie Jacobson,*
Ginger Knowlton, Marilyn E. Marlow,
Maureen Walters
Film, TV, Audio Rights *Timothy Knowlton,*
Jess Taylor, Chris McKerrow
Translation *Dave Barbor*

FOUNDED 1914. *Handles* general fiction and
non-fiction. Also scripts for film, TV, theatre and
radio. No unsolicited mss; queries only, with
IRCs for reply. No reading fee. *Overseas associates*
representatives in all major foreign countries.

Aleta M. Daley/Maximilian Becker Agency
444 East 82nd Street, New York NY 10028
☎001 212 744 1453

Contact *Aleta M. Daley*

FOUNDED 1950. *Handles* non-fiction and fiction; also scripts for film and TV. No unsolicited mss. Send query letter in the first
instance with sample chapters or a proposal.
No reading fee, but handling fee is charged to
cover postage, telephone, etc. *Commission*
Home 15%; UK 20%.

Joan Daves Agency
21 West 26th Street, New York
NY 10010-1003
☎001 212 685 2663   Fax 001 212 685 1781

Contact *Jennifer Lyons*

FOUNDED 1952. Trade fiction and non-fiction.
No romance or textbooks. No scripts. Send
query letter in the first instance. 'A detailed
synopsis seems valuable only for non-fiction
work. Material submitted should specify the
author's background, publishing credits and
similar pertinent information.' No reading fee.
CLIENTS include Frederick Franck, Frank
Browning, Suzy McKee Charnas and the
estates of Isaac Babel, Heinrich Böll and Martin
Luther King Jr. *Commission* Home 15%;
Dramatic 10–25%; Foreign 20%.

Elaine Davie Literary Agency
620 Park Avenue, Rochester NY 14607
☎001 716 442 0830

President *Elaine Davie*

FOUNDED 1986. *Handles* all types of adult fiction
and non-fiction, specialising in books by and for
women. Particularly interested in commercial
genre fiction. No scripts. No short stories,
anthologies, poetry or children's. Submit synopsis and sample chapters or complete mss together
with IRCs. No reading fee. CLIENTS include
Marcia Evanick, Jane Kidder, Merline Lovelace,
Maggie Shayne, Christina Skye. *Commission*
Home 15%; Dramatic & Translation 20%.

The Deering Literary Agency
1153 Alabama Road, Ste. 104, Acworth
GA 30101-2506
☎001 404 591 2051   Fax 001 404 591 0369

Director *Dorothy Deering*
Manager *Charles F. Deering*

FOUNDED 1989. *Handles* non-fiction (all subjects) and fiction: historical, mystery, romance,
literary, religious, horror, science fiction and fantasy. Unsolicited mss welcome. *Specialises* in new
authors. Reading fee of $90 (under 100,000
words); $105 (over 100,000). CLIENTS include
Lyle Howard, Daniel Marder, Theodore J.
Nottingham, Chris Scott. *Commission* Home
12%; Dramatic 18%; Foreign & Translation 15%.

Anita Diamant Literary Agency
Suite 1105, 310 Madison Avenue, New York
NY 10017
☎001 212 687 1122

Contact *Anita Diamant, Robin Rue*

FOUNDED 1917. *Handles* fiction and non-fiction.
No academic, children's, science fiction and fantasy, poetry, articles, short stories, screenplays or teleplays. Works in association with Hollywood film agent. No unsolicited mss. Write with description of work, short synopsis and details of publishing background. No reading fee.
CLIENTS include V. C. Andrews, Elliott Baker, Carol Brennan, James Elward, Oscar Fraley, Pat Hagan, Linda Howard, Richard Lederer, Mark McGarrity, Andrew Neiderman, Penny Thornton. *Commission* Home & Dramatic 15%; Translation 20%. *Overseas associates* **A. M. Heath & Co. Ltd**, London.

Sandra Dijkstra Literary Agency
1155 Camino del Mar, Suite 515, Del Mar
CA 92014
☎001 619 755 3115

Contact *Debra Ginsberg*

FOUNDED 1981. *Handles* quality and commercial non-fiction and fiction, including some genre fiction. No scripts. No westerns, contemporary romance or poetry. Willing to look at children's projects. *Specialises* in quality fiction, mystery/thrillers, psychology, self-help, science, health, business, memoirs, biography. Dedicated to promoting new and original voices and ideas. For fiction: send brief synopsis (1 page) and first 50 pages; for non-fiction: send proposal with overview, chapter outline, author biog. and two sample chapters. All submissions should be accompanied by IRCs. No reading fee. CLIENTS include Diane Mott Davidson, Maxine Hong Kingston, Susan Faludi, Abigail Padgett, Max De Pree, Amy Tan, Deb Waterhouse. *Commission* Home 15%; Translation 20%. *Overseas associates* **Abner Stein**, London; Agence Hoffman, Germany; Monic Heyum, Scandinavia; Luigi Bernabo, Italy; M. Casanovas, Spain; M. Kling (La Nouvelle Agence), France; The English Agency, Japan.

Robert Ducas Literary Agency
See **Caroline Davidson & Robert Ducas Literary Agency (UK Agents)**

Dykeman Associates, Inc.
4115 Rawlins, Dallas TX 75219-3661
☎001 214 528 2991   Fax 001 214 528 0241

Contact *Alice Dykeman*

FOUNDED 1974. *Handles* non-fiction, namely celebrity profiles and biographies, fiction and movie scripts. No unsolicited mss; send outline or synopsis. Reading fee of $250 charged for manuscripts (not movie scripts). *Commission* 15%.

Jane Dystel Literary Management
One Union Square West, Suite 904,
New York NY 10003
☎001 212 627 9100   Fax 001 212 627 9313

Contact *Jane Dystel, Miriam Goderich*

FOUNDED 1975. *Handles* non-fiction and fiction. *Specialises* in politics, history, biography, cookbooks, current affairs, celebrities, commercial and literary fiction. No reading fee. CLIENTS include Lorene Cary, Thomas French, Lynne Rossetto Kasper, Gus Lee, Alice Medrich, Michael Tucker.

Educational Design Services, Inc.
PO Box 253, Wantagh NY 11793
☎001 718 539 4107/516 221 0995

President *Bertram Linder*
Vice President *Edwin Selzer*

FOUNDED 1979. *Specialises* in educational material and textbooks for sale to school markets. IRCs must accompany submissions. *Commission* Home 15%; Foreign 25%.

Elek International Rights Agents
457 Broome Street, New York NY 10013
☎001 212 431 9368   Fax 001 212 966 5768

Contact *Debbie Miketta*

FOUNDED 1979. *Handles* adult non-fiction and children's picture books. No scripts, novels, psychology, New Age, poetry, short stories or autobiography. No unsolicited mss; send letter of enquiry with IRCs for reply; include résumé, credentials, brief synopsis. No reading fee. CLIENTS Tedd Arnold, Dr Robert Ballard, Patrick Brogan, Robert Bateman, Laura Cornell, Chris Dodd, Sally Placksin. *Commission* Home 15%; Dramatic & Foreign 20%. *Overseas associates* **Vardey & Brunton Associates**, London.

Ann Elmo Agency, Inc.
60 East 42nd Street, New York NY 10165
☎001 212 661 2880/1 Fax 001 212 661 2883

Contact *Lettie Lee, Mari Cronin, Andree Abecassis*

FOUNDED in the 1940s. *Handles* literary and romantic fiction, mysteries and mainstream; also non-fiction in all subjects, including biography and self-help. Some children's (8–12-year-olds) and young adult. Query letter with outline of project in the first instance. No reading fee. *Commission* Home 15–20%. *Overseas associates* John Johnson Ltd, London.

Florence Feiler Literary Agency
1524 Sunset Plaza Drive, Los Angeles
CA 90069
☎001 310 652 6920   Fax 001 310 659 0945
Contact *Florence Feiler*

FOUNDED 1967. *Specialises* in fiction, non-fiction, how-to textbooks, translations, TV and film scripts/tapes. No short stories or pornography. No unsolicited mss. First approach by letter. No reading fee. CLIENTS include literary estates of Isak Dinesen (*Out of Africa* and *Babette's Feast*) and Bess Streeter Aldrich. Submission procedure: letter of enquiry, samples of previously published work, if recommended by an editor or another client, or if you have heard Ms Feiler lecture. No multiple submissions accepted. Will consider negotiating contracts and sales but, 'First I must read the material. Nothing leaves this office unless I have read it first and approve mailing under my name. I suggest the craft be taken seriously and severe editing be accomplished before submission. I do not wish to hear from writers who think they have good ideas and are Sunday writers'.

Commission 10% text domestic; 20% foreign. No other fees unless another agent is used, then 15%.

Frieda Fishbein Ltd
2556 Hubbard Street, Brooklyn NY 11235
☎001 212 247 4398
President *Janice Fishbein*
Associates *Heidi Carlson, Douglas Michael*

FOUNDED 1925. Eager to work with new/unpublished writers. *Specialises* in historical romance, historical adventure, male adventure, mysteries, thrillers, family sagas, 'non-reporting' and how-to. Also non-fiction, plays and screenplays. No poetry, magazine articles, short stories or young children's. First approach with query letter. No reading fee for outlines at our request or for published authors working in the same genre. CLIENTS include Gary Bohlke, Alan Brandt, Herbert Fisher, David Gilman, Jeanne Mackin, Robert Simpson, Alicen White. *Commission* Home & Dramatic 10%; Foreign 20%.

Flannery, White & Stone
1675 Larimer Street, Suite 410, Denver
CO 80202
☎001 303 571 4001   Fax 001 303 534 0577

Contact *Robin Ann Barrett, Connie Solowiej*

FOUNDED 1987. *Handles* literary and mainstream fiction, children's, general non-fiction and business. Also screenplays for motion pictures. No theatre or radio. No pornography. Call or write with query in first instance. No unsolicited mss. CLIENTS include Reginald McKnight, Maxine Schur, David Seals. *Commission* Home 15%; Dramatic & Translation 20%.

ForthWrite Literary Agency
3579 E. Foothill Boulevard, Suite 327,
Pasadena CA 91107
☎001 818 798 0793
Contact *Wendy L. Zhorne*

FOUNDED 1988. *Specialises* in non-fiction, especially business, marketing, crisis management, alternative health, popular psychology, history (English and Scottish), self-help, home and health, crafts, religious (devotional, inspirational, theology and study guides), how-to, illustrated, animal care, and juvenile. Send query letter with IRCs. Reading fee charged in some cases. 'A dedicated, zealous agency' which only represents 'quality material we are enthusiastic about'. *Commission* Home & Dramatic 15%; Translation 20%.

Robert A. Freedman Dramatic Agency, Inc.
Suite 2310, 1501 Broadway, New York
NY 10036
☎001 212 840 5760
President *Robert A. Freedman*
Vice President *Selma Luttinger*

FOUNDED 1928 as Brandt & Brandt Dramatic Department, Inc. Took its present name in 1984. Works mostly with established authors. *Specialises* in plays, film and TV scripts. Unsolicited mss not read. *Commission* Dramatic 10%.

Jay Garon-Brooke Associates, Inc.
101 West 55th Street, Suite 5K, New York
NY 10019
☎001 212 581 8300   Fax 001 212 581 8397
President/Executive Agent *Jay Garon*
Vice President *Jean Free*
Agent *Nancy Coffey*

FOUNDED 1951. Fiction and non-fiction: history and historical romance, suspense/thrillers, political intrigue, horror/occult, self-help. No category romance, westerns or mysteries. No unsolicited mss. First approach by query letter. No reading fee. CLIENTS include Virginia Coffman, Elizabeth Gage, Curtis Gathje, John

Grisham, Eric Harry, Patricia Matthews. *Commission* Home 15%; Dramatic 10–15%; Foreign 30%. *Overseas associates* **Abner Stein**, London; Translation: Bernard Kurman.

Max Gartenberg, Literary Agent

521 Fifth Avenue, Suite 1700, New York NY 10175
☎001 212 860 8451   Fax 001 201 535 5033
Contact *Max Gartenberg*

FOUNDED 1954. Works mostly with established/published authors. *Specialises* in non-fiction and trade fiction. No reading fee for outlines. CLIENTS include William Ashworth, Linda Davis, Ralph Hickok, Charles Little, Howard Owen, David Roberts. *Commission* Home & Dramatic 10%; Foreign 15%.

Gelfman Schneider Literary Agents, Inc.

250 West 57th Street, Suite 2515, New York NY 10107
☎001 212 245 1993   Fax 001 212 245 8678
Contact *Deborah Schneider, Jane Gelfman*

FOUNDED 1919 (London), 1980 (New York). Formerly John Farquharson Ltd. Works mostly with established/published authors. *Specialises* in general trade fiction and non-fiction. No poetry, short stories or screenplays. No reading fee for outlines. Submissions must be accompanied by IRCs. *Commission* Home 15%; Dramatic 10%; Foreign 20%. *Overseas associates* **Curtis Brown Group Ltd**, London.

Gelles-Cole Literary Enterprises

Woodstock Towers, 320 East 42nd Street, New York NY 10017
☎001 212 573 9857   Fax 001 914 735 8860
President *Sandi Gelles-Cole*

FOUNDED 1983. *Specialises* in general commercial fiction and women's business books. No scripts. No science fiction and fantasy. No unsolicited mss; query first. Reading fee charged. Editorial service available, including mss evaluation, character and plot development.

Lucianne Goldberg Literary Agents, Inc.

255 West 84th Street, New York NY 10024
☎001 212 799 1260
Editorial Director *Kathrine Butler*

FOUNDED 1974. *Handles* fiction and non-fiction. No unsolicited mss. Send query letter describing work in the first instance. No read-

ing fee. *Commission* Home 10%; UK 20%. *Overseas associate* Peter Knight, London.

Sanford J. Greenburger Associates

15th Floor, 55 Fifth Avenue, New York NY 10003
☎001 212 206 5600   Fax 001 212 463 8718
Contact *Francis Greenburger, Heide Lange, Faith Hamlin*

Handles fiction and non-fiction. No unsolicited mss. First approach with query letter, sample chapter and synopsis. No reading fee.

The Charlotte Gusay Literary Agency

10532 Blythe Avenue, Los Angeles CA 90064
☎001 310 559 0831   Fax 001 310 559 2639
Contact *Charlotte Gusay*

FOUNDED 1988. *Handles* fiction, both literary and commercial, plus non-fiction: children's and adult humour, parenting, gardening, women's and men's issues, feminism, psychology, memoirs, biography, travel. No science fiction, horror, short pieces or collections of stories. No unsolicited mss; send query letter first with succinct outline and three sample chapters for fiction, or proposal for non-fiction. No response without IRCs. No reading fee. *Commission* Home 15%; Dramatic 10%; Translation & Foreign 25%.

Joy Harris Literary Agency
See **Robert Lantz**

John Hawkins & Associates, Inc.

71 West 23rd Street, Suite 1600, New York NY 10010
☎001 212 807 7040   Fax 001 212 807 9555
Contact *John Hawkins, William Reiss*

FOUNDED 1893. *Handles* film and TV rights and software. No unsolicited mss; send queries with 1–3 page outline and 1-page c.v. IRCs necessary for response. No reading fee. *Commission* Apply for rates. *UK associates* **Murray Pollinger** London.

Heacock Literary Agency

1523 Sixth Street, Suite 14, Santa Monica CA 90401–12514
☎001 310 393 6227/451 8523
Fax 001 310 451 8524
President *Rosalie G. Heacock*

FOUNDED 1978. Works with a small number of new/unpublished authors. *Specialises* in non-fiction on a wide variety of subjects: new ideas, new ways of solving problems, futurism, art criticism and techniques, health, nutrition, beauty, women's studies, popular psychology, crafts, business expertise, alternative health concepts, contemporary celebrity biographies. Also novels by established authors and film/TV scripts by full-time professionals and members of the Writer's Guild. No unsolicited mss. Queries with IRCs only. No reading fee. CLIENTS include Dr Joseph Bark, Larry D. Brimner, Dr Allan Chinen, Dr Arnold Fox & Barry Fox, John Goldhammer, Paul Horn, Don & Audrey Wood. *Commission* Home 15% on first $50,000 each year, 10% thereafter; Foreign 15% if sold direct, 25% if agent used.

The Jeff Herman Agency, Inc.
500 Greenwich Street, Suite 501C,
New York NY 10013
☎001 212 941 0540   Fax 001 212 941 0614
Contact *Jeffrey H. Herman*

Handles non-fiction, textbooks and reference. No scripts. No unsolicited mss. Query letter with IRCs in the first instance. No reading fee. Jeff Herman publishes a useful reference guide to the book trade called *The Insider's Guide to Book Editors, Publishers & Literary Agents* (Prima/St Martin's Press). *Commission* Home 15%; Translation 10%.

Susan Herner Rights Agency, Inc.
PO Box 303, Scarsdale NY 10583
☎001 914 725 8967   Fax 001 914 725 8969
Contact *Susan N. Herner, Sue P. Yuen*

FOUNDED 1987. Adult fiction and non-fiction in all areas. No children's books. *Handles* film and TV rights and software. Send query letter with outline and sample chapters. No reading fee. *Commission* Home 15%; Dramatic & Translation 20%. *Overseas associates* **David Grossman Literary Agency Ltd**, London.

Frederick Hill Associates
1842 Union Street, San Francisco
CA 94123
☎001 415 921 2910   Fax 001 415 921 2802
Contact *Fred Hill, Bonnie Nadell*

FOUNDED 1979. General fiction and non-fiction. No scripts. Send query letter detailing past publishing history if any. IRCs required. CLIENTS include Katherine Neville, Richard North Patterson, Randy Shilts. *Commission* Home & Dramatic 15%; Foreign 20%. *Overseas associates* **Mary Clemmey**, London.

Hull House Literary Agency
240 East 82nd Street, New York NY 10028
☎001 212 988 0725   Fax 001 212 794 8758
President *David Stewart Hull*
Associate *Lydia Mortimer*

FOUNDED 1987. *Handles* commercial fiction, mystery, biography, military history and true crime. No scripts, poetry, short stories, romance, science fiction and fantasy, children's or young adult. No unsolicited mss; send single-page letter describing project briefly, together with short biographical note and list of previous publications if any. IRCs essential. No reading fee. *Commission* Home 15%; Translation 20%.

IMG-Julian Bach Literary Agency
22 East 71st Street, New York NY 10021
☎001 212 772 8900   Fax 001 212 772 2617
Contact *Julian Bach, Trish Lande, Carolyn Krupp*

FOUNDED 1959. *Handles* non-fiction and fiction. No science fiction, fantasy, poetry or photography. No scripts. Query first. Submissions should include brief synopsis (typed), sample chapters (50 pp maximum), publishing history, etc. Send IRCs for return. CLIENTS include Jerry Baker, Pat Conroy, Jan Morris, Liz Nickles, Hedrick Smith, Adam Ulam, Robin Winks. *Commission* Home & Dramatic 15%; Foreign 25%. *Overseas associates* worldwide.

Kidde, Hoyt & Picard Literary Agency
333 East 51st Street, New York NY 10022
☎001 212 755 9461/9465   Fax 001 212 593 4688
Chief Associate *Katharine Kidde*
Associate *Laura Langlie*

FOUNDED 1981. *Specialises* in mainstream and literary fiction, romantic fiction (historical and contemporary), and quality non-fiction in humanities and social sciences (biography, history, current affairs, the arts). No reading fee. Query first, include s.a.e. CLIENTS include Michael Cadnum, Jim Oliver, Patricia Robinson, Frank Sherry. *Commission* 10%.

Daniel P. King
5125 North Cumberland Boulevard,
Whitefish Bay WI 53217
☎001 414 964 2903   Fax 001 414 964 6860
President *Daniel P. King*

FOUNDED 1974. *Specialises* in mystery and non-fiction books on crime and espionage. Also handles mainstream fiction including crime/ mystery and science fiction. Scripts handled by representative office in Beverly Hills, California. No unsolicited mss. Send synopsis or sample chapter first or (and preferably) a concise letter (1–2 pages) describing the book. No reading fee unless an author wants a critique on his material. CLIENTS include John Bonnet, Ella Griffiths, Cyril Joyce. *Commission* Home & Dramatic 10%; Foreign 20%.

Kirchoff/Wohlberg, Inc.
866 United Nations Plaza, 525, New York NY 10017
☎001 212 644 2020   Fax 001 212 223 4387
Authors' Representative *Elizabeth Pulitzer-Voges*
FOUNDED 1930. *Handles* books for children and young adults, specialising in children's picture books. No adult material. No scripts for TV, radio, film or theatre. Send letter of enquiry with synopsis or outline and IRCs for reply or return. No reading fee. CLIENTS Lizi Boyd, Lois Ehlert, Suçie Stevenson, Gloria Whelan.

Paul Kohner, Inc.
9169 Sunset Boulevard, Los Angeles CA 90069
☎001 310 550 1060   Fax 001 310 276 1083
Contact *Gary Salt*
FOUNDED 1938. *Handles* a broad range of books for subsidiary rights sales to film and TV. Few direct placements with publishers as film and TV scripts are the major part of the business. No short stories, poetry, science fiction or gothic. Unsolicited material will be returned unread, if accompanied by s.a.e. Approach via a third-party reference or send query letter with professional résumé. No reading fee. *Commission* Home & Dramatic 10%; Publishing 15%.

Barbara S. Kouts, Literary Agent
PO Box 558, Bellport NY 11713
☎001 516 286 1278   Fax 001 516 286 1538
Contact *Barbara S. Kouts*
FOUNDED 1980. *Handles* fiction, non-fiction and children's. No romance, science fiction or scripts. No unsolicited mss. Query letter in the first instance. No reading fee. CLIENTS include Hal Gieseking, Nancy Mairs, Robert San Souci. *Commission* Home 10%; Foreign 20%. *Overseas associates* **Murray Pollinger**, London.

Lucy Kroll Agency
390 West End Avenue, New York NY 10024
☎001 212 877 0627   Fax 001 212 769 2832
Contact *Lucy Kroll, Barbara Hogenson*
FOUNDED in 1949. *Handles* non-fiction: science, travel, art, humanities and psychiatry. Handles film and TV rights. No unsolicited mss. Recommendations from clients are preferred but unsolicited queries welcome and should be accompanied by IRCs. No reading fee. *Commission* Home & Dramatic 10%; Translation 20%.

Peter Lampack Agency, Inc.
551 Fifth Avenue, Suite 1613, New York NY 10176
☎001 212 687 9106   Fax 001 212 687 9109
Contact *Peter Lampack, Sandra Blanton, Deborah T. Brown*
FOUNDED in 1977. *Handles* commercial fiction: male action and adventure, contemporary relationships, historical, mysteries and suspense, literary fiction; also non-fiction from recognised experts in a given field, plus biographies, autobiographies. Also handles theatrical, motion picture, and TV rights from book properties. No original scripts or screenplays, series or episodic material or category novels, particularly science fiction, horror and romance. Best approach by letter in first instance. 'We will respond within three weeks and invite the submission of manuscripts which we would like to examine.' No reading fee. CLIENTS include J. M. Coetzee, Clive Cussler, Judith Kelman, Johanna Kingsley, David Osborn, Jessica March, Doris Mortman, Fred Mustard Stewart, Derek Van Arman. *Commission* Home & Dramatic 15%; Translation & UK 20%.

Robert Lantz/Joy Harris Literary Agency, Inc.
156 Fifth Avenue, Suite 617, New York NY 10010-617
☎001 212 924 6269   Fax 001 212 924 6609
Contact *Joy Harris*
Handles adult non-fiction and fiction. No unsolicited mss. Query letter in the first instance. No reading fee. *Commission* Home & Dramatic 15%; Foreign 20%. *Overseas associates* Michael Meller, Germany; **Abner Stein**, London; Tuttle Mori, Japan/China; Rosemarie Buchman, Scandinavia/ Spain; Eliane Benisti, France.

The Lazear Agency, Inc.
430 First Avenue North, Suite 416,
Minneapolis MN 55401
☎001 612 332 8640   Fax 001 612 332 4648

Contact *Jonathon Lazear, Eric Vrooman,
Susanne Moncur, Dennis Cass, Sarah Nelson
Hunter*

FOUNDED 1984. *Handles* fiction: mysteries, suspense, young adult and literary; also true crime, addiction recovery, biography, travel, children's picture books, business, and scripts for film and TV, CD-ROM and CD-I, broad band interactive television. No poetry or stage plays. Approach by letter, with description of mss, short autobiography and IRCs. No reading fee. CLIENTS include Noah Adams, Andrei Codrescu, Al Franken, Merrill Lynch, Harvey Mackay, Gary Paulsen, The Pillsbury Co., Will Weaver, Bailey White. *Commission* Home & Dramatic 15%; Translation 10%.

L. Harry Lee Literary Agency
PO Box 203, Rocky Point NY 11778
☎001 516 744 1188

Contacts *Charles Rothery* (science fiction), *Sue Hollister Barr* (adventure/humour/westerns), *Patti Roenbeck* (romance/mainstream/mystery/suspense), *Diane Clerke* (historical/fantasy), *Cami Calligos* (horror/erotica), *Colin James* (mainstream/military/war), *Katie Polk* (mystery/detective), *Mary Lee Gaylor* (mainstream/contemporary), *James Kingston* (motion pictures), *Stacy Parker/Anastassia Evereaux* (TV, episodic), *Vitor Brenna* (plays)

FOUNDED 1979. *Handles* adventure, westerns, horror, romance, mainstream/contemporary, science fiction, humour, detective, military, war, historical, erotica, fantasy, occult, suspense, plays, literature. Also scripts for film, TV and theatre: handles a lot of material which goes into motion pictures/TV. No gay, lesbian, feminist, confessional, religious, poetry, how-to, children's, biographies, cookery, picture or textbooks. Strictly fiction. Keen on comedy and currently looking for comedy screenplays. No unsolicited mss; query letter first with IRCs, details, a page or two, on project and one-page autobiography. Response time two weeks. Critique fee charged depending on appraisal ($215 screenplays; $115 novels, first 70–75 pp; $1.10 per page plays). CLIENTS include Luis Anguilar, James Colaneri, Steve Blower, Anastassia Evereaux, Dennis Glover, James G. Kingston, John Lubas, Charlie Purpura, Bill Tyman, Fay Van. *Commission* Novels 15%; Film & Drama 10%.

Lee Allan Agency
PO Box 18617, Milwaukee WI 53218
☎001 414 357 7708   Fax 001 414 357 7708

Contact *Lee A. Matthias, Andrea Knickerbocker*

FOUNDED 1983. *Handles* fiction: science fiction, fantasy, mystery, horror, thrillers, men's adventure, historical, westerns and mainstream. No poetry or textbooks. Also handles feature film screenplays properly formatted to the Writer's Guild of America guidelines. No unsolicited mss. Send query letters first, with IRCs, giving length/word count. Novels – min. 50,000 words; scripts – min. 90 pp, max. 140 pp. No reading fee. *Commission* Home 15%; Dramatic 10%; Foreign up to 20%.

Levant & Wales, Literary Agency, Inc.
108 Hayes Street, Seattle WA 98109
☎001 206 284 7114   Fax 001 206 284 0190

Contact *Dan Levant, Elizabeth Wales, Valerie Griffith*

FOUNDED 1988. *Handles* quality fiction and non-fiction. No scripts except via sub-agents. No genre fiction, westerns, romance, science fiction or horror. Special interest in local (Pacific Northwest) clients. No unsolicited mss; send query letter with publication list and writing sample. No reading fee. *Commission* Home 15%; Dramatic & Translation 25%.

Ellen Levine, Literary Agency, Inc.
Suite 1801, 15 East 26th Street, New York
NY 10010-1505
☎001 212 899 0620   Fax 001 212 725 4501

Contact *Ellen Levine*

FOUNDED 1980. *Handles* all types of books. No scripts. Strongly prefers UK authors to have representation initially with UK agent. No unsolicited mss, nor any other material unless requested. No telephone calls. First approach by letter; send US postage or IRCs for reply. Material not returned. No reading fee. *Commission* Home 15%; Dramatic 10%; Foreign 20%. *Overseas associates* **A. P. Watt Ltd**, London.

Ray Lincoln Literary Agency
Elkins Park House, Suite 107-B, 7900 Old
York Road, Elkins Park PA 19117
☎001 215 635 0827

Contact *Mrs Ray Lincoln*

FOUNDED 1974. *Handles* adult and children's fiction and non-fiction: biography, science, nature, popular medicine, psychology and psychiatry, history. Scripts as spin-offs from book mss only. No poetry or plays unless adaptations from published book. Keenly interested in adult biography, in all types of children's books (age five and upwards, not illustrated), in fine adult fiction, science and nature. No unsolicited mss; send query letter first, including IRCs for response. If interested, material will then be requested. No reading fee. Postage fee for projects handled by the agency. *Commission* Home & Dramatic 15%; Translation 20%.

Literary & Creative Artists Agency
3539 Albemarle Street NW,
Washington DC 20008
☎001 202 362 4688   Fax 001 202 362 4688
Contact *Muriel G. Nellis, Jane F. Roberts, Karen S. Gerwin*

FOUNDED 1981. *Specialises* in broad range of non-fiction, including politics, health and real life/human drama. No poetry, pornography, academic or educational textbooks. No unsolicited mss; query letter in the first instance. Include IRCs for response. No reading fee. *Commission* Home 15%; Dramatic 20%; Translation 20–25%.

The Literary Group International
270 Lafayette Street, Suite 1505, New York NY 10012
☎001 212 274 1616   Fax 001 212 274 9876
President *Frank Weimann*
Associates *James Hornfischer, Jessica Wainwright*

FOUNDED 1987. *Handles* true crime, biography, self-help and fiction. *Specialises* in organised crime and exposés. No scripts or textbooks. Unsolicited mss, synopses and ideas welcome. Submit first three chapters only. No reading fee. CLIENTS include Sam Giancana, Joe Lansdale, Joseph Starita. *Commission* Home 15%; UK 20% (including sub-agent's fee).

Sterling Lord Literistic, Inc.
One Madison Avenue, New York NY 10010
☎001 212 696 2800
Contact *Peter Matson, Sterling Lord*

FOUNDED 1979. *Handles* all genres, fiction and non-fiction, plus scripts for TV, radio, film and theatre. Unsolicited mss will be considered. Prefer letter outlining all non-fiction. No reading fee. *Commission* Home 15%; UK & Translation 20%. *Overseas associates* **Peters Fraser & Dunlop Group Ltd**, London.

Donald MacCampbell, Inc.
12 East 41st Street, New York NY 10017
☎001 212 683 5580
President *Donald MacCampbell*
Editor *Maureen Moran*

FOUNDED 1940. *Handles* women's fiction only. No scripts, non-fiction, science fiction, westerns or suspense. *Specialises* in romance. No unsolicited mss; approach by letter. No reading fee. *Commission* US Book Sales 10%; First Novels US 15%.

Denise Marcil Literary Agency, Inc.
685 West End Avenue, Suite 9C, New York NY 10025
☎001 212 932 3110
President *Denise Marcil*

FOUNDED 1977. *Specialises* in non-fiction: money, business, health, popular reference, childcare, parenting, self-help and how-to; and commercial fiction, especially women's, and psychological suspense. Query letters only, with IRCs. CLIENTS include Rosanne Bittner, Carol Kane, Clare McNally. *Commission* Home & Dramatic 15%; Foreign 20%.

Barbara Markowitz Literary Agency
117 North Mansfield Avenue, Los Angeles CA 90036
☎001 213 939 5927   Fax 001 213 937 9006
President *Barbara Markowitz*
Associate *Judith Rosenthal*

FOUNDED 1979. *Handles* contemporary adult fiction, including murder mysteries and thrillers; also contemporary and historical fiction for children aged 8–12. No illustrated books for pre-school or early readers. No poetry, short stories or science fiction. No scripts. Send query letter with IRCs giving some idea of the size of the project, or submit first three chapters only for consideration. No reading fee. CLIENTS include Henry Garfield, Kristiana Gregory, Cynthia Lawrence, Ellen Jaffe McClain, Geoffrey Miller. *Commission* Home 15%; UK 20%.

Betty Marks
176 East 77th Street, Apt. 9F, New York NY 10021
☎001 212 535 8388
Contact *Betty Marks*

FOUNDED 1969. Works mostly with established/published authors. *Specialises* in journalists' non-fiction and novels. No unsolicited mss. Query letter and outline in the first instance. No reading fee for outlines. *Commission* Home 15%; Foreign 20%. *Overseas associates* **Abner Stein**, London; Mohrbooks, Germany; International Editors, Spain & Portugal; Rosemary Buchman, Europe; Tuttle Mori, Japan.

The Evan Marshall Agency
6 Tristram Place, Pine Brook NJ 07058–9445
☎001 201 882 1122   Fax 001 201 882 3099
Contact *Evan Marshall, Martha Jewett*

FOUNDED 1987. *Handles* general adult fiction and non-fiction, and scripts for film and television. No unsolicited mss; send query letter first. Handling fee charged to unpublished authors. *Commission* Home 15%; UK & Translation 20%.

Richard P. McDonough, Literary Agent
551 Franklin Street, Cambridge MA 02139
☎001 617 354 6440   Fax 001 617 354 6607
Contact *Richard P. McDonough*

FOUNDED 1986. General non-fiction and literary fiction. No scripts. No genre fiction except mysteries and thrillers. No unsolicited mss; query first with three sample chapters and include IRCs. No reading fee. CLIENTS John Dufresne, Peter Guralnick, Jane Holtz Kay, M. R. Montgomery. *Commission* 15%.

McIntosh & Otis, Inc.
310 Madison Avenue, New York
NY 10017
☎001 212 687 7400   Fax 001 212 687 6894
President *Eugene H. Winick*
Adult Books *Julie Fallowfield, Louise Quayle*
Children's *Dorothy Markinko, Renée Cho*

FOUNDED 1928. Adult and juvenile literary fiction and non-fiction. No textbooks or scripts. No unsolicited mss. Query letter indicating nature of the work plus details of background. IRCs for response. No reading fee. CLIENTS include Mary Higgins Clark, Shirley Hazzard, Victoria Holt, Harper Lee. *Commission* Home & Dramatic 15%; Foreign 20%. *Overseas associates* **A. M. Heath & Co. Ltd**, London.

Mews Books Ltd
c/o Sidney B. Kramer, 20 Bluewater Hill,
Westport CT 06880
☎001 203 227 1836   Fax 001 203 227 1144
Contact *Sidney B. Kramer, Fran Pollak*

FOUNDED 1970. *Handles* adult fiction and non-fiction, children's, pre-school and young adult. No scripts, short stories or novellas (unless by established authors). *Specialises* in cookery, medical, health and nutrition, scientific non-fiction, children's and young adult. Also handles electronic rights to published books and represents publisher purchasing electronic rights. Unsolicited material welcome. Presentation must be professional. Partial submissions should include summary of plot/characters, one or two sample chapters, personal credentials and brief on target market. No reading fee. If material is accepted, agency asks $350 circulation fee (4–5 publishers), which will be applied against commissions (waived for published authors). Charges for photocopying, postage expenses, telephone calls and other direct costs. Principal agent is an attorney and former publisher. Offers consultation service through which writers can get advice on a contract or on publishing problems.
    Commission Home 15%; Film & Translation 20%. *Overseas associates* **Abner Stein**, London.

Robert P. Mills
See **Richard Curtis Associates, Inc./ The Content Company**

Howard Morhaim Literary Agency
175 Fifth Avenue, Suite 709, New York
NY 10010
☎001 212 529 4433   Fax 001 212 995 1112
Contact *Howard Morhaim, Allison Mullen*

FOUNDED 1979. *Handles* general adult fiction and non-fiction. No scripts. No children's or young adult material, poetry or religious. No unsolicited mss. Send query letter with synopsis and sample chapters for fiction; query letter with outline or proposal for non-fiction. No reading fee. *Commission* Home 15%; UK & Translation 20%. *Overseas associates* worldwide.

Henry Morrison, Inc.
PO Box 235, 320 McLain Street, Bedford
Hills NY 10507
☎001 914 666 3500   Fax 001 914 241 7846
Contact *Henry Morrison, Joan Gurgold*

FOUNDED 1965. *Handles* general fiction, crime and science fiction, and non-fiction. No scripts unless by established writers. Unsolicited material welcome; send query letter with outline of proposal (1–5 pp). No reading fee. CLIENTS Beverly Byrne, Joe Gores, Robert Ludlum. *Commission* Home 15%; UK & Translation 20%.

Multimedia Product Development, Inc.

410 South Michigan Avenue, Suite 724, Chicago IL 60605
☎001 312 922 3063   Fax 001 312 922 1905

Contact *Jane Jordan Browne*

FOUNDED 1971. *Handles* biography, history, current affairs, mainstream fiction, genre novels, science, psychology, social science, how-to. No autobiography (except celebrities). No poetry or scripts. No unsolicited mss. Send query letter with IRCs. No reading fee. CLIENTS include D.C. Brod, Jackie Hyman, James Kahn, Axel Madsen, Helen Hooven Santmyer, Donald A. Stanwood, Susan Sussman, J. Patrick Wright. *Commission* Home & Dramatic 15%; Foreign 20%. *Overseas associates* **A. M. Heath & Co. Ltd.**

Ruth Nathan Agency

80 Fifth Avenue, Suite 706, New York NY 10011
☎001 212 675 6063   Fax 001 212 675 6063

FOUNDED 1984. *Specialises* in illustrated books, fine art & decorative arts, biography in those areas, true crime, showbiz. No unsolicited mss. Query first. No reading fee. *Commission* 15%.

B. K. Nelson Literary Agency

84 Woodland Road, Pleasantville NY 10570–1322
☎001 914 741 1322   Fax 001 914 741 1324

President *Bonita K. Nelson*

FOUNDED 1979. *Specialises* in business, self-help, how-to, political, autobiography, celebrity biography. Major motion picture and TV documentary success. No unsolicited mss. Letter of inquiry. Reading fee charged. *Commission* 20%. Lecture Bureau for Authors founded 1994.

New Age World Services & Books

62091 Valley View Circle, Joshua Tree CA 92252
☎001 619 366 2833

Contact *Victoria E. Vandertuin*

FOUNDED 1957. New Age fiction and non-fiction, young adult fiction and non-fiction, and poetry. No scripts, drama, missionary, biography, sports, erotica, humour, travel or cookbooks. *Specialises* in New Age, self-help, health and beauty, meditation, yoga, channelling, how-to, metaphysical, occult, psychology, religion, lost continents, time travel. Unsolicited mss and queries welcome. Reading fee charged. *Commission* Home 15%; Foreign 20%.

New England Publishing Associates, Inc.

Box 5, Chester CT 06412
☎001 203 345 7323   Fax 001 203 345 3660

Contact *Elizabeth Frost Knappman, Edward W. Knappman*

FOUNDED 1983. *Handles* non-fiction. *Specialises* in current affairs, history, science, women's studies, reference, psychology, biography, true crime. No textbooks or anthologies. No scripts. Unsolicited mss considered but query letter or phone call preferred first. No reading fee. CLIENTS include Kathryn Cullen-Du Pont, Sharon Edwards, Elizabeth Lewin, Lary Bloom, Philip Ginsburg, William Packard, Carl Rollyson, Ian Tattersall, Orion Magazine, Claude Summers. *Commission* Home 15%. *Overseas associates* throughout Europe and Japan; Scott-Ferris, UK.

The Betsy Nolan Literary Agency

224 West 29th Street, 15th Floor, New York NY 10001
☎001 212 967 8200   Fax 001 212 967 7292

Contact *Betsy Nolan, Carla Glasser, Donald Lehr*

FOUNDED 1980. *Specialises* in non-fiction: popular culture, music, gardening, childcare, cooking, how-to. Some fiction, film & TV rights. No unsolicited mss. Send query letter with synopsis first. No reading fee. *Commission* Home 15%; Foreign 20%.

The Otte Co

9 Goden Street, Belmont MA 02178–3002
☎001 617 484 8505

Contact *Jane H. Otte*

FOUNDED 1973. *Handles* adult fiction and non-fiction. No scripts. No unsolicited mss. Approach by letter. No reading fee. *Commission* Home 15%; Dramatic 7½%; Foreign 20%.

Richard Parks Agency

138 East 16th Street, Suite 5B, New York NY 10003
☎001 212 254 9067

Contact *Richard Parks*

FOUNDED 1989. *Handles* general trade fiction and non-fiction: literary novels, mysteries and thrillers, commercial fiction, science fiction and fantasy, biography, pop culture, psychology, self-help, parenting, medical, cooking, gardening, etc. No scripts. No technical or academic. No unsolicited mss. Fiction read by referral only. No reading fee. CLIENTS include

Richard W. Langer, Jonathan Lethem, Abraham Rodriguez Jr, Audrey Schulman, Susan Straight. *Commission* Home 15%; UK & Translation 20%. *Overseas associates* **Marsh & Sheil Ltd, Barbara Levy Literary Agency.**

Pegasus International
PO Box 5470, Winter Park FL 32793-5470
☎001 407 699 1299
Director *Gene Lovitz*
FOUNDED 1987. 'We work with unpublished authors. Once an author comes aboard we work together to accomplish a marketable work, and never abandon the author once she or he is accepted as a client. Accordingly, we are rather selective in whom we represent.' *Handles* non-fiction and fiction: regency and historical romances, horror, New Age, fantasy and magic, gothic, science fiction, war, mystery, plus film/TV scripts. *Specialises* in science fiction, the 'intellectual novel', and translations into English. No hard-core pornography or verse. 'We will accept erotica done on the level of Anaïs Nin, making a distinction between pornography and erotica.' Approach in writing with proposal. Reading fee charged but reimbursed upon publication. *Commission* 15%.

Penmarin Books
PO Box 286, Woodacre CA 94973
☎001 415 488 1628   Fax 001 415 488 1123
Contact *Hal Lockwood*
FOUNDED 1987. *Handles* projects for popular trade publication, both fiction and non-fiction. No poetry or children's; no school, scholarly or academic books. Unsolicited mss welcome; initial approach in writing preferred: send professional/personal background details, project outline or synopsis (2–3 pp), sample of past or current writing (5–8 pp) and pre-paid return postage. No reading fee for initial reading. *Commission* 15%.

Perkins Literary Agency
PO Box 48, Childs MD 21916-0048
☎001 410 398 2647
Contact *Esther R. Perkins*
FOUNDED 1979. *Handles* fiction only: men's interest, mysteries, regencies and mainstream. No scripts, non-fiction, children's or poetry. No unsolicited mss. Send query letter. Reading fee charged. CLIENTS Karla Hocker, Barbara Reeves, Jeanne Savery. *Commission* Home 15%; UK & Translation 20%. *Overseas associates* Lennart Sane.

James Peter Associates, Inc.
PO Box 772, Tenafly NJ 07670
☎001 201 568 0760   Fax 001 201 568 2959
Contact *Bert Holtje*
FOUNDED 1971. Non-fiction only. 'Many of our authors are historians, psychologists, physicians – all are writing trade books for general readers.' No scripts. No fiction or children's books. *Specialises* in history, popular culture, health, biography and politics. No unsolicited mss. Send query letter first, with brief project outline, samples and biographical information. No reading fee. CLIENTS include Alan Axelrod, Kim Dae Jung, Charles Phillips, David Stutz, Carol Turkington. A member of the Association of Author's Representatives. *Commission* 15%.

Alison J. Picard Literary Agent
PO Box 2000, Cotuit MA 02635
☎001 508 477 7192   Fax 001 508 420 0762
Contact *Alison Picard*
FOUNDED 1985. *Handles* mainstream and literary fiction, contemporary and historical romance, children's and young adult, mysteries and thrillers; plus non-fiction. No short stories unless suitable for major national publications, and no poetry. Rarely any science fiction and fantasy. Particularly interested in expanding non-fiction titles. Approach with written query. No reading fee. *Commission* 15%. *Overseas associates* **A. M. Heath & Co. Ltd**, London.

Arthur Pine Associates, Inc.
250 West 57th Street, New York NY 10107
☎001 212 265 7330   Fax 001 212 265 4650
Contact *Richard S. Pine, Lori Andiman*
FOUNDED 1970. *Handles* fiction and non-fiction (adult books only). No scripts, children's, autobiographical (unless celebrity), textbooks or scientific. No unsolicited mss. Send query letter with synopsis, including IRCs in first instance. Reading fee charged. *Commission* 15%.

PMA Literary & Film Management, Inc.
220 West 19th Street, Suite 501, New York NY 10011
☎001 212 929 1222   Fax 001 212 206 0238
President *Peter Miller*
Vice President *Jennifer Robinson*
Associates *Harrison McGuigan, Eric Wilinski, Elizabeth Rufenacht, Yuri Skujins, John Stryder, Giselle Dean Miller*
FOUNDED 1976. Commercial fiction, non-fiction and screenplays. *Specialises* in books with

motion picture and television potential, and in true crime. No poetry, pornography, non-commercial or academic. No unsolicited mss. Approach by letter with one-page synopsis. Reading fee for unpublished authors (non-obligatory). Fee recoupable out of first monies earned. CLIENTS include Vincent T. Bugliosi, Jay R. Bonansinga, Martin Caidin, Michael Eberhardt, Christopher Cook Gilmore, Sarah Lovett, Michael Peak, Nancy Taylor Rosenberg, Ted Sennett, Gene Walden, Steven Yount. *Commission* Home 15%; Dramatic 10–15%; Foreign 20–25%.

Susan Ann Protter Literary Agent
Suite 1408, 110 West 40th Street, New York NY 10018
☎001 212 840 0480
Contact *Susan Protter*

FOUNDED 1971. *Handles* general fiction, mysteries, thrillers, science fiction and fantasy; also non-fiction: history, general reference, biography, science, health and parenting. No romantic fiction, poetry, religious, children's or sport manuals. No scripts. First approach with letter, including IRCs. No reading fee. CLIENTS include Lydia Adamson, Terry Bisson, David G. Hartwell, Robert Edwin Herzstein, Kathleen McCoy PhD, Lynn Armistead McKee, Rudy Rucker, Barbara C. Unell. *Commission* Home & Dramatic 15%; Foreign 25%. *Overseas associates* **Abner Stein**, London.

Puddingstone Literary/ SBC Enterprises, Inc.
11 Mabro Drive, Denville NJ 07834–9607
☎001 201 366 3622
Contact *Alec Bernard, Eugenia Cohen*

FOUNDED 1972. Works with new/unpublished writers as well as with established ones. *Handles* trade fiction, non-fiction, film and telemovies. No unsolicited mss. Send query letter with IRCs. No reading fee. *Commission* varies.

Quicksilver Books, Literary Agents
50 Wilson Street, Hartsdale NY 10530
☎001 914 946 8748
President *Bob Silverstein*

FOUNDED 1987. *Handles* literary fiction and mainstream commercial fiction: blockbuster, suspense, thriller, contemporary, mystery and historical; and general non-fiction, including self-help, psychology, holistic healing, ecology, environmental, biography, fact crime, New Age, health, nutrition, enlightened wisdom and spirituality. No scripts, science fiction and fantasy, pornographic, children's or romance. UK material being submitted must have universal appeal for the US market. Unsolicited material welcome but must be accompanied by IRCs for response, together with biographical details, covering letter, etc. No reading fee. CLIENTS include John Harricharan, Susan S. Lang, Brad Steiger, Grace Speare, Melvin van Peebles. *Commission* Home & Dramatic 15%; Translation 20%.

Helen Rees Literary Agency
308 Commonwealth Avenue, Boston MA 02115
☎001 617 262 2401   Fax 001 617 262 2401
Contact *Joan Mazmanian*

FOUNDED 1982. *Specialises* in books on health and business; also handles biography, autobiography and history; quality fiction. No scholarly, academic or technical books. No scripts. No unsolicited mss. Send query letter with IRCs. No reading fee. CLIENTS include Donna Carpenter, Alan Dershowitz, Alexander Dubcek, Harry Figgie Jr, Senator Barry Goldwater, Mitchell Kapor, Sandra Mackey, Price Waterhouse, Chet Raymo. *Commission* Home 15%; Foreign 20%.

Rights Unlimited, Inc.
101 West 55th Street, New York NY 10019
☎001 212 246 0900   Fax 001 212 246 2114
Contact *Bernard Kurman*

FOUNDED 1985. *Handles* fiction, non-fiction, business and children's picture books. No scripts, poetry, short stories, educational or literary works. Unsolicited mss welcome; query letter with synopsis preferred in the first instance. Reading fee $50. CLIENTS Charles Berlitz, Gyo Fujikawa, Norman Lang. *Commission* Home 15%; Translation 20%.

Rosenstone/Wender
3 East 48th Street, 4th Floor, New York NY 10017
☎001 212 832 8330   Fax 001 212 759 4524
Contact *Phyllis Wender, Susan Perlman Cohen*

FOUNDED 1981. *Handles* fiction, non-fiction, children's and scripts for film, TV and theatre. No material for radio. No unsolicited mss. Send letter outlining the project, credits, etc. No reading fee. *Commission* Home 15%; Dramatic 10%; Foreign 20%. *Overseas associates* La Nouvelle Agence, France; Andrew Nurnberg, Netherlands; The English Agency, Japan; Mohrbooks, Germany; Ole Licht, Scandinavia.

Shyama Ross Agency

2000 North Ivar Avenue, Suite 3, Hollywood
CA 90068
☎001 213 465 2630

Contact *Shyama Ross*

FOUNDED 1979. *Handles* non-fiction trade
books: New Age, health and fitness, philosophy, psychology, trends, humour, business,
mysticism; also fiction: thrillers, romance, suspense, mystery, contemporary. No scripts. No
Christian evangelical, travel, sleazy sex or children's. *Specialises* in health, how-to, mainstream
fiction, healing and women's issues. New writers welcome. Query by letter with brief outline
of contents and background (plus IRCs). Fee
charged ($95 for up to 50,000 words) for
detailed analysis of mss. Professional editing also
available (rates per page or hour). *Commission*
Home & Film rights 15%; Translation 20%.

Jane Rotrosen Agency

318 East 51st Street, New York NY 10022
☎001 212 593 4330   Fax 001 212 935 6985

Branch office: PO Box 1331, Taos, NM 87571
☎001 505 758 5991   Fax: 001 505 758 7108

Contact *Meg Ruley, Andrea Cirillo, Ruth Kagle
(New York); Stephanie Tade (Taos)*

Handles commercial fiction: romance, horror,
mysteries, thrillers and fantasy and popular non-
fiction. No scripts, educational, professional or
belles lettres. No unsolicited mss; send query letter in the first instance. No reading fee. CLIENTS
include Barbara Bickmore, Julie Garwood,
Tami Hoag, Judith Michael, Michael Palmer,
John Saul, Norman Spinrad. *Commission* Home
15%; UK & Translation 20%. *Overseas associates*
worldwide and film agents on the West Coast.

Victoria Sanders Literary Agency

241 Avenue of the Americas, New York
NY 10014
☎001 212 633 8811   Fax 001 212 633 0525

Contact *Victoria Sanders, Diane Dickensheid*

FOUNDED 1993. *Handles* general trade fiction
and non-fiction, plus ancillary film and televi-
sion rights. CLIENTS Connie Briscoe, Katherine
Eban Finkelstein, Colin Kersey, Estate of
Darrell Yates Rist, J. M. Redmann. *Commission*
Home & Dramatic 15%; Translation 20%.

Sandum & Associates

144 East 84th Street, New York NY 10028
☎001 212 737 2011

Contact *Howard E. Sandum*

FOUNDED 1987. *Handles* all categories of general

adult non-fiction, plus commercial and literary
fiction. No scripts. No children's, poetry or
short stories. No unsolicited mss. Third-party
referral preferred but direct approach by letter,
with synopsis, brief biography and IRCs, is
accepted. No reading fee. CLIENTS include
James Cowan, Charles Kutcher, Ward
Morehouse III, Silvia Sanza. *Commission* Home
& Dramatic 15%; Translation & Foreign 20%.
Overseas associates Scott Ferris Associates.

SBC Enterprises, Inc.
See **Puddingstone Literary**

Jack Scagnetti Literary Agency

5118 Vineland Avenue, Suite 102, North
Hollywood CA 91601
☎001 818 762 3871

Contact *Jack Scagnetti*

FOUNDED 1974. Works mostly with estab-
lished/published authors. *Handles* non-fiction,
fiction, film and TV scripts. No reading fee for
outlines. *Commission* Home & Dramatic 10%;
Foreign 15%.

Susan Schulman, A Literary Agency

454 West 44th Street, New York NY 10036
☎001 212 713 1633/4/5
Fax 001 212 581 8830

FOUNDED 1979. *Specialises* in non-fiction of all
types but particularly in psychology-based self-
help for men, women and families. Other
interests include business, the social sciences,
science, language and linguistics. Fiction interests include contemporary fiction, including
women's, mysteries, soft horror and thrillers
'with a cutting edge'. Always looking for
'something original and fresh'. No unsolicited
mss. Query first including outline and three
sample chapters with IRCs. No reading fee.
Represents properties for film and television,
and works with agents in appropriate territories
for translation rights. *Commission* Home &
Dramatic 15%; Translation 20%. *Overseas associates* Plays: **Rosica Colin Ltd**, London; Film:
Michelle Kass Associates, London;
Children's books: Marilyn Malin, London,
Commercial fiction: **MBA Literary Agents**
London.

Shapiro-Lichtman Talent Agency

8827 Beverly Boulevard, Los Angeles
CA 90048
☎001 310 859 8877   Fax 001 310 859 7153

FOUNDED 1969. Works mostly with established/
published authors. *Handles* film and TV scripts.

Unsolicited mss will not be read. *Commission* Home & Dramatic 10%; Foreign 20%.

The Shepard Agency
Pawling Savings Bank Building, Suite 3, Southeast Plaza, Brewster NY 10509
☎001 914 279 2900/3236
Fax 001 914 279 3239
Contact *Jean Shepard, Lance Shepard*
FOUNDED 1987. *Handles* non-fiction: business, food, self-help and travel; some fiction: adult, children's and young adult and the occasional script. No pornography. *Specialises* in business. Send query letter, table of contents, sample chapters and IRCs for response. No reading fee. *Commission* Home & Dramatic 15%; Translation 20%.

Lee Shore Agency
440 Friday Road, Pittsburgh PA 15209
☎001 412 821 0440   Fax 001 412 821 6099
Contact *Cynthia Sterling, Megan Davidson, Patrick Freeman*
FOUNDED 1988. *Handles* non-fiction, including textbooks, and mass-market fiction: horror, romance, mystery, westerns, science fiction. Also some young adult and, more recently, screenplays. *Specialises* in New Age, self-help, how-to and quality fiction. No children's. No unsolicited mss. Send IRCs for guidelines before submitting work. Reading fee charged. CLIENTS include Mel Blount, Francisco Cruz, Dr Laura Essen, Dr Lynn Hawker, Susan Sheppard. *Commission* Home 15%; Dramatic 20%.

Bobbe Siegel Literary Agency
41 West 83rd Street, New York NY 10024
☎001 212 877 4985   Fax 001 212 877 4985
Contact *Bobbe Siegel*
FOUNDED 1975. Works mostly with established/published authors. *Specialises* in literary fiction, detective, suspense, historical, fantasy, biography, how-to, women's interest, fitness, health, beauty, sports, pop psychology. No scripts. No cookbooks, crafts, children's, short stories or humour. First approach with letter including IRCs for response. No reading fee. Critiques given if the writer is taken on for representation. CLIENTS include Tom De Frank, John De Santis, Margaret Mitchell Dukore, Graham Landrum, Primo Levi, Curt Smith, Bonnie Tucker. *Commission* Home 15%; Dramatic & Foreign 20%. (Foreign/ Dramatic split 50/50 with sub-agent.) *Overseas associates* **John Pawsey**, London; others in other countries.

The Evelyn Singer Literary Agency, Inc.
PO Box 594, White Plains NY 10602
☎001 914 949 1147/914 631 5160
Contact *Evelyn Singer*
FOUNDED 1951. Works mostly with established/published authors. *Handles* fiction and non-fiction, both adult and children's. Adult: health, medicine, how-to, diet, biography, celebrity, conservation, political, serious novels, suspense and mystery. Children's: educational non-fiction for all ages and fiction for the middle/teen levels. No picture books unless the author is or has an experienced book illustrator. No formula romance, poetry, sex, occult, textbooks or specialised material unsuitable for trade market. No scripts. No unsolicited mss. First approach with letter giving writing background, credits, publications, including date of publication and publisher. IRCs essential. No phone calls. No reading fee. CLIENTS include John Armistead, Mary Elting, Franklin Folsom, William F. Hallstead, Rose Wyler. *Commission* Home 15%; Dramatic 20%; Foreign 25%. *Overseas associates* **Laurence Pollinger Ltd**, London.

Singer Media Corporation
Seaview Business Park, 1030 Calle Cordillera, Unit 106, San Clemente CA 92673
☎001 714 498 7227   Fax 001 714 498 2162
Contact *Helen J. Lee*
FOUNDED 1940. *Handles* contemporary romance, non-fiction and biographies. *Specialises* in business books and psychological self-help. No scripts or personal adventure novels. No unsolicited mss. Letter first. Reading fee for unpublished authors of $350 for a complete critique and suggestions. Packages mass market books for supermarkets and discount stores. Licences US books to foreign publishers. CLIENTS include Dr Frank S. Caprio, Dr Muriel Oberleder, C. Northcote Parkinson, W.E.D. Ross. *Commission* Home 15%; Foreign 20%.

Michael Snell Literary Agency
PO Box 1206, Truro MA 02666–1206
☎001 508 349 3718
President *Michael Snell*
Vice President *Patricia Smith*
FOUNDED 1980. Eager to work with new/ unpublished writers. *Specialises* in business and computer books (professional and reference to popular trade how-to); general how-to and self-help on all topics, from diet and exercise to

sex, psychology and personal finance, plus literary and suspense fiction. No unsolicited mss. Send outline and sample chapter with return postage for reply. No reading fee for outlines. Brochure available on how to write a book proposal. Rewriting, developmental editing, collaborating and ghostwriting services available on a fee basis. Send IRCs. *Commission* Home 15%.

Southern Writers
5120 Prytania Street, New Orleans LA 70115
☎001 504 899 5889

President *Helen Dietrich*
Vice President *William Griffin*

FOUNDED 1979. *Handles* fiction and non-fiction of general interest. No scripts, short stories, poetry, autobiography or articles. No unsolicited mss. Approach in writing with query. Reading fee charged to authors unpublished in the field. *Commission* Home 15%; Dramatic & Translation 20%.

Spieler Literary Agency
154 West 57th Street, Room 135, New York NY 10019
☎001 212 757 4439   Fax 001 212 333 2019

The Spieler Agency/West, 1760 Solano Avenue, Suite 300, Berkeley, CA 94707
☎001 510 528 0946   Fax 001 510 528 8117

Contact *Joseph Spieler, Lisa M. Ross, John Thornton (New York); Victoria Shoemaker (Berkeley)*

FOUNDED 1980. *Handles* literary fiction and non-fiction. No how-to or genre romance. *Specialises* in history, science, ecology, social issues and business. No scripts. Approach in writing with IRCs. No reading fee. CLIENTS include James Chace, Amy Ehrlich, Paul Hawken, Joe Kane, Walter Laqueur, Catherine MacCoun, Akio Morita, Marc Reisner. *Commission* Home & Dramatic 15%; Translation 20%. *Overseas associates* **Abner Stein**, **The Marsh Agency**, **Marsh & Sheil Ltd**, London.

Philip G. Spitzer Literary Agency
50 Talmage Farm Lane, East Hampton NY 11937
☎001 516 329 3650   Fax 001 516 329 3651

Contact *Philip Spitzer*

FOUNDED 1969. Works mostly with established/published authors. *Specialises* in general non-fiction and fiction – thrillers. No reading fee for outlines. *Commission* Home & Dramatic 15%; Foreign 20%.

Lyle Steele & Co. Ltd
511 East 73rd Street, Suite 6, New York NY 10021
☎001 212 288 2981

President *Lyle Steele*
Vice President *Stan Sitarski*

FOUNDED 1985. *Handles* general non-fiction and category fiction, including mysteries (anxious to see good British mysteries), thrillers, horror and occult. Also North American rights to titles published by major English publishers. *Specialises* in history, parenting, children's activities, social and political issues, health, self-help and business. No scripts unless derived from books already being handled. No romance. No unsolicited mss: query with IRCs in first instance. No reading fee. *Commission* 10%. *Overseas associates* worldwide.

Gloria Stern Agency
2929 Buffalo Speedway, Suite 2111, Houston TX 77098
☎001 713 963 8360   Fax 001 713 963 8460

Contact *Gloria Stern*

FOUNDED 1976. *Specialises* in non-fiction, including biography, history, politics, women's issues, self-help, health, science and education; also adult fiction. No scripts, how-to, poetry, short stories or first fiction from unpublished authors. First approach by letter stating content of book, including one chapter, list of competing books, qualifications as author and IRCs. No reading fee. *Commission* Home 10–15%; Dramatic 10%; Foreign 15% shared; Translation 20% shared. *Overseas associates* **A. M. Heath & Co. Ltd**, London, and worldwide.

Gloria Stern Agency (Hollywood)
12535 Chandler Boulevard, Suite 3, North Hollywood CA 91607
☎001 818 508 6296   Fax 001 818 508 6296

Contact *Gloria Stern*

FOUNDED 1984. *Handles* film scripts, genre (romance, detective, thriller and sci-fi) and mainstream fiction. 'No books containing gratuitous violence.' Approach with letter, biography and synopsis. Reading fee charged by the hour. *Commission* Home 15%; Offshore 20%.

Jo Stewart Agency
201 East 66th Street, Suite 18G, New York NY 10021
☎001 212 879 1301

Contact *Jo Stewart*

FOUNDED 1978. *Handles* fiction and non-fiction. No scripts. No unsolicited mss; send query letter first. No reading fee. *Commission* Home 10%; Foreign 20%; Unpublished 15%. *Overseas associates* **Murray Pollinger**, London.

Gunther Stuhlmann Author's Representative

PO Box 276, Becket MA 01223
☎001 413 623 5170

Contact *Gunther Stuhlmann, Barbara Ward*

FOUNDED 1954. *Handles* literary fiction, biography and serious non-fiction. No film/TV scripts unless from established clients. No short stories, detective, romance, adventure, poetry, technical or computers. *Specialises* in 20th-century literature, translations of Japanese and Spanish literature and modern American writers. Query first with IRCs, including sample chapters and synopsis of project. 'We take on few new clients.' No reading fee. CLIENTS include Kenneth Bernard, Julieta Campos, B. H. Friedman, Anaïs Nin, Richard Powers, Otto Rank. *Commission* Home 10%; Foreign 15%; Translation 20%.

H. N. Swanson, Inc.

8523 Sunset Boulevard, Los Angeles CA 90069
☎001 310 652 5385   Fax 001 310 652 3690

Owner *N. V. Swanson*
President *Thomas J. Shanks*
Literary Associates *Jim Anderson, Gail Barrick, Anna Courtney, Steven Fisher, Larry Kennar*

FOUNDED 1934. Fiction; film and TV rights. No unsolicited mss. Send query letter with IRCs in the first instance. No reading fee. *Commission* Home 10–15%.

The Tantleff Office

375 Greenwich Street, Suite 700, New York NY 10013
☎001 212 941 3939   Fax 001 212 941 3948

Contact *Jack Tantleff, John B. Santoianni, Jill Bock, Anthony Gardner, Charmaine Ferenczi*

FOUNDED 1986. *Handles* primarily scripts for TV, film and theatre. Also fiction and non-fiction books. No unsolicited mss; queries only. No reading fee. CLIENTS include Brian Friel, Howard Korder, Marsha Norman, Mark O'Donnell. *Commission* Scripts 10%; Books 15%.

2M Communications Ltd

121 West 27th Street, Suite 601, New York NY 10001
☎001 212 741 1509   Fax 001 212 691 4460

Contact *Madeleine Morel*

FOUNDED 1982. *Handles* non-fiction only: everything from pop psychology and health to cookery books, biographies and pop culture. No scripts. No fiction, children's, computers or science. No unsolicited mss; send letter with sample pages and IRCs. No reading fee. CLIENTS include David Steinman, Janet Wolfe, Donald Woods. *Commission* Home & Dramatic 15%; Translation 20%. *Overseas associates* **Gregory & Radice Authors' Agents**, London; Thomas Schluck Agency, Germany; Asano Agency, Japan; Bengt Nordin Agency, Scandinavia; EAIS, France; Living Literary Agency, Italy; Nueva Agencia Literaria Internacional, Spain.

Susan P. Urstadt, Inc.

PO Box 1676, New Canaan CT 06840
☎001 203 966 6111   Fax 001 203 966 2249

President *Susan P. Urstadt*

FOUNDED 1975. *Specialises* in decorative arts, antiques, architecture, gardening, cookery, biography, history, performing arts, sports, current affairs, natural history and environment, lifestyle, current living trends and popular reference. Query with outline, sample chapter, author biography and IRCs to cover return postage. CLIENTS include Emyl Jenkins, Thomas Powers, Elizabeth Stillinger. *Commission* Home 15%; Dramatic & Foreign 20%.

Van der Leun & Associates

22 Division Street, Easton CT 06612
☎001 203 259 4897

Contact *Patricia Van der Leun*

FOUNDED 1984. *Handles* fiction and non-fiction. No scripts. No science fiction or fantasy romance. *Specialises* in art and architecture, science, biography and fiction. No unsolicited mss; query first, with proposal and short biography. No reading fee. CLIENTS include David Darling, Robert Fulghum, Marion Winik. *Commission* 15%. *Overseas associates* **Abner Stein**, UK; Michelle Lapautre, France; English Agency, Japan; Carmen Balcells, Spain; Lijnkamp Associates, The Netherlands; Karin Schindler, South America; Susanna Zevi, Italy.

Bess Wallace Literary Agency

PO Box 972, Duchesne UT 84021
☎001 801 738 2317

Contact *Bess Wallace*

FOUNDED 1977. *Handles* non-fiction only. No eroticism or poetry. No scripts. Unsolicited mss welcome but query first. No reading fee. *Commission* Home 15%; Dramatic & Translation 10%.

Wallace Literary Agency, Inc.
177 East 70th Street, New York NY 10021
☎001 212 570 9090   Fax 001 212 772 8979
Contact *Lois Wallace, Thomas C. Wallace*
FOUNDED 1988. No unsolicited mss. No faxed queries. *Commission* Rates upon application. *UK representative* **A.M. Heath & Co. Ltd**; *European representatives* Michelle Lapautre, France; **Andrew Nurnberg Associates**, UK.

Gerry B. Wallerstein Agency
2315 Powell Avenue, Suite 12, Erie
PA 16506
☎001 814 833 5511   Fax 001 814 833 6260
Contact *Gerry B. Wallerstein*
FOUNDED 1984. Adult fiction and non-fiction. No scripts unless by established clients. No children's, textbooks, esoteric or autobiographical (unless celebrity). Broad range of clients, main interest being marketability of material. No unsolicited mss. Send IRCs for information regarding submissions. Reading fee charged for non-established authors. CLIENTS include Carl Caiati, Jack D. Coombe, Nan DeVincentis-Hayes, Gregory Janicki, Sandy Dengler. *Commission* Home & Dramatic 15%; Translation 20%.

John A. Ware Literary Agency
392 Central Park West, New York NY 10025
☎001 212 866 4733   Fax 001 212 866 4734
Contact *John Ware*
FOUNDED 1978. *Specialises* in non-fiction: biography, history, current affairs, investigative journalism, science, inside looks at phenomena, medicine and psychology (academic credentials required). Also handles literary fiction: mysteries/thrillers, sport, oral history, Americana and folklore. Unsolicited mss not read. Send query letter first with IRCs to cover return postage. No reading fee. CLIENTS include Alfie Kohn, Jon Krakauer, Jack Womack. *Commission* Home & Dramatic 15%; Foreign 20%.

Waterside Productions, Inc.
2191 San Elijo Avenue, Cardiff by the Sea
CA 92007-1839
☎001 619 632 9190   Fax 001 619 632 9295
Contact *William Gladstone*
FOUNDED 1982. *Handles* mainstream and category fiction, and general non-fiction: computers and technology, psychology, science, women's issues, business. All types of multimedia. No science fiction or horror. No unsolicited mss; send query letter. No reading fee.

Commission Home 15%; Dramatic 20%; Translation 25%. *Overseas associates* **Serafina Clarke**, England; Asano Agency, Japan; Ulla Lohren, Sweden; Ruth Liepman, Germany; Vera Le Marie, EAIS, France; Bardon Chinese Media Agency, China; Grandi & Vitali, Italy; DRT, Korea; Mercedes Casanovas, Spain.

Watkins Loomis Agency, Inc.
133 East 35th Street, Suite 1, New York
NY 10016
☎001 212 532 0080   Fax 001 212 889 0506
Contact *Lily Oei*
FOUNDED 1904. *Handles* fiction and non-fiction, political and cultural. No scripts for film, radio, TV or theatre. No science fiction, fantasy or horror. No reading fee. No unsolicited mss. Approach in writing with enquiry or proposal. CLIENTS include Maureen Howard, Walter Mosley, Arianna Stassinopoulos Huffington. *Commission* Home 15%; UK & Translation 20%. *Overseas associates* **Abner Stein**; **Marsh & Sheil Ltd**, London.

Wecksler-Incomco
170 West End Avenue, New York NY 10023
☎001 212 787 2239   Fax 001 212 496 7035
Contact *Sally Wecksler, Joann Amparan*
FOUNDED 1971. *Handles* fiction and non-fiction (biographies, performing arts), heavily illustrated books and reference. Film and TV rights. No unsolicited mss; queries only. No reading fee. *Commission* Home 15%; Translation 20% and British rights 20%.

Cherry Weiner Literary Agency
28 Kipling Way, Manalapan NJ 07726
☎001 908 446 2096
Fax 001 908 446 2096 (3★)
Contact *Cherry Weiner*
FOUNDED 1977. *Handles* more or less all types of genre fiction: science fiction and fantasy, romance, mystery, westerns. No scripts. No non-fiction. No unsolicited mss. No submissions except through referral. No reading fee. *Commission* 15%. *Overseas associates* **Abner Stein**, London; Thomas Schluck, Germany.

Wieser & Wieser, Inc.
118 East 25th Street, New York NY 10010
☎001 212 260 0860   Fax 001 212 505 7186
Contact *Olga B. Wieser, George J. Wieser, Jake Elwell*
FOUNDED 1976. Works mostly with established/published authors. *Specialises* in literary

and mainstream fiction, serious and popular historical fiction, and general non-fiction: business, finance, aviation, sports, photography, cookbooks, travel and popular medicine. No poetry, children's, science fiction or religious. No unsolicited mss. First approach by letter with IRCs. No reading fee for outlines. *Commission* Home & Dramatic 15%; Foreign 20%.

Ruth Wreschner, Authors' Representative

10 West 74th Street, New York
NY 10023
☎001 212 877 2605   Fax 001 212 595 5843
Contact *Ruth Wreschner*

FOUNDED 1981. Works mostly with established/published authors but 'will consider very good first novels, both mainstream and genre, particularly British mystery writers'. *Specialises* in popular medicine, psychology, health, self-help, business. No screenplays or dramatic plays. First approach with query letter and IRCs. For fiction, send a synopsis and first 100 pp; for non-fiction, an outline and two sample chapters. No reading fee. *Commission* Home 15%; Foreign 20%.

Ann Wright Representatives

165 West 46th Street, Suite 1105, New York
NY 10036–2501
☎001 212 764 6770   Fax 001 212 764 5125
Contact *Dan Wright*

FOUNDED 1961. *Specialises* in screenplays for film and TV. Also handles novels, drama and fiction. No academic, scientific or scholarly. Approach by letter; no reply without IRCs. Include outline and credits only. New film and TV writers encouraged. No reading fee. CLIENTS include Theodore Bonnet, Liam Burke, Tom Dempsey, Owen McKevit, Taber McMordie, Edmund Naughton, John Peer Nugent, Brian Reich, Joseph H. Sheehy. Signatory to the Writers Guild of America Agreement. *Commission* Home varies according to current trend (10–20%); Dramatic 10% of gross.

Writers House, Inc.

21 West 26th Street, New York NY 10010
☎001 212 685 2400   Fax 001 212 685 1781
Contact *Albert Zuckerman, Amy Berkower, Merrilee Heifetz, Susan Cohen, Susan Ginsburg, Liza Landsman*

FOUNDED 1974. *Handles* all types of fiction, including children's and young adult, plus narrative non-fiction: history, biography, popular science, pop and rock culture. Also represents designers and developers of CD-ROM computer games. *Specialises* in popular fiction, women's novels, thrillers and children's. No scripts. No professional or scholarly. For consideration of unsolicited mss, send letter of enquiry, 'explaining why your book is wonderful, briefly what it's about and outlining your writing background'. No reading fee. CLIENTS include Ken Follett, Eileen Goudge, Stephen Hawking, Michael Lewis, Robin McKinley, Ann Martin, Francine Pascal, Ridley Pearson, Craig Thomas, Cynthia Voigt, F. Paul Wilson. *Commission* Home & Dramatic 15%; Foreign 20%. *Overseas associates* **Blake Friedmann Literary Agency Ltd**, London. Albert Zuckerman is author of *Writing the Blockbuster Novel*, published by **Little, Brown & Co**.

Susan Zeckendorf Associates, Inc.

171 West 57th Street, Suite 11B, New York
NY 10019
☎001 212 245 2928   Fax 001 212 977 2643
President *Susan Zeckendorf*

FOUNDED 1979. Works with new/unpublished writers. *Specialises* in literary fiction, commercial women's fiction, international espionage, thrillers and mysteries. Non-fiction interests: science, parenting, music and self-help. No category romance, science fiction or scripts. No unsolicited mss. Send query letter describing mss. No reading fee. CLIENTS include Linda Dahl, James N. Frey, Una-Mary Parker, Jerry E. Patterson, Boyce Rensberger, Katherine Wallace King. *Commission* Home & Dramatic 15%; Foreign 20%. *Overseas associates* **Abner Stein**, London; V. K. Rosemarie Buckman, Europe, South America; Tom Mori, Japan, Taiwan.

US Press, Journals and Broadcasting

ABC News
8 Carburton Street, London W1P 7DT
☎0171 637 9222   Fax 0171 631 5084
Director, News Coverage, Europe,
  Middle East & Africa *Ned Warwick*

Associated Press
12 Norwich Street, London EC4A 1BP
☎0171 353 1515   Fax 0171 353 8118
Chief of Bureau/Managing Director
  Myron L. Belkind

Baltimore Sun
10 Bolt Court, Fleet Street, London EC4A 3DB
☎0171 353 3531   Fax 0171 353 5331
Bureau Chief *Bill Glauber*

Bloomberg Business News
City Gate House, 39–45 Finsbury Square,
London EC2A 1PX
☎0171 256 7500   Fax 0171 374 6138
European Bureau Chief *Douglas McGill*

Business Week
34 Dover Street, London W1X 4BR
☎0171 491 8985   Fax 0171 409 7152
Bureau Manager *Paula Dwyer*

Cable News International Inc.
CNN House, 19–22 Rathbone Place, London
W1P 1DF
☎0171 637 6800   Fax 0171 637 6868
Bureau Chief *David Feingold*

CBC Television
43/51 Great Titchfield Street,
London W1P 8DD
☎0171 412 9200   Fax 0171 631 3095
Bureau Chief *John Owen*

CBS News
68 Knightsbridge, London SW1X 7LL
☎0171 581 4801   Fax 0171 581 4431
Bureau Chief *Al Ortiz*

Chicago Tribune Press Service
169 Piccadilly, London W1V 9DD
☎0171 499 8769   Fax 0171 499 8781
Chief European Correspondent *Ray Moseley*

The Christian Science Monitor
49 Chartfield Avenue, London SW15 6HW
☎0181 543 9393   Fax 0181 545 0392
British Isles Correspondent *Alexander*
  Macleod

CNBC
8 Bedford Avenue, London WC1B 3NQ
☎0171 927 6759   Fax 0171 636 2628
Correspondent *Sissel McCarthy*

Forbes Magazine
51 Charles Street, London W1X 7PA
☎0171 465 0120   Fax 0171 465 0121
European Bureau Manager *Peter Fuhrman*

Fortune Magazine
Brettenham House, Lancaster Place, London
WC2E 7TL
☎0171 499 4080
European Editor *Carla Rapoport*

The Globe and Mail
The Quadrangle, PO Box 4YG,
180 Wardour Street, London W1A 4YG
☎0171 396 4116   Fax 0171 734 0561
European Correspondent *Paul Koring*

International Herald Tribune
63 Long Acre, London WC2E 9JH
☎0171 836 4802   Fax 0171 240 2254
London Correspondent *Erik Ipsen*

Journal of Commerce
Totara Park House, 3rd Floor, 34/36 Gray's
Inn Road, London WC1X 8HR
☎0171 430 2495   Fax 0171 837 2168
Chief European Correspondent *Janet Porter*

Life Magazine
Brettenham House, Lancaster Place, London
WC2E 7TL
☎0171 499 4080   Fax 0171 322 1021
Contact *Gail Ridgwell*

Los Angeles Times
150 Brompton Road, London SW3 1HX
☎0171 823 7315   Fax 0171 823 7308
Bureau Chief *Dan Fisher*

Market News Service Inc.
Wheatsheaf House, 4 Carmelite Street,
London EC4Y 0BN
☎0171 353 4462   Fax 0171 353 9122
Bureau Chief *Jon Hurdle*

National Public Radio
Room G-10 East Wing, Bush House, Strand,
London WC2B 4PH
☎0171 257 8086   Fax 0171 379 6486
London Bureau Chief *Andrew Bowers*

NBC News
8 Bedford Avenue, London WC1B 2NQ
☎0171 637 8655   Fax 0171 636 2628
Bureau Chief *Karen Curry*

The New York Times
66 Buckingham Gate, London SW1E 6AU
☎0171 799 5050   Fax 0171 799 2962
Chief Correspondent *John Darnton*

Newsweek
18 Park Street, London W1Y 4HH
☎0171 629 8361   Fax 0171 408 1403
Bureau Chief *Daniel Pedersen*

People Magazine
Brettenham House, Lancaster Place,
London WC2E 7TL
☎0171 499 4080   Fax 0171 322 1125
Special Correspondent *Jerene Jones*

Philadelphia Inquirer
14 Queen's Grove, London NW8 6EL
☎0171 483 3766   Fax 0171 483 3766
Correspondent *Dick Polman*

Reader's Digest Association Ltd
Berkeley Square House, Berkeley Square,
London W1X 6AB
☎0171 629 8144   Fax 0171 408 0748
Editor-in-Chief, British Edition *Russell Twisk*

Time Magazine
Brettenham House, Lancaster Place,
London WC2E 7TL
☎0171 499 4080   Fax 0171 322 1230
Bureau Chief *Barry Hillenbrand*

United Press International
408 Strand, London WC2R 0NE
☎0171 333 0999   Fax 0171 333 1690
Bureau Chief *Michael Collins*

US News and World Report
169 Piccadilly, London W1V 9DD
☎0171 493 4643   Fax 0171 493 8308
Senior European Editor *Robin Knight*

Voice of America
IPC, 76 Shoe Lane, London EC4A 3JB
☎0171 410 0960   Fax 0171 410 0966
Senior Editor *Mark Hopkins*

Wall Street Journal
10 Fleet Place, London EC4M 7RB
☎0171 832 9200   Fax 0171 832 9201
London Bureau Chief *Lawrence Ingrassia*

Washington Post
18 Park Street, London W1Y 4HH
☎0171 629 8958   Fax 0171 629 0050
Bureau Chief *Fred Barbash*

Copyright and Wrong

British copyright is enshrined in the 1988 Copyright Designs and Patents Act, an updating which almost immediately became outdated as European legislators got to work. Having reaffirmed the Berne Convention rule that copyright protection lasts for 50 years from the author's death, the Government is now trying to fall in line with a Community directive extending copyright to 70 years. There is no inherent logic to this figure. It is merely part of a general tidying up process which the highest figure on offer (in this case, for German copyright) is judged to be the common standard. By the same reasoning, the Italians are having to change their copyright on musical recordings from 30 to 50 years to match the British law.

There is something wonderfully ironic, not say typically bureaucratic, in adding on to copyright at a time when the information revolution is putting the whole concept under threat. But the immediate concern is the confusion caused by the prospect of works that have recently entered the public domain going back into copyright.

Who precisely owns the extra twenty years? Hugh Jones, a lawyer member of the Publishers' Association's Publishing Law and Copyright Committee, advises a close look 'at the terms of each publishing contract, the true intention of the parties at the time they entered into it'. He goes on, 'Where the grant of rights to the publisher is for the full term of copyright "including all renewals, reversions, and extensions thereof", the publisher would certainly benefit from any 20-year extension. But these words are by no means always present: the most common phrase in publishing contracts refers simply to "the full legal term of copyright". Arguably, what the parties meant by this was no more than the current term at the time the contract was signed, almost certainly life plus 50 years. . . In the absence of any hard evidence of what the parties actually meant, it may well be that the present publisher cannot simply assume that his licence will continue, and will have to revert to the copyright owner to agree an extension and, if necessary settle new terms.'

This is connected to a worry of the Society of Authors, that copyright will be used to restrict legitimate research and creative enterprise. Historians and biographers are most at risk. Examples are already cropping up of studies cut short or circumscribed by the reassertion of copyright.

A suitable cooling off period in which work in progress might be completed without hindrance or charge might serve the cause of natural justice. A complimentary amendment, recommended by the Society of Authors, is for the restoration of copyright to be limited to an equitable fee for material used. For the add-on period of 20 years, copyright holders would not be able to withhold rights of access or permission to quote. Many writers feel that this concession (still a matter of consultation, incidentally, and by no means certain of adoption) should apply across the board. Even if it is accepted that an author's beneficiaries should enjoy an unearned income for half a century after the funeral, it is not at all clear that they are necessarily suitable guardians of the literary estate. Copyright, of whatever duration, can be an oppressive law used to stifle debate and to block the spread of knowledge.

Copyright applies to all written work, unpublished as well as published. For works not published during the author's lifetime, the period of copyright runs from the date of publication. For a published work of joint authorship, protection extends from the end of the year of the death of the author who dies last.

In most books a copyright notice appears on one of the front pages. In its simplest form this is the symbol © followed by the name of the copyright owner and the year of first publication. The assertion of copyright may be emphasised by the phrase 'All rights reserved', and in case there are any lingering doubts the reader may be warned that 'No part of this publication may be reproduced or transmitted in any form or by any means without permission'.

But this is to overstate the case. It is perfectly legitimate for a writer to quote from someone else's work for 'purposes of criticism or review' as long as 'sufficient acknowledgement' is given. What he must not do is to lift 'a substantial part' of. In one case, four lines from a thirty-two line poem were held to amount to 'a substantial part'. On the other hand, even a 'substantial' quotation from a copyright work may be acceptable if a student or critic is engaged in 'fair dealing with a literary work for the purposes of research or music study'.

Some years ago the Society of Authors and the Publishers' Association stated that they would usually regard as 'fair dealing' the use of a single extract of up to 400 words, or a series of extracts (of which none exceeds 300 words) to a total of 800 words from a prose work, or of extracts to a total of 40 lines from a poem, provided that this did not exceed a quarter of the poem.

Titles and trademarks

Technically, there is no copyright in a title. But where a title is inseparable from the work of a particular author, proceedings for 'passing off' are likely to be successful. Everything depends on the nature of the rival works, the methods by which they are exploited and the extent to which the title is essentially distinctive.

The singularity of letters

The copyright status of a letter is something of a curiosity. The actual document belongs to the recipient, but the copyright remains with the writer and after his or her death, to the writer's estate. This has caused difficulty for some biographers who have assumed that it is the owners of letters who are empowered to give permission to quote from them. This only applies if the writer has assigned copyright.

Copyright in lectures and speeches

The pre-1988 rule was unnecessarily complicated and depended, for example, on whether the lecturer was speaking from prepared notes. Now, even if a speaker talks without notes, copyright exists in a lecture as soon as it is recorded (in writing or otherwise) but not until then. The copyright belongs to the person who spoke the words, whether or not the recording was made by, or with the permission of, the speaker.

Copyright on ideas

Writers trying to sell ideas should start on the assumption that it is almost impossible to stake an exclusive claim. So much unsolicited material comes the way of publishers and script departments, duplication of ideas is inevitable.

Frequent complaints of plagiarism have led publishers and production companies to point out the risks whenever they acknowledge an unsolicited synopsis or script, warning correspondents, 'it is often the case that we are currently considering or have already considered ideas that may be similar to your own'.

The fact is that to succeed in an action for infringement of copyright on an idea or on the bare bones of a plot, the copying of 'a combination or series of dramatic events' must be very close indeed. Proceedings have failed because incidents common to two works have been stock incidents or revolving around stock characters common to many works. Furthermore, as copyright is not a monopoly, it is a perfectly good defence if a later author can show that he had no knowledge of an earlier author's work.

The best way of protecting ideas, says solicitor Carolyn Jennings, is to 'get anyone who sees your work to sign a letter confirming that they will not disclose the ideas behind your work to anyone else, and will not use those ideas except by arrangement with you'. The catch, as Ms Jennings readily concedes is that 'it is very difficult to get broadcasters or film companies to sign such a letter'. In a highly competitive, fast moving industry, it is likely that many synopses or scripts based on similar ideas are floating around though created entirely independently.

Minimum security is in refusing to discuss ideas before they are written down. If there is still a worry that a proposal could end up in the wrong hands, copy the manuscript, send it to yourself by registered post, then deposit the package and dated receipt at a bank or other safe place. At least then no one can fault memory on essential details.

Permissions

A quotation of a 'substantial' extract from a copyright work or for any quotation of copyright material, however short, for an anthology must be approved by the publishers of the original work.

It is in the author's interest to deal with permissions as early as possible. Last-minute requests just before a book goes to press can lead to embarrassing difficulties if fees are too high or if permission is refused.

Anthology and quotation rates

The Society of Authors and the Publishers' Association have recently revised their recommendations for 'basic *minimum* fees' for quotation and anthology use of copyright material.

Prose

The suggested rate is £82–£96 per 1,000 words for world rights. The rate for the UK and Commonwealth or the USA alone is usually half of the world rate. For an individual country (e.g. Canada, Australia or New Zealand): one quarter of the world rate.

Where an extract is complete in itself (e.g. a chapter or short story) publishers sometimes charge an additional fee at half the rate applicable for 1,000 words.

There is pressure from some publishers and agents to increase permission rates by up to 50 per cent. Authors have mixed feelings. They like it when the money comes to them but they are less keen to pay out. The likely compromise is a 20 per cent increase.

Further information

A booklet entitled *The Law of Copyright and Rights in Performances* is available from The British Copyright Council, Copyright House, 29-33 Berners Street, London W1P 4AA.

For any queries on copyright contact: The Department of Trade and Industry, Intellectual Property Policy Directorate, Copyright Enquiries, Room 4/5, Hazlitt House, 45 Southampton Buildings, London WC2A 1AR (Tel: 0171 438 4778).

Professional Associations

Alliance of Literary Societies
Birmingham and Midland Institute, Margaret Street, Birmingham B3 3BS
☎0121 236 3591
President *Gabriel Woolf*
Chairman *J. Hunt*
Honorary Secretary *P. A. Fisher*
FOUNDED 1974. Acts as a liaison body between member societies and, when necessary, as a pressure group. Deals with enquiries and assists in preserving buildings and places with literary connections. Over 40 societies hold membership. A directory of literary societies is maintained and the ALS produces an annual fanzine, *Chapter One*, which is distributed to affiliated societies, carrying news of personalities, activities and events. Details from Kenneth Oultram, Editor, Chapter One, Clatterwick Hall, Little Leigh, Northwich, Cheshire CW8 4RJ (Tel: 01606 891303).

Arvon Foundation
Totleigh Barton, Sheepwash, Beaworthy, Devon EX21 5NS
☎0140 923338
Lumb Bank, Heptonstall, Hebden Bridge, West Yorkshire HX7 6DF
☎01422 843714.
Moniack Mhor, Moniack, Kirkhill, Inverness IV5 7PQ
☎01463 8336
Co-Presidents *Terry Hands, Ted Hughes OBE*
Chairman *Professor Brian Cox, CBE*
FOUNDED 1968. Offers people of any age (16+) and any background the opportunity to live and work with professional writers. Five-day residential courses are held throughout the year at Arvon's two main centres, covering poetry, narrative, drama, writing for children, songwriting and the performing arts. A number of bursaries towards the cost of course fees are available for those on low incomes, the unemployed, students and pensioners. Runs a biennial poetry competition (see under **Prizes**) and a pilot scheme of courses in the Scottish Highlands, near Inverness.

Association for Business Sponsorship of the Arts (ABSA)
Nutmeg House, 60 Gainsford Street, Butlers Wharf, London SE1 2NY
☎0171 378 8143   Fax 0171 407 7527

ABSA is the independent national association that exists to promote and encourage partnerships between the private sector and the arts to their mutual benefit and to that of the community at large. ABSA represents the interests of the business sponsor, in particular those of its business members, and also advises and trains the arts community both individually and corporately on the development of private sector support. A major initiative of ABSA is *Business in the Arts* which encourages business men and women to share their management skills with the arts to their mutual benefit. It also adminsters the *Business Sponsorship Incentive Scheme* on behalf of the Department of National Heritage.

Association of American Correspondents in London
12 Norwich Street, London EC4A 1BP
☎0171 353 1515   Fax 0171 936 2229
Contact *Sandra Marshall*
Subscription £90 (Organisations)
FOUNDED 1919 to serve the professional interests of its member organisations, promote social cooperation among them, and maintain the ethical standards of the profession. (An extra £30 is charged for each department of an organisation which requires separate listing in the Association's handbook.)

Association of Authors' Agents
c/o Greene & Heaton Ltd, 37 Goldhawk Road, London W12 8QQ
☎0181 749 0315   Fax 0181 749 0318
Secretary *Carol Heaton*
Membership £50 p.a.
FOUNDED 1974. Membership voluntary. The AAA maintains a code of practice, provides a forum for discussion, and represents its members in issues affecting the profession.

Association of British Editors
Broadvision, 49 Frederick Road, Edgbaston, Birmingham B15 1HN
☎0121 455 7949   Fax 0121 454 6187
Executive Director/Honorary Secretary
  Jock Gallagher
Subscription £50 p.a.
FOUNDED 1985. Independent organisation for the study and enhancement of journalism world-

wide. Established to protect and promote the freedom of the Press. Members are expected to 'maintain the dignity and rights of the profession; consider and sustain standards of professional conduct; exchange ideas for the advancement of professional ideals; work for the solution of common problems.' Membership is limited, but open to persons who have immediate charge of editorial or news policies in all media.

Association of British Science Writers (ABSW)

c/o British Association for the Advancement of Science, Fortress House, 23 Savile Row, London W1X 2NB
☎0171 439 1205   Fax 0171 734 1658
Administrator *Barbara Drillsma*
Membership £20 p.a.; £15 (Associate)

ABSW has played a central role in improving the standards of science journalism in the UK over the last 40 years. The Association seeks to improve standards by means of networking, lectures and organised visits to institutional laboratories and industrial research centres. Puts members in touch with major projects in the field and with experts worldwide. A member of the European Union of Science Journalists' Associations, ABSW is able to offer heavily subsidised places on visits to research centres in most other European countries and hosts reciprocal visits to Britain by European journalists. Membership open to those who are considered to be *bona fide* science writers/editors, or their film/TV/radio equivalents, who earn a substantial part of their income by promoting public interest in and understanding of science. Runs the administration and judging of the **Glaxo Science Writers' Awards**, for outstanding science journalism in newspapers, journals and broadcasting.

Association of Golf Writers

c/o Sports Desk, Daily Express, Blackfriars Road, London SE1 9UX
☎0171 922 7118   Fax 0171 922 7974
Contact *Frances Jennings*

FOUNDED 1938. Aims to co-operate with golfing bodies to ensure best possible working conditions.

Association of Illustrators

29 Bedford Square, London WC1B 3EG
☎0171 636 4100   Fax 0171 580 2338
Contact *Gina Morley*

FOUNDED 1973 to promote illustration and illustrators' rights, and encourage professional stan-

dards. The AOI is a non-profit making trade association dedicated to its members, to protecting their interests and promoting their work. Talks, seminars, a newsletter, regional groups, legal and portfolio advice as well as a number of related publications such as *Rights*, *The Illustrator's Guide to Professional Practice*, and *Survive*, *The Illustrator's Guide to a Professional Career*.

Association of Independent Libraries

Birmingham and Midland Institute, Margaret Street, Birmingham B3 3BS
☎0121 236 3591
Secretary *Philip Fisher*

Established to 'further the advancement, conservation and restoration of a little-known but important living portion of our cultural heritage'. Members include the **London Library, Devon & Exeter Institution, Linen Hall Library** and **Plymouth Proprietary Library**.

Association of Independent Radio Companies

Radio House, 46 Westbourne Grove, London W2 5SH
☎0171 727 2646   Fax 0171 229 0352
Director *Brian West*
Research Officer *James Galpin*

The AIRC is the trade association of the independent radio companies. It represents members' interests to Government, the Radio Authority, trade unions, copyright organisations and other bodies.

Association of Learned and Professional Society Publishers

48 Kelsey Lane, Beckenham, Kent BR3 3NE
☎0181 658 0459   Fax 0181 663 3583
Secretary-General *Bernard Donovan*

FOUNDED 1972 to foster the publishing activities of learned societies and academic and professional bodies. Membership is limited to such organisations, those publishing on behalf of member organisations and those closely associated with the work of academic publishers.

Association of Little Presses

30 Greenhill, Hampstead High Street, London NW3 5UA
☎0171 435 1889
Coordinator *Stan Trevor*
Subscription £12.50 p.a.

FOUNDED 1966 as a loosely knit association of individuals running little presses, who grouped together for mutual self-help and encouragement. First acted as a pressure group to extend the availability of grant aid to small presses and later became more of an information exchange, advice centre and general promoter of small press publishing. Currently represents over 300 publishers and associates throughout Britain. Membership is open to presses and magazines as well as to individuals and institutions.

ALP publishes a twice-yearly magazine, *Poetry and Little Press Information* (PALPI); a *Catalogue of Little Press Books in Print*; information booklets such as *Getting Your Poetry Published* (over 35,000 copies sold since 1973) and *Publishing Yourself: Not Too Difficult After All* which advises those who are thinking of self-publishing; and a regular newsletter. A full list of little presses (some of which, like **Bloodaxe Books**, are now sufficiently established and successful to be considered in the mainstream of the business) is available from ALP.

ALP organises bookfairs twice-yearly. Its main focus, that of supporting members' presses, brings it into contact with organisations worldwide. Over 80% of all new poetry in Britain is published by small presses and magazines but the Association is by no means solely devoted to publishers of poetry; its members produce everything from comics to cookery, novels and naval history.

Association of Scottish Motoring Writers
c/o 85 East King Street, Helensburgh, Dunbartonshire G84 7RG
☎01436 672187   Fax 01436 672187
Contact *Ross Finlay*
Subscription £35 (Full); £20 (Associate)
FOUNDED 1961. Aims to co-ordinate the activities of, and provide shared facilities for, motoring writers resident in Scotland as well as creating opportunities for them to keep in touch when working outside of Scotland. Membership is by invitation only.

Author–Publisher Enterprise
12 Mercers, Hawkhurst, Kent TN18 4LH
☎01580 753346
Chairman *John Dawes*
Secretary *Trevor Lockwood*
Subscription £25 (p.a.)
FOUNDED 1993. The association aims to provide an active forum for writers publishing their own work. An information network of ideas and opportunities for self-publishers. Regular newsletter, seminars and workshops, etc.

Authors North
c/o The Society of Authors, 84 Drayton Gardens, London SW10 9SB
☎0171 373 6642
Secretary *Ray Dunbobbin*
A group within **The Society of Authors** which organises meetings for members living in the North of England.

The Authors' Club
40 Dover Street, London W1X 3RB
☎0171 499 8581   Fax 0171 409 0913
Secretary *Mrs Ann Carter*
Entry Fee £250
FOUNDED 1891 by Sir Walter Besant. For men and women writers and those with literary interests. Apply to the Secretary for current subscription rates.

Authors' Licensing and Collecting Society
74 New Oxford Street, London WC1A 1EF
☎0171 255 2034   Fax 0171 323 0486
Secretary General *Janet Hurrell*
Subscription £5.88 incl. VAT (free to members of **The Society of Authors** and **The Writers' Guild**); £7 (Overseas)
A non-profit making society collecting and distributing payment to writers in areas where they are unable to administer the rights themselves, such as reprography, certain lending rights, private and off-air recording and simultaneous cabling. Open to writers and their heirs.

The Bibliographical Society
c/o The National Art Library, Victoria & Albert Museum, London SW7 2RLG
☎0171 938 8312   Fax 0171 938 8461
President *P. Isaac*
Honorary Secretary *D. Pearson*
Subscription £28 p.a.
Aims to promote and encourage the study and research of historical, analytical, descriptive and textual bibliography, and the history of printing, publishing, bookselling, bookbinding and collecting; to hold meetings at which papers are read and discussed; to print and publish works concerned with bibliography; to form a bibliographical library. Awards grants and bursaries for bibliographical research. *Publishes* a quarterly magazine called *The Library*.

Book Development Council
See **The Publishers Association**

Book Packagers Association

93A Blenheim Crescent, London W11 2EQ
☎0171 221 9089
Secretary *Rosemary Pettit*
Subscription £150 p.a.; Associate
membership £75 p.a.

Aims to provide members with a forum for the exchange of information, to improve the image of packaging and to represent the interests of members. Activities include meetings, seminars, the provision of standard contracts and a joint stand at London Book Fair.

Book Trust

Book House, 45 East Hill, London SW18 2QZ
☎0181 870 9055   Fax 0181 874 4790
Chief Executive *Brian Perman*
Subscription £25 p.a.; £28 (Overseas)

FOUNDED 1925. The Trust, while continuing its commitment to children's reading, plans to do more for the adult reader in future. The former Children's Book Foundation has been absorbed into the Trust under the title of Young Book Trust. Children's Book Week will continue to take place. The Trust offers a free book information service to the public (written enquiries only) and a trade service on subscription. Other aspects of its work include organising touring exhibitions; administering literary prizes (including the **Booker**); carrying out surveys for publication. *Publishes* a number of useful reference books (books about books, writers, prizes, education, etc.), and continues to house the **Book Trust Children's Reference Library**. Catalogue available.

Book Trust Scotland

The Scottish Book Centre, 137 Dundee Street, Edinburgh EH11 1BG
☎0131 229 3663   Fax 0131 228 4293
Contact *Lindsey Fraser*

FOUNDED 1956. Book Trust Scotland works with schools, libraries, writers, artists, publishers, bookshops and individuals to promote the pleasures of reading to people of all ages. It provides a book information service which draws on the children's reference library (a copy of every children's book published in the previous twelve months), the Scottish children's book collection, a range of press cuttings on Scottish literary themes and a number of smaller collections of Scottish books. Book Trust Scotland administers the **Kathleen Fidler Award** and the **McVitie's Prize for the Scottish Writer of the Year**; and pub-*lishes* guides to Scottish books and writers, both adult and children's. Book Trust Scotland also produces a range of children's reading posters and Scottish poetry posters.

Booksellers Association of Great Britain & Ireland

272 Vauxhall Bridge Road, London SW1V 1BA
☎0171 834 5477   Fax 0171 834 8812
Chief Executive *Tim Godfray*

FOUNDED 1895. The BA helps 3,300 independent, chain and multiple members to sell more books and reduce costs. It represents members' interests to publishers, Government, authors and others in the trade as well as offering marketing assistance, running training courses, conferences, seminars and exhibitions. *Publishes* directories, catalogues, surveys and various other publications connected with the book trade and administers the **Whitbread Book of the Year and Literary Awards**.

BAFTA (British Academy of Film and Television Arts)

195 Piccadilly, London W1V 0LN
☎0171 734 0022   Fax 0171 734 1792
Chief Executive *Harry Manley*
Subscription £140 p.a.; £72.50 (Country)

FOUNDED 1947. Membership limited to 'those who have contributed to the industry' over a minimum period of three years. Provides facilities for screening and discussions; encourages research and experimentation; lobbies Parliament; and makes annual awards.

BASCA (British Academy of Songwriters, Composers and Authors)

34 Hanway Street, London W1P 9DE
☎0171 436 2261   Fax 0171 436 1913
Contact *Amanda Harcourt*
Subscription from £35 + VAT p.a.

FOUNDED 1947. The Academy offers advice and support for songwriters and composers and represents members' interests to the music industry. It also issues a standard contract between publishers and writers and a collaborators' agreement. Members receive the Academy's quarterly magazine, and can attend fortnightly legal and financial seminars and creative workshops. The Academy administers Britain's annual awards for composers, the Ivor Novello Awards, now in their 40th year. BASCA is a member of the Alliance of Composer Organisations, ACO.

British Amateur Press Association

Michaelmas, Cimarron Close, South
Woodham Ferrers, Essex CM3 5PB
Secretary/Treasurer *L. E. Linford*

A non-profit making, non-sectarian hobby
organisation founded in 1890 to 'promote the
fellowship of amateur writers, artists, editors,
printers, publishers and other craftspeople. To
encourage them to edit, print and publish, *as a
hobby*, magazines and newsletters, etc' by letterpress and other processes, including photocopiers and computer DTP/word-processors.
Not an outlet for placing work commercially,
only with other members in their private publications circulated within the society and friends.
A fraternity providing contacts between amateur
writers, poets, editors, artists, etc. Postal enquiries
only, please enclose first class stamp.

British American Arts Association

116 Commercial Street, London E1 6NF
☎0171 247 5385   Fax 0171 247 5256
Director *Jennifer Williams*

The BAAA acts as a catalyst for transatlantic
cultural exchange. It offers advice and counselling in all arts disciplines, runs a conference
programme and takes on special projects.
Emphasis is on the non-profit sector. The
BAAA is not a grant-giving organisation.

British Association of Industrial Editors

3 Locks Yard, High Street, Sevenoaks, Kent
TN13 1LT
☎01732 459331   Fax 01732 461757

FOUNDED 1949. The professional association
for people in corporate internal communication and related functions. Provides a wide
range of services to its members, including
workshops, seminars and courses, conferences
and publications.

British Association of Journalists

99 Fleet Street, London EC4Y 1DE
☎0171 353 3003   Fax 0171 353 2310
General Secretary *Steve Turner*
Subscription National newspaper staff, national
    broadcasting staff, national news agency staff:
    £12.50 a month. Other seniors, including
    magazine journalists, PRs and freelancers
    who earn the majority of their income from
    journalism: £7.50 a month. Journalists under
    24: £5 a month. Student journalists: Free.

FOUNDED 1992. Aims to protect and promote
the professional interests of journalists.

BAPLA (British Association of Picture Libraries and Agencies)

13 Woodberry Crescent, London N10 1PJ
☎0181 444 7913   Fax 0181 883 9215
Administrator *Sal Shuel*

An association of more than 300 picture
libraries and agencies, who between them handle more than 300 million images: 'black and
white, colour, very old, very new, scientific,
absurd, news, kittens in furry slippers, aard-
varks, Zulus, and almost everything in
between'. *The Directory* (obtainable from the
above address, price £10) is a guide to who has
what and where they are. The Association also
offers advice on costs, etc., and produces an
entertaining journal.

British Copyright Council

Copyright House, 29–33 Berners Street,
London W1P 4AA
☎0171 359 1895   Fax 0171 359 1895
Secretary *Geoffrey Adams*

Works for the national and international acceptance of copyright and acts as a lobby/watch-
dog organisation on behalf of creators, publishers and performers on copyright and associated
matters. Publications include *Guide to the Law
of Copyright and Rights in Performances in the UK*;
Photocopying from Books and Journals. An
umbrella organisation which does not deal
with individual enquiries.

The British Council

10 Spring Gardens, London SW1A 2BN
☎0171 930 8466/Press Office: 389 4878   Fax
0171 389 4971
Head of Literature *Neil Gilroy-Scott*

The British Council promotes Britain abroad.
It provides access to British ideas, talents,
expertise and experience in education and
training, books and periodicals, the English
language, literature and the arts, sciences and
technology. An independent, non-political
organisation, the British Council works in 228
cities in 108 countries.

British Equestrian Writers' Association

Priory House, Station Road, Swavesey,
Cambridge CB4 5QJ
☎01954 232084   Fax 01954 231362
Contact *Gillian Newsum*
Subscription £10

FOUNDED 1973. Aims to further the interests of
equestrian sport and improve, wherever possible,

the working conditions of the equestrian press. Membership is by invitation of the committee. Candidates for membership must be nominated and seconded by full members and receive a majority vote of the committee.

British Film Commission
70 Baker Street, London W1M 1DJ
☎0171 224 5000   Fax 0171 224 1013
Chief Executive *Andrew Patrick*
FOUNDED 1991 the BFC is funded through the Department of National Heritage. Its remit is to promote the United Kingdom as an international production centre, to encourage the use of British personnel, technical services, facilities and locations and to provide wide ranging support to those filming and contemplating filming in the UK.

British Film Institute
21 Stephen Street, London W1P 2LN
☎0171 255 1444   Fax 0171 436 7950
Membership from £11.95–£56.45 p.a.
(concessions available)
FOUNDED 1933. Exists to encourage the development of film, television and video in the UK. Its divisions include: National Film and Television Archive; BFI on the South Bank (National Film Theatre and Museum of the Moving Image); **BFI Production**; **BFI Library and Information Services**; and BFI Research & Education (including Publishing, Sight and Sound). It also provides programming support to a regional network of 40 film theatres.

British Guild of Beer Writers
PO Box 900, Hemel Hempstead,
Hertfordshire HP3 0RJ
☎01442 834900   Fax 01442 834901
Contact *Peter Coulson*
Subscription £25.00 p.a.
FOUNDED 1988. Aims to improve standards in beer writing and at the same time extend public knowledge of beers and brewing. Publishes a directory of members with details of their publications and their particular areas of interest; this is then circulated to newspapers, magazines, trade press and broadcasting organisations. As part of the plan to improve writing standards and to achieve a higher profile for beer, the Guild offers annual awards, The Gold and Silver Tankard Awards, to the members judged to have made the most valuable contribution towards this end in their work. Meetings are held regularly.

British Guild of Travel Writers
90 Corringway, London W5 3HA
☎0181 998 2223
Chairman *John Bell*
Honorary Secretary *John Harrison*
Subscription £50 p.a.

The professional association of travel writers, broadcasters, photographers and editors which aims to serve its membership's interest professionally and acts as a forum for debate and discussion, with monthly meetings. Members are required to earn the majority of their income from travel reporting. The Guild represents its members to the BTA.

British Science Fiction Association
52 Woodhill Drive, Grove, Wantage, Oxon OX12 0DF
Membership Secretary *Ms Alison Cook*
Subscription £18 p.a.

FOUNDED originally in 1958 by a group of authors, readers, publishers and booksellers interested in science fiction. With a worldwide membership, the Association aims to promote the reading, writing and publishing of science fiction and to encourage SF fans to maintain contact with each other. Also offers postal writers workshop, a magazine chain and an information service. *Publishes Matrix* bimonthly newsletter with comment and opinions, news of conventions, etc. Contributions from members welcomed; *Vector* bi-monthly critical journal – reviews of books and magazines. Edited by Catie Cary; *Focus* bi-annual magazine with articles, original fiction and letters column. Edited by Carol Ann Green.

British Screen Finance
14–17 Wells Mews, London W1P 3FL
☎0171 323 9080   Fax 0171 323 0092
Contact *Simon Perry, Stephen Cleary*

A private company aided by government grant; shareholders are Rank, **Channel 4**, **Granada** and Pathé. Exists to invest in British films specifically intended for cinema release in the UK and worldwide. Divided into two functions: project development (contact *Stephen Cleary*), and production investment (contact *Simon Perry*). British Screen also manages the European Co-production Fund which exists to support feature films co-produced by the UK with other European countries. British Screen develops around 40 projects per year, and has invested in 115 British feature film productions in the last nine years.

British Society of Magazine Editors (BSME)
8 Brockley Avenue, Stanmore, Middlesex
HA7 4LXN
☎0181 905 4147
Contact *Gill Branston*
FOUNDED 1960, aims to represent interests and needs of magazine editors in the UK from both business and consumer sectors.

Broadcasting Press Guild
Tiverton, The Ridge, Woking, Surrey
GU22 7EQ
☎01483 764895   Fax 01483 764895
Membership Secretary *Richard Last*
Subscription £15 p.a.
FOUNDED 1973 to promote the professional interests of journalists specialising in writing or broadcasting about the media. Organises monthly lunches addressed by top broadcasting executives, and annual TV and radio awards.

Campaign for Press and Broadcasting Freedom
8 Cynthia Street, London N1 9JF
☎0171 278 4430   Fax 0171 837 8868
Subscription £12 p.a. (concessions available); £25 p.a. (Institutions); £20 p.a. (Organisations)
Broadly-based pressure group working for more accountable and accessible media in Britain. Advises on right of reply and takes up the issue of the portrayal of minorities. Members receive *Free Press* (bi-monthly), discounts on publications and news of campaign progress.

The Caravan Writers' Guild
Hillside House, Beach Road, Benllech, Anglesey, Gwynedd LL74 8SW
☎01248 852248   Fax 01248 852107
Contact *The Chairman*
Subscription £5 joining fee plus £10 p.a.
Guild for writers active in the specialist fields of caravan and camping journalism.

Careers Writers' Association
Manor Farm Lodge, Upper Wield, Alresford, Hampshire SO24 9RU
☎01420 562046
Membership Secretary *Katherine Lea*
FOUNDED 1979. The association aims to promote high standards of careers writing, improve access to sources of information, provide a network for members to exchange information and experience, hold meetings on topics of relevance and interest to members. Also produces a regular newsletter and maintains a membership list. Forges links with organisations sharing related interests, and maintains regular contact with national education and training bodies, government agencies and publishers.

Chartered Institute of Journalists
2 Dock Offices, Surrey Quays Road, London SE16 2XL
☎0171 252 1187   Fax 0171 232 2302
General Secretary *Christopher Underwood*
Subscription £105–£170 (by assessment)
FOUNDED 1884. The Chartered Institute is concerned with professional journalistic standards and with safeguarding the freedom of the media. It is open to writers, broadcasters and journalists (including self-employed) in all media. Affiliation is available to part-time or occasional practitioners and to overseas journalists who can join the Institute's International Division. Members also belong to the IOJ (Institute of Journalists), an independent trade union which protects, advises and represents them in their employment or freelance work; negotiates on their behalf and provides legal assistance and support. The IOJ (TU) is a certificated trade union which represents members' interests in the workplace.

Children's Book Circle
c/o Hamish Hamilton, 27 Wrights Lane, London W8 5TZ
☎0171 416 3000   Fax 0171 416 3099
Contact *Anna Trenter*
The Children's Book Circle provides a discussion forum for anybody involved with children's books. Monthly meetings are addressed by a panel of invited speakers and topics focus on current and controversial issues. Administers the **Children's Book Circle Eleanor Farjeon Award**.

Children's Book Foundation
See **Book Trust**

Circle of Wine Writers
44 Oaklands Avenue, Droitwich, Worcestershire WR9 7BT
☎01905 773707   Fax 01905 773707
Vice Chairman *Philippe Boucheron*
Membership £25 p.a.
FOUNDED 1962. Open to all *bona fide* authors, broadcasters, journalists, lecturers and tutors

who are engaged in, or earn a significant part of their income from, communicating about wine and spirits. Aims to improve the standard of writing, broadcasting and lecturing about wine; to contribute to the growth of knowledge and interest in wine; to promote wine of quality in the UK and to comment adversely on faulty products or dubious practices which could lead to a fall in consumption; to establish and maintain good relations between the Circle and the wine trade in the best interests of the consumer.

Clé, The Irish Book Publishers Association

The Writers' Centre, 19 Parnell Square,
Dublin 1, Republic of Ireland
☎00 353 1 8729090   Fax 00 353 1 8722035

President *John Spillane*
Administrator *Hilary Kennedy*

FOUNDED 1970 to promote Irish publishing, protect members' interests and train the industry.

Comedy Writers' Association of Great Britain

61 Parry Road, Ashmore Park,
Wolverhampton, West Midlands WV11 2PS
☎01902 722729   Fax 01902 722729

Contact *Ken Rock*

FOUNDED 1981 to assist and promote the work of comedy writers. The Association is a self-help group designed to encourage and advise its members to sell their work. It is an international organisation with representatives in Britain, Germany, Cyprus, Sweden, Belgium, Luxembourg, Czechoslovakia, Denmark, Finland and Canada. International seminar with videos of foreign TV comedy programmes, bookshop and business club where members can discuss opportunities. Members often come together to work jointly on a variety of comedy projects for British and overseas productions. *Publishes* regular magazines and monthly market information.

Comics Creators Guild (formerly Society for Strip Illustration)

7 Dilke Street, London SW3 4JE

Since 1977 the Guild has offered a service to professional comic creators. Open to artists, writers, editors, colourists, publishers, journalists and comics retailers, and anyone professionally concerned with comics, newspaper strips and strip illustration. Also welcomes enthusiasts and those working in the 'small' or 'independent' press who publish comics. Holds

monthly meetings, issues a monthly newsletter and publishes *Comics Forum*, *Directory of Members' Work*, *Collected Submission Guidelines*, *Sample Scripts*, *Guide to Contracts* and *Getting Started in Comics*.

The Copyright Licensing Agency Ltd

90 Tottenham Court Road,
London W1P 9HE
☎0171 436 5931   Fax 0171 436 3986

Chief Executive/Secretary *Colin P. Hadley*
Office Manager *Kate Gardner*

FOUNDED 1982 by the **Authors' Licensing and Collecting Society (ALCS)** and the **Publishers Licensing Society Ltd (PLS)**, the CLA administers collectively photocopying and other copying rights that it is uneconomic for writers and publishers to administer for themselves. The Agency issues collective and transactional licences, and the fees it collects, after the deduction of its operating costs, are distributed at regular intervals to authors and publishers via their respective societies (i.e. PLS or ALCS). Since 1987 the CLA has distributed over £20 million.

Council for British Archaeology

Bowes Morrell House, 111 Walmgate, York
YO1 2UA
☎01904 671417   Fax 01904 671384

Information Officer *Mike Heyworth*

FOUNDED 1944 to represent and promote archaeology at all levels. Its aims are to improve the public's awareness in and understanding of Britain's past; to carry out research; to survey, guide and promote the teaching of archaeology at all levels of education; to publish a wide range of academic, educational, general and bibliographical works (see **CBA Publishing**).

Council of Academic and Professional Publishers

See **The Publishers Association**

Crime Writers' Association (CWA)

PO Box 172, Tring, Hertfordshire HP23 5LP

Secretary *Anthea Fraser*
Membership £40 (Town); £35 (Country)

Full membership is limited to professional crime writers, but publishers, literary agents, booksellers, etc., who specialise in crime are eligible for Associate membership. Meetings are held monthly in Soho, with informative talks frequently given by police, scenes of crime officers, lawyers, etc., and a weekend conference is held annually in different parts of the country. Produces a monthly newsletter for members called *Red Herrings* and presents various annual awards.

The Critics' Circle
c/o The Stage & Television Today, 47 Bermondsey Street, London SE1 3XT
☎0171 403 1818   Fax 0171 403 1418
President *Stephen Pettitt*
Honorary General Secretary *Peter Hepple*
Subscription £12 p.a.

Membership by invitation only. Aims to uphold and promote the art of criticism (and the commercial rates of pay thereof) and preserve the interests of its members: professionals involved in criticism of film, drama, music and dance.

Department of National Heritage
2–4 Cockspur Street, London SW1Y 5DH
☎0171 211 6000   Fax 0171 211 6210
Senior Press Officer, Arts *Toby Sargent*

The Department of National Heritage has responsibilities for Government policies relating to the arts, museums and galleries, public libraries, sport, broadcasting, Press standards, film, the built heritage, tourism and the National Lottery. It funds **The Arts Council**, national museums and galleries, **The British Library** (including the new library building at St Pancras), the Public Lending Right and the Royal Commission on Historical Manuscripts. It is responsible within Government for the public library service in England, and for library and information matters generally, where they are not the responsibility of other departments.

Directory Publishers Association
93A Blenheim Crescent, London W11 2EQ
☎0171 221 9089
Contact *Rosemary Pettit*
Subscription £100–£600 p.a.

FOUNDED 1970 to promote the interests of *bona fide* directory publishers and protect the public from disreputable and fraudulent practices. The objectives of the Association are to maintain a code of professional practice to safeguard public interest; to raise the standard and status of directory publishing throughout the UK; to promote business directories as a medium for advertising; to protect the legal and statutory interests of directory publishers; to foster bonds of common interest among responsible directory publishers and provide for the exchange of technical, commercial and management information between members. Meetings, seminars, conference, newsletter and representation at book fairs.

Drama Association of Wales
The Library, Singleton Road, Splott, Cardiff CF2 2ET
☎01222 452200   Fax 01222 452277
Contact *Aled Rhys-Jones*

Runs a large playscript lending library; holds an annual playwriting competition (see under **Prizes**); offers a script reading service (£10 per script) which usually takes three months from receipt of play to issue of reports. From plays submitted to the reading service, selected scripts are considered for publication of a short run (250–750 copies). Writers receive a percentage of the cover price on sales and a percentage of the performance fees.

East Anglian Writers
47 Christchurch Road, Norwich, Norfolk NR2 3NE
☎01603 455503   Fax 01603 455503
Chairman *Michael Pollard*

A group of professional writers living in Norfolk and Suffolk. Business and social meetings and informal contacts with regional publishers and other organisations interested in professional writing.

Edinburgh Bibliographical Society
New College Library, Mound Place, Edinburgh EH1 2LU
☎0131 650 8956   Fax 0131 650 6579
Honorary Secretary *Dr M. Simpson*
Subscription £7; £5 (Students)

FOUNDED 1890. Organises lectures on bibliographical topics and visits to libraries. *Publishes* a biennial journal called *Transactions*, which is free to members, and other occasional publications.

Educational Publishers Council
See **The Publishers Association**

Educational Television Association
37 Monkgate, York YO3 7PB
☎01904 639212   Fax 01904 639212
Administrator *Josie Key*

An umbrella organisation for individuals and organisations using television and other media for education and training. Annual awards scheme (video competition), and annual conferences. New members always welcome.

The English Association

University of Leicester, 128 Regent Road,
Leicester LE1 7PA
☎0116 2525927

Secretary *Helen Lucas*

FOUNDED 1906 to promote understanding and
appreciation of the English language and its literature. Activities include sponsoring a number
of publications and organising lectures and
conferences for teachers, plus annual sixth-
form conferences. Publications include *Year's
Work in Critical and Cultural Theory, English,
Use of English, Primary English, Essays and Studies.*

European Association for the Promotion of Poetry

See **Organisations of Interest to Poets**

Federation of Entertainment Unions

1 Highfield, Twyford, Nr Winchester,
Hampshire SO21 1QR
☎01962 713134

Secretary *Mrs S. Harris*

Consists of two committees: one concerned
with media; the other with live entertainment.
Represents the following unions: British
Actors' Equity Association; Broadcasting
Entertainment Cinematograph and Theatre
Union; Film Artistes' Association; Musicians'
Union; **National Union of Journalists**; **The
Writers' Guild of Great Britain**.

Federation of Worker Writers and Community Publishers (FWWCP)

PO Box 540, Burslem, Stoke on Trent,
Staffordshire ST6 6DR
☎01782 822327

Administrator/Coordinator *Tim Diggles*

The FWWCP is a federation of writing groups
who are committed to writing and publishing
based on working-class experience and creativity. The FWWCP is the membership's collective
national voice and has for some time been given
funding by **The Arts Council**. It was founded
in 1976 and comprises around 50 member
groups, each one with its own identity, reflecting
its community and membership, offering a
wealth of experience and support. The membership includes groups involved with community
history, poetry, adult learners, local publishing,
Black publishing, lesbian and gay writing,
women's writing as well as open writers' groups.
The main activities include a series of regional
training days to learn and share skills, a twice-
yearly magazine, a major annual festival of writing, networking between member organisations
and a manuscript reading service. The FWWCP
has published a number of anthologies and is
willing to work with other organisations on publishing projects. Membership is only open to
groups but individuals will be put in touch with
groups which can help them.

Foreign Press Association in London

11 Carlton House Terrace, London SW1Y 5AJ
☎0171 930 0445   Fax 171 925 0469

Contact *Davina Crole, Catherine Flury*
Membership (not incl. VAT) £88 p.a. (Full);
£81 (Associate Journalists); £98 (Associate
Non-Journalists)

FOUNDED 1888. Non-profit making service
association for foreign correspondents based in
London. Provides various press-related services.

The Gaelic Books Council (Comhairle nan Leabhraichean)

Department of Celtic, University of Glasgow,
Glasgow G12 8QQ
☎0141 330 5190

Chairman *Professor Donald MacAulay*
Chief Executive *Ian MacDonald*

FOUNDED 1968. Encourages and promotes
Gaelic publishing by offering grants to publishers and writers; providing editorial services;
retailing and cataloguing Gaelic books; and
answering enquiries related to them.

The Garden Writers' Guild

c/o Institute of Horticulture, 14/15 Belgrave
Square, London SW1X 8PS
☎0171 245 6943

Contact *Angela Clarke*
Subscription £15; (£10 to Institute of
Horticulture members)

FOUNDED 1990. Aims to revise the status and
standing of gardening communicators. Administers an annual Awards scheme. Operates a mailing service and organises press briefing days.

General Practitioner Writers' Association

Jasmine Cottage, Hampton Lucy, Warwick
CV35 8BE
☎01789 840509

Contact *Dr F. M. Hull*
Subscription £20 p.a.; £30 (Joint)

FOUNDED 1986 to promote and improve writing
activities within and for general practices. Open

to general practitioners, practice managers, nurses, etc. and professional journalists writing on anything pertaining to general practice. Very keen to develop input from interested parties who work mainly outside the profession. Regular workshops, discussions and a twice-yearly newsletter.

Guild of Agricultural Journalists

The Farmers Club, 3 Whitehall Court, London SW1A 2EL
☎0171 930 3557   Fax 0171 839 7864
Honorary General Secretary *Don Gomery*
Subscription £25 p.a.

FOUNDED 1944 to promote a high professional standard among journalists who specialise in agriculture, horticulture and allied subjects. Represents members' interests with representative bodies in the industry; provides a forum through meetings and social activities for members to meet eminent people in the industry; maintains contact with associations of agricultural journalists overseas; promotes schemes for the education of members and for the provision of suitable entrants into agricultural journalism.

Guild of British Newspaper Editors

See **The Newspaper Society**

Guild of Motoring Writers

30 The Cravens, Smallfield, Surrey RH6 9QS
☎01342 843294   Fax 01342 844093
General Secretary *Sharon Scott-Fairweather*

FOUNDED 1944. Represents members' interests and provides a forum for members to exchange information.

The Guild of Regional Film Writers

22 Gray Court, Gray Road, Sunderland, Tyne & Wear SR2 8DU
☎0191 565 0395
Secretary *Bernice Saltzer*
Subscription £30 p.a.

FOUNDED 1986. Aims to strengthen the voice of the regional film writers and broadcasters within the industry. Works with the publicists and attends screenings and press conferences with major stars. Members are invited to 'cinema days' and weekends. Would-be members have to supply cuttings/tapes to prove they work in the industry.

Humberside Writers' Association (HWA)

'Fairoaks', West Promenade, Driffield, East Yorkshire YO25 7TZ
☎01377 255542
Chairman *Glynn S. Russell*
Annual membership fee £2

FOUNDED 1987 by local writers, would-be writers and people interested in new writing who gathered together with the backing of their regional arts association to create a platform for local scribblers, published or otherwise. Organises and promotes writing-related events and workshops within the Humberside area. *Publishes* information about events, competitions, workshops, publications and any other news, local or national, about opportunities of interest to members. Regular meetings (last Wednesday of the month) to which writers, publishers and agents are invited; plus day schools, readings, newsletter and library/resource unit.

Independent Publishers Guild

25 Cambridge Road, Hampton, Middlesex TW12 2JL
☎0181 979 0250   Fax 0181 979 6393
Secretary *Yvonne Messenger*
Subscription approx. £75 p.a.

FOUNDED 1962. Membership open to independent publishers, packagers and suppliers, i.e. professionals in allied fields. Regular meetings, conferences, seminars, a bulletin and regional groups.

Independent Television Association

See **ITV Network Centre**

Independent Theatre Council

12 The Leathermarket, Weston Street, London SE1 3ER
☎0171 403 1727 Fax 0171 403 6698 (training)
Contact *Charlotte Jones*

The management association and representative body for small/middle-scale theatres (up to around 350 seats) and touring theatre companies. Negotiates contracts and has established standard agreements with Equity on behalf of all professionals working in the theatre. Negotiations with the **Theatre Writers' Union** and **The Writers' Guild** for a contractual agreement covering rights and fee structure for playwrights reached their conclusion in 1991. Copies of the minimum terms agreement can be obtained from The Writers' Guild. Recently produced a booklet giving guidance to writers on how to submit scripts to theatres and guidance to theatres on how to deal with them, called *A Practical Guide for Writers and Companies* (£3.50 plus p&p).

Institute of Translation and Interpreting
377 City Road, London EC1V 1NA
☎0171 713 7600   Fax 0171 713 7650

Membership is open to those who satisfy stringent admission criteria and can provide evidence of adequate professional translation or interpreting experience. Offers affiliation and student membership. Benefits include listing in an index which specifies the skills and languages of each member. *Publishes* a bi-monthly bulletin and a *Directory of Translators & Interpreters*, listing qualified members of both the ITI and the **Translators Association**.

International Cultural Desk
6 Belmont Crescent, Glasgow G12 8ES
☎0141 339 0090   Fax 0141 337 2271
Development Manager *Hilde Bollen*
Information Assistant *Anne Robb*
FOUNDED 1994. Aims to assist the Scottish cultural community to operate more effectively in an international context by providing timely and targeted information and advice. The Desk provides and disseminates information on funding sources, international opportunities and cultural policy development in Europe, and also assists with establishing contacts internationally. The Desk is not a funding agency.

Irish Book Publishers Association
See **Clé**

Irish Copyright Licensing Agency Ltd
19 Parnell Square, Dublin 1,
Republic of Ireland
☎00 353 1 872 9090
Fax 00 353 1 872 2035

FOUNDED 1992 by writers and publishers in Ireland to provide a scheme through which rights holders can give permission, and users of copyright material can obtain permission, to copy. Established with the support of and advice from **The Copyright Licensing Agency Ltd** of the UK, and has a reciprocal agreement with CLA for an exchange of repertoires.

Irish Writers' Union
19 Parnell Square, Dublin 1
Republic of Ireland
☎00 353 1 872 1302   Fax 00 353 1 872 6282
Secretary *Clairr O'Connor*
Administrator *Jacinta Douglas*
Subscription £20 p.a.
FOUNDED 1986 to promote the interests and protect the rights of writers in Ireland.

Isle of Man Authors
24 Laurys Avenue, Ramsey, Isle of Man
IM8 2HE
☎01624 815634
Secretary *Mrs Beryl Sandwell*
Subscription £7 p.a. (Free to members of the Society of Authors)
An association of writers living on the Isle of Man, which has links with **The Society of Authors**.

ITV Network Centre
200 Gray's Inn Road, London W1X 8HF
☎0171 843 8000   Fax 0171 843 8158

The ITV Network Centre, wholly owned by the ITV companies, independently commissions and schedules the television programmes which are shown across the ITV network. As a successor to the Independent Television Association, it also provides a range of services to the ITV companies where a common approach is required.

IVCA Writers' Group
Bolsover House, 5–6 Clipstone Street,
London W1P 8LD
☎0171 580 0962   Fax 0171 436 2606

The special interest group within the IVCA (International Visual Communication Association) which represents scriptwriters in the corporate and non-broadcast film and video industry.

The Library Association
7 Ridgmount Street, London WC1E 7AE
☎0171 636 7543   Fax 0171 436 7218
Chief Executive *Ross Shimmon*
The professional body for librarians and information managers, with 25,000 individual and institutional members. **Library Association Publishing** produces 25 new titles each year and has over 200 in print. The *LA Record* is the monthly magazine for members.

The Media Society

Church Cottage, East Rudham, Norfolk
PE31 8QZ
☎01485 528664   Fax 01485 528155
Contact *Rodney Bennett-England*
Subscription £25 p.a.; £10 entry fee
FOUNDED 1973. A registered charity which aims
to provide a forum for the exchange of knowledge and opinion between those in public and
political life, the professions, industry, education.
Meetings (about 6 a year in London) are usually
in the form of luncheons or dinners with invited
speakers. The society also acts as a 'think tank',
submitting reports/observations to royal commissions, select committees and review bodies.

Medical Journalists' Association

Old Barley Mow, 185 High Street, Stony
Stratford, Milton Keynes MK11 1AP
☎01908 564623
Chairman *Michael Jeffries*
Secretary *Gwen Yates*
Subscription £20 p.a.
FOUNDED 1966/7. Aims to improve the quality and practice of medical journalism and to
improve relationships and understanding
between medical journalists and the health and
medical professions. Regular meetings with
senior figures in medicine and medico politics;
teach-ins on particular subjects to help journalists with background information; weekend
symposium for an invited audience of members
and people with newsworthy stories in the
field; awards for medical journalists offered by
various commercial sponsors, plus MJA's own
award financed by members. *Publishes* a
detailed directory of members and freelances.

Medical Writers' Group

The Society of Authors, 84 Drayton Gardens,
London SW10 9SB
☎0171 373 6642   Fax 0171 373 5768
Contact *Jacqueline Granger-Taylor*
FOUNDED 1980. A specialist group within **The
Society of Authors** offering advice and help
to authors of medical books. Administers the
Royal Society of Medicine Prizes.

National Association of Writers in Education

PO Box 1, Sheriff Hutton, York YO6 7YU
☎01653 618429   Fax 01653 618429
Contact *Paul Munden*
Subscription £12 p.a.
FOUNDED 1991. Aims to promote the contribution of living writers to education and to
encourage both the practice and the critical
appreciation of creative writing. Has over 400
members. Organises national conferences and
training courses. *Publishes* a directory of writers
who work in schools, colleges and the community and a magazine, *Writing in Education*,
issued free to members three times per year.

National Campaign for the Arts

Francis House, Francis Street, London
SW1P 1DE
☎0171 828 4448   Fax 0171 931 9959
Director *Jennifer Edwards*
FOUNDED 1984 to represent the cultural sector
in Britain and to make sure that the problems
facing the arts are properly put to Government,
whether at local, national or international level.
The NCA is an independent body relying on
finance from its members. Involved in all issues
which affect the arts: public finance, education,
broadcasting and media affairs, the fight against
censorship, the monitoring of European legislation, the rights of artists, the place of the arts
on the public agenda and structures for supporting culture. Membership open to all arts
organisations (except government agencies)
and to individuals. Overseas Associate
Membership available.

National Poetry Foundation

See **Organisations of Interest to Poets**

The National Small Press Centre

Small Press Centre, Middlesex University,
All Saints Site, White Hart Lane,
London N17 8HR
☎0181 362 6058
Centre Director *John Nicholson*
The National Small Press Centre is committed
to small presses in Britain, providing a focal
point while actively raising the profile of small
presses. Formerly known as the Small Press
Group of Britain, it continues to raise public
awareness of small presses and provides a programme of events which not only takes place at
Middlesex University but also travels around
Britain and abroad. Promotes small presses as a
whole with exhibitions, talks, courses, workshops, conferences, regional small press fairs,
small press-athons, small press studies, etc. The
SPC Yearbook has been replaced by a series of
National Small Press Centre Handbooks which
give extensive information on presses and their
publications. *Publishes Small Press Listings* and
News From the Centre (see under **Magazines**).

National Union of Journalists

Acorn House, 314 Gray's Inn Road, London
WC1X 8DP
☎0171 278 7916   Fax 0171 837 8143

General Secretary *John Foster*
Subscription £135 p.a. (Freelance) or 1% of
annual income if lower

Represents journalists in all sectors of publishing, print and broadcast. Responsible for wages and conditions agreements which apply across the industry. Provides advice and representation for its members, as well as administering unemployment and other benefits. *Publishes* various guides and magazines: *Freelance Directory, Fees Guide, The Journalist* and *The Freelance* (see **Magazines**).

New Playwrights Trust

Interchange Studios, 15 Dalby Street,
London NW5 3NQ
☎0171 284 2818   Fax 0171 482 5292

Contact *Ben Payne*
Subscription (information on rates available
by post)

New Playwrights Trust is the national research and development organisation for writing for all forms of live and recorded performance. *Publishes* a range of information pertinent to writers on all aspects of development and production in the form of pamphlets, and a six-weekly journal which also includes articles and interviews on aesthetic and practical issues. NPT also runs a script reading service and a link service between writers and producers, organises seminars and conducts research projects. The latter includes research into the use of bilingual techniques in playwriting (*Two Tongues*), documentation of training programmes for writers (*Black Theatre Co-operative*) and an investigation of the relationship between live art and writing *Writing Live*.

New Producers Alliance (NPA)

1st Floor, 2 Lexington Street, Soho,
London W1R 3HS
☎0171 437 5624   Fax 0171 437 3614

Contact *Jackie Elliman*

FOUNDED 1992. Aims to encourage the production of commercial feature films for an international audience and to educate and inform feature film producers in the UK. The NPA does not produce films so please do not send scripts or treatments.

The New SF Alliance (NSFA)

c/o BBR Magazine, PO Box 625, Sheffield,
South Yorkshire S1 3GY
Contact *Chris Reed*

FOUNDED 1989. Committed to supporting the work of new writers and artists by promoting independent and small press publications worldwide. 'Help with finding the right market for your material by providing a mail-order service which allows you to sample magazines, and various publications including *BBR* magazine and *Scavenger's Newsletter*, which features the latest market news and tips.'

Newspaper Conference

See **The Newspaper Society**

The Newspaper Society

Bloomsbury House, 74–77 Great Russell
Street, London WC1B 3DA
☎0171 636 7014   Fax 0171 631 5119

Director *Dugal Nisbet-Smith*
Young Newspaper Executives'
  Association *Joanne Butcher*

The association of publishers of the regional and local Press, representing 1300 regional daily and weekly, paid and free, newspaper titles in the UK. The Newspaper Conference is an organisation within the Society for London editors and representatives of regional newspapers. Bloomsbury House is also home to the Guild of British Newspaper Editors and to the Young Newspaper Executives' Association.

Outdoor Writers Guild

27 Camwood, Clayton Green, Bamber
Bridge, Preston, Lancashire PR5 8LA
☎01772 321243

Honorary Secretary *Terry Marsh*
Subscription £20 p.a.

FOUNDED 1980 to promote a high professional standard among writers who specialise in outdoor activities; to represent members' interests with representatives of the outdoor leisure industry; to circulate members with news of writing opportunities. Presents awards for excellence to members.

PACT (Producers Alliance for Cinema and Television)

Gordon House, Greencoat Place, London
SW1P 1PH
☎0171 233 6000   Fax 0171 233 8935

Chief Executive *John Woodward*
Membership Officer *Susan Finlayson-Sitch*

FOUNDED 1992. PACT is the trade association of the UK independent television and feature film production sector and is a key contact point for foreign producers seeking British co-production, co-finance partners and distributors. Works for producers in the industry at every level and operates a members' regional network throughout the UK with a divisional office in Scotland. Membership services include: a dedicated industrial relations unit; discounted legal advice; a varied calendar of events; business advice; representation at international film and television markets; a comprehensive research programme; various publications: a monthly magazine, an annual members' directory; affiliation with European and international producers' organisations; extensive information and production advice. Lobbies actively with broadcasters, financiers and governments to ensure that the producer's voice is heard and understood in Britain and Europe on all matters affecting the film and television industry.

PEN

7 Dilke Street, London SW3 4JE
☎0171 352 6303   Fax 0171 351 0220
General Secretary Gilly Vincent
Membership £35 (London/Overseas);
    £30 (members living over 50 miles from London)

English PEN is part of International PEN, a worldwide association of writers which fights for freedom of expression and speaks out for writers who are imprisoned or harassed for having criticised their governments, or for publishing other unpopular views. FOUNDED in London in 1921, International PEN now consists of 124 centres in 90 countries. PEN originally stood for poets, essayists and novelists, but membership is now also open to published playwrights, editors, translators and journalists. A programme of talks and discussions is supplemented by the publication of a twice-yearly magazine.

The Penman Club

185 Daws Heath Road, Benfleet,
Essex SS7 2TF
☎01702 557431

Subscription £15 in the first year;
    £8.25 thereafter

FOUNDED 1950. Writers' society offering criticism of members' work and general advice. Send s.a.e. for prospectus to the General Secretary.

Performing Right Society

29–33 Berners Street, London W1P 4AA
☎0171 580 5544   Fax 0171 631 4138

Collects and distributes royalties arising from the performance and broadcast of copyright music on behalf of its composer, lyricist and music publisher members and members of affiliated societies worldwide.

Periodical Publishers Association (PPA)

Imperial House, 15–19 Kingsway, London WC2B 6UN
☎0171 379 6268   Fax 0171 379 5661
Contact Nicholas Mazur

FOUNDED 1913 to promote and protect the interests of magazine publishers in the UK.

The Personal Managers' Association Ltd

1 Summer Road, East Molesey, Surrey KT8 9LX
☎0181 398 9796

Co-chairs Jane Annakin, Marc Berlin, David
    Wilkinson
Secretary Angela Adler
Subscription £200 p.a.

An association of artists' and dramatists' agents (membership not open to individuals). Monthly meetings for exchange of information and discussion. Maintains a code of conduct and acts as a lobby when necessary. Applicants screened. A high proportion of play agents are members of the PMA.

Player–Playwrights

9 Hillfield Park, London N10 3QT
☎0181 883 0371

President Jack Rosenthal
Contact Peter Thompson
Subscription £5 p.a., plus £1 per attendance

FOUNDED 1948. A society for newcomers to play and television writing. Membership includes established writers and actors. Meets on Monday evenings; members' scripts are read or performed and a discussion follows.

Playwrights' Workshop

22 Brown Street, Altrincham, Cheshire WA14 2EU
☎0161 928 3095

Honorary Secretary Robert Coupland
Subscription £2 p.a.

FOUNDED 1949. The Society meets monthly in Manchester and aims to support playwrights of all kinds who are interested in furthering their work. Guest speakers on all aspects of the theatre. Past members include Michael Dines and Harry Kershaw. Provides reading service with report by private reader (reasonable terms).

Poetry Association of Scotland
See **Organisations of Interest to Poets**

Poetry Book Society
See **Organisations of Interest to Poets**

Poetry Ireland
See **Organisations of Interest to Poets**

The Poetry Society
See **Organisations of Interest to Poets**

Private Libraries Association
16 Brampton Grove, Kenton, Harrow, Middlesex HA3 8LG
☎0181 907 6802   Fax 0181 907 6802
Honorary Secretary *Frank Broomhead*
Membership £25 p.a.

FOUNDED 1956. An international society of book collectors. The Association's objectives are to promote and encourage the awareness of the benefits of book ownership, and the study of books, their production, and ownership; to publish works concerned with this, particularly those which are not commercially profitable, to hold meetings at which papers on cognate subjects can be read and discussed. Lectures and exhibitions are open to non-members.

The Publishers Association
19 Bedford Square, London WC1B 3HJ
☎0171 580 6321-5/580 7761/323 1548
Fax 0171 636 5375
Chief Executive *Clive Bradley*

The national UK trade association with around 300 member companies in the industry. Very much a trade body representing the industry to Government and the European Commission, and providing services to publishers. *Publishes* the *Directory of Publishing* in association with **Cassell**. Also home of The Book Development Council (the PA's International Division), the Educational Publishers Council (school books) and the Council of Academic and Professional Publishers.

Publishers Licensing Society Ltd
90 Tottenham Court Road, London W1P 9HE
☎0171 436 5931   Fax 0171 436 3986
Manager *Caroline Elmslie*

FOUNDED 1981 to exercise and enforce on behalf of publishers the rights of copyright and other rights of a similar nature; to authorise the granting of licences for the making of reprographic copies; and to receive and distribute to the relevant publisher and copyright proprietors the sums accruing from such licensed use.

Publishers Publicity Circle
48 Crabtree Lane, London SW6 6LW
☎0171 385 3708   Fax 0171 385 3708
Contact *Christina Thomas*

Enables book publicists from both publishing houses and freelance PR agencies to meet and share information regularly. Meetings are held monthly in central London which provide a forum for press journalists, television and radio researchers and producers to meet publicists collectively. A directory of the PPC membership is published each year and distributed to over 2000 media contacts.

The Romantic Novelists' Association
35 Ruddlesway, Windsor, Berkshire SL4 5SF
☎01753 867100
Secretary *Joyce Bell*
Subscription £20 p.a.

Membership is open to published writers of romantic novels, or two or more full-length serials. Associate membership is open to publishers, editors, literary agents, booksellers, librarians and others having a close connection with novel writing and publishing. Meetings are held in London and guest speakers are often invited. *RNA News* is published quarterly and issued free to members. The Association makes two annual awards. **The Major Award** for the Romantic Novel of the Year, and **The New Writers Award**

Royal Society of Literature
1 Hyde Park Gardens, London W2 2LT
☎0171 723 5104   Fax 0171 402 0199
President *Lord Jenkins of Hillhead*
Subscription £25 p.a.

FOUNDED 1823. Membership by application to the Secretary. Fellowships are conferred by the Society on the proposal of two Fellows. Membership benefits include journal *Letters*, lectures, discussion meetings and poetry readings in the Society's rooms. Lecturers have included Alan Ayckbourn, Victoria Glendinning, Denis Healey, Vikram Seth and Muriel Spark. Presents the **W. H. Heinemann Prize** and the **Winifred Holtby Memorial Prize**.

Royal Television Society

Holborn Hall, 100 Gray's Inn Road,
London WC1X 8AL
☎0171 430 1000   Fax 0171 430 0924

Subscription £60; £72 surface/£90 airmail
(Overseas)

FOUNDED 1927. Covers all disciplines involved in the television industry. Provides a forum for debate and conferences on technical, social and cultural aspects of the medium. Presents various awards including journalism, programmes, technology, design and commericals. *Publishes Television Magazine* eight times a year for members and subscribers.

Science Fiction Foundation

c/o Liverpool University Library,
PO Box 123, Liverpool L69 3DA
☎0151 794 2733/2696   Fax 0151 794 2681

The SFF, a national academic body for the furtherance of science fiction studies, publishes a thrice-yearly magazine, *Foundation* (see under **Magazines**), which features academic articles and reviews of new fiction. It also has a reference library (see under **Library Services**), now housed at Liverpool University.

Scottsh Library Association

Motherwell Business Centre, Coursington Road, Motherwell, Strathclyde ML1 1PW
☎01698 252526   Fax 01698 252057

Director *Robert Craig*

FOUNDED 1908 to bring together everyone engaged in or interested in library work in Scotland. The Association has over 2300 members, covering all aspects of library and information work. Its main aims are the promotion of library services and the qualifications and status of librarians.

Scottish Newspaper Publishers' Association

48 Palmerston Place, Edinburgh EH12 5DE
☎0131 220 4353   Fax 0131 220 4344

Director *Mr J. B. Raeburn*

FOUNDED around 1905. The representative body for the publishers of paid-for weekly and associated free newspapers in Scotland. Represents the interests of the industry to Government, public and other bodies and provides a range of services including industrial relations, education and training, and advertising. It is an active supporter of the Press Complaints Commission.

Scottish Print Employers' Federation

48 Palmerston Place, Edinburgh EH12 5DE
☎0131 220 4353   Fax 0131 220 4344

Director *Mr J. B. Raeburn*

FOUNDED 1910. Employers' organisation and trade association for the Scottish printing industry. Represents the interests of the industry to Government, public and other bodies and provides a range of services including industrial relations. Negotiates a national wages and conditions agreement with the Graphical, Paper and Media Union, as well as education, training and commercial activities. The Federation is a member of Intergraf, the international confederation for employers' associations in the printing industry. In this capacity its views are channelled on the increasing number of matters affecting print businesses emanating from the European Union.

The Scottish Publishers Association

Scottish Book Centre, Fountainbridge Library,
137 Dundee Street, Edinburgh EH11 1BG
☎0131 228 6866   Fax 0131 228 3220

Director *Lorraine Fannin*
Administrator *Neil Gowans*

The Association represents nearly 70 Scottish publishers, from multinationals to very small presses, in a number of capacities, but primarily in the cooperative promotion and marketing of their books. The SPA also acts as an information and advice centre for both the trade and general public. *Publishes* seasonal catalogues, membership lists, a directory of publishing in Scotland and regular newsletters. Represents members at international book fairs; provides opportunities for publishers' training; carries out market research; and encourages export initiatives.

'Sean Dorman' Manuscript Society

Cherry Trees, Crosemere Road, Cockshutt,
Ellesmere, Shropshire SY12 0JP
☎01939 270293

Director *Mary Driver*
Subscription £6.50 p.a.

FOUNDED 1957. The Society provides mutual help among writers and aspiring writers in England, Wales and Scotland. By means of circulating manuscript parcels, members receive constructive criticism of their own work and read and comment on the work of others. Each

'Circulator' has up to nine participants and members' contributions may be in any medium: short stories, chapters of a novel, poetry, magazine articles etc. Members may join two such circulators if they wish. Each circulator has a technical section and a letters section in which friendly communication between members is encouraged, and all are of a general nature apart from one, specialising in manuscripts for the Christian market. Full details and application forms available on receipt of a s.a.e.

Small Press Group of Great Britain
See **National Small Press Centre**

Society for Strip Illustration
See **Comics Creators Guild**

The Society of Authors in Scotland
24 March Hall Crescent, Edinburgh EH16 5HL
☎0131 667 5230
Secretary *Alanna Knight*

The Scottish branch of **The Society of Authors**, which organises business meetings and social events in Scotland.

The Society of Authors
84 Drayton Gardens, London SW10 9SB
☎0171 373 6642　　　　Fax 0171 373 5768
General Secretary *Mark Le Fanu*
Subscription £60/65 p.a.

FOUNDED 1884. The Society of Authors is an independent trade union with some 5500 members. It advises on negotiations with publishers, broadcasting organisations, theatre managers and film companies; takes up complaints and pursues legal action for breach of contract, copyright infringement, etc. Together with **The Writers' Guild**, the Society has played a major role in advancing the Minimum Terms Agreement for authors. Among the Society's publications are *The Author* (a quarterly journal), *The Electronic Author* (twice yearly) and the *Quick Guides* series to various aspects of writing (all free of charge to members). Other services include emergency funds for writers and various special discounts. There are groups within the Society for scriptwriters, children's writers and illustrators, educational writers, medical writers and translators. Authors under 35, who are not yet earning a significant income from their writing, may apply for membership at a lower subscrip-

tion of £47. Contact the Society for a free booklet giving further information.

Society of Civil Service Authors
4 Top Street, Wing, Nr Oakham, Rutland LE15 8SE
Membership Secretary *Mrs Joan Hykin*
Subscription £12 p.a.

FOUNDED 1935. Aims to encourage authorship by present and past members of the Civil Service and to provide opportunities for social and cultural relationships between civil servants who are authors or who aspire to be authors. Annual competitions, open to members only, are held for short stories, poetry, sonnets, travel articles, humour, etc. Members receive *The Civil Service Author*, a bi-monthly magazine. Occasional meetings in London, two weekends outside London.

Society of Freelance Editors and Proofreaders (SFEP)
c/o SFEP Office, 38 Rochester Road, London NW1 9JJ
☎0171 813 3113
Chair *Michèle Clarke*
Vice-chair *Eric Smith*
Secretary *Valerie Elliston*
Subscription £27.50 p.a. (Individuals); £7.50 (Students); £17.50 (Joint); £70 or £95 (Corporate, depending on size of company); plus £10 registration fee for new members

FOUNDED 1988 in response to the growing number of freelance editors and their increasing importance to the publishing industry. Aims to promote high editorial standards by disseminating information and through advice and training, and to achieve recognition of the professional status of its members. The Society also supports moves towards recognised standards of training and qualifications, and is currently putting in place accredited and registered membership of SFEP.

Society of Indexers
38 Rochester Road, London NW1 9JJ
☎0171 916 7809
Secretary *Claire Troughton*
Subscription £25 p.a.; £30 (Institutions)

FOUNDED 1957. Publishes *The Indexer* (bi-annual, April and October) and a quarterly newsletter. Issues an annual list of members and the *(IA) Indexers Available*, which lists members and their subject expertise. In addition the Society runs an open-learning course entitled

Training in Indexing and recommends rates of pay (currently £11 per hour).

Society of Picture Researchers & Editors (SPRED)

BM Box 259, London WC1N 3XX
☎0171 404 5011

Subscription Members: Intermediate £30; Full £40. Magazine only: £22.50 per year quarterly

FOUNDED 1977 as a professional body for picture researchers and picture editors. Not a trade union but a society for those who wish to share problems and exchange information on all aspects dealing with illustration. The Society's main aims are to promote the recognition of picture research as a profession; to promote and maintain professional standards; to bring together those involved in the research and publication of visual material and provide a forum for the exchange of information; to encourage the use of trained researchers throughout publishing and other media; and to provide guidance to its members. Monthly meetings and a quarterly magazine.

Society of Sussex Authors

Bookends, Lewes Road, Horsted Keynes, Haywards Heath, West Sussex RH17 7DP
☎01825 790755   Fax 01825 790755

Contact *Michael Legat*
Subscription £8 p.a.

FOUNDED 1968 to promote the interests of its members and of literature, particularly within the Sussex area. Regular meetings and exchange of information; plus social events. Membership restricted to writers who live in Sussex and who have had at least one book commercially published. Meetings are held six times a year in Lewes.

Society of Women Writers and Journalists

110 Whitehall Road, London E4 6DW
☎0181 529 0886

Honorary Secretary *Jean Hawkes*
Subscription £21 (Country); £18 (Regional); £12 (Overseas). £10 joining fee

FOUNDED 1894. The first of its kind to be run as an association of women engaged in journalism. Aims to encourage literary achievement, uphold professional standards, and establish social contacts with other writers. Lectures given at monthly lunchtime meetings. Offers advice to members and has regular seminars, etc. *Publishes* a quarterly society journal, *The Woman Journalist*.

Society of Young Publishers

12 Dyott Street, London WC1A 1DF
Subscription £20 p.a.

Provides facilities whereby members can increase their knowledge and widen their experience of all aspects of publishing. Open to those in related occupations, with associate membership available for over-35s. *Publishes* a monthly newsletter called *Inprint* and holds meetings on the last Wednesday of each month at **The Publishers Association**.

The South and Mid-Wales Association of Writers (S.A.M.W.A.W)

c/o I.M.C. Consulting Group, Denham House, Lambourne Crescent, Cardiff CF4 5ZW
☎01222 761170   Fax 01222 761304

Contact *Julian Rosser*
Subscription £7 (Single); £12 (Joint)

FOUNDED 1971 to foster the art and craft of writing in all its forms. Provides a common meeting ground for writers, critics, editors, adjudicators from all over the UK and abroad. Organises an annual residential weekend conference and a day seminar in May and October respectively. Holds competitions – two for members only and two which are open to the public – **The Gooding Award for Short Story Writing** and The Oriel Competition for Poetry.

South Bank Board Literature Office

Artistic Projects Department, Royal Festival Hall, South Bank Centre, London SE1 8XX
☎0171 921 0907   Fax 0171 928 2049

Head of Literature *Antonia Byatt*

The South Bank presents a year-round literature programme covering all aspects of writing. Literature events are now programmed in the Purcell Room, the Queen Elizabeth Hall, and in the Voice Box. The South Bank also has a Writer-in-Residence.

South Eastern Writers' Association

47 Sunningdale Avenue, Leigh-on-Sea, Essex SS9 1JY
☎01702 77083   Fax 01702 77083

President *Marion Hough*

FOUNDED 1989 to bring together writers, both experienced and novice, in an informative but informal atmosphere. A non-profit making organisation, the Association holds a weekend residential conference in March each year and a one-day seminar in Autumn at the Colchester Mill Hotel. Recent guest speakers: Simon Brett, Jonathan Gash, George Layton, Maureen Lipman, Terry Pratchett, Jack Rosenthal.

Sports Writers' Association of Great Britain

c/o Sports Council Press Office, 16 Upper Woburn Place, London WC1H 0QP
☎0171 387 9415   Fax 0171 383 0273
Secretary *Mary Fitzhenry*
Subscription £15 p.a.

FOUNDED 1948 to promote and maintain a high professional standard among journalists who specialise in sport in all its branches and to serve members' interests.

Sussex Playwrights' Club

2 Princes Avenue, Hove, East Sussex BN3 4GD
☎01273 734985
Secretary *Mrs Constance Cox*
Subscription £5 p.a.

FOUNDED 1935. Aims to encourage the writing of plays for stage, radio and TV by giving monthly dramatic readings of members' work by experienced actors, mainly from local drama groups. Gives constructively criticised suggestions as to how work might be improved, and suggests possible marketing. Membership is not confined to writers but to all who are interested in theatre in all its forms, and all members are invited to take part in such discussions. Guests are always welcome at a nominal 50p. Meetings held at New Venture Theatre, Bedford Place, Brighton, East Sussex.

Television History Centre

27 Old Gloucester Street, Queen Square, London WC1N 3XX
☎0171 405 6627   Fax 0171 242 1426
Contact *Sharon Goulds, Marilyn Wheatcroft*

Home of the television history workshop. Provides a range of resources (including a catalogue of videos available for sale or hire), materials, information and assistance to help people record their own history.

Theatre Writers' Union

c/o The Actors' Centre, 1A Tower Street, London WC2H 9ND
☎0181 673 6636
Chair *David Edgar*
Administrator *Suzy Gilmour*

Formed in the mid 1970s. Specialises in the concerns of all who write for theatre, of whatever kind. Has national branch network. Actively seeks a membership which represents the diversity of playwriting today. Many members are also active in other media: radio, TV, film and video. Responsible for the very first standard agreements on minimum pay and conditions for playwrights working in British theatre. Any playwright who has written a play is eligible to join. Annual subscription is related to income from playwriting. Members may receive legal and professional advice, copies of standard contracts and regular newsletters. As affiliates to the General Federation of Trade Unions, TWU has access to their legal and education services.

The Translators Association

84 Drayton Gardens, London SW10 9SB
☎0171 373 6642   Fax 0171 373 5768
Contact *Gordon Fielden*

FOUNDED 1958 as a subsidiary group within **The Society of Authors** to deal exclusively with the special problems of literary translators into the English language. Members are entitled to all the benefits and services of the parent Society without extra charge. The Association offers them free legal and general advice and assistance on all matters relating to translators' work, including the vetting of contracts and information about improvements in fees. Membership is normally confined to translators who have had their work published in volume or serial form or produced in this country for stage, television or radio. Translators of technical work for industrial firms or government departments are in certain cases admitted to membership if their work, though not on general sale, is published by the organisation commissioning the work.

The Union of Welsh Writers

Botacho Wyn, Nefyn, Pwllheli, Gwynedd LL53 6HA
Secretary *M. P. Jones*
Membership £5 p.a.

FOUNDED 1974. Aims to provide a comprehensive service and support for members: mainly authors who publish a wide variety of material written predominantly in Welsh. Members include novelists, poets, short story writers and children's authors.

Ver Poets

Haycroft, 61–63 Chiswell Green Lane, St Albans, Hertfordshire AL2 3AL
☎01727 867005
Chairman *Ray Badman*
Editor/Organiser *May Badman*

Membership £10 p.a.; £12.50 or US$25
(Overseas)

FOUNDED 1966 to promote poetry and to help poets. Holds meetings in St Albans; runs a poetry bookstall for members' books and publications from other groups; publishes members' work in magazines; and organises poetry competitions, including its own **Ver Poets Open**. Gives help and advice whenever they are sought; and makes information available to members about other poetry groups, events and opportunities for publication.

Voice of the Listener and Viewer

101 Kings Drive, Gravesend, Kent DA12 5BQ
☎01474 352835

Voluntary association and consumer body speaking for viewers and listeners on all broadcasting issues.

Welsh Academy

3rd Floor, Mount Stuart House, Mount Stuart Square, Cardiff CF1 6DQ
☎01222 492025   Fax 01222 492930
Director *Kevin Thomas*

FOUNDED 1968. The Welsh Academy is the English Language section of **Yr Academi Gymreig**, the national society of Welsh writers. The Academy exists to promote English literature in Wales. Organises readings, an annual conference (usually held in May) and literary events such as the **Cardiff Literature Festival**. There are three tiers of membership: Fellow (max. 12, an honorary position offered to those who have made an outstanding contribution to the literature of Wales over a number of years); Member (open to all who are deemed to have made a contribution to the literature of Wales whether writers, editors or critics); Associate Member (open to all who are interested in the Academy's work). Publications include: *BWA*, the Academy's newsletter; *The Oxford Companion to the Literature of Wales*; *Writing in Wales*; *The Literature of Wales in Secondary Schools; How the Earth Was Formed Quiz And Other Poems and Stories by Children; The New Welsh Review; A Bibliography of Anglo-Welsh Literature; Interweave*.

Welsh Books Council (Cyngor Llyfrau Cymraeg)

Castell Brychan, Aberystwyth, Dyfed SY23 2JB
☎01970 624151   Fax 01970 625385
Director *Gwerfyl Pierce Jones*
Head of Editorial Department *Dewi Morris Jones*

FOUNDED 1961 to stimulate interest in Welsh literature and to support authors. The Council distributes the government grant for Welsh language publications and promotes and fosters all aspects of both Welsh and Welsh interest book production. Its Editorial, Design, Marketing and Children's Books departments and wholesale distribution centre offer central services to publishers in Wales. Writers in Welsh and English are welcome to approach the Editorial Department for advice on how to get their manuscripts published. *Books in Wales/Llais Llyfrau* is a quarterly publication which includes book lists, reviews and articles on various aspects of Welsh writing and publishing (see under **Magazines**).

Welsh Union of Writers

13 Richmond Road, Roath, Cardiff CF2 3AQ
Secretary *John Harrison*
Subscription £10 p.a.; £5 joining fee

FOUNDED 1982. Independent union. Membership by application to persons born or working in Wales with at least one publication in a quality journal or other outlet. Lobbies for writing in Wales, represents members in disputes; annual conference and occasional events and publications.

West Country Writers' Association

Malvern View, Garway Hill, Hereford, Hereford & Worcester HR2 8EZ
☎01981 580495
President *Christopher Fry*
Honorary Secretary *Mrs Anne Double*
Subscription £10 p.a.

FOUNDED 1951 in the interest of published authors with an interest in the West Country. Meets to discuss news and views and to listen to talks. Conference and newsletters.

Women in Publishing

c/o The Bookseller, 12 Dyott Street, London WC1A 1DF
Contact *Information Officer*
Membership £15 p.a. (Individuals); £10 (Unwaged); £20 (if paid for by company)

Aims to promote the status of women working within the publishing industry and related trades, to encourage networking, and to provide training for career and personal development. Meetings held on the second Wednesday of the month at **The Publishers Association** (see entry for address) at 6.30 pm. Monthly newsletter.

Women Writers Network (WWN)
23 Prospect Road, London NW2 2JU
☎0171 794 5861
Membership Secretary *Cathy Smith*
Subscription £25 p.a.; £30 p.a. (Overseas)
FOUNDED 1985. Provides a forum for the exchange of information, support, career and networking opportunities for working women writers. Meetings, seminars, excursions, newsletter and directory. Branches in the north east and north west of England; details from the Membership Secretary at the above address.

Writers in Oxford
Cauldwell's Castle, Folly Bridge, Oxford OX1 4LB
☎01865 727254
Contact *Matthew Kneale*
Subscription £15 p.a.
FOUNDED 1992. Open to published authors, playwrights, poets and journalists. Linked to **The Society of Authors** but organised locally. Arranges a programme of meetings, seminars and functions. *Publishes* quarterly newsletter, *The Oxford Writer*.

The Writers' Guild of Great Britain
430 Edgware Road, London W2 1EH
☎0171 723 8074   Fax 0171 706 2413
General Secretary *Alison V. Gray*
Annual subscription 1% of that part of the author's income earned in the areas in which the Guild operates, with a basic subscription of £70 and a maximum of £920
FOUNDED 1959. The Writers' Guild is the writers' trade union, affiliated to the TUC. It represents writers in film, radio, television, theatre and publishing. The Guild has negotiated agreements on which writers' contracts are based with the BBC, Independent Television companies, and **PACT** (the Producers' Alliance for Cinema and Television). Those agreements are regularly renegotiated, both in terms of finance and conditions.

In 1979, together with the **Theatre Writers' Union**, the Guild negotiated the first ever industrial agreement for theatre writers, the TNC Agreement which covers the Royal National Theatre, the RSC, and the English Stage Company. Further agreements have been negotiated with the **Theatre Management Association** which covers regional theatre and the **Independent Theatre Council**, the organisation which covers small theatres and the Fringe.

The Guild initiated a campaign over ten years ago which achieved the first ever publishing agreement for writers with the publisher W. H. Allen. Jointly with **The Society of Authors**, that campaign has continued and each year sees new agreements with more publishers. Perhaps the most important breakthrough came with **Penguin** on 20 July 1990. The Guild now also has agreements covering **HarperCollins** and the **Random House Group**.

The Guild regularly provides individual help and advice to members on contracts, conditions of work, and matters which affect a member's life as a professional writer. Members are given the opportunity of meeting at craft meetings, which are held on a regular basis throughout the year. Membership is by a points system. One major piece of work (a full-length book, an hour-long television or radio play, a feature film, etc.) entitles the author to full membership; writers who do not qualify for Full Membership may qualify for Temporary Membership; they currently pay the basic subscription only of £70.

Yachting Journalists' Association
3 Friar's Lane, Maldon, Essex CM9 6AG
☎01245 223189   Fax 01245 223189
Honorary Secretary *Peter Cook*
Subscription £30 p.a.
To further the interest of yachting, sail and power, and to provide support and assistance to journalists in the field. A handbook listing members' details available free of charge.

Young Newspaper Executives' Association
See **The Newspaper Society**

Yr Academi Gymreig
3rd Floor, Mount Stuart House, Mount Stuart Square, Cardiff CF1 6DQ
☎01222 492064   Fax 01222 492930
Director *Dafydd Rogers*
FOUNDED 1959. National society of Welsh writers. Aims to encourage writing in Welsh. *Publishes Taliesin*, plus books on Welsh literature and an English/Welsh dictionary. Organises readings, conferences and general literary events. Various tiers of membership available.

Rules of the Game – Libel

The standard definition of libel is the publication of a statement which tends to lower a person's reputation in the estimation of 'right thinking members of society'. Twenty years ago the Faulkes Committee on Defamation suggested minimising the value judgement implied by 'right thinking' by relying instead on the estimation of 'reasonable people'. But the arcane form of words survives, presumably, on the assumption that in our muddled world and despite all contrary evidence, 'right thinking' is still an identifiable attribute.

The distinction between libel and slander is explained by Peter Marsh, a barrister specialising in defamation.

'Whether or not the publication is in a permanent form determines whether it is libel or slander. Films, broadcasting and matter published in newspapers falls into the category of libel. On the other hand, if I gossip with work colleagues about a person's sexual proclivities in derogatory terms that amounts to slander.'

Another important difference is that in libel there is no obligation to prove that any actual damage as opposed to hurt to reputation has been suffered while in slander cases it is necessary to show that the plaintiff has suffered material damage.

It may be that the defendant in a libel case did not intend harm. No matter. All that the plaintiff need show is that the offending statement would be understood by right thinking people to refer to him. There is a clear warning here for fiction writers not to venture too close to real life. It may seem a neat idea to introduce friends and neighbours into a story – it is so much easier to describe people you know – but if one of them is cast as a villain and recognises himself, albeit in an unlikely role, then a solicitor's letter will surely follow.

Names, too, can be a trap for the unwary. If a novel features a corrupt member of parliament, a financier who fiddles his tax or a vicar with an obsessive interest in choirboys, it is as well to check that the names given to these characters do not correspond to flesh and blood people. Often, the more unlikely the name, the greater the risk. You may think you are on safe ground when you relate the dubious practices of the Reverend Harbottle Tiddles Grimston, but Sod's Law dictates that as soon as the book is in the shops, a curious coincidence will be drawn to your attention. The problem is accentuated by the sure knowledge that much of what appears in novels does relate to real life, even if the writer is not immediately aware of it. It is extraordinary what can be dredged up from the subconscious. One well-known writer recalls the awful embarrassment of realising, too late, that the name of the leading protagonist in his steaming sex saga happened to be that of his fiancée. He avoided a libel action but she sent back his engagement ring.

A precaution Mark Le Fanu of the **Society of Authors** urges on all fiction writers is to check with the relevant directories before picking characters' names.

'For example, if the author has invented a corrupt landlord living in Paddington he should look up the invented name in the London telephone directory and substitute a safe one, if there is someone of that name with a Paddington telephone number. If one of the characters is a bishop of doubtful sanctity, the author should look in *Crockford's* to make sure that there is no bishop of that name.'

Paul Watkins has cause to regret not checking the list of Old Etonians. His novel *Stand Up Before Your God* based on his schooldays at Eton featured an undesirable called Wilbraham. It was a name he had picked at random from a New York telephone directory. Unfortunately, it happened also to be the name of an Eton contemporary. Neither the author nor the real Wilbraham could remember ever having met. It was an unfortunate misunderstanding which nonetheless ended with Paul Watkins and his publisher **Faber** paying damages in the region of £15,000.

In 1956 an actress, June Sylvaine, sued the publishers of Antonia White's novel *The Sugar House* because it included a character called June Sylvaine, who was described as 'fat'. Both sides agreed that the coincidence of names was accidental, and the real Sylvaine admitted that it had done her no discernible harm. Nevertheless, she was awarded damages.

Since one cannot libel the dead, a valuable and safe source of names is *Who Was Who?*

Biographers of contemporary, or near-contemporary figures tread the narrowest line. To state a known fact about an individual, that he behaved deviously or dishonestly for example, may raise questions about his friends, associates or family which they feel bound to contest.

A film star who was famous for his stories of licentious adventures, usually with the wives of other film stars, was never so much as challenged by his victims. But when he died and his biographer got to work, the writs began to fly. In such cases the best hope for the writer is the plaintiff's awareness that publicity generated by his action will cause him yet more pain. As Dr Johnson reminds us, 'Few attacks either of ridicule or invective make much noise but with the help of those they provoke'.

Where libel has been committed unintentionally or 'innocently', it is possible to alleviate the consequences by an 'offer to make amends'. This usually involves a published apology and a settlement of costs. Otherwise, unless it can be established that a statement, however defamatory, is true in substance and fact (a difficult trick to pull off), the defence against libel will probably turn on the assertion that the words complained of are fair comment on a matter of public interest. The defence will fail if the defendant is shown to have been activated by malice or if the facts on which he based the comment are shown to be untrue.

This is where the wheel turns full circle because writers, who are themselves inclined to rush to law when they feel aggrieved, often hear the 'fair comment' defence from their critics. The perimeters of 'fair comment' are wide enough to protect, in essence, the principles of free speech, so that, according to precedent, 'However wrong the opinion expressed may be in point of truth, or however prejudiced the writer, it may still be within the prescribed limit'. In other words, it is one thing to argue that a person's *views* are lunatic but quite another to assert that *he* is a lunatic.

The scope of 'fair comment' was defined recently when a libel action against a reviewer in the *Sunday Telegraph* was withdrawn after the complainant who felt that the 'severe criticisms of his works were quite unwarrantable', was persuaded that his castigator was 'doing no more than expressing his honest opinion, which he has a right to do'.

Since there is no legal aid for libel action, reflecting, as one lawyer puts it, 'an unspoken feeling that reputation matters more to those who are important or among the better off in society', the headline cases are reserved for the very rich or the very determined, while a plaintiff of modest means is generally urged to try for an out-of-court settlement. This way he will at least save time (a full bloodied libel case can take up to three years to get to court) and avoid risking his life's savings.

Every writer is responsible for his own work. But this should not mean that when he makes mistakes he alone carries the can.

Journalists are usually covered by their employers who take on the whole cost of a libel action. Authors, on the other hand, are more exposed to the rigours of legal censorship. A typical publishing contract includes a warranty clause which entitles the publisher to be indemnified by the author against damages and costs if any part of the work turns out to be libellous.

Publishers excuse their weakness of backbone by arguing that only the author is in a position to know whether or not a work is libellous and that the onus should be on the author to check facts before they are published. But why, asks Mark Le Fanu of the Society of Authors, should the risk be borne by the author alone when a publisher deliberately gambles on making money out of a book.

'While it is true that a writer of fiction is much more likely than the publisher to know whether or not a person has been defamed (whether intentionally or unintentionally), the issue is much less clear-cut with non-fiction. Authors are not experts in the arcane mysteries of the 'fair comment' defence to a libel claim. Publishers are well aware that certain sorts of books (eg biographies of the living, business exposés, etc) inevitably carry a libel risk.'

In fairness, it must be said that the indemnity is rarely invoked unless a publisher feels he has been deceived or misled. But, at the very least, the author should insist that his publisher has the manuscript read for libel and that his contract does not specify unlimited liability.

In 1972 David Irving, whose book *The Destruction of Convoy PQ17* had been the subject of a successful libel action, was in turn sued by his publishers,

Cassell, who sought to recover the libel damages and costs they had paid out. The claim was for £100,000. But fortunately for Irving he had taken the advice of the Society of Authors and amended his contract. He was liable only for breaches of his warranty that the book was free of libel unknown to the publisher. Irving argued that Cassell knew all the relevant facts before an action was brought. In the end, Cassell did not proceed with the claim.

Libel insurance offers some sort of safeguard and a publisher who is insured is clearly preferable to one who is not. But most insurance policies carry severe limitations, not least a ceiling on the payout of damages. Also, reading for libel can be expensive for a book that is in any way controversial. As Richard West discovered when he wrote an investigative volume, 'the lawyer who read it for libel got £1000. The lawyer who wrote in to the publisher to complain on behalf of his client was probably paid about £5000'.

Since West himself earned about £500 for his efforts he concluded, not unreasonably, that authorship was a mug's game.

There are many cases where a cost-conscious publisher has played safe by amending a text to a point where it loses its cutting edge and thus its sales appeal. It is not unknown for an entire book to be jettisoned to save on lawyers' bills.

Another limitation on libel insurance is that few policies extend to the US market, where claims and awards can take off like Concorde. There, a thriving libel industry has been made yet more prosperous by enterprising lawyers who assess fees as a percentage of whatever they can persuade juries to award. The consolation for defendants is that while the law of libel in the States is similar to the law here, in practical terms it is more favourable to authors, in that the reputations of public figures are thought to be in less need of protection. A politician, say, who sues for libel is ridiculed as a bad sport. Whoever puts his head above the parapet, goes the argument, should expect to be shot at. Judges are more understanding of ordinary citizens particularly when there is an invasion-of-privacy claim but as a general rule, for libel damages to be awarded in an American court, someone must publish untruths knowing them to be untrue. Even then, there is plenty of leeway.

Early in 1988 a conservative-led Supreme Court allowed an appeal to overturn $200,000 damages awarded to Jerry Falwell against Larry Flynt. The peculiar fascination of the case comes from knowing the identity of the contenders. Falwell is the Reverend Jerry Falwell, founded of the Moral Majority while Flynt is the supremo of soft porn magazines. The action arose when Falwell was parodied in a cartoon which suggested that he had gained his first sexual experience with his mother. He sued for libel, invasion of privacy and emotional distress. In striking down the decision of a lower court to declare in favour of the Baptist minister, Chief Justice William Rehnquist argued that even when cartoons are 'harsh, indecent or indecorous', they are within the bounds of America's 'robust political and social satire'.

There is a consequent danger, as Lord Goodman argued of individuals suffering persecution by rumour, but can this be worse than the state of affairs in

Britain where a statement which is genuinely believed to be true and, indeed, *is* true in part, may still be libellous? It is for this reason that impure reputations, such as that of the late Robert Maxwell, survive public scrutiny.

Peter Marsh offers these tips for writers about to embark on a controversial project.

'If the subject or subjects of critical comment are still alive, beware; if you are writing a book about real life incidents but have changed names to avoid identification, take extreme care in the choice of names for your characters; remember that damage to a person's reputation can be caused by innuendo. For example, to write of someone that most people thought he was taking advantage of the Inland Revenue may suggest some improper and unethical practice. If a living person is going to be the subject of comment which is expressly or implicitly derogatory, make absolutely sure your facts are correct and can be substantiated. Otherwise, your publisher is going to be propelled into the courtroom naked of a defence.'

In one important respect, authors and publishers suffer more than anyone from the application of the libel laws. At the root of the problem is the case with which determined plaintiffs can get a book withdrawn from circulation. The process, successfully used by Sir James Goldsmith in his litigation against *Private Eye*, was given a shot in the arm by Maxwell in his tussles with Tom Bower over a biography of which Maxwell did not approve. David Hooper, author of *Public Scandal, Odium and Contempt* points out that the position of distributors in such situations is extremely perilous: 'They have no means of knowing whether the book is in fact libellous. All they know is that any profit they might have made – and more – will find its way smartly into the hands of their lawyers.'

The remedy, says David Hooper, is for anyone seeking to get a book withdrawn to be required to undertake to pay damages if their claims turn out to be without substance.

Is there anything to be said for those who bring libel actions? No better summary of the risks and tribulations for all but the excessively rich appears in Adam Raphael's absorbing indictment, *Grotesque Libels*.

'The problems of a libel action can be stated quite simply. The law is highly technical and the pleadings so complex that even its skilled practitioners often differ on the most basic questions. The costs of the lawyers involved are so high that they make the fees charged by any other profession appear to be a mere bagatelle. The opportunities for obstruction and delay are such that it can take as long as five years to bring a libel action to court. When it eventually does reach the court, the damages left to the whim of a jury are so uncertain that the result is often no sounder than a dodgy fruit machine. A libel action has in fact more in common with a roulette wheel than justice. The net result for both plaintiffs and defendants is that such actions are a nightmare with only the lawyers able to sleep soundly.'

No wonder Bernard Levin asserts 'If I were libelled (I have frequently been) and were given the choice of suing or having all my toenails pulled out with red-hot pincers while listening to *Pelléas et Mélisande*, I think it would be a close run thing'.

As for those who are unable to keep out of the courts, the best advice comes from Tom Crone in his book on Law and the Media. The libel litigant, he says, must possess two prime qualities – 'a strong nerve and a deep pocket'.

Literary Societies

Most literary societies exist on a shoestring budget; it is a good idea to enclose an A5 s.a.e. with all correspondence needing a reply.

The Abbey Chronicle
30 Sidford High Street, Sidford, Devon
EX10 9SL
Contact *Mrs Monica Godfrey*
Subscription £6 p.a.
FOUNDED 1989 to promote the works of Elsie J. Oxenham. Publishes three newsletters a year.

Margery Allingham Society
3 Corringham Road, Wembley, Middlesex
HA9 9PX
☎0181 904 5994
Contact *Mrs Pat Wat*
Subscription £7 p.a.
FOUNDED 1988 to promote interest in and study of the works of Margery Allingham. The London Society branch *publishes* two newsletters yearly, *The Bottle Street Gazette*; and distributes those of its American branch to members. Contributions welcome. Two social events a year. Open membership.

Jane Austen Society
Carton House, Redwood Lane, Medstead, Alton, Hampshire GU34 5PE
☎01420 562469
Honorary Secretary *Susan McCartan*
Subscription UK: £10 (Annual);
£15 (Joint); £30 (Corporate); £150 (Life);
Overseas: £12 (Annual); £18 (Joint);
£33 (Corporate); £180 (Life)
FOUNDED 1940 to promote interest in and enjoyment of Jane Austen's novels and letters. The society has branches in Bath & Bristol, Midlands, London, Oxford, Kent and Hampshire. Overseas branches in North America and Australia.

William Barnes Society
51 Binghams Road, Crossways, Dorchester, Dorset DT2 8BW
☎01305 853338   Fax 01305 854212
Contact *Mrs J. R. Bryant*
Subscription £4 p.a.
FOUNDED 1983 to provide a forum in which admirers of the Dorset poet could share fellowship and pleasure in his work. William Barnes (1801–86) is best known as the writer of Dorset dialect poetry. His interest in dialect prompted him to become a learned philologist and he published many papers in defence of native English against the incursions of French and Latin. Quarterly meetings and newsletter.

The Baskerville Hounds
6 Bramham Moor, Hill Head, Fareham, Hampshire PO14 3RU
☎01329 667325
Chairman *Philip Weller*
Subscription £7.00 p.a.
FOUNDED 1989. An international Sherlock Holmes society specialising solely in studies of *The Hound of the Baskervilles* and its Dartmoor associations. The society publishes a quarterly newsletter, an annual journal, and specialist monographs. It also organises many social functions, usually on Dartmoor. Open membership.

Arnold Bennett Society
106 Scotia Road, Burslem, Stoke on Trent, Staffordshire ST6 4ET
☎01782 816311
Secretary *Mrs Jean Potter*
Subscription £5 (Single); £6 (Family);
£4 (Unwaged)
Re-formed in 1954 to promote interest in the life and works of 'Five Towns' author Arnold Bennett and other North Staffordshire writers. Annual dinner and other events. Quarterly newsletter. Open membership.

E. F. Benson Society
88 Tollington Park, London N4 3RA
☎0171 272 3375   Fax 0171 580 0763
Secretary *Allan Downend*
Subscription £7.50 (UK/Europe);
£12.50 (Overseas)
FOUNDED 1985 to promote the life and work of E. F. Benson and the Benson family. Organises social and literary events, exhibitions and talks. *Publishes* a quarterly newsletter and annual journal, *The Dodo*, postcards and reprints of E. F. Benson articles and short stories. Holds an archive which includes the Seckersen Collec-

tion (transcriptions of the Benson collection at the Bodleian Library in Oxford).

E. F. Benson/The Tilling Society

Martello Bookshop, 26 High Street, Rye, East Sussex TN31 7JJ
☎01797 222242   Fax 01797 227335
Contact *Cynthia Reavell*
Subscription Full starting membership (members receive all back newsletters) £17 (UK); £22 (Overseas); or Annual Membership (members receive only current year's newsletters) £7 (UK); £9 (Overseas).

FOUNDED 1982 for the exchange of news, information and speculation about E. F. Benson and his *Mapp & Lucia* novels. Readings, discussions and twice-yearly newsletter. Acts as a clearing house for every sort of news and activity concerning E. F. Benson.

The Betjeman Society

35 Eaton Court, Boxgrove Avenue, Guildford, Surrey GU1 1XH
☎01483 560882

Contact *Secretary*
Subscription £7 (Individual); £9 (Family); £3 (Student); £2 extra each category for overseas members

Aims to promote the study and appreciation of the work and life of Sir John Betjeman. Annual programme includes poetry reading, lectures, discussions, visits to places associated with Betjeman, and various social events. Meetings are held in London and other centres. Regular newsletter and annual journal, *The Betjemanian*.

The Bewick Society

c/o The Dean's Office, Faculty of Arts and Design, University of Northumbria, Squires Building, Sandyford Road, Newcastle upon Tyne NE1 8ST
Chairman *Kenneth McConkey*
Subscription £7 p.a.

FOUNDED 1988 to promote an interest in the life and work of Thomas Bewick, wood-engraver and naturalist (1753–1828). Organises related events and meetings, and is associated with the Bewick birthplace museum.

Biggles & Co

8 The Heath, Leighton Buzzard, Bedfordshire LU7 7HL
☎01525 382669

Contact *Paul Marriott*
Subscription £12 p.a.

The W. E. Johns Society. Four newsletters per year and an annual meeting.

Birmingham Central Literary Association

c/o Birmingham & Midland Institute, Margaret Street, Birmingham B3 3DS
Contact *The Honorary Secretary*

Holds fortnightly meetings at the Birmingham Midland Institute to discuss the lives and work of authors and poets. Holds an annual dinner to celebrate Shakespeare's birthday.

Enid Blyton Book and Ephemera Collectors Society

69 Yew Tree Drive, Bredbury, Stockport, Cheshire SK6 2HH
Contact *Richard Walker*
Subscription £9 p.a.

Enid Blyton society. Organises bi-monthly meetings and newsletters.

Enid Blyton

See **Green Hedges**

The George Borrow Society

The Gables, 112 Irchester Road, Rushden, Northants NN10 9XQ
☎01933 312965   Fax 01933 312965
President *Sir Angus Fraser, KCB TD*
Honorary Secretary *James H. Reading*
Honorary Treasurer *Mrs Ena R. J. Reading*
Subscription £7 p.a.

FOUNDED 1991 to promote knowledge of the life and works of George Borrow (1803–81), traveller, linguist and writer. The Society holds biennial conferences (with published proceedings) and informal intermediate gatherings, all at places associated with Borrow. *Publishes* the *George Borrow Bulletin* twice yearly, a newsletter containing scholarly articles, publications relating to Borrow, reports of past events and news of forthcoming events. Member of the Alliance of Literary Societies and corporate associate member of the Centre of East Anglian Studies (CEAS) at the University of East Anglia, Norwich (Borrow's home city for many years).

Elinor Brent-Dyer

See **Friends of the Chalet School**

British Fantasy Society

2 Harwood Street, Heaton Norris, Stockport, Cheshire SK4 1JJ
☎0161 476 5368

President *Ramsey Campbell*
Vice-President *Mike Chim*
Secretary *Robert Parkinson*
Subscription from £15 p.a. (Apply to secretary.)

FOUNDED 1971 for devotees of fantasy, horror and related fields in literature, art and the cinema. *Publishes* a regular newsletter with information and reviews of new books and films, plus related fiction and non-fiction magazines. Annual conference at which the **British Fantasy Awards** are presented.

The Brontë Society

Brontë Parsonage Museum, Haworth, Keighley, West Yorkshire BD22 8DR
☎01535 642323   Fax 01535 647131
Contact *Executive Secretary*
Subscription £12 p.a. (UK/Europe); £7.50 (Student); £5 (Junior – up to age 14); £17 (Overseas); joint subscriptions and life membership also available

FOUNDED 1893. Aims and activities include the preservation of manuscripts and other objects related to or connected with the Brontë family, and the maintenance and development of the museum and library at Haworth. The society holds regular meetings, lectures and exhibitions; and *publishes* information relating to the family, a bi-annual society journal *Transactions* and a bi-annual *Gazette*. Freelance contributions for either publication should be sent to the Publications Secretary at the address above.

The Browning Society

100 Townshend Court, Mackennal Street, London NW8 6LD
Honorary Secretary *Mairi Calcraft-Rennie*
Subscription £10 p.a.

FOUNDED 1969 to promote an interest in the lives and poetry of Robert and Elizabeth Barrett Browning. Meetings are arranged in the London area.

The Burns Federation

The Dick Institute, Elmbank Avenue, Kilmarnock, Strathclyde KA1 3BU
☎01563 526401   Fax 01563 529661
Honorary Secretary *Allister Anderson*
Subscription £12 p.a.

FOUNDED 1885 to encourage interest in the life and work of Robert Burns and keep alive the old Scottish Tongue. The Society's interests go beyond Burns himself in its commitment to the development of Scottish literature, music and arts in general. *Publishes* the quarterly *Burns Chronicle/Burnsian*.

The Byron Society/International Byron Society

The Byron Society, Byron House, 6 Gertrude Street, London SW10 0JN
☎0171 352 5112
Honorary Director, Byron Society
    Mrs Elma Dangerfield OBE
Joint International Secretary *Mrs Maureen Crisp*
Subscription £15 p.a.

Also at: International Byron Society, Newstead Abbey, Newstead Abbey Park, Nottingham NG15 8GE. Tel: 01623 797392

FOUNDED 1876; revived in 1971. Aims to promote knowledge and discussion of Lord Byron's life and works, and those of his contemporaries, through lectures, readings, concerts, performances and international conferences.

Randolph Caldecott Society

Clatterwick Hall, Little Leigh, Northwich, Cheshire CW8 4RJ
☎01606 891303
Honorary Secretary *Kenneth N. Oultram*
Subscription £7–£10 p.a.

FOUNDED 1983 to promote the life and work of artist/book illustrator Randolph Caldecott. Meetings held in the spring and autumn in Caldecott's birthplace, Chester. Guest speakers, outings, newsletter, exchanges with the society's American counterpart. (Caldecott died and was buried in St Augustine, Florida.) A medal in his memory is awarded annually in the US for children's book illustration.

The Carlyle Society, Edinburgh

15 Lennox Street, Edinburgh EH4 1QB
☎0131 332 2854
Honorary Secretary *Dr C. P. Lowther*
Subscription £2 p.a.; £10 (Life); $20 (US)

FOUNDED 1929 to examine the lives of Thomas Carlyle and his wife Jane, his writings, contemporaries, and influences. Meetings are held about six times a year, and an annual members' journal is published.

Lewis Carroll Society

Little Folly, 105 The Street, Willesborough, Ashford, Kent TN24 0NB
☎01233 623919
Secretary *Sarah Stanfield*
Subscription £10 (Individual); £12 (Institutions); £6 (Concessions)

FOUNDED 1969 to bring together people with

an interest in Charles Dodgson and promote research into his life and works. *Publishes* quarterly journal *Jabberwocky*, featuring scholarly articles and reviews; plus a newsletter (*Bandersnatch*) which reports on Carrollian events and the Society's activities. Regular meetings held in London with lectures, talks, outings, etc.

Lewis Carroll Society (Daresbury)
Clatterwick Hall, Little Leigh, Northwich, Cheshire CW8 4RJ
☎01606 891303

Honorary Secretary *Kenneth N. Oultram*
Subscription £5 p.a.

FOUNDED 1970. To promote the life and work of Charles Dodgson, author of the world-famous *Alice's Adventures*. Holds regular meetings in the spring and autumn in Carroll's birthplace, Daresbury, in Cheshire. Guest speakers, theatre visits and a newsletter.

Friends of the Chalet School
4 Rock Terrace, Coleford, Bath, Avon BA3 5NF
☎01373 812705   Fax 01373 813517

Contact *Ann Mackie-Hunter, Clarissa Cridland*
Subscription £6 p.a.; £5 (Under-18);
   Outside Europe: details on application

FOUNDED 1989 to promote the works of Elinor Brent-Dyer. The society has members worldwide and is run by a team of five. Publishes four newsletters a year, runs a lending library and organises social events.

The Chesterton Society
11 Lawrence Leys, Bloxham, Near Banbury, Oxfordshire OX15 4NU
☎01295 720869

Secretary *Robert Hughes*
Subscription £17 p.a.

FOUNDED 1964 to promote the ideas and writings of G. K. Chesterton.

The Children's Books History Society
25 Field Way, Hoddesdon, Hertfordshire EN11 0QN
☎01992 464885

Membership Secretary *Mrs Pat Garrett*
Subscription £7.50 p.a.

ESTABLISHED 1969. Aims to promote an appreciation of children's books and to study their history, bibliography and literary content. The Society holds approximately six meetings per year in London and a Summer meeting to a collection, or to a location with a children's book connection. Two to three newsletters issued annually. The Society constitutes the British branch of the Friends of the Osborne and Lillian H. Smith Collections in Toronto, Canada, and also liaises with the **Library Association**.

The John Clare Society
The Stables, 1A West Street, Helpston, Peterborough PE6 7DU
☎01733 252678

Honorary Secretary *Mrs J. Mary Moyse*
Subscription £9.50 (Individual); £12.50 (Joint); £7.50 (Fully Retired); £9 (Joint Retired); £10 (Group/Library); £3 (Student, Full-time); £12.50 sterling draft/$25 (Overseas)

FOUNDED 1981 to promote a wider appreciation of the life and works of the poet John Clare (1793–1864). Organises an annual festival in Helpston in July; arranges exhibitions, poetry readings and conferences; and *publishes* an annual society journal and quarterly newsletter.

Wilkie Collins Society
104 Tibberton Square, Islington, London N1 8SF

Secretary *Andrew Gasson*
Membership Secretary *Louise Marchant (at above address)*
Subscription £7.50 (UK); $10 (US)

FOUNDED 1980 to provides information on and promote interest in the life and works of Wilkie Collins, one of the first English novelists to deal with the detection of crime. *The Woman in White* appeared in 1860 and *The Moonstone* in 1868. *Publishes* newsletters, a journal and reprints of Collins' work.

The Arthur Conan Doyle Society
Ashcroft, 2 Abbottsford Drive, Penyffordd, Chester CH4 0JG
☎01244 545210

Contact *Christopher Roden, Barbara Roden*
Subscription £14 (UK); £16 (Overseas); family rates available

FOUNDED 1989 to promote the study and discussion of the life and works of Sir Arthur Conan Doyle. Occasional meetings, functions and visits. *Publishes* an annual journal and twice-yearly news magazine, together with reprints of Conan Doyle's writings.

The Dickens Fellowship
48 Doughty Street, London WC1N 2LF
☎0171 405 2127   Fax 0171 831 5175
Honorary General Secretary *Edward G. Preston*

FOUNDED 1902. The society's particular aims and objectives are: to bring together lovers of Charles Dickens; to spread the message of Dickens, his love of humanity ('the keynote of all his work'); to remedy social injustice for the poor and oppressed; to assist in the preservation of material and buildings associated with Dickens. Annual conference. *Publishes* journal called *The Dickensian*. Branches worldwide.

Early English Text Society
Christ Church, Oxford OX1 1DP
Fax 01865 794199

Executive Secretary *R. F. S. Hamer*
Editorial Secretary *Dr H. L. Spencer*
  (at Exeter College, Oxford OX1 3DP)
Subscription £15 p.a.; $30 (US);
  $35 (Canada)

FOUNDED 1864. Concerned with the publication of early English texts. Members receive annual publications (one or two a year) or may select titles from the backlist in lieu.

The Eighteen Nineties Society
97D Brixton Road, London SW9 6EE
☎0171 582 4690

Contact *Honorary Secretary*
Subscription £10 p.a. (UK); $25 (US)

FOUNDED 1963 to bring together admirers of the work of Francis Thompson, the Society widened its scope in 1972 to embrace the artistic and literary scene of the entire decade (Impressionism, Realism, Naturalism, Symbolism). Assists members' research into the literature and art of the period; mounts exhibitions; and *publishes* an annual journal and quarterly newsletter.

The George Eliot Fellowship
71 Stepping Stones Road, Coventry,
Warwickshire CV5 8JT
☎01203 592231

Contact *Mrs Kathleen Adams*
Subscription £8 p.a.; £80 (Life); concessions
  for pensioners

FOUNDED 1930. Exists to honour George Eliot and promote interest in her life and works. Readings, memorial lecture, birthday luncheon and functions. Issues a quarterly newsletter and an annual journal.

Folly (Fans of Light Literature for the Young)
21 Warwick Road, Pokesdown,
Bournemouth, Dorset BH7 6JW
Contact *Mrs Sue Sims*
Subscription £6 p.a. (UK); £7 (Europe);
  £8.50 (Worldwide)

FOUNDED 1990 to promote interest in a wide variety of children's authors – with a bias towards writers of girls' books and school stories. *Publishes* three newsletters a year.

The Franco-Midland Hardware Company
6 Bramham Moor, Hill Head, Fareham,
Hampshire PO14 3RU
☎01329 667325

Chairman *Philip Weller*
Subscription £14 p.a.

FOUNDED 1989. 'The world's leading Sherlock Holmes correspondence study group and the most active Holmesian society in Britain.' The Society *publishes* a quarterly journal and at least six specialist monographs a year. It provides certificated self-study courses and organises functions at Holmes-associated locations. Open membership.

The Friars' Club
271 Firs Lane, Palmers Green,
London N13 5QH
Contact *Colin Cole*
Subscription £7.50 p.a.

FOUNDED 1983. Primarily concerned with the works of Charles Hamilton, alias Frank Richards, Martin Clifford, etc. – the creator of Billy Bunter and Greyfriars School. *Publishes* a quarterly magazine and holds about four meetings a year, usually in the London/Southeast area.

The Gaskell Society
Far Yew Tree House, Over Tabley,
Knutsford, Cheshire WA16 0HN
☎01565 634668

Honorary Secretary *Joan Leach*
Subscription £7 p.a.; £10 (Overseas)

FOUNDED 1985 to promote and encourage the study and appreciation of the life and works of Elizabeth Cleghorn Gaskell. Meetings held in Knutsford, Manchester and London; residential study weekends and visits; annual journal and bi-annual newsletter.

The Ghost Story Society

Ashcroft, 2 Abbottsford Drive, Penyffordd,
Chester CH4 0JG
☎01244 545210

Contacts *Barbara Roden, Christopher Roden*
Subscription £12.50 (UK); £14.50
(Overseas) currency options available

FOUNDED 1988. Devoted mainly to supernatural fiction in the literary tradition of M. R. James, Walter de la Mare, Algernon Blackwood, E. F. Benson, A. N. L. Murphy, R. H. Malden, etc. *Publishes* a thrice-yearly journal, *All Hallows*, which includes new fiction in the genre and non-fiction of relevance to the genre.

The Gothic Society

Chatham House, Gosshill Road, Chislehurst,
Kent BR7 5NS
☎0181 467 8475   Fax 0181 295 1967

Contact *Jennie Gray*
Subscription £18 p.a.; £21 (Overseas)

FOUNDED 1990 for the amusement of 'those who delight in morbid, macabre and black-hued themes, both ancient and modern Gothick!' *Publishes* high-quality paperbacks on related subjects, and four large-format illustrated magazines yearly. Some scope for original and imaginative fiction, but main preference is for history, biography and intelligent but amusing essays on the arts. Members have a definite advantage over writers outside the Society. (Also see **Small Presses**).

Green Hedges

16 Edward Street, Anstey, Leicestershire
LE7 7DP
☎0116 2350941

Contact *Michael Rouse*
Subscription £5 p.a.

The society for Enid Blyton fans. Publishes four newsletters a year.

Rider Haggard Appreciation Society

27 Deneholm, Whitley Bay, Tyne & Wear
NE25 9AU
☎0191 252 4516

Contact *Roger Allen*
Subscription £7 p.a. (UK); £8 (Overseas)

FOUNDED 1985 to promote appreciation of the life and works of Sir Henry Rider Haggard, English novelist, 1856–1925. News/books exchange, and meetings every two years.

The Thomas Hardy Society

PO Box 1438, Dorchester, Dorset DT1 1YH
☎01305 251501

Honorary Secretary *Mrs Helen Gibson*
Subscription £12 (Individual); £16
(Corporate); £15 (Individual Overseas);
£20 (Corporate Overseas)

FOUNDED 1967 to promote the reading and study of the works and life of Thomas Hardy. Thrice-yearly journal, events and a biennial conference.

The Henty Society

Fox Hall, Kelshall, Royston, Hertfordshire
SG8 9SE
☎01763 287208

Honorary Secretary *Mrs Ann J. King*
Subscription £12 p.a. (UK); £15 (Overseas)

FOUNDED 1977 to study the life and work of George Alfred Henty, and to publish research, bibliographical data and lesser known works, namely short stories. Organises conferences and social gatherings in the UK and Canada, and *publishes* quarterly bulletins to members.

Sherlock Holmes Society (Northern Musgraves)

Overdale, 69 Greenhead Road, Huddersfield,
West Yorkshire HD1 4ER
☎01484 426957

Contact *David Stuart Davies*
Subscription £13.50 p.a. (UK)

FOUNDED 1987 to promote enjoyment and study of Sir Arthur Conan Doyle's *Sherlock Holmes* through publications and meetings. One of the largest Sherlock Holmes societies in Great Britain. Honorary members include Jeremy Brett, Edward Hardwicke and Dame Jean Conan Doyle. Open membership. Consultation on matters relating to Holmes and Conan Doyle available.

The Sherlock Holmes Society of London

3 Outram Road, Southsea, Hampshire
PO5 1QP
☎01705 812104

Honorary Secretary *G. S. Stavert*
Subscription £9.50 p.a. (Associate); £14 (Full)

FOUNDED 1951 to promote the study of the life and work of Sherlock Holmes and Dr Watson, and their creator, Sir Arthur Conan Doyle. Offers correspondence and liaison with international societies, plus a bi-annual society journal.

Sherlock Holmes
See **The Franco-Midland Hardware Company**

Hopkins Society
Daniel Owen Centre, Earl Road, Mold, Clwyd CH7 1AP
☎01352 758403   Fax 01352 700236
Contact *Sandra Wynne*
Subscription £5 p.a.

FOUNDED 1990 to celebrate the life and work of Gerard Manley Hopkins; to inform members of any publications, courses or events about the poet. Holds an annual lecture on Hopkins in the spring; produces two newsletters a year; sponsors and organises educational projects based on Hopkins' life and works.

W. W. Jacobs Appreciation Society
3 Roman Road, Southwick, West Sussex BN42 4TP
☎01273 871017   Fax 01273 871017
Contact *A. R. James*

FOUNDED 1988 to encourage and promote the enjoyment of the works of W. W. Jacobs, and stimulate research into his life and works. *Publishes* a quarterly newsletter free to those who send s.a.e. (9in x 4in). Contributions welcome but no payment made. Preferred lengths 600–1200 words. No subscription charge. Biography, bibliography, directories of plays and films are available for purchase.

Richard Jefferies Society
45 Kemerton Walk, Swindon, Wiltshire SN3 2EA
☎01793 521512
Honorary Secretary *Cyril F. Wright*
Membership Secretary *Sheila Povey*
Subscription £5 p.a. (Individual); £6 (Joint); life membership for those over 50

FOUNDED 1950 to promote understanding of the work of Richard Jefferies, nature/country writer, novelist and mystic (1848–87). Produces newsletters, reports and an annual journal; organises talks, discussions and readings. Library and archives. Assists in maintaining museum in Jefferies' birthplace at Coate near Swindon. Membership applications to *Sheila Povey*, 20 Farleigh Crescent, Swindon, Wiltshire SN3 1JY.

Jerome K. Jerome Society
The Birthplace Museum, Belsize House, Bradford Street, Walsall, West Midlands WS1 1PN
☎01922 27686   Fax 01922 721065
Honorary Secretary *Tony Gray*
Subscription £5 p.a. (Ordinary); £25 (Corporate); £6 (Joint); £2.50 (Under 21/Over 65)

FOUNDED 1984 to stimulate interest in Jerome K. Jerome's life and works (1859–1927). One of the Society's principal activities is the support of a small museum in the author's birthplace, Walsall. Meetings, lectures, events and a twice-yearly newsletter *Idle Thoughts*. Annual dinner in Walsall near Jerome's birth date (2nd May).

Johnson Society
Johnson Birthplace Museum, Breadmarket Street, Lichfield, Staffordshire WS13 6LG
☎01543 264972
Contact *Mrs Rita M. Willard*
Subscription £5 p.a.; £7 (Joint)

FOUNDED 1910 to encourage the study of the life, works and times of Samuel Johnson (1709–1784) and his contemporaries. The Society is committed to the preservation of the Johnson Birthplace Museum and Johnson memorials.

Johnson Society of London
255 Baring Road, Grove Park, London SE12 0BQ
☎0181 851 0173
Honorary Secretary *Mrs Z. E. O'Donnell*
Subscription £6 p.a.; £7 (Joint)

FOUNDED 1928 to promote the knowledge and appreciation of Dr Samuel Johnson (1709–1784) and his works. Regular meetings from October to May in London on the third Saturday of each month, and a commemoration ceremony around the anniversary of Johnson's death, held in Westminster Abbey.

The Just William Society
15 St James' Avenue, Bexhill-on-Sea, East Sussex TN40 2DN
☎01424 216065
Secretary *Michael Vigar*
Treasurer *Phil Woolley*
Subscription £7 p.a. (UK); £10 (Overseas); £5 (Juvenile/Student); £15 (Family)

FOUNDED 1994 to further knowledge of Richmal Crompton's *William* and *Jimmy* books. An annual 'William' meeting is held in April, although this is not currently organised by the Society. The Honorary President of the Society is Richmal Crompton's niece, Richmal Ashby.

The Keats–Shelley Memorial Association

1 Lewis Road, Radford Semele, Warwickshire CV31 1UB

Contact *Honorary Treasurer* (at 10 Lansdowne Rd, Tunbridge Wells, Kent TN1 2NJ. Tel 01892 533452 Fax 01892 519142)

Subscription £10 p.a.; £100 (Life)

FOUNDED 1909 to promote appreciation of the works of Keats and Shelley, and their contemporaries. One of the Society's main tasks is the preservation of 26 Piazza di Spagna in Rome as a memorial to the British Romantic poets in Italy, particularly Keats and Shelley. *Publishes* an annual review of Romantic Studies called the *Keats-Shelley Review* and arranges events and lectures for Friends. The review is edited by *Angus Graham-Campbell*, c/o Eton College, Windsor, Berkshire SL4 6DL.

Kent & Sussex Poetry Society

Costens, Carpenters Lane, Hadlow, Kent TN11 0EY
☎01732 851404

Contact *Mrs Doriel Hulse*
Subscription £5 p.a.; £3 (Country)

FOUNDED 1946 to promote the enjoyment of poetry. Monthly meetings, including readings by major poets, and a monthly workshop. Produces an annual folio of members' work, adjudicated and commented upon by a major poet; and runs an open poetry competition (see **Prizes**) annually.

The Kilvert Society

The Old Forge, Kinnersley, Hereford HR3 6OB

Secretary *Mrs M. Sharp*
Subscription £5 p.a.; £50 (Life)

FOUNDED 1948 to foster an interest in the Diary, the diarist and the countryside he loved. *Publishes* three newsletters each year; during the summer holds three weekends of walks, commemoration services and talks.

The Kipling Society

P.O. Box 68, Haslemere, Surrey GU27 2YR
☎01428 652709

Secretary *Norman Entract*
Subscription £20 p.a.

FOUNDED 1927. The Society's main activities are: maintaining a specialised library; answering enquiries from the public (schools, publishers, writers and the media); arranging a regular programme of lectures and an annual luncheon with guest speaker; and issuing a quarterly journal. Open to anyone interested in the prose and verse, life and times of Rudyard Kipling (1865–1936). Approach in writing; no visits.

The Kitley Trust

Toadstone Cottage, Edge View, Litton, Derbyshire SK17 8QU
☎01298 871564

Contact *Rosie Ford*

FOUNDED 1990 by a teacher in Sheffield to promote the art of creative writing, in memory of her mother, Jessie Kitley. Activities include: bi-annual poetry competitions; a 'Get Poetry' Day (distribution of children's poems in shopping malls); annual sponsorship of a writer for a school; campaigns; organising conferences for writers and teachers of writing. Funds are provided by donations and profits (if any) from competitions.

Charles Lamb Society

1A Royston Road, Richmond, Surrey TW10 6LT
☎0181 940 3837

General Secretary *Mrs M. R. Huxstep*
Membership Secretary *Mrs Audrey Moore*
Subscription £12 p.a. (Single); £18 (Joint & Corporate); $28 (Overseas personal); $42 (Overseas corporate)

FOUNDED 1935 to promote the study of the life, works and times of English essayist Charles Lamb (1775–1834). Holds regular monthly meetings and lectures in London and organises society events over the summer. *Publishes* a quarterly bulletin, *The Charles Lamb Bulletin*. Contributions of Elian interest are welcomed by the editor *Dr Duncan Wu* at 58 Chaucer Road, Acton, London W3 6DP. Tel: 0181 993 6873. Membership applications should be sent to the Membership Secretary at Shelley Cottage, 108 West Street, Marlow, Buckinghamshire SL7 2BP. The Society's library is housed in the **Guildhall Library**, Aldermanbury, London EC2P 2EJ (Tel: 0171 606 3030). Registered Charity No: 803222.

Lancashire Authors' Association

Heatherslade, 5 Quakerfields, Westhoughton, Bolton, Lancashire BL5 2BJ
☎01942 816785

General Secretary *Eric Holt*
Membership £7 p.a.; £10 (Joint); £1 (Junior)

FOUNDED 1909 for writers and lovers of Lancashire literature and history. Aims to foster and stimulate interest in Lancashire history and literature as well as in the preservation of the

Lancashire dialect. Meets four times a year on Saturday at various locations. *Publishes* a quarterly journal called *The Record* which is issued free to members and holds eight annual competitions (open to members only) for both verse and prose. Comprehensive library with access for research to members.

The T. E. Lawrence Society
8 Staverton Road, Flat 3, Oxford OX2 6XJ
☎01865 510319

Secretary & Librarian *Mrs A. Horsfield*
Subscription £14 p.a.

FOUNDED 1985 to advance the education of the public in the life and works of T. E. Lawrence, and to promote and publish research into both areas.

The Leamington Literary Society
15 Church Hill, Leamington Spa,
Warwickshire CV32 5AZ
☎01926 425733

Honorary Secretary *Mrs Margaret Watkins*
Subscription £5 p.a.

FOUNDED 1912 to promote the study and appreciation of literature and the arts. Holds regular meetings every second Tuesday of the month (except August) at the Regent Hotel, Leamington Spa, and lectures. The Society has published various books of local interest.

Wyndham Lewis Society
8 Montgomery Road, Chiswick,
London W4 5LZ
☎0181 995 4457

Contact *Anthony Wilcock*
Subscription £5.60 p.a. (UK/Europe);
    £7.30 p.a. (Institutions); $16–21 (Elsewhere)
    (dollar subs to be sent to Prof. Reed Way
    Dasenbrock, English Dept. Box 3E/NMSU,
    Las Cruces, New Mexico 88013, USA)

FOUNDED 1974 to promote recognition of the value of Lewis's works and encourage scholarly research on the man, his painting and his writing. *Publishes* inaccessible Lewis writings; the annual society journal *The Wyndham Lewis Annual* plus two newsletters; and reproduces Lewis's paintings. The journal is edited by *Paul Edwards*, 77A Newbridge Road, Bath, Avon BA1 3HF.

Arthur Machen Literary Society
19 Cross Street, Caerleon, Gwent NP6 1AF
☎01633 422520   Fax 01633 421055

President *Barry Humphries*
Patron *Julian Lloyd Webber*

Contact *Rita Tait*
Subscription £15 (UK); £18 (Overseas)

Exists to honour the life and work of writer Arthur Machen (1863–1947). *Publishes* a newsletter *The Silurist* and a journal *Avallaunius*, both twice yearly; also hardback books by and about Machen and his circle, under its own Green Round Press imprint. Gives assistance to researchers on the 1890s mystery and imagination genre of which Machen was part.

The Monday Literary Club
c/o 12 Little East Street, Lewes, East Sussex
BN7 2NU
☎01273 472658

Honorary Secretary *Mrs Christine Mason*
Subscription £9 p.a.

FOUNDED 1948, the Club meets on the last Monday of each month from October to April at the White Hart Hotel, Lewes, where the eighteenth-century Headstrong Club had its headquarters and Tom Paine was a keen debater. Today the Club offers talks and informal discussion on a wide range of subjects to do with the literary scene: from the construction of the new British Library to a poetry reading. Membership is regulated by the fire regulations of the White Hart to around 100 members. Currently a short waiting list.

William Morris Society
Kelmscott House, 26 Upper Mall,
Hammersmith, London W6 9TA
☎0181 741 3735

Contact *David Rodgers*
Subscription £13.50 p.a.

FOUNDED 1953 to promote interest in the life, work and ideas of William Morris (1834–1923), English poet and craftsman.

Violet Needham Society
c/o 19 Ashburnham Place, London SE10 8TZ
☎0181 692 4562

Honorary Secretary *R. H. A. Cheffins*
Subscription £6 p.a. (UK & Europe);
    £9 (outside Europe)

FOUNDED 1985 to celebrate the work of children's author Violet Needham and stimulate critical awareness of her work. *Publishes* thrice-yearly *Souvenir*, the Society journal with an accompanying newsletter; organises meetings and excursions to places associated with the author and her books. The journal includes articles about other children's writers of the 1940s and 50s. Contributions welcome.

The Wilfred Owen Association

17 Belmont, Shrewsbury, Shropshire
SY1 1TE
☎01743 235904
Chairman *Helen McPhail*
Subscription Adults £4 (£6 Overseas);
£2 (Senior Citizens, Students,
Unemployed); £10 (Groups/Institutions)

FOUNDED 1989 to commemorate the life and
works of Wilfred Owen by promoting readings, talks and performances relating to Owen
and his work. Membership is international
with 650 members in 16 countries. *Publishes* a
newsletter two or three times a year. Contact
the Association for information on their activities or on Owen. Speakers are available for
schools or clubs etc. In 1993 (the centenary of
Owen's birth and the 75th anniversary of his
death) the Association established permanent
memorials to Owen in Shropshire.

Thomas Paine Society U.K.

43 Wellington Gardens, Selsey, West Sussex
PO20 0RF
☎01243 605730
President *The Rt. Hon. Michael Foot*
Honorary Secretary/Treasurer *Eric Paine*
Subscription (Minimum) £5 p.a.

FOUNDED 1963 to promote the life and work
of Thomas Paine, and continues to expound
his ideals. Meetings, newsletters, lectures and
research assistance. Membership badge. The
Society has members worldwide and keeps in
touch with American and French Thomas
Paine associations. *Publishes* annual magazine
Bulletin.

The Polidori Society

Ebenezer House, 31 Ebenezer Street, Langley
Mill, Nottinghamshire NG16 4DA
☎0181 994 5902   Fax 0181 995 3275
Founder & President *Franklin C. Bishop*
Membership Secretary *Kathy McGrath*
Subscription £10 p.a. (Individual or Joint
Husband/Wife) £6 (Students)

FOUNDED 1990 to promote and encourage
appreciation of the life and works of John
William Polidori (1795–1821). Author of
the seminal work *The Vampyre – A Tale* (1819),
Polidori thus introduced into literature the
enduring icon of the vampire portrayed as an
aristocrat and a seducer; evil, cynical and hand-
some. As well as being a novelist, Polidori was
a poet, tragedian, philosopher, diarist, essayist,
traveller and one of the youngest students to

obtain a medical degree (at the age of 19). He
was one-time travelling companion and private
physician to Lord Byron and took part in the
infamous Villa Diodati 'ghost story' sessions in
which he assisted Mary Shelley in her creation
of Frankenstein. Members receive exclusive
newsletters, including unique publications and
invitations to special events. International
membership.

The Beatrix Potter Society

High Banks, 26 Stoneborough Lane, Budleigh
Salterton, Devon EX9 6HL
Membership Secretary *Irene Whalley*
Subscription UK: £7 p.a. (Individual);
£10 (Institutional); Overseas: £14 (Or
US$25/Can.$27.50/Aus.$30) (Individual);
£20 (US$35/Can.$40/Aus.$45)
(Institutional)

FOUNDED 1980 to promote the study and
appreciation of the life and works of Beatrix
Potter (1866–1943). Potter was not only the
author of *The Tale of Peter Rabbit* and other
classics of children's literature; she was also a
landscape and natural history artist, diarist,
farmer and conservationist, and was responsible
for the preservation of large areas of the Lake
District through her gifts to the National Trust.
The Society upholds and protects the integrity
of the inimitable and unique work of the lady,
her aims and bequests. Holds regular talks and
meetings in London with visits to places connected with Beatrix Potter. Biennial International Study Conferences are held in the UK
and occasionally in the USA.

The Powys Society

Keeper's Cottage, Montacute, Somerset
TA15 6XN
☎01935 824077
Hon. Secretary *John Batten*
Subscription £13.50 (UK); £16 (Overseas)

The Society aims to promote public education
and recognition of the writings, thought and
contribution to the arts of the Powys family;
particularly of John Cowper, Theodore and
Llewelyn, but also of the other members of the
family and their close associates. The Society
holds two major collections of Powys published works, letters, manuscripts and memorabilia. *Publishes* the *Powys Society Newsletter* in
April, June and November and *The Powys
Journal* in August. Organises an annual conference as well as lectures and meetings in Powys
places.

The Arthur Ransome Society

Abbot Hall Art Gallery, Kirkland, Kendal,
Cumbria LA9 5AL
☎01539 722464   Fax 01539 722494
Chairman *M. Temple*
Secretary *Dr K. Cochrane*
Contact *E. King*
Subscription £5 (Junior); £10 (Student);
   £15 (Adult); £20 (Family/Overseas); £40
   (Corporate); concessions for retired persons

FOUNDED 1990 to celebrate the life and promote
the works and ideas of Arthur Ransome, author
of the world-famous *Swallows and Amazons* titles
for children and biographer of Oscar Wilde.
TARS seeks to encourage children and adults to
engage in adventurous pursuits, to educate the
public about Ransome and his works, and to
sponsor research into his literary works and life.

Frank Richards

See **The Friars' Club**

The Followers of Rupert

31 Whiteley, Windsor, Berkshire SL4 5PJ
☎01753 865562
Membership Secretary *Mrs Shirley Reeves*
Subscription UK: £7; £9 (Joint);
   Overseas: £7.50/£10 (Surface/Airmail);
   £9.50/£12 (Joint)

FOUNDED in 1983. The Society caters for the
growing interest in the Rupert Bear stories,
past, present and future. *Publishes* the *Nutwood
Newsletter* quarterly which gives up-to-date
news of Rupert and information on Society
activities. A national get-together of members
– the Followers Annual – is held during the
autumn in venues around the country.

The Ruskin Society of London

351 Woodstock Road, Oxford OX2 7NX
☎01865 310987 or 515962
Honorary Secretary *Miss O. E. Forbes-Madden*
Subscription £10 p.a.

FOUNDED 1986 to promote interest in John
Ruskin (1819–1900) and various aspects of
Ruskiana. Functions held in London. *Publishes*
the annual *Ruskin Gazette*, a learned journal
concerned with Ruskin's influence in England
and abroad.

The Dorothy L. Sayers Society

Rose Cottage, Malthouse Lane,
Hurstpierpoint, West Sussex BN6 9JY
☎01273 833444
Contact *Christopher Dean*

Subscription £9 p.a.

FOUNDED 1976 to promote the study of the
life, works and thoughts of Dorothy Sayers; to
encourage the performance of her plays and
publication of her books and books about her;
to preserve original material and provide assistance to researchers. Acts as a forum and information centre, providing material for study
purposes which would otherwise be unavailable. Annual seminars and other meetings.
Publications.

The Robert Southey Society

16 Rhydhir, Longford, Neath Abbey, Neath,
West Glamorgan SA10 7HP
☎01792 814783
Contact *Robert King*
Subscription £10 p.a.

FOUNDED 1990 to promote the work of
Robert Southey. *Publishes* an annual newsletter
and arranges talks on his life and work. Open
membership.

Robert Louis Stevenson Club

5 Albyn Place, Edinburgh EH2 4NJ
☎0131 225 6665   Fax 0131 220 1015
Contact *Alistair J. R. Ferguson*
Subscription £3 p.a. (Individual); £15 (Life)

FOUNDED 1920 to promote the memory of
Robert Louis Stevenson and interest in his
works.

The R. S. Surtees Society

Riverside House, Nunney, Near Frome,
Somerset BA11 4NH
☎01373 836646
Contact *Mrs C. de Planta, Sir Charles Pickthorn*
Subscription £10

FOUNDED 1979 to republish the works of R. S.
Surtees and others.

The Tennyson Society

Central Library, Free School Lane, Lincoln
LN2 1EZ
☎01522 552866   Fax 01522 552858
Honorary Secretary *Miss K. Jefferson*
Subscription £8 p.a. (Individual); £10
   (Family); £15 (Corporate); £125 (Life)

FOUNDED 1960. An international society with
membership worldwide. Exists to promote the
study and understanding of the life and work of
Alfred, Lord Tennyson. The Society is concerned with the work of the Tennyson
Research Centre, probably the most significant
collection of mss, family papers and books in

the world. *Publishes* annually the *Tennyson Research Bulletin*, which contains articles and critical reviews; and organises lectures, visits and seminars. Annual memorial service at Somersby in Lincolnshire.

Angela Thirkell Society
14 Stanhope Avenue, Horsforth, Leeds, West Yorkshire LS18 5AR
☎0113 2582241
Honorary Secretary *Mrs Valerie Ramsden*
Contact *Mrs J. E. Self*
Subscription £5 p.a.

FOUNDED 1979 to honour the memory of writer Angela Thirkell and promote her work to future generations. *Publishes* an annual journal and encourages the study of Thirkell's writing through lectures.

The Edward Thomas Fellowship
Butlers Cottage, Halswell House, Goathurst, Bridgwater, Somerset TA5 2DH
☎01278 662856
Secretary *Richard Emeny*
Subscription £5 p.a. (Single); £7 p.a. (Joint)

FOUNDED 1980 to perpetuate and promote the memory of Edward Thomas and to encourage an appreciation of his life and work. The Fellowship holds a commemorative birthday walk on the Sunday nearest the poet's birthday, 3 March; issues newsletters and holds various events.

The Trollope Society
9A North Street, Clapham, London SW4 9HY
☎0171 720 6789   Fax 0171 978 1815
Contacts *John Letts, Phyllis Eden*

FOUNDED 1987 to study and promote Anthony Trollope's works. Linked with the publication of the first complete edition of his novels.

Edgar Wallace Society
9 Hurst Rise Road, North Hinksey, Oxford OX2 9HE
☎01865 863655
Organiser *Neil Clark*
Subscription £8 p.a.; £10 (Overseas); £5.50 (Senior Citizens)

FOUNDED 1969 by Edgar's daughter, Penelope, to bring together all who have an interest in Edgar Wallace. Members receive a brief biography of her father by Penelope Wallace, with a complete list of all published book titles. A 24-page quarterly newsletter, *Crimson Circle*, is issued

in February, May, August and November. The Society is organised by the racing journalist and author, Neil Clark.

The Walmsley Society
23 Lennard Road, Dunton Green, Sevenoaks, Kent TN13 2UU
☎01732 462536
Honorary Secretary *Fred Lane*
Subscription £7 p.a.; £8 (Family); £6 (Students/Senior Citizens)

FOUNDED 1985 to promote interest in the art and writings of Ulric and Leo Walmsley. Two annual meetings, one held in Robin Hood's Bay on the East Yorkshire coast, spiritual home of the author Leo Walmsley. The Society also seeks to foster appreciation of the work of his father Ulric Walmsley. *Publishes* a journal twice-yearly and newsletters, and is involved in other publications which benefit the aims of the Society.

Mary Webb Society
15 Melbourne Rise, Gains Park, Shrewsbury, Shropshire SY3 5DA
Secretary *Mrs J.M. Palmer*
Subscription £5 p.a.

FOUNDED 1972 to further the reading and appreciation of the works of Mary Webb; to foster appreciation of the countryside about which she wrote; and to liaise with other organisations in encouraging scholarship and education in the spirit of Mary Webb. Talks, lectures, events, summer school.

H. G. Wells Society
75 Wellmeadow Road, Blackheath, London SE13 6TA
☎0181 461 4583
Honorary Membership Secretary *Mary Mayer*
Subscription £12 (UK/EU); £18 (Overseas); £20 (Corporate); £6 (Concessions)

FOUNDED 1960 to promote an interest in and appreciation of the life, work and thought of Herbert George Wells.

The Charles Williams Society
26 Village Road, London N3 1TL
Contact *Honorary Secretary*

FOUNDED 1975 to promote interest in, and provide a means for, the exchange of views and information on the life and work of Charles Williams.

The Henry Williamson Society

16 Doran Drive, Redhill, Surrey RH1 6AX
☎01737 763228

Membership Secretary *Mrs Margaret Murphy*
Subscription £8 p.a.; £10 (Family);
£4 (Students)

FOUNDED 1980 to encourage, by all appropriate means, a wider readership and deeper understanding of the literary heritage left by the 20th-century English writer Henry Williamson (1895–1977). Twice-yearly journal.

The Wodehouse Society

108 Balmoral Road, Northampton NN2 6JZ
☎01604 710500

Contact *Richard Morris*
Subscription £10 p.a. (Individual); £50 (Life)

Society to promote the prose and lyricism of the Master – particularly his theatrical works and musical comedies. Will deal with all enquiries on PGW through an eminent network of contacts. *Publishes* quarterly journal for which unsolicited mss are accepted, not necessarily to do with the author but must have a Wodehousean style; maximum 1000 words. Society patrons include Richard Briers, Stephen Fry, Tom Sharpe and Richard Usborne.

Parson Woodforde Society

Priddles Hill House, Hadspen, Castle Cary, Somerset BA7 7LX
☎01963 350462

Chairman *G. H. Bunting*
Subscription £10 p.a. (UK); £20 (Overseas)

FOUNDED 1968 to promote education in the social and domestic history of 18th-century England, with special reference to the life and work of James Woodforde.

WW2 HMSO PPBKS Society

3 Roman Road, Southwick, West Sussex BN42 4TP
☎01273 871017   Fax 01273 871017

Contact *A.R. James*
Subscription £2 p.a.

FOUNDED 1994 to encourage collectors of, and promote research into HM Stationery Office's World War II series of paperbacks, most of which were written by well-known authors, although, in many cases, anonymously. *Publishes* quarterly newsletter for those who send s.a.e. (9in x 4in). Contributors welcome; preferred length 600 – 1200 words but no payment made. Bibliography available for purchase (£3.20 post paid).

Yorkshire Dialect Society

Farfields, Weeton Lane, Weeton, Near Leeds, West Yorkshire LS17 0AN
☎01423 734377

Secretary *Stanley Ellis*
Subscription £6 p.a.

FOUNDED 1897 to promote interest in and preserve a record of the Yorkshire dialect. *Publishes* dialect verse and prose writing. Two journals to members annually. Details of publications are available from the Librarian, YDS, School of English, University of Leeds, LS2 9JT.

Francis Brett Young Society

52 Park Road, Hagley, Near Stourbridge, West Midlands DY9 0QF
☎01562 882973

Honorary Secretary *Mrs Jean Pritchard*
Subscription £5 p.a. (Individuals);
£7 (Married couples sharing a journal);
£3 (Students); £5 (Organisations/Overseas);
£45 (Life)

FOUNDED 1979. Aims to provide a forum for those interested in the life and works of English novelist Francis Brett Young and to collate research on him. Promotes lectures, exhibitions and readings; *publishes* a regular newsletter; and seeks to support writers born in Young's birthplace, Halesowen.

Arts Councils and Regional Arts Boards

The Arts Council of England

14 Great Peter Street, London SW1P 3NQ
☎0171 333 0100 Fax 0171 973 6590

Chairman *Lord Gowrie*
Secretary General *Mary Allen*

The 1995/96 grant dispensed by the Arts Council stands at approximately £191 million. From this fund the Arts Council supports arts organisations, artists, performers and others: grants can also be made for particular productions, exhibitions and projects. Grants available to individuals are detailed in the free Arts Council folder: *Projects, Schemes and Awards 1995-96*. The total amount set aside for literature in 1995/96 is £1,723,000, an increase of around 12.8% on the previous year's figure.

Drama Director *Nick Jones* New writing is supported through *Theatre Writing Allocations* (contact the Drama Department for more details).

Literature Director *Alastair Niven* The Literature Department has defined support for writers, education, access to literature including the touring of authors and literary exhibitions, cultural diversity, and an international view of writing including more translation into English among its top priorities. Michael Holroyd is chairman of the Literature Advisory Panel. This year the Arts Council will be giving at least 15 grants of £7,000 each to individual writers. Applicants must have at least one published book. Details available from the Literature Department from July 1995.

The Arts Council, Ireland

An Chomhairle Ealaíon, 70 Merrion Square, Dublin 2
☎00 353 1 6611840 Fax 00 353 1 6761302

Literature Officer *Laurence Cassidy*

The Irish Arts Council has programmes under six headings to assist in the area of literature and the book world: a) Writers; b) Literary Organisations; c) Publishers; d) Literary Magazines; e) Participation Programmes; f) Foreign Representation. It also gives a number of annual bursaries (see **Arts Council Literature Bursaries, Ireland**) and organises the **Dublin International Writers' Festival**.

The Arts Council of Northern Ireland

185 Stranmillis Road, Belfast BT9 5DU
☎01232 381591 Fax 01232 661715

Literature Officer *Ciaran Carson*

Funds book production by established publishers, programmes of readings, literary festivals, writers-in-residence schemes and literary magazines and periodicals. Occasional schools programmes and anthologies of children's writing are produced. Annual awards and bursaries for writers are available. Holds information also on various groups associated with local arts, workshops and courses.

Scottish Arts Council

12 Manor Place, Edinburgh EH3 7DD
☎0131 226 6051 Fax 0131 225 9833

Literature Director *Walter Cairns*
Literature Officer *Shonagh Irvine*
Literature Secretary *Catherine Allan*

The Council's work for Scottish-based professional writers who have a track record of publication includes: bursaries (considered twice yearly); travel and research grants (considered three times yearly); writing fellowships (posts usually advertised) and an international writing fellowship (organised reciprocally with the Canada Council); and two schemes: *Writers in Schools* and *Writers in · Public* (the Writer's Register is a list of writers willing to participate in the schemes). Also publishes lists of Scottish writers' groups, workshops, circles, awards and literary agents.

The Arts Council of Wales

Museum Place, Cardiff CF1 3NX
☎01222 394711 Fax 01222 221447

Literature Director *Tony Bianchi*
Drama Director *Michael Baker*

Funds literary magazines and book production; *Writers on Tour* and bursary schemes; **Welsh Academy, Welsh Books Council, Hay-on-Wye Literature Festival, Cardiff Literature Festival**, and Tŷ newydd Writers' Centre at Criccieth; also children's literature, annual awards. The Council's Drama Board aims to develop theatrical experience in Wales-based writers through various schemes: in particular, by funding them on year-long attachments.

Arts Council of Wales – North Wales Office

10 Wellfield House, Bangor, Gwynedd LL57 1ER
☎01248 353248   Fax 01248 351077
Regional Director *Sandra Wynne*
Arts Officer (Literature) *J. Clifford Jones*
The region includes Gwynedd, Clwyd and the Montgomeryshire district of Powys. The Regional Board's role in the field of literature is fourfold: to highlight all aspects of the literary heritage in both English and Welsh; to foster an understanding and appreciation of this tradition; to stimulate others to develop these traditions; to encourage promising new initiatives. Priorities include the *Authors in Residence, Authors on Video* and *Writers on Tour* schemes, and the support of literary circles, Eisteddfodau and community newspapers. Can supply list of names and addresses of regional groups and circles in the region. Contact the Literature Officer.

Arts Council of Wales – South East Wales Office

Victoria Street, Cwmbran, Gwent NP44 3YT
☎01633 875075   Fax 01633 875389
Literature Officer *Bob Mole*
Can supply names and addresses of local groups, workshops and writing courses, and information on local writing schemes, and writers.

Arts Council of Wales – West Wales Office

3 Red Street, Carmarthen, Dyfed SA31 1QL
☎01267 234248   Fax 01267 233084
Literature Officer *Elsie Reynolds*
ACW West Wales covers Dyfed and West Glamorgan. It supports a network of writers' groups through the **Arts Council of Wales** *Writers on Tour* scheme and organises an ongoing series of community writing projects. Writers receive additional support through their participation in residencies and other activities in the education and healthcare sectors. In conjunction with the Welsh Language Board, the ACW also supports a network of Welsh language community newspapers. Publishing ventures are referred to other agencies. Supplies a list of names and addresses of over 20 groups in Dyfed and West Glamorgan, including groups like **Carmarthen Writers' Circle**.

English Regional Arts Boards

5 City Road, Winchester, Hampshire SO23 8SD
☎01962 851063   Fax 01962 842033
Chief Executive *Christopher Gordon*
Assistant *Carolyn Nixson*
English Regional Arts Boards is the representative body for the 10 Regional Arts Boards (RABs) in England. Its Winchester secretariat provides project management, services and information for the members, and acts on their behalf in appropriate circumstances. Scotland, Northern Ireland and Wales have their own Arts Councils. The three Welsh Regional Arts Associations are now absorbed into the Welsh Arts Council. RABs are support and development agencies for the arts in the regions. Policies are developed in response to regional demand, and to assist new initiatives in areas of perceived need; they may vary from region to region.

DIRECT GRANTS FOR WRITERS
While most of the RABs designate part of their budget for allocation direct to writers, this is often a minor proportion, which new or aspiring playwrights stand little chance of receiving. Money is more readily available for the professional, though because of the emphasis on community access to the arts in many of the boards, this is often allocated to writers' appearances in schools and community settings, theatre workshops, etc., rather than to support the writer at the typewriter. New writing is also encouraged through the funding of small presses and grants to theatre companies for play commissions. Details of schemes available from individual boards.

Cleveland Arts

7–9 Eastbourne Road, Linthorpe, Middlesbrough, Cleveland TS5 6QS
☎01642 812288   Fax 01642 813388
Contact *Literature Development Officer*
Cleveland Arts is an independent arts development agency working in the county of Cleveland. The company works in partnership with local authorities, public agencies, the business sector, schools, colleges, individuals and organisations to coordinate, promote and develop the arts – crafts, film, video, photography, music, drama, dance, literature, public arts, disability, Black arts, community arts. The Literature Development Officer promotes writing classes, poetry readings and cabarets, issues a free newsletter and assists publishers and writers.

East Midlands Arts

Mountfields House, Epinal Way,
Loughborough, Leicestershire LE11 0QE
☎01509 218292   Fax 01509 262214
Literature Officer *Debbie Hicks*
Drama Officer *Helen Flach*

Covers Leicestershire, Nottinghamshire, Derbyshire (excluding the High Peak district) and
Northamptonshire. A comprehensive information service for regional writers includes an
extensive *Writers' Information Pack*, with details
of local groups, workshops, residential writing
retreats, publishers and publishing information,
regional magazines which offer a market for
work, advice on approaching the media, on
unions, courses and grants. Also available is a
directory of writers, primarily to aid people
using the *Artists At Your Service* scheme and to
establish *Writers' Attachments*. Writers' bursaries
are granted for work on a specific project – all
forms of writing are eligible except for local history and biography. Writing for the theatre can
come under the aegis of both Literature and
Drama. A list of writers' groups is available, plus
Foreword, the literature newsletter.

Eastern Arts Board

Cherry Hinton Hall, Cambridge
CB1 4DW
☎01223 215355   Fax 01223 248075
Literature Officer *Don Watson*
Drama Officer *Alan Orme*
Director (Performing Arts) *Sandy Bailey*

Covers Bedfordshire, Cambridgeshire, Essex,
Hertfordshire, Norfolk, Suffolk and Lincolnshire. Policy emphasises quality and access. As a
self-styled arts development agency, great stress
is placed upon work with publishers within the
region and on literature in performance. With
regard to drama, emphasis is placed on plays
into performance and companies are funded
either directly or through project support to
commission new work. EAB is currently inves-
tigating ways of directly supporting playwrights. In literature, support is given to projects which develop an audience for literature,
festivals and performances, and publishing. The
Board organises a critical reading service which
runs on a first come, first served basis while
funds last, and it also offers a range of bursaries
annually for individual published writers.
Supplies a list of literary groups, workshops and
local writing courses. Currently in the process
of setting up a year-long course aimed at writers aspiring to publication which will run from
a number of centres throughout the region.

London Arts Board

Elme House, 3rd Floor, 133 Long Acre,
London WC2E 9AF
☎0171 240 1313/Help Line: 0171 240 4578
Fax 0171 240 4580

Principal Literature Officer *John Hampson*
Principal Drama Officer *Sue Timothy*

The London Arts Board is the Regional Arts
Board for the Capital, covering the 32 boroughs
and the City of London. Potential applicants for
support for literature and other arts projects
should contact the Board for information.

North West Arts Board

4th Floor, 12 Harter Street, Manchester
M1 6HY
☎0161 228 3062   Fax 0161 236 5361
Literature Officers *Christine Bridgwood, Marc
    Collett*
Theatre Officer *Sue Williams*

Covers Cheshire, Greater Manchester, Merseyside, Lancashire and the High Peak district of
Derbyshire. Gives financial assistance to a great
variety of organisations and schemes, including
Lancaster Literature Festival, Commonword (a community publishing and writing
development organisation), and writers' bursary schemes. The *Residencies and Placements*
scheme subsidises writers' placements in schools,
community organisations, etc. The *Live Writing*
scheme assists literature promoters with the
cost of organising readings and performance.
For information sheets and further details of
what is available, contact the Literature
Assistant. NWAB publishes a directory of local
groups and a directory of writers.

Northern Arts Board

9–10 Osborne Terrace, Jesmond, Newcastle
upon Tyne NE2 1NZ
☎0191 281 6334   Fax 0191 281 3276
Head of Published and Broadcast Arts
    John Bradshaw

Covers Cleveland, Cumbria, Durham, Northumberland and Tyne and Wear, and was the first
regional arts association in the country to be set
up by local authorities. It supports both organisations and writers and aims to stimulate public
interest in artistic events. Offers Writers Awards
for published writers to release them from work
or other commitments for short periods of time
to enable them to concentrate on specific literary
projects. It also has a film/TV script development fund operated through the Media
Investment Fund. A separate scheme for playwrights is operated by the Northern Playwrights

Society. Northern Arts makes drama awards to producers only. Also funds writers' residencies, and has a fund for publications. Contact list of regional groups and workshops available.

South East Arts

10 Mount Ephraim, Tunbridge Wells, Kent TN4 8AS
☎01892 515210　　　　Fax 01892 549383
Literature Officer *Celia Hunt*
Drama Officer *Linda Lewis*

Covers Kent, Surrey, East and West Sussex (excluding the London boroughs). The literature programme aims to raise the profile of contemporary literature across the region and to support new and established writers. Priorities include writers' residencies, *Writers-in-Education* and *Live Literature* schemes; also the continued support of literature festivals in the region. For a small fee, new writers from the region can have their work assessed by professional readers under the *Reader Service*. New writers are also supported by the *Bursary Scheme*. A regular newsletter is available (£3 p.a./£5 to those outside the region).

South West Arts

Bradninch Place, Gandy Street, Exeter, Devon EX4 3LS
☎01392 218188　　　　Fax 01392 413554
Director of Media & Published Arts *David Drake*
Director of Performing Arts *Nick Capaldi*
Administrator *Sara Fasey*

Covers Avon, Cornwall, Devon, much of Dorset, Gloucestershire and Somerset. 'The central theme running through the Board's aims are access, awareness and quality.' The literature policy aims to promote a healthy environment for writers of all kinds and to encourage a high standard of new writing. There is direct investment in small presses, publishers and community groups. Literary festivals, societies and arts centres are encouraged. The theatre department aims to support the development of theatre writing by funding the development of literary management programmes of dramaturgy and seasons of new plays. List of regional groups and workshops available from the Information Service.

Southern Arts

13 St Clement Street, Winchester, Hampshire SO23 9DQ
☎01962 855099　　　　Fax 01962 861186
Literature Officer *Keiren Phelan*
Film, Video & Broadcasting Officer *Jane Gerson*

Theatre Officer *Sheena Wrigley*

Covers Berkshire, Buckinghamshire, Hampshire, the Isle of Wight, Oxfordshire, Wiltshire and South East Dorset. The Literature Department funds fiction and poetry readings, festivals, magazines, bursaries, a literature prize, publications, residencies and two schemes: *Write Connections*, which subsidises writers working in education and the community, and *Write Reactions*, a manuscript appraisal service aimed at helping new and unpublished writers within the region.

West Midlands Arts

82 Granville Street, Birmingham B1 2LH
☎0121 631 3121　　　　Fax 0121 643 7239
Literature Officer *David Hart*

There are special criteria across the art forms, so contact the Information Office for details of *New Work & Production* and other schemes as well as for the *Reading (Correspondence Mss Advice) Service*. There are contact lists of writers, storytellers, writing groups etc. Their magazine of new writing, *People to People*, is now published independently under the new title *Heart Throb*. Contact 95 Spencer Street, Birmingham B18 6DA for details.

Yorkshire & Humberside Arts

21 Bond Street, Dewsbury, West Yorkshire WF13 1AY
☎01924 455555　　　　Fax 01924 466522
Literature Officer *Steve Dearden*
Drama Officer *Shea Connolly*
Administrator *Jill Leahy*

'Libraries, publishing houses, local authorities and the education service all make major contributions to the support of literature. Recognising the resources these agencies command, Yorkshire & Humberside Arts actively seeks ways of acting in partnership with them, whilst at the same time retaining its particular responsibility for the living writer and the promotion of activities currently outside the scope of these agencies.' Funding goes to the Black Literature Project; **Yorkshire Art Circus** (community publishing); *Live Writing*, which subsidises projects involving professional writers and students at all levels as well as community groups; and to awards for local independent publishers. Also offers support for literature in performance and for the **Ilkley Literature Festival**, **Huddersfield Poetry Festival** and *Bête Noire* magazine. Holds a list of workshops and writers' groups throughout the region, and publishes a writers' directory. Contact the Literature Officer.

Independent Postal Workshops

Book Folio
17 Andrews Crescent, Peterborough, Cambridgeshire PE4 7XL
Contact *Kate Dean*

For writers who have a complete draft of a book which needs revision. Maximum number on the rota is six and each member receives one mss per week, to be read, criticised and passed on by first post the following Monday. Not interested in porn or experimental fiction. The system demands dedicated writers who will guarantee to deal with one mss per week for as long as it takes. Also runs a Manuscript folio, which arrives with six–eight mss. Kate Dean is willing to act as liaison between other genre groups, to put interested novelists of the same genre in touch with each other. Send s.a.e., plus two second-class stamps for further details.

Concordant Poets Folios
87 Brookhouse Road, Farnborough, Hampshire GU14 0BU

FOUNDED through popular demand several years ago to encourage and assist poets, while studying techniques and possible marketing outlets. Each poem included is discussed and advised upon from several different viewpoints, with poets gaining valuable knowledge while building (via postal method) a circle of friends with mutual interests. Whether beginner, intermediate or advanced, there is a suitable place in one of the eight folios. For details and enrolment form please send s.a.e.

Croftspun
Drakemyre Croft, Cairnorrie, Methlick, Ellon, Aberdeenshire AB41 0JN
☎01651 806252

Publishes a small booklet entitled *The Cottage Guide to Writers' Postal Workshops*, a directory giving the contact names and addresses of postal folios for writers (£1.50 post free).

Historical Novel Folio
17 Purbeck Heights, Mount Road, Parkstone, Poole, Dorset BH14 0QP
☎01202 741897

Contact *Doris Myall-Harris*

A single folio dealing with any period before World War II. Send s.a.e. for details.

Anna Owens Dragons – Fantasy Folio
17 Andrews Crescent, Peterborough, Cambridgeshire PE4 7XL
Contact *Kate Dean*

For adult novels only. Not interested in porn or experimental ficton. Send s.a.e. for details.

Partners in Crime
159 All Saints Road, Burton-on-Trent, Staffordshire DE14 3PL
Contact *Stella A Milner*

Postal workshops for dedicated crime writers, published or unpublished (novels only please). 'We offer honest criticism and a friendly exchange of advice, plus news and views in general.' Send s.a.e. for details.

Scribo
Flat 1, 31 Hamilton Road, Boscombe, Bournemouth, Dorset BH1 4EQ
☎01202 302533

Contact *K. Sylvester, P. A. Sylvester*

FOUNDED in the early 70s, Scribo circulates folios (published and unpublished work) to its members, who currently number about 40 and rising. The only criteria for joining is that you must be actively engaged in writing novels. Forum folios discuss anything of interest to novelists; problems are shared and information exchanged. Manuscript folios offer friendly criticism and advice. Besides 'general' mss folios there are three specialist folios: crime; aga-saga/saga/ romance; fantasy/science-fiction. Now a new folio specifically for the more literary novelist has been launched. Members – mostly graduates, published and unpublished – would welcome a few similarly dedicated serious novelists. 'No pornography.'

Trick or Treat?

Michèle Roche enters the minefield of creative writing courses

I could have swept Richard Francis off his feet when he offered me a place on the new MA programme in Novel Writing at Manchester last summer. The Gods were out in force on my behalf that day; even the sun was shining.

This was the only MA course of its kind in the UK, the only one dedicated to the art of the novel. I was struggling with the form, I was struggling with structure, and was despairing of not moving on. I felt I needed a gun to my head. This was it.

In the months leading up to my acceptance in Manchester, I had been hurdling my way towards the creative writing course at Norwich, fantasising about discussing writing with Malcolm Bradbury and Rose Tremain, and with so many other potential contributors: Ian McEwan, Ishiguro and Philip McCann, all names I associated with UEA. But alas it was not to be. Not there and not like that. At the last UEA hurdle, I fell. . .

Devastated, I listened through a haze of gloom as the UEA secretary gave me the news, thinking of the months of solitary ahead. I think she sensed the depth of my disappointment. Why not try Manchester? There was a new MA course there.

This time, it couldn't have been easier. There were no long anxious weeks of waiting or indecision. From my first call of enquiry to acceptance took less than a fortnight. I couldn't believe my luck, despite a nagging concern about quality. This was an infant course - I was to be among the second year's intake. Still, I was prepared to gamble £2300 in fees, reckoning that the odds must surely be in my favour. I wasn't asking for much: a critical eye, a little guidance, communing with like minds, that kind of thing. Fairly fundamental stuff, I thought.

At my interview I met Dr Richard Francis, Senior Lecturer in American Literature and Creative Writing, one of the two people who convene this course. The other is Michael Schmidt of Carcanet fame, also Senior Lecturer in Poetry at Manchester. He was unable to attend the interview. We met for the first time on the day classes began.

The day of registration finally came. It was badly organised. This was an ill omen, but one I missed at the time. We were aged between 22 and 67, and were fourteen in number - which made for a big circle in the longer-than-it-is-wide Writing Centre, where all the classes and workshops were held. It was not a room particularly conducive to thought and imagination, being rather untidy much of the time, with chairs left scattered from one class to the next.

We met over nine months for two sessions a week, each lasting a couple of hours: one a workshop, the other a lecture or seminar on the thirty or so novels we had to read. Two novels were discovered to be out-of-print, despite one being a Carcanet edition.

The reading list was distinguished by an emphasis on novels in translation. We came across some wonderful novels, some wonderful translations, we might otherwise never have read. Among the best: José Saramago's *The Life and Death of Ricardo Reis* (trans. Pontiero); Lampedusa's *The Leopard* (Colquhoun); Bulgakov's *The Master and Margarita* (Ginsberg); Clarice Lispector's *The Hour of the Star* (Pontiero). But the reading commitment was heavy – to the point of intrusion for many on the creative writing element of the course, which for everyone was the primary concern.

The workshops were the opportunity to talk about our novels in progress. We each had half-hour sessions, two in each of the two semesters. Writing commands about a quarter of the course's attention, which reflects roughly the amount of time you can spend on it. I harbour misgivings about the workshop method – its success depends so much on people's ability to communicate, their critical judgement, their sensibilities. Such diversities can be restrictive, and some among us did not feel in any way stretched or challenged. But what I found invaluable was being forced to meet deadlines and to let go of a piece of work. It is also a useful exercise in coming up against reactions to your work. A writing course can toughen you up. If you are trying to do something different, you need to have confidence in your direction and faith in your voice. Tension got the better of people at times and, occasionally, there was something of a showdown. A stamping of feet.

At worst, workshops can sometimes turn out to be more destructive than productive, but Manchester's creative writing course is, in the main, a soft-touch approach in my opinion.

One of the most rewarding aspects of the course was the chance to meet with fellow students and other writers. There were regular readings organised in the Writing Centre as well as opportunities to talk with visiting writers such as Paul Bailey, Stuart Hood, Elaine Feinstein, Jane Rogers, Mimi Khalvati, José Saramago, and literary agent Giles Gordon. All you had to do was turn up. In terms of bringing you into touch, a course can be helpful.

At Manchester you meet with plenty of enthusiasm and *general* support from both Richard Francis and Michael Schmidt. You will not find much in the way of demand on you in terms of the theory or history of the novel as form. It is expected that you already have a grasp on all this. Do not expect anything in the way of practical individual teaching on the craft of writing. The course doesn't set itself up to teach you how to write a novel, but it does introduce you to the various stages of publication.

Was it all worth it? All the sweating over applications, the trials and the treats? I can't say I got all I was hoping for and expecting, but everyone comes to a course with different expectations. It was certainly preferable to struggling alone. This said, after 15 years away from academia, it wasn't long before I was thinking to myself: Christ, what's academia like? Can we get real here, please, someone? I feel like I'm floating around in space, with almost two-and-a-half grand floating round with me. Please Sirs! More direction and focus. More sense of purpose. These elements to my mind were amiss.

Writers Courses, Circles and Workshops

Courses

Courses are listed alphabetically under country and county.

England

Avon
Bath College of Higher Education
Newton Park, Bath, Avon BA2 9BN
☎01225 873701

Postgraduate Diploma/MA in Creative Writing. Includes poetry, fiction, playwriting and script-writing. Visiting writers have included Roy Fisher, Marion Lomax, William Stafford and Fay Weldon.

University of Bristol
Department for Continuing Education, 8–10 Berkeley Square, Bristol, Avon BS8 1HH
☎0117 9287172   Fax 0117 9254975

Courses in Bristol and the surrounding counties (Avon, Dorset, Gloucestershire, Somerset and Wiltshire). *Women and Writing*, for women who write or would like to begin to write (poetry, fiction, non-fiction, journals); *Certificate in Creative Writing*. Detailed brochure available.

Bucks, Berks & Oxon
National Film & Television School
Beaconsfield Studios, Station Road, Beaconsfield, Buckinghamshire HP9 1LG
☎01494 671234   Fax 01494 674042

Writers' course designed for students who already have experience of writing in other fields. The course is divided into two parts: a self-contained intensive five-week course, concentrating on the fundamentals of screenwriting, and an 18-month course for 8–10 students selected from the one-month course: intensive programme of writing and analysis combined with an understanding of the practical stages involved in the making of film and television drama.

University of Reading
Department of Extended Education, London Road, Reading, Berkshire RG1 5AQ
☎01734 318347

Creative writing courses have included *Life into Fiction*; *Poetry Workshop*;. *Getting Started*; *Writers*

Helping Writers (with **Southern Arts'** help, the course includes visits from well-known writers); *Writing Popular Fiction*. There is also a support group for teachers of creative writing, a public lecture by a writer, and a reading by students of their own work. Fees vary depending on the length of the course. Concessions available.

Cambridgeshire
National Extension College
18 Brooklands Avenue, Cambridge CB2 2HN
☎01223 316644

Runs a number of home-study courses on writing. Courses include: *Essential Editing; Creative Writing; Writing for Money; Copywriting; Essential Desktop Publishing; Essential Design.* Contact the NEC for copy of the guide to courses which includes details of fees.

PMA Training
The Old Anchor, Church Street, Hemmingford Grey, Cambridgeshire PE18 9DF
☎01480 300653   Fax 01480 496022

One-/two-/three-day editorial, PR, design and publishing courses held in central London. High-powered, intensive courses run by Fleet Street journalists and magazine editors. Courses include: *News Writing, Journalistic Style, Feature Writing, Investigative Reporting, Basic Writing Skills.* Fees range from £150 to £495 plus VAT. Special rates for freelancers.

Cheshire
Distance Learning Course
The College of Technical Authorship, PO Box 7, Cheadle, Cheshire SK8 3BT
☎0161 437 4235

Distance learning courses for City & Guilds Tech 536, Part 1, Technical Communication Techniques, and Part 2, Technical Authorship. Individual tuition by correspondence and fax, for qualifications from a world-renowned institute. Includes some practical work done at home. Contact: John Crossley, DipDistEd, DipM, MCIM, MISTC, LCGI.

Cleveland

University of Leeds
Adult Education Centre, 37 Harrow Road,
Middlesbrough, Cleveland TS5 5NT
☎01642 814987

Creative writing courses held in the autumn,
spring and summer terms. Contact Rebecca
O'Rourke for details.

Cumbria

Higham Hall College
Bassenthwaite Lake, Cockermouth, Cumbria
CA13 9SH
☎017687 76276   Fax 017687 76013

Residential courses. Summer 1994 programme
included *Creative Writing* and *Memoir Writing*.
Detailed brochure available.

Devon

Dartington College of Arts
Totnes, Devon TW9 6EJ
☎01803 862224

BA(Hons) course in *Performance Writing*.
Contact John Hall, Vice-Principal.

Exeter & Devon Arts Centre
Bradninch Place, Gandy Street, Exeter, Devon
EX4 3LS
☎01392 219741

Hold weekly courses: *Poetry Project and Advanced
Poetry; Writing for Television*; also occasional writers' workshops. A copy of their quarterly programme of events is available from the Centre.

University of Exeter
Exeter, Devon EX4 4QW
☎01392 264580

BA(Hons) in Drama with a third-year option in
Playwriting. Contact Professor Peter Thomson.

Dorset

Bournemouth University
Talbot Circus, Fern Barrow, Poole, Dorset
BY12 5BB
☎01202 524111

Three-year, full-time BA(Hons) course in
Scriptwriting for Film and Television. Contact
Frank Matthews-Finn.

Essex

**National Council for the
Training of Journalists**
Latton Bush Centre, Southern Way, Harlow,
Essex CM18 7BL
☎01279 430009   Fax 01279 438008

For details of journalism courses, both full-time
and via distance learning, please write to the
NCTJ enclosing a large s.a.e.

Hampshire

Highbury College of Technology
Dovercourt Road, Cosham, Portsmouth,
Hampshire PO6 2SA
☎01705 383131

Courses include: one-year *Pre-entry Magazine
Journalism* course (mainly post-graduate intake).
Run under the auspices of the Periodicals
Training Council. One-year *Pre-entry Newspaper
Journalism* course, under the auspices of the
National Council for Training of Journalists.
One-year course in   *Broadcasting Journalism*.
Contact Mrs Paulette Miller, Faculty Secretary,
Tel: 01705 283287.

King Alfred's College
Winchester, Hampshire SO22 4NR
☎01962 841515

Three-year course on *Drama, Theatre and
Television Studies*, including *Writing for Devised
Community Theatre* and *Writing for Television
Documentary*. Contact Tim Prentki.

School of Creative Writing
Weavers Press Publishing Ltd.,
113 Abbotts Ann Down, Andover,
Hampshire SP11 7BX
☎01264 710701

A correspondence course for beginners, covering all the basics of writing articles, features,
short stories, novels, non-fiction, marketing
and writing for publication. Assignments are
assessed and advice is given by an experienced
writer. Contact: Allan Travell.

University of Southampton
Department of Adult Continuing Education,
Southampton SO17 1BJ
☎01703 592833

Creative writing courses and writers' workshops. Courses are held in local/regional centres.

Humberside

Hull College of Further Education
Queen's Gardens, Hull, North Humberside
HU1 3DG
☎01482 29943   Fax 01482 219079

Offers part-time day/evening writing courses,
including *Fiction Writing, Novel Writing, Short
Story Writing*, at various centres within the city.
Most courses begin each academic term and
last for a period of ten weeks. Publishes an

anthology of students' work each year entitled, *Embryo*. Contact Ed Strauss.

Kent
Rose Bruford College of Speech and Drama
Lamorbey Park, Sidcup, Kent DA15 9DF
☎0181 300 3024

BA(Hons) Theatre Degree: Writers' Course. Aims to produce skilled theatre writers and prepare them for work in film, radio and television. Not a 'creative writing' course but training as a theatre professional. Contact Mary Gillam.

International Forum
The Oast House, Plaxtol, Sevenoaks, Kent TN15 0QG
☎01732 810925

Wide range of courses (one-/two-/three-day) on screenwriting and other key creative roles in film and television. Courses run throughout the year and concessions are available for members of certain trade organisations. Contact: Joan Harrison.

University of Kent at Canterbury
School of Continuing Education, Rutherford College, Canterbury, Kent CT2 7NX
☎01227 823662

Creative writing courses. Contact: Vicki Inge.

Lancashire
Lancaster University
Department of Creative Writing, Lonsdale College, Bailrigg, Lancaster LA1 4YN
☎01524 594169

Offers practical graduate and undergraduate courses in writing fiction, poetry and scripts. All based on group workshops – students' work-in-progress is circulated and discussed. Visiting writers have included: Carol Ann Duffy, Kazuo Ishiguro, Bernard MacLaverty, David Pownall. Contact Linda Anderson for details.

London
The Central School of Speech and Drama
Embassy Theatre, Eton Avenue, London NW3 3HY
☎0171 722 8183

Advanced Diploma in *Creative Theatre*. One-year, full-time course aimed at providing a grounding in three areas of professional theatre practices: *Directing, New Writing* and *Performance*. Entrants to *New Writing* are required to submit two pieces of writing together with completed application form. Prospectus available.

City University
Northampton Square, London EC1V 0HB
☎0171 477 8268

Creative writing classes include: *Writer's Workshop; Wordshop* (poetry); *Writer's Craft; Writing Fiction; Writing Comedy; Playwright's Workshop; Writing Freelance Articles for Newspapers; Women Writer's Workshop; Creative Writing*. Contact: Courses for Adults.

London College of Printing & Distributive Trades
School of Media Studies, Back Hill, London EC1R 5EN
☎0171 514 6500

Courses in journalism. Part-time: *Writing for Magazines; English for Journalists; Sub-editing and Layout*. Full-time: *BAHons. in Journalism; HND in Periodical Journalism; Periodical Journalism for Graduates*. Prospectus and information leaflets available.

London School of Journalism
22 Upbrook Mews, London W2 3HG
☎0171 706 3536/01225 444774 (Admin)
Fax 0171 706 3780/01225 313986 (Admin)

Correspondence courses with an individual and personal approach. Students remain with the same tutor throughout their course. Options include: *Short Story Writing; Writing for Children; Poetry; Freelance Journalism; Improve Your English; English for Business; Journalism and Newswriting*. Fees vary but range from £145 for *Poetry* to £360 for *Journalism and Newswriting*. Contact Antoinette Winckworth at the Administration Office, PO Box 1745, Bath, Avon BA2 6YE.

Middlesex University
School of English Cultural and Communication Studies, White Hart Lane, London N17 8HR
☎0181 362 5000   Fax 0181 362 6299

BA course in writing and publishing. Modules include *Writing for Media Presentation, Writing for Radio, Writing for the Screen*. Contact Susanne Gladwin.

Roehampton Institute
Senate House, Roehampton Lane, London SW15 5PU
☎0181 392 3000

Three-year BA(Hons) course in *Drama and Theatre Studies* which includes writing for the theatre and associated media. Contact Jeremy Ridgman.

Scriptwriters Tutorials

65 Lancaster Road, London N4 4PL
☎0171 272 2335/720 7047

Offers professional *one-to-one* scriptwriting tuition by working writers in film, television, radio or stage. Beginners, intermediate and advanced courses. Script evaluation service and correspondence courses. Also holds an annual writers retreat in Gascony.

Thames University

St Mary's Road, London W5 5RF
☎0181 231 2271

Offers a course in *Scriptwriting for Television, Stage and Radio*. Aims to provide the fundamental principles of the craft of script writing. Contact Tony Dinner.

University of Westminster

Short Courses Unit, 35 Marylebone Road, London NW1 5LS
☎0171 911 5000

Short courses in writing, including *Basic News and Feature Writing*.

Writing School

29 Turnpike Lane, London N8 0EP
☎0181 342 8980

Correspondence course covering writing for articles, short stories, books, plays and scripts, with a strong emphasis on writing to sell. Fee £269 (1995). Contact the Director of Studies for enrolment details.

Manchester

Manchester Metropolitan University

Dept of Arts, Design and Performance, Crewe & Alsager Faculty, Hassall Road, Alsager, Stoke on Trent, Staffordshire ST7 2HL
☎01270 500661

BA Creative Arts course with *Writing for Performance* as one of the options. Contact John Singleton or Liz Allen.

University of Manchester

Department of American Studies, Arts Building, Oxford Road, Manchester M13 9PL
☎0161 275 3055

Offers a one-year MA in *Novel Writing*. Contact Richard Francis.

Password Training

23 New Mount Street, Manchester M4 4DE
☎0161 953 4009   Fax 0161 953 4090

Two-day courses in publishing held in Manchester or London. A *Foundation* course for those new to publishing, and *Marketing in Publishing* for those with a more advanced knowledge. Grants are available. Contact Claire Turner, Training Co-ordinator for further information.

The Writers Bureau

Sevendale House, 7 Dale Street, Manchester M1 1JB
☎0161 228 2362   Fax 0161 228 3533

Comprehensive home-study writing course with personal tuition service from professional writers (fee approx. £219); Professional Business Writing Course which covers the writing of letters, memos, reports, minutes etc. (fee £199); and a Poetry Course which covers all aspects of writing poetry (fee £119).

Merseyside

University of Liverpool

Centre for Continuing Education, 19 Abercromby Square, Liverpool L69 3BX
☎0151 794 6900 (24 hours)

General creative writing courses for beginners. *Poetry, Writing and Performance; The Short Story and the Novel; Scripting for Television, Radio, Comedy, Including Stand Up; Women's Writing; Asian Voices, Asian Lives; Writing for Children; Chinese and South East Asia Writing; An Introduction to Journalism; Feature Writing for Magazines and Newspapers; The Art and Craft of Songwriting*. Most courses are run in the evening over 10 or 20 weeks. Weekend and residential courses in the summer. No pre-entry qualifications required. Fees vary; some courses may be free. Further information and copy of current prospectus, phone or write to Keith Birch, Academic Organiser, Creative Arts (address as above).

Writing in Merseyside

c/o Writing Liaison Office, Toxteth Library, Windsor Street, Liverpool L8 1XF
☎0151 708 0143

A mini-directory which lists facilities, resources and opportunities in the Merseyside area. Excellent publication for putting writers in touch with what's available in their area. Everything from workshops and courses to competitions, research and library facilities, plus tips. Comprehensive course information on all areas of writing is provided.

Norfolk

University of East Anglia

School of English & American Studies, Norwich, Norfolk NR4 7TJ
☎01603 593262

UEA has a history of concern with contemporary literary culture. Among its MA programmes is one in *Creative Writing*, Stream 1: Prose Fiction; Stream 2: Script and Screenwriting.

Northamptonshire
Swanwick Writers' Summer School
The New Vicarage, Parson's Street, Woodford Halse, Daventry, Northants NN11 3RE
☎01327 261477

A week-long summer school held at The Hayes, Swanwick, Derbyshire. Lectures, informal talks and discussion groups, forums, panels, quizzes and competitions, and 'a lot of fun'. Open to everyone, from absolute beginners to published authors. Held in August from late Saturday to Friday morning. Cost (1995) £185+, all inclusive. Contact the Secretary, Brenda Courtie at the above address.

Staffordshire
Keele University
Adult and Continuing Education, Keele University, (Freepost ST1666), Newcastle under Lyme, Staffordshire ST5 5BR
☎01782 625116

Weekend courses on literature and creative writing. The 1995 programme included a fiction writing weekend and a poetry weekend.

Suffolk
Fen Farm
10 Angel Hill, Bury St Edmunds, Suffolk IP33 1UZ
☎01284 753110

Five-day residential courses from late afternoon Monday to Saturday morning. Courses have included *Beginning to Write; Short Stories; Plays; Novels; Journalism*. Open to all over 16 who have a desire to write. Fee (including food, tuition and accommodation) £270. Sponsored by Channel 4. Grants may be available for those in the region on low incomes.

Write on Course
1 Waterloo Road, Ipswich, Suffolk IP1 2NY
☎01473 210199

A variety of one-day and weekend residential courses on topics such as *Ways to Make Money from Spare-time Writing, Self-Publishing, Erotic Writing, Writing Short Stories*, and *Getting into Technical Writing*. Courses are held in East Anglia and other parts of the country.

Surrey
Royal Holloway and Bedford New College
University of London, Egham Hill, Egham, Surrey TW20 0EX
☎01784 443922

Three-year BA course in *Theatre Studies* during which playwriting can be studied as an option in the second and third years. Contact Dan Rebellato or David Wiles.

University of Surrey
Department of Educational Studies, Guildford, Surrey GU2 5XH
☎01483 259754

The programme 'Courses For All' includes a *Creative writing* course, held at the University, the Guildford Institute and throughout the county. Contact Maureen Russell-Pope for details.

Sussex
University of Sussex
Centre for Continuing Education Centre, Education Development Building, Falmer, Brighton, East Sussex BN1 9RG
☎01273 678040   Fax 01273 678848

Courses in creative writing, autobiographical writing, and dramatic writing. Day and evening courses. Concessions available.

Tyne & Wear
University of Newcastle upon Tyne
Centre for Continuing Education, Newcastle upon Tyne NE1 7RU
☎0191 222 6542

Writing-related courses include: *Writing From the Inside Out; Dramatic Writing for Film, TV and Radio*. Contact the Secretary, Adult Education Programme.

Warwickshire
University of Warwick
Open Studies, Continuing Education Dept, Coventry, Warwickshire CV4 7AL
☎01203 523831

Creative writing courses held at the university or in regional centres. Subjects have included: *Starting to Write; Creative Writing; Express Yourself in Writing*. A two-year certificate in *Creative Writing* is available.

West Midlands
University of Birmingham
School of Continuing Studies, Edgbaston, Birmingham B15 2TT
☎0121 414 5606/7/8

Day and weekend classes, including creative writing, writing for radio and television. Courses are held at locations throughout Birmingham, the West Midlands, Hereford & Worcester and Shropshire. Detailed course brochure available from the above address.

The University also offers an MA course in *Playwriting Studies* established by David Edgar in 1970. Contact Julietta MacDonald at the Department of Drama and Theatre Arts (Tel 0121 414 5998).

Sandwell College
High Street, West Bromwich, Birmingham B70 8DW
☎0121 556 6000

Creative writing courses held afternoons/ evenings, from September to July. Script writing, poetry, etc. Contact Dave Richmond.

Worcestershire
Lord Ryan Writers
Loch Ryan Hotel, 119 Sidbury, Worcester WR5 2DH
☎01905 351143   Fax 01905 764407

Weekend residential writing workshops throughout the year. Emphasis on poetry, but also prose and drama. Contact Gwynneth Royce for details and all-inclusive prices.

Yorkshire
ARTTS International
Highfield Grange, Bubwith, North Yorkshire YO8 7DP
☎01757 288088

Theatre, television, film and radio courses. Two-week introductory courses, including *Scriptwriting for Stage and Screen*.

The Northern School of Film and Television
Leeds Metropolitan University, 2–8 Merrion Way, Leeds, West Yorkshire LS2 8BT
☎0113 2833193   Fax 0113 2833194

A relatively new film school, the NSFT offers a Postgraduate Diploma/MA course in *Fiction Scriptwriting*. Currently one-year, full-time but planning to offer a part-time option over two years. Contact Ian Macdonald.

Open College of the Arts
Houndhill, Worsbrough, Barnsley, South Yorkshire S70 6TU
☎01226 730495

The OCA correspondence course, *Starting to Write*, offers help and stimulus, without an emphasis on commercial success, from experienced writers/tutors. Subsequent levels available include specialist poetry and fiction writing courses.

University College, Scarborough
North Riding College, Filey Road, Scarborough, North Yorkshire YO11 3AZ
☎01723 362393

BA Combined Arts Degree in which *Theatre Studies* contains modules in *Writing for Theatre* and *Writing and the Writer*. Contact Eric Prince.

University of Sheffield
Division of Adult Continuing Education, 196–198 Wear Street, Sheffield S1 4ET
☎0115 2825400

Creative writing courses and workshops. Day/evening classes, residential courses.

Northern Ireland
Queen's University of Belfast
Institute of Continuing Education, Belfast BT7 1NN
☎01232 245133 ext. 3326

Courses have included *Creative Writing*.

University of Ulster (Belfast/Jordanstown)
Continuing Education, Belfast BT37 0QB
☎01232 365131 ext. 2835 (Belfast)/ ext. 6680 (Jordanstown)

Creative writing course/workshop of ten sessions. Group discussions and individual readings. Prose, plays or poetry will be considered. Concessions available. Contact the Administrative Officer.

University of Ulster (Londonderry)
Magee College, Londonderry
☎01504 372073

Creative Writing for Beginners, a 10-session course providing a useful foundation for anyone interested in writing poetry, drama, etc. Explores different methods and devices available to writers.

Creative Writing, a 10-session course particularly aimed at those interested in writing poetry and prose for the stage. Provides a critical forum in which the writing is read, discussed and developed 'supportively and rigorously'.

Scotland

University of Aberdeen
Centre for Continuing Education, Regent
Building, Regent Walk, Aberdeen AB9 1FX
☎01224 272448
Creative writing evening class held weekly.

University of Dundee
Centre for Continuing Education, Perth
Road, Dundee DD1 3HN
☎01382 344128
Various creative writing courses held at the
University and elsewhere in the Dundee area.
Detailed course brochure available.

Edinburgh University
Centre for Continuing Education,
11 Buccleuch Place, Edinburgh EH8 9LW
☎0131 650 4400   Fax 0131 667 6097
Several writing-orientated courses and summer
schools. Beginners welcome. Publishes a series
of occasional papers – eg: *No. 4 – Creative
Writing: Towards a Framework for Evaluation* by
Graham Hartill, available from the above address
(£2). Course brochure available.

University of Glasgow
Department of Adult and Continuing
Education, 59 Oakfield Avenue,
Glasgow G12 8LW
☎0141 330 4032/4394 (Brochure/Enquiries)
In Spring 1995 ran *Write Around*, 'a friendly and
positive look at students' own writing, aimed at
refining style and discovering what you really
want to write'. Four morning classes; Fee £12.

University of St Andrews
School of English, The University,
St Andrews, Fife KY16 9AL
☎01334 462666   Fax 01334 462655
Offers postgraduate study in *Creative Writing*.
Candidates choose two topics from: *Fiction:
The Novel; Craft and Technique in Poetry; The
Short Story; Twentieth-Century Scottish Poetry*.

University of St Andrews
(Special Interest Courses)
66 North Street, St Andrews,
Fife KY16 9AH
☎01334 462202
Week-long summer courses, occupying most
mornings and afternoons, with the occasional

evening. Courses have included *Creative Writing
for Beginners*.

Wales

University of Glamorgan
Treforest, Pontypridd CF37 1DL
☎01443 482551
MA in Writing – a two-year part-time Master
of Arts degree for writers of fiction and poets.
ESTABLISHED 1993. Contact Professor Tony
Curtis at the School of Humanities and Social
Sciences. Also, BA in Theatre and Media
Drama. Modules include *Scriptwriting: Theatre,
Radio, TV and Video*. Contact Steven Blandford.

Pro Forma Skilled Writing
PO Box 29, Neath, West Glamorgan
SA11 1WL
A correspondence course, tailored to individual
needs. £12 for initial in-depth appraisal with
suggestions, guidelines and details of assignments and support material. Send s.a.e.

Taliesin Trust
Tŷ Newydd, Llanystumdwy, Criccieth,
Gwynedd LL52 0LW
☎01766 522811   Fax 01766 523095
Residential writers' centre set up by the Trust
and supported by the **Arts Council of Wales** to
encourage and promote writing in both English
and Welsh. Most courses run from Monday
evening to Saturday morning. Each course has
two tutors and takes up to 16 participants. The
centre offers a wide range of specific courses.
1995 course tutors included Gillian Clarke, Liz
Lochhead, Roger McGough and Adrian
Mitchell. Early booking essential. Fee £250
inclusive; weekend courses available £100 inclusive. People on low incomes may be eligible for
a grant or bursary. Course leaflet available.

Tre Fechan
Tre Fechan Arts Centre, Pennant Melangell,
Nr Llangynog, Powys SY10 0EU
☎01691 860346
Residential courses held in North Wales. Short
story writing, biography, poetry, getting published, and writing for television. Applicants are
asked to submit 1,000 words to give an indication of their style. Contact Tom and Michelle
Haycraft for details.

Circles and Workshops

Directory of Writers' Circles
Oldacre, Horderns Park road, Chapel en le Frith, Derbyshire SK12 6SY
☎01298 812305

Comprehensive directory of writers' circles, containing contacts and addresses of hundreds of groups and circles including postal circles, meeting throughout the country. Some overseas entries too. Available from Jill Dick at the above address. £4 post free.

Basement Writers
7 Aylward House, Dupont Street, London E14 7QE
☎0171 790 4803

Small group of writers meeting every Tuesday evening at St George's Town Hall, Shadwell from 7.00–9.00pm. Running for over 20 years. Also publishers of the group's material. Contact Frances Lane (Secretary)

Chiltern Writers' Group
31 Cressex Road, High Wycombe HP12 4PG
☎01494 520375

Invites writers, publishers, editors and agents to speak at its monthly meetings at Wendover Public Library. Regular newsletter and competitions. Annual subscription: £10. Trial meeting: £2. Contact Karen Hemmingham at the above address.

The Cotswold Writers' Circle
Dar-es-Salaam, Beeches Park, Hampton Fields, Minchinhampton, Gloucestershire GL6 9BA

Contact *Charles Hooker*, Honorary Treasurer, for details of the Circle's activities.

Equinoxe Screenwriting Workshops (in association with the Sundance Institute)
Association Equinoxe, 85–89 Quai André Citroën, 75711 Paris, France
☎00 33 1 4425 7146   Fax 00 33 1 4425 7142

FOUNDED 1993, with Jeanne Moreau as president, to promote screenwriting and to establish a link between European and American film production. In adapting the Sundance Institute's concept (founded by Robert Redford), Equinoxe supports young writers of all nationalities by creating a screenwriting community capable of appealing to an international audience. For selected professional screenwriters able to speak either English or French fluently. Contact Claire Dubert.

Gay Authors Workshop
BM Box 5700, London WC1N 3XX
☎0181 520 5223

Established 1978 to encourage and support lesbian/gay writers. Regular meetings and a newsletter. Contact Kathryn Byrd. Membership £5; £2 unwaged.

London Screenwriters' Workshop
84 Wardour Street, London W1V 3LF
☎0171 434 0942

Established by writers in 1983 as a forum for contact, information and tuition. LSW helps new and established writers in the film, TV and video industries. Organises a continuous programme of workshops, events with industry figures, seminars and courses. Contact Paul Gallagher or Andrew Fish. Membership £18 p.a.

NWP (North West Playwrights)
Contact Theatre, Oxford Road, Manchester M15 6JA
☎& Fax 0161 274 4418

FOUNDED 1982. Award-winning organisation whose primary aim is to promote new writing for the theatre in the North West of England. Offers a script-reading service, six writing bursaries a year in the region, regular newsletter and a series of workshops with selected scripts for a festival each year. Previous participants have included Kevin Fegan, Charlotte Keatley, Lavinia Murray and James Stock. Co-ordinator Jonquil Panting

Nottingham Writers Contact
W.E.A. Centre, 16 Shakespeare Street, Nottingham NG1 4GF
☎01159 288913

A group of professional and amateur writers which meets every third Saturday in the month at the W.E.A. Centre, 10.00am – 12.30pm. 'If you are visiting the city contact Keith Taylor at the above telephone number.'

Playwrights' Workshop
22 Brown Street, Altrincham, Cheshire WA14 2EU
☎0161 928 3095

Monthly meetings, readings, guest speakers, etc.

SOURCES Script Development Workshops
Jan Luykenstraat 92, 1071 CT Amsterdam, The Netherlands
☎00 31 20 6720801   Fax 00 31 20 6720399

The aim of SOURCES is to contribute to a higher standard of European film and television production by means of script-development workshops for professional screenwriters. Each workshop consists of two group sessions of seven days, each situated in a different European country. An intermediate period of approximately 12 weeks is used for rewrites. English is the working language for all workshops. Participation is subject to selection on the basis of the creative quality of the script/treatment submitted. For further information contact Dick Willemsen, Secretary General.

Southport Writers' Circle
53 Richmond Road, Birkdale, Southport, Merseyside PR8 4SB

Runs a poetry competition (see **Prizes**). Contact Alison Chisholm.

Speakeasy
14 Langcliffe Drive, Heelands, Milton Keynes MK13 7AL
☎01908 318722

Invites poets and writers to Milton Keynes most months. Also runs workshops according to demand. Monthly meetings are held where people can read their own work. Contact Anita Packwood.

University of Stirling
Continuing Education, Airthrey Castle, Stirling FK9 4LA
☎01786 473171

Holds writers' workshop at Airthrey Castle one evening per week for eight weeks. Covers writing short stories, poetry, novels, letters, diaries, drama, newspaper articles, biography and autobiography, etc.

Workers' Educational Association
National Office: Temple House, 17 Victoria Park Square, London E2 9BB
☎0181 983 1515   Fax 0181 983 4840
FOUNDED in 1903, the WEA is a voluntary body with members drawn from all walks of life. It runs writing courses and workshops throughout the country and all courses are open to everyone. Branches in most towns and many villages, with 13 district offices in England and 1 in Scotland. Contact your district WEA office for courses in your region. All correspondence should be addressed to the District Secretary.

Cheshire, Merseyside & West Lancashire: 7/8 Bluecoat Chambers, School Lane, Liverpool L1 3BX (☎0151 709 8023)

Eastern: Botolph House, 17 Botolph Lane, Cambridge CB2 3RE (☎01223 350978).

East Midlands: 16 Shakespeare Street, Nottingham NG1 4GF (☎01159 9475162).

London: 44–46 Crowndale Road, London NW1 1TR (☎0171 388 7261).

Northern: 51 Grainger Street, Newcastle upon Tyne NE1 5JE (☎0191 232 3957)

North Western: 4th Floor, Crawford House, University Precinct Centre, Oxford Road, Manchester M13 9GH (☎0161 273 7652).

South Eastern: 4 Castle Hill, Rochester, Kent ME1 1QQ (☎01631 842140).

South Western: Martin's Gate Annexe, Bretonside, Plymouth, Devon PL4 0AT (Tel: 01752 664989).

Thames & Solent: 6 Brewer Street Oxford OX1 1QN (☎01865 246270).

Western: 40 Morse Road, Redfield, Bristol, Avon BS5 9LB (☎01179 351764).

West Mercia: 78–80 Sherlock Street, Birmingham B5 6LT (Tel: 0121 666 6101).

Yorkshire North: 7 Woodhouse Square, Leeds, W. Yorkshire LS3 1AD (☎01132 453304).

Yorkshire South: Chantry Buildings, Corporation Street, Rotherham S60 1NG (Tel: 01709 837001).

Scotland: Riddle's Court, 322 Lawnmarket, Edinburgh EH1 3PG (☎0131 226 3456).

The Writers' Workshop
23 Upper Ashlyns Road, Berkhamsted, Hertfordshire HP4 3BW
☎01442 871004

The Writers' Workshop at Frieth, near High Wycombe, offers classes in creative writing, plus workshop opportunities. Professional assessments optional. Now publishes a twice-yearly literary magazine, *Rivet*, and holds an annual poetry competition. Contact Maggie Prince at the above address.

Editorial Research and other Services

Lesley & Roy Adkins
Longstone Lodge, Aller, Langport, Somerset
TA10 0QT
☎01458 250075   Fax 01458 250858
Contact *Lesley Adkins, Roy Adkins*

Offers indexing, research, copy-editing, manuscript criticism/advice, contract writing for publishers, rewriting, book reviews and feature writing. *Special interests* archaeology (worldwide), history and heritage. See also **Lesley & Roy Adkins Picture Library**.

Anagram Editorial Service
26 Wherwell Road, Guildford, Surrey
GU2 5JR
☎01483 33497   Fax 01483 306848
Contact *Martyn Bramwell*

Full range of editorial services available from project development through commissioning, editing and proof-reading to production of finished books. Specialises in earth sciences, natural history, environment, general science and technology. Also author of over 30 non-fiction titles for young readers. Clients include UK, German and American publishers, United Nations agencies (UNEP, FAO) and international conservation organisations.

Arioma Editorial Services
Gloucester House, High Street, Borth, Dyfed
SY24 5HZ
☎01970 871296   Fax 01970 871296
Contact *Moira Smith*

FOUNDED 1987. Staffed by ex-London journalists, who work mainly with authors wanting to self-publish. Editing, indexing, ghost writing, cover design, plus initial help with marketing and publicity. Sample chapter and synopsis required. All types of book welcome, but work must be of a 'sufficiently high standard'. No reading fee. Rates on application. Please send s.a.e. with all submissions.

Ascribe
112 Mildred Avenue, Watford, Hertfordshire
WD1 7DX
☎01923 238899
Contact *Mary Baginsky*

Complete book production services for charities, small societies and individuals, as well as editorial, writing, rewriting, research and any emergency projects. Specialist areas include education, law, criminology and other social sciences.

Astron Appointments Ltd
20–24 Uxbridge Street, London W8 7TA
☎0171 229 9171   Fax 0171 221 7594
Contact *Deborah Rea*

In addition to a long-standing register of permanent job-seekers within publishing, Astron has a freelance register with details of a large number of experienced people available to undertake all types of freelance assignments within the publishing field.

Authors' Research Services (ARS)
32 Oak Village, London NW5 4QN
☎0171 284 4316
Contact *Richard Wright*

Research and document supply service, particularly to authors, academics and others without easy access to London libraries and sources of information. Also indexing of books and journals. Rates negotiable.

Black Ace Enterprises
Ellemford Farmhouse, Duns, Berwickshire
TD11 3SG
☎01361 890370   Fax 01361 890287
Directors *Hunter Steele, Boo Wood*

Book production and text processing, including scanning, editing, proofing, printing and binding, artwork and design. Can offer complete packages including promotion and distribution.

D. Buckmaster
Wayfarer House, 51 Chatsworth Road,
Torquay, Devon TQ1 3BJ
☎01803 294663
Contact *Mrs D. Buckmaster*

General editing of mss, specialising in traditional themes in religious, metaphysical and esoteric subjects. Also success and inspirational books or articles.

Graham Burn Productions

9–13 Soulbury Road, Linslade, Leighton
Buzzard, Bedfordshire LU7 2RL
☎01525 377963/376390   Fax 01525 382498

Offers complete production services to writers
wishing to publish their own material, and pre-
press services to other publishers.

Carter Rae Communications

15 Moray Place, Edinburgh EH3 6DT
☎0131 225 9979   Fax 0131 220 2895

Contact *Jenny Carter, Janet Rae*

Specialises in the production of newspapers and
magazines for commerce and industry. Full
editorial and production service: writing, editing, proof-reading, typesetting, layout, etc.
Rates on application.

CIRCA Research and Reference Information Ltd

13–17 Sturton Street, Cambridge
CB1 2SN
☎01223 568017   Fax 01223 354643

An editorial cooperative
Approx. turnover £500,000

ESTABLISHED 1989. Specialises in researching,
writing and editing of reference works on
international politics and economics, including
*Keesing's Record of World Events; Keesing's
UK Record; People in Power*. All work is fee-
based.

Creative Communications

11 Belhaven Terrace, Glasgow
G12 0TG
☎0141 334 9577   Fax 0141 334 9577

Contact *Ronnie Scott*

Creative Comunications delivers professional
corporate communication services to leading
Scottish organisations. It also provides effective
writing (including copywriting and script writing), editing and newspaper design, and con-
sults on all aspects of communications.

E. Glyn Davies

Cartref, 21 Claremont Avenue, Bishopston,
Bristol, Avon BS7 8JD
☎0117 9445438   Fax 0117 9248065

Contact *E. Glyn Davies*

Proof-reading, indexing, revision and rewriting service, assistance with theses. *Specialises* in
travel, guide books, health care and psychology, religion, translation into English (from
French, Italian and Welsh). Quotations on
request.

Deeson Editorial Services

Ewell House, Faversham, Kent ME13 8UP
☎01795 535468   Fax 01795 535469

Also at: 100 Grove Vale, London SE22 8DR.
☎0181 693 3383   Fax: 0181 299 0862

Contact *Dr Tony Deeson, Dominic Deeson*

ESTABLISHED 1959. A comprehensive research/
writing/editing service for books, magazines,
newspapers, articles, annual reports, submissions,
presentations. Design and production facilities.
Specialists in scientific, technical, industrial and
business-to-business subjects including company
histories.

Fern House Publications

19 High Street, Haddenham, Ely,
Cambridgeshire CB6 3XA
☎01353 741229   Fax 01353 741601

Contact *Rodney Dale*

Extensively published author, editor, producer of
published matter, and series editor for *Discoveries
& Inventions* for the British Library. Fern House
offers a consultancy service and practical help to
achieve publication. Example: producing a biography for the Bryan Green Society: *Bryan Green
– Parson-Evangelist*.

Flair for Words

5 Delavall Walk, Eastbourne, East Sussex
BN23 6ER
☎01323 640646

Directors *Cass and Janie Jackson*

ESTABLISHED 1988. Offers wide range of services to writers, whether beginners or professional, through the Flair Network. Offers
assessment, editing and advisory service. Publishes bi-monthly newsletter, handbooks on all
aspects of writing, and audio tapes. Organises
residential writing weekends.

F. G. & K. M. Gill

11 Cranmore Close, Aldershot, Hampshire
GU11 3BH
☎01252 25881/24067   Fax 01252 25881

Contacts *Fred and Kathie Gill*

ESTABLISHED over 15 years. Proof-reading, copy
editing and indexing services. Fiction and non-
fiction (all subjects). Clients include UK, North
American and continental publishers. Rates on
application.

Valerie Grosvenor Myer

34 West End, Haddenham, Cambridge
CB7 3TE
☎01353 740748   Fax 01353 740738

Contact *Valerie Grosvenor Myer*

Copy-editing of manuscripts and typescripts for publication. Research in English literature, post-15th century. Learned periodical articles and bibliographies a speciality. Experienced indexer. Hourly fees by agreement.

Ink Inc. Ltd

1 Anglesea Road, Kingston on Thames, Surrey KT1 2EW
☎0181 549 3174   Fax 0181 546 2415
Managing Director *Richard Parkes*
Editorial Head *Barbara Leedham*

Publishing consultants. Clients range from very small dtp operations through to large plcs. Advise on every aspect of publishing including production, design, editorial, marketing, distribution and finance. Also take on editorial, design, production and project management work.

J G Editorial

54 Mount Street, Lincoln LN1 3JG
☎01522 530758   Fax 01522 575679
Contact *Jenni Goss*

ESTABLISHED 1988. Freelance editors with 19 years' experience offering full editorial service to authors and typesetters. Independent critique service for fiction, general non-fiction and academic/business (no poetry) – includes structure and presentation; rewriting/ghosting; word processing/presentation/keying; project management; editorial reports; copy and disk editing (IBM/AppleMac); proofreading. Quotations on request.

Gordon Jarvie Editorial

81 Comiston Drive, Edinburgh EH10 5QT
☎0131 447 3417   Fax 0131 452 8595
Contact *Gordon Jarvie, Frances Jarvie*

Full range of general editorial and research services, including authorship, editing, proof-reading, blurb writing, indexing, market analyses, etc. No science or technology.

LJC Permission Services

11 Monkswell Lane, Chipstead, Coulsdon, Surrey CR5 3SX
☎01737 833536   Fax 01737 833004
Contacts *Louisa Clements, Robert Young*

A copyright clearing agency used widely by publishers and authors who wish to reproduce copyright material. The agency undertakes to obtain permission for articles, photographs, artwork and music to be reproduced in another publication or on cassettes. Part of the service includes preparing acknowledgement copy if requested and negotiating the reproduction fee with the copyright holder. Full breakdown of costs on larger projects. Large database of copyright sources. Multimedia permissions also undertaken. Fixed fee per permission.

Deborah Manley

57 Plantation Road, Oxford OX2 6JE
☎01865 310284   Fax 01865 59671
Contact *Deborah Manley*

Offers (to publishers) project management, editorial reports, copy-editing, writing, rewriting, research, anthologising, indexing, proofreading and caption copy. Specialises mainly in educational, English Language Teaching, children's, reference and travel. NUJ rates.

Duncan McAra

30 Craighall Crescent, Edinburgh EH6 4RZ
☎0131 552 1558
Contact *Duncan McAra*

Consultancy on all aspects of general trade publishing: editing, rewriting, copy-editing, proofreading. *Specialises* in art, architecture, archaeology, biography, film, military and travel. Also runs a literary agency (see **UK Agents**).

Minett Media

25 Campbell Drive, Gunthorpe, Peterborough PE4 7JZ
☎01733 327671   Fax 01733 327864
Contact *Dr Steve Minett, Gunnel Minett*

Specialises in the production of press releases and feature articles for multi-national business-to-business companies, offering a comprehensive editorial service (including site visits anywhere in Europe, writing draft text, securing approval and best effort at publication in the international trade press). Also offers management of press relations with the international business-to-business trade press, complete package production of business-to-business, multi-language customer magazines (including translation, design, artwork, repro, printing and distribution) and enquiry database management. Clients include ITT Flygt, Anglian Water Processes, IMO, Celleco-Hedemora (part of Alfa Laval).

Murder Files

Marienau, Brimley Road, Bovey Tracey, Devon TQ13 9DH
☎01626 833487   Fax 01626 835797
Contact *Paul Williams*

Crime writer and researcher specialising in UK murders. Can provide information on thousands of well-known and less well-known cases dating from 1400. Copies of press cuttings relating to murder available for cases from 1920 onwards. Research also undertaken for general enquirers, writers, TV, radio, video, etc. Rates on application.

Northern Writers Advisory Services (NWAS)

77 Marford Crescent, Sale, Cheshire M33 4DN
☎0161 969 1573

Contact *Jill Groves*

Offers publishing services such as copy-editing, proof-reading, word-processing and desktop publishing (with laser printing). Does much of its work with societies (mainly local history), and small presses. NWAS's specialist subject is history of all types, but especially local and family history. Also handles biographies and leisure books. No computer software material. Rates on application, but very reasonable.

James A. Oliver Consultants

69–76 Long Acre, London WC2E 9JH
☎0171 379 3939   Fax 0171 497 3708

Contact *James A. Oliver*

Authorship, research and editorial consultants to an international clientèle. Company newsletters and journals; corporate literature; training; expeditions; brochures; conference proceedings; communications strategies; confidential reports. Member of **The Society of Authors** and **The Writers Guild of Great Britain**. Associates in UK, USA, Europe, and Asia-Pacific.

Ormrod Research Services

Weeping Birch, Burwash, East Sussex TN19 7HG
☎01435 882541   Fax 01435 882541

Contact *Richard Ormrod*

ESTABLISHED 1982. Comprehensive research service: literary, historical, academic, biographical, commercial. Critical reading with report, editing, indexing, proof-reading, ghosting. Verbal quotations available.

Out of Print Book Service

13 Pantbach Road, Birchgrove, Cardiff CF4 1TU
☎01222 627703

Contact *L. A. Foulkes*

FOUNDED 1971. Covers all subjects including fiction and non-fiction. No charge for search. Send s.a.e for details.

Pages Editorial & Publishing Services

Ballencrieff Cottage, Ballencrieff Toll, Bathgate, West Lothian EH48 4LD
☎01506 632728   Fax 01506 632728

Contact *Susan Coon*

Contract publishing service for magazines and newsletters, including journalism, editing, advertising, production and mailing. Also editorial advice, word processing and desktop publishing service for authors.

Roger Palmer Limited, Media Contracts and Copyright

18 Maddox Street, Mayfair, London W1R 9PL
☎0171 499 8875   Fax 0171 499 9580

Contact *Roger Palmer, Stephen Aucutt*

ESTABLISHED 1933. Drafts, advises on and negotiates all media contracts (on a regular or *ad hoc* basis) for publishers, agents, packagers, charities and others; there is also a small list of private clients. Manages and operates clients' complete contracts and copyright functions, undertakes contractual audits, devises contracts systems, advises on copyright and related issues and provides training and seminars. Roger Palmer (Managing Director) was for many years Contracts and Intellectual Property Director of the Hodder & Stoughton Group; Stephen Aucutt (Senior Consultant) was previously Contracts Manager for Reed Children's Books.

Penman Literary Service

185 Daws Heath Road, Benfleet, Essex SS7 2TF
☎01702 557431

Contact *Mark Sorrell*

ESTABLISHED 1950. Advisory, editorial and typing service for authors. Rewriting, ghosting, proof-reading; critical assessment of mss.

Perfect English

11 Hill Square, Upper Cam, Dursley, Gloucestershire GL11 5NJ
☎01453 547320   Fax 01453 521525

Contact *James Alexander*

'Meticulous reading and editing to remove errors of spelling, grammar, punctuation, word choice and meaning. Mss returned fully checked and as perfect as possible within the structure and style of the original material.' Rates on application.

Plain Words (Business Writers)
96 Wellmeadow Road, London SE6 1HW
☎0181 698 5269/697 3227 Fax 0181 461 5705
Contact *Henry Galgut, Judy Byrne*

Writing, editing, design and production services for industrial, commercial, public and other organisations: house journals, newsletters, brochures, books, manuals, directives, publicity material, press releases.

Reading & Righting (Robert Lambolle Services)
618B Finchley Road, London NW11 7RR
☎0181 455 4564   Fax 0171 431 7636
Contact *Robert Lambolle*

Reader/literary editor, with agency, publishing and theatre experience. Offers detailed manuscript evaluation, analysis of prospects and next-step guidelines. Fiction, non-fiction, drama and screenplays. Special interests include cinema, the performing arts, popular culture, psychotherapy and current affairs. Also editorial services, creative writing workshops and lectures. Services do not include representing writers in an agent's capacity.

Scottish Script Centre
c/o Pine Trees, Greenbank, Falkirk FK1 5PU
☎01324 636265   Fax 01324 636265
Contact *Anne-Marie Barth*

A joint theatre initiative (Edinburgh **Traverse** and Royal Lyceum) set up to provide a script-reading service for Scottish theatres as a whole. Promises a fast, professional service to writers (fee charged to cover costs) and two reports on any script handled. Also able to offer advice about outlets and showcasing workshops for the most highly recommended scripts. Theatres will be in touch with the Script Centre and its operations and will assist in the showcasing of the best scripts, with a view towards the possibility of full production.

Scriptmate
20 Shepherds Hill, London N6 5AH
☎0181 341 7650
Contact *Ann Kritzinger*

Writers' advisory service. Professional editing and readers-for-writers service. Associated with **Book-in-Hand Ltd** production service.

Strand Editorial Services
16 Mitchley View, South Croydon, Surrey CR2 9HQ
☎0181 657 1247   Fax 0181 657 1247

Contact *Derek Bradley*

All stages of editorial production of house journals, magazines, newsletters, publicity material, etc. Short-term, long-term and emergency projects. Sub-editing and proof-reading, and book reviews (educational, training and business). Reasonable rates (negotiable).

Teral Research Services
45 Forest View Road, Moordown, Bournemouth, Dorset BH9 3BH
☎01202 516834   Fax 01202 519220
Contact *Terry C. Treadwell*

All aspects of research undertaken but specialises in all military, aviation, naval and defence subjects, both past and present. Extensive book and photographic library, including one of the best collections of World War One aviation photographs. Terms by arrangement.

WORDSmith
2 The Island, Thames Ditton, Surrey KT7 0SH
☎0181 339 0945   Fax 0181 339 0945
Contact *Michael Russell*

Conventional copy-editing service, with on-screen revision and computer setting. Specialises in improving badly-written text, and abridging instruction sheets for appliance operation and toy/furniture assembly into something useful. Everything from 1000 to 200,000 words. Phone for details.

Writerlink
Production House, 59 Marlborough Hill, Harrow, Middlesex HA1 1TX
☎0181 863 4491   Fax 0181 863 4491
Contact *Paul Usiskin*

Offers professional reading and report service, editing advice, contacts with publishers. Rates on application.

The Writers Advice Centre for Children's Books
Thames Wharf Studios, Rainville Road, London W6 9HA
☎0181 874 7347
Contact *Louise Jordan*

Offers editorial and marketing advice to children's writers – both published and unpublished – by Readers who are all currently connected with children's publishing. Plus personal introductions to publishers/agents where appropriate. Also runs courses.

The Writers' Exchange
14 Yewdale, Clifton Green, Swinton
M27 8GN
Contact *The Secretary*

FOUNDED 1978. Reading and appraisal service for writers preparing to submit material to, or having had material rejected by, literary agents and/or publishers. Offers 'constructive, objec tive evaluation service, particularly for those who can't get past the standard rejection slip barrier, or who have had mss rejected by publishers and need an impartial view of why it did not sell.' Novels, short stories, film, TV, radio, and stage plays. Reading fee £4.00 per 1000 words; Initial Appraisal £40 (maximum wordage 10,000). Send s.a.e. for details.

Press Cuttings Agencies

The Broadcast Monitoring Company/Lincoln Hannah Ltd

89½ Worship Street, London EC2A 2BE
☎0171 377 1742/247 1166
Fax 0171 377 6103

Television, radio, national and European press monitoring agency. Cuttings from national and all major European press available seven days a week, with early morning delivery. Also monitoring of all news and current affairs programmes – national, international and satellite. Retrospective research service and free telephone notification. Sponsorship evaluation from all media sources.

Durrant's Press Cuttings

103 Whitecross Street, London EC1Y 8QT
☎0171 588 3671   Fax 0171 374 8171

Covers national/London dailies, London/Greater London weeklies, provincial dailies, weeklies and Sundays, Scottish/Welsh/Channel Isles papers, free sheets, consumer magazines, specialised and trade publications, and foreign press in association with agencies abroad. Cuttings are posted twice weekly by first-class mail. Rates are fully comprehensive; no additional charges such as reading fee. Minimum rate (about £150 plus VAT) covers 100 cuttings or lasts 6 months, whichever is sooner.

International Press-Cutting Bureau

224–236 Walworth Road,
London SE17 1JE
☎0171 708 2113   Fax 0171 701 4489

Contact *Robert Podro*

Covers national, provincial, trade, technical and magazine press. Cuttings are normally sent twice weekly by first-class post and there are no additional service charges or reading fees. Subscriptions for 100 and 250 cuttings are valid for six months. Larger subscriptions expire after one year even if the total number of cuttings subscribed for has not been reached. 100 cuttings (£136, plus VAT); 200 (£260, plus VAT).

Premium Press Monitoring

139 Tooley Street, London SE1 2HZ
☎0171 403 6033   Fax 0171 407 5857

Contact *Sandra Appleyard*

Offers an overnight national press monitoring service with same day, early morning delivery. Also coverage of regional papers and weekly/monthly business/trade magazines. Rates on application.

Romeike & Curtice

Hale House, 290–296 Green Lanes, London N13 5TP
☎0181 882 0155   Fax 0181 882 6716

Contact *Angela Webb*

Covers national and international dailies and Sundays, provincial papers, consumer magazines, trade and technical journals, national radio/TV logs and teletext services. Back research and advertising checking services are also available.

We Find It (Press Clippings)

103 South Parade, Belfast BT7 2GN
☎01232 646008

Contact *Avril Forsythe*

Specialises in Northern Ireland press and magazines, both national and provincial. Rates on application.

Bursaries, Fellowships and Grants

Aosdána Scheme

An Chomhairle Ealaíon (The Arts Council),
70 Merrion Square, Dublin 2,
Republic of Ireland
☎00 353 1 6611840   Fax 00 353 1 6761302

Literature Officer *Laurence Cassidy*

Aosdána is an affiliation of creative artists engaged in literature, music and the visual arts, and consists of not more than 200 artists who have gained a reputation for achievement and distinction. Membership is by competitive sponsored selection and is open to Irish citizens or residents only. Members are eligible to receive an annuity for a five-year term to assist them in pursuing their art full-time.

Award IR£8000 (annuity).

Arts Council Literature Bursaries, Ireland

An Chomhairle Ealaíon, 70 Merrion Square,
Dublin 2, Republic of Ireland
☎00 353 1 6611840   Fax 00 353 1 6761302

Literature Officer *Laurence Cassidy*

Bursaries in literature awarded to creative writers of fiction, poetry and drama in Irish and English to enable concentration on, or completion of, specific projects. A limited number of bursaries may be given to non-fiction projects. Open to Irish citizens or residents only. Final entry date 8 April.

Award IR£2000–£8000.

Arts Council Theatre Writing Bursaries

Arts Council of England, 14 Great Peter Street, London SW1P 3NQ
☎0171 333 0100   Fax 0171 973 6590

Contact *Drama Director*

Intended to provide experienced playwrights with an opportunity to research and develop a play for the theatre independently of financial pressures and free from the need to write for a particular market. Bursaries are also available for theatre translation projects. Writers must be resident in England. Writers resident in Wales, Scotland or Northern Ireland should approach their own Arts Council. Final entry date 9 January 1996.

Award £3000.

Arts Council Writers' Awards

14 Great Peter Street, London SW1P 3NQ
☎0171 333 0100   Fax 0171 973 6590

Contact *Literature Department*

The Arts Council offers 15 bursaries a year. Applications should be accompanied by a c.v., description and sample of work in progress, statement of annual income and three copies of a previously published creative work. Judges will make their choices principally on the grounds of artistic quality, basing that judgment on their reading of work in progress and evidence before them of the writer's past achievement. Past winners include: Susan Hill, Kazuo Ishiguro, Jean Rhys, Salman Rushdie, Graham Swift, Rose Tremain, Gerard Woodward. Final entry date 30 September.

Award up to £7000.

The Authors' Contingency Fund

The Society of Authors, 84 Drayton Gardens,
London SW10 9SB
☎0171 373 6642   Fax 0171 373 5768

This fund makes modest grants to published authors who find themselves in sudden financial difficulties.

The Authors' Foundation

The Society of Authors, 84 Drayton Gardens,
London SW10 9SB
☎0171 373 6642   Fax 0171 373 5768

Annual grants to writers whose publisher's advance is insufficient to cover the costs of research involved. Application by letter to The Authors' Foundation giving details, in confidence, of the advance and royalties, together with the reasons for needing additional funding. Grants are sometimes given even if there is no commitment by a publisher, so long as the work will almost certainly be published. £75,000 was distributed in 1994. Contact the Society of Authors for an information sheet. Final entry date 30 April.

The K. Blundell Trust

The Society of Authors, 84 Drayton Gardens,
London SW10 9SB
☎0171 373 6642   Fax 0171 373 5768

Annual grants to writers whose publisher's

advance is insufficient to cover the costs of research. Author must be under 40, has to submit copy of his/her previous book and the work must 'contribute to the greater understanding of existing social and economic organisation'. Application by letter. Contact the Society of Authors for an information sheet. Final entry date 30 April. Total of £15,000 available.

Alfred Bradley Bursary Award
c/o Network Radio Drama, BBC North,
New Broadcasting House, Oxford Road,
Manchester M60 1SJ
☎0161 200 2020
Contact *Kate Rowland*

ESTABLISHED 1992. Biennial award in commemoration of the life and work of the distinguished radio producer Alfred Bradley. Aims to encourage and develop new writing talent in the **BBC North** region. There is a change of focus for each award; in 1995 it was for drama, and details of the theme for the next award (1997) will be available in 1996. Entrants must live or work in the North region. The award is given to help authors to pursue a career in writing for radio. Support and guidance is given from regional BBC radio producers. Previous winners: Lee Hall, Julie Clark.

Award not less than £3000 a year for 2 years.

British Academy Publication Subventions
20–21 Cornwall Terrace, London NW1 4QP
☎0171 487 5966   Fax 0171 224 3807
Contact *Assistant Secretary, Research Grants*

Thrice-yearly award to help defray production costs of scholarly publications which might otherwise not succeed in finding a publisher. Work to be published must be a serious contribution to scholarship and the manuscript must have been completed and accepted by a publisher prior to application. Subventions do not normally exceed 25% (up to a maximum of £2000) of the direct costs of production, excluding any element of publisher's overheads.

British Academy Small Personal Research Grants
20–21 Cornwall Terrace, London NW1 4QP
☎0171 487 5966   Fax 0171 224 3807
Contact *Assistant Secretary, Research Grants*

Quarterly award to further original creative research at postdoctoral level in the humanities

and social sciences. Entrants must no longer be registered for postgraduate study, and must be resident in the UK. Final entry dates end of September, November, February and April.

Award maximum £5000.

Cholmondeley Awards
The Society of Authors, 84 Drayton Gardens,
London SW10 9SB
☎0171 373 6642   Fax 0171 373 5768

FOUNDED 1965 by the late Dowager Marchioness of Cholmondeley. Annual noncompetitive awards for the benefit and encouragement of poets of any age, sex or nationality, for which submissions are not required. Presentation date June. 1994 winners: Ruth Fainlight, Gwen Harwood, Elizabeth Jennings, John Mole.

Award (total) £8000, usually shared.

The Economist/Richard Casement Internship
The Economist, 25 St James's Street,
London SW1A 1HG
☎0171 839 7000
Contact *Business Affairs Editor (re. Casement Internship)*

For a journalist under 24 to spend three months in the summer writing for *The Economist* about science and technology. Applicants should write a letter of introduction along with an article of approximately 600 words suitable for inclusion in the Science and Technology Section. Competition details normally announced in the magazine late January and 5–6 weeks allowed for application.

Fulbright T. E. B. Clarke Fellowship in Screenwriting
The Fulbright Commission,
Fulbright House, 62 Doughty Street,
London WC1N 2LS
☎0171 404 6880   Fax 0171 404 6834
Contact *Programme Director*

Award offered to a young (normally, under 35) British film screenwriter to spend nine months in the US developing his/her expertise and experience. The successful candidate will follow postgraduate courses in screenwriting at a US institution, attend real-life story conferences and write a screenplay and some treatments during the award period. Final entry date end February.

Award air travel and grant of £18,000 plus approved tuition fees.

Fulton Fellowship

David Fulton (Publishers) Ltd, 2 Barbon
Close, Great Ormond Street, London
WC1N 3JX
☎0171 405 5606   Fax 0171 831 48400
Contact *David Fulton*

ESTABLISHED 1995. Annual award to support
research in special educational needs. Recipients will have the opportunity to publish their
work in a form accessible to teachers with the
help of the publisher, David Fulton and the
Centre of the Study of Special Education at
Westminster College, Oxford. 1995 winner:
Erica Brown.

Funding for Script Development

39C Highbury Place, London N5 1QP
☎0171 226 9903   Fax 0171 354 2706
Contact *Philip Hughes*

ESTABLISHED 1989. Four awards schemes,
including a biannual award to provide financial
support for writers. Open to residents in the
EU, EFTA and Hungary.

Eric Gregory Trust Fund

The Society of Authors, 84 Drayton Gardens,
London SW10 9SB
☎0171 373 6642   Fax 0171 373 5768

Annual competitive awards of varying amounts
are made each year for the encouragement of
young poets under the age of 30 who can show
that they are likely to benefit from an opportunity to give more time to writing. Open only
to British-born subjects resident in the UK.
Final entry date 31 October. Presentation date
June. Contact The Society of Authors for further information. 1994 winners: Julia Copus,
Alice Oswald, Giles Goodland, Steven Blyth,
Kate Clanchy.
    Award (total) £30,000.

The Guardian Research Fellowship

Nuffield College, Oxford OX1 1NF
☎01865 278520   Fax 01865 278676
Contact *Warden's Secretary*

One-year fellowship endowed by the Scott
Trust, owner of *The Guardian*, to give someone
working in the media the chance to put their
experience into a new perspective, publish the
outcome and give a *Guardian* lecture.
Applications welcomed from journalists and
management members, in newspapers, periodicals or broadcasting. Research or study proposals should be directly related to experience of
working in the media. Accommodation and
meals in college will be provided, and a 'modest' supplementary stipend might be arranged
to ensure the Fellow does not lose out from the
stay. Advertised annually in November.

Francis Head Bequest

The Society of Authors, 84 Drayton Gardens,
London SW10 9SB
☎0171 373 6642   Fax 0171 373 5768

Provides grants to published British authors
over the age of 35 who need financial help
during a period of illness, disablement or temporary financial crisis.

The Independent Student Journalist Bursary

1 Canada Square, Canary Wharf,
London E14 5AP
☎0171 293 2000   Fax 0171 293 2145
Contact *Personnel Officer*

Occasional bursaries for graduate trainee journalists. Due to changes in management, *The
Independent* is to review the possibility of granting these from year to year.

Ralph Lewis Award

University of Sussex Library, Brighton, East
Sussex BN1 9QL
☎01273 678158   Fax 01273 678441

ESTABLISHED 1985. Triennial award set up by
Ralph Lewis, a Brighton author and art collector who left money to fund awards for promising manuscripts which would not otherwise be
published. The award is given in the form of a
grant to a UK-based publisher in respect of an
agreed three-year programme of publication of
literary works by new authors or by established
authors using new styles or forms. No direct
applications from writers. At the time of going
to press, the 1995 award had been postponed,
subject to review. Previous winners: **Peterloo
Poets** (1989-91); **Serpent's Tail** (1992-94).

London Arts Board Publishing New Writing Fund

Elme House, 133 Long Acre,
London WC2E 9AF
☎0171 240 1313   Fax 0171 240 4580

Aims to support and develop small presses and
literary magazines in the publishing of new or
under-represented fiction and poetry. This
fund is only open to groups for whom publishing is a central activity. Contact the Principal
Literature Officer for further details and deadline.

Macaulay Fellowship

An Chomhairle Ealaíon (The Arts Council),
70 Merrion Square, Dublin 2,
Republic of Ireland
☎00 353 1 6611840   Fax 00 353 1 6761302
Literature Officer *Laurence Cassidy*

To further the liberal education of a young
creative artist. Candidates for this triennial
award must be under 30 on 30 June, or 35 in
exceptional circumstances, and must be Irish
citizens or residents. Last awarded 1993.
Award IR£4000.

The John Masefield
Memorial Trust

The Society of Authors, 84 Drayton Gardens,
London SW10 9SB
☎0171 373 6642   Fax 0171 373 5768

This trust makes occasional grants to professional poets (or to their immediate dependants)
who are faced with sudden financial problems.

Somerset Maugham Trust Fund

The Society of Authors, 84 Drayton Gardens,
London SW10 9SB
☎0171 373 6642   Fax 0171 373 5768

The annual awards arising from this Fund are
designed to encourage young writers to travel
and to acquaint themselves with the manners
and customs of other countries. Candidates
must be under 35 and their publishers must
submit a published literary work in volume
form in English. They must be British subjects
by birth. Final entry date 31 December.
Presentation in June. 1994 winners: Jackie Kay,
A.L. Kennedy, Philip Marsden.
Award £5000 each.

Mobil Bursary

See **Mobil Playwriting Competition**
under **Prizes**

National Poetry
Foundation Grants

27 Mill Road, Fareham, Hampshire
PO16 0TH
☎01329 822218
Contact *Johnathon Clifford*

The **National Poetry Foundation** considers
applications for grant aid of up to £1000
where other funding is not available and the
product will benefit poetry in general. Send
details together with s.a.e. to NPF (Grants) at
the above address.

The Airey Neave Trust

40 Charles Street, London WC1X 7PB
☎0171 495 0554   Fax 0171 491 1118
Contact *Hannah Scott*

INITIATED 1989. Annual research fellowships
for up to three years – towards a book or paper
– for serious research connected with national
and international law, and human freedom.
Must be attached to a particular university in
Britain. Interested applicants should come forward with ideas, preferably before March in
any year.

Newspaper Press Fund

Dickens House, 35 Wathen Road, Dorking,
Surrey RH4 1JY
☎01306 887511   Fax 01306 876104
Director/Secretary *Peter Evans*

Aims to relieve distress among journalists and
their dependants. Limited help available to non-
member journalists. Continuous and/or occasional financial grants; also retirement homes for
eligible beneficiaries. Information and subscription details available from The Secretary.

Northern Arts Literary Fellowship

Northern Arts, 10 Osborne Terrace, Jesmond,
Newcastle upon Tyne NE2 1NZ
☎0191 281 6334   Fax 0191 281 3276
Contact *Published & Broadcast Arts Department*

A competitive fellowship tenable at and co-
sponsored by the universities of Durham and
Newcastle upon Tyne for a period of two academic years. Next Fellowship will begin in 1996.
Award £14,000 p.a.

Northern Arts Writers Awards

Northern Arts, 10 Osborne Terrace, Jesmond,
Newcastle upon Tyne NE2 1NZ
☎0191 281 6334   Fax 0191 281 3276
Contact *Published & Broadcast Arts Department*

Awards are offered to established authors resi-
dent in the **Northern Arts** area on the basis of
literary merit. Application spring/summer.
Also available, one-month residencies at
Tyrone Guthrie Centre, Ireland.
Award variable.

Oppenheim John Downes
Memorial Trust

36 Whitefriars Street, London EC4Y 8BH

Grants to writers and artists of all descriptions
who are over the age of 30 and unable to pursue
their vocation by reason of their poverty.
Applicants must be British by birth and of British

parents and grandparents. Awards made annually in December. Final entry date 1 November. Application forms available from 1 September each year; send written request and enclose s.a.e.

Grant variable, but usually between £50 and £1500.

The PAWS (Public Awareness of Science) Drama Script Fund

The PAWS Office, OMNI Communications, Osborne House, 11 Bartholomew Road, London NW5 2BJ

☎0171 267 2555   Fax 0171 482 2394

Contacts *Barrie Whatley, Andrew Millington*

ESTABLISHED 1994. Annual award aimed at encouraging television scriptwriters to include science and engineering scenarios in their work. Grants (currently £2000) are given to selected writers to develop their script ideas into full treatments; Prizes are awarded for the best of these treatments (Grand Prix £5000). The Fund holds meetings enabling writers to meet scientists and engineers and also offers a contacts service to put writers in 'one-to-one' contact with specialists who can help them develop their ideas.

The Margaret Rhondda Award

The Society of Authors, 84 Drayton Gardens, London SW10 9SB

☎0171 373 6642   Fax 0171 373 5768

Competitive award given to a woman writer as a grant-in-aid towards the expenses of a research project in journalism. Triennial (next award 1996). Final entry date 31 December 1995. Presentation date June.

Award (total) approx. £1000.

The Royal Literary Fund

144 Temple Chambers, Temple Avenue, London EC4Y 0DA

☎0171 353 7150

Secretary *Mrs Fiona Clark*

Grants and pensions are awarded to published authors in financial need, or to their dependants. Examples of author's works are needed for assessment by Committee. Write for further details and application form.

Southern Arts Literature Bursaries

13 St Clement Street, Winchester, Hampshire SO23 9DQ

☎01962 855099   Fax 01962 861186

Contact *Literature Officer*

Offers an annual award of £3,500 to a published writer living in the region to assist a

specific project. Awards can be used to cover a period of unpaid leave while writing from home, to finance necessary research and travel, or to purchase equipment. Final entry date: mid-August.

Laurence Stern Fellowship

Graduate Centre for Journalism, City University, Northampton Square, London EC1V 0HB

☎0171 477 8224   Fax 0171 477 8574

Contact *Robert Jones*

Awarded to a young journalist experienced enough to work on national stories. It gives them the chance to work on the national desk of the *Washington Post*. Benjamin Bradlee, the *Post*'s Vice-President, selects from a shortlist drawn up in March/April. 1994 winner: Rebecca Fowler of *The Sunday Times*.

The Sunday Times Fellowship

The Sunday Times, 1 Pennington Street, London E1 9XW

Contact *John Witherow* (Editor)

For anyone from an African, Asian or Caribbean background, *The Sunday Times* is offering a fellowship to help develop journalistic skills. Applications are sought from young people who have already started on a journalistic career or from graduates leaving university with experience of student newspapers. Formal training and practical experience alongside staff journalists will be given.

Thames Television Theatre Writers' Scheme

Teddington Lock, Teddington, Middlesex TW11 9NT

☎0181 948 1154

Contact *Jack Andrews*

Awards bursaries to playwrights. Applicants must be sponsored by a theatre which then submits the play for consideration by a panel. Each award allows the playwright a twelve-month attachment. Applications invited via theatres at the end of 1995 and the end of 1996. For up-to-date information, contact Jack Andrews.

David Thomas Prize

The Financial Times (L), 1 Southwark Bridge, London SE1 9HL

☎0171 873 3000   Fax 0171 873 3924

Managing Editor *Robin Pauley*

FOUNDED 1991. Annual award in memory of David Thomas, *FT* journalist killed on assignment in Kuwait in April 1991, whose 'life was characterised by original and radical thinking coupled with a search for new subjects and orthodoxies to challenge'. The award will provide an annual study/travel grant to enable the recipient to take a career break to explore a theme in the fields of industrial policy, Third World development or the environment. Entrants may be of any nationality; age limits vary. A given theme which changes from year to year is announced in the early autumn. The 1995 theme was: Does free trade threaten the environment? Entrants should submit up to 1000 words on the theme, together with a brief c.v. and proposal outlining how the award could be used to explore the theme further. Award winners will be required to write an essay of 1500–2000 words at the end of the study period which will be considered for publication in the newspaper. Final entry date end December/early January.

Prize £3000 travel grant.

Tom-Gallon Trust
The Society of Authors, 84 Drayton Gardens, London SW10 9SB
☎0171 373 6642   Fax 0171 373 5768

A biennial award is made from the Trust Fund to fiction writers of limited means who have had at least one short story accepted. Authors wishing to enter should send a list of their already published fiction, giving the name of the publisher or periodical in each case and the approximate date of publication; one published short story; a brief statement of their financial position; an undertaking that they intend to devote a substantial amount of time to the writing of fiction as soon as they are financially able to do so; and an s.a.e. for the return of work submitted. Final entry date 20 September 1996. Presentation date June.

Award £600.

The Betty Trask Awards
The Society of Authors, 84 Drayton Gardens, London SW10 9SB
☎0171 373 6642   Fax 0171 373 5768

These annual awards are for authors who are under 35 and Commonwealth citizens, awarded on the strength of a first novel (published or unpublished) of a traditional or romantic (rather than experimental) nature. The awards must be used for a period or periods of foreign travel. Final entry date 31 January. Presentation June. Contact The Society of Authors for an information sheet. 1994 winners: Colin Bateman *Divorcing Jack*; Nadeem Aslam *Season of the Rainbirds*; Guy Burt *After the Hole*; Frances Liardet *The Game*; Jonathan Rix *Some Hope*.

Award (total) £25,000+.

The Travelling Scholarships
The Society of Authors, 84 Drayton Gardens, London SW10 9SB
☎0171 373 6642   Fax 0171 373 5768

Annual, non-competitive awards for the benefit of British authors, to enable them to travel abroad. 1994 winners: Maurice Leitch, Peter Levi, Bernard MacLaverty.

Award (total) £6000.

UEA Writing Fellowship
University of East Anglia, University Plain, Norwich NR4 7TJ
☎01603 592734   Fax 01603 593522
Director of Personnel & Registry Services
J. R. L. Beck

ESTABLISHED 1971. Awarded to a writer of established reputation in any field for a period of six months, January to end June. The duties of the Fellowship are discussed at an interview. It is assumed that one activity will be the pursuit of the Fellow's own writing. In addition the Fellow will be expected to (a) offer an undergraduate creative writing course in the School of English and American Studies during the Spring semester, and to read and grade work received; (b) offer 15 less formal sessions of one hour or more made up of readings, workshops, tutorials, and/or visits to seminars; (c) arrange, with help from UEA and **Eastern Arts**, additional visits and readings by other writers from outside the university; (d) make contact with groups around the county, and participate with Eastern Arts in organising off-campus visits for writers from the performance programme. A handbook including guidelines for this scheme and all the necessary form letters will be provided by EAB; (e) take part in a project on the future of undergraduate creative writing teaching in the School of English and American Studies, and, after discussion with relevant faculty, write a brief report. It is hoped that (b), (c) and (d) above will involve students from the University as a whole, as well as participants from the city and the region. An office and some limited secretarial assistance will be provided, and some additional funds will be available to help the Fellow with the activities described above. Applications for the fellowship should be lodged with the Director of Personnel & Registry Services in the autumn; candidates should submit at least two examples of recent work. Previous winner: Carol Morin.

Award £5000 plus free flat on campus.

Prizes

ABSW/Glaxo Science Writers' Awards

Association of British Science Writers, c/o British Association for the Advancement of Science, 23 Savile Row, London W1X 2NB
☎0171 439 1205   Fax 0171 734 1658
ABSW Administrator *Barbara Drillsma*

A series of annual awards for outstanding science journalism in newspapers, journals and broadcasting.

J. R. Ackerley Prize

English Centre of International PEN, 7 Dilke Street, London SW3 4JE
☎0171 352 6303   Fax 0171 351 0220

Commemorating the novelist/autobiographer J. R. Ackerley, this prize is awarded for a literary autobiography, written in English and published in the year preceding the award. Previous winners include: Paul Binding *St Martin's Ride*; Germaine Greer *Daddy, We Hardly Knew You*; John Osborne *Almost a Gentleman*; Barry Humphries *More Please*; Blake Morrison *And When Did You Last See Your Father?*.
Prize £2000.

The Acorn Award

See **Nottinghamshire Children's Book Award**

Aldeburgh Poetry Festival Prize

Goldings, Goldings Lane, Leiston, Suffolk IP16 4EB
☎01728 830631   Fax 01728 832029
Festival Coordinator *Michael Laskey*

ESTABLISHED 1989 by the Aldeburgh Poetry Trust. Sponsored jointly by Waterstone's and the Aldeburgh Bookshop for the best first collection published in Britain or the Republic of Ireland in the preceding twelve months. Open to any first collection of poetry of at least 40 pp. Final entry date 1 October. Previous winners: Mark Roper, Donald Atkinson, Susan Wicks, Sue Stewart.
Prize £500, plus an invitation to read at the following year's festival.

Alexander Prize

Royal Historical Society, University College London, Gower Street, London WC1E 6BT
☎0171 387 7532   Fax 0171 387 7532

Contact *Literary Director*
Awarded for a historical essay of not more than 8000 words. Competitors may choose their own subject for the essay, but must submit their choice for approval in the first instance to the Literary Director of the Royal Historical Society.
Prize £250.

An Duais don bhFilíocht i nGaeilge

An Chomhairle Ealaíon (The Arts Council), 70 Merrion Square, Dublin 2, Republic of Ireland
☎00 353 1 6611840   Fax 00 353 1 6761302
Literature Officer *Laurence Cassidy*

Triennial award for the best book of Irish poetry. Works must have been published in the Irish language in the preceding three years. Last award 1995.
Prize £1500.

Hans Christian Andersen Awards

IBBY, Nonnenweg 12, Postfach CH-4003, Basle, Switzerland
☎00 41 61 272 2917   Fax 00 41 61 272 2757
Executive Director *Leena Maissen*

The highest international prizes for children's literature: The Hans Christian Andersen Award for Writing ESTABLISHED 1956; The Hans Christian Andersen Award for Illustration ESTABLISHED 1966. Candidates are nominated by National Sections of IBBY (The International Board on Books for Young Children). Biennial prizes are awarded, in even-numbered years, to an author and an illustrator whose body of work has made a lasting contribution to children's literature. Next award 1996. Previous winners: Award for Writing: Michio Mado (Japan), Virginia Hamilton (USA); Award for Illustration: Jörg Müller (Switzerland), Kvĕta Pacovská (Czech Republic).
Award Gold medals.

Eileen Anderson Central Television Drama Award

Central Broadcasting, Central House, Broad Street, Birmingham B1 2JP
☎0121 643 9898   Fax 0121 634 4137
Manager, Corporate PR & Promotions *Kevin Johnson*

ESTABLISHED 1987 with money left by the late Dr Eileen Anderson and contributed to by **Central Television**, this is an annual award to encourage new theatre writing in the Midlands. Open to all new plays or an adaptation commissioned or premièred by a building-based theatre company in the Central region. Previous winners include: Sean Street *Honest John* (premièred on Community Tour by the Royal Theatre Northampton); Vilma Hollingbery & Michael Napier Brown *Is This the Day?* (premièred at the Royal Theatre Northampton); Lucy Gannon *Wicked Old Nellie* (Derby Playhouse); Timberlake Wertenbaker *The Love of the Nightingale* (commissioned by the Royal Shakespeare Company's The Other Place in Stratford); Pam Gem's *The Blue Angel* (premièred at the Royal Shakespeare Company's The Other Place) and Rod Dungate for *Playing By The Rules* (premièred at the Birmingham Repertory Theatre).

Prize £1500, plus trophy worth an additional £500 designed each year by a local college of education. A plaque is awarded to the theatre which commissioned the work.

The Aristeion Prize

Commission of the European Communities, Culture Unit, Rue de la Loi 200, B–1049 Brussels, Belgium
☎00 32 22 99 92 40   Fax 00 32 22 99 92 83
Contact *The Culture Unit*

ESTABLISHED 1990 to bring knowledge and appreciation of European literature to a wider public and to celebrate the strength and diversity of the European literary tradition. Member countries of the EC nominate their best works of literature and translation from the last three years. Sponsored by the Commission. 1994 winners: Juan Marse *El Embrujo de Shangai* (Literary Prize); Giovanni Raboni *Alla Ricerca del Tempo Perduto* (Translation Prize).

Prize 20,000 ecus (about £14,000) for each category.

Rosemary Arthur Award

National Poetry Foundation, 27 Mill Road, Fareham, Hampshire PO16 0TH
Contact *Johnathon Clifford*

ESTABLISHED 1989. Annual award to get poets of merit published in book form. Anyone resident in the UK who has not previously had a book published may submit 40 poems together with s.a.e. and £5 reading fee at any time during the year. Winners are announced in February.

Award Complete funding for a book of the poet's work, plus £100 and an engraved carriage clock.

Arvon Foundation International Poetry Competition

Kilnhurst, Kilnhurst Road, Todmorden, Lancashire OL14 6AX
☎01706 816582   Fax 01706 816359
Contact *David Pease*

ESTABLISHED 1980. Biennial competition (odd years) for poems written in English and not previously broadcast or published. There are no restrictions on the number of lines, themes, age of entrants or nationality. No limit to the number of entries. Entry fee: £3.50 per poem. Previous winner Don Paterson *A Private Bottling*.

Prize (1st) £5000 and £5000 worth of other prizes sponsored by *The Observer* and Duncan Lawrie Limited.

AT & T Non-Fiction Award

AT & T, 206 Marylebone Road, London NW1 6LY
☎0171 723 7070   Fax 0171 724 6519
Contact *The Administrator*

ESTABLISHED 1987 (first award made 1988), the AT & T Non-Fiction Award is for a book written in English by a living writer from Britain, the Commonwealth or Republic of Ireland, and published in the UK. One of the UK's single most valuable annual book prizes, with a total prize money of £29,500, and the only major prize specifically for non-fiction. Publishers only may submit titles, limited to three per imprint. The award covers all areas of adult non-fiction except academic, guidebooks and practical listings (such as cookery books). Titles must be published in the 12 months between 1 April and 31 March. A shortlist of four books is announced in mid-April and the winning book in early/mid-May. The aim of the award is to stimulate interest in non-fiction writing, reading and publishing in the UK. 1995 winner: Mark Hudson *Coming Back Brockens: A Year in a Mining Village*;

Prizes(1st) £25,000 and computer equipment; three runners-up shortlisted £1500.

Authors' Club First Novel Award

The Authors' Club, 40 Dover Street, London W1X 3RB
☎0171 499 8581   Fax 0171 409 0913
Contact *Mrs Ann Carter*

ESTABLISHED 1954. This award is made for the most promising work published in Britain by a

British author, and is presented at a dinner held at the Authors' Club. Entries for the award are accepted from publishers and must be full-length – short stories are not eligible. Previous winners: Nadeem Aslam *Season of the Rainbirds*; David Park *The Healing*.
Award £750.

BAAL Book Prize
BAAL Publications Secretary, CLAC, School of Education, Open University, Milton Keynes MK7 6AA
☎01908 653383   Fax 01908 654111
Contact *David Graddol*

Annual award made by the British Association for Applied Linguistics to an outstanding book in the field of applied linguistics. Final entry at the end of February. Nominations from publishers only. Previous winners: Ruth Lesser and Lesley Milroy *Linguistics and Aphasia*; *Dictionary of British Sign Language*; Susan Berk-Seligson *The Bilingual Courtroom*; Joshua A. Fishman *Reversing Language Shift*.

Barclays Bank Prize
See **Lakeland Book of the Year Awards**

Verity Bargate Award
The Soho Theatre Company, The Cockpit Theatre, Gateforth Street, London NW8 8EH
☎0171 262 7907   Fax 0171 723 8146
Contact *Paul Syrett*

To commemorate the late Verity Bargate, founder and director of the **Soho Theatre Company**. This award is presented annually for a new and unperformed full-length play. Send s.a.e. for details; if submitting scripts, enclose one s.a.e. script-size and one standard-size. The Soho Theatre Company also runs many courses for new writers. Previous winners: Mick Mahoney, Gillian Plowman, Lyndon Morgans, Diane Samuels, Judy Upton, Angela Meredith.
Award £1500, plus production by the Soho Theatre Company.

H. E. Bates Short Story Competition
Events Team, Directorate of Environment Services, Northampton Borough Council, Cliftonville House, Bedford Road, Northampton NN4 7NR
☎01604 233500   Fax 01604 29571
Contact *Liz Carroll*

Named after the late H. E. Bates, one of the masters of the short story form. Entries should preferably be typed, 2000 words maximum on any subject. Any writer resident in Great Britain is eligible and there are categories for children under 11 and under 16.
Prize (1st) £100.

BBC Wildlife Magazine Awards for Nature Writing
BBC WILDLIFE Magazine, Broadcasting House, Whiteladies Road, Bristol, Avon BS8 2LR
☎0117 9732211   Fax 0117 9467075
Editor *Rosamund Kidman Cox*

Annual competition for professional and amateur writers. Entries should be a single essay, either on personal observations of or thoughts about nature – general or specific – or about reflections on human relationships with nature. Entry forms published usually in the late spring and early summer issues of the magazine.
Prizes £1000 for best essay by a professional or amateur writer; £400 for best essay by an amateur writer (only if a professional writer wins the top award); £200 for best essay by a young writer aged between 13 and 17; £100 for best essay by a young writer aged 12 or under.

Samuel Beckett Award
c/o Faber & Faber, 3 Queen Square, London WC1N 3AU
☎0171 465 0045   Fax 0171 465 0034
Contact *Editorial Department*

This award aims to give support and encouragement to new playwrights at a crucial stage of their careers. Rules of eligibility currently under review.

David Berry Prize
Royal Historical Society, University College London, Gower Street, London WC1E 6BT
☎0171 387 7532   Fax 0171 387 7532

Triennial award (next in 1997) for an essay of not more than 10,000 words on Scottish history within the period of James I to James VI. Candidates may select any subject from the relevant period, providing it has been submitted to, and approved by, the Council of the Royal Historical Society.
Prize £250.

James Tait Black Memorial Prizes
University of Edinburgh, David Hume Tower, George Square, Edinburgh EH8 9JX
☎0131 650 3619   Fax 0131 650 6898
Contact *Department of English Literature*

ESTABLISHED 1918 in memory of a partner of

the publishing firm of **A. & C. Black Ltd** and supported since 1979 by the **Scottish Arts Council**. Two prizes, one for biography and one for fiction. Each prize is awarded for a book published in Britain in the previous twelve months. Prize winners are announced in November each year. Previous winners include: Caryl Phillips *Crossing the River;* Richard Holmes *Dr Johnson and Mr Savage.*

Prizes £1500 each.

Boardman Tasker Award

14 Pine Lodge, Dairyground Road, Bramhall, Stockport, Cheshire SK7 2HS
☎0161 439 4624
Contact *Dorothy Boardman*

ESTABLISHED 1983, this award is given for a work of fiction, non-fiction or poetry, whose central theme is concerned with the mountain environment and which can be said to have made an outstanding contribution to mountain literature. Authors of any nationality are eligible, but the book must have been published or distributed in the UK for the first time between 1 November 1994 and 31 October 1995. Entries from publishers only. Previous winners: Dermot Somers *At the Rising of the Moon;* Will McLewin *In Monte Viso's Horizon;* Alison Fell *Mer de Glace;* Jeff Long *The Ascent.*

Prize £2000 (at Trustees' discretion).

Booker Prize for Fiction

Book Trust, Book House, 45 East Hill, London SW18 2QZ
☎0181 870 9055   Fax 0181 874 4790
Contact *Sandra Vince*

The leading British literary prize, set up in 1968 by Booker McConnell Ltd, with the intention of rewarding merit, raising the stature of the author in the eyes of the public and increasing the sale of the books. The announcement of the winner has been televised live since 1981, and all books on the shortlist experience a substantial increase in sales. Eligible novels must be written in English by a citizen of Britain, the Commonwealth, the Republic of Ireland or South Africa, and must be published in the UK for the first time between 1 October and 30 September of the year of the prize. Entries are accepted from UK publishers who may each submit not more than three novels within the appropriate scheduled publication dates. The judges may also ask for certain other eligible novels to be submitted to them. Annual award. Previous winners include: James Kelman *How Late It Was, How Late;* Ben Okri *The Famished Road;* Michael Ondaatje *The English*

Patient; Barry Unsworth *Sacred Hunger;* Roddy Doyle, *Paddy Clarke Ha, Ha, Ha.*

Prize £20,000.

Author of the Year Award
Booksellers Association of Great Britain and Ireland

272 Vauxhall Bridge Road, London SW1V 1BA
☎0171 834 5477
Contact *Administrator*

Founded as part of BA Annual Conference to involve authors more closely in the event. Authors must be British, Irish, or resident in the UK. Not an award open to entry but voted on by the membership. 1994 winner: Alan Bennett.

Award £1000 plus trophy.

Border Television Prize
See **Lakeland Book of the Year Awards**

Bournemouth International Festival Open Poetry Competition

2 Digby Chambers, Post Office Road, Bournemouth, Dorset BH1 1BA
☎01202 297327   Fax 01202 552510
Contact *Julian Robbins*

A feature of the **Bournemouth International Festival**, the annual open poetry competition attracts hundreds of entries from all over the world. There are two categories, Adult Section (19+) and Junior Section (12–18 years). 1994 winners: C. Millington (Adult); Paul Groves (Junior). Write enclosing s.a.e. for more information and entry form.

Prizes Adult class, 1st prize £200; Junior class 1st prize £150; 2nd & 3rd place cash prizes plus poetry books for runners-up. All award winning poets are invited to read their poems at the Festival.

The Michaél Breathnach Literary Memorial Award

Cló Iar-Chonnachta Teo, Indreabhán, Conamara, Co. Galway Republic of Ireland
☎00 353 91 93307   Fax 00 353 91 93362
Literature & Music Editor *Nóirín Ní Ghrádaigh*

As part of their 10-year celebration, **Cló Iar-Chonnachta** have established an annual award for the best work in any literary form; novel, drama, poetry collection or short story collection. Open to writers under 30 years of age.

Prize IR£1000.

Bridport Arts Centre
The Bridport Prize

Arts Centre, South Street, Bridport, Dorset
DT6 3NR
☎01308 427183   Fax 01308 427183

Contact *Bridport Prize Administrator*

Annual competition for poetry and short story
writing. Unpublished work only, written in
English. Winning stories are read by leading
London literary agent and an anthology of
prize-winning entries is published. Also runs a
young writers competition with variable prizes.
Final entry date 30 June (early April for young
writers award). Send s.a.e. for entry forms.

Prizes £2,500, £1000 & £500 in each category, plus supplementary runners-up prizes.

Katharine Briggs Folklore Award

The Folklore Society, University College
London, Gower Street, London WC1E 6BT
☎0171 387 5894

Contact *The Convener*

An annual award in November for the book,
published in Britain between 1 June and 30
May in the previous calendar year, which has
made the most distinguished non-fiction contribution to folklore studies. Intended to
encourage serious research in the field which
Katharine Briggs did so much to establish. The
term folklore studies is interpreted broadly to
include all aspects of traditional and popular
culture, narrative, belief, custom and folk arts.
Previous winners include: Simon Charley *Rites
of Marrying, The Wedding in Scotland.*

Prize £50, plus engraved goblet.

British Book Awards

Publishing News, 43 Museum Street, London
WC1A 1LY
☎0171 404 0304   Fax 0171 242 0762

ESTABLISHED 1988. A mixed bag of annual
trade awards: Children's Author; Illustrated
Children's Book; Distributor; Editor; Fantasy
and SF Author; Chain Bookseller; Independent
Bookseller; Marketing Campaign; Book of the
Year; Author of the Year; Publisher of the
Year. The top author prizes are awarded (in
February) to the authors who have made the
greatest impact in the book trade during the
previous year. Winners receive mounted brass
pen nibs – the Nibbies are equivalent to
Oscars. Previous winners have included: Jung
Chang *Wild Swans*; Roddy Doyle; Anne Fine;
Terry Pratchett; **Transworld Publishers Ltd**
(Publisher of the Year). For further informa-

tion contact: Merric Davidson, Oakwood,
Ashley Park, Tunbridge Wells, Kent TN4
8UA (Tel 01892 514282).

British Comparative Literature Association Translation Prizes

St John's College, Oxford OX1 3JP
☎01865 277381   Fax 01865 277435

Contact *Dr Nicholas Crowe*

ESTABLISHED 1983. Annual competition open
to literary translations from all languages.
Special prizes for translations from Hebrew,
Yiddish and other languages on a Jewish
theme; and Swedish (biennial). Final entry date
15 December.

Prizes (1st) £350; (2nd) £150; plus publication for all winning entries in the Association's
annual journal *Comparative Criticism.*

British Fantasy Awards

2 Harwood Street, Heaton Norris, Stockport,
Cheshire SK4 1JJ
☎0161 476 5368 (after 6 p.m.)

Secretary *Robert Parkinson*

Awarded by the **British Fantasy Society** at its
annual conference for Best Novel and Best
Short Story categories, among others. Previous
winners include: Piers Anthony, Clive Barker,
Ken Bulmer, Ramsey Campbell.

British Literature Prize

See **David Cohen British Literature Prize**

British Science Fiction (Association) Award

c/o 275 Lonsdale Avenue, Intake, Doncaster,
South Yorkshire DN2 6HJ
☎01302 367556

Award Administrator *Nicholas Mahoney*

ESTABLISHED 1966. The BSFA awards a trophy
each year in three categories – novel, short fic-
tion and artwork – published in the preceding
year. Winners in 1994 were Christopher Evans
Aztec Century (Novel); Robert Holdstock and
Garry Kilworth *The Ragthom* (Short Fiction);
Jim Burns for the cover of *Red Dust* by Paul J.
McAuley (Artwork).

James Cameron Award

City University, Department of Journalism,
Northampton Square, London EC1V 0HB
☎0171 477 8221   Fax 0171 477 8594

Contact *The Administrator*

Annual award for journalism to a reporter of any
nationality, working for the British media, whose

work is judged to have contributed most during the year to the continuance of the Cameron tradition. Administered by City University Department of Journalism. 1995 winner: George Alagiah, BBC South Africa correspondent.

The City of Cardiff International Poetry Competition

The Welsh Academy, 3rd Floor, Mount Stuart House, Mount Stuart Square, Cardiff CF1 6DQ
☎01222 492025   Fax 01222 492930
Contact *Kevin Thomas*

ESTABLISHED 1986. An annual competition for unpublished poems in English of up to 50 lines. Launched in the spring with a summer closing date.
Prize (total) £4000.

Carey Award

Society of Indexers, 38 Rochester Road, London NW1 9JJ
☎0171 916 7809
Secretary *Claire Troughton*

A private award made by the Society to a member who has given outstanding services to indexing. The recipient is selected by Council with no recommendations considered from elsewhere.

Carmarthen Writers' Circle Short Story Competition

79 Bronwydd Road, Carmarthen, Dyfed SA31 2AP
☎01267 230900
Contact *Madeline Mayne*

ESTABLISHED 1990. Annual. All stories must be unpublished and not yet accepted for publication. Entries must be anonymous and an entry form, giving titles of all stories, must be attached to submissions. Any number may be submitted; entry fee £4 per story. Stories must be typed in double-spacing on one side of A4 paper. Send s.a.e. for details.
Prizes (1st) £100; (2nd) £75; (3rd) £50. All prize winners will be put on tape for the Talking Newspaper.

Cheltenham Prize

Cheltenham Festival of Literature, Town Hall, Imperial Square, Cheltenham, Gloucestershire GL50 1QA
☎01242 521621   Fax 01242 256457
Contact *Nicola Bennett*

ESTABLISHED 1978. The Cheltenham Prize is awarded annually to the author of a work of literature, which is deemed in the opinion of an independent judge to have made an outstanding contribution to the previous year's literature and which has not yet received the critical attention it deserves.
Prize £500.

Children's Book Award

The Federation of Children's Book Groups, 30 Senneleys Park Road, Birmingham B31 1AL
☎0121 427 4860   Fax 0121 643 3152
Contact *Jenny Blanch*

ESTABLISHED 1980. Awarded annually for best book of fiction suitable for children. Unique in that it is judged by the children themselves. Previous winners include: Ian Strachan *The Boy in the Bubble*; Mick Inkpen *Threadbear*; Robert Swindells *Room 13*; Elizabeth Laird *Kiss the Dust*; and Jaqueline Wilson *The Suitcase Kid*. 1995 winner: Dick King-Smith *Harriet's Hare*.

Award A splendid silver and oak sculpture made by Graham Stewart and Tim Stead, plus portfolio of letters, drawings and comments from the children who took part in the judging; category winners receive silver bowls designed by the same artists and portfolios.

Children's Book Circle Eleanor Farjeon Award

c/o Hamish Hamilton Ltd, 27 Wrights Lane, London W8 5TZ
☎0171 416 3000   Fax 0171 416 3099
Contact *Anna Trenter*

This award, named in memory of the much-loved children's writer, is for distinguished services to children's books either in this country or overseas, and may be given to a librarian, teacher, publisher, bookseller, author, artist, reviewer, television producer, etc. Nominations from members of the **Children's Book Circle**. 1995 winner: Helen Paiba.
Award £500.

Arthur C. Clarke Award for Science Fiction

60 Bournemouth Road, Folkestone, Kent CT19 5AZ
☎01303 252939
Administrator *Paul Kincaid*

ESTABLISHED 1986. The Arthur C. Clarke Award is given yearly to the best science fiction novel with first UK publication in the previous calendar year. Both hardcover and paperback books qualify. Made possible by a generous donation from Arthur C. Clarke, this award is selected by a

rotating panel of six judges nominated by the **British Science Fiction Association**, the International Science Policy Foundation and the **Science Fiction Foundation**. Previous winners include: Jeff Noon *Vurt*; Marge Piercy *Body of Glass*; Pat Cadigan *Synners*; Colin Greenland *Take Back Plenty*.
Award £1000 plus trophy.

The Cló Iar-Chonnachta Literary Award

Cló Iar-Chonnachta Teo, Indreabhán, Conamara, Co. Galway Republic of Ireland
☎00 353 91 93307   Fax 00 353 91 93362
Literature & Music Editor *Nóirín Ní Ghrádaigh*

As part of their 10-year celebration, **Cló Iar-Chonnachta** have established an annual prize for a newly-written and unpublished work in the Irish language. Awarded in 1995 for the best novel, 1996 for the best poetry collection, and 1997 for the best short story collection or drama.
Prize IR£5000.

David Cohen British Literature Prize in the English Language

Arts Council of Great Britain, 14 Great Peter Street, London SW1P 3NQ
☎0171 333 0100   Fax 0171 973 6590
Literature Director *Dr Alastair Niven*
Literature Assistant *Anne Bendall*

ESTABLISHED 1993. By far the most valuable literature prize in Britain, the British Literature Prize, launched by the **Arts Council**, will be awarded biennially. Anyone is eligible to suggest candidates and the award recognises writers who use the English language and who are British citizens, encompassing dramatists as well as novelists, poets and essayists. The prize is for a lifetime's achievement rather than a single play or book and is donated by the David Cohen Family Charitable Trust in association with Coutts Bank. The David Cohen Trust was set up in 1980 by David Cohen, general practitioner son of a property developer. The Trust has helped composers, choreographers, dancers, poets, playwrights and actors. The Council is providing a further £10,000 to enable the winner to commission new work, with the dual aim of encouraging young writers and readers. Next award 1997. 1995 winner: Harold Pinter; 1993 winner: V. S. Naipaul.
Award £30,000, plus £10,000 towards new work.

Collins Biennial Religious Book Award

HarperCollins Publishers, 77-85 Fulham Palace Road, London W6 8JB
☎0181 741 7070   Fax 0181 307 4064
Contact *Lesley Walmsley*

Biennial award given for the book which has made the most distinguished contribution to the relevance of Christianity in the modern world, written by a living citizen of the Commonwealth, the Republic of Ireland or South Africa. Previous winners include: John MacQuarrie *Jesus Christ in Modern Thought*.
Award £5000.

The Constable Trophy

Constable Publishers Ltd, 3 The Lanchesters, 162 Fulham Palace Road, London W6 9ER
☎0181 741 3663   Fax 0181 748 7562

Biennial competition, supported by the northern-based regional arts associations, for a previously unpublished novel by a writer living in the North of England. Winning entry may be considered for publication by **Constable & Co. Ltd**. Next award 1996.
Prize (1st) £1000, and £1000 in advance of royalties on acceptance for publication by Constable.

The Thomas Cook/Daily Telegraph Travel Book Award

The Thomas Cook Group, 45 Berkeley Street, London W1A 1EB
☎0171 408 4218   Fax 0171 408 4551
Contact *Alexis Coles, Corporate Affairs*

Annual award given to encourage the art of narrative travel writing. Previous winners: William Dalrymple *City of Djinns*; Nik Cohn *The Heart of the World*.
Award £7500.

Catherine Cookson Fiction Prize

Transworld Publishers Ltd, 61–63 Uxbridge Road, London W5 5SA
☎0181 579 2652   Fax 0181 579 5479
Contact *Catherine Cookson Fiction Prize Administrator*

ESTABLISHED 1992 by **Transworld Publishers Ltd**, in celebration of the achievement of Catherine Cookson. Annual award for a novel, of at least 70,000 words, which possesses strong characterisation, authentic background and storytelling quality, which are the mark of Cookson's work. The work may be contemporary or historical. Submissions must be in English and original (no translations), and must not have been previously published in any form. Final entry date 31 May; winner announced in Autumn. First winner: Valerie Wood *The Hungry Tide*.

Award £10,000, plus publication by Transworld. Runners-up may be offered publication on terms to be negotiated.

The Duff Cooper Prize

54 St Maur Road, London SW6 4DP
☎0171 736 3729   Fax 0171 731 7638
Contact *Artemis Cooper*

An annual award for a literary work of biography or history, published by a recognised publisher (member of **The Publishers Association**) during the previous 12 months. The book must be submitted by the publisher, not the author. Financed by the interest from a trust fund commemorating Duff Cooper, first Viscount Norwich (1890–1954). 1995 winner: David Gilmour *Curzon*.

Prize £500.

Rose Mary Crawshay Prize

The British Academy, 20–21 Cornwall Terrace, London NW1 4QP
☎0171 487 5966   Fax 0171 224 3807
Contact *British Academy Secretary*

ESTABLISHED 1888 by Rose Mary Crawshay, this prize is given for a historical or critical work by a woman of any nationality on English literature, with particular preference for a work on Keats, Byron or Shelley. The work must have been published in the preceding three years.

Prize normally two prizes of approximately £300 each.

Crime Writers' Association (Gold Dagger Award for Non-Fiction)

Crime Writers' Association, PO Box 172, Tring, Hertfordshire HP23 5LP
Contact *The Secretary*

Annual award for the best non-fiction crime book published during the year. Previous winners: David Canter *Criminal Shadows*; Alexandra Artley *Murder in the Heart*; Charles Nicholl *The Reckoning*; John Bossy *Giordano Bruno and the Embassy Affair*.

Award Dagger, plus cheque (sum varies).

Crime Writers' Association (Gold, Silver & Diamond Dagger Awards for Fiction)

Crime Writers' Association, PO Box 172, Tring, Hertfordshire HP23 5LP
Contact *The Secretary*

Three annual awards: Gold and Silver for the best crime fiction published during the year; Diamond for outstanding contribution to the genre. Nominations for Gold Dagger from publishers only. Previous winners: Michael Gilbert, Ellis Peters (Diamond); Minette Walters *The Scold's Bridle*, Patricia Cornwell *Cruel and Unusual* (Gold); Peter Høeg *Miss Smilla's Feeling for Snow*, Sarah Dunant *Fatlands* (Silver).

Award Dagger, plus cheque (sum varies).

Crime Writers' Association (John Creasey Memorial Award)

Crime Writers' Association, PO Box 172, Tring, Hertfordshire HP23 5LP
Contact *The Secretary*

ESTABLISHED 1973 following the death of crime writer John Creasey, founder of the **Crime Writers' Association**. This award is given annually for the best crime novel by an author who has not previously published a full-length work of fiction. Nominations from publishers only. Previous winners include: Doug J. Swanson *Big Town*; Walter Mosley *Devil in a Blue Dress*.

Award Cheque, plus magnifying glass.

Crime Writers' Association (Last Laugh Award)

Crime Writers' Association, PO Box 172, Tring, Hertfordshire HP23 5LP
Contact *The Secretary*

Annual award for the funniest crime novel published during the year. Nominations from publishers only. Previous winners: Simon Shaw *The Villain of the Earth*; Michael Pearce *The Mamur Zapt and the Spoils of Egypt*; Carl Hiassen *Native Tongue*; Mike Ripley *Angels in Arms*.

Award Gold-plated fountain pen.

Crime Writers' Association (The Macallan Short Story Award)

6 Ainscow Avenue, Lostock, Bolton, Lancashire BL6 4LR
Contact *Val McDermid*

ESTABLISHED 1993. An award for a published crime story. Publishers should submit three copies of the story to the address above by 30

September 1995. 1994 winner: Ian Rankin *A Deep Hole*.

Prize £200 and a silver-plated brooch/tie-pin of crossed daggers.

The Daily Telegraph National Power Young Science Writer Awards

Electric Echo, 334A Goswell Road, London EC1V 7LQ
☎0171 713 5525

Contact *Gerry Fallon*

ESTABLISHED 1988. The awards are open to anyone aged between 16–28 for a short article (max. 700 words) on any scientific or science-related subject suitable for publication in *The Daily Telegraph*. Two age groups: 16–19 and 20–28. Substantial prizes include a trip to the US for the annual meeting of the American Association for the Advancement of Science. Entry details from the above address. Final entry date in April.

Hunter Davies Prize

See **Lakeland Book of the Year Awards**

Rhys Davies Contemporary Short Story Competition

Welsh Academy, 3rd Floor,
Mount Stuart House, Mount Stuart Square,
Cardiff CF1 6DQ
☎01222 492025   Fax 01222 492930

Contact *Kevin Thomas*

ESTABLISHED 1993. Open to Welsh nationals or residents only, the award is for unpublished short stories in English of up to 3,000 words which reflect Welsh life or experience since 1960.

Prizes £1000 (1st); 12 prizes of £250.

Isaac & Tamara Deutscher Memorial Prize

157 Fortis Green Road, London N10 3AX
☎0181 883 7063

Secretary *Ann Jungmann*

An annual award in recognition of, and as encouragement to, outstanding research in the Marxist tradition of Isaac Deutscher. Made to the author of an essay or full-scale work published or in manuscript. Final entry date 1 May.

Award £500.

George Devine Award

17A South Villas, London NW1 9BS
☎0171 267 9793 (evenings)

Contact *Christine Smith*

Annual award for a promising new playwright

writing for the stage in memory of George Devine, artistic director of the **Royal Court Theatre,** who died in 1965. The play does not need to have been produced. Send two copies of the script to Christine Smith by March. Information leaflet available.

Prize £5000.

Denis Devlin Memorial Award for Poetry

An Chomhairle Ealaíon (The Arts Council),
70 Merrion Square, Dublin 2,
Republic of Ireland
☎00 353 1 6611840   Fax 00 353 1 6761302

Literature Officer *Laurence Cassidy*

Triennial award for the best book of poetry in English by an Irish poet, published in the preceding three years. Last award 1994.

Award £1500.

Dog Watch Open Poetry Competition

267 Hillbury Road, Warlingham,
Surrey CR6 9TL
☎01883 622121

Contact *Michaela Edridge*

ESTABLISHED 1993. Dog Watch is a charity that rescues and finds new homes for badly abused dogs. The annual prize is awarded only to authors of unpublished works. Final entry date is 1 January each year and entrants should send £1 entry fee and s.a.e. for details.

Prize (1st) £25 (to be increased as entries increase).

Drama Association of Wales Playwriting Competition

The Library, Singleton Road, Splott,
Cardiff CF2 2ET
☎01222 452200   Fax 01222 452277

Contact *Aled Rhys-Jones*

Annual competition held to promote the writing of one act plays in English and Welsh of between 20 and 45 minutes playing time. The theme of the competition is changed each year – the 1995 title was *Closed Doors*. Application forms from the above address.

Prizes £100; £50; £25, plus a special prize for the most outstanding author under 25 years of age; performance at 'dramaffest', the National Drama Festival; publication by DAWS Publications.

Earthworm Award

Friends of the Earth, 26–28 Underwood Street, London N1 7JQ

☎0171 490 4734   Fax 0171 490 0881

Contact *The Earthworm Award Administrator*

Set up in 1987 by Friends of the Earth and the first children's book prize of its kind. Aims to promote and reward environmental awareness and sensitivity in literature for children of all ages. Looking for books of every kind, fact and fiction, which promote an awareness and appreciation of the natural world; encourage an overall sense of environmental responsibility; present concepts and facts accurately and clearly where appropriate. Entries need to express a sympathetic and positive approach and need not present an explicit Green message. Applications are invited from publishers for books published or distributed in the previous year. Closing date end April. 1994 winner: Sian Lewis *Red Kite*.

Eccles Prize

Columbia Business School, 810 Uris Hall, New York NY 10027, USA

☎001 212 854 2747   Fax 001 212 678 0825

Contact *Office of Public Affairs*

ESTABLISHED 1986 by Spencer F. Eccles in commemoration of his uncle, George S. Eccles, a 1922 graduate of the Business School. Annual award for excellence in economic writing. One of the US's most prestigious book prizes. Books must have a business theme and be written for a general audience. Previous winners: *The Warbugs* Ron Chernow; *The New Palgrave Dictionary of Money and Finance* ed. Peter Newman, Murray Milgate and John Eatwell; *The Prize* Daniel Yergin.

The T.S. Eliot Prize

The Poetry Book Society, Book House, 45 East Hill, London SW18 2QZ

☎0181 870 8403/874 6361

Contacts *Martha Smart, Betty Redpath, Alex Heald*

ESTABLISHED 1993. Annual award named after T.S. Eliot, one of the founders of the Poetry Book Society. Open to books of new poetry published in the UK and Republic of Ireland during the year and over 32 pages in length. At least 75 per cent of the collection must be previously unpublished in book form. Final entry date is in September/October. Previous winners: *First Language* Ciaran Carson; *The Annals of Chile* Paul Muldoon.

The Encore Award

The Society of Authors, 84 Drayton Gardens, London SW10 9SB

☎0171 373 6642   Fax 0171 373 5768

ESTABLISHED 1990. Awarded to an author who has had one (and only one) novel previously published. Details from **The Society of Authors**. 1995 winner: Dermot Healy *A Goat's Song*.

Prize (total) £7500.

Envoi Poetry Competition

Envoi, 44 Rudyard Road, Biddulph Moor, Stoke on Trent, Staffordshire ST8 7JN

☎01782 517892

Contact *David Bowes*

Run by *Envoi* poetry magazine. Competitions are featured regularly, with prizes of £200, plus three annual subscriptions to *Envoi*. Winning poems along with full adjudication report are published. Send s.a.e. to Competition Manager, David Bowes, 17 Millcroft, Bishops Stortford, Hertfordshire CM23 2BP.

Esquire/Volvo/ Waterstone's Non-Fiction Award

National Magazine Co Ltd, 72 Broadwick Street, London W1V 2BP

☎0171 439 5000   Fax 0171 439 5067

Editor *Rosie Boycott*

ESTABLISHED 1993 by *Esquire* as a major annual literary award. The award 'seeks to reflect an exciting new spirit in non-fiction writing', and is open to any work published by a British publisher between November of one year and October of the following. The final entry date is end of September. The winner in 1994 was Tobias Wolff *In Pharoah's Army*.

Prizes (1st) £5000; (5 finalists) £1000 each.

European Literary Prize/European Translation Prize

See **The Aristeion Prize**

Geoffrey Faber Memorial Prize

Faber & Faber Ltd, 3 Queen Square, London WC1N 3AU

☎0171–465 0045   Fax 0171–465 0034

ESTABLISHED 1963 as a memorial to the founder and first chairman of **Faber & Faber**, this prize is awarded in alternate years for the volume of verse and the volume of prose fiction published in the UK in the preceding two years, which is judged to be of greatest literary merit. Authors must be under 40 at the time of publication and citizens of the UK, Commonwealth, Republic of Ireland or South Africa. 1995 winner: Livi Michael *Their Angel Reach*.

Prize £1000.

Prudence Farmer Award

New Statesman and Society,
Foundation House, Perseverance Works,
38 Kingsland Road, London E2 8DQ
☎0171–739 3211   Fax 0171–739 9307
Contact *Boyd Tonkin*

For the best poem to have been published in the *New Statesman and Society* during the previous year.

Award £100.

Fawcett Society Book Prize

New Light on Women's Lives, 46 Harleyford Road, London SE11 5AY
☎0171 587 1287   Fax 0171 793 0451
Contact *Charlotte Burt*

Awarded annually to the author of the book which gives us a greater understanding of women's lives, whether it be a book of fiction, non-fiction, biography, etc. All works submitted for the prize are placed in the **Fawcett Library** at London Guildhall University. Previous winners: Jung Chang *Wild Swans*; Margaret Forster *Daphne du Maurier*.

Prize £2000.

The Kathleen Fidler Award

c/o Book Trust Scotland, The Scottish Book Centre, 137 Dundee Street, Edinburgh EH11 1BG
☎0131 229 3663   Fax 0131 228 4293

For an unpublished novel for children aged 8–12, to encourage authors new to writing for this age group. Authors should not previously have had a novel published for this age group. The award is sponsored by Blackie Children's Books, now owned by **Penguin**, and is administered by **Book Trust Scotland**. Final entry date end October. Previous winners: Theresa Breslin *Simon's Challenge*; Mij Kelly *48 Hours with Franklin*.

Award £1000, plus publication.

Sir Banister Fletcher Award

The Authors' Club, 40 Dover Street, London W1X 3RB
☎0171 499 8581   Fax 0171 409 0913
Contact *Mrs Ann Carter*

This award was created by Sir Bannister Fletcher, who was president of **The Authors' Club** for many years. The prize is donated by Nelson Hurst & Marsh, insurance brokers and is presented annually for the best book on architecture or the fine arts published in the preceding year. Submissions: Fletcher Award Committee, RIBA, 66 Portland Place, London W1N 4AD. Previous winners: Professor Thomas Markus *Building and Power*; John Onians *Bearers of Meaning: Classical Orders in Antiquity*; Sir Michael Levey *Giambattista Tiepolo: His Life and Art;* John Allan *Berthold Lubetkin – Architecture and The Tradition of Progress.*

Award £750.

The John Florio Prize

The Translators Association, 84 Drayton Gardens, London SW10 9SB
☎0171 373 6642   Fax 0171 373 5768
Contact *Kate Pool*

ESTABLISHED 1963 under the auspices of the Italian Institute and the British-Italian Society, this prize is awarded biennially for the best translation into English of a twentieth-century Italian work of literary merit and general interest, published by a British publisher in the two years preceding the prize. Previous winners include: Tim Parks for *The Road to San Giovanni* by Italo Calvino.

Prize £1000.

The Forward Prizes for Poetry

Book Trust, Book House, 45 East Hill, London SW18 2QZ
☎0181 870 9055   Fax 0181 874 4790
Contact *Sandra Vince*

ESTABLISHED 1992. Three awards, sponsored by Forward Publishing, for the best collection of poetry, the best first collection of poetry, and the best poem published but not as part of a collection. Open to poets of any nationality; collections or poems must be published. Previous winners: Thom Gunn, Simon Armitage, Jackie Kay, Carol Ann Duffy, Don Paterson, Vicki Feaver, Alan Jenkins, Kwarne Dawes, Iain Crichton Smith.

Prizes £10,000 for best collection; £5000 for best first collection; £1000 for best poem.

Anne Frankel Prize

c/o Critics' Circle, 47 Bermondsey Street, London SE1 3XT
☎0171 403 1818   Fax 0171 403 1418
Contact *Peter Hepple*

ESTABLISHED 1991. Annual prize for young film critics in memory of the late Anne Frankel, who wrote on film. Set up by her father William

Frankel, former editor and now chairman of the *Jewish Chronicle*. Age limit for entrants is 25. Entries should be self-submitted and have been published in a local/national/student newspaper or periodical. Submit three examples of work, sending four copies of each to the above address. Final entry date usually end August.

Prize £500.

The Frogmore Poetry Prize
The Frogmore Press, 42 Morehall Avenue, Folkestone, Kent CT19 4EF
Contact *Jeremy Page*

ESTABLISHED 1987. Awarded annually and sponsored by the Frogmore Foundation. The winning poem, runners-up and short-listed entries are all published in the magazine. Previous winners have been: David Satherley, Caroline Price, Bill Headdon, John Latham, Diane Brown.

Prize The winner receives 100 guineas and a life subscription to the biannual literary magazine *The Frogmore Papers*.

David Gemmell Cup
Hastings Writers Group, 39 Emmanuel Road, Hastings, East Sussex TN34 3LB
☎01424 442471

Contact *Mrs R. Bartholomew* (for entry form)

ESTABLISHED 1988. Annual award to encourage writers of short fiction (1500 words) resident in East and West Sussex, Kent and Surrey. Final entry date end August. The competition is organised by Hastings Writers' Group and is presented by its sponsor David Gemmell. Previous winners: Stella Radford, Carol Bostock, Sarah Mills.

Prizes 1st £200 plus David Gemmell Cup; 2nd £150; 3rd £100; 4th £50; 5th £30; 6th £20. Additionally, certificates of commendation issued at the discretion of the judge, David Gemmell.

Glenfiddich Awards
10 Stukeley Street, London WC2B 5LQ
☎0171 405 8638   Fax 0171 405 6328

A series of awards to writers and broadcasters who have contributed most to the civilised appreciation of food and drink through articles, books, illustration and photography published in the UK. Also covers TV and radio programmes, as well as a Special Award for outstanding work or event. 1995 winners: Food Book of the Year: *Roast Chicken and Other Stories* Simon Hopkinson with Lindsey Bareham; Drink Book of the Year: *The Oxford Companion to Wine* Jancis Robinson; Food Writer of the Year: Philippa Davenport for work in the *Financial Times* and *Country Living*; Drink Writer of the Year: Andrew Jefford for work in *Wine* and the *Evening Standard*; Cookery Writer of the Year: Nigel Slater for work in *The Observer*; Restaurant Writer of the Year: John McKenna for work in *The Irish Times*; Whisky Writer of the Year: Andrew Jefford for work in the *Evening Standard* and *Spirits*, a *Wine* magazine supplement; Regional Writer of the Year: Catherine Brown for work in *The Herald* (Glasgow) and A Taste of Scotland's Food, *Cultural Tourism*; Magazine of the Year: *Sainsbury's: The Magazine*; Television Programme of the Year: *Pigs* written and presented by Jonathan Meades, directed by Russell England and produced by David Turnbull for BBC TV; Radio Programme of the Year: *The Indian Spice Trail*, presented by Leslie Forbes and produced by Matt Thompson for BBC Radio Features Unit, BBC Radio 3; Visual Award: Kevin Summers and Nigel Slater for work in *The Observer*; 1995 Special Awards: Delia Smith, 'for her profound impact as an educator and her unrivalled influence on the Nation's cooking and eating habits'; Common Ground 'for its achievement in raising awareness about Britain's orchards and informing consumers about the breadth, diversity and benefits of apples'; 1995 Glenfiddich Trophy Winner: Nigel Slater.

Award Overall winner (chosen from the category winners) £3000, plus the Glenfiddich Trophy (which is held for one year); category winners £800 each, plus a case of Glenfiddich Single Malt Scotch Whisky and an engraved commemorative quaich.

The Gooding Award for Short Story Writing
95 Celyn Avenue, Lakeside, Cardiff CF2 6EL
Competition Secretary *Mrs Betty Persen*
Organiser *Philip Beynon*

ESTABLISHED 1986 by A. J. Gooding, O.B.E. to provide sponsorship and promote Wales and its writers. Competition open to all writers in English; the final entry date is 1 March each year.

Prizes (1st) £600; (2 runners-up) £250 each.

Edgar Graham Book Prize
School of Oriental and African Studies, Thornhaugh Street, Russell Square, London WC1H 0XG
☎0171 637 2388   Fax 0171 436 3844

Contact *Centre for Development Studies*

ESTABLISHED 1984. Biennial award in memory of Edgar Graham. Aims to encourage research work in Third World agricultural and industrial

development. Open to published works of original scholarship on agricultural and/or industrial development in Asia and/or Africa. No edited volumes. Next award 1996; final entry date 30 September 1995.
Prize £1500.

The Guardian Children's Fiction Award

The Guardian, 119 Farringdon Road, London EC1R 3ER
☎0171 278 2332   Fax 0171 837 2114
Children's Book Editor *Joanna Carey*

Annual award for an outstanding work of fiction for children by a British or Commonwealth author, first published in the UK in the preceding year, excluding picture books and previous winners. Final entry date end December. Previous winners: Rachel Anderson *Paper Faces*; Hilary McKay *The Exiles*; William Mayne *Low Tide*; 1994 winner: Sylvia Waugh *The Mennyms*.
Award £1000.

The Guardian Fiction Prize

The Guardian, 119 Farringdon Road, London EC1R 3ER
☎0171 278 2332   Fax 0171 837 2114
Contact *Literary Editor*

ESTABLISHED 1965. An annual award for a novel published by a British, Irish or Commonwealth writer, which is chosen by the literary editor in conjunction with the paper's regular reviewers of fiction. Previous winners: Candia McWilliam *Debatable Land*; Alasdair Gray *Poor Things*; Alan Judd *The Devil's Own Work*; Pat Barker *The Eye in the Door*.
Prize £2000.

W. H. Heinemann Prize

Royal Society of Literature, 1 Hyde Park Gardens, London W2 2LT
☎0171 723 5104   Fax 0171 402 0199

Works of any kind of literature may be submitted by publishers under this award, which aims to encourage genuine contributions to literature. Books must be written in the English language and have been published in the previous year; translations are not eligible for consideration. Preference tends to be given to publications which are unlikely to command large sales: poetry, biography, criticism, philosophy, history. Final entry date 31 October. Up to three awards may be given. Previous winners: John Hale *The Civilisation of Europe In the Renaissance*; John Gross *Shylock*; Nicholas Boyle *The Poet and the Age*.

Felicia Hemans Prize for Lyrical Poetry

University of Liverpool, PO Box 147, Liverpool, Merseyside L69 3BX
☎0151 794 2458   Fax 0151 708 6502
Contact *The Registrar*

ESTABLISHED 1899. Annual award for published or unpublished verse. Open to past or present members and students of the University of Liverpool. One poem per entrant only. Closing date 1 May.
Prize £30.

Heywood Hill Literary Prize

10 Curzon Street, London W1Y 7FJ
☎0171 629 0647
Contact *John Saumarez Smith*

ESTABLISHED 1995 by the Duke of Devonshire to reward a lifetime's contribution to the enjoyment of books. No recommendations are considered for this annual award.
Prize £10,000.

David Higham Prize for Fiction

c/o Book Trust, Book House, 45 East Hill, London SW18 2QZ
☎0181 870 9055   Fax 0181 874 4790
Contact *Sandra Vince*

An annual award for a first novel or book of short stories published in the UK in the year of the award by an author who is a citizen of Britain, the Commonwealth, the Republic of Ireland or South Africa. Previous winners: Fred D'Aguiar *The Longest Memory*; Nicola Barker *Love Your Enemies*; John Loveday *Halo*; Elspeth Barker *O Caledonia*.
Award £1000.

William Hill Sports Book of the Year

c/o Lay & Partners, 1 Chelsea Manor Gardens, London SW3 5PN
☎0181 365 7211 (Graham Sharpe)/
0171 349 5075 (Tim Fordham-Moss)
Fax 0171 352 624
Contact *Graham Sharpe, Tim Fordham-Moss*

ESTABLISHED 1989. Annual award introduced by Graham Sharpe of bookmakers William Hill. Sponsored by William Hill and thus dubbed the 'bookie' prize, it is the first, and only, Sports Book of the Year award. Final entry date September. Previous winners: Simon Kuper *Football Against the Enemy*; Stephen Jones *Endless Winter*; Nick Hornby *Fever Pitch: A Fan's Life*.
Prize (reviewed annually) £6000 package

including £3500 cash, hand-bound copy, free bet and a day at the races.

Calvin & Rose G. Hoffman Prize

King's School, Canterbury, Kent CT1 2ES
☎01227 595501

Contact *The Headmaster*

Annual award for distinguished publication on Christopher Marlowe, established by the late Calvin Hoffman, author of *The Man Who was Shakespeare* (1955) as a memorial to himself and his wife. For essays of at least 5000 words written in English for their scholarly contribution to the study of Christopher Marlowe and his relationship to William Shakespeare. Final entry date September. Previous winners: Prof. Dr Kurt Tetzeli von Rosador, Dr R. Dutton, Prof. R. Danson, Prof. T. Cartelli, Dr. David Pascoe, Dr Lisa Hopkins, Prof. J. Shapiro. *Prize* not less than £6,500.

Winifred Holtby Memorial Prize

Royal Society of Literature, 1 Hyde Park Gardens, London W2 2LT
☎0171 723 5104   Fax 0171 402 0199

ESTABLISHED 1986 by Vera Brittain who gave a sum of money to the RSL to provide an annual prize in honour of Winifred Holtby who died at the age of 37. Administered by the **Royal Society of Literature**. The prize is for the best regional novel of the year written in the English language. The writer must be of British or Irish nationality, or a citizen of the Commonwealth. Translations, unless made by the author himself of his own work, are not eligible for consideration. If in any year it is considered that no regional novel is of sufficient merit the prize money may be awarded to an author, qualified as aforesaid, of a literary work of non-fiction or poetry, concerning a regional subject. Publishers are invited to submit works (one copy of each) published during the current year to the Secretary, labelled 'Winifred Holtby Prize'. Final entry date 31 October. Previous winners: Carl MacDougall *The Lights Below*; Adam Thorpe *Ulverton*; Elspeth Barker *O Caledonia*. *Prize* £750.

The Richard Imison Memorial Award

The Society of Authors, 84 Drayton Gardens, London SW10 9SB
☎0171 373 6642   Fax 0171 373 5768

Contact *The Secretary, The Broadcasting Committee*

Annual award established 'to perpetuate the memory of Richard Imison, to acknowledge the encouragement he gave to writers working in the medium of radio, and in memory of the support and friendship he invariably offered writers in general, and radio writers in particular'. Administered by the Society of Authors and sponsored most recently by *The Times*, the purpose is 'to encourage new talent and high standards in writing for radio by selecting the radio drama by a writer new to radio which, in the opinion of the judges, is the best of those submitted. An adaptation for radio of a piece originally written for the stage, television or film will not be eligible. Any radio drama first transmitted in the UK between 1 January and 31 December by a writer or writers new to radio, is eligible, provided the work is an original piece for radio and it is the first dramatic work by the writer(s) that has been broadcast. Submission may be made by any party to the production in the form of two copies of an audio cassette (not-returnable) accompanied by a nomination form. Final entry date is end of the first week January 1996. *Prize* £1000.

The Independent Foreign Fiction Award

The Independent, 1 Canada Square, Canary Wharf, London E14 5DL
☎0171 293 2693   Fax 0171 293 2010

Contact *Catriona Luke*

ESTABLISHED 1990. Full-length novel or collection of short stories, translated into English and published in the UK in the year preceding the award. 'To reward and promote the best fiction from abroad translated into English for the first time.' Six bi-monthly awards to produce a shortlist of six books for the annual award announced in June. No cash prize for monthly awards. 1994 winner: *Sorrow of War* Bao Ninh, translated by Phan Thanh Hao *Award* £10,000.

The Independent/Scholastic Story of the Year

Postal box address changes each year (see below)

ESTABLISHED 1993. Open competition for the best short story for children aged 6–9. One story per entrant (between 1500–2000 words). Details of the competition, including the postal box address are published in *The Independent* in April of each year. *Prize* £2000; two runners-up of £500 each. The winning story will be published in the newspaper and in an anthology published by **Scholastic Children's Books**, along with a selection of the best entries.

International Reading Association Literacy Award

International Reading Association, 800 Barksdale Road, PO Box 8139, Newark Delaware 19714-8139, USA
☎001 302 731 1600   Fax 001 302 731 1057
Marketing Manager *Tracy Webb*

The International Reading Association is a non-profit education organisation devoted to improving reading instruction and promoting literacy worldwide. In addition to the US $10,000 award presented each year on International Literacy Day (September 8), the organisation gives more than 25 awards in recognition of achievement in reading research, writing for children, media coverage of literacy, and literacy instruction.

Irish Times International Fiction Prize

Irish Times Ltd, 10–16 D'Olier Street, Dublin 2, Republic of Ireland
☎00 353 1 679 2022   Fax 00 353 1 670 9383
Administrator, Book Prizes *Gerard Cavanagh*

FOUNDED 1989. Biennial award to the author of a work of fiction written in the English language and published in Ireland, the UK or the US in the two years of the award. Next award to be announced in October 1995, the short list having been announced in September. Books are nominated by literary critics and editors only. Previous winners: Annie Proulx *The Shipping News*; Norman Rush *Mating*; Louis Begley *Wartime Lies*.
Prize IR£7500.

Irish Times Irish Literature Prizes

Irish Times Ltd, 10–16 D'Olier Street, Dublin 2, Republic of Ireland
☎00 353 1 679 2022   Fax 00 353 1 670 9383
Administrator, Book Prizes *Gerard Cavanagh*

FOUNDED 1989. Biennial prizes awarded in three different categories: fiction (a novel, novella or collection of short stories), non-fiction prose (history, biography, autobiography, criticism, politics, sociological interest, travel, current affairs and belles-lettres), and poetry (collection or a long poem or a sequence of poems, or a revised/updated edition of a previously published selection/collection). The author must have been born in Ireland or be an Irish citizen, but may live in any part of the world. Books are nominated by literary editors and critics, and are then called in from publishers. Previous winners: Brian Keenan *An Evil Cradling*; John MacKenna *The Fallen and Other Stories*; Patrick McCabe *The Butcher Boy*; Derek Mahon *Selected Poems*.
Prizes IR£5,000 each category.

Jewish Quarterly Literary Prizes

PO Box 1148, London NW5 2AZ
☎0171 485 4062
Contact *Andrew Franklin*

Formerly the H. H. Wingate Prize. Annual awards (one for fiction, one for non-fiction and one for poetry) for works which best stimulate an interest in and awareness of themes of Jewish interest. Books must have been published in the UK in the year of the award and be written in English by an author resident in Britain, Commonwealth, Israel, Republic of Ireland or South Africa. Previous winners: Amos Oz *Black Box*; Anton Gill *The Journey Back from Hell*; Bernice Rubens *Kingdom Come*; Leo Abse *Wotan My Enemy*; Ronald Harwood *Home*.
Prizes Fiction: £4000; Non-fiction: £3000; Poetry: £1000.

Mary Vaughan Jones Award

Cyngor Llyfrau Cymraeg (Welsh Books Council), Castell Brychan, Aberystwyth, Dyfed SY23 2JB
☎01970 624151   Fax 01970 625385
Contact *The Administrator*

Triennial award for distinguished services in the field of children's literature in Wales over a considerable period of time.
Award Silver trophy to the value of £750.

Kent & Sussex Poetry Society Open Competition

7 Southfield Road, Tunbridge Wells, Kent TN4 9UH
Contact *Susan Collins*

Open poetry competition. Entry fee £2 per poem. Poems should be in English, unpublished and not accepted for publication elsewhere, and should not have been entered for any other current poetry competition. Maximum 40 lines on any subject, in any form and style. Presentation details should be checked before submitting anything. Final entry date 31 January 1996. Attracts around 2000 entries a year.
Prizes (1st) £300; (2nd) £100; (3rd) £50; (4th) 5 prizes of £20.

The Sir Peter Kent Conservation Book Prize

Book Trust, Book House, 45 East Hill, London SW18 2QZ
☎0181 870 9055   Fax 0181 874 4790
Contact *Sandra Vince*

ESTABLISHED by BP Exploration for a book on creative conservation of the environment. Entries from UK publishers only. Previous winners: Oliver Rackham *The Illustrated History of the Countryside*; Edward O. Wilson *The Diversity of Life*; Jo Readman *Muck and Magic*; Philip Wayne *Operation Otter*; Jonathan Kingdon *Island Africa*; George Monbiot *Amazon Watershed*; Iain & Oria Douglas-Hamilton *Battle for the Elephants*.

Prizes (1st) £5000; £2000 prize for book on conservation for 8–14-year-olds.

Kent Short Story Competition

Kent Literature Festival, The Metropole Arts Centre, The Leas, Folkestone, Kent CT20 2LS
☎01303 255070
Contact *Ann Fearey*

ESTABLISHED 1992. For a short story of up to 3000 words by anyone over the age of 16. Sponsored by **South East Arts**, Kent County Council Arts & Libraries and Shepway District Council. Entry forms available from March.

Prizes (1st) £250; (2nd) £125; (3rd) £75.

Kent Young Writers of the Year Award

Kent Literature Festival, The Metropole Arts Centre, The Leas, Folkestone, Kent CT20 2LS
☎01303 255070
Contact *David Stone, Ann Fearey*

FOUNDED 1990. Funded by **South East Arts**, Kent County Council Arts & Libraries, Shepway District Council and the Metropole Arts Centre Trust. Annual award for nine young writers aged between 5–18 years, whereby their writing will be brought to the attention of the public at the **Kent Literature Festival** at the end of September.

Lakeland Book of the Year Awards

Cumbria Tourist Board, Ashleigh, Holly Road, Windermere, Cumbria LA23 2AQ
☎015394 44444   Fax 015394 44041
Contact *Regional Publicity Officer*

Four annual awards set up by Cumbrian author Hunter Davies and the Cumbria Tourist Board. The **Hunter Davies Prize** was established in 1984 and is awarded for the book which best helps visitors or residents enjoy a greater love or understanding of any aspect of life in Cumbria and the Lake District. Three further awards were set up in 1993 with funding from the private sector: the **Tullie House Prize** is for the book which best helps develop a greater appreciation of the built and/or natural environment of Cumbria; the **Barclays Bank Prize** is for the best small book on any aspect of Cumbrian life, its people or culture; and the **Border Television Prize** is for the book which best illustrates the beauty and character of Cumbria. Final entry date mid-March. Previous winners: Hunter Davies Prize: Grevel Lindop *A Literary Guide to the Lake District*; Border Television Prize: Colin Shelbourn, Stirling Moss and David Ward *Great Drives in the Lakes and Dales*; Barclays Bank Prize: Sheila Richardson *Tales of a Lakeland Poacher*; Tullie House Prize: A. Wainwright and Ed Geldard *Wainwright's Tour in the Lake District – Whitsuntide 1931*.

Prize £100 and certificate.

Lancashire County Library/NWB Children's Book of the Year Award

Lancashire County Library Headquarters, 143 Corporation Street, Preston, Lancashire PR1 2UQ
☎01772 264010   Fax 01772 555919
Assistant County Librarian, Education & Reader Services *D. G. Lightfoot*

ESTABLISHED 1986. Annual award sponsored by the National Westminster Bank for a work of original fiction suitable for 11–14-year-olds. The winner is chosen by 13–14-year-old secondary school pupils in Lancashire. Books must have been published between 1 September and 31 August in the year of the award and authors must be UK residents. Final entry date 1 September each year. Previous winners: Brian Jacques *Mattimeo*; Robin Jarvis *Whitby Witches*; Robert Westall *Gulf*; Ian Strachan *The Boy in the Bubble*.

Prize £300 plus engraved glass decanter.

D.H. Lawrence/GPT Short Story Competition

Broxtowe Borough Council, Technical & Leisure Services, Council Offices, Foster Avenue, Beeston, Nottingham NG9 1AB
☎0115 9254891 ext. 4654
Contacts *Mrs Joan Wildgust, Miss Kaye Needham*

Annual short story awards. ESTABLISHED in 1980, the year of the 50th anniversary of the death of D.H. Lawrence. The competition aims to encourage young writers between the ages of 13 and 19 years of age. Stories must be no more than 5000 words in length and on any topic of local relevance. Entrants must live in Nottinghamshire or a district adjacent to Broxtow Borough. Final entry date is the last day of June.

Prizes a trophy in the form of a Phoenix, made by Plessey apprentices for the school with the best level of entries; book tokens for individuals.

The Library Association Besterman Medal

7 Ridgmount Street, London WC1E 7AE
☎0171 636 7543   Fax 0171 436 7218

Awarded annually for an outstanding bibliography or guide to literature first published in the UK during the preceding year. Recommendations for the award are invited from members of **The Library Association**. Among criteria taken into consideration in making the award are: authority of the work and quality of articles or entries; accessibility and arrangement of the information; scope and coverage; quality of indexing; adequacy of references; accuracy of information; physical presentation; and the originality of the work. Previous winners include: Katharine Pantzer, *A Short-title Catalogue of Books 1475–1640 Volume 3*; Eileen Harris and Nicholas Savage *British Architectural Books and Writers*; William Ringler *Bibliography and Index of English Verse printed 1476–1558*.
Award Medal.

The Library Association Carnegie Medal

7 Ridgmount Street, London WC1E 7AE
☎0171 636 7543   Fax 0171 436 7218

ESTABLISHED 1936. Sponsored by Peters Library Service. Presented for an outstanding book for children written in English and first published in the UK during the preceding year. This award is not necessarily restricted to books of an imaginative nature. Previous winners include: Berlie Doherty *Dear Nobody*; Geraldine McCaughrean *A Pack of Lies*.
Award Medal.

The Library Association Kate Greenaway Medal

7 Ridgmount Street, London WC1E 7AE
☎0171 636 7543   Fax 0171 436 7218

ESTABLISHED 1955. Sponsored by Peters Library Service. Presented annually for the most distin-

guished work in the illustration of children's books first published in the UK during the preceding year. Previous winners include: Adrienne Kennaway *Crafty Chameleon*; Janet & Allan Ahlberg *The Jolly Christmas Postman*.
Award Medal.

The Library Association McColvin Medal

7 Ridgmount Street, London WC1E 7AE
☎0171 636 7543   Fax 0171 436 7218

Annual award for an outstanding reference book first published in the UK during the preceding year. Books eligible for consideration include: encyclopedias, general and special; dictionaries, general and special; biographical dictionaries; annuals, yearbooks and directories; handbooks and compendia of data; atlases. Recommendations invited from members of **The Library Association**. Previous winners include: Michael Brooke and Tim Birkhead eds *The Cambridge Encyclopedia of Ornithology*; Christopher Hibbert, ed. *The Encyclopaedia of Oxford; The Oxford English Dictionary*, 2nd ed.
Award Medal.

The Library Association Wheatley Medal

7 Ridgmount Street, London WC1E 7AE
☎0171 636 7543   Fax 0171 436 7218

Annual award for an outstanding index first published in the UK during the preceding three years. Whole work must have originated in the UK and recommendations for the award are invited from members of **The Library Association**, the **Society of Indexers**, publishers and others. Previous winners include: Elizabeth Moys *British Tax Encyclopedia*; Bobby Burke *Halsbury's Laws of England*, 4th ed; Richard Raper *The Works of Charles Darwin*.
Award Medal.

Lichfield Prize

c/o Tourist Information Centre, Donegal House, Bore Street, Lichfield, Staffordshire WS13 6NE
☎01543 252109   Fax 01543 417308
Contact *Mrs D. Broach* at above or *Mr S. Smith* at Lichfield District Council on 01543 414000 ext. 2027

ESTABLISHED 1988. Biennial award initiated by Lichfield District Council to coincide with the Lichfield Festival. Run in conjunction with James Redshaw Books Ltd. Awarded for a previously unpublished novel based upon the geographical area of Lichfield district, contemporary or historical, but not futuristic. Previous winners include: Valerie Kershaw *Rockabye*; Gary Coyne *A Short Caution*; John Caine *A Nest of Singing Birds*. Next award 1997. Final entry date in May of that year.

Prize £5000, plus possible publication.

Literary Review Grand Poetry Competition
See *Literary Review* under **Magazines**

Lloyds Private Banking Playwright of the Year Award
Tony Ball Associates Plc, 174–178 North Gower Street, London NW1 2NB
☎0171 380 0953   Fax 0171 387 9004
Contact *Stephen Harrison*

LAUNCHED in February 1994. The Award aims to provide support and encouragement for writing talent to flourish and gain greater recognition, as well as to help widen interest in regional and London theatres. Playwrights must be of British or Irish nationality and have written a new play which was first performed in the previous year. Nominations are made by theatre critics from which a shortlist of ten is selected. The winner is announced in March. 1995 winner: Terry Johnson.

Prize £25,000.

London Writers Competition
See **Wandsworth London Writers Competition**

Sir William Lyons Award
The Guild of Motoring Writers, 30 The Cravens, Smallfield, Surrey RH6 9QS
☎01342 843294   Fax 01342 844093
Contact *Sharon Scott-Fairweather*

An annual competitive award to encourage young people in automotive journalism and to foster interests in motoring and the motor industry. Entrance by two essays and interview with Awards Committee. Applicants must be British, aged 17–23 and resident in UK. Final entry date 1 August. Presentation date December.

Award £1000 plus trophy.

Agnes Mure Mackenzie Award
The Saltire Society, 9 Fountain Close, 22 High Street, Edinburgh EH1 1TF
☎0131 556 1836   Fax 0131 557 1675
Administrator *Kathleen Munro*

ESTABLISHED 1965. Triennial award in memory of the late Dr Agnes Mure Mackenzie for a published work of distinguished Scottish historical research of scholarly importance (including intellectual history and the history of science). Editions of texts are not eligible. The 1995 award was open to books published between 1st January 1992 and 31st December 1994. Nominations are invited and should be sent to the Administrator.

Prize Bound and inscribed copy of the winning publication.

W. J. M. Mackenzie Book Prize
Political Studies Association, Dept of Politics, Queen's University, Belfast BT7 1NN
☎01232 245133 ext. 3224   Fax 01232 235373
PSA Administrative Secretary *Lynn Corken*

ESTABLISHED 1987. Annual award to best work of political science published in the UK during the previous year. Submissions from publishers only. Final entry date in March. Previous winners: James Mayall *Nationalism and International Society*; Brian Barry *Theories of Justice;* Avi Shlaim *Collusion Across the Jordan*; Colin Crouch *Industrial Relation and European State Tradition*; Iain Hampsher-Monk *A History of Modern Political Thought*; Patrick Dunleavy *Democracy, Bureaucracy and Public Choice*.

Prize £100 plus travel/attendance at three-day annual conference.

Francis McManus Short Story Competition
RTE Radio 1, Dublin 4, Republic of Ireland
Contact *The Administrator*

ESTABLISHED in 1985 in memory of the late Francis McManus, writer and broadcaster. Open to people born or resident in Ireland, the stories (in English or Irish) should be written for radio and unpublished. Entries should be between 1,850 and 1,950 words in length. Closing date is in September.

Prizes IR£1500 and commemorative award (1st); IR£750 (2nd); IR£500 (3rd); IR£250 (4th). RTE Radio have the right to one broadcast of each of the prize-winning entries.

Macmillan Prize for a Children's Picture Book
Pan Macmillan Ltd, 18–21 Cavaye Place, London SW10 9PG
☎0171 373 6070   Fax 0171 370 0746
Contact *Marketing Dept., Macmillan Children's Books*

Set up in order to stimulate new work from young illustrators in art schools, and to help them start their professional lives. Fiction or non-fiction. **Macmillan** have the option to publish any of the prize winners. 1994 winner: Ross Collins.

Prizes (1st) £1000; (2nd) £500; (3rd) £250.

Macmillan Silver PEN Award
The English Centre of International PEN, 7 Dilke Street, London SW3 4JE
☎0171 352 6303   Fax 0171 351 0220

An annual award for a volume of short stories written in English by a British author and published in the UK in the year preceding the prize. Nominations by the PEN Executive Committee only. Previous winners: Nicola Barker *Love Your Enemies*; Clive Collins *Misunderstandings*; John Arden *Cogs Tyrannic*; Pauline Melville *Shape-Shifter*; George Steiner *Proofs and Three Parables*.

Prize £500, plus silver pen.

The Mail on Sunday Novel Competition
The Mail on Sunday, PO Box 2, Central Way, Feltham, Middlesex TW14 0TG
☎0171 938 6000

Annual award ESTABLISHED 1983. Judges look for a story/character that springs to life in the 'tantalising opening 50–150 words of a novel'. Previous winners: Jill Roe, Judy Astley, Simon Levack, Sarah Cooper, Terry Eccles, Jillian Hart.

Awards (1st) £400 book tokens and a weekend writing course at the **Arvon Foundation**; (2nd) £300 tokens; (3rd) £200 tokens; three runners-up receive £150 tokens each.

The Mail on Sunday/John Llewellyn Rhys Prize
Book Trust, Book House, 45 East Hill, London SW18 2QZ
☎0181 870 9055   Fax 0181 874 4790
Contact *Sandra Vince*

An annual young writer's award for a memorable work of any kind. Entrants must be under the age of 35 at the time of publication; books must have been published in the UK in the year of the award. The author must be a citizen of Britain or the Commonwealth, writing in English. Previous winners: Matthew Kneale *Sweet Thames*; Jason Goodwin *On Foot to the Golden Horn*. 1995 winner: Jonathan Coe *What a Carve Up!*

Prize £5000 (1st); £500 for shortlisted entries.

Marsh Award for Children's Literature in Translation
The Authors' Club, 40 Dover Street, London W1X 3RB
☎0171 499 8581   Fax 0171 409 0913
Contact *Mrs Ann Carter*

ESTABLISHED 1995 and sponsored by the Marsh Christian Trust, the award aims to encourage translation of foreign children's books into English. It is a biennial award (first year: 1996), open to British translators of books for 4–16-year-olds, published in the UK by a British publisher. Final entry date is March 1996. Any category will be considered with the exception of encyclopedias/reference. No electronic books.

Prize £750.

Marsh Biography Award
The Authors' Club, 40 Dover Street, London W1X 3RB
☎0171 499 8581   Fax 0171 409 0913
Contact *Mrs Ann Carter*

A biennial award for the most significant biography published over a two-year period by a British publisher. Previous winners: Hugh & Mirabel Cecil *Clever Hearts*; Patrick Marnham *The Man who Wasn't Maigret*. Next award October 1995.

Award £3000, plus silver trophy presented at a dinner.

Kurt Maschler Award
Book Trust, Book House, 45 East Hill, London SW18 2QZ
☎0181 870 9055   Fax 0181 874 4790
Contact *Sandra Vince*

For 'a work of imagination in the children's field in which text and illustration are of excellence and so presented that each enhances, yet balances the other'. Books published in the current year in the UK by a British author and/or artist, or by someone resident for ten years, are eligible. Previous winners: Raymond Briggs *The Man*; Colin McNaughton *Have You Seen Who's Just Moved in Next Door to Us?* Karen Wallace & Mike Bostock *Think of an Eel*; Trish Cooke, illus. Helen Oxenbury *So Much*.

Award £1000 plus bronze Emil trophy.

McKitterick Prize
Society of Authors, 84 Drayton Gardens, London SW10 9SB
☎0171 373 6642   Fax 0171 373 5768
Contact *Awards Secretary*

Annual award for a full-length work in the

English language, first published in the UK or unpublished. Open to writers over 40 who have not had any adult novel published other than the one submitted. Closing date 16 December. 1994 winner: Helen Dunmore *Zennor in Darkness*.
Prize £5000.

Enid McLeod Prize

Franco-British Society, Room 623, Linen Hall, 162–168 Regent Street, London W1R 5TB
☎0171 734 0815   Fax 0171 734 0815
Executive Secretary *Mrs Marian Clarke*

ESTABLISHED 1982. Annual award to the author of the work of literature published in the UK which, in the opinion of the judges, has contributed most to Franco-British understanding. Any full-length work written in English by a citizen of the UK, Commonwealth, Republic of Ireland, Pakistan, Bangladesh and South Africa. Nominations from publishers for books published between 1 January and 31 December of the year of the prize. Previous winners: Allan Massie *A Question of Loyalties*; Frank Giles *The Locust Years*; Margaret Crosland *Simone de Beauvoir – The Woman and Her Work*.
Prize Copy of Enid McLeod's memoirs, plus cheque.

The McVitie's Prize for the Scottish Writer of the Year

c/o Book Trust Scotland, The Scottish Book Centre, 137 Dundee Street, Edinburgh EH11 1BG
☎0131 229 3663   Fax 0131 228 4293
Contact *Kathryn Ross*

ESTABLISHED 1987. Sponsored by United Biscuits (Holdings) plc for the best substantial work of an imaginative nature, including TV and radio scripts and writing for children, first published, performed, filmed or transmitted between 1st August and 31st July. Writers born in Scotland, or who have Scottish parents, or who have been resident in Scotland for a considerable period, or who take Scotland as their inspiration are all eligible. Submissions accepted in English, Scots or Gaelic. Recent winners: Janice Galloway, John Prebble, and William Boyd.
Prize £10,000, plus £1,000 to each of the other four shortlisted writers.

Meyer-Whitworth Award

Arts Council of England, 14 Great Peter Street, London SW1P 3NQ
☎0171 333 0100   Fax 0171 973 6590
Contact *The Drama Director*

In 1908 the movement for a National Theatre joined forces with that to create a memorial to William Shakespeare. The result was the Shakespeare Memorial National Theatre Committee, the embodiment of the campaign for a National Theatre. This award, bearing the name of but two protagonists in the movement, has been established to commemorate all those who worked for the SMNT. Endowed by residual funds of the SMNT, the award is intended to help further the careers of UK playwrights who are not yet established, and to draw contemporary theatre writers to the public's attention. The award is given to the writer whose play most nearly satisfies the following criteria: a play which embodies Geoffrey Whitworth's dictum that 'drama is important in so far as it reveals the truth about the relationships of human beings with each other and the world at large'; a play which shows promise of a developing new talent; a play in which the writing is of individual quality. Nominations from professional theatre companies. Plays must have been written in the English language and produced professionally in the UK in the 12 months preceding the award.
Award £8000.

MIND Book of the Year/Allen Lane Award

Granta House, 15–19 Broadway, London E15 4BQ
☎0181 519 2122 ext. 225   Fax 0181 522 1725

ESTABLISHED 1981. Annual award, in memory of Sir Allen Lane, for the author of a book published in the current year (fiction or non-fiction), which furthers public understanding of mental health problems.
Award £1000.

The Mitchell Prize for Art History/The Eric Mitchell Prize

c/o The Burlington Magazine, 14–16 Duke's Road, London WC1H 9AD
☎0171 388 1228   Fax 0171 388 1230
Executive Director *Caroline Elam*

ESTABLISHED 1977 by art collector, philanthropist and businessman, Jan Mitchell, to draw attention to exceptional achievements in the history of art. Consists of two prizes: The Mitchell Prize, given for an outstanding and original contribution to the study and understanding of visual arts, and The Eric Mitchell Prize, given for the most outstanding first book in this field. The prizes are awarded to authors of books in English that have been published in the previous 12 months (i.e. 1 January–31 December 1995 for the 1996 award). Books are submitted by publishers before the end of February. Previous winners: The Mitchell Prize: *Colour and Culture* John Gage; The Eric Mitchell Prize: *Fra Angelico at San Marco* William Hood.

Prizes $15,000 (Mitchell Prize); $5000 (Eric Mitchell Prize)

Mobil Playwriting Competition

Royal Exchange Theatre, St Ann's Square, Manchester M2 7DH

☎0161 833 9333   Fax 0161 832 0881

Both the **Mobil Bursary** and the Playwriting Competition are currently under review, subject to an announcement later in 1995.

Scott Moncrieff Prize

The Translators' Association, 84 Drayton Gardens, London SW10 9SB

☎0171 373 6642

Contact *Kate Pool*

An annual award for the best translation published by a British publisher during the previous year of a French work which must have been published within the last 150 years of literary merit and general interest. Previous winners: Barbara Wright for *The Midnight Love Feast* by Michel Tournier; James Kirkup for *Painted Shadows* by Jean-Baptiste Niel.

Prize £1000.

The Montagu of Beaulieu Trophy Sponsored by Classic Cars Magazine

Guild of Motoring Writers, 30 The Cravens, Smallfield, Surrey RH6 9QS

☎01342 843294   Fax 01342 844093

Contact *Sharon Scott-Fairweather*

First presented by Lord Montagu on the occasion of the opening of the National Motor Museum at Beaulieu in 1972. Awarded annually to a member of the **Guild of Motoring Writers** who, in the opinion of the nominated jury, has made the greatest contribution to recording in the English language the history of motoring or motor cycling in a published book or article, film, television or radio script, or research manuscript available to the public.

Prize Trophy and £1000 given by *Classic Cars Magazine*.

The Mother Goose Award

Books for Children, 4 Furzeground Way, Stockley Park, Uxbridge, Middlesex UB11 1DP

☎0181 606 3061   Fax 0181 606 3099

Contact *Sian Hardy, Editorial Manager*

For the most exciting newcomer to British children's book illustration. 1994 winner: Lisa Flather *Where the Great Bear Watches.*

Prize £1000, plus Golden Egg trophy.

NASEN Special Educational Needs Award

See **Times Educational Supplement/NASEN Special Educational Needs Award**

Natural World Book of the Year Award

Natural World Magazine, 20 Upper Ground, London SE1 9PF

☎0171 928 2111   Fax 0171 620 1594

Contact *Linda Bennett*

ESTABLISHED 1987. Annual award to encourage the publication of high-quality natural history books. Open to books published between 1 October and 30 September about British and European wildlife or countryside. Final entry date end of August. Previous winners: Oliver Rackham *The Illustrated History of the Countryside*; Sir Peter Scott *Images from a Lifetime*; Jeremy Thomas *The Butterflies of Britain & Ireland*. Administered by *Natural World* magazine.

Prize £500, plus magazine promotion feature of book.

NCR Book Award for Non-Fiction

See **AT & T Non-Fiction Award**

Nobel Prize

The Nobel Foundation, Box 5232/Sturegatan 14, Stockholm, Sweden S–10245

☎00 46 8 663 0920   Fax 00 46 8 660 3847

Contact *Information Section*

Awarded yearly for outstanding achievement in physics, chemistry, physiology or medicine, literature and peace. FOUNDED by Alfred Nobel, a chemist who proved his creative ability by inventing dynamite. In general, individuals cannot nominate someone for a Nobel Prize. The rules vary from prize to prize but the following are eligible to do so for Literature: members of the Swedish Academy and of other academies, institutions and societies similar to it in membership and aims; professors of history of literature or of languages at universities or colleges; Nobel Laureates in Literature; presidents of authors' organisations which are representative of the literary activities of their respective countries. British winners of the literature prize, first granted in 1901, include Rudyard Kipling, John Galsworthy and Winston Churchill.

Recent winners: Camilio Jose Cela (Spain); Octavio Paz (Mexico); Nadine Gordimer (South Africa); Derek Walcott (St Lucia); Toni Morrison (USA); Kenzaburo Oe (Japan).

Prize 1994: SEK7,000,000 (about £550,000), increasing each year to cover inflation.

Northern Short Stories Competition

ARC Publications, Nanholme Mill,
Shaw Wood Road, Todmorden, Lancashire
OL14 6DA
☎01706 812338   Fax 01706 818948

Contact *Rosemary Jones*

ESTABLISHED 1988. Annual award set up to stimulate the writing and reading of quality short fiction. Open to all living in the area covered by the three Northern regional arts boards (**North West Arts, Northern Arts, Yorkshire & Humberside Arts**). Final entry date 30 June. Please send s.a.e. for entry form.

Prize Guaranteed same-year publication in anthology, plus small cash prize.

Nottinghamshire Children's Book Award

Nottinghamshire County Council, Education Library Service, Glaisdale Parkway,
Nottingham NG8 4GP
☎0115 9854200   Fax 0115 9286400

Contact *Ann Fairbairn* (Library)

ESTABLISHED 1989. Annual award jointly organised and promoted by Nottingham Libraries and Dillons Bookstore, who sponsor the award. The aim is to encourage reading and draw attention to the exciting range of children's books available. The award is given in two categories: **The Acorn Award**, for an outstanding book written and illustrated for the 0–7 age group; and **The Oak Tree Award**, for an outstanding book written and illustrated for the 8–12 age group. Books must have been published for the first time in the UK in the preceding year. Shortlist drawn up by librarians and bookshop staff. Previous winners: Helen Cresswell *The Watchers*; David Morgan and David Parkins: *Blooming Cats*.

Award £250 (each category).

The Oak Tree Award

See **Nottinghamshire Children's Book Award**

C. B. Oldman Prize

Aberdeen University Library, Queen Mother Library, Meston Walk, Aberdeen AB9 2UE
☎01224 272592   Fax 01224 487048

Contact *Richard Turbet*

ESTABLISHED 1989 by the International Association of Music Libraries, UK Branch. Annual award for best book of music bibliography, librarianship or reference published the year before last (i.e. books published in 1992 considered for the 1994 prize). Previous winners: Andrew Ashbee, Michael Talbot, Donald Clarke, John Parkinson, John Wagstaff, Stanley Sadie.

Prize £150.

One Voice Monologue Competition

c/o Pro Forma, Box 29, Neath, West Glamorgan SA11 1WL

Contact *Nicola Davies*

ESTABLISHED 1992. An international competition run by playwright Nicola Davies with the support of a team of writers/actors. Annual award sponsored by Canon UK and Filofax. The competition has been supported by Sir Anthony Hopkins, Simon Callow and Miriam Margolyes. Finalists' work is broadcast and published in an illustrated designed book. There are now three categories: Monologue, Story, Letter. Entries must be previously unpublished and unperformed. Please send s.a.e. for entry form. Final entry date May 1996.

Prizes in 1996 are anticipated as being a total of £6000 (£2000 in each category).

Outposts Poetry Competition

Outposts, 22 Whitewell Road, Frome, Somerset BA11 4EL
☎01373 466653

Contact *Roland John*

Annual competition for an unpublished poem of not more than 40 lines run by **Hippopotamus Press**.

Prize £1000.

OWG/COLA Awards for Excellence

Outdoor Writers' Guild, 27 Camwood, Clayton Green, Bamber Bridge, Preston, Lancashire PR5 8LA
☎01772 321243

Contact *Terry Marsh*

ESTABLISHED 1990. Annual award by the **Outdoor Writers' Guild** and the Camping & Outdoor Leisure Association to raise the standard of outdoor writing, journalism and broadcasting. Winning categories include best book, best guidebook, best feature, best technical report. Open to OWG members only. Final entry date February. Previous winners include: Leigh Hatts, Nick Crane, Steve Venables, Hazel Constance, Catherine Moore, John and Anne Nuttal, Roland Smith, Terry Marsh.

Prize (total) £1250.

Catherine Pakenham Award

The Sunday Telegraph, 1 Canada Square, Canary Wharf, London E14 5DT
☎0171 538 5000   Fax 0171 538 6242
Contact *Joanne Henwood*

ESTABLISHED 1970, this is an annual award in memory of Lady Catherine Pakenham, and is given for a non-fiction article (750–2000 words) by a woman aged between 18 and 25, resident in Britain and involved in or intending to take up a career in journalism. 1995 winner: Esther Oxford, feature writer for *The Independent.*

Award £1000 and a writing commission with one of the Telegraph publications; three runner-up prizes of £200 each.

Peer Petry Competition

Box 26/100, Arlington House, Bath Street, Bath, Somerset Avon BA1 1QU
Contact *Competition Editor*

Bi-annual open competition for one or more poems up to 120 lines in total. Unpublished poems only. All qualifying poems will be printed in *Peer Poetry.* Send s.a.e. for rules and qualifying details. Closing date 30 October.

Prizes £120 (1st); £60 (2nd); £30 (3rd).

PEN Awards

See **Macmillan Silver PEN Award**; **Time-Life Silver PEN Award**;

Peterloo Poets Open Poetry Competition

2 Kelly Gardens, Calstock, Cornwall PL18 9SA
☎01822 833473
Contact *Lynn Chambers*

ESTABLISHED 1986. Annual competition sponsored by Marks & Spencer for unpublished English language poems of not more than 40 lines. Final entry date end February. Previous winners: David Craig, Rodney Pybus, Debjani Chatterjee, Donald Atkinson, Romesh Gunesekera.

Prize £3000 (1st).

Poetry Business Competition

The Studio, Byram Arcade, Westgate, Huddersfield, West Yorkshire HD1 1ND
☎01484 434840   Fax 01484 426566
Contact *The Competition Administrator*

ESTABLISHED 1986. Annual award which aims to discover and publish new writers. Entrants should submit 24 pp of poems. Entry fee £15. Winners will have their work published by the **Poetry Business** under the Smith/Doorstop imprint. Final entry date end of October. Previous winners include: Pauline Stainer, Michael Laskey, Mimi Khalvati, David Morley, Julia Casterton, Liz Cashdan, Moniza Alvi. Send s.a.e. for full details.

No cash prize; 20 complimentary copies.

Poetry Life Poetry Competition

Poetry Life, 14 Pennington Oval, Lymington, Hampshire SO41 8BQ
Contact *Adrian Bishop*

ESTABLISHED 1990. Open competition for original poems in any style which have not been published in a book. Maximum length of 80 lines. Entry fee of £2 per poem (£10 for seven poems).

Prize £500 (1st); £100 (2nd); £50 each (3rd & 4th).

The Poetry Society's National Poetry Competition

The Poetry Society, 22 Betterton Street, London WC2H 9BU
☎0171 240 4810   Fax 0171 240 4818
Contact *Competition Organiser*

One of Britian's major open poetry competitions. Closing date 31 October 1995. Special category for poems of 40–100 lines. For rules and entry form send s.a.e. to the Competition Organiser at the above address.

Prize (1st) £3000; (2nd) £1000; (3rd) £500; (Special category) £1000.

The Portico Prize

See **The Royal Bank of Scotland Portico Prize**

The Dennis Potter Television Play of the Year Award

BBC Television Centre, Wood Lane, London, W12 7RJ
☎0181 743 8000

ESTABLISHED 1994 in memory of the late television playwright to 'bring out courageous and imaginative voices'. Annual award for writers who have not had single plays produced on television. Nominees are put forward by independent and BBC producers.

Prize commission worth £10,000.

Michael Powell Book Award

British Film Institute, 21 Stephen Street,
London W1P 1PL
☎0171 255 1444   Fax 0171 436 7950
Contact *BFI Press Office*

Annual award given by the **British Film
Institute** for a book by a British author on film
or television which is both innovative and acces-
sible, with a lively approach to the media. Pre-
vious winners include: Tony Richardson *Long
Distance Runner, A Memoir*; John Boorman &
Walter Donohue *Projections: A Forum for
Filmmakers*; David Thomson *Showman: The Life
of David O Selznick.*
Award varies.

Pro Dogs National Charity Open Creative Writing & Photographic Awards

Pro Dogs National Charity, Rocky Bank, 4
New Road, Ditton, Aylesford, Maidstone,
Kent ME20 6AD

ESTABLISHED 1988 to help publicise Pro Dogs
National Charity. Biennial awards in three cat-
egories: best poem; best story; best photo.
Entry qualifications: poems up to 32 lines; sto-
ries up to 1000 words, photos black and white
or colour. Send s.a.e. for entry form/details.
Final entry date 1 October 1995.
Prize (total) £250.

Pulitzer Prizes

The Pulitzer Prize Board, 702 Journalism,
Columbia University, New York
NY 10027, USA
☎001 212 854 3841/2
Contact *The Administrator*

Awards for journalism in US newspapers, and for
literature, drama and music by American nationals. Deadline 1 February (journalism); 1 March
(music); 1 March (drama); 1 July for books published between 1 Jan–30 June, and 1 Nov for
books published between 1 July–31 Dec (literature). 1995 winners included: Carol Shields *The
Stone Diaries*. Previous winners: E. Annie Proulx
The Shipping News; David Levering Lewis *W. E.
B. DuBois*; David Remnick *Lenin's Tomb: The
Last Days of the Soviet Empire.*

The Questors Theatre Student Playwright Competition

12 Mattock Lane, Ealing, London W5 5BQ
☎0181 567 0011   Fax 0181 567 8736
Theatre Manager *Elaine Orchard*
ESTABLISHED 1985. Annual award. The win-

ning play, and sometimes the runner-up, is/are
performed at Questors Theatre. Deadline for
entries 31st March.
Prize £1000.

Raconteur Short Story Competition
See *Raconteur* under **Magazines**

Trevor Reese Memorial Prize

Institute of Commonwealth Studies,
University of London, 28 Russell Square,
London WC1B 5DS
☎0171 580 5876   Fax 0171 255 2160
Contact *Seminar Secretary*

ESTABLISHED 1979 with the proceeds of contributions to a memorial fund to Dr Trevor Reese,
Reader in Commonwealth Studies at the
Institute and a distinguished scholar of imperial
history (d.1976). Biennial award (next award
1996) for a scholarly work by a single author in
the field of Imperial and Commonwealth
History published in the preceding two years.
All correspondence relating to the prize should
be marked *Trevor Reese Memorial Prize*. Previous
winner: Dr Avner Offer *The First World War: an
Agrarian Interpretation.*
Prize £1000.

Regional Press Awards

UK Press Gazette, EMAP Business
Communications, Chalk Lane, Cockfosters
Road, Barnet, Herts EN4 0BU
☎0181 242 3093   Fax 0181 242 3088

Comprehensive range of journalist and newspaper awards for the regional press. Five newspapers of the year, by circulation and frequency, and a full list of journalism categories.
Open to all regional journalists, whether freelance or staff. Final entry date 31 January. Run
by the *UK Press Gazette* and sponsored by the
Post Office.

Renault UK Journalist of the Year Award

Guild of Motoring Writers, 30 The Cravens,
Smallfield, Surrey RH6 9QS
☎01342 843294   Fax 01342 844093
Contact *Sharon Scott-Fairweather*

Originally the Pierre Dreyfus Award and ESTAB-
LISHED 1977. Awarded annually by Renault UK
Ltd in honour of Pierre Dreyfus, president
director general of Renault 1955–75, to the
member of the **Guild of Motoring Writers**

who is judged to have made the most outstanding journalistic effort during the year.
Prizes 1st £1000, plus trophy; 2nd £500; 3rd £250.

The Rhône-Poulenc Prizes for Science Books

COPUS, c/o The Royal Society, 6 Carlton House Terrace, London SW1Y 5AG
☎0171 839 5561 ext. 266 Fax 0171 930 2170
Contact *Jill A. Nelson*

ESTABLISHED 1987 by COPUS (Committee on the Public Understanding of Science) with the Science Museum. Sponsored by Rhône-Poulenc. Annual awards for popular non-fiction science and technology books judged to contribute most to the public understanding of science. Books must be published during the previous calendar year in their first English edition in the UK. The prizes, totalling £20,000, are divided between two categories: the Rhône-Poulenc Prize awarded for a book for general readership; and the Junior Prize for books written primarily for young people. Final entry date January. 1995 winners: John Emsley *The Consumer's Good Chemical Guide*; Jay Young *The Most Amazing Pop-up Science Book* (Junior prize).
Prizes Rhône-Poulenc Prize £10,000; Junior Prize £10,000.

Rhyme International Prize

c/o Orbis Magazine, 199 The Long Shoot, Nuneaton, Warwickshire CV11 6JQ
☎01203 327440   Fax 01203 327440
Contact *Mike Shields*

ESTABLISHED 1982. Annual competition aimed at promoting rhyming poetry. Minimum entry fee £5 (£2.50 per poem). Entries may fall into two categories: rhymed poems of less than 50 lines; or formal: sonnet, villanelle, etc. Final entry date end September.
Prize (1994 total) £1200.

John Llewellyn Rhys Prize

See **The Mail on Sunday/John Llewellyn Rhys Prize**

The Rivet Poetry Competition

74 Walton Drive, High Wycombe, Buckinghamshire HP13 6TT
Contact *Fleur Adcock*

Competition for poetry on any subject and in any style or form. 40 lines maximum; entry fee of £3 per poem. Closing date for entries is in April. Winning poems are published in *Rivet*

magazine. Information and entry forms available from the above address.
Prizes £100 (1st); £50 (2nd); £25 (3rd).

Rogers Prize

Scholarships Section, Room 21A, University of London, Senate House, London WC1E 7HU
☎0171 636 8000 ext. 3042
Contact *Mrs M. Praulins*

Annual award for an essay or dissertation on alternately a medical or surgical subject, which is named and appointed by the University of London on the advice of the relevant Board of Studies. Essays and dissertations must be in English and shall be typewritten or printed.
Prize £250.

Romantic Novelists' Association Major Award

3 Arnesby Lane, Peatling Magna, Leicester LE8 5UN
☎0116 2478330
Organiser *Jean Chapman*

Annual award for the best romantic novel of the year, open to non-members as well as members of the **Romantic Novelists' Association**. Novels must be published between specified dates which vary year to year. Authors must be based in the UK. Previous winners include: June Knox-Mawer *Sandstorm*; Susan Kay *Phantom*; Reay Tannahill *Passing Glory*; Elizabeth Buchan *Consider the Lily*. Contact the Organiser for entry form.
Award £5000.

Romantic Novelists' Association New Writers Award

RNA, 35 Ruddlesway, Windsor, Berkshire SL4 5SF
☎01753 867100
Secretary *Joyce Bell*

The award is for unpublished writers in the field of the romantic novel. Entrants are required to join the Association as probationary members. Mss entered for this award must be specifically written for it.

Rooney Prize for Irish Literature

Rooney Prize, Strathin, Templecarrig, Delgany, Co. Wicklow, Republic of Ireland
☎00 353 1 287 4769   Fax 00 353 1 287 4769
Contact *Jim Sherwin*

ESTABLISHED 1976. Annual award to encourage young Irish writing to develop and con-

tinue. Authors must be Irish, under 40 and published. A non-competitive award with no application procedure.
Prize IR£5000.

Routledge Ancient History Prize
c/o Richard Stoneman, Senior Editor, Routledge, 11 New Fetter Lane, London EC4P 4EE
☎0171 842 2160   Fax 0171 842 2302

Annual award presented to the author of the best contribution in English to the understanding of the history of the classical world. Typescripts (70,000–120,000 words) should be submitted by 31 July each year. No editions or commentaries. Works submitted should not normally be such as to require extensive photographic illustration or extensive typesetting in foreign alphabets. Funded by **Routledge** who will also publish the winning title. No restriction on age, nationality or status of candidates. Previous winner: Ray Laurence *Roman Pompeii.*
Prize £500, plus publication.

Rover Group Award
Guild of Motoring Writers, 30 The Cravens, Smallfield, Surrey RH6 9QS
☎01342 843294   Fax 01342 844093
Contact *Sharon Scott-Fairweather*

Awarded annually to the Guild member judged to have done most towards improving reader understanding of the issues affecting the vehicle industry.
Prize £1000.

The Royal Bank of Scotland Portico Prize
The Portico Library, 57 Mosley Street, Manchester M2 3HY
☎0161 236 6785
Contact *Mrs Jo Francis*

ESTABLISHED 1985. Administered by the Portico Library in Manchester. Biennial award (odd-numbered years) for a published work of fiction or non-fiction set wholly or mainly in the North-West/Cumbria. Previous winners include: Alan Hankinson *Coleridge Walks the Fells;* Jenny Uglow *Elizabeth Gaskell: A Habit of Stories.*
Prize £2500.

Royal Economic Society Prize
c/o University of York, York YO1 5DD
☎01904 433575   Fax 01904 433575
Contact *Prof. John D. Hey*

Biennial award for the best article published in

The Economic Journal. Open to members of the Royal Economic Society only. Next award 1996. Final entry date December 1995. Previous winners: Drs O. P. Attanasio & Guglielmo Weber; Prof. M. H. Pesaran; Prof. J. Pemberton.
Prize £1000.

Royal Society of Literature Awards
See **Winifred Holtby Memorial Prize** and **W. H. Heinemann Prize**

The Royal Society of Medicine Prizes
The Society of Authors, 84 Drayton Gardens, London SW10 9SB
☎0171 373 6642   Fax 0171 373 5768
Contact *Jacqueline Granger-Taylor*

Annual award in four categories: textbook, illustrated textbook, atlas and electronic format, published in the UK in the year preceding the award. Previous winners: R. J. Trent *Molecular Medicine;* A. R. Mundy and Philip Wilson *Urodynamic and Reconstructive Surgery of the Lower Urinary Tract;* Clifford M. Lawrence and Neil H. Cox *Physical Signs in Dermatology.*
Prizes £1000 (each category).

The RTZ David Watt Memorial Prize
RTZ Corporation plc, 6 St James's Square, London SW1Y 4LD
☎0171 930 2399   Fax 0171 930 3249

INITIATED 1987 to commemorate the life and work of David Watt. Annual award, open to writers currently engaged in writing for newspapers and journals, in the English language, on international and political affairs. The winners are judged as having made 'outstanding contributions towards the greater understanding and promotion of national and international political issues'. Entries must have been published during the year preceding the award. Final entry date 31 March. The 1994 winner was David Rose of the *Observer.* Previous winners include: Martin Woollacott of *The Guardian;* Dr Avi Shlaim for an article on Israel and the Gulf published in the *London Review of Books;* Neil Ascherson for an article in the *Independent on Sunday* headlined 'A Breath of Foul Air'.
Prize £5000.

Runciman Award
Anglo-Hellenic League, Flat 4, 68 Elm Park Gardens, London SW10 9PB
☎0171 352 2676   Fax 0171 351 5657
Contact *Mrs N. White-Gaze*

ESTABLISHED 1985. Annual award, founded by the Anglo-Hellenic League and funded by the Onassis Foundation, to promote Anglo-Greek understanding and friendship. Named after Sir Steven Runciman, former chairman of the Anglo-Hellenic League. Awarded to a work wholly about Greece or the Hellenic scene: fiction, poetry, translation, drama or non-fiction (guidebook), provided it is concerned (academically or non-academically) with history of any period, biography or autobiography, the arts, archaeology, the country, etc. Books must have been published in their first English edition in the UK during the calendar year. Final entry date end February; awards presented in May/June. 1994 winner: Paul Magdalino *The Empire of Mannell I Komnenos 1143–1180*. Previous winners: *Greece and the Inter-War Economic Crisis* Dr Mark Mazower; *Crete: the Battle and the Resistance* Antony Beevor; *A Concise History of Greece* Richard Clogg.
Award (total) £1000.

The SAGA Prize

Book Trust, Book House, 45 East Hill, London SW18 2QZ
☎0181 870 9055   Fax 0181 874 4790
Contact *Sandra Vince*

ESTABLISHED 1995. Annual award for the best unpublished novel by a black writer born in Great Britain or the Republic of Ireland and having a black African ancestor. Established by Marsha Hunt and sponsored by The SAGA Group. Mss must be unpublished and of no more than 80,000 words. Entry fee of £10 per mss. Final entry date is in May.
Prize £3000 plus publication by **Virago Press**.

Sagittarius Prize

Society of Authors, 84 Drayton Gardens, London SW10 9SB
☎0171 373 6642   Fax 0171 373 5768

ESTABLISHED 1990. For first published novel by an author over the age of 60. Final entry date mid December. 1994 winner: G. B. Hummer *Red Branch*.
Prize £2000.

The Salaman Prize for Non-Fiction

29 Allendale, Woodthorpe, York YO2 2SF
☎01904 708201
Contact *W.H. Bradley*

ESTABLISHED 1994. Annual award for the best published work of non-fiction by writers living in, born in, or writing about the North of England. Named after Redcliffe Salaman, author of *The History & Social Influence of the Potato*, the prize is awarded in association with the York and District Writers Circle. £4 administration fee for each entry; further details and entry forms from the above address. Final entry date is in April. Previous winner: *Charlotte Brontë and Her 'Dearest Nell'* E. Whitehead.
Prize £150, trophy and certificate.

The Saltire Literary Awards

Saltire Society, 9 Fountain Close, 22 High Street, Edinburgh EH1 1TF
☎0131 556 1836   Fax 0131 557 1675
Administrator *Kathleen Munro*

ESTABLISHED 1982. Annual awards, one for Book of the Year, the other for Best First Book by an author publishing for the first time. Open to any author of Scottish descent or living in Scotland, or to anyone who has written a book which deals with either the work and life of a Scot or with a Scottish problem, event or situation. Nominations are invited from editors of leading newspapers, magazines and periodicals. Previous winners: Scottish Book of the Year: *Beside the Ocean of Time* George Mackay Brown; *Collected Poems* Iain Crichton Smith; Best First Book: *Music, In a Foreign Language* Andrew Crumey; *The Adoption Papers* Jackie Kay; *Uirsgeul Myth* (poems in Gaelic with English translations) Le Crisdean Whyte.
Cash prize.

Schlegel-Tieck Prize

The Translators Association, 84 Drayton Gardens, London SW10 9SB
☎0171 373 6642   Fax 0171 373 5768
Contact *Kate Pool*

An annual award for the best translation of a German 20th-century work of literary merit and interest published by a British publisher during the preceding year. Previous winners include: Krishna Winston for *Goebbels* by Rolf Georg Reuth.
Prize £2200.

Scottish Arts Council Book Awards

Scottish Arts Council, 12 Manor Place, Edinburgh EH3 7DD
☎0131 226 6051   Fax 0131 225 9833
Literature Officer *Shonagh Irvine*

A number of awards are given biannually to authors of published books in recognition of high standards in new writing from new and established writers. Authors should be Scottish, resident in Scotland or have published books of Scottish interest. Applications from publishers only.

Award £1000 each.

Scottish Book of the Year
See **The Saltire Literary Awards**

SCSE Book Prizes
Department of Education Studies,
University of Reading, Bulmershe Court,
Reading, Berkshire RG6 1HY
☎01734 318861   Fax 01734 352080
Contact *Professor P. Croll*

Annual awards given by the Standing Conference on Studies in Education for the best book on education published during the preceding year and for the best book by a new author. Nomination by members of the Standing Conference and publishers.

Prizes £1000 and £500.

Bernard Shaw Translation Prize
The Translators Association, 84 Drayton Gardens, London SW10 9SB
☎0171 373 6642
Contact *Kate Pool*

ESTABLISHED 1990. Triennial award funded by the Anglo-Swedish Literary Foundation for the best translation of a Swedish work published in the UK in the three years preceding the closing date. Final entry date 31 December 1996 for 1997 award. Winners include: David McDuff for *A Valley in the Midst of Violence* by Gösta Åren.

Signal Poetry for Children Award
Thimble Press, Lockwood, Station Road,
South Woodchester, Stroud, Gloucestershire
GL5 5EQ
☎01453 873716/872208   Fax 01453 878599
Contact *Nancy Chambers*

This award is given annually for particular excellence in one of the following areas: single-poet collections published for children; poetry anthologies published for children; the body of work of a contemporary poet; critical or educational activity promoting poetry for children. All books for children published in Britain are eligible regardless of the original country of publication. Unpublished work is not eligible. Previous winners include: James Berry *When I Dance*; Jackie Kay *Two's Company*.

Award £100 plus certificate designed by Michael Harvey.

André Simon Memorial Fund Book Awards
5 Sion Hill Place, Bath, Avon BA1 5SJ
☎01225 336305   Fax 01225 421862
Contact *Tessa Hayward*

Three awards given annually for the best book on drink, best on food and special commendation in either.

Awards £2000 (best books); £1000 (special commendation); £200 to shortlisted books.

Smarties Prize for Children's Books
Book Trust, Book House, 45 East Hill,
London SW18 2QZ
☎0181 870 9055   Fax 0181 874 4790
Contact *Sandra Vince*

ESTABLISHED 1985 to encourage high standards and stimulate interest in books for children, this prize is given for a children's book (fiction), written in English by a citizen of the UK or an author resident in the UK, and published in the UK in the year ending 31 October. There are three age-group categories: 0–5, 6–8 and 9–11. An overall winner from these categories is chosen for the Smarties Book Prize. Previous winners include: Trish Cooke (illus. Helen Oxenbury) *So Much* (0–5); Henrietta Branford *Dimanche Diller* (6–8); Hilary McKay *The Exiles at Home* (9–11 and overall winner).

Prizes £8000 (overall winner); £2000 (other categories).

W. H. Smith Literary Award
W. H. Smith, Strand House, 7 Holbein Place,
London SW1W 8NR
☎0171 824 5458   Fax 0171 730 0195
Contact *Michael Mackenzie*

Annual prize awarded to a UK, Republic of Ireland or Commonwealth citizen for the most oustanding contribution to English literature, published in English in UK in the preceding year. Writers cannot submit work themselves. Previous winners include: Vikram Seth *A Suitable Boy*; Michèle Robert *Daughters of the House*; Thomas Pakenham *The Scramble for Africa*; Derek Walcott *Omeros*.

Prize £10,000.

W. H. Smith's Mind Boggling Books Award
Scope Communications, Tower House,
8–14 Southampton Street, London
WC2E 7HA
☎0171 379 3234   Fax 0171 240 7729
Public Relations Manager *Serena De Morgan*

ESTABLISHED 1993. Annual award. The six shortlisted books are chosen by a panel of ten children aged between nine and twelve. Authors must be British and have had their book published in paperback during the previous year. Like Smith's Thumping Good Read Award for adult fiction, this award focuses on 'the type of book which will really appeal to the majority of our customers'. 1994 winner: Malorie Blackman *Hacker*.

Award £5000.

W. H. Smith's Thumping Good Read Award

Scope Communications, Tower House, 8–14 Southampton Street, London WC2E 7HA
☎0171 379 3234   Fax 0171 240 7729
Public Relations Executive *Clare McKeown*

ESTABLISHED 1992 to promote new writers of popular fiction. Books must have appeared on W. H. Smith's bestseller list for the first time and must have been published in the 12 months preceding the award. Submissions, made by publishers, are judged by a panel of customers to be the most un-put-down-able from a shortlist of six. Final entry date February each year. Previous winners: Dominick Dunne *A Season in Purgatory*; Robert Harris *Fatherland*.

Award £5000.

W. H. Smith's Young Writers' Competition

W. H. Smith, Strand House, 7 Holbein Place, London SW1W 8NR
☎0171 824 5456   Fax 0171 730 0195
Contact *Lois Beeson*

Annual awards for poems or prose by anyone in the UK under the age of 17. There are three age groups. Over 60 individual winners have their work included in a paperback every year.

Prize (total) over £7000.

Smith Corona Prize

3A High Street, Rickmansworth, Hertfordshire WD3 1HP
☎01923 777111   Fax 01923 896370
Contact *Debra Simpson*

Quarterly competition sponsored by Smith Corona (UK) Ltd (manufacturers of electronic typewriters, personal word processors and other office equipment) for a short story or piece of writing on a selected topic. Featured in *Writers Monthly* magazine.

Prize Personal word processor or electronic typewriter.

Sony Radio Awards

Zazer, 47–48 Chagford Street, London NW1 6EB
☎0171 723 0106
Contact *Francesca Watt, Suzy Langford*

ESTABLISHED 1981 by the **Society of Authors**. Sponsored by Sony. Annual awards to recognise excellence in radio broadcasting. Entries must have been broadcast in the UK between 1 January and 31 December in the year preceding the award. The categories for the awards are reviewed each year. 1995 Awards: The Society of Authors Award for Original Drama; Creative Writing Award.

Southern Arts Literature Prize

Southern Arts, 13 St Clement Street, Winchester, Hampshire SO23 9DQ
☎01962 855099   Fax 01962 861186
Contact *Literature Officer*

This prize is awarded annually to an author living in the **Southern Arts** region for the most promising work of prose or poetry published during the year. The 1995 prize will be awarded for literary non-fiction. Previous winner: Jamie McKendrick *The Kiosk on the Brink* (poetry). Final entry date late October.

Prize £1000, plus a craft commission to the value of £600.

Southport Writers' Circle Poetry Competition

53 Richmond Road, Birkdale, Southport, Merseyside PR8 4SB
Contact *Mrs Alison Chisholm*

For previously unpublished work which has not been entered in any other current competition. Entry fee £1.50 first poem, plus £1 for each subsequent entry. Maximum 40 lines on any subject and in any form. Closing date end April. Poems must be entered under a pseudonym, accompanied by a sealed envelope marked with the pseudonym and title of poem, containing s.a.e. Entries must be typed on A4 paper and be accompanied by the appropriate fee payable to Southport Writers' Circle. No application form is required. Envelopes should be marked 'Poetry Competition'. Postal enquiries only. No calls.

Prizes (1st) £100; (2nd) £50; (3rd) £25.

Ian St James Awards

c/o The New Writers' Club, PO Box 101, Tunbridge Wells, Kent TN4 8YD
☎01892 511322   Fax 01892 514282

ESTABLISHED 1989. Administered by the New

Writers Club. Presented annually to twenty writers of short stories: ten awards in the under 3000-word category; ten in the above 3000-word category. These awards are 'an opportunity for talented and as yet unpublished writers to achieve recognition'. Ian St James is a successful novelist who hopes to attract both literary and commercial fiction from aspiring writers. Winning entries are published in a paperback anthology by **HarperCollins** in the autumn. The Ian St James Awards are open to international writers who have not had a novel or novella previously published. Final entry date 28 February each year. 1994 top prize winners: Joshua Davidson *The Saviour*, Anna McGrail *The Welfare of the Patient* Entry forms available from around October in most bookshops or from above address.

Award (total) cash and pens to the value of £26,000. 60 runners-up are published throughout the year in *Acclaim* magazine.

Stand Magazine Short Story Competition

Stand Magazine, 179 Wingrove Road,
Newcastle upon Tyne NE4 9DA
☎0191 273 3280

Contact *The Administrator*

Biennial award for short stories written in English and not yet published, broadcast or under consideration elsewhere. Next award 1997. Send s.a.e. for entry form.

Prize (total) £2250.

Staple First Editions Project 1995–96

Tor Cottage, 81 Cavendish Road, Matlock, Derbyshire DE4 3HD
☎01629 582764

Contact *Donald Measham*

Biennial open competition for collections (poetry, prose) run by *Staple* magazine. Final entry date March 1996. Publication of winning monograph, July 1996; of shared collection, July 1997.

Prize share of £400, complimentary copies, publication and distribution.

Steinbeck Award

The Society of Authors, 84 Drayton Gardens, London SW10 9SB
☎0171 373 6642   Fax 0171 373 5768

Contact *The Awards Secretary*

ESTABLISHED 1994. Annual award, sponsored by **William Heinemann** to support a young writer (under 40) for a new full-length work of fiction, first published in the UK, and written in the spirit of the works of John Steinbeck. Final closing date end of October 1995. Entries are submitted by publishers and not authors. Information sheet available. 1995 winner: Pinckney Benedict *Dogs of God*.

Prizes £10,000, of which £5000 is donated to a charity chosen by the winner.

Sunday Express Book of the Year Award

Ludgate House, 245 Blackfriars Road, London SE1 9UX
☎0171 928 8000   Fax 0171 922 7599

INITIATED 1987. An award for a work of fiction published in the current year. Books are nominated by a panel of judges. No entries from publishers or authors. Previous winners: Hilary Mantel *A Place of Greater Safety*; Michael Frayn *A Landing on the Sun*; William Boyd *The Blue Afternoon*; William Trevor *Felicia's Journey*.

Prize £20,000.

Sunday Times Award for Small Publishers

Independent Publishers Guild, 25 Cambridge Road, Hampton, Middlesex TW12 2JL
☎0181 979 0250   Fax 0181 979 6393

Contact *Yvonne Messenger*

ESTABLISHED 1988, the first winner was **Fourth Estate**. Open to any publisher producing between five and forty titles a year, which must primarily be original titles, not reprints. Entrants are invited to submit their catalogues for the last twelve months, together with two representative titles. Previous winners: **Polygon**; **Blackstaff Press Ltd**. 1994 winner: **Nick Hern Books**.

Sunday Times Special Award for Excellence in Writing

The Sunday Times, 1 Pennington Street, London E1 9XW
☎0171 782 5774   Fax 0171 782 5120

Contact *The Literary Editor*

ESTABLISHED 1987. Annual award to fiction and non-fiction writers. The panel consists of *Sunday Times* journalists, publishers and other figures from the book world. Previous winners: Anthony Burgess, Seamus Heaney, Stephen Hawking, Ruth Rendell, Muriel Spark, William Trevor and Martin Amis.

Award Silver trophy in the shape of a book, inscribed with the winner's name.

Edith & Joseph Sunlight Award

Balfour Diamond Jubilee Trust, Balfour House, 741 High Road, London N12 0BQ
☎0181 343 9541   Fax 0181 343 7309
Executive Director *Norman H. Morris, FRSA*

The award, presented in Manchester, takes the form of an inscribed crystal glass bowl which is awarded for literary works, the content of which enhances cultural relations between the UK and the state of Israel. Previous winners include: Martin Gilbert, Dr Conor Cruise O'Brien, Paul Johnson and Abba Eban. Further information from the above address.

Reginald Taylor and Lord Fletcher Essay Prize

Journal of the British Archaeological Association, Institute of Archaelogy, 36 Beaumont Street, Oxford OX1 2PG
Contact *Dr Martin Henig*

A biennial prize, in memory of the late E. Reginald Taylor and of Lord Fletcher, for the best unpublished essay, not exceeding 7500 words, on a subject of archaeological, art history or antiquarian interest within the period from the Roman era to AD 1830. The essay should show *original* research on its chosen subject, and the author will be invited to read the essay before the Association. Closing date for entries 31 October 1996. In addition, the essay may be published in the journal of the Association if approved by the Editorial Committee. All enquiries by post please. No phone calls. Send s.a.e. for details.
Prize £300.

The Teixeira Gomes Prize

The Translators Association, 84 Drayton Gardens, London SW10 9SB
☎0171 373 6642   Fax 0171 373 5768
Contact *Kate Pool*

ESTABLISHED 1989. Triennial award funded by the Calouste Gulbenkian Foundation and the Portuguese Book Institute for the best translation of a work by a Portugues national published in the UK in the three years preceding the closing date, or unpublished. Final entry date is 31 December 1997 for 1998 award.

Anne Tibble Poetry Competition

Events Team, Directorate of Environment Services, Northampton, Cliftonville House, Bedford Road, Northampton NN4 7NR
☎01604 233500   Fax 01604 29571
Contact *Liz Carroll*

Entries should preferably be typed on one side of paper only and must not exceed 20 lines. Any writer resident in Great Britain is eligible, and there are categories for children: under 11; under 16.
Prize (1st) £100.

Time-Life Silver PEN Award

English Centre of International PEN, 7 Dilke Street, London SW3 4JE
☎0171 352 6303   Fax 0171 351 0220

An annual award, the winner being nominated by the PEN Executive Committee, for an outstanding work of non-fiction written in English and published in England in the year preceding the prize. Previous winners: Susan Richards *Epics of Everyday Life*; William St Clair *The Godwins and the Shelleys*; Alan Bullock *Hitler and Stalin*; Brian Keenan *An Evil Cradling*. 1994 winner: John Hale *The Civilization of Europe in the Renaissance*.
Prize £1000, plus silver pen.

The Times Educational Supplement Book Awards

Times Educational Supplement, Admiral House, 66–68 East Smithfield, London E1 9XY
☎0171 782 3000   Fax 0171 782 3200
Contact *Literary Editor*

ESTABLISHED 1973. Two annual awards made for the best books used in schools. The books must have been published in Britain or the Commonwealth. Previous winners: Junior Information Book Award: *Think of an Eel* Karen Wallace, illus. Mike Bostock; Senior Information Book Award: *Getting Physical* Dr Aric Sigman; Primary Schoolbook Award: *Bathtime* Gill Tanner and Tim Wood; Secondary Schoolbook Award: *Discovering Medieval Realms* Colin Shephard and Alan Large.

The Times Educational Supplement/NASEN Special Educational Needs Award

The Educational Publishers Council, The Publishers Association, 19 Bedford Square, London WC1B 3HJ
☎0171 580 6321   Fax 0171 636 5375

ESTABLISHED 1992. Organised by the *TES*, the National Association for Special Educational Needs (NASEN) and the **Educational Publishers Council**. Two awards: the *Academic Book Award*, for a book which enhances the knowledge and understanding of those engaged in the education of children with special needs; the *Children's Book Award*, for a book written for children under the age of 16 which does most to put forward a positive image of children with special education needs. Books must have been published in the UK in the two years preceding the award. Previous winners: Paul Greenhalgh *Emotional Growth and Learning* (Academic); David Hill *See ya, Simon* (Children's).

Prize £500 plus £1000 advertising space in the *TES* for the winning publisher.

The Tir Na N-Og Award
Welsh Books Council, Castell Brychan, Aberystwyth, Dyfed SY23 2JB
☎01970 624151   Fax 01970 625385

An annual award given to the best original book published for children. There are three categories: Best Welsh Fiction; Best Welsh Non-fiction; Best English Book with an authentic Welsh background.

Award £1000 (each category).

Marten Toonder Award
An Chomhairle Ealaíon (The Arts Council), 70 Merrion Square, Dublin 2, Republic of Ireland
☎00 353 1 6611840   Fax 00 353 1 6761302
Literature Officer *Laurence Cassidy*

A triennial award for creative writing. Awarded in 1995. Given to an established writer in recognition of achievement. Open to Irish citizens or residents only.

Award IR£3500.

John Tripp Award
The Welsh Academy, 3rd Floor, Mount Stuart House, Mount Stuart Square, Cardiff CF1 6DQ
☎01222 492025   Fax 01222 492930
Contact *Kevin Thomas*

ESTABLISHED 1990. Open to Welsh nationals or residents only. Usually launched in the spring with closing date in summer. Themes and rules vary from year to year. Send s.a.e. for details.

Tullie House Prize
See **Lakeland Book of the Year Awards**

Dorothy Tutin Award
National Poetry Foundation, 27 Mill Road, Fareham, Hampshire PO16 0TH
Contact *Johnathon Clifford*

ESTABLISHED 1979. An occasional award to the person whom it is felt has done the most to encourage the writing of poetry throughout the UK. By recommendation only.

Award Engraved carriage clock.

UNESCO/PEN Short Story Competition
English Centre of International PEN, 7 Dilke Street, London SW3 4JE
☎0171 352 6303

ESTABLISHED 1993. Biennial award, funded by UNESCO and administered by the English Centre of PEN. It is intended to reward the efforts of those who write in English despite the fact that it is not their mother tongue (the Irish, Scots and Welsh are not eligible). Entries in the form of short stories not exceeding 1500 words should be submitted to the writer's home country PEN centre. The top three entries are then forwarded to the English PEN centre for final judging. Final entry date end December of year preceding award. First awarded March 1993. Winner 1993: John Auerbach *The Owl*.

Prizes (1st) $3000; (2nd) $2000; (3rd) $500.

Unicorn Arts Theatre National Young Playwrights' Competition
Unicorn Theatre for Children, Arts Theatre, Great Newport Street, London WC2H 7JB
☎0171 379 3280   Fax 0171 836 5366
Contact *Dorothy Wooder*

Annual awards to young playwrights aged 4–12 for plays on a theme decided by the theatre. Three age groups: 4–6; 7–9; 10–12. The plays are judged by a committee of writers. The winners take part in workshops on the plays with members of the Unicorn Theatre for Children Club in preparation for performances on stage the following spring. Final entry date end December. 1994 award winners: Paul De Araujo *Paul Goes to Africa* (4–6); Anne Briggs *Wizards on the Move* (7–9); Aditya Basrur *People on the Move* (10–12).

T. E. Utley Memorial Award
38 Aldridge Road Villas, London W11 1BW
Contact *The Secretary*

ESTABLISHED 1988 in memory of the political journalist Peter Utley. In 1995, two awards were given for unpublished essays by aspiring journalists who were still at school or university.

Prizes £2500 (under 25); £1500 (under 18).

Vauxhall Trophy
Guild of Motoring Writers, 30 The Cravens, Smallfield, Surrey RH6 9QS
☎01342 843294   Fax 01342 844093
Contact *Sharon Scott-Fairweather*

Awarded annually to the Guild member judged to have written the best article(s) explaining

any aspect of automotive design or technology.
Prize Trophy, plus £750.

Ver Poets Open Competition

Haycroft, 61–63 Chiswell Green Lane, St
Albans, Hertfordshire AL2 3AL
☎01727 867005

Contact *May Badman*

Various competitions are organised by **Ver
Poets**, the main one being the annual Open
for unpublished poems of no more than 30
lines written in English. Entry fee £2 per
poem. Entries must be made under a pseudonym, with name and address on form or separate sheet. An anthology of winning and
selected poems as well as the adjudicators'
report is normally available from mid-June.
Final entry date 30 April.
Prizes Open: (1st) £500; (2nd) £300; two
runners-up £100.

Vogue Talent Contest

Vogue, Vogue House, Hanover Square,
London W1R 0AD
☎0171 499 9080   Fax 0171 408 0559

Contact *Frances Bentley*

ESTABLISHED 1951. Annual award for young
writers and journalists (under 25 on 1 January
in the year of the contest). Final entry date
beginning May. Entrants must write three
pieces of journalism on given subjects.
Prizes £1000, plus a month's work experience with *Vogue*; (2nd) £500.

Wadsworth Prize for Business History

Business Archives Council, The Clove
Building, 4 Maguire Street, London SE1 2NQ
☎0171 407 6110

Contact *Wadsworth Prize Coordinator*

Annual award for scholarly contribution to the
history of British business and commercial
affairs. Previous winner: Sir Peter Thompson
Sharing the Success: The Story of NFC.
Prize £200.

Arts Council of Wales Book of the Year Awards

Arts Council of Wales, Museum Place, Cardiff
CF1 3NX
☎01222 394711   Fax 01222 221447

Contact *Tony Bianchi*

Annual non-competitive prizes awarded for
works of exceptional literary merit written by
Welsh authors (by birth or residence), published in Welsh or English during the previous
calendar year. There is one major prize in
English, the Book of the Year Award, and one
major prize in Welsh, Gwobr Llyfr y
Flwyddyn. Shortlists of three titles in each language are announced in April; winners
announced in May.
Prizes £3000 (each); £1000 to each of four
runners-up.

Wandsworth London Writers Competition

Room 224, Town Hall, Wandsworth High
Street, London SW18 2PU
☎0181 871 7037   Fax 0181 871 7560

Contact *Arts Office*

An annual competition, open to all writers of
16 and over who live, work or study in the
Greater London Area. There are two categories, all for previously unpublished work, in
poetry and short story.
Prizes £1000 for each class, divided between
the top three in each category; plus two runners-up in each class.

Whitbread Book of the Year and Literary Awards

Minster House, 272 Vauxhall Bridge Road,
London SW1V 1BA
☎0171 834 5477   Fax 0171 834 8812

Contact *Gillian Cronin*

Publishers are invited to submit books for this
annual competition designed for writers who
have been resident in Great Britain or the
Republic of Ireland for three years or more.
The awards are made in two stages. First, nominations are selected in five categories: novel,
first novel, biography, children's novel and
poetry. One of these is then voted by the panel
of judges as Whitbread Book of the Year. 1994
winners: William Trevor *Felicia's Journey* (novel
and Book of the Year); Fred D'Aguiar *The
Longest Memory* (first novel); James Fenton *Out
of Danger* (poetry); Brenda Maddox *The Married
Man: A Life of D. H. Lawrence* (biography);
Geraldine McCaughrean *Gold Dust* (Beefeater
Children's Novel Award).
Awards £21,000 (Book of the Year); £2000
(all nominees).

Whitfield Prize

Royal Historical Society, University College
London, Gower Street, London WC1E 6BT
☎0171 387 7532   Fax 0171 387 7532

Contact *Literary Director*

An annual award for the best new work within

a field of British history, published in the UK in the preceding calendar year. The book must be the author's first (solely written) history book and be an original and scholarly work of historical research. Final entry date end December.

Prize £1000.

John Whiting Award
Arts Council of England, 14 Great Peter Street, London SW1P 3NQ
☎0171 333 0100   Fax 0171 973 6590
Contact *The Drama Director*

FOUNDED 1965. Annual award to commemorate the life and work of the playwright John Whiting (*The Devils, A Penny for a Song*). Any writer who has received during the previous two calendar years an award through the **Arts Council's Theatre Writing Schemes** or who has had a première production by a theatre company in receipt of annual subsidy is eligible to apply. Awarded to the writer whose play most nearly satisfies the following criteria: a play in which the writing is of special quality; a play of relevance and importance to contemporary life; a play of potential value to the British theatre. Previous joint winners: Helen Edmundson and Jonathan Harvey.

Prize £6000.

Alfred and Mary Wilkins Memorial Poetry Competition
Birmingham & Midland Institute, 9 Margaret Street, Birmingham B3 3BS
☎0121 236 3591
Administrator *J. Hunt, MA*

An annual competition for an unpublished poem not exceeding 40 lines, written in English by an author over the age of 15 and living, working or studying in the UK. The poem should not have been entered for any other poetry competition. Six prizes awarded in all.

Prize (total) £475.

Griffith John Williams Memorial Prize
3rd Floor, Mount Stuart House, Mount Stuart Square, Cardiff CF1 6DQ
☎01222 492064   Fax 01222 492930
Contact *Dafydd Rogers*

FOUNDED 1965. Biennial award in honour of the first president of the **Welsh Academy** which aims to promote writing in Welsh. Entries must be the first published work of authors or poets writing in Welsh. Work must

have been published in the two-year period preceding the award.

Award £400.

Raymond Williams Community Publishing Prize
Literature Dept, Arts Council of England, 14 Great Peter Street, London SW1P 3NQ
☎0171 973 6442   Fax 0171 973 6590
Contact *Anne Bendall*

ESTABLISHED 1990. Award for published work which exemplifies the values of ordinary people and their lives – as often embodied in Raymond Williams' own work. Submissions may be in the form of poetry, fiction, biography, autobiography, drama or even local history, providing they are literary in quality and intent. They are likely to be produced by small community or cooperative presses, but other forms of publication will be considered. Final entry date end April. Winner announced in July. 1994 winner: *Memories of Childhood on the Isle of Dogs.*

Prizes (1st) £3000; runner-up £2000. Prizes are divided between publisher and author.

H. H. Wingate Prize
See **Jewish Quarterly Literary Prize**

Wolfson History Awards
Wolfson Foundation, 18–22 Haymarket, London SW1Y 4DQ
☎0171 930 1057   Fax 0171 930 1036
Contact *The Director*

ESTABLISHED 1972. An award made annually to authors of published historical works, with the object of encouraging historians to communicate with general readers as well as with their professional colleagues. Previous winners include: Fiona MacCarthy *William Morris*; John G. C. Rohl *The Kaiser and His Court: Wilhelm II and the Government of Germany*; Lord Skidelsky *John Maynard Keynes: The Economist as Saviour 1920–1937*; Professor Linda Colley *Britons: Forging the Nation 1707–1837.*

Award (total) £20,000.

Woolwich Young Radio Playwrights' Competition
Independent Radio Drama Productions Ltd, PO Box 518, Manningtree, Essex CO11 1XD
Contact *Marja Giejgo*

ESTABLISHED 1990 and sponsored by the Woolwich Building Society, with writer and broadcaster Melvyn Bragg as patron. This is a national scheme which aims to discover and professionally produce radio drama writing talent among young people aged 25 and under. The competition involves national and regional script writing competitions with various workshop programmes at independent and BBC local radio stations. Send s.a.e. for further details. Writers selected for production receive a **Writers' Guild** approved contract.

The Writers Bureau Poetry and Short Story Competition

The Writers Bureau, Sevendale House, 7 Dale Street, Manchester M1 1JB
☎0161 228 2362

Competition Secretary *Angela Cox*

ESTABLISHED 1994. Annual award. Poems should be no longer than 40 lines and short stories no more than 2000 words. £3.50 entry fee. Previous winners: Kathy Miles (Poetry); Susan Smith Barrie (Short Story).

Prizes in each category: £250 (1st); £150 (2nd); £75 (3rd).

The Writers' Guild Awards

430 Edgware Road, London W2 1EH
☎0171 723 8074   Fax 0171 706 2413

Originally ESTABLISHED 1961 and relaunched in 1991. Five categories of awards: radio (drama, comedy, dramatisations, children's); theatre (West End, fringe, regional); books (non-fiction, fiction, children's); film (best screenplay); television (play/film, original drama serial, dramatised serial, original drama series, dramatised series, situation comedy, light entertainment, children's). There is also a Lifetime Achievement Award (won by Dennis Potter in 1994). The various short-lists are prepared by a different jury in each category and presented to the full Guild membership for its final vote.

Xenos Short Story Competition
See **See Xenos** under **Magazines**

Yorkshire Open Poetry Competition

c/o Ilkley Literature Festival, Manor House Museum, Ilkley, West Yorkshire LS29 9DT
☎01943 601210

Contact *David Porter*

Annual open poetry competition run by the **Ilkley Literature Festival**. Final entry date August each year. Previous winners: Anthony Dunn, John Sewell.

Prize (total) £500.

Yorkshire Post Art and Music Awards

Yorkshire Post, PO Box 168, Wellington Street, Leeds, West Yorkshire LS1 1RF
☎0113 2432701

Contact *Margaret Brown*

Two annual awards made to the authors whose work has contributed most to the understanding and appreciation of art and music. Books should have been published in the preceding year in the UK. Previous winners: Charles Hemming *British Landscape Painters: A History and Gazetteer;* David Cairns *Berlioz: The Making of An Artist.*
Award £1000 each.

Yorkshire Post Best First Work Awards

Yorkshire Post, PO Box 168, Wellington Street, Leeds, West Yorkshire LS1 1RF
☎0113 2432701

Contact *Margaret Brown*

An annual award for a work by a new author published during the preceding year. Previous winners include: Harriet O'Brien *Forgotten Land.*
Prize £1000.

Yorkshire Post Book of the Year Award

Yorkshire Post, PO Box 168, Wellington Street, Leeds, West Yorkshire LS1 1RF
☎0113 2432701

Contact *Margaret Brown*

An annual award for the book (either fiction or non-fiction) which, in the opinion of the judges, is the best work published in the preceding year. Previous winner: Corelli Barnett *Engage the Enemy More Closely.*
Prize £1200.

Yorkshire Post Yorkshire Author of the Year Award

Yorkshire Post, PO Box 168, Wellington Street, Leeds, West Yorkshire LS1 1RF
☎0113 2432701

Contact *Margaret Brown*

Award sponsored by Marriott Hotel, Leeds. Author must have been born in Yorkshire. Fiction and non-fiction accepted. Previous winner: Leslie Glaister *Limestone and Clay.*
Prize £1000.

Young Science Writer Awards
See **The Daily Telegraph National Power Young Science Writer Awards**

Borrowers versus Lenders

The Libraries are in a poor way but so too are authors

What are libraries for? A decade ago the question could only have come from a philistine with sawn off nerve ends. Libraries were cultural storehouses open to all. If the soul of civilisation was to be found anywhere, a well-stocked library was its likeliest location.

All that changed in the 80s when respect for hallowed institutions went out of fashion. It is customary to blame Margaret Thatcher and her cost cutting hatchet for all the subsequent woes suffered by the libraries. But there is more to it than that.

Sophisticated marketing of books, notably the exploitation of the cheap paperback have turned people away from the libraries and into the bookshops. (Twice as many Britons buy books from bookshops as borrow them from libraries.) Of those who continue to use the libraries a high proportion make a beeline for the popular and adult fiction. To draw on the latest statistics, of the twenty most borrowed books, one is by Barbara Taylor Bradford, two by Dick Francis, six by Danielle Steel and no less than eleven by Catherine Cookson. Whatever the qualities of these writers they fall a long way short of the founding ideal of public libraries – to put the ordinary citizen in reach of higher learning and the finest literary endeavours. One does not have to be a right wing radical to wonder at the allocation of public resources to promote thrillers and light romance.

What of the serried shelves of non-fiction? Certainly there are more quality books to be found there; books, moreover, that are either not easily obtainable, from high street shops or obtainable only at a price that is more than the average reader can afford. But even here there are doubts that the libraries are serving the best interests of their customers.

Money is at the root of the problem – not so much the getting as the spending. Ignore for a moment the siren voices raised against government and local authority parsimony; consider instead the manner in which libraries administer their budgets. For the most part, book ordering is handled by library suppliers. Like everyone else in bookselling their terms of trade are circumvented by the Net Book Agreement which allows publishers to fix the price at which their books are sold. There are arguments for and against the NBA, but suffice for this discussion, booksellers and publishers are largely in favour. And looking at the way they use the library system as a milch cow, it is easy to see why.

It was in the late 70s and the recession of the early 80s, when publishers were looking to ways of maintaining their profit margins, that it occurred to them that if they bumped up the prices of hardbacks there was little the libraries could do about it. True, there was some leeway within the NBA – a library discount 'not exceeding' 10 per cent, conditional on 'prompt settlement'. But thereafter there could be 'no consideration in cash or kind' and supplementary services such as plastic jacketing had to be 'charged and paid for at not less than the actual cost to the bookseller'. In other words, the libraries had sacrificed their freedom to manage their own businesses. The 10 per cent discount held no terror for publishers. That could be accommodated easily within their inflated price structure.

So it was that hardback books that had cost £5 jumped to £7.50 then £10 and beyond. The race was led by academic books which seemed to double in price every season. Since nobody in their right mind was ready to pay for a £30 or £40 monograph out of their own pockets, the mega-priced titles all but disappeared from the bookshops. But no matter, the libraries continued to fork out. Print runs fell while more titles appeared - a paradoxical but none the less highly profitable equation. Many academic books were limited to just two or three hundred copies, all or nearly all sold to libraries.

Interestingly, a contrasting pattern developed for school books which are traditionally outside the scope of the NBA and are sold non-net, i.e. at prices determined by market forces. Here, costs were held down by education authorities making best use of their purchasing muscle to strike favourable deals. Deprived of that freedom, libraries remained submissive to accountancy games – until the day of judgement when, in the late-80s, the government gave notice that automatic increases in funding were to end. It was then that the librarians started reassessing their buying policy. To make the available money go further, within the restraints of the NBA, they now buy more paperbacks and fewer hardbacks. (It is not altogether fanciful to believe that, as this shift continues, hardbacks will disappear completely as the entire publishing industry goes over to softback covers.) Other economies – cutting down on opening hours, closing smaller branch libraries – smack of defeatism. The strategy of the Library Association seems to rely on accompanying highly visible cutbacks with a chorus of appeals for sympathy, hoping that, eventually, the government will be forced to open its wallet.

A more realistic policy would require libraries to get their marketing act together to put pressure on publishers and suppliers to bring down prices. They should concentrate on providing books not easily available elsewhere and they should be leading the way in the use of the new information technology, as urged in the recent Department of National Heritage review. Above all, they should make more of an effort to provide a service that matches that of the best bookshops. This means opening at times convenient to customers and making them feel welcome and comfortable. Library assistants need not behave like commissars. A happy smile and a cheerful greeting would not come amiss. Certainly we could do with more sensitivity than my own local library showed when, without warning, it shut down for a day. A notice stuck up in the window explained that staff were at a meeting – to protest against library closures.

What do authors have to say about all this? Well, of course, no one bothers to ask. Authors provide the books but otherwise are expected to remain minor participants in the great game, and minor beneficiaries in the distribution of resources. Look at the figures.

We take out 550 million books a year at a collected cost of around £740 million or over 12 per head for every man, woman and child in the United Kingdom. This puts us far ahead of most other developed countries with the exception in Europe only of the Netherlands and Denmark. Now for the breakdown. Close on 50 per cent of expenditure is allocated to labour – not of writing the books, of course, but of handing them back and forth across the counter. After other administrative costs, 14 per cent or £112 million is spent on acquisitions and of this, averaging out royalty payments, just £10 million goes to authors.

Or rather it would if it were not for Public Lending Right, which allows for a modest payment to authors (writers, translators and illustrators) whose books are lent out from public libraries. The amount they receive is proportional to the number of borrowings credited to their titles over a year.

The first payments under PLR were made in 1984 when £1.5 million was divided between 6000 authors. The latest funding (for 1994-95) was just short of £5 million but now 23,000 authors are registered. Of these, around three quarters had books borrowed often enough to qualify for payment. Most were down in the lower levels with 14,000 getting under £100. 116 authors came in at £6000, the highest permitted payout (nearly all writers of crime, romance and children's fiction whose fans consume a lot very quickly) and just over 1700 authors made in excess of £500.

These are the ground rules for PLR:

To qualify, an author must be resident in the United Kingdom or Germany (the latter as part of a reciprocal deal). For a book to be eligible it must be printed, bound and put on sale. It must not be mistaken for a newspaper or periodical, or be a musical score. Crown copyright is excluded, also books where authorship is attributed to a company or association. But – and this is where mistakes often occur – the author does not have to own copyright to be eligible for PLR. Anyone who has disclaimed copyright as part of a flat fee commission, for instance, will still have a claim if his name is on the title page.

Under PLR, the sole writer of a book may not be its sole author. Others named on the title page, such as illustrators, translators, compilers, editors and revisers, may have a claim to authorship. Where there are joint authors – two writers, say, or a writer and illustrator – they can strike their own bargain on how their entitlement is to be split. But translators may apply, without reference to other authors, for a 30 per cent fixed share (to be divided equally between joint translators). Similarly, an editor or compiler may register a 20 per cent share provided he has written 10 per cent of the book or at least ten pages of text. Joint editors or compilers must divide the 20 per cent share equally.

Authors and books can be registered for PLR only when application is made during the author's lifetime. However, once an author is registered, the PLR on his books continues for the period of copyright. If he wishes, an author can assign PLR to other people and bequeath it by will. If a co-author is dead or untraceable, the remaining co-author can still register for a share of PLR so long as he provides supporting evidence as to why he alone is making application.

Three years ago the criteria for eligibility were amended slightly to allow for cases where an author's name is not given on the title page, or where a book lacks a conventional title page. In these instances, it will now be possible for a writer to register if he is named elsewhere in the book and where he can show that his contribution would normally merit a title page credit. Alternatively, proof of a royalty payment is acceptable. Where there are several writers, one of whom cannot prove eligibility, the co-authors can provide a signed statement testifying to their colleague's right to a share of the PLR payment.

The other significant change to eligibility concerns the former rule that books were disqualified if more than three authors were named on the title page. This has been abolished and there is now no maximum limit on the number of authors who can apply for part-shares.

One limiting factor has been introduced. Authors can no longer register books that do not have an ISBN. Tracing them was simply too expensive.

A note on German PLR. Some authors are wondering why their payments are so small. The answer is that under the German system after the 10 per cent deduction for administrative costs, a further 10 per cent is paid into a 'social fund', which is set aside for making *ex gratia* payments to authors who are in need, and yet another 45 per cent is paid into a 'social security' fund. Foreign authors, however, are not entitled to benefit from either fund. After the 65 per cent deductions, the remaining amount is divided between the authors (who take 70 per cent) and the publishers (who take 30 per cent). Furthermore, under German law, the translator is entitled to 50 per cent of the author's share, and if there are editors involved, they are also entitled to a percentage of the fee.

There are various ideas for extending PLR. Much thought, for example, has gone into the question of rewarding authors of reference books which are consulted on library premises but rarely taken out on loan. Complex sampling procedures have been rejected as too expensive and time consuming. Instead, payment is likely to be based on the average number of loans of a book in the lending stock. Also, there is a good argument for extending PLR to all authors living in the European Union. This might persuade other European countries to follow Germany's example with reciprocity payments to UK authors.

Next in line for a claim on PLR are the authors and presenters of talking books. The only reason why the spoken word is currently excluded from PLR is that the producers of talking books are also the exclusive copyright holders. But a directive from the European Community suggests that copyright in audio and visual productions can be reclaimed by those responsible for creative input. Expect a settlement for the spoken word before long. Doubtless, this will start a debate on PLR for computer books. The queue of potential supplicants is never-ending.

Trouble is, unless funding is increased, which seems unlikely in the short run, more claimants means less money per author. One possible corrective is to raise the minimum payment level from £1 to £10 or possibly £20. But redistribution which favours the better off is not likely to go down well with the writers' associations. For now, they will not go above £5 as a minimum payment. Another possible saving is to cut the retention time for unclaimed PLR payments from six to two years. But we are talking peanuts here.

Maybe the solution rests with the libraries themselves. Once they have got their own economic house in order by winning concessions from publishers, say, or saving on administration, there might be a little left over from their £740 million budget to support hard pressed writers.

PLR application forms and details can be obtained from: The Registrar, PLR Office, Bayheath House, Prince Regent Street, Stockton on Tees, Cleveland TS18 1DF (Tel: 01642 604699)

Libraries

City of Aberdeen District Council Arts & Recreation Division, Libraries Department

Central Library, Rosemount Viaduct,
Aberdeen AB9 1GU
☎01224 634622 Fax 01224 641985

Reference Services Librarian *James A. Pratt*
Open 9.00 am to 8.00 pm Monday to Friday
(Reference & Local Studies 9.00 am to 9.00 pm); 9.00 am to 5.00 pm Saturday. Branch library opening times vary.

Open access

General reference and loans. Books, pamphlets, periodicals and newspapers; videos, CDs, records and cassettes; arts equipment lending service; recording studio; DTP for public access; photographs of the Aberdeen area; census records, maps; on-line database, patents and standards. The library is supported by a mobile library and offers special services to housebound readers. In the belief that extension activities now form a prominent part of the library's role in modern-day society, a publishing and recording dimension has recently been adopted, thereby heightening the profile of arts in the community.

Armitt Library

Ambleside, Cumbria LA22 0BZ
☎015394 33949

Open 10.00 am to 12.30 pm & 1.30 pm to 4.00 pm Monday, Tuesday, Wednesday, Friday.

Access By arrangement (phone or write)

A small but unique reference library of rare books, manuscripts, pictures, antiquarian prints and museum items, mainly about the Lake District. It includes early guidebooks and topographical works, books and papers relating to Wordsworth, Ruskin, H. Martineau and others; fine art including work by W. Green, J. B. Pyne, John Harden, K. Schwitters, and Victorian photographs by Herbert Bell; also a major collection of Beatrix Potter's scientific watercolour drawings and microscope studies.

Art & Design Department, Westminster Reference Library

2nd Floor, Westminster Reference Library,
St Martin's Street, London WC2H 7HP
☎0171 798 2038 Fax 0171 798 2040

Open 10.00 am to 7.00 pm Monday to Friday; 10.00 am to 5.00 pm Saturday

Access For reference only (stacks are closed to the public)

Located on the second floor of the City of Westminster's main reference library. An excellent reference source for fine and applied arts, including antiques, architecture, ceramics, coins, costume, crafts, design, furniture, garden history, interior decoration, painting, sculpture, textiles. Complete runs of major English Language periodicals such as *Studio*; exhibition catalogues; guidebooks to historic houses, castles, gardens and churches. Some older books and most periodicals earlier than 1980 are in storage and at least three days' notice is required before they can be obtained. ART-XTRA fee-based desk research service (☎0171 798 2039).

The Athenaeum, Liverpool

Church Alley, Liverpool L1 3DD
☎0151 709 7770

Open 9.00 am to 5.00 pm Monday to Friday

Access To club members; researchers by application only

General collection, with books dating from the 15th century, now concentrated mainly on local history with a long run of Liverpool directories and guides. *Special collections* Liverpool playbills; William Roscoe; Blanco White; Robert Gladstone; 18th-century plays; 19th-century economic pamphlets; the Norris books; Bibles; Yorkshire and other genealogy. Some original drawings, portraits, topographical material and local maps.

Avon Library & Information Service

P.O Box 1037, Avon House North, St James, Barton, Bristol, Avon BS99 1VR
☎0117 875160 Fax 0117 875168

Central Library Open 10.00 am to 7.30 pm Monday to Thursday; 9.30 am to 7.30 pm Friday; 9.30 am to 5.00 pm Saturday

There are a total of 59 libraries under the aegis of the Avon Library & Information Service. Lending, reference, art, music, commerce and local studies are particularly strong.

Bank of England Library and Information Services

Threadneedle Street, London EC2R 8AH
☎0171 601 4715   Fax 0171 601 4356
Open 9.30 am to 5.30 pm Monday to Friday

Access For research workers by prior arrangement only, when material is not readily available elsewhere
    50,000 volumes of books and periodicals. 3000 periodicals taken. UK and overseas coverage of banking, finance and economics. *Special collections* Central bank reports; UK 17th–19th-century economic tracts; Government reports in the field of banking.

Barbican Library

Barbican Centre, London EC2Y 8DS
☎0171 638 0569
Librarian *Barry Cropper*
Open 9.30 am to 5.30 pm Monday, Wednesday, Thursday, Friday; 9.30 am to 7.30 pm Tuesday; 9.30 am to 12.30 pm Saturday
Open access
    Situated on Level 7 of the Barbican Centre, this is the Corporation of London's largest lending library. Limited study facilities are available. In addition to a large general lending library, the library seeks to reflect the Centre's emphasis on the arts and includes strong collections, including videos, on painting, sculpture, theatre, cinema and ballet, as well as a large music library with books, scores, cassettes and CDs (sound recording loans available at a small charge). Also houses the City's main children's library and has special collections on finance, natural resources, conservation, socialism and the history of London. Service available for housebound readers.

Barnsley Public Library

Central Library, Shambles Street, Barnsley, South Yorkshire S70 2JF
☎01226 773930   Fax 01226 773955
Acting Librarian *Mr I.B. Ireland*
Open 9.30 am to 8.00 pm Monday and Wednesday; 9.30 am to 6.00 pm Tuesday, Thursday, Friday; 9.30 am to 5.00 pm Saturday; Archive Collection: 9.30 am to 1.00 pm and 2.00 pm to 6.00 pm (closed all day Thursday and Saturday afternoon)
Open access
    General library, lending and reference. Archive collection of family history and local firms; local studies: coalmining, local authors,

Yorkshire and Barnsley; European Business Information Unit; music library (books, CDs, records, tapes); large junior library. (Specialist departments are closed on certain weekday evenings and Saturday afternoons.)

BBC Written Archives Centre

Peppard Road, Caversham Park, Reading, Berkshire RG4 8TZ
☎01734 472742 ext. 280/1/2/3
Fax 01734 461145
Contact *Jacqueline Kavanagh*
Open 9.45 am to 5.15 pm Wednesday to Friday

Access For reference, by appointment only
    Holds the written records of the BBC, including internal papers from 1922 to 1969 and published material to date. Charges for certain services.

Belfast Public Libraries: Central Library

Royal Avenue, Belfast BT1 1EA
☎01232 243233   Fax 01232 332819
Chief Librarian *J. N. Montgomery*
Open 9.30 am to 8.00 pm Monday and Thursday; 9.30 am to 5.30 pm Tuesday, Wednesday, Friday; 9.30 am to 1.00 pm Saturday

Open access To lending libraries; reference libraries by application only
    Over 2 million volumes for lending and reference. *Special collections* United Nations/Unesco depository; complete British Patent Collection; Northern Ireland Newspaper Library; British and Irish government publications. The Central Library offers the following reference departments: Humanities and General Reference; Irish and Local Studies; Business and Law; Science and Technology; Fine Arts, Language and Literature; Music and Recorded Sound. The lending library, supported by twenty branch libraries and two mobile libraries, offers special services to hospitals, prisons and housebound readers.

BFI Library and Information Services

21 Stephen Street, London W1P 2LN
☎0171 255 1444   Fax 0171 436 7950
Open 10.30 am to 5.30 pm Monday and Friday; 10.30 am to 8.00 pm Tuesday and Thursday; 1.00 pm to 8.00 pm Wednesday; Telephone Enquiry Service operates from 10.00 am to 5.00 pm

Access For reference only; annual and limited day membership available

The world's largest collection of information on film and television including periodicals, cuttings, scripts, related documentation, personal papers. Information available through SIFT (Summary of Information on Film and Television).

Birmingham and Midland Institute
Margaret Street, Birmingham B3 3BS
☎0121 236 3591   Fax 0121 233 4946
Administrator *W.E. Stober, MA(Cantab)*
Access For research, to students (loans restricted to members)

ESTABLISHED 1855. Later merged with the Birmingham Library (now renamed the Priestley Library), which was founded in 1779. The Priestley Library specialises in the humanities, with approximately 100,000 volumes in stock. Headquarters and founder member of the **Association of Independent Libraries** and headquarters of the **Alliance of Literary Societies**. Meeting-place of many affiliated societies including many devoted to poetry and literature.

Birmingham Library Services
Central Library, Chamberlain Square, Birmingham B3 3HQ
☎0121 235 2615   Fax 0121 233 4458
Open 9.00 am to 8.00 pm Monday to Friday; 9.00 am to 5.00 pm Saturday

Open access
600,000 volumes. *Special collections* include the Shakespeare Library; War Poetry Collection; Parker Collection of Early Children's Books; Joseph Priestley Collection; Johnson Collection; Early and Fine Printing Collection; British Topography; and *Life in Birmingham*, plus the archive of the Birmingham Repertory Theatre and Sir Barry Jackson Library.

Book Trust Children's Reference Library
Book House, 45 East Hill, London SW18 2QZ
☎0181 870 9055   Fax 0181 874 4790
Open 9.00 am to 5.00 pm Monday to Friday
Access For reference only

A comprehensive collection of children's literature, related books and periodicals. Aims to hold all children's titles published within the last two years. An information service covers all aspects of children's literature, including profiles of authors and illustrators. Reading room facilities.

Bradford Central Library
Princes Way, Bradford, West Yorkshire BD1 1NN
☎01274 753600   Fax 01274 395108
Open 9.00 am to 7.30 pm Monday to Friday; 9.00 am to 5.00 pm Saturday

Open access
Wide range of books and media loan services, including major local history collections. Comprehensive reference and information facilities. Specialised business information service. Study facilities and publishing programme. Runs *In Your Own Write*, a creative writing scheme, including DTP/word processing facilities for writers.

Brighton Reference Library
Church Street, Brighton, East Sussex BN1 1UE
☎01273 691195   Fax 01273 695882
Library Manager *Elaine Jewell*
Open 10.00 am to 7.00 pm Monday to Friday (closed Wednesday); 10.00 am to 4.00 pm Saturday

Access Limited stock on open access; all material for reference use only

FOUNDED 1869, the library has a large stock covering most subjects. Specialisations include art and antiques, history of Brighton and Sussex, family history, local illustrations, HMSO, business and large bequests of antiquarian books and ecclesiastical history.

British Architectural Library
Royal Institute of British Architects, 66 Portland Place, London W1N 4AD
☎0171 580 5533 ext. 4320 Fax 0171 631 1802
Open 1.30 pm to 5.00 pm Monday; 10.00 am to 8.00 pm Tuesday; 10.00 am to 5.00 pm Wednesday, Thursday, Friday; 10.00 am to 1.30 pm Saturday

Access Free to RIBA members; non-members must buy a day ticket (£10/£5 concessions but on Tuesday between 5–8.00 pm and Saturday £5/£2.50); annual membership (£90/£45.00 concessions); loans available to RIBA and library members only

Collection of books, drawings, manuscripts, photographs and periodicals, 400 of which are indexed. All aspects of architecture, current and historical. Material both technical and aesthetic, covering related fields including: interior design, landscape architecture, topography, the construction industry and applied arts. Brochure available; queries by telephone, letter or in person. Charge for research £40 per hour (min. charge £10).

British Library Business Information Service

25 Southampton Buildings, Chancery Lane, London WC2A 1AW
☎0171 412 7454(Free)/0171 412 7457(Priced Enquiry Service)   Fax 0171 412 7453

Open 9.30 am to 9.00 pm Monday to Friday; 10.00 am to 1.00 pm Saturday; Free Enquiry Service 9.30 am to 5.30 pm Monday to Friday; Priced Enquiry Service 9.30 am to 5.00 pm Monday to Friday

Open access
A resource facility for those engaged in all aspects of business.

British Library Information Sciences Service

7 Ridgmount Street, London WC1E 7AE
☎0171 412 7688   Fax 0171 412 7691

Open 9.00 am to 6.00 pm Monday and Wednesday; 9.00 am to 8.00 pm Tuesday and Thursday; 9.00 am to 5.00 pm Friday. Mid July–September: 9.00 am to 6.00 pm Monday to Thursday; 9.00 am 5.00 pm Friday

Access For reference only (loans restricted to members of the Library Association, Book Trust, Society of Indexers, or by British Library form)
Provides British and foreign material on librarianship, information science and related subjects. *Special collections* theses on librarianship.

British Library Manuscript Collections

Great Russell Street, London WC1B 3DG
☎0171 412 7513/4   Fax 0171 412 7745

Open 10.00 am to 4.45 pm Monday to Saturday; enquiries and applications up to 4.30 pm (closed one week in November)

Access Reading facilities only, by British Library reader's pass
Two useful publications, *Index of Manuscripts in the British Library*, Cambridge 1984–6, 10 vols, and *The British Library: Guide to the Catalogues and Indexes of the Department of Manuscripts* by M. A. E. Nickson, help to guide the researcher through this vast collection of manuscripts dating from Ancient Greece to the present day. Approximately 250,000 mss, charters, papyri and seals are housed here.

British Library Map Library

Great Russell Street, London WC1B 3DG
☎0171 412 7700   Fax 0171 412 7780

Open 10.00 am to 4.30 pm Monday to Saturday

Access By British Library reader's pass or Map Library day pass
A collection of two million maps, charts and globes with particular reference to the history of British cartography. Maps for all parts of the world in wide range of scales and dates, including the most comprehensive collection of Ordnance Survey maps and plans. *Special collections* King George III Topographical Collection and Maritime Collection, and the Crace Collection of maps and plans of London. Also satellite imagery microfiche catalogue and browse film.

British Library Music Library

Great Russell Street, London WC1B 3DG
☎0171 412 7527   Fax 0171 412 7751

Open 9.30 am to 4.45 pm Monday to Friday; on Saturday material is made available 10.00 am to 4.45 pm in the Manuscripts students' room

Access By British Library reader's pass
Special collections The Royal Music Library (containing almost all Handel's surviving autograph scores) and the Paul Hirsch Music Library. Also a large collection (about one and a quarter million items) of printed music, both British and foreign.

British Library National Sound Archive

29 Exhibition Road, London SW7 2AS
☎0171 412 7440   Fax 0171 412 7416

Open 10.00 am to 5.00 pm Monday to Friday (Thursday till 9.00 pm)
Listening service (by appointment) 10.00 am to 5.00 pm Monday to Friday (Thursday till 9.00 pm)
Northern Listening Service
British Library Document Supply Centre, Boston Spa, West Yorkshire: 9.15 am to 4.30 pm Monday to Friday

Open access
An archive of over 900,000 discs and more than 125,000 tape recordings, including all types of music, oral history, drama, wildlife, selected BBC broadcasts and BBC Sound Archive material. Produces a thrice-yearly newsletter, *Playback*.

British Library Newspaper Library

Colindale Avenue, London NW9 5HE

☎0171 412 7353   Fax 0171 412 7379

Open 10.00 am to 4.45 pm Monday to Saturday (last newspaper issue 4.15 pm)

Access By British Library reader's pass or Newspaper Library day pass (available from and valid only for Colindale Avenue)

English provincial, Scottish, Welsh, Irish, Commonwealth and foreign newspapers from *c.*1700 are housed here. London newspapers from 1801 and many weekly periodicals are also in stock as well as selected newspapers from overseas. (London newspapers pre-dating 1801 are housed in Great Russell Street.) Readers are advised to check availability of material in advance.

British Library Official Publications and Social Sciences Service

Great Russell Street, London WC1B 3DG

☎0171 412 7536

Open 9.30 am to 4.45 pm (last admissions 4.30pm) Monday to Friday

Access By British Library reader's pass

Provides access to current and historical official publications from all countries, plus publications of intergovernmental bodies, including House of Commons sessional papers from 1715, UK legislation, current and back numbers of UK electoral registers, and up-to-date reference books on official publications and on the social sciences.

British Library Oriental and India Office Collections

Orbit House, 197 Blackfriars Road, London SE1 8NG

☎0171 412 7873   Fax 0171 412 7843

Open 9.30 am to 5.45 pm Monday to Friday; 9.30 am to 12.45 pm Saturday

Open access By British Library reader's pass or day pass (identification required)

A comprehensive collection of printed volumes and manuscripts in the languages of North Africa, the Near and Middle East and all of Asia, plus official records of the East India Company and British government in India until 1947. Also prints, drawings and paintings by British artists of India.

British Library Reading Room

Great Russell Street, London WC1B 3DG

☎0171 412 7677 (Admissions)

Fax 0171 412 7736

☎0171–412 7676 (Bibliographical holdings enquiries)

Open 9.00 am to 5.00 pm Monday, Friday, Saturday; 9.00 am to 9.00 pm Tuesday, Wednesday, Thursday (closed week following the last complete week in October). The Admissions Office is open 9.00 am to 4.30 pm Monday, Friday, Saturday; 10.00 am to 6.00 pm Tuesday, Wednesday, Thursday.

Access By British Library reader's pass

Large and comprehensive stock of books and periodicals relating to the humanities and social sciences for reference and research which cannot easily be done elsewhere. Leaflet *Applying for a Reader's Pass* available for guidance. Also exhibitions on literary and historical figures and a permanent exhibition on the history of printing and binding. Telephone enquiries welcome.

British Library Science Reference and Information Service

25 Southampton Buildings, London WC2A 1AW

☎0171 412 7494/7496 (General Enquiries)

Fax 0171 412 7495

Also at: 9 Kean Street, London WC2B 4AT. (Life sciences enquiries)

☎0171 412 7288 Fax 0171 412 7290.

And: Chancery House Reading Room, Chancery Lane, London WC2A 1AW

☎0171 412 7902 Fax 0171 412 7480

Open Southampton Buildings: 9.30 am to 9.00 pm Monday to Friday; 10.00 am to 1.00 pm Saturday. Kean Street and Chancery House Reading Room: 9.30 am to 5.30 pm Monday to Friday.

General enquiries tel as above; British and EPO Patent enquiries: 0171 412 7919; Foreign Patent enquiries: 0171 412 7902; Business enquiries: 0171 412 7454/7977.

Open access

The national library for modern science, technology, business, patents, trade marks and designs, it is the most comprehensive reference collection in Western Europe of such literature from the whole world. The primary purpose is to make this information readily accessible, so no prior arrangement or reader's ticket is necessary. The library has enquiry and referral services and priced services (especially in business information, the environment, and industrial property); online database search; photocopy and linguistic aid services; runs courses and seminars; and publishes a wide range of publications from newsletters to definitive bibliographies.

PRICED RESEARCH SERVICE CONTRACT DETAILS:
Business Information Service:
☎0171 412 7457   Fax 0171 412 7453.
Environmental Information Service:
☎0171 412 7955   Fax 0171 412 7954.
Science and Technology Information Service:
☎0171 412 7477   Fax 0171 412 7954.

British Psychological Society Library
c/o Psychology Library, University of London, Senate House, Malet Street, London WC1E 7HU
☎0171 636 8000 ext. 5060Fax 0171 436 1494

Open Term-time: 9.30 am to 9.00 pm Monday to Thursday; 9.30 am to 6.30 pm Friday; 9.30 am to 5.30 pm Saturday (holidays: 9.30 am to 5.30 pm Monday to Saturday)

Access Members only
Reference library, containing the British Psychological Society collection of periodicals – over 140 current titles housed alongside the University of London's collection of books and journals. Largely for academic research. General queries referred to **Swiss Cottage Library** which has a very good psychology collection.

CAA Central Library
Aviation House, Gatwick Airport, West Sussex RH6 0YR
☎01293 573725   Fax 01293 573999
Open 1.00 pm to 4.30 pm Monday to Friday
Open Access
Books, periodicals and reports on air transport, air traffic control, electronics, radar and computing.

Cambridge Central Library (Reference Library & Information Service)
7 Lion Yard, Cambridge CB2 3QD
☎01223 65252   Fax 01223 62786
Open 9.30 am to 7.00 pm Monday to Friday; 9.00 am to 5.00 pm Saturday
Access Open

Large stock of books, periodicals, newspapers, maps, plus comprehensive collection of directories and annuals covering UK, Europe and the world. Microfilm and fiche reading and printing services. On-line access to news and business databases.

Camomile Street Library
12–20 Camomile Street, London EC3A 7EX
☎0171 247 8895   Fax 0171 377 2972
Open 9.30 am to 5.30 pm Monday to Friday
Open access
The new City of London lending library, replacing the Bishopsgate Library. Wide range of fiction and non-fiction books and language courses on cassette, foreign fiction, paperbacks, maps and guides for travel at home and abroad, children's books, a selection of large print, and collections of music CDs and of videos.

Cardiff Central Library
Frederick Street, St David's Link, Cardiff, South Glamorgan CF1 4DT
☎01222 382116   Fax 01222 238642
Open 9.00 am to 6.00 pm Monday, Tuesday, Friday; 9.00 am to 8.00 pm Wednesday and Thursday; 9.00 am to 5.30 pm Saturday
General lending library with the following departments: leisure, music, children's, local studies, information, science and humanities. Kurzweil reader available for those with visual handicap.

Carmarthen Public Library
St Peter's Street, Carmarthen, Dyfed SA31 1LN
☎01267 233333 ext. 4833 Fax 01267 221839
Senior Co-ordinating Librarian *Dewi Thomas*
Open 10.00 am to 7.00 pm Monday to Friday; 10.00 am to 1.00 pm Saturday.
Open access
Comprehensive range of fiction, non-fiction, children's books and reference works in English and in Welsh. Large local history library – newspapers/census returns on microfilm. Large Print books, books on tape, CDs, cassettes, and videos available for loan.

Catholic Central Library
47 Francis Street, London SW1P 1QR
☎0171 834 6128
Librarian *J. Bond*
Open 10.00 am to 5.00 pm Monday to Friday; 10.00 am to 1.30 pm Saturday
Open access For reference (non-members must sign in; loans restricted to members)

Contains books, many not readily available elsewhere, on theology, religions worldwide, scripture and the history of churches of all denominations.

Central Music Library (Westminster)

Victoria Library, 160 Buckingham Palace Road, London SW1W 9UD
☎0171 798 2192   Fax 0171 798 2181
Open 1.00 pm to 7.00 pm Monday to Friday; 10 am to 5.00 pm Saturday

Open access
Located at Victoria Library, this is the largest public music library in the South of England, with extensive coverage of all aspects of music, including books, periodicals and printed scores. No recorded material, notated only. Lending library includes a small collection of CDs, cassettes and videos.

City Business Library

1 Brewers Hall Garden, London EC2V 5BX
☎0171 638 8215   Fax 0171 332 1847
☎0171 480 7638 (recorded information)
Open 9.30 am to 5.00 pm Monday to Friday

Open access Local authority public reference library run by the Corporation of London.

Books, pamphlets, periodicals and newspapers of current business interest, mostly financial. Aims to satisfy the day-to-day information needs of the City's business community, and in so doing has become one of the leading public resource centres in Britain in its field. Strong collection of directories for both the UK and overseas, plus companies information, market research sources, management, law, banking, insurance, statistics and investment.

City of London Libraries

See **Barbican Library; Camomile Street Library; City Business Library; Guildhall**

Commonwealth Institute

Kensington High Street, London W8 6NQ
☎0171 603 4535   Fax 0171 602 7374
Senior Librarian *Karen Peters*
Open 11.00 am to 4.00 pm Tuesday to Friday; 1.00 pm to 4.45 pm Saturday

Access For reference
Special collection Books and periodicals on Commonwealth countries. Also a collection of directories and reference books on the Commonwealth and information on arts, geography, history and literature, cultural

organisations and bibliography. The Commonwealth Literature Library includes fiction, poems, drama and critical writings.

Commonwealth Secretariat Library

10 Carlton House Terrace, London SW1Y 5AH
☎0171 747 6164   Fax 0171 747 6235
Open 9.15 am to 5.00 pm Monday to Friday

Access For reference only, by appointment
Extensive reference source concerned with economy, development, trade, production and industry of Commonwealth countries; also sub-library specialising in human resources including women, youth, health, management and education.

Cornwall County Library

County Hall, Truro, Cornwall TR1 3AY
☎01872 74282   Fax 01872 70340
Open 9.30 am to 5.00 pm Monday to Friday
Books, cassettes, CDs and videos for loan through branch or mobile networks. Reference, local studies, music and drama. *Special collections* on the visual arts and maritime studies. Opening hours vary at branch libraries throughout the county.

Coventry Central Library

Smithford Way, Coventry, Warwickshire CV1 1FY
☎01203 832321   Fax 01203 833163
Open 9.00 am to 8.00 pm Monday, Tuesday, Thursday, Friday; 9.30 am to 8.00 pm Wednesday; 9.00 am to 4.30 pm Saturday

Open access
Located in the middle of the city's main shopping centre. Approximately 120,000 items (books, records, cassettes and CDs) for loan; plus reference collection of business information and local history. *Special collections* Cycling and motor industries; George Eliot; Angela Brazil; Tom Mann Collection (trade union and labour studies); local newspapers on microfilm from 1740 onwards. Over 500 periodicals taken. Kurzweil reader and CCTV available for people with visual handicap. 'Peoplelink' community information database available.

Derby Central Library

Wardwick, Derby DE1 1HS
☎01332 255389   Fax 01332 369570
Central Librarian *Bernard Haigh*
Open 9.30 am to 7.00 pm Monday, Tuesday,

Thursday, Friday; 9.30 am to 1.00 pm
Wednesday and Saturday
LOCAL STUDIES LIBRARY
25B Irongate, Derby DE1 3GL
Open 9.30 am to 7.00 pm Monday and
Tuesday; 9.30 am to 5.00 pm Wednesday,
Thursday, Friday; 9.30 am to 1.00 pm
Saturday

Open access
General library for lending, information and
Children's Services. The Central Library also
houses specialist private libraries: Derbyshire
Archaeological Society; Derby Philatelic
Society. The Local Studies Library houses the
largest multimedia collection of resources in
existence relating to Derby and Derbyshire.
The collection includes mss deeds, family
papers, business records including the Derby
Canal Company, Derby Board of Guardians
and the Derby China Factory.

Devon & Exeter Institution Library
7 Cathedral Close, Exeter, Devon EX1 1EZ
☎01392 74727

Librarian *Sheila Stirling*
Open 9.00 am to 5.00 pm Monday to Friday

Access Members only
FOUNDED 1813. Contains over 36,000 volumes, including long runs of 19th-century
journals, theology, history, topography, early
science, biography and literature. A large and
growing collection of books, journals, newspapers, prints and maps relating to the South-
West.

Dorchester Library
Colliton Park, Dorchester, Dorset DT1 1XJ
☎01305 224440/224448   Fax 01305 266120

Open 10.00 am to 7.00 pm Monday; 9.30 am
to 7.00 pm Tuesday, Wednesday, Friday;
9.30 am to 5.00 pm Thursday; 9.00 am to
1.00 pm Saturday

Open Access
General lending and reference library,
including Local Studies Collection, special collections on Thomas Hardy, The Powys Family
and T. E. Lawrence. Periodicals, children's
library, playsets.

Dundee District Libraries
Central Library, The Wellgate, Dundee
DD1 1DB
☎01382 434318   Fax 01382 434642
Chief Librarian *John Ramage*

Open Lending Departments: 9.30 am to 7.00
pm Monday to Friday; 9.30 am to 5.00 pm
Saturday. General Reference Department:
9.30 am to 9.00 pm Monday to Friday; 9.30
am to 5.00 pm Saturday. Local History
Department: 9.30 am to 5.00 pm Monday,
Tuesday, Friday, Saturday; 9.30 am to 7.00
pm Wednesday and Thursday.

Access Reference services available to all;
lending services to those who live, work or
study within the City of Dundee District
Adult lending, reference and children's services. Art, music, audio and video lending services. Schools service (Agency). Housebound
and mobile services. *Special collections*: The
Ivory Collection; The Sturrock Collection;
The Wighton Collection of National Music;
The Wilson Photographic Collection; The
Lamb Collection.
The Steps Film Theatre, a regional film theatre, is based in the Central Library under the
licence of the Chief Librarian.

English Nature
Northminster House, Peterborough,
Cambridgeshire PE1 1UA
☎01733 340345   Fax 01733 68834

Open 10.00 am to 12.00 pm and 2.00 pm to
4.00 pm Monday to Friday

Access To *bona fide* students only. Telephone
for appointment
Information on nature conservation, nature
reserves, SSSIs, planning, legislation, etc.

Equal Opportunities Commission Library
Overseas House, Quay Street, Manchester
M3 3HN
☎0161 833 9244   Fax 0161 835 1657

Open 9.00 am to 5.00 pm Monday to Friday

Access For reference (loans available)
Books and pamphlets on equal opportunities
and gender issues. Non-sexist children's books
and Equal Opportunities Commission publications. Also an information service with periodicals and press cuttings.

Essex County Council Libraries
Colchester Central Library, Trinity Square,
Colchester, Essex CO1 1JB
☎01206 562243/Minicom 01206 549676
Fax 01206 562413

Open 9.00 am to 7.30 pm Monday, Tuesday,
Wednesday, Friday; 9.00 am to 5.00 pm
Thursday and Saturday

Open access

A comprehensive collection of books, newspapers and periodicals for lending and reference use; recorded sound items in audio cassette and CD format; language-learning tapes and a large video collection. *Special collections* include the County Music Library and the Local Studies Library. Microform and CD-ROM material available. On-line computer cataloguing and information service.

Farming Information Centre

National Farmers' Union, 22 Long Acre, London WC2E 9LY
☎0171 331 7293   Fax 0171 331 7382
Open 10.00 am to 4.30 pm Monday to Thursday
Access For reference only (telephone first)
The politics of agriculture rather than technical aspects, and union affairs. Houses a small picture library.

The Fawcett Library

London Guildhall University, Calcutta House, Old Castle Street, London E1 7NT
☎0171 320 1189   Fax 0171 320 1117
Open Term-time: 11.00 am to 8.00 pm Monday; 10.00 am to 5.00 pm Wednesday to Friday (holidays: 10.00 am to 5.00 pm Monday, Wednesday to Friday)
Open access to non-university members on payment of fee; contact the library for current rates
The leading library for feminist studies and research into all other aspects of women's history with emphasis on social sciences and the humanities. Contains extensive stocks of books, pamphlets, photographs and archive materials. Limited loans to members. The **Mary Evans Picture Library** acts as agent for the Fawcett Library's pictorial material.

Foreign and Commonwealth Office Library

King Charles Street, London SW1A 2AH
☎0171 270 3925   Fax 0171 930 2364
Access By appointment only
An extensive stock of books, pamphlets and other reference material on all aspects of historical, socio-economic and political subjects relating to countries covered by the Foreign and Commonwealth Office. Particularly strong on colonial history, early works on travel and photograph collections, mainly of Commonwealth countries and former colonies, *c.* 1850s–1960s.

French Institute Library

17 Queensberry Place, London SW7 2DT
☎0171 589 6211   Fax 0171 581 5127
Contact *Odile Grandet*
Open 11.00 am to 7.00 pm Monday, Tuesday, Wednesday, Friday; 12.00 pm to 3.00 pm Saturday
Open access For reference (loans restricted to members)
Annual membership £19; students and OAPs £14
A collection of over 83,000 volumes mainly centred on French cultural interests with special emphasis on language, literature and history. Video library and children's library (8000 books); plus 3500 press cutting files.

Gloucestershire County Library Arts & Museums Service

Quayside House, Shire Hall, Gloucester GL1 2HY
☎01452 425020   Fax 01452 425042
County Library Arts & Museums Officer *Linda Hopkins ALA*
Open access
The service includes 39 local libraries – telephone number above for opening hours; and seven mobile libraries telephone 01452 425039 for timetable/route enquiries

Goethe-Institut Library

50 Princes Gate, Exhibition Road, London SW7 2PH
☎0171 411 3452   Fax 0171 584 3180
Librarian *Regine Friederici*
Open 10.00 am to 8.00 pm Monday to Thursday; 10.00 am to 1.00 pm Saturday
Library specialising in German literature and books/ audiovisual material on German culture and history: 27,000 books (4,800 of them in English), 169 periodicals, 17 newspapers, 2,750 audiovisual-media (including 800 videos), selected press clippings on German affairs from the German and UK press, information service, photocopier, video facility for six viewers. Also German language teaching material for teachers and students of German.

Greater London Record Library

40 Northampton Road, London EC1R 0HB
☎0171 332 3822   Fax 0171 833 9136
Open 9.30 am to 7.30 pm Tuesday; 9.30 am to 4.45 pm Wednesday to Friday
Access For reference only
Covers all aspects of the life and development of London, specialising in the history and

organisation of local government in general, and London in particular. Books on London history and topography, covering many subjects. Also London directories dating back to 1677, plus other source material including Acts of Parliament, Hansard reports, statistical returns, atlases, yearbooks and many complete sets of newspapers and magazines.

Guildford Institute of University of Surrey Library

Ward Street, Guildford, Surrey GU1 4LH
☎01483 62142

Librarian *Mrs Patricia Chapman*

Open 10.00 am to 3.00 pm Monday to Friday (under review and occasionally closed at lunchtime)

Open access To members only

FOUNDED 1834. Some 10,000 volumes of which 7500 were printed before the First World War. The remaining stock consists of recently published works of fiction, biography and travel. Newspapers and periodicals also available. *Special collections* include an almost complete run of the *Illustrated London News* from 1843-1906, a collection of Victorian scrapbooks, and about 400 photos and other pictures relating to the Institute's history and the town of Guildford.

Guildhall Library

Aldermanbury, London EC2P 2EJ
☎0171 332 1839   Fax 0171 600 3384

Access For reference (but much of the material is kept in storage areas and is supplied to readers on request; proof of identity is required for consultation of certain categories of stock)

Part of the Corporation of London libraries. Seeks to provide a basic general reference service but its major strength, acknowledged worldwide, is in its historical collections. The library is divided into three sections, each with its own catalogues and enquiry desks. These are: Printed Books; Manuscripts; the Print Room.

PRINTED BOOKS

Open 9.30 am to 5 pm Monday to Saturday.
☎0171 332 1868/1870

Strong on all aspects of London history, with wide holdings of English history, topography and genealogy, including local directories, poll books and parish register transcripts. Also good collections of English statutes, law reports, parliamentary debates and journals, and House of Commons papers. Home of several important

collections deposited by London institutions: the Marine collection of the Corporation of Lloyd's, the Stock Exchange's historical files of reports and prospectuses, the Clockmakers' Company library and museum, the Gardeners' Company, Fletchers' Company, the Institute of Masters of Wine, International Wine and Food Society and Gresham College.

MANUSCRIPTS

Open 9.30 am to 4.45 pm Monday to Saturday (no requests for records after 4.30 pm). ☎0171 332 1863

The official repository for historical records relating to the City of London (except those of the Corporation of London itself, which are housed at the Corporation Records Office). Records date from the 11th century to the present day. They include archives of most of the City's parishes, wards and livery companies, and of many individuals, families, estates, schools, societies and other institutions, notably the Diocese of London and St Paul's Cathedral, as well as the largest collection of business archives in any public repository in the UK. Although mainly of City interest, holdings include material for the London area as a whole and beyond.

PRINT ROOM

Open 9.30 am to 5.00 pm Monday to Friday.
☎0171 332 1839

An unrivalled collection of prints and drawings relating to London and the adjacent counties. The emphasis is on topography, but there are strong collections of portraits and satirical prints. The map collection includes maps from the capital from the mid-16th century to the present day and various classes of Ordnance Survey maps. Other material includes photographs, theatre bills and programmes, trade cards, book plates and playing cards as well as a sizeable collection of Old Master prints.

Health Information Library (Westminster)

Marylebone Library, Marylebone Road, London NW1 5PS
☎0171 798 1039   Fax 0171 798 1044

Open 10.00 am to 7.00 pm Monday; 9.30 am to 7.00 pm Tuesday to Friday; 9.30 am to 5.00 pm Saturday

Open access

Located in Westminster's Marylebone public library. Books, pamphlets and periodicals covering all aspects of medicine and the health services.

Hereford & Worcester County Libraries

Libraries Department, County Hall, Spetchley Road, Worcester WR5 2NP
☎01905 766240   Fax 01905 763000

Open Opening hours vary in branches across the county; all full-time libraries open at least one evening a week until 7.00 pm or 8.00 pm, and on Saturday until 4 pm

Access For reference; loans to members only (membership criteria: resident, educated, working, or an elector in the county or neighbouring authorities; temporary membership to other visitors. Proof of identity and address required)

Reference and lending libraries. Non-fiction and fiction for all age groups, including large print, sound recordings (CD, cassette, vinyl), video collection, maps, local history. *Special collections* Carpets and Textiles; Needles & Needlemaking; Stuart Period; Cidermaking; Beekeeping; Housman and John Masefield.

University of Hertfordshire Library

College Lane, Hatfield, Hertfordshire AL10 9AD
☎01707 284677   Fax 01707 284670

Open Term-time: 8.45 am to 9.30 pm Monday to Thursday; 8.45 am to 7.00 pm Friday; 2.00 pm to 5.00 pm Saturday; 2.00 pm to 7.00 pm Sunday; Holidays: 9.00 am to 5.00 pm Monday to Friday

Access For reference; loans available to members of HERTIS.

280,000 volumes and 2000 journals in science technology and social science, including law, across all three of the university's campuses. There are two other site libraries, one at Hertford (business), the other at Wall Hall, near Radlett (education and humanities). Desk research, postal interlibrary loans and consultancy undertaken by HERTIS Information and Research Unit which is based at Hatfield and has capacity for up to 300 subscribing companies and organisations.

HERTIS

See **University of Hertfordshire Library**

Highgate Literary and Scientific Institution Library

11 South Grove, London N6 6BS
☎0181 340 3343

Open 10.00 am to 5.00 pm Tuesday to Friday; 10.00 am to 4.00 pm Saturday (closed Monday)

Annual membership £30 single; £46 household

40,000 volumes of general fiction and non-fiction, with a children's section and extensive archives. *Special collections* on local history, London, and local poets Coleridge, Leonard Clark, Manley Hopkins, Housman and Betjeman.

Highland Libraries, Highland Regional Council, Department of Libraries and Leisure Services

Central Services, 31A Harbour Road, Inverness IV1 1UA
☎01463 235713   Fax 01463 236986

Regional Librarian M. G. O'Brien

Open Administration and support services: 8.00 am to 6.00 pm Monday to Friday; Libraries open to suit local needs

Open access

Comprehensive range of lending and reference stock: books, pamphlets, periodicals, newspapers, compact discs, audio and video cassettes, maps, census records, genealogical records, photographs, educational materials, etc. Highland Libraries provides the public library service throughout the Highland Region with a network of 41 static and 12 mobile libraries.

Holborn Library

32–38 Theobalds Road, London WC1X 8PA
☎0171 413 6345/6

Open 10.00 am to 7.00 pm Monday and Thursday; 10.00 am to 6.00 pm Tuesday and Friday; 10.00 am to 5.00 pm Saturday (closed all day Wednesday)

Open access

London Borough of Camden public library, specialising in law.

Sherlock Holmes Collection (Westminster)

Marylebone Library, Marylebone Road, London NW1 5PS
☎0171 798 1206   Fax 0171 798 1019

Open 10.00 am to 7.00 pm Monday; 9.30 am to 7.00 pm Tuesday to Friday; 9.30 am to 5.00 pm Saturday

Telephone for Access By appointment only

Located in Westminster's Marylebone Library. An extensive collection of material from all over the world, covering Sherlock Holmes and Sir Arthur Conan Doyle. Books, pamphlets, journals, newspaper cuttings and photos, much of which is otherwise unavailable in this country. Some background material.

Imperial College Library
See **Science Museum Library**

Imperial War Museum
Department of Printed Books, Lambeth Road, London SE1 6HZ
☎0171 416 5000   Fax 0171 416 5374

Open 10.00 am to 5.00 pm Monday to Saturday (restricted service Saturday; closed on Bank Holiday Saturdays)

Access For reference (but at least 24 hours' notice must be given for intended visits)

A large collection of material on 20th-century life with detailed coverage of the two world wars and other conflicts. Books, pamphlets and periodicals, including many produced for short periods in unlikely wartime settings; also maps, biographies and privately printed memoirs, and foreign language material. Research material available in the following departments: Art, Documents, Exhibits and Firearms, Film, Sound Records, Photographs. Active publishing programme based on reprints of rare books held in library. Catalogue available.

Instituto Cervantes
22 Manchester Square, London W1M 5AP
☎0171 235 1484   Fax 0171 235 4115

Open 9.30 am to 1.00 pm and 2.00 pm to 5.00 pm Monday to Friday

Open access For reference
Spanish literature, history, art, philosophy. Books, slides, tapes, records and films.

Italian Institute Library
39 Belgrave Square, London SW1X 8NX
☎0171 235 1461   Fax 0171 235 4618

Open 10.00 am to 1.00 pm and 2.00 pm to 5.00 pm Monday to Friday

Open access For reference
A collection of over 26,000 volumes relating to all aspects of Italian culture. Texts are mostly in Italian, with some in English.

Jersey Library
Halkett Place, St Helier, Jersey JE2 4UH
☎01534 59991 (Lending)/59992 (Reference)
Fax 01534 69444

Open 9.30 am to 5.30 pm Monday, Wednesday, Thursday, Friday; 9.30 am to 7.00 pm Tuesday; 9.30 am to 4.00 pm Saturday

Access Open
Books, periodicals, newspapers, CDs, cassettes, CD-ROMs, microfilm, specialised local studies collection.

Kent Central Lending Library
Kent County Council Arts & Libraries, Springfield, Maidstone, Kent ME14 2LH
☎01622 696511   Fax 01622 663575

Open 10.00 am to 6.00 pm Monday, Tuesday, Wednesday, Friday; 10.00 am to 7.00 pm Thursday; 9.00 am to 4.00 pm Saturday

Open access
300,000 volumes of non-fiction, mostly academic. English literature, poetry, classical literature, drama (including playsets), music (including music sets). Strong, too, in sociology, art and history. Loans to all who live or work in Kent; those who do not may consult stock for reference or arrange loans via their own local library service.

Lansdowne Library
Meyrick Road, Bournemouth, Dorset BH1 3DJ
☎01202 556603   Fax 01202 291781

Open 10.00 am to 7.00 pm Monday; 9.30 am to 7.00 pm Tuesday, Thursday, Friday; 9.30 am to 5.00 pm Wednesday; 9.00 am to 1.00 pm Saturday

Open access
General lending and reference library, County Music Library, collection of Government publications. Children's section, periodicals.

The Law Society
50 Chancery Lane, London WC2A 1SX
☎0171 320 5810/11/12   Fax 0171 242 1309

Press Officer *Catherine Slaytor*
Head of Press & Parliamentary Unit *Sue Stapely (LLB. Hons/Solicitor)*

Open 8.30 am to 5.30 pm with out-of-house answerphone and mobile phone back-up

Access Library restricted to solicitors/members but press office available to all journalists for advice, information and assistance.
Provides all information about solicitors, the legal profession in general, law reform issues etc.

Leeds Central Library
Calverley Street, Leeds, West Yorkshire LS1 3AB
☎0113 2478274   Fax 0113 2478268

Open 9.00 am to 8.00 pm Monday and

Wednesday; 9.00 am to 5.30 pm Tuesday, Thursday, Friday; 9.00 am to 4.00 pm Saturday

Open Access to lending libraries; Reference material on request

Lending Library covering all subjects.

Music Library contains scores, books and audio.

Information for Business Library holds company information, market research, statistics, directories, journals and computer-based information.

Art Library (in Art Gallery) has a major collection of material on fine and applied arts.

Local & Family History Library contains an extensive collection on Leeds and Yorkshire, including maps, books, pamphlets, local newspapers, illustrations and playbills. Census returns for the whole of Yorkshire also available. International Genealogical Index and parish registers.

Reference Library with over 270,000 volumes, including extensive files of newspapers and periodicals plus all government publications since 1960. *Special collections* include military history, Judaic, early gardening books, and mountaineering.

Leeds City Libraries has an extensive network of 65 branch and mobile libraries.

Leeds Library

18 Commercial Street, Leeds, West Yorkshire LS1 6AL
☎0113 2453071

Open 9.00 am to 5.00 pm Monday to Friday

Access To members; research use upon application to the librarian

FOUNDED 1768. Contains over 120,000 books and periodicals from the 15th century to the present day. *Special collections* include Reformation pamphlets, Civil War tracts, Victorian and Edwardian children's books and fiction, European language material, spiritualism and psychical research, plus local material.

Lincoln Central Library

Greyfriars Museum Building, Broadgate, Lincoln LN2 1HQ
☎01522 549160 (Reference)/510800(Lending)
Fax 01522 535882

Reference Librarian *Sarah H. Medd*

Open 9.00 am to 7.00 pm Monday, Tuesday, Thursday, Friday; 9.00 am to 1.00 pm Wednesday; 9.00 am to 12.30 pm Saturday

Linen Hall Library

17 Donegall Square North, Belfast BT1 5GD
☎01232 321707   Fax 01232 438586

Librarian *John Gray*

Open 9.30 am to 5.30 pm Monday, Tuesday, Wednesday, Friday; 9.30 am to 8.30 pm Thursday (5.30 pm in July and August); 9.30 am to 4.00 pm Saturday

Open access For reference (loans restricted to members)

FOUNDED 1788. Contains about 200,000 books. As well as general stock, there is a substantial Irish and local studies collection, with over 80,000 items.

Literary & Philosophical Society of Newcastle upon Tyne

23 Westgate Road, Newcastle upon Tyne NE1 1SE
☎0191 232 0192

Open 9.30 am to 7.00 pm Monday, Wednesday, Thursday, Friday; 9.30 am to 8.00 pm Tuesday; 9.30 am to 1.00 pm Saturday

Access Members; research facilities for *bona fide* scholars on application to the Librarian

200-year-old library of 140,000 volumes, periodicals (including 130 current titles), classical music on vinyl recordings and CD, plus a collection of scores. A programme of lectures and recitals provided. Recent publications include: *History of the Literary and Philosophical Society of Newcastle upon Tyne, Vol. 2 (1896–1989)* Charles Parish; *Bicentenary Lectures 1993* ed. John Philipson.

Liverpool City Libraries

William Brown Street, Liverpool LE3 8EW
☎0151 225 5429   Fax 0151 207 1342

Open 9.00 am to 7.30 pm Monday to Thursday; 9.00 am to 5.00 pm Friday and Saturday

Open access

Arts and Recreations Library 50,000 volumes covering all subjects in arts and recreation.

Business & Information Library Business and trade directories, plus all UK statutes and law reports. Serves as a depository library for UN and EC reports.

General & Social Sciences/Hornby Library Contains stock of 68,000 volumes and 24,000 maps, plus book plates, prints and autographed letters. *Special collections* Walter Crane and Edward Lear illustrations.

International Library Open-shelf and reserve stocks on language, literature, geography and history. *Special collection* British history, with much on politicians and statesmen. 20,000 copies of British, American and European plays, plus language tapes in twenty languages.

Music Library Extensive stock relating to all aspects of music. Includes 128,000 volumes and music scores, 18,500 records and over 3000 cassettes and CDs. *Special collections* Carl Rosa Opera Company Collection and Earl of Sefton's early printed piano music.

Record Office and Local History Department Printed and audiovisual material relating to Liverpool, Merseyside, Lancashire and Cheshire, together with archive material mainly on Liverpool. Some restrictions on access, with 30-year rule applying to archives.

Science and Technology Library Extensive stock dealing with all aspects of science and technology, including British and European standards and patents.

London College of Printing & Distributive Trades: Department of Learning Resources
Elephant and Castle, London SE1 6SB
☎0171 514 6500

Access By arrangement
The Department of Learning Resources operates from the three sites of the college at: Elephant & Castle; Davies Street (W1); Back Hill (Clerkenwell). Books, periodicals, slides, CD-ROM, videos and computer software on all aspects of the art of the book: printing, management, film/photograph, graphic arts, plus historical retailing. *Special collections* Private Press books and the history and development of printing and books.

The London Library
14 St James's Square, London SW1Y 4LG
☎0171 930 7705/6   Fax 0171 930 0436
Librarian *A. S. Bell*
Open 9.30 am to 5.30 pm Monday to Saturday (Thursday till 7.30 pm)

Access For members only (£100 p.a. 1995 price)
With over a million books and 8300 members, The London Library 'is the most distinguished private library in the world; probably the largest, certainly the best loved'. Founded in 1841, it is wholly independent of public funding. There are few restrictions on membership; anybody can apply and at present there is no waiting list. Members can take home up to ten books; fifteen if the member lives more than twenty miles from St James's Square. The library offers a comfortable reading room and an annexe for users of personal computers, where compact disc editions of *The Times* and *Sunday Times* (1990 onwards) and of *English Poetry Full-Text Database* are available. The library specialises in the humanities and includes works in most European languages as well as in English. Science and technology, medicine and law are excluded.

The London Library Trust was founded in 1952 with the object of making the resources of the Library accessible to scholars and students who cannot afford the full annual membership fee; making grants for original research work at the Library; and purchasing works of scholarship for the Library which it might not otherwise acquire.

Lord Louis Library
Orchard Street, Newport, Isle of Wight
PO30 1LL
☎01983 527655/823800 (Reference Library)
Fax 01983 825972
Open 9.30 am to 5.30 pm Monday to Friday (Saturday till 5.00 pm)

Open access
General adult and junior fiction and non-fiction collections; local history collection and periodicals. Also the county's main reference library.

Manchester Central Library
St Peters Square, Manchester M2 5PD
☎0161 234 1900   Fax 0161 234 1963
Open 10.00 am to 8.00 pm Monday to Thursday; 10.00 am to 5.00 pm Friday and Saturday; Commercial and European Units: 10.00 am to 6.00 pm Monday to Thursday; 10.00 am to 5.00 pm Friday and Saturday

Open access
One of the country's leading reference libraries with extensive collections covering all subjects. Subject departments include: Commercial, European, Technical, Social Sciences, Arts, Music, Local Studies, Chinese, General Readers, Language & Literature. Large lending stock and VIP (visually impaired) service available.

Marylebone Library (Westminster)
See **Health Information Library; Sherlock Holmes Collection**

Ministry of Agriculture, Fisheries and Food

Whitehall Place Library, 3 Whitehall Place, London SW1A 2HH

☎0171 270 8000/8421   Fax 0171 270 8419

MAFF Helpline 0645 335577 (local call rate) – general contact point which can provide information on the work of MAFF, either directly or by referring callers to appropriate contacts. Available 9.00 am to 5.00 pm Monday to Friday (excluding Bank Holidays)

Open 9.30 am to 5.00 pm Monday to Friday

Access For reference (but at least 24 hours notice must be given for intended visits)

Large stock of volumes on temperate agriculture.

The Mitchell Library

North Street, Glasgow G3 7DN

☎0141 305 2999   Fax 0141 305 2815

Contact *Mrs F. MacPherson*

Open 9.30 am to 9.00 pm Monday to Friday; 9.30 am to 5.00 pm Saturday

Open access

Europe's largest public reference library with stock of over 1,200,000 volumes. It subscribes to 46 newspapers and more than 2,000 periodicals. There are collections in microform, records, tapes and videos, as well as CD-ROM, illustrations, photographs, postcards etc.

The library is divided into a number of subject departments including the language & literature department which contains a number of special collections, eg the Robert Burns Collection (4,000 vols), the Scottish Poetry Collection (10,000 items) and the Scottish Drama Collection (1,600 items).

National Library of Scotland

George IV Bridge, Edinburgh EH1 1EW

☎0131 226 4531/459 4531

Fax 0131 220 6662

Open Main Reading Room: 9.30 am to 8.30 pm Monday, Tuesday, Thursday, Friday; 10.00 am to 8.30 pm Wednesday; 9.30 am to 1.00 pm Saturday.
Map Library: 9.30 am to 5.00 pm Monday, Tuesday, Thursday, Friday; 10.00 am to 5.00 pm Wednesday; 9.30 am to 1.00 pm Saturday.
Scottish Science Library: 9.30 am to 5.00 pm Monday, Tuesday, Thursday, Friday; 10.00 am to 8.30 pm Wednesday.

Access To reading rooms and Map Library, for research not easily done elsewhere, by reader's ticket

Collection of over 6 million volumes. The library receives all British and Irish publications. Large stock of newspapers and periodicals. Many special collections, including early Scottish books, theology, polar studies, baking, phrenology and liturgies. Also large collections of maps, music and manuscripts including personal archives of notable Scottish persons.

National Library of Wales

Aberystwyth, Dyfed SY23 3BU

☎01970 623816   Fax 01970 615709

Open 9.30 am to 6.00 pm Monday to Friday; 9.30 am to 5.00 pm Saturday (closed Bank Holidays and first week of October)

Access To reading rooms and map room by reader's ticket, available on application

Collection of over 3 million books including large collections of periodicals, maps and manuscripts. Particular emphasis on humanities in foreign material, and on Wales and other Celtic areas in all collections.

Natural History Museum Library

Cromwell Road, London SW7 5BD

☎0171 938 9191   Fax 0171 938 9290

Open 10.00 am to 4.30 pm Monday to Friday

Access To *bona fide* researchers, by reader's ticket (telephone first to make an appointment)

The library is in five sections: general; botany; zoology; entomology; palaeontology and mineralogy. The sub-department of ornithology is housed at Zoological Museum, Akeman Street, Tring, Herts HP23 6AP (Tel 01442 834181). Resources available include books, journals, maps, manuscripts, drawings and photographs covering all aspects of natural history, including palaeontology and mineralogy, from the 14th century to the present day. Also archives and an historical collection on the museum itself.

Newcastle Literary and Philosophical Society Library

Westgate Road, Newcastle upon Tyne NE1 1SE

☎0191 232 0192

Librarian *Margaret Norwell*

Open 9.30 am to 7.00 pm (Tuesdays till 8.00 pm; Saturdays till 1.00 pm)

Access To members; scholars on application

Over 140,000 volumes, many of them old and rare. *Special collections* 19th-century science and technology, history, exploration and travel, biography, literature, music, and local history.

Newcastle upon Tyne Central Library

Princess Square, Newcastle upon Tyne
NE99 1DX
☎0191 261 0691   Fax 0191 261 1435

Open 9.30 am to 8.00 pm Monday and
Thursday; 9.30 am to 5.00 pm Tuesday,
Wednesday, Friday; 9.00 am to 5.00 pm
Saturday

Open access
Extensive local studies collection, including
newspapers, illustrations and genealogy. Also
business, science, humanities and arts, educational guidance unit, open learning resource
centre, marketing advice centre. Patents advice
centre.

Norfolk Library & Information Service

Norwich Central Library, Central Lending
Service, 71 Ber Street, Norwich, Norfolk
NR1 3AD
☎01603 222222

**Central Reference & Information Service
and Norfolk Studies**
Gildengate House, Upper Green Lane,
Norwich, Norfolk NR3 1AX
☎01603 222222

Open Leisure & Learning and Information &
Research depts: 10.00 am to 8.00 pm
Monday to Friday; 9.00 am to 5.00 pm
Saturday. Local Studies: 10.00 am to 5.00 pm
Monday to Friday; 9.00 am to 5.00 pm
Saturday

Open access
Reference and lending library with wide
range of stock for loan, including books,
recorded music, music scores, plays and videos.
(The collections were severely damaged by fire
in August 1994 and are in the process of being
rebuilt.) Houses the 2nd Air Division Memorial
Library and has a strong Local Studies Library.
Extensive range of reference stock including
business information. On-line database and
CD-ROM services. Public fax and colour photocopying. Information brokerage provides in-
depth research services.

Northamptonshire Libraries & Information Service

Library HQ, PO Box 259, 27 Guildhall Road,
Northampton NN1 1BA
☎01604 20262   Fax 01604 26789

Since 1991 the Library and Information

Service has run two programmes of literary
events for adults each year between April and
July, and October and March. Programmes so
far have included visiting authors, poetry readings, workshops and other events and activities.
The programmes are supported by regular
touring fiction displays, writers' advice sessions
and dedicated notice boards in libraries across
the country.

Northumberland Central Library

The Willows, Morpeth, Northumberland
NE61 1TA
☎01670 512385   Fax 01670 519985

Open 10.00 am to 8.00 pm Monday,
Tuesday, Wednesday, Friday; 9.30 am to
12.30 pm Saturday (closed Thursday)

Open access
Books, periodicals, newspapers, cassettes,
CDs, video, microcomputers, CD-ROM,
prints, microforms, vocal scores, playsets, community resource equipment. *Special collections*
Northern Arts Poetry Library: 12,000 volumes of modern poetry (see entry: **Organisations of Interest to Poets**); cinema: comprehensive collection of about 5000 volumes
covering all aspects of the cinema; family history.

Nottingham Central Library

Angel Row, Nottingham NG1 6HP
☎0115 9412121   Fax 0115 9504207

Open 9.30 am to 8.00 pm Monday to Friday;
9.00 am to 1.00 pm Saturday

Open access
General public lending library: business
information, the arts, local studies, religion, literature. Videos, periodicals, spoken word,
recorded music. *Special collection* on D. H.
Lawrence. Extensive back-up reserve stocks.
Drama and music sets for loan to groups.

Nottingham Subscription Library Ltd

Bromley House, Angel Row, Nottingham
NG1 6HL
☎0115 9473134

Librarian *Jane Corbett*
Open 9.30 am to 5.00 pm Monday to Friday;
also first Saturday of each month from
10.00 am to 12.30 pm for members only

FOUNDED 1816. Collection of 30,000 books
including local history, topography, biography,
travel and fiction.

Office of Population Censuses & Surveys Library

Library Services and Central Enquiry Unit, St Catherine's House, 10 Kingsway, London WC2B 6JP
☎0171 396 2235(Library)/2828(OPCS Data)
Fax 0171 396 2467

Open 9.30 am to 4.30 pm Monday to Friday

Access By appointment only
All published Census data from 1801 onwards for the UK. Population and health statistics from 1837 onwards. Foreign censuses and statistics (incomplete; most are out-housed and require one week's notice for retrieval). International statistics (WHO, UN, etc). Government Social Survey reports, 1941 onwards. Small stock of books on demography, vital registration, epidemology, survey methodology, census taking.

Orkney Library

Laing Street, Kirkwall, Orkney KW15 1NW
☎01856 873166   Fax 01856 875260

Chief Librarian *R. K. Leslie*

Open 9.00 am to 8.00 pm Monday to Friday; 9.00 am to 5.00 pm Saturday. Archives: 9.00 am to 1.00 pm and 2.00 pm to 4.45 pm Monday to Friday

Open access
Local studies collection. Archive includes sound and photographic departments.

Oxford Central Library

Westgate, Oxford OX1 1DJ
☎01865 815549   Fax 01865 721694

Open 9.15 am to 7.00 pm Monday, Tuesday, Thursday, Friday (Wednesday and Saturday till 5.00 pm)
General lending and reference library including the Centre for Oxfordshire Studies. Also periodicals, music library, children's library and Business Information Point.

Penzance Library

Morrab House, Morrab Gardens, Penzance, Cornwall TR18 4DQ
☎01736 64474

Librarian *L. Lowdon*

Open 10.00 am to 4.00 pm Tuesday to Friday; 10.00 am to 1.00 pm Saturday

Access Non-members may use the library for a small daily fee, but may not borrow books
A private subscription lending library of over 60,000 volumes covering virtually all subjects except modern science and technology, with large collections on history, literature and religion. There is a comprehensive Cornish collection of books, newspapers and manuscripts including the Borlase letters; a West Cornwall photographic archive; many runs of 18th- and 19th-century periodicals; a collection of over 2000 books published before 1800.

Plymouth Proprietary Library

Alton Terrace, 111 North Hill, Plymouth, Devon PL4 8JY
☎01752 660515

Librarian *Camilla M. Blackman*

Open Monday to Saturday from 9.30 am (closing time varies)

Access To members; visitors by appointment only
FOUNDED 1810. The library contains approximately 17,000 volumes of mainly 20th-century work. Member of the Association of Independent Libraries.

The Poetry Library

See under **Organisations of Interest to Poets**

Polish Library

238–246 King Street, London W6 0RF
☎0181 741 0474   Fax 0181 746 3798

Open 10.00 am to 8.00 pm Monday and Wednesday; 10.00 am to 5.00 pm Friday; 10.00 am to 1.00 pm Saturday (library closed Tuesday and Thursday)

Access For reference to all interested in Polish affairs; limited loans to members and *bona fide* scholars only through inter-library loans
Books, pamphlets, periodicals, maps, music, photographs on all aspects of Polish history and culture. *Special collections* Emigré publications; Joseph Conrad and related works; Polish underground publications; bookplates.

Poole Central Library

Dolphin Centre, Poole, Dorset BH15 1QE
☎01202 673910   Fax 01202 670253

Open 10.00 am to 7.00 pm Monday; 9.30 am to 7.00 pm Tuesday to Friday; 9.00 am to 1.00 pm Saturday

Open access
General lending and reference library, including Healthpoint health information centre, HATRICS business information centre, children's library, periodicals.

Press Association Library

85 Fleet Street, London EC4P 4BE
☎0171 353 7440   Fax 0171 936 8093(News)/
353 0784(Pics.)

Open News Library: 8.00 am to 8.00 pm
Monday to Friday; 8.00 am to 6.00 pm
Saturday; 9.00 am to 5.00 pm Sunday.
Picture Library: personal callers 9.00 am to
5.00 pm Monday to Friday

The national news agency offers public
access to over 14 million news cuttings on
every subject from 1926 onwards, and over 5
million colour and b&w photographs from
1902 to the present day. Personal callers welcome or research undertaken by in-house staff.

Harry Price Library of Magical Literature

University of London Library, Senate House,
Malet Street, London WC1E 7HU
☎0171 636 4514   Fax 0171 636 5841

Open Term-time: 10.00 am to 6.30 pm
Monday to Friday; 10.00 am to 5.30 pm
Saturday (holidays: 10.00 am to 5.30 pm
Monday to Saturday)

Open access For reference only, restricted to
members of the University and accredited
research students (apply in writing)

Over 14,000 volumes and pamphlets on psychic phenomena and pseudo-phenomena;
books relating to spiritualism and its history, to
hypnotism, telepathy, astrology, conjuring and
quackery.

Public Record Office

Ruskin Avenue, Kew, Richmond, Surrey
TW9 4DU
☎0181 876 3444   Fax 0181 878 8905

Also at: Chancery Lane, London WC2A 1LR
Open 9.30 am to 5.00 pm Monday to Friday

Access For reference, by reader's ticket, available free of charge on production of proof of
identity (UK citizens: banker's card or driving
licence; non-UK: passport or national identity
card. Telephone for further information)

Over 90 miles of shelving house the national
repository of records of central Government in
the UK and law courts of England and Wales,
which extend in time from the 11th–20th century. Medieval records and the records of the
State Paper Office from the early 16th–late 18th
century, plus the records of the Privy Council
Office and the Lord Chamberlain's and Lord
Steward's departments, together with the
records of the decennial censuses, 1841–1891,

are held at Chancery Lane. Modern government department records, together with those
of the Copyright Office, are held at Kew; these
date mostly from the late 18th century. Under
the Public Records Act, records are normally
only open to inspection when they are 30 years
old. Chancery Lane also houses a small permanent exhibition of records (open 10.00 am to
5.00 pm Monday to Friday; Census Rooms also
open 9.30 am to 5.00 pm Saturday).

Reading Central Library

Abbey Square, Reading, Berkshire RG1 3BQ
☎01734 509245   Fax 01734 589039

Open 9.30 am to 5.00 pm Monday,
Wednesday; 9.30 am to 7.00 pm Tuesday,
Thursday, Friday; 9.30 am to 4.00 pm
Saturday

Open access

Lending library; county reference library;
county local studies library, bringing together
every aspect of the local environment and
human activity in Berkshire; county business
library; county music and drama library.
Special collections: Mary Russell Mitford; local
illustrations.

Public meeting room available.

Religious Society of Friends Library

Friends House, 173 Euston Road, London
NW1 2BJ
☎0171 387 3601   Fax 0171 388 1977

Open 10.00 am to 5.00 pm Tuesday to Friday
(closed last full week November and week
preceding Spring Bank Holiday)

Access For reference, to members of the
Society of Friends and to *bona fide* researchers
on introduction or letter of recommendation

Quaker history, thought and activities from
the 17th century onwards. Supporting collections on peace, anti-slavery and other subjects
in which Quakers have maintained long-standing interest. Also archives and manuscripts
relating to the Society of Friends.

Richmond Central Reference Library

Old Town Hall, Whittaker Avenue,
Richmond, Surrey TW9 1TP
☎0181 940 5529   Fax 0181 940 6899

Principal Reference Librarian *Diana
Howard*

Open 10.00 am to 6.00 pm Monday,
Thursday, Friday (Tuesday till 1.00 pm;

Wednesday till 8.00 pm and Saturday till
5.00 pm)

Open access
General reference library serving the needs
of local residents and organisations.

Royal Geographical Society Library
1 Kensington Gore, London SW7 2AR
☎0171 589 5466   Fax 0171 584 4447

Open 10.00 am to 5.00 pm Monday to Friday

Access To the Map Room and picture library;
library and reading rooms restricted to use by
Fellows and members
Books and periodicals on geography, topography, cartography, voyages and travels. The
Map Room houses map sheets, atlases and
expedition reports. Photographs on travel and
exploration are housed in the picture library.

Royal Society Library
6 Carlton House Terrace, London SW1Y 5AG
☎0171 839 5561   Fax 0171 930 2170

Open 10.00 am to 5.00 pm Monday to Friday

Access For research only, to *bona fide*
researchers on application to the librarian
Science, history of science, scientists' biographies, science policy reports, and publications
of international scientific unions and national
academies from all over the world.

RSA (Royal Society for the Encouragement of Arts, Manufacturers & Commerce)
8 John Adam Street, London WC2N 6EZ
☎0171 930 5115   Fax 0171 839 5805

Library Administrator *Susan Bennett*
Open 10.00 am to 1.00 pm Monday to
Thursday and 2.00–5.00 pm Wednesdays
only

Access to fellows of RSA; by application and
appointment to non-fellows (£6.00 for a yearly
ticket)
Archives of the Society since 1754.
International exhibition material.

Royal Society of Medicine Library
1 Wimpole Street, London W1M 8AE
☎0171 290 2940   Fax 0171 290 2939

Open 9.00 am to 9.30 pm Monday to Friday;
10.00 am to 5.00 pm Saturday

Access For reference only, on introduction by
Fellow of the Society (temporary membership
may also be granted)

Books and periodicals on general medicine,
biochemistry and biomedical science. Extensive historical material.

Royal Statistical Society Library
University College London, Gower Street,
London WC1E 6BT
☎0171 387 7050 ext. 2628
Fax 0171 380 7727/7373

Contact *D Chatarji*

Access RSS fellows registered with University
College London Library
Statistics (theory and methodology), mathematical statistics, applied statistics, econometrics.

Science Fiction Foundation Research Library
Liverpool University Library, PO Box 123,
Liverpool L69 3DA
☎0151 794 2733/2696   Fax 0151 794 2681

Access For research, by appointment only
(telephone first)
The largest collection outside the US of science fiction and related material, including autobiographies and critical works. *Special collection* of
'pulp' magazines dating back to the 1920s.
Foreign-language material (including a large
Russian collection), and the papers of the Flat
Earth Society. The collection features a growing
range of archive and manuscript material.

Science Museum Library
Imperial Institute Road, off Exhibition Road,
London SW7 5NH
☎0171 938 8234   Fax 0171 938 8213

Open 9.30 am to 9.00 pm Monday to Friday
(closes 5.30 pm outside academic terms);
9.30 am to 5.30 pm Saturday

Open access Reference only; no loans
National reference library for the history and
public understanding of science and technology, with a large collection of source material.
Operates jointly with Imperial College Central
Library.

Scottish Poetry Library
See under **Organisations of Interest to Poets**

Sheffield Libraries and Information Services
Central Library, Surrey Street, Sheffield S1 1XZ
☎0114 2734711   Fax 0114 2735009

Sheffield Archives
52 Shoreham Street, Sheffield S1 4SP
☎0114 2734756

Open 9.30 am to 5.30 pm Monday to Thursday; 9.00 am to 1.00 pm & 2.00 pm to 4.30 pm Saturday (documents should be ordered by 5.00 pm Thursday for Saturday)

Access By reader's pass

Holds documents relating to Sheffield and South Yorkshire, dating from the 12th century to the present day, including records of the City Council, churches, businesses, landed estates, families and individuals, institutions and societies.

Arts and Social Sciences Reference Service
☎0114 2734756

Open 10.00 am to 8.00 pm Monday; 10.00 am to 5.30 pm Tuesday, Thursday and Friday; 1.00 pm to 8.00 pm Wednesday; 9.30 am to 4.30 pm Saturday

Access For reference only

A comprehensive collection of books, periodicals and newspapers covering all aspects of arts (excluding music) and social sciences.

Music and Video Service
☎0114 2734733

Open as for Arts and Social Services above

Access For reference (loans to ticket holders only)

An extensive range of books, records, CDs, cassettes, scores, etc. related to music. Also a video cassette loan service.

Local Studies Service
☎0114 2734753

Open as for Arts & Social Sciences above (except Wednesday 1.00 pm to 5.30 pm)

Access For reference (but advance notice advisable)

Extensive material covering all aspects of Sheffield and its population, including maps, photos and taped oral histories.

Business, Science and Technology Reference Service
☎0114 2734736/7 (Business); 0114 2734742/3 (Science & Technology)

Open as for Arts & Social Sciences above

Access For reference only

Extensive coverage of science and technology as well as commerce and commercial law. British patents and British and European standards with emphasis on metals. Hosts the World Metal Index. The business section holds a large stock of business and trade directories, plus overseas telephone directories and reference works with business emphasis.

Sheffield Information Service
☎0114 2734760/1

Open 10.00 am to 1.00 pm & 2.00 pm to 5.30 pm Monday, Tuesday and Friday; 1.00 pm to 5.30 pm Wednesday and Thursday; 9.30 am to 1.00 pm Saturday

Full local information service covering all aspects of the Sheffield community.

Shetland Library
Lower Hillhead, Lerwick, Shetland ZE1 0EL
☎01595 693868   Fax 01595 694430

Chief Librarian D. G. *Hunter*

Open 10.00 am to 7.00 pm Monday, Wednesday, Friday; 10.00 am to 5.00 pm Tuesday, Thursday, Saturday

General lending and reference library; extensive local interest collection including complete set of *The Shetland Times, The Shetland News* and other local newspapers on microfilm and many old and rare books; audio collection including *Linguaphone* courses and talking books/newspapers. Junior room for children and a weekly storytime for pre-school children. Disabled access and Housebound Readers Service (delivery to reader's home). Mobile library services to rural areas. Open Learning Service. Overnight photocopying service.

Shoe Lane Library
Hill House, Little New Street, London EC4A 3JR
☎0171 583 7178

Open 9.30 am to 5.30 pm Monday, Wednesday, Thursday, Friday; 9.30 am to 6.30 pm Tuesday

Open access

City of London general lending library, with a comprehensive stock of 48,000 volumes, more than half of which are on display. Some specialisation in graphics, advertising and illustrated works.

Shrewsbury Library
Castlegates, Shrewsbury, Shropshire SY1 2AS
☎01743 255300   Fax 01743 255309

Open 9.30 am to 5.00 pm Monday and Wednesday; 9.30am to 1.00 pm Thursday; 9.30am to 7.30 pm Tuesday and Friday; 9.30 am to 4.00 pm Saturday

Open access

The largest public lending library in Shropshire. Books, cassettes, CDs, talking books, videos, language courses. Strong literature and art book collection. Reference library, performing arts library and local studies library. (Plans to move these departments at the time of going to press. Telephone for details.)

Spanish Institute Library
See **Instituto Cervantes**

St Bride Printing Library
Bride Lane, London EC4Y 8EE
☎0171 353 4660   Fax 0171 583 7073
Open 9.30 am to 5.30 pm Monday to Friday
Open access
   Corporation of London public reference library. Appointments advisable for consultation of special collections. Every aspect of printing and related matters: publishing and bookselling, newspapers and magazines, graphic design, calligraphy and type, paper-making and bookbinding. One of the world's largest specialist collections in its field, with over 40,000 volumes, over 2000 periodicals (200 current titles), and extensive collection of drawings, manuscripts, prospectuses, patents and materials for printing and typefounding. Noted for its comprehensive holdings of historical and early technical literature.

Suffolk County Council Libraries & Heritage
St Andrew House, County Hall, St Helens Street, Ipswich, Suffolk IP4 2JS
☎01473 230000   Fax 01473 225491
Open Details on application to St Andrew House above. Major libraries open six days a week
Access A single user registration card gives access to the lending service of 41 libraries across the county
   Full range of lending and reference services. *Special collections* include Suffolk Archives and Local History Collection; Benjamin Britten Collection; Edward Fitzgerald Collection; Seckford Collection and Racing Collection (Newmarket). The Suffolk Infolink service gives details of local groups and societies and is available in libraries throughout the county.

Sunderland City Library and Arts Centre
28–30 Fawcett Street, Sunderland, Tyne & Wear SR1 1RE
☎0191 514 1235   Fax 0191 514 8444
Open 9.30 am to 7.30 pm Monday and Wednesday; 9.30 am to 5.00 pm Tuesday, Thursday, Friday; 9.30 am to 4.00 pm Saturday
   The city's main lending and reference library. Local studies and children's sections, plus sound and vision department (CDs, cas-settes, videos, talking books). The City of Sunderland maintains a further nineteen branch libraries. Special services available to housebound readers, hospitals and schools, plus two mobile libraries.

Swansea Central Reference Library
Alexandra Road, Swansea, West Glamorgan SA1 5DX
☎01792 655521   Fax 01792 645751
Open 9.00 am to 7.00 pm Monday, Tuesday, Wednesday, Friday; 9.00 am to 5.00 pm Thursday and Saturday. The library has a lending service but hours tend to be shorter – check in advance.
Access For reference only (Local Studies closed access: items must be requested on forms provided)
   General reference material (approx. 50,000 volumes); also British standards, statutes, company information, maps, etc. Local studies: comprehensive collections on Wales; Swansea & Gower; Dylan Thomas. Local maps, periodicals, illustrations, local newspapers from 1804. B&w and colour photocopying facilities and microfilm/microfiche copying facility.

Swiss Cottage Library
88 Avenue Road, London NW3 3HA
☎0171 413 6533/4
Open 10.00 am to 7.00 pm Monday and Thursday; 10.00 am to 6.00 pm Tuesday and Friday; 10.00 am to 5.00 pm Saturday (closed all day Wednesday)
Open access
   Over 60,000 volumes and 400 periodical titles. Home of the London Borough of Camden's Information and Reference Services.

Theatre Museum Library & Archive
1e Tavistock Street, London WC2E 7PA
☎0171 836 7891   Fax 0171 836 5148
Open 10.30 am to 4.30 pm Tuesday to Friday
Access By appointment only
   The Theatre Museum was founded as a separate department of the Victoria & Albert Museum in 1974 and moved to its own building in Covent Garden in 1987. The museum (open Tuesday to Sunday 11.00 am to 7.00 pm) houses permanent displays, temporary exhibitions, a studio theatre, and organises a programme of special events, performances, lectures and guided visits. The library houses the UK's largest performing arts research collec-

tions, including books, photographs, designs, engravings, programmes, press cuttings, etc. All the performing arts are covered but strengths are in the areas of theatre history, ballet, circus and stage design. The Theatre Museum has acquired much of the British Theatre Association's library and is providing reference access to its collections of play texts and critical works.

Trades Union Congress Library

Congress House, Great Russell Street, London WC1B 3LS
☎0171 636 4030 ext. 1298 Fax 0171 636 0632
Librarian *Christine Coates*
Open 10.00 am to 5.00 pm Monday to Friday
Access For research, by appointment only
Industrial relations, wages and conditions of employment, trade unions, economics, occupational health, international trade union activities and other areas covered by TUC policy. Also a small collection of photographs.

United Nations London Information Centre and Reference Library

18 Buckingham Gate, London SW1E 6LB
☎0171 630 1981   Fax 0171 976 6478
Open Information Centre: 9.30 am to 1.00 pm and 2.00 pm to 5.30 pm Monday to Friday. Reference Library: 10.00 am to 1.00 pm and 2.00 pm to 5.00 pm Monday, Wednesday, Thursday
Open access To Information Centre only; Reference Library by appointment only
A full stock of official publications and documentation from the United Nations.

Victoria Library (Westminster)

See **Central Music Library**

Western Isles Libraries

Public Library, Keith Street, Stornoway, Isle of Lewis HS1 2QG
☎01851 703064   Fax 01851 705657
Open 10.00 am to 5.00 pm Monday to Thursday; 10.00 am to 7.00 pm Friday; 10.00 am to 1.00 pm Saturday
Open access
General public library stock, plus local history and Gaelic collections including maps, printed music and cassettes; census records and Council minutes; music collection (cassettes). Branch libraries on the isles of Barra, Benbecula, Harris and Lewis.

City of Westminster Archive

10 St Ann's Street, London SW1P 2XR
☎0171 798 2180   Fax 0171 798 2179
Open 9.30 am to 7.00 pm Monday to Friday; 9.30 am to 5.00 pm Saturday
Access For reference
Comprehensive coverage of the history of Westminster and selective coverage of general London history. 22,000 books, together with a large stock of maps, prints, photographs, and theatre programmes.

Westminster Reference Library

35 St Martin's Street, London WC2H 7HP
☎0171 798 2036 (General & Performing Arts)
Fax 0171 798 2040
Librarian *Derrick Fernandes*
Business and Official Publications:
☎0171 798 2034
Information for Business Service:
☎0171 976 1285
Open 10.00 am to 7.00 pm Monday to Friday; 10.00 am to 5.00 pm Saturday
Access For reference only
A general reference library with emphasis on the following: Art & Design (see separate entry); Performing Arts – theatre, cinema, radio, television and dance; Official Publications – major collection of HMSO publications from 1947, plus parliamentary papers dating back to 1906, and a ten-year file of key statistical publications from OECD, UN, Unesco, EU, etc.; Maps – an excellent map and town plan collection for Britain, plus international material; Business – UK directories, trade directories, company and market data; Periodicals – long files of many titles. Two working days' notice is required for some monographs and most older periodicals. Online computer service. Official EU depository library – carries all official EU material.

The Wiener Library

4 Devonshire Street, London W1N 2BH
☎0171 636 7247   Fax 0171 436 6428
Open 10.00 am to 5.30 pm Monday to Friday
Access By letter of introduction (readers needing to use the Library for any length of time should become members)
Private library – one of the leading research centres on European history since the First World War, with special reference to the era of totalitarianism and to Jewish affairs. Founded by Dr Alfred Wiener in Amsterdam in 1933, it holds material that is not available elsewhere.

Books, periodicals, press archives, documents, pamphlets, leaflets and brochures. Much of the material can be consulted on microfilm.

Vaughan Williams Memorial Library

English Folk Dance and Song Society, Cecil Sharp House, 2 Regent's Park, London NW1 7AY

☎0171 284 0523   Fax 0171 284 0523

Open 9.30 am to 5.30 pm Monday to Friday

Access For reference to the general public, on payment of a daily fee; members may borrow books and use the library free of charge

A multi-media collection: books, periodicals, manuscripts, tapes, records, CDs, films, videos. Mostly British folk culture and how this has developed around the world. Some foreign language material, and some books in English about foreign cultures. Also, the history of the English Folk Dance and Song Society.

Dr Williams's Library

14 Gordon Square, London WC1H 0AG
☎0171 387 3727

Open 10.00 am to 5.00 pm Monday, Wednesday, Friday; 10.00 am to 6.30 pm Tuesday and Thursday

Open access To reading room (loans restricted to subscribers)

Annual subscription £10; ministers of religion and certain students £5

Primarily a library of theology, religion and ecclesiastical history. Also philosophy, history (English and Byzantine). Particularly important for the study of English Nonconformity.

Wolverhampton Central Library

Snow Hill, Wolverhampton WV1 3AX
☎01902 312025   Fax 01902 714579

Open 10.00 am to 7.00 pm Monday to Thursday; 10.00 am to 5.00 pm Friday and Saturday

Archives & Local Studies Collection 10.00

am to 5.00 pm Monday to Saturday (Limited archive production between 12.00 pm and 2.00 pm; Archives must be booked in advance on Saturdays)

General lending and reference libraries, plus children's library and the Archives & Local Studies library. Also audio visual library holding cassettes, CDs, videos and music scores.

York Central Library (North Yorkshire County Library)

Museum Street, York YO1 2DS
☎01904 655631/654144 (reference library)
Fax 01904 611025

Open 9.30 am to 8.00 pm Monday, Tuesday, Friday; 9.30 am to 1.00 pm Wednesday; 9.30 am to 5.30 pm Thursday; 9.30 am to 4.00 pm Saturday

Reference Library 9.00 am to 8.00 pm Monday, Tuesday, Wednesday, Friday; 9.00 am to 5.30 pm Thursday; 9.00 am to 1.00 pm Saturday

General lending library plus reference library incorporating local organisations database; local studies library for York and surrounding area; business information service; microfilm/fiche readers for national and local newspapers; census returns and family history resource; general reference collection. Maintains strong links with other local history resource centres, namely the Borthwick Institute, York City Archive and York Minster Library. Audio books service and music library.

Zoological Society Library

Regent's Park, London NW1 4RY
☎0171 722 3333 ext. 293 Fax 0171 586 5743

Open 9.30 am to 5.30 pm Monday to Friday

Access To members and staff; non-members by application and on payment of fee

160,000 volumes on zoology including 5000 journals (1300 current) and a wide range of books on animals and particular habitats. Slide collection available and many historic zoological prints.

Picture Libraries

A–Z Botanical Collection Ltd

Bedwell Lodge, Cucumber Lane, Essendon, Hatfield, Hertfordshire AL9 6JB

☎01707 649091   Fax 01707 649091

Contact *Jeremy Finlay*

150,000 transparencies, specialising in plants and related subjects.

Action Plus

54–58 Tanner Street, London SE1 3LL

☎0171 403 1558   Fax 0171 403 1526

Specialist sports and action library with a vast and comprehensive collection of small format colour and b&w images covering all aspects of over 120 professional and amateur sports from around the world. As well as personalities, events, venues etc, also covers themes such as success, celebration, dejection, teamwork, effort and exhaustion. Offers same day despatch of pictures or alternatively, clients with Macintosh and modem or ISDN links can receive digital images direct.

Lesley & Roy Adkins Picture Library

Longstone Lodge, Aller, Langport, Somerset TA10 0QT

☎01458 250075   Fax 01458 250858

Colour coverage of archaeology, heritage and related subjects (UK and Europe), prehistoric, Roman, medieval and recent sites and monuments, landscapes and countryside, housing, art and architecture, towns, villages and religious monuments. Prompt service. No service charge if any pictures are used. Catalogue available.

The Advertising Archives

45 Lyndale Avenue, London NW2 2QB

☎0171 435 6540   Fax 0171 794 6584

Contact *Suzanne or Larry Viner*

With half a million images, the largest collection of British and American press ads and magazine cover illustrations in Europe. Visitors by appointment. Research undertaken; rapid service, competitive rates.

AFP (Agence France Presse)

See **Popperfoto**

AKG London Ltd, Arts and History Picture Library

10 Plato Place, 72 – 74 St Dionis Road, London SW6 4TU

☎0171 610 6103   Fax 0171 610 6125

Contact *Julia Engelhardt*

Collection of 10,000 images with computerised access to eight million more kept in the Berlin AKG Library. Specialises in art, archaeology, history, topography, music, personalities and film.

Bryan & Cherry Alexander Photography

Higher Cottage, Manston, Sturminster Newton, Dorset DT10 1EZ

☎01258 473006   Fax 01258 473333

Contact *Cherry Alexander*

70,000 colour transparencies, specialising in polar regions, with emphasis on the wildlife and native peoples of the Arctic.

Allsport (UK) Ltd

Allsport House, 3 Greenlea Park, Prince George's Road, London SW19 2JD

☎0181 685 1010   Fax 0181 648 5240

Contact *Lee Martin*

A large specialist library with 6 million colour transparencies, covering 130 different sports and top sports personalities. Represented in 27 countries worldwide. Large studio and digital wiring facilities through Macintosh picture desk.

Alvey & Towers

9 Rosebank Road, Countesthorpe, Leicestershire LE8 5YA

☎0116 2779184   Fax 0116 2779184

Contact *Emma Alvey*

Collection of approximately 10,000 transparencies, mainly of the modern railway industry and all related supporting industries. In addition, also covers architecture, gardens, industry people, scenics, transport and travel.

Andes Press Agency

26 Padbury Court, London E2 7EH

☎0171 739 3159   Fax 0171 739 3159

Contact *Val Baker, Carlos Reyes*

80,000 colour transparencies and 300,000

b&w, specialising in social documentary, world religions, Latin America and Britain.

Animal Photography
4 Marylebone Mews, New Cavendish Street, London W1M 7LF
☎0171 935 0503   Fax 0171 487 3038

Colour and b&w coverage of horses, dogs, cats, zoos, the Galapagos Islands, East Africa. Commissions undertaken.

Aquarius Picture Library
PO Box 5, Hastings, East Sussex TN34 1HR
☎01424 721196   Fax 01424 717704
Contact *David Corkill*

Over one million images specialising in cinema, past and present, television, pop music, ballet, opera, theatre, etc. The library includes various American showbiz collections. Film stills date back to the beginning of the century. Interested in film stills, the older the better. Current material is supplied by own suppliers.

Aquila Photographics
PO Box 1, Studley, Warwickshire B80 7AN
☎0152785 2357   Fax 0152785 7507

Colour and b&w natural history library specialising in birds, British and European wildlife, North America, Africa and Australia, environmental subjects, farming, habitats and related subjects, domestic animals and pets.

Arcaid
The Factory, 2 Acre Road, Kingston upon Thames, Surrey KT2 6EF
☎0181 546 4352   Fax 0181 541 5230

The built environment, historic and contemporary architecture and interior design by leading architectural photographers. Covers international and British subjects, single images and series, with background information. Visitors welcome by appointment. Commissions undertaken.

Architectural Association Photo Library
34–36 Bedford Square, London WC1B 3ES
☎0171 636 0974   Fax 0171 414 0782
Contact *Valerie Bennett*

100,000 35 mm transparencies on architecture, historical and contemporary. Archive of large-format b&w negatives from the 1920s and 1930s.

Ardea London Ltd
35 Brodrick Road, London SW17 7DX
☎0181 672 2067   Fax 0181 672 8787

Wildlife, natural history, conservation and environmental topics in colour and b&w. Animals, birds, plants and fish in their natural habitat worldwide.

Art Directors Photo Library
Image House, 86 Haverstock Hill, London NW3 2BD
☎0171 485 9325/267 6930
Fax 0171 485 7776

Work from international photographers which includes computer graphics, medical, hi-tech, industry, business, space, personalities, lifestyles, travel, skies, still life, entertainment, fashion, cars (vintage and modern), the USA, Europe, Asia, Africa and the Tropics. Catalogue available.

Artbank Illustration Library
8 Woodcroft Avenue, London NW7 2AG
☎0181 906 2288   Fax 0181 906 2289

Illustration and art library holding thousands of images by many renowned artists. Large-format transparencies. Catalogue available on faxed request. Represents a diverse group of UK and American illustrators for commissioned work. Portfolios available for viewing.

Aspect Picture Library Ltd
40 Rostrevor Road, London SW6 5AD
☎0171 736 1998/731 7362
Fax 0171 731 7362

Colour and b&w worldwide coverage of countries, events, industry and travel, with large files on art, namely paintings, space, China and the Middle East.

Audio Visual Services
St Mary's Hospital Medical School, London W2 1PG
☎0171 725 1739   Fax 0171 724 7349
Contact *B. Tallon*

Colour and b&w, mostly 35 mm colour. Clinical medicine, contemporary and historical, including HIV-AIDS material and history of penicillin. Commissions undertaken.

Autosport Photographic
60 Waldegrave Road, Teddington, Middlesex TW11 8LG
☎0181 943 5918   Fax 0181 943 5977
Contact *Jed Leicester*

Collection of one million images of Formula 1, touring and club cars. Now incorporates Classic & Sportscar.

Aviation Images – Mark Wagner

42B Queens Road,
London SW19 8LR
☎0181 944 5225   Fax 0181 944 5335
Contact *Mark Wagner*

100,000+ aviation images, technical and generic.
Mark Wagner is the photographer for *Flight International* magazine. Member of **BAPLA**.

Aviation Photographs International

15 Downs View Road, Swindon, Wiltshire
SN3 1NS
☎01793 497179   Fax 01793 497179

The 200,000 colour photos comprise a comprehensive coverage of army, naval and airforce hardware ranging from early pistols to the latest ships. Extensive coverage of military and civil aviation includes modern together with many air-to-air views of vintage/warbird types. Commissions undertaken for additional photography and research.

Aviation Picture Library

35 Kingsley Avenue, London W13 0EQ
☎0181 566 7712   Fax 0181 566 7714
Contact *Austin John Brown, Chris Savill*

Specialists in the aviation field but also a general library which includes travel, architecture, transport, landscapes and skyscapes. Special collections: aircraft and all aspects of the aviation industry; aerial obliques of Europe, USA, Caribbean and West Africa; architectural and town planning. Commissions undertaken on the ground and in the air.

Axel Poignant Archive

115 Bedford Court Mansions, Bedford
Avenue, London WC1B 3AG
☎0171 636 2555   Fax 0171 636 2555

Anthropological and ethnographic subjects, especially Australia and the South Pacific. Also Scandinavia (early history and mythology), Sicily and England.

Axiom Picture Library

58–60 Lowesmoor, Worcester WR1 2SE
☎01905 616412   Fax 01905 25573
Contact *David Newham*

20,000 images of UK scenics: landscapes, cities, villages, towns, coastlines, tourist attractions; plus smaller sections on agriculture, transport, military aviation, backgrounds, flora, people and leisure.

Barnaby's Picture Library

Barnaby House, 19 Rathbone Street, London
W1P 1AF
☎0171 636 6128   Fax 0171 637 4317
Contact *Mary Buckland*

Colour and b&w coverage of a wide range of subjects: nature, transport, industry and historical, including a collection on Hitler. Commissions undertaken.

Barnardos Photographic and Film Archive

Tanners Lane, Barkingside, Ilford,
Essex IG6 1QG
☎0181 550 8822   Fax 0181 551 6870
Contact *John Kirkham*

Specialises in social history (1874 to present day), child care, education, war years, emigration/migration. Half a million prints, slides, negatives. Images are mainly b&w, colour since late 1940s/early 50s. Archive of 200 films dating back to 1905. Visitors by appointment Mon–Fri 9.30 am to 4.30 pm.

Colin Baxter Photography Limited

Woodlands Industrial Estate, Grantown-on-Spey PH26 3NA
☎01479 873999   Fax 01479 873888
Contact *M. Rensner*

Over 50,000 images specialising in Scotland. Also the Lake District, Yorkshire, the Cotswolds, France, Iceland and a special collection on Charles Rennie Mackintosh's work.

The Photographic Library Beamish, The North of England Open Air Museum

Beamish, The North of England Open Air
Museum, Beamish, County Durham DH9 0RG
☎01207 231811   Fax 01207 290933
Assistant Keeper, Resource Collections
Jim Lawson

Comprehensive collection; images relate to the North East of England and cover agricultural, industrial, topography, advertising and shop scenes, people at work and play. Also on laser disc for rapid searching. Visitors by appointment weekdays.

Ivan J. Belcher Colour Picture Library

57 Gibson Close, Abingdon, Oxfordshire
OX14 1XS
☎01235 521524   Fax 01235 521524

Extensive colour picture library specialising in top quality medium format transparencies depicting the British scene. Particular emphasis on tourist, holiday and heritage locations, including famous cities, towns, picturesque harbours, rivers, canals, castles, cottages, rural scenes and traditions photographed throughout the seasons. Mainly of recent origin, and constantly updated.

The Berlitz Collection
33 Albury Avenue, Isleworth, Middlesex TW7 5HY
☎0181 847 3777   Fax 0181 568 2402
Contact *Brigitte Arora*

An extensive travel photography archive, commissioned specifically for the famous Berlitz travel list (*Berlitz Pocket Guides* and *Discovery* series). Covers destinations world-wide; comprehensive not only in its coverage of tourist attractions but also in its insight into local culture and lifestyle.

Andrew Besley PhotoLibrary
3 Pen-Tye, Relistian Lane, Gwinear, Nr Hayle, Cornwall TR27 5HL
☎01736 850086   Fax 01736 756555
Contact *Andrew Besley*

Specialist library of 20,000 images of West Country faces, places and moods.

John Bethell Photography
89 Fishpool Street, St Albans, Hertfordshire AL3 4RU
☎01727 850112   Fax 01727 850112
Contact *John Bethell*

10,000 colour transparencies of architecture in Britain and abroad including country house interiors, castles, gardens, churches and townscapes; plus landscapes. All material is shot on the versatile 6x9 cm roll film format. Incorporates Bernard Cox's 35mm Kodachromes of architectural subjects worldwide. Eastern Europe and the Middle East are particular strengths.

BFI Stills, Posters and Designs
British Film Institute, 21 Stephen Street, London W1P 2LN
☎0171 255 1444   Fax 0171 323 9260
Contact *Bridget Kinally*

Holds images from more than 60,000 films and TV programmes on 6 million b&w prints and over 500,000 colour transparencies. A further 20,000 files hold portraits of film and TV personalities and cover related general subjects such as studios, equipment, awards. Also holds original posters and set and costume designs. Visitors welcome by appointment only (from 10.00 am to 6.00 pm).

Blackwoods Picture Library
See **Geoslides Photography**

Anthony Blake Photo Library
54 Hill Rise, Richmond, Surrey TW10 6UB
☎0181 940 7583   Fax 0181 948 1224

Leading source of coverage on food and wine including farming, fishing, vineyards, restaurants, raw ingredients and finished dishes. Brochure available. Commissions undertaken.

Chris Bonington Picture Library
Badger Hill, Nether Row, Hesket Newmarket, Wigton, Cumbria CA7 8LA
☎016974 78286   Fax 016974 78238
Contact *Frances Daltrey*

Based on the personal collection of climber and author Chris Bonington and his extensive travels and mountaineering achievements; also work by Doug Scott and other climbers, including the Peter Boardman and Joe Tasker Collections. Full coverage of the world's mountains from British hills to Everest depicting expedition planning and management stages, the approach march showing inhabitants of the area, flora and fauna, local architecture and climbing action shots on some of the world's highest mountains.

Bridgeman Art Library
17–19 Garway Road, London W2 4PH
☎0171 727 4065   Fax 0171 792 8509
Marketing Manager *Sarah Pooley*

Fine art photo archive acting as an agent to more than 600 museums, galleries and picture owners around the world. Large-format colour transparencies of paintings, sculptures, prints, manuscripts, antiquities and the decorative arts. The library is currently expanding at the rate of 100 new images every working day and recent additions include the collections of the National Galleries of Scotland, the Courtauld Institute Galleries and San Diego Museum. Catalogues of stock are available in printed form and on CD-ROM. Please call for a free brochure.

British Library Reproductions
British Library, Great Russell Street, London WC1B 3DG
☎0171 412 7614   Fax 0171 412 7771

Twelve million books and approximately five million other items available for photography.

Generally, photographs are made to order. Material should be ordered as far in advance as possible. All photography is done in-house by staff only. Specialist subjects include illuminated manuscripts, both Western and Oriental, maps, botanical and zoological illustration, portraits of historical figures, history of India and South-East Asia.

Brooklands Museum Picture Library

Brooklands Museum, The Clubhouse, Brooklands Road, Weybridge, Surrey KT13 0QN

☎01932 857381   Fax 01932 855465

Contact *John Pulford, Curator of Collections*

About 40,000 b&w and colour prints and slides. Subjects include: Brooklands Motor Racing 1907–1939; British Aeroplanes 1908–1920; Vickers Aeroplanes 1911–1964; British Aircraft Corporation Aeroplanes 1964–1977; British Aerospace Aeroplanes 1977–1988; Sopwith Aeroplanes 1910–1920; Hawker Aeroplanes 1920–1964; Civil Aeroplanes of the World 1945–1990.

Hamish Brown Scottish Photographic

21 Carlin Craig, Kinghorn, Fife KY3 9RX
☎01592 890422

Contact *Hamish M. Brown*

Colour and b&w coverage of most topics and areas of Scotland (sites, historic, buildings, landscape, mountains), also travel and mountains abroad, Ireland and Morocco. Commissions undertaken.

Bubbles Photolibrary

23A Benwell Road, London N7 7BL
☎0171 609 4547   Fax 0171 607 1410

Pregnancy, babies, children, teenagers, general lifestyle, health, old age, medical, still lives of food.

Cable & Wireless Visual Resource

124 Theobalds Road, London WC1X 8RX
☎0171 315 4885   Fax 0171 315 5052

Contact *Philippa Bridge, Claire Nicol*

Telecommunications collection, plus worldwide scenics, street scenes, the Far East, Caribbean, USA and Pacific. Over 30,000 transparencies on 35 mm. Visitors by appointment.

Camera Press

21 Queen Elizabeth Street, London SE1 2PD
☎0171 378 1300   Fax 0171 278 5126

High-quality photofeatures and up-to-date coverage of international events, celebrities, royals, fashion and beauty, and general stock.

Camera Ways Ltd Picture Library

Court View, Stonebridge Green Road, Egerton, Ashford, Kent TN27 9AN
☎01233 756454   Fax 01233 756454

Contacts *Derek, Caryl, Jonathan, Steve*

Founded by award-winning film-maker and photographer, Derek Budd, the library specialises in rural activities and natural history. It contains 35mm and 6x4.5mm, colour and b&w images as well as 16mm film and video footage on Beta SP. Coverage includes: wildlife habitats, flora and fauna of Britain and Europe, traditional country crafts and people, village scenes, landscapes, gardens, coastal and aquatic life, dinosaurs, aerial surveys, storm damage and M.O.D. reserves. A creative service is available from their Technical Artist & Wildlife Illustrator; commissions undertaken in all aspects of commercial multi-media photography, 16mm film, broadcast and corporate video production.

Capital Pictures

54a Clerkenwell Road, London EC1M 5PS
☎0171 253 1122   Fax 0171 253 1414

Contact *Jane Sherwood, Phil Loftus*

300,000 images. Specialises in showbusiness, rock & pop, film & television, politics and royalty.

The Casement Collection

Erin Lodge, Jigs Lane South, Warfield, Berkshire RG12 6DP
☎01344 302067   Fax 01344 303158

Colour and b&w travel library, particularly strong on North America and the Gulf. Not just beaches and palm trees. Based on Jack Casement's collection, with additions by other photographers. Digitised images available.

J. Allan Cash Ltd

74 South Ealing Road, London W5 4QB
☎0181 840 4141   Fax 0181 566 2568

Colour and b&w coverage of travel, natural history, people, space, sport, industry, agriculture and many other subjects. New material regularly contributed by 300 plus photographers.

CEPHAS Picture Library

20 Bedster Gardens, West Molesey, Surrey
KT8 1SZ
☎0181 979 8647   Fax 0181 224 8095

The wine industry and vineyards of the world is the subject on which Cephas has made its reputation. Around 50,000 images, mainly original 6x7 transparencies, make this the most comprehensive and up-to-date archive in Britain. Almost all the wine-producing countries of the world are covered in depth along with all aspects of the industry. CEPHAS also has a rapidly expanding food and drink department and a worldwide travel section which incorporates a major collection on France. Visitors welcome by appointment.

Christel Clear Marine Photography

Roselea, Church Lane, Awbridge,
Near Romsey, Hampshire SO51 0HN
☎01794 341081   Fax 01794 340890

Contact *Nigel Dowden, Christel Dowden*

Over 50,000 images on 35mm and 645 transparency: yachting and boating from Grand Prix sailing to small dinghies, cruising locations and harbours. Recent additions include angling, fly fishing and travel. Visitors by appointment.

Christian Aid Photo Library

PO Box 100, London SE1 7RT
☎0171 620 4444   Fax 0171 620 0719

Pictures from Africa, Asia and Latin America, relating to small-scale, community-based programmes. Mostly development themes: agriculture, health, education, urban and rural life.

Christie's Images

1 Langley Lane, London SW8 1TH
☎0171 582 1282   Fax 0171 582 5638

Contact *Edward Schneider*

130,000 images of fine and decorative art; the largest collection of its kind in the UK.

The Cinema Museum

The Old Fire Station, 46 Renfrew Road,
London SE11 4NA
☎0171 820 9991   Fax 0171 793 0849

Colour and b&w coverage (including stills) of the motion picture industry throughout its history, including the Ronald Grant Archive. Small collections on theatre, variety, television and popular music.

John Cleare/Mountain Camera

Hill Cottage, Fonthill Gifford, Salisbury,
Wiltshire SP3 6QW
☎01747 820320   Fax 01747 820320

Colour and b&w coverage of mountains and wild places, climbing, trekking, expeditions, wilderness travel, landscapes and people from all continents. Geographical features, the Himalaya and the British countryside are specialities. Commissions and consultancy work undertaken in all these fields. Researchers welcome by appointment.

Close-Up Picture Library

14 Burnham Wood, Fareham, Hampshire
PO16 7UD
☎01329 239053

Director *David Stent*

Specialises in the close-up angle of all aspects of life: people, places, animal and bird-life and the environment in general. Also a wide range of pictures covering travel in Europe and the Orient, multicultural, ethnic and educational issues. Photographers with quality material always welcome: no minimum initial submission; 50% commission on 35mm.

Stephanie Colasanti

38 Hillside Court, 409 Finchley Road,
London NW3 6HQ
☎0171 435 3695   Fax 0171 435 9995

Colour coverage of Europe, Africa, Asia, United Arab Emirates, the Caribbean, USA, Australia, New Zealand, the Pacific Islands and South America: people, animals, towns, agriculture, landscapes, carnivals, markets, archaeology, religion and ancient civilisations. Travel assignments undertaken. Medium-format transparencies (2" square).

Michael Cole Camerawork

The Coach House, 27 The Avenue,
Beckenham, Kent BR3 2DP
☎0181 658 6120   Fax 0181 658 6120

Contact *Michael Cole, Derrick Bentley*

Probably the largest and most comprehensive collection of tennis pictures in the world; incorporating the library of Le Roye Productions, a company which covered Wimbledon from 1945–70, and MCC coverage of all major tennis events, worldwide, since 1970. Also small travel picture library: English countryside, Venice, Moscow, US etc. 200,000 35mm colour slides, 3,600 2¼" and 6x7cm colour transparencies, 270,000 b&w negatives and a vast quantity of b&w movie film.

Collections

13 Woodberry Crescent, London N10 1PJ

☎0181 883 0083   Fax 0181 883 9215

Contact *Laura Boswell, Brian Shuel*

250,000 colour and b&w images making a collection of collections about the British Isles. 'Our "area" collections aim to cover Great Britain, Ireland and the many smaller islands eventually – and we are doing well so far.' Subjects include two of Britain's major collections on pregnancy, birth, childhood and education by Anthea Sieveking and Sandra Lousada, the customs of Britain by Brian Shuel, landscapes by Fay Godwin, large collections of castles, waterways, railways, bridges and London, and a large variety of smaller specialities. Also building an unusual collection on the emergency services. Visitors welcome by appointment.

The Complete Picture

Princes House, Elephant Lane, London SE14 4JD

☎0171 237 8660   Fax 0171 237 6860

Contacts *Christina Vaughan, Joanne Stiffell*

Collection of over 100,000 contemporary colour and b&w images. Specialises in people-related images: beauty, lifestyle, health, sports, corporate and family, as well as wildlife, nature, travel, landscapes and industry. Call for free catalogue. No search fees.

COMSTOCK Photolibrary

28 Chelsea Wharf, 15 Lots Road, London SW10 0QQ

☎0171 351 4448   Fax 0171 352 8414

Contact *Helena Kovac*

Extensive coverage of business, people, industry, science, futuristic, world travel, landscapes, medical and natural history. Also desktop photography and CD-ROM. Free catalogue on request. Provides access to over four million images.

Conway Picture Library

See **The Victory Archive**

Sylvia Cordaiy Photo Library

72 East Ham Road, Littlehampton, West Sussex BN17 7BQ

☎01903 715297   Fax 01903 715297

Contact *Sylvia Cordaiy*

Growing collection on all formats, colour and b&w: architecture, world travel, wildlife, global environmental topics, landscapes, cities and rural scenes, veterinary work, the RSPCA at work with both wild and domestic animals, ocean racing. Huge files of card/calendar material and an archive of 17,000 b&w negatives. Visitors welcome.

Country Life Picture Library

King's Reach Tower, Stamford Street, London SE1 9LS

☎0171 261 6337   Fax 0171 261 6216

Contact *Camilla Costello*

Over 150,000 b&w negatives and 15,000 colour transparencies dating back to 1897. Country houses, stately homes, churches and town houses in Britain and abroad, interiors of architectural interest (ceilings, fireplaces, furniture, paintings, sculpture), and exteriors showing many landscaped gardens. Visitors by appointment. Open Tuesday to Friday.

County Visuals

The Design Studio, Professional Services Dept, Kent County Council, Springfield, Maidstone, Kent ME14 2LT

☎01622 696209   Fax 01622 696444

Contact *Tony Hemsted*

Scenes across the county of Kent: attractions, activities, general countryside, villages, coastline and developments such as the Channel Tunnel and high-speed rail link.

Philip Craven Worldwide Photo-Library

Surrey Studios, 21 Nork Way, Nork, Banstead, Surrey SM7 1PB

☎01737 373737   Fax 01737 373737

Contact *Philip Craven*

Extensive coverage of British scenes, cities, villages, English countryside, gardens, historic buildings and wildlife. Worldwide travel and wildlife subjects on medium and large format transparencies.

CTC Picture Library

CTC Publicity, Longfield, Midhurst Road, Fernhurst, Haslemere, Surrey GU27 3HA

☎01428 65500   Fax 01428 641071

Contact *Neil Crighton*

One of the biggest specialist libraries in the UK with 250,000 slides covering world and UK agriculture, horticulture, and environmental subjects. Also a small section on travel.

Sue Cunningham Photographic

56 Chatham Road, Kingston upon Thames, Surrey KT1 3AA

☎0181 541 3024   Fax 0181 541 5388

Extensive specialist collection on Brazil. Expanding coverage of other areas including Peru, Bolivia, Tanzania, Burundi, Zambia, Portugal, Spain, Hungary, Poland, Czech Republic and the UK. Colour and b&w. Member of **BAPLA**.

James Davis Travel Photography
30 Hengistbury Road, New Milton, Hampshire BH25 7LU
☎01425 610328   Fax 01425 638402

Travel collection: people, places, emotive scenes and tourism. Constantly updated by James Davis and a team of photographers, both at home and abroad. Same-day service available.

Douglas Dickins Photo Library
2 Wessex Gardens, Golders Green, London NW11 9RT
☎0181 455 6221

Worldwide colour and b&w coverage, specialising in Asia, particularly India, Indonesia and Japan. Meeting educational requirements on landscape, archaeology, history, religions, customs, people and folklore.

C M Dixon
The Orchard, Marley Lane, Kingston, Canterbury, Kent CT4 6HJ
☎01227 830075   Fax 01227 831135

Colour coverage of ancient civilisations, archaeology and art, ethnology, mythology, world religion, museum objects, geography, geology, meteorology, landscapes, people and places from many countries including most of Europe, former USSR, Ethiopia, Iceland, Jordan, Morocco, Sri Lanka, Tunisia, Turkey, Egypt, Uzbekistan.

Dominic Photography
4B Moore Park Road, London SW6 2JT
☎0171 381 0007   Fax 0171 381 0008
Contact *Zoë Dominic, Catherine Ashmore*

Colour and b&w coverage of the entertainment world from 1957 onwards: dance, opera, theatre, ballet, musicals and personalities.

Philip Dunn Picture Library
Jasmine Cottage, Marston, Church Eaton, Staffordshire ST20 0AS
☎01785 840674/0860 523599
Fax 01785 840674
Contact *Philip Dunn*

Constantly expanding collection of some 50,000 b&w/colour images of travel, people, activities and places in Britain and overseas. Commissions undertaken.

Patrick Eagar Photography
5 Ennerdale Road, Kew Gardens, Surrey TW9 3PG
☎0181 940 9269   Fax 0181 332 1229

Colour and b&w coverage of cricket from 1965. Test matches, overseas tours and all aspects of the sport. Also a constantly expanding wine library (colour) of vineyards, grapes, cellars and winemakers of France, Italy, Germany, Australia, New Zealand, South Africa (and England).

Ecoscene
The Oasts, Headley Lane, Passfield, Liphook, Hampshire GU30 7RX
☎01428 751056   Fax 01428 751057
Contact *Sally Morgan*

Expanding colour library of over 80,000 transparencies specialising in all aspects of the environment: pollution, conservation, recycling, restoration, natural history, habitats, education, landscapes, industry and agriculture. All parts of the globe are covered with specialist collections covering Antarctica, Australia, North America. Sally Morgan, who runs the library, is a professional ecologist and expert source of information on all environmental topics. Photographic and writing commissions undertaken.

Edifice
14 Doughty Street, London WC1N 2PL
☎0171 405 9395   Fax 0171 267 3632
Contact *Philippa Lewis, Gillian Darley*

Colour coverage of architecture, buildings of all possible descriptions, gardens, urban and rural landscape. Specialises in details of ornament, period style and material. British Isles, USA, Africa, Europe and Japan all covered. Detailed list available, visits by appointment.

English Heritage Photographic Library
23 Savile Row, London W1X 1AB
☎0171 973 3338   Fax 0171 973 3001
Contact *Lucy Bunning, Celia Sterne*

Images of English castles, abbeys, houses, gardens, Roman remains, ancient monuments, battlefields, industrial and post-war buildings, interiors, paintings, artifacts.

The Environmental Picture Library Ltd
5 Baker's Row, London EC1R 3DB
☎0171 833 1355   Fax 0171 833 1383
Contacts *Daphne Christelis, Liz Somerville*

Rapidly growing stock of pictures on all environmental issues to illustrate the real problems as well as positive practices from local to global. Now supplying the Greenpeace collection. Colour transparencies and black & white prints.

EPA (European Pressphoto Agency)
See **Popperfoto**

Greg Evans International Photo Library
91 Charlotte Street, London W1P 1LB
☎0171 636 8238 (4 lines) Fax 0171 637 1439
Colour coverage of a wide range of subjects including travel, winter skiing, UK scenery, families, industry, business, sport, abstracts, natural history. Visitors welcome. Commissions undertaken. Colour catalogue available.

Mary Evans Picture Library
59 Tranquil Vale, Blackheath,
London SE3 0BS
☎0181 318 0034   Fax 0181 852 7211
General, international, historical collection from ancient times to recent past. Prints, photographs, periodicals and ephemera. *Special collections* include Sigmund Freud; Psychical Research; Fawcett Library (women's rights); Bruce Castle Museum (London daily life); Ernst Dryden illustration archive; Roger Mayne, Thurston Hopkins & Grace Robertson (1950s and 1960s documentation); Ida Kar & Jeffrey Morgan (portraits); Institution of Civil Engineers: Town & Country Planning; Meledin Collection (Russian history). Holds reciprocal arrangement with Explorer Archives in Paris. Brochure available on request.

Express Newspapers Syndication
Ludgate House, 245 Blackfriars Road, London SE1 9UX
☎0171 922 7902/3/4/5/6 Fax 0171 922 7871
Syndication Manager *Jamie Maskey*
One and a half million images updated daily, with strong collections on personalities, royalty, showbiz, sport, fashion, nostalgia and events. Electronic transmission available.

Eye Ubiquitous
65 Brighton Road, Shoreham, East Sussex BN43 6RE
☎01273 440113   Fax 01273 440116
Contact *Paul Seheult*
General stock specialising in social documentary worldwide, including the work of Tim Page.

Chris Fairclough Colour Library
Studio 65, Smithbrook Kilns, Cranleigh, Surrey GU6 8JJ
☎01483 277992   Fax 01483 267984
Contact *Chris Fairclough, Bridget Sherlock*
General colour library with special collections on religion, education, travel, children, people and places. Commissions undertaken and studio facility.

Falklands Pictorial
Vision House, 16 Broadfield Road, Heeley, Sheffield, South Yorkshire S8 0XJ
☎0114 2589299   Fax 0114 2550113
Colour and b&w photographs showing all aspects of Falklands life from 1880 to the present day.

Famous Pictures and Features
Studio 4, Limehouse Cut, 46 Morris Road, London E14 6NQ
☎0171 537 7055   Fax 0171 537 7056
Approximately 30,000 colour photos of music, film and television celebrities. Pictures date back to 1985 and include party, live concerts and portrait shots.

Farmers Weekly Picture Library
Farmers Weekly, Room L614, Quadrant House, The Quadrant, Sutton, Surrey SM2 5AS
☎0181 652 4914   Fax 0181 652 4005
Library Manager *Barry Dixon*
'Europe's largest agricultural picture library' containing 2.5 million transparencies on all aspects of farming and country life. The collection is constantly updated.

The Fencing Photo Library
30 Crowhurst Mead, Godstone, Surrey RH9 8BF
☎01883 744134   Fax 01883 744134
Contact *Karina Hoskyns, Graham Morrison*
More than 30,000 images covering over 1000 fencers worldwide (b&w up to 1988; colour thereafter), including major international tournaments from 1983, world championships from 1981, and the Seoul and Barcelona Olympic Games.

Ffotograff
10 Kyveilog Street, Pontcanna, Cardiff CF1 9JA
☎01222 236879   Fax 01222 229326
Contact *Patricia Aithie*
Approximately 100,000 images. Specialist sub-

jects include Wales, the Middle and Far East (China, Hong Kong, India, Jordan, Thailand, Taiwan, United Arab Emirates, Yemen, etc), travel, exploration, the arts, foreign cultures, people, architecture and the natural environment. Other countries covered include Australia, Cyprus, Russia, Spain. Commissions undertaken.

Fine Art Photographic Library Ltd
2A Milner Street, London SW3 2PU
☎0171 589 3127   Fax 0171 584 1944

Contact *Linda Hammerbeck, Lyndsey Price*

Over 15,000 large-format transparencies, with a specialist collection of 19th-century paintings.

Fogden Natural History Photos
Mid Cambushinnie Cottage, Kinbuck,
Dunblane, Perthshire FK15 9JU
☎01786 822069   Fax 01786 822069

Contact *Susan Fogden*

Natural history collection, with special reference to rain forests and deserts. Emphasis on quality rather than quantity; growing collection of around 10,000 images.

Food Features
Unit 3P, Leroy House, 436 Essex Road,
London N1 3QP
☎0171 226 8707   Fax 0171 359 4167

Contacts *Steve Moss, Alex Barker*

Specialised high-quality food and drink photography, features and tested recipes. Clients' specific requirements can be incorporated into regular shooting schedules.

Ron & Christine Foord Colour Picture Library
155B City Way, Rochester, Kent ME1 2BE
☎01634 847348   Fax 01634 847348

Specialist library with over 1000 species of British and European wild flowers, plus garden flowers, trees, indoor plants, pests and diseases, mosses, lichen, cacti and the majority of larger British insects.

Forest Life Picture Library
231 Corstorphine Road, Edinburgh EH12 7AT
☎0131 334 0303   Fax 0131 334 4473

Contact *Douglas Green, Donald Peden*

The official image bank of the Forestry Commission with 20,000 countryside images on 35mm colour transparencies. Provides a comprehensive, single source for all aspects of forestry, conservation and recreation.

Werner Forman Archive Ltd
36 Camden Square,
London NW1 9XA
☎0171 267 1034   Fax 0171 267 6026

Colour and b&w coverage of ancient civilisations, the Near and Far East and primitive societies around the world. A number of rare collections. Subject lists available.

Format Partners Photo Library
19 Arlington Way,
London EC1R 1UY
☎0171 833 0292   Fax 0171 833 0381

Contact *Dale Eru*

Social documentary photographic library with worldwide coverage in colour and b&w. Specialisations include women's issues, work, health, education, disability, Asian and Black community, gay issues, housing, homelessness, the elderly and the very young.

Robert Forsythe Picture Library
16 Lime Grove, Prudhoe, Northumberland
NE42 6PR
☎01661 834511

Contact *Robert Forsythe, Fiona Forsythe*

25,000 transparencies of industrial and transport heritage; plus a unique collection of 50,000 items of related publicity ephemera from 1945. Image finding service available. Robert Forsythe is a transport/industrial heritage historian and consultant. Nationwide coverage, particularly strong on Northern Britain. A bibliography of published material is available.

Fortean Picture Library
Henblas, Mwrog Street, Ruthin,
Clwyd LL15 1LG
☎01824 707278   Fax 01824 705324

Contact *Janet Bord*

30,000 colour and 45,000 b&w images: mysteries and strange phenomena worldwide, including ghosts, UFOs, witchcraft and monsters; also antiquities, folklore and mythology. Subject list available.

The Fotomas Index
12 Pickhurst Rise, West Wickham,
Kent BR4 0AL
☎0181 776 2772   Fax 0181 776 2772

Contact *Arthur Allan*

General historical collection, mostly pre-1900. Subjects include London, topography, art, satirical, social and political history.

Galaxy Picture Library

1 Milverton Drive, Ickenham, Uxbridge,
Middlesex UB10 8PP
☎01895 637463   Fax 01895 623277
Contact *Robin Scagell*

Specialises in astronomy, space, telescopes, observatories, the sky, clouds and sunsets. Composites of foregrounds, stars, moon and planets prepared to commission. Editorial service available.

Garden and Wildlife Matters Photo Library

'Marlham', Henley's Down, Battle,
East Sussex TN33 9BN
☎01424 830566   Fax 01424 830224
Contact *Dr John Feltwell*

Collection of 80,000 6x4 and 35mm images. General gardening techniques and design; cottage gardens and USA designer gardens. Flowers, wild and house plants, trees and crops. Environmental, ecological and conservation pictures, including sea, air, noise and freshwater pollution and Eastern Europe. Recycling in all its forms, agriculture, forestry, horticulture and oblique aerial habitat shots from Europe, USA and SE Asian rainforests.

The Garden Picture Library

Unit 30, Ransome's Dock, 35 Parkgate Road,
London SW11 4NP
☎0171 228 4332   Fax 0171 924 3267
Contact *Sally Wood*

Original colour transparencies featuring inspirational images of gardens, plants, outdoor living, people in the garden, swimming pools, conservatories, patios, indoor planting, water features, decorative details, landscapes and seasonal aspects on 35mm and medium formats. Special collections include al fresco food and the still life photography of Linda Burgess. In-house picture research can be undertaken on request and visitors are welcome by appointment. Promotional literature available on request.

Leslie Garland Picture Library

69 Fern Avenue, Jesmond, Newcastle upon
Tyne, Tyne & Wear NE2 2QU
☎0191 281 3442   Fax 0191 281 3442
Contact *Leslie Garland, ABIPP, ARPS*

The only general picture library between Leeds and Edinburgh, it contains images from North Yorkshire to the Scottish border, and from the North Sea to the Irish Sea. As well as covering the major cities, sights and scenes, the library also stocks images of an applied science, engineering and industrial nature. There is also a growing collection on Norway. Much of the work is on medium format. Brochure available on request. Qualified photographers available for commissioned work.

Ed Geldard Picture Collection

7 Ellergreen House, Nr Burnside, Kendal,
Cumbria LA9 5SD
☎01539 728609
Contact *Ed Geldard*

Approximately 10,000 colour transparencies and b&w negs, all by Ed Geldard, specialising in mountain landscapes: particularly the mountain regions of the Lake District; and the Yorkshire limestone areas, from valley to summit. Commissions undertaken. Books published: *Wainwright's Tour of the Lake District* and *Wainwright in the Limestone Dales*.

Genesis Space Photo Library

Peppercombe Lodge, Horns Cross, Devon
EX39 5DH
☎01237 451 756   Fax 01237 451 600
Contact *Tim Furniss*

Contemporary and historical colour and b&w spaceflight collection including rockets, spacecraft, spacemen, Earth, moon and planets. Stock list available on request.

Geo Aerial Photography

4 Christian Fields, London SW16 3JZ
☎0181 764 6292
Fax 0181 764 6292/0115 9815474
Contact *Kelly White*

Established 1990 and now a growing collection of aerial oblique photographs from the UK, Scandinavia and Asia – landscapes, buildings, industrial sites etc. Commissions undertaken.

Geonex UK Ltd

See **NRSC – Air Photo Group**

GeoScience Features

6 Orchard Drive, Wye, Kent TN25 5AU
☎01233 812707   Fax 01233 812707
Fully computerised and comprehensive library containing the world's principal source of volcanic phenomena. Extensive collections, providing scientific detail with technical quality, of rocks, minerals, fossils, microsections of botanical and animal tissues, animals, biology, birds, botany, chemistry, earth science, ecology,

environment, geology, geography, habitats, landscapes, macro/microbiology, peoples, sky, weather, wildlife and zoology. Over 220,000 original colour transparencies in medium- and 35 mm-format. Subject lists available on application.

Geoslides Photography
4 Christian Fields, London SW16 3JZ
☎0181 764 6292   Fax 0181 764 6292
Contact *John Douglas*

Established in 1968. Specialist collections of geographical images: British India (the Raj) and Boer War. Also landscape and human interest subjects from the Arctic, Antarctica, Scandinavia, UK, Africa (south of Sahara), Middle East, Asia (south and southeast); also Australia, via Blackwoods Picture Library.

Glamour International
16 Broadfield Road, Sheffield, South Yorkshire S8 0XJ
☎0114 2589299   Fax 0114 2550113
Contact *Dave Muscroft, Scott Ward*

The UK's only specialist glamour library: dressed glamour, head shots, boy-girl, beauty, lifestyle and Page 3 models.

Martin and Dorothy Grace
40 Clipstone Avenue, Mapperley, Nottingham NG3 5JZ
☎0115 9208248   Fax 0115 9626802

Colour coverage of Britain's natural history, specialising in trees, shrubs and wild flowers. Also birds and butterflies, habitats, landscapes, ecology. Subject lists available. Member of **BAPLA**.

Ronald Grant Archive
See **The Cinema Museum**

Greater London Photograph Library
Greater London Record Office & History Library, 40 Northampton Road, London EC1R 0HB
☎0171 332 3823   Fax 0171 833 9136
Contact *The Photograph Librarian*

A large collection on London, mostly topographical and architectural. Subjects include education, local authority housing, transport, the Thames, parks, churches, hospitals, war damage, pubs, theatres and cinemas. Also major redevelopments like the South Bank, The City, Covent Garden and Docklands.

Sally and Richard Greenhill
357A Liverpool Road, London N1 1NL
☎0171 607 8549   Fax 0171 607 7151

Colour and b&w photos of a social documentary nature: child development, pregnancy and birth, education and urban scenes in London and Northern England. Also Modern China 1971–89, Hong Kong, USA, longhouse life in Sarawak, and other material from around the world.

Greenpeace Communications
See **Environmental Picture Library**

V. K. Guy Ltd
Silver Birches, Troutbeck, Windermere, Cumbria LA23 1PN
☎015394 33519   Fax 015394 32971
Contact *Vic Guy, Pauline Guy, Mike Guy, Paul Guy, Nicola Guy*

British landscapes and architectural heritage. 20,000 5x4in transparencies, suitable for tourism brochures. Colour catalogue available.

Tom Hanley
61 Stephendale Road, London SW6 2LT
☎0171 731 3525   Fax 0171 731 3525

Colour and b&w coverage of London, England, Europe, Canada, India, the Philippines, Brazil, China, Japan, Korea, Taiwan, the Seychelles, Cayman Islands, USA. Also pop artists of the 60s, First World War trenches, removal of London Bridge to America, and much more. Current preoccupation with Greece, Turkey, Spain and Egypt, ancient and modern.

Robert Harding Picture Library
58–59 Great Marlborough Street, London W1V 1DD
☎0171 287 5414   Fax 0171 631 1070

Two million colour images covering wide range of subjects – people, beauty, art, architecture, cities, computer graphics, fashion, landscapes, lifestyle, space, sport, technology and travel. Many specialist collections, including: Tutankhamun, Chinese Exhibition, Beauty Bank, FPG B/W Historical Selects. Syndication of 25 titles from IPC Magazines, BBC Magazines and Burda Group.

Harpur Garden Library
44 Roxwell Road, Chelmsford, Essex CM1 2NB
☎01245 257527   Fax 01245 344101
Contact *Jerry and Marcus Harpur*

Jerry Harpur's personal collection of gardens in Britain, France, Australia, South Africa, the US,

Morocco and Japan (35mm and 6x7, colour). Inspired partly by contemporary designers and horticulturalists but also includes historic gardens: formal gardens, front and back gardens, plant associations, gardens in all four seasons, garden containers, fences, hedges, herbs, hillsides, seaside, lawns, paths, paving, rock, arbours, scented, fruit and vegetables, ornaments, water and integrated gardens.

Jim Henderson AMPA Photographer

Crooktree, Kincardine O'Neil, Aboyne, Aberdeenshire AB34 4JD
☎01339 882149   Fax 01339 882149
Contact *Jim Henderson, AMPA*

Scenic and general activity coverage of the North-east Scotland-Grampian region for tourist, holiday and activity illustration. Specialist collection of over 100 Aurora Borealis displays from 1989–1995 in Grampian. Large collection of recent images of Egypt: Cairo through to Abu-Simbel. Commissions undertaken.

Heritage and Natural History Photographic Library

37 Plainwood Close, Summersdale, Chichester, West Sussex PO19 4YB
☎01243 533822
Contact *Dr John B. Free*

Specialises in insects (particularly bees and beekeeping), tropical and temperate agriculture and crops, archaeology and history worldwide.

John Heseltine Picture Library

44 Nailsworth Mills, Nailsworth, Gloucestershire GL6 0BS
☎01453 835792   Fax 01453 835792
Contact *John Heseltine*

90,000 colour transparencies of landscapes, food and travel.

Hobbs Golf Collection

5 Winston Way, New Ridley, Stocksfield, Northumberland NE43 7RF
☎01661 842933   Fax 01661 842933
Contact *Michael Hobbs*

Specialist golf collection: players, courses, art, memorabilia and historical topics (1300–present). Commissions undertaken.

David Hoffman Photo Library

21 Norman Grove, London E3 5EG
☎0181 981 5041   Fax 0181 980 2041
Contact *David Hoffman*

Social documentary library covering drugs, policing, disorder, strikes, racism, homelessness, protest and related social issues. Colour and b&w images since the late 1970s, with recent pictures on ecology, environmental and pollution issues. Also a range of specialist files covering subjects from cycling to local authority services.

Holt Studios International Ltd

The Courtyard, 24 High Street, Hungerford, Berkshire RG17 0NF
☎01488 683523   Fax 01488 683511
Commercial Director *Andy Morant*

World agriculture and horticulture both from a pictorial and a technical point of view. Commissions undertaken worldwide.

Kit Houghton Photography

Radlet Cottage, Spaxton, Bridgwater, Somerset TA5 1DE
☎01278 671362   Fax 01278 671739
Contact *Kit Houghton, Debbie Cook*

Specialist equestrian library of 100,000 colour transparencies/negatives and b&w material. All aspects of the horse world from competitive to instructional.

Chris Howes/ Wild Places Photography

51 Timbers Square, Roath, Cardiff CF2 3SH
☎01222 486557   Fax 01222 486557
Contact *Chris Howes, Judith Calford*

Expanding collection of over 50,000 colour transparencies and b&w prints covering travel, topography and natural history worldwide, plus action sports such as climbing. Specialist areas include caves, caving and mines (with historical coverage using engravings and early photographs), wildlife and the environment, including pollution and conservation. Europe (including Britain), USA, Africa and Australia are all well represented within the collection.

The Hulton Deutsch Collection

Unique House, 21–31 Woodfield Road, London W9 2BA
☎0171 266 2662   Fax 0171 289 6392

The Hulton Deutsch Collection, the largest picture resource in Europe, holds over 15 million images from ancient history through the early years of photography up to present day. News events, sport, royalty, war, social history, people and places – photos, lithographs, etchings, engravings, woodcuts. A unique source of visual and reference material which includes the Keystone, Three Lions, Fox Photos and Central Press collections. Manages Mirror Syndication International and represents Reuter News Picture Service. Also publishes material on CD-ROM (both Windows and Macintosh). Catalogue available.

The Robert Hunt Library

2nd Floor, 19 Phipp Street,
London EC2A 4NP
☎0171 739 3536   Fax 0171 729 5188

Colour and b&w coverage of warfare, arts, film stars, animals, sport, crime, disasters and royalty (British, European, Middle Eastern, Asian and tribal). Visitors welcome. Subject list available.

Jacqui Hurst

66 Richford Street, Hammersmith,
London W6 7HP
☎0181 743 2315/0860 563484
Fax 0181 743 2315

Contact *Jacqui Hurst*

Approximately 6000 colour transparencies of British gardens and plant portraits, regional foods and crafts, and India. Fish-smokers, mussel gatherers, millers and bakers, chocolatiers, markets, fruit picking, salmon netting, farmhouse cheeses, soft cheeses, goats and ewes cheese, cheese shops, woven fabrics, smocking and quilting, paper crafts, pottery, thatching, blockmaking and printing, rugmaking, tie & dye, screen printing, Rajasthan villages, sarees, Indian wall painting, camel fairs, markets, and much more.

The Hutchison Library

118B Holland Park Avenue,
London W11 4UA
☎0171 229 2743 (3 lines)
Fax 0171 792 0259

Colour and b&w worldwide coverage of agriculture, architecture, industry, landscape, transport, ecology, energy, environment, families, festivals, human relationships, pregnancy, birth, leisure, modern life, peoples and religions, technology, lifestyles, travel, urban and country life, weather, wildlife. Collections include: Durrell-McKenna (birth, babies and human relationships); Disappearing World (ethnic minorities); Puttkamer (Amazon Indians); Long Search (world religions); Felix Greene (China, North Vietnam, Tibet); Tribal Eye; Shogun Experience; Spirit of Asia; New Pacific.

Illustrated London News Picture Library

20 Upper Ground, London SE1 9PF
☎0171 928 2111 ext. 4141/2
Fax 0171 928 8144

Engravings, photographs and illustrations from 1842 to the present day, taken from magazines published by Illustrated Newspapers: *Illustrated London News; Graphic; Sphere; Tatler; Sketch; Illustrated Sporting and Dramatic News; Illustrated War News 1914–18; Bystander; Britannia & Eve.* Social history, London, Industrial Revolution, wars, travel. Brochure available. Visitors by appointment.

The Image Bank

17 Conway Street, London W1P 6EE
☎0171 312 0300   Fax 0171 391 9111

4 Jordan Street, Manchester M15 4PX.
☎0161 236 9226 Fax 0161 236 8723.

And: 14 Alva Street, Edinburgh EH2 4QG
☎0131 225 1770 Fax 0131 225 1660.

Contact, London *Paul Walker*
Contact, Manchester *Rowan Sykes*
Contact, Edinburgh *Roddy McRae*

Stock photography, illustration and film footage. Over 20 million constantly updated images from 450 photographers and 337 illustrators. Free catalogue available. Creative advertising, editorial and corporate commissions undertaken. For magazines, partworks and books, contact the publishing department. Visitors welcome.

Image Resource Ltd

Heritage House, Wreakes Lane, Dronfield,
Sheffield S18 6PN
☎01246 290966   Fax 01246 290959

Contact *Barry Marshall*

CD-ROM publisher of images from specialist archive sources.

Image Select/Ann Ronan Picture Library

Kebbell House, Delta Gain, Carpenders Park,
Watford, Hertfordshire WD1 5BE
☎0181 421 3131   Fax 0181 421 3896

Astronomy, economic history, *Illustrated London News* 1844 – 1901, music, personalities, politics, *Punch* 1848 – 1928, rail, royalty, science, society, space, technology, war, and world history.

Images Colour Library

15/17 High Court Lane, The Calls, Leeds,
West Yorkshire LS2 7EU
☎0113 2433389   Fax 0113 2425605

12–14 Argyll Street, London W1V 1AB
☎0171 734 7344   Fax 0171 287 3933

A general contemporary library specialising in
top-quality advertising, editorial and travel
photography. Catalogues available. Visitors
welcome. See also **Landscape Only**.

Images of Africa Photobank

11 The Windings, Lichfield, Staffordshire
WS13 7EX
☎01543 262898   Fax 01543 417154

Contact *David Keith Jones, ABIPP, FRPS*

Over 120,000 images covering eleven African
countries: Botswana, Egypt, Ethiopia, Kenya,
Rwanda, South Africa, Tanzania, Uganda,
Zaire, Zambia and Zimbabwe. 'Probably the
best collection of photographs of Kenya in
Europe.' Very strong on African wildlife with
over 80 species of mammals including many
sequences showing action and behaviour.
Popular animals like lions and elephants are covered in encyclopedic detail. Over 100 species of
birds and many reptiles are included. Other
strengths include National Parks & Reserves,
natural beauty, tourism facilities, tradition and
modern people. Most work is by David Keith
Jones, ABIPP, FRPS; several other photographers are represented. Colour brochure available.

Imagetransfer/The Archive

Suite 212, Business Design Centre, Islington
Green, London N1 0QH
☎0171 288 6080   Fax 0171 288 6094

Extensive worldwide coverage of many subjects. One of the world's largest collections of
pictures of England.

Imperial War Museum Department of Photographs

Lambeth Road, London SE1 6HZ
☎0171 416 5333   Fax 0171 416 5379

A national archive of photographs of war in
this century. Mostly the two world wars but
also other conflicts involving Britain and the
Commonwealth. Mostly b&w. Visitors welcome. Appointments preferred.

International Photobank

Loscombe Barn Farmhouse, West Knighton,
Dorchester, Dorset DT2 8LS
☎01305 854145   Fax 01305 853065

Over 275,000 transparencies, mostly medium-
format, colour coverage of travel subjects: places,
people, folklore, events. Assignments undertaken
for guide books/brochure photography.

Joel Photographic Library

Unit 105, Blackfriars Foundry Annexe,
65 Glasshill Street, London SE1 0QR
☎0171 721 7274   Fax 0171 721 7276

Contact *Patrick Skinner, Emma Aylett*

90,000 images of travel, people, situations, skies
and general. Commissions undertaken worldwide.

Trevor Jones Thoroughbred Photography

The Hornbeams, 2 The Street, Worlington,
Suffolk IP28 8RU
☎01638 713944   Fax 01638 713945

Contact *Trevor Jones, Gillian Jones*

Extensive library of high-quality colour transparencies depicting all aspects of thoroughbred
horse racing dating from 1987. Major group
races, English classics, studs, stallions, mares and
foals, early morning scenes, personalities, jock-
eys, trainers and prominent owners. Also international work: USA Breeders Cup, Arc de
Triomphe, French Classics; and more unusual
scenes such as racing on the sands at low tide,
Ireland, and on the frozen lake at St Moritz.
Visitors by appointment.

The Keystone Collection

See **Hulton Deutsch Collection**

David King Collection

90 St Pauls Road, London N1 2QP
☎0171 226 0149   Fax 0171 354 8264

Contact *David King*

250,000 b&w original and copy photographs and
colour transparencies of historical and present-
day images. Russian history and the Soviet
Union from 1900 to the fall of Khrushchev; the
lives of Lenin, Trotsky and Stalin; the Tzars,
Russo-Japanese War, 1917 Revolution, World
War I, Red Army, Great Patriotic War etc.
Special collections on China, Eastern Europe,
the Weimar Republic, American labour strug-
gles, Spanish Civil War. Open to qualified researchers by appointment, Monday to Friday,
10–6. Staff will undertake research; negotiable
fee for long projects.

The Kobal Collection

4th Floor, 184 Drummond Street, London
NW1 3HP
☎0171 383 0011   Fax 0171 383 0044

Colour and b&w coverage of Hollywood films: portraits, stills, publicity shots, posters, ephemera. Visitors by appointment.

Kodak Motoring Picture Library
National Motor Museum, Beaulieu,
Hampshire SO42 7ZN
☎01590 612345   Fax 01590 612655
Contact *Lynda Springate, Jonathan Day*

A quarter of a million b&w images, plus 50,000 colour transparencies covering all forms of motoring history from the 1880s to the present day. Commissions undertaken. Own studio.

Kos Picture Source Ltd
The Glider Centre, Bishop's Waltham,
Hampshire SO32 1BA
☎01489 896311   Fax 01489 892416
Managing Director *Lizzie Green*

Worldwide marine subjects from yachting to seascapes. Constantly updated, covering all aspects of water-based subjects.

Landscape Only
12–14 Argyll Street, London W1V 1AB
☎0171 734 7344   Fax 0171 287 3933

Premier landscape collection, featuring the work of top photographers Charlie Waite, Nick Meers, Joe Cornish and many others. Colour brochure available.

Frank Lane Picture Agency Ltd
Pages Green House, Wetheringsett,
Stowmarket, Suffolk IP14 5QA
☎01728 860789   Fax 01728 860222

Colour and b&w coverage of natural history and weather. Represents Silvestris Fotoservice, Germany, and works closely with Eric and David Hosking, plus 200 freelance photographers.

André Laubier Picture Library
4 St James Park, Bath, Avon BA1 2SS
☎01225 420688

An extensive library of photographs from 1935 to the present day in 35 mm and medium format. Main subjects are: archaeology and architecture; art and artists (wood carving, sculptures, contemporary glass); botany; historical buildings, sites and events; landscapes; nature; leisure sports; events; experimental artwork and photography; people; and travel. Substantial stock of many other subjects including: birds, buildings and cities, folklore, food and drink, gardens, transport. Special collection *Images*

d'Europe (Austria, Britain, France, Greece, Italy, Spain, Turkey and former Yugoslavia). Private collection: World War II to D-Day. List available on request. Photo assignments, artwork, design, and line drawings undertaken. Visitors by appointment only. Correspondence welcome in English, French or German.

The Erich Lessing Archive of Fine Art & Culture
c/o AKG London Ltd, Arts and History Picture Library, 10 Plato Place,
72–74 St Dionis Road, London SW6 4TU
☎0171 610 6103   Fax 0171 610 6125

Computerised archive of large-format transparencies depicting the contents of many of the world's finest art galleries as well as ancient archaeological and biblical sites. Over 70,000 pictures can be viewed on microfiche. Represented by AKG London Ltd.

Link Picture Library
33 Greyhound Road, London W6 8NH
☎0171 381 2261/2433   Fax 0171 385 6244
Contacts *Orde Eliason, Ivan Coleman*

20,000 images of South Africa, India, Vietnam; also international musicians. Link Picture Library has an international network and can source material not in its file from Japan, USA, Holland, Scandinavia, Germany and South Africa. Original photographic commissions also undertaken.

London Aerial Photo Library
PO Box 25, Ashwellthorpe, Norwich,
Norfolk NR16 1HL
☎01508 488320   Fax 01508 488282
Contact *Sandy Stockwell*

56,000 colour negatives of aerial photographs covering most of Britain, with particular emphasis on London and surrounding counties. No search fee. Photocopies of library prints are supplied free of charge to enquirers. Welcome enquiries in respect of either general subjects or specific sites and buildings.

The Ludvigsen Library Limited
73 Collier Street, London N1 3LS
☎0171 837 1700   Fax 0171 837 1776
Contact *Christine Lalla*

Approximately 250,000 images (chiefly b&w with some colour transparencies) of automobiles and motorsport, mainly dating from the 1950s. Glass plate negatives from the early 1900s; Formula One, Le Mans, motor car shows, vintage, antique and classic cars from all countries. Includes the Dalton-Watson Collection and noted photographers such as Max le Grand and Rodolfo Mailander. Extensive research facilities.

Lupe Cunha Photos
19 Ashfields Parade, London N14 5EH
☎0181 882 6441   Fax 0181 882 6303

Children, health, pregnancy and general women's interest. Also special collection on Brazil. Commissions undertaken.

MacQuitty International Photographic Collection
7 Elm Lodge, River Gardens, Stevenage Road, London SW6 6NZ
☎0171 385 6031/384 1781
Fax 0171 384 1781

Contact *Dr Miranda MacQuitty*

Colour and b&w collection on aspects of life in over 70 countries: dancing, music, religion, death, archaeology, buildings, transport, food, drink, nature. Visitors by appointment.

Magnum Photos Ltd
Moreland Buildings, 2nd Floor, 5 Old Street, London EC1V 9HL
☎0171 490 1771   Fax 0171 608 0020

Head of Library *Heather Vickers*

FOUNDED 1947 by Cartier Bresson, George Rodger, Robert Capa and David 'Chim' Seymour. Represents over 50 of the world's leading photo-journalists. Coverage of all major world events from the Spanish Civil War to present day. Also a large collection of personalities.

The Raymond Mander & Joe Mitchenson Theatre Collection
The Mansion, Beckenham Place Park, Beckenham, Kent BR3 2BP
☎0181 658 7725   Fax 0181 663 0313

Contact *Richard Mangan*

Enormous collection covering all aspects of the theatre: plays, actors, dramatists, music hall, theatres, singers, composers, etc. Visitors welcome by appointment.

The Martin Library
45 Stainforth Road, Newbury Park, Ilford, Essex IG2 7EL
☎0181 590 4144/518 0961
Fax 0181 518 0961

Wildlife, travel, environment and general stock library.

S & O Mathews Photography
Stitches Farm House, Eridge, East Sussex TN3 9JB
☎01892 852848   Fax 01892 853314

Landscapes, gardens and flowers.

MC Picture Library
119 Wardour Street, London W1V 3TD
☎0171 734 6710   Fax 0171 494 1839

Contact *Julia Cooper*

Leisure-related subjects – cookery, gardening, needlecraft, antiques, health and sex. Related text is often available.

Institution of Mechanical Engineers
1 Birdcage Walk, London SW1H 9JJ
☎0171 973 1289   Fax 0171 222 4557

Contact *Public Affairs Department*

800 contemporary images on mechanical engineering can be borrowed free of charge.

Lee Miller Archives
Burgh Hill House, Chiddingly, Near Lewes, East Sussex BN8 6JF
☎01825 872691   Fax 01825 872733

The work of Lee Miller (1907–77). As a writer she covered the war in Europe from early in 1944 to VE Day with further reporting from the Balkans. Collection includes photographic portraits of prominent Surrealist artists: Ernst, Eluard, Miró, Picasso, Penrose, Carrington, Tanning, and others. Surrealist and contemporary art, poets and writers, fashion, the Middle East, Egypt, the Balkans in the 1930s, London during the Blitz, war in Europe and the liberation of Dachau and Buchenwald.

Mirror Syndication International
Unique House, 21-31 Woodfield Road, London W9 2BA
☎0171 266 1133   Fax 0171 266 2563

Head of Operations *Alastair Fuad-Luke*

Major photo library specialising in current affairs, personalities, royalty, sport, pop and glamour. Extensive British and world travel pictures, including the British Tourist Authority collection. Specialist film archive, the Picture Goer. Agents for Mirror Group Newspapers. Syndicator of photos and text for news/features. Managed by the **Hulton Deutsch Collection Limited**.

Monitor Syndication

17 Old Street, London EC1V 9HL
☎0171 253 7071   Fax 0171 250 0966

Colour and b&w coverage of leading international personalities. Politics, entertainment, royals, judicial, commerce, religion, trade unions, well-known buildings. Syndication to international, national and local media.

Moroccan Scapes

Seend Park, Seend, Wiltshire SN12 6NZ
☎01380 828533   Fax 01380 828630

Contact *Chris Lawrence*

Specialist collection of Moroccan and Greek material: scenery, towns, people, markets and places, plus the Atlas Mountains. Over 16,000 images.

James H. Morris Picture Library

4 Mozart Street, London W10 4LA
☎0181 969 9481   Fax 0181 964 8440

Contacts *J.H. Morris, G. Gaetani*

50,000 images of architecture, travel, human issues, environment from Europe, Asia and Africa.

Motoring Picture Library

National Motor Museum, Trust Centre,
Beaulieu, Hampshire SO42 7ZN
☎01590 612345   Fax 01590 612655

Contacts *Mrs Lynda Springate, Jonathan Day*

Half-a-million b&w photographs and 60,000 transparencies on all aspects of motoring from the 1890s to the present day. The collection includes cars commercial and motorcycles.

Mountain Camera

See **John Cleare**

Moving Image Research & Library Services

91–101 Oxford Street, London W1R 1RA
☎0171 437 5688   Fax 0171 437 5649

Contact *Liz Fay*

Includes TV-AM library, 'Fun in the Sun' holiday locations from all over the world. Extensive Fleet Street at work material.

Museum of Antiquities Picture Library

University and Society of Antiquaries of Newcastle upon Tyne, Newcastle upon Tyne NE1 7RU
☎0191 222 7846   Fax 0191 261 1182

Contact *Lindsay Allason-Jones*

25,000 images, mostly b&w, of special collections including: Hadrian's Wall Archive (b&ws taken over the last 100 years); Gertrude Bell Archive (during her travels in the Near East, 1900–26); and aerial photographs of archaeological sites in the North of England. Visitors welcome by appointment.

Museum of London Picture Library

London Wall, London EC2Y 5HN
☎0171 600 3699 ext. 254 Fax 0171 600 1058

Contact *Gavin Morgan*

Comprehensive coverage of the history and archaeology of London represented in paintings, photographs and historic artefacts. Special files include Roman and medieval archaeology, costume, Suffragettes and Port of London.

National Galleries of Scotland Picture Library

National Galleries of Scotland, Belford Road, Edinburgh EH4 3DR
☎0131 556 8921, ext 319 Fax 0131 315 2963

Contacts *Deborah Hunter, Katharine May*

Over 30,000 b&w and several thousand images in colour of works of art from the Renaissance to present day. Specialist subjects cover fine art (painting, sculpture, drawing), portraits, Scottish, historical, still life, photography and landscape. Colour leaflet, scale of charges and application forms available on request.

National Maritime Museum Picture Library

Greenwich, London SE10 9NF
☎0181 312 6631   Fax 0181 312 6632

Manager *Chris Gray*

Over 3 million maritime-related images and artefacts, including oil paintings from the 16th century to present day, prints and drawings, historic photographs, plans of ships built in the UK since the beginning of the 18th Century, models, rare maps and charts, instruments, etc. Over 50,000 items within the collection are now photographed and with the Historic Photographs Collection form the basis of the picture library's stock.

National Medical Slide Bank

Wellcome Centre Medical Photo Library, 210 Euston Road, London NW1 2BE
☎0171 611 8746   Fax 0171 611 8577

Contact *Julie Dorrington*

Specialist section of the **Wellcome Centre**

Medical Photographic Library, it comprises 15,000 slides covering clinical and general medicine with associated pathology and medical imaging. 12,000 images on videodisc.

National Monuments Record
National Monuments Record Centre,
Kemble Drive, Swindon, Wiltshire SN2 2GZ
☎01793 414600   Fax 01793 414606
The National Monuments Record is the first stop for photographs of the built environment of England. Over 6.5 million photographs are held in three main collections. English architecture from the first days of photography to the present, air photographs covering every inch of England from the first days of flying to the present and key archaeological sites. The London office specialises in the architecture of the capital city – for more information phone 0171 208 8200.

National Portrait Gallery Picture Library
St Martin's Place, London WC2H 0HE
☎0171 306 0055   Fax 0171 306 0056/0092
Contact *Shruti Patel*
Over 700,000 images – portraits of famous British men and women dating from medieval times to the present day. Various formats/media.

National Railway Museum Picture Library
Leeman Road, York, North Yorkshire YO2 4XJ
☎01904 621261   Fax 01904 611112
1.5 million images, mainly b&w, covering every aspect of railways from 1866 to the present day. Visitors by appointment.

The National Trust Photographic Library
36 Queen Anne's Gate, London SW1H 9AS
☎0171 222 9251   Fax 0171 222 5097
Contact *Gayle Mault*
Collection of mixed format transparencies covering landscape and coastline throughout England, Wales and Northern Ireland; also architecture, interiors, gardens, painting and conservation. Brochure available on request. Profits from the picture library are reinvested in continuing the work of the Trust.

Natural History Museum Picture Library
Cromwell Road, London SW7 5BD
☎0171 938 9122/9035   Fax 0171 938 9169
Contact *Martin Pulsford, Lodvina Mascarenhas*
12,000 large-format transparencies on natural history and related subjects: extinct animals, dinosaurs, fossils, anthropology, minerals, gemstones, fauna and flora. Commissions of museum specimens undertaken.

Natural History Photographic Agency
See **NHPA (Natural History Photographic Agency)**

Natural Science Photos
33 Woodland Drive, Watford, Hertfordshire WD1 3BY
☎01923 245265   Fax 01923 246067
Colour coverage of natural history subjects worldwide. The work of some 100 photographers, it includes animals, birds, reptiles, amphibia, fish, insects and other invertebrates, habitats, plants, fungi, geography, weather, scenics, horticulture, agriculture, farm animals and registered dog breeds. Researched by experienced scientists Peter and Sondra Ward. Visits by appointment. Commissions undertaken.

Nature Photographers Ltd
West Wit, New Road, Little London,
Basingstoke, Hampshire RG26 5EU
☎01256 850661   Fax 01256 851157
Contact *Dr Paul Sterry*
Over 150,000 images on worldwide natural history and environmental subjects. The library is run by a trained biologist and experienced author on his subject.

Peter Newark's Pictures
3 Barton Buildings, Queen Square, Bath,
Avon BA1 2JR
☎01225 334213   Fax 01225 334213
Over 1 million images covering world history from ancient times to the present day. Incorporates two special collections: American history in general with strong Wild West collection; and the military collection: military/naval personalities and events. Subject list available. Visitors welcome by appointment.

NHPA (Natural History Photographic Agency)

Little Tye, 57 High Street, Ardingly,
West Sussex RH17 6TB
☎01444 892514   Fax 01444 892168
Library Manager *Tim Harris*

High-quality colour and b&w coverage of natural history worldwide. Specialist files include: Bushman culture; high-speed subjects (flying and leaping creatures, splashes, explosions, etc.); extensive files on African and North/South American wildlife; the ANT collection of Australasian subjects. Loans are generally made direct to publishers; individual writers must request material via their publisher.

The Northern Picture Library

Greenheys Business Centre, 10 Pencroft Way,
Manchester M15 6JJ
☎0161 226 2007   Fax 0161 226 2022

Wide selection of subjects from the UK and abroad. Mostly colour, some b&w. Industry, business, sport, farming, scenic, personalities, jazz musicians (and some classical), space, and many more. Special collection on the North West of England. Commissions undertaken.

NRSC – Air Photo Group

Arthur Street, Barwell, Leicestershire
LE9 8GZ
☎01455 844513   Fax 01455 841785

Leading supplier of colour aerial photography in the UK. Commissions undertaken.

Observer Colour Library

PO Box 33, Edenbridge, Kent TN8 5PB
☎01342 850313   Fax 01342 850244

Half a million pictures from the *Observer* magazine, from 1962 to end 1992.

Only Horses Picture Agency

27 Greenway Gardens, Greenford, Middlesex
UB6 9AF
☎0181 578 9047   Fax 0181 575 7531

Colour and b&w coverage of all aspects of the horse. Foaling, retirement, racing, show jumping, eventing, veterinary, polo, breeds, personalities.

George Outram Picture Library

195 Albion Street, Glasgow G1 1QP
☎0141 552 6255   Fax 0141 553 3587

Over 6 million images: b&w and colour photographs from *c*.1900 from the *Herald* (Glasgow) and *Evening Times*. Current affairs, Scotland, Glasgow, Clydeside shipbuilding and engineering, personalities, World Wars I and II, sport.

Oxford Picture Library

1 North Hinksey Village,
Oxford OX2 0NA
☎01865 723404   Fax 01865 725294
Contact *Annabel Webb, Chris Andrews*

Specialist collection on Oxford: the city, university and colleges, events, people, spires and shires; also the Cotswolds, architecture and landscape from Stratford-upon-Avon down to Bath; the Chilterns and Henley on Thames, with aerial views of all of the above; plus Channel Islands, especially Guernsey and Sark. General collection includes wildlife, trees, plants, clouds, sun, sky and water. Commissions undertaken.

Oxford Scientific Films Photo Library

Long Hanborough, Witney, Oxfordshire
OX8 8LL
☎01993 881881   Fax 01993 882808
Contact *Sandra Berry, Photo Library Manager*

Natural history subjects photographed by 250 photographers worldwide: animals, plants, histology, embryology, landscapes, conservation, pollution, high speed and time lapse. Commissions undertaken. Visits by appointment. Recently merged with the Survival Anglia Photo Library.

Hugh Palmer

Knapp House, Shenington, Near Banbury,
Oxfordshire OX15 6NE
☎01295 670433   Fax 01295 670709

Extensive coverage of gardens from Britain and Europe, stately homes, conservatories and garden buildings. Medium-format transparencies from numerous specialist commissions for books and magazines.

Panos Pictures

9 White Lion Street, London N1 9PD
☎0171 837 7505/0171 278 1111
Fax 0171 278 0345

Documentary colour and b&w library specialising in Third World and Eastern Europe, with emphasis on environment and development issues. Leaflet available. All profits from this library go to the Panos Institute to further its work in international sustainable development.

Papilio Natural History Library
44 Palestine Grove, Merton,
London SW19 2QN
☎0181 687 2202   Fax 0181 687 2202
Contact *Robert Pickett, Justine Bowler, Michele Murray*

20,000 colour transparencies of natural history, including birds, animals, insects, flowers, plants, fungi and landscapes; plus travel. Commissions undertaken. Member of **BAPLA**.

David Paterson Photo-Library
88 Cavendish Road,
London SW12 0DF
☎0181 673 2414   Fax 0181 675 9197

Travel, landscapes, nature, mountains from the UK, Europe, North Africa, the Himalayas, Japan and Scotland.

Ann & Bury Peerless Slide Resources & Picture Library
St David's, 22 King's Avenue, Minnis Bay,
Birchington-on-Sea, Kent CT7 9QL
☎01843 841428   Fax 01843 848321
Contact *Ann or Bury Peerless*

Specialist collection on world religions: Hinduism, Buddhism, Jainism, Christianity, Sikhism. Geographical areas covered: India, Pakistan, Bangladesh, Sri Lanka, Thailand, Russia, Republic of China, Spain. 10,000 35mm colour transparencies.

Performing Arts Library
52 Agate Road, London W6 0AH
☎0181 748 2002   Fax 0181 563 0538

Colour and b&w pictures of all aspects of the performing arts, including classical music, opera, theatre, ballet and contemporary dance, musicals, concert halls, opera houses and festivals.

Photo Flora
46 Jacoby Place, Priory Road, Edgbaston,
Birmingham B5 7UN
☎0121 471 3300

Specialist in British and European wild plants, with colour coverage of most British and many European species (rare and common) and habitats; also travel in India, Nepal, Egypt, China, Thailand and Tibet.

Photo Library International Ltd
PO Box 75, Leeds, West Yorkshire LS7 3NZ
☎0113 2623005   Fax 0113 2625366
Contemporary colour coverage of most subjects, including industry.

Photo Press Defence Pictures
Glider House, 14 Addison Road, Plymouth,
Devon PL4 8LL
☎01752 251271/491534   Fax 01752 222482
Contact *David Reynolds, Jessica Kelly*

Leading source of military photography covering all areas of the UK Armed Forces, supported by a research agency of facts and figures. More than 100,000 images. Campaigns in Aden, the Falklands, Ulster, the Gulf and Yugoslavia covered. Specialist collections include the Royal Marine Commandos and Parachute Regiment training. Visitors welcome by appointment.

Photo Resources
The Orchard, Marley Lane, Kingston,
Canterbury, Kent CT4 6JH
☎01227 830075   Fax 01227 831135

Colour and b&w coverage of archaeology, art, ancient art, ethnology, mythology, world religion, museum objects.

Photofusion
17A Electric Lane, London SW9 8LA
☎0171 738 5774   Fax 0171 738 5509
Contact *Janis Austin*

Colour and b&w coverage of contemporary social issues including babies and children, disablement, education, the elderly, environment, family, health, housing, homelessness, people general and work. List available.

The Photographers' Library
81A Endell Street, London WC2H 9AJ
☎0171 836 5591   Fax 0171 379 4650

Covers worldwide travel destinations, industry, sport, people, landscapes, health. Brochure available.

Photomax
118–122 Magdalen Road, Oxford OX4 1RQ
☎01865 241825   Fax 01865 794511
Contact *Max Gibbs, Sarah Giles, Barry Allday*

All aspects of the aquarium hobby are covered: aquarium fish, tropical freshwater, tropical marine, coldwater, marine invertebrates (tropical); aquarium plants; water lilies. Expanding. Commissions undertaken.

Photos Horticultural
169 Valley Road, Ipswich, Suffolk IP1 4PJ
☎01473 257329   Fax 01473 233974
Colour coverage of all aspects of gardening in Britain and abroad, including extensive files on plants in cultivation and growing wild.

PictureBank Photo Library Ltd
Parman House, 30–36 Fife Road, Kingston upon Thames, Surrey KT1 1SY
☎0181 547 2344   Fax 0181 974 5652

250,000 colour transparencies covering people (girls, couples, families, children), travel and scenic (UK and world), moods (sunsets, seascapes, deserts, etc.), industry and technology, environments and general. Commissions undertaken. Visitors welcome. Member of **BAPLA**. New material on medium/large format welcome.

Picturepoint Ltd
See **Topham Picturepoint**

Pictures Colour Library
10A Neal's Yard, London WC2H 9DP
☎0171 497 2034   Fax 0171 497 3070

Location, lifestyle, food, still life, sport, animals, industry and business. Visitors welcome.

Pitkin Pictorials Ltd
Healey House, Dene Road, Andover, Hampshire SP10 2AA
☎01264 334303   Fax 01264 334110
Contact *Sarah Pickering*

Colour transparencies of English cathedrals; plus a large collection of b&w prints. Also London and a few other cities. No visitors.

Popperfoto
The Old Mill, Overstone Farm, Overstone, Northampton NN6 0AB
☎01604 670670   Fax 01604 670635

Includes early colour from 1940s and b&w from 1870 to the present day. Subjects include Scott's 1910–12 Antarctic expedition, wars, royalty, sport, politics, transport, crime, topography, history and social conditions worldwide. Houses the EPA (European Pressphoto Agency), AFP (Agence France Presse), Reuter and UPI collections: worldwide news events, European politics and news in depth. The UPI collection commences 1932; Reuter from its start in 1985 to the present day. Also represents Bob Thomas Sports Photography.

Premaphotos Wildlife
Amberstone, 1 Kirland Road, Bodmin, Cornwall PL30 5JQ
☎01208 78258   Fax 01208 72302
Contact *Jean Preston-Mafham, Library Manager*

Natural history worldwide. Subjects include flowering and non-flowering plants, fungi, slime moulds, fruits and seeds, galls, leaf mines, seashore life, mammals, birds, reptiles, amphibians, insects, spiders, habitats, scenery and cultivated cacti. Commissions undertaken. Visitors welcome.

Press Association
See **Library Services**

Professional Sport
8 Apollo Studios, Charlton Kings Mews, London NW5 2SA
☎0171 482 2311   Fax 0171 482 2441

Colour and b&w coverage of tennis, soccer, athletics, golf, cricket, boxing, winter sports and many minor sports. Major international events including the Olympic Games, World Cup soccer and all Grand Slam tennis events. Also news and feature material supplied worldwide. Computerised library with in-house processing and studio facilities; Macintosh photo transmission services available for editorial and advertising.

Railfotos
Millbrook House Ltd., Calthorpe House, 30 Hagley Road, Edgbaston, Birmingham B16 8QY
☎0121 454 1308   Fax 0121 454 4224 quote Millbrook House

One of the largest specialist libraries dealing comprehensively with railway subjects worldwide. Colour and b&w dating from the turn of the century to present day. Up-to-date material on UK, South America and Far East (except Japan), especially China. Visitors by appointment.

Raleigh International Picture Library
Raleigh House, 27 Parsons Green Lane, London SW6 4HZ
☎0171 371 8585   Fax 0171 371 5116
Contact *Annabel James*

Colour coverage of worldwide locations and subjects. Commissions undertaken worldwide.

Range Pictures Limited
First Floor, 6 Paddington Street, London W1M 3LA
☎0171 486 4086   Fax 0171 935 4791
Contacts *Helen Menzies, Anna Calvert*

Access to one of the world's largest picture sources, Bettmann. With over 17 million images, the archive is home to scores of individual collections including two of the most important news libraries: UPI (1907–1990) and Reuters (1985 to the present day, from the original negatives). Specialist subjects include news events, sports, cinema, war, social history, entertainment, people, geography, and early coverage of the Wild West, native Americans and the American Civil War. Other major components provide comprehensive coverage of world history from woodcuts and engravings to early photographs. A 6000-image directory has been published and a free catalogue is available.

Redferns
7 Bramley Road, London W10 6SZ
☎0171 792 9914   Fax 0171 792 0921
Music picture library covering every aspect of popular music from 1920s jazz to present day. Over 7,000 artists on file plus other subjects including musical instruments, recording studios, crowd scenes, festivals, etc. List and brochure available.

Reed Consumer Books Picture Library
Michelin House, 81 Fulham Road, London SW3 6RB
☎0171 225 9212   Fax 0171 225 9053
Contact *Sally Claxton*
400,000 images of cookery, gardening, crafts and interiors.

Reflections PhotoLibrary
The Bath Brewery, Toll Bridge Road, Bath, Avon BA1 7DE
☎01225 852790   Fax 01225 852791
Contact *Colin Bowers, Jennie Woodcock*
Family life, maternity, babies, childcare, teenagers, education and health.

Remote Source
See **Royal Geographical Society Picture Library**

Retna Pictures Ltd
1 Fitzroy Mews, Cleveland Street, London W1P 5DQ
☎0171 388 3444   Fax 0171 383 7151
Colour and b&w coverage of international rock and pop performers, actors, actresses, entertainers and celebrities. Also a general stock library covering a wide range of subjects, including travel, people, sport and leisure, flora and fauna, and the environment.

Retrograph Archive Ltd
164 Kensington Park Road, London W11 2ER
☎0171 727 9378/9426   Fax 0171 229 3395
Contact *Jilliana Ranicar-Breese*
'Number One for nostalgia!' A vast archive of commercial and decorative art (1860–1960). Worldwide labels and packaging for food, wine, chocolate, soap, perfume, cigars and cigarettes; fine art and commercial art journals, fashion magazines, posters, Victorian greeting cards, Christmas and Edwardian postcards, wallpaper and gift wrap sample books, music sheets, folios of decorative design and ornament – Art Nouveau and Deco; hotel, airline and shipping labels; memorabilia, tourism, leisure, poster art, postcards, food and drink, transport and entertainment. Originals viewed then photographed to order. Lasers for book dummies, packaging, mock-ups, film/TV action props. Colour brochure on request. Medium format. Colour, b&w and illustration. Picture research service. Design consultancy service. Victorian style montages conceived, designed and styled.

Reuters Television
40 Cumberland Avenue, London NW10 7EH
☎0171 510 5647/5603   Fax 0171 510 8568
Colour coverage of international political leaders, personalities and locations on 35mm colour transparencies. Videoprints available from Reuters' international coverage.

Rex Features Ltd
18 Vine Hill, London EC1R 5DX
☎0171 278 7294/3362   Fax 0171 696 0974
Established in the 1950s. Colour and b&w coverage of news, politics, personalities, show business, glamour, humour, art, medicine, science, landscapes, royalty, etc.

RIDA Photo Library
29 Camrose Avenue, Hanworth, Feltham, Middlesex TW13 7DA
☎0181 890 5353   Fax 0181 890 5353
Contact *David Bayliss*
Geological and geographical collection: fossils, rocks, minerals, field and economic geology and geography.

Royal Air Force Museum
Grahame Park Way, Hendon, London NW9 5LL
☎0181 205 2266   Fax 0181 200 1751
Contact *Christine Gregory*
About a quarter of a million images, mostly

b&w, with around 1500 colour in all formats, on the history of aviation. Particularly strong on the activities of the Royal Air Force from the 1870s to 1970s.

The Royal Collection
Windsor Castle, Windsor, Berks SL4 1NJ
☎01753 868286   Fax 01753 620046
Contact *Gwyneth Campling, Nicole Tetzner*

Photographic material of items in the Royal Collection, particularly oil paintings, drawings and watercolours, works of art, and interiors and exteriors of royal residences. 35,000 colour transparencies plus 25,000 b&w negatives.

Royal Geographical Society Picture Library
1 Kensington Gore, London SW7 2AR
☎0171 584 4381 ext. 152 Fax 0171 584 4381
Contact *Joanna Scadden, Victoria Keble-Williams*

A strong source of geographical and historical images, both archival and modern, showing the world through the eyes of photographers and explorers dating from the 1830s to the present day. The 'Remote Source Collection' provides up-to-date transparencies from around the world, highlighting aspects of cultural activity, environmental phenomena, anthropology, architectural design, travel, mountaineering and exploration. Offers a professional and comprehensive service for both commercial and academic use.

Royal Opera House Archives
Royal Opera House, Covent Garden, London WC2E 9DD
☎0171 240 1200   Fax 0171 836 1762
Contact *Francesca Franchi, Jane Jackson*

Information and illustrations covering the history of the three Covent Garden Theatres, 1732 to the present, including the three Royal Opera House Companies – The Birmingham Royal Ballet, The Royal Ballet and The Royal Opera. Visitors welcome by appointment.

The Royal Photographic Society
The Octagon, Milsom Street, Bath, Avon BA1 1DN
☎01225 462841   Fax 01225 448688
Contact *Debbie Ireland*

History of photography, with an emphasis on pictorial photography as an art rather than a documentary record. Photographic processes and cameras, landscape, portraiture, architecture, India, Victorian and Edwardian life.

RSPB Picture Library
The Lodge, Sandy, Bedfordshire SG19 2DL
☎01767 680551   Fax 01767 692365
Contact *Chris Sargeant*

Colour and b&w images of birds, butterflies, moths, mammals, reptiles and their habitats. Also colour images of all RSPB reserves. Growing selection of various habitats. Total number of slides now 65,000.

Russia and Republics Photolibrary
Conifers House, Cheapside Lane, Denham, Uxbridge, Middlesex UB9 5AE
☎01895 834814/0956 304384 (mobile)
Fax 01895 834028

Images of Russia and the Republics: cities, museums, cathedrals, markets, landmarks, landscapes, resorts, traditional costumes and dances, craftsmen at work.

Peter Sanders Photography
9 Meades Lane, Chesham, Buckinghamshire HP5 1ND
☎01494 773674   Fax 01494 773674
Contact *Peter Sanders, Hafsa Garwatuk*

The world of Islam in all its aspects from religion and industry to culture and arts. Areas included are Saudi Arabia, Africa, Asia, Europe and USA. Now expanding to all religions.

Science and Society Picture Library
Science Museum, Exhibition Road, London SW7 2DD
☎0171 938 9750   Fax 0171 938 9751
Contact *Angela Murphy, Venita Paul, Ivor Gwilliams*

25,000 reference prints and 100,000 colour transparencies, incorporating many from collections at the Science Museum, the National Railway Museum and the National Museum of Film, Photography and Television. Collections illustrate the history of: science, industry, technology, medicine, transport and the media. Plus three archives documenting British society in the twentieth century.

The Scottish Highland Photo Library
Unit 5, Castle Avenue Industrial Estate, Invergordon, Ross-shire IV18 0PQ
☎01349 852144   Fax 01349 852144
Contact *Hugh Webster*

100,000 colour transparencies of the Scottish

Highlands and Islands. Not just a travel library; images cover industry, agriculture, fisheries and many other subjects of the Highlands and Islands. Submissions from photographers welcome. Commissions undertaken.

Select Photos

N5 Studios, Metropolitan Wharf, Wapping Wall, London E1 9SS
☎0171 265 1422   Fax 0171 265 1421
Contact *Shirley Berry, Julius Domoney*

Colour and b&w coverage of environmental issues, current affairs, news and political subjects. New travel section. Commissions undertaken. Representatives for European and US agencies.

Mick Sharp Photography

Eithinog, Waun, Penisarwaun, Caernarfon, Gwynedd LL55 3PW
☎01286 872425   Fax 01286 872425
Contacts *Mick Sharp, Jean Williamson*

Colour transparencies (6″x4.5″ and 35mm) and black & white prints (5″x4″ and 6″x4.5″ negatives) of subjects connected with archaeology, ancient monuments, buildings, churches, countryside, environment, history, landscape, past cultures and topography from Britain and abroad. Photographs by Mick Sharp and Jean Williamson, plus access to other specialist collections on related subjects. Commissions undertaken.

Phil Sheldon Golf Picture Library

40 Manor Road, Barnet, Hertfordshire EN5 2JQ
☎0181 440 1986   Fax 0181 440 9348

Over 300,000 colour and b&w photos dating from 1976 including detailed coverage of 42 major championships, eight Ryder Cup matches and over 300 other tournaments. Expanding collection which includes player action, portraits, instruction material, trophies and over 200 courses from around the world. Also classic 1960s collection by photographer Sidney Harris. Commissions undertaken.

Skishoot Offshoot

28 Dalebury Road, London SW17 7HH
☎0181 767 0059   Fax 0181 767 6680
Contact *Caroline Ellerby*

Predominantly skiing and ski-related subjects, but also a travel library specialising in offbeat images. Commissions undertaken.

Skyscan Balloon Photography

Oak House, Toddington, Cheltenham, Gloucestershire GL54 5BY
☎01242 621357   Fax 01242 621343

Unusual aerial views taken from a tethered balloon flown at heights of 80 to 800 feet all on medium format transparency. This photo library of unique low level pictures of British city and rural landscapes has a special collection of Heritage sites, the Cotswolds, London and the Thames Valley. Commissions undertaken.

SOA (Sabine Oppenländer Associates)

H Welbeck Mansions, Inglewood Road, London NW6 1QX
☎0171 794 4567   Fax 0171 431 5385
Contact *Sabine Oppenländer*

50,000 colour slides, 5,000 b&w photos covering *Stern* productions, celebrities, sports, travel & geographic, advertising, social subjects. Own in-house productions (text & photos).

Solo Syndication Ltd

49-53 Kensington High Street, London W8 5ED
☎0171 376 2166   Fax 0171 938 3165
Contact *Trevor York*

Access to three million images from *Daily Mail* and *Evening Standard* libraries. Leading collections of royalty and celebrity pictures, also crime portfolio. Available by bromide prints or by electronic transmission.

Sotheby's Transparency Library

34-35 New Bond Street, London W1A 2AA
☎0171 408 5383   Fax 0171 408 5062
Contact *Joanna Ling*

A new source of images. Recently set up, the library mainly consists of several thousand selected transparencies of pictures sold at Sotheby's. Images from the 15th to the 20th century. Oils, drawings, watercolours and prints. 'Happy to do searches or, alternatively, visitors are welcome by appointment.'

South American Pictures

48 Station Road, Woodbridge, Suffolk IP12 4AT
☎01394 383963/383279   Fax 01394 380176
Contact *Marion Morrison*

Colour and b&w images of South/Central America, Cuba and Mexico, including archaeology and the Amazon. Frequently updated.

There is an archival section, with pictures and documents from most countries.

Spectrum Colour Library
41–42 Berners Street, London W1P 3AA
☎0171 637 1587   Fax 0171 637 3681

A large collection including travel, sport, people, pets, scenery, industry, British and European cities, etc. All pictures are also available in digital format. Visitors welcome by appointment.

Frank Spooner Pictures Ltd
Unit B7, Hatton Square, 16–16A Baldwin's Gardens, London EC1N 7US
☎0171 405 9943   Fax 0171 831 2483

Subjects include current affairs, show business, fashion, politics, travel, adventure, sport, personalities, films, animals and the Middle East. Represented in more than 30 countries and handles UK distribution of Harry Benson, and Gamma Presse Images of Paris. Commissions undertaken.

The Still Moving Picture Co.
67A Logie Green Road, Edinburgh EH7 4HF
☎0131 557 9697   Fax 0131 557 9699
Contact *John Hutchinson, Sue Hall*

250,000 colour, b&w and 16mm film coverage of Scotland and sport. The largest photo and film library in Scotland, holding the Scottish Tourist Board library among its files. Scottish agents for **Allsport (UK) Ltd.**

Stockfile
PO Box 605, Virginia Water, Surrey GU25 4SS
☎01344 844395   Fax 01344 843513
Contact *Jill Behr, Steven Behr*

Specialist cycling- and skiing-based collection covering most aspects of these activities, with emphasis on mountain biking. Expanding adventure sports section.

Survival Anglia Photo Library
See **Oxford Scientific Films**

Telegraph Colour Library
The Innovation Centre, 225 Marsh Wall, London E14 9FX
☎0171 987 1212   Fax 0171 538 3309
Contact *Joanne Onion*

Leading stock photography agency covering a wide subject range: business, sport, people, industry, animals, medical, nature, space, travel and graphics. Free catalogue available. Same-day service to UK clients.

Teral Research Services
See **Editorial, Research and Other Services**

Patrick Thurston Photolibrary
10 Willis Road, Cambridge CB1 2AQ
☎01223 352547   Fax 01223 66274

Colour photography of Britain: scenery, people, museums, churches, coastline. Also various countries abroad. Commissions undertaken.

Topham Picturepoint
PO Box 33, Edenbridge, Kent TN8 5PB
☎01342 850313   Fax 01342 850244
Contact *Alan Smith*

Eight million contemporary and historical images, ideal for advertisers, publishers and the travel trade. Delivery on line.

B. M. Totterdell Photography
Constable Cottage, Burlings Lane, Knockholt, Kent TN14 7PE
☎01959 532001
Contact *Barbara Totterdell*

Specialist volleyball library covering all aspects of the sport.

Trades Union Congress Picture Library
See **Library Services**

Tessa Traeger
7 Rossetti Studios, 72 Flood Street, London SW3 5TF
☎0171 352 3641   Fax 0171 352 4846

Food, gardens, travel and artists.

Travel Ink Photo & Feature Library
The Old Coach House, 14 High Street, Goring on Thames, Nr Reading, Berkshire RG8 9AR
☎01491 873011   Fax 01491 875558
Contact *Abbie Enock*

Around 35,000 colour images on-site covering about 100 countries (including the UK). With associate library in London, has access to nearly 200,000 transparencies. Topics range across travel, tourism, lifestyles, business, industry, transport, children, history activities. Specialist collections on Hong Kong and North Wales.

Peter Trenchard's Image Store Ltd

The Studio, West Hill, St Helier, Jersey,
Channel Islands JE2 3HB
☎01534 869933   Fax 01534 889191

Contact *Peter Trenchard*

Colour coverage of the Channel Islands –
mainly tourist and financial-related. Commissions undertaken.

Tropix Photographic Library

156 Meols Parade, Meols, Wirral, Merseyside
L47 6AN
☎0151 632 1698   Fax 0151 632 1698

Contact *Veronica Birley*

Leading specialists on the developing world in
all its aspects. Environmental topics widely
covered. Assignment photography undertaken
at home and overseas. New collections welcome, especially parts of Africa and Latin
America, and environmental; please write for
details enclosing s.a.e. All submissions (35
mm+ colour transparencies only) must be
accompanied by detailed accurate captions,
prepared according to Tropix specifications.

Ulster Museum

Botanic Gardens, Belfast BT9 5AB
☎01232 381251   Fax 01232 665510

Contact *Mrs Pat McLean*

Affectionately known as the 'treasure house of
Ulster', the Ulster Museum is a national
museum for Northern Ireland. Specialist subjects: archaeology, ethnography, treasures from
the Armada shipwrecks, geology, botany, zoology, local history and industrial archaeology.
Commissions welcome for objects not already
photographed.

Universal Pictorial Press & Agency Ltd

29–31 Saffron Hill, London EC1N 8FH
☎0171 421 6000   Fax 0171 421 6006

News Editor *Peter Dare*

Photo archive dates back to 1944 and contains
approximately four million pictures. Colour
and b&w coverage of news, royalty, politics,
sport, arts, and many other subjects. Commissions undertaken for press and public relations. Fully interactive digital photo archive
accessible by Apple Mac via ISDN or modem.
Full scanning and wire facilities for analogue
and digital.

UPI

See **Popperfoto**

V & A Picture Library

Victoria and Albert Museum, South
Kensington, London SW7 2RL
☎0171 938 8352/8354   Fax 0171 938 8353

30,000 colour and half a million b&w photos
of decorative and applied arts, including
ceramics, ivories, furniture, costumes, textiles,
stage, musical instruments, toys, Indian, Far
Eastern, Islamic objects, sculpture, painting and
prints, from medieval to present day.

The Victory Archive

c/o Popperfoto, The Old Mill, Overstone
Farm, Northampton NN6 0AB
☎01604 670670   Fax 01604 670635

Formerly the Conway Picture Library.
Magazine photo collections from women's
journals 1940s–1960s. Colour and b&w coverage of personalities, fashion and features, plus a
transport section, which includes naval shipping from the 19th century. Excellent World
War II material.

Viewfinder Colour Photo Library

3 Northload Street, Glastonbury, Somerset
BA6 9JJ
☎01458 832600   Fax 01458 832850

Quality colour coverage of occupations, industry, leisure, people, scenics, transport, travel,
British Isles, agriculture, sport.

The Vintage Magazine Company Ltd

203–213 Mare Street, London E8 3QE
☎0181 533 7588   Fax 0181 533 7283

A large collection of movie stills and photographs covering music, glamour, social history,
theatre posters, ephemera, postcards.

The Charles Walker Collection

12–14 Argyll Street, London W1V 1AB
☎0171 734 7344   Fax 0171 287 3933

One of the foremost collections in the world
on subjects popularly listed as 'Mystery, myth
and magic'. The collection includes astrology,
occultism, witchcraft and many other related
areas. Catalogue available.

John Walmsley Photo Library

April Cottage, Warners Lane, Albury Heath,
Guildford, Surrey GU5 9DE
☎01483 203846   Fax 01483 203846

Specialist library of learning-training-working
subjects. Comprehensive coverage of learning
environments such as playgroups, schools,
colleges, universities and skills centres. Images

reflect a multi-racial Britain. Plus a section on complementary medicine with over 30 therapies from acupuncture and yoga to more unusual treatments like moxibustion and metamorphic technique. Commissions undertaken. Subject list available on request.

Waterways Photo Library
39 Manor Court Road, Hanwell,
London W7 3EJ
☎0181 840 1659   Fax 0181 567 0605

A specialist photo library on all aspects of Britain's inland waterways. Top quality 35mm and medium format colour transparencies, plus a large collection of b&w. Rivers and canals, bridges, locks, aqueducts, tunnels and waterside buildings. Town and countryside scenes, canal art, waterway holidays, boating, fishing, windmills, watermills, watersports and wildlife.

Wellcome Centre Medical Photographic Library
183 Euston Road, London NW1 2BE
☎0171 611 8888   Fax 0171 611 8577
Contact *Catherine Draycott, Clare Dunne, Michele Minto, Julie Dorrington*

Approximately 120,000 images on the history of medicine and human culture worldwide, including modern clinical medicine. Incorporates the **National Medical Slide Bank**.

Eric Whitehead Photography
PO Box 33, Kendal, Cumbria LA9 4SU
☎015396 21002

Incorporates the Cumbria Picture Library. The agency covers local news events, PR and commercial material.

Derek G. Widdicombe-Worldwide Photographic Library
Oldfield, High Street, Clayton West,
Huddersfield, West Yorkshire HD8 9NS
☎01484 862638   Fax 01484 862638
Contact *Derek G. Widdicombe*

Around 150,000 images (mostly the work of Derek Widdicombe) in colour and b&w. Landscapes, seascapes, human interest, architecture, moods and seasons, buildings and natural features in Britain and abroad.

Wilderness Photographic Library
Mill Barn, Broad Raine, Sedbergh, Cumbria
LA10 5ED
☎015396 20196   Fax 015396 21293
Contact *John Noble*

Striking colour images from around the world, from polar wastes to the Himalayas and Amazon jungle. Subjects: mountains, Arctic, deserts, icebergs, wildlife, rainforests, glaciers, geysers, exploration, caves, rivers, eco-tourism, people and cultures, canyons, seascapes, marine life, weather, volcanoes, mountaineering, skiing, geology, conservation, adventure sports, national parks, the Antarctic and Amazonia.

David Williams Picture Library
50 Burlington Avenue, Glasgow G12 0LH
☎0141 339 7823   Fax 0141 337 3031

Colour coverage of Scotland and Iceland. Smaller collections of the Faroes, France and Western USA. Landscapes, historical sites, buildings, geology and physical geography. Medium format and 35 mm. Catalogue available. Commissions undertaken.

Vaughan Williams Memorial Library
English Folk Dance and Song Society,
Cecil Sharp House, 2 Regent's Park Road,
London NW1 7AY
☎0171 284 0523   Fax 0171 284 0523

Mainly b&w coverage of traditional/folk music, dance and customs worldwide, focusing on Britain and other English-speaking nations. Photographs date from late 19th century to the 1970s.

Windrush Photos, Wildlife and Travel Picture Agency
99 Noah's Ark, Kemsing, Sevenoaks, Kent
TN15 6PD
☎01732 763486   Fax 01732 763285
Contact *David Tipling*

The whole environmental spectrum is covered. Specialist subjects include birds from around the world, and British wildlife. Worldwide wildlife and landscapes. Asian travel includes landscapes, people and tourist destinations from the region. A large collection of black and white images covering British wildlife and angling, and shooting scenes dating back to the 1930s. High quality photographic and features commissions are regularly undertaken for publications in the UK and overseas.

The Wingfield Sporting Art Library
The Old Nunnery, 191 Battersea Bridge
Road, London SW11 3AS
☎0171 978 5990   Fax 0171 978 5990
Contact *Mary Ann Wingfield*

Sporting works of art, both historical and contemporary, covering 50 different sports. Commissions undertaken.

World Pictures
85a Great Portland Street, London
W1N 5RA
☎0171 437 2121   Fax 0171 439 1307
Contacts *David Brenes, Carlo Irek*

600,000 colour transparencies of travel and emotive material.

WWF UK Photolibrary
Panda House, Weyside Park, Catteshall Lane, Godalming, Surrey GU7 1XR
☎01483 426444   Fax 01483 426409
Contact *Heidi Cameron, Andrea Ballard*

Specialist library covering natural history, endangered species, conservation, environment, forests, habitats, habitat destruction, and pollution in the UK and abroad. 9,000 colour slides (35mm), 550 medium format, 500 b&w prints, 100 b&w line drawings.

York Archaeological Trust Picture Library
Piccadilly House, 55 Piccadilly, York
YO1 1PL
☎01904 663032/663000   Fax 01904 640029

Specialist library of rediscovered artifacts, historic buildings and excavations, presented by the creators of the highly acclaimed Jorvik Viking Centre. The main emphasis is on the Roman, Anglo-Saxon and Viking periods.

John Robert Young Collection
61 De Montfort Road, Lewes, East Sussex
BN7 1SS
☎01273 475216   Fax 01273 475216
Contact *Jennifer Barrett*

50,000 transparencies on travel, religion and military subjects.

Balancing the Books –
Tax and the Writer

'No man in this country is under the smallest obligation, moral or other, to arrange his affairs as to enable the Inland Revenue to put the largest possible shovel in his stores.

'The Inland Revenue is not slow, and quite rightly, to take every advantage which is open to it . . . for the purpose of depleting the taxpayer's pockets. And the taxpayer is, in like manner, entitled to be astute to prevent as far as he honestly can the depletion of his means by the Inland Revenue.'

Lord Clyde, *Ayrshire Pullman v Inland Revenue Commissioners, 1929.*

Income Tax

What is a professional writer for tax purposes?

Writers are professionals while they are writing regularly with the intention of making a profit; or while they are gathering material, researching or otherwise preparing a publication.

A professional freelance writer is taxed under Case II of Schedule D of the *Income and Corporation Taxes Act 1988*. The taxable income is the amount received, either directly or by an agent, on his behalf, less expenses wholly and exclusively laid out for the purposes of the profession. If expenses exceed income, the loss can either be carried forward and set against future income from writing or set against other income which is subject to tax in the same year. If tax has been paid on that other income, a repayment can be obtained, or the sum can be offset against other tax liabilities. Special loss relief can apply in the opening year of the profession. Losses made in the first four years can be set against income of up to five earlier years.

Where a writer receives very occasional payments for isolated articles, it may not be possible to establish that these are profits arising from carrying on a continuing profession. In such circumstances these 'isolated transactions' may be assessed under Case VI of Schedule D of the *Income and Corporation Taxes Act 1988*. Again, expenses may be deducted in arriving at the taxable income, but, if expenses exceed income, the loss can only be set against the profits from future isolated transactions, or other income assessable under Case VI.

Expenses

A writer can normally claim the following expenses:

(a) Secretarial, typing, proofreading, research. Where payment for these are made to the author's wife or husband, they should be recorded and entered in the spouse's tax return as earned income which is subject to the usual personal allowances. If payments reach taxable levels, PAYE should be operated.

(b) Telephone, telegrams, postage, stationery, printing, maintenance, insurance, dictation tapes, batteries, any equipment or office requisites used for the profession.

(c) Periodicals, books (including presentation copies and reference books) and other publications necessary for the profession, but amounts received from the sale of books should be deducted. Some inspectors of tax allow only capital allowances on books (see (l) below).

(d) Hotels, fares, car running expenses (including repairs, petrol, oil, garaging, parking, cleaning, insurance, licence, road fund tax, depreciation), hire of cars or taxis in connection with:

    (i)   business discussions with agents, publishers, co-authors, collaborators, researchers, illustrators, etc.

    (ii) travel at home and abroad to collect background material.

(e) Publishing and advertising expenses, including costs of proof corrections, indexing, photographs, etc.

(f) Subscriptions to societies and associations, press cutting agencies, libraries, etc., incurred wholly for the purpose of the profession.

(g) Premiums to pension schemes such as the *Society of Authors Retirement Benefits Scheme*. Depending on age, up to 40% of net earned income can be paid into a personal pension plan.

(h) Rent, council tax and water rates, etc., the proportion being determined by the ratio which the number of rooms are used exclusively for the profession bears to the total number of rooms in the residence. But see note on *Capital Gains Tax* below.

(i) Lighting, heating and cleaning. A carefully estimated figure of the business use of these costs can be claimed as a proportion of the total.

(j) Accountancy charges and legal charges incurred wholly in the course of the profession including cost of defending libel actions, damages in so far as they are not covered by insurance and libel insurance premiums. However, where in a libel case, damages are awarded to punish the author for having acted maliciously the action becomes quasi-criminal and costs and damages may not be allowed.

(k) TV and video rental (which may be apportioned for private use), and cinema or theatre tickets, if wholly for the purpose of the profession, e.g. playwriting.

(l) Capital allowances for equipment, e.g. car, TV, radio, hi-fi sets, tape and video recorders, dictaphones, typewriters, desks, bookshelves, filing cabinets, photographic equipment. Allowances vary in the Finance Acts depending upon political and economic views prevailing. At present they are set at 25%. On motor cars the allowance is 25% in the first year and

25% of the reduced balance in each successive year limited to £2000 each year. In the case of motor cars bought after 11 March 1992 the limit is £3000 each year. The total allowances in the case of all assets must not exceed the difference between cost and eventual sale price. Allowances will be reduced to exclude personal (non-professional) use where necessary.

(m) Lease rent. The cost of lease rent of equipment is allowable; also on cars, subject to restrictions for private use and for expensive cars.

(n) Tax relief is available for three-year (minimum) covenants to charities. With effect from 1 October 1990 individuals can obtain tax relief on one-off charitable gifts subject to certain generous limits.

NB It is always advisable to keep detailed records. Diary entries of appointments, notes of fares and receipted bills are much more convincing to the Inland Revenue than round figure estimates.

It has recently been announced that there is a fundamental change in the method of assessment of income of the self-employed to the 'current year' basis. This will operate for most existing businesses with effect from 1996/7 but anyone who is just starting to write for profit should take professional advice as regards the date to choose for their accounting year end.

Capital Gains Tax

The exemption from Capital Gains Tax which applies to an individual's main residence does not apply to any part of that residence which is used exclusively for business purposes. The effect of this is that the appropriate proportion of any increase in value of the residence since 31 March 1982 can be taxed, when the residence is sold, at the maximum rate of 40% (at present).

Writers who own their houses should bear this in mind before claiming expenses for the use of a room for writing purposes. Arguments in favour of making such claims are that they afford some relief now, while Capital Gains Tax in its present form may not stay for ever. Also, where a new house is bought in place of an old one, the gain made on the sale of the first study may be set off against the cost of the study in the new house, thus postponing the tax payment until the final sale. For this relief to apply, each house must have a study, and the author must continue his profession throughout. On death there is an exemption of the total Capital Gains of the estate. Some relief from tax will be given on Council Tax.

NB Writers can claim that their use is non-exclusive and restrict their claim to the cost of extra lighting, heating and cleaning to avoid Capital Gains Tax liability.

Can a writer average out his income over a number of years for tax purposes?

Under Section 534 of the *Income and Corporation Taxes Act 1988,* a writer may in certain circumstances spread over two or three fiscal years lump sum payments, whenever received, and royalties received during two years from the date of first publication or performance of work. Points to note are:

(a) The relief can only be claimed if the writer has been engaged in preparing and collecting material and writing the book for more than twelve months.

(b) If the period of preparing and writing the work exceeds twelve months but does not exceed twenty-four months, one-half of the advances and/or royalties will be regarded as income from the year preceding that of receipt. If the period of preparing and writing exceeds twenty-four months, one-third of the amount received would be regarded as income from each of the two years preceding that of receipt.

(c) For a writer on a very large income, who otherwise fulfils the conditions required, a claim under these sections could result in a tax saving. If his income is not large he should consider the implication, in the various fiscal years concerned, of possible loss of benefit from personal and other allowances and changes in the standard rate of income tax.

It is also possible to average out income within the terms of publishers' contracts, but professional advice should be taken before signature. Where a husband and wife collaborate as writers, advice should be taken as to whether a formal partnership agreement should be made or whether the publishing agreement should be in joint names.

Is a lump sum paid for an outright sale of the copyright or part of the copyright exempt from tax?

No. All the money received from the marketing of literary work, by whatever means, is taxable. Some writers, in spite of clear judicial decisions to the contrary, still seem to think that an outright sale of, for instance, the film rights in a book is not subject to tax.

Is there any relief where old copyrights are sold?

Section 535 of the *Income and Corporation Taxes Act 1988* gives relief where not less than ten years after the first publication of the work the author of a literary, dramatic, musical or artistic work assigns the copyright therein wholly or partially, or grants any interest in the copyright by licence, and:

(a) the consideration for the assignment or grant consists wholly or partially of a lump sum payment, the whole amount of which would, but for this section, be included in computing the amount of his/her profits or gains for a single year of assessment, and

(b) the copyright or interest is not assigned or granted for a period of less than two years.

In such cases, the amount received may be spread forward in equal yearly instalments for a maximum of six years, or, where the copyright or interest is assigned or granted for a period of less than six years, for the number of whole years in that period. A 'lump sum payment' is defined to include a non-returnable advance on account of royalties.

It should be noted that a claim may not be made under this section in respect of a payment if a prior claim has been made under Section 534 of the *Income and*

Corporation Taxes Act 1988 (see section on spreading lump sum payments over two or three years) or vice versa.

Are royalties payable on publication of a book abroad subject to both foreign tax as well as UK tax?

Where there is a Double Taxation Agreement between the country concerned and the UK, then on the completion of certain formalities no tax is deductible at source by the foreign payer, but such income is taxable in the UK in the ordinary way. When there is no Double Taxation agreement, credit will be given against UK tax for overseas tax paid. A complete list of countries with which the UK has conventions for the avoidance of double taxation may be obtained from the Inspector of Foreign Dividends, Lynwood Road, Thames Ditton, Surrey KT7 0DP, or the local tax office.

Residence Abroad

Writers residing abroad will, of course, be subject to the tax laws ruling in their country of residence, and as a general rule royalty income paid from the United Kingdom can be exempted from deduction of UK tax at source, providing the author is carrying on his profession abroad. A writer who is intending to go and live abroad should make early application for future royalties to be paid without deduction of tax to HM Inspector of Taxes, Foreign Division, Prudential Building, 72 Maid Marian, Nottingham NG1 6AS. In certain circumstances writers resident in the Irish Republic are exempt from Irish Income Tax on their authorship earnings.

Are grants or prizes taxable?

The law is uncertain. Some Arts Council grants are now deemed to be taxable, whereas most prizes and awards are not, though it depends on the conditions in each case. When submitting a statement of income and expenses, such items should be excluded, but reference made to them in a covering letter to the Inspector of Taxes.

What if I disagree with a tax assessment?

Income Tax law requires the Inspector of Taxes to make an assessment each year calculating the amount of income tax payable on the 'profits' of the profession. Even though accounts may have already been submitted the assessment can quite possibly be estimated and overstated.

The taxpayer has the right of appeal within 30 days of receipt of the assessment and can request that the tax payable should be reduced to the correct liability which he must estimate as accurately as possible. However, if he underestimates the amount, interest can become payable on the amount by which he underpays when the correct liability is known.

What is the item 'Class 4 N.I.C.' which appears on my tax assessment?

All taxpayers who are self-employed pay an additional national insurance contribution if their earned income exceeds a figure which is varied each year. This contribution is described as Class 4 and is calculated in the tax assessment. It is additional to the self-employed Class 2 (stamp) contribution but confers no additional benefits and is a form of levy. It applies to men aged under 65 and women under 60. Tax relief is given on half the Class 4 contributions.

Value Added Tax

Value Added Tax (VAT) is a tax currently levied at 17.5% on:
  (a)   the total value of taxable goods and services supplied to consumers,
  (b)   the importation of goods into the UK,
  (c)   certain services from abroad if a taxable person receives them in the UK for the purpose of their business.

Who is Taxable?
A writer resident in the UK whose turnover from writing and any other business, craft or art on a self-employed basis is greater than £46,000 annually, before deducting agent's commission, must register with HM Customs & Excise as a taxable person. A business is required to register:
  – at the end of any month if the value of taxable supplies in the past 12 months has exceeded the annual threshold; or
  – if there are reasonable grounds for believing that the value of taxable supplies in the next 12 months will exceed the annual threshold.
  Penalties will be claimed in the case of late registration. A writer whose turnover is below these limits is exempt from the requirements to register for VAT, but may apply for voluntary registration, and this will be allowed at the discretion of HM Customs & Excise.
  A taxable person collects VAT on outputs (turnover) and deducts VAT paid on inputs (taxable expenses) and where VAT collected exceeds VAT paid, must remit the difference to HM Customs & Excise. In the event that input exceeds output, the difference will be repaid by HM Customs & Excise.

Outputs (Turnover)
A writer's outputs are taxable services supplied to publishers, broadcasting organisations, theatre managements, film companies, educational institutions, etc. A taxable writer must invoice, i.e. collect from, all the persons (either individuals or organisations) in the UK for whom supplies have been made, for fees, royalties or other considerations plus VAT. An unregistered writer cannot and must not invoice for VAT. A taxable writer is not obliged to collect VAT on royalties or other fees paid by publishers or others overseas. In practice, agents usually collect VAT for the registered author.

Remit to Customs
The taxable writer adds up the VAT which has been paid on taxable inputs, deducts it from the VAT received and remits the balance to Customs. Business

with HM Customs is conducted through the local VAT Offices of HM Customs which are listed in local telephone directories, except for tax returns which are sent direct to the Customs and Excise VAT Central Unit, Alexander House, 21 Victoria Avenue, Southend on Sea, Essex SS99 IAA.

Accounting

A taxable writer is obliged to account to HM Customs & Excise at quarterly intervals. Returns must be completed and sent to VAT Central Unit by the dates shown on the return. Penalties can be charged if the returns are late.

It is possible to account for the VAT liability under the Cash Accounting Scheme (Note 731), whereby the author accounts for the output tax when the

Taxable at the standard rate	*Taxable at the zero or special rate*	*Exempt*
Rent of certain commercial premises	Books (zero)	Rent of non-commercial premises
Advertisements in newspapers, magazines, journals and periodicals	Periodicals (zero)	Council Tax
	Coach, rail, and air travel (zero)	Postage
Agent's commission (unless it relates to monies from overseas, when it is zero-rated)	From 1.4.94 electricity (8%)	Services supplied by unregistered persons
Accountant's fees	Gas (8%)	Subscriptions to the Society of Authors, PEN, NUJ, etc.
Solicitor's fees *re* business matters	Other fuel (8%)	Wages and salaries
Agency services (typing, copying, etc.)		Insurance
Word processors, typewriters and stationery		Taxicab fares
Artists' materials		
Photographic equipment		
Tape recorders and tapes		
Hotel accommodation		*Outside the scope of VAT*
Motor-car expenses		PLR (Public Lending Right)
Telephone		Profit shares
Theatres and concerts		Investment income

NB This list is not exhaustive.

invoice is paid or royalties, etc., are received. The same applies to the input tax, but as most purchases are probably on a 'cash basis', this will not make a considerable difference to the author's input tax. This scheme is only applicable to those with a taxable turnover of less than £350,000 and, therefore, is available to the majority of authors. The advantage of this scheme is that the author does not have to account for VAT before receiving payment, thereby relieving the author of a cash flow problem.

It is also possible to pay VAT by nine estimated direct debits, with a final balance at the end of the year (see leaflet 732).

Registration

A writer will be given a VAT registration number which must be quoted on all VAT correspondence. It is the responsibility of those registered to inform those to whom they make supplies of their registration number. From 1 May 1994, the taxable turnover limit which determines whether a person who is registered for VAT may apply for cancellation of registration is £44,000.

Voluntary Registration

A writer whose turnover is below the limits may apply to register. If the writer is paying a relatively large amount of VAT on taxable inputs – agent's commissions, accountant's fees, equipment, materials, or agency services, etc. – it may make a significant improvement in the net income to be able to offset the VAT on these inputs. An author who pays relatively little VAT may find it easier, and no more expensive, to remain unregistered.

Fees and Royalties

A taxable writer must notify those to whom he makes supplies of the Tax Registration Number at the first opportunity. One method of accounting for and paying VAT on fees and royalties is the use of multiple stationery for 'self-billing', one copy of the royalty statement being used by the author as the VAT invoice. A second method is for the recipient of taxable outputs to pay fees, including authors' royalties, without VAT. The taxable author then renders a tax invoice for the VAT element and a second payment, of the VAT element, will be made. This scheme is cumbersome but will involve only taxable authors. Fees and royalties from abroad will count as payments for exported services and will accordingly be zero-rated.

Agents and Accountants

A writer is responsible to HM Customs for making VAT returns and payments. Neither an agent nor an accountant nor a solicitor can remove the responsibility, although they can be helpful in preparing and keeping VAT returns and accounts. Their professional fees or commission will, except in rare cases where the adviser or agent is himself unregistered, be taxable at the standard rate and will represent some of a writer's taxable inputs.

Income Tax – Schedule D

An unregistered writer can claim some of the VAT paid on taxable inputs as a business expense allowable against income tax. However, certain taxable inputs fall into categories which cannot be claimed under the income tax regulations. A taxable writer, who has already offset VAT on inputs, cannot charge it as a business expense for the purposes of income tax.

Certain Services From Abroad

A taxable author who resides in the United Kingdom and who receives certain services from abroad must account for VAT on those services at the appropriate tax rate on the sum paid for them. Examples of the type of services concerned include: services of lawyers, accountants, consultants, provisions of information and copyright permissions.

Inheritance Tax

Inheritance Tax was introduced in 1984 to replace Capital Transfer Tax, which had in turn replaced Estate Duty, the first of the death taxes of recent times. Paradoxically, Inheritance Tax has reintroduced a number of principles present under the old Estate Duty.

The general principle now is that all legacies on death are chargeable to tax (currently 40%), except for legacies between spouses which are exempt, as are the first £150,000 of legacies to others. Gifts made more than seven years before death are exempt, but those made within this period are taxed on a sliding scale. No tax is payable at the time of making the gift.

In addition, each individual may currently make gifts of up to £3000 in any year and these will be considered to be exempt. A further exemption covers any number of annual gifts not exceeding £250 to any one person.

If the £3000 is not utilised in one year it, or the unused balance, can be given in the following year (but no later), plus that year's exemptions. Gifts out of income, which means those which do not reduce one's capital or one's living standards, are also exempt if they are part of one's normal expenditure.

At death all assets are valued: they will include any property, investments, life policies, furniture and personal possessions, bank balances and, in the case of authors, the value of their copyrights. All, with the sole exception of copyrights, are capable (as assets) of accurate valuation, and, if necessary, can be turned into cash. The valuation of copyright is, of course, complicated, and frequently gives rise to difficulty. Except where they are bequeathed to the owner's husband or wife, very real problems can be left behind by the author.

Experience has shown that a figure based on two to three years' past royalties may be proposed by the Inland Revenue in their valuation of copyright. However, it all depends. If a book is running out of print or if, as in the case of educational books, it may need revision at the next reprint, these factors must be taken into account. In many cases the fact that the author is no longer alive and able to make personal appearances, or provide publicity, or write further works, will result in lower or slower sales. Obviously this is an area in which help can be given by the publishers, and in particular one needs to know what their future intentions are, what stocks of the books remain, and what likelihood there will be of reprinting.

There is a further relief available to authors who have established that they have been carrying on a business, normally assessable under Case II of Schedule D, for at least two years prior to death. It has been possible to establish that copyrights are treated as business property and in these circumstances, 'business property relief' is available. This relief at present is at 100% on business assets including copyrights, so that the tax saving can be quite substantial. The Inland Revenue may wish to be assured that the business is continuing and consideration should therefore be given to the appointment, in the author's will, of a literary executor who should be a qualified business person or, in certain circumstances, the formation of a partnership between the author and his or her spouse, or other relative, to ensure that it is established that the business is continuing after the author's death.

If the author has sufficient income, consideration should be given to building up a fund to cover future liabilities. One of a number of ways would be to take out a whole life assurance policy which is assigned to the children, or other beneficiaries, the premiums on which are within the annual exemption of £3000. The capital sum payable on the death of the assured is exempt from inheritance tax.

Anyone wondering how best to order his affairs for tax purposes, should consult an accountant with specialised knowledge in this field. Experience shows that a good accountant is well worth his fee which, incidentally, so far as it relates to matters other than personal tax work, is an allowable expense.

The information contained in this section is adapted from **The Society of Authors** *Quick Guides to Taxation* (Nos 4 and 7), with the kind help of A. P. Kernon, FCA.

Index of Companies

The following codes have been used to classify the index entries:

British Science Fiction (Association) Award **T** 532
British Science Fiction Association **Q** 463
British Screen Finance **Q** 463
British Society of Magazine Editors (BSME) **Q** 464
BRMB FM/XTRA am **K** 322
Broadcast **I** 235
Broadcast Communications **L** 333
Broadcast Monitoring Company, The/Lincoln Hannah Ltd **YY** 521
Broadcasting Press Guild **Q** 464
Broadland 102 **K** 322
Brockhampton Press, The **A** 18
Brombergs Bokförlag AB **AA** 405
Bromley (Rosemary) Literary Agency **F** 167
Brontë Society, The **Z** 488
Brooklands Museum Picture Library **V** 595
Brooks (Clive) **L** 334
Brown (Hamish) Scottish Photographic **V** 595
Brown (W. C. B.) **A** 18
Brown Son & Ferguson Ltd **A** 19
Brown Watson Ltd **A** 19
Brown Wells and Jacobs Ltd **E** 160
Browndeer Press **N** 411
Browne (Pema) Ltd **O** 432
Brownie **I** 235
Browning Society, The **Z** 488
Bruford (Rose) College of Speech and Drama **AB** 507
Bruna (A.W.) Uitgevers **AA** 401
Brunel Classic Gold **K** 322
Bryan (Felicity) **F** 167
Bryant (Peter) (Writers) **F** 167
Bubbles Photolibrary **V** 595
Buckmaster (D.) **Y** 515
Bucknell **A** 19
Building **I** 235
Bulfinch Press **N** 411
Bulzoni Editore SRL (Le Edizioni Universitarie d'Italia) **AA** 400
Burke (Edmund) Publisher **A1** 97
Burlington Magazine, The **I** 235
Burn (Graham) Productions **Y** 516
Burns & Oates **A** 19
Burns Federation, The **Z** 488
Burston (Diane) Literary Agency **F** 167
Burton Mail **H** 207
Bush Theatre **M** 367
Business Education Publishers Ltd **A** 19
Business Innovations Research **W** 142
Business Life **I** 236
Business Television **L** 334
Business Traveller **I** 236
Business Video Communications Ltd **L** 334
Business Week **P** 452
Businesslike Publishing **W** 143
Butterworth **A** 19
Butterworth Ireland Limited **A1** 97
Buxton Opera Festival **X** 386
Bycornute Books **F** 168
Bykofsky (Sheree) Associates, Inc. **O** 432
Byron Society, The/International Byron Society **Z** 488
BZZTÔH (Uitgeverij) **AA** 401
CAA Central Library **U** 573
Cable & Wireless Visual Resource **V** 595
Cable News International Inc. **P** 452
Cadogan Books plc **A** 19
Cakebreads Publications **W** 143

Caldecott (Randolph) Society **Z** 488
Calder Publications Ltd **A** 19
Caledonian Television Ltd **L** 334
California (University of) Press **N** 411
California University Press **A** 19
Calmann & King Ltd **E** 160
Calmann-Lévy (Editions) SA **AA** 397
Cambridge Central Library (Reference Library & Information Service) **U** 573
Cambridge Evening News **H** 207
Cambridge Theatre Company **M** 367
Cambridge University Press **A** 19
Camcorder User **I** 236
Camden Large Print **A** 20
Camera Press **V** 595
Camera Ways Ltd Picture Library **V** 595
Cameron (James) Award **T** 532
Cameron Books (Production) Ltd **E** 160
Camerson a.v. **L** 334
Caminho (Editorial) SARL **AA** 403
Camomile Street Library **U** 573
Campaign **I** 236
Campaign for Press and Broadcasting Freedom **Q** 464
Campbell (David) Publishers Ltd **A** 20
Campbell Books **A** 20
Campbell Thomson & McLaughlin Ltd **F** 168
Camping and Caravanning **I** 236
Camping Magazine **I** 236
Canal and Riverboat **I** 236
Candelabrum Poetry Magazine **C** 130
Canongate Audio **AU** 104
Canongate Books Ltd **A** 20
Canterbury Festival **X** 386
Canterbury Press Norwich **W** 143
Canterbury Press Norwich/Chansitor Publications **A** 20
Canto **A** 21
Cape (Jonathan) Ltd **A** 21
Capital FM/Capital Gold **K** 322
Capital Gay **I** 237
Capital Pictures **V** 595
Cappelens (J. W.) Forlag A/S **AA** 402
Cappelli (Nuova Casa Editrice Licinio) SRL GEM **AA** 400
Car Mechanics **I** 237
Caravan Life **I** 237
Caravan Magazine **I** 237
Caravan Writers' Guild, The **Q** 464
Caravel Film Techniques Ltd **L** 334
Carcanet Press **B** 125
Carcanet Press Ltd **A** 21
Cardiff (The City of) International Poetry Competition **T** 533
Cardiff Central Library **U** 573
Cardiff Literature Festival **X** 386
Careers Writers' Association **Q** 464
Caress Newsletter **I** 237
Carey Award **T** 533
Caribbean Times/Asian Times **I** 237
Carlsen Verlag GmbH **AA** 398
Carlton **J** 308
Carlton Books Ltd **A** 21
Carlton UK Productions **L** 334
Carlyle Society, Edinburgh, The **Z** 488
Carmarthen Public Library **U** 573
Carmarthen Writers' Circle Short Story Competition **T** 533
Carnell Literary Agency **F** 168
Carnival **C** 130
Carnival (Films & Theatre) Ltd **L** 334, **M** 367

Carnival Press **B** 125
Carnivorous Arpeggio (Press) **B** 125
Carol Publishing **N** 411
Carolrhoda Books, Inc. **N** 411
Carroll & Graf Publishers, Inc. **N** 411
Carroll (Lewis) Society **Z** 488
Carroll (Lewis) Society (Daresbury) **Z** 489
Cars and Car Conversions Magazine **I** 237
Carter Rae Communications **Y** 516
Cartwn Cymru **L** 334
Carvainis (Maria) Agency, Inc. **O** 432
Casarotto Ramsay Ltd **F** 168
Cascando **C** 130
Casement Collection, The **V** 595
Cash (J. Allan) Ltd **V** 595
Cass (Frank) & Co Ltd **A** 21
Cassandra Editions **N** 411
Cassell **A** 21
Casselman (Martha), Literary Agent **O** 432
Cat World **I** 238
Catalog Literary Agency, The **O** 432
Catch **I** 238
Catesby Press **A** 22
Cathie (Kyle) Ltd **A** 22
Catholic Central Library **U** 573
Catholic Herald **I** 238
Catholic Truth Society **A** 22
Catlin (Pearl) Associates **L** 335
Causeway Press Ltd **A** 22
Causeway Video **L** 335
Cavalcade Story Cassettes **AU** 104
CBA Publishing **A** 23
CBC Television **P** 452
CBD Research Ltd **A** 23
CBS News **P** 452
CCC Wadlow Productions Ltd **L** 335
Celador Productions Ltd **L** 335
Celtic Pen **C** 130
Cencrastus – The Curly Snake **C** 130
Centaur Press **A** 23
Central **J** 308
Central Music Library (Westminster) **U** 574
Central Office of Information **HH** 301
Central Office of Information Productions **L** 335
Central School of Speech and Drama, The **AB** 508
Century Books **A** 23
Century Radio **K** 322
CEPHAS Picture Library **V** 596
Certified Accountant **I** 238
CFM **K** 322
Chadwyck-Healey Ltd **A** 23
Chalet School (Friends of) **Z** 489
Challenge **I** 238
Chambers Harrap Ltd **A** 23
Champs Elysées **AU** 104
Champs-Elysées **I** 238
Chancerel International Publishers Ltd **E** 161
Chancery House Press **A** 23
Channel 4 **J** 308
Channel 5 **J** 308
Channel One Television Ltd **J** 312
Channel Television **J** 309
Channel X **L** 335
Chansitor Publications Ltd **A** 23
Chapman **A** 23, **C** 130, **I** 239
Chapman (Geoffrey) **A** 24
Chapman (Paul) Publishing Ltd **A** 24
Chapman Press **B** 125
Chapmans Publishers **A** 24
Chapter One **I** 239

Subject Index